GNU Emacs Lisp Reference Manual

For Emacs Version 25.2
Revision 3.1, October 2014

by Bil Lewis, Dan LaLiberte, Richard Stallman,
the GNU Manual Group, et al.

This is edition 3.1 of the *GNU Emacs Lisp Reference Manual*,
corresponding to Emacs version 25.2.

Published by the Free Software Foundation
51 Franklin St, Fifth Floor
Boston, MA 02110-1301
USA
ISBN 1-882114-74-4

Cover art by Etienne Suvasa.

Short Contents

Table of Contents

22 Major and Minor Modes 429

25   Backups and Auto-Saving 539

26   Buffers 550

27   Windows 567

1 Introduction

Most of the GNU Emacs text editor is written in the programming language called Emacs Lisp. You can write new code in Emacs Lisp and install it as an extension to the editor. However, Emacs Lisp is more than a mere extension language; it is a full computer programming language in its own right. You can use it as you would any other programming language.

Because Emacs Lisp is designed for use in an editor, it has special features for scanning and parsing text as well as features for handling files, buffers, displays, subprocesses, and so on. Emacs Lisp is closely integrated with the editing facilities; thus, editing commands are functions that can also conveniently be called from Lisp programs, and parameters for customization are ordinary Lisp variables.

This manual attempts to be a full description of Emacs Lisp. For a beginner's introduction to Emacs Lisp, see *An Introduction to Emacs Lisp Programming*, by Bob Chassell, also published by the Free Software Foundation. This manual presumes considerable familiarity with the use of Emacs for editing; see *The GNU Emacs Manual* for this basic information.

Generally speaking, the earlier chapters describe features of Emacs Lisp that have counterparts in many programming languages, and later chapters describe features that are peculiar to Emacs Lisp or relate specifically to editing.

This is edition 3.1 of the *GNU Emacs Lisp Reference Manual*, corresponding to Emacs version 25.2.

1.1 Caveats

This manual has gone through numerous drafts. It is nearly complete but not flawless. There are a few topics that are not covered, either because we consider them secondary (such as most of the individual modes) or because they are yet to be written. Because we are not able to deal with them completely, we have left out several parts intentionally.

The manual should be fully correct in what it does cover, and it is therefore open to criticism on anything it says—from specific examples and descriptive text, to the ordering of chapters and sections. If something is confusing, or you find that you have to look at the sources or experiment to learn something not covered in the manual, then perhaps the manual should be fixed. Please let us know.

As you use this manual, we ask that you mark pages with corrections so you can later look them up and send them to us. If you think of a simple, real-life example for a function or group of functions, please make an effort to write it up and send it in. Please reference any comments to the chapter name, section name, and function name, as appropriate, since page numbers and chapter and section numbers will change and we may have trouble finding the text you are talking about. Also state the version of the edition you are criticizing.

Please send comments and corrections using *M-x report-emacs-bug*.

1.2 Lisp History

Lisp (LISt Processing language) was first developed in the late 1950s at the Massachusetts Institute of Technology for research in artificial intelligence. The great power of the Lisp language makes it ideal for other purposes as well, such as writing editing commands.

Dozens of Lisp implementations have been built over the years, each with its own idiosyncrasies. Many of them were inspired by Maclisp, which was written in the 1960s at MIT's Project MAC. Eventually the implementers of the descendants of Maclisp came together and developed a standard for Lisp systems, called Common Lisp. In the meantime, Gerry Sussman and Guy Steele at MIT developed a simplified but very powerful dialect of Lisp, called Scheme.

GNU Emacs Lisp is largely inspired by Maclisp, and a little by Common Lisp. If you know Common Lisp, you will notice many similarities. However, many features of Common Lisp have been omitted or simplified in order to reduce the memory requirements of GNU Emacs. Sometimes the simplifications are so drastic that a Common Lisp user might be very confused. We will occasionally point out how GNU Emacs Lisp differs from Common Lisp. If you don't know Common Lisp, don't worry about it; this manual is self-contained.

A certain amount of Common Lisp emulation is available via the `cl-lib` library. See Section "Overview" in *Common Lisp Extensions*.

Emacs Lisp is not at all influenced by Scheme; but the GNU project has an implementation of Scheme, called Guile. We use it in all new GNU software that calls for extensibility.

1.3 Conventions

This section explains the notational conventions that are used in this manual. You may want to skip this section and refer back to it later.

1.3.1 Some Terms

Throughout this manual, the phrases "the Lisp reader" and "the Lisp printer" refer to those routines in Lisp that convert textual representations of Lisp objects into actual Lisp objects, and vice versa. See Section 2.1 [Printed Representation], page 8, for more details. You, the person reading this manual, are thought of as the programmer and are addressed as "you". The user is the person who uses Lisp programs, including those you write.

Examples of Lisp code are formatted like this: `(list 1 2 3)`. Names that represent metasyntactic variables, or arguments to a function being described, are formatted like this: *first-number*.

1.3.2 `nil` and `t`

In Emacs Lisp, the symbol `nil` has three separate meanings: it is a symbol with the name 'nil'; it is the logical truth value *false*; and it is the empty list—the list of zero elements. When used as a variable, `nil` always has the value `nil`.

As far as the Lisp reader is concerned, '()' and 'nil' are identical: they stand for the same object, the symbol `nil`. The different ways of writing the symbol are intended entirely for human readers. After the Lisp reader has read either '()' or 'nil', there is no way to determine which representation was actually written by the programmer.

In this manual, we write () when we wish to emphasize that it means the empty list, and we write `nil` when we wish to emphasize that it means the truth value *false*. That is a good convention to use in Lisp programs also.

```
(cons 'foo ())              ; Emphasize the empty list
(setq foo-flag nil)         ; Emphasize the truth value false
```

In contexts where a truth value is expected, any non-**nil** value is considered to be *true*. However, **t** is the preferred way to represent the truth value *true*. When you need to choose a value that represents *true*, and there is no other basis for choosing, use **t**. The symbol **t** always has the value **t**.

In Emacs Lisp, **nil** and **t** are special symbols that always evaluate to themselves. This is so that you do not need to quote them to use them as constants in a program. An attempt to change their values results in a **setting-constant** error. See Section 11.2 [Constant Variables], page 157.

booleanp *object*   [Function]
     Return non-**nil** if *object* is one of the two canonical boolean values: **t** or **nil**.

1.3.3 Evaluation Notation

A Lisp expression that you can evaluate is called a *form*. Evaluating a form always produces a result, which is a Lisp object. In the examples in this manual, this is indicated with '⇒':

```
(car '(1 2))
     ⇒ 1
```

You can read this as "(car '(1 2)) evaluates to 1".

When a form is a macro call, it expands into a new form for Lisp to evaluate. We show the result of the expansion with '↦'. We may or may not show the result of the evaluation of the expanded form.

```
(third '(a b c))
     ↦ (car (cdr (cdr '(a b c))))
     ⇒ c
```

To help describe one form, we sometimes show another form that produces identical results. The exact equivalence of two forms is indicated with '≡'.

```
(make-sparse-keymap)  ≡  (list 'keymap)
```

1.3.4 Printing Notation

Many of the examples in this manual print text when they are evaluated. If you execute example code in a Lisp Interaction buffer (such as the buffer *scratch*), the printed text is inserted into the buffer. If you execute the example by other means (such as by evaluating the function **eval-region**), the printed text is displayed in the echo area.

Examples in this manual indicate printed text with '⊣', irrespective of where that text goes. The value returned by evaluating the form follows on a separate line with '⇒'.

```
(progn (prin1 'foo) (princ "\n") (prin1 'bar))
     ⊣ foo
     ⊣ bar
     ⇒ bar
```

1.3.5 Error Messages

Some examples signal errors. This normally displays an error message in the echo area. We show the error message on a line starting with ' error '. Note that ' error ' itself does not appear in the echo area.

```
(+ 23 'x)
```
error   Wrong type argument: number-or-marker-p, x

1.3.6 Buffer Text Notation

Some examples describe modifications to the contents of a buffer, by showing the before and after versions of the text. These examples show the contents of the buffer in question between two lines of dashes containing the buffer name. In addition, '⋆' indicates the location of point. (The symbol for point, of course, is not part of the text in the buffer; it indicates the place *between* two characters where point is currently located.)

```
---------- Buffer: foo ----------
This is the ⋆contents of foo.
---------- Buffer: foo ----------

(insert "changed ")
     ⇒ nil
---------- Buffer: foo ----------
This is the changed ⋆contents of foo.
---------- Buffer: foo ----------
```

1.3.7 Format of Descriptions

Functions, variables, macros, commands, user options, and special forms are described in this manual in a uniform format. The first line of a description contains the name of the item followed by its arguments, if any. The category—function, variable, or whatever—is printed next to the right margin. The description follows on succeeding lines, sometimes with examples.

1.3.7.1 A Sample Function Description

In a function description, the name of the function being described appears first. It is followed on the same line by a list of argument names. These names are also used in the body of the description, to stand for the values of the arguments.

The appearance of the keyword **&optional** in the argument list indicates that the subsequent arguments may be omitted (omitted arguments default to **nil**). Do not write **&optional** when you call the function.

The keyword **&rest** (which must be followed by a single argument name) indicates that any number of arguments can follow. The single argument name following **&rest** receives, as its value, a list of all the remaining arguments passed to the function. Do not write **&rest** when you call the function.

Here is a description of an imaginary function **foo**:

foo *integer1* **&optional** *integer2* **&rest** *integers*   [Function]
     The function **foo** subtracts *integer1* from *integer2*, then adds all the rest of the arguments to the result. If *integer2* is not supplied, then the number 19 is used by default.

```
(foo 1 5 3 9)
     ⇒ 16
(foo 5)
     ⇒ 14
```

More generally,

```
(foo w x y...)
≡
(+ (- x w) y...)
```

By convention, any argument whose name contains the name of a type (e.g., *integer*, *integer1* or *buffer*) is expected to be of that type. A plural of a type (such as *buffers*) often means a list of objects of that type. An argument named *object* may be of any type. (For a list of Emacs object types, see Chapter 2 [Lisp Data Types], page 8.) An argument with any other sort of name (e.g., *new-file*) is specific to the function; if the function has a documentation string, the type of the argument should be described there (see Chapter 23 [Documentation], page 485).

See Section 12.2 [Lambda Expressions], page 188, for a more complete description of arguments modified by **&optional** and **&rest**.

Command, macro, and special form descriptions have the same format, but the word 'Function' is replaced by 'Command', 'Macro', or 'Special Form', respectively. Commands are simply functions that may be called interactively; macros process their arguments differently from functions (the arguments are not evaluated), but are presented the same way.

The descriptions of macros and special forms use a more complex notation to specify optional and repeated arguments, because they can break the argument list down into separate arguments in more complicated ways. '[*optional-arg*]' means that *optional-arg* is optional and '*repeated-args*...' stands for zero or more arguments. Parentheses are used when several arguments are grouped into additional levels of list structure. Here is an example:

count-loop (*var* [*from to* [*inc*]]) *body*...   [Special Form]
    This imaginary special form implements a loop that executes the *body* forms and then increments the variable *var* on each iteration. On the first iteration, the variable has the value *from*; on subsequent iterations, it is incremented by one (or by *inc* if that is given). The loop exits before executing *body* if *var* equals *to*. Here is an example:

```
(count-loop (i 0 10)
  (prin1 i) (princ " ")
  (prin1 (aref vector i))
  (terpri))
```

If *from* and *to* are omitted, *var* is bound to **nil** before the loop begins, and the loop exits if *var* is non-**nil** at the beginning of an iteration. Here is an example:

```
(count-loop (done)
  (if (pending)
      (fixit)
    (setq done t)))
```

In this special form, the arguments *from* and *to* are optional, but must both be present or both absent. If they are present, *inc* may optionally be specified as well. These arguments are grouped with the argument *var* into a list, to distinguish them from *body*, which includes all remaining elements of the form.

1.3.7.2 A Sample Variable Description

A *variable* is a name that can be *bound* (or *set*) to an object. The object to which a variable is bound is called a *value*; we say also that variable holds that value. Although nearly all variables can be set by the user, certain variables exist specifically so that users can change them; these are called *user options*. Ordinary variables and user options are described using a format like that for functions, except that there are no arguments.

Here is a description of the imaginary `electric-future-map` variable.

`electric-future-map`   [Variable]

> The value of this variable is a full keymap used by Electric Command Future mode. The functions in this map allow you to edit commands you have not yet thought about executing.

User option descriptions have the same format, but 'Variable' is replaced by 'User Option'.

1.4 Version Information

These facilities provide information about which version of Emacs is in use.

`emacs-version &optional` *here*   [Command]

> This function returns a string describing the version of Emacs that is running. It is useful to include this string in bug reports.
>
> ```
> (emacs-version)
>     ⇒ "GNU Emacs 24.5.1 (x86_64-unknown-linux-gnu, GTK+ Version 3.16)
>             of 2015-06-01"
> ```
>
> If *here* is non-`nil`, it inserts the text in the buffer before point, and returns `nil`. When this function is called interactively, it prints the same information in the echo area, but giving a prefix argument makes *here* non-`nil`.

`emacs-build-time`   [Variable]

> The value of this variable indicates the time at which Emacs was built. It is a list of four integers, like the value of `current-time` (see Section 38.5 [Time of Day], page 999).
>
> ```
>     emacs-build-time
>        ⇒ (20614 63694 515336 438000)
> ```

`emacs-version`   [Variable]

> The value of this variable is the version of Emacs being run. It is a string such as `"23.1.1"`. The last number in this string is not really part of the Emacs release version number; it is incremented each time Emacs is built in any given directory. A value with four numeric components, such as `"22.0.91.1"`, indicates an unreleased test version.

`emacs-major-version`   [Variable]

> The major version number of Emacs, as an integer. For Emacs version 23.1, the value is 23.

`emacs-minor-version`   [Variable]
>   The minor version number of Emacs, as an integer. For Emacs version 23.1, the value
>   is 1.

1.5 Acknowledgments

This manual was originally written by Robert Krawitz, Bil Lewis, Dan LaLiberte, Richard M. Stallman and Chris Welty, the volunteers of the GNU manual group, in an effort extending over several years. Robert J. Chassell helped to review and edit the manual, with the support of the Defense Advanced Research Projects Agency, ARPA Order 6082, arranged by Warren A. Hunt, Jr. of Computational Logic, Inc. Additional sections have since been written by Miles Bader, Lars Brinkhoff, Chong Yidong, Kenichi Handa, Lute Kamstra, Juri Linkov, Glenn Morris, Thien-Thi Nguyen, Dan Nicolaescu, Martin Rudalics, Kim F. Storm, Luc Teirlinck, and Eli Zaretskii, and others.

Corrections were supplied by Drew Adams, Juanma Barranquero, Karl Berry, Jim Blandy, Bard Bloom, Stephane Boucher, David Boyes, Alan Carroll, Richard Davis, Lawrence R. Dodd, Peter Doornbosch, David A. Duff, Chris Eich, Beverly Erlebacher, David Eckelkamp, Ralf Fassel, Eirik Fuller, Stephen Gildea, Bob Glickstein, Eric Hanchrow, Jesper Harder, George Hartzell, Nathan Hess, Masayuki Ida, Dan Jacobson, Jak Kirman, Bob Knighten, Frederick M. Korz, Joe Lammens, Glenn M. Lewis, K. Richard Magill, Brian Marick, Roland McGrath, Stefan Monnier, Skip Montanaro, John Gardiner Myers, Thomas A. Peterson, Francesco Potortì, Friedrich Pukelsheim, Arnold D. Robbins, Raul Rockwell, Jason Rumney, Per Starbäck, Shinichirou Sugou, Kimmo Suominen, Edward Tharp, Bill Trost, Rickard Westman, Jean White, Eduard Wiebe, Matthew Wilding, Carl Witty, Dale Worley, Rusty Wright, and David D. Zuhn.

For a more complete list of contributors, please see the relevant change log entries in the Emacs source repository.

2 Lisp Data Types

A Lisp *object* is a piece of data used and manipulated by Lisp programs. For our purposes, a *type* or *data type* is a set of possible objects.

Every object belongs to at least one type. Objects of the same type have similar structures and may usually be used in the same contexts. Types can overlap, and objects can belong to two or more types. Consequently, we can ask whether an object belongs to a particular type, but not for *the* type of an object.

A few fundamental object types are built into Emacs. These, from which all other types are constructed, are called *primitive types*. Each object belongs to one and only one primitive type. These types include *integer*, *float*, *cons*, *symbol*, *string*, *vector*, *hash-table*, *subr*, and *byte-code function*, plus several special types, such as *buffer*, that are related to editing. (See Section 2.4 [Editing Types], page 24.)

Each primitive type has a corresponding Lisp function that checks whether an object is a member of that type.

Lisp is unlike many other languages in that its objects are *self-typing*: the primitive type of each object is implicit in the object itself. For example, if an object is a vector, nothing can treat it as a number; Lisp knows it is a vector, not a number.

In most languages, the programmer must declare the data type of each variable, and the type is known by the compiler but not represented in the data. Such type declarations do not exist in Emacs Lisp. A Lisp variable can have any type of value, and it remembers whatever value you store in it, type and all. (Actually, a small number of Emacs Lisp variables can only take on values of a certain type. See Section 11.14 [Variables with Restricted Values], page 183.)

This chapter describes the purpose, printed representation, and read syntax of each of the standard types in GNU Emacs Lisp. Details on how to use these types can be found in later chapters.

2.1 Printed Representation and Read Syntax

The *printed representation* of an object is the format of the output generated by the Lisp printer (the function `prin1`) for that object. Every data type has a unique printed representation. The *read syntax* of an object is the format of the input accepted by the Lisp reader (the function `read`) for that object. This is not necessarily unique; many kinds of object have more than one syntax. See Chapter 18 [Read and Print], page 302.

In most cases, an object's printed representation is also a read syntax for the object. However, some types have no read syntax, since it does not make sense to enter objects of these types as constants in a Lisp program. These objects are printed in *hash notation*, which consists of the characters '#<', a descriptive string (typically the type name followed by the name of the object), and a closing '>'. For example:

```
(current-buffer)
     ⇒ #<buffer objects.texi>
```

Hash notation cannot be read at all, so the Lisp reader signals the error `invalid-read-syntax` whenever it encounters '#<'.

In other languages, an expression is text; it has no other form. In Lisp, an expression is primarily a Lisp object and only secondarily the text that is the object's read syntax. Often there is no need to emphasize this distinction, but you must keep it in the back of your mind, or you will occasionally be very confused.

When you evaluate an expression interactively, the Lisp interpreter first reads the textual representation of it, producing a Lisp object, and then evaluates that object (see Chapter 9 [Evaluation], page 124). However, evaluation and reading are separate activities. Reading returns the Lisp object represented by the text that is read; the object may or may not be evaluated later. See Section 18.3 [Input Functions], page 304, for a description of **read**, the basic function for reading objects.

2.2 Comments

A *comment* is text that is written in a program only for the sake of humans that read the program, and that has no effect on the meaning of the program. In Lisp, a semicolon (';') starts a comment if it is not within a string or character constant. The comment continues to the end of line. The Lisp reader discards comments; they do not become part of the Lisp objects which represent the program within the Lisp system.

The '#@*count*' construct, which skips the next *count* characters, is useful for program-generated comments containing binary data. The Emacs Lisp byte compiler uses this in its output files (see Chapter 16 [Byte Compilation], page 260). It isn't meant for source files, however.

See Section D.7 [Comment Tips], page 1062, for conventions for formatting comments.

2.3 Programming Types

There are two general categories of types in Emacs Lisp: those having to do with Lisp programming, and those having to do with editing. The former exist in many Lisp implementations, in one form or another. The latter are unique to Emacs Lisp.

2.3.1 Integer Type

The range of values for an integer depends on the machine. The minimum range is $-536{,}870{,}912$ to $536{,}870{,}911$ (30 bits; i.e., -2^{29} to $2^{29} - 1$) but many machines provide a wider range. Emacs Lisp arithmetic functions do not check for integer overflow. Thus (1+ 536870911) is $-536{,}870{,}912$ if Emacs integers are 30 bits.

The read syntax for integers is a sequence of (base ten) digits with an optional sign at the beginning and an optional period at the end. The printed representation produced by the Lisp interpreter never has a leading '+' or a final '.'.

```
-1          ; The integer -1.
1           ; The integer 1.
1.          ; Also the integer 1.
+1          ; Also the integer 1.
```

As a special exception, if a sequence of digits specifies an integer too large or too small to be a valid integer object, the Lisp reader reads it as a floating-point number (see Section 2.3.2 [Floating-Point Type], page 10). For instance, if Emacs integers are 30 bits, 536870912 is read as the floating-point number 536870912.0.

See Chapter 3 [Numbers], page 34, for more information.

2.3.2 Floating-Point Type

Floating-point numbers are the computer equivalent of scientific notation; you can think of a floating-point number as a fraction together with a power of ten. The precise number of significant figures and the range of possible exponents is machine-specific; Emacs uses the C data type `double` to store the value, and internally this records a power of 2 rather than a power of 10.

The printed representation for floating-point numbers requires either a decimal point (with at least one digit following), an exponent, or both. For example, '1500.0', '+15e2', '15.0e+2', '+1500000e-3', and '.15e4' are five ways of writing a floating-point number whose value is 1500. They are all equivalent.

See Chapter 3 [Numbers], page 34, for more information.

2.3.3 Character Type

A *character* in Emacs Lisp is nothing more than an integer. In other words, characters are represented by their character codes. For example, the character *A* is represented as the integer 65.

Individual characters are used occasionally in programs, but it is more common to work with *strings*, which are sequences composed of characters. See Section 2.3.8 [String Type], page 18.

Characters in strings and buffers are currently limited to the range of 0 to 4194303—twenty two bits (see Section 32.5 [Character Codes], page 765). Codes 0 through 127 are ASCII codes; the rest are non-ASCII (see Chapter 32 [Non-ASCII Characters], page 761). Characters that represent keyboard input have a much wider range, to encode modifier keys such as Control, Meta and Shift.

There are special functions for producing a human-readable textual description of a character for the sake of messages. See Section 23.4 [Describing Characters], page 490.

2.3.3.1 Basic Char Syntax

Since characters are really integers, the printed representation of a character is a decimal number. This is also a possible read syntax for a character, but writing characters that way in Lisp programs is not clear programming. You should *always* use the special read syntax formats that Emacs Lisp provides for characters. These syntax formats start with a question mark.

The usual read syntax for alphanumeric characters is a question mark followed by the character; thus, '?A' for the character *A*, '?B' for the character *B*, and '?a' for the character a.

For example:

        ?Q ⇒ 81   ?q ⇒ 113

You can use the same syntax for punctuation characters, but it is often a good idea to add a '\' so that the Emacs commands for editing Lisp code don't get confused. For example, '?\(' is the way to write the open-paren character. If the character is '\', you *must* use a second '\' to quote it: '?\\'.

You can express the characters control-g, backspace, tab, newline, vertical tab, formfeed, space, return, del, and escape as '?\a', '?\b', '?\t', '?\n', '?\v', '?\f', '?\s', '?\r', '?\d', and '?\e', respectively. ('?\s' followed by a dash has a different meaning—it applies the Super modifier to the following character.) Thus,

```
?\a ⇒ 7               ; control-g, C-g
?\b ⇒ 8               ; backspace, BS, C-h
?\t ⇒ 9               ; tab, TAB, C-i
?\n ⇒ 10              ; newline, C-j
?\v ⇒ 11              ; vertical tab, C-k
?\f ⇒ 12              ; formfeed character, C-l
?\r ⇒ 13              ; carriage return, RET, C-m
?\e ⇒ 27              ; escape character, ESC, C-[
?\s ⇒ 32              ; space character, SPC
?\\ ⇒ 92              ; backslash character, \
?\d ⇒ 127             ; delete character, DEL
```

These sequences which start with backslash are also known as *escape sequences*, because backslash plays the role of an escape character; this has nothing to do with the character ESC. '\s' is meant for use in character constants; in string constants, just write the space.

A backslash is allowed, and harmless, preceding any character without a special escape meaning; thus, '?\+' is equivalent to '?+'. There is no reason to add a backslash before most characters. However, you should add a backslash before any of the characters '()\|;'`"#.,' to avoid confusing the Emacs commands for editing Lisp code. You can also add a backslash before whitespace characters such as space, tab, newline and formfeed. However, it is cleaner to use one of the easily readable escape sequences, such as '\t' or '\s', instead of an actual whitespace character such as a tab or a space. (If you do write backslash followed by a space, you should write an extra space after the character constant to separate it from the following text.)

2.3.3.2 General Escape Syntax

In addition to the specific escape sequences for special important control characters, Emacs provides several types of escape syntax that you can use to specify non-ASCII text characters.

Firstly, you can specify characters by their Unicode values. ?\u*nnnn* represents a character with Unicode code point 'U+*nnnn*', where *nnnn* is (by convention) a hexadecimal number with exactly four digits. The backslash indicates that the subsequent characters form an escape sequence, and the 'u' specifies a Unicode escape sequence.

There is a slightly different syntax for specifying Unicode characters with code points higher than U+*ffff*: ?\U00*nnnnnn* represents the character with code point 'U+*nnnnnn*', where *nnnnnn* is a six-digit hexadecimal number. The Unicode Standard only defines code points up to 'U+*10ffff*', so if you specify a code point higher than that, Emacs signals an error.

Secondly, you can specify characters by their hexadecimal character codes. A hexadecimal escape sequence consists of a backslash, 'x', and the hexadecimal character code. Thus, '?\x41' is the character A, '?\x1' is the character C-a, and ?\xe0 is the character à (a with grave accent). You can use any number of hex digits, so you can represent any character code in this way.

Thirdly, you can specify characters by their character code in octal. An octal escape sequence consists of a backslash followed by up to three octal digits; thus, '?\101' for the character *A*, '?\001' for the character *C-a*, and ?\002 for the character *C-b*. Only characters up to octal code 777 can be specified this way.

These escape sequences may also be used in strings. See Section 2.3.8.2 [Non-ASCII in Strings], page 19.

2.3.3.3 Control-Character Syntax

Control characters can be represented using yet another read syntax. This consists of a question mark followed by a backslash, caret, and the corresponding non-control character, in either upper or lower case. For example, both '?\^I' and '?\^i' are valid read syntax for the character *C-i*, the character whose value is 9.

Instead of the '^', you can use 'C-'; thus, '?\C-i' is equivalent to '?\^I' and to '?\^i':

   ?\^I $\Rightarrow$ 9   ?\C-I $\Rightarrow$ 9

In strings and buffers, the only control characters allowed are those that exist in ASCII; but for keyboard input purposes, you can turn any character into a control character with 'C-'. The character codes for these non-ASCII control characters include the 2^{26} bit as well as the code for the corresponding non-control character. Ordinary text terminals have no way of generating non-ASCII control characters, but you can generate them straightforwardly using X and other window systems.

For historical reasons, Emacs treats the **DEL** character as the control equivalent of *?*:

   ?\^? $\Rightarrow$ 127   ?\C-? $\Rightarrow$ 127

As a result, it is currently not possible to represent the character *Control-?*, which is a meaningful input character under X, using '\C-'. It is not easy to change this, as various Lisp files refer to **DEL** in this way.

For representing control characters to be found in files or strings, we recommend the '^' syntax; for control characters in keyboard input, we prefer the 'C-' syntax. Which one you use does not affect the meaning of the program, but may guide the understanding of people who read it.

2.3.3.4 Meta-Character Syntax

A *meta character* is a character typed with the **META** modifier key. The integer that represents such a character has the 2^{27} bit set. We use high bits for this and other modifiers to make possible a wide range of basic character codes.

In a string, the 2^7 bit attached to an ASCII character indicates a meta character; thus, the meta characters that can fit in a string have codes in the range from 128 to 255, and are the meta versions of the ordinary ASCII characters. See Section 20.7.15 [Strings of Events], page 372, for details about **META**-handling in strings.

The read syntax for meta characters uses '\M-'. For example, '?\M-A' stands for *M-A*. You can use '\M-' together with octal character codes (see below), with '\C-', or with any other syntax for a character. Thus, you can write *M-A* as '?\M-A', or as '?\M-\101'. Likewise, you can write *C-M-b* as '?\M-\C-b', '?\C-\M-b', or '?\M-\002'.

2.3.3.5 Other Character Modifier Bits

The case of a graphic character is indicated by its character code; for example, ASCII distinguishes between the characters 'a' and 'A'. But ASCII has no way to represent whether a control character is upper case or lower case. Emacs uses the 2^{25} bit to indicate that the shift key was used in typing a control character. This distinction is possible only when you use X terminals or other special terminals; ordinary text terminals do not report the distinction. The Lisp syntax for the shift bit is '\S-'; thus, '?\C-\S-o' or '?\C-\S-O' represents the shifted-control-o character.

The X Window System defines three other modifier bits that can be set in a character: *hyper*, *super* and *alt*. The syntaxes for these bits are '\H-', '\s-' and '\A-'. (Case is significant in these prefixes.) Thus, '?\H-\M-\A-x' represents *Alt-Hyper-Meta-x*. (Note that '\s' with no following '-' represents the space character.) Numerically, the bit values are 2^{22} for alt, 2^{23} for super and 2^{24} for hyper.

2.3.4 Symbol Type

A *symbol* in GNU Emacs Lisp is an object with a name. The symbol name serves as the printed representation of the symbol. In ordinary Lisp use, with one single obarray (see Section 8.3 [Creating Symbols], page 117), a symbol's name is unique—no two symbols have the same name.

A symbol can serve as a variable, as a function name, or to hold a property list. Or it may serve only to be distinct from all other Lisp objects, so that its presence in a data structure may be recognized reliably. In a given context, usually only one of these uses is intended. But you can use one symbol in all of these ways, independently.

A symbol whose name starts with a colon (':') is called a *keyword symbol*. These symbols automatically act as constants, and are normally used only by comparing an unknown symbol with a few specific alternatives. See Section 11.2 [Constant Variables], page 157.

A symbol name can contain any characters whatever. Most symbol names are written with letters, digits, and the punctuation characters '-+=*/'. Such names require no special punctuation; the characters of the name suffice as long as the name does not look like a number. (If it does, write a '\' at the beginning of the name to force interpretation as a symbol.) The characters '_~!@$%^&:<>{}?' are less often used but also require no special punctuation. Any other characters may be included in a symbol's name by escaping them with a backslash. In contrast to its use in strings, however, a backslash in the name of a symbol simply quotes the single character that follows the backslash. For example, in a string, '\t' represents a tab character; in the name of a symbol, however, '\t' merely quotes the letter 't'. To have a symbol with a tab character in its name, you must actually use a tab (preceded with a backslash). But it's rare to do such a thing.

> **Common Lisp note:** In Common Lisp, lower case letters are always folded to upper case, unless they are explicitly escaped. In Emacs Lisp, upper case and lower case letters are distinct.

Here are several examples of symbol names. Note that the '+' in the fourth example is escaped to prevent it from being read as a number. This is not necessary in the sixth example because the rest of the name makes it invalid as a number.

```
foo                      ; A symbol named 'foo'.
FOO                      ; A symbol named 'FOO', different from 'foo'.
```

```
1+                      ; A symbol named '1+'
                        ;    (not '+1', which is an integer).
\+1                     ; A symbol named '+1'
                        ;    (not a very readable name).
\(*\ 1\ 2\)             ; A symbol named '(* 1 2)' (a worse name).
+-*/_~!@$%^&=:<>{}       ; A symbol named '+-*/_~!@$%^&=:<>{}'.
                        ;    These characters need not be escaped.
```

As an exception to the rule that a symbol's name serves as its printed representation, '##' is the printed representation for an interned symbol whose name is an empty string. Furthermore, '#:*foo*' is the printed representation for an uninterned symbol whose name is *foo*. (Normally, the Lisp reader interns all symbols; see Section 8.3 [Creating Symbols], page 117.)

2.3.5 Sequence Types

A *sequence* is a Lisp object that represents an ordered set of elements. There are two kinds of sequence in Emacs Lisp: *lists* and *arrays*.

Lists are the most commonly-used sequences. A list can hold elements of any type, and its length can be easily changed by adding or removing elements. See the next subsection for more about lists.

Arrays are fixed-length sequences. They are further subdivided into strings, vectors, char-tables and bool-vectors. Vectors can hold elements of any type, whereas string elements must be characters, and bool-vector elements must be t or nil. Char-tables are like vectors except that they are indexed by any valid character code. The characters in a string can have text properties like characters in a buffer (see Section 31.19 [Text Properties], page 732), but vectors do not support text properties, even when their elements happen to be characters.

Lists, strings and the other array types also share important similarities. For example, all have a length *l*, and all have elements which can be indexed from zero to *l* minus one. Several functions, called sequence functions, accept any kind of sequence. For example, the function **length** reports the length of any kind of sequence. See Chapter 6 [Sequences Arrays Vectors], page 89.

It is generally impossible to read the same sequence twice, since sequences are always created anew upon reading. If you read the read syntax for a sequence twice, you get two sequences with equal contents. There is one exception: the empty list () always stands for the same object, **nil**.

2.3.6 Cons Cell and List Types

A *cons cell* is an object that consists of two slots, called the CAR slot and the CDR slot. Each slot can *hold* any Lisp object. We also say that the CAR of this cons cell is whatever object its CAR slot currently holds, and likewise for the CDR.

A *list* is a series of cons cells, linked together so that the CDR slot of each cons cell holds either the next cons cell or the empty list. The empty list is actually the symbol **nil**. See Chapter 5 [Lists], page 67, for details. Because most cons cells are used as part of lists, we refer to any structure made out of cons cells as a *list structure*.

A note to C programmers: a Lisp list thus works as a *linked list* built up of cons cells. Because pointers in Lisp are implicit, we do not distinguish between a cons cell slot holding a value versus pointing to the value.

Because cons cells are so central to Lisp, we also have a word for an object which is not a cons cell. These objects are called *atoms*.

The read syntax and printed representation for lists are identical, and consist of a left parenthesis, an arbitrary number of elements, and a right parenthesis. Here are examples of lists:

```
(A 2 "A")            ; A list of three elements.
()                   ; A list of no elements (the empty list).
nil                  ; A list of no elements (the empty list).
("A ()")             ; A list of one element: the string "A ()".
(A ())               ; A list of two elements: A and the empty list.
(A nil)              ; Equivalent to the previous.
((A B C))            ; A list of one element
                     ;    (which is a list of three elements).
```

Upon reading, each object inside the parentheses becomes an element of the list. That is, a cons cell is made for each element. The CAR slot of the cons cell holds the element, and its CDR slot refers to the next cons cell of the list, which holds the next element in the list. The CDR slot of the last cons cell is set to hold nil.

The names CAR and CDR derive from the history of Lisp. The original Lisp implementation ran on an IBM 704 computer which divided words into two parts, the address and the decrement; CAR was an instruction to extract the contents of the address part of a register, and CDR an instruction to extract the contents of the decrement. By contrast, cons cells are named for the function **cons** that creates them, which in turn was named for its purpose, the construction of cells.

2.3.6.1 Drawing Lists as Box Diagrams

A list can be illustrated by a diagram in which the cons cells are shown as pairs of boxes, like dominoes. (The Lisp reader cannot read such an illustration; unlike the textual notation, which can be understood by both humans and computers, the box illustrations can be understood only by humans.) This picture represents the three-element list (**rose violet buttercup**):

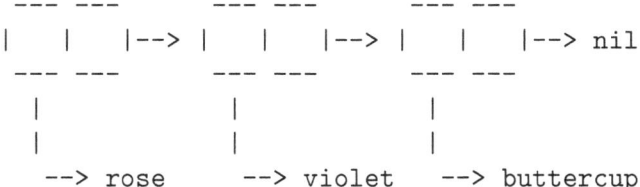

```
        --- ---         --- ---         --- ---
       |   |   |-->    |   |   |-->    |   |   |--> nil
        --- ---         --- ---         --- ---
         |               |               |
         |               |               |
         --> rose        --> violet      --> buttercup
```

In this diagram, each box represents a slot that can hold or refer to any Lisp object. Each pair of boxes represents a cons cell. Each arrow represents a reference to a Lisp object, either an atom or another cons cell.

In this example, the first box, which holds the CAR of the first cons cell, refers to or holds **rose** (a symbol). The second box, holding the CDR of the first cons cell, refers to the next pair of boxes, the second cons cell. The CAR of the second cons cell is `violet`, and its CDR is the third cons cell. The CDR of the third (and last) cons cell is `nil`.

Here is another diagram of the same list, `(rose violet buttercup)`, sketched in a different manner:

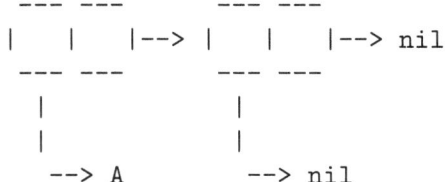

A list with no elements in it is the *empty list*; it is identical to the symbol `nil`. In other words, `nil` is both a symbol and a list.

Here is the list `(A ())`, or equivalently `(A nil)`, depicted with boxes and arrows:

Here is a more complex illustration, showing the three-element list, `((pine needles) oak maple)`, the first element of which is a two-element list:

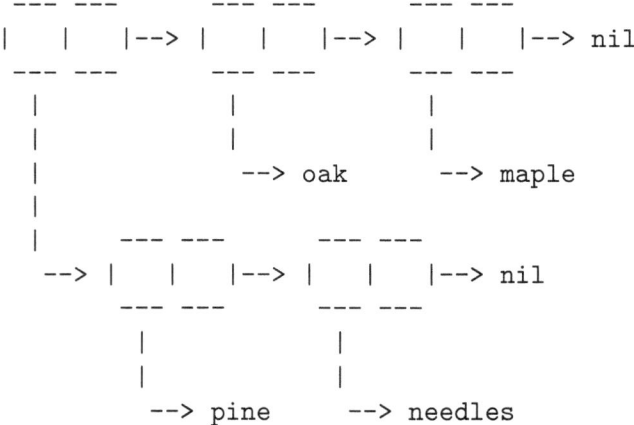

The same list represented in the second box notation looks like this:

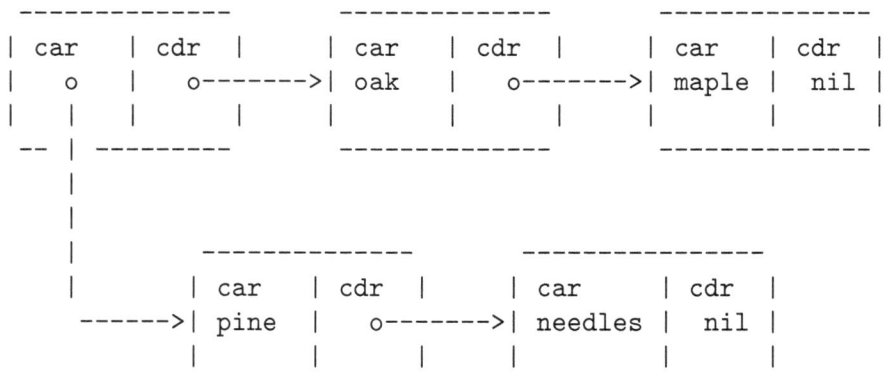

2.3.6.2 Dotted Pair Notation

Dotted pair notation is a general syntax for cons cells that represents the CAR and CDR explicitly. In this syntax, `(a . b)` stands for a cons cell whose CAR is the object *a* and whose CDR is the object *b*. Dotted pair notation is more general than list syntax because the CDR does not have to be a list. However, it is more cumbersome in cases where list syntax would work. In dotted pair notation, the list '`(1 2 3)`' is written as '`(1 . (2 . (3 . nil)))`'. For `nil`-terminated lists, you can use either notation, but list notation is usually clearer and more convenient. When printing a list, the dotted pair notation is only used if the CDR of a cons cell is not a list.

Here's an example using boxes to illustrate dotted pair notation. This example shows the pair (`rose . violet`):

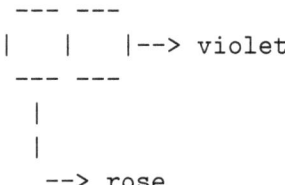

You can combine dotted pair notation with list notation to represent conveniently a chain of cons cells with a non-`nil` final CDR. You write a dot after the last element of the list, followed by the CDR of the final cons cell. For example, (`rose violet . buttercup`) is equivalent to (`rose . (violet . buttercup)`). The object looks like this:

The syntax (`rose . violet . buttercup`) is invalid because there is nothing that it could mean. If anything, it would say to put `buttercup` in the CDR of a cons cell whose CDR is already used for `violet`.

The list (`rose violet`) is equivalent to (`rose . (violet)`), and looks like this:

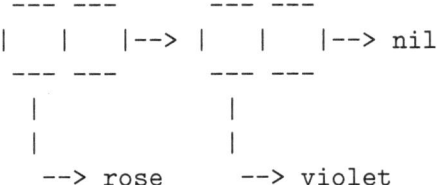

Similarly, the three-element list (`rose violet buttercup`) is equivalent to (`rose . (violet . (buttercup)))`.

2.3.6.3 Association List Type

An *association list* or *alist* is a specially-constructed list whose elements are cons cells. In each element, the CAR is considered a *key*, and the CDR is considered an *associated value*. (In some cases, the associated value is stored in the CAR of the CDR.) Association lists are often used as stacks, since it is easy to add or remove associations at the front of the list.

For example,

```
(setq alist-of-colors
      '((rose . red) (lily . white) (buttercup . yellow)))
```

sets the variable `alist-of-colors` to an alist of three elements. In the first element, `rose` is the key and `red` is the value.

See Section 5.8 [Association Lists], page 83, for a further explanation of alists and for functions that work on alists. See Chapter 7 [Hash Tables], page 110, for another kind of lookup table, which is much faster for handling a large number of keys.

2.3.7 Array Type

An *array* is composed of an arbitrary number of slots for holding or referring to other Lisp objects, arranged in a contiguous block of memory. Accessing any element of an array takes approximately the same amount of time. In contrast, accessing an element of a list requires time proportional to the position of the element in the list. (Elements at the end of a list take longer to access than elements at the beginning of a list.)

Emacs defines four types of array: strings, vectors, bool-vectors, and char-tables.

A string is an array of characters and a vector is an array of arbitrary objects. A bool-vector can hold only `t` or `nil`. These kinds of array may have any length up to the largest integer. Char-tables are sparse arrays indexed by any valid character code; they can hold arbitrary objects.

The first element of an array has index zero, the second element has index 1, and so on. This is called *zero-origin* indexing. For example, an array of four elements has indices 0, 1, 2, and 3. The largest possible index value is one less than the length of the array. Once an array is created, its length is fixed.

All Emacs Lisp arrays are one-dimensional. (Most other programming languages support multidimensional arrays, but they are not essential; you can get the same effect with nested one-dimensional arrays.) Each type of array has its own read syntax; see the following sections for details.

The array type is a subset of the sequence type, and contains the string type, the vector type, the bool-vector type, and the char-table type.

2.3.8 String Type

A *string* is an array of characters. Strings are used for many purposes in Emacs, as can be expected in a text editor; for example, as the names of Lisp symbols, as messages for the user, and to represent text extracted from buffers. Strings in Lisp are constants: evaluation of a string returns the same string.

See Chapter 4 [Strings and Characters], page 49, for functions that operate on strings.

2.3.8.1 Syntax for Strings

The read syntax for a string is a double-quote, an arbitrary number of characters, and another double-quote, `"like this"`. To include a double-quote in a string, precede it with a backslash; thus, `"\""` is a string containing just one double-quote character. Likewise, you can include a backslash by preceding it with another backslash, like this: `"this \\ is a single embedded backslash"`.

The newline character is not special in the read syntax for strings; if you write a new line between the double-quotes, it becomes a character in the string. But an escaped newline—one that is preceded by '\'—does not become part of the string; i.e., the Lisp reader ignores an escaped newline while reading a string. An escaped space '\ ' is likewise ignored.

```
"It is useful to include newlines
in documentation strings,
but the newline is \
ignored if escaped."
     ⇒ "It is useful to include newlines
in documentation strings,
but the newline is ignored if escaped."
```

2.3.8.2 Non-ASCII Characters in Strings

There are two text representations for non-ASCII characters in Emacs strings: multibyte and unibyte (see Section 32.1 [Text Representations], page 761). Roughly speaking, unibyte strings store raw bytes, while multibyte strings store human-readable text. Each character in a unibyte string is a byte, i.e., its value is between 0 and 255. By contrast, each character in a multibyte string may have a value between 0 to 4194303 (see Section 2.3.3 [Character Type], page 10). In both cases, characters above 127 are non-ASCII.

You can include a non-ASCII character in a string constant by writing it literally. If the string constant is read from a multibyte source, such as a multibyte buffer or string, or a file that would be visited as multibyte, then Emacs reads each non-ASCII character as a multibyte character and automatically makes the string a multibyte string. If the string constant is read from a unibyte source, then Emacs reads the non-ASCII character as unibyte, and makes the string unibyte.

Instead of writing a character literally into a multibyte string, you can write it as its character code using an escape sequence. See Section 2.3.3.2 [General Escape Syntax], page 11, for details about escape sequences.

If you use any Unicode-style escape sequence '\uNNNN' or '\UOONNNNNN' in a string constant (even for an ASCII character), Emacs automatically assumes that it is multibyte.

You can also use hexadecimal escape sequences ('\xn') and octal escape sequences ('\n') in string constants. **But beware:** If a string constant contains hexadecimal or octal escape sequences, and these escape sequences all specify unibyte characters (i.e., less than 256), and there are no other literal non-ASCII characters or Unicode-style escape sequences in the string, then Emacs automatically assumes that it is a unibyte string. That is to say, it assumes that all non-ASCII characters occurring in the string are 8-bit raw bytes.

In hexadecimal and octal escape sequences, the escaped character code may contain a variable number of digits, so the first subsequent character which is not a valid hexadecimal or octal digit terminates the escape sequence. If the next character in a string could be interpreted as a hexadecimal or octal digit, write '\ ' (backslash and space) to terminate the escape sequence. For example, '\xe0\ ' represents one character, 'a' with grave accent. '\ ' in a string constant is just like backslash-newline; it does not contribute any character to the string, but it does terminate any preceding hex escape.

2.3.8.3 Nonprinting Characters in Strings

You can use the same backslash escape-sequences in a string constant as in character literals (but do not use the question mark that begins a character constant). For example, you can write a string containing the nonprinting characters tab and *C-a*, with commas and spaces between them, like this: `"\t, \C-a"`. See Section 2.3.3 [Character Type], page 10, for a description of the read syntax for characters.

However, not all of the characters you can write with backslash escape-sequences are valid in strings. The only control characters that a string can hold are the ASCII control characters. Strings do not distinguish case in ASCII control characters.

Properly speaking, strings cannot hold meta characters; but when a string is to be used as a key sequence, there is a special convention that provides a way to represent meta versions of ASCII characters in a string. If you use the '\M-' syntax to indicate a meta character in a string constant, this sets the 2^7 bit of the character in the string. If the string is used in **define-key** or **lookup-key**, this numeric code is translated into the equivalent meta character. See Section 2.3.3 [Character Type], page 10.

Strings cannot hold characters that have the hyper, super, or alt modifiers.

2.3.8.4 Text Properties in Strings

A string can hold properties for the characters it contains, in addition to the characters themselves. This enables programs that copy text between strings and buffers to copy the text's properties with no special effort. See Section 31.19 [Text Properties], page 732, for an explanation of what text properties mean. Strings with text properties use a special read and print syntax:

```
#("characters" property-data...)
```

where *property-data* consists of zero or more elements, in groups of three as follows:

```
beg end plist
```

The elements *beg* and *end* are integers, and together specify a range of indices in the string; *plist* is the property list for that range. For example,

```
#("foo bar" 0 3 (face bold) 3 4 nil 4 7 (face italic))
```

represents a string whose textual contents are 'foo bar', in which the first three characters have a **face** property with value **bold**, and the last three have a **face** property with value **italic**. (The fourth character has no text properties, so its property list is **nil**. It is not actually necessary to mention ranges with **nil** as the property list, since any characters not mentioned in any range will default to having no properties.)

2.3.9 Vector Type

A *vector* is a one-dimensional array of elements of any type. It takes a constant amount of time to access any element of a vector. (In a list, the access time of an element is proportional to the distance of the element from the beginning of the list.)

The printed representation of a vector consists of a left square bracket, the elements, and a right square bracket. This is also the read syntax. Like numbers and strings, vectors are considered constants for evaluation.

```
[1 "two" (three)]        ; A vector of three elements.
     ⇒ [1 "two" (three)]
```

See Section 6.4 [Vectors], page 102, for functions that work with vectors.

2.3.10 Char-Table Type

A *char-table* is a one-dimensional array of elements of any type, indexed by character codes. Char-tables have certain extra features to make them more useful for many jobs that involve assigning information to character codes—for example, a char-table can have a parent to inherit from, a default value, and a small number of extra slots to use for special purposes. A char-table can also specify a single value for a whole character set.

The printed representation of a char-table is like a vector except that there is an extra '#^' at the beginning.[1]

See Section 6.6 [Char-Tables], page 104, for special functions to operate on char-tables. Uses of char-tables include:

- Case tables (see Section 4.9 [Case Tables], page 64).
- Character category tables (see Section 34.8 [Categories], page 829).
- Display tables (see Section 37.22.2 [Display Tables], page 974).
- Syntax tables (see Chapter 34 [Syntax Tables], page 816).

2.3.11 Bool-Vector Type

A *bool-vector* is a one-dimensional array whose elements must be `t` or `nil`.

The printed representation of a bool-vector is like a string, except that it begins with '#&' followed by the length. The string constant that follows actually specifies the contents of the bool-vector as a bitmap—each character in the string contains 8 bits, which specify the next 8 elements of the bool-vector (1 stands for `t`, and 0 for `nil`). The least significant bits of the character correspond to the lowest indices in the bool-vector.

```
(make-bool-vector 3 t)
     ⇒ #&3"^G"
(make-bool-vector 3 nil)
     ⇒ #&3"^@"
```

These results make sense, because the binary code for 'C-g' is 111 and 'C-@' is the character with code 0.

If the length is not a multiple of 8, the printed representation shows extra elements, but these extras really make no difference. For instance, in the next example, the two bool-vectors are equal, because only the first 3 bits are used:

```
(equal #&3"\377" #&3"\007")
     ⇒ t
```

2.3.12 Hash Table Type

A hash table is a very fast kind of lookup table, somewhat like an alist in that it maps keys to corresponding values, but much faster. The printed representation of a hash table specifies its properties and contents, like this:

```
(make-hash-table)
     ⇒ #s(hash-table size 65 test eql rehash-size 1.5
```

---

[1] You may also encounter '#^^', used for sub-char-tables.

```
rehash-threshold 0.8 data ())
```
See Chapter 7 [Hash Tables], page 110, for more information about hash tables.

2.3.13 Function Type

Lisp functions are executable code, just like functions in other programming languages. In Lisp, unlike most languages, functions are also Lisp objects. A non-compiled function in Lisp is a lambda expression: that is, a list whose first element is the symbol `lambda` (see Section 12.2 [Lambda Expressions], page 188).

In most programming languages, it is impossible to have a function without a name. In Lisp, a function has no intrinsic name. A lambda expression can be called as a function even though it has no name; to emphasize this, we also call it an *anonymous function* (see Section 12.7 [Anonymous Functions], page 198). A named function in Lisp is just a symbol with a valid function in its function cell (see Section 12.4 [Defining Functions], page 192).

Most of the time, functions are called when their names are written in Lisp expressions in Lisp programs. However, you can construct or obtain a function object at run time and then call it with the primitive functions `funcall` and `apply`. See Section 12.5 [Calling Functions], page 194.

2.3.14 Macro Type

A *Lisp macro* is a user-defined construct that extends the Lisp language. It is represented as an object much like a function, but with different argument-passing semantics. A Lisp macro has the form of a list whose first element is the symbol `macro` and whose CDR is a Lisp function object, including the `lambda` symbol.

Lisp macro objects are usually defined with the built-in `defmacro` macro, but any list that begins with `macro` is a macro as far as Emacs is concerned. See Chapter 13 [Macros], page 217, for an explanation of how to write a macro.

Warning: Lisp macros and keyboard macros (see Section 20.16 [Keyboard Macros], page 389) are entirely different things. When we use the word "macro" without qualification, we mean a Lisp macro, not a keyboard macro.

2.3.15 Primitive Function Type

A *primitive function* is a function callable from Lisp but written in the C programming language. Primitive functions are also called *subrs* or *built-in functions*. (The word "subr" is derived from "subroutine".) Most primitive functions evaluate all their arguments when they are called. A primitive function that does not evaluate all its arguments is called a *special form* (see Section 9.1.7 [Special Forms], page 128).

It does not matter to the caller of a function whether the function is primitive. However, this does matter if you try to redefine a primitive with a function written in Lisp. The reason is that the primitive function may be called directly from C code. Calls to the redefined function from Lisp will use the new definition, but calls from C code may still use the built-in definition. Therefore, **we discourage redefinition of primitive functions**.

The term *function* refers to all Emacs functions, whether written in Lisp or C. See Section 2.3.13 [Function Type], page 22, for information about the functions written in Lisp.

Primitive functions have no read syntax and print in hash notation with the name of the subroutine.

```
(symbol-function 'car)              ; Access the function cell
                                    ;    of the symbol.
        ⇒ #<subr car>
(subrp (symbol-function 'car))      ; Is this a primitive function?
        ⇒ t                         ; Yes.
```

2.3.16 Byte-Code Function Type

Byte-code function objects are produced by byte-compiling Lisp code (see Chapter 16 [Byte Compilation], page 260). Internally, a byte-code function object is much like a vector; however, the evaluator handles this data type specially when it appears in a function call. See Section 16.7 [Byte-Code Objects], page 266.

The printed representation and read syntax for a byte-code function object is like that for a vector, with an additional '#' before the opening '['.

2.3.17 Autoload Type

An *autoload object* is a list whose first element is the symbol `autoload`. It is stored as the function definition of a symbol, where it serves as a placeholder for the real definition. The autoload object says that the real definition is found in a file of Lisp code that should be loaded when necessary. It contains the name of the file, plus some other information about the real definition.

After the file has been loaded, the symbol should have a new function definition that is not an autoload object. The new definition is then called as if it had been there to begin with. From the user's point of view, the function call works as expected, using the function definition in the loaded file.

An autoload object is usually created with the function `autoload`, which stores the object in the function cell of a symbol. See Section 15.5 [Autoload], page 249, for more details.

2.3.18 Finalizer Type

A *finalizer object* helps Lisp code clean up after objects that are no longer needed. A finalizer holds a Lisp function object. When a finalizer object becomes unreachable after a garbage collection pass, Emacs calls the finalizer's associated function object. When deciding whether a finalizer is reachable, Emacs does not count references from finalizer objects themselves, allowing you to use finalizers without having to worry about accidentally capturing references to finalized objects themselves.

Errors in finalizers are printed to `*Messages*`. Emacs runs a given finalizer object's associated function exactly once, even if that function fails.

make-finalizer *function*   [Function]
> Make a finalizer that will run *function*. *function* will be called after garbage collection when the returned finalizer object becomes unreachable. If the finalizer object is reachable only through references from finalizer objects, it does not count as reachable for the purpose of deciding whether to run *function*. *function* will be run once per finalizer object.

2.4 Editing Types

The types in the previous section are used for general programming purposes, and most of them are common to most Lisp dialects. Emacs Lisp provides several additional data types for purposes connected with editing.

2.4.1 Buffer Type

A *buffer* is an object that holds text that can be edited (see Chapter 26 [Buffers], page 550). Most buffers hold the contents of a disk file (see Chapter 24 [Files], page 495) so they can be edited, but some are used for other purposes. Most buffers are also meant to be seen by the user, and therefore displayed, at some time, in a window (see Chapter 27 [Windows], page 567). But a buffer need not be displayed in any window. Each buffer has a designated position called *point* (see Chapter 29 [Positions], page 673); most editing commands act on the contents of the current buffer in the neighborhood of point. At any time, one buffer is the *current buffer*.

The contents of a buffer are much like a string, but buffers are not used like strings in Emacs Lisp, and the available operations are different. For example, you can insert text efficiently into an existing buffer, altering the buffer's contents, whereas inserting text into a string requires concatenating substrings, and the result is an entirely new string object.

Many of the standard Emacs functions manipulate or test the characters in the current buffer; a whole chapter in this manual is devoted to describing these functions (see Chapter 31 [Text], page 696).

Several other data structures are associated with each buffer:
- a local syntax table (see Chapter 34 [Syntax Tables], page 816);
- a local keymap (see Chapter 21 [Keymaps], page 391); and,
- a list of buffer-local variable bindings (see Section 11.10 [Buffer-Local Variables], page 171).
- overlays (see Section 37.9 [Overlays], page 904).
- text properties for the text in the buffer (see Section 31.19 [Text Properties], page 732).

The local keymap and variable list contain entries that individually override global bindings or values. These are used to customize the behavior of programs in different buffers, without actually changing the programs.

A buffer may be *indirect*, which means it shares the text of another buffer, but presents it differently. See Section 26.11 [Indirect Buffers], page 564.

Buffers have no read syntax. They print in hash notation, showing the buffer name.

```
(current-buffer)
     ⇒ #<buffer objects.texi>
```

2.4.2 Marker Type

A *marker* denotes a position in a specific buffer. Markers therefore have two components: one for the buffer, and one for the position. Changes in the buffer's text automatically relocate the position value as necessary to ensure that the marker always points between the same two characters in the buffer.

Markers have no read syntax. They print in hash notation, giving the current character position and the name of the buffer.

```
(point-marker)
     ⇒ #<marker at 10779 in objects.texi>
```

See Chapter 30 [Markers], page 687, for information on how to test, create, copy, and move markers.

2.4.3 Window Type

A *window* describes the portion of the terminal screen that Emacs uses to display a buffer. Every window has one associated buffer, whose contents appear in the window. By contrast, a given buffer may appear in one window, no window, or several windows.

Though many windows may exist simultaneously, at any time one window is designated the *selected window*. This is the window where the cursor is (usually) displayed when Emacs is ready for a command. The selected window usually displays the current buffer (see Section 26.2 [Current Buffer], page 550), but this is not necessarily the case.

Windows are grouped on the screen into frames; each window belongs to one and only one frame. See Section 2.4.4 [Frame Type], page 25.

Windows have no read syntax. They print in hash notation, giving the window number and the name of the buffer being displayed. The window numbers exist to identify windows uniquely, since the buffer displayed in any given window can change frequently.

```
(selected-window)
     ⇒ #<window 1 on objects.texi>
```

See Chapter 27 [Windows], page 567, for a description of the functions that work on windows.

2.4.4 Frame Type

A *frame* is a screen area that contains one or more Emacs windows; we also use the term "frame" to refer to the Lisp object that Emacs uses to refer to the screen area.

Frames have no read syntax. They print in hash notation, giving the frame's title, plus its address in core (useful to identify the frame uniquely).

```
(selected-frame)
     ⇒ #<frame emacs@psilocin.gnu.org 0xdac80>
```

See Chapter 28 [Frames], page 630, for a description of the functions that work on frames.

2.4.5 Terminal Type

A *terminal* is a device capable of displaying one or more Emacs frames (see Section 2.4.4 [Frame Type], page 25).

Terminals have no read syntax. They print in hash notation giving the terminal's ordinal number and its TTY device file name.

```
(get-device-terminal nil)
     ⇒ #<terminal 1 on /dev/tty>
```

2.4.6 Window Configuration Type

A *window configuration* stores information about the positions, sizes, and contents of the windows in a frame, so you can recreate the same arrangement of windows later.

Window configurations do not have a read syntax; their print syntax looks like '`#<window-configuration>`'. See Section 27.25 [Window Configurations], page 623, for a description of several functions related to window configurations.

2.4.7 Frame Configuration Type

A *frame configuration* stores information about the positions, sizes, and contents of the windows in all frames. It is not a primitive type—it is actually a list whose CAR is `frame-configuration` and whose CDR is an alist. Each alist element describes one frame, which appears as the CAR of that element.

See Section 28.13 [Frame Configurations], page 660, for a description of several functions related to frame configurations.

2.4.8 Process Type

The word *process* usually means a running program. Emacs itself runs in a process of this sort. However, in Emacs Lisp, a process is a Lisp object that designates a subprocess created by the Emacs process. Programs such as shells, GDB, ftp, and compilers, running in subprocesses of Emacs, extend the capabilities of Emacs. An Emacs subprocess takes textual input from Emacs and returns textual output to Emacs for further manipulation. Emacs can also send signals to the subprocess.

Process objects have no read syntax. They print in hash notation, giving the name of the process:

```
(process-list)
     ⇒ (#<process shell>)
```

See Chapter 36 [Processes], page 839, for information about functions that create, delete, return information about, send input or signals to, and receive output from processes.

2.4.9 Stream Type

A *stream* is an object that can be used as a source or sink for characters—either to supply characters for input or to accept them as output. Many different types can be used this way: markers, buffers, strings, and functions. Most often, input streams (character sources) obtain characters from the keyboard, a buffer, or a file, and output streams (character sinks) send characters to a buffer, such as a `*Help*` buffer, or to the echo area.

The object `nil`, in addition to its other meanings, may be used as a stream. It stands for the value of the variable `standard-input` or `standard-output`. Also, the object `t` as a stream specifies input using the minibuffer (see Chapter 19 [Minibuffers], page 313) or output in the echo area (see Section 37.4 [The Echo Area], page 888).

Streams have no special printed representation or read syntax, and print as whatever primitive type they are.

See Chapter 18 [Read and Print], page 302, for a description of functions related to streams, including parsing and printing functions.

2.4.10 Keymap Type

A *keymap* maps keys typed by the user to commands. This mapping controls how the user's command input is executed. A keymap is actually a list whose CAR is the symbol **keymap**.

See Chapter 21 [Keymaps], page 391, for information about creating keymaps, handling prefix keys, local as well as global keymaps, and changing key bindings.

2.4.11 Overlay Type

An *overlay* specifies properties that apply to a part of a buffer. Each overlay applies to a specified range of the buffer, and contains a property list (a list whose elements are alternating property names and values). Overlay properties are used to present parts of the buffer temporarily in a different display style. Overlays have no read syntax, and print in hash notation, giving the buffer name and range of positions.

See Section 37.9 [Overlays], page 904, for information on how you can create and use overlays.

2.4.12 Font Type

A *font* specifies how to display text on a graphical terminal. There are actually three separate font types—*font objects*, *font specs*, and *font entities*—each of which has slightly different properties. None of them have a read syntax; their print syntax looks like '`#<font-object>`', '`#<font-spec>`', and '`#<font-entity>`' respectively. See Section 37.12.12 [Low-Level Font], page 932, for a description of these Lisp objects.

2.5 Read Syntax for Circular Objects

To represent shared or circular structures within a complex of Lisp objects, you can use the reader constructs '`#n=`' and '`#n#`'.

Use `#n=` before an object to label it for later reference; subsequently, you can use `#n#` to refer the same object in another place. Here, n is some integer. For example, here is how to make a list in which the first element recurs as the third element:

```
(#1=(a) b #1#)
```

This differs from ordinary syntax such as this

```
((a) b (a))
```

which would result in a list whose first and third elements look alike but are not the same Lisp object. This shows the difference:

```
(prog1 nil
  (setq x '(#1=(a) b #1#)))
(eq (nth 0 x) (nth 2 x))
     ⇒ t
(setq x '((a) b (a)))
(eq (nth 0 x) (nth 2 x))
     ⇒ nil
```

You can also use the same syntax to make a circular structure, which appears as an element within itself. Here is an example:

```
#1=(a #1#)
```

This makes a list whose second element is the list itself. Here's how you can see that it really works:

```
(prog1 nil
  (setq x '#1=(a #1#)))
(eq x (cadr x))
    ⇒ t
```

The Lisp printer can produce this syntax to record circular and shared structure in a Lisp object, if you bind the variable `print-circle` to a non-`nil` value. See Section 18.6 [Output Variables], page 310.

2.6 Type Predicates

The Emacs Lisp interpreter itself does not perform type checking on the actual arguments passed to functions when they are called. It could not do so, since function arguments in Lisp do not have declared data types, as they do in other programming languages. It is therefore up to the individual function to test whether each actual argument belongs to a type that the function can use.

All built-in functions do check the types of their actual arguments when appropriate, and signal a `wrong-type-argument` error if an argument is of the wrong type. For example, here is what happens if you pass an argument to + that it cannot handle:

```
(+ 2 'a)
```
        `error`   **Wrong type argument: number-or-marker-p, a**

If you want your program to handle different types differently, you must do explicit type checking. The most common way to check the type of an object is to call a *type predicate* function. Emacs has a type predicate for each type, as well as some predicates for combinations of types.

A type predicate function takes one argument; it returns `t` if the argument belongs to the appropriate type, and `nil` otherwise. Following a general Lisp convention for predicate functions, most type predicates' names end with 'p'.

Here is an example which uses the predicates `listp` to check for a list and `symbolp` to check for a symbol.

```
(defun add-on (x)
  (cond ((symbolp x)
          ;; If X is a symbol, put it on LIST.
          (setq list (cons x list)))
         ((listp x)
          ;; If X is a list, add its elements to LIST.
          (setq list (append x list)))
         (t
          ;; We handle only symbols and lists.
          (error "Invalid argument %s in add-on" x))))
```

Here is a table of predefined type predicates, in alphabetical order, with references to further information.

`atom`   See Section 5.2 [List-related Predicates], page 67.

`arrayp`   See Section 6.3 [Array Functions], page 101.

`bool-vector-p`
         See Section 6.7 [Bool-Vectors], page 106.

`bufferp`   See Section 26.1 [Buffer Basics], page 550.

`byte-code-function-p`
         See Section 2.3.16 [Byte-Code Type], page 23.

`case-table-p`
         See Section 4.9 [Case Tables], page 64.

`char-or-string-p`
         See Section 4.2 [Predicates for Strings], page 50.

`char-table-p`
         See Section 6.6 [Char-Tables], page 104.

`commandp`   See Section 20.3 [Interactive Call], page 352.

`consp`   See Section 5.2 [List-related Predicates], page 67.

`custom-variable-p`
         See Section 14.3 [Variable Definitions], page 228.

`floatp`   See Section 3.3 [Predicates on Numbers], page 36.

`fontp`   See Section 37.12.12 [Low-Level Font], page 932.

`frame-configuration-p`
         See Section 28.13 [Frame Configurations], page 660.

`frame-live-p`
         See Section 28.7 [Deleting Frames], page 655.

`framep`   See Chapter 28 [Frames], page 630.

`functionp`
         See Chapter 12 [Functions], page 186.

`hash-table-p`
         See Section 7.4 [Other Hash], page 114.

`integer-or-marker-p`
         See Section 30.2 [Predicates on Markers], page 688.

`integerp`   See Section 3.3 [Predicates on Numbers], page 36.

`keymapp`   See Section 21.4 [Creating Keymaps], page 394.

`keywordp`   See Section 11.2 [Constant Variables], page 157.

`listp`   See Section 5.2 [List-related Predicates], page 67.

`markerp`   See Section 30.2 [Predicates on Markers], page 688.

`wholenump`
         See Section 3.3 [Predicates on Numbers], page 36.

`nlistp`   See Section 5.2 [List-related Predicates], page 67.

`numberp`   See Section 3.3 [Predicates on Numbers], page 36.

`number-or-marker-p`
               See Section 30.2 [Predicates on Markers], page 688.

`overlayp`   See Section 37.9 [Overlays], page 904.

`processp`   See Chapter 36 [Processes], page 839.

`sequencep`
               See Section 6.1 [Sequence Functions], page 89.

`stringp`   See Section 4.2 [Predicates for Strings], page 50.

`subrp`   See Section 12.9 [Function Cells], page 202.

`symbolp`   See Chapter 8 [Symbols], page 115.

`syntax-table-p`
               See Chapter 34 [Syntax Tables], page 816.

`vectorp`   See Section 6.4 [Vectors], page 102.

`window-configuration-p`
               See Section 27.25 [Window Configurations], page 623.

`window-live-p`
               See Section 27.7 [Deleting Windows], page 584.

`windowp`   See Section 27.1 [Basic Windows], page 567.

`booleanp`   See Section 1.3.2 [nil and t], page 2.

`string-or-null-p`
               See Section 4.2 [Predicates for Strings], page 50.

The most general way to check the type of an object is to call the function `type-of`. Recall that each object belongs to one and only one primitive type; `type-of` tells you which one (see Chapter 2 [Lisp Data Types], page 8). But `type-of` knows nothing about non-primitive types. In most cases, it is more convenient to use type predicates than `type-of`.

`type-of` *object*   [Function]
     This function returns a symbol naming the primitive type of *object*. The value is one of the symbols `bool-vector`, `buffer`, `char-table`, `compiled-function`, `cons`, `finalizer`, `float`, `font-entity`, `font-object`, `font-spec`, `frame`, `hash-table`, `integer`, `marker`, `overlay`, `process`, `string`, `subr`, `symbol`, `vector`, `window`, or `window-configuration`.

```
(type-of 1)
     ⇒ integer
(type-of 'nil)
     ⇒ symbol
(type-of '())    ; () is nil.
     ⇒ symbol
(type-of '(x))
     ⇒ cons
```

2.7 Equality Predicates

Here we describe functions that test for equality between two objects. Other functions test equality of contents between objects of specific types, e.g., strings. For these predicates, see the appropriate chapter describing the data type.

eq *object1 object2*   [Function]

This function returns **t** if *object1* and *object2* are the same object, and **nil** otherwise.

If *object1* and *object2* are integers with the same value, they are considered to be the same object (i.e., **eq** returns **t**). If *object1* and *object2* are symbols with the same name, they are normally the same object—but see Section 8.3 [Creating Symbols], page 117, for exceptions. For other types (e.g., lists, vectors, strings), two arguments with the same contents or elements are not necessarily **eq** to each other: they are **eq** only if they are the same object, meaning that a change in the contents of one will be reflected by the same change in the contents of the other.

```
(eq 'foo 'foo)
    ⇒ t

(eq 456 456)
    ⇒ t

(eq "asdf" "asdf")
    ⇒ nil

(eq "" "")
    ⇒ t
;; This exception occurs because Emacs Lisp
;; makes just one multibyte empty string, to save space.

(eq '(1 (2 (3))) '(1 (2 (3))))
    ⇒ nil

(setq foo '(1 (2 (3))))
    ⇒ (1 (2 (3)))
(eq foo foo)
    ⇒ t
(eq foo '(1 (2 (3))))
    ⇒ nil

(eq [(1 2) 3] [(1 2) 3])
    ⇒ nil

(eq (point-marker) (point-marker))
    ⇒ nil
```

The **make-symbol** function returns an uninterned symbol, distinct from the symbol that is used if you write the name in a Lisp expression. Distinct symbols with the same name are not **eq**. See Section 8.3 [Creating Symbols], page 117.

```
(eq (make-symbol "foo") 'foo)
    ⇒ nil
```

equal *object1 object2*   [Function]

This function returns `t` if *object1* and *object2* have equal components, and `nil` otherwise. Whereas `eq` tests if its arguments are the same object, `equal` looks inside nonidentical arguments to see if their elements or contents are the same. So, if two objects are `eq`, they are `equal`, but the converse is not always true.

```
(equal 'foo 'foo)
    ⇒ t

(equal 456 456)
    ⇒ t

(equal "asdf" "asdf")
    ⇒ t
(eq "asdf" "asdf")
    ⇒ nil

(equal '(1 (2 (3))) '(1 (2 (3))))
    ⇒ t
(eq '(1 (2 (3))) '(1 (2 (3))))
    ⇒ nil

(equal [(1 2) 3] [(1 2) 3])
    ⇒ t
(eq [(1 2) 3] [(1 2) 3])
    ⇒ nil

(equal (point-marker) (point-marker))
    ⇒ t

(eq (point-marker) (point-marker))
    ⇒ nil
```

Comparison of strings is case-sensitive, but does not take account of text properties—it compares only the characters in the strings. See Section 31.19 [Text Properties], page 732. Use `equal-including-properties` to also compare text properties. For technical reasons, a unibyte string and a multibyte string are `equal` if and only if they contain the same sequence of character codes and all these codes are either in the range 0 through 127 (ASCII) or 160 through 255 (`eight-bit-graphic`). (see Section 32.1 [Text Representations], page 761).

```
(equal "asdf" "ASDF")
    ⇒ nil
```

However, two distinct buffers are never considered `equal`, even if their textual contents are the same.

The test for equality is implemented recursively; for example, given two cons cells x and y, (equal x y) returns t if and only if both the expressions below return t:

    (equal (car x) (car y))
    (equal (cdr x) (cdr y))

Because of this recursive method, circular lists may therefore cause infinite recursion (leading to an error).

equal-including-properties *object1 object2*   [Function]

This function behaves like equal in all cases but also requires that for two strings to be equal, they have the same text properties.

        (equal "asdf" (propertize "asdf" 'asdf t))
            ⇒ t
        (equal-including-properties "asdf"
                                    (propertize "asdf" 'asdf t))

            ⇒ nil

3 Numbers

GNU Emacs supports two numeric data types: *integers* and *floating-point numbers*. Integers are whole numbers such as −3, 0, 7, 13, and 511. Floating-point numbers are numbers with fractional parts, such as −4.5, 0.0, and 2.71828. They can also be expressed in exponential notation: '`1.5e2`' is the same as '`150.0`'; here, '`e2`' stands for ten to the second power, and that is multiplied by 1.5. Integer computations are exact, though they may overflow. Floating-point computations often involve rounding errors, as the numbers have a fixed amount of precision.

3.1 Integer Basics

The range of values for an integer depends on the machine. The minimum range is −536,870,912 to 536,870,911 (30 bits; i.e., -2^{29} to $2^{29} - 1$), but many machines provide a wider range. Many examples in this chapter assume the minimum integer width of 30 bits.

The Lisp reader reads an integer as a sequence of digits with optional initial sign and optional final period. An integer that is out of the Emacs range is treated as a floating-point number.

```
1                       ; The integer 1.
1.                      ; The integer 1.
+1                      ; Also the integer 1.
-1                      ; The integer −1.
9000000000000000000
                        ; The floating-point number 9e18.
0                       ; The integer 0.
-0                      ; The integer 0.
```

The syntax for integers in bases other than 10 uses '`#`' followed by a letter that specifies the radix: '`b`' for binary, '`o`' for octal, '`x`' for hex, or '`radix r`' to specify radix *radix*. Case is not significant for the letter that specifies the radix. Thus, '`#b`*integer*' reads *integer* in binary, and '`#`*radix*`r`*integer*' reads *integer* in radix *radix*. Allowed values of *radix* run from 2 to 36. For example:

```
#b101100 ⇒ 44
#o54 ⇒ 44
#x2c ⇒ 44
#24r1k ⇒ 44
```

To understand how various functions work on integers, especially the bitwise operators (see Section 3.8 [Bitwise Operations], page 43), it is often helpful to view the numbers in their binary form.

In 30-bit binary, the decimal integer 5 looks like this:

```
0000...000101 (30 bits total)
```

(The '`...`' stands for enough bits to fill out a 30-bit word; in this case, '`...`' stands for twenty 0 bits. Later examples also use the '`...`' notation to make binary integers easier to read.)

The integer −1 looks like this:

```
1111...111111 (30 bits total)
```

−1 is represented as 30 ones. (This is called *two's complement* notation.)

Subtracting 4 from −1 returns the negative integer −5. In binary, the decimal integer 4 is 100. Consequently, −5 looks like this:

```
1111...111011 (30 bits total)
```

In this implementation, the largest 30-bit binary integer is 536,870,911 in decimal. In binary, it looks like this:

```
0111...111111 (30 bits total)
```

Since the arithmetic functions do not check whether integers go outside their range, when you add 1 to 536,870,911, the value is the negative integer −536,870,912:

```
(+ 1 536870911)
    ⇒ -536870912
    ⇒ 1000...000000 (30 bits total)
```

Many of the functions described in this chapter accept markers for arguments in place of numbers. (See Chapter 30 [Markers], page 687.) Since the actual arguments to such functions may be either numbers or markers, we often give these arguments the name *number-or-marker*. When the argument value is a marker, its position value is used and its buffer is ignored.

`most-positive-fixnum`   [Variable]
> The value of this variable is the largest integer that Emacs Lisp can handle. Typical values are $2^{29} - 1$ on 32-bit and $2^{61} - 1$ on 64-bit platforms.

`most-negative-fixnum`   [Variable]
> The value of this variable is the smallest integer that Emacs Lisp can handle. It is negative. Typical values are -2^{29} on 32-bit and -2^{61} on 64-bit platforms.

In Emacs Lisp, text characters are represented by integers. Any integer between zero and the value of (`max-char`), inclusive, is considered to be valid as a character. See Section 32.5 [Character Codes], page 765.

3.2 Floating-Point Basics

Floating-point numbers are useful for representing numbers that are not integral. The range of floating-point numbers is the same as the range of the C data type `double` on the machine you are using. On all computers currently supported by Emacs, this is double-precision IEEE floating point.

The read syntax for floating-point numbers requires either a decimal point, an exponent, or both. Optional signs ('+' or '-') precede the number and its exponent. For example, '1500.0', '+15e2', '15.0e+2', '+1500000e-3', and '.15e4' are five ways of writing a floating-point number whose value is 1500. They are all equivalent. Like Common Lisp, Emacs Lisp requires at least one digit after any decimal point in a floating-point number; '1500.' is an integer, not a floating-point number.

Emacs Lisp treats `-0.0` as numerically equal to ordinary zero with respect to `equal` and `=`. This follows the IEEE floating-point standard, which says `-0.0` and `0.0` are numerically equal even though other operations can distinguish them.

The IEEE floating-point standard supports positive infinity and negative infinity as floating-point values. It also provides for a class of values called NaN, or "not a number"; numerical functions return such values in cases where there is no correct answer. For example, (/ 0.0 0.0) returns a NaN. Although NaN values carry a sign, for practical purposes there is no other significant difference between different NaN values in Emacs Lisp.

Here are read syntaxes for these special floating-point values:

infinity   '1.0e+INF' and '-1.0e+INF'

not-a-number
            '0.0e+NaN' and '-0.0e+NaN'

The following functions are specialized for handling floating-point numbers:

isnan *x*   [Function]
> This predicate returns **t** if its floating-point argument is a NaN, **nil** otherwise.

frexp *x*   [Function]
> This function returns a cons cell (**s . e**), where *s* and *e* are respectively the significand and exponent of the floating-point number *x*.
>
> If *x* is finite, then *s* is a floating-point number between 0.5 (inclusive) and 1.0 (exclusive), *e* is an integer, and $x = s2^e$. If *x* is zero or infinity, then *s* is the same as *x*. If *x* is a NaN, then *s* is also a NaN. If *x* is zero, then *e* is 0.

ldexp *s e*   [Function]
> Given a numeric significand *s* and an integer exponent *e*, this function returns the floating point number $s2^e$.

copysign *x1 x2*   [Function]
> This function copies the sign of *x2* to the value of *x1*, and returns the result. *x1* and *x2* must be floating point.

logb *x*   [Function]
> This function returns the binary exponent of *x*. More precisely, the value is the logarithm base 2 of $|x|$, rounded down to an integer.
>
> ```
> (logb 10)
>     ⇒ 3
> (logb 10.0e20)
>     ⇒ 69
> ```

3.3 Type Predicates for Numbers

The functions in this section test for numbers, or for a specific type of number. The functions **integerp** and **floatp** can take any type of Lisp object as argument (they would not be of much use otherwise), but the **zerop** predicate requires a number as its argument. See also **integer-or-marker-p** and **number-or-marker-p**, in Section 30.2 [Predicates on Markers], page 688.

floatp *object*   [Function]
> This predicate tests whether its argument is floating point and returns **t** if so, **nil** otherwise.

integerp *object*   [Function]

> This predicate tests whether its argument is an integer, and returns **t** if so, **nil** otherwise.

numberp *object*   [Function]

> This predicate tests whether its argument is a number (either integer or floating point), and returns **t** if so, **nil** otherwise.

natnump *object*   [Function]

> This predicate (whose name comes from the phrase "natural number") tests to see whether its argument is a nonnegative integer, and returns **t** if so, **nil** otherwise. 0 is considered non-negative.
>
> **wholenump** is a synonym for **natnump**.

zerop *number*   [Function]

> This predicate tests whether its argument is zero, and returns **t** if so, **nil** otherwise. The argument must be a number.
>
> (**zerop** x) is equivalent to (= x 0).

3.4 Comparison of Numbers

To test numbers for numerical equality, you should normally use =, not **eq**. There can be many distinct floating-point objects with the same numeric value. If you use **eq** to compare them, then you test whether two values are the same *object*. By contrast, = compares only the numeric values of the objects.

In Emacs Lisp, each integer is a unique Lisp object. Therefore, **eq** is equivalent to = where integers are concerned. It is sometimes convenient to use **eq** for comparing an unknown value with an integer, because **eq** does not report an error if the unknown value is not a number—it accepts arguments of any type. By contrast, = signals an error if the arguments are not numbers or markers. However, it is better programming practice to use = if you can, even for comparing integers.

Sometimes it is useful to compare numbers with **equal**, which treats two numbers as equal if they have the same data type (both integers, or both floating point) and the same value. By contrast, = can treat an integer and a floating-point number as equal. See Section 2.7 [Equality Predicates], page 31.

There is another wrinkle: because floating-point arithmetic is not exact, it is often a bad idea to check for equality of floating-point values. Usually it is better to test for approximate equality. Here's a function to do this:

```
(defvar fuzz-factor 1.0e-6)
(defun approx-equal (x y)
  (or (= x y)
      (< (/ (abs (- x y))
            (max (abs x) (abs y)))
         fuzz-factor)))
```

Common Lisp note: Comparing numbers in Common Lisp always requires = because Common Lisp implements multi-word integers, and two distinct integer objects can have the same numeric value. Emacs Lisp can have just one integer object for any given value because it has a limited range of integers.

= *number-or-marker* **&rest** *number-or-markers*   [Function]
> This function tests whether all its arguments are numerically equal, and returns `t` if
> so, `nil` otherwise.

eql *value1* *value2*   [Function]
> This function acts like `eq` except when both arguments are numbers. It compares
> numbers by type and numeric value, so that (`eql 1.0 1`) returns `nil`, but (`eql 1.0
> 1.0`) and (`eql 1 1`) both return `t`.

/= *number-or-marker1* *number-or-marker2*   [Function]
> This function tests whether its arguments are numerically equal, and returns `t` if they
> are not, and `nil` if they are.

< *number-or-marker* **&rest** *number-or-markers*   [Function]
> This function tests whether each argument is strictly less than the following argument.
> It returns `t` if so, `nil` otherwise.

<= *number-or-marker* **&rest** *number-or-markers*   [Function]
> This function tests whether each argument is less than or equal to the following
> argument. It returns `t` if so, `nil` otherwise.

> *number-or-marker* **&rest** *number-or-markers*   [Function]
> This function tests whether each argument is strictly greater than the following ar-
> gument. It returns `t` if so, `nil` otherwise.

>= *number-or-marker* **&rest** *number-or-markers*   [Function]
> This function tests whether each argument is greater than or equal to the following
> argument. It returns `t` if so, `nil` otherwise.

max *number-or-marker* **&rest** *numbers-or-markers*   [Function]
> This function returns the largest of its arguments. If any of the arguments is floating
> point, the value is returned as floating point, even if it was given as an integer.
>
>   (max 20)
>   ⇒ 20
>   (max 1 2.5)
>   ⇒ 2.5
>   (max 1 3 2.5)
>   ⇒ 3.0

min *number-or-marker* **&rest** *numbers-or-markers*   [Function]
> This function returns the smallest of its arguments. If any of the arguments is floating
> point, the value is returned as floating point, even if it was given as an integer.
>
>   (min -4 1)
>   ⇒ -4

abs *number*   [Function]
> This function returns the absolute value of *number*.

3.5 Numeric Conversions

To convert an integer to floating point, use the function `float`.

float *number*   [Function]
> This returns *number* converted to floating point. If *number* is already floating point,
> `float` returns it unchanged.

There are four functions to convert floating-point numbers to integers; they differ in
how they round. All accept an argument *number* and an optional argument *divisor*. Both
arguments may be integers or floating-point numbers. *divisor* may also be `nil`. If *divisor*
is `nil` or omitted, these functions convert *number* to an integer, or return it unchanged if
it already is an integer. If *divisor* is non-`nil`, they divide *number* by *divisor* and convert
the result to an integer. If *divisor* is zero (whether integer or floating point), Emacs signals
an `arith-error` error.

truncate *number* **&optional** *divisor*   [Function]
> This returns *number*, converted to an integer by rounding towards zero.
>
>   (truncate 1.2)
>   ⇒ 1
>   (truncate 1.7)
>   ⇒ 1
>   (truncate -1.2)
>   ⇒ -1
>   (truncate -1.7)
>   ⇒ -1

floor *number* **&optional** *divisor*   [Function]
> This returns *number*, converted to an integer by rounding downward (towards nega-
> tive infinity).
>
> If *divisor* is specified, this uses the kind of division operation that corresponds to `mod`,
> rounding downward.
>
>   (floor 1.2)
>   ⇒ 1
>   (floor 1.7)
>   ⇒ 1
>   (floor -1.2)
>   ⇒ -2
>   (floor -1.7)
>   ⇒ -2
>   (floor 5.99 3)
>   ⇒ 1

ceiling *number* **&optional** *divisor*   [Function]
> This returns *number*, converted to an integer by rounding upward (towards positive
> infinity).
>
>   (ceiling 1.2)
>   ⇒ 2

```
(ceiling 1.7)
     ⇒ 2
(ceiling -1.2)
     ⇒ -1
(ceiling -1.7)
     ⇒ -1
```

round *number* **&optional** *divisor*   [Function]

This returns *number*, converted to an integer by rounding towards the nearest integer. Rounding a value equidistant between two integers returns the even integer.

```
(round 1.2)
     ⇒ 1
(round 1.7)
     ⇒ 2
(round -1.2)
     ⇒ -1
(round -1.7)
     ⇒ -2
```

3.6 Arithmetic Operations

Emacs Lisp provides the traditional four arithmetic operations (addition, subtraction, multiplication, and division), as well as remainder and modulus functions, and functions to add or subtract 1. Except for %, each of these functions accepts both integer and floating-point arguments, and returns a floating-point number if any argument is floating point.

Emacs Lisp arithmetic functions do not check for integer overflow. Thus (1+ 536870911) may evaluate to −536870912, depending on your hardware.

1+ *number-or-marker*   [Function]

This function returns *number-or-marker* plus 1. For example,

```
(setq foo 4)
     ⇒ 4
(1+ foo)
     ⇒ 5
```

This function is not analogous to the C operator ++—it does not increment a variable. It just computes a sum. Thus, if we continue,

```
foo
     ⇒ 4
```

If you want to increment the variable, you must use **setq**, like this:

```
(setq foo (1+ foo))
     ⇒ 5
```

1- *number-or-marker*   [Function]

This function returns *number-or-marker* minus 1.

+ **&rest** *numbers-or-markers*   [Function]

This function adds its arguments together. When given no arguments, + returns 0.

```
(+)
```

```
                        ⇒ 0
        (+ 1)
                        ⇒ 1
        (+ 1 2 3 4)
                        ⇒ 10
```

– &optional *number-or-marker* **&rest** *more-numbers-or-markers*   [Function]

The – function serves two purposes: negation and subtraction. When – has a single argument, the value is the negative of the argument. When there are multiple arguments, – subtracts each of the *more-numbers-or-markers* from *number-or-marker*, cumulatively. If there are no arguments, the result is 0.

```
        (- 10 1 2 3 4)
                        ⇒ 0
        (- 10)
                        ⇒ -10
        (-)
                        ⇒ 0
```

∗ &rest *numbers-or-markers*   [Function]

This function multiplies its arguments together, and returns the product. When given no arguments, ∗ returns 1.

```
        (*)
                        ⇒ 1
        (* 1)
                        ⇒ 1
        (* 1 2 3 4)
                        ⇒ 24
```

/ *number* **&rest** *divisors*   [Function]

With one or more *divisors*, this function divides *number* by each divisor in *divisors* in turn, and returns the quotient. With no *divisors*, this function returns 1/*number*, i.e., the multiplicative inverse of *number*. Each argument may be a number or a marker.

If all the arguments are integers, the result is an integer, obtained by rounding the quotient towards zero after each division.

```
        (/ 6 2)
                        ⇒ 3
        (/ 5 2)
                        ⇒ 2
        (/ 5.0 2)
                        ⇒ 2.5
        (/ 5 2.0)
                        ⇒ 2.5
        (/ 5.0 2.0)
                        ⇒ 2.5
        (/ 4.0)
                        ⇒ 0.25
        (/ 4)
                        ⇒ 0
```

```
(/ 25 3 2)
     ⇒ 4
(/ -17 6)
     ⇒ -2
```

If you divide an integer by the integer 0, Emacs signals an **arith-error** error (see Section 10.6.3 [Errors], page 148). Floating-point division of a nonzero number by zero yields either positive or negative infinity (see Section 3.2 [Float Basics], page 35).

% *dividend divisor* [Function]

This function returns the integer remainder after division of *dividend* by *divisor*. The arguments must be integers or markers.

For any two integers *dividend* and *divisor*,

```
(+ (% dividend divisor)
   (* (/ dividend divisor) divisor))
```

always equals *dividend* if *divisor* is nonzero.

```
(% 9 4)
     ⇒ 1
(% -9 4)
     ⇒ -1
(% 9 -4)
     ⇒ 1
(% -9 -4)
     ⇒ -1
```

mod *dividend divisor* [Function]

This function returns the value of *dividend* modulo *divisor*; in other words, the remainder after division of *dividend* by *divisor*, but with the same sign as *divisor*. The arguments must be numbers or markers.

Unlike %, mod permits floating-point arguments; it rounds the quotient downward (towards minus infinity) to an integer, and uses that quotient to compute the remainder.

If *divisor* is zero, mod signals an **arith-error** error if both arguments are integers, and returns a NaN otherwise.

```
(mod 9 4)
     ⇒ 1
(mod -9 4)
     ⇒ 3
(mod 9 -4)
     ⇒ -3
(mod -9 -4)
     ⇒ -1
(mod 5.5 2.5)
     ⇒ .5
```

For any two numbers *dividend* and *divisor*,

```
(+ (mod dividend divisor)
   (* (floor dividend divisor) divisor))
```

always equals *dividend*, subject to rounding error if either argument is floating point and to an `arith-error` if *dividend* is an integer and *divisor* is 0. For `floor`, see Section 3.5 [Numeric Conversions], page 39.

3.7 Rounding Operations

The functions `ffloor`, `fceiling`, `fround`, and `ftruncate` take a floating-point argument and return a floating-point result whose value is a nearby integer. `ffloor` returns the nearest integer below; `fceiling`, the nearest integer above; `ftruncate`, the nearest integer in the direction towards zero; `fround`, the nearest integer.

`ffloor` *float*   [Function]
> This function rounds *float* to the next lower integral value, and returns that value as a floating-point number.

`fceiling` *float*   [Function]
> This function rounds *float* to the next higher integral value, and returns that value as a floating-point number.

`ftruncate` *float*   [Function]
> This function rounds *float* towards zero to an integral value, and returns that value as a floating-point number.

`fround` *float*   [Function]
> This function rounds *float* to the nearest integral value, and returns that value as a floating-point number. Rounding a value equidistant between two integers returns the even integer.

3.8 Bitwise Operations on Integers

In a computer, an integer is represented as a binary number, a sequence of *bits* (digits which are either zero or one). A bitwise operation acts on the individual bits of such a sequence. For example, *shifting* moves the whole sequence left or right one or more places, reproducing the same pattern moved over.

The bitwise operations in Emacs Lisp apply only to integers.

`lsh` *integer1 count*   [Function]
> `lsh`, which is an abbreviation for *logical shift*, shifts the bits in *integer1* to the left *count* places, or to the right if *count* is negative, bringing zeros into the vacated bits. If *count* is negative, `lsh` shifts zeros into the leftmost (most-significant) bit, producing a positive result even if *integer1* is negative. Contrast this with `ash`, below.
>
> Here are two examples of `lsh`, shifting a pattern of bits one place to the left. We show only the low-order eight bits of the binary pattern; the rest are all zero.

```
(lsh 5 1)
     ⇒ 10
;; Decimal 5 becomes decimal 10.
00000101 ⇒ 00001010
```

```
(lsh 7 1)
     ⇒ 14
;; Decimal 7 becomes decimal 14.
00000111 ⇒ 00001110
```

As the examples illustrate, shifting the pattern of bits one place to the left produces a number that is twice the value of the previous number.

Shifting a pattern of bits two places to the left produces results like this (with 8-bit binary numbers):

```
(lsh 3 2)
     ⇒ 12
;; Decimal 3 becomes decimal 12.
00000011 ⇒ 00001100
```

On the other hand, shifting one place to the right looks like this:

```
(lsh 6 -1)
     ⇒ 3
;; Decimal 6 becomes decimal 3.
00000110 ⇒ 00000011
```

```
(lsh 5 -1)
     ⇒ 2
;; Decimal 5 becomes decimal 2.
00000101 ⇒ 00000010
```

As the example illustrates, shifting one place to the right divides the value of a positive integer by two, rounding downward.

The function lsh, like all Emacs Lisp arithmetic functions, does not check for overflow, so shifting left can discard significant bits and change the sign of the number. For example, left shifting 536,870,911 produces -2 in the 30-bit implementation:

```
(lsh 536870911 1)              ; left shift
     ⇒ -2
```

In binary, the argument looks like this:

```
;; Decimal 536,870,911
0111...111111 (30 bits total)
```

which becomes the following when left shifted:

```
;; Decimal -2
1111...111110 (30 bits total)
```

ash *integer1 count*   [Function]
> ash (*arithmetic shift*) shifts the bits in *integer1* to the left *count* places, or to the right if *count* is negative.

ash gives the same results as lsh except when *integer1* and *count* are both negative. In that case, ash puts ones in the empty bit positions on the left, while lsh puts zeros in those bit positions.

Thus, with ash, shifting the pattern of bits one place to the right looks like this:

```
(ash -6 -1) ⇒ -3
;; Decimal −6 becomes decimal −3.
1111...111010 (30 bits total)
       ⇒
1111...111101 (30 bits total)
```

In contrast, shifting the pattern of bits one place to the right with lsh looks like this:

```
(lsh -6 -1) ⇒ 536870909
;; Decimal −6 becomes decimal 536,870,909.
1111...111010 (30 bits total)
       ⇒
0111...111101 (30 bits total)
```

Here are other examples:

```
                        ;      30-bit binary values

(lsh 5 2)               ;  5  =  0000...000101
       ⇒ 20             ;     =  0000...010100
(ash 5 2)
       ⇒ 20
(lsh -5 2)              ; -5  =  1111...111011
       ⇒ -20            ;     =  1111...101100
(ash -5 2)
       ⇒ -20
(lsh 5 -2)              ;  5  =  0000...000101
       ⇒ 1              ;     =  0000...000001
(ash 5 -2)
       ⇒ 1
(lsh -5 -2)             ; -5  =  1111...111011
       ⇒ 268435454
                        ;     =  0011...111110
(ash -5 -2)             ; -5  =  1111...111011
       ⇒ -2             ;     =  1111...111110
```

logand &rest *ints-or-markers*   [Function]

This function returns the bitwise AND of the arguments: the nth bit is 1 in the result if, and only if, the nth bit is 1 in all the arguments.

For example, using 4-bit binary numbers, the bitwise AND of 13 and 12 is 12: 1101 combined with 1100 produces 1100. In both the binary numbers, the leftmost two bits are both 1 so the leftmost two bits of the returned value are both 1. However, for the rightmost two bits, each is 0 in at least one of the arguments, so the rightmost two bits of the returned value are both 0.

Therefore,

```
(logand 13 12)
       ⇒ 12
```

If `logand` is not passed any argument, it returns a value of −1. This number is an identity element for `logand` because its binary representation consists entirely of ones. If `logand` is passed just one argument, it returns that argument.

```
                        ;       30-bit binary values

(logand 14 13)     ; 14  =  0000...001110
                   ; 13  =  0000...001101
        ⇒ 12       ; 12  =  0000...001100

(logand 14 13 4)   ; 14  =  0000...001110
                   ; 13  =  0000...001101
                   ;  4  =  0000...000100
        ⇒ 4        ;  4  =  0000...000100

(logand)
        ⇒ -1       ; -1  =  1111...111111
```

logior &rest *ints-or-markers*   [Function]

This function returns the bitwise inclusive OR of its arguments: the nth bit is 1 in the result if, and only if, the nth bit is 1 in at least one of the arguments. If there are no arguments, the result is 0, which is an identity element for this operation. If `logior` is passed just one argument, it returns that argument.

```
                        ;       30-bit binary values

(logior 12 5)      ; 12  =  0000...001100
                   ;  5  =  0000...000101
        ⇒ 13       ; 13  =  0000...001101

(logior 12 5 7)    ; 12  =  0000...001100
                   ;  5  =  0000...000101
                   ;  7  =  0000...000111
        ⇒ 15       ; 15  =  0000...001111
```

logxor &rest *ints-or-markers*   [Function]

This function returns the bitwise exclusive OR of its arguments: the nth bit is 1 in the result if, and only if, the nth bit is 1 in an odd number of the arguments. If there are no arguments, the result is 0, which is an identity element for this operation. If `logxor` is passed just one argument, it returns that argument.

```
                        ;       30-bit binary values

(logxor 12 5)      ; 12  =  0000...001100
                   ;  5  =  0000...000101
        ⇒ 9        ;  9  =  0000...001001

(logxor 12 5 7)    ; 12  =  0000...001100
                   ;  5  =  0000...000101
                   ;  7  =  0000...000111
        ⇒ 14       ; 14  =  0000...001110
```

lognot *integer*   [Function]

This function returns the bitwise complement of its argument: the nth bit is one in the result if, and only if, the nth bit is zero in *integer*, and vice-versa.

```
(lognot 5)
        ⇒ -6
```

```
;;   5  =   0000...000101 (30 bits total)
;;  becomes
;;  -6  =   1111...111010 (30 bits total)
```

3.9 Standard Mathematical Functions

These mathematical functions allow integers as well as floating-point numbers as arguments.

sin *arg*   [Function]
cos *arg*   [Function]
tan *arg*   [Function]
    These are the basic trigonometric functions, with argument *arg* measured in radians.

asin *arg*   [Function]
    The value of (**asin arg**) is a number between $-\pi/2$ and $\pi/2$ (inclusive) whose sine is *arg*. If *arg* is out of range (outside $[-1, 1]$), **asin** returns a NaN.

acos *arg*   [Function]
    The value of (**acos arg**) is a number between 0 and π (inclusive) whose cosine is *arg*. If *arg* is out of range (outside $[-1, 1]$), **acos** returns a NaN.

atan *y* **&optional** *x*   [Function]
    The value of (**atan y**) is a number between $-\pi/2$ and $\pi/2$ (exclusive) whose tangent is *y*. If the optional second argument *x* is given, the value of (**atan y x**) is the angle in radians between the vector [*x, y*] and the **X** axis.

exp *arg*   [Function]
    This is the exponential function; it returns *e* to the power *arg*.

log *arg* **&optional** *base*   [Function]
    This function returns the logarithm of *arg*, with base *base*. If you don't specify *base*, the natural base *e* is used. If *arg* or *base* is negative, **log** returns a NaN.

expt *x y*   [Function]
    This function returns *x* raised to power *y*. If both arguments are integers and *y* is positive, the result is an integer; in this case, overflow causes truncation, so watch out. If *x* is a finite negative number and *y* is a finite non-integer, **expt** returns a NaN.

sqrt *arg*   [Function]
    This returns the square root of *arg*. If *arg* is finite and less than zero, **sqrt** returns a NaN.

    In addition, Emacs defines the following common mathematical constants:

float-e   [Variable]
    The mathematical constant *e* (2.71828...).

float-pi   [Variable]
    The mathematical constant *pi* (3.14159...).

3.10 Random Numbers

A deterministic computer program cannot generate true random numbers. For most purposes, *pseudo-random numbers* suffice. A series of pseudo-random numbers is generated in a deterministic fashion. The numbers are not truly random, but they have certain properties that mimic a random series. For example, all possible values occur equally often in a pseudo-random series.

Pseudo-random numbers are generated from a *seed value*. Starting from any given seed, the **random** function always generates the same sequence of numbers. By default, Emacs initializes the random seed at startup, in such a way that the sequence of values of **random** (with overwhelming likelihood) differs in each Emacs run.

Sometimes you want the random number sequence to be repeatable. For example, when debugging a program whose behavior depends on the random number sequence, it is helpful to get the same behavior in each program run. To make the sequence repeat, execute `(random "")`. This sets the seed to a constant value for your particular Emacs executable (though it may differ for other Emacs builds). You can use other strings to choose various seed values.

random &optional *limit*   [Function]

> This function returns a pseudo-random integer. Repeated calls return a series of pseudo-random integers.
>
> If *limit* is a positive integer, the value is chosen to be nonnegative and less than *limit*. Otherwise, the value might be any integer representable in Lisp, i.e., an integer between `most-negative-fixnum` and `most-positive-fixnum` (see Section 3.1 [Integer Basics], page 34).
>
> If *limit* is `t`, it means to choose a new seed as if Emacs were restarting, typically from the system entropy. On systems lacking entropy pools, choose the seed from less-random volatile data such as the current time.
>
> If *limit* is a string, it means to choose a new seed based on the string's contents.

4 Strings and Characters

A string in Emacs Lisp is an array that contains an ordered sequence of characters. Strings are used as names of symbols, buffers, and files; to send messages to users; to hold text being copied between buffers; and for many other purposes. Because strings are so important, Emacs Lisp has many functions expressly for manipulating them. Emacs Lisp programs use strings more often than individual characters.

See Section 20.7.15 [Strings of Events], page 372, for special considerations for strings of keyboard character events.

4.1 String and Character Basics

A character is a Lisp object which represents a single character of text. In Emacs Lisp, characters are simply integers; whether an integer is a character or not is determined only by how it is used. See Section 32.5 [Character Codes], page 765, for details about character representation in Emacs.

A string is a fixed sequence of characters. It is a type of sequence called a *array*, meaning that its length is fixed and cannot be altered once it is created (see Chapter 6 [Sequences Arrays Vectors], page 89). Unlike in C, Emacs Lisp strings are *not* terminated by a distinguished character code.

Since strings are arrays, and therefore sequences as well, you can operate on them with the general array and sequence functions documented in Chapter 6 [Sequences Arrays Vectors], page 89. For example, you can access or change individual characters in a string using the functions `aref` and `aset` (see Section 6.3 [Array Functions], page 101). However, note that `length` should *not* be used for computing the width of a string on display; use `string-width` (see Section 37.10 [Size of Displayed Text], page 912) instead.

There are two text representations for non-ASCII characters in Emacs strings (and in buffers): unibyte and multibyte. For most Lisp programming, you don't need to be concerned with these two representations. See Section 32.1 [Text Representations], page 761, for details.

Sometimes key sequences are represented as unibyte strings. When a unibyte string is a key sequence, string elements in the range 128 to 255 represent meta characters (which are large integers) rather than character codes in the range 128 to 255. Strings cannot hold characters that have the hyper, super or alt modifiers; they can hold ASCII control characters, but no other control characters. They do not distinguish case in ASCII control characters. If you want to store such characters in a sequence, such as a key sequence, you must use a vector instead of a string. See Section 2.3.3 [Character Type], page 10, for more information about keyboard input characters.

Strings are useful for holding regular expressions. You can also match regular expressions against strings with `string-match` (see Section 33.4 [Regexp Search], page 803). The functions `match-string` (see Section 33.6.2 [Simple Match Data], page 808) and `replace-match` (see Section 33.6.1 [Replacing Match], page 807) are useful for decomposing and modifying strings after matching regular expressions against them.

Like a buffer, a string can contain text properties for the characters in it, as well as the characters themselves. See Section 31.19 [Text Properties], page 732. All the Lisp primitives that copy text from strings to buffers or other strings also copy the properties of the characters being copied.

See Chapter 31 [Text], page 696, for information about functions that display strings or copy them into buffers. See Section 2.3.3 [Character Type], page 10, and Section 2.3.8 [String Type], page 18, for information about the syntax of characters and strings. See Chapter 32 [Non-ASCII Characters], page 761, for functions to convert between text representations and to encode and decode character codes.

4.2 Predicates for Strings

For more information about general sequence and array predicates, see Chapter 6 [Sequences Arrays Vectors], page 89, and Section 6.2 [Arrays], page 100.

stringp *object*   [Function]
> This function returns t if *object* is a string, nil otherwise.

string-or-null-p *object*   [Function]
> This function returns t if *object* is a string or nil. It returns nil otherwise.

char-or-string-p *object*   [Function]
> This function returns t if *object* is a string or a character (i.e., an integer), nil otherwise.

4.3 Creating Strings

The following functions create strings, either from scratch, or by putting strings together, or by taking them apart.

make-string *count character*   [Function]
> This function returns a string made up of *count* repetitions of *character*. If *count* is negative, an error is signaled.
>
>   (make-string 5 ?x)
>   ⇒ "xxxxx"
>   (make-string 0 ?x)
>   ⇒ ""
>
> Other functions to compare with this one include make-vector (see Section 6.4 [Vectors], page 102) and make-list (see Section 5.4 [Building Lists], page 71).

string &rest *characters*   [Function]
> This returns a string containing the characters *characters*.
>
>   (string ?a ?b ?c)
>   ⇒ "abc"

substring *string* &optional *start end*   [Function]
> This function returns a new string which consists of those characters from *string* in the range from (and including) the character at the index *start* up to (but excluding) the character at the index *end*. The first character is at index zero. With one argument, this function just copies *string*.
>
>   (substring "abcdefg" 0 3)
>   ⇒ "abc"

In the above example, the index for 'a' is 0, the index for 'b' is 1, and the index for 'c' is 2. The index 3—which is the fourth character in the string—marks the character position up to which the substring is copied. Thus, 'abc' is copied from the string "abcdefg".

A negative number counts from the end of the string, so that -1 signifies the index of the last character of the string. For example:

```
(substring "abcdefg" -3 -1)
     ⇒ "ef"
```

In this example, the index for 'e' is -3, the index for 'f' is -2, and the index for 'g' is -1. Therefore, 'e' and 'f' are included, and 'g' is excluded.

When nil is used for *end*, it stands for the length of the string. Thus,

```
(substring "abcdefg" -3 nil)
     ⇒ "efg"
```

Omitting the argument *end* is equivalent to specifying nil. It follows that (substring *string* 0) returns a copy of all of *string*.

```
(substring "abcdefg" 0)
     ⇒ "abcdefg"
```

But we recommend copy-sequence for this purpose (see Section 6.1 [Sequence Functions], page 89).

If the characters copied from *string* have text properties, the properties are copied into the new string also. See Section 31.19 [Text Properties], page 732.

substring also accepts a vector for the first argument. For example:

```
(substring [a b (c) "d"] 1 3)
     ⇒ [b (c)]
```

A wrong-type-argument error is signaled if *start* is not an integer or if *end* is neither an integer nor nil. An args-out-of-range error is signaled if *start* indicates a character following *end*, or if either integer is out of range for *string*.

Contrast this function with buffer-substring (see Section 31.2 [Buffer Contents], page 697), which returns a string containing a portion of the text in the current buffer. The beginning of a string is at index 0, but the beginning of a buffer is at index 1.

substring-no-properties *string* &optional *start end*   [Function]
> This works like substring but discards all text properties from the value. Also, *start* may be omitted or nil, which is equivalent to 0. Thus, (substring-no-properties *string*) returns a copy of *string*, with all text properties removed.

concat &rest *sequences*   [Function]
> This function returns a new string consisting of the characters in the arguments passed to it (along with their text properties, if any). The arguments may be strings, lists of numbers, or vectors of numbers; they are not themselves changed. If concat receives no arguments, it returns an empty string.
>
> ```
> (concat "abc" "-def")
>      ⇒ "abc-def"
> ```

```
(concat "abc" (list 120 121) [122])
     ⇒ "abcxyz"
;; nil is an empty sequence.
(concat "abc" nil "-def")
     ⇒ "abc-def"
(concat "The " "quick brown " "fox.")
     ⇒ "The quick brown fox."
(concat)
     ⇒ ""
```

This function always constructs a new string that is not `eq` to any existing string, except when the result is the empty string (to save space, Emacs makes only one empty multibyte string).

For information about other concatenation functions, see the description of `mapconcat` in Section 12.6 [Mapping Functions], page 196, `vconcat` in Section 6.5 [Vector Functions], page 102, and `append` in Section 5.4 [Building Lists], page 71. For concatenating individual command-line arguments into a string to be used as a shell command, see Section 36.2 [Shell Arguments], page 841.

split-string *string* **&optional** *separators omit-nulls trim*   [Function]
This function splits *string* into substrings based on the regular expression *separators* (see Section 33.3 [Regular Expressions], page 793). Each match for *separators* defines a splitting point; the substrings between splitting points are made into a list, which is returned.

If *omit-nulls* is `nil` (or omitted), the result contains null strings whenever there are two consecutive matches for *separators*, or a match is adjacent to the beginning or end of *string*. If *omit-nulls* is `t`, these null strings are omitted from the result.

If *separators* is `nil` (or omitted), the default is the value of `split-string-default-separators`.

As a special case, when *separators* is `nil` (or omitted), null strings are always omitted from the result. Thus:

```
(split-string "  two words ")
     ⇒ ("two" "words")
```

The result is not `("" "two" "words" "")`, which would rarely be useful. If you need such a result, use an explicit value for *separators*:

```
(split-string "  two words "
              split-string-default-separators)
     ⇒ ("" "two" "words" "")
```

More examples:

```
(split-string "Soup is good food" "o")
     ⇒ ("S" "up is g" "" "d f" "" "d")
(split-string "Soup is good food" "o" t)
     ⇒ ("S" "up is g" "d f" "d")
(split-string "Soup is good food" "o+")
     ⇒ ("S" "up is g" "d f" "d")
```

Empty matches do count, except that `split-string` will not look for a final empty match when it already reached the end of the string using a non-empty match or when *string* is empty:

```
(split-string "aooob" "o*")
    ⇒ ("" "a" "" "b" "")
(split-string "ooaboo" "o*")
    ⇒ ("" "" "a" "b" "")
(split-string "" "")
    ⇒ ("")
```

However, when *separators* can match the empty string, *omit-nulls* is usually `t`, so that the subtleties in the three previous examples are rarely relevant:

```
(split-string "Soup is good food" "o*" t)
    ⇒ ("S" "u" "p" " " "i" "s" " " "g" "d" " " "f" "d")
(split-string "Nice doggy!" "" t)
    ⇒ ("N" "i" "c" "e" " " "d" "o" "g" "g" "y" "!")
(split-string "" "" t)
    ⇒ nil
```

Somewhat odd, but predictable, behavior can occur for certain "non-greedy" values of *separators* that can prefer empty matches over non-empty matches. Again, such values rarely occur in practice:

```
(split-string "ooo" "o*" t)
    ⇒ nil
(split-string "ooo" "\\|o+" t)
    ⇒ ("o" "o" "o")
```

If the optional argument *trim* is non-`nil`, it should be a regular expression to match text to trim from the beginning and end of each substring. If trimming makes the substring empty, it is treated as null.

If you need to split a string into a list of individual command-line arguments suitable for `call-process` or `start-process`, see Section 36.2 [Shell Arguments], page 841.

split-string-default-separators   [Variable]
> The default value of *separators* for `split-string`. Its usual value is `"[ \f\t\n\r\v]+"`.

4.4 Modifying Strings

The most basic way to alter the contents of an existing string is with `aset` (see Section 6.3 [Array Functions], page 101). (`aset` *string idx char*) stores *char* into *string* at index *idx*. Each character occupies one or more bytes, and if *char* needs a different number of bytes from the character already present at that index, `aset` signals an error.

A more powerful function is `store-substring`:

store-substring *string idx obj*   [Function]
> This function alters part of the contents of the string *string*, by storing *obj* starting at index *idx*. The argument *obj* may be either a character or a (smaller) string.

Since it is impossible to change the length of an existing string, it is an error if *obj* doesn't fit within *string*'s actual length, or if any new character requires a different number of bytes from the character currently present at that point in *string*.

To clear out a string that contained a password, use `clear-string`:

`clear-string` *string*   [Function]
    This makes *string* a unibyte string and clears its contents to zeros. It may also change *string*'s length.

4.5 Comparison of Characters and Strings

`char-equal` *character1 character2*   [Function]
    This function returns `t` if the arguments represent the same character, `nil` otherwise. This function ignores differences in case if `case-fold-search` is non-`nil`.

```
(char-equal ?x ?x)
    ⇒ t
(let ((case-fold-search nil))
  (char-equal ?x ?X))
    ⇒ nil
```

`string=` *string1 string2*   [Function]
    This function returns `t` if the characters of the two strings match exactly. Symbols are also allowed as arguments, in which case the symbol names are used. Case is always significant, regardless of `case-fold-search`.

    This function is equivalent to `equal` for comparing two strings (see Section 2.7 [Equality Predicates], page 31). In particular, the text properties of the two strings are ignored; use `equal-including-properties` if you need to distinguish between strings that differ only in their text properties. However, unlike `equal`, if either argument is not a string or symbol, `string=` signals an error.

```
(string= "abc" "abc")
    ⇒ t
(string= "abc" "ABC")
    ⇒ nil
(string= "ab" "ABC")
    ⇒ nil
```

For technical reasons, a unibyte and a multibyte string are `equal` if and only if they contain the same sequence of character codes and all these codes are either in the range 0 through 127 (ASCII) or 160 through 255 (`eight-bit-graphic`). However, when a unibyte string is converted to a multibyte string, all characters with codes in the range 160 through 255 are converted to characters with higher codes, whereas ASCII characters remain unchanged. Thus, a unibyte string and its conversion to multibyte are only `equal` if the string is all ASCII. Character codes 160 through 255 are not entirely proper in multibyte text, even though they can occur. As a consequence, the situation where a unibyte and a multibyte string are `equal` without both being all ASCII is a technical oddity that very few Emacs Lisp programmers ever get confronted with. See Section 32.1 [Text Representations], page 761.

string-equal *string1 string2*   [Function]

   string-equal is another name for **string=**.

string-collate-equalp *string1 string2* **&optional** *locale ignore-case*   [Function]

   This function returns **t** if *string1* and *string2* are equal with respect to collation rules.
   A collation rule is not only determined by the lexicographic order of the characters
   contained in *string1* and *string2*, but also further rules about relations between these
   characters. Usually, it is defined by the *locale* environment Emacs is running with.

   For example, characters with different coding points but the same meaning might be
   considered as equal, like different grave accent Unicode characters:

   > (string-collate-equalp (string ?\uFF40) (string ?\u1FEF))
   >   ⇒ t

   The optional argument *locale*, a string, overrides the setting of your current locale
   identifier for collation. The value is system dependent; a *locale* **"en_US.UTF-8"** is applicable on POSIX systems, while it would be, e.g., **"enu_USA.1252"** on MS-Windows
   systems.

   If *ignore-case* is non-**nil**, characters are converted to lower-case before comparing
   them.

   To emulate Unicode-compliant collation on MS-Windows systems, bind
   w32-collate-ignore-punctuation to a non-**nil** value, since the codeset part of
   the locale cannot be **"UTF-8"** on MS-Windows.

   If your system does not support a locale environment, this function behaves like
   string-equal.

   Do *not* use this function to compare file names for equality, as filesystems generally
   don't honor linguistic equivalence of strings that collation implements.

string< *string1 string2*   [Function]

   This function compares two strings a character at a time. It scans both the strings at
   the same time to find the first pair of corresponding characters that do not match. If
   the lesser character of these two is the character from *string1*, then *string1* is less, and
   this function returns **t**. If the lesser character is the one from *string2*, then *string1* is
   greater, and this function returns **nil**. If the two strings match entirely, the value is
   nil.

   Pairs of characters are compared according to their character codes. Keep in mind
   that lower case letters have higher numeric values in the ASCII character set than
   their upper case counterparts; digits and many punctuation characters have a lower
   numeric value than upper case letters. An ASCII character is less than any non-ASCII
   character; a unibyte non-ASCII character is always less than any multibyte non-ASCII
   character (see Section 32.1 [Text Representations], page 761).

   > (string< "abc" "abd")
   >   ⇒ t
   > (string< "abd" "abc")
   >   ⇒ nil
   > (string< "123" "abc")
   >   ⇒ t

When the strings have different lengths, and they match up to the length of *string1*, then the result is `t`. If they match up to the length of *string2*, the result is `nil`. A string of no characters is less than any other string.

```
(string< "" "abc")
     ⇒ t
(string< "ab" "abc")
     ⇒ t
(string< "abc" "")
     ⇒ nil
(string< "abc" "ab")
     ⇒ nil
(string< "" "")
     ⇒ nil
```

Symbols are also allowed as arguments, in which case their print names are compared.

`string-lessp` *string1* *string2*   [Function]
> `string-lessp` is another name for `string<`.

`string-greaterp` *string1* *string2*   [Function]
> This function returns the result of comparing *string1* and *string2* in the opposite order, i.e., it is equivalent to calling (`string-lessp` *string2* *string1*).

`string-collate-lessp` *string1* *string2* **&optional** *locale ignore-case*   [Function]
> This function returns `t` if *string1* is less than *string2* in collation order. A collation order is not only determined by the lexicographic order of the characters contained in *string1* and *string2*, but also further rules about relations between these characters. Usually, it is defined by the *locale* environment Emacs is running with.
>
> For example, punctuation and whitespace characters might be ignored for sorting (see Section 6.1 [Sequence Functions], page 89):
> ```
> (sort '("11" "12" "1 1" "1 2" "1.1" "1.2") 'string-collate-lessp)
>      ⇒ ("11" "1 1" "1.1" "12" "1 2" "1.2")
> ```

This behavior is system-dependent; e.g., punctuation and whitespace are never ignored on Cygwin, regardless of locale.

The optional argument *locale*, a string, overrides the setting of your current locale identifier for collation. The value is system dependent; a *locale* `"en_US.UTF-8"` is applicable on POSIX systems, while it would be, e.g., `"enu_USA.1252"` on MS-Windows systems. The *locale* value of `"POSIX"` or `"C"` lets `string-collate-lessp` behave like `string-lessp`:
```
(sort '("11" "12" "1 1" "1 2" "1.1" "1.2")
      (lambda (s1 s2) (string-collate-lessp s1 s2 "POSIX")))
     ⇒ ("1 1" "1 2" "1.1" "1.2" "11" "12")
```

If *ignore-case* is non-`nil`, characters are converted to lower-case before comparing them.

To emulate Unicode-compliant collation on MS-Windows systems, bind `w32-collate-ignore-punctuation` to a non-`nil` value, since the codeset part of the locale cannot be `"UTF-8"` on MS-Windows.

If your system does not support a locale environment, this function behaves like `string-lessp`.

`string-prefix-p` *string1 string2* **&optional** *ignore-case*   [Function]
This function returns non-`nil` if *string1* is a prefix of *string2*; i.e., if *string2* starts with *string1*. If the optional argument *ignore-case* is non-`nil`, the comparison ignores case differences.

`string-suffix-p` *suffix string* **&optional** *ignore-case*   [Function]
This function returns non-`nil` if *suffix* is a suffix of *string*; i.e., if *string* ends with *suffix*. If the optional argument *ignore-case* is non-`nil`, the comparison ignores case differences.

`compare-strings` *string1 start1 end1 string2 start2 end2* **&optional**   [Function]
  ignore-case
This function compares a specified part of *string1* with a specified part of *string2*. The specified part of *string1* runs from index *start1* (inclusive) up to index *end1* (exclusive); `nil` for *start1* means the start of the string, while `nil` for *end1* means the length of the string. Likewise, the specified part of *string2* runs from index *start2* up to index *end2*.

The strings are compared by the numeric values of their characters. For instance, *str1* is considered less than *str2* if its first differing character has a smaller numeric value. If *ignore-case* is non-`nil`, characters are converted to upper-case before comparing them. Unibyte strings are converted to multibyte for comparison (see Section 32.1 [Text Representations], page 761), so that a unibyte string and its conversion to multibyte are always regarded as equal.

If the specified portions of the two strings match, the value is `t`. Otherwise, the value is an integer which indicates how many leading characters agree, and which string is less. Its absolute value is one plus the number of characters that agree at the beginning of the two strings. The sign is negative if *string1* (or its specified portion) is less.

`assoc-string` *key alist* **&optional** *case-fold*   [Function]
This function works like `assoc`, except that *key* must be a string or symbol, and comparison is done using `compare-strings`. Symbols are converted to strings before testing. If *case-fold* is non-`nil`, *key* and the elements of *alist* are converted to upper-case before comparison. Unlike `assoc`, this function can also match elements of the alist that are strings or symbols rather than conses. In particular, *alist* can be a list of strings or symbols rather than an actual alist. See Section 5.8 [Association Lists], page 83.

See also the function `compare-buffer-substrings` in Section 31.3 [Comparing Text], page 700, for a way to compare text in buffers. The function `string-match`, which matches a regular expression against a string, can be used for a kind of string comparison; see Section 33.4 [Regexp Search], page 803.

4.6 Conversion of Characters and Strings

This section describes functions for converting between characters, strings and integers. `format` (see Section 4.7 [Formatting Strings], page 59) and `prin1-to-string` (see Section 18.5 [Output Functions], page 308) can also convert Lisp objects into strings. `read-from-string` (see Section 18.3 [Input Functions], page 304) can convert a string representation of a Lisp object into an object. The functions `string-to-multibyte` and `string-to-unibyte` convert the text representation of a string (see Section 32.3 [Converting Representations], page 763).

See Chapter 23 [Documentation], page 485, for functions that produce textual descriptions of text characters and general input events (`single-key-description` and `text-char-description`). These are used primarily for making help messages.

`number-to-string` *number*   [Function]
> This function returns a string consisting of the printed base-ten representation of *number*. The returned value starts with a minus sign if the argument is negative.
>
> ```
> (number-to-string 256)
>     ⇒ "256"
> (number-to-string -23)
>     ⇒ "-23"
> (number-to-string -23.5)
>     ⇒ "-23.5"
> ```
>
> `int-to-string` is a semi-obsolete alias for this function.
>
> See also the function `format` in Section 4.7 [Formatting Strings], page 59.

`string-to-number` *string* &optional *base*   [Function]
> This function returns the numeric value of the characters in *string*. If *base* is non-`nil`, it must be an integer between 2 and 16 (inclusive), and integers are converted in that base. If *base* is `nil`, then base ten is used. Floating-point conversion only works in base ten; we have not implemented other radices for floating-point numbers, because that would be much more work and does not seem useful. If *string* looks like an integer but its value is too large to fit into a Lisp integer, `string-to-number` returns a floating-point result.
>
> The parsing skips spaces and tabs at the beginning of *string*, then reads as much of *string* as it can interpret as a number in the given base. (On some systems it ignores other whitespace at the beginning, not just spaces and tabs.) If *string* cannot be interpreted as a number, this function returns 0.
>
> ```
> (string-to-number "256")
>     ⇒ 256
> (string-to-number "25 is a perfect square.")
>     ⇒ 25
> (string-to-number "X256")
>     ⇒ 0
> (string-to-number "-4.5")
>     ⇒ -4.5
> (string-to-number "1e5")
>     ⇒ 100000.0
> ```

`string-to-int` is an obsolete alias for this function.

`char-to-string` *character*   [Function]

> This function returns a new string containing one character, *character*. This function is semi-obsolete because the function `string` is more general. See Section 4.3 [Creating Strings], page 50.

`string-to-char` *string*   [Function]

> This function returns the first character in *string*. This mostly identical to `(aref string 0)`, except that it returns 0 if the string is empty. (The value is also 0 when the first character of *string* is the null character, ASCII code 0.) This function may be eliminated in the future if it does not seem useful enough to retain.

Here are some other functions that can convert to or from a string:

`concat`   This function converts a vector or a list into a string. See Section 4.3 [Creating Strings], page 50.

`vconcat`   This function converts a string into a vector. See Section 6.5 [Vector Functions], page 102.

`append`   This function converts a string into a list. See Section 5.4 [Building Lists], page 71.

`byte-to-string`

> This function converts a byte of character data into a unibyte string. See Section 32.3 [Converting Representations], page 763.

4.7 Formatting Strings

Formatting means constructing a string by substituting computed values at various places in a constant string. This constant string controls how the other values are printed, as well as where they appear; it is called a *format string*.

Formatting is often useful for computing messages to be displayed. In fact, the functions `message` and `error` provide the same formatting feature described here; they differ from `format-message` only in how they use the result of formatting.

`format` *string* **&rest** *objects*   [Function]

> This function returns a new string that is made by copying *string* and then replacing any format specification in the copy with encodings of the corresponding *objects*. The arguments *objects* are the computed values to be formatted.

> The characters in *string*, other than the format specifications, are copied directly into the output, including their text properties, if any.

`format-message` *string* **&rest** *objects*   [Function]

> This function acts like `format`, except it also converts any curved single quotes in *string* as per the value of `text-quoting-style`, and treats grave accent (') and apostrophe (') as if they were curved single quotes.

> A format that quotes with grave accents and apostrophes `'like this'` typically generates curved quotes `'like this'`. In contrast, a format that quotes with only

apostrophes `'like this'` typically generates two closing curved quotes `'like this'`, an unusual style in English. See Section 23.3 [Keys in Documentation], page 488, for how the `text-quoting-style` variable affects generated quotes.

A format specification is a sequence of characters beginning with a '%'. Thus, if there is a '%d' in *string*, the `format` function replaces it with the printed representation of one of the values to be formatted (one of the arguments *objects*). For example:

```
(format "The value of fill-column is %d." fill-column)
     ⇒ "The value of fill-column is 72."
```

Since `format` interprets '%' characters as format specifications, you should *never* pass an arbitrary string as the first argument. This is particularly true when the string is generated by some Lisp code. Unless the string is *known* to never include any '%' characters, pass `"%s"`, described below, as the first argument, and the string as the second, like this:

```
(format "%s" arbitrary-string)
```

If *string* contains more than one format specification, the format specifications correspond to successive values from *objects*. Thus, the first format specification in *string* uses the first such value, the second format specification uses the second such value, and so on. Any extra format specifications (those for which there are no corresponding values) cause an error. Any extra values to be formatted are ignored.

Certain format specifications require values of particular types. If you supply a value that doesn't fit the requirements, an error is signaled.

Here is a table of valid format specifications:

'%s'   Replace the specification with the printed representation of the object, made without quoting (that is, using `princ`, not `prin1`—see Section 18.5 [Output Functions], page 308). Thus, strings are represented by their contents alone, with no '"' characters, and symbols appear without '\' characters.

            If the object is a string, its text properties are copied into the output. The text properties of the '%s' itself are also copied, but those of the object take priority.

'%S'   Replace the specification with the printed representation of the object, made with quoting (that is, using `prin1`—see Section 18.5 [Output Functions], page 308). Thus, strings are enclosed in '"' characters, and '\' characters appear where necessary before special characters.

'%o'   Replace the specification with the base-eight representation of an unsigned integer.

'%d'   Replace the specification with the base-ten representation of a signed integer.

'%x'
'%X'   Replace the specification with the base-sixteen representation of an unsigned integer. '%x' uses lower case and '%X' uses upper case.

'%c'   Replace the specification with the character which is the value given.

'%e'   Replace the specification with the exponential notation for a floating-point number.

'%f'   Replace the specification with the decimal-point notation for a floating-point number.

'%g'   Replace the specification with notation for a floating-point number, using either exponential notation or decimal-point notation. The exponential notation is used if the exponent would be less than -4 or greater than or equal to the precision (default: 6). By default, trailing zeros are removed from the fractional portion of the result and a decimal-point character appears only if it is followed by a digit.

'%%'   Replace the specification with a single '%'. This format specification is unusual in that it does not use a value. For example, (format "%% %d" 30) returns "% 30".

Any other format character results in an 'Invalid format operation' error.

Here are several examples, which assume the typical text-quoting-style settings:

```
(format "The octal value of %d is %o,
         and the hex value is %x." 18 18 18)
    ⇒ "The octal value of 18 is 22,
         and the hex value is 12."


(format-message
 "The name of this buffer is '%s'." (buffer-name))
    ⇒ "The name of this buffer is 'strings.texi'."


(format-message
 "The buffer object prints as `%s'." (current-buffer))
    ⇒ "The buffer object prints as 'strings.texi'."
```

A specification can have a *width*, which is a decimal number between the '%' and the specification character. If the printed representation of the object contains fewer characters than this width, format extends it with padding. The width specifier is ignored for the '%%' specification. Any padding introduced by the width specifier normally consists of spaces inserted on the left:

```
(format "%5d is padded on the left with spaces" 123)
    ⇒ "  123 is padded on the left with spaces"
```

If the width is too small, format does not truncate the object's printed representation. Thus, you can use a width to specify a minimum spacing between columns with no risk of losing information. In the following two examples, '%7s' specifies a minimum width of 7. In the first case, the string inserted in place of '%7s' has only 3 letters, and needs 4 blank spaces as padding. In the second case, the string "specification" is 13 letters wide but is not truncated.

```
(format "The word '%7s' has %d letters in it."
        "foo" (length "foo"))
    ⇒ "The word '    foo' has 3 letters in it."
(format "The word '%7s' has %d letters in it."
        "specification" (length "specification"))
    ⇒ "The word 'specification' has 13 letters in it."
```

Immediately after the '%' and before the optional width specifier, you can also put certain *flag characters*.

The flag '+' inserts a plus sign before a positive number, so that it always has a sign. A space character as flag inserts a space before a positive number. (Otherwise, positive numbers start with the first digit.) These flags are useful for ensuring that positive numbers and negative numbers use the same number of columns. They are ignored except for '%d', '%e', '%f', '%g', and if both flags are used, '+' takes precedence.

The flag '#' specifies an alternate form which depends on the format in use. For '%o', it ensures that the result begins with a '0'. For '%x' and '%X', it prefixes the result with '0x' or '0X'. For '%e' and '%f', the '#' flag means include a decimal point even if the precision is zero. For '%g', it always includes a decimal point, and also forces any trailing zeros after the decimal point to be left in place where they would otherwise be removed.

The flag '0' ensures that the padding consists of '0' characters instead of spaces. This flag is ignored for non-numerical specification characters like '%s', '%S' and '%c'. These specification characters accept the '0' flag, but still pad with *spaces*.

The flag '-' causes the padding inserted by the width specifier, if any, to be inserted on the right rather than the left. If both '-' and '0' are present, the '0' flag is ignored.

```
(format "%06d is padded on the left with zeros" 123)
    ⇒ "000123 is padded on the left with zeros"

(format "'%-6d' is padded on the right" 123)
    ⇒ "'123   ' is padded on the right"

(format "The word '%-7s' actually has %d letters in it."
        "foo" (length "foo"))
    ⇒ "The word 'foo    ' actually has 3 letters in it."
```

All the specification characters allow an optional *precision* before the character (after the width, if present). The precision is a decimal-point '.' followed by a digit-string. For the floating-point specifications ('%e' and '%f'), the precision specifies how many digits following the decimal point to show; if zero, the decimal-point itself is also omitted. For '%g', the precision specifies how many significant digits to show (significant digits are the first digit before the decimal point and all the digits after it). If the precision of %g is zero or unspecified, it is treated as 1. For '%s' and '%S', the precision truncates the string to the given width, so '%.3s' shows only the first three characters of the representation for *object*. For other specification characters, the effect of precision is what the local library functions of the `printf` family produce.

4.8 Case Conversion in Lisp

The character case functions change the case of single characters or of the contents of strings. The functions normally convert only alphabetic characters (the letters 'A' through 'Z' and 'a' through 'z', as well as non-ASCII letters); other characters are not altered. You can specify a different case conversion mapping by specifying a case table (see Section 4.9 [Case Tables], page 64).

These functions do not modify the strings that are passed to them as arguments.

The examples below use the characters 'X' and 'x' which have ASCII codes 88 and 120 respectively.

`downcase` *string-or-char*   [Function]

This function converts *string-or-char*, which should be either a character or a string, to lower case.

When *string-or-char* is a string, this function returns a new string in which each letter in the argument that is upper case is converted to lower case. When *string-or-char* is a character, this function returns the corresponding lower case character (an integer); if the original character is lower case, or is not a letter, the return value is equal to the original character.

```
(downcase "The cat in the hat")
     ⇒ "the cat in the hat"


(downcase ?X)
     ⇒ 120
```

`upcase` *string-or-char*   [Function]

This function converts *string-or-char*, which should be either a character or a string, to upper case.

When *string-or-char* is a string, this function returns a new string in which each letter in the argument that is lower case is converted to upper case. When *string-or-char* is a character, this function returns the corresponding upper case character (an integer); if the original character is upper case, or is not a letter, the return value is equal to the original character.

```
(upcase "The cat in the hat")
     ⇒ "THE CAT IN THE HAT"


(upcase ?x)
     ⇒ 88
```

`capitalize` *string-or-char*   [Function]

This function capitalizes strings or characters. If *string-or-char* is a string, the function returns a new string whose contents are a copy of *string-or-char* in which each word has been capitalized. This means that the first character of each word is converted to upper case, and the rest are converted to lower case.

The definition of a word is any sequence of consecutive characters that are assigned to the word constituent syntax class in the current syntax table (see Section 34.2.1 [Syntax Class Table], page 817).

When *string-or-char* is a character, this function does the same thing as `upcase`.

```
(capitalize "The cat in the hat")
     ⇒ "The Cat In The Hat"


(capitalize "THE 77TH-HATTED CAT")
     ⇒ "The 77th-Hatted Cat"


(capitalize ?x)
     ⇒ 88
```

`upcase-initials` *string-or-char*   [Function]

> If *string-or-char* is a string, this function capitalizes the initials of the words in *string-or-char*, without altering any letters other than the initials. It returns a new string whose contents are a copy of *string-or-char*, in which each word has had its initial letter converted to upper case.
>
> The definition of a word is any sequence of consecutive characters that are assigned to the word constituent syntax class in the current syntax table (see Section 34.2.1 [Syntax Class Table], page 817).
>
> When the argument to `upcase-initials` is a character, `upcase-initials` has the same result as `upcase`.
>
> ```
> (upcase-initials "The CAT in the hAt")
>      ⇒ "The CAT In The HAt"
> ```

See Section 4.5 [Text Comparison], page 54, for functions that compare strings; some of them ignore case differences, or can optionally ignore case differences.

4.9 The Case Table

You can customize case conversion by installing a special *case table*. A case table specifies the mapping between upper case and lower case letters. It affects both the case conversion functions for Lisp objects (see the previous section) and those that apply to text in the buffer (see Section 31.18 [Case Changes], page 730). Each buffer has a case table; there is also a standard case table which is used to initialize the case table of new buffers.

A case table is a char-table (see Section 6.6 [Char-Tables], page 104) whose subtype is `case-table`. This char-table maps each character into the corresponding lower case character. It has three extra slots, which hold related tables:

upcase   The upcase table maps each character into the corresponding upper case character.

canonicalize
> The canonicalize table maps all of a set of case-related characters into a particular member of that set.

equivalences
> The equivalences table maps each one of a set of case-related characters into the next character in that set.

In simple cases, all you need to specify is the mapping to lower-case; the three related tables will be calculated automatically from that one.

For some languages, upper and lower case letters are not in one-to-one correspondence. There may be two different lower case letters with the same upper case equivalent. In these cases, you need to specify the maps for both lower case and upper case.

The extra table *canonicalize* maps each character to a canonical equivalent; any two characters that are related by case-conversion have the same canonical equivalent character. For example, since 'a' and 'A' are related by case-conversion, they should have the same canonical equivalent character (which should be either 'a' for both of them, or 'A' for both of them).

The extra table *equivalences* is a map that cyclically permutes each equivalence class (of characters with the same canonical equivalent). (For ordinary ASCII, this would map 'a' into 'A' and 'A' into 'a', and likewise for each set of equivalent characters.)

When constructing a case table, you can provide **nil** for *canonicalize*; then Emacs fills in this slot from the lower case and upper case mappings. You can also provide **nil** for *equivalences*; then Emacs fills in this slot from *canonicalize*. In a case table that is actually in use, those components are non-**nil**. Do not try to specify *equivalences* without also specifying *canonicalize*.

Here are the functions for working with case tables:

case-table-p *object* [Function]
> This predicate returns non-**nil** if *object* is a valid case table.

set-standard-case-table *table* [Function]
> This function makes *table* the standard case table, so that it will be used in any buffers created subsequently.

standard-case-table [Function]
> This returns the standard case table.

current-case-table [Function]
> This function returns the current buffer's case table.

set-case-table *table* [Function]
> This sets the current buffer's case table to *table*.

with-case-table *table body...* [Macro]
> The **with-case-table** macro saves the current case table, makes *table* the current case table, evaluates the *body* forms, and finally restores the case table. The return value is the value of the last form in *body*. The case table is restored even in case of an abnormal exit via **throw** or error (see Section 10.6 [Nonlocal Exits], page 145).

Some language environments modify the case conversions of ASCII characters; for example, in the Turkish language environment, the ASCII capital I is downcased into a Turkish dotless i ('ı'). This can interfere with code that requires ordinary ASCII case conversion, such as implementations of ASCII-based network protocols. In that case, use the **with-case-table** macro with the variable *ascii-case-table*, which stores the unmodified case table for the ASCII character set.

ascii-case-table [Variable]
> The case table for the ASCII character set. This should not be modified by any language environment settings.

The following three functions are convenient subroutines for packages that define non-ASCII character sets. They modify the specified case table *case-table*; they also modify the standard syntax table. See Chapter 34 [Syntax Tables], page 816. Normally you would use these functions to change the standard case table.

set-case-syntax-pair *uc lc case-table* [Function]
> This function specifies a pair of corresponding letters, one upper case and one lower case.

`set-case-syntax-delims` *l r case-table* [Function]

This function makes characters *l* and *r* a matching pair of case-invariant delimiters.

`set-case-syntax` *char syntax case-table* [Function]

This function makes *char* case-invariant, with syntax *syntax*.

`describe-buffer-case-table` [Command]

This command displays a description of the contents of the current buffer's case table.

5 Lists

A *list* represents a sequence of zero or more elements (which may be any Lisp objects). The important difference between lists and vectors is that two or more lists can share part of their structure; in addition, you can insert or delete elements in a list without copying the whole list.

5.1 Lists and Cons Cells

Lists in Lisp are not a primitive data type; they are built up from *cons cells* (see Section 2.3.6 [Cons Cell Type], page 14). A cons cell is a data object that represents an ordered pair. That is, it has two slots, and each slot *holds*, or *refers to*, some Lisp object. One slot is known as the CAR, and the other is known as the CDR. (These names are traditional; see Section 2.3.6 [Cons Cell Type], page 14.) CDR is pronounced "could-er".

We say that "the CAR of this cons cell is" whatever object its CAR slot currently holds, and likewise for the CDR.

A list is a series of cons cells chained together, so that each cell refers to the next one. There is one cons cell for each element of the list. By convention, the CARs of the cons cells hold the elements of the list, and the CDRs are used to chain the list (this asymmetry between CAR and CDR is entirely a matter of convention; at the level of cons cells, the CAR and CDR slots have similar properties). Hence, the CDR slot of each cons cell in a list refers to the following cons cell.

Also by convention, the CDR of the last cons cell in a list is `nil`. We call such a `nil`-terminated structure a *true list*. In Emacs Lisp, the symbol `nil` is both a symbol and a list with no elements. For convenience, the symbol `nil` is considered to have `nil` as its CDR (and also as its CAR).

Hence, the CDR of a true list is always a true list. The CDR of a nonempty true list is a true list containing all the elements except the first.

If the CDR of a list's last cons cell is some value other than `nil`, we call the structure a *dotted list*, since its printed representation would use dotted pair notation (see Section 2.3.6.2 [Dotted Pair Notation], page 17). There is one other possibility: some cons cell's CDR could point to one of the previous cons cells in the list. We call that structure a *circular list*.

For some purposes, it does not matter whether a list is true, circular or dotted. If a program doesn't look far enough down the list to see the CDR of the final cons cell, it won't care. However, some functions that operate on lists demand true lists and signal errors if given a dotted list. Most functions that try to find the end of a list enter infinite loops if given a circular list.

Because most cons cells are used as part of lists, we refer to any structure made out of cons cells as a *list structure*.

5.2 Predicates on Lists

The following predicates test whether a Lisp object is an atom, whether it is a cons cell or is a list, or whether it is the distinguished object `nil`. (Many of these predicates can be defined in terms of the others, but they are used so often that it is worth having them.)

consp *object*   [Function]
> This function returns **t** if *object* is a cons cell, **nil** otherwise. **nil** is not a cons cell, although it *is* a list.

atom *object*   [Function]
> This function returns **t** if *object* is an atom, **nil** otherwise. All objects except cons cells are atoms. The symbol **nil** is an atom and is also a list; it is the only Lisp object that is both.
>
>> (atom *object*) ≡ (not (consp *object*))

listp *object*   [Function]
> This function returns **t** if *object* is a cons cell or **nil**. Otherwise, it returns **nil**.
>
>> (listp '(1))
>>> ⇒ t
>> (listp '())
>>> ⇒ t

nlistp *object*   [Function]
> This function is the opposite of **listp**: it returns **t** if *object* is not a list. Otherwise, it returns **nil**.
>
>> (listp *object*) ≡ (not (nlistp *object*))

null *object*   [Function]
> This function returns **t** if *object* is **nil**, and returns **nil** otherwise. This function is identical to **not**, but as a matter of clarity we use **null** when *object* is considered a list and **not** when it is considered a truth value (see **not** in Section 10.3 [Combining Conditions], page 141).
>
>> (null '(1))
>>> ⇒ nil
>> (null '())
>>> ⇒ t

5.3 Accessing Elements of Lists

car *cons-cell*   [Function]
> This function returns the value referred to by the first slot of the cons cell *cons-cell*. In other words, it returns the CAR of *cons-cell*.
>
> As a special case, if *cons-cell* is **nil**, this function returns **nil**. Therefore, any list is a valid argument. An error is signaled if the argument is not a cons cell or **nil**.
>
>> (car '(a b c))
>>> ⇒ a
>> (car '())
>>> ⇒ nil

cdr *cons-cell*   [Function]
> This function returns the value referred to by the second slot of the cons cell *cons-cell*. In other words, it returns the CDR of *cons-cell*.

As a special case, if *cons-cell* is `nil`, this function returns `nil`; therefore, any list is a valid argument. An error is signaled if the argument is not a cons cell or `nil`.

```
(cdr '(a b c))
     ⇒ (b c)
(cdr '())
     ⇒ nil
```

car-safe *object*   [Function]

This function lets you take the CAR of a cons cell while avoiding errors for other data types. It returns the CAR of *object* if *object* is a cons cell, `nil` otherwise. This is in contrast to `car`, which signals an error if *object* is not a list.

```
(car-safe object)
≡
(let ((x object))
  (if (consp x)
      (car x)
    nil))
```

cdr-safe *object*   [Function]

This function lets you take the CDR of a cons cell while avoiding errors for other data types. It returns the CDR of *object* if *object* is a cons cell, `nil` otherwise. This is in contrast to `cdr`, which signals an error if *object* is not a list.

```
(cdr-safe object)
≡
(let ((x object))
  (if (consp x)
      (cdr x)
    nil))
```

pop *listname*   [Macro]

This macro provides a convenient way to examine the CAR of a list, and take it off the list, all at once. It operates on the list stored in *listname*. It removes the first element from the list, saves the CDR into *listname*, then returns the removed element.

In the simplest case, *listname* is an unquoted symbol naming a list; in that case, this macro is equivalent to `(prog1 (car listname) (setq listname (cdr listname)))`.

```
x
     ⇒ (a b c)
(pop x)
     ⇒ a
x
     ⇒ (b c)
```

More generally, *listname* can be a generalized variable. In that case, this macro saves into *listname* using `setf`. See Section 11.15 [Generalized Variables], page 183.

For the `push` macro, which adds an element to a list, See Section 5.5 [List Variables], page 74.

nth *n list*   [Function]

This function returns the *n*th element of *list*. Elements are numbered starting with zero, so the CAR of *list* is element number zero. If the length of *list* is *n* or less, the value is `nil`.

```
(nth 2 '(1 2 3 4))
     ⇒ 3
(nth 10 '(1 2 3 4))
     ⇒ nil
```

```
(nth n x) ≡ (car (nthcdr n x))
```

The function `elt` is similar, but applies to any kind of sequence. For historical reasons, it takes its arguments in the opposite order. See Section 6.1 [Sequence Functions], page 89.

nthcdr *n list*   [Function]

This function returns the *n*th CDR of *list*. In other words, it skips past the first *n* links of *list* and returns what follows.

If *n* is zero, `nthcdr` returns all of *list*. If the length of *list* is *n* or less, `nthcdr` returns `nil`.

```
(nthcdr 1 '(1 2 3 4))
     ⇒ (2 3 4)
(nthcdr 10 '(1 2 3 4))
     ⇒ nil
(nthcdr 0 '(1 2 3 4))
     ⇒ (1 2 3 4)
```

last *list* **&optional** *n*   [Function]

This function returns the last link of *list*. The `car` of this link is the list's last element. If *list* is null, `nil` is returned. If *n* is non-`nil`, the *n*th-to-last link is returned instead, or the whole of *list* if *n* is bigger than *list*'s length.

safe-length *list*   [Function]

This function returns the length of *list*, with no risk of either an error or an infinite loop. It generally returns the number of distinct cons cells in the list. However, for circular lists, the value is just an upper bound; it is often too large.

If *list* is not `nil` or a cons cell, `safe-length` returns 0.

The most common way to compute the length of a list, when you are not worried that it may be circular, is with `length`. See Section 6.1 [Sequence Functions], page 89.

caar *cons-cell*   [Function]

This is the same as `(car (car cons-cell))`.

cadr *cons-cell*   [Function]

This is the same as `(car (cdr cons-cell))` or `(nth 1 cons-cell)`.

cdar *cons-cell*   [Function]

This is the same as `(cdr (car cons-cell))`.

cddr *cons-cell*   [Function]
> This is the same as (cdr (cdr *cons-cell*)) or (nthcdr 2 *cons-cell*).

butlast *x* &optional *n*   [Function]
> This function returns the list *x* with the last element, or the last *n* elements, removed.
> If *n* is greater than zero it makes a copy of the list so as not to damage the original
> list. In general, (append (butlast *x n*) (last *x n*)) will return a list equal to *x*.

nbutlast *x* &optional *n*   [Function]
> This is a version of butlast that works by destructively modifying the cdr of the
> appropriate element, rather than making a copy of the list.

5.4 Building Cons Cells and Lists

Many functions build lists, as lists reside at the very heart of Lisp. cons is the fundamental
list-building function; however, it is interesting to note that list is used more times in the
source code for Emacs than cons.

cons *object1* *object2*   [Function]
> This function is the most basic function for building new list structure. It creates a
> new cons cell, making *object1* the CAR, and *object2* the CDR. It then returns the new
> cons cell. The arguments *object1* and *object2* may be any Lisp objects, but most
> often *object2* is a list.
>
>   (cons 1 '(2))
>   ⇒ (1 2)
>   (cons 1 '())
>   ⇒ (1)
>   (cons 1 2)
>   ⇒ (1 . 2)
>
> cons is often used to add a single element to the front of a list. This is called *consing
> the element onto the list*.[1] For example:
>
>   (setq list (cons newelt list))
>
> Note that there is no conflict between the variable named list used in this example
> and the function named list described below; any symbol can serve both purposes.

list &rest *objects*   [Function]
> This function creates a list with *objects* as its elements. The resulting list is always
> nil-terminated. If no *objects* are given, the empty list is returned.
>
>   (list 1 2 3 4 5)
>   ⇒ (1 2 3 4 5)
>   (list 1 2 '(3 4 5) 'foo)
>   ⇒ (1 2 (3 4 5) foo)
>   (list)
>   ⇒ nil

---

[1] There is no strictly equivalent way to add an element to the end of a list. You can use (append *listname*
(list *newelt*)), which creates a whole new list by copying *listname* and adding *newelt* to its end. Or
you can use (nconc *listname* (list *newelt*)), which modifies *listname* by following all the CDRs and
then replacing the terminating nil. Compare this to adding an element to the beginning of a list with
cons, which neither copies nor modifies the list.

make-list *length object*   [Function]

This function creates a list of *length* elements, in which each element is *object*. Compare **make-list** with **make-string** (see Section 4.3 [Creating Strings], page 50).

```
(make-list 3 'pigs)
     ⇒ (pigs pigs pigs)
(make-list 0 'pigs)
     ⇒ nil
(setq l (make-list 3 '(a b)))
     ⇒ ((a b) (a b) (a b))
(eq (car l) (cadr l))
     ⇒ t
```

append *&rest sequences*   [Function]

This function returns a list containing all the elements of *sequences*. The *sequences* may be lists, vectors, bool-vectors, or strings, but the last one should usually be a list. All arguments except the last one are copied, so none of the arguments is altered. (See **nconc** in Section 5.6.3 [Rearrangement], page 79, for a way to join lists with no copying.)

More generally, the final argument to **append** may be any Lisp object. The final argument is not copied or converted; it becomes the CDR of the last cons cell in the new list. If the final argument is itself a list, then its elements become in effect elements of the result list. If the final element is not a list, the result is a dotted list since its final CDR is not **nil** as required in a true list.

Here is an example of using **append**:

```
(setq trees '(pine oak))
     ⇒ (pine oak)
(setq more-trees (append '(maple birch) trees))
     ⇒ (maple birch pine oak)

trees
     ⇒ (pine oak)
more-trees
     ⇒ (maple birch pine oak)
(eq trees (cdr (cdr more-trees)))
     ⇒ t
```

You can see how **append** works by looking at a box diagram. The variable **trees** is set to the list (pine oak) and then the variable **more-trees** is set to the list (maple birch pine oak). However, the variable **trees** continues to refer to the original list:

```
more-trees                   trees
 |                            |
 |   --- ---     --- ---   -> --- ---     --- ---
 --> |   |   |--> |   |   |--> |   |   |--> |   |   |--> nil
     --- ---     --- ---     --- ---     --- ---
      |           |           |           |
      |           |           |           |
     --> maple   -->birch     --> pine    --> oak
```

An empty sequence contributes nothing to the value returned by **append**. As a consequence of this, a final **nil** argument forces a copy of the previous argument:

```
trees
     ⇒ (pine oak)
(setq wood (append trees nil))
     ⇒ (pine oak)
wood
     ⇒ (pine oak)
(eq wood trees)
     ⇒ nil
```

This once was the usual way to copy a list, before the function **copy-sequence** was invented. See Chapter 6 [Sequences Arrays Vectors], page 89.

Here we show the use of vectors and strings as arguments to **append**:

```
(append [a b] "cd" nil)
     ⇒ (a b 99 100)
```

With the help of **apply** (see Section 12.5 [Calling Functions], page 194), we can append all the lists in a list of lists:

```
(apply 'append '((a b c) nil (x y z) nil))
     ⇒ (a b c x y z)
```

If no *sequences* are given, **nil** is returned:

```
(append)
     ⇒ nil
```

Here are some examples where the final argument is not a list:

```
(append '(x y) 'z)
     ⇒ (x y . z)
(append '(x y) [z])
     ⇒ (x y . [z])
```

The second example shows that when the final argument is a sequence but not a list, the sequence's elements do not become elements of the resulting list. Instead, the sequence becomes the final CDR, like any other non-list final argument.

copy-tree *tree* **&optional** *vecp*   [Function]

> This function returns a copy of the tree **tree**. If *tree* is a cons cell, this makes a new cons cell with the same CAR and CDR, then recursively copies the CAR and CDR in the same way.

> Normally, when *tree* is anything other than a cons cell, **copy-tree** simply returns *tree*. However, if *vecp* is non-**nil**, it copies vectors too (and operates recursively on their elements).

number-sequence *from* **&optional** *to separation*   [Function]

> This returns a list of numbers starting with *from* and incrementing by *separation*, and ending at or just before *to*. *separation* can be positive or negative and defaults to 1. If *to* is **nil** or numerically equal to *from*, the value is the one-element list (*from*). If *to* is less than *from* with a positive *separation*, or greater than *from* with a negative *separation*, the value is **nil** because those arguments specify an empty sequence.

If *separation* is 0 and *to* is neither `nil` nor numerically equal to *from*, `number-sequence` signals an error, since those arguments specify an infinite sequence.

All arguments are numbers. Floating-point arguments can be tricky, because floating-point arithmetic is inexact. For instance, depending on the machine, it may quite well happen that (`number-sequence` 0.4 0.6 0.2) returns the one element list (0.4), whereas (`number-sequence` 0.4 0.8 0.2) returns a list with three elements. The *n*th element of the list is computed by the exact formula (+ *from* (* *n* *separation*)). Thus, if one wants to make sure that *to* is included in the list, one can pass an expression of this exact type for *to*. Alternatively, one can replace *to* with a slightly larger value (or a slightly more negative value if *separation* is negative).

Some examples:

```
(number-sequence 4 9)
    ⇒ (4 5 6 7 8 9)
(number-sequence 9 4 -1)
    ⇒ (9 8 7 6 5 4)
(number-sequence 9 4 -2)
    ⇒ (9 7 5)
(number-sequence 8)
    ⇒ (8)
(number-sequence 8 5)
    ⇒ nil
(number-sequence 5 8 -1)
    ⇒ nil
(number-sequence 1.5 6 2)
    ⇒ (1.5 3.5 5.5)
```

5.5 Modifying List Variables

These functions, and one macro, provide convenient ways to modify a list which is stored in a variable.

push *element listname*   [Macro]

This macro creates a new list whose CAR is *element* and whose CDR is the list specified by *listname*, and saves that list in *listname*. In the simplest case, *listname* is an unquoted symbol naming a list, and this macro is equivalent to (`setq` *listname* (`cons` *element* *listname*)).

```
(setq l '(a b))
    ⇒ (a b)
(push 'c l)
    ⇒ (c a b)
l
    ⇒ (c a b)
```

More generally, `listname` can be a generalized variable. In that case, this macro does the equivalent of (`setf` *listname* (`cons` *element* *listname*)). See Section 11.15 [Generalized Variables], page 183.

For the **pop** macro, which removes the first element from a list, See Section 5.3 [List Elements], page 68.

Two functions modify lists that are the values of variables.

add-to-list *symbol element* **&optional** *append compare-fn*   [Function]

This function sets the variable *symbol* by consing *element* onto the old value, if *element* is not already a member of that value. It returns the resulting list, whether updated or not. The value of *symbol* had better be a list already before the call. **add-to-list** uses *compare-fn* to compare *element* against existing list members; if *compare-fn* is **nil**, it uses **equal**.

Normally, if *element* is added, it is added to the front of *symbol*, but if the optional argument *append* is non-**nil**, it is added at the end.

The argument *symbol* is not implicitly quoted; **add-to-list** is an ordinary function, like **set** and unlike **setq**. Quote the argument yourself if that is what you want.

Here's a scenario showing how to use **add-to-list**:

```
(setq foo '(a b))
     ⇒ (a b)

(add-to-list 'foo 'c)       ; ; Add c.
     ⇒ (c a b)

(add-to-list 'foo 'b)       ; ; No effect.
     ⇒ (c a b)

foo                         ; ; foo was changed.
     ⇒ (c a b)
```

An equivalent expression for (**add-to-list** '*var value*) is this:

```
(or (member value var)
    (setq var (cons value var)))
```

add-to-ordered-list *symbol element* **&optional** *order*   [Function]

This function sets the variable *symbol* by inserting *element* into the old value, which must be a list, at the position specified by *order*. If *element* is already a member of the list, its position in the list is adjusted according to *order*. Membership is tested using **eq**. This function returns the resulting list, whether updated or not.

The *order* is typically a number (integer or float), and the elements of the list are sorted in non-decreasing numerical order.

order may also be omitted or **nil**. Then the numeric order of *element* stays unchanged if it already has one; otherwise, *element* has no numeric order. Elements without a numeric list order are placed at the end of the list, in no particular order.

Any other value for *order* removes the numeric order of *element* if it already has one; otherwise, it is equivalent to **nil**.

The argument *symbol* is not implicitly quoted; **add-to-ordered-list** is an ordinary function, like **set** and unlike **setq**. Quote the argument yourself if necessary.

The ordering information is stored in a hash table on *symbol*'s **list-order** property.

Here's a scenario showing how to use `add-to-ordered-list`:

```
(setq foo '())
     ⇒ nil

(add-to-ordered-list 'foo 'a 1)        ;; Add a.
     ⇒ (a)

(add-to-ordered-list 'foo 'c 3)        ;; Add c.
     ⇒ (a c)

(add-to-ordered-list 'foo 'b 2)        ;; Add b.
     ⇒ (a b c)

(add-to-ordered-list 'foo 'b 4)        ;; Move b.
     ⇒ (a c b)

(add-to-ordered-list 'foo 'd)          ;; Append d.
     ⇒ (a c b d)

(add-to-ordered-list 'foo 'e)          ;; Add e.
     ⇒ (a c b e d)

foo                                    ;; foo was changed.
     ⇒ (a c b e d)
```

5.6 Modifying Existing List Structure

You can modify the CAR and CDR contents of a cons cell with the primitives `setcar` and
`setcdr`. These are destructive operations because they change existing list structure.

> **Common Lisp note:** Common Lisp uses functions `rplaca` and `rplacd` to alter
> list structure; they change structure the same way as `setcar` and `setcdr`, but
> the Common Lisp functions return the cons cell while `setcar` and `setcdr` return
> the new CAR or CDR.

5.6.1 Altering List Elements with `setcar`

Changing the CAR of a cons cell is done with `setcar`. When used on a list, `setcar` replaces
one element of a list with a different element.

`setcar` *cons object*   [Function]
> This function stores *object* as the new CAR of *cons*, replacing its previous CAR. In
> other words, it changes the CAR slot of *cons* to refer to *object*. It returns the value
> *object*. For example:
>
> ```
> (setq x '(1 2))
>      ⇒ (1 2)
> (setcar x 4)
>      ⇒ 4
> ```

```
          x
              ⇒ (4 2)
```

When a cons cell is part of the shared structure of several lists, storing a new CAR into the cons changes one element of each of these lists. Here is an example:

```
;; Create two lists that are partly shared.
(setq x1 '(a b c))
     ⇒ (a b c)
(setq x2 (cons 'z (cdr x1)))
     ⇒ (z b c)

;; Replace the CAR of a shared link.
(setcar (cdr x1) 'foo)
     ⇒ foo
x1                              ; Both lists are changed.
     ⇒ (a foo c)
x2
     ⇒ (z foo c)

;; Replace the CAR of a link that is not shared.
(setcar x1 'baz)
     ⇒ baz
x1                              ; Only one list is changed.
     ⇒ (baz foo c)
x2
     ⇒ (z foo c)
```

Here is a graphical depiction of the shared structure of the two lists in the variables x1 and x2, showing why replacing b changes them both:

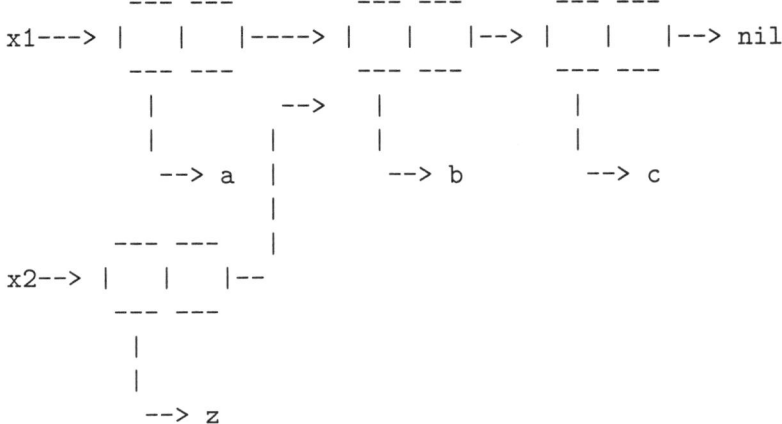

Here is an alternative form of box diagram, showing the same relationship:

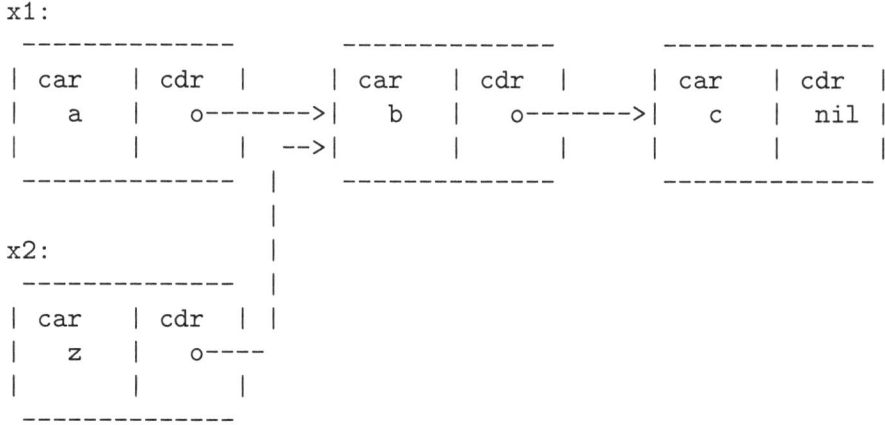

5.6.2 Altering the CDR of a List

The lowest-level primitive for modifying a CDR is `setcdr`:

setcdr *cons object*   [Function]
> This function stores *object* as the new CDR of *cons*, replacing its previous CDR. In other words, it changes the CDR slot of *cons* to refer to *object*. It returns the value *object*.

Here is an example of replacing the CDR of a list with a different list. All but the first element of the list are removed in favor of a different sequence of elements. The first element is unchanged, because it resides in the CAR of the list, and is not reached via the CDR.

```
(setq x '(1 2 3))
     ⇒ (1 2 3)
(setcdr x '(4))
     ⇒ (4)
x
     ⇒ (1 4)
```

You can delete elements from the middle of a list by altering the CDRs of the cons cells in the list. For example, here we delete the second element, b, from the list (a b c), by changing the CDR of the first cons cell:

```
(setq x1 '(a b c))
     ⇒ (a b c)
(setcdr x1 (cdr (cdr x1)))
     ⇒ (c)
x1
     ⇒ (a c)
```

Here is the result in box notation:

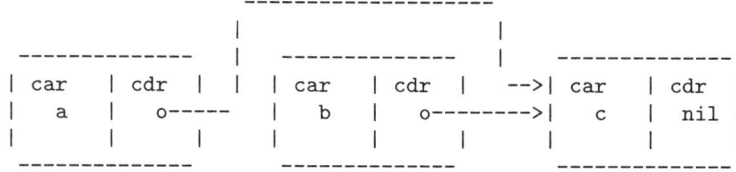

The second cons cell, which previously held the element b, still exists and its CAR is still b, but it no longer forms part of this list.

It is equally easy to insert a new element by changing CDRs:

```
(setq x1 '(a b c))
     ⇒ (a b c)
(setcdr x1 (cons 'd (cdr x1)))
     ⇒ (d b c)
x1
     ⇒ (a d b c)
```

Here is this result in box notation:

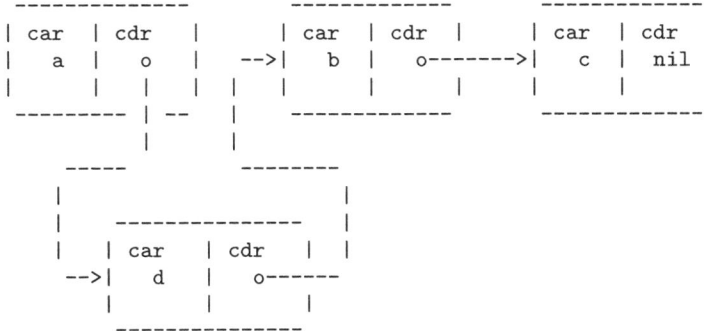

5.6.3 Functions that Rearrange Lists

Here are some functions that rearrange lists destructively by modifying the CDRs of their component cons cells. These functions are destructive because they chew up the original lists passed to them as arguments, relinking their cons cells to form a new list that is the returned value.

The function **delq** in the following section is another example of destructive list manipulation.

nconc &rest *lists*   [Function]

This function returns a list containing all the elements of *lists*. Unlike **append** (see Section 5.4 [Building Lists], page 71), the *lists* are *not* copied. Instead, the last CDR of each of the *lists* is changed to refer to the following list. The last of the *lists* is not altered. For example:

```
(setq x '(1 2 3))
     ⇒ (1 2 3)
(nconc x '(4 5))
     ⇒ (1 2 3 4 5)
x
     ⇒ (1 2 3 4 5)
```

Since the last argument of **nconc** is not itself modified, it is reasonable to use a constant list, such as '(4 5), as in the above example. For the same reason, the last argument need not be a list:

```
(setq x '(1 2 3))
     ⇒ (1 2 3)
```

```
(nconc x 'z)
     ⇒ (1 2 3 . z)
x
     ⇒ (1 2 3 . z)
```

However, the other arguments (all but the last) must be lists.

A common pitfall is to use a quoted constant list as a non-last argument to `nconc`. If you do this, your program will change each time you run it! Here is what happens:

```
(defun add-foo (x)           ; We want this function to add
  (nconc '(foo) x))          ;    foo to the front of its arg.

(symbol-function 'add-foo)
     ⇒ (lambda (x) (nconc (quote (foo)) x))

(setq xx (add-foo '(1 2)))   ; It seems to work.
     ⇒ (foo 1 2)
(setq xy (add-foo '(3 4)))   ; What happened?
     ⇒ (foo 1 2 3 4)
(eq xx xy)
     ⇒ t

(symbol-function 'add-foo)
     ⇒ (lambda (x) (nconc (quote (foo 1 2 3 4) x)))
```

5.7 Using Lists as Sets

A list can represent an unordered mathematical set—simply consider a value an element of a set if it appears in the list, and ignore the order of the list. To form the union of two sets, use `append` (as long as you don't mind having duplicate elements). You can remove `equal` duplicates using `delete-dups`. Other useful functions for sets include `memq` and `delq`, and their `equal` versions, `member` and `delete`.

> **Common Lisp note:** Common Lisp has functions `union` (which avoids duplicate elements) and `intersection` for set operations. Although standard GNU Emacs Lisp does not have them, the `cl-lib` library provides versions. See Section "Lists as Sets" in *Common Lisp Extensions*.

`memq` *object list*   [Function]

    This function tests to see whether *object* is a member of *list*. If it is, `memq` returns a list starting with the first occurrence of *object*. Otherwise, it returns `nil`. The letter 'q' in `memq` says that it uses `eq` to compare *object* against the elements of the list. For example:

```
(memq 'b '(a b c b a))
     ⇒ (b c b a)
(memq '(2) '((1) (2)))     ; (2) and (2) are not eq.
     ⇒ nil
```

`delq` *object list*   [Function]

    This function destructively removes all elements `eq` to *object* from *list*, and returns the resulting list. The letter 'q' in `delq` says that it uses `eq` to compare *object* against the elements of the list, like `memq` and `remq`.

Typically, when you invoke `delq`, you should use the return value by assigning it to the variable which held the original list. The reason for this is explained below.

The `delq` function deletes elements from the front of the list by simply advancing down the list, and returning a sublist that starts after those elements. For example:

```
(delq 'a '(a b c)) ≡ (cdr '(a b c))
```

When an element to be deleted appears in the middle of the list, removing it involves changing the CDRs (see Section 5.6.2 [Setcdr], page 78).

```
(setq sample-list '(a b c (4)))
     ⇒ (a b c (4))
(delq 'a sample-list)
     ⇒ (b c (4))
sample-list
     ⇒ (a b c (4))
(delq 'c sample-list)
     ⇒ (a b (4))
sample-list
     ⇒ (a b (4))
```

Note that (`delq 'c sample-list`) modifies `sample-list` to splice out the third element, but (`delq 'a sample-list`) does not splice anything—it just returns a shorter list. Don't assume that a variable which formerly held the argument *list* now has fewer elements, or that it still holds the original list! Instead, save the result of `delq` and use that. Most often we store the result back into the variable that held the original list:

```
(setq flowers (delq 'rose flowers))
```

In the following example, the (4) that `delq` attempts to match and the (4) in the `sample-list` are not `eq`:

```
(delq '(4) sample-list)
     ⇒ (a c (4))
```

If you want to delete elements that are `equal` to a given value, use `delete` (see below).

`remq` *object list*   [Function]

    This function returns a copy of *list*, with all elements removed which are `eq` to *object*. The letter 'q' in `remq` says that it uses `eq` to compare *object* against the elements of `list`.

```
(setq sample-list '(a b c a b c))
     ⇒ (a b c a b c)
(remq 'a sample-list)
     ⇒ (b c b c)
sample-list
     ⇒ (a b c a b c)
```

`memql` *object list*   [Function]

    The function `memql` tests to see whether *object* is a member of *list*, comparing members with *object* using `eql`, so floating-point elements are compared by value. If *object* is a member, `memql` returns a list starting with its first occurrence in *list*. Otherwise, it returns `nil`.

Compare this with `memq`:

```
(memql 1.2 '(1.1 1.2 1.3))   ; 1.2 and 1.2 are eql.
     ⇒ (1.2 1.3)
(memq 1.2 '(1.1 1.2 1.3))    ; 1.2 and 1.2 are not eq.
     ⇒ nil
```

The following three functions are like `memq`, `delq` and `remq`, but use `equal` rather than `eq` to compare elements. See Section 2.7 [Equality Predicates], page 31.

member *object list*   [Function]

The function `member` tests to see whether *object* is a member of *list*, comparing members with *object* using `equal`. If *object* is a member, `member` returns a list starting with its first occurrence in *list*. Otherwise, it returns `nil`.

Compare this with `memq`:

```
(member '(2) '((1) (2)))   ; (2) and (2) are equal.
     ⇒ ((2))
(memq '(2) '((1) (2)))     ; (2) and (2) are not eq.
     ⇒ nil
;; Two strings with the same contents are equal.
(member "foo" '("foo" "bar"))
     ⇒ ("foo" "bar")
```

delete *object sequence*   [Function]

This function removes all elements `equal` to *object* from *sequence*, and returns the resulting sequence.

If *sequence* is a list, `delete` is to `delq` as `member` is to `memq`: it uses `equal` to compare elements with *object*, like `member`; when it finds an element that matches, it cuts the element out just as `delq` would. As with `delq`, you should typically use the return value by assigning it to the variable which held the original list.

If `sequence` is a vector or string, `delete` returns a copy of `sequence` with all elements `equal` to `object` removed.

For example:

```
(setq l '((2) (1) (2)))
(delete '(2) l)
     ⇒ ((1))
l
     ⇒ ((2) (1))
;; If you want to change l reliably,
;; write (setq l (delete '(2) l)).
(setq l '((2) (1) (2)))
(delete '(1) l)
     ⇒ ((2) (2))
l
     ⇒ ((2) (2))
;; In this case, it makes no difference whether you set l,
;; but you should do so for the sake of the other case.
```

```
(delete '(2) [(2) (1) (2)])
    ⇒ [(1)]
```

remove *object sequence*   [Function]

> This function is the non-destructive counterpart of `delete`. It returns a copy of *sequence*, a list, vector, or string, with elements `equal` to *object* removed. For example:
>
> ```
> (remove '(2) '((2) (1) (2)))
>     ⇒ ((1))
> (remove '(2) [(2) (1) (2)])
>     ⇒ [(1)]
> ```
>
> **Common Lisp note:** The functions `member`, `delete` and `remove` in GNU Emacs Lisp are derived from Maclisp, not Common Lisp. The Common Lisp versions do not use `equal` to compare elements.

member-ignore-case *object list*   [Function]

> This function is like `member`, except that *object* should be a string and that it ignores differences in letter-case and text representation: upper-case and lower-case letters are treated as equal, and unibyte strings are converted to multibyte prior to comparison.

delete-dups *list*   [Function]

> This function destructively removes all `equal` duplicates from *list*, stores the result in *list* and returns it. Of several `equal` occurrences of an element in *list*, `delete-dups` keeps the first one.

See also the function `add-to-list`, in Section 5.5 [List Variables], page 74, for a way to add an element to a list stored in a variable and used as a set.

5.8 Association Lists

An *association list*, or *alist* for short, records a mapping from keys to values. It is a list of cons cells called *associations*: the CAR of each cons cell is the *key*, and the CDR is the *associated value*.[2]

Here is an example of an alist. The key `pine` is associated with the value `cones`; the key `oak` is associated with `acorns`; and the key `maple` is associated with `seeds`.

```
((pine . cones)
 (oak . acorns)
 (maple . seeds))
```

Both the values and the keys in an alist may be any Lisp objects. For example, in the following alist, the symbol `a` is associated with the number `1`, and the string `"b"` is associated with the *list* `(2 3)`, which is the CDR of the alist element:

```
((a . 1) ("b" 2 3))
```

Sometimes it is better to design an alist to store the associated value in the CAR of the CDR of the element. Here is an example of such an alist:

```
((rose red) (lily white) (buttercup yellow))
```

---

[2] This usage of "key" is not related to the term "key sequence"; it means a value used to look up an item in a table. In this case, the table is the alist, and the alist associations are the items.

Here we regard `red` as the value associated with `rose`. One advantage of this kind of alist is that you can store other related information—even a list of other items—in the CDR of the CDR. One disadvantage is that you cannot use `rassq` (see below) to find the element containing a given value. When neither of these considerations is important, the choice is a matter of taste, as long as you are consistent about it for any given alist.

The same alist shown above could be regarded as having the associated value in the CDR of the element; the value associated with `rose` would be the list `(red)`.

Association lists are often used to record information that you might otherwise keep on a stack, since new associations may be added easily to the front of the list. When searching an association list for an association with a given key, the first one found is returned, if there is more than one.

In Emacs Lisp, it is *not* an error if an element of an association list is not a cons cell. The alist search functions simply ignore such elements. Many other versions of Lisp signal errors in such cases.

Note that property lists are similar to association lists in several respects. A property list behaves like an association list in which each key can occur only once. See Section 5.9 [Property Lists], page 87, for a comparison of property lists and association lists.

assoc *key alist*   [Function]

This function returns the first association for *key* in *alist*, comparing *key* against the alist elements using `equal` (see Section 2.7 [Equality Predicates], page 31). It returns `nil` if no association in *alist* has a CAR `equal` to *key*. For example:

```
(setq trees '((pine . cones) (oak . acorns) (maple . seeds)))
     ⇒ ((pine . cones) (oak . acorns) (maple . seeds))
(assoc 'oak trees)
     ⇒ (oak . acorns)
(cdr (assoc 'oak trees))
     ⇒ acorns
(assoc 'birch trees)
     ⇒ nil
```

Here is another example, in which the keys and values are not symbols:

```
(setq needles-per-cluster
      '((2 "Austrian Pine" "Red Pine")
        (3 "Pitch Pine")
        (5 "White Pine")))

(cdr (assoc 3 needles-per-cluster))
     ⇒ ("Pitch Pine")
(cdr (assoc 2 needles-per-cluster))
     ⇒ ("Austrian Pine" "Red Pine")
```

The function `assoc-string` is much like `assoc` except that it ignores certain differences between strings. See Section 4.5 [Text Comparison], page 54.

rassoc *value alist*   [Function]

This function returns the first association with value *value* in *alist*. It returns `nil` if no association in *alist* has a CDR `equal` to *value*.

`rassoc` is like `assoc` except that it compares the CDR of each *alist* association instead of the CAR. You can think of this as reverse `assoc`, finding the key for a given value.

assq *key alist*   [Function]

>   This function is like **assoc** in that it returns the first association for *key* in *alist*, but
>   it makes the comparison using **eq** instead of **equal**. **assq** returns **nil** if no association
>   in *alist* has a CAR eq to *key*. This function is used more often than **assoc**, since **eq**
>   is faster than **equal** and most alists use symbols as keys. See Section 2.7 [Equality
>   Predicates], page 31.
>
>   ```
>   (setq trees '((pine . cones) (oak . acorns) (maple . seeds)))
>        ⇒ ((pine . cones) (oak . acorns) (maple . seeds))
>   (assq 'pine trees)
>        ⇒ (pine . cones)
>   ```
>
>   On the other hand, **assq** is not usually useful in alists where the keys may not be
>   symbols:
>
>   ```
>   (setq leaves
>         '(("simple leaves" . oak)
>           ("compound leaves" . horsechestnut)))
>
>   (assq "simple leaves" leaves)
>        ⇒ nil
>   (assoc "simple leaves" leaves)
>        ⇒ ("simple leaves" . oak)
>   ```

alist-get *key alist* **&optional** *default remove*   [Function]

>   This function is like **assq**, but instead of returning the entire association for *key* in
>   *alist*, (**key** . **value**), it returns just the *value*. If *key* is not found in *alist*, it returns
>   *default*.
>
>   This is a generalized variable (see Section 11.15 [Generalized Variables], page 183)
>   that can be used to change a value with **setf**. When using it to set a value, optional
>   argument *remove* non-**nil** means to remove *key* from *alist* if the new value is **eql** to
>   *default*.

rassq *value alist*   [Function]

>   This function returns the first association with value *value* in *alist*. It returns **nil** if
>   no association in *alist* has a CDR eq to *value*.
>
>   **rassq** is like **assq** except that it compares the CDR of each *alist* association instead
>   of the CAR. You can think of this as reverse **assq**, finding the key for a given value.
>
>   For example:
>
>   ```
>   (setq trees '((pine . cones) (oak . acorns) (maple . seeds)))
>
>   (rassq 'acorns trees)
>        ⇒ (oak . acorns)
>   (rassq 'spores trees)
>        ⇒ nil
>   ```
>
>   **rassq** cannot search for a value stored in the CAR of the CDR of an element:
>
>   ```
>   (setq colors '((rose red) (lily white) (buttercup yellow)))
>
>   (rassq 'white colors)
>        ⇒ nil
>   ```
>
>   In this case, the CDR of the association (**lily white**) is not the symbol **white**, but
>   rather the list (**white**). This becomes clearer if the association is written in dotted
>   pair notation:
>
>   ```
>   (lily white) ≡ (lily . (white))
>   ```

assoc-default *key alist* **&optional** *test default*   [Function]

> This function searches *alist* for a match for *key*. For each element of *alist*, it compares
> the element (if it is an atom) or the element's CAR (if it is a cons) against *key*, by
> calling *test* with two arguments: the element or its CAR, and *key*. The arguments are
> passed in that order so that you can get useful results using **string-match** with an
> alist that contains regular expressions (see Section 33.4 [Regexp Search], page 803).
> If *test* is omitted or **nil**, **equal** is used for comparison.
>
> If an alist element matches *key* by this criterion, then **assoc-default** returns a value
> based on this element. If the element is a cons, then the value is the element's CDR.
> Otherwise, the return value is *default*.
>
> If no alist element matches *key*, **assoc-default** returns **nil**.

copy-alist *alist*   [Function]

> This function returns a two-level deep copy of *alist*: it creates a new copy of each
> association, so that you can alter the associations of the new alist without changing
> the old one.
>
> ```
> (setq needles-per-cluster
>       '((2 . ("Austrian Pine" "Red Pine"))
>         (3 . ("Pitch Pine"))
>         (5 . ("White Pine"))))
> ⇒
> ((2 "Austrian Pine" "Red Pine")
>  (3 "Pitch Pine")
>  (5 "White Pine"))
>
> (setq copy (copy-alist needles-per-cluster))
> ⇒
> ((2 "Austrian Pine" "Red Pine")
>  (3 "Pitch Pine")
>  (5 "White Pine"))
>
> (eq needles-per-cluster copy)
>     ⇒ nil
> (equal needles-per-cluster copy)
>     ⇒ t
> (eq (car needles-per-cluster) (car copy))
>     ⇒ nil
> (cdr (car (cdr needles-per-cluster)))
>     ⇒ ("Pitch Pine")
> (eq (cdr (car (cdr needles-per-cluster)))
>     (cdr (car (cdr copy))))
>     ⇒ t
> ```
>
> This example shows how **copy-alist** makes it possible to change the associations of
> one copy without affecting the other:
>
> ```
> (setcdr (assq 3 copy) '("Martian Vacuum Pine"))
> (cdr (assq 3 needles-per-cluster))
>     ⇒ ("Pitch Pine")
> ```

assq-delete-all *key alist*   [Function]

> This function deletes from *alist* all the elements whose CAR is **eq** to *key*, much as
> if you used **delq** to delete each such element one by one. It returns the shortened

alist, and often modifies the original list structure of *alist*. For correct results, use the return value of `assq-delete-all` rather than looking at the saved value of *alist*.

```
(setq alist '((foo 1) (bar 2) (foo 3) (lose 4)))
     ⇒ ((foo 1) (bar 2) (foo 3) (lose 4))
(assq-delete-all 'foo alist)
     ⇒ ((bar 2) (lose 4))
alist
     ⇒ ((foo 1) (bar 2) (lose 4))
```

`rassq-delete-all` *value alist*   [Function]
  This function deletes from *alist* all the elements whose CDR is `eq` to *value*. It returns the shortened alist, and often modifies the original list structure of *alist*. `rassq-delete-all` is like `assq-delete-all` except that it compares the CDR of each *alist* association instead of the CAR.

5.9 Property Lists

A *property list* (*plist* for short) is a list of paired elements. Each of the pairs associates a property name (usually a symbol) with a property or value. Here is an example of a property list:

```
(pine cones numbers (1 2 3) color "blue")
```

This property list associates `pine` with `cones`, `numbers` with (1 2 3), and `color` with `"blue"`. The property names and values can be any Lisp objects, but the names are usually symbols (as they are in this example).

Property lists are used in several contexts. For instance, the function `put-text-property` takes an argument which is a property list, specifying text properties and associated values which are to be applied to text in a string or buffer. See Section 31.19 [Text Properties], page 732.

Another prominent use of property lists is for storing symbol properties. Every symbol possesses a list of properties, used to record miscellaneous information about the symbol; these properties are stored in the form of a property list. See Section 8.4 [Symbol Properties], page 119.

5.9.1 Property Lists and Association Lists

Association lists (see Section 5.8 [Association Lists], page 83) are very similar to property lists. In contrast to association lists, the order of the pairs in the property list is not significant, since the property names must be distinct.

Property lists are better than association lists for attaching information to various Lisp function names or variables. If your program keeps all such information in one association list, it will typically need to search that entire list each time it checks for an association for a particular Lisp function name or variable, which could be slow. By contrast, if you keep the same information in the property lists of the function names or variables themselves, each search will scan only the length of one property list, which is usually short. This is why the documentation for a variable is recorded in a property named `variable-documentation`. The byte compiler likewise uses properties to record those functions needing special treatment.

However, association lists have their own advantages. Depending on your application, it may be faster to add an association to the front of an association list than to update a property. All properties for a symbol are stored in the same property list, so there is a possibility of a conflict between different uses of a property name. (For this reason, it is a good idea to choose property names that are probably unique, such as by beginning the property name with the program's usual name-prefix for variables and functions.) An association list may be used like a stack where associations are pushed on the front of the list and later discarded; this is not possible with a property list.

5.9.2 Property Lists Outside Symbols

The following functions can be used to manipulate property lists. They all compare property names using `eq`.

`plist-get` *plist property*   [Function]

> This returns the value of the *property* property stored in the property list *plist*. It accepts a malformed *plist* argument. If *property* is not found in the *plist*, it returns `nil`. For example,

```
(plist-get '(foo 4) 'foo)
    ⇒ 4
(plist-get '(foo 4 bad) 'foo)
    ⇒ 4
(plist-get '(foo 4 bad) 'bad)
    ⇒ nil
(plist-get '(foo 4 bad) 'bar)
    ⇒ nil
```

`plist-put` *plist property value*   [Function]

> This stores *value* as the value of the *property* property in the property list *plist*. It may modify *plist* destructively, or it may construct a new list structure without altering the old. The function returns the modified property list, so you can store that back in the place where you got *plist*. For example,

```
(setq my-plist '(bar t foo 4))
    ⇒ (bar t foo 4)
(setq my-plist (plist-put my-plist 'foo 69))
    ⇒ (bar t foo 69)
(setq my-plist (plist-put my-plist 'quux '(a)))
    ⇒ (bar t foo 69 quux (a))
```

`lax-plist-get` *plist property*   [Function]

> Like `plist-get` except that it compares properties using `equal` instead of `eq`.

`lax-plist-put` *plist property value*   [Function]

> Like `plist-put` except that it compares properties using `equal` instead of `eq`.

`plist-member` *plist property*   [Function]

> This returns non-`nil` if *plist* contains the given *property*. Unlike `plist-get`, this allows you to distinguish between a missing property and a property with the value `nil`. The value is actually the tail of *plist* whose `car` is *property*.

6 Sequences, Arrays, and Vectors

The *sequence* type is the union of two other Lisp types: lists and arrays. In other words, any list is a sequence, and any array is a sequence. The common property that all sequences have is that each is an ordered collection of elements.

An *array* is a fixed-length object with a slot for each of its elements. All the elements are accessible in constant time. The four types of arrays are strings, vectors, char-tables and bool-vectors.

A list is a sequence of elements, but it is not a single primitive object; it is made of cons cells, one cell per element. Finding the *n*th element requires looking through *n* cons cells, so elements farther from the beginning of the list take longer to access. But it is possible to add elements to the list, or remove elements.

The following diagram shows the relationship between these types:

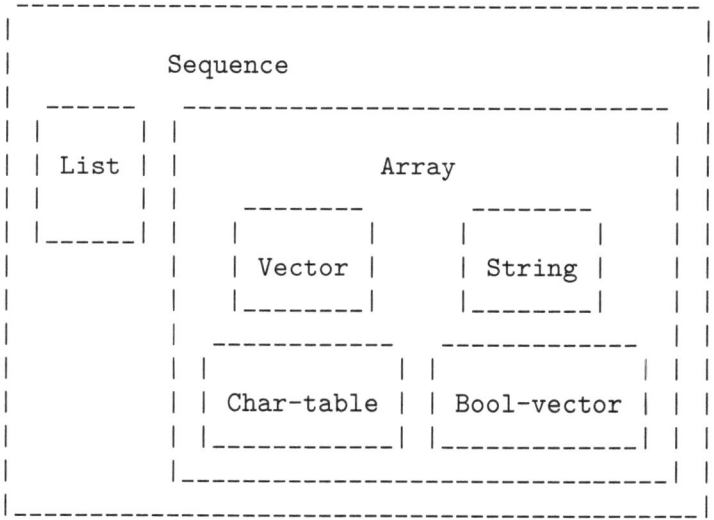

6.1 Sequences

This section describes functions that accept any kind of sequence.

sequencep *object*   [Function]
    This function returns **t** if *object* is a list, vector, string, bool-vector, or char-table, **nil** otherwise.

length *sequence*   [Function]
    This function returns the number of elements in *sequence*. If *sequence* is a dotted list, a **wrong-type-argument** error is signaled. Circular lists may cause an infinite loop. For a char-table, the value returned is always one more than the maximum Emacs character code.

    See [Definition of safe-length], page 70, for the related function **safe-length**.

```
(length '(1 2 3))
    ⇒ 3
```

```
(length ())
     ⇒ 0
(length "foobar")
     ⇒ 6
(length [1 2 3])
     ⇒ 3
(length (make-bool-vector 5 nil))
     ⇒ 5
```

See also **string-bytes**, in Section 32.1 [Text Representations], page 761.

If you need to compute the width of a string on display, you should use **string-width** (see Section 37.10 [Size of Displayed Text], page 912), not **length**, since **length** only counts the number of characters, but does not account for the display width of each character.

elt *sequence index*   [Function]
 This function returns the element of *sequence* indexed by *index*. Legitimate values of *index* are integers ranging from 0 up to one less than the length of *sequence*. If *sequence* is a list, out-of-range values behave as for **nth**. See [Definition of nth], page 70. Otherwise, out-of-range values trigger an **args-out-of-range** error.

```
(elt [1 2 3 4] 2)
     ⇒ 3
(elt '(1 2 3 4) 2)
     ⇒ 3
;; We use string to show clearly which character elt returns.
(string (elt "1234" 2))
     ⇒ "3"
(elt [1 2 3 4] 4)
     error   Args out of range: [1 2 3 4], 4
(elt [1 2 3 4] -1)
     error   Args out of range: [1 2 3 4], -1
```

This function generalizes **aref** (see Section 6.3 [Array Functions], page 101) and **nth** (see [Definition of nth], page 70).

copy-sequence *sequence*   [Function]
 This function returns a copy of *sequence*. The copy is the same type of object as the original sequence, and it has the same elements in the same order.

Storing a new element into the copy does not affect the original *sequence*, and vice versa. However, the elements of the new sequence are not copies; they are identical (**eq**) to the elements of the original. Therefore, changes made within these elements, as found via the copied sequence, are also visible in the original sequence.

If the sequence is a string with text properties, the property list in the copy is itself a copy, not shared with the original's property list. However, the actual values of the properties are shared. See Section 31.19 [Text Properties], page 732.

This function does not work for dotted lists. Trying to copy a circular list may cause an infinite loop.

See also `append` in Section 5.4 [Building Lists], page 71, `concat` in Section 4.3 [Creating Strings], page 50, and `vconcat` in Section 6.5 [Vector Functions], page 102, for other ways to copy sequences.

```
(setq bar '(1 2))
      ⇒ (1 2)
(setq x (vector 'foo bar))
      ⇒ [foo (1 2)]
(setq y (copy-sequence x))
      ⇒ [foo (1 2)]

(eq x y)
      ⇒ nil
(equal x y)
      ⇒ t
(eq (elt x 1) (elt y 1))
      ⇒ t

;; Replacing an element of one sequence.
(aset x 0 'quux)
x ⇒ [quux (1 2)]
y ⇒ [foo (1 2)]

;; Modifying the inside of a shared element.
(setcar (aref x 1) 69)
x ⇒ [quux (69 2)]
y ⇒ [foo (69 2)]
```

reverse *sequence*   [Function]

This function creates a new sequence whose elements are the elements of *sequence*, but in reverse order. The original argument *sequence* is *not* altered. Note that char-tables cannot be reversed.

```
(setq x '(1 2 3 4))
      ⇒ (1 2 3 4)
(reverse x)
      ⇒ (4 3 2 1)
x
      ⇒ (1 2 3 4)
(setq x [1 2 3 4])
      ⇒ [1 2 3 4]
(reverse x)
      ⇒ [4 3 2 1]
x
      ⇒ [1 2 3 4]
(setq x "xyzzy")
      ⇒ "xyzzy"
```

```
(reverse x)
      ⇒ "yzzyx"
x
      ⇒ "xyzzy"
```

nreverse *sequence*   [Function]

This function reverses the order of the elements of *sequence*. Unlike **reverse** the original *sequence* may be modified.

For example:

```
(setq x '(a b c))
      ⇒ (a b c)
x
      ⇒ (a b c)
(nreverse x)
      ⇒ (c b a)
;; The cons cell that was first is now last.
x
      ⇒ (a)
```

To avoid confusion, we usually store the result of **nreverse** back in the same variable which held the original list:

```
(setq x (nreverse x))
```

Here is the **nreverse** of our favorite example, (a b c), presented graphically:

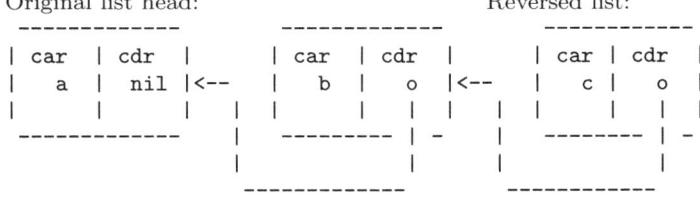

For the vector, it is even simpler because you don't need setq:

```
(setq x [1 2 3 4])
      ⇒ [1 2 3 4]
(nreverse x)
      ⇒ [4 3 2 1]
x
      ⇒ [4 3 2 1]
```

Note that unlike **reverse**, this function doesn't work with strings. Although you can alter string data by using **aset**, it is strongly encouraged to treat strings as immutable.

sort *sequence predicate*   [Function]

This function sorts *sequence* stably. Note that this function doesn't work for all sequences; it may be used only for lists and vectors. If *sequence* is a list, it is modified destructively. This functions returns the sorted *sequence* and compares elements using *predicate*. A stable sort is one in which elements with equal sort keys maintain their relative order before and after the sort. Stability is important when successive sorts are used to order elements according to different criteria.

The argument *predicate* must be a function that accepts two arguments. It is called with two elements of *sequence*. To get an increasing order sort, the *predicate* should return non-`nil` if the first element is "less" than the second, or `nil` if not.

The comparison function *predicate* must give reliable results for any given pair of arguments, at least within a single call to `sort`. It must be *antisymmetric*; that is, if *a* is less than *b*, *b* must not be less than *a*. It must be *transitive*—that is, if *a* is less than *b*, and *b* is less than *c*, then *a* must be less than *c*. If you use a comparison function which does not meet these requirements, the result of `sort` is unpredictable.

The destructive aspect of `sort` for lists is that it rearranges the cons cells forming *sequence* by changing CDRs. A nondestructive sort function would create new cons cells to store the elements in their sorted order. If you wish to make a sorted copy without destroying the original, copy it first with `copy-sequence` and then sort.

Sorting does not change the CARs of the cons cells in *sequence*; the cons cell that originally contained the element `a` in *sequence* still has `a` in its CAR after sorting, but it now appears in a different position in the list due to the change of CDRs. For example:

```
(setq nums '(1 3 2 6 5 4 0))
     ⇒ (1 3 2 6 5 4 0)
(sort nums '<)
     ⇒ (0 1 2 3 4 5 6)
nums
     ⇒ (1 2 3 4 5 6)
```

Warning: Note that the list in `nums` no longer contains 0; this is the same cons cell that it was before, but it is no longer the first one in the list. Don't assume a variable that formerly held the argument now holds the entire sorted list! Instead, save the result of `sort` and use that. Most often we store the result back into the variable that held the original list:

```
(setq nums (sort nums '<))
```

For the better understanding of what stable sort is, consider the following vector example. After sorting, all items whose `car` is 8 are grouped at the beginning of `vector`, but their relative order is preserved. All items whose `car` is 9 are grouped at the end of `vector`, but their relative order is also preserved:

```
(setq
  vector
  (vector '(8 . "xxx") '(9 . "aaa") '(8 . "bbb") '(9 . "zzz")
          '(9 . "ppp") '(8 . "ttt") '(8 . "eee") '(9 . "fff")))
     ⇒ [(8 . "xxx") (9 . "aaa") (8 . "bbb") (9 . "zzz")
         (9 . "ppp") (8 . "ttt") (8 . "eee") (9 . "fff")]
(sort vector (lambda (x y) (< (car x) (car y))))
     ⇒ [(8 . "xxx") (8 . "bbb") (8 . "ttt") (8 . "eee")
         (9 . "aaa") (9 . "zzz") (9 . "ppp") (9 . "fff")]
```

See Section 31.15 [Sorting], page 722, for more functions that perform sorting. See `documentation` in Section 23.2 [Accessing Documentation], page 486, for a useful example of `sort`.

The `seq.el` library provides the following additional sequence manipulation macros and functions, prefixed with `seq-`. To use them, you must first load the `seq` library.

All functions defined in this library are free of side-effects; i.e., they do not modify any sequence (list, vector, or string) that you pass as an argument. Unless otherwise stated, the result is a sequence of the same type as the input. For those functions that take a predicate, this should be a function of one argument.

The `seq.el` library can be extended to work with additional types of sequential data-structures. For that purpose, all functions are defined using `cl-defgeneric`. See Section 12.8 [Generic Functions], page 199, for more details about using `cl-defgeneric` for adding extensions.

`seq-elt` *sequence index* [Function]
> This function returns the element of *sequence* at the specified *index*, which is an integer whose valid value range is zero to one less than the length of *sequence*. For out-of-range values on built-in sequence types, `seq-elt` behaves like `elt`. For the details, see [Definition of elt], page 90.
>
>> ```
>> (seq-elt [1 2 3 4] 2)
>> ⇒ 3
>> ```
>
> `seq-elt` returns places settable using `setf` (see Section 11.15.1 [Setting Generalized Variables], page 184).
>
>> ```
>> (setq vec [1 2 3 4])
>> (setf (seq-elt vec 2) 5)
>> vec
>> ⇒ [1 2 5 4]
>> ```

`seq-length` *sequence* [Function]
> This function returns the number of elements in *sequence*. For built-in sequence types, `seq-length` behaves like `length`. See [Definition of length], page 89.

`seqp` *sequence* [Function]
> This function returns non-`nil` if *sequence* is a sequence (a list or array), or any additional type of sequence defined via `seq.el` generic functions.
>
>> ```
>> (seqp [1 2])
>> ⇒ t
>> (seqp 2)
>> ⇒ nil
>> ```

`seq-drop` *sequence n* [Function]
> This function returns all but the first *n* (an integer) elements of *sequence*. If *n* is negative or zero, the result is *sequence*.
>
>> ```
>> (seq-drop [1 2 3 4 5 6] 3)
>> ⇒ [4 5 6]
>> (seq-drop "hello world" -4)
>> ⇒ "hello world"
>> ```

`seq-take` *sequence n* [Function]
> This function returns the first *n* (an integer) elements of *sequence*. If *n* is negative or zero, the result is `nil`.

```
(seq-take '(1 2 3 4) 3)
⇒ (1 2 3)
(seq-take [1 2 3 4] 0)
⇒ []
```

seq-take-while *predicate sequence*   [Function]

This function returns the members of *sequence* in order, stopping before the first one for which *predicate* returns `nil`.

```
(seq-take-while (lambda (elt) (> elt 0)) '(1 2 3 -1 -2))
⇒ (1 2 3)
(seq-take-while (lambda (elt) (> elt 0)) [-1 4 6])
⇒ []
```

seq-drop-while *predicate sequence*   [Function]

This function returns the members of *sequence* in order, starting from the first one for which *predicate* returns `nil`.

```
(seq-drop-while (lambda (elt) (> elt 0)) '(1 2 3 -1 -2))
⇒ (-1 -2)
(seq-drop-while (lambda (elt) (< elt 0)) [1 4 6])
⇒ [1 4 6]
```

seq-do *function sequence*   [Function]

This function applies *function* to each element of *sequence* in turn (presumably for side effects), and returns *sequence*.

seq-map *function sequence*   [Function]

This function returns the result of applying *function* to each element of *sequence*. The returned value is a list.

```
(seq-map #'1+ '(2 4 6))
⇒ (3 5 7)
(seq-map #'symbol-name [foo bar])
⇒ ("foo" "bar")
```

seq-mapn *function* **&rest** *sequences*   [Function]

This function returns the result of applying *function* to each element of *sequences*. The arity (see Section 12.1 [What Is a Function], page 186) of *function* must match the number of sequences. Mapping stops at the end of the shortest sequence, and the returned value is a list.

```
(seq-mapn #'+ '(2 4 6) '(20 40 60))
⇒ (22 44 66)
(seq-mapn #'concat '("moskito" "bite") ["bee" "sting"])
⇒ ("moskitobee" "bitesting")
```

seq-filter *predicate sequence*   [Function]

This function returns a list of all the elements in *sequence* for which *predicate* returns non-`nil`.

```
(seq-filter (lambda (elt) (> elt 0)) [1 -1 3 -3 5])
⇒ (1 3 5)
```

```
(seq-filter (lambda (elt) (> elt 0)) '(-1 -3 -5))
⇒ nil
```

seq-remove *predicate sequence*   [Function]
> This function returns a list of all the elements in *sequence* for which *predicate* returns
> nil.
>
> ```
> (seq-remove (lambda (elt) (> elt 0)) [1 -1 3 -3 5])
> ⇒ (-1 -3)
> (seq-remove (lambda (elt) (< elt 0)) '(-1 -3 -5))
> ⇒ nil
> ```

seq-reduce *function sequence initial-value*   [Function]
> This function returns the result of calling *function* with *initial-value* and the first
> element of *sequence*, then calling *function* with that result and the second element
> of *sequence*, then with that result and the third element of *sequence*, etc. *function*
> should be a function of two arguments. If *sequence* is empty, this returns *initial-value*
> without calling *function*.
>
> ```
> (seq-reduce #'+ [1 2 3 4] 0)
> ⇒ 10
> (seq-reduce #'+ '(1 2 3 4) 5)
> ⇒ 15
> (seq-reduce #'+ '() 3)
> ⇒ 3
> ```

seq-some *predicate sequence*   [Function]
> This function returns the first non-nil value returned by applying *predicate* to each
> element of *sequence* in turn.
>
> ```
> (seq-some #'numberp ["abc" 1 nil])
> ⇒ t
> (seq-some #'numberp ["abc" "def"])
> ⇒ nil
> (seq-some #'null ["abc" 1 nil])
> ⇒ t
> (seq-some #'1+ [2 4 6])
> ⇒ 3
> ```

seq-find *predicate sequence* **&optional** *default*   [Function]
> This function returns the first element in *sequence* for which *predicate* returns non-
> nil. If no element matches *predicate*, the function returns *default*.
>
> Note that this function has an ambiguity if the found element is identical to *default*,
> as in that case it cannot be known whether an element was found or not.
>
> ```
> (seq-find #'numberp ["abc" 1 nil])
> ⇒ 1
> (seq-find #'numberp ["abc" "def"])
> ⇒ nil
> ```

`seq-every-p` *predicate sequence*   [Function]

This function returns non-`nil` if applying *predicate* to every element of *sequence* returns non-`nil`.

```
(seq-every-p #'numberp [2 4 6])
⇒ t
(seq-some #'numberp [2 4 "6"])
⇒ nil
```

`seq-empty-p` *sequence*   [Function]

This function returns non-`nil` if *sequence* is empty.

```
(seq-empty-p "not empty")
⇒ nil
(seq-empty-p "")
⇒ t
```

`seq-count` *predicate sequence*   [Function]

This function returns the number of elements in *sequence* for which *predicate* returns non-`nil`.

```
(seq-count (lambda (elt) (> elt 0)) [-1 2 0 3 -2])
⇒ 2
```

`seq-sort` *function sequence*   [Function]

This function returns a copy of *sequence* that is sorted according to *function*, a function of two arguments that returns non-`nil` if the first argument should sort before the second.

`seq-contains` *sequence elt* **&optional** *function*   [Function]

This function returns the first element in *sequence* that is equal to *elt*. If the optional argument *function* is non-`nil`, it is a function of two arguments to use instead of the default `equal`.

```
(seq-contains '(symbol1 symbol2) 'symbol1)
⇒ symbol1
(seq-contains '(symbol1 symbol2) 'symbol3)
⇒ nil
```

`seq-position` *sequence elt* **&optional** *function*   [Function]

This function returns the index of the first element in *sequence* that is equal to *elt*. If the optional argument *function* is non-`nil`, it is a function of two arguments to use instead of the default `equal`.

```
(seq-position '(a b c) 'b)
⇒ 1
(seq-position '(a b c) 'd)
⇒ nil
```

`seq-uniq` *sequence* **&optional** *function*   [Function]

This function returns a list of the elements of *sequence* with duplicates removed. If the optional argument *function* is non-`nil`, it is a function of two arguments to use instead of the default `equal`.

```
(seq-uniq '(1 2 2 1 3))
⇒ (1 2 3)
(seq-uniq '(1 2 2.0 1.0) #'=)
⇒ [3 4]
```

seq-subseq *sequence start* **&optional** *end*   [Function]

This function returns a subset of *sequence* from *start* to *end*, both integers (*end* defaults to the last element). If *start* or *end* is negative, it counts from the end of *sequence*.

```
(seq-subseq '(1 2 3 4 5) 1)
⇒ (2 3 4 5)
(seq-subseq '[1 2 3 4 5] 1 3)
⇒ [2 3]
(seq-subseq '[1 2 3 4 5] -3 -1)
⇒ [3 4]
```

seq-concatenate *type* **&rest** *sequences*   [Function]

This function returns a sequence of type *type* made of the concatenation of *sequences*. *type* may be: `vector`, `list` or `string`.

```
(seq-concatenate 'list '(1 2) '(3 4) [5 6])
⇒ (1 2 3 4 5 6)
(seq-concatenate 'string "Hello " "world")
⇒ "Hello world"
```

seq-mapcat *function sequence* **&optional** *type*   [Function]

This function returns the result of applying `seq-concatenate` to the result of applying *function* to each element of *sequence*. The result is a sequence of type *type*, or a list if *type* is `nil`.

```
(seq-mapcat #'seq-reverse '((3 2 1) (6 5 4)))
⇒ (1 2 3 4 5 6)
```

seq-partition *sequence n*   [Function]

This function returns a list of the elements of *sequence* grouped into sub-sequences of length *n*. The last sequence may contain less elements than *n*. *n* must be an integer. If *n* is a negative integer or 0, the return value is `nil`.

```
(seq-partition '(0 1 2 3 4 5 6 7) 3)
⇒ ((0 1 2) (3 4 5) (6 7))
```

seq-intersection *sequence1 sequence2* **&optional** *function*   [Function]

This function returns a list of the elements that appear both in *sequence1* and *sequence2*. If the optional argument *function* is non-`nil`, it is a function of two arguments to use to compare elements instead of the default `equal`.

```
(seq-intersection [2 3 4 5] [1 3 5 6 7])
⇒ (3 5)
```

seq-difference *sequence1 sequence2* **&optional** *function*   [Function]

This function returns a list of the elements that appear in *sequence1* but not in *sequence2*. If the optional argument *function* is non-`nil`, it is a function of two arguments to use to compare elements instead of the default `equal`.

```
(seq-difference '(2 3 4 5) [1 3 5 6 7])
⇒ (2 4)
```

seq-group-by *function sequence*   [Function]

This function separates the elements of *sequence* into an alist whose keys are the result of applying *function* to each element of *sequence*. Keys are compared using `equal`.

```
(seq-group-by #'integerp '(1 2.1 3 2 3.2))
⇒ ((t 1 3 2) (nil 2.1 3.2))
(seq-group-by #'car '((a 1) (b 2) (a 3) (c 4)))
⇒ ((b (b 2)) (a (a 1) (a 3)) (c (c 4)))
```

seq-into *sequence type*   [Function]

This function converts the sequence *sequence* into a sequence of type *type*. *type* can be one of the following symbols: `vector`, `string` or `list`.

```
(seq-into [1 2 3] 'list)
⇒ (1 2 3)
(seq-into nil 'vector)
⇒ []
(seq-into "hello" 'vector)
⇒ [104 101 108 108 111]
```

seq-min *sequence*   [Function]

This function returns the smallest element of *sequence*. The elements of *sequence* must be numbers or markers (see Chapter 30 [Markers], page 687).

```
(seq-min [3 1 2])
⇒ 1
(seq-min "Hello")
⇒ 72
```

seq-max *sequence*   [Function]

This function returns the largest element of *sequence*. The elements of *sequence* must be numbers or markers.

```
(seq-max [1 3 2])
⇒ 3
(seq-max "Hello")
⇒ 111
```

seq-doseq (*var sequence*) *body*...   [Macro]

This macro is like `dolist` (see Section 10.4 [Iteration], page 142), except that *sequence* can be a list, vector or string. This is primarily useful for side-effects.

seq-let *arguments sequence body*...   [Macro]

This macro binds the variables defined in *arguments* to the elements of *sequence*. *arguments* can themselves include sequences, allowing for nested destructuring.

The *arguments* sequence can also include the `&rest` marker followed by a variable name to be bound to the rest of `sequence`.

```
(seq-let [first second] [1 2 3 4]
  (list first second))
⇒ (1 2)
(seq-let (_ a _ b) '(1 2 3 4)
  (list a b))
⇒ (2 4)
(seq-let [a [b [c]]] [1 [2 [3]]]
  (list a b c))
⇒ (1 2 3)
(seq-let [a b &rest others] [1 2 3 4]
  others)
⇒ [3 4]
```

6.2 Arrays

An *array* object has slots that hold a number of other Lisp objects, called the elements of the array. Any element of an array may be accessed in constant time. In contrast, the time to access an element of a list is proportional to the position of that element in the list.

Emacs defines four types of array, all one-dimensional: *strings* (see Section 2.3.8 [String Type], page 18), *vectors* (see Section 2.3.9 [Vector Type], page 20), *bool-vectors* (see Section 2.3.11 [Bool-Vector Type], page 21), and *char-tables* (see Section 2.3.10 [Char-Table Type], page 21). Vectors and char-tables can hold elements of any type, but strings can only hold characters, and bool-vectors can only hold t and nil.

All four kinds of array share these characteristics:

- The first element of an array has index zero, the second element has index 1, and so on. This is called *zero-origin* indexing. For example, an array of four elements has indices 0, 1, 2, and 3.

- The length of the array is fixed once you create it; you cannot change the length of an existing array.

- For purposes of evaluation, the array is a constant—i.e., it evaluates to itself.

- The elements of an array may be referenced or changed with the functions aref and aset, respectively (see Section 6.3 [Array Functions], page 101).

When you create an array, other than a char-table, you must specify its length. You cannot specify the length of a char-table, because that is determined by the range of character codes.

In principle, if you want an array of text characters, you could use either a string or a vector. In practice, we always choose strings for such applications, for four reasons:

- They occupy one-fourth the space of a vector of the same elements.

- Strings are printed in a way that shows the contents more clearly as text.

- Strings can hold text properties. See Section 31.19 [Text Properties], page 732.

- Many of the specialized editing and I/O facilities of Emacs accept only strings. For example, you cannot insert a vector of characters into a buffer the way you can insert a string. See Chapter 4 [Strings and Characters], page 49.

By contrast, for an array of keyboard input characters (such as a key sequence), a vector may be necessary, because many keyboard input characters are outside the range that will fit in a string. See Section 20.8.1 [Key Sequence Input], page 373.

6.3 Functions that Operate on Arrays

In this section, we describe the functions that accept all types of arrays.

arrayp *object*   [Function]
> This function returns t if *object* is an array (i.e., a vector, a string, a bool-vector or a char-table).
>
> ```
> (arrayp [a])
>      ⇒ t
> (arrayp "asdf")
>      ⇒ t
> (arrayp (syntax-table))    ;; A char-table.
>      ⇒ t
> ```

aref *array index*   [Function]
> This function returns the *index*th element of *array*. The first element is at index zero.
>
> ```
> (setq primes [2 3 5 7 11 13])
>      ⇒ [2 3 5 7 11 13]
> (aref primes 4)
>      ⇒ 11
> (aref "abcdefg" 1)
>      ⇒ 98              ; 'b' is ASCII code 98.
> ```
>
> See also the function elt, in Section 6.1 [Sequence Functions], page 89.

aset *array index object*   [Function]
> This function sets the *index*th element of *array* to be *object*. It returns *object*.
>
> ```
> (setq w [foo bar baz])
>      ⇒ [foo bar baz]
> (aset w 0 'fu)
>      ⇒ fu
> w
>      ⇒ [fu bar baz]
>
> (setq x "asdfasfd")
>      ⇒ "asdfasfd"
> (aset x 3 ?Z)
>      ⇒ 90
> x
>      ⇒ "asdZasfd"
> ```
>
> If *array* is a string and *object* is not a character, a wrong-type-argument error results. The function converts a unibyte string to multibyte if necessary to insert a character.

fillarray *array object*   [Function]

>This function fills the array *array* with *object*, so that each element of *array* is *object*.
>It returns *array*.
>
>```
>(setq a [a b c d e f g])
>      ⇒ [a b c d e f g]
>(fillarray a 0)
>      ⇒ [0 0 0 0 0 0 0]
>a
>      ⇒ [0 0 0 0 0 0 0]
>(setq s "When in the course")
>      ⇒ "When in the course"
>(fillarray s ?-)
>      ⇒ "------------------"
>```
>
>If *array* is a string and *object* is not a character, a `wrong-type-argument` error results.

The general sequence functions `copy-sequence` and `length` are often useful for objects known to be arrays. See Section 6.1 [Sequence Functions], page 89.

6.4 Vectors

A *vector* is a general-purpose array whose elements can be any Lisp objects. (By contrast, the elements of a string can only be characters. See Chapter 4 [Strings and Characters], page 49.) Vectors are used in Emacs for many purposes: as key sequences (see Section 21.1 [Key Sequences], page 391), as symbol-lookup tables (see Section 8.3 [Creating Symbols], page 117), as part of the representation of a byte-compiled function (see Chapter 16 [Byte Compilation], page 260), and more.

Like other arrays, vectors use zero-origin indexing: the first element has index 0.

Vectors are printed with square brackets surrounding the elements. Thus, a vector whose elements are the symbols `a`, `b` and `a` is printed as `[a b a]`. You can write vectors in the same way in Lisp input.

A vector, like a string or a number, is considered a constant for evaluation: the result of evaluating it is the same vector. This does not evaluate or even examine the elements of the vector. See Section 9.1.1 [Self-Evaluating Forms], page 125.

Here are examples illustrating these principles:

```
(setq avector [1 two '(three) "four" [five]])
      ⇒ [1 two (quote (three)) "four" [five]]
(eval avector)
      ⇒ [1 two (quote (three)) "four" [five]]
(eq avector (eval avector))
      ⇒ t
```

6.5 Functions for Vectors

Here are some functions that relate to vectors:

vectorp *object*   [Function]

>This function returns `t` if *object* is a vector.

```
(vectorp [a])
    ⇒ t
(vectorp "asdf")
    ⇒ nil
```

vector **&rest** *objects*   [Function]

This function creates and returns a vector whose elements are the arguments, *objects*.

```
(vector 'foo 23 [bar baz] "rats")
    ⇒ [foo 23 [bar baz] "rats"]
(vector)
    ⇒ []
```

make-vector *length object*   [Function]

This function returns a new vector consisting of *length* elements, each initialized to *object*.

```
(setq sleepy (make-vector 9 'Z))
    ⇒ [Z Z Z Z Z Z Z Z Z]
```

vconcat **&rest** *sequences*   [Function]

This function returns a new vector containing all the elements of *sequences*. The arguments *sequences* may be true lists, vectors, strings or bool-vectors. If no *sequences* are given, the empty vector is returned.

The value is either the empty vector, or is a newly constructed nonempty vector that is not **eq** to any existing vector.

```
(setq a (vconcat '(A B C) '(D E F)))
    ⇒ [A B C D E F]
(eq a (vconcat a))
    ⇒ nil
(vconcat)
    ⇒ []
(vconcat [A B C] "aa" '(foo (6 7)))
    ⇒ [A B C 97 97 foo (6 7)]
```

The **vconcat** function also allows byte-code function objects as arguments. This is a special feature to make it easy to access the entire contents of a byte-code function object. See Section 16.7 [Byte-Code Objects], page 266.

For other concatenation functions, see **mapconcat** in Section 12.6 [Mapping Functions], page 196, **concat** in Section 4.3 [Creating Strings], page 50, and **append** in Section 5.4 [Building Lists], page 71.

The **append** function also provides a way to convert a vector into a list with the same elements:

```
(setq avector [1 two (quote (three)) "four" [five]])
    ⇒ [1 two (quote (three)) "four" [five]]
(append avector nil)
    ⇒ (1 two (quote (three)) "four" [five])
```

6.6 Char-Tables

A char-table is much like a vector, except that it is indexed by character codes. Any valid character code, without modifiers, can be used as an index in a char-table. You can access a char-table's elements with **aref** and **aset**, as with any array. In addition, a char-table can have *extra slots* to hold additional data not associated with particular character codes. Like vectors, char-tables are constants when evaluated, and can hold elements of any type.

Each char-table has a *subtype*, a symbol, which serves two purposes:

- The subtype provides an easy way to tell what the char-table is for. For instance, display tables are char-tables with **display-table** as the subtype, and syntax tables are char-tables with **syntax-table** as the subtype. The subtype can be queried using the function **char-table-subtype**, described below.

- The subtype controls the number of *extra slots* in the char-table. This number is specified by the subtype's **char-table-extra-slots** symbol property (see Section 8.4 [Symbol Properties], page 119), whose value should be an integer between 0 and 10. If the subtype has no such symbol property, the char-table has no extra slots.

A char-table can have a *parent*, which is another char-table. If it does, then whenever the char-table specifies **nil** for a particular character *c*, it inherits the value specified in the parent. In other words, (**aref** *char-table c*) returns the value from the parent of *char-table* if *char-table* itself specifies **nil**.

A char-table can also have a *default value*. If so, then (**aref** *char-table c*) returns the default value whenever the char-table does not specify any other non-**nil** value.

make-char-table *subtype* **&optional** *init*   [Function]

> Return a newly-created char-table, with subtype *subtype* (a symbol). Each element is initialized to *init*, which defaults to **nil**. You cannot alter the subtype of a char-table after the char-table is created.
>
> There is no argument to specify the length of the char-table, because all char-tables have room for any valid character code as an index.
>
> If *subtype* has the **char-table-extra-slots** symbol property, that specifies the number of extra slots in the char-table. This should be an integer between 0 and 10; otherwise, **make-char-table** raises an error. If *subtype* has no **char-table-extra-slots** symbol property (see Section 5.9 [Property Lists], page 87), the char-table has no extra slots.

char-table-p *object*   [Function]

> This function returns **t** if *object* is a char-table, and **nil** otherwise.

char-table-subtype *char-table*   [Function]

> This function returns the subtype symbol of *char-table*.

There is no special function to access default values in a char-table. To do that, use **char-table-range** (see below).

char-table-parent *char-table*   [Function]

> This function returns the parent of *char-table*. The parent is always either **nil** or another char-table.

set-char-table-parent *char-table new-parent* [Function]
> This function sets the parent of *char-table* to *new-parent*.

char-table-extra-slot *char-table n* [Function]
> This function returns the contents of extra slot *n* (zero based) of *char-table*. The number of extra slots in a char-table is determined by its subtype.

set-char-table-extra-slot *char-table n value* [Function]
> This function stores *value* in extra slot *n* (zero based) of *char-table*.

A char-table can specify an element value for a single character code; it can also specify a value for an entire character set.

char-table-range *char-table range* [Function]
> This returns the value specified in *char-table* for a range of characters *range*. Here are the possibilities for *range*:
>
> nil
> > Refers to the default value.
>
> *char*
> > Refers to the element for character *char* (supposing *char* is a valid character code).
>
> (*from . to*)
> > A cons cell refers to all the characters in the inclusive range '[*from..to*]'.

set-char-table-range *char-table range value* [Function]
> This function sets the value in *char-table* for a range of characters *range*. Here are the possibilities for *range*:
>
> nil
> > Refers to the default value.
>
> t
> > Refers to the whole range of character codes.
>
> *char*
> > Refers to the element for character *char* (supposing *char* is a valid character code).
>
> (*from . to*)
> > A cons cell refers to all the characters in the inclusive range '[*from..to*]'.

map-char-table *function char-table* [Function]
> This function calls its argument *function* for each element of *char-table* that has a non-nil value. The call to *function* is with two arguments, a key and a value. The key is a possible *range* argument for **char-table-range**—either a valid character or a cons cell (*from . to*), specifying a range of characters that share the same value. The value is what (**char-table-range** *char-table key*) returns.
>
> Overall, the key-value pairs passed to *function* describe all the values stored in *char-table*.
>
> The return value is always nil; to make calls to **map-char-table** useful, *function* should have side effects. For example, here is how to examine the elements of the syntax table:

```
(let (accumulator)
  (map-char-table
```

```
                #'(lambda (key value)
                    (setq accumulator
                          (cons (list
                                  (if (consp key)
                                      (list (car key) (cdr key))
                                    key)
                                  value)
                                accumulator)))
              (syntax-table))
            accumulator)
     ⇒
     (((2597602 4194303) (2)) ((2597523 2597601) (3))
      ... (65379 (5 . 65378)) (65378 (4 . 65379)) (65377 (1))
      ... (12 (0)) (11 (3)) (10 (12)) (9 (0)) ((0 8) (3)))
```

6.7 Bool-vectors

A bool-vector is much like a vector, except that it stores only the values t and nil. If you try to store any non-nil value into an element of the bool-vector, the effect is to store t there. As with all arrays, bool-vector indices start from 0, and the length cannot be changed once the bool-vector is created. Bool-vectors are constants when evaluated.

Several functions work specifically with bool-vectors; aside from that, you manipulate them with same functions used for other kinds of arrays.

make-bool-vector *length initial*   [Function]
    Return a new bool-vector of *length* elements, each one initialized to *initial*.

bool-vector **&rest** *objects*   [Function]
    This function creates and returns a bool-vector whose elements are the arguments, *objects*.

bool-vector-p *object*   [Function]
    This returns t if *object* is a bool-vector, and nil otherwise.

There are also some bool-vector set operation functions, described below:

bool-vector-exclusive-or *a b* **&optional** *c*   [Function]
    Return *bitwise exclusive or* of bool vectors *a* and *b*. If optional argument *c* is given, the result of this operation is stored into *c*. All arguments should be bool vectors of the same length.

bool-vector-union *a b* **&optional** *c*   [Function]
    Return *bitwise or* of bool vectors *a* and *b*. If optional argument *c* is given, the result of this operation is stored into *c*. All arguments should be bool vectors of the same length.

bool-vector-intersection *a b* **&optional** *c*   [Function]
    Return *bitwise and* of bool vectors *a* and *b*. If optional argument *c* is given, the result of this operation is stored into *c*. All arguments should be bool vectors of the same length.

bool-vector-set-difference *a b* **&optional** *c* [Function]

 Return *set difference* of bool vectors *a* and *b*. If optional argument *c* is given, the result of this operation is stored into *c*. All arguments should be bool vectors of the same length.

bool-vector-not *a* **&optional** *b* [Function]

 Return *set complement* of bool vector *a*. If optional argument *b* is given, the result of this operation is stored into *b*. All arguments should be bool vectors of the same length.

bool-vector-subsetp *a b* [Function]

 Return `t` if every `t` value in *a* is also `t` in *b*, `nil` otherwise. All arguments should be bool vectors of the same length.

bool-vector-count-consecutive *a b i* [Function]

 Return the number of consecutive elements in *a* equal *b* starting at *i*. *a* is a bool vector, *b* is `t` or `nil`, and *i* is an index into `a`.

bool-vector-count-population *a* [Function]

 Return the number of elements that are `t` in bool vector *a*.

The printed form represents up to 8 boolean values as a single character:

```
(bool-vector t nil t nil)
     ⇒ #&4"^E"
(bool-vector)
     ⇒ #&0""
```

You can use `vconcat` to print a bool-vector like other vectors:

```
(vconcat (bool-vector nil t nil t))
     ⇒ [nil t nil t]
```

Here is another example of creating, examining, and updating a bool-vector:

```
(setq bv (make-bool-vector 5 t))
     ⇒ #&5"^_"
(aref bv 1)
     ⇒ t
(aset bv 3 nil)
     ⇒ nil
bv
     ⇒ #&5"^W"
```

These results make sense because the binary codes for control-_ and control-W are 11111 and 10111, respectively.

6.8 Managing a Fixed-Size Ring of Objects

A *ring* is a fixed-size data structure that supports insertion, deletion, rotation, and modulo-indexed reference and traversal. An efficient ring data structure is implemented by the `ring` package. It provides the functions listed in this section.

Note that several rings in Emacs, like the kill ring and the mark ring, are actually implemented as simple lists, *not* using the `ring` package; thus the following functions won't work on them.

make-ring *size*   [Function]

    This returns a new ring capable of holding *size* objects. *size* should be an integer.

ring-p *object*   [Function]

    This returns `t` if *object* is a ring, `nil` otherwise.

ring-size *ring*   [Function]

    This returns the maximum capacity of the *ring*.

ring-length *ring*   [Function]

    This returns the number of objects that *ring* currently contains. The value will never exceed that returned by `ring-size`.

ring-elements *ring*   [Function]

    This returns a list of the objects in *ring*, in order, newest first.

ring-copy *ring*   [Function]

    This returns a new ring which is a copy of *ring*. The new ring contains the same (`eq`) objects as *ring*.

ring-empty-p *ring*   [Function]

    This returns `t` if *ring* is empty, `nil` otherwise.

The newest element in the ring always has index 0. Higher indices correspond to older elements. Indices are computed modulo the ring length. Index -1 corresponds to the oldest element, -2 to the next-oldest, and so forth.

ring-ref *ring index*   [Function]

    This returns the object in *ring* found at index *index*. *index* may be negative or greater than the ring length. If *ring* is empty, `ring-ref` signals an error.

ring-insert *ring object*   [Function]

    This inserts *object* into *ring*, making it the newest element, and returns *object*.

    If the ring is full, insertion removes the oldest element to make room for the new element.

ring-remove *ring* **&optional** *index*   [Function]

    Remove an object from *ring*, and return that object. The argument *index* specifies which item to remove; if it is `nil`, that means to remove the oldest item. If *ring* is empty, `ring-remove` signals an error.

ring-insert-at-beginning *ring object*   [Function]

    This inserts *object* into *ring*, treating it as the oldest element. The return value is not significant.

    If the ring is full, this function removes the newest element to make room for the inserted element.

If you are careful not to exceed the ring size, you can use the ring as a first-in-first-out queue. For example:

```
(let ((fifo (make-ring 5)))
```

```
(mapc (lambda (obj) (ring-insert fifo obj))
      '(0 one "two"))
(list (ring-remove fifo) t
      (ring-remove fifo) t
      (ring-remove fifo)))
   ⇒ (0 t one t "two")
```

7 Hash Tables

A hash table is a very fast kind of lookup table, somewhat like an alist (see Section 5.8 [Association Lists], page 83) in that it maps keys to corresponding values. It differs from an alist in these ways:

- Lookup in a hash table is extremely fast for large tables—in fact, the time required is essentially *independent* of how many elements are stored in the table. For smaller tables (a few tens of elements) alists may still be faster because hash tables have a more-or-less constant overhead.

- The correspondences in a hash table are in no particular order.

- There is no way to share structure between two hash tables, the way two alists can share a common tail.

Emacs Lisp provides a general-purpose hash table data type, along with a series of functions for operating on them. Hash tables have a special printed representation, which consists of '#s' followed by a list specifying the hash table properties and contents. See Section 7.1 [Creating Hash], page 110. (Hash notation, the initial '#' character used in the printed representations of objects with no read representation, has nothing to do with hash tables. See Section 2.1 [Printed Representation], page 8.)

Obarrays are also a kind of hash table, but they are a different type of object and are used only for recording interned symbols (see Section 8.3 [Creating Symbols], page 117).

7.1 Creating Hash Tables

The principal function for creating a hash table is `make-hash-table`.

`make-hash-table &rest` *keyword-args*   [Function]

> This function creates a new hash table according to the specified arguments. The arguments should consist of alternating keywords (particular symbols recognized specially) and values corresponding to them.
>
> Several keywords make sense in `make-hash-table`, but the only two that you really need to know about are `:test` and `:weakness`.
>
> `:test` *test*
>> This specifies the method of key lookup for this hash table. The default is `eql`; `eq` and `equal` are other alternatives:
>>
>> `eql`   Keys which are numbers are the same if they are `equal`, that is, if they are equal in value and either both are integers or both are floating point; otherwise, two distinct objects are never the same.
>>
>> `eq`   Any two distinct Lisp objects are different as keys.
>>
>> `equal`   Two Lisp objects are the same, as keys, if they are equal according to `equal`.
>>
>> You can use `define-hash-table-test` (see Section 7.3 [Defining Hash], page 113) to define additional possibilities for *test*.

:weakness *weak*

> The weakness of a hash table specifies whether the presence of a key or value in the hash table preserves it from garbage collection.
>
> The value, *weak*, must be one of `nil`, `key`, `value`, `key-or-value`, `key-and-value`, or `t` which is an alias for `key-and-value`. If *weak* is `key` then the hash table does not prevent its keys from being collected as garbage (if they are not referenced anywhere else); if a particular key does get collected, the corresponding association is removed from the hash table.
>
> If *weak* is `value`, then the hash table does not prevent values from being collected as garbage (if they are not referenced anywhere else); if a particular value does get collected, the corresponding association is removed from the hash table.
>
> If *weak* is `key-and-value` or `t`, both the key and the value must be live in order to preserve the association. Thus, the hash table does not protect either keys or values from garbage collection; if either one is collected as garbage, that removes the association.
>
> If *weak* is `key-or-value`, either the key or the value can preserve the association. Thus, associations are removed from the hash table when both their key and value would be collected as garbage (if not for references from weak hash tables).
>
> The default for *weak* is `nil`, so that all keys and values referenced in the hash table are preserved from garbage collection.

:size *size*

> This specifies a hint for how many associations you plan to store in the hash table. If you know the approximate number, you can make things a little more efficient by specifying it this way. If you specify too small a size, the hash table will grow automatically when necessary, but doing that takes some extra time.
>
> The default size is 65.

:rehash-size *rehash-size*

> When you add an association to a hash table and the table is full, it grows automatically. This value specifies how to make the hash table larger, at that time.
>
> If *rehash-size* is an integer, it should be positive, and the hash table grows by adding that much to the nominal size. If *rehash-size* is floating point, it had better be greater than 1, and the hash table grows by multiplying the old size by that number.
>
> The default value is 1.5.

:rehash-threshold *threshold*

> This specifies the criterion for when the hash table is full (so it should be made larger). The value, *threshold*, should be a positive floating-point number, no greater than 1. The hash table is full whenever the actual

number of entries exceeds this fraction of the nominal size. The default for *threshold* is 0.8.

You can also create a new hash table using the printed representation for hash tables. The Lisp reader can read this printed representation, provided each element in the specified hash table has a valid read syntax (see Section 2.1 [Printed Representation], page 8). For instance, the following specifies a new hash table containing the keys `key1` and `key2` (both symbols) associated with `val1` (a symbol) and `300` (a number) respectively.

```
#s(hash-table size 30 data (key1 val1 key2 300))
```

The printed representation for a hash table consists of '`#s`' followed by a list beginning with '`hash-table`'. The rest of the list should consist of zero or more property-value pairs specifying the hash table's properties and initial contents. The properties and values are read literally. Valid property names are `size`, `test`, `weakness`, `rehash-size`, `rehash-threshold`, and `data`. The `data` property should be a list of key-value pairs for the initial contents; the other properties have the same meanings as the matching `make-hash-table` keywords (`:size`, `:test`, etc.), described above.

Note that you cannot specify a hash table whose initial contents include objects that have no read syntax, such as buffers and frames. Such objects may be added to the hash table after it is created.

7.2 Hash Table Access

This section describes the functions for accessing and storing associations in a hash table. In general, any Lisp object can be used as a hash key, unless the comparison method imposes limits. Any Lisp object can also be used as the value.

gethash *key table* **&optional** *default*   [Function]

> This function looks up *key* in *table*, and returns its associated *value*—or *default*, if *key* has no association in *table*.

puthash *key value table*   [Function]

> This function enters an association for *key* in *table*, with value *value*. If *key* already has an association in *table*, *value* replaces the old associated value.

remhash *key table*   [Function]

> This function removes the association for *key* from *table*, if there is one. If *key* has no association, `remhash` does nothing.
>
> **Common Lisp note:** In Common Lisp, `remhash` returns non-`nil` if it actually removed an association and `nil` otherwise. In Emacs Lisp, `remhash` always returns `nil`.

clrhash *table*   [Function]

> This function removes all the associations from hash table *table*, so that it becomes empty. This is also called *clearing* the hash table.
>
> **Common Lisp note:** In Common Lisp, `clrhash` returns the empty *table*. In Emacs Lisp, it returns `nil`.

maphash *function table*   [Function]

> This function calls *function* once for each of the associations in *table*. The function *function* should accept two arguments—a *key* listed in *table*, and its associated *value*. `maphash` returns `nil`.

7.3 Defining Hash Comparisons

You can define new methods of key lookup by means of **define-hash-table-test**. In order to use this feature, you need to understand how hash tables work, and what a *hash code* means.

You can think of a hash table conceptually as a large array of many slots, each capable of holding one association. To look up a key, **gethash** first computes an integer, the hash code, from the key. It reduces this integer modulo the length of the array, to produce an index in the array. Then it looks in that slot, and if necessary in other nearby slots, to see if it has found the key being sought.

Thus, to define a new method of key lookup, you need to specify both a function to compute the hash code from a key, and a function to compare two keys directly.

define-hash-table-test *name test-fn hash-fn*   [Function]
> This function defines a new hash table test, named *name*.
>
> After defining *name* in this way, you can use it as the *test* argument in **make-hash-table**. When you do that, the hash table will use *test-fn* to compare key values, and *hash-fn* to compute a hash code from a key value.
>
> The function *test-fn* should accept two arguments, two keys, and return non-**nil** if they are considered the same.
>
> The function *hash-fn* should accept one argument, a key, and return an integer that is the hash code of that key. For good results, the function should use the whole range of integers for hash codes, including negative integers.
>
> The specified functions are stored in the property list of *name* under the property **hash-table-test**; the property value's form is (*test-fn hash-fn*).

sxhash *obj*   [Function]
> This function returns a hash code for Lisp object *obj*. This is an integer which reflects the contents of *obj* and the other Lisp objects it points to.
>
> If two objects *obj1* and *obj2* are equal, then (**sxhash** *obj1*) and (**sxhash** *obj2*) are the same integer.
>
> If the two objects are not equal, the values returned by **sxhash** are usually different, but not always; once in a rare while, by luck, you will encounter two distinct-looking objects that give the same result from **sxhash**.

This example creates a hash table whose keys are strings that are compared case-insensitively.

```
(defun case-fold-string= (a b)
  (eq t (compare-strings a nil nil b nil nil t)))
(defun case-fold-string-hash (a)
  (sxhash (upcase a)))

(define-hash-table-test 'case-fold
  'case-fold-string= 'case-fold-string-hash)

(make-hash-table :test 'case-fold)
```

Here is how you could define a hash table test equivalent to the predefined test value `equal`. The keys can be any Lisp object, and equal-looking objects are considered the same key.

```
(define-hash-table-test 'contents-hash 'equal 'sxhash)
```

```
(make-hash-table :test 'contents-hash)
```

7.4 Other Hash Table Functions

Here are some other functions for working with hash tables.

`hash-table-p` *table*   [Function]
> This returns non-`nil` if *table* is a hash table object.

`copy-hash-table` *table*   [Function]
> This function creates and returns a copy of *table*. Only the table itself is copied—the keys and values are shared.

`hash-table-count` *table*   [Function]
> This function returns the actual number of entries in *table*.

`hash-table-test` *table*   [Function]
> This returns the *test* value that was given when *table* was created, to specify how to hash and compare keys. See `make-hash-table` (see Section 7.1 [Creating Hash], page 110).

`hash-table-weakness` *table*   [Function]
> This function returns the *weak* value that was specified for hash table *table*.

`hash-table-rehash-size` *table*   [Function]
> This returns the rehash size of *table*.

`hash-table-rehash-threshold` *table*   [Function]
> This returns the rehash threshold of *table*.

`hash-table-size` *table*   [Function]
> This returns the current nominal size of *table*.

8 Symbols

A *symbol* is an object with a unique name. This chapter describes symbols, their components, their property lists, and how they are created and interned. Separate chapters describe the use of symbols as variables and as function names; see Chapter 11 [Variables], page 157, and Chapter 12 [Functions], page 186. For the precise read syntax for symbols, see Section 2.3.4 [Symbol Type], page 13.

You can test whether an arbitrary Lisp object is a symbol with `symbolp`:

symbolp *object*   [Function]
> This function returns `t` if *object* is a symbol, `nil` otherwise.

8.1 Symbol Components

Each symbol has four components (or "cells"), each of which references another object:

Print name
> The symbol's name.

Value   The symbol's current value as a variable.

Function   The symbol's function definition. It can also hold a symbol, a keymap, or a keyboard macro.

Property list
> The symbol's property list.

The print name cell always holds a string, and cannot be changed. Each of the other three cells can be set to any Lisp object.

The print name cell holds the string that is the name of a symbol. Since symbols are represented textually by their names, it is important not to have two symbols with the same name. The Lisp reader ensures this: every time it reads a symbol, it looks for an existing symbol with the specified name before it creates a new one. To get a symbol's name, use the function `symbol-name` (see Section 8.3 [Creating Symbols], page 117).

The value cell holds a symbol's value as a variable, which is what you get if the symbol itself is evaluated as a Lisp expression. See Chapter 11 [Variables], page 157, for details about how values are set and retrieved, including complications such as *local bindings* and *scoping rules*. Most symbols can have any Lisp object as a value, but certain special symbols have values that cannot be changed; these include `nil` and `t`, and any symbol whose name starts with ':' (those are called *keywords*). See Section 11.2 [Constant Variables], page 157.

The function cell holds a symbol's function definition. Often, we refer to "the function `foo`" when we really mean the function stored in the function cell of `foo`; we make the distinction explicit only when necessary. Typically, the function cell is used to hold a function (see Chapter 12 [Functions], page 186) or a macro (see Chapter 13 [Macros], page 217). However, it can also be used to hold a symbol (see Section 9.1.4 [Function Indirection], page 126), keyboard macro (see Section 20.16 [Keyboard Macros], page 389), keymap (see Chapter 21 [Keymaps], page 391), or autoload object (see Section 9.1.8 [Autoloading], page 129). To get the contents of a symbol's function cell, use the function `symbol-function` (see Section 12.9 [Function Cells], page 202).

The property list cell normally should hold a correctly formatted property list. To get a symbol's property list, use the function `symbol-plist`. See Section 8.4 [Symbol Properties], page 119.

The function cell or the value cell may be *void*, which means that the cell does not reference any object. (This is not the same thing as holding the symbol `void`, nor the same as holding the symbol `nil`.) Examining a function or value cell that is void results in an error, such as 'Symbol's value as variable is void'.

Because each symbol has separate value and function cells, variables names and function names do not conflict. For example, the symbol `buffer-file-name` has a value (the name of the file being visited in the current buffer) as well as a function definition (a primitive function that returns the name of the file):

```
buffer-file-name
     ⇒ "/gnu/elisp/symbols.texi"
(symbol-function 'buffer-file-name)
     ⇒ #<subr buffer-file-name>
```

8.2 Defining Symbols

A *definition* is a special kind of Lisp expression that announces your intention to use a symbol in a particular way. It typically specifies a value or meaning for the symbol for one kind of use, plus documentation for its meaning when used in this way. Thus, when you define a symbol as a variable, you can supply an initial value for the variable, plus documentation for the variable.

`defvar` and `defconst` are special forms that define a symbol as a *global variable*—a variable that can be accessed at any point in a Lisp program. See Chapter 11 [Variables], page 157, for details about variables. To define a customizable variable, use the `defcustom` macro, which also calls `defvar` as a subroutine (see Chapter 14 [Customization], page 225).

In principle, you can assign a variable value to any symbol with `setq`, whether not it has first been defined as a variable. However, you ought to write a variable definition for each global variable that you want to use; otherwise, your Lisp program may not act correctly if it is evaluated with lexical scoping enabled (see Section 11.9 [Variable Scoping], page 166).

`defun` defines a symbol as a function, creating a lambda expression and storing it in the function cell of the symbol. This lambda expression thus becomes the function definition of the symbol. (The term "function definition", meaning the contents of the function cell, is derived from the idea that `defun` gives the symbol its definition as a function.) `defsubst` and `defalias` are two other ways of defining a function. See Chapter 12 [Functions], page 186.

`defmacro` defines a symbol as a macro. It creates a macro object and stores it in the function cell of the symbol. Note that a given symbol can be a macro or a function, but not both at once, because both macro and function definitions are kept in the function cell, and that cell can hold only one Lisp object at any given time. See Chapter 13 [Macros], page 217.

As previously noted, Emacs Lisp allows the same symbol to be defined both as a variable (e.g., with `defvar`) and as a function or macro (e.g., with `defun`). Such definitions do not conflict.

These definitions also act as guides for programming tools. For example, the `C-h f` and `C-h v` commands create help buffers containing links to the relevant variable, function, or macro definitions. See Section "Name Help" in *The GNU Emacs Manual*.

8.3 Creating and Interning Symbols

To understand how symbols are created in GNU Emacs Lisp, you must know how Lisp reads them. Lisp must ensure that it finds the same symbol every time it reads the same set of characters. Failure to do so would cause complete confusion.

When the Lisp reader encounters a symbol, it reads all the characters of the name. Then it hashes those characters to find an index in a table called an *obarray*. Hashing is an efficient method of looking something up. For example, instead of searching a telephone book cover to cover when looking up Jan Jones, you start with the J's and go from there. That is a simple version of hashing. Each element of the obarray is a *bucket* which holds all the symbols with a given hash code; to look for a given name, it is sufficient to look through all the symbols in the bucket for that name's hash code. (The same idea is used for general Emacs hash tables, but they are a different data type; see Chapter 7 [Hash Tables], page 110.)

If a symbol with the desired name is found, the reader uses that symbol. If the obarray does not contain a symbol with that name, the reader makes a new symbol and adds it to the obarray. Finding or adding a symbol with a certain name is called *interning* it, and the symbol is then called an *interned symbol*.

Interning ensures that each obarray has just one symbol with any particular name. Other like-named symbols may exist, but not in the same obarray. Thus, the reader gets the same symbols for the same names, as long as you keep reading with the same obarray.

Interning usually happens automatically in the reader, but sometimes other programs need to do it. For example, after the `M-x` command obtains the command name as a string using the minibuffer, it then interns the string, to get the interned symbol with that name.

No obarray contains all symbols; in fact, some symbols are not in any obarray. They are called *uninterned symbols*. An uninterned symbol has the same four cells as other symbols; however, the only way to gain access to it is by finding it in some other object or as the value of a variable.

Creating an uninterned symbol is useful in generating Lisp code, because an uninterned symbol used as a variable in the code you generate cannot clash with any variables used in other Lisp programs.

In Emacs Lisp, an obarray is actually a vector. Each element of the vector is a bucket; its value is either an interned symbol whose name hashes to that bucket, or 0 if the bucket is empty. Each interned symbol has an internal link (invisible to the user) to the next symbol in the bucket. Because these links are invisible, there is no way to find all the symbols in an obarray except using `mapatoms` (below). The order of symbols in a bucket is not significant.

In an empty obarray, every element is 0, so you can create an obarray with (`make-vector` *length* 0). **This is the only valid way to create an obarray.** Prime numbers as lengths tend to result in good hashing; lengths one less than a power of two are also good.

Do not try to put symbols in an obarray yourself. This does not work—only `intern` can enter a symbol in an obarray properly.

Common Lisp note: Unlike Common Lisp, Emacs Lisp does not provide for interning a single symbol in several obarrays.

Most of the functions below take a name and sometimes an obarray as arguments. A `wrong-type-argument` error is signaled if the name is not a string, or if the obarray is not a vector.

symbol-name *symbol*   [Function]

This function returns the string that is *symbol*'s name. For example:

```
(symbol-name 'foo)
     ⇒ "foo"
```

Warning: Changing the string by substituting characters does change the name of the symbol, but fails to update the obarray, so don't do it!

make-symbol *name*   [Function]

This function returns a newly-allocated, uninterned symbol whose name is *name* (which must be a string). Its value and function definition are void, and its property list is `nil`. In the example below, the value of `sym` is not `eq` to `foo` because it is a distinct uninterned symbol whose name is also 'foo'.

```
(setq sym (make-symbol "foo"))
     ⇒ foo
(eq sym 'foo)
     ⇒ nil
```

intern *name* **&optional** *obarray*   [Function]

This function returns the interned symbol whose name is *name*. If there is no such symbol in the obarray *obarray*, `intern` creates a new one, adds it to the obarray, and returns it. If *obarray* is omitted, the value of the global variable `obarray` is used.

```
(setq sym (intern "foo"))
     ⇒ foo
(eq sym 'foo)
     ⇒ t


(setq sym1 (intern "foo" other-obarray))
     ⇒ foo
(eq sym1 'foo)
     ⇒ nil
```

Common Lisp note: In Common Lisp, you can intern an existing symbol in an obarray. In Emacs Lisp, you cannot do this, because the argument to `intern` must be a string, not a symbol.

intern-soft *name* **&optional** *obarray*   [Function]

This function returns the symbol in *obarray* whose name is *name*, or `nil` if *obarray* has no symbol with that name. Therefore, you can use `intern-soft` to test whether a symbol with a given name is already interned. If *obarray* is omitted, the value of the global variable `obarray` is used.

The argument *name* may also be a symbol; in that case, the function returns *name* if *name* is interned in the specified obarray, and otherwise `nil`.

```
(intern-soft "frazzle")          ; No such symbol exists.
     ⇒ nil
(make-symbol "frazzle")          ; Create an uninterned one.
     ⇒ frazzle
(intern-soft "frazzle")          ; That one cannot be found.
     ⇒ nil
(setq sym (intern "frazzle"))    ; Create an interned one.
     ⇒ frazzle
(intern-soft "frazzle")          ; That one can be found!
     ⇒ frazzle
(eq sym 'frazzle)                ; And it is the same one.
     ⇒ t
```

`obarray`   [Variable]
This variable is the standard obarray for use by `intern` and `read`.

`mapatoms` *function* **&optional** *obarray*   [Function]
This function calls *function* once with each symbol in the obarray *obarray*. Then it returns `nil`. If *obarray* is omitted, it defaults to the value of `obarray`, the standard obarray for ordinary symbols.

```
(setq count 0)
     ⇒ 0
(defun count-syms (s)
  (setq count (1+ count)))
     ⇒ count-syms
(mapatoms 'count-syms)
     ⇒ nil
count
     ⇒ 1871
```

See `documentation` in Section 23.2 [Accessing Documentation], page 486, for another example using `mapatoms`.

`unintern` *symbol obarray*   [Function]
This function deletes *symbol* from the obarray *obarray*. If `symbol` is not actually in the obarray, `unintern` does nothing. If *obarray* is `nil`, the current obarray is used.

If you provide a string instead of a symbol as *symbol*, it stands for a symbol name. Then `unintern` deletes the symbol (if any) in the obarray which has that name. If there is no such symbol, `unintern` does nothing.

If `unintern` does delete a symbol, it returns `t`. Otherwise it returns `nil`.

8.4 Symbol Properties

A symbol may possess any number of *symbol properties*, which can be used to record miscellaneous information about the symbol. For example, when a symbol has a `risky-local-variable` property with a non-`nil` value, that means the variable which the symbol names is a risky file-local variable (see Section 11.11 [File Local Variables], page 177).

Each symbol's properties and property values are stored in the symbol's property list cell (see Section 8.1 [Symbol Components], page 115), in the form of a property list (see Section 5.9 [Property Lists], page 87).

8.4.1 Accessing Symbol Properties

The following functions can be used to access symbol properties.

get *symbol property*   [Function]

> This function returns the value of the property named *property* in *symbol*'s property list. If there is no such property, it returns **nil**. Thus, there is no distinction between a value of **nil** and the absence of the property.
>
> The name *property* is compared with the existing property names using **eq**, so any object is a legitimate property.
>
> See **put** for an example.

put *symbol property value*   [Function]

> This function puts *value* onto *symbol*'s property list under the property name *property*, replacing any previous property value. The **put** function returns *value*.
>
> ```
> (put 'fly 'verb 'transitive)
>      ⇒'transitive
> (put 'fly 'noun '(a buzzing little bug))
>      ⇒ (a buzzing little bug)
> (get 'fly 'verb)
>      ⇒ transitive
> (symbol-plist 'fly)
>      ⇒ (verb transitive noun (a buzzing little bug))
> ```

symbol-plist *symbol*   [Function]

> This function returns the property list of *symbol*.

setplist *symbol plist*   [Function]

> This function sets *symbol*'s property list to *plist*. Normally, *plist* should be a well-formed property list, but this is not enforced. The return value is *plist*.
>
> ```
> (setplist 'foo '(a 1 b (2 3) c nil))
>      ⇒ (a 1 b (2 3) c nil)
> (symbol-plist 'foo)
>      ⇒ (a 1 b (2 3) c nil)
> ```

For symbols in special obarrays, which are not used for ordinary purposes, it may make sense to use the property list cell in a nonstandard fashion; in fact, the abbrev mechanism does so (see Chapter 35 [Abbrevs], page 832).

You could define **put** in terms of **setplist** and **plist-put**, as follows:

```
(defun put (symbol prop value)
  (setplist symbol
            (plist-put (symbol-plist symbol) prop value)))
```

function-get *symbol property* **&optional** *autoload* [Function]
> This function is identical to `get`, except that if *symbol* is the name of a function alias, it looks in the property list of the symbol naming the actual function. See Section 12.4 [Defining Functions], page 192. If the optional argument *autoload* is non-`nil`, and *symbol* is auto-loaded, this function will try to autoload it, since autoloading might set *property* of *symbol*. If *autoload* is the symbol `macro`, only try autoloading if *symbol* is an auto-loaded macro.

function-put *function property value* [Function]
> This function sets *property* of *function* to *value*. *function* should be a symbol. This function is preferred to calling `put` for setting properties of a function, because it will allow us some day to implement remapping of old properties to new ones.

8.4.2 Standard Symbol Properties

Here, we list the symbol properties which are used for special purposes in Emacs. In the following table, whenever we say "the named function", that means the function whose name is the relevant symbol; similarly for "the named variable" etc.

`:advertised-binding`
> This property value specifies the preferred key binding, when showing documentation, for the named function. See Section 23.3 [Keys in Documentation], page 488.

`char-table-extra-slots`
> The value, if non-`nil`, specifies the number of extra slots in the named chartable type. See Section 6.6 [Char-Tables], page 104.

`customized-face`
`face-defface-spec`
`saved-face`
`theme-face`
> These properties are used to record a face's standard, saved, customized, and themed face specs. Do not set them directly; they are managed by `defface` and related functions. See Section 37.12.2 [Defining Faces], page 918.

`customized-value`
`saved-value`
`standard-value`
`theme-value`
> These properties are used to record a customizable variable's standard value, saved value, customized-but-unsaved value, and themed values. Do not set them directly; they are managed by `defcustom` and related functions. See Section 14.3 [Variable Definitions], page 228.

`disabled` If the value is non-`nil`, the named function is disabled as a command. See Section 20.14 [Disabling Commands], page 388.

`face-documentation`
> The value stores the documentation string of the named face. This is set automatically by `defface`. See Section 37.12.2 [Defining Faces], page 918.

history-length

> The value, if non-**nil**, specifies the maximum minibuffer history length for the named history list variable. See Section 19.4 [Minibuffer History], page 318.

interactive-form

> The value is an interactive form for the named function. Normally, you should not set this directly; use the **interactive** special form instead. See Section 20.3 [Interactive Call], page 352.

menu-enable

> The value is an expression for determining whether the named menu item should be enabled in menus. See Section 21.17.1.1 [Simple Menu Items], page 416.

mode-class

> If the value is **special**, the named major mode is special. See Section 22.2.1 [Major Mode Conventions], page 432.

permanent-local

> If the value is non-**nil**, the named variable is a buffer-local variable whose value should not be reset when changing major modes. See Section 11.10.2 [Creating Buffer-Local], page 172.

permanent-local-hook

> If the value is non-**nil**, the named function should not be deleted from the local value of a hook variable when changing major modes. See Section 22.1.2 [Setting Hooks], page 430.

pure

> If the value is non-**nil**, the named function is considered to be side-effect free. Calls with constant arguments can be evaluated at compile time. This may shift run time errors to compile time.

risky-local-variable

> If the value is non-**nil**, the named variable is considered risky as a file-local variable. See Section 11.11 [File Local Variables], page 177.

safe-function

> If the value is non-**nil**, the named function is considered generally safe for evaluation. See Section 12.16 [Function Safety], page 215.

safe-local-eval-function

> If the value is non-**nil**, the named function is safe to call in file-local evaluation forms. See Section 11.11 [File Local Variables], page 177.

safe-local-variable

> The value specifies a function for determining safe file-local values for the named variable. See Section 11.11 [File Local Variables], page 177.

side-effect-free

> A non-**nil** value indicates that the named function is free of side-effects, for determining function safety (see Section 12.16 [Function Safety], page 215) as well as for byte compiler optimizations. Do not set it.

`variable-documentation`

If non-`nil`, this specifies the named variable's documentation string. This is set automatically by `defvar` and related functions. See Section 37.12.2 [Defining Faces], page 918.

9 Evaluation

The *evaluation* of expressions in Emacs Lisp is performed by the *Lisp interpreter*—a program that receives a Lisp object as input and computes its *value as an expression*. How it does this depends on the data type of the object, according to rules described in this chapter. The interpreter runs automatically to evaluate portions of your program, but can also be called explicitly via the Lisp primitive function `eval`.

A Lisp object that is intended for evaluation is called a *form* or *expression*[1]. The fact that forms are data objects and not merely text is one of the fundamental differences between Lisp-like languages and typical programming languages. Any object can be evaluated, but in practice only numbers, symbols, lists and strings are evaluated very often.

In subsequent sections, we will describe the details of what evaluation means for each kind of form.

It is very common to read a Lisp form and then evaluate the form, but reading and evaluation are separate activities, and either can be performed alone. Reading per se does not evaluate anything; it converts the printed representation of a Lisp object to the object itself. It is up to the caller of `read` to specify whether this object is a form to be evaluated, or serves some entirely different purpose. See Section 18.3 [Input Functions], page 304.

Evaluation is a recursive process, and evaluating a form often involves evaluating parts within that form. For instance, when you evaluate a *function call* form such as `(car x)`, Emacs first evaluates the argument (the subform `x`). After evaluating the argument, Emacs *executes* the function (`car`), and if the function is written in Lisp, execution works by evaluating the *body* of the function (in this example, however, `car` is not a Lisp function; it is a primitive function implemented in C). See Chapter 12 [Functions], page 186, for more information about functions and function calls.

Evaluation takes place in a context called the *environment*, which consists of the current values and bindings of all Lisp variables (see Chapter 11 [Variables], page 157).[2] Whenever a form refers to a variable without creating a new binding for it, the variable evaluates to the value given by the current environment. Evaluating a form may also temporarily alter the environment by binding variables (see Section 11.3 [Local Variables], page 158).

Evaluating a form may also make changes that persist; these changes are called *side effects*. An example of a form that produces a side effect is `(setq foo 1)`.

Do not confuse evaluation with command key interpretation. The editor command loop translates keyboard input into a command (an interactively callable function) using the active keymaps, and then uses `call-interactively` to execute that command. Executing the command usually involves evaluation, if the command is written in Lisp; however, this step is not considered a part of command key interpretation. See Chapter 20 [Command Loop], page 345.

---

[1] It is sometimes also referred to as an *S-expression* or *sexp*, but we generally do not use this terminology in this manual.

[2] This definition of "environment" is specifically not intended to include all the data that can affect the result of a program.

9.1 Kinds of Forms

A Lisp object that is intended to be evaluated is called a *form* (or an *expression*). How Emacs evaluates a form depends on its data type. Emacs has three different kinds of form that are evaluated differently: symbols, lists, and all other types. This section describes all three kinds, one by one, starting with the other types, which are self-evaluating forms.

9.1.1 Self-Evaluating Forms

A *self-evaluating form* is any form that is not a list or symbol. Self-evaluating forms evaluate to themselves: the result of evaluation is the same object that was evaluated. Thus, the number 25 evaluates to 25, and the string `"foo"` evaluates to the string `"foo"`. Likewise, evaluating a vector does not cause evaluation of the elements of the vector—it returns the same vector with its contents unchanged.

```
'123                    ; A number, shown without evaluation.
    ⇒ 123
123                     ; Evaluated as usual—result is the same.
    ⇒ 123
(eval '123)             ; Evaluated "by hand"—result is the same.
    ⇒ 123
(eval (eval '123))      ; Evaluating twice changes nothing.
    ⇒ 123
```

It is common to write numbers, characters, strings, and even vectors in Lisp code, taking advantage of the fact that they self-evaluate. However, it is quite unusual to do this for types that lack a read syntax, because there's no way to write them textually. It is possible to construct Lisp expressions containing these types by means of a Lisp program. Here is an example:

```
;; Build an expression containing a buffer object.
(setq print-exp (list 'print (current-buffer)))
    ⇒ (print #<buffer eval.texi>)
;; Evaluate it.
(eval print-exp)
    ⊣ #<buffer eval.texi>
    ⇒ #<buffer eval.texi>
```

9.1.2 Symbol Forms

When a symbol is evaluated, it is treated as a variable. The result is the variable's value, if it has one. If the symbol has no value as a variable, the Lisp interpreter signals an error. For more information on the use of variables, see Chapter 11 [Variables], page 157.

In the following example, we set the value of a symbol with `setq`. Then we evaluate the symbol, and get back the value that `setq` stored.

```
(setq a 123)
    ⇒ 123
(eval 'a)
    ⇒ 123
a
    ⇒ 123
```

The symbols **nil** and **t** are treated specially, so that the value of **nil** is always **nil**, and the value of **t** is always **t**; you cannot set or bind them to any other values. Thus, these two symbols act like self-evaluating forms, even though **eval** treats them like any other symbol. A symbol whose name starts with ':' also self-evaluates in the same way; likewise, its value ordinarily cannot be changed. See Section 11.2 [Constant Variables], page 157.

9.1.3 Classification of List Forms

A form that is a nonempty list is either a function call, a macro call, or a special form, according to its first element. These three kinds of forms are evaluated in different ways, described below. The remaining list elements constitute the *arguments* for the function, macro, or special form.

The first step in evaluating a nonempty list is to examine its first element. This element alone determines what kind of form the list is and how the rest of the list is to be processed. The first element is *not* evaluated, as it would be in some Lisp dialects such as Scheme.

9.1.4 Symbol Function Indirection

If the first element of the list is a symbol then evaluation examines the symbol's function cell, and uses its contents instead of the original symbol. If the contents are another symbol, this process, called *symbol function indirection*, is repeated until it obtains a non-symbol. See Section 12.3 [Function Names], page 191, for more information about symbol function indirection.

One possible consequence of this process is an infinite loop, in the event that a symbol's function cell refers to the same symbol. Otherwise, we eventually obtain a non-symbol, which ought to be a function or other suitable object.

More precisely, we should now have a Lisp function (a lambda expression), a byte-code function, a primitive function, a Lisp macro, a special form, or an autoload object. Each of these types is a case described in one of the following sections. If the object is not one of these types, Emacs signals an **invalid-function** error.

The following example illustrates the symbol indirection process. We use **fset** to set the function cell of a symbol and **symbol-function** to get the function cell contents (see Section 12.9 [Function Cells], page 202). Specifically, we store the symbol **car** into the function cell of **first**, and the symbol **first** into the function cell of **erste**.

```
;; Build this function cell linkage:
;;    --------------        -----        -------        -------
;;   | #<subr car> | <-- | car |  <-- | first |  <-- | erste |
;;    --------------        -----        -------        -------
(symbol-function 'car)
     ⇒ #<subr car>
(fset 'first 'car)
     ⇒ car
(fset 'erste 'first)
     ⇒ first
(erste '(1 2 3))    ; Call the function referenced by erste.
     ⇒ 1
```

By contrast, the following example calls a function without any symbol function indirection, because the first element is an anonymous Lisp function, not a symbol.

```
((lambda (arg) (erste arg))
 '(1 2 3))
     ⇒ 1
```

Executing the function itself evaluates its body; this does involve symbol function indirection when calling `erste`.

This form is rarely used and is now deprecated. Instead, you should write it as:

```
(funcall (lambda (arg) (erste arg))
         '(1 2 3))
```

or just

```
(let ((arg '(1 2 3))) (erste arg))
```

The built-in function `indirect-function` provides an easy way to perform symbol function indirection explicitly.

indirect-function *function* **&optional** *noerror*   [Function]
> This function returns the meaning of *function* as a function. If *function* is a symbol, then it finds *function*'s function definition and starts over with that value. If *function* is not a symbol, then it returns *function* itself.
>
> This function returns `nil` if the final symbol is unbound. It signals a `cyclic-function-indirection` error if there is a loop in the chain of symbols.
>
> The optional argument *noerror* is obsolete, kept for backward compatibility, and has no effect.
>
> Here is how you could define `indirect-function` in Lisp:
>
> ```
> (defun indirect-function (function)
>   (if (symbolp function)
>       (indirect-function (symbol-function function))
>     function))
> ```

9.1.5 Evaluation of Function Forms

If the first element of a list being evaluated is a Lisp function object, byte-code object or primitive function object, then that list is a *function call*. For example, here is a call to the function `+`:

```
(+ 1 x)
```

The first step in evaluating a function call is to evaluate the remaining elements of the list from left to right. The results are the actual argument values, one value for each list element. The next step is to call the function with this list of arguments, effectively using the function `apply` (see Section 12.5 [Calling Functions], page 194). If the function is written in Lisp, the arguments are used to bind the argument variables of the function (see Section 12.2 [Lambda Expressions], page 188); then the forms in the function body are evaluated in order, and the value of the last body form becomes the value of the function call.

9.1.6 Lisp Macro Evaluation

If the first element of a list being evaluated is a macro object, then the list is a *macro call*. When a macro call is evaluated, the elements of the rest of the list are *not* initially evaluated. Instead, these elements themselves are used as the arguments of the macro. The macro definition computes a replacement form, called the *expansion* of the macro, to be evaluated in place of the original form. The expansion may be any sort of form: a self-evaluating constant, a symbol, or a list. If the expansion is itself a macro call, this process of expansion repeats until some other sort of form results.

Ordinary evaluation of a macro call finishes by evaluating the expansion. However, the macro expansion is not necessarily evaluated right away, or at all, because other programs also expand macro calls, and they may or may not evaluate the expansions.

Normally, the argument expressions are not evaluated as part of computing the macro expansion, but instead appear as part of the expansion, so they are computed when the expansion is evaluated.

For example, given a macro defined as follows:

```
(defmacro cadr (x)
  (list 'car (list 'cdr x)))
```

an expression such as `(cadr (assq 'handler list))` is a macro call, and its expansion is:

```
(car (cdr (assq 'handler list)))
```

Note that the argument `(assq 'handler list)` appears in the expansion.

See Chapter 13 [Macros], page 217, for a complete description of Emacs Lisp macros.

9.1.7 Special Forms

A *special form* is a primitive function specially marked so that its arguments are not all evaluated. Most special forms define control structures or perform variable bindings—things which functions cannot do.

Each special form has its own rules for which arguments are evaluated and which are used without evaluation. Whether a particular argument is evaluated may depend on the results of evaluating other arguments.

If an expression's first symbol is that of a special form, the expression should follow the rules of that special form; otherwise, Emacs's behavior is not well-defined (though it will not crash). For example, `((lambda (x) x . 3) 4)` contains a subexpression that begins with `lambda` but is not a well-formed `lambda` expression, so Emacs may signal an error, or may return 3 or 4 or `nil`, or may behave in other ways.

`special-form-p` *object*   [Function]
> This predicate tests whether its argument is a special form, and returns `t` if so, `nil` otherwise.

Here is a list, in alphabetical order, of all of the special forms in Emacs Lisp with a reference to where each is described.

`and`   see Section 10.3 [Combining Conditions], page 141,

`catch`   see Section 10.6.1 [Catch and Throw], page 145,

`cond`   see Section 10.2 [Conditionals], page 136,

`condition-case`
> see Section 10.6.3.3 [Handling Errors], page 150,

`defconst`   see Section 11.5 [Defining Variables], page 161,

`defvar`   see Section 11.5 [Defining Variables], page 161,

`function`   see Section 12.7 [Anonymous Functions], page 198,

`if`   see Section 10.2 [Conditionals], page 136,

`interactive`
              see Section 20.3 [Interactive Call], page 352,

`lambda`   see Section 12.2 [Lambda Expressions], page 188,

`let`
`let*`   see Section 11.3 [Local Variables], page 158,

`or`   see Section 10.3 [Combining Conditions], page 141,

`prog1`
`prog2`
`progn`   see Section 10.1 [Sequencing], page 135,

`quote`   see Section 9.2 [Quoting], page 130,

`save-current-buffer`
              see Section 26.2 [Current Buffer], page 550,

`save-excursion`
              see Section 29.3 [Excursions], page 683,

`save-restriction`
              see Section 29.4 [Narrowing], page 684,

`setq`   see Section 11.8 [Setting Variables], page 165,

`setq-default`
              see Section 11.10.2 [Creating Buffer-Local], page 172,

`track-mouse`
              see Section 28.14 [Mouse Tracking], page 660,

`unwind-protect`
              see Section 10.6 [Nonlocal Exits], page 145,

`while`   see Section 10.4 [Iteration], page 142,

> **Common Lisp note:** Here are some comparisons of special forms in GNU Emacs Lisp and Common Lisp. `setq`, `if`, and `catch` are special forms in both Emacs Lisp and Common Lisp. `save-excursion` is a special form in Emacs Lisp, but doesn't exist in Common Lisp. `throw` is a special form in Common Lisp (because it must be able to throw multiple values), but it is a function in Emacs Lisp (which doesn't have multiple values).

9.1.8 Autoloading

The *autoload* feature allows you to call a function or macro whose function definition has not yet been loaded into Emacs. It specifies which file contains the definition. When an autoload object appears as a symbol's function definition, calling that symbol as a function automatically loads the specified file; then it calls the real definition loaded from that file. The way to arrange for an autoload object to appear as a symbol's function definition is described in Section 15.5 [Autoload], page 249.

9.2 Quoting

The special form `quote` returns its single argument, as written, without evaluating it. This provides a way to include constant symbols and lists, which are not self-evaluating objects, in a program. (It is not necessary to quote self-evaluating objects such as numbers, strings, and vectors.)

`quote` *object*   [Special Form]
    This special form returns *object*, without evaluating it.

Because `quote` is used so often in programs, Lisp provides a convenient read syntax for it. An apostrophe character ('') followed by a Lisp object (in read syntax) expands to a list whose first element is `quote`, and whose second element is the object. Thus, the read syntax `'x` is an abbreviation for (`quote x`).

Here are some examples of expressions that use `quote`:

```
(quote (+ 1 2))
     ⇒ (+ 1 2)
(quote foo)
     ⇒ foo
'foo
     ⇒ foo
''foo
     ⇒ (quote foo)
'(quote foo)
     ⇒ (quote foo)
['foo]
     ⇒ [(quote foo)]
```

Other quoting constructs include `function` (see Section 12.7 [Anonymous Functions], page 198), which causes an anonymous lambda expression written in Lisp to be compiled, and '`' (see Section 9.3 [Backquote], page 130), which is used to quote only part of a list, while computing and substituting other parts.

9.3 Backquote

Backquote constructs allow you to quote a list, but selectively evaluate elements of that list. In the simplest case, it is identical to the special form `quote` For example, these two forms yield identical results:

```
`(a list of (+ 2 3) elements)
     ⇒ (a list of (+ 2 3) elements)
'(a list of (+ 2 3) elements)
     ⇒ (a list of (+ 2 3) elements)
```

The special marker ',' inside of the argument to backquote indicates a value that isn't constant. The Emacs Lisp evaluator evaluates the argument of ',', and puts the value in the list structure:

```
`(a list of ,(+ 2 3) elements)
     ⇒ (a list of 5 elements)
```

Substitution with ',' is allowed at deeper levels of the list structure also. For example:

```
`(1 2 (3 ,(+ 4 5)))
     ⇒ (1 2 (3 9))
```

You can also *splice* an evaluated value into the resulting list, using the special marker ',@'. The elements of the spliced list become elements at the same level as the other elements of the resulting list. The equivalent code without using '`' is often unreadable. Here are some examples:

```
(setq some-list '(2 3))
     ⇒ (2 3)
(cons 1 (append some-list '(4) some-list))
     ⇒ (1 2 3 4 2 3)
`(1 ,@some-list 4 ,@some-list)
     ⇒ (1 2 3 4 2 3)

(setq list '(hack foo bar))
     ⇒ (hack foo bar)
(cons 'use
  (cons 'the
    (cons 'words (append (cdr list) '(as elements)))))
     ⇒ (use the words foo bar as elements)
`(use the words ,@(cdr list) as elements)
     ⇒ (use the words foo bar as elements)
```

9.4 Eval

Most often, forms are evaluated automatically, by virtue of their occurrence in a program being run. On rare occasions, you may need to write code that evaluates a form that is computed at run time, such as after reading a form from text being edited or getting one from a property list. On these occasions, use the `eval` function. Often `eval` is not needed and something else should be used instead. For example, to get the value of a variable, while `eval` works, `symbol-value` is preferable; or rather than store expressions in a property list that then need to go through `eval`, it is better to store functions instead that are then passed to `funcall`.

The functions and variables described in this section evaluate forms, specify limits to the evaluation process, or record recently returned values. Loading a file also does evaluation (see Chapter 15 [Loading], page 244).

It is generally cleaner and more flexible to store a function in a data structure, and call it with `funcall` or `apply`, than to store an expression in the data structure and evaluate it. Using functions provides the ability to pass information to them as arguments.

`eval` *form* **&optional** *lexical*   [Function]
> This is the basic function for evaluating an expression. It evaluates *form* in the current environment, and returns the result. The type of the *form* object determines how it is evaluated. See Section 9.1 [Forms], page 125.

The argument *lexical* specifies the scoping rule for local variables (see Section 11.9 [Variable Scoping], page 166). If it is omitted or `nil`, that means to evaluate *form* using the default dynamic scoping rule. If it is `t`, that means to use the lexical scoping rule. The value of *lexical* can also be a non-empty alist specifying a particular *lexical environment* for lexical bindings; however, this feature is only useful for specialized purposes, such as in Emacs Lisp debuggers. See Section 11.9.3 [Lexical Binding], page 168.

Since `eval` is a function, the argument expression that appears in a call to `eval` is evaluated twice: once as preparation before `eval` is called, and again by the `eval` function itself. Here is an example:

```
(setq foo 'bar)
     ⇒ bar
(setq bar 'baz)
     ⇒ baz
;; Here eval receives argument foo
(eval 'foo)
     ⇒ bar
;; Here eval receives argument bar, which is the value of foo
(eval foo)
     ⇒ baz
```

The number of currently active calls to `eval` is limited to `max-lisp-eval-depth` (see below).

`eval-region` *start end* **&optional** *stream read-function*   [Command]
    This function evaluates the forms in the current buffer in the region defined by the positions *start* and *end*. It reads forms from the region and calls `eval` on them until the end of the region is reached, or until an error is signaled and not handled.

    By default, `eval-region` does not produce any output. However, if *stream* is non-`nil`, any output produced by output functions (see Section 18.5 [Output Functions], page 308), as well as the values that result from evaluating the expressions in the region are printed using *stream*. See Section 18.4 [Output Streams], page 306.

    If *read-function* is non-`nil`, it should be a function, which is used instead of `read` to read expressions one by one. This function is called with one argument, the stream for reading input. You can also use the variable `load-read-function` (see [How Programs Do Loading], page 246) to specify this function, but it is more robust to use the *read-function* argument.

    `eval-region` does not move point. It always returns `nil`.

`eval-buffer` **&optional** *buffer-or-name stream filename unibyte*   [Command]
    print
    This is similar to `eval-region`, but the arguments provide different optional features. `eval-buffer` operates on the entire accessible portion of buffer *buffer-or-name* (see Section "Narrowing" in *The GNU Emacs Manual*). *buffer-or-name* can be a buffer, a buffer name (a string), or `nil` (or omitted), which means to use the current buffer. *stream* is used as in `eval-region`, unless *stream* is `nil` and *print* non-`nil`. In that case, values that result from evaluating the expressions are still discarded, but the

output of the output functions is printed in the echo area. *filename* is the file name to use for `load-history` (see Section 15.9 [Unloading], page 257), and defaults to `buffer-file-name` (see Section 26.4 [Buffer File Name], page 554). If *unibyte* is non-`nil`, `read` converts strings to unibyte whenever possible.

`eval-current-buffer` is an alias for this command.

`max-lisp-eval-depth` [User Option]

This variable defines the maximum depth allowed in calls to `eval`, `apply`, and `funcall` before an error is signaled (with error message `"Lisp nesting exceeds max-lisp-eval-depth"`).

This limit, with the associated error when it is exceeded, is one way Emacs Lisp avoids infinite recursion on an ill-defined function. If you increase the value of `max-lisp-eval-depth` too much, such code can cause stack overflow instead. On some systems, this overflow can be handled. In that case, normal Lisp evaluation is interrupted and control is transferred back to the top level command loop (`top-level`). Note that there is no way to enter Emacs Lisp debugger in this situation. See Section 17.1.1 [Error Debugging], page 270.

The depth limit counts internal uses of `eval`, `apply`, and `funcall`, such as for calling the functions mentioned in Lisp expressions, and recursive evaluation of function call arguments and function body forms, as well as explicit calls in Lisp code.

The default value of this variable is 400. If you set it to a value less than 100, Lisp will reset it to 100 if the given value is reached. Entry to the Lisp debugger increases the value, if there is little room left, to make sure the debugger itself has room to execute.

`max-specpdl-size` provides another limit on nesting. See [Local Variables], page 160.

`values` [Variable]

The value of this variable is a list of the values returned by all the expressions that were read, evaluated, and printed from buffers (including the minibuffer) by the standard Emacs commands which do this. (Note that this does *not* include evaluation in `*ielm*` buffers, nor evaluation using *C-j*, *C-x C-e*, and similar evaluation commands in `lisp-interaction-mode`.) The elements are ordered most recent first.

```
(setq x 1)
     ⇒ 1
(list 'A (1+ 2) auto-save-default)
     ⇒ (A 3 t)
values
     ⇒ ((A 3 t) 1 ...)
```

This variable is useful for referring back to values of forms recently evaluated. It is generally a bad idea to print the value of `values` itself, since this may be very long. Instead, examine particular elements, like this:

```
;; Refer to the most recent evaluation result.
(nth 0 values)
     ⇒ (A 3 t)
```

```
;; That put a new element on,
;;    so all elements move back one.
(nth 1 values)
     ⇒ (A 3 t)
;; This gets the element that was next-to-most-recent
;;    before this example.
(nth 3 values)
     ⇒ 1
```

10 Control Structures

A Lisp program consists of a set of *expressions*, or *forms* (see Section 9.1 [Forms], page 125). We control the order of execution of these forms by enclosing them in *control structures*. Control structures are special forms which control when, whether, or how many times to execute the forms they contain.

The simplest order of execution is sequential execution: first form *a*, then form *b*, and so on. This is what happens when you write several forms in succession in the body of a function, or at top level in a file of Lisp code—the forms are executed in the order written. We call this *textual order*. For example, if a function body consists of two forms *a* and *b*, evaluation of the function evaluates first *a* and then *b*. The result of evaluating *b* becomes the value of the function.

Explicit control structures make possible an order of execution other than sequential.

Emacs Lisp provides several kinds of control structure, including other varieties of sequencing, conditionals, iteration, and (controlled) jumps—all discussed below. The built-in control structures are special forms since their subforms are not necessarily evaluated or not evaluated sequentially. You can use macros to define your own control structure constructs (see Chapter 13 [Macros], page 217).

10.1 Sequencing

Evaluating forms in the order they appear is the most common way control passes from one form to another. In some contexts, such as in a function body, this happens automatically. Elsewhere you must use a control structure construct to do this: `progn`, the simplest control construct of Lisp.

A `progn` special form looks like this:

```
(progn a b c ...)
```

and it says to execute the forms *a*, *b*, *c*, and so on, in that order. These forms are called the *body* of the `progn` form. The value of the last form in the body becomes the value of the entire `progn`. `(progn)` returns `nil`.

In the early days of Lisp, `progn` was the only way to execute two or more forms in succession and use the value of the last of them. But programmers found they often needed to use a `progn` in the body of a function, where (at that time) only one form was allowed. So the body of a function was made into an implicit `progn`: several forms are allowed just as in the body of an actual `progn`. Many other control structures likewise contain an implicit `progn`. As a result, `progn` is not used as much as it was many years ago. It is needed now most often inside an `unwind-protect`, `and`, `or`, or in the *then*-part of an `if`.

`progn` *forms...*   [Special Form]
> This special form evaluates all of the *forms*, in textual order, returning the result of the final form.

```
(progn (print "The first form")
       (print "The second form")
       (print "The third form"))
     ⊣ "The first form"
     ⊣ "The second form"
     ⊣ "The third form"
  ⇒ "The third form"
```

Two other constructs likewise evaluate a series of forms but return different values:

prog1 *form1 forms...*   [Special Form]

    This special form evaluates *form1* and all of the *forms*, in textual order, returning the result of *form1*.

```
(prog1 (print "The first form")
       (print "The second form")
       (print "The third form"))
     ⊣ "The first form"
     ⊣ "The second form"
     ⊣ "The third form"
  ⇒ "The first form"
```

    Here is a way to remove the first element from a list in the variable x, then return the value of that former element:

```
(prog1 (car x) (setq x (cdr x)))
```

prog2 *form1 form2 forms...*   [Special Form]

    This special form evaluates *form1*, *form2*, and all of the following *forms*, in textual order, returning the result of *form2*.

```
(prog2 (print "The first form")
       (print "The second form")
       (print "The third form"))
     ⊣ "The first form"
     ⊣ "The second form"
     ⊣ "The third form"
  ⇒ "The second form"
```

10.2 Conditionals

Conditional control structures choose among alternatives. Emacs Lisp has four conditional forms: `if`, which is much the same as in other languages; `when` and `unless`, which are variants of `if`; and `cond`, which is a generalized case statement.

if *condition then-form else-forms...*   [Special Form]

    `if` chooses between the *then-form* and the *else-forms* based on the value of *condition*. If the evaluated *condition* is non-`nil`, *then-form* is evaluated and the result returned. Otherwise, the *else-forms* are evaluated in textual order, and the value of the last one is returned. (The *else* part of `if` is an example of an implicit `progn`. See Section 10.1 [Sequencing], page 135.)

If *condition* has the value `nil`, and no *else-forms* are given, `if` returns `nil`.

`if` is a special form because the branch that is not selected is never evaluated—it is ignored. Thus, in this example, `true` is not printed because `print` is never called:

```
(if nil
    (print 'true)
  'very-false)
⇒ very-false
```

when *condition then-forms. . .*   [Macro]

This is a variant of `if` where there are no *else-forms*, and possibly several *then-forms*. In particular,

```
(when condition a b c)
```

is entirely equivalent to

```
(if condition (progn a b c) nil)
```

unless *condition forms. . .*   [Macro]

This is a variant of `if` where there is no *then-form*:

```
(unless condition a b c)
```

is entirely equivalent to

```
(if condition nil
  a b c)
```

cond *clause. . .*   [Special Form]

`cond` chooses among an arbitrary number of alternatives. Each *clause* in the `cond` must be a list. The CAR of this list is the *condition*; the remaining elements, if any, the *body-forms*. Thus, a clause looks like this:

```
(condition body-forms...)
```

`cond` tries the clauses in textual order, by evaluating the *condition* of each clause. If the value of *condition* is non-`nil`, the clause succeeds; then `cond` evaluates its *body-forms*, and returns the value of the last of *body-forms*. Any remaining clauses are ignored.

If the value of *condition* is `nil`, the clause fails, so the `cond` moves on to the following clause, trying its *condition*.

A clause may also look like this:

```
(condition)
```

Then, if *condition* is non-`nil` when tested, the `cond` form returns the value of *condition*.

If every *condition* evaluates to `nil`, so that every clause fails, `cond` returns `nil`.

The following example has four clauses, which test for the cases where the value of `x` is a number, string, buffer and symbol, respectively:

```
(cond ((numberp x) x)
      ((stringp x) x)
      ((bufferp x)
       (setq temporary-hack x) ; multiple body-forms
       (buffer-name x))        ; in one clause
      ((symbolp x) (symbol-value x)))
```

Often we want to execute the last clause whenever none of the previous clauses was successful. To do this, we use `t` as the *condition* of the last clause, like this: `(t body-forms)`. The form `t` evaluates to `t`, which is never `nil`, so this clause never fails, provided the `cond` gets to it at all. For example:

```
(setq a 5)
(cond ((eq a 'hack) 'foo)
      (t "default"))
⇒ "default"
```

This `cond` expression returns `foo` if the value of `a` is `hack`, and returns the string `"default"` otherwise.

Any conditional construct can be expressed with `cond` or with `if`. Therefore, the choice between them is a matter of style. For example:

```
(if a b c)
≡
(cond (a b) (t c))
```

10.2.1 Pattern matching case statement

The `cond` form lets you choose between alternatives using predicate conditions that compare values of expressions against specific values known and written in advance. However, sometimes it is useful to select alternatives based on more general conditions that distinguish between broad classes of values. The `pcase` macro allows you to choose between alternatives based on matching the value of an expression against a series of patterns. A pattern can be a literal value (for comparisons to literal values you'd use `cond`), or it can be a more general description of the expected structure of the expression's value.

pcase *expression* **&rest** *clauses*   [Macro]

Evaluate *expression* and choose among an arbitrary number of alternatives based on the value of *expression*. The possible alternatives are specified by *clauses*, each of which must be a list of the form `(pattern body-forms...)`. `pcase` tries to match the value of *expression* to the *pattern* of each clause, in textual order. If the value matches, the clause succeeds; `pcase` then evaluates its *body-forms*, and returns the value of the last of *body-forms*. Any remaining *clauses* are ignored.

The *pattern* part of a clause can be of one of two types: *QPattern*, a pattern quoted with a backquote; or a *UPattern*, which is not quoted. UPatterns are simpler, so we describe them first.

Note: In the description of the patterns below, we use "the value being matched" to refer to the value of the *expression* that is the first argument of `pcase`.

A UPattern can have the following forms:

`'val`   Matches if the value being matched is `equal` to *val*.

`atom`   Matches any *atom*, which can be a keyword, a number, or a string. (These are self-quoting, so this kind of UPattern is actually a shorthand for `'atom`.) Note that a string or a float matches any string or float with the same contents/value.

`_`   Matches any value. This is known as *don't care* or *wildcard*.

symbol   Matches any value, and additionally let-binds *symbol* to the value it matched, so that you can later refer to it, either in the *body-forms* or also later in the pattern.

(pred *predfun*)
      Matches if the predicate function *predfun* returns non-**nil** when called with the value being matched as its argument. *predfun* can be one of the possible forms described below.

(guard *boolean-expression*)
      Matches if *boolean-expression* evaluates to non-**nil**. This allows you to include in a UPattern boolean conditions that refer to symbols bound to values (including the value being matched) by previous UPatterns. Typically used inside an **and** UPattern, see below. For example, (and x (guard (< x 10))) is a pattern which matches any number smaller than 10 and let-binds the variable x to that number.

(let *upattern expression*)
      Matches if the specified *expression* matches the specified *upattern*. This allows matching a pattern against the value of an *arbitrary* expression, not just the expression that is the first argument to **pcase**. (It is called **let** because *upattern* can bind symbols to values using the *symbol* UPattern. For example: ((or `(key . ,val) (let val 5)) val).)

(app *function upattern*)
      Matches if *function* applied to the value being matched returns a value that matches *upattern*. This is like the **pred** UPattern, except that it tests the result against *upattern*, rather than against a boolean truth value. The *function* call can use one of the forms described below.

(or *upattern1 upattern2*...)
      Matches if one the argument UPatterns matches. As soon as the first matching UPattern is found, the rest are not tested. For this reason, if any of the UPatterns let-bind symbols to the matched value, they should all bind the same symbols.

(and *upattern1 upattern2*...)
      Matches if all the argument UPatterns match.

The function calls used in the **pred** and **app** UPatterns can have one of the following forms:

function symbol, like **integerp**
      In this case, the named function is applied to the value being matched.

lambda-function (lambda (*arg*) *body*)
      In this case, the lambda-function is called with one argument, the value being matched.

(*func args*...)
      This is a function call with *n* specified arguments; the function is called with these *n* arguments and an additional *n*+1-th argument that is the value being matched.

Here's an illustrative example of using UPatterns:

```
(pcase (get-return-code x)
  ('success        (message "Done!"))
  ('would-block    (message "Sorry, can't do it now"))
  ('read-only      (message "The shmliblick is read-only"))
  ('access-denied  (message "You do not have the needed rights"))
  (code            (message "Unknown return code %S" code)))
```

In addition, you can use backquoted patterns that are more powerful. They allow matching the value of the *expression* that is the first argument of **pcase** against specifications of its *structure*. For example, you can specify that the value must be a list of 2 elements whose first element is a specific string and the second element is any value with a backquoted pattern like `("first" ,second-elem)`.

Backquoted patterns have the form `qpattern` where *qpattern* can have the following forms:

(*qpattern1* . *qpattern2*)
> Matches if the value being matched is a cons cell whose **car** matches *qpattern1* and whose **cdr** matches *qpattern2*. This readily generalizes to backquoted lists as in (*qpattern1* *qpattern2* ...).

[*qpattern1* *qpattern2* ... *qpatternm*]
> Matches if the value being matched is a vector of length *m* whose 0..(*m*-1)th elements match *qpattern1*, *qpattern2* ... *qpatternm*, respectively.

atom
> Matches if corresponding element of the value being matched is **equal** to the specified *atom*.

,upattern
> Matches if the corresponding element of the value being matched matches the specified *upattern*.

Note that uses of QPatterns can be expressed using only UPatterns, as QPatterns are implemented on top of UPatterns using **pcase-defmacro**, described below. However, using QPatterns will in many cases lead to a more readable code.

Here is an example of using **pcase** to implement a simple interpreter for a little expression language (note that this example requires lexical binding, see Section 11.9.3 [Lexical Binding], page 168):

```
(defun evaluate (exp env)
  (pcase exp
    (`(add ,x ,y)     (+ (evaluate x env) (evaluate y env)))
    (`(call ,fun ,arg) (funcall (evaluate fun env) (evaluate arg env)))
    (`(fn ,arg ,body)  (lambda (val)
                          (evaluate body (cons (cons arg val) env))))
    ((pred numberp)   exp)
    ((pred symbolp)   (cdr (assq exp env)))
    (_                (error "Unknown expression %S" exp))))
```

Here `` `(add ,x ,y) `` is a pattern that checks that `exp` is a three-element list starting with the literal symbol `add`, then extracts the second and third elements and binds them to the variables `x` and `y`. Then it evaluates `x` and `y` and adds the results. The `call` and `fn` patterns similarly implement two flavors of function calls. `(pred numberp)` is a pattern that simply checks that `exp` is a number and if so, evaluates it. `(pred symbolp)` matches symbols, and returns their association. Finally, `_` is the catch-all pattern that matches anything, so it's suitable for reporting syntax errors.

Here are some sample programs in this small language, including their evaluation results:

```
(evaluate '(add 1 2) nil)               ;=> 3
(evaluate '(add x y) '((x . 1) (y . 2)))  ;=> 3
(evaluate '(call (fn x (add 1 x)) 2) nil) ;=> 3
(evaluate '(sub 1 2) nil)               ;=> error
```

Additional UPatterns can be defined using the `pcase-defmacro` macro.

pcase-defmacro *name args* **&rest** *body*   [Macro]
> Define a new kind of UPattern for `pcase`. The new UPattern will be invoked as (*name actual-args*). The *body* should describe how to rewrite the UPattern *name* into some other UPattern. The rewriting will be the result of evaluating *body* in an environment where *args* are bound to *actual-args*.

10.3 Constructs for Combining Conditions

This section describes three constructs that are often used together with `if` and `cond` to express complicated conditions. The constructs `and` and `or` can also be used individually as kinds of multiple conditional constructs.

not *condition*   [Function]
> This function tests for the falsehood of *condition*. It returns `t` if *condition* is `nil`, and `nil` otherwise. The function `not` is identical to `null`, and we recommend using the name `null` if you are testing for an empty list.

and *conditions...*   [Special Form]
> The **and** special form tests whether all the *conditions* are true. It works by evaluating the *conditions* one by one in the order written.

> If any of the *conditions* evaluates to `nil`, then the result of the **and** must be `nil` regardless of the remaining *conditions*; so **and** returns `nil` right away, ignoring the remaining *conditions*.

> If all the *conditions* turn out non-`nil`, then the value of the last of them becomes the value of the **and** form. Just (**and**), with no *conditions*, returns `t`, appropriate because all the *conditions* turned out non-`nil`. (Think about it; which one did not?)

> Here is an example. The first condition returns the integer 1, which is not `nil`. Similarly, the second condition returns the integer 2, which is not `nil`. The third condition is `nil`, so the remaining condition is never evaluated.

```
(and (print 1) (print 2) nil (print 3))
          ⊣ 1
          ⊣ 2
    ⇒ nil
```

Here is a more realistic example of using **and**:

```
(if (and (consp foo) (eq (car foo) 'x))
    (message "foo is a list starting with x"))
```

Note that `(car foo)` is not executed if `(consp foo)` returns **nil**, thus avoiding an error.

and expressions can also be written using either **if** or **cond**. Here's how:

```
(and arg1 arg2 arg3)
≡
(if arg1 (if arg2 arg3))
≡
(cond (arg1 (cond (arg2 arg3))))
```

or *conditions...*   [Special Form]

The **or** special form tests whether at least one of the *conditions* is true. It works by evaluating all the *conditions* one by one in the order written.

If any of the *conditions* evaluates to a non-**nil** value, then the result of the **or** must be non-**nil**; so **or** returns right away, ignoring the remaining *conditions*. The value it returns is the non-**nil** value of the condition just evaluated.

If all the *conditions* turn out **nil**, then the **or** expression returns **nil**. Just `(or)`, with no *conditions*, returns **nil**, appropriate because all the *conditions* turned out **nil**. (Think about it; which one did not?)

For example, this expression tests whether **x** is either **nil** or the integer zero:

```
(or (eq x nil) (eq x 0))
```

Like the **and** construct, **or** can be written in terms of **cond**. For example:

```
(or arg1 arg2 arg3)
≡
(cond (arg1)
      (arg2)
      (arg3))
```

You could almost write **or** in terms of **if**, but not quite:

```
(if arg1 arg1
  (if arg2 arg2
    arg3))
```

This is not completely equivalent because it can evaluate *arg1* or *arg2* twice. By contrast, `(or arg1 arg2 arg3)` never evaluates any argument more than once.

10.4 Iteration

Iteration means executing part of a program repetitively. For example, you might want to repeat some computation once for each element of a list, or once for each integer from 0 to *n*. You can do this in Emacs Lisp with the special form **while**:

while *condition forms...*   [Special Form]

while first evaluates *condition*. If the result is non-**nil**, it evaluates *forms* in textual order. Then it reevaluates *condition*, and if the result is non-**nil**, it evaluates *forms* again. This process repeats until *condition* evaluates to **nil**.

There is no limit on the number of iterations that may occur. The loop will continue until either *condition* evaluates to `nil` or until an error or `throw` jumps out of it (see Section 10.6 [Nonlocal Exits], page 145).

The value of a `while` form is always `nil`.

```
(setq num 0)
     ⇒ 0
(while (< num 4)
  (princ (format "Iteration %d." num))
  (setq num (1+ num)))
     ⊣ Iteration 0.
     ⊣ Iteration 1.
     ⊣ Iteration 2.
     ⊣ Iteration 3.
     ⇒ nil
```

To write a repeat-until loop, which will execute something on each iteration and then do the end-test, put the body followed by the end-test in a `progn` as the first argument of `while`, as shown here:

```
(while (progn
          (forward-line 1)
          (not (looking-at "^$"))))
```

This moves forward one line and continues moving by lines until it reaches an empty line. It is peculiar in that the `while` has no body, just the end test (which also does the real work of moving point).

The `dolist` and `dotimes` macros provide convenient ways to write two common kinds of loops.

dolist (*var list* [*result*]) *body*...   [Macro]

    This construct executes *body* once for each element of *list*, binding the variable *var* locally to hold the current element. Then it returns the value of evaluating *result*, or `nil` if *result* is omitted. For example, here is how you could use `dolist` to define the `reverse` function:

```
(defun reverse (list)
  (let (value)
    (dolist (elt list value)
      (setq value (cons elt value)))))
```

dotimes (*var count* [*result*]) *body*...   [Macro]

    This construct executes *body* once for each integer from 0 (inclusive) to *count* (exclusive), binding the variable *var* to the integer for the current iteration. Then it returns the value of evaluating *result*, or `nil` if *result* is omitted. Here is an example of using `dotimes` to do something 100 times:

```
(dotimes (i 100)
  (insert "I will not obey absurd orders\n"))
```

10.5 Generators

A *generator* is a function that produces a potentially-infinite stream of values. Each time the function produces a value, it suspends itself and waits for a caller to request the next value.

iter-defun *name args* [*doc*] [*declare*] [*interactive*] *body...*   [Macro]
    iter-defun defines a generator function. A generator function has the same signature as a normal function, but works differently. Instead of executing *body* when called, a generator function returns an iterator object. That iterator runs *body* to generate values, emitting a value and pausing where **iter-yield** or **iter-yield-from** appears. When *body* returns normally, **iter-next** signals **iter-end-of-sequence** with *body*'s result as its condition data.

    Any kind of Lisp code is valid inside *body*, but **iter-yield** and **iter-yield-from** cannot appear inside **unwind-protect** forms.

iter-lambda *args* [*doc*] [*interactive*] *body...*   [Macro]
    iter-lambda produces an unnamed generator function that works just like a generator function produced with **iter-defun**.

iter-yield *value*   [Macro]
    When it appears inside a generator function, **iter-yield** indicates that the current iterator should pause and return *value* from **iter-next**. **iter-yield** evaluates to the **value** parameter of next call to **iter-next**.

iter-yield-from *iterator*   [Macro]
    iter-yield-from yields all the values that *iterator* produces and evaluates to the value that *iterator*'s generator function returns normally. While it has control, *iterator* receives values sent to the iterator using **iter-next**.

To use a generator function, first call it normally, producing a *iterator* object. An iterator is a specific instance of a generator. Then use **iter-next** to retrieve values from this iterator. When there are no more values to pull from an iterator, **iter-next** raises an **iter-end-of-sequence** condition with the iterator's final value.

It's important to note that generator function bodies only execute inside calls to **iter-next**. A call to a function defined with **iter-defun** produces an iterator; you must drive this iterator with **iter-next** for anything interesting to happen. Each call to a generator function produces a *different* iterator, each with its own state.

iter-next *iterator value*   [Function]
    Retrieve the next value from *iterator*. If there are no more values to be generated (because *iterator*'s generator function returned), **iter-next** signals the **iter-end-of-sequence** condition; the data value associated with this condition is the value with which *iterator*'s generator function returned.

    value is sent into the iterator and becomes the value to which **iter-yield** evaluates. *value* is ignored for the first **iter-next** call to a given iterator, since at the start of *iterator*'s generator function, the generator function is not evaluating any **iter-yield** form.

iter-close *iterator*   [Function]
>   If *iterator* is suspended inside an `unwind-protect`'s `bodyform` and becomes unreach-
>   able, Emacs will eventually run unwind handlers after a garbage collection pass. (Note
>   that `iter-yield` is illegal inside an `unwind-protect`'s `unwindforms`.) To ensure that
>   these handlers are run before then, use `iter-close`.

Some convenience functions are provided to make working with iterators easier:

iter-do (*var iterator*) *body* ...   [Macro]
>   Run *body* with *var* bound to each value that *iterator* produces.

The Common Lisp loop facility also contains features for working with iterators. See
See Section "Loop Facility" in *Common Lisp Extensions*.

The following piece of code demonstrates some important principles of working with
iterators.

```
(require 'generator)
(iter-defun my-iter (x)
  (iter-yield (1+ (iter-yield (1+ x))))
   ;; Return normally
  -1)

(let* ((iter (my-iter 5))
       (iter2 (my-iter 0)))
  ;; Prints 6
  (print (iter-next iter))
  ;; Prints 9
  (print (iter-next iter 8))
  ;; Prints 1; iter and iter2 have distinct states
  (print (iter-next iter2 nil))

  ;; We expect the iter sequence to end now
  (condition-case x
      (iter-next iter)
    (iter-end-of-sequence
     ;; Prints -1, which my-iter returned normally
     (print (cdr x)))))
```

10.6 Nonlocal Exits

A *nonlocal exit* is a transfer of control from one point in a program to another remote point.
Nonlocal exits can occur in Emacs Lisp as a result of errors; you can also use them under
explicit control. Nonlocal exits unbind all variable bindings made by the constructs being
exited.

10.6.1 Explicit Nonlocal Exits: `catch` and `throw`

Most control constructs affect only the flow of control within the construct itself. The
function `throw` is the exception to this rule of normal program execution: it performs a

nonlocal exit on request. (There are other exceptions, but they are for error handling only.) `throw` is used inside a `catch`, and jumps back to that `catch`. For example:

```
(defun foo-outer ()
  (catch 'foo
    (foo-inner)))

(defun foo-inner ()
  ...
  (if x
      (throw 'foo t))
  ...)
```

The `throw` form, if executed, transfers control straight back to the corresponding `catch`, which returns immediately. The code following the `throw` is not executed. The second argument of `throw` is used as the return value of the `catch`.

The function `throw` finds the matching `catch` based on the first argument: it searches for a `catch` whose first argument is `eq` to the one specified in the `throw`. If there is more than one applicable `catch`, the innermost one takes precedence. Thus, in the above example, the `throw` specifies `foo`, and the `catch` in `foo-outer` specifies the same symbol, so that `catch` is the applicable one (assuming there is no other matching `catch` in between).

Executing `throw` exits all Lisp constructs up to the matching `catch`, including function calls. When binding constructs such as `let` or function calls are exited in this way, the bindings are unbound, just as they are when these constructs exit normally (see Section 11.3 [Local Variables], page 158). Likewise, `throw` restores the buffer and position saved by `save-excursion` (see Section 29.3 [Excursions], page 683), and the narrowing status saved by `save-restriction`. It also runs any cleanups established with the `unwind-protect` special form when it exits that form (see Section 10.6.4 [Cleanups], page 155).

The `throw` need not appear lexically within the `catch` that it jumps to. It can equally well be called from another function called within the `catch`. As long as the `throw` takes place chronologically after entry to the `catch`, and chronologically before exit from it, it has access to that `catch`. This is why `throw` can be used in commands such as `exit-recursive-edit` that throw back to the editor command loop (see Section 20.13 [Recursive Editing], page 386).

> **Common Lisp note:** Most other versions of Lisp, including Common Lisp, have several ways of transferring control nonsequentially: `return`, `return-from`, and `go`, for example. Emacs Lisp has only `throw`. The `cl-lib` library provides versions of some of these. See Section "Blocks and Exits" in *Common Lisp Extensions*.

catch *tag body...*   [Special Form]
> `catch` establishes a return point for the `throw` function. The return point is distinguished from other such return points by *tag*, which may be any Lisp object except `nil`. The argument *tag* is evaluated normally before the return point is established.
>
> With the return point in effect, `catch` evaluates the forms of the *body* in textual order. If the forms execute normally (without error or nonlocal exit) the value of the last body form is returned from the `catch`.

If a `throw` is executed during the execution of *body*, specifying the same value *tag*, the `catch` form exits immediately; the value it returns is whatever was specified as the second argument of `throw`.

`throw` *tag value*   [Function]

The purpose of `throw` is to return from a return point previously established with `catch`. The argument *tag* is used to choose among the various existing return points; it must be `eq` to the value specified in the `catch`. If multiple return points match *tag*, the innermost one is used.

The argument *value* is used as the value to return from that `catch`.

If no return point is in effect with tag *tag*, then a `no-catch` error is signaled with data (*tag value*).

10.6.2 Examples of `catch` and `throw`

One way to use `catch` and `throw` is to exit from a doubly nested loop. (In most languages, this would be done with a `goto`.) Here we compute (`foo i j`) for *i* and *j* varying from 0 to 9:

```
(defun search-foo ()
  (catch 'loop
    (let ((i 0))
      (while (< i 10)
        (let ((j 0))
          (while (< j 10)
            (if (foo i j)
                (throw 'loop (list i j)))
            (setq j (1+ j))))
        (setq i (1+ i))))))
```

If `foo` ever returns non-`nil`, we stop immediately and return a list of *i* and *j*. If `foo` always returns `nil`, the `catch` returns normally, and the value is `nil`, since that is the result of the `while`.

Here are two tricky examples, slightly different, showing two return points at once. First, two return points with the same tag, `hack`:

```
(defun catch2 (tag)
  (catch tag
    (throw 'hack 'yes)))
⇒ catch2

(catch 'hack
  (print (catch2 'hack))
  'no)
⊣ yes
⇒ no
```

Since both return points have tags that match the `throw`, it goes to the inner one, the one established in `catch2`. Therefore, `catch2` returns normally with value `yes`, and this value is printed. Finally the second body form in the outer `catch`, which is `'no`, is evaluated and returned from the outer `catch`.

Now let's change the argument given to `catch2`:

```
(catch 'hack
  (print (catch2 'quux))
  'no)
⇒ yes
```

We still have two return points, but this time only the outer one has the tag `hack`; the inner one has the tag `quux` instead. Therefore, `throw` makes the outer `catch` return the value `yes`. The function `print` is never called, and the body-form `'no` is never evaluated.

10.6.3 Errors

When Emacs Lisp attempts to evaluate a form that, for some reason, cannot be evaluated, it *signals* an *error*.

When an error is signaled, Emacs's default reaction is to print an error message and terminate execution of the current command. This is the right thing to do in most cases, such as if you type *C-f* at the end of the buffer.

In complicated programs, simple termination may not be what you want. For example, the program may have made temporary changes in data structures, or created temporary buffers that should be deleted before the program is finished. In such cases, you would use `unwind-protect` to establish *cleanup expressions* to be evaluated in case of error. (See Section 10.6.4 [Cleanups], page 155.) Occasionally, you may wish the program to continue execution despite an error in a subroutine. In these cases, you would use `condition-case` to establish *error handlers* to recover control in case of error.

Resist the temptation to use error handling to transfer control from one part of the program to another; use `catch` and `throw` instead. See Section 10.6.1 [Catch and Throw], page 145.

10.6.3.1 How to Signal an Error

Signaling an error means beginning error processing. Error processing normally aborts all or part of the running program and returns to a point that is set up to handle the error (see Section 10.6.3.2 [Processing of Errors], page 150). Here we describe how to signal an error.

Most errors are signaled automatically within Lisp primitives which you call for other purposes, such as if you try to take the CAR of an integer or move forward a character at the end of the buffer. You can also signal errors explicitly with the functions `error` and `signal`.

Quitting, which happens when the user types *C-g*, is not considered an error, but it is handled almost like an error. See Section 20.11 [Quitting], page 382.

Every error specifies an error message, one way or another. The message should state what is wrong ("File does not exist"), not how things ought to be ("File must exist"). The convention in Emacs Lisp is that error messages should start with a capital letter, but should not end with any sort of punctuation.

error *format-string* **&rest** *args*   [Function]
> This function signals an error with an error message constructed by applying `format-message` (see Section 4.7 [Formatting Strings], page 59) to *format-string* and *args*.

These examples show typical uses of **error**:

```
(error "That is an error -- try something else")
     error   That is an error -- try something else


(error "Invalid name `%s'" "A%%B")
     error   Invalid name 'A%%B'
```

error works by calling **signal** with two arguments: the error symbol **error**, and a list containing the string returned by **format-message**.

The **text-quoting-style** variable controls what quotes are generated; See Section 23.3 [Keys in Documentation], page 488. A call using a format like "Missing '%s'" with grave accents and apostrophes typically generates a message like "Missing 'foo'" with matching curved quotes. In contrast, a call using a format like "Missing '%s'" with only apostrophes typically generates a message like "Missing 'foo'" with only closing curved quotes, an unusual style in English.

Warning: If you want to use your own string as an error message verbatim, don't just write (**error** *string*). If *string string* contains '%', '`', or ''' it may be reformatted, with undesirable results. Instead, use (**error** "%s" *string*).

signal *error-symbol data*   [Function]

This function signals an error named by *error-symbol*. The argument *data* is a list of additional Lisp objects relevant to the circumstances of the error.

The argument *error-symbol* must be an *error symbol*—a symbol defined with **define-error**. This is how Emacs Lisp classifies different sorts of errors. See Section 10.6.3.4 [Error Symbols], page 154, for a description of error symbols, error conditions and condition names.

If the error is not handled, the two arguments are used in printing the error message. Normally, this error message is provided by the **error-message** property of *error-symbol*. If *data* is non-**nil**, this is followed by a colon and a comma separated list of the unevaluated elements of *data*. For **error**, the error message is the CAR of *data* (that must be a string). Subcategories of **file-error** are handled specially.

The number and significance of the objects in *data* depends on *error-symbol*. For example, with a **wrong-type-argument** error, there should be two objects in the list: a predicate that describes the type that was expected, and the object that failed to fit that type.

Both *error-symbol* and *data* are available to any error handlers that handle the error: **condition-case** binds a local variable to a list of the form (*error-symbol* . *data*) (see Section 10.6.3.3 [Handling Errors], page 150).

The function **signal** never returns.

```
(signal 'wrong-number-of-arguments '(x y))
     error   Wrong number of arguments: x, y


(signal 'no-such-error '("My unknown error condition"))
     error   peculiar error: "My unknown error condition"
```

user-error *format-string* **&rest** *args*   [Function]

This function behaves exactly like **error**, except that it uses the error symbol **user-error** rather than **error**. As the name suggests, this is intended to report errors on the part of the user, rather than errors in the code itself. For example, if you try to use the command **Info-history-back** (*1*) to move back beyond the start of your Info browsing history, Emacs signals a **user-error**. Such errors do not cause entry to the debugger, even when **debug-on-error** is non-**nil**. See Section 17.1.1 [Error Debugging], page 270.

Common Lisp note: Emacs Lisp has nothing like the Common Lisp concept of continuable errors.

10.6.3.2 How Emacs Processes Errors

When an error is signaled, **signal** searches for an active *handler* for the error. A handler is a sequence of Lisp expressions designated to be executed if an error happens in part of the Lisp program. If the error has an applicable handler, the handler is executed, and control resumes following the handler. The handler executes in the environment of the **condition-case** that established it; all functions called within that **condition-case** have already been exited, and the handler cannot return to them.

If there is no applicable handler for the error, it terminates the current command and returns control to the editor command loop. (The command loop has an implicit handler for all kinds of errors.) The command loop's handler uses the error symbol and associated data to print an error message. You can use the variable **command-error-function** to control how this is done:

command-error-function   [Variable]

This variable, if non-**nil**, specifies a function to use to handle errors that return control to the Emacs command loop. The function should take three arguments: *data*, a list of the same form that **condition-case** would bind to its variable; *context*, a string describing the situation in which the error occurred, or (more often) **nil**; and *caller*, the Lisp function which called the primitive that signaled the error.

An error that has no explicit handler may call the Lisp debugger. The debugger is enabled if the variable **debug-on-error** (see Section 17.1.1 [Error Debugging], page 270) is non-**nil**. Unlike error handlers, the debugger runs in the environment of the error, so that you can examine values of variables precisely as they were at the time of the error.

10.6.3.3 Writing Code to Handle Errors

The usual effect of signaling an error is to terminate the command that is running and return immediately to the Emacs editor command loop. You can arrange to trap errors occurring in a part of your program by establishing an error handler, with the special form **condition-case**. A simple example looks like this:

```
(condition-case nil
    (delete-file filename)
  (error nil))
```

This deletes the file named *filename*, catching any error and returning **nil** if an error occurs. (You can use the macro **ignore-errors** for a simple case like this; see below.)

The `condition-case` construct is often used to trap errors that are predictable, such as failure to open a file in a call to `insert-file-contents`. It is also used to trap errors that are totally unpredictable, such as when the program evaluates an expression read from the user.

The second argument of `condition-case` is called the *protected form*. (In the example above, the protected form is a call to `delete-file`.) The error handlers go into effect when this form begins execution and are deactivated when this form returns. They remain in effect for all the intervening time. In particular, they are in effect during the execution of functions called by this form, in their subroutines, and so on. This is a good thing, since, strictly speaking, errors can be signaled only by Lisp primitives (including `signal` and `error`) called by the protected form, not by the protected form itself.

The arguments after the protected form are handlers. Each handler lists one or more *condition names* (which are symbols) to specify which errors it will handle. The error symbol specified when an error is signaled also defines a list of condition names. A handler applies to an error if they have any condition names in common. In the example above, there is one handler, and it specifies one condition name, `error`, which covers all errors.

The search for an applicable handler checks all the established handlers starting with the most recently established one. Thus, if two nested `condition-case` forms offer to handle the same error, the inner of the two gets to handle it.

If an error is handled by some `condition-case` form, this ordinarily prevents the debugger from being run, even if `debug-on-error` says this error should invoke the debugger.

If you want to be able to debug errors that are caught by a `condition-case`, set the variable `debug-on-signal` to a non-nil value. You can also specify that a particular handler should let the debugger run first, by writing `debug` among the conditions, like this:

```
(condition-case nil
    (delete-file filename)
  ((debug error) nil))
```

The effect of `debug` here is only to prevent `condition-case` from suppressing the call to the debugger. Any given error will invoke the debugger only if `debug-on-error` and the other usual filtering mechanisms say it should. See Section 17.1.1 [Error Debugging], page 270.

`condition-case-unless-debug` *var protected-form handlers. . .*   [Macro]
    The macro `condition-case-unless-debug` provides another way to handle debugging of such forms. It behaves exactly like `condition-case`, unless the variable `debug-on-error` is non-`nil`, in which case it does not handle any errors at all.

Once Emacs decides that a certain handler handles the error, it returns control to that handler. To do so, Emacs unbinds all variable bindings made by binding constructs that are being exited, and executes the cleanups of all `unwind-protect` forms that are being exited. Once control arrives at the handler, the body of the handler executes normally.

After execution of the handler body, execution returns from the `condition-case` form. Because the protected form is exited completely before execution of the handler, the handler cannot resume execution at the point of the error, nor can it examine variable bindings that were made within the protected form. All it can do is clean up and proceed.

Error signaling and handling have some resemblance to `throw` and `catch` (see Section 10.6.1 [Catch and Throw], page 145), but they are entirely separate facilities. An error cannot be caught by a `catch`, and a `throw` cannot be handled by an error handler (though using `throw` when there is no suitable `catch` signals an error that can be handled).

condition-case *var protected-form handlers...*   [Special Form]

This special form establishes the error handlers *handlers* around the execution of *protected-form*. If *protected-form* executes without error, the value it returns becomes the value of the `condition-case` form; in this case, the `condition-case` has no effect. The `condition-case` form makes a difference when an error occurs during *protected-form*.

Each of the *handlers* is a list of the form (*conditions body...*). Here *conditions* is an error condition name to be handled, or a list of condition names (which can include `debug` to allow the debugger to run before the handler); *body* is one or more Lisp expressions to be executed when this handler handles an error. Here are examples of handlers:

```
(error nil)

(arith-error (message "Division by zero"))

((arith-error file-error)
 (message
  "Either division by zero or failure to open a file"))
```

Each error that occurs has an *error symbol* that describes what kind of error it is, and which describes also a list of condition names (see Section 10.6.3.4 [Error Symbols], page 154). Emacs searches all the active `condition-case` forms for a handler that specifies one or more of these condition names; the innermost matching `condition-case` handles the error. Within this `condition-case`, the first applicable handler handles the error.

After executing the body of the handler, the `condition-case` returns normally, using the value of the last form in the handler body as the overall value.

The argument *var* is a variable. `condition-case` does not bind this variable when executing the *protected-form*, only when it handles an error. At that time, it binds *var* locally to an *error description*, which is a list giving the particulars of the error. The error description has the form (*error-symbol . data*). The handler can refer to this list to decide what to do. For example, if the error is for failure opening a file, the file name is the second element of *data*—the third element of the error description.

If *var* is `nil`, that means no variable is bound. Then the error symbol and associated data are not available to the handler.

Sometimes it is necessary to re-throw a signal caught by `condition-case`, for some outer-level handler to catch. Here's how to do that:

```
(signal (car err) (cdr err))
```

where `err` is the error description variable, the first argument to `condition-case` whose error condition you want to re-throw. See [Definition of signal], page 149.

error-message-string *error-descriptor*   [Function]
> This function returns the error message string for a given error descriptor. It is useful if you want to handle an error by printing the usual error message for that error. See [Definition of signal], page 149.

Here is an example of using **condition-case** to handle the error that results from dividing by zero. The handler displays the error message (but without a beep), then returns a very large number.

```
(defun safe-divide (dividend divisor)
  (condition-case err
      ;; Protected form.
      (/ dividend divisor)
    ;; The handler.
    (arith-error                     ; Condition.
     ;; Display the usual message for this error.
     (message "%s" (error-message-string err))
     1000000)))
⇒ safe-divide


(safe-divide 5 0)
     ⊣ Arithmetic error: (arith-error)
⇒ 1000000
```

The handler specifies condition name **arith-error** so that it will handle only division-by-zero errors. Other kinds of errors will not be handled (by this **condition-case**). Thus:

```
(safe-divide nil 3)
     error  Wrong type argument: number-or-marker-p, nil
```

Here is a **condition-case** that catches all kinds of errors, including those from **error**:

```
(setq baz 34)
     ⇒ 34


(condition-case err
    (if (eq baz 35)
        t
      ;; This is a call to the function error.
      (error "Rats!  The variable %s was %s, not 35" 'baz baz))
  ;; This is the handler; it is not a form.
  (error (princ (format "The error was: %s" err))
         2))
⊣ The error was: (error "Rats!  The variable baz was 34, not 35")
⇒ 2
```

ignore-errors *body*...   [Macro]
> This construct executes *body*, ignoring any errors that occur during its execution. If the execution is without error, **ignore-errors** returns the value of the last form in *body*; otherwise, it returns **nil**.

Here's the example at the beginning of this subsection rewritten using `ignore-errors`:

```
(ignore-errors
 (delete-file filename))
```

`with-demoted-errors` *format body...*   [Macro]

This macro is like a milder version of `ignore-errors`. Rather than suppressing errors altogether, it converts them into messages. It uses the string *format* to format the message. *format* should contain a single '%'-sequence; e.g., `"Error: %S"`. Use `with-demoted-errors` around code that is not expected to signal errors, but should be robust if one does occur. Note that this macro uses `condition-case-unless-debug` rather than `condition-case`.

10.6.3.4 Error Symbols and Condition Names

When you signal an error, you specify an *error symbol* to specify the kind of error you have in mind. Each error has one and only one error symbol to categorize it. This is the finest classification of errors defined by the Emacs Lisp language.

These narrow classifications are grouped into a hierarchy of wider classes called *error conditions*, identified by *condition names*. The narrowest such classes belong to the error symbols themselves: each error symbol is also a condition name. There are also condition names for more extensive classes, up to the condition name `error` which takes in all kinds of errors (but not `quit`). Thus, each error has one or more condition names: `error`, the error symbol if that is distinct from `error`, and perhaps some intermediate classifications.

`define-error` *name message* **&optional** *parent*   [Function]

In order for a symbol to be an error symbol, it must be defined with `define-error` which takes a parent condition (defaults to `error`). This parent defines the conditions that this kind of error belongs to. The transitive set of parents always includes the error symbol itself, and the symbol `error`. Because quitting is not considered an error, the set of parents of `quit` is just (`quit`).

In addition to its parents, the error symbol has a *message* which is a string to be printed when that error is signaled but not handled. If that message is not valid, the error message 'peculiar error' is used. See [Definition of signal], page 149.

Internally, the set of parents is stored in the `error-conditions` property of the error symbol and the message is stored in the `error-message` property of the error symbol.

Here is how we define a new error symbol, `new-error`:

```
(define-error 'new-error "A new error" 'my-own-errors)
```

This error has several condition names: `new-error`, the narrowest classification; `my-own-errors`, which we imagine is a wider classification; and all the conditions of `my-own-errors` which should include `error`, which is the widest of all.

The error string should start with a capital letter but it should not end with a period. This is for consistency with the rest of Emacs.

Naturally, Emacs will never signal `new-error` on its own; only an explicit call to `signal` (see [Definition of signal], page 149) in your code can do this:

```
(signal 'new-error '(x y))
    error  A new error: x, y
```

This error can be handled through any of its condition names. This example handles `new-error` and any other errors in the class `my-own-errors`:

```
(condition-case foo
    (bar nil t)
  (my-own-errors nil))
```

The significant way that errors are classified is by their condition names—the names used to match errors with handlers. An error symbol serves only as a convenient way to specify the intended error message and list of condition names. It would be cumbersome to give `signal` a list of condition names rather than one error symbol.

By contrast, using only error symbols without condition names would seriously decrease the power of `condition-case`. Condition names make it possible to categorize errors at various levels of generality when you write an error handler. Using error symbols alone would eliminate all but the narrowest level of classification.

See Appendix F [Standard Errors], page 1091, for a list of the main error symbols and their conditions.

10.6.4 Cleaning Up from Nonlocal Exits

The `unwind-protect` construct is essential whenever you temporarily put a data structure in an inconsistent state; it permits you to make the data consistent again in the event of an error or throw. (Another more specific cleanup construct that is used only for changes in buffer contents is the atomic change group; Section 31.27 [Atomic Changes], page 758.)

unwind-protect *body-form cleanup-forms.* . .   [Special Form]

> `unwind-protect` executes *body-form* with a guarantee that the *cleanup-forms* will be evaluated if control leaves *body-form*, no matter how that happens. *body-form* may complete normally, or execute a `throw` out of the `unwind-protect`, or cause an error; in all cases, the *cleanup-forms* will be evaluated.
>
> If *body-form* finishes normally, `unwind-protect` returns the value of *body-form*, after it evaluates the *cleanup-forms*. If *body-form* does not finish, `unwind-protect` does not return any value in the normal sense.
>
> Only *body-form* is protected by the `unwind-protect`. If any of the *cleanup-forms* themselves exits nonlocally (via a `throw` or an error), `unwind-protect` is *not* guaranteed to evaluate the rest of them. If the failure of one of the *cleanup-forms* has the potential to cause trouble, then protect it with another `unwind-protect` around that form.
>
> The number of currently active `unwind-protect` forms counts, together with the number of local variable bindings, against the limit `max-specpdl-size` (see [Local Variables], page 160).

For example, here we make an invisible buffer for temporary use, and make sure to kill it before finishing:

```
(let ((buffer (get-buffer-create " *temp*")))
  (with-current-buffer buffer
    (unwind-protect
        body-form
      (kill-buffer buffer))))
```

You might think that we could just as well write (kill-buffer (current-buffer)) and dispense with the variable buffer. However, the way shown above is safer, if *body-form* happens to get an error after switching to a different buffer! (Alternatively, you could write a save-current-buffer around *body-form*, to ensure that the temporary buffer becomes current again in time to kill it.)

Emacs includes a standard macro called with-temp-buffer which expands into more or less the code shown above (see [Current Buffer], page 552). Several of the macros defined in this manual use unwind-protect in this way.

Here is an actual example derived from an FTP package. It creates a process (see Chapter 36 [Processes], page 839) to try to establish a connection to a remote machine. As the function ftp-login is highly susceptible to numerous problems that the writer of the function cannot anticipate, it is protected with a form that guarantees deletion of the process in the event of failure. Otherwise, Emacs might fill up with useless subprocesses.

```
(let ((win nil))
  (unwind-protect
      (progn
        (setq process (ftp-setup-buffer host file))
        (if (setq win (ftp-login process host user password))
            (message "Logged in")
          (error "Ftp login failed")))
    (or win (and process (delete-process process)))))
```

This example has a small bug: if the user types *C-g* to quit, and the quit happens immediately after the function ftp-setup-buffer returns but before the variable process is set, the process will not be killed. There is no easy way to fix this bug, but at least it is very unlikely.

11 Variables

A *variable* is a name used in a program to stand for a value. In Lisp, each variable is represented by a Lisp symbol (see Chapter 8 [Symbols], page 115). The variable name is simply the symbol's name, and the variable's value is stored in the symbol's value cell[1]. See Section 8.1 [Symbol Components], page 115. In Emacs Lisp, the use of a symbol as a variable is independent of its use as a function name.

As previously noted in this manual, a Lisp program is represented primarily by Lisp objects, and only secondarily as text. The textual form of a Lisp program is given by the read syntax of the Lisp objects that constitute the program. Hence, the textual form of a variable in a Lisp program is written using the read syntax for the symbol representing the variable.

11.1 Global Variables

The simplest way to use a variable is *globally*. This means that the variable has just one value at a time, and this value is in effect (at least for the moment) throughout the Lisp system. The value remains in effect until you specify a new one. When a new value replaces the old one, no trace of the old value remains in the variable.

You specify a value for a symbol with `setq`. For example,

```
(setq x '(a b))
```

gives the variable `x` the value `(a b)`. Note that `setq` is a special form (see Section 9.1.7 [Special Forms], page 128); it does not evaluate its first argument, the name of the variable, but it does evaluate the second argument, the new value.

Once the variable has a value, you can refer to it by using the symbol itself as an expression. Thus,

```
x ⇒ (a b)
```

assuming the `setq` form shown above has already been executed.

If you do set the same variable again, the new value replaces the old one:

```
x
     ⇒ (a b)
(setq x 4)
     ⇒ 4
x
     ⇒ 4
```

11.2 Variables that Never Change

In Emacs Lisp, certain symbols normally evaluate to themselves. These include `nil` and `t`, as well as any symbol whose name starts with ':' (these are called *keywords*). These symbols cannot be rebound, nor can their values be changed. Any attempt to set or bind `nil` or `t` signals a `setting-constant` error. The same is true for a keyword (a symbol

---

[1] To be precise, under the default *dynamic scoping* rule, the value cell always holds the variable's current value, but this is not the case under the *lexical scoping* rule. See Section 11.9 [Variable Scoping], page 166, for details.

whose name starts with ':'), if it is interned in the standard obarray, except that setting such a symbol to itself is not an error.

```
nil  ≡  'nil
       ⇒ nil
(setq nil 500)
```
error Attempt to set constant symbol: nil

keywordp *object*   [Function]
> function returns **t** if *object* is a symbol whose name starts with ':', interned in the standard obarray, and returns **nil** otherwise.

These constants are fundamentally different from the constants defined using the **defconst** special form (see Section 11.5 [Defining Variables], page 161). A **defconst** form serves to inform human readers that you do not intend to change the value of a variable, but Emacs does not raise an error if you actually change it.

11.3 Local Variables

Global variables have values that last until explicitly superseded with new values. Sometimes it is useful to give a variable a *local value*—a value that takes effect only within a certain part of a Lisp program. When a variable has a local value, we say that it is *locally bound* to that value, and that it is a *local variable*.

For example, when a function is called, its argument variables receive local values, which are the actual arguments supplied to the function call; these local bindings take effect within the body of the function. To take another example, the **let** special form explicitly establishes local bindings for specific variables, which take effect within the body of the **let** form.

We also speak of the *global binding*, which is where (conceptually) the global value is kept.

Establishing a local binding saves away the variable's previous value (or lack of one). We say that the previous value is *shadowed*. Both global and local values may be shadowed. If a local binding is in effect, using **setq** on the local variable stores the specified value in the local binding. When that local binding is no longer in effect, the previously shadowed value (or lack of one) comes back.

A variable can have more than one local binding at a time (e.g., if there are nested **let** forms that bind the variable). The *current binding* is the local binding that is actually in effect. It determines the value returned by evaluating the variable symbol, and it is the binding acted on by **setq**.

For most purposes, you can think of the current binding as the innermost local binding, or the global binding if there is no local binding. To be more precise, a rule called the *scoping rule* determines where in a program a local binding takes effect. The default scoping rule in Emacs Lisp is called *dynamic scoping*, which simply states that the current binding at any given point in the execution of a program is the most recently-created binding for that variable that still exists. For details about dynamic scoping, and an alternative scoping rule called *lexical scoping*, See Section 11.9 [Variable Scoping], page 166.

The special forms **let** and **let*** exist to create local bindings:

let (*bindings...*) *forms...*   [Special Form]

> This special form sets up local bindings for a certain set of variables, as specified by *bindings*, and then evaluates all of the *forms* in textual order. Its return value is the value of the last form in *forms*.
>
> Each of the *bindings* is either (i) a symbol, in which case that symbol is locally bound to `nil`; or (ii) a list of the form (`symbol value-form`), in which case *symbol* is locally bound to the result of evaluating *value-form*. If *value-form* is omitted, `nil` is used.
>
> All of the *value-form*s in *bindings* are evaluated in the order they appear and *before* binding any of the symbols to them. Here is an example of this: `z` is bound to the old value of `y`, which is 2, not the new value of `y`, which is 1.
>
> ```
> (setq y 2)
>      ⇒ 2
> ```
>
> ```
> (let ((y 1)
>       (z y))
>   (list y z))
>      ⇒ (1 2)
> ```
>
> On the other hand, the order of *bindings* is unspecified: in the following example, either 1 or 2 might be printed.
>
> ```
> (let ((x 1)
>       (x 2))
>   (print x))
> ```
>
> Therefore, avoid binding a variable more than once in a single `let` form.

let* (*bindings...*) *forms...*   [Special Form]

> This special form is like `let`, but it binds each variable right after computing its local value, before computing the local value for the next variable. Therefore, an expression in *bindings* can refer to the preceding symbols bound in this `let*` form. Compare the following example with the example above for `let`.
>
> ```
> (setq y 2)
>      ⇒ 2
> ```
>
> ```
> (let* ((y 1)
>        (z y))        ; Use the just-established value of y.
>   (list y z))
>      ⇒ (1 1)
> ```

Here is a complete list of the other facilities that create local bindings:

- Function calls (see Chapter 12 [Functions], page 186).
- Macro calls (see Chapter 13 [Macros], page 217).
- `condition-case` (see Section 10.6.3 [Errors], page 148).

Variables can also have buffer-local bindings (see Section 11.10 [Buffer-Local Variables], page 171); a few variables have terminal-local bindings (see Section 28.2 [Multiple Terminals], page 631). These kinds of bindings work somewhat like ordinary local bindings, but they are localized depending on where you are in Emacs.

`max-specpdl-size`   [User Option]

> This variable defines the limit on the total number of local variable bindings and **unwind-protect** cleanups (see Section 10.6.4 [Cleaning Up from Nonlocal Exits], page 155) that are allowed before Emacs signals an error (with data `"Variable binding depth exceeds max-specpdl-size"`).
>
> This limit, with the associated error when it is exceeded, is one way that Lisp avoids infinite recursion on an ill-defined function. `max-lisp-eval-depth` provides another limit on depth of nesting. See [Eval], page 133.
>
> The default value is 1300. Entry to the Lisp debugger increases the value, if there is little room left, to make sure the debugger itself has room to execute.

11.4 When a Variable is Void

We say that a variable is void if its symbol has an unassigned value cell (see Section 8.1 [Symbol Components], page 115).

Under Emacs Lisp's default dynamic scoping rule (see Section 11.9 [Variable Scoping], page 166), the value cell stores the variable's current (local or global) value. Note that an unassigned value cell is *not* the same as having **nil** in the value cell. The symbol **nil** is a Lisp object and can be the value of a variable, just as any other object can be; but it is still a value. If a variable is void, trying to evaluate the variable signals a **void-variable** error, instead of returning a value.

Under the optional lexical scoping rule, the value cell only holds the variable's global value—the value outside of any lexical binding construct. When a variable is lexically bound, the local value is determined by the lexical environment; hence, variables can have local values even if their symbols' value cells are unassigned.

`makunbound` *symbol*   [Function]

> This function empties out the value cell of *symbol*, making the variable void. It returns *symbol*.
>
> If *symbol* has a dynamic local binding, **makunbound** voids the current binding, and this voidness lasts only as long as the local binding is in effect. Afterwards, the previously shadowed local or global binding is reexposed; then the variable will no longer be void, unless the reexposed binding is void too.
>
> Here are some examples (assuming dynamic binding is in effect):
>
> ```
> (setq x 1)               ; Put a value in the global binding.
>      ⇒ 1
> (let ((x 2))             ; Locally bind it.
>   (makunbound 'x)        ; Void the local binding.
>   x)
> error  Symbol's value as variable is void: x
> x                        ; The global binding is unchanged.
>      ⇒ 1
>
> (let ((x 2))             ; Locally bind it.
>   (let ((x 3))           ; And again.
>     (makunbound 'x)      ; Void the innermost-local binding.
>     x))                  ; And refer: itfls void.
> error  Symbol's value as variable is void: x
> ```

```
(let ((x 2))
  (let ((x 3))
    (makunbound 'x))      ; Void inner binding, then remove it.
  x)                      ; Now outer let binding is visible.
    ⇒ 2
```

boundp *variable*   [Function]

> This function returns **t** if *variable* (a symbol) is not void, and **nil** if it is void.
>
> Here are some examples (assuming dynamic binding is in effect):

```
(boundp 'abracadabra)         ; Starts out void.
    ⇒ nil
(let ((abracadabra 5))        ; Locally bind it.
  (boundp 'abracadabra))
    ⇒ t
(boundp 'abracadabra)         ; Still globally void.
    ⇒ nil
(setq abracadabra 5)          ; Make it globally nonvoid.
    ⇒ 5
(boundp 'abracadabra)
    ⇒ t
```

11.5 Defining Global Variables

A *variable definition* is a construct that announces your intention to use a symbol as a global variable. It uses the special forms **defvar** or **defconst**, which are documented below.

A variable definition serves three purposes. First, it informs people who read the code that the symbol is *intended* to be used a certain way (as a variable). Second, it informs the Lisp system of this, optionally supplying an initial value and a documentation string. Third, it provides information to programming tools such as **etags**, allowing them to find where the variable was defined.

The difference between **defconst** and **defvar** is mainly a matter of intent, serving to inform human readers of whether the value should ever change. Emacs Lisp does not actually prevent you from changing the value of a variable defined with **defconst**. One notable difference between the two forms is that **defconst** unconditionally initializes the variable, whereas **defvar** initializes it only if it is originally void.

To define a customizable variable, you should use **defcustom** (which calls **defvar** as a subroutine). See Section 14.3 [Variable Definitions], page 228.

defvar *symbol* [*value* [*doc-string*]]   [Special Form]

> This special form defines *symbol* as a variable. Note that *symbol* is not evaluated; the symbol to be defined should appear explicitly in the **defvar** form. The variable is marked as *special*, meaning that it should always be dynamically bound (see Section 11.9 [Variable Scoping], page 166).
>
> If *value* is specified, and *symbol* is void (i.e., it has no dynamically bound value; see Section 11.4 [Void Variables], page 160), then *value* is evaluated and *symbol* is set to the result. But if *symbol* is not void, *value* is not evaluated, and *symbol*'s value is left unchanged. If *value* is omitted, the value of *symbol* is not changed in any case.
>
> If *symbol* has a buffer-local binding in the current buffer, **defvar** acts on the default value, which is buffer-independent, rather than the buffer-local binding. It sets the

default value if the default value is void. See Section 11.10 [Buffer-Local Variables], page 171.

If *symbol* is already lexically bound (e.g., if the `defvar` form occurs in a `let` form with lexical binding enabled), then `defvar` sets the dynamic value. The lexical binding remains in effect until its binding construct exits. See Section 11.9 [Variable Scoping], page 166.

When you evaluate a top-level `defvar` form with *C-M-x* in Emacs Lisp mode (`eval-defun`), a special feature of `eval-defun` arranges to set the variable unconditionally, without testing whether its value is void.

If the *doc-string* argument is supplied, it specifies the documentation string for the variable (stored in the symbol's `variable-documentation` property). See Chapter 23 [Documentation], page 485.

Here are some examples. This form defines `foo` but does not initialize it:

```
(defvar foo)
    ⇒ foo
```

This example initializes the value of `bar` to 23, and gives it a documentation string:

```
(defvar bar 23
  "The normal weight of a bar.")
      ⇒ bar
```

The `defvar` form returns *symbol*, but it is normally used at top level in a file where its value does not matter.

defconst *symbol value [doc-string]*   [Special Form]

This special form defines *symbol* as a value and initializes it. It informs a person reading your code that *symbol* has a standard global value, established here, that should not be changed by the user or by other programs. Note that *symbol* is not evaluated; the symbol to be defined must appear explicitly in the `defconst`.

The `defconst` form, like `defvar`, marks the variable as *special*, meaning that it should always be dynamically bound (see Section 11.9 [Variable Scoping], page 166). In addition, it marks the variable as risky (see Section 11.11 [File Local Variables], page 177).

`defconst` always evaluates *value*, and sets the value of *symbol* to the result. If *symbol* does have a buffer-local binding in the current buffer, `defconst` sets the default value, not the buffer-local value. (But you should not be making buffer-local bindings for a symbol that is defined with `defconst`.)

An example of the use of `defconst` is Emacs's definition of `float-pi`—the mathematical constant *pi*, which ought not to be changed by anyone (attempts by the Indiana State Legislature notwithstanding). As the second form illustrates, however, `defconst` is only advisory.

```
(defconst float-pi 3.141592653589793 "The value of Pi.")
      ⇒ float-pi
(setq float-pi 3)
      ⇒ float-pi
float-pi
      ⇒ 3
```

Warning: If you use a `defconst` or `defvar` special form while the variable has a local binding (made with `let`, or a function argument), it sets the local binding rather than the global binding. This is not what you usually want. To prevent this, use these special forms at top level in a file, where normally no local binding is in effect, and make sure to load the file before making a local binding for the variable.

11.6 Tips for Defining Variables Robustly

When you define a variable whose value is a function, or a list of functions, use a name that ends in '`-function`' or '`-functions`', respectively.

There are several other variable name conventions; here is a complete list:

'`...-hook`'
> The variable is a normal hook (see Section 22.1 [Hooks], page 429).

'`...-function`'
> The value is a function.

'`...-functions`'
> The value is a list of functions.

'`...-form`'
> The value is a form (an expression).

'`...-forms`'
> The value is a list of forms (expressions).

'`...-predicate`'
> The value is a predicate—a function of one argument that returns non-`nil` for success and `nil` for failure.

'`...-flag`'
> The value is significant only as to whether it is `nil` or not. Since such variables often end up acquiring more values over time, this convention is not strongly recommended.

'`...-program`'
> The value is a program name.

'`...-command`'
> The value is a whole shell command.

'`...-switches`'
> The value specifies options for a command.

When you define a variable, always consider whether you should mark it as safe or risky; see Section 11.11 [File Local Variables], page 177.

When defining and initializing a variable that holds a complicated value (such as a keymap with bindings in it), it's best to put the entire computation of the value into the `defvar`, like this:

```
(defvar my-mode-map
  (let ((map (make-sparse-keymap)))
    (define-key map "\C-c\C-a" 'my-command)
```

```
       . . .
     map)
   docstring)
```

This method has several benefits. First, if the user quits while loading the file, the variable is either still uninitialized or initialized properly, never in-between. If it is still uninitialized, reloading the file will initialize it properly. Second, reloading the file once the variable is initialized will not alter it; that is important if the user has run hooks to alter part of the contents (such as, to rebind keys). Third, evaluating the `defvar` form with *C-M-x* will reinitialize the map completely.

Putting so much code in the `defvar` form has one disadvantage: it puts the documentation string far away from the line which names the variable. Here's a safe way to avoid that:

```
(defvar my-mode-map nil
  docstring)
(unless my-mode-map
  (let ((map (make-sparse-keymap)))
    (define-key map "\C-c\C-a" 'my-command)
    . . .
    (setq my-mode-map map)))
```

This has all the same advantages as putting the initialization inside the `defvar`, except that you must type *C-M-x* twice, once on each form, if you do want to reinitialize the variable.

11.7 Accessing Variable Values

The usual way to reference a variable is to write the symbol which names it. See Section 9.1.2 [Symbol Forms], page 125.

Occasionally, you may want to reference a variable which is only determined at run time. In that case, you cannot specify the variable name in the text of the program. You can use the `symbol-value` function to extract the value.

symbol-value *symbol*   [Function]

This function returns the value stored in *symbol*'s value cell. This is where the variable's current (dynamic) value is stored. If the variable has no local binding, this is simply its global value. If the variable is void, a `void-variable` error is signaled.

If the variable is lexically bound, the value reported by `symbol-value` is not necessarily the same as the variable's lexical value, which is determined by the lexical environment rather than the symbol's value cell. See Section 11.9 [Variable Scoping], page 166.

```
(setq abracadabra 5)
     ⇒ 5
(setq foo 9)
     ⇒ 9
```

```
;; Here the symbol abracadabra
;;    is the symbol whose value is examined.
(let ((abracadabra 'foo))
  (symbol-value 'abracadabra))
      ⇒ foo

;; Here, the value of abracadabra,
;;    which is foo,
;;    is the symbol whose value is examined.
(let ((abracadabra 'foo))
  (symbol-value abracadabra))
      ⇒ 9

(symbol-value 'abracadabra)
      ⇒ 5
```

11.8 Setting Variable Values

The usual way to change the value of a variable is with the special form setq. When you need to compute the choice of variable at run time, use the function set.

setq [*symbol form*]...   [Special Form]

> This special form is the most common method of changing a variable's value. Each *symbol* is given a new value, which is the result of evaluating the corresponding *form*. The current binding of the symbol is changed.
>
> setq does not evaluate *symbol*; it sets the symbol that you write. We say that this argument is *automatically quoted*. The 'q' in setq stands for "quoted".
>
> The value of the setq form is the value of the last *form*.
>
> ```
> (setq x (1+ 2))
>       ⇒ 3
> x                          ; x now has a global value.
>       ⇒ 3
> (let ((x 5))
>   (setq x 6)              ; The local binding of x is set.
>   x)
>       ⇒ 6
> x                          ; The global value is unchanged.
>       ⇒ 3
> ```
>
> Note that the first *form* is evaluated, then the first *symbol* is set, then the second *form* is evaluated, then the second *symbol* is set, and so on:
>
> ```
> (setq x 10              ; Notice that x is set before
>       y (1+ x))         ;    the value of y is computed.
>       ⇒ 11
> ```

`set` *symbol value*   [Function]

> This function puts *value* in the value cell of *symbol*. Since it is a function rather than a special form, the expression written for *symbol* is evaluated to obtain the symbol to set. The return value is *value*.
>
> When dynamic variable binding is in effect (the default), `set` has the same effect as `setq`, apart from the fact that `set` evaluates its *symbol* argument whereas `setq` does not. But when a variable is lexically bound, `set` affects its *dynamic* value, whereas `setq` affects its current (lexical) value. See Section 11.9 [Variable Scoping], page 166.
>
> ```
> (set one 1)
> ```
> error   Symbol's value as variable is void: one
> ```
> (set 'one 1)
>      ⇒ 1
> (set 'two 'one)
>      ⇒ one
> (set two 2)              ; two evaluates to symbol one.
>      ⇒ 2
> one                     ; So it is one that was set.
>      ⇒ 2
> (let ((one 1))          ; This binding of one is set,
>   (set 'one 3)          ;    not the global value.
>   one)
>      ⇒ 3
> one
>      ⇒ 2
> ```
>
> If *symbol* is not actually a symbol, a `wrong-type-argument` error is signaled.
>
> ```
> (set '(x y) 'z)
> ```
> error   Wrong type argument: symbolp, (x y)

11.9 Scoping Rules for Variable Bindings

When you create a local binding for a variable, that binding takes effect only within a limited portion of the program (see Section 11.3 [Local Variables], page 158). This section describes exactly what this means.

Each local binding has a certain *scope* and *extent*. *Scope* refers to *where* in the textual source code the binding can be accessed. *Extent* refers to *when*, as the program is executing, the binding exists.

By default, the local bindings that Emacs creates are *dynamic bindings*. Such a binding has *dynamic scope*, meaning that any part of the program can potentially access the variable binding. It also has *dynamic extent*, meaning that the binding lasts only while the binding construct (such as the body of a `let` form) is being executed.

Emacs can optionally create *lexical bindings*. A lexical binding has *lexical scope*, meaning that any reference to the variable must be located textually within the binding construct[2]. It also has *indefinite extent*, meaning that under some circumstances the binding can live on

---

[2] With some exceptions; for instance, a lexical binding can also be accessed from the Lisp debugger.

even after the binding construct has finished executing, by means of special objects called *closures*.

The following subsections describe dynamic binding and lexical binding in greater detail, and how to enable lexical binding in Emacs Lisp programs.

11.9.1 Dynamic Binding

By default, the local variable bindings made by Emacs are dynamic bindings. When a variable is dynamically bound, its current binding at any point in the execution of the Lisp program is simply the most recently-created dynamic local binding for that symbol, or the global binding if there is no such local binding.

Dynamic bindings have dynamic scope and extent, as shown by the following example:

```
(defvar x -99)    ; x receives an initial value of −99.

(defun getx ()
  x)              ; x is used free in this function.

(let ((x 1))      ; x is dynamically bound.
  (getx))
    ⇒ 1


;; After the let form finishes, x reverts to its
;; previous value, which is −99.

(getx)
    ⇒ -99
```

The function `getx` refers to x. This is a *free* reference, in the sense that there is no binding for x within that `defun` construct itself. When we call `getx` from within a `let` form in which x is (dynamically) bound, it retrieves the local value (i.e., 1). But when we call `getx` outside the `let` form, it retrieves the global value (i.e., −99).

Here is another example, which illustrates setting a dynamically bound variable using `setq`:

```
(defvar x -99)         ; x receives an initial value of −99.

(defun addx ()
  (setq x (1+ x)))     ; Add 1 to x and return its new value.

(let ((x 1))
  (addx)
  (addx))
    ⇒ 3                ; The two addx calls add to x twice.


;; After the let form finishes, x reverts to its
;; previous value, which is −99.

(addx)
    ⇒ -98
```

Dynamic binding is implemented in Emacs Lisp in a simple way. Each symbol has a value cell, which specifies its current dynamic value (or absence of value). See Section 8.1 [Symbol Components], page 115. When a symbol is given a dynamic local binding, Emacs records the contents of the value cell (or absence thereof) in a stack, and stores the new local value in the value cell. When the binding construct finishes executing, Emacs pops the old value off the stack, and puts it in the value cell.

11.9.2 Proper Use of Dynamic Binding

Dynamic binding is a powerful feature, as it allows programs to refer to variables that are not defined within their local textual scope. However, if used without restraint, this can also make programs hard to understand. There are two clean ways to use this technique:

- If a variable has no global definition, use it as a local variable only within a binding construct, such as the body of the `let` form where the variable was bound. If this convention is followed consistently throughout a program, the value of the variable will not affect, nor be affected by, any uses of the same variable symbol elsewhere in the program.

- Otherwise, define the variable with `defvar`, `defconst`, or `defcustom`. See Section 11.5 [Defining Variables], page 161. Usually, the definition should be at top-level in an Emacs Lisp file. As far as possible, it should include a documentation string which explains the meaning and purpose of the variable. You should also choose the variable's name to avoid name conflicts (see Section D.1 [Coding Conventions], page 1053).

Then you can bind the variable anywhere in a program, knowing reliably what the effect will be. Wherever you encounter the variable, it will be easy to refer back to the definition, e.g., via the *C-h v* command (provided the variable definition has been loaded into Emacs). See Section "Name Help" in *The GNU Emacs Manual*.

For example, it is common to use local bindings for customizable variables like `case-fold-search`:

```
(defun search-for-abc ()
  "Search for the string \"abc\", ignoring case differences."
  (let ((case-fold-search nil))
    (re-search-forward "abc")))
```

11.9.3 Lexical Binding

Lexical binding was introduced to Emacs, as an optional feature, in version 24.1. We expect its importance to increase in the future. Lexical binding opens up many more opportunities for optimization, so programs using it are likely to run faster in future Emacs versions. Lexical binding is also more compatible with concurrency, which we want to add to Emacs in the future.

A lexically-bound variable has *lexical scope*, meaning that any reference to the variable must be located textually within the binding construct. Here is an example (see the next subsection, for how to actually enable lexical binding):

```
(let ((x 1))      ; x is lexically bound.
  (+ x 3))
      ⇒ 4

(defun getx ()
  x)                ; x is used free in this function.

(let ((x 1))      ; x is lexically bound.
  (getx))
error  Symbol's value as variable is void: x
```

Here, the variable x has no global value. When it is lexically bound within a let form, it can be used in the textual confines of that let form. But it can *not* be used from within a getx function called from the let form, since the function definition of getx occurs outside the let form itself.

Here is how lexical binding works. Each binding construct defines a *lexical environment*, specifying the variables that are bound within the construct and their local values. When the Lisp evaluator wants the current value of a variable, it looks first in the lexical environment; if the variable is not specified in there, it looks in the symbol's value cell, where the dynamic value is stored.

(Internally, the lexical environment is an alist of symbol-value pairs, with the final element in the alist being the symbol t rather than a cons cell. Such an alist can be passed as the second argument to the eval function, in order to specify a lexical environment in which to evaluate a form. See Section 9.4 [Eval], page 131. Most Emacs Lisp programs, however, should not interact directly with lexical environments in this way; only specialized programs like debuggers.)

Lexical bindings have indefinite extent. Even after a binding construct has finished executing, its lexical environment can be "kept around" in Lisp objects called *closures*. A closure is created when you define a named or anonymous function with lexical binding enabled. See Section 12.10 [Closures], page 204, for details.

When a closure is called as a function, any lexical variable references within its definition use the retained lexical environment. Here is an example:

```
(defvar my-ticker nil)   ; We will use this dynamically bound
                          ; variable to store a closure.

(let ((x 0))              ; x is lexically bound.
  (setq my-ticker (lambda ()
                    (setq x (1+ x)))))
    ⇒ (closure ((x . 0) t) ()
          (setq x (1+ x)))

(funcall my-ticker)
    ⇒ 1

(funcall my-ticker)
    ⇒ 2
```

```
(funcall my-ticker)
    ⇒ 3
```

   x   ; Note that x has no global value.
    [error] Symbol's value as variable is void: x

The `let` binding defines a lexical environment in which the variable x is locally bound to
0. Within this binding construct, we define a lambda expression which increments x by one
and returns the incremented value. This lambda expression is automatically turned into a
closure, in which the lexical environment lives on even after the `let` binding construct has
exited. Each time we evaluate the closure, it increments x, using the binding of x in that
lexical environment.

Note that unlike dynamic variables which are tied to the symbol object itself, the relationship between lexical variables and symbols is only present in the interpreter (or compiler).
Therefore, functions which take a symbol argument (like `symbol-value`, `boundp`, and `set`)
can only retrieve or modify a variable's dynamic binding (i.e., the contents of its symbol's
value cell).

11.9.4 Using Lexical Binding

When loading an Emacs Lisp file or evaluating a Lisp buffer, lexical binding is enabled if
the buffer-local variable `lexical-binding` is non-`nil`:

`lexical-binding`   [Variable]
    If this buffer-local variable is non-`nil`, Emacs Lisp files and buffers are evaluated
    using lexical binding instead of dynamic binding. (However, special variables are still
    dynamically bound; see below.) If `nil`, dynamic binding is used for all local variables.
    This variable is typically set for a whole Emacs Lisp file, as a file local variable (see
    Section 11.11 [File Local Variables], page 177). Note that unlike other such variables,
    this one must be set in the first line of a file.

When evaluating Emacs Lisp code directly using an `eval` call, lexical binding is enabled if
the *lexical* argument to `eval` is non-`nil`. See Section 9.4 [Eval], page 131.

Even when lexical binding is enabled, certain variables will continue to be dynamically
bound. These are called *special variables*. Every variable that has been defined with
`defvar`, `defcustom` or `defconst` is a special variable (see Section 11.5 [Defining Variables],
page 161). All other variables are subject to lexical binding.

`special-variable-p` *symbol*   [Function]
    This function returns non-`nil` if *symbol* is a special variable (i.e., it has a `defvar`,
    `defcustom`, or `defconst` variable definition). Otherwise, the return value is `nil`.

The use of a special variable as a formal argument in a function is discouraged. Doing so
gives rise to unspecified behavior when lexical binding mode is enabled (it may use lexical
binding sometimes, and dynamic binding other times).

Converting an Emacs Lisp program to lexical binding is easy. First, add a file-local
variable setting of `lexical-binding` to `t` in the header line of the Emacs Lisp source file
(see Section 11.11 [File Local Variables], page 177). Second, check that every variable in

the program which needs to be dynamically bound has a variable definition, so that it is not inadvertently bound lexically.

A simple way to find out which variables need a variable definition is to byte-compile the source file. See Chapter 16 [Byte Compilation], page 260. If a non-special variable is used outside of a `let` form, the byte-compiler will warn about reference or assignment to a free variable. If a non-special variable is bound but not used within a `let` form, the byte-compiler will warn about an unused lexical variable. The byte-compiler will also issue a warning if you use a special variable as a function argument.

(To silence byte-compiler warnings about unused variables, just use a variable name that start with an underscore. The byte-compiler interprets this as an indication that this is a variable known not to be used.)

11.10 Buffer-Local Variables

Global and local variable bindings are found in most programming languages in one form or another. Emacs, however, also supports additional, unusual kinds of variable binding, such as *buffer-local* bindings, which apply only in one buffer. Having different values for a variable in different buffers is an important customization method. (Variables can also have bindings that are local to each terminal. See Section 28.2 [Multiple Terminals], page 631.)

11.10.1 Introduction to Buffer-Local Variables

A buffer-local variable has a buffer-local binding associated with a particular buffer. The binding is in effect when that buffer is current; otherwise, it is not in effect. If you set the variable while a buffer-local binding is in effect, the new value goes in that binding, so its other bindings are unchanged. This means that the change is visible only in the buffer where you made it.

The variable's ordinary binding, which is not associated with any specific buffer, is called the *default binding*. In most cases, this is the global binding.

A variable can have buffer-local bindings in some buffers but not in other buffers. The default binding is shared by all the buffers that don't have their own bindings for the variable. (This includes all newly-created buffers.) If you set the variable in a buffer that does not have a buffer-local binding for it, this sets the default binding, so the new value is visible in all the buffers that see the default binding.

The most common use of buffer-local bindings is for major modes to change variables that control the behavior of commands. For example, C mode and Lisp mode both set the variable `paragraph-start` to specify that only blank lines separate paragraphs. They do this by making the variable buffer-local in the buffer that is being put into C mode or Lisp mode, and then setting it to the new value for that mode. See Section 22.2 [Major Modes], page 431.

The usual way to make a buffer-local binding is with `make-local-variable`, which is what major mode commands typically use. This affects just the current buffer; all other buffers (including those yet to be created) will continue to share the default value unless they are explicitly given their own buffer-local bindings.

A more powerful operation is to mark the variable as *automatically buffer-local* by calling `make-variable-buffer-local`. You can think of this as making the variable local in all buffers, even those yet to be created. More precisely, the effect is that setting the variable automatically makes the variable local to the current buffer if it is not already so. All buffers start out by sharing the default value of the variable as usual, but setting the variable creates a buffer-local binding for the current buffer. The new value is stored in the buffer-local binding, leaving the default binding untouched. This means that the default value cannot be changed with `setq` in any buffer; the only way to change it is with `setq-default`.

Warning: When a variable has buffer-local bindings in one or more buffers, `let` rebinds the binding that's currently in effect. For instance, if the current buffer has a buffer-local value, `let` temporarily rebinds that. If no buffer-local bindings are in effect, `let` rebinds the default value. If inside the `let` you then change to a different current buffer in which a different binding is in effect, you won't see the `let` binding any more. And if you exit the `let` while still in the other buffer, you won't see the unbinding occur (though it will occur properly). Here is an example to illustrate:

```
(setq foo 'g)
(set-buffer "a")
(make-local-variable 'foo)
(setq foo 'a)
(let ((foo 'temp))
  ;; foo ⇒ 'temp   ; let binding in buffer 'a'
  (set-buffer "b")
  ;; foo ⇒ 'g      ; the global value since foo is not local in 'b'
  body...)
foo ⇒ 'g            ; exiting restored the local value in buffer 'a',
                    ; but we donflt see that in buffer 'b'
(set-buffer "a")    ; verify the local value was restored
foo ⇒ 'a
```

Note that references to `foo` in *body* access the buffer-local binding of buffer 'b'.

When a file specifies local variable values, these become buffer-local values when you visit the file. See Section "File Variables" in *The GNU Emacs Manual*.

A buffer-local variable cannot be made terminal-local (see Section 28.2 [Multiple Terminals], page 631).

11.10.2 Creating and Deleting Buffer-Local Bindings

`make-local-variable` *variable*   [Command]
> This function creates a buffer-local binding in the current buffer for *variable* (a symbol). Other buffers are not affected. The value returned is *variable*.
>
> The buffer-local value of *variable* starts out as the same value *variable* previously had. If *variable* was void, it remains void.
>
> ```
>         ;; In buffer 'b1':
>         (setq foo 5)                    ; Affects all buffers.
>              ⇒ 5
>         (make-local-variable 'foo)      ; Now it is local in 'b1'.
>              ⇒ foo
> ```

```
foo                           ; That did not change
    ⇒ 5                       ;   the value.
(setq foo 6)                  ; Change the value
    ⇒ 6                       ;   in 'b1'.
foo
    ⇒ 6


;; In buffer 'b2', the value hasnflt changed.
(with-current-buffer "b2"
  foo)
    ⇒ 5
```

Making a variable buffer-local within a `let`-binding for that variable does not work reliably, unless the buffer in which you do this is not current either on entry to or exit from the `let`. This is because `let` does not distinguish between different kinds of bindings; it knows only which variable the binding was made for.

If the variable is terminal-local (see Section 28.2 [Multiple Terminals], page 631), this function signals an error. Such variables cannot have buffer-local bindings as well.

Warning: do not use `make-local-variable` for a hook variable. The hook variables are automatically made buffer-local as needed if you use the *local* argument to `add-hook` or `remove-hook`.

`setq-local` *variable value*   [Macro]

> This macro creates a buffer-local binding in the current buffer for *variable*, and gives it the buffer-local value *value*. It is equivalent to calling `make-local-variable` followed by `setq`. *variable* should be an unquoted symbol.

`make-variable-buffer-local` *variable*   [Command]

> This function marks *variable* (a symbol) automatically buffer-local, so that any subsequent attempt to set it will make it local to the current buffer at the time. Unlike `make-local-variable`, with which it is often confused, this cannot be undone, and affects the behavior of the variable in all buffers.

> A peculiar wrinkle of this feature is that binding the variable (with `let` or other binding constructs) does not create a buffer-local binding for it. Only setting the variable (with `set` or `setq`), while the variable does not have a `let`-style binding that was made in the current buffer, does so.

> If *variable* does not have a default value, then calling this command will give it a default value of `nil`. If *variable* already has a default value, that value remains unchanged. Subsequently calling `makunbound` on *variable* will result in a void buffer-local value and leave the default value unaffected.

> The value returned is *variable*.

> **Warning:** Don't assume that you should use `make-variable-buffer-local` for user-option variables, simply because users *might* want to customize them differently in different buffers. Users can make any variable local, when they wish to. It is better to leave the choice to them.

> The time to use `make-variable-buffer-local` is when it is crucial that no two buffers ever share the same binding. For example, when a variable is used for internal

purposes in a Lisp program which depends on having separate values in separate buffers, then using `make-variable-buffer-local` can be the best solution.

`defvar-local` *variable value* **&optional** *docstring* [Macro]

This macro defines *variable* as a variable with initial value *value* and *docstring*, and marks it as automatically buffer-local. It is equivalent to calling `defvar` followed by `make-variable-buffer-local`. *variable* should be an unquoted symbol.

`local-variable-p` *variable* **&optional** *buffer* [Function]

This returns `t` if *variable* is buffer-local in buffer *buffer* (which defaults to the current buffer); otherwise, `nil`.

`local-variable-if-set-p` *variable* **&optional** *buffer* [Function]

This returns `t` if *variable* either has a buffer-local value in buffer *buffer*, or is automatically buffer-local. Otherwise, it returns `nil`. If omitted or `nil`, *buffer* defaults to the current buffer.

`buffer-local-value` *variable buffer* [Function]

This function returns the buffer-local binding of *variable* (a symbol) in buffer *buffer*. If *variable* does not have a buffer-local binding in buffer *buffer*, it returns the default value (see Section 11.10.3 [Default Value], page 175) of *variable* instead.

`buffer-local-variables` **&optional** *buffer* [Function]

This function returns a list describing the buffer-local variables in buffer *buffer*. (If *buffer* is omitted, the current buffer is used.) Normally, each list element has the form (`sym` . `val`), where *sym* is a buffer-local variable (a symbol) and *val* is its buffer-local value. But when a variable's buffer-local binding in *buffer* is void, its list element is just *sym*.

```
(make-local-variable 'foobar)
(makunbound 'foobar)
(make-local-variable 'bind-me)
(setq bind-me 69)
(setq lcl (buffer-local-variables))
    ;; First, built-in variables local in all buffers:
⇒ ((mark-active . nil)
   (buffer-undo-list . nil)
   (mode-name . "Fundamental")
   ...
   ;; Next, non-built-in buffer-local variables.
   ;; This one is buffer-local and void:
   foobar
   ;; This one is buffer-local and nonvoid:
   (bind-me . 69))
```

Note that storing new values into the CDRs of cons cells in this list does *not* change the buffer-local values of the variables.

`kill-local-variable` *variable* [Command]

This function deletes the buffer-local binding (if any) for *variable* (a symbol) in the current buffer. As a result, the default binding of *variable* becomes visible in this buffer. This typically results in a change in the value of *variable*, since the default value is usually different from the buffer-local value just eliminated.

If you kill the buffer-local binding of a variable that automatically becomes buffer-local when set, this makes the default value visible in the current buffer. However, if you set the variable again, that will once again create a buffer-local binding for it.

`kill-local-variable` returns *variable*.

This function is a command because it is sometimes useful to kill one buffer-local variable interactively, just as it is useful to create buffer-local variables interactively.

`kill-all-local-variables`   [Function]

This function eliminates all the buffer-local variable bindings of the current buffer except for variables marked as permanent and local hook functions that have a non-nil `permanent-local-hook` property (see Section 22.1.2 [Setting Hooks], page 430). As a result, the buffer will see the default values of most variables.

This function also resets certain other information pertaining to the buffer: it sets the local keymap to `nil`, the syntax table to the value of (`standard-syntax-table`), the case table to (`standard-case-table`), and the abbrev table to the value of `fundamental-mode-abbrev-table`.

The very first thing this function does is run the normal hook `change-major-mode-hook` (see below).

Every major mode command begins by calling this function, which has the effect of switching to Fundamental mode and erasing most of the effects of the previous major mode. To ensure that this does its job, the variables that major modes set should not be marked permanent.

`kill-all-local-variables` returns `nil`.

`change-major-mode-hook`   [Variable]

The function `kill-all-local-variables` runs this normal hook before it does anything else. This gives major modes a way to arrange for something special to be done if the user switches to a different major mode. It is also useful for buffer-specific minor modes that should be forgotten if the user changes the major mode.

For best results, make this variable buffer-local, so that it will disappear after doing its job and will not interfere with the subsequent major mode. See Section 22.1 [Hooks], page 429.

A buffer-local variable is *permanent* if the variable name (a symbol) has a `permanent-local` property that is non-nil. Such variables are unaffected by `kill-all-local-variables`, and their local bindings are therefore not cleared by changing major modes. Permanent locals are appropriate for data pertaining to where the file came from or how to save it, rather than with how to edit the contents.

11.10.3 The Default Value of a Buffer-Local Variable

The global value of a variable with buffer-local bindings is also called the *default* value, because it is the value that is in effect whenever neither the current buffer nor the selected frame has its own binding for the variable.

The functions `default-value` and `setq-default` access and change a variable's default value regardless of whether the current buffer has a buffer-local binding. For example, you could use `setq-default` to change the default setting of `paragraph-start` for most buffers; and this would work even when you are in a C or Lisp mode buffer that has a buffer-local value for this variable.

The special forms `defvar` and `defconst` also set the default value (if they set the variable at all), rather than any buffer-local value.

`default-value` *symbol*   [Function]

> This function returns *symbol*'s default value. This is the value that is seen in buffers and frames that do not have their own values for this variable. If *symbol* is not buffer-local, this is equivalent to `symbol-value` (see Section 11.7 [Accessing Variables], page 164).

`default-boundp` *symbol*   [Function]

> The function `default-boundp` tells you whether *symbol*'s default value is nonvoid. If `(default-boundp 'foo)` returns `nil`, then `(default-value 'foo)` would get an error.
>
> `default-boundp` is to `default-value` as `boundp` is to `symbol-value`.

`setq-default` [*symbol form*]...   [Special Form]

> This special form gives each *symbol* a new default value, which is the result of evaluating the corresponding *form*. It does not evaluate *symbol*, but does evaluate *form*. The value of the `setq-default` form is the value of the last *form*.
>
> If a *symbol* is not buffer-local for the current buffer, and is not marked automatically buffer-local, `setq-default` has the same effect as `setq`. If *symbol* is buffer-local for the current buffer, then this changes the value that other buffers will see (as long as they don't have a buffer-local value), but not the value that the current buffer sees.

```
;; In buffer 'foo':
(make-local-variable 'buffer-local)
     ⇒ buffer-local
(setq buffer-local 'value-in-foo)
     ⇒ value-in-foo
(setq-default buffer-local 'new-default)
     ⇒ new-default
buffer-local
     ⇒ value-in-foo
(default-value 'buffer-local)
     ⇒ new-default

;; In (the new) buffer 'bar':
buffer-local
     ⇒ new-default
(default-value 'buffer-local)
     ⇒ new-default
(setq buffer-local 'another-default)
     ⇒ another-default
```

```
(default-value 'buffer-local)
     ⇒ another-default

;; Back in buffer 'foo':
buffer-local
     ⇒ value-in-foo
(default-value 'buffer-local)
     ⇒ another-default
```

set-default *symbol value*   [Function]

This function is like `setq-default`, except that *symbol* is an ordinary evaluated argument.

```
(set-default (car '(a b c)) 23)
     ⇒ 23
(default-value 'a)
     ⇒ 23
```

A variable can be let-bound (see Section 11.3 [Local Variables], page 158) to a value. This makes its global value shadowed by the binding; `default-value` will then return the value from that binding, not the global value, and `set-default` will be prevented from setting the global value (it will change the let-bound value instead). The following two functions allow to reference the global value even if it's shadowed by a let-binding.

default-toplevel-value *symbol*   [Function]

This function returns the *top-level* default value of *symbol*, which is its value outside of any let-binding.

```
(defvar variable 'global-value)
     ⇒ variable
(let ((variable 'let-binding))
  (default-value 'variable))
     ⇒ let-binding
(let ((variable 'let-binding))
  (default-toplevel-value 'variable))
     ⇒ global-value
```

set-default-toplevel-value *symbol value*   [Function]

This function sets the top-level default value of *symbol* to the specified *value*. This comes in handy when you want to set the global value of *symbol* regardless of whether your code runs in the context of *symbol*'s let-binding.

11.11 File Local Variables

A file can specify local variable values; Emacs uses these to create buffer-local bindings for those variables in the buffer visiting that file. See Section "Local Variables in Files" in *The GNU Emacs Manual*, for basic information about file-local variables. This section describes the functions and variables that affect how file-local variables are processed.

If a file-local variable could specify an arbitrary function or Lisp expression that would be called later, visiting a file could take over your Emacs. Emacs protects against this by automatically setting only those file-local variables whose specified values are known to be safe. Other file-local variables are set only if the user agrees.

For additional safety, `read-circle` is temporarily bound to `nil` when Emacs reads file-local variables (see Section 18.3 [Input Functions], page 304). This prevents the Lisp reader from recognizing circular and shared Lisp structures (see Section 2.5 [Circular Objects], page 27).

`enable-local-variables`   [User Option]
 This variable controls whether to process file-local variables. The possible values are:

  `t` (the default)
    Set the safe variables, and query (once) about any unsafe variables.

  `:safe` Set only the safe variables and do not query.

  `:all` Set all the variables and do not query.

  `nil` Don't set any variables.

  anything else
    Query (once) about all the variables.

`inhibit-local-variables-regexps`   [Variable]
 This is a list of regular expressions. If a file has a name matching an element of this list, then it is not scanned for any form of file-local variable. For examples of why you might want to use this, see Section 22.2.2 [Auto Major Mode], page 435.

`hack-local-variables` &optional *mode-only*   [Function]
 This function parses, and binds or evaluates as appropriate, any local variables specified by the contents of the current buffer. The variable `enable-local-variables` has its effect here. However, this function does not look for the '`mode:`' local variable in the '`-*-`' line. `set-auto-mode` does that, also taking `enable-local-variables` into account (see Section 22.2.2 [Auto Major Mode], page 435).

 This function works by walking the alist stored in `file-local-variables-alist` and applying each local variable in turn. It calls `before-hack-local-variables-hook` and `hack-local-variables-hook` before and after applying the variables, respectively. It only calls the before-hook if the alist is non-`nil`; it always calls the other hook. This function ignores a '`mode`' element if it specifies the same major mode as the buffer already has.

 If the optional argument *mode-only* is non-`nil`, then all this function does is return a symbol specifying the major mode, if the '`-*-`' line or the local variables list specifies one, and `nil` otherwise. It does not set the mode nor any other file-local variable.

`file-local-variables-alist`   [Variable]
 This buffer-local variable holds the alist of file-local variable settings. Each element of the alist is of the form (*var* . *value*), where *var* is a symbol of the local variable and *value* is its value. When Emacs visits a file, it first collects all the file-local variables into this alist, and then the `hack-local-variables` function applies them one by one.

`before-hack-local-variables-hook`   [Variable]

> Emacs calls this hook immediately before applying file-local variables stored in `file-local-variables-alist`.

`hack-local-variables-hook`   [Variable]

> Emacs calls this hook immediately after it finishes applying file-local variables stored in `file-local-variables-alist`.

You can specify safe values for a variable with a `safe-local-variable` property. The property has to be a function of one argument; any value is safe if the function returns non-`nil` given that value. Many commonly-encountered file variables have `safe-local-variable` properties; these include `fill-column`, `fill-prefix`, and `indent-tabs-mode`. For boolean-valued variables that are safe, use `booleanp` as the property value.

When defining a user option using `defcustom`, you can set its `safe-local-variable` property by adding the arguments `:safe` *function* to `defcustom` (see Section 14.3 [Variable Definitions], page 228).

`safe-local-variable-values`   [User Option]

> This variable provides another way to mark some variable values as safe. It is a list of cons cells (*var* . *val*), where *var* is a variable name and *val* is a value which is safe for that variable.
>
> When Emacs asks the user whether or not to obey a set of file-local variable specifications, the user can choose to mark them as safe. Doing so adds those variable/value pairs to `safe-local-variable-values`, and saves it to the user's custom file.

`safe-local-variable-p` *sym val*   [Function]

> This function returns non-`nil` if it is safe to give *sym* the value *val*, based on the above criteria.

Some variables are considered *risky*. If a variable is risky, it is never entered automatically into `safe-local-variable-values`; Emacs always queries before setting a risky variable, unless the user explicitly allows a value by customizing `safe-local-variable-values` directly.

Any variable whose name has a non-`nil` `risky-local-variable` property is considered risky. When you define a user option using `defcustom`, you can set its `risky-local-variable` property by adding the arguments `:risky` *value* to `defcustom` (see Section 14.3 [Variable Definitions], page 228). In addition, any variable whose name ends in any of '-command', '-frame-alist', '-function', '-functions', '-hook', '-hooks', '-form', '-forms', '-map', '-map-alist', '-mode-alist', '-program', or '-predicate' is automatically considered risky. The variables 'font-lock-keywords', 'font-lock-keywords' followed by a digit, and 'font-lock-syntactic-keywords' are also considered risky.

`risky-local-variable-p` *sym*   [Function]

> This function returns non-`nil` if *sym* is a risky variable, based on the above criteria.

`ignored-local-variables`   [Variable]

> This variable holds a list of variables that should not be given local values by files. Any value specified for one of these variables is completely ignored.

The 'Eval:' "variable" is also a potential loophole, so Emacs normally asks for confirmation before handling it.

enable-local-eval   [User Option]
> This variable controls processing of 'Eval:' in '-*-' lines or local variables lists in files being visited. A value of t means process them unconditionally; nil means ignore them; anything else means ask the user what to do for each file. The default value is maybe.

safe-local-eval-forms   [User Option]
> This variable holds a list of expressions that are safe to evaluate when found in the 'Eval:' "variable" in a file local variables list.

If the expression is a function call and the function has a safe-local-eval-function property, the property value determines whether the expression is safe to evaluate. The property value can be a predicate to call to test the expression, a list of such predicates (it's safe if any predicate succeeds), or t (always safe provided the arguments are constant).

Text properties are also potential loopholes, since their values could include functions to call. So Emacs discards all text properties from string values specified for file-local variables.

11.12 Directory Local Variables

A directory can specify local variable values common to all files in that directory; Emacs uses these to create buffer-local bindings for those variables in buffers visiting any file in that directory. This is useful when the files in the directory belong to some *project* and therefore share the same local variables.

There are two different methods for specifying directory local variables: by putting them in a special file, or by defining a *project class* for that directory.

dir-locals-file   [Constant]
> This constant is the name of the file where Emacs expects to find the directory-local variables. The name of the file is .dir-locals.el[3]. A file by that name in a directory causes Emacs to apply its settings to any file in that directory or any of its subdirectories (optionally, you can exclude subdirectories; see below). If some of the subdirectories have their own .dir-locals.el files, Emacs uses the settings from the deepest file it finds starting from the file's directory and moving up the directory tree. The file specifies local variables as a specially formatted list; see Section "Per-directory Local Variables" in *The GNU Emacs Manual*, for more details.

hack-dir-local-variables   [Function]
> This function reads the .dir-locals.el file and stores the directory-local variables in file-local-variables-alist that is local to the buffer visiting any file in the directory, without applying them. It also stores the directory-local settings in dir-locals-class-alist, where it defines a special class for the directory in which .dir-locals.el file was found. This function works by calling dir-locals-set-class-variables and dir-locals-set-directory-class, described below.

---

[3] The MS-DOS version of Emacs uses _dir-locals.el instead, due to limitations of the DOS filesystems.

`hack-dir-local-variables-non-file-buffer`   [Function]

> This function looks for directory-local variables, and immediately applies them in the current buffer. It is intended to be called in the mode commands for non-file buffers, such as Dired buffers, to let them obey directory-local variable settings. For non-file buffers, Emacs looks for directory-local variables in `default-directory` and its parent directories.

`dir-locals-set-class-variables` *class variables*   [Function]

> This function defines a set of variable settings for the named *class*, which is a symbol. You can later assign the class to one or more directories, and Emacs will apply those variable settings to all files in those directories. The list in *variables* can be of one of the two forms: (*major-mode* . *alist*) or (*directory* . *list*). With the first form, if the file's buffer turns on a mode that is derived from *major-mode*, then the all the variables in the associated *alist* are applied; *alist* should be of the form (*name* . *value*). A special value `nil` for *major-mode* means the settings are applicable to any mode. In *alist*, you can use a special *name*: `subdirs`. If the associated value is `nil`, the alist is only applied to files in the relevant directory, not to those in any subdirectories.

> With the second form of *variables*, if *directory* is the initial substring of the file's directory, then *list* is applied recursively by following the above rules; *list* should be of one of the two forms accepted by this function in *variables*.

`dir-locals-set-directory-class` *directory class* **&optional** *mtime*   [Function]

> This function assigns *class* to all the files in `directory` and its subdirectories. Thereafter, all the variable settings specified for *class* will be applied to any visited file in *directory* and its children. *class* must have been already defined by `dir-locals-set-class-variables`.

> Emacs uses this function internally when it loads directory variables from a `.dir-locals.el` file. In that case, the optional argument *mtime* holds the file modification time (as returned by `file-attributes`). Emacs uses this time to check stored local variables are still valid. If you are assigning a class directly, not via a file, this argument should be `nil`.

`dir-locals-class-alist`   [Variable]

> This alist holds the class symbols and the associated variable settings. It is updated by `dir-locals-set-class-variables`.

`dir-locals-directory-cache`   [Variable]

> This alist holds directory names, their assigned class names, and modification times of the associated directory local variables file (if there is one). The function `dir-locals-set-directory-class` updates this list.

`enable-dir-local-variables`   [Variable]

> If `nil`, directory-local variables are ignored. This variable may be useful for modes that want to ignore directory-locals while still respecting file-local variables (see Section 11.11 [File Local Variables], page 177).

11.13 Variable Aliases

It is sometimes useful to make two variables synonyms, so that both variables always have the same value, and changing either one also changes the other. Whenever you change the name of a variable—either because you realize its old name was not well chosen, or because its meaning has partly changed—it can be useful to keep the old name as an *alias* of the new one for compatibility. You can do this with `defvaralias`.

defvaralias *new-alias base-variable* **&optional** *docstring*   [Function]
> This function defines the symbol *new-alias* as a variable alias for symbol *base-variable*. This means that retrieving the value of *new-alias* returns the value of *base-variable*, and changing the value of *new-alias* changes the value of *base-variable*. The two aliased variable names always share the same value and the same bindings.
>
> If the *docstring* argument is non-`nil`, it specifies the documentation for *new-alias*; otherwise, the alias gets the same documentation as *base-variable* has, if any, unless *base-variable* is itself an alias, in which case *new-alias* gets the documentation of the variable at the end of the chain of aliases.
>
> This function returns *base-variable*.

Variable aliases are convenient for replacing an old name for a variable with a new name. `make-obsolete-variable` declares that the old name is obsolete and therefore that it may be removed at some stage in the future.

make-obsolete-variable *obsolete-name current-name when*   [Function]
    &optional *access-type*
> This function makes the byte compiler warn that the variable *obsolete-name* is obsolete. If *current-name* is a symbol, it is the variable's new name; then the warning message says to use *current-name* instead of *obsolete-name*. If *current-name* is a string, this is the message and there is no replacement variable. *when* should be a string indicating when the variable was first made obsolete (usually a version number string).
>
> The optional argument *access-type*, if non-`nil`, should specify the kind of access that will trigger obsolescence warnings; it can be either `get` or `set`.

You can make two variables synonyms and declare one obsolete at the same time using the macro `define-obsolete-variable-alias`.

define-obsolete-variable-alias *obsolete-name current-name*   [Macro]
    &optional *when docstring*
> This macro marks the variable *obsolete-name* as obsolete and also makes it an alias for the variable *current-name*. It is equivalent to the following:
>
> ```
> (defvaralias obsolete-name current-name docstring)
> (make-obsolete-variable obsolete-name current-name when)
> ```

indirect-variable *variable*   [Function]
> This function returns the variable at the end of the chain of aliases of *variable*. If *variable* is not a symbol, or if *variable* is not defined as an alias, the function returns *variable*.
>
> This function signals a `cyclic-variable-indirection` error if there is a loop in the chain of symbols.

```
(defvaralias 'foo 'bar)
(indirect-variable 'foo)
      ⇒ bar
(indirect-variable 'bar)
      ⇒ bar
(setq bar 2)
bar
      ⇒ 2
foo
      ⇒ 2
(setq foo 0)
bar
      ⇒ 0
foo
      ⇒ 0
```

11.14 Variables with Restricted Values

Ordinary Lisp variables can be assigned any value that is a valid Lisp object. However, certain Lisp variables are not defined in Lisp, but in C. Most of these variables are defined in the C code using `DEFVAR_LISP`. Like variables defined in Lisp, these can take on any value. However, some variables are defined using `DEFVAR_INT` or `DEFVAR_BOOL`. See [Writing Emacs Primitives], page 1077, in particular the description of functions of the type `syms_of_filename`, for a brief discussion of the C implementation.

Variables of type `DEFVAR_BOOL` can only take on the values `nil` or `t`. Attempting to assign them any other value will set them to `t`:

```
(let ((display-hourglass 5))
  display-hourglass)
      ⇒ t
```

`byte-boolean-vars`   [Variable]
> This variable holds a list of all variables of type `DEFVAR_BOOL`.

Variables of type `DEFVAR_INT` can take on only integer values. Attempting to assign them any other value will result in an error:

```
(setq undo-limit 1000.0)
   error   Wrong type argument: integerp, 1000.0
```

11.15 Generalized Variables

A *generalized variable* or *place form* is one of the many places in Lisp memory where values can be stored. The simplest place form is a regular Lisp variable. But the CARs and CDRs of lists, elements of arrays, properties of symbols, and many other locations are also places where Lisp values are stored.

Generalized variables are analogous to lvalues in the C language, where 'x = a[i]' gets an element from an array and 'a[i] = x' stores an element using the same notation. Just as certain forms like a[i] can be lvalues in C, there is a set of forms that can be generalized variables in Lisp.

11.15.1 The `setf` Macro

The `setf` macro is the most basic way to operate on generalized variables. The `setf` form is like `setq`, except that it accepts arbitrary place forms on the left side rather than just symbols. For example, `(setf (car a) b)` sets the car of `a` to `b`, doing the same operation as `(setcar a b)`, but without having to remember two separate functions for setting and accessing every type of place.

`setf` [*place form*]...   [Macro]
> This macro evaluates *form* and stores it in *place*, which must be a valid generalized variable form. If there are several *place* and *form* pairs, the assignments are done sequentially just as with `setq`. `setf` returns the value of the last *form*.

The following Lisp forms will work as generalized variables, and so may appear in the *place* argument of `setf`:

- A symbol naming a variable. In other words, `(setf x y)` is exactly equivalent to `(setq x y)`, and `setq` itself is strictly speaking redundant given that `setf` exists. Many programmers continue to prefer `setq` for setting simple variables, though, purely for stylistic or historical reasons. The macro `(setf x y)` actually expands to `(setq x y)`, so there is no performance penalty for using it in compiled code.

- A call to any of the following standard Lisp functions:

aref	cddr	symbol-function
car	elt	symbol-plist
caar	get	symbol-value
cadr	gethash	
cdr	nth	
cdar	nthcdr	

- A call to any of the following Emacs-specific functions:

alist-get	process-get
frame-parameter	process-sentinel
terminal-parameter	window-buffer
keymap-parent	window-display-table
match-data	window-dedicated-p
overlay-get	window-hscroll
overlay-start	window-parameter
overlay-end	window-point
process-buffer	window-start
process-filter	default-value

`setf` signals an error if you pass a *place* form that it does not know how to handle.

Note that for `nthcdr`, the list argument of the function must itself be a valid *place* form. For example, `(setf (nthcdr 0 foo) 7)` will set `foo` itself to 7.

The macros `push` (see Section 5.5 [List Variables], page 74) and `pop` (see Section 5.3 [List Elements], page 68) can manipulate generalized variables, not just lists. `(pop place)` removes and returns the first element of the list stored in *place*. It is analogous to `(prog1 (car place) (setf place (cdr place)))`, except that it takes care to evaluate all subforms only once. `(push x place)` inserts *x* at the front of the list stored in *place*. It is analogous to `(setf place (cons x place))`, except for evaluation of the subforms. Note that `push` and `pop` on an `nthcdr` place can be used to insert or delete at any position in a list.

The `cl-lib` library defines various extensions for generalized variables, including additional `setf` places. See Section "Generalized Variables" in *Common Lisp Extensions*.

11.15.2 Defining new `setf` forms

This section describes how to define new forms that `setf` can operate on.

gv-define-simple-setter *name setter* **&optional** *fix-return*   [Macro]

This macro enables you to easily define `setf` methods for simple cases. *name* is the name of a function, macro, or special form. You can use this macro whenever *name* has a directly corresponding *setter* function that updates it, e.g., (**gv-define-simple-setter** car setcar).

This macro translates a call of the form

        (setf (*name args...*) *value*)

into

        (*setter args... value*)

Such a `setf` call is documented to return *value*. This is no problem with, e.g., **car** and **setcar**, because **setcar** returns the value that it set. If your *setter* function does not return *value*, use a non-**nil** value for the *fix-return* argument of **gv-define-simple-setter**. This expands into something equivalent to

        (let ((temp *value*))
          (*setter args... temp*)
          temp)

so ensuring that it returns the correct result.

gv-define-setter *name arglist* **&rest** *body*   [Macro]

This macro allows for more complex `setf` expansions than the previous form. You may need to use this form, for example, if there is no simple setter function to call, or if there is one but it requires different arguments to the place form.

This macro expands the form (**setf** (*name args...*) *value*) by first binding the `setf` argument forms (*value args...*) according to *arglist*, and then executing *body*. *body* should return a Lisp form that does the assignment, and finally returns the value that was set. An example of using this macro is:

        (gv-define-setter caar (val x) `(setcar (car ,x) ,val))

For more control over the expansion, see the macro **gv-define-expander**. The macro **gv-letplace** can be useful in defining macros that perform similarly to `setf`; for example, the **incf** macro of Common Lisp. Consult the source file **gv.el** for more details.

> **Common Lisp note:** Common Lisp defines another way to specify the `setf` behavior of a function, namely `setf` functions, whose names are lists (**setf** *name*) rather than symbols. For example, (**defun** (**setf** foo) ...) defines the function that is used when `setf` is applied to **foo**. Emacs does not support this. It is a compile-time error to use `setf` on a form that has not already had an appropriate expansion defined. In Common Lisp, this is not an error since the function (**setf** *func*) might be defined later.

12 Functions

A Lisp program is composed mainly of Lisp functions. This chapter explains what functions are, how they accept arguments, and how to define them.

12.1 What Is a Function?

In a general sense, a function is a rule for carrying out a computation given input values called *arguments*. The result of the computation is called the *value* or *return value* of the function. The computation can also have side effects, such as lasting changes in the values of variables or the contents of data structures.

In most computer languages, every function has a name. But in Lisp, a function in the strictest sense has no name: it is an object which can *optionally* be associated with a symbol (e.g., `car`) that serves as the function name. See Section 12.3 [Function Names], page 191. When a function has been given a name, we usually also refer to that symbol as a "function" (e.g., we refer to "the function `car`"). In this manual, the distinction between a function name and the function object itself is usually unimportant, but we will take note wherever it is relevant.

Certain function-like objects, called *special forms* and *macros*, also accept arguments to carry out computations. However, as explained below, these are not considered functions in Emacs Lisp.

Here are important terms for functions and function-like objects:

lambda expression
> A function (in the strict sense, i.e., a function object) which is written in Lisp. These are described in the following section.

primitive
> A function which is callable from Lisp but is actually written in C. Primitives are also called *built-in functions*, or *subrs*. Examples include functions like `car` and `append`. In addition, all special forms (see below) are also considered primitives.
>
> Usually, a function is implemented as a primitive because it is a fundamental part of Lisp (e.g., `car`), or because it provides a low-level interface to operating system services, or because it needs to run fast. Unlike functions defined in Lisp, primitives can be modified or added only by changing the C sources and recompiling Emacs. See Section E.7 [Writing Emacs Primitives], page 1075.

special form
> A primitive that is like a function but does not evaluate all of its arguments in the usual way. It may evaluate only some of the arguments, or may evaluate them in an unusual order, or several times. Examples include `if`, `and`, and `while`. See Section 9.1.7 [Special Forms], page 128.

macro
> A construct defined in Lisp, which differs from a function in that it translates a Lisp expression into another expression which is to be evaluated instead of the original expression. Macros enable Lisp programmers to do the sorts of things that special forms can do. See Chapter 13 [Macros], page 217.

command   An object which can be invoked via the `command-execute` primitive, usually due to the user typing in a key sequence *bound* to that command. See Section 20.3 [Interactive Call], page 352. A command is usually a function; if the function is written in Lisp, it is made into a command by an `interactive` form in the function definition (see Section 20.2 [Defining Commands], page 346). Commands that are functions can also be called from Lisp expressions, just like other functions.

Keyboard macros (strings and vectors) are commands also, even though they are not functions. See Section 20.16 [Keyboard Macros], page 389. We say that a symbol is a command if its function cell contains a command (see Section 8.1 [Symbol Components], page 115); such a *named command* can be invoked with *M-x*.

closure   A function object that is much like a lambda expression, except that it also encloses an environment of lexical variable bindings. See Section 12.10 [Closures], page 204.

byte-code function
A function that has been compiled by the byte compiler. See Section 2.3.16 [Byte-Code Type], page 23.

autoload object
A place-holder for a real function. If the autoload object is called, Emacs loads the file containing the definition of the real function, and then calls the real function. See Section 15.5 [Autoload], page 249.

You can use the function `functionp` to test if an object is a function:

`functionp` *object*   [Function]
This function returns **t** if *object* is any kind of function, i.e., can be passed to `funcall`. Note that `functionp` returns **t** for symbols that are function names, and returns **nil** for special forms.

Unlike `functionp`, the next three functions do *not* treat a symbol as its function definition.

`subrp` *object*   [Function]
This function returns **t** if *object* is a built-in function (i.e., a Lisp primitive).

```
(subrp 'message)          ; message is a symbol,
    ⇒ nil                 ;    not a subr object.
(subrp (symbol-function 'message))
    ⇒ t
```

`byte-code-function-p` *object*   [Function]
This function returns **t** if *object* is a byte-code function. For example:

```
(byte-code-function-p (symbol-function 'next-line))
    ⇒ t
```

`subr-arity` *subr*   [Function]
This function provides information about the argument list of a primitive, *subr*. The returned value is a pair (**min . max**). *min* is the minimum number of args. *max* is the maximum number or the symbol **many**, for a function with **&rest** arguments, or the symbol **unevalled** if *subr* is a special form.

12.2 Lambda Expressions

A lambda expression is a function object written in Lisp. Here is an example:

```
(lambda (x)
   "Return the hyperbolic cosine of X."
   (* 0.5 (+ (exp x) (exp (- x)))))
```

In Emacs Lisp, such a list is a valid expression which evaluates to a function object.

A lambda expression, by itself, has no name; it is an *anonymous function*. Although lambda expressions can be used this way (see Section 12.7 [Anonymous Functions], page 198), they are more commonly associated with symbols to make *named functions* (see Section 12.3 [Function Names], page 191). Before going into these details, the following subsections describe the components of a lambda expression and what they do.

12.2.1 Components of a Lambda Expression

A lambda expression is a list that looks like this:

```
(lambda (arg-variables...)
   [documentation-string]
   [interactive-declaration]
   body-forms...)
```

The first element of a lambda expression is always the symbol `lambda`. This indicates that the list represents a function. The reason functions are defined to start with `lambda` is so that other lists, intended for other uses, will not accidentally be valid as functions.

The second element is a list of symbols—the argument variable names. This is called the *lambda list*. When a Lisp function is called, the argument values are matched up against the variables in the lambda list, which are given local bindings with the values provided. See Section 11.3 [Local Variables], page 158.

The documentation string is a Lisp string object placed within the function definition to describe the function for the Emacs help facilities. See Section 12.2.4 [Function Documentation], page 190.

The interactive declaration is a list of the form (`interactive code-string`). This declares how to provide arguments if the function is used interactively. Functions with this declaration are called *commands*; they can be called using *M-x* or bound to a key. Functions not intended to be called in this way should not have interactive declarations. See Section 20.2 [Defining Commands], page 346, for how to write an interactive declaration.

The rest of the elements are the *body* of the function: the Lisp code to do the work of the function (or, as a Lisp programmer would say, "a list of Lisp forms to evaluate"). The value returned by the function is the value returned by the last element of the body.

12.2.2 A Simple Lambda Expression Example

Consider the following example:

```
(lambda (a b c) (+ a b c))
```

We can call this function by passing it to `funcall`, like this:

```
(funcall (lambda (a b c) (+ a b c))
         1 2 3)
```

This call evaluates the body of the lambda expression with the variable a bound to 1, b bound to 2, and c bound to 3. Evaluation of the body adds these three numbers, producing the result 6; therefore, this call to the function returns the value 6.

Note that the arguments can be the results of other function calls, as in this example:

```
(funcall (lambda (a b c) (+ a b c))
         1 (* 2 3) (- 5 4))
```

This evaluates the arguments 1, (* 2 3), and (- 5 4) from left to right. Then it applies the lambda expression to the argument values 1, 6 and 1 to produce the value 8.

As these examples show, you can use a form with a lambda expression as its CAR to make local variables and give them values. In the old days of Lisp, this technique was the only way to bind and initialize local variables. But nowadays, it is clearer to use the special form let for this purpose (see Section 11.3 [Local Variables], page 158). Lambda expressions are mainly used as anonymous functions for passing as arguments to other functions (see Section 12.7 [Anonymous Functions], page 198), or stored as symbol function definitions to produce named functions (see Section 12.3 [Function Names], page 191).

12.2.3 Other Features of Argument Lists

Our simple sample function, (lambda (a b c) (+ a b c)), specifies three argument variables, so it must be called with three arguments: if you try to call it with only two arguments or four arguments, you get a wrong-number-of-arguments error (see Section 10.6.3 [Errors], page 148).

It is often convenient to write a function that allows certain arguments to be omitted. For example, the function substring accepts three arguments—a string, the start index and the end index—but the third argument defaults to the *length* of the string if you omit it. It is also convenient for certain functions to accept an indefinite number of arguments, as the functions list and + do.

To specify optional arguments that may be omitted when a function is called, simply include the keyword &optional before the optional arguments. To specify a list of zero or more extra arguments, include the keyword &rest before one final argument.

Thus, the complete syntax for an argument list is as follows:

```
(required-vars...
 [&optional optional-vars...]
 [&rest rest-var])
```

The square brackets indicate that the &optional and &rest clauses, and the variables that follow them, are optional.

A call to the function requires one actual argument for each of the *required-vars*. There may be actual arguments for zero or more of the *optional-vars*, and there cannot be any actual arguments beyond that unless the lambda list uses &rest. In that case, there may be any number of extra actual arguments.

If actual arguments for the optional and rest variables are omitted, then they always default to nil. There is no way for the function to distinguish between an explicit argument of nil and an omitted argument. However, the body of the function is free to consider nil an abbreviation for some other meaningful value. This is what substring does; nil as the third argument to substring means to use the length of the string supplied.

> **Common Lisp note:** Common Lisp allows the function to specify what default
> value to use when an optional argument is omitted; Emacs Lisp always uses
> `nil`. Emacs Lisp does not support `supplied-p` variables that tell you whether
> an argument was explicitly passed.

For example, an argument list that looks like this:

```
(a b &optional c d &rest e)
```

binds `a` and `b` to the first two actual arguments, which are required. If one or two more
arguments are provided, `c` and `d` are bound to them respectively; any arguments after the
first four are collected into a list and `e` is bound to that list. If there are only two arguments,
`c` is `nil`; if two or three arguments, `d` is `nil`; if four arguments or fewer, `e` is `nil`.

There is no way to have required arguments following optional ones—it would not make
sense. To see why this must be so, suppose that `c` in the example were optional and `d`
were required. Suppose three actual arguments are given; which variable would the third
argument be for? Would it be used for the c, or for d? One can argue for both possibilities.
Similarly, it makes no sense to have any more arguments (either required or optional) after
a `&rest` argument.

Here are some examples of argument lists and proper calls:

```
(funcall (lambda (n) (1+ n))        ; One required:
         1)                         ; requires exactly one argument.
    ⇒ 2
(funcall (lambda (n &optional n1)   ; One required and one optional:
         (if n1 (+ n n1) (1+ n)))   ; 1 or 2 arguments.
         1 2)
    ⇒ 3
(funcall (lambda (n &rest ns)       ; One required and one rest:
         (+ n (apply '+ ns)))       ; 1 or more arguments.
         1 2 3 4 5)
    ⇒ 15
```

12.2.4 Documentation Strings of Functions

A lambda expression may optionally have a *documentation string* just after the lambda
list. This string does not affect execution of the function; it is a kind of comment, but
a systematized comment which actually appears inside the Lisp world and can be used
by the Emacs help facilities. See Chapter 23 [Documentation], page 485, for how the
documentation string is accessed.

It is a good idea to provide documentation strings for all the functions in your program,
even those that are called only from within your program. Documentation strings are like
comments, except that they are easier to access.

The first line of the documentation string should stand on its own, because `apropos`
displays just this first line. It should consist of one or two complete sentences that summarize
the function's purpose.

The start of the documentation string is usually indented in the source file, but since
these spaces come before the starting double-quote, they are not part of the string. Some
people make a practice of indenting any additional lines of the string so that the text lines
up in the program source. *That is a mistake.* The indentation of the following lines is inside

the string; what looks nice in the source code will look ugly when displayed by the help commands.

You may wonder how the documentation string could be optional, since there are required components of the function that follow it (the body). Since evaluation of a string returns that string, without any side effects, it has no effect if it is not the last form in the body. Thus, in practice, there is no confusion between the first form of the body and the documentation string; if the only body form is a string then it serves both as the return value and as the documentation.

The last line of the documentation string can specify calling conventions different from the actual function arguments. Write text like this:

```
\(fn arglist)
```

following a blank line, at the beginning of the line, with no newline following it inside the documentation string. (The '\' is used to avoid confusing the Emacs motion commands.) The calling convention specified in this way appears in help messages in place of the one derived from the actual arguments of the function.

This feature is particularly useful for macro definitions, since the arguments written in a macro definition often do not correspond to the way users think of the parts of the macro call.

12.3 Naming a Function

A symbol can serve as the name of a function. This happens when the symbol's *function cell* (see Section 8.1 [Symbol Components], page 115) contains a function object (e.g., a lambda expression). Then the symbol itself becomes a valid, callable function, equivalent to the function object in its function cell.

The contents of the function cell are also called the symbol's *function definition*. The procedure of using a symbol's function definition in place of the symbol is called *symbol function indirection*; see Section 9.1.4 [Function Indirection], page 126. If you have not given a symbol a function definition, its function cell is said to be *void*, and it cannot be used as a function.

In practice, nearly all functions have names, and are referred to by their names. You can create a named Lisp function by defining a lambda expression and putting it in a function cell (see Section 12.9 [Function Cells], page 202). However, it is more common to use the `defun` special form, described in the next section.

We give functions names because it is convenient to refer to them by their names in Lisp expressions. Also, a named Lisp function can easily refer to itself—it can be recursive. Furthermore, primitives can only be referred to textually by their names, since primitive function objects (see Section 2.3.15 [Primitive Function Type], page 22) have no read syntax.

A function need not have a unique name. A given function object *usually* appears in the function cell of only one symbol, but this is just a convention. It is easy to store it in several symbols using `fset`; then each of the symbols is a valid name for the same function.

Note that a symbol used as a function name may also be used as a variable; these two uses of a symbol are independent and do not conflict. (This is not the case in some dialects of Lisp, like Scheme.)

12.4 Defining Functions

We usually give a name to a function when it is first created. This is called *defining a function*, and it is done with the **defun** macro.

defun *name args* [*doc*] [*declare*] [*interactive*] *body. . .*   [Macro]

> **defun** is the usual way to define new Lisp functions. It defines the symbol *name* as a function with argument list *args* and body forms given by *body*. Neither *name* nor *args* should be quoted.
>
> *doc*, if present, should be a string specifying the function's documentation string (see Section 12.2.4 [Function Documentation], page 190). *declare*, if present, should be a **declare** form specifying function metadata (see Section 12.14 [Declare Form], page 212). *interactive*, if present, should be an **interactive** form specifying how the function is to be called interactively (see Section 20.3 [Interactive Call], page 352).
>
> The return value of **defun** is undefined.
>
> Here are some examples:
>
> ```
> (defun foo () 5)
> (foo)
>      ⇒ 5
>
> (defun bar (a &optional b &rest c)
>     (list a b c))
> (bar 1 2 3 4 5)
>      ⇒ (1 2 (3 4 5))
> (bar 1)
>      ⇒ (1 nil nil)
> (bar)
> error  Wrong number of arguments.
>
> (defun capitalize-backwards ()
>   "Upcase the last letter of the word at point."
>   (interactive)
>   (backward-word 1)
>   (forward-word 1)
>   (backward-char 1)
>   (capitalize-word 1))
> ```
>
> Be careful not to redefine existing functions unintentionally. **defun** redefines even primitive functions such as **car** without any hesitation or notification. Emacs does not prevent you from doing this, because redefining a function is sometimes done deliberately, and there is no way to distinguish deliberate redefinition from unintentional redefinition.

defalias *name definition* **&optional** *doc*   [Function]

> This function defines the symbol *name* as a function, with definition *definition* (which can be any valid Lisp function). Its return value is *undefined*.
>
> If *doc* is non-**nil**, it becomes the function documentation of *name*. Otherwise, any documentation provided by *definition* is used.

Internally, `defalias` normally uses `fset` to set the definition. If *name* has a `defalias-fset-function` property, however, the associated value is used as a function to call in place of `fset`.

The proper place to use `defalias` is where a specific function name is being defined—especially where that name appears explicitly in the source file being loaded. This is because `defalias` records which file defined the function, just like `defun` (see Section 15.9 [Unloading], page 257).

By contrast, in programs that manipulate function definitions for other purposes, it is better to use `fset`, which does not keep such records. See Section 12.9 [Function Cells], page 202.

You cannot create a new primitive function with `defun` or `defalias`, but you can use them to change the function definition of any symbol, even one such as `car` or `x-popup-menu` whose normal definition is a primitive. However, this is risky: for instance, it is next to impossible to redefine `car` without breaking Lisp completely. Redefining an obscure function such as `x-popup-menu` is less dangerous, but it still may not work as you expect. If there are calls to the primitive from C code, they call the primitive's C definition directly, so changing the symbol's definition will have no effect on them.

See also `defsubst`, which defines a function like `defun` and tells the Lisp compiler to perform inline expansion on it. See Section 12.13 [Inline Functions], page 212.

Alternatively, you can define a function by providing the code which will inline it as a compiler macro. The following macros make this possible.

`define-inline` *name args* [*doc*] [*declare*] *body*. . .   [Macro]
> Define a function *name* by providing code that does its inlining, as a compiler macro. The function will accept the argument list *args* and will have the specified *body*.
>
> If present, *doc* should be the function's documentation string (see Section 12.2.4 [Function Documentation], page 190); *declare*, if present, should be a `declare` form (see Section 12.14 [Declare Form], page 212) specifying the function's metadata.

Functions defined via `define-inline` have several advantages with respect to macros defined by `defsubst` or `defmacro`:

- They can be passed to `mapcar` (see Section 12.6 [Mapping Functions], page 196).
- They are more efficient.
- They can be used as *place forms* to store values (see Section 11.15 [Generalized Variables], page 183).
- They behave in a more predictable way than `cl-defsubst` (see Section "Argument Lists" in *Common Lisp Extensions for GNU Emacs Lisp*).

Like `defmacro`, a function inlined with `define-inline` inherits the scoping rules, either dynamic or lexical, from the call site. See Section 11.9 [Variable Scoping], page 166.

The following macros should be used in the body of a function defined by `define-inline`.

`inline-quote` *expression*   [Macro]
> Quote *expression* for `define-inline`. This is similar to the backquote (see Section 9.3 [Backquote], page 130), but quotes code and accepts only `,`, not `,@`.

inline-letevals (*bindings...*) *body...*   [Macro]

> This is is similar to `let` (see Section 11.3 [Local Variables], page 158): it sets up local variables as specified by *bindings*, and then evaluates *body* with those bindings in effect. Each element of *bindings* should be either a symbol or a list of the form (*var expr*); the result is to evaluate *expr* and bind *var* to the result. The tail of *bindings* can be either `nil` or a symbol which should hold a list of arguments, in which case each argument is evaluated, and the symbol is bound to the resulting list.

inline-const-p *expression*   [Macro]

> Return non-`nil` if the value of *expression* is already known.

inline-const-val *expression*   [Macro]

> Return the value of *expression*.

inline-error *format* **&rest** *args*   [Macro]

> Signal an error, formatting *args* according to *format*.

Here's an example of using `define-inline`:

```
(define-inline myaccessor (obj)
  (inline-letevals (obj)
    (inline-quote (if (foo-p ,obj) (aref (cdr ,obj) 3) (aref ,obj 2)))))
```

This is equivalent to

```
(defsubst myaccessor (obj)
  (if (foo-p obj) (aref (cdr obj) 3) (aref obj 2)))
```

12.5 Calling Functions

Defining functions is only half the battle. Functions don't do anything until you *call* them, i.e., tell them to run. Calling a function is also known as *invocation*.

The most common way of invoking a function is by evaluating a list. For example, evaluating the list (`concat "a" "b"`) calls the function `concat` with arguments `"a"` and `"b"`. See Chapter 9 [Evaluation], page 124, for a description of evaluation.

When you write a list as an expression in your program, you specify which function to call, and how many arguments to give it, in the text of the program. Usually that's just what you want. Occasionally you need to compute at run time which function to call. To do that, use the function `funcall`. When you also need to determine at run time how many arguments to pass, use `apply`.

funcall *function* **&rest** *arguments*   [Function]

> `funcall` calls *function* with *arguments*, and returns whatever *function* returns.

> Since `funcall` is a function, all of its arguments, including *function*, are evaluated before `funcall` is called. This means that you can use any expression to obtain the function to be called. It also means that `funcall` does not see the expressions you write for the *arguments*, only their values. These values are *not* evaluated a second time in the act of calling *function*; the operation of `funcall` is like the normal procedure for calling a function, once its arguments have already been evaluated.

> The argument *function* must be either a Lisp function or a primitive function. Special forms and macros are not allowed, because they make sense only when given the

unevaluated argument expressions. `funcall` cannot provide these because, as we saw above, it never knows them in the first place.

If you need to use `funcall` to call a command and make it behave as if invoked interactively, use `funcall-interactively` (see Section 20.3 [Interactive Call], page 352).

```
(setq f 'list)
     ⇒ list
(funcall f 'x 'y 'z)
     ⇒ (x y z)
(funcall f 'x 'y '(z))
     ⇒ (x y (z))
(funcall 'and t nil)
     error  Invalid function: #<subr and>
```

Compare these examples with the examples of `apply`.

apply *function* **&rest** *arguments*   [Function]

> `apply` calls *function* with *arguments*, just like `funcall` but with one difference: the last of *arguments* is a list of objects, which are passed to *function* as separate arguments, rather than a single list. We say that `apply` *spreads* this list so that each individual element becomes an argument.

> `apply` returns the result of calling *function*. As with `funcall`, *function* must either be a Lisp function or a primitive function; special forms and macros do not make sense in `apply`.

```
(setq f 'list)
     ⇒ list
(apply f 'x 'y 'z)
     error  Wrong type argument: listp, z
(apply '+ 1 2 '(3 4))
     ⇒ 10
(apply '+ '(1 2 3 4))
     ⇒ 10

(apply 'append '((a b c) nil (x y z) nil))
     ⇒ (a b c x y z)
```

> For an interesting example of using `apply`, see [Definition of mapcar], page 196.

Sometimes it is useful to fix some of the function's arguments at certain values, and leave the rest of arguments for when the function is actually called. The act of fixing some of the function's arguments is called *partial application* of the function[1]. The result is a new function that accepts the rest of arguments and calls the original function with all the arguments combined.

Here's how to do partial application in Emacs Lisp:

apply-partially *func* **&rest** *args*   [Function]

> This function returns a new function which, when called, will call *func* with the list of arguments composed from *args* and additional arguments specified at the time of

---

[1] This is related to, but different from *currying*, which transforms a function that takes multiple arguments in such a way that it can be called as a chain of functions, each one with a single argument.

the call. If *func* accepts *n* arguments, then a call to `apply-partially` with *m* < *n* arguments will produce a new function of *n* − *m* arguments.

Here's how we could define the built-in function `1+`, if it didn't exist, using `apply-partially` and `+`, another built-in function:

```
(defalias '1+ (apply-partially '+ 1)
  "Increment argument by one.")
(1+ 10)
     ⇒ 11
```

It is common for Lisp functions to accept functions as arguments or find them in data structures (especially in hook variables and property lists) and call them using `funcall` or `apply`. Functions that accept function arguments are often called *functionals*.

Sometimes, when you call a functional, it is useful to supply a no-op function as the argument. Here are two different kinds of no-op function:

`identity` *arg*   [Function]
> This function returns *arg* and has no side effects.

`ignore` **&rest** *args*   [Function]
> This function ignores any arguments and returns `nil`.

Some functions are user-visible *commands*, which can be called interactively (usually by a key sequence). It is possible to invoke such a command exactly as though it was called interactively, by using the `call-interactively` function. See Section 20.3 [Interactive Call], page 352.

12.6 Mapping Functions

A *mapping function* applies a given function (*not* a special form or macro) to each element of a list or other collection. Emacs Lisp has several such functions; this section describes `mapcar`, `mapc`, and `mapconcat`, which map over a list. See [Definition of mapatoms], page 119, for the function `mapatoms` which maps over the symbols in an obarray. See [Definition of maphash], page 112, for the function `maphash` which maps over key/value associations in a hash table.

These mapping functions do not allow char-tables because a char-table is a sparse array whose nominal range of indices is very large. To map over a char-table in a way that deals properly with its sparse nature, use the function `map-char-table` (see Section 6.6 [Char-Tables], page 104).

`mapcar` *function sequence*   [Function]
> `mapcar` applies *function* to each element of *sequence* in turn, and returns a list of the results.

> The argument *sequence* can be any kind of sequence except a char-table; that is, a list, a vector, a bool-vector, or a string. The result is always a list. The length of the result is the same as the length of *sequence*. For example:

```
(mapcar 'car '((a b) (c d) (e f)))
     ⇒ (a c e)
(mapcar '1+ [1 2 3])
     ⇒ (2 3 4)
(mapcar 'string "abc")
     ⇒ ("a" "b" "c")

;; Call each function in my-hooks.
(mapcar 'funcall my-hooks)

(defun mapcar* (function &rest args)
  "Apply FUNCTION to successive cars of all ARGS.
Return the list of results."
  ;; If no list is exhausted,
  (if (not (memq nil args))
      ;; apply function to CARs.
      (cons (apply function (mapcar 'car args))
            (apply 'mapcar* function
                   ;; Recurse for rest of elements.
                   (mapcar 'cdr args)))))

(mapcar* 'cons '(a b c) '(1 2 3 4))
     ⇒ ((a . 1) (b . 2) (c . 3))
```

mapc *function sequence*   [Function]

mapc is like mapcar except that *function* is used for side-effects only—the values it returns are ignored, not collected into a list. mapc always returns *sequence*.

mapconcat *function sequence separator*   [Function]

mapconcat applies *function* to each element of *sequence*; the results, which must be sequences of characters (strings, vectors, or lists), are concatenated into a single string return value. Between each pair of result sequences, mapconcat inserts the characters from *separator*, which also must be a string, or a vector or list of characters. See Chapter 6 [Sequences Arrays Vectors], page 89.

The argument *function* must be a function that can take one argument and returns a sequence of characters: a string, a vector, or a list. The argument *sequence* can be any kind of sequence except a char-table; that is, a list, a vector, a bool-vector, or a string.

```
(mapconcat 'symbol-name
           '(The cat in the hat)
           " ")
     ⇒ "The cat in the hat"

(mapconcat (function (lambda (x) (format "%c" (1+ x))))
           "HAL-8000"
           "")
     ⇒ "IBM.9111"
```

12.7 Anonymous Functions

Although functions are usually defined with `defun` and given names at the same time, it is sometimes convenient to use an explicit lambda expression—an *anonymous function*. Anonymous functions are valid wherever function names are. They are often assigned as variable values, or as arguments to functions; for instance, you might pass one as the *function* argument to `mapcar`, which applies that function to each element of a list (see Section 12.6 [Mapping Functions], page 196). See [describe-symbols example], page 486, for a realistic example of this.

When defining a lambda expression that is to be used as an anonymous function, you can in principle use any method to construct the list. But typically you should use the `lambda` macro, or the `function` special form, or the `#'` read syntax:

`lambda` *args* [*doc*] [*interactive*] *body*. . .   [Macro]

> This macro returns an anonymous function with argument list *args*, documentation string *doc* (if any), interactive spec *interactive* (if any), and body forms given by *body*.
>
> In effect, this macro makes `lambda` forms self-quoting: evaluating a form whose CAR is `lambda` yields the form itself:
>
>  ```
>  (lambda (x) (* x x))
>       ⇒ (lambda (x) (* x x))
>  ```
>
> The `lambda` form has one other effect: it tells the Emacs evaluator and byte-compiler that its argument is a function, by using `function` as a subroutine (see below).

`function` *function-object*   [Special Form]

> This special form returns *function-object* without evaluating it. In this, it is similar to `quote` (see Section 9.2 [Quoting], page 130). But unlike `quote`, it also serves as a note to the Emacs evaluator and byte-compiler that *function-object* is intended to be used as a function. Assuming *function-object* is a valid lambda expression, this has two effects:
>
> - When the code is byte-compiled, *function-object* is compiled into a byte-code function object (see Chapter 16 [Byte Compilation], page 260).
> - When lexical binding is enabled, *function-object* is converted into a closure. See Section 12.10 [Closures], page 204.

The read syntax `#'` is a short-hand for using `function`. The following forms are all equivalent:

```
(lambda (x) (* x x))
(function (lambda (x) (* x x)))
#'(lambda (x) (* x x))
```

In the following example, we define a `change-property` function that takes a function as its third argument, followed by a `double-property` function that makes use of `change-property` by passing it an anonymous function:

```
(defun change-property (symbol prop function)
  (let ((value (get symbol prop)))
    (put symbol prop (funcall function value))))
```

```
(defun double-property (symbol prop)
  (change-property symbol prop (lambda (x) (* 2 x))))
```

Note that we do not quote the `lambda` form.

If you compile the above code, the anonymous function is also compiled. This would not happen if, say, you had constructed the anonymous function by quoting it as a list:

```
(defun double-property (symbol prop)
  (change-property symbol prop '(lambda (x) (* 2 x))))
```

In that case, the anonymous function is kept as a lambda expression in the compiled code. The byte-compiler cannot assume this list is a function, even though it looks like one, since it does not know that `change-property` intends to use it as a function.

12.8 Generic Functions

Functions defined using `defun` have a hard-coded set of assumptions about the types and expected values of their arguments. For example, a function that was designed to handle values of its argument that are either numbers or lists of numbers will fail or signal an error if called with a value of any other type, such as a vector or a string. This happens because the implementation of the function is not prepared to deal with types other than those assumed during the design.

By contrast, object-oriented programs use *polymorphic functions*: a set of specialized functions having the same name, each one of which was written for a certain specific set of argument types. Which of the functions is actually called is decided at run time based on the types of the actual arguments.

Emacs provides support for polymorphism. Like other Lisp environments, notably Common Lisp and its Common Lisp Object System (CLOS), this support is based on *generic functions*. The Emacs generic functions closely follow CLOS, including use of similar names, so if you have experience with CLOS, the rest of this section will sound very familiar.

A generic function specifies an abstract operation, by defining its name and list of arguments, but (usually) no implementation. The actual implementation for several specific classes of arguments is provided by *methods*, which should be defined separately. Each method that implements a generic function has the same name as the generic function, but the method's definition indicates what kinds of arguments it can handle by *specializing* the arguments defined by the generic function. These *argument specializers* can be more or less specific; for example, a `string` type is more specific than a more general type, such as `sequence`.

Note that, unlike in message-based OO languages, such as C++ and Simula, methods that implement generic functions don't belong to a class, they belong to the generic function they implement.

When a generic function is invoked, it selects the applicable methods by comparing the actual arguments passed by the caller with the argument specializers of each method. A method is applicable if the actual arguments of the call are compatible with the method's specializers. If more than one method is applicable, they are combined using certain rules, described below, and the combination then handles the call.

cl-defgeneric *name arguments* [*documentation*]   [Macro]
    [*options-and-methods*...] **&rest** *body*

This macro defines a generic function with the specified *name* and *arguments*. If *body* is present, it provides the default implementation. If *documentation* is present (it should always be), it specifies the documentation string for the generic function, in the form (`:documentation` *docstring*). The optional *options-and-methods* can be one of the following forms:

(`declare` *declarations*)
    A declare form, as described in Section 12.14 [Declare Form], page 212.

(`:argument-precedence-order` **&rest** *args*)
    This form affects the sorting order for combining applicable methods. Normally, when two methods are compared during combination, method arguments are examined left to right, and the first method whose argument specializer is more specific will come before the other one. The order defined by this form overrides that, and the arguments are examined according to their order in this form, and not left to right.

(`:method` [*qualifiers*...] `args` **&rest** `body`)
    This form defines a method like `cl-defmethod` does.

cl-defmethod *name* [*qualifier*] *arguments* **&rest** [*docstring*] *body*   [Macro]

This macro defines a particular implementation for the generic function called *name*. The implementation code is given by *body*. If present, *docstring* is the documentation string for the method. The *arguments* list, which must be identical in all the methods that implement a generic function, and must match the argument list of that function, provides argument specializers of the form (`arg spec`), where *arg* is the argument name as specified in the `cl-defgeneric` call, and *spec* is one of the following specializer forms:

type   This specializer requires the argument to be of the given *type*, one of the types from the type hierarchy described below.

(`eql` *object*)
    This specializer requires the argument be `eql` to the given *object*.

(`head` *object*)
    The argument must be a cons cell whose `car` is `eql` to *object*.

struct-tag
    The argument must be an instance of a class named *struct-tag* defined with `cl-defstruct` (see Section "Structures" in *Common Lisp Extensions for GNU Emacs Lisp*), or of one of its parent classes.

Alternatively, the argument specializer can be of the form `&context` (*expr spec*), in which case the value of *expr* must be compatible with the specializer provided by *spec*; *spec* can be any of the forms described above. In other words, this form of specializer uses the value of *expr* instead of arguments for the decision whether the method is applicable. For example, `&context` (`overwrite-mode` (`eql t`)) will make the method compatible only when `overwrite-mode` is turned on.

The type specializer, (**arg type**), can specify one of the *system types* in the following list. When a parent type is specified, an argument whose type is any of its more specific child types, as well as grand-children, grand-grand-children, etc. will also be compatible.

integer   Parent type: number.

number

null   Parent type: symbol

symbol

string   Parent type: array.

array   Parent type: sequence.

cons   Parent type: list.

list   Parent type: sequence.

marker

overlay

float   Parent type: number.

window-configuration
process

window

subr

compiled-function
buffer

char-table
            Parent type: array.

bool-vector
            Parent type: array.

vector   Parent type: array.

frame

hash-table
font-spec
font-entity
font-object

The optional *qualifier* allows combining several applicable methods. If it is not present, the defined method is a *primary* method, responsible for providing the primary implementation of the generic function for the specialized arguments. You can also define *auxiliary methods*, by using one of the following values as *qualifier*:

:before   This auxiliary method will run before the primary method. More accurately, all the :before methods will run before the primary, in the most-specific-first order.

:after   This auxiliary method will run after the primary method. More accurately, all such methods will run after the primary, in the most-specific-last order.

:around   This auxiliary method will run *instead* of the primary method. The most specific of such methods will be run before any other method. Such methods normally use `cl-call-next-method`, described below, to invoke the other auxiliary or primary methods.

:extra *string*
             This allows you to add more methods, distinguished by *string*, for the same specializers and qualifiers.

Each time a generic function is called, it builds the *effective method* which will handle this invocation by combining the applicable methods defined for the function. The process of finding the applicable methods and producing the effective method is called *dispatch*. The applicable methods are those all of whose specializers are compatible with the actual arguments of the call. Since all of the arguments must be compatible with the specializers, they all determine whether a method is applicable. Methods that explicitly specialize more than one argument are called *multiple-dispatch methods*.

The applicable methods are sorted into the order in which they will be combined. The method whose left-most argument specializer is the most specific one will come first in the order. (Specifying `:argument-precedence-order` as part of `cl-defmethod` overrides that, as described above.) If the method body calls `cl-call-next-method`, the next most-specific method will run. If there are applicable `:around` methods, the most-specific of them will run first; it should call `cl-call-next-method` to run any of the less specific `:around` methods. Next, the `:before` methods run in the order of their specificity, followed by the primary method, and lastly the `:after` methods in the reverse order of their specificity.

cl-call-next-method &rest *args*   [Function]
             When invoked from within the lexical body of a primary or an `:around` auxiliary method, call the next applicable method for the same generic function. Normally, it is called with no arguments, which means to call the next applicable method with the same arguments that the calling method was invoked. Otherwise, the specified arguments are used instead.

cl-next-method-p   [Function]
             This function, when called from within the lexical body of a primary or an `:around` auxiliary method, returns non-`nil` if there is a next method to call.

12.9 Accessing Function Cell Contents

The *function definition* of a symbol is the object stored in the function cell of the symbol. The functions described here access, test, and set the function cell of symbols.

See also the function `indirect-function`. See [Definition of indirect-function], page 127.

symbol-function *symbol*   [Function]
             This returns the object in the function cell of *symbol*. It does not check that the returned object is a legitimate function.

If the function cell is void, the return value is `nil`. To distinguish between a function cell that is void and one set to `nil`, use `fboundp` (see below).

```
(defun bar (n) (+ n 2))
(symbol-function 'bar)
     ⇒ (lambda (n) (+ n 2))
(fset 'baz 'bar)
     ⇒ bar
(symbol-function 'baz)
     ⇒ bar
```

If you have never given a symbol any function definition, we say that that symbol's function cell is *void*. In other words, the function cell does not have any Lisp object in it. If you try to call the symbol as a function, Emacs signals a `void-function` error.

Note that void is not the same as `nil` or the symbol `void`. The symbols `nil` and `void` are Lisp objects, and can be stored into a function cell just as any other object can be (and they can be valid functions if you define them in turn with `defun`). A void function cell contains no object whatsoever.

You can test the voidness of a symbol's function definition with `fboundp`. After you have given a symbol a function definition, you can make it void once more using `fmakunbound`.

fboundp *symbol*   [Function]

>   This function returns `t` if the symbol has an object in its function cell, `nil` otherwise. It does not check that the object is a legitimate function.

fmakunbound *symbol*   [Function]

>   This function makes *symbol*'s function cell void, so that a subsequent attempt to access this cell will cause a `void-function` error. It returns *symbol*. (See also `makunbound`, in Section 11.4 [Void Variables], page 160.)

```
(defun foo (x) x)
(foo 1)
     ⇒1
(fmakunbound 'foo)
     ⇒ foo
(foo 1)
```
|error| Symbol's function definition is void: foo

fset *symbol definition*   [Function]

>   This function stores *definition* in the function cell of *symbol*. The result is *definition*. Normally *definition* should be a function or the name of a function, but this is not checked. The argument *symbol* is an ordinary evaluated argument.

>   The primary use of this function is as a subroutine by constructs that define or alter functions, like `defun` or `advice-add` (see Section 12.11 [Advising Functions], page 204). You can also use it to give a symbol a function definition that is not a function, e.g., a keyboard macro (see Section 20.16 [Keyboard Macros], page 389):

```
;; Define a named keyboard macro.
(fset 'kill-two-lines "\^u2\^k")
     ⇒ "\^u2\^k"
```

It you wish to use `fset` to make an alternate name for a function, consider using `defalias` instead. See [Definition of defalias], page 192.

12.10 Closures

As explained in Section 11.9 [Variable Scoping], page 166, Emacs can optionally enable lexical binding of variables. When lexical binding is enabled, any named function that you create (e.g., with `defun`), as well as any anonymous function that you create using the `lambda` macro or the `function` special form or the `#'` syntax (see Section 12.7 [Anonymous Functions], page 198), is automatically converted into a *closure*.

A closure is a function that also carries a record of the lexical environment that existed when the function was defined. When it is invoked, any lexical variable references within its definition use the retained lexical environment. In all other respects, closures behave much like ordinary functions; in particular, they can be called in the same way as ordinary functions.

See Section 11.9.3 [Lexical Binding], page 168, for an example of using a closure.

Currently, an Emacs Lisp closure object is represented by a list with the symbol `closure` as the first element, a list representing the lexical environment as the second element, and the argument list and body forms as the remaining elements:

```
;; lexical binding is enabled.
(lambda (x) (* x x))
      ⇒ (closure (t) (x) (* x x))
```

However, the fact that the internal structure of a closure is exposed to the rest of the Lisp world is considered an internal implementation detail. For this reason, we recommend against directly examining or altering the structure of closure objects.

12.11 Advising Emacs Lisp Functions

When you need to modify a function defined in another library, or when you need to modify a hook like *foo-function*, a process filter, or basically any variable or object field which holds a function value, you can use the appropriate setter function, such as `fset` or `defun` for named functions, `setq` for hook variables, or `set-process-filter` for process filters, but those are often too blunt, completely throwing away the previous value.

The *advice* feature lets you add to the existing definition of a function, by *advising the function*. This is a cleaner method than redefining the whole function.

Emacs's advice system provides two sets of primitives for that: the core set, for function values held in variables and object fields (with the corresponding primitives being `add-function` and `remove-function`) and another set layered on top of it for named functions (with the main primitives being `advice-add` and `advice-remove`).

For example, in order to trace the calls to the process filter of a process *proc*, you could use:

```
(defun my-tracing-function (proc string)
  (message "Proc %S received %S" proc string))

(add-function :before (process-filter proc) #'my-tracing-function)
```

This will cause the process's output to be passed to `my-tracing-function` before being passed to the original process filter. `my-tracing-function` receives the same arguments as the original function. When you're done with it, you can revert to the untraced behavior with:

```
(remove-function (process-filter proc) #'my-tracing-function)
```

Similarly, if you want to trace the execution of the function named `display-buffer`, you could use:

```
(defun his-tracing-function (orig-fun &rest args)
  (message "display-buffer called with args %S" args)
  (let ((res (apply orig-fun args)))
    (message "display-buffer returned %S" res)
    res))


(advice-add 'display-buffer :around #'his-tracing-function)
```

Here, `his-tracing-function` is called instead of the original function and receives the original function (additionally to that function's arguments) as argument, so it can call it if and when it needs to. When you're tired of seeing this output, you can revert to the untraced behavior with:

```
(advice-remove 'display-buffer #'his-tracing-function)
```

The arguments `:before` and `:around` used in the above examples specify how the two functions are composed, since there are many different ways to do it. The added function is also called a piece of *advice*.

12.11.1 Primitives to manipulate advices

add-function *where place function* **&optional** *props*   [Macro]

> This macro is the handy way to add the advice *function* to the function stored in *place* (see Section 11.15 [Generalized Variables], page 183).
>
> *where* determines how *function* is composed with the existing function, e.g., whether *function* should be called before, or after the original function. See Section 12.11.3 [Advice combinators], page 208, for the list of available ways to compose the two functions.
>
> When modifying a variable (whose name will usually end with `-function`), you can choose whether *function* is used globally or only in the current buffer: if *place* is just a symbol, then *function* is added to the global value of *place*. Whereas if *place* is of the form (`local` *symbol*), where *symbol* is an expression which returns the variable name, then *function* will only be added in the current buffer. Finally, if you want to modify a lexical variable, you will have to use (`var` *variable*).
>
> Every function added with **add-function** can be accompanied by an association list of properties *props*. Currently only two of those properties have a special meaning:

> name   This gives a name to the advice, which `remove-function` can use to identify which function to remove. Typically used when *function* is an anonymous function.

> depth   This specifies how to order the advice, should several pieces of advice be present. By default, the depth is 0. A depth of 100 indicates that

this piece of advice should be kept as deep as possible, whereas a depth of -100 indicates that it should stay as the outermost piece. When two pieces of advice specify the same depth, the most recently added one will be outermost.

For `:before` advice, being outermost means that this advice will be run first, before any other advice, whereas being innermost means that it will run right before the original function, with no other advice run between itself and the original function. Similarly, for `:after` advice innermost means that it will run right after the original function, with no other advice run in between, whereas outermost means that it will be run right at the end after all other advice. An innermost `:override` piece of advice will only override the original function and other pieces of advice will apply to it, whereas an outermost `:override` piece of advice will override not only the original function but all other advice applied to it as well.

If *function* is not interactive, then the combined function will inherit the interactive spec, if any, of the original function. Else, the combined function will be interactive and will use the interactive spec of *function*. One exception: if the interactive spec of *function* is a function (rather than an expression or a string), then the interactive spec of the combined function will be a call to that function with as sole argument the interactive spec of the original function. To interpret the spec received as argument, use `advice-eval-interactive-spec`.

Note: The interactive spec of *function* will apply to the combined function and should hence obey the calling convention of the combined function rather than that of *function*. In many cases, it makes no difference since they are identical, but it does matter for `:around`, `:filter-args`, and `filter-return`, where *function*.

remove-function *place function*   [Macro]
This macro removes *function* from the function stored in *place*. This only works if *function* was added to *place* using `add-function`.

function is compared with functions added to *place* using `equal`, to try and make it work also with lambda expressions. It is additionally compared also with the `name` property of the functions added to *place*, which can be more reliable than comparing lambda expressions using `equal`.

advice-function-member-p *advice function-def*   [Function]
Return non-`nil` if *advice* is already in *function-def*. Like for `remove-function` above, instead of *advice* being the actual function, it can also be the `name` of the piece of advice.

advice-function-mapc *f function-def*   [Function]
Call the function *f* for every piece of advice that was added to *function-def*. *f* is called with two arguments: the advice function and its properties.

advice-eval-interactive-spec *spec*   [Function]
Evaluate the interactive *spec* just like an interactive call to a function with such a spec would, and then return the corresponding list of arguments that was built. E.g., (`advice-eval-interactive-spec "r\nP"`) will return a list of three elements, containing the boundaries of the region and the current prefix argument.

12.11.2 Advising Named Functions

A common use of advice is for named functions and macros. You could just use `add-function` as in:

```
(add-function :around (symbol-function 'fun) #'his-tracing-function)
```

But you should use `advice-add` and `advice-remove` for that instead. This separate set of functions to manipulate pieces of advice applied to named functions, offers the following extra features compared to `add-function`: they know how to deal with macros and autoloaded functions, they let `describe-function` preserve the original docstring as well as document the added advice, and they let you add and remove advice before a function is even defined.

`advice-add` can be useful for altering the behavior of existing calls to an existing function without having to redefine the whole function. However, it can be a source of bugs, since existing callers to the function may assume the old behavior, and work incorrectly when the behavior is changed by advice. Advice can also cause confusion in debugging, if the person doing the debugging does not notice or remember that the function has been modified by advice.

For these reasons, advice should be reserved for the cases where you cannot modify a function's behavior in any other way. If it is possible to do the same thing via a hook, that is preferable (see Section 22.1 [Hooks], page 429). If you simply want to change what a particular key does, it may be better to write a new command, and remap the old command's key bindings to the new one (see Section 21.13 [Remapping Commands], page 409). In particular, Emacs's own source files should not put advice on functions in Emacs. (There are currently a few exceptions to this convention, but we aim to correct them.)

Special forms (see Section 9.1.7 [Special Forms], page 128) cannot be advised, however macros can be advised, in much the same way as functions. Of course, this will not affect code that has already been macro-expanded, so you need to make sure the advice is installed before the macro is expanded.

It is possible to advise a primitive (see Section 12.1 [What Is a Function], page 186), but one should typically *not* do so, for two reasons. Firstly, some primitives are used by the advice mechanism, and advising them could cause an infinite recursion. Secondly, many primitives are called directly from C, and such calls ignore advice; hence, one ends up in a confusing situation where some calls (occurring from Lisp code) obey the advice and other calls (from C code) do not.

define-advice *symbol* (*where lambda-list* **&optional** *name depth*)   [Macro]
      &rest *body*

    This macro defines a piece of advice and adds it to the function named *symbol*. The advice is an anonymous function if *name* is nil or a function named `symbol@name`. See `advice-add` for explanation of other arguments.

advice-add *symbol where function* **&optional** *props*   [Function]

    Add the advice *function* to the named function *symbol*. *where* and *props* have the same meaning as for `add-function` (see Section 12.11.1 [Core Advising Primitives], page 205).

`advice-remove` *symbol function*   [Function]

> Remove the advice *function* from the named function *symbol*. *function* can also be the **name** of a piece of advice.

`advice-member-p` *function symbol*   [Function]

> Return non-**nil** if the advice *function* is already in the named function *symbol*. *function* can also be the **name** of a piece of advice.

`advice-mapc` *function symbol*   [Function]

> Call *function* for every piece of advice that was added to the named function *symbol*. *function* is called with two arguments: the advice function and its properties.

12.11.3 Ways to compose advice

Here are the different possible values for the *where* argument of **add-function** and **advice-add**, specifying how the advice *function* and the original function should be composed.

`:before`   Call *function* before the old function. Both functions receive the same arguments, and the return value of the composition is the return value of the old function. More specifically, the composition of the two functions behaves like:

```
(lambda (&rest r) (apply function r) (apply oldfun r))
```

        (add-function :before *funvar function***)** is comparable for single-function hooks to **(add-hook '**hookvar function**)** for normal hooks.

`:after`   Call *function* after the old function. Both functions receive the same arguments, and the return value of the composition is the return value of the old function. More specifically, the composition of the two functions behaves like:

```
(lambda (&rest r) (prog1 (apply oldfun r) (apply function r)))
```

        (add-function :after *funvar function***)** is comparable for single-function hooks to **(add-hook '**hookvar function **'append)** for normal hooks.

`:override`

> This completely replaces the old function with the new one. The old function can of course be recovered if you later call **remove-function**.

`:around`   Call *function* instead of the old function, but provide the old function as an extra argument to *function*. This is the most flexible composition. For example, it lets you call the old function with different arguments, or many times, or within a let-binding, or you can sometimes delegate the work to the old function and sometimes override it completely. More specifically, the composition of the two functions behaves like:

```
(lambda (&rest r) (apply function oldfun r))
```

`:before-while`

> Call *function* before the old function and don't call the old function if *function* returns **nil**. Both functions receive the same arguments, and the return value of the composition is the return value of the old function. More specifically, the composition of the two functions behaves like:

```
(lambda (&rest r) (and (apply function r) (apply oldfun r)))
```

(add-function :before-while *funvar function*) is comparable for single-function hooks to (add-hook '*hookvar function*) when *hookvar* is run via run-hook-with-args-until-failure.

:before-until

Call *function* before the old function and only call the old function if *function* returns nil. More specifically, the composition of the two functions behaves like:

(lambda (&rest r) (or (apply *function* r) (apply *oldfun* r)))

(add-function :before-until *funvar function*) is comparable for single-function hooks to (add-hook '*hookvar function*) when *hookvar* is run via run-hook-with-args-until-success.

:after-while

Call *function* after the old function and only if the old function returned non-nil. Both functions receive the same arguments, and the return value of the composition is the return value of *function*. More specifically, the composition of the two functions behaves like:

(lambda (&rest r) (and (apply *oldfun* r) (apply *function* r)))

(add-function :after-while *funvar function*) is comparable for single-function hooks to (add-hook '*hookvar function* 'append) when *hookvar* is run via run-hook-with-args-until-failure.

:after-until

Call *function* after the old function and only if the old function returned nil. More specifically, the composition of the two functions behaves like:

(lambda (&rest r) (or (apply *oldfun* r) (apply *function* r)))

(add-function :after-until *funvar function*) is comparable for single-function hooks to (add-hook '*hookvar function* 'append) when *hookvar* is run via run-hook-with-args-until-success.

:filter-args

Call *function* first and use the result (which should be a list) as the new arguments to pass to the old function. More specifically, the composition of the two functions behaves like:

(lambda (&rest r) (apply *oldfun* (funcall *function* r)))

:filter-return

Call the old function first and pass the result to *function*. More specifically, the composition of the two functions behaves like:

(lambda (&rest r) (funcall *function* (apply *oldfun* r)))

12.11.4 Adapting code using the old defadvice

A lot of code uses the old defadvice mechanism, which is largely made obsolete by the new advice-add, whose implementation and semantics is significantly simpler.

An old piece of advice such as:

(defadvice previous-line (before next-line-at-end

```
                                    (&optional arg try-vscroll))
        "Insert an empty line when moving up from the top line."
        (if (and next-line-add-newlines (= arg 1)
                 (save-excursion (beginning-of-line) (bobp)))
            (progn
              (beginning-of-line)
              (newline))))
```

could be translated in the new advice mechanism into a plain function:

```
(defun previous-line--next-line-at-end (&optional arg try-vscroll)
  "Insert an empty line when moving up from the top line."
  (if (and next-line-add-newlines (= arg 1)
           (save-excursion (beginning-of-line) (bobp)))
      (progn
        (beginning-of-line)
        (newline))))
```

Obviously, this does not actually modify `previous-line`. For that the old advice needed:

```
(ad-activate 'previous-line)
```

whereas the new advice mechanism needs:

```
(advice-add 'previous-line :before #'previous-line--next-line-at-end)
```

Note that `ad-activate` had a global effect: it activated all pieces of advice enabled for that specified function. If you wanted to only activate or deactivate a particular piece, you needed to *enable* or *disable* it with `ad-enable-advice` and `ad-disable-advice`. The new mechanism does away with this distinction.

Around advice such as:

```
(defadvice foo (around foo-around)
  "Ignore case in `foo'."
  (let ((case-fold-search t))
    ad-do-it))
(ad-activate 'foo)
```

could translate into:

```
(defun foo--foo-around (orig-fun &rest args)
  "Ignore case in `foo'."
  (let ((case-fold-search t))
    (apply orig-fun args)))
(advice-add 'foo :around #'foo--foo-around)
```

Regarding the advice's *class*, note that the new `:before` is not quite equivalent to the old `before`, because in the old advice you could modify the function's arguments (e.g., with `ad-set-arg`), and that would affect the argument values seen by the original function, whereas in the new `:before`, modifying an argument via `setq` in the advice has no effect on the arguments seen by the original function. When porting `before` advice which relied on this behavior, you'll need to turn it into new `:around` or `:filter-args` advice instead.

Similarly old `after` advice could modify the returned value by changing `ad-return-value`, whereas new `:after` advice cannot, so when porting such old `after` advice, you'll need to turn it into new `:around` or `:filter-return` advice instead.

12.12 Declaring Functions Obsolete

You can mark a named function as *obsolete*, meaning that it may be removed at some point in the future. This causes Emacs to warn that the function is obsolete whenever it byte-compiles code containing that function, and whenever it displays the documentation for that function. In all other respects, an obsolete function behaves like any other function.

The easiest way to mark a function as obsolete is to put a (`declare` (`obsolete` ...)) form in the function's `defun` definition. See Section 12.14 [Declare Form], page 212. Alternatively, you can use the `make-obsolete` function, described below.

A macro (see Chapter 13 [Macros], page 217) can also be marked obsolete with `make-obsolete`; this has the same effects as for a function. An alias for a function or macro can also be marked as obsolete; this makes the alias itself obsolete, not the function or macro which it resolves to.

`make-obsolete` *obsolete-name current-name* **&optional** *when*   [Function]
> This function marks *obsolete-name* as obsolete. *obsolete-name* should be a symbol naming a function or macro, or an alias for a function or macro.
>
> If *current-name* is a symbol, the warning message says to use *current-name* instead of *obsolete-name*. *current-name* does not need to be an alias for *obsolete-name*; it can be a different function with similar functionality. *current-name* can also be a string, which serves as the warning message. The message should begin in lower case, and end with a period. It can also be `nil`, in which case the warning message provides no additional details.
>
> If provided, *when* should be a string indicating when the function was first made obsolete—for example, a date or a release number.

`define-obsolete-function-alias` *obsolete-name current-name*   [Macro]
> **&optional** *when doc*
> This convenience macro marks the function *obsolete-name* obsolete and also defines it as an alias for the function *current-name*. It is equivalent to the following:
>
>   (defalias *obsolete-name current-name doc*)
>   (make-obsolete *obsolete-name current-name when*)

In addition, you can mark a certain a particular calling convention for a function as obsolete:

`set-advertised-calling-convention` *function signature when*   [Function]
> This function specifies the argument list *signature* as the correct way to call *function*. This causes the Emacs byte compiler to issue a warning whenever it comes across an Emacs Lisp program that calls *function* any other way (however, it will still allow the code to be byte compiled). *when* should be a string indicating when the variable was first made obsolete (usually a version number string).
>
> For instance, in old versions of Emacs the `sit-for` function accepted three arguments, like this
>
>   (sit-for seconds milliseconds nodisp)
>
> However, calling `sit-for` this way is considered obsolete (see Section 20.10 [Waiting], page 382). The old calling convention is deprecated like this:
>
>   (set-advertised-calling-convention

```
'sit-for '(seconds &optional nodisp) "22.1")
```

12.13 Inline Functions

An *inline function* is a function that works just like an ordinary function, except for one thing: when you byte-compile a call to the function (see Chapter 16 [Byte Compilation], page 260), the function's definition is expanded into the caller. To define an inline function, use `defsubst` instead of `defun`.

`defsubst` *name args* [*doc*] [*declare*] [*interactive*] *body...*   [Macro]
>   This macro defines an inline function. Its syntax is exactly the same as `defun` (see Section 12.4 [Defining Functions], page 192).

Making a function inline often makes its function calls run faster. But it also has disadvantages. For one thing, it reduces flexibility; if you change the definition of the function, calls already inlined still use the old definition until you recompile them.

Another disadvantage is that making a large function inline can increase the size of compiled code both in files and in memory. Since the speed advantage of inline functions is greatest for small functions, you generally should not make large functions inline.

Also, inline functions do not behave well with respect to debugging, tracing, and advising (see Section 12.11 [Advising Functions], page 204). Since ease of debugging and the flexibility of redefining functions are important features of Emacs, you should not make a function inline, even if it's small, unless its speed is really crucial, and you've timed the code to verify that using `defun` actually has performance problems.

After an inline function is defined, its inline expansion can be performed later on in the same file, just like macros.

It's possible to use `defsubst` to define a macro to expand into the same code that an inline function would execute (see Chapter 13 [Macros], page 217). But the macro would be limited to direct use in expressions—a macro cannot be called with `apply`, `mapcar` and so on. Also, it takes some work to convert an ordinary function into a macro. To convert it into an inline function is easy; just replace `defun` with `defsubst`. Since each argument of an inline function is evaluated exactly once, you needn't worry about how many times the body uses the arguments, as you do for macros.

As an alternative to `defsubst`, you can use `define-inline` to define functions via their exhaustive compiler macro. See Section 12.4 [Defining Functions], page 192.

12.14 The `declare` Form

`declare` is a special macro which can be used to add meta properties to a function or macro: for example, marking it as obsolete, or giving its forms a special `TAB` indentation convention in Emacs Lisp mode.

`declare` *specs...*   [Macro]
>   This macro ignores its arguments and evaluates to `nil`; it has no run-time effect. However, when a `declare` form occurs in the *declare* argument of a `defun` or `defsubst` function definition (see Section 12.4 [Defining Functions], page 192) or a `defmacro`

macro definition (see Section 13.4 [Defining Macros], page 219), it appends the properties specified by *specs* to the function or macro. This work is specially performed by `defun`, `defsubst`, and `defmacro`.

Each element in *specs* should have the form (*property args...*), which should not be quoted. These have the following effects:

`(advertised-calling-convention `*`signature when`*`)`

> This acts like a call to `set-advertised-calling-convention` (see Section 12.12 [Obsolete Functions], page 211); *signature* specifies the correct argument list for calling the function or macro, and *when* should be a string indicating when the old argument list was first made obsolete.

`(debug `*`edebug-form-spec`*`)`

> This is valid for macros only. When stepping through the macro with Edebug, use *edebug-form-spec*. See Section 17.2.15.1 [Instrumenting Macro Calls], page 292.

`(doc-string `*`n`*`)`

> This is used when defining a function or macro which itself will be used to define entities like functions, macros, or variables. It indicates that the *n*th argument, if any, should be considered as a documentation string.

`(indent `*`indent-spec`*`)`

> Indent calls to this function or macro according to *indent-spec*. This is typically used for macros, though it works for functions too. See Section 13.6 [Indenting Macros], page 224.

`(interactive-only `*`value`*`)`

> Set the function's `interactive-only` property to *value*. See [The interactive-only property], page 346.

`(obsolete `*`current-name when`*`)`

> Mark the function or macro as obsolete, similar to a call to `make-obsolete` (see Section 12.12 [Obsolete Functions], page 211). *current-name* should be a symbol (in which case the warning message says to use that instead), a string (specifying the warning message), or `nil` (in which case the warning message gives no extra details). *when* should be a string indicating when the function or macro was first made obsolete.

`(compiler-macro `*`expander`*`)`

> This can only be used for functions, and tells the compiler to use *expander* as an optimization function. When encountering a call to the function, of the form (*function args...*), the macro expander will call *expander* with that form as well as with *args...*, and *expander* can either return a new expression to use instead of the function call, or it can return just the form unchanged, to indicate that the function call should be left alone. *expander* can be a symbol, or it can be a form (`lambda (`*`arg`*`) ` *`body`*`)` in which case *arg* will hold the original function call expression, and the (unevaluated) arguments to the function can be accessed using the function's formal arguments.

> (gv-expander *expander*)
>> Declare *expander* to be the function to handle calls to the macro (or function) as a generalized variable, similarly to `gv-define-expander`. *expander* can be a symbol or it can be of the form (`lambda` (*arg*) *body*) in which case that function will additionally have access to the macro (or function)'s arguments.

> (gv-setter *setter*)
>> Declare *setter* to be the function to handle calls to the macro (or function) as a generalized variable. *setter* can be a symbol in which case it will be passed to `gv-define-simple-setter`, or it can be of the form (`lambda` (*arg*) *body*) in which case that function will additionally have access to the macro (or function)'s arguments and it will passed to `gv-define-setter`.

12.15 Telling the Compiler that a Function is Defined

Byte-compiling a file often produces warnings about functions that the compiler doesn't know about (see Section 16.6 [Compiler Errors], page 265). Sometimes this indicates a real problem, but usually the functions in question are defined in other files which would be loaded if that code is run. For example, byte-compiling `fortran.el` used to warn:

```
In end of data:
fortran.el:2152:1:Warning: the function 'gud-find-c-expr' is not
    known to be defined.
```

In fact, `gud-find-c-expr` is only used in the function that Fortran mode uses for the local value of `gud-find-expr-function`, which is a callback from GUD; if it is called, the GUD functions will be loaded. When you know that such a warning does not indicate a real problem, it is good to suppress the warning. That makes new warnings which might mean real problems more visible. You do that with `declare-function`.

All you need to do is add a `declare-function` statement before the first use of the function in question:

```
(declare-function gud-find-c-expr "gud.el" nil)
```

This says that `gud-find-c-expr` is defined in `gud.el` (the '.el' can be omitted). The compiler takes for granted that that file really defines the function, and does not check.

The optional third argument specifies the argument list of `gud-find-c-expr`. In this case, it takes no arguments (`nil` is different from not specifying a value). In other cases, this might be something like (`file &optional overwrite`). You don't have to specify the argument list, but if you do the byte compiler can check that the calls match the declaration.

declare-function *function file* **&optional** *arglist fileonly*   [Macro]
> Tell the byte compiler to assume that *function* is defined, with arguments *arglist*, and that the definition should come from the file *file*. *fileonly* non-`nil` means only check that *file* exists, not that it actually defines *function*.

To verify that these functions really are declared where `declare-function` says they are, use `check-declare-file` to check all `declare-function` calls in one source file, or use `check-declare-directory` check all the files in and under a certain directory.

These commands find the file that ought to contain a function's definition using `locate-library`; if that finds no file, they expand the definition file name relative to the directory of the file that contains the `declare-function` call.

You can also say that a function is a primitive by specifying a file name ending in '.c' or '.m'. This is useful only when you call a primitive that is defined only on certain systems. Most primitives are always defined, so they will never give you a warning.

Sometimes a file will optionally use functions from an external package. If you prefix the filename in the `declare-function` statement with 'ext:', then it will be checked if it is found, otherwise skipped without error.

There are some function definitions that 'check-declare' does not understand (e.g., `defstruct` and some other macros). In such cases, you can pass a non-`nil` *fileonly* argument to `declare-function`, meaning to only check that the file exists, not that it actually defines the function. Note that to do this without having to specify an argument list, you should set the *arglist* argument to `t` (because `nil` means an empty argument list, as opposed to an unspecified one).

12.16 Determining whether a Function is Safe to Call

Some major modes, such as SES, call functions that are stored in user files. (See Info file `ses`, node 'Top', for more information on SES.) User files sometimes have poor pedigrees—you can get a spreadsheet from someone you've just met, or you can get one through email from someone you've never met. So it is risky to call a function whose source code is stored in a user file until you have determined that it is safe.

unsafep *form* **&optional** *unsafep-vars* [Function]

> Returns `nil` if *form* is a *safe* Lisp expression, or returns a list that describes why it might be unsafe. The argument *unsafep-vars* is a list of symbols known to have temporary bindings at this point; it is mainly used for internal recursive calls. The current buffer is an implicit argument, which provides a list of buffer-local bindings.

Being quick and simple, `unsafep` does a very light analysis and rejects many Lisp expressions that are actually safe. There are no known cases where `unsafep` returns `nil` for an unsafe expression. However, a safe Lisp expression can return a string with a `display` property, containing an associated Lisp expression to be executed after the string is inserted into a buffer. This associated expression can be a virus. In order to be safe, you must delete properties from all strings calculated by user code before inserting them into buffers.

12.17 Other Topics Related to Functions

Here is a table of several functions that do things related to function calling and function definitions. They are documented elsewhere, but we provide cross references here.

apply   See Section 12.5 [Calling Functions], page 194.

autoload   See Section 15.5 [Autoload], page 249.

call-interactively
> See Section 20.3 [Interactive Call], page 352.

`called-interactively-p`
> See Section 20.4 [Distinguish Interactive], page 354.

`commandp`   See Section 20.3 [Interactive Call], page 352.

`documentation`
> See Section 23.2 [Accessing Documentation], page 486.

`eval`   See Section 9.4 [Eval], page 131.

`funcall`   See Section 12.5 [Calling Functions], page 194.

`function`   See Section 12.7 [Anonymous Functions], page 198.

`ignore`   See Section 12.5 [Calling Functions], page 194.

`indirect-function`
> See Section 9.1.4 [Function Indirection], page 126.

`interactive`
> See Section 20.2.1 [Using Interactive], page 346.

`interactive-p`
> See Section 20.4 [Distinguish Interactive], page 354.

`mapatoms`   See Section 8.3 [Creating Symbols], page 117.

`mapcar`   See Section 12.6 [Mapping Functions], page 196.

`map-char-table`
> See Section 6.6 [Char-Tables], page 104.

`mapconcat`
> See Section 12.6 [Mapping Functions], page 196.

`undefined`
> See Section 21.11 [Functions for Key Lookup], page 404.

13 Macros

Macros enable you to define new control constructs and other language features. A macro is defined much like a function, but instead of telling how to compute a value, it tells how to compute another Lisp expression which will in turn compute the value. We call this expression the *expansion* of the macro.

Macros can do this because they operate on the unevaluated expressions for the arguments, not on the argument values as functions do. They can therefore construct an expansion containing these argument expressions or parts of them.

If you are using a macro to do something an ordinary function could do, just for the sake of speed, consider using an inline function instead. See Section 12.13 [Inline Functions], page 212.

13.1 A Simple Example of a Macro

Suppose we would like to define a Lisp construct to increment a variable value, much like the ++ operator in C. We would like to write (inc x) and have the effect of (setq x (1+ x)). Here's a macro definition that does the job:

```
(defmacro inc (var)
  (list 'setq var (list '1+ var)))
```

When this is called with (inc x), the argument *var* is the symbol x—*not* the *value* of x, as it would be in a function. The body of the macro uses this to construct the expansion, which is (setq x (1+ x)). Once the macro definition returns this expansion, Lisp proceeds to evaluate it, thus incrementing x.

macrop *object* [Function]
> This predicate tests whether its argument is a macro, and returns t if so, nil otherwise.

13.2 Expansion of a Macro Call

A macro call looks just like a function call in that it is a list which starts with the name of the macro. The rest of the elements of the list are the arguments of the macro.

Evaluation of the macro call begins like evaluation of a function call except for one crucial difference: the macro arguments are the actual expressions appearing in the macro call. They are not evaluated before they are given to the macro definition. By contrast, the arguments of a function are results of evaluating the elements of the function call list.

Having obtained the arguments, Lisp invokes the macro definition just as a function is invoked. The argument variables of the macro are bound to the argument values from the macro call, or to a list of them in the case of a &rest argument. And the macro body executes and returns its value just as a function body does.

The second crucial difference between macros and functions is that the value returned by the macro body is an alternate Lisp expression, also known as the *expansion* of the macro. The Lisp interpreter proceeds to evaluate the expansion as soon as it comes back from the macro.

Since the expansion is evaluated in the normal manner, it may contain calls to other macros. It may even be a call to the same macro, though this is unusual.

Note that Emacs tries to expand macros when loading an uncompiled Lisp file. This is not always possible, but if it is, it speeds up subsequent execution. See Section 15.1 [How Programs Do Loading], page 244.

You can see the expansion of a given macro call by calling `macroexpand`.

macroexpand *form &optional environment*   [Function]

> This function expands *form*, if it is a macro call. If the result is another macro call, it is expanded in turn, until something which is not a macro call results. That is the value returned by `macroexpand`. If *form* is not a macro call to begin with, it is returned as given.
>
> Note that `macroexpand` does not look at the subexpressions of *form* (although some macro definitions may do so). Even if they are macro calls themselves, `macroexpand` does not expand them.
>
> The function `macroexpand` does not expand calls to inline functions. Normally there is no need for that, since a call to an inline function is no harder to understand than a call to an ordinary function.
>
> If *environment* is provided, it specifies an alist of macro definitions that shadow the currently defined macros. Byte compilation uses this feature.
>
> ```
> (defmacro inc (var)
>     (list 'setq var (list '1+ var)))
>
> (macroexpand '(inc r))
>     ⇒ (setq r (1+ r))
>
> (defmacro inc2 (var1 var2)
>     (list 'progn (list 'inc var1) (list 'inc var2)))
>
> (macroexpand '(inc2 r s))
>     ⇒ (progn (inc r) (inc s))   ; inc not expanded here.
> ```

macroexpand-all *form &optional environment*   [Function]

> `macroexpand-all` expands macros like `macroexpand`, but will look for and expand all macros in *form*, not just at the top-level. If no macros are expanded, the return value is `eq` to *form*.
>
> Repeating the example used for `macroexpand` above with `macroexpand-all`, we see that `macroexpand-all` *does* expand the embedded calls to `inc`:
>
> ```
> (macroexpand-all '(inc2 r s))
>     ⇒ (progn (setq r (1+ r)) (setq s (1+ s)))
> ```

macroexpand-1 *form &optional environment*   [Function]

> This function expands macros like `macroexpand`, but it only performs one step of the expansion: if the result is another macro call, `macroexpand-1` will not expand it.

13.3 Macros and Byte Compilation

You might ask why we take the trouble to compute an expansion for a macro and then evaluate the expansion. Why not have the macro body produce the desired results directly? The reason has to do with compilation.

When a macro call appears in a Lisp program being compiled, the Lisp compiler calls the macro definition just as the interpreter would, and receives an expansion. But instead of evaluating this expansion, it compiles the expansion as if it had appeared directly in the program. As a result, the compiled code produces the value and side effects intended for the macro, but executes at full compiled speed. This would not work if the macro body computed the value and side effects itself—they would be computed at compile time, which is not useful.

In order for compilation of macro calls to work, the macros must already be defined in Lisp when the calls to them are compiled. The compiler has a special feature to help you do this: if a file being compiled contains a `defmacro` form, the macro is defined temporarily for the rest of the compilation of that file.

Byte-compiling a file also executes any `require` calls at top-level in the file, so you can ensure that necessary macro definitions are available during compilation by requiring the files that define them (see Section 15.7 [Named Features], page 253). To avoid loading the macro definition files when someone *runs* the compiled program, write `eval-when-compile` around the `require` calls (see Section 16.5 [Eval During Compile], page 264).

13.4 Defining Macros

A Lisp macro object is a list whose CAR is `macro`, and whose CDR is a function. Expansion of the macro works by applying the function (with `apply`) to the list of *unevaluated* arguments from the macro call.

It is possible to use an anonymous Lisp macro just like an anonymous function, but this is never done, because it does not make sense to pass an anonymous macro to functionals such as `mapcar`. In practice, all Lisp macros have names, and they are almost always defined with the `defmacro` macro.

defmacro *name args* [*doc*] [*declare*] *body...*   [Macro]
    `defmacro` defines the symbol *name* (which should not be quoted) as a macro that looks like this:

        `(macro lambda `*args*` . `*body*`)`

    (Note that the CDR of this list is a lambda expression.) This macro object is stored in the function cell of *name*. The meaning of *args* is the same as in a function, and the keywords `&rest` and `&optional` may be used (see Section 12.2.3 [Argument List], page 189). Neither *name* nor *args* should be quoted. The return value of `defmacro` is undefined.

    doc, if present, should be a string specifying the macro's documentation string. *declare*, if present, should be a `declare` form specifying metadata for the macro (see Section 12.14 [Declare Form], page 212). Note that macros cannot have interactive declarations, since they cannot be called interactively.

Macros often need to construct large list structures from a mixture of constants and nonconstant parts. To make this easier, use the '`' syntax (see Section 9.3 [Backquote], page 130). For example:

```
(defmacro t-becomes-nil (variable)
  `(if (eq ,variable t)
       (setq ,variable nil)))

(t-becomes-nil foo)
     ≡ (if (eq foo t) (setq foo nil))
```

13.5 Common Problems Using Macros

Macro expansion can have counterintuitive consequences. This section describes some important consequences that can lead to trouble, and rules to follow to avoid trouble.

13.5.1 Wrong Time

The most common problem in writing macros is doing some of the real work prematurely—while expanding the macro, rather than in the expansion itself. For instance, one real package had this macro definition:

```
(defmacro my-set-buffer-multibyte (arg)
  (if (fboundp 'set-buffer-multibyte)
      (set-buffer-multibyte arg)))
```

With this erroneous macro definition, the program worked fine when interpreted but failed when compiled. This macro definition called `set-buffer-multibyte` during compilation, which was wrong, and then did nothing when the compiled package was run. The definition that the programmer really wanted was this:

```
(defmacro my-set-buffer-multibyte (arg)
  (if (fboundp 'set-buffer-multibyte)
      `(set-buffer-multibyte ,arg)))
```

This macro expands, if appropriate, into a call to `set-buffer-multibyte` that will be executed when the compiled program is actually run.

13.5.2 Evaluating Macro Arguments Repeatedly

When defining a macro you must pay attention to the number of times the arguments will be evaluated when the expansion is executed. The following macro (used to facilitate iteration) illustrates the problem. This macro allows us to write a for-loop construct.

```
(defmacro for (var from init to final do &rest body)
  "Execute a simple \"for\" loop.
For example, (for i from 1 to 10 do (print i))."
  (list 'let (list (list var init))
        (cons 'while
              (cons (list '<= var final)
                    (append body (list (list 'inc var)))))))
```

```
(for i from 1 to 3 do
   (setq square (* i i))
   (princ (format "\n%d %d" i square)))
↦
(let ((i 1))
  (while (<= i 3)
    (setq square (* i i))
    (princ (format "\n%d %d" i square))
    (inc i)))

     ⊣1        1
     ⊣2        4
     ⊣3        9
⇒ nil
```

The arguments `from`, `to`, and `do` in this macro are syntactic sugar; they are entirely ignored. The idea is that you will write noise words (such as `from`, `to`, and `do`) in those positions in the macro call.

Here's an equivalent definition simplified through use of backquote:

```
(defmacro for (var from init to final do &rest body)
  "Execute a simple \"for\" loop.
For example, (for i from 1 to 10 do (print i))."
  `(let ((,var ,init))
     (while (<= ,var ,final)
       ,@body
       (inc ,var))))
```

Both forms of this definition (with backquote and without) suffer from the defect that *final* is evaluated on every iteration. If *final* is a constant, this is not a problem. If it is a more complex form, say `(long-complex-calculation x)`, this can slow down the execution significantly. If *final* has side effects, executing it more than once is probably incorrect.

A well-designed macro definition takes steps to avoid this problem by producing an expansion that evaluates the argument expressions exactly once unless repeated evaluation is part of the intended purpose of the macro. Here is a correct expansion for the **for** macro:

```
(let ((i 1)
      (max 3))
  (while (<= i max)
    (setq square (* i i))
    (princ (format "%d      %d" i square))
    (inc i)))
```

Here is a macro definition that creates this expansion:

```
(defmacro for (var from init to final do &rest body)
  "Execute a simple for loop: (for i from 1 to 10 do (print i))."
  `(let ((,var ,init)
         (max ,final))
     (while (<= ,var max)
       ,@body
       (inc ,var))))
```

Unfortunately, this fix introduces another problem, described in the following section.

13.5.3 Local Variables in Macro Expansions

The new definition of for has a new problem: it introduces a local variable named max which the user does not expect. This causes trouble in examples such as the following:

```
(let ((max 0))
  (for x from 0 to 10 do
    (let ((this (frob x)))
      (if (< max this)
          (setq max this)))))
```

The references to max inside the body of the for, which are supposed to refer to the user's binding of max, really access the binding made by for.

The way to correct this is to use an uninterned symbol instead of max (see Section 8.3 [Creating Symbols], page 117). The uninterned symbol can be bound and referred to just like any other symbol, but since it is created by for, we know that it cannot already appear in the user's program. Since it is not interned, there is no way the user can put it into the program later. It will never appear anywhere except where put by for. Here is a definition of for that works this way:

```
(defmacro for (var from init to final do &rest body)
  "Execute a simple for loop: (for i from 1 to 10 do (print i))."
  (let ((tempvar (make-symbol "max")))
    `(let ((,var ,init)
           (,tempvar ,final))
       (while (<= ,var ,tempvar)
         ,@body
         (inc ,var)))))
```

This creates an uninterned symbol named max and puts it in the expansion instead of the usual interned symbol max that appears in expressions ordinarily.

13.5.4 Evaluating Macro Arguments in Expansion

Another problem can happen if the macro definition itself evaluates any of the macro argument expressions, such as by calling eval (see Section 9.4 [Eval], page 131). If the argument is supposed to refer to the user's variables, you may have trouble if the user happens to use a variable with the same name as one of the macro arguments. Inside the macro body, the macro argument binding is the most local binding of this variable, so any references inside the form being evaluated do refer to it. Here is an example:

```
(defmacro foo (a)
  (list 'setq (eval a) t))
```

```
(setq x 'b)
(foo x) ↦ (setq b t)
     ⇒ t                      ; and b has been set.
;; but
(setq a 'c)
(foo a) ↦ (setq a t)
     ⇒ t                      ; but this set a, not c.
```

It makes a difference whether the user's variable is named **a** or **x**, because **a** conflicts with the macro argument variable **a**.

Another problem with calling `eval` in a macro definition is that it probably won't do what you intend in a compiled program. The byte compiler runs macro definitions while compiling the program, when the program's own computations (which you might have wished to access with `eval`) don't occur and its local variable bindings don't exist.

To avoid these problems, **don't evaluate an argument expression while computing the macro expansion**. Instead, substitute the expression into the macro expansion, so that its value will be computed as part of executing the expansion. This is how the other examples in this chapter work.

13.5.5 How Many Times is the Macro Expanded?

Occasionally problems result from the fact that a macro call is expanded each time it is evaluated in an interpreted function, but is expanded only once (during compilation) for a compiled function. If the macro definition has side effects, they will work differently depending on how many times the macro is expanded.

Therefore, you should avoid side effects in computation of the macro expansion, unless you really know what you are doing.

One special kind of side effect can't be avoided: constructing Lisp objects. Almost all macro expansions include constructed lists; that is the whole point of most macros. This is usually safe; there is just one case where you must be careful: when the object you construct is part of a quoted constant in the macro expansion.

If the macro is expanded just once, in compilation, then the object is constructed just once, during compilation. But in interpreted execution, the macro is expanded each time the macro call runs, and this means a new object is constructed each time.

In most clean Lisp code, this difference won't matter. It can matter only if you perform side-effects on the objects constructed by the macro definition. Thus, to avoid trouble, **avoid side effects on objects constructed by macro definitions**. Here is an example of how such side effects can get you into trouble:

```
(defmacro empty-object ()
  (list 'quote (cons nil nil)))

(defun initialize (condition)
  (let ((object (empty-object)))
    (if condition
        (setcar object condition))
    object))
```

If `initialize` is interpreted, a new list `(nil)` is constructed each time `initialize` is called. Thus, no side effect survives between calls. If `initialize` is compiled, then the macro `empty-object` is expanded during compilation, producing a single constant `(nil)` that is reused and altered each time `initialize` is called.

One way to avoid pathological cases like this is to think of `empty-object` as a funny kind of constant, not as a memory allocation construct. You wouldn't use `setcar` on a constant such as `'(nil)`, so naturally you won't use it on `(empty-object)` either.

13.6 Indenting Macros

Within a macro definition, you can use the `declare` form (see Section 13.4 [Defining Macros], page 219) to specify how `TAB` should indent calls to the macro. An indentation specification is written like this:

        (declare (indent *indent-spec*))

This results in the `lisp-indent-function` property being set on the macro name.

Here are the possibilities for *indent-spec*:

nil   This is the same as no property—use the standard indentation pattern.

defun   Handle this function like a 'def' construct: treat the second line as the start of
            a *body*.

an integer, *number*

            The first *number* arguments of the function are *distinguished* arguments; the
            rest are considered the body of the expression. A line in the expression is
            indented according to whether the first argument on it is distinguished or not.
            If the argument is part of the body, the line is indented `lisp-body-indent`
            more columns than the open-parenthesis starting the containing expression. If
            the argument is distinguished and is either the first or second argument, it is
            indented *twice* that many extra columns. If the argument is distinguished and
            not the first or second argument, the line uses the standard pattern.

a symbol, *symbol*

            symbol should be a function name; that function is called to calculate the in-
            dentation of a line within this expression. The function receives two arguments:

            pos   The position at which the line being indented begins.

            state   The value returned by `parse-partial-sexp` (a Lisp primitive for
                        indentation and nesting computation) when it parses up to the
                        beginning of this line.

            It should return either a number, which is the number of columns of indentation
            for that line, or a list whose car is such a number. The difference between
            returning a number and returning a list is that a number says that all following
            lines at the same nesting level should be indented just like this one; a list says
            that following lines might call for different indentations. This makes a difference
            when the indentation is being computed by *C-M-q*; if the value is a number,
            C-M-q need not recalculate indentation for the following lines until the end of
            the list.

14 Customization Settings

Users of Emacs can customize variables and faces without writing Lisp code, by using the Customize interface. See Section "Easy Customization" in *The GNU Emacs Manual*. This chapter describes how to define *customization items* that users can interact with through the Customize interface.

Customization items include customizable variables, which are defined with the `defcustom` macro; customizable faces, which are defined with `defface` (described separately in Section 37.12.2 [Defining Faces], page 918); and *customization groups*, defined with `defgroup`, which act as containers for groups of related customization items.

14.1 Common Item Keywords

The customization declarations that we will describe in the next few sections—`defcustom`, `defgroup`, etc.—all accept keyword arguments (see Section 11.2 [Constant Variables], page 157) for specifying various information. This section describes keywords that apply to all types of customization declarations.

All of these keywords, except `:tag`, can be used more than once in a given item. Each use of the keyword has an independent effect. The keyword `:tag` is an exception because any given item can only display one name.

`:tag label`

> Use *label*, a string, instead of the item's name, to label the item in customization menus and buffers. **Don't use a tag which is substantially different from the item's real name; that would cause confusion.**

`:group group`

> Put this customization item in group *group*. If this keyword is missing from a customization item, it'll be placed in the same group that was last defined (in the current file).
>
> When you use `:group` in a `defgroup`, it makes the new group a subgroup of *group*.
>
> If you use this keyword more than once, you can put a single item into more than one group. Displaying any of those groups will show this item. Please don't overdo this, since the result would be annoying.

`:link link-data`

> Include an external link after the documentation string for this item. This is a sentence containing a button that references some other documentation.
>
> There are several alternatives you can use for *link-data*:
>
> `(custom-manual info-node)`
>
> > Link to an Info node; *info-node* is a string which specifies the node name, as in `"(emacs)Top"`. The link appears as '[Manual]' in the customization buffer and enters the built-in Info reader on *info-node*.
>
> `(info-link info-node)`
>
> > Like `custom-manual` except that the link appears in the customization buffer with the Info node name.

> (url-link *url*)
>> Link to a web page; *url* is a string which specifies the URL. The link appears in the customization buffer as *url* and invokes the WWW browser specified by `browse-url-browser-function`.
>
> (emacs-commentary-link *library*)
>> Link to the commentary section of a library; *library* is a string which specifies the library name. See Section D.8 [Library Headers], page 1063.
>
> (emacs-library-link *library*)
>> Link to an Emacs Lisp library file; *library* is a string which specifies the library name.
>
> (file-link *file*)
>> Link to a file; *file* is a string which specifies the name of the file to visit with `find-file` when the user invokes this link.
>
> (function-link *function*)
>> Link to the documentation of a function; *function* is a string which specifies the name of the function to describe with `describe-function` when the user invokes this link.
>
> (variable-link *variable*)
>> Link to the documentation of a variable; *variable* is a string which specifies the name of the variable to describe with `describe-variable` when the user invokes this link.
>
> (custom-group-link *group*)
>> Link to another customization group. Invoking it creates a new customization buffer for *group*.

> You can specify the text to use in the customization buffer by adding `:tag` *name* after the first element of the *link-data*; for example, (`info-link :tag "foo"` `"(emacs)Top"`) makes a link to the Emacs manual which appears in the buffer as 'foo'.

> You can use this keyword more than once, to add multiple links.

`:load` *file*

> Load file *file* (a string) before displaying this customization item (see Chapter 15 [Loading], page 244). Loading is done with `load`, and only if the file is not already loaded.

`:require` *feature*

> Execute (`require '`*feature*) when your saved customizations set the value of this item. *feature* should be a symbol.

> The most common reason to use `:require` is when a variable enables a feature such as a minor mode, and just setting the variable won't have any effect unless the code which implements the mode is loaded.

`:version` *version*

> This keyword specifies that the item was first introduced in Emacs version *version*, or that its default value was changed in that version. The value *version* must be a string.

`:package-version '(`*package* `. `*version*`)`

> This keyword specifies that the item was first introduced in *package* version *version*, or that its meaning or default value was changed in that version. This keyword takes priority over `:version`.
>
> *package* should be the official name of the package, as a symbol (e.g., MH-E). *version* should be a string. If the package *package* is released as part of Emacs, *package* and *version* should appear in the value of `customize-package-emacs-version-alist`.

Packages distributed as part of Emacs that use the `:package-version` keyword must also update the `customize-package-emacs-version-alist` variable.

`customize-package-emacs-version-alist`   [Variable]

> This alist provides a mapping for the versions of Emacs that are associated with versions of a package listed in the `:package-version` keyword. Its elements are:
>
> > (*package* (*pversion* . *eversion*)...)
>
> For each *package*, which is a symbol, there are one or more elements that contain a package version *pversion* with an associated Emacs version *eversion*. These versions are strings. For example, the MH-E package updates this alist with the following:
>
> ```
> (add-to-list 'customize-package-emacs-version-alist
>              '(MH-E ("6.0" . "22.1") ("6.1" . "22.1") ("7.0" . "22.1")
>                     ("7.1" . "22.1") ("7.2" . "22.1") ("7.3" . "22.1")
>                     ("7.4" . "22.1") ("8.0" . "22.1")))
> ```
>
> The value of *package* needs to be unique and it needs to match the *package* value appearing in the `:package-version` keyword. Since the user might see the value in an error message, a good choice is the official name of the package, such as MH-E or Gnus.

14.2 Defining Customization Groups

Each Emacs Lisp package should have one main customization group which contains all the options, faces and other groups in the package. If the package has a small number of options and faces, use just one group and put everything in it. When there are more than twenty or so options and faces, then you should structure them into subgroups, and put the subgroups under the package's main customization group. It is OK to put some of the options and faces in the package's main group alongside the subgroups.

The package's main or only group should be a member of one or more of the standard customization groups. (To display the full list of them, use *M-x customize*.) Choose one or more of them (but not too many), and add your group to each of them using the `:group` keyword.

The way to declare new customization groups is with `defgroup`.

defgroup *group members doc [keyword value]. . .*   [Macro]
> Declare *group* as a customization group containing *members*. Do not quote the symbol *group*. The argument *doc* specifies the documentation string for the group.
>
> The argument *members* is a list specifying an initial set of customization items to be members of the group. However, most often *members* is **nil**, and you specify the group's members by using the **:group** keyword when defining those members.
>
> If you want to specify group members through *members*, each element should have the form (**name widget**). Here *name* is a symbol, and *widget* is a widget type for editing that symbol. Useful widgets are **custom-variable** for a variable, **custom-face** for a face, and **custom-group** for a group.
>
> When you introduce a new group into Emacs, use the **:version** keyword in the **defgroup**; then you need not use it for the individual members of the group.
>
> In addition to the common keywords (see Section 14.1 [Common Keywords], page 225), you can also use this keyword in **defgroup**:
>
> **:prefix** *prefix*
>> If the name of an item in the group starts with *prefix*, and the customizable variable **custom-unlispify-remove-prefixes** is non-**nil**, the item's tag will omit *prefix*. A group can have any number of prefixes.

custom-unlispify-remove-prefixes   [User Option]
> If this variable is non-**nil**, the prefixes specified by a group's **:prefix** keyword are omitted from tag names, whenever the user customizes the group.
>
> The default value is **nil**, i.e., the prefix-discarding feature is disabled. This is because discarding prefixes often leads to confusing names for options and faces.

14.3 Defining Customization Variables

Customizable variables, also called *user options*, are global Lisp variables whose values can be set through the Customize interface. Unlike other global variables, which are defined with **defvar** (see Section 11.5 [Defining Variables], page 161), customizable variables are defined using the **defcustom** macro. In addition to calling **defvar** as a subroutine, **defcustom** states how the variable should be displayed in the Customize interface, the values it is allowed to take, etc.

defcustom *option standard doc [keyword value]. . .*   [Macro]
> This macro declares *option* as a user option (i.e., a customizable variable). You should not quote *option*.
>
> The argument *standard* is an expression that specifies the standard value for *option*. Evaluating the **defcustom** form evaluates *standard*, but does not necessarily bind the option to that value. If *option* already has a default value, it is left unchanged. If the user has already saved a customization for *option*, the user's customized value is installed as the default value. Otherwise, the result of evaluating *standard* is installed as the default value.
>
> Like **defvar**, this macro marks **option** as a special variable, meaning that it should always be dynamically bound. If *option* is already lexically bound, that lexical binding

remains in effect until the binding construct exits. See Section 11.9 [Variable Scoping], page 166.

The expression *standard* can be evaluated at various other times, too—whenever the customization facility needs to know *option*'s standard value. So be sure to use an expression which is harmless to evaluate at any time.

The argument *doc* specifies the documentation string for the variable.

If a `defcustom` does not specify any `:group`, the last group defined with `defgroup` in the same file will be used. This way, most `defcustom` do not need an explicit `:group`.

When you evaluate a `defcustom` form with `C-M-x` in Emacs Lisp mode (`eval-defun`), a special feature of `eval-defun` arranges to set the variable unconditionally, without testing whether its value is void. (The same feature applies to `defvar`, see Section 11.5 [Defining Variables], page 161.) Using `eval-defun` on a defcustom that is already defined calls the `:set` function (see below), if there is one.

If you put a `defcustom` in a pre-loaded Emacs Lisp file (see Section E.1 [Building Emacs], page 1067), the standard value installed at dump time might be incorrect, e.g., because another variable that it depends on has not been assigned the right value yet. In that case, use `custom-reevaluate-setting`, described below, to re-evaluate the standard value after Emacs starts up.

In addition to the keywords listed in Section 14.1 [Common Keywords], page 225, this macro accepts the following keywords:

`:type` *type*

> Use *type* as the data type for this option. It specifies which values are legitimate, and how to display the value (see Section 14.4 [Customization Types], page 232). Every `defcustom` should specify a value for this keyword.

`:options` *value-list*

> Specify the list of reasonable values for use in this option. The user is not restricted to using only these values, but they are offered as convenient alternatives.
>
> This is meaningful only for certain types, currently including `hook`, `plist` and `alist`. See the definition of the individual types for a description of how to use `:options`.

`:set` *setfunction*

> Specify *setfunction* as the way to change the value of this option when using the Customize interface. The function *setfunction* should take two arguments, a symbol (the option name) and the new value, and should do whatever is necessary to update the value properly for this option (which may not mean simply setting the option as a Lisp variable); preferably, though, it should not modify its value argument destructively. The default for *setfunction* is `set-default`.
>
> If you specify this keyword, the variable's documentation string should describe how to do the same job in hand-written Lisp code.

`:get` *getfunction*

> Specify *getfunction* as the way to extract the value of this option. The function *getfunction* should take one argument, a symbol, and should return whatever

customize should use as the current value for that symbol (which need not be the symbol's Lisp value). The default is `default-value`.

You have to really understand the workings of Custom to use `:get` correctly. It is meant for values that are treated in Custom as variables but are not actually stored in Lisp variables. It is almost surely a mistake to specify *getfunction* for a value that really is stored in a Lisp variable.

`:initialize` *function*

> *function* should be a function used to initialize the variable when the `defcustom` is evaluated. It should take two arguments, the option name (a symbol) and the value. Here are some predefined functions meant for use in this way:

> `custom-initialize-set`
>
>> Use the variable's `:set` function to initialize the variable, but do not reinitialize it if it is already non-void.

> `custom-initialize-default`
>
>> Like `custom-initialize-set`, but use the function `set-default` to set the variable, instead of the variable's `:set` function. This is the usual choice for a variable whose `:set` function enables or disables a minor mode; with this choice, defining the variable will not call the minor mode function, but customizing the variable will do so.

> `custom-initialize-reset`
>
>> Always use the `:set` function to initialize the variable. If the variable is already non-void, reset it by calling the `:set` function using the current value (returned by the `:get` method). This is the default `:initialize` function.

> `custom-initialize-changed`
>
>> Use the `:set` function to initialize the variable, if it is already set or has been customized; otherwise, just use `set-default`.

> `custom-initialize-safe-set`
> `custom-initialize-safe-default`
>
>> These functions behave like `custom-initialize-set` (`custom-initialize-default`, respectively), but catch errors. If an error occurs during initialization, they set the variable to `nil` using `set-default`, and signal no error.
>>
>> These functions are meant for options defined in pre-loaded files, where the *standard* expression may signal an error because some required variable or function is not yet defined. The value normally gets updated in `startup.el`, ignoring the value computed by `defcustom`. After startup, if one unsets the value and reevaluates the `defcustom`, the *standard* expression can be evaluated without error.

`:risky` *value*

> Set the variable's `risky-local-variable` property to *value* (see Section 11.11 [File Local Variables], page 177).

:safe *function*

>   Set the variable's `safe-local-variable` property to *function* (see Section 11.11 [File Local Variables], page 177).

:set-after *variables*

>   When setting variables according to saved customizations, make sure to set the variables *variables* before this one; i.e., delay setting this variable until after those others have been handled. Use :set-after if setting this variable won't work properly unless those other variables already have their intended values.

It is useful to specify the :require keyword for an option that turns on a certain feature. This causes Emacs to load the feature, if it is not already loaded, whenever the option is set. See Section 14.1 [Common Keywords], page 225. Here is an example, from the library `saveplace.el`:

```
(defcustom save-place nil
  "Non-nil means automatically save place in each file..."
  :type 'boolean
  :require 'saveplace
  :group 'save-place)
```

If a customization item has a type such as `hook` or `alist`, which supports :options, you can add additional values to the list from outside the `defcustom` declaration by calling `custom-add-frequent-value`. For example, if you define a function `my-lisp-mode-initialization` intended to be called from `emacs-lisp-mode-hook`, you might want to add that to the list of reasonable values for `emacs-lisp-mode-hook`, but not by editing its definition. You can do it thus:

```
(custom-add-frequent-value 'emacs-lisp-mode-hook
  'my-lisp-mode-initialization)
```

custom-add-frequent-value *symbol value*   [Function]

>   For the customization option *symbol*, add *value* to the list of reasonable values.

>   The precise effect of adding a value depends on the customization type of *symbol*.

Internally, `defcustom` uses the symbol property `standard-value` to record the expression for the standard value, `saved-value` to record the value saved by the user with the customization buffer, and `customized-value` to record the value set by the user with the customization buffer, but not saved. See Section 8.4 [Symbol Properties], page 119. These properties are lists, the car of which is an expression that evaluates to the value.

custom-reevaluate-setting *symbol*   [Function]

>   This function re-evaluates the standard value of *symbol*, which should be a user option declared via `defcustom`. If the variable was customized, this function re-evaluates the saved value instead. Then it sets the user option to that value (using the option's :set property if that is defined).

>   This is useful for customizable options that are defined before their value could be computed correctly. For example, during startup Emacs calls this function for some user options that were defined in pre-loaded Emacs Lisp files, but whose initial values depend on information available only at run-time.

custom-variable-p *arg* [Function]

This function returns non-**nil** if *arg* is a customizable variable. A customizable variable is either a variable that has a **standard-value** or **custom-autoload** property (usually meaning it was declared with **defcustom**), or an alias for another customizable variable.

14.4 Customization Types

When you define a user option with **defcustom**, you must specify its *customization type*. That is a Lisp object which describes (1) which values are legitimate and (2) how to display the value in the customization buffer for editing.

You specify the customization type in **defcustom** with the **:type** keyword. The argument of **:type** is evaluated, but only once when the **defcustom** is executed, so it isn't useful for the value to vary. Normally we use a quoted constant. For example:

```
(defcustom diff-command "diff"
  "The command to use to run diff."
  :type '(string)
  :group 'diff)
```

In general, a customization type is a list whose first element is a symbol, one of the customization type names defined in the following sections. After this symbol come a number of arguments, depending on the symbol. Between the type symbol and its arguments, you can optionally write keyword-value pairs (see Section 14.4.4 [Type Keywords], page 238).

Some type symbols do not use any arguments; those are called *simple types*. For a simple type, if you do not use any keyword-value pairs, you can omit the parentheses around the type symbol. For example just **string** as a customization type is equivalent to (**string**).

All customization types are implemented as widgets; see Section "Introduction" in *The Emacs Widget Library*, for details.

14.4.1 Simple Types

This section describes all the simple customization types. For several of these customization types, the customization widget provides inline completion with *C-M-i* or *M-TAB*.

sexp   The value may be any Lisp object that can be printed and read back. You can use **sexp** as a fall-back for any option, if you don't want to take the time to work out a more specific type to use.

integer   The value must be an integer.

number   The value must be a number (floating point or integer).

float   The value must be floating point.

string   The value must be a string. The customization buffer shows the string without delimiting '"' characters or '\' quotes.

regexp   Like **string** except that the string must be a valid regular expression.

character

The value must be a character code. A character code is actually an integer, but this type shows the value by inserting the character in the buffer, rather than by showing the number.

file   The value must be a file name. The widget provides completion.

(file :must-match t)

The value must be a file name for an existing file. The widget provides completion.

directory

The value must be a directory name. The widget provides completion.

hook   The value must be a list of functions. This customization type is used for hook variables. You can use the :options keyword in a hook variable's defcustom to specify a list of functions recommended for use in the hook; See Section 14.3 [Variable Definitions], page 228.

symbol   The value must be a symbol. It appears in the customization buffer as the symbol name. The widget provides completion.

function   The value must be either a lambda expression or a function name. The widget provides completion for function names.

variable   The value must be a variable name. The widget provides completion.

face   The value must be a symbol which is a face name. The widget provides completion.

boolean   The value is boolean—either nil or t. Note that by using choice and const together (see the next section), you can specify that the value must be nil or t, but also specify the text to describe each value in a way that fits the specific meaning of the alternative.

key-sequence

The value is a key sequence. The customization buffer shows the key sequence using the same syntax as the *kbd* function. See Section 21.1 [Key Sequences], page 391.

coding-system

The value must be a coding-system name, and you can do completion with *M-TAB*.

color   The value must be a valid color name. The widget provides completion for color names, as well as a sample and a button for selecting a color name from a list of color names shown in a *Colors* buffer.

14.4.2 Composite Types

When none of the simple types is appropriate, you can use composite types, which build new types from other types or from specified data. The specified types or data are called the *arguments* of the composite type. The composite type normally looks like this:

        (constructor arguments...)

but you can also add keyword-value pairs before the arguments, like this:

        (constructor {keyword value}... arguments...)

Here is a table of constructors and how to use them to write composite types:

(cons `car-type` `cdr-type`)

> The value must be a cons cell, its CAR must fit `car-type`, and its CDR must fit `cdr-type`. For example, (cons string symbol) is a customization type which matches values such as ("foo" . foo).
>
> In the customization buffer, the CAR and CDR are displayed and edited separately, each according to their specified type.

(list `element-types`...)

> The value must be a list with exactly as many elements as the `element-types` given; and each element must fit the corresponding `element-type`.
>
> For example, (list integer string function) describes a list of three elements; the first element must be an integer, the second a string, and the third a function.
>
> In the customization buffer, each element is displayed and edited separately, according to the type specified for it.

(group `element-types`...)

> This works like list except for the formatting of text in the Custom buffer. list labels each element value with its tag; group does not.

(vector `element-types`...)

> Like list except that the value must be a vector instead of a list. The elements work the same as in list.

(alist :key-type `key-type` :value-type `value-type`)

> The value must be a list of cons-cells, the CAR of each cell representing a key of customization type `key-type`, and the CDR of the same cell representing a value of customization type `value-type`. The user can add and delete key/value pairs, and edit both the key and the value of each pair.
>
> If omitted, `key-type` and `value-type` default to sexp.
>
> The user can add any key matching the specified key type, but you can give some keys a preferential treatment by specifying them with the :options (see Section 14.3 [Variable Definitions], page 228). The specified keys will always be shown in the customize buffer (together with a suitable value), with a checkbox to include or exclude or disable the key/value pair from the alist. The user will not be able to edit the keys specified by the :options keyword argument.
>
> The argument to the :options keywords should be a list of specifications for reasonable keys in the alist. Ordinarily, they are simply atoms, which stand for themselves. For example:
>
>   :options '("foo" "bar" "baz")
>
> specifies that there are three known keys, namely "foo", "bar" and "baz", which will always be shown first.
>
> You may want to restrict the value type for specific keys, for example, the value associated with the "bar" key can only be an integer. You can specify this by using a list instead of an atom in the list. The first element will specify the key, like before, while the second element will specify the value type. For example:

```
:options '("foo" ("bar" integer) "baz")
```

Finally, you may want to change how the key is presented. By default, the key is simply shown as a `const`, since the user cannot change the special keys specified with the `:options` keyword. However, you may want to use a more specialized type for presenting the key, like `function-item` if you know it is a symbol with a function binding. This is done by using a customization type specification instead of a symbol for the key.

```
:options '("foo"
           ((function-item some-function) integer)
           "baz")
```

Many alists use lists with two elements, instead of cons cells. For example,

```
(defcustom list-alist
  '(("foo" 1) ("bar" 2) ("baz" 3))
  "Each element is a list of the form (KEY VALUE).")
```

instead of

```
(defcustom cons-alist
  '(("foo" . 1) ("bar" . 2) ("baz" . 3))
  "Each element is a cons-cell (KEY . VALUE).")
```

Because of the way lists are implemented on top of cons cells, you can treat `list-alist` in the example above as a cons cell alist, where the value type is a list with a single element containing the real value.

```
(defcustom list-alist '(("foo" 1) ("bar" 2) ("baz" 3))
  "Each element is a list of the form (KEY VALUE)."
  :type '(alist :value-type (group integer)))
```

The `group` widget is used here instead of `list` only because the formatting is better suited for the purpose.

Similarly, you can have alists with more values associated with each key, using variations of this trick:

```
(defcustom person-data '(("brian"  50 t)
                         ("dorith" 55 nil)
                         ("ken"    52 t))
  "Alist of basic info about people.
Each element has the form (NAME AGE MALE-FLAG)."
  :type '(alist :value-type (group integer boolean)))
```

`(plist :key-type key-type :value-type value-type)`

> This customization type is similar to `alist` (see above), except that (i) the information is stored as a property list, (see Section 5.9 [Property Lists], page 87), and (ii) key-type, if omitted, defaults to `symbol` rather than `sexp`.

`(choice alternative-types...)`

> The value must fit one of alternative-types. For example, `(choice integer string)` allows either an integer or a string.
>
> In the customization buffer, the user selects an alternative using a menu, and can then edit the value in the usual way for that alternative.

Normally the strings in this menu are determined automatically from the choices; however, you can specify different strings for the menu by including the `:tag` keyword in the alternatives. For example, if an integer stands for a number of spaces, while a string is text to use verbatim, you might write the customization type this way,

```
(choice (integer :tag "Number of spaces")
        (string :tag "Literal text"))
```

so that the menu offers 'Number of spaces' and 'Literal text'.

In any alternative for which `nil` is not a valid value, other than a `const`, you should specify a valid default for that alternative using the `:value` keyword. See Section 14.4.4 [Type Keywords], page 238.

If some values are covered by more than one of the alternatives, customize will choose the first alternative that the value fits. This means you should always list the most specific types first, and the most general last. Here's an example of proper usage:

```
(choice (const :tag "Off" nil)
        symbol (sexp :tag "Other"))
```

This way, the special value `nil` is not treated like other symbols, and symbols are not treated like other Lisp expressions.

(radio *element-types*...**)**

This is similar to `choice`, except that the choices are displayed using radio buttons rather than a menu. This has the advantage of displaying documentation for the choices when applicable and so is often a good choice for a choice between constant functions (`function-item` customization types).

(const *value***)**

The value must be *value*—nothing else is allowed.

The main use of `const` is inside of `choice`. For example, `(choice integer (const nil))` allows either an integer or `nil`.

`:tag` is often used with `const`, inside of `choice`. For example,

```
(choice (const :tag "Yes" t)
        (const :tag "No" nil)
        (const :tag "Ask" foo))
```

describes a variable for which `t` means yes, `nil` means no, and `foo` means "ask".

(other *value***)**

This alternative can match any Lisp value, but if the user chooses this alternative, that selects the value *value*.

The main use of `other` is as the last element of `choice`. For example,

```
(choice (const :tag "Yes" t)
        (const :tag "No" nil)
        (other :tag "Ask" foo))
```

describes a variable for which `t` means yes, `nil` means no, and anything else means "ask". If the user chooses 'Ask' from the menu of alternatives, that specifies the value `foo`; but any other value (not `t`, `nil` or `foo`) displays as 'Ask', just like `foo`.

`(function-item function)`

    Like `const`, but used for values which are functions. This displays the documentation string as well as the function name. The documentation string is either the one you specify with `:doc`, or *function*'s own documentation string.

`(variable-item variable)`

    Like `const`, but used for values which are variable names. This displays the documentation string as well as the variable name. The documentation string is either the one you specify with `:doc`, or *variable*'s own documentation string.

`(set types...)`

    The value must be a list, and each element of the list must match one of the *types* specified.

    This appears in the customization buffer as a checklist, so that each of *types* may have either one corresponding element or none. It is not possible to specify two different elements that match the same one of *types*. For example, `(set integer symbol)` allows one integer and/or one symbol in the list; it does not allow multiple integers or multiple symbols. As a result, it is rare to use nonspecific types such as `integer` in a `set`.

    Most often, the *types* in a `set` are `const` types, as shown here:

```
(set (const :bold) (const :italic))
```

    Sometimes they describe possible elements in an alist:

```
(set (cons :tag "Height" (const height) integer)
     (cons :tag "Width" (const width) integer))
```

    That lets the user specify a height value optionally and a width value optionally.

`(repeat element-type)`

    The value must be a list and each element of the list must fit the type *element-type*. This appears in the customization buffer as a list of elements, with '`[INS]`' and '`[DEL]`' buttons for adding more elements or removing elements.

`(restricted-sexp :match-alternatives criteria)`

    This is the most general composite type construct. The value may be any Lisp object that satisfies one of *criteria*. *criteria* should be a list, and each element should be one of these possibilities:

- A predicate—that is, a function of one argument that has no side effects, and returns either `nil` or non-`nil` according to the argument. Using a predicate in the list says that objects for which the predicate returns non-`nil` are acceptable.

- A quoted constant—that is, `'object`. This sort of element in the list says that *object* itself is an acceptable value.

    For example,

```
(restricted-sexp :match-alternatives
                 (integerp 't 'nil))
```

allows integers, `t` and `nil` as legitimate values.

The customization buffer shows all legitimate values using their read syntax, and the user edits them textually.

Here is a table of the keywords you can use in keyword-value pairs in a composite type:

`:tag` *tag*   Use *tag* as the name of this alternative, for user communication purposes. This is useful for a type that appears inside of a `choice`.

`:match-alternatives` *criteria*

> Use *criteria* to match possible values. This is used only in `restricted-sexp`.

`:args` *argument-list*

> Use the elements of *argument-list* as the arguments of the type construct. For instance, `(const :args (foo))` is equivalent to `(const foo)`. You rarely need to write `:args` explicitly, because normally the arguments are recognized automatically as whatever follows the last keyword-value pair.

14.4.3 Splicing into Lists

The `:inline` feature lets you splice a variable number of elements into the middle of a `list` or `vector` customization type. You use it by adding `:inline t` to a type specification which is contained in a `list` or `vector` specification.

Normally, each entry in a `list` or `vector` type specification describes a single element type. But when an entry contains `:inline t`, the value it matches is merged directly into the containing sequence. For example, if the entry matches a list with three elements, those become three elements of the overall sequence. This is analogous to '`,@`' in a backquote construct (see Section 9.3 [Backquote], page 130).

For example, to specify a list whose first element must be `baz` and whose remaining arguments should be zero or more of `foo` and `bar`, use this customization type:

```
(list (const baz) (set :inline t (const foo) (const bar)))
```

This matches values such as `(baz)`, `(baz foo)`, `(baz bar)` and `(baz foo bar)`.

When the element-type is a `choice`, you use `:inline` not in the `choice` itself, but in (some of) the alternatives of the `choice`. For example, to match a list which must start with a file name, followed either by the symbol `t` or two strings, use this customization type:

```
(list file
       (choice (const t)
               (list :inline t string string)))
```

If the user chooses the first alternative in the choice, then the overall list has two elements and the second element is `t`. If the user chooses the second alternative, then the overall list has three elements and the second and third must be strings.

14.4.4 Type Keywords

You can specify keyword-argument pairs in a customization type after the type name symbol. Here are the keywords you can use, and their meanings:

`:value` *default*

> Provide a default value.

If `nil` is not a valid value for the alternative, then it is essential to specify a valid default with `:value`.

If you use this for a type that appears as an alternative inside of `choice`; it specifies the default value to use, at first, if and when the user selects this alternative with the menu in the customization buffer.

Of course, if the actual value of the option fits this alternative, it will appear showing the actual value, not *default*.

`:format` *format-string*

This string will be inserted in the buffer to represent the value corresponding to the type. The following '%' escapes are available for use in *format-string*:

'%[*button*%]'

Display the text *button* marked as a button. The `:action` attribute specifies what the button will do if the user invokes it; its value is a function which takes two arguments—the widget which the button appears in, and the event.

There is no way to specify two different buttons with different actions.

'%{*sample*%}'

Show *sample* in a special face specified by `:sample-face`.

'%v'   Substitute the item's value. How the value is represented depends on the kind of item, and (for variables) on the customization type.

'%d'   Substitute the item's documentation string.

'%h'   Like '%d', but if the documentation string is more than one line, add a button to control whether to show all of it or just the first line.

'%t'   Substitute the tag here. You specify the tag with the `:tag` keyword.

'%%'   Display a literal '%'.

`:action` *action*

Perform *action* if the user clicks on a button.

`:button-face` *face*

Use the face *face* (a face name or a list of face names) for button text displayed with '%[...%]'.

`:button-prefix` *prefix*
`:button-suffix` *suffix*

These specify the text to display before and after a button. Each can be:

nil   No text is inserted.

a string   The string is inserted literally.

a symbol   The symbol's value is used.

`:tag` *tag*   Use *tag* (a string) as the tag for the value (or part of the value) that corresponds to this type.

:doc *doc*   Use *doc* as the documentation string for this value (or part of the value) that corresponds to this type. In order for this to work, you must specify a value for :format, and use '%d' or '%h' in that value.

> The usual reason to specify a documentation string for a type is to provide more information about the meanings of alternatives inside a :choice type or the parts of some other composite type.

:help-echo *motion-doc*

> When you move to this item with widget-forward or widget-backward, it will display the string *motion-doc* in the echo area. In addition, *motion-doc* is used as the mouse help-echo string and may actually be a function or form evaluated to yield a help string. If it is a function, it is called with one argument, the widget.

:match *function*

> Specify how to decide whether a value matches the type. The corresponding value, *function*, should be a function that accepts two arguments, a widget and a value; it should return non-nil if the value is acceptable.

:validate *function*

> Specify a validation function for input. *function* takes a widget as an argument, and should return nil if the widget's current value is valid for the widget. Otherwise, it should return the widget containing the invalid data, and set that widget's :error property to a string explaining the error.

14.4.5 Defining New Types

In the previous sections we have described how to construct elaborate type specifications for defcustom. In some cases you may want to give such a type specification a name. The obvious case is when you are using the same type for many user options: rather than repeat the specification for each option, you can give the type specification a name, and use that name each defcustom. The other case is when a user option's value is a recursive data structure. To make it possible for a datatype to refer to itself, it needs to have a name.

Since custom types are implemented as widgets, the way to define a new customize type is to define a new widget. We are not going to describe the widget interface here in details, see Section "Introduction" in *The Emacs Widget Library*, for that. Instead we are going to demonstrate the minimal functionality needed for defining new customize types by a simple example.

```
(define-widget 'binary-tree-of-string 'lazy
  "A binary tree made of cons-cells and strings."
  :offset 4
  :tag "Node"
  :type '(choice (string :tag "Leaf" :value "")
                 (cons :tag "Interior"
                       :value ("" . "")
                       binary-tree-of-string
                       binary-tree-of-string)))

(defcustom foo-bar ""
```

```
"Sample variable holding a binary tree of strings."
:type 'binary-tree-of-string)
```

The function to define a new widget is called **define-widget**. The first argument is the symbol we want to make a new widget type. The second argument is a symbol representing an existing widget, the new widget is going to be defined in terms of difference from the existing widget. For the purpose of defining new customization types, the **lazy** widget is perfect, because it accepts a **:type** keyword argument with the same syntax as the keyword argument to **defcustom** with the same name. The third argument is a documentation string for the new widget. You will be able to see that string with the *M-x widget-browse RET binary-tree-of-string RET* command.

After these mandatory arguments follow the keyword arguments. The most important is **:type**, which describes the data type we want to match with this widget. Here a **binary-tree-of-string** is described as being either a string, or a cons-cell whose car and cdr are themselves both **binary-tree-of-string**. Note the reference to the widget type we are currently in the process of defining. The **:tag** attribute is a string to name the widget in the user interface, and the **:offset** argument is there to ensure that child nodes are indented four spaces relative to the parent node, making the tree structure apparent in the customization buffer.

The **defcustom** shows how the new widget can be used as an ordinary customization type.

The reason for the name **lazy** is that the other composite widgets convert their inferior widgets to internal form when the widget is instantiated in a buffer. This conversion is recursive, so the inferior widgets will convert *their* inferior widgets. If the data structure is itself recursive, this conversion is an infinite recursion. The **lazy** widget prevents the recursion: it convert its **:type** argument only when needed.

14.5 Applying Customizations

The following functions are responsible for installing the user's customization settings for variables and faces, respectively. When the user invokes 'Save for future sessions' in the Customize interface, that takes effect by writing a **custom-set-variables** and/or a **custom-set-faces** form into the custom file, to be evaluated the next time Emacs starts.

custom-set-variables &rest *args*   [Function]

  This function installs the variable customizations specified by *args*. Each argument in *args* should have the form

    (*var expression* [*now* [*request* [*comment*]]])

  var is a variable name (a symbol), and *expression* is an expression which evaluates to the desired customized value.

  If the **defcustom** form for *var* has been evaluated prior to this **custom-set-variables** call, *expression* is immediately evaluated, and the variable's value is set to the result. Otherwise, *expression* is stored into the variable's **saved-value** property, to be evaluated when the relevant **defcustom** is called (usually when the library defining that variable is loaded into Emacs).

  The *now*, *request*, and *comment* entries are for internal use only, and may be omitted. *now*, if non-**nil**, means to set the variable's value now, even if the variable's **defcustom** form has not been evaluated. *request* is a list of features to be loaded immediately (see Section 15.7 [Named Features], page 253). *comment* is a string describing the customization.

custom-set-faces **&rest** *args* [Function]

This function installs the face customizations specified by *args*. Each argument in *args* should have the form

> (*face spec* [*now* [*comment*]])

face is a face name (a symbol), and *spec* is the customized face specification for that face (see Section 37.12.2 [Defining Faces], page 918).

The *now* and *comment* entries are for internal use only, and may be omitted. *now*, if non-**nil**, means to install the face specification now, even if the **defface** form has not been evaluated. *comment* is a string describing the customization.

14.6 Custom Themes

Custom themes are collections of settings that can be enabled or disabled as a unit. See Section "Custom Themes" in *The GNU Emacs Manual*. Each Custom theme is defined by an Emacs Lisp source file, which should follow the conventions described in this section. (Instead of writing a Custom theme by hand, you can also create one using a Customize-like interface; see Section "Creating Custom Themes" in *The GNU Emacs Manual*.)

A Custom theme file should be named *foo*-theme.el, where *foo* is the theme name. The first Lisp form in the file should be a call to **deftheme**, and the last form should be a call to **provide-theme**.

deftheme *theme* **&optional** *doc* [Macro]

This macro declares *theme* (a symbol) as the name of a Custom theme. The optional argument *doc* should be a string describing the theme; this is the description shown when the user invokes the **describe-theme** command or types **?** in the '*Custom Themes*' buffer.

Two special theme names are disallowed (using them causes an error): **user** is a dummy theme that stores the user's direct customization settings, and **changed** is a dummy theme that stores changes made outside of the Customize system.

provide-theme *theme* [Macro]

This macro declares that the theme named *theme* has been fully specified.

In between **deftheme** and **provide-theme** are Lisp forms specifying the theme settings: usually a call to **custom-theme-set-variables** and/or a call to **custom-theme-set-faces**.

custom-theme-set-variables *theme* **&rest** *args* [Function]

This function specifies the Custom theme *theme*'s variable settings. *theme* should be a symbol. Each argument in *args* should be a list of the form

> (*var expression* [*now* [*request* [*comment*]]])

where the list entries have the same meanings as in **custom-set-variables**. See Section 14.5 [Applying Customizations], page 241.

`custom-theme-set-faces` *theme* **&rest** *args*   [Function]

> This function specifies the Custom theme *theme*'s face settings. *theme* should be a symbol. Each argument in *args* should be a list of the form
>
> (*face spec* [*now* [*comment*]])
>
> where the list entries have the same meanings as in `custom-set-faces`. See Section 14.5 [Applying Customizations], page 241.

In theory, a theme file can also contain other Lisp forms, which would be evaluated when loading the theme, but that is bad form. To protect against loading themes containing malicious code, Emacs displays the source file and asks for confirmation from the user before loading any non-built-in theme for the first time.

The following functions are useful for programmatically enabling and disabling themes:

`custom-theme-p` *theme*   [Function]

> This function return a non-`nil` value if *theme* (a symbol) is the name of a Custom theme (i.e., a Custom theme which has been loaded into Emacs, whether or not the theme is enabled). Otherwise, it returns `nil`.

`custom-known-themes`   [Variable]

> The value of this variable is a list of themes loaded into Emacs. Each theme is represented by a Lisp symbol (the theme name). The default value of this variable is a list containing two dummy themes: (`user changed`). The `changed` theme stores settings made before any Custom themes are applied (e.g., variables set outside of Customize). The `user` theme stores settings the user has customized and saved. Any additional themes declared with the `deftheme` macro are added to the front of this list.

`load-theme` *theme* **&optional** *no-confirm no-enable*   [Command]

> This function loads the Custom theme named *theme* from its source file, looking for the source file in the directories specified by the variable `custom-theme-load-path`. See Section "Custom Themes" in *The GNU Emacs Manual*. It also *enables* the theme (unless the optional argument *no-enable* is non-`nil`), causing its variable and face settings to take effect. It prompts the user for confirmation before loading the theme, unless the optional argument *no-confirm* is non-`nil`.

`enable-theme` *theme*   [Command]

> This function enables the Custom theme named *theme*. It signals an error if no such theme has been loaded.

`disable-theme` *theme*   [Command]

> This function disables the Custom theme named *theme*. The theme remains loaded, so that a subsequent call to `enable-theme` will re-enable it.

15 Loading

Loading a file of Lisp code means bringing its contents into the Lisp environment in the form of Lisp objects. Emacs finds and opens the file, reads the text, evaluates each form, and then closes the file. Such a file is also called a *Lisp library*.

The load functions evaluate all the expressions in a file just as the `eval-buffer` function evaluates all the expressions in a buffer. The difference is that the load functions read and evaluate the text in the file as found on disk, not the text in an Emacs buffer.

The loaded file must contain Lisp expressions, either as source code or as byte-compiled code. Each form in the file is called a *top-level form*. There is no special format for the forms in a loadable file; any form in a file may equally well be typed directly into a buffer and evaluated there. (Indeed, most code is tested this way.) Most often, the forms are function definitions and variable definitions.

Emacs can also load compiled dynamic modules: shared libraries that provide additional functionality for use in Emacs Lisp programs, just like a package written in Emacs Lisp would. When a dynamic module is loaded, Emacs calls a specially-named initialization function which the module needs to implement, and which exposes the additional functions and variables to Emacs Lisp programs.

For on-demand loading of external libraries which are known in advance to be required by certain Emacs primitives, see Section 38.21 [Dynamic Libraries], page 1022.

15.1 How Programs Do Loading

Emacs Lisp has several interfaces for loading. For example, `autoload` creates a placeholder object for a function defined in a file; trying to call the autoloading function loads the file to get the function's real definition (see Section 15.5 [Autoload], page 249). `require` loads a file if it isn't already loaded (see Section 15.7 [Named Features], page 253). Ultimately, all these facilities call the `load` function to do the work.

`load` *filename* **&optional** *missing-ok nomessage nosuffix must-suffix*   [Function]
> This function finds and opens a file of Lisp code, evaluates all the forms in it, and closes the file.
>
> To find the file, `load` first looks for a file named *filename*`.elc`, that is, for a file whose name is *filename* with the extension '`.elc`' appended. If such a file exists, it is loaded. If there is no file by that name, then `load` looks for a file named *filename*`.el`. If that file exists, it is loaded. If Emacs was compiled with support for dynamic modules (see Section 15.11 [Dynamic Modules], page 258), `load` next looks for a file named *filename*`.ext`, where *ext* is a system-dependent file-name extension of shared libraries. Finally, if neither of those names is found, `load` looks for a file named *filename* with nothing appended, and loads it if it exists. (The `load` function is not clever about looking at *filename*. In the perverse case of a file named `foo.el.el`, evaluation of (`load "foo.el"`) will indeed find it.)
>
> If Auto Compression mode is enabled, as it is by default, then if `load` can not find a file, it searches for a compressed version of the file before trying other file names. It decompresses and loads it if it exists. It looks for compressed versions by appending

each of the suffixes in `jka-compr-load-suffixes` to the file name. The value of this variable must be a list of strings. Its standard value is (".gz").

If the optional argument *nosuffix* is non-`nil`, then `load` does not try the suffixes '.elc' and '.el'. In this case, you must specify the precise file name you want, except that, if Auto Compression mode is enabled, `load` will still use `jka-compr-load-suffixes` to find compressed versions. By specifying the precise file name and using `t` for *nosuffix*, you can prevent file names like `foo.el.el` from being tried.

If the optional argument *must-suffix* is non-`nil`, then `load` insists that the file name used must end in either '.el' or '.elc' (possibly extended with a compression suffix) or the shared-library extension, unless it contains an explicit directory name.

If the option `load-prefer-newer` is non-`nil`, then when searching suffixes, `load` selects whichever version of a file ('.elc', '.el', etc.) has been modified most recently.

If *filename* is a relative file name, such as `foo` or `baz/foo.bar`, `load` searches for the file using the variable `load-path`. It appends *filename* to each of the directories listed in `load-path`, and loads the first file it finds whose name matches. The current default directory is tried only if it is specified in `load-path`, where `nil` stands for the default directory. `load` tries all three possible suffixes in the first directory in `load-path`, then all three suffixes in the second directory, and so on. See Section 15.3 [Library Search], page 247.

Whatever the name under which the file is eventually found, and the directory where Emacs found it, Emacs sets the value of the variable `load-file-name` to that file's name.

If you get a warning that `foo.elc` is older than `foo.el`, it means you should consider recompiling `foo.el`. See Chapter 16 [Byte Compilation], page 260.

When loading a source file (not compiled), `load` performs character set translation just as Emacs would do when visiting the file. See Section 32.10 [Coding Systems], page 773.

When loading an uncompiled file, Emacs tries to expand any macros that the file contains (see Chapter 13 [Macros], page 217). We refer to this as *eager macro expansion*. Doing this (rather than deferring the expansion until the relevant code runs) can significantly speed up the execution of uncompiled code. Sometimes, this macro expansion cannot be done, owing to a cyclic dependency. In the simplest example of this, the file you are loading refers to a macro defined in another file, and that file in turn requires the file you are loading. This is generally harmless. Emacs prints a warning ('`Eager macro-expansion skipped due to cycle...`') giving details of the problem, but it still loads the file, just leaving the macro unexpanded for now. You may wish to restructure your code so that this does not happen. Loading a compiled file does not cause macroexpansion, because this should already have happened during compilation. See Section 13.3 [Compiling Macros], page 219.

Messages like '`Loading foo...`' and '`Loading foo...done`' appear in the echo area during loading unless *nomessage* is non-`nil`.

Any unhandled errors while loading a file terminate loading. If the load was done for the sake of `autoload`, any function definitions made during the loading are undone.

If `load` can't find the file to load, then normally it signals the error `file-error` (with 'Cannot open load file *filename*'). But if *missing-ok* is non-`nil`, then `load` just returns `nil`.

You can use the variable `load-read-function` to specify a function for `load` to use instead of `read` for reading expressions. See below.

`load` returns `t` if the file loads successfully.

`load-file` *filename*   [Command]

> This command loads the file *filename*. If *filename* is a relative file name, then the current default directory is assumed. This command does not use `load-path`, and does not append suffixes. However, it does look for compressed versions (if Auto Compression Mode is enabled). Use this command if you wish to specify precisely the file name to load.

`load-library` *library*   [Command]

> This command loads the library named *library*. It is equivalent to `load`, except for the way it reads its argument interactively. See Section "Lisp Libraries" in *The GNU Emacs Manual*.

`load-in-progress`   [Variable]

> This variable is non-`nil` if Emacs is in the process of loading a file, and it is `nil` otherwise.

`load-file-name`   [Variable]

> When Emacs is in the process of loading a file, this variable's value is the name of that file, as Emacs found it during the search described earlier in this section.

`load-read-function`   [Variable]

> This variable specifies an alternate expression-reading function for `load` and `eval-region` to use instead of `read`. The function should accept one argument, just as `read` does.
>
> By default, this variable's value is `read`. See Section 18.3 [Input Functions], page 304.
>
> Instead of using this variable, it is cleaner to use another, newer feature: to pass the function as the *read-function* argument to `eval-region`. See [Eval], page 132.

For information about how `load` is used in building Emacs, see Section E.1 [Building Emacs], page 1067.

15.2 Load Suffixes

We now describe some technical details about the exact suffixes that `load` tries.

`load-suffixes`   [Variable]

> This is a list of suffixes indicating (compiled or source) Emacs Lisp files. It should not include the empty string. `load` uses these suffixes in order when it appends Lisp suffixes to the specified file name. The standard value is (`".elc" ".el"`) which produces the behavior described in the previous section.

`load-file-rep-suffixes` [Variable]

> This is a list of suffixes that indicate representations of the same file. This list should normally start with the empty string. When `load` searches for a file it appends the suffixes in this list, in order, to the file name, before searching for another file.
>
> Enabling Auto Compression mode appends the suffixes in `jka-compr-load-suffixes` to this list and disabling Auto Compression mode removes them again. The standard value of `load-file-rep-suffixes` if Auto Compression mode is disabled is (`""`). Given that the standard value of `jka-compr-load-suffixes` is (`".gz"`), the standard value of `load-file-rep-suffixes` if Auto Compression mode is enabled is (`""` `".gz"`).

`get-load-suffixes` [Function]

> This function returns the list of all suffixes that `load` should try, in order, when its *must-suffix* argument is non-`nil`. This takes both `load-suffixes` and `load-file-rep-suffixes` into account. If `load-suffixes`, `jka-compr-load-suffixes` and `load-file-rep-suffixes` all have their standard values, this function returns (`".elc"` `".elc.gz"` `".el"` `".el.gz"`) if Auto Compression mode is enabled and (`".elc"` `".el"`) if Auto Compression mode is disabled.

To summarize, `load` normally first tries the suffixes in the value of (`get-load-suffixes`) and then those in `load-file-rep-suffixes`. If *nosuffix* is non-`nil`, it skips the former group, and if *must-suffix* is non-`nil`, it skips the latter group.

`load-prefer-newer` [User Option]

> If this option is non-`nil`, then rather than stopping at the first suffix that exists, `load` tests them all, and uses whichever file is the newest.

15.3 Library Search

When Emacs loads a Lisp library, it searches for the library in a list of directories specified by the variable `load-path`.

`load-path` [Variable]

> The value of this variable is a list of directories to search when loading files with `load`. Each element is a string (which must be a directory name) or `nil` (which stands for the current working directory).

When Emacs starts up, it sets up the value of `load-path` in several steps. First, it initializes `load-path` using default locations set when Emacs was compiled. Normally, this is a directory something like

> `"/usr/local/share/emacs/version/lisp"`

(In this and the following examples, replace /usr/local with the installation prefix appropriate for your Emacs.) These directories contain the standard Lisp files that come with Emacs. If Emacs cannot find them, it will not start correctly.

If you run Emacs from the directory where it was built—that is, an executable that has not been formally installed—Emacs instead initializes `load-path` using the `lisp` directory in the directory containing the sources from which it was built. If you built Emacs in a separate directory from the sources, it also adds the lisp directories from the build directory. (In all cases, elements are represented as absolute file names.)

Unless you start Emacs with the `--no-site-lisp` option, it then adds two more `site-lisp` directories to the front of `load-path`. These are intended for locally installed Lisp files, and are normally of the form:

```
"/usr/local/share/emacs/version/site-lisp"
```

and

```
"/usr/local/share/emacs/site-lisp"
```

The first one is for locally installed files for a specific Emacs version; the second is for locally installed files meant for use with all installed Emacs versions. (If Emacs is running uninstalled, it also adds `site-lisp` directories from the source and build directories, if they exist. Normally these directories do not contain `site-lisp` directories.)

If the environment variable `EMACSLOADPATH` is set, it modifies the above initialization procedure. Emacs initializes `load-path` based on the value of the environment variable.

The syntax of `EMACSLOADPATH` is the same as used for `PATH`; directory names are separated by ':' (or ';', on some operating systems). Here is an example of how to set `EMACSLOADPATH` variable (from a `sh`-style shell):

```
export EMACSLOADPATH=/home/foo/.emacs.d/lisp:
```

An empty element in the value of the environment variable, whether trailing (as in the above example), leading, or embedded, is replaced by the default value of `load-path` as determined by the standard initialization procedure. If there are no such empty elements, then `EMACSLOADPATH` specifies the entire `load-path`. You must include either an empty element, or the explicit path to the directory containing the standard Lisp files, else Emacs will not function. (Another way to modify `load-path` is to use the −L command-line option when starting Emacs; see below.)

For each directory in `load-path`, Emacs then checks to see if it contains a file `subdirs.el`, and if so, loads it. The `subdirs.el` file is created when Emacs is built/installed, and contains code that causes Emacs to add any subdirectories of those directories to `load-path`. Both immediate subdirectories and subdirectories multiple levels down are added. But it excludes subdirectories whose names do not start with a letter or digit, and subdirectories named `RCS` or `CVS`, and subdirectories containing a file named `.nosearch`.

Next, Emacs adds any extra load directories that you specify using the −L command-line option (see Section "Action Arguments" in *The GNU Emacs Manual*). It also adds the directories where optional packages are installed, if any (see Section 39.1 [Packaging Basics], page 1026).

It is common to add code to one's init file (see Section 38.1.2 [Init File], page 988) to add one or more directories to `load-path`. For example:

```
(push "~/.emacs.d/lisp" load-path)
```

Dumping Emacs uses a special value of `load-path`. If you use a `site-load.el` or `site-init.el` file to customize the dumped Emacs (see Section E.1 [Building Emacs], page 1067), any changes to `load-path` that these files make will be lost after dumping.

`locate-library` *library* **&optional** *nosuffix path interactive-call*   [Command]

> This command finds the precise file name for library *library*. It searches for the library in the same way `load` does, and the argument *nosuffix* has the same meaning as in `load`: don't add suffixes '`.elc`' or '`.el`' to the specified name *library*.
>
> If the *path* is non-`nil`, that list of directories is used instead of `load-path`.
>
> When `locate-library` is called from a program, it returns the file name as a string. When the user runs `locate-library` interactively, the argument *interactive-call* is `t`, and this tells `locate-library` to display the file name in the echo area.

`list-load-path-shadows` **&optional** *stringp*   [Command]

> This command shows a list of *shadowed* Emacs Lisp files. A shadowed file is one that will not normally be loaded, despite being in a directory on `load-path`, due to the existence of another similarly-named file in a directory earlier on `load-path`.
>
> For instance, suppose `load-path` is set to
>
> ```
> ("/opt/emacs/site-lisp" "/usr/share/emacs/23.3/lisp")
> ```
>
> and that both these directories contain a file named `foo.el`. Then (`require 'foo`) never loads the file in the second directory. Such a situation might indicate a problem in the way Emacs was installed.
>
> When called from Lisp, this function prints a message listing the shadowed files, instead of displaying them in a buffer. If the optional argument `stringp` is non-`nil`, it instead returns the shadowed files as a string.

15.4 Loading Non-ASCII Characters

When Emacs Lisp programs contain string constants with non-ASCII characters, these can be represented within Emacs either as unibyte strings or as multibyte strings (see Section 32.1 [Text Representations], page 761). Which representation is used depends on how the file is read into Emacs. If it is read with decoding into multibyte representation, the text of the Lisp program will be multibyte text, and its string constants will be multibyte strings. If a file containing Latin-1 characters (for example) is read without decoding, the text of the program will be unibyte text, and its string constants will be unibyte strings. See Section 32.10 [Coding Systems], page 773.

In most Emacs Lisp programs, the fact that non-ASCII strings are multibyte strings should not be noticeable, since inserting them in unibyte buffers converts them to unibyte automatically. However, if this does make a difference, you can force a particular Lisp file to be interpreted as unibyte by writing '`coding: raw-text`' in a local variables section. With that designator, the file will unconditionally be interpreted as unibyte. This can matter when making keybindings to non-ASCII characters written as `?vliteral`.

15.5 Autoload

The *autoload* facility lets you register the existence of a function or macro, but put off loading the file that defines it. The first call to the function automatically loads the proper library, in order to install the real definition and other associated code, then runs the real definition as if it had been loaded all along. Autoloading can also be triggered by looking up the documentation of the function or macro (see Section 23.1 [Documentation Basics], page 485).

There are two ways to set up an autoloaded function: by calling `autoload`, and by writing a "magic" comment in the source before the real definition. `autoload` is the low-level primitive for autoloading; any Lisp program can call `autoload` at any time. Magic comments are the most convenient way to make a function autoload, for packages installed along with Emacs. These comments do nothing on their own, but they serve as a guide for the command `update-file-autoloads`, which constructs calls to `autoload` and arranges to execute them when Emacs is built.

`autoload` *function filename* **&optional** *docstring interactive type*   [Function]
> This function defines the function (or macro) named *function* so as to load automatically from *filename*. The string *filename* specifies the file to load to get the real definition of *function*.
>
> If *filename* does not contain either a directory name, or the suffix `.el` or `.elc`, this function insists on adding one of these suffixes, and it will not load from a file whose name is just *filename* with no added suffix. (The variable `load-suffixes` specifies the exact required suffixes.)
>
> The argument *docstring* is the documentation string for the function. Specifying the documentation string in the call to `autoload` makes it possible to look at the documentation without loading the function's real definition. Normally, this should be identical to the documentation string in the function definition itself. If it isn't, the function definition's documentation string takes effect when it is loaded.
>
> If *interactive* is non-`nil`, that says *function* can be called interactively. This lets completion in `M-x` work without loading *function*'s real definition. The complete interactive specification is not given here; it's not needed unless the user actually calls *function*, and when that happens, it's time to load the real definition.
>
> You can autoload macros and keymaps as well as ordinary functions. Specify *type* as `macro` if *function* is really a macro. Specify *type* as `keymap` if *function* is really a keymap. Various parts of Emacs need to know this information without loading the real definition.
>
> An autoloaded keymap loads automatically during key lookup when a prefix key's binding is the symbol *function*. Autoloading does not occur for other kinds of access to the keymap. In particular, it does not happen when a Lisp program gets the keymap from the value of a variable and calls `define-key`; not even if the variable name is the same symbol *function*.
>
> If *function* already has a non-void function definition that is not an autoload object, this function does nothing and returns `nil`. Otherwise, it constructs an autoload object (see Section 2.3.17 [Autoload Type], page 23), and stores it as the function definition for *function*. The autoload object has this form:
>
> > `(autoload filename docstring interactive type)`
>
> For example,
>
> > `(symbol-function 'run-prolog)`
> >   ⇒ `(autoload "prolog" 169681 t nil)`
>
> In this case, `"prolog"` is the name of the file to load, 169681 refers to the documentation string in the `emacs/etc/DOC` file (see Section 23.1 [Documentation Basics], page 485), `t` means the function is interactive, and `nil` that it is not a macro or a keymap.

autoloadp *object*   [Function]

   This function returns non-**nil** if *object* is an autoload object. For example, to check
   if **run-prolog** is defined as an autoloaded function, evaluate

```
(autoloadp (symbol-function 'run-prolog))
```

The autoloaded file usually contains other definitions and may require or provide one
or more features. If the file is not completely loaded (due to an error in the evaluation of
its contents), any function definitions or **provide** calls that occurred during the load are
undone. This is to ensure that the next attempt to call any function autoloading from this
file will try again to load the file. If not for this, then some of the functions in the file might
be defined by the aborted load, but fail to work properly for the lack of certain subroutines
not loaded successfully because they come later in the file.

If the autoloaded file fails to define the desired Lisp function or macro, then an error is
signaled with data "Autoloading failed to define function *function-name*".

A magic autoload comment (often called an *autoload cookie*) consists of
';;;###autoload', on a line by itself, just before the real definition of the function
in its autoloadable source file. The command *M-x update-file-autoloads* writes a
corresponding **autoload** call into **loaddefs.el**. (The string that serves as the autoload
cookie and the name of the file generated by **update-file-autoloads** can be changed
from the above defaults, see below.) Building Emacs loads **loaddefs.el** and thus calls
autoload. *M-x update-directory-autoloads* is even more powerful; it updates autoloads
for all files in the current directory.

The same magic comment can copy any kind of form into **loaddefs.el**. The form
following the magic comment is copied verbatim, *except* if it is one of the forms which the
autoload facility handles specially (e.g., by conversion into an **autoload** call). The forms
which are not copied verbatim are the following:

Definitions for function or function-like objects:
   defun and **defmacro**; also **cl-defun** and **cl-defmacro** (see Section "Argument
   Lists" in *Common Lisp Extensions*), and **define-overloadable-function** (see
   the commentary in **mode-local.el**).

Definitions for major or minor modes:
   define-minor-mode, **define-globalized-minor-mode**, **define-generic-
   mode**, **define-derived-mode**, **easy-mmode-define-minor-mode**,
   easy-mmode-define-global-mode, **define-compilation-mode**, and
   define-global-minor-mode.

Other definition types:
   defcustom, **defgroup**, **defclass** (see *EIEIO*), and **define-skeleton** (see
   Autotyping).

You can also use a magic comment to execute a form at build time *without* executing
it when the file itself is loaded. To do this, write the form *on the same line* as the magic
comment. Since it is in a comment, it does nothing when you load the source file; but
M-x update-file-autoloads copies it to **loaddefs.el**, where it is executed while building
Emacs.

The following example shows how **doctor** is prepared for autoloading with a magic
comment:

```
;;;###autoload
(defun doctor ()
  "Switch to *doctor* buffer and start giving psychotherapy."
  (interactive)
  (switch-to-buffer "*doctor*")
  (doctor-mode))
```

Here's what that produces in `loaddefs.el`:

```
(autoload (quote doctor) "doctor" "\
Switch to *doctor* buffer and start giving psychotherapy.
```

```
\(fn)" t nil)
```

The backslash and newline immediately following the double-quote are a convention used only in the preloaded uncompiled Lisp files such as `loaddefs.el`; they tell `make-docfile` to put the documentation string in the `etc/DOC` file. See Section E.1 [Building Emacs], page 1067. See also the commentary in `lib-src/make-docfile.c`. '(fn)' in the usage part of the documentation string is replaced with the function's name when the various help functions (see Section 23.5 [Help Functions], page 491) display it.

If you write a function definition with an unusual macro that is not one of the known and recognized function definition methods, use of an ordinary magic autoload comment would copy the whole definition into `loaddefs.el`. That is not desirable. You can put the desired `autoload` call into `loaddefs.el` instead by writing this:

```
;;;###autoload (autoload 'foo "myfile")
(mydefunmacro foo
  ...)
```

You can use a non-default string as the autoload cookie and have the corresponding autoload calls written into a file whose name is different from the default `loaddefs.el`. Emacs provides two variables to control this:

generate-autoload-cookie   [Variable]

> The value of this variable should be a string whose syntax is a Lisp comment. *M-x update-file-autoloads* copies the Lisp form that follows the cookie into the autoload file it generates. The default value of this variable is "`;;;###autoload`".

generated-autoload-file   [Variable]

> The value of this variable names an Emacs Lisp file where the autoload calls should go. The default value is `loaddefs.el`, but you can override that, e.g., in the local variables section of a `.el` file (see Section 11.11 [File Local Variables], page 177). The autoload file is assumed to contain a trailer starting with a formfeed character.

The following function may be used to explicitly load the library specified by an autoload object:

autoload-do-load *autoload* **&optional** *name macro-only*   [Function]

> This function performs the loading specified by *autoload*, which should be an autoload object. The optional argument *name*, if non-nil, should be a symbol whose function value is *autoload*; in that case, the return value of this function is the symbol's new function value. If the value of the optional argument *macro-only* is `macro`, this function avoids loading a function, only a macro.

15.6 Repeated Loading

You can load a given file more than once in an Emacs session. For example, after you have rewritten and reinstalled a function definition by editing it in a buffer, you may wish to return to the original version; you can do this by reloading the file it came from.

When you load or reload files, bear in mind that the `load` and `load-library` functions automatically load a byte-compiled file rather than a non-compiled file of similar name. If you rewrite a file that you intend to save and reinstall, you need to byte-compile the new version; otherwise Emacs will load the older, byte-compiled file instead of your newer, non-compiled file! If that happens, the message displayed when loading the file includes, '(compiled; note, source is newer)', to remind you to recompile it.

When writing the forms in a Lisp library file, keep in mind that the file might be loaded more than once. For example, think about whether each variable should be reinitialized when you reload the library; `defvar` does not change the value if the variable is already initialized. (See Section 11.5 [Defining Variables], page 161.)

The simplest way to add an element to an alist is like this:

```
(push '(leif-mode " Leif") minor-mode-alist)
```

But this would add multiple elements if the library is reloaded. To avoid the problem, use `add-to-list` (see Section 5.5 [List Variables], page 74):

```
(add-to-list 'minor-mode-alist '(leif-mode " Leif"))
```

Occasionally you will want to test explicitly whether a library has already been loaded. If the library uses `provide` to provide a named feature, you can use `featurep` earlier in the file to test whether the `provide` call has been executed before (see Section 15.7 [Named Features], page 253). Alternatively, you could use something like this:

```
(defvar foo-was-loaded nil)

(unless foo-was-loaded
  execute-first-time-only
  (setq foo-was-loaded t))
```

15.7 Features

`provide` and `require` are an alternative to `autoload` for loading files automatically. They work in terms of named *features*. Autoloading is triggered by calling a specific function, but a feature is loaded the first time another program asks for it by name.

A feature name is a symbol that stands for a collection of functions, variables, etc. The file that defines them should *provide* the feature. Another program that uses them may ensure they are defined by *requiring* the feature. This loads the file of definitions if it hasn't been loaded already.

To require the presence of a feature, call `require` with the feature name as argument. `require` looks in the global variable `features` to see whether the desired feature has been provided already. If not, it loads the feature from the appropriate file. This file should call `provide` at the top level to add the feature to `features`; if it fails to do so, `require` signals an error.

For example, in `idlwave.el`, the definition for `idlwave-complete-filename` includes the following code:

```
(defun idlwave-complete-filename ()
  "Use the comint stuff to complete a file name."
  (require 'comint)
  (let* ((comint-file-name-chars "~/A-Za-z0-9+@:_.$#%={}\\-")
         (comint-completion-addsuffix nil)
         ...)
    (comint-dynamic-complete-filename)))
```

The expression `(require 'comint)` loads the file `comint.el` if it has not yet been loaded, ensuring that `comint-dynamic-complete-filename` is defined. Features are normally named after the files that provide them, so that `require` need not be given the file name. (Note that it is important that the `require` statement be outside the body of the `let`. Loading a library while its variables are let-bound can have unintended consequences, namely the variables becoming unbound after the let exits.)

The `comint.el` file contains the following top-level expression:

```
(provide 'comint)
```

This adds `comint` to the global `features` list, so that `(require 'comint)` will henceforth know that nothing needs to be done.

When `require` is used at top level in a file, it takes effect when you byte-compile that file (see Chapter 16 [Byte Compilation], page 260) as well as when you load it. This is in case the required package contains macros that the byte compiler must know about. It also avoids byte compiler warnings for functions and variables defined in the file loaded with `require`.

Although top-level calls to `require` are evaluated during byte compilation, `provide` calls are not. Therefore, you can ensure that a file of definitions is loaded before it is byte-compiled by including a `provide` followed by a `require` for the same feature, as in the following example.

```
(provide 'my-feature)   ; Ignored by byte compiler,
                        ;   evaluated by load.
(require 'my-feature)   ; Evaluated by byte compiler.
```

The compiler ignores the `provide`, then processes the `require` by loading the file in question. Loading the file does execute the `provide` call, so the subsequent `require` call does nothing when the file is loaded.

provide *feature* **&optional** *subfeatures*   [Function]
> This function announces that *feature* is now loaded, or being loaded, into the current Emacs session. This means that the facilities associated with *feature* are or will be available for other Lisp programs.
>
> The direct effect of calling `provide` is to add *feature* to the front of `features` if it is not already in that list and call any `eval-after-load` code waiting for it (see Section 15.10 [Hooks for Loading], page 257). The argument *feature* must be a symbol. `provide` returns *feature*.
>
> If provided, *subfeatures* should be a list of symbols indicating a set of specific subfeatures provided by this version of *feature*. You can test the presence of a subfeature

using `featurep`. The idea of subfeatures is that you use them when a package (which is one *feature*) is complex enough to make it useful to give names to various parts or functionalities of the package, which might or might not be loaded, or might or might not be present in a given version. See Section 36.17.3 [Network Feature Testing], page 875, for an example.

```
features
     ⇒ (bar bish)

(provide 'foo)
     ⇒ foo
features
     ⇒ (foo bar bish)
```

When a file is loaded to satisfy an autoload, and it stops due to an error in the evaluation of its contents, any function definitions or `provide` calls that occurred during the load are undone. See Section 15.5 [Autoload], page 249.

`require` *feature* **&optional** *filename noerror*   [Function]

This function checks whether *feature* is present in the current Emacs session (using (`featurep` *feature*); see below). The argument *feature* must be a symbol.

If the feature is not present, then `require` loads *filename* with `load`. If *filename* is not supplied, then the name of the symbol *feature* is used as the base file name to load. However, in this case, `require` insists on finding *feature* with an added '`.el`' or '`.elc`' suffix (possibly extended with a compression suffix); a file whose name is just *feature* won't be used. (The variable `load-suffixes` specifies the exact required Lisp suffixes.)

If *noerror* is non-`nil`, that suppresses errors from actual loading of the file. In that case, `require` returns `nil` if loading the file fails. Normally, `require` returns *feature*.

If loading the file succeeds but does not provide *feature*, `require` signals an error, '`Required feature feature was not provided`'.

`featurep` *feature* **&optional** *subfeature*   [Function]

This function returns `t` if *feature* has been provided in the current Emacs session (i.e., if *feature* is a member of `features`.) If *subfeature* is non-`nil`, then the function returns `t` only if that subfeature is provided as well (i.e., if *subfeature* is a member of the `subfeature` property of the *feature* symbol.)

`features`   [Variable]

The value of this variable is a list of symbols that are the features loaded in the current Emacs session. Each symbol was put in this list with a call to `provide`. The order of the elements in the `features` list is not significant.

15.8 Which File Defined a Certain Symbol

`symbol-file` *symbol* **&optional** *type*   [Function]

This function returns the name of the file that defined *symbol*. If *type* is `nil`, then any kind of definition is acceptable. If *type* is `defun`, `defvar`, or `defface`, that specifies function definition, variable definition, or face definition only.

The value is normally an absolute file name. It can also be `nil`, if the definition is not associated with any file. If *symbol* specifies an autoloaded function, the value can be a relative file name without extension.

The basis for `symbol-file` is the data in the variable `load-history`.

`load-history`   [Variable]

> The value of this variable is an alist that associates the names of loaded library files with the names of the functions and variables they defined, as well as the features they provided or required.
>
> Each element in this alist describes one loaded library (including libraries that are preloaded at startup). It is a list whose CAR is the absolute file name of the library (a string). The rest of the list elements have these forms:
>
> *var*   The symbol *var* was defined as a variable.
>
> `(defun . fun)`
> > The function *fun* was defined.
>
> `(t . fun)`   The function *fun* was previously an autoload before this library redefined it as a function. The following element is always `(defun . fun)`, which represents defining *fun* as a function.
>
> `(autoload . fun)`
> > The function *fun* was defined as an autoload.
>
> `(defface . face)`
> > The face *face* was defined.
>
> `(require . feature)`
> > The feature *feature* was required.
>
> `(provide . feature)`
> > The feature *feature* was provided.
>
> `(cl-defmethod method specializers)`
> > The named *method* was defined by using `cl-defmethod`, with *specializers* as its specializers.
>
> `(define-type . type)`
> > The type *type* was defined.
>
> The value of `load-history` may have one element whose CAR is `nil`. This element describes definitions made with `eval-buffer` on a buffer that is not visiting a file.

The command `eval-region` updates `load-history`, but does so by adding the symbols defined to the element for the file being visited, rather than replacing that element. See Section 9.4 [Eval], page 131.

15.9 Unloading

You can discard the functions and variables loaded by a library to reclaim memory for other Lisp objects. To do this, use the function `unload-feature`:

unload-feature *feature* **&optional** *force*   [Command]

> This command unloads the library that provided feature *feature*. It undefines all functions, macros, and variables defined in that library with `defun`, `defalias`, `defsubst`, `defmacro`, `defconst`, `defvar`, and `defcustom`. It then restores any autoloads formerly associated with those symbols. (Loading saves these in the `autoload` property of the symbol.)
>
> Before restoring the previous definitions, `unload-feature` runs `remove-hook` to remove functions in the library from certain hooks. These hooks include variables whose names end in '`-hook`' (or the deprecated suffix '`-hooks`'), plus those listed in `unload-feature-special-hooks`, as well as `auto-mode-alist`. This is to prevent Emacs from ceasing to function because important hooks refer to functions that are no longer defined.
>
> Standard unloading activities also undoes ELP profiling of functions in that library, unprovides any features provided by the library, and cancels timers held in variables defined by the library.
>
> If these measures are not sufficient to prevent malfunction, a library can define an explicit unloader named *feature*`-unload-function`. If that symbol is defined as a function, `unload-feature` calls it with no arguments before doing anything else. It can do whatever is appropriate to unload the library. If it returns `nil`, `unload-feature` proceeds to take the normal unload actions. Otherwise it considers the job to be done.
>
> Ordinarily, `unload-feature` refuses to unload a library on which other loaded libraries depend. (A library *a* depends on library *b* if *a* contains a `require` for *b*.) If the optional argument *force* is non-`nil`, dependencies are ignored and you can unload any library.

The `unload-feature` function is written in Lisp; its actions are based on the variable `load-history`.

unload-feature-special-hooks   [Variable]

> This variable holds a list of hooks to be scanned before unloading a library, to remove functions defined in the library.

15.10 Hooks for Loading

You can ask for code to be executed each time Emacs loads a library, by using the variable `after-load-functions`:

after-load-functions   [Variable]

> This abnormal hook is run after loading a file. Each function in the hook is called with a single argument, the absolute filename of the file that was just loaded.

If you want code to be executed when a *particular* library is loaded, use the macro `with-eval-after-load`:

`with-eval-after-load` *library body. . .*   [Macro]

> This macro arranges to evaluate *body* at the end of loading the file *library*, each time
> *library* is loaded. If *library* is already loaded, it evaluates *body* right away.
>
> You don't need to give a directory or extension in the file name *library*. Normally,
> you just give a bare file name, like this:
>
> > `(with-eval-after-load "edebug" (def-edebug-spec c-point t))`
>
> To restrict which files can trigger the evaluation, include a directory or an extension
> or both in *library*. Only a file whose absolute true name (i.e., the name with all
> symbolic links chased out) matches all the given name components will match. In the
> following example, `my_inst.elc` or `my_inst.elc.gz` in some directory `. . . ./foo/bar`
> will trigger the evaluation, but not `my_inst.el`:
>
> > `(with-eval-after-load "foo/bar/my_inst.elc" ...)`
>
> *library* can also be a feature (i.e., a symbol), in which case *body* is evaluated at the
> end of any file where (`provide` *library*) is called.
>
> An error in *body* does not undo the load, but does prevent execution of the rest of
> *body*.

Normally, well-designed Lisp programs should not use `with-eval-after-load`. If you
need to examine and set the variables defined in another library (those meant for outside
use), you can do it immediately—there is no need to wait until the library is loaded. If you
need to call functions defined by that library, you should load the library, preferably with
`require` (see Section 15.7 [Named Features], page 253).

15.11 Emacs Dynamic Modules

A *dynamic Emacs module* is a shared library that provides additional functionality for use
in Emacs Lisp programs, just like a package written in Emacs Lisp would.

Functions that load Emacs Lisp packages can also load dynamic modules. They recognize
dynamic modules by looking at their file-name extension, a.k.a. "suffix". This suffix is
platform-dependent.

`module-file-suffix`   [Variable]

> This variable holds the system-dependent value of the file-name extension of the
> module files. Its value is `.so` on Posix hosts and `.dll` on MS-Windows.

Every dynamic module should export a C-callable function named `emacs_module_init`,
which Emacs will call as part of the call to `load` or `require` which loads the module. It
should also export a symbol named `plugin_is_GPL_compatible` to indicate that its code
is released under the GPL or compatible license; Emacs will refuse to load modules that
don't export such a symbol.

If a module needs to call Emacs functions, it should do so through the API defined and
documented in the header file `emacs-module.h` that is part of the Emacs distribution.

Modules can create `user-ptr` Lisp objects that embed pointers to C struct's defined by
the module. This is useful for keeping around complex data structures created by a module,
to be passed back to the module's functions. User-ptr objects can also have associated
finalizers – functions to be run when the object is GC'ed; this is useful for freeing any

resources allocated for the underlying data structure, such as memory, open file descriptors, etc.

user-ptrp *object* [Function]

    This function returns `t` if its argument is a `user-ptr` object.

Loadable modules in Emacs are enabled by using the `--with-modules` option at configure time.

16 Byte Compilation

Emacs Lisp has a *compiler* that translates functions written in Lisp into a special representation called *byte-code* that can be executed more efficiently. The compiler replaces Lisp function definitions with byte-code. When a byte-code function is called, its definition is evaluated by the *byte-code interpreter*.

Because the byte-compiled code is evaluated by the byte-code interpreter, instead of being executed directly by the machine's hardware (as true compiled code is), byte-code is completely transportable from machine to machine without recompilation. It is not, however, as fast as true compiled code.

In general, any version of Emacs can run byte-compiled code produced by recent earlier versions of Emacs, but the reverse is not true.

If you do not want a Lisp file to be compiled, ever, put a file-local variable binding for `no-byte-compile` into it, like this:

```
;; -*-no-byte-compile: t; -*-
```

16.1 Performance of Byte-Compiled Code

A byte-compiled function is not as efficient as a primitive function written in C, but runs much faster than the version written in Lisp. Here is an example:

```
(defun silly-loop (n)
  "Return the time, in seconds, to run N iterations of a loop."
  (let ((t1 (float-time)))
    (while (> (setq n (1- n)) 0))
    (- (float-time) t1)))
⇒ silly-loop

(silly-loop 50000000)
⇒ 10.235304117202759

(byte-compile 'silly-loop)
⇒ [Compiled code not shown]

(silly-loop 50000000)
⇒ 3.705854892730713
```

In this example, the interpreted code required 10 seconds to run, whereas the byte-compiled code required less than 4 seconds. These results are representative, but actual results may vary.

16.2 Byte-Compilation Functions

You can byte-compile an individual function or macro definition with the `byte-compile` function. You can compile a whole file with `byte-compile-file`, or several files with `byte-recompile-directory` or `batch-byte-compile`.

Sometimes, the byte compiler produces warning and/or error messages (see Section 16.6 [Compiler Errors], page 265, for details). These messages are normally recorded in a buffer called *Compile-Log*, which uses Compilation mode. See Section "Compilation Mode" in *The GNU Emacs Manual*. However, if the variable `byte-compile-debug` is non-nil, error message will be signaled as Lisp errors instead (see Section 10.6.3 [Errors], page 148).

Be careful when writing macro calls in files that you intend to byte-compile. Since macro calls are expanded when they are compiled, the macros need to be loaded into Emacs or the byte compiler will not do the right thing. The usual way to handle this is with `require` forms which specify the files containing the needed macro definitions (see Section 15.7 [Named Features], page 253). Normally, the byte compiler does not evaluate the code that it is compiling, but it handles `require` forms specially, by loading the specified libraries. To avoid loading the macro definition files when someone *runs* the compiled program, write `eval-when-compile` around the `require` calls (see Section 16.5 [Eval During Compile], page 264). For more details, See Section 13.3 [Compiling Macros], page 219.

Inline (`defsubst`) functions are less troublesome; if you compile a call to such a function before its definition is known, the call will still work right, it will just run slower.

byte-compile *symbol*   [Function]

This function byte-compiles the function definition of *symbol*, replacing the previous definition with the compiled one. The function definition of *symbol* must be the actual code for the function; `byte-compile` does not handle function indirection. The return value is the byte-code function object which is the compiled definition of *symbol* (see Section 16.7 [Byte-Code Objects], page 266).

```
(defun factorial (integer)
  "Compute factorial of INTEGER."
  (if (= 1 integer) 1
    (* integer (factorial (1- integer)))))
⇒ factorial

(byte-compile 'factorial)
⇒
#[(integer)
  "^H\301U\203^H^@\301\207\302^H\303^HS!\"\207"
  [integer 1 * factorial]
  4 "Compute factorial of INTEGER."]
```

If *symbol*'s definition is a byte-code function object, `byte-compile` does nothing and returns **nil**. It does not compile the symbol's definition again, since the original (non-compiled) code has already been replaced in the symbol's function cell by the byte-compiled code.

The argument to `byte-compile` can also be a `lambda` expression. In that case, the function returns the corresponding compiled code but does not store it anywhere.

compile-defun &**optional** *arg*   [Command]

This command reads the defun containing point, compiles it, and evaluates the result. If you use this on a defun that is actually a function definition, the effect is to install a compiled version of that function.

`compile-defun` normally displays the result of evaluation in the echo area, but if *arg* is non-**nil**, it inserts the result in the current buffer after the form it compiled.

byte-compile-file *filename* **&optional** *load*   [Command]

This function compiles a file of Lisp code named *filename* into a file of byte-code. The output file's name is made by changing the '.el' suffix into '.elc'; if *filename* does not end in '.el', it adds '.elc' to the end of *filename*.

Compilation works by reading the input file one form at a time. If it is a definition of a function or macro, the compiled function or macro definition is written out. Other forms are batched together, then each batch is compiled, and written so that its compiled code will be executed when the file is read. All comments are discarded when the input file is read.

This command returns **t** if there were no errors and **nil** otherwise. When called interactively, it prompts for the file name.

If *load* is non-**nil**, this command loads the compiled file after compiling it. Interactively, *load* is the prefix argument.

```
$ ls -l push*
-rw-r--r-- 1 lewis lewis 791 Oct  5 20:31 push.el


(byte-compile-file "~/emacs/push.el")
     ⇒ t


$ ls -l push*
-rw-r--r-- 1 lewis lewis 791 Oct  5 20:31 push.el
-rw-rw-rw- 1 lewis lewis 638 Oct  8 20:25 push.elc
```

byte-recompile-directory *directory* **&optional** *flag force*   [Command]

This command recompiles every '.el' file in *directory* (or its subdirectories) that needs recompilation. A file needs recompilation if a '.elc' file exists but is older than the '.el' file.

When a '.el' file has no corresponding '.elc' file, *flag* says what to do. If it is **nil**, this command ignores these files. If *flag* is 0, it compiles them. If it is neither **nil** nor 0, it asks the user whether to compile each such file, and asks about each subdirectory as well.

Interactively, **byte-recompile-directory** prompts for *directory* and *flag* is the prefix argument.

If *force* is non-**nil**, this command recompiles every '.el' file that has a '.elc' file.

The returned value is unpredictable.

batch-byte-compile **&optional** *noforce*   [Function]

This function runs **byte-compile-file** on files specified on the command line. This function must be used only in a batch execution of Emacs, as it kills Emacs on completion. An error in one file does not prevent processing of subsequent files, but no output file will be generated for it, and the Emacs process will terminate with a nonzero status code.

If *noforce* is non-**nil**, this function does not recompile files that have an up-to-date '.elc' file.

```
$ emacs -batch -f batch-byte-compile *.el
```

16.3 Documentation Strings and Compilation

When Emacs loads functions and variables from a byte-compiled file, it normally does not load their documentation strings into memory. Each documentation string is dynamically loaded from the byte-compiled file only when needed. This saves memory, and speeds up loading by skipping the processing of the documentation strings.

This feature has a drawback: if you delete, move, or alter the compiled file (such as by compiling a new version), Emacs may no longer be able to access the documentation string of previously-loaded functions or variables. Such a problem normally only occurs if you build Emacs yourself, and happen to edit and/or recompile the Lisp source files. To solve it, just reload each file after recompilation.

Dynamic loading of documentation strings from byte-compiled files is determined, at compile time, for each byte-compiled file. It can be disabled via the option `byte-compile-dynamic-docstrings`.

`byte-compile-dynamic-docstrings` [User Option]

> If this is non-`nil`, the byte compiler generates compiled files that are set up for dynamic loading of documentation strings.

> To disable the dynamic loading feature for a specific file, set this option to `nil` in its header line (see Section "Local Variables in Files" in *The GNU Emacs Manual*), like this:

> ```
> -*-byte-compile-dynamic-docstrings: nil;-*-
> ```

> This is useful mainly if you expect to change the file, and you want Emacs sessions that have already loaded it to keep working when the file changes.

Internally, the dynamic loading of documentation strings is accomplished by writing compiled files with a special Lisp reader construct, '`#@count`'. This construct skips the next *count* characters. It also uses the '`#$`' construct, which stands for the name of this file, as a string. Do not use these constructs in Lisp source files; they are not designed to be clear to humans reading the file.

16.4 Dynamic Loading of Individual Functions

When you compile a file, you can optionally enable the *dynamic function loading* feature (also known as *lazy loading*). With dynamic function loading, loading the file doesn't fully read the function definitions in the file. Instead, each function definition contains a place-holder which refers to the file. The first time each function is called, it reads the full definition from the file, to replace the place-holder.

The advantage of dynamic function loading is that loading the file becomes much faster. This is a good thing for a file which contains many separate user-callable functions, if using one of them does not imply you will probably also use the rest. A specialized mode which provides many keyboard commands often has that usage pattern: a user may invoke the mode, but use only a few of the commands it provides.

The dynamic loading feature has certain disadvantages:

- If you delete or move the compiled file after loading it, Emacs can no longer load the remaining function definitions not already loaded.

- If you alter the compiled file (such as by compiling a new version), then trying to load any function not already loaded will usually yield nonsense results.

These problems will never happen in normal circumstances with installed Emacs files. But they are quite likely to happen with Lisp files that you are changing. The easiest way to prevent these problems is to reload the new compiled file immediately after each recompilation.

The byte compiler uses the dynamic function loading feature if the variable `byte-compile-dynamic` is non-`nil` at compilation time. Do not set this variable globally, since dynamic loading is desirable only for certain files. Instead, enable the feature for specific source files with file-local variable bindings. For example, you could do it by writing this text in the source file's first line:

```
-*-byte-compile-dynamic: t;-*-
```

`byte-compile-dynamic`   [Variable]
> If this is non-`nil`, the byte compiler generates compiled files that are set up for dynamic function loading.

`fetch-bytecode` *function*   [Function]
> If *function* is a byte-code function object, this immediately finishes loading the byte code of *function* from its byte-compiled file, if it is not fully loaded already. Otherwise, it does nothing. It always returns *function*.

16.5 Evaluation During Compilation

These features permit you to write code to be evaluated during compilation of a program.

`eval-and-compile` *body...*   [Special Form]
> This form marks *body* to be evaluated both when you compile the containing code and when you run it (whether compiled or not).
>
> You can get a similar result by putting *body* in a separate file and referring to that file with `require`. That method is preferable when *body* is large. Effectively `require` is automatically `eval-and-compile`, the package is loaded both when compiling and executing.
>
> `autoload` is also effectively `eval-and-compile` too. It's recognized when compiling, so uses of such a function don't produce "not known to be defined" warnings.
>
> Most uses of `eval-and-compile` are fairly sophisticated.
>
> If a macro has a helper function to build its result, and that macro is used both locally and outside the package, then `eval-and-compile` should be used to get the helper both when compiling and then later when running.
>
> If functions are defined programmatically (with `fset` say), then `eval-and-compile` can be used to have that done at compile-time as well as run-time, so calls to those functions are checked (and warnings about "not known to be defined" suppressed).

`eval-when-compile` *body...*   [Special Form]
> This form marks *body* to be evaluated at compile time but not when the compiled program is loaded. The result of evaluation by the compiler becomes a constant which

appears in the compiled program. If you load the source file, rather than compiling it, *body* is evaluated normally.

If you have a constant that needs some calculation to produce, `eval-when-compile` can do that at compile-time. For example,

```
(defvar my-regexp
  (eval-when-compile (regexp-opt '("aaa" "aba" "abb"))))
```

If you're using another package, but only need macros from it (the byte compiler will expand those), then `eval-when-compile` can be used to load it for compiling, but not executing. For example,

```
(eval-when-compile
  (require 'my-macro-package))
```

The same sort of thing goes for macros and `defsubst` functions defined locally and only for use within the file. They are needed for compiling the file, but in most cases they are not needed for execution of the compiled file. For example,

```
(eval-when-compile
  (unless (fboundp 'some-new-thing)
    (defmacro 'some-new-thing ()
      (compatibility code))))
```

This is often good for code that's only a fallback for compatibility with other versions of Emacs.

Common Lisp Note: At top level, `eval-when-compile` is analogous to the Common Lisp idiom `(eval-when (compile eval) ...)`. Elsewhere, the Common Lisp '#.' reader macro (but not when interpreting) is closer to what `eval-when-compile` does.

16.6 Compiler Errors

Error and warning messages from byte compilation are printed in a buffer named `*Compile-Log*`. These messages include file names and line numbers identifying the location of the problem. The usual Emacs commands for operating on compiler output can be used on these messages.

When an error is due to invalid syntax in the program, the byte compiler might get confused about the error's exact location. One way to investigate is to switch to the buffer `*Compiler Input*`. (This buffer name starts with a space, so it does not show up in the Buffer Menu.) This buffer contains the program being compiled, and point shows how far the byte compiler was able to read; the cause of the error might be nearby. See Section 17.3 [Syntax Errors], page 299, for some tips for locating syntax errors.

A common type of warning issued by the byte compiler is for functions and variables that were used but not defined. Such warnings report the line number for the end of the file, not the locations where the missing functions or variables were used; to find these, you must search the file manually.

If you are sure that a warning message about a missing function or variable is unjustified, there are several ways to suppress it:

- You can suppress the warning for a specific call to a function *func* by conditionalizing it on an `fboundp` test, like this:

```
(if (fboundp 'func) ...(func ...)...)
```

The call to *func* must be in the *then-form* of the `if`, and *func* must appear quoted in the call to `fboundp`. (This feature operates for `cond` as well.)

- Likewise, you can suppress the warning for a specific use of a variable *variable* by conditionalizing it on a `boundp` test:

  ```
  (if (boundp 'variable) ...variable...)
  ```

  The reference to *variable* must be in the *then-form* of the `if`, and *variable* must appear quoted in the call to `boundp`.

- You can tell the compiler that a function is defined using `declare-function`. See Section 12.15 [Declaring Functions], page 214.

- Likewise, you can tell the compiler that a variable is defined using `defvar` with no initial value. (Note that this marks the variable as special.) See Section 11.5 [Defining Variables], page 161.

You can also suppress any and all compiler warnings within a certain expression using the construct `with-no-warnings`:

with-no-warnings *body...*   [Special Form]

In execution, this is equivalent to (`progn` *body...*), but the compiler does not issue warnings for anything that occurs inside *body*.

We recommend that you use this construct around the smallest possible piece of code, to avoid missing possible warnings other than one you intend to suppress.

Byte compiler warnings can be controlled more precisely by setting the variable `byte-compile-warnings`. See its documentation string for details.

16.7 Byte-Code Function Objects

Byte-compiled functions have a special data type: they are *byte-code function objects*. Whenever such an object appears as a function to be called, Emacs uses the byte-code interpreter to execute the byte-code.

Internally, a byte-code function object is much like a vector; its elements can be accessed using `aref`. Its printed representation is like that for a vector, with an additional '#' before the opening '['. It must have at least four elements; there is no maximum number, but only the first six elements have any normal use. They are:

argdesc   The descriptor of the arguments. This can either be a list of arguments, as described in Section 12.2.3 [Argument List], page 189, or an integer encoding the required number of arguments. In the latter case, the value of the descriptor specifies the minimum number of arguments in the bits zero to 6, and the maximum number of arguments in bits 8 to 14. If the argument list uses `&rest`, then bit 7 is set; otherwise it's cleared.

                If *argdesc* is a list, the arguments will be dynamically bound before executing the byte code. If *argdesc* is an integer, the arguments will be instead pushed onto the stack of the byte-code interpreter, before executing the code.

byte-code   The string containing the byte-code instructions.

constants   The vector of Lisp objects referenced by the byte code. These include symbols used as function names and variable names.

stacksize   The maximum stack size this function needs.

docstring   The documentation string (if any); otherwise, `nil`. The value may be a number or a list, in case the documentation string is stored in a file. Use the function `documentation` to get the real documentation string (see Section 23.2 [Accessing Documentation], page 486).

interactive

The interactive spec (if any). This can be a string or a Lisp expression. It is `nil` for a function that isn't interactive.

Here's an example of a byte-code function object, in printed representation. It is the definition of the command `backward-sexp`.

```
#[256
  "\211\204^G^@\300\262^A\301^A[!\207"
  [1 forward-sexp]
  3
  1793299
  "^p"]
```

The primitive way to create a byte-code object is with `make-byte-code`:

`make-byte-code` **&rest** *elements*   [Function]

This function constructs and returns a byte-code function object with *elements* as its elements.

You should not try to come up with the elements for a byte-code function yourself, because if they are inconsistent, Emacs may crash when you call the function. Always leave it to the byte compiler to create these objects; it makes the elements consistent (we hope).

16.8 Disassembled Byte-Code

People do not write byte-code; that job is left to the byte compiler. But we provide a disassembler to satisfy a cat-like curiosity. The disassembler converts the byte-compiled code into human-readable form.

The byte-code interpreter is implemented as a simple stack machine. It pushes values onto a stack of its own, then pops them off to use them in calculations whose results are themselves pushed back on the stack. When a byte-code function returns, it pops a value off the stack and returns it as the value of the function.

In addition to the stack, byte-code functions can use, bind, and set ordinary Lisp variables, by transferring values between variables and the stack.

`disassemble` *object* **&optional** *buffer-or-name*   [Command]

This command displays the disassembled code for *object*. In interactive use, or if *buffer-or-name* is `nil` or omitted, the output goes in a buffer named `*Disassemble*`. If *buffer-or-name* is non-`nil`, it must be a buffer or the name of an existing buffer. Then the output goes there, at point, and point is left before the output.

The argument *object* can be a function name, a lambda expression (see Section 12.2 [Lambda Expressions], page 188), or a byte-code object (see Section 16.7 [Byte-Code Objects], page 266). If it is a lambda expression, `disassemble` compiles it and disassembles the resulting compiled code.

Here are two examples of using the `disassemble` function. We have added explanatory comments to help you relate the byte-code to the Lisp source; these do not appear in the output of `disassemble`.

```
(defun factorial (integer)
  "Compute factorial of an integer."
  (if (= 1 integer) 1
    (* integer (factorial (1- integer)))))
      ⇒ factorial

(factorial 4)
      ⇒ 24

(disassemble 'factorial)
      ⊣ byte-code for factorial:
 doc: Compute factorial of an integer.
 args: (integer)
```

```
0   varref   integer        ; Get the value of integer and
                            ;   push it onto the stack.
1   constant 1              ; Push 1 onto stack.
2   eqlsign                 ; Pop top two values off stack, compare
                            ;   them, and push result onto stack.
3   goto-if-nil 1           ; Pop and test top of stack;
                            ;   if nil, go to 1, else continue.
6   constant 1              ; Push 1 onto top of stack.
7   return                  ; Return the top element of the stack.
8:1 varref   integer        ; Push value of integer onto stack.
9   constant factorial      ; Push factorial onto stack.
10  varref   integer        ; Push value of integer onto stack.
11  sub1                    ; Pop integer, decrement value,
                            ;   push new value onto stack.
12  call     1              ; Call function factorial using first
                            ;   (i.e., top) stack element as argument;
                            ;   push returned value onto stack.

13 mult                     ; Pop top two values off stack, multiply
                            ;   them, and push result onto stack.
14 return                   ; Return the top element of the stack.
```

The `silly-loop` function is somewhat more complex:

```
(defun silly-loop (n)
  "Return time before and after N iterations of a loop."
  (let ((t1 (current-time-string)))
    (while (> (setq n (1- n))
             0))
    (list t1 (current-time-string))))
      ⇒ silly-loop
```

```
(disassemble 'silly-loop)
    ⊣ byte-code for silly-loop:
 doc: Return time before and after N iterations of a loop.
 args: (n)
```

0	constant current-time-string	;	Push current-time-string
		;	onto top of stack.
1	call	0	; Call current-time-string with no
		;	argument, push result onto stack.
2	varbind	t1	; Pop stack and bind t1 to popped value.
3:1	varref	n	; Get value of n from the environment
		;	and push the value on the stack.
4	sub1		; Subtract 1 from top of stack.
5	dup		; Duplicate top of stack; i.e., copy the top
		;	of the stack and push copy onto stack.
6	varset	n	; Pop the top of the stack,
		;	and bind n to the value.

```
;; (In effect, the sequence dup varset copies the top of the stack
;; into the value of n without popping it.)
```

7	constant	0	; Push 0 onto stack.
8	gtr		; Pop top two values off stack,
		;	test if *n* is greater than 0
		;	and push result onto stack.
9	goto-if-not-nil 1		; Goto 1 if n > 0
		;	(this continues the while loop)
		;	else continue.
12	varref	t1	; Push value of t1 onto stack.
13	constant current-time-string	;	Push current-time-string
		;	onto the top of the stack.
14	call	0	; Call current-time-string again.
15	unbind	1	; Unbind t1 in local environment.
16	list2		; Pop top two elements off stack, create a
		;	list of them, and push it onto stack.
17	return		; Return value of the top of stack.

17 Debugging Lisp Programs

There are several ways to find and investigate problems in an Emacs Lisp program.

- If a problem occurs when you run the program, you can use the built-in Emacs Lisp debugger to suspend the Lisp evaluator, and examine and/or alter its internal state.

- You can use Edebug, a source-level debugger for Emacs Lisp.

- If a syntactic problem is preventing Lisp from even reading the program, you can locate it using Lisp editing commands.

- You can look at the error and warning messages produced by the byte compiler when it compiles the program. See Section 16.6 [Compiler Errors], page 265.

- You can use the Testcover package to perform coverage testing on the program.

- You can use the ERT package to write regression tests for the program. See *ERT: Emacs Lisp Regression Testing*.

- You can profile the program to get hints about how to make it more efficient.

Other useful tools for debugging input and output problems are the dribble file (see Section 38.13 [Terminal Input], page 1010) and the `open-termscript` function (see Section 38.14 [Terminal Output], page 1011).

17.1 The Lisp Debugger

The ordinary *Lisp debugger* provides the ability to suspend evaluation of a form. While evaluation is suspended (a state that is commonly known as a *break*), you may examine the run time stack, examine the values of local or global variables, or change those values. Since a break is a recursive edit, all the usual editing facilities of Emacs are available; you can even run programs that will enter the debugger recursively. See Section 20.13 [Recursive Editing], page 386.

17.1.1 Entering the Debugger on an Error

The most important time to enter the debugger is when a Lisp error happens. This allows you to investigate the immediate causes of the error.

However, entry to the debugger is not a normal consequence of an error. Many commands signal Lisp errors when invoked inappropriately, and during ordinary editing it would be very inconvenient to enter the debugger each time this happens. So if you want errors to enter the debugger, set the variable `debug-on-error` to non-`nil`. (The command `toggle-debug-on-error` provides an easy way to do this.)

`debug-on-error`   [User Option]

> This variable determines whether the debugger is called when an error is signaled and not handled. If `debug-on-error` is `t`, all kinds of errors call the debugger, except those listed in `debug-ignored-errors` (see below). If it is `nil`, none call the debugger.
>
> The value can also be a list of error conditions (see Section 10.6.3.1 [Signaling Errors], page 148). Then the debugger is called only for error conditions in this list (except those also listed in `debug-ignored-errors`). For example, if you set `debug-on-error` to the list (`void-variable`), the debugger is only called for errors about a variable that has no value.

Note that `eval-expression-debug-on-error` overrides this variable in some cases; see below.

When this variable is non-`nil`, Emacs does not create an error handler around process filter functions and sentinels. Therefore, errors in these functions also invoke the debugger. See Chapter 36 [Processes], page 839.

`debug-ignored-errors`   [User Option]

This variable specifies errors which should not enter the debugger, regardless of the value of `debug-on-error`. Its value is a list of error condition symbols and/or regular expressions. If the error has any of those condition symbols, or if the error message matches any of the regular expressions, then that error does not enter the debugger.

The normal value of this variable includes `user-error`, as well as several errors that happen often during editing but rarely result from bugs in Lisp programs. However, "rarely" is not "never"; if your program fails with an error that matches this list, you may try changing this list to debug the error. The easiest way is usually to set `debug-ignored-errors` to `nil`.

`eval-expression-debug-on-error`   [User Option]

If this variable has a non-`nil` value (the default), running the command `eval-expression` causes `debug-on-error` to be temporarily bound to to `t`. See Section "Evaluating Emacs-Lisp Expressions" in *The GNU Emacs Manual*.

If `eval-expression-debug-on-error` is `nil`, then the value of `debug-on-error` is not changed during `eval-expression`.

`debug-on-signal`   [User Option]

Normally, errors caught by `condition-case` never invoke the debugger. The `condition-case` gets a chance to handle the error before the debugger gets a chance.

If you change `debug-on-signal` to a non-`nil` value, the debugger gets the first chance at every error, regardless of the presence of `condition-case`. (To invoke the debugger, the error must still fulfill the criteria specified by `debug-on-error` and `debug-ignored-errors`.)

For example, setting this variable is useful to get a backtrace from code evaluated by emacsclient's `--eval` option. If Lisp code evaluated by emacsclient signals an error while this variable is non-`nil`, the backtrace will popup in the running Emacs.

Warning: Setting this variable to non-`nil` may have annoying effects. Various parts of Emacs catch errors in the normal course of affairs, and you may not even realize that errors happen there. If you need to debug code wrapped in `condition-case`, consider using `condition-case-unless-debug` (see Section 10.6.3.3 [Handling Errors], page 150).

`debug-on-event`   [User Option]

If you set `debug-on-event` to a special event (see Section 20.9 [Special Events], page 381), Emacs will try to enter the debugger as soon as it receives this event, bypassing `special-event-map`. At present, the only supported values correspond to the signals `SIGUSR1` and `SIGUSR2` (this is the default). This can be helpful when `inhibit-quit` is set and Emacs is not otherwise responding.

debug-on-message   [Variable]

> If you set **debug-on-message** to a regular expression, Emacs will enter the debugger if it displays a matching message in the echo area. For example, this can be useful when trying to find the cause of a particular message.

To debug an error that happens during loading of the init file, use the option '--debug-init'. This binds **debug-on-error** to **t** while loading the init file, and bypasses the **condition-case** which normally catches errors in the init file.

17.1.2 Debugging Infinite Loops

When a program loops infinitely and fails to return, your first problem is to stop the loop. On most operating systems, you can do this with *C-g*, which causes a *quit*. See Section 20.11 [Quitting], page 382.

Ordinary quitting gives no information about why the program was looping. To get more information, you can set the variable **debug-on-quit** to non-**nil**. Once you have the debugger running in the middle of the infinite loop, you can proceed from the debugger using the stepping commands. If you step through the entire loop, you may get enough information to solve the problem.

Quitting with *C-g* is not considered an error, and **debug-on-error** has no effect on the handling of *C-g*. Likewise, **debug-on-quit** has no effect on errors.

debug-on-quit   [User Option]

> This variable determines whether the debugger is called when **quit** is signaled and not handled. If **debug-on-quit** is non-**nil**, then the debugger is called whenever you quit (that is, type *C-g*). If **debug-on-quit** is **nil** (the default), then the debugger is not called when you quit.

17.1.3 Entering the Debugger on a Function Call

To investigate a problem that happens in the middle of a program, one useful technique is to enter the debugger whenever a certain function is called. You can do this to the function in which the problem occurs, and then step through the function, or you can do this to a function called shortly before the problem, step quickly over the call to that function, and then step through its caller.

debug-on-entry *function-name*   [Command]

> This function requests *function-name* to invoke the debugger each time it is called.

> Any function or macro defined as Lisp code may be set to break on entry, regardless of whether it is interpreted code or compiled code. If the function is a command, it will enter the debugger when called from Lisp and when called interactively (after the reading of the arguments). You can also set debug-on-entry for primitive functions (i.e., those written in C) this way, but it only takes effect when the primitive is called from Lisp code. Debug-on-entry is not allowed for special forms.

> When **debug-on-entry** is called interactively, it prompts for *function-name* in the minibuffer. If the function is already set up to invoke the debugger on entry, **debug-on-entry** does nothing. **debug-on-entry** always returns *function-name*.

Here's an example to illustrate use of this function:

```
(defun fact (n)
  (if (zerop n) 1
      (* n (fact (1- n))))))
     ⇒ fact
(debug-on-entry 'fact)
     ⇒ fact
(fact 3)


------ Buffer: *Backtrace* ------
Debugger entered--entering a function:
* fact(3)
  eval((fact 3))
  eval-last-sexp-1(nil)
  eval-last-sexp(nil)
  call-interactively(eval-last-sexp)
------ Buffer: *Backtrace* ------
```

`cancel-debug-on-entry` **&optional** *function-name*   [Command]

This function undoes the effect of `debug-on-entry` on *function-name*. When called interactively, it prompts for *function-name* in the minibuffer. If *function-name* is omitted or `nil`, it cancels break-on-entry for all functions. Calling `cancel-debug-on-entry` does nothing to a function which is not currently set up to break on entry.

17.1.4 Explicit Entry to the Debugger

You can cause the debugger to be called at a certain point in your program by writing the expression `(debug)` at that point. To do this, visit the source file, insert the text '`(debug)`' at the proper place, and type *C-M-x* (`eval-defun`, a Lisp mode key binding). **Warning:** if you do this for temporary debugging purposes, be sure to undo this insertion before you save the file!

The place where you insert '`(debug)`' must be a place where an additional form can be evaluated and its value ignored. (If the value of `(debug)` isn't ignored, it will alter the execution of the program!) The most common suitable places are inside a **progn** or an implicit **progn** (see Section 10.1 [Sequencing], page 135).

If you don't know exactly where in the source code you want to put the debug statement, but you want to display a backtrace when a certain message is displayed, you can set `debug-on-message` to a regular expression matching the desired message.

17.1.5 Using the Debugger

When the debugger is entered, it displays the previously selected buffer in one window and a buffer named `*Backtrace*` in another window. The backtrace buffer contains one line for each level of Lisp function execution currently going on. At the beginning of this buffer is a message describing the reason that the debugger was invoked (such as the error message and associated data, if it was invoked due to an error).

The backtrace buffer is read-only and uses a special major mode, Debugger mode, in which letters are defined as debugger commands. The usual Emacs editing commands are available; thus, you can switch windows to examine the buffer that was being edited at the time of the error, switch buffers, visit files, or do any other sort of editing. However, the debugger is a recursive editing level (see Section 20.13 [Recursive Editing], page 386) and it is wise to go back to the backtrace buffer and exit the debugger (with the q command) when you are finished with it. Exiting the debugger gets out of the recursive edit and buries the backtrace buffer. (You can customize what the q command does with the backtrace buffer by setting the variable debugger-bury-or-kill. For example, set it to kill if you prefer to kill the buffer rather than bury it. Consult the variable's documentation for more possibilities.)

When the debugger has been entered, the debug-on-error variable is temporarily set according to eval-expression-debug-on-error. If the latter variable is non-nil, debug-on-error will temporarily be set to t. This means that any further errors that occur while doing a debugging session will (by default) trigger another backtrace. If this is not what you want, you can either set eval-expression-debug-on-error to nil, or set debug-on-error to nil in debugger-mode-hook.

The backtrace buffer shows you the functions that are executing and their argument values. It also allows you to specify a stack frame by moving point to the line describing that frame. (A stack frame is the place where the Lisp interpreter records information about a particular invocation of a function.) The frame whose line point is on is considered the *current frame*. Some of the debugger commands operate on the current frame. If a line starts with a star, that means that exiting that frame will call the debugger again. This is useful for examining the return value of a function.

If a function name is underlined, that means the debugger knows where its source code is located. You can click with the mouse on that name, or move to it and type RET, to visit the source code.

The debugger itself must be run byte-compiled, since it makes assumptions about how many stack frames are used for the debugger itself. These assumptions are false if the debugger is running interpreted.

17.1.6 Debugger Commands

The debugger buffer (in Debugger mode) provides special commands in addition to the usual Emacs commands. The most important use of debugger commands is for stepping through code, so that you can see how control flows. The debugger can step through the control structures of an interpreted function, but cannot do so in a byte-compiled function. If you would like to step through a byte-compiled function, replace it with an interpreted definition of the same function. (To do this, visit the source for the function and type C-M-x on its definition.) You cannot use the Lisp debugger to step through a primitive function.

Here is a list of Debugger mode commands:

c   Exit the debugger and continue execution. This resumes execution of the program as if the debugger had never been entered (aside from any side-effects that you caused by changing variable values or data structures while inside the debugger).

d Continue execution, but enter the debugger the next time any Lisp function is called. This allows you to step through the subexpressions of an expression, seeing what values the subexpressions compute, and what else they do.

    The stack frame made for the function call which enters the debugger in this way will be flagged automatically so that the debugger will be called again when the frame is exited. You can use the *u* command to cancel this flag.

b Flag the current frame so that the debugger will be entered when the frame is exited. Frames flagged in this way are marked with stars in the backtrace buffer.

u Don't enter the debugger when the current frame is exited. This cancels a *b* command on that frame. The visible effect is to remove the star from the line in the backtrace buffer.

j Flag the current frame like *b*. Then continue execution like *c*, but temporarily disable break-on-entry for all functions that are set up to do so by **debug-on-entry**.

e Read a Lisp expression in the minibuffer, evaluate it (with the relevant lexical environment, if applicable), and print the value in the echo area. The debugger alters certain important variables, and the current buffer, as part of its operation; *e* temporarily restores their values from outside the debugger, so you can examine and change them. This makes the debugger more transparent. By contrast, *M-:* does nothing special in the debugger; it shows you the variable values within the debugger.

R Like *e*, but also save the result of evaluation in the buffer ***Debugger-record***.

q Terminate the program being debugged; return to top-level Emacs command execution.

    If the debugger was entered due to a *C-g* but you really want to quit, and not debug, use the *q* command.

r Return a value from the debugger. The value is computed by reading an expression with the minibuffer and evaluating it.

    The *r* command is useful when the debugger was invoked due to exit from a Lisp call frame (as requested with *b* or by entering the frame with *d*); then the value specified in the *r* command is used as the value of that frame. It is also useful if you call **debug** and use its return value. Otherwise, *r* has the same effect as *c*, and the specified return value does not matter.

    You can't use *r* when the debugger was entered due to an error.

l Display a list of functions that will invoke the debugger when called. This is a list of functions that are set to break on entry by means of **debug-on-entry**.

v Toggle the display of local variables of the current stack frame.

17.1.7 Invoking the Debugger

Here we describe in full detail the function **debug** that is used to invoke the debugger.

debug &rest *debugger-args*   [Command]

This function enters the debugger. It switches buffers to a buffer named *Backtrace* (or *Backtrace*<2> if it is the second recursive entry to the debugger, etc.), and fills it with information about the stack of Lisp function calls. It then enters a recursive edit, showing the backtrace buffer in Debugger mode.

The Debugger mode *c*, *d*, *j*, and *r* commands exit the recursive edit; then **debug** switches back to the previous buffer and returns to whatever called **debug**. This is the only way the function **debug** can return to its caller.

The use of the *debugger-args* is that **debug** displays the rest of its arguments at the top of the *Backtrace* buffer, so that the user can see them. Except as described below, this is the *only* way these arguments are used.

However, certain values for first argument to **debug** have a special significance. (Normally, these values are used only by the internals of Emacs, and not by programmers calling **debug**.) Here is a table of these special values:

lambda
: A first argument of **lambda** means **debug** was called because of entry to a function when **debug-on-next-call** was non-**nil**. The debugger displays 'Debugger entered--entering a function:' as a line of text at the top of the buffer.

debug
: **debug** as first argument means **debug** was called because of entry to a function that was set to debug on entry. The debugger displays the string 'Debugger entered--entering a function:', just as in the **lambda** case. It also marks the stack frame for that function so that it will invoke the debugger when exited.

t
: When the first argument is **t**, this indicates a call to **debug** due to evaluation of a function call form when **debug-on-next-call** is non-**nil**. The debugger displays 'Debugger entered--beginning evaluation of function call form:' as the top line in the buffer.

exit
: When the first argument is **exit**, it indicates the exit of a stack frame previously marked to invoke the debugger on exit. The second argument given to **debug** in this case is the value being returned from the frame. The debugger displays 'Debugger entered--returning value:' in the top line of the buffer, followed by the value being returned.

error
: When the first argument is **error**, the debugger indicates that it is being entered because an error or **quit** was signaled and not handled, by displaying 'Debugger entered--Lisp error:' followed by the error signaled and any arguments to **signal**. For example,

```
(let ((debug-on-error t))
  (/ 1 0))


------ Buffer: *Backtrace* ------
Debugger entered--Lisp error: (arith-error)
  /(1 0)
...
------ Buffer: *Backtrace* ------
```

If an error was signaled, presumably the variable `debug-on-error` is non-`nil`. If `quit` was signaled, then presumably the variable `debug-on-quit` is non-`nil`.

nil   Use `nil` as the first of the *debugger-args* when you want to enter the debugger explicitly. The rest of the *debugger-args* are printed on the top line of the buffer. You can use this feature to display messages—for example, to remind yourself of the conditions under which `debug` is called.

17.1.8 Internals of the Debugger

This section describes functions and variables used internally by the debugger.

debugger   [Variable]
The value of this variable is the function to call to invoke the debugger. Its value must be a function of any number of arguments, or, more typically, the name of a function. This function should invoke some kind of debugger. The default value of the variable is `debug`.

The first argument that Lisp hands to the function indicates why it was called. The convention for arguments is detailed in the description of `debug` (see Section 17.1.7 [Invoking the Debugger], page 275).

backtrace   [Command]
This function prints a trace of Lisp function calls currently active. This is the function used by `debug` to fill up the *Backtrace* buffer. It is written in C, since it must have access to the stack to determine which function calls are active. The return value is always `nil`.

In the following example, a Lisp expression calls `backtrace` explicitly. This prints the backtrace to the stream `standard-output`, which, in this case, is the buffer 'backtrace-output'.

Each line of the backtrace represents one function call. The line shows the values of the function's arguments if they are all known; if they are still being computed, the line says so. The arguments of special forms are elided.

```
(with-output-to-temp-buffer "backtrace-output"
  (let ((var 1))
    (save-excursion
      (setq var (eval '(progn
                          (1+ var)
                          (list 'testing (backtrace)))))))))

     ⇒ (testing nil)


----------- Buffer: backtrace-output -----------
backtrace()
(list ...computing arguments...)
(progn ...)
eval((progn (1+ var) (list (quote testing) (backtrace))))
(setq ...)
(save-excursion ...)
(let ...)
(with-output-to-temp-buffer ...)
eval((with-output-to-temp-buffer ...))
```

```
        eval-last-sexp-1(nil)
        eval-last-sexp(nil)
        call-interactively(eval-last-sexp)
----------- Buffer: backtrace-output ------------
```

debug-on-next-call   [Variable]

> If this variable is non-`nil`, it says to call the debugger before the next `eval`, `apply` or `funcall`. Entering the debugger sets `debug-on-next-call` to `nil`.
>
> The *d* command in the debugger works by setting this variable.

backtrace-debug *level flag*   [Function]

> This function sets the debug-on-exit flag of the stack frame *level* levels down the stack, giving it the value *flag*. If *flag* is non-`nil`, this will cause the debugger to be entered when that frame later exits. Even a nonlocal exit through that frame will enter the debugger.
>
> This function is used only by the debugger.

command-debug-status   [Variable]

> This variable records the debugging status of the current interactive command. Each time a command is called interactively, this variable is bound to `nil`. The debugger can set this variable to leave information for future debugger invocations during the same command invocation.
>
> The advantage of using this variable rather than an ordinary global variable is that the data will never carry over to a subsequent command invocation.
>
> This variable is obsolete and will be removed in future versions.

backtrace-frame *frame-number*   [Function]

> The function `backtrace-frame` is intended for use in Lisp debuggers. It returns information about what computation is happening in the stack frame *frame-number* levels down.
>
> If that frame has not evaluated the arguments yet, or is a special form, the value is (`nil` *function* *arg-forms*...).
>
> If that frame has evaluated its arguments and called its function already, the return value is (`t` *function* *arg-values*...).
>
> In the return value, *function* is whatever was supplied as the CAR of the evaluated list, or a `lambda` expression in the case of a macro call. If the function has a `&rest` argument, that is represented as the tail of the list *arg-values*.
>
> If *frame-number* is out of range, `backtrace-frame` returns `nil`.

17.2 Edebug

Edebug is a source-level debugger for Emacs Lisp programs, with which you can:

- Step through evaluation, stopping before and after each expression.
- Set conditional or unconditional breakpoints.
- Stop when a specified condition is true (the global break event).
- Trace slow or fast, stopping briefly at each stop point, or at each breakpoint.

- Display expression results and evaluate expressions as if outside of Edebug.
- Automatically re-evaluate a list of expressions and display their results each time Edebug updates the display.
- Output trace information on function calls and returns.
- Stop when an error occurs.
- Display a backtrace, omitting Edebug's own frames.
- Specify argument evaluation for macros and defining forms.
- Obtain rudimentary coverage testing and frequency counts.

The first three sections below should tell you enough about Edebug to start using it.

17.2.1 Using Edebug

To debug a Lisp program with Edebug, you must first *instrument* the Lisp code that you want to debug. A simple way to do this is to first move point into the definition of a function or macro and then do *C-u C-M-x* (`eval-defun` with a prefix argument). See Section 17.2.2 [Instrumenting], page 280, for alternative ways to instrument code.

Once a function is instrumented, any call to the function activates Edebug. Depending on which Edebug execution mode you have selected, activating Edebug may stop execution and let you step through the function, or it may update the display and continue execution while checking for debugging commands. The default execution mode is step, which stops execution. See Section 17.2.3 [Edebug Execution Modes], page 281.

Within Edebug, you normally view an Emacs buffer showing the source of the Lisp code you are debugging. This is referred to as the *source code buffer*, and it is temporarily read-only.

An arrow in the left fringe indicates the line where the function is executing. Point initially shows where within the line the function is executing, but this ceases to be true if you move point yourself.

If you instrument the definition of `fac` (shown below) and then execute `(fac 3)`, here is what you would normally see. Point is at the open-parenthesis before `if`.

```
      (defun fac (n)
    =>*(if (< 0 n)
          (* n (fac (1- n)))
        1))
```

The places within a function where Edebug can stop execution are called *stop points*. These occur both before and after each subexpression that is a list, and also after each variable reference. Here we use periods to show the stop points in the function `fac`:

```
      (defun fac (n)
        .(if .(< 0 n.).
            .(* n.  .(fac .(1- n.).).).
          1).)
```

The special commands of Edebug are available in the source code buffer in addition to the commands of Emacs Lisp mode. For example, you can type the Edebug command SPC to execute until the next stop point. If you type SPC once after entry to `fac`, here is the display you will see:

```
      (defun fac (n)
```

```
=>(if *(< 0 n)
      (* n (fac (1- n)))
   1))
```

When Edebug stops execution after an expression, it displays the expression's value in the echo area.

Other frequently used commands are *b* to set a breakpoint at a stop point, *g* to execute until a breakpoint is reached, and *q* to exit Edebug and return to the top-level command loop. Type *?* to display a list of all Edebug commands.

17.2.2 Instrumenting for Edebug

In order to use Edebug to debug Lisp code, you must first *instrument* the code. Instrumenting code inserts additional code into it, to invoke Edebug at the proper places.

When you invoke command *C-M-x* (`eval-defun`) with a prefix argument on a function definition, it instruments the definition before evaluating it. (This does not modify the source code itself.) If the variable `edebug-all-defs` is non-`nil`, that inverts the meaning of the prefix argument: in this case, *C-M-x* instruments the definition *unless* it has a prefix argument. The default value of `edebug-all-defs` is `nil`. The command *M-x edebug-all-defs* toggles the value of the variable `edebug-all-defs`.

If `edebug-all-defs` is non-`nil`, then the commands `eval-region`, `eval-current-buffer`, and `eval-buffer` also instrument any definitions they evaluate. Similarly, `edebug-all-forms` controls whether `eval-region` should instrument *any* form, even non-defining forms. This doesn't apply to loading or evaluations in the minibuffer. The command *M-x edebug-all-forms* toggles this option.

Another command, *M-x edebug-eval-top-level-form*, is available to instrument any top-level form regardless of the values of `edebug-all-defs` and `edebug-all-forms`. `edebug-defun` is an alias for `edebug-eval-top-level-form`.

While Edebug is active, the command *I* (`edebug-instrument-callee`) instruments the definition of the function or macro called by the list form after point, if it is not already instrumented. This is possible only if Edebug knows where to find the source for that function; for this reason, after loading Edebug, `eval-region` records the position of every definition it evaluates, even if not instrumenting it. See also the *i* command (see Section 17.2.4 [Jumping], page 282), which steps into the call after instrumenting the function.

Edebug knows how to instrument all the standard special forms, `interactive` forms with an expression argument, anonymous lambda expressions, and other defining forms. However, Edebug cannot determine on its own what a user-defined macro will do with the arguments of a macro call, so you must provide that information using Edebug specifications; for details, see Section 17.2.15 [Edebug and Macros], page 292.

When Edebug is about to instrument code for the first time in a session, it runs the hook `edebug-setup-hook`, then sets it to `nil`. You can use this to load Edebug specifications associated with a package you are using, but only when you use Edebug.

To remove instrumentation from a definition, simply re-evaluate its definition in a way that does not instrument. There are two ways of evaluating forms that never instrument them: from a file with `load`, and from the minibuffer with `eval-expression` (*M-:*).

If Edebug detects a syntax error while instrumenting, it leaves point at the erroneous code and signals an `invalid-read-syntax` error.

See Section 17.2.9 [Edebug Eval], page 286, for other evaluation functions available inside of Edebug.

17.2.3 Edebug Execution Modes

Edebug supports several execution modes for running the program you are debugging. We call these alternatives *Edebug execution modes*; do not confuse them with major or minor modes. The current Edebug execution mode determines how far Edebug continues execution before stopping—whether it stops at each stop point, or continues to the next breakpoint, for example—and how much Edebug displays the progress of the evaluation before it stops.

Normally, you specify the Edebug execution mode by typing a command to continue the program in a certain mode. Here is a table of these commands; all except for *S* resume execution of the program, at least for a certain distance.

S   Stop: don't execute any more of the program, but wait for more Edebug commands (`edebug-stop`).

SPC   Step: stop at the next stop point encountered (`edebug-step-mode`).

n   Next: stop at the next stop point encountered after an expression (`edebug-next-mode`). Also see `edebug-forward-sexp` in Section 17.2.4 [Jumping], page 282.

t   Trace: pause (normally one second) at each Edebug stop point (`edebug-trace-mode`).

T   Rapid trace: update the display at each stop point, but don't actually pause (`edebug-Trace-fast-mode`).

g   Go: run until the next breakpoint (`edebug-go-mode`). See Section 17.2.6.1 [Breakpoints], page 283.

c   Continue: pause one second at each breakpoint, and then continue (`edebug-continue-mode`).

C   Rapid continue: move point to each breakpoint, but don't pause (`edebug-Continue-fast-mode`).

G   Go non-stop: ignore breakpoints (`edebug-Go-nonstop-mode`). You can still stop the program by typing *S*, or any editing command.

In general, the execution modes earlier in the above list run the program more slowly or stop sooner than the modes later in the list.

When you enter a new Edebug level, Edebug will normally stop at the first instrumented function it encounters. If you prefer to stop only at a break point, or not at all (for example, when gathering coverage data), change the value of `edebug-initial-mode` from its default `step` to `go`, or `Go-nonstop`, or one of its other values (see Section 17.2.16 [Edebug Options], page 297). You can do this readily with *C-x C-a C-m* (`edebug-set-initial-mode`):

`edebug-set-initial-mode`   [Command]
          This command, bound to *C-x C-a C-m*, sets `edebug-initial-mode`. It prompts you for a key to indicate the mode. You should enter one of the eight keys listed above, which sets the corresponding mode.

Note that you may reenter the same Edebug level several times if, for example, an instrumented function is called several times from one command.

While executing or tracing, you can interrupt the execution by typing any Edebug command. Edebug stops the program at the next stop point and then executes the command you typed. For example, typing *t* during execution switches to trace mode at the next stop point. You can use *S* to stop execution without doing anything else.

If your function happens to read input, a character you type intending to interrupt execution may be read by the function instead. You can avoid such unintended results by paying attention to when your program wants input.

Keyboard macros containing the commands in this section do not completely work: exiting from Edebug, to resume the program, loses track of the keyboard macro. This is not easy to fix. Also, defining or executing a keyboard macro outside of Edebug does not affect commands inside Edebug. This is usually an advantage. See also the `edebug-continue-kbd-macro` option in Section 17.2.16 [Edebug Options], page 297.

`edebug-sit-for-seconds`   [User Option]
>   This option specifies how many seconds to wait between execution steps in trace mode or continue mode. The default is 1 second.

17.2.4 Jumping

The commands described in this section execute until they reach a specified location. All except *i* make a temporary breakpoint to establish the place to stop, then switch to go mode. Any other breakpoint reached before the intended stop point will also stop execution. See Section 17.2.6.1 [Breakpoints], page 283, for the details on breakpoints.

These commands may fail to work as expected in case of nonlocal exit, as that can bypass the temporary breakpoint where you expected the program to stop.

h   Proceed to the stop point near where point is (`edebug-goto-here`).

f   Run the program for one expression (`edebug-forward-sexp`).

o   Run the program until the end of the containing sexp (`edebug-step-out`).

i   Step into the function or macro called by the form after point (`edebug-step-in`).

The *h* command proceeds to the stop point at or after the current location of point, using a temporary breakpoint.

The *f* command runs the program forward over one expression. More precisely, it sets a temporary breakpoint at the position that `forward-sexp` would reach, then executes in go mode so that the program will stop at breakpoints.

With a prefix argument *n*, the temporary breakpoint is placed *n* sexps beyond point. If the containing list ends before *n* more elements, then the place to stop is after the containing expression.

You must check that the position `forward-sexp` finds is a place that the program will really get to. In `cond`, for example, this may not be true.

For flexibility, the *f* command does `forward-sexp` starting at point, rather than at the stop point. If you want to execute one expression *from the current stop point*, first type *w* (`edebug-where`) to move point there, and then type *f*.

The *o* command continues out of an expression. It places a temporary breakpoint at the end of the sexp containing point. If the containing sexp is a function definition itself, *o* continues until just before the last sexp in the definition. If that is where you are now, it returns from the function and then stops. In other words, this command does not exit the currently executing function unless you are positioned after the last sexp.

The *i* command steps into the function or macro called by the list form after point, and stops at its first stop point. Note that the form need not be the one about to be evaluated. But if the form is a function call about to be evaluated, remember to use this command before any of the arguments are evaluated, since otherwise it will be too late.

The *i* command instruments the function or macro it's supposed to step into, if it isn't instrumented already. This is convenient, but keep in mind that the function or macro remains instrumented unless you explicitly arrange to deinstrument it.

17.2.5 Miscellaneous Edebug Commands

Some miscellaneous Edebug commands are described here.

?   Display the help message for Edebug (`edebug-help`).

C-]   Abort one level back to the previous command level (`abort-recursive-edit`).

q   Return to the top level editor command loop (`top-level`). This exits all recursive editing levels, including all levels of Edebug activity. However, instrumented code protected with `unwind-protect` or `condition-case` forms may resume debugging.

Q   Like *q*, but don't stop even for protected code (`edebug-top-level-nonstop`).

r   Redisplay the most recently known expression result in the echo area (`edebug-previous-result`).

d   Display a backtrace, excluding Edebug's own functions for clarity (`edebug-backtrace`).

                You cannot use debugger commands in the backtrace buffer in Edebug as you would in the standard debugger.

                The backtrace buffer is killed automatically when you continue execution.

You can invoke commands from Edebug that activate Edebug again recursively. Whenever Edebug is active, you can quit to the top level with *q* or abort one recursive edit level with *C-]*. You can display a backtrace of all the pending evaluations with *d*.

17.2.6 Breaks

Edebug's step mode stops execution when the next stop point is reached. There are three other ways to stop Edebug execution once it has started: breakpoints, the global break condition, and source breakpoints.

17.2.6.1 Edebug Breakpoints

While using Edebug, you can specify *breakpoints* in the program you are testing: these are places where execution should stop. You can set a breakpoint at any stop point, as defined in Section 17.2.1 [Using Edebug], page 279. For setting and unsetting breakpoints, the stop point that is affected is the first one at or after point in the source code buffer. Here are the Edebug commands for breakpoints:

b   Set a breakpoint at the stop point at or after point (`edebug-set-breakpoint`). If you use a prefix argument, the breakpoint is temporary—it turns off the first time it stops the program.

u   Unset the breakpoint (if any) at the stop point at or after point (`edebug-unset-breakpoint`).

x condition RET
             Set a conditional breakpoint which stops the program only if evaluating *condition* produces a non-`nil` value (`edebug-set-conditional-breakpoint`). With a prefix argument, the breakpoint is temporary.

B   Move point to the next breakpoint in the current definition (`edebug-next-breakpoint`).

While in Edebug, you can set a breakpoint with *b* and unset one with *u*. First move point to the Edebug stop point of your choice, then type *b* or *u* to set or unset a breakpoint there. Unsetting a breakpoint where none has been set has no effect.

Re-evaluating or reinstrumenting a definition removes all of its previous breakpoints.

A *conditional breakpoint* tests a condition each time the program gets there. Any errors that occur as a result of evaluating the condition are ignored, as if the result were `nil`. To set a conditional breakpoint, use *x*, and specify the condition expression in the minibuffer. Setting a conditional breakpoint at a stop point that has a previously established conditional breakpoint puts the previous condition expression in the minibuffer so you can edit it.

You can make a conditional or unconditional breakpoint *temporary* by using a prefix argument with the command to set the breakpoint. When a temporary breakpoint stops the program, it is automatically unset.

Edebug always stops or pauses at a breakpoint, except when the Edebug mode is Go-nonstop. In that mode, it ignores breakpoints entirely.

To find out where your breakpoints are, use the *B* command, which moves point to the next breakpoint following point, within the same function, or to the first breakpoint if there are no following breakpoints. This command does not continue execution—it just moves point in the buffer.

17.2.6.2 Global Break Condition

A *global break condition* stops execution when a specified condition is satisfied, no matter where that may occur. Edebug evaluates the global break condition at every stop point; if it evaluates to a non-`nil` value, then execution stops or pauses depending on the execution mode, as if a breakpoint had been hit. If evaluating the condition gets an error, execution does not stop.

The condition expression is stored in `edebug-global-break-condition`. You can specify a new expression using the *X* command from the source code buffer while Edebug is active, or using *C-x X X* from any buffer at any time, as long as Edebug is loaded (`edebug-set-global-break-condition`).

The global break condition is the simplest way to find where in your code some event occurs, but it makes code run much more slowly. So you should reset the condition to `nil` when not using it.

17.2.6.3 Source Breakpoints

All breakpoints in a definition are forgotten each time you reinstrument it. If you wish to make a breakpoint that won't be forgotten, you can write a *source breakpoint*, which is simply a call to the function `edebug` in your source code. You can, of course, make such a call conditional. For example, in the `fac` function, you can insert the first line as shown below, to stop when the argument reaches zero:

```
(defun fac (n)
  (if (= n 0) (edebug))
  (if (< 0 n)
      (* n (fac (1- n)))
    1))
```

When the `fac` definition is instrumented and the function is called, the call to `edebug` acts as a breakpoint. Depending on the execution mode, Edebug stops or pauses there.

If no instrumented code is being executed when `edebug` is called, that function calls `debug`.

17.2.7 Trapping Errors

Emacs normally displays an error message when an error is signaled and not handled with `condition-case`. While Edebug is active and executing instrumented code, it normally responds to all unhandled errors. You can customize this with the options `edebug-on-error` and `edebug-on-quit`; see Section 17.2.16 [Edebug Options], page 297.

When Edebug responds to an error, it shows the last stop point encountered before the error. This may be the location of a call to a function which was not instrumented, and within which the error actually occurred. For an unbound variable error, the last known stop point might be quite distant from the offending variable reference. In that case, you might want to display a full backtrace (see Section 17.2.5 [Edebug Misc], page 283).

If you change `debug-on-error` or `debug-on-quit` while Edebug is active, these changes will be forgotten when Edebug becomes inactive. Furthermore, during Edebug's recursive edit, these variables are bound to the values they had outside of Edebug.

17.2.8 Edebug Views

These Edebug commands let you view aspects of the buffer and window status as they were before entry to Edebug. The outside window configuration is the collection of windows and contents that were in effect outside of Edebug.

v   Switch to viewing the outside window configuration (`edebug-view-outside`). Type *C-x X w* to return to Edebug.

p   Temporarily display the outside current buffer with point at its outside position (`edebug-bounce-point`), pausing for one second before returning to Edebug. With a prefix argument *n*, pause for *n* seconds instead.

w   Move point back to the current stop point in the source code buffer
              (`edebug-where`).

              If you use this command in a different window displaying the same buffer, that
              window will be used instead to display the current definition in the future.

W   Toggle whether Edebug saves and restores the outside window configuration
              (`edebug-toggle-save-windows`).

              With a prefix argument, W only toggles saving and restoring of the selected
              window. To specify a window that is not displaying the source code buffer, you
              must use *C-x X W* from the global keymap.

You can view the outside window configuration with *v* or just bounce to the point in the
current buffer with *p*, even if it is not normally displayed.

After moving point, you may wish to jump back to the stop point. You can do that with
w from a source code buffer. You can jump back to the stop point in the source code buffer
from any buffer using *C-x X w*.

Each time you use W to turn saving *off*, Edebug forgets the saved outside window
configuration—so that even if you turn saving back *on*, the current window configuration
remains unchanged when you next exit Edebug (by continuing the program). However, the
automatic redisplay of `*edebug*` and `*edebug-trace*` may conflict with the buffers you
wish to see unless you have enough windows open.

17.2.9 Evaluation

While within Edebug, you can evaluate expressions as if Edebug were not running. Edebug
tries to be invisible to the expression's evaluation and printing. Evaluation of expressions
that cause side effects will work as expected, except for changes to data that Edebug explicitly saves and restores. See Section 17.2.14 [The Outside Context], page 290, for details
on this process.

e exp RET   Evaluate expression *exp* in the context outside of Edebug (`edebug-eval-`
              `expression`). That is, Edebug tries to minimize its interference with the
              evaluation.

M-: exp RET
              Evaluate expression *exp* in the context of Edebug itself (`eval-expression`).

C-x C-e   Evaluate the expression before point, in the context outside of Edebug
              (`edebug-eval-last-sexp`).

Edebug supports evaluation of expressions containing references to lexically bound
symbols created by the following constructs in `cl.el`: `lexical-let`, `macrolet`, and
`symbol-macrolet`.

17.2.10 Evaluation List Buffer

You can use the *evaluation list buffer*, called `*edebug*`, to evaluate expressions interactively.
You can also set up the *evaluation list* of expressions to be evaluated automatically each
time Edebug updates the display.

E   Switch to the evaluation list buffer `*edebug*` (`edebug-visit-eval-list`).

In the `*edebug*` buffer you can use the commands of Lisp Interaction mode (see Section "Lisp Interaction" in *The GNU Emacs Manual*) as well as these special commands:

`C-j`   Evaluate the expression before point, in the outside context, and insert the value in the buffer (`edebug-eval-print-last-sexp`).

`C-x C-e`   Evaluate the expression before point, in the context outside of Edebug (`edebug-eval-last-sexp`).

`C-c C-u`   Build a new evaluation list from the contents of the buffer (`edebug-update-eval-list`).

`C-c C-d`   Delete the evaluation list group that point is in (`edebug-delete-eval-item`).

`C-c C-w`   Switch back to the source code buffer at the current stop point (`edebug-where`).

You can evaluate expressions in the evaluation list window with `C-j` or `C-x C-e`, just as you would in `*scratch*`; but they are evaluated in the context outside of Edebug.

The expressions you enter interactively (and their results) are lost when you continue execution; but you can set up an *evaluation list* consisting of expressions to be evaluated each time execution stops.

To do this, write one or more *evaluation list groups* in the evaluation list buffer. An evaluation list group consists of one or more Lisp expressions. Groups are separated by comment lines.

The command `C-c C-u` (`edebug-update-eval-list`) rebuilds the evaluation list, scanning the buffer and using the first expression of each group. (The idea is that the second expression of the group is the value previously computed and displayed.)

Each entry to Edebug redisplays the evaluation list by inserting each expression in the buffer, followed by its current value. It also inserts comment lines so that each expression becomes its own group. Thus, if you type `C-c C-u` again without changing the buffer text, the evaluation list is effectively unchanged.

If an error occurs during an evaluation from the evaluation list, the error message is displayed in a string as if it were the result. Therefore, expressions using variables that are not currently valid do not interrupt your debugging.

Here is an example of what the evaluation list window looks like after several expressions have been added to it:

```
(current-buffer)
#<buffer *scratch*>
;-----------------------------------------------------------
(selected-window)
#<window 16 on *scratch*>
;-----------------------------------------------------------
(point)
196
;-----------------------------------------------------------
bad-var
"Symbol's value as variable is void: bad-var"
;-----------------------------------------------------------
(recursion-depth)
0
;-----------------------------------------------------------
this-command
```

```
eval-last-sexp
;----------------------------------------------------------------
```

To delete a group, move point into it and type *C-c C-d*, or simply delete the text for the group and update the evaluation list with *C-c C-u*. To add a new expression to the evaluation list, insert the expression at a suitable place, insert a new comment line, then type *C-c C-u*. You need not insert dashes in the comment line—its contents don't matter.

After selecting *edebug*, you can return to the source code buffer with *C-c C-w*. The *edebug* buffer is killed when you continue execution, and recreated next time it is needed.

17.2.11 Printing in Edebug

If an expression in your program produces a value containing circular list structure, you may get an error when Edebug attempts to print it.

One way to cope with circular structure is to set `print-length` or `print-level` to truncate the printing. Edebug does this for you; it binds `print-length` and `print-level` to the values of the variables `edebug-print-length` and `edebug-print-level` (so long as they have non-`nil` values). See Section 18.6 [Output Variables], page 310.

`edebug-print-length`   [User Option]
> If non-`nil`, Edebug binds `print-length` to this value while printing results. The default value is 50.

`edebug-print-level`   [User Option]
> If non-`nil`, Edebug binds `print-level` to this value while printing results. The default value is 50.

You can also print circular structures and structures that share elements more informatively by binding `print-circle` to a non-`nil` value.

Here is an example of code that creates a circular structure:

```
(setq a '(x y))
(setcar a a)
```

Custom printing prints this as 'Result: #1=(#1# y)'. The '#1=' notation labels the structure that follows it with the label '1', and the '#1#' notation references the previously labeled structure. This notation is used for any shared elements of lists or vectors.

`edebug-print-circle`   [User Option]
> If non-`nil`, Edebug binds `print-circle` to this value while printing results. The default value is `t`.

Other programs can also use custom printing; see `cust-print.el` for details.

17.2.12 Trace Buffer

Edebug can record an execution trace, storing it in a buffer named *edebug-trace*. This is a log of function calls and returns, showing the function names and their arguments and values. To enable trace recording, set `edebug-trace` to a non-`nil` value.

Making a trace buffer is not the same thing as using trace execution mode (see Section 17.2.3 [Edebug Execution Modes], page 281).

When trace recording is enabled, each function entry and exit adds lines to the trace buffer. A function entry record consists of ':::::{', followed by the function name and argument values. A function exit record consists of ':::::}', followed by the function name and result of the function.

The number of ':'s in an entry shows its recursion depth. You can use the braces in the trace buffer to find the matching beginning or end of function calls.

You can customize trace recording for function entry and exit by redefining the functions `edebug-print-trace-before` and `edebug-print-trace-after`.

edebug-tracing *string body...*   [Macro]
>   This macro requests additional trace information around the execution of the *body*
>   forms. The argument *string* specifies text to put in the trace buffer, after the '{' or
>   '}'. All the arguments are evaluated, and `edebug-tracing` returns the value of the
>   last form in *body*.

edebug-trace *format-string* **&rest** *format-args*   [Function]
>   This function inserts text in the trace buffer. It computes the text with (`apply`
>   `'format` *format-string format-args*). It also appends a newline to separate en-
>   tries.

`edebug-tracing` and `edebug-trace` insert lines in the trace buffer whenever they are called, even if Edebug is not active. Adding text to the trace buffer also scrolls its window to show the last lines inserted.

17.2.13 Coverage Testing

Edebug provides rudimentary coverage testing and display of execution frequency.

Coverage testing works by comparing the result of each expression with the previous result; each form in the program is considered covered if it has returned two different values since you began testing coverage in the current Emacs session. Thus, to do coverage testing on your program, execute it under various conditions and note whether it behaves correctly; Edebug will tell you when you have tried enough different conditions that each form has returned two different values.

Coverage testing makes execution slower, so it is only done if `edebug-test-coverage` is non-`nil`. Frequency counting is performed for all executions of an instrumented function, even if the execution mode is Go-nonstop, and regardless of whether coverage testing is enabled.

Use *C-x X* = (`edebug-display-freq-count`) to display both the coverage information and the frequency counts for a definition. Just = (`edebug-temp-display-freq-count`) displays the same information temporarily, only until you type another key.

edebug-display-freq-count   [Command]
>   This command displays the frequency count data for each line of the current definition.
>
>   It inserts frequency counts as comment lines after each line of code. You can undo
>   all insertions with one **undo** command. The counts appear under the '(' before an
>   expression or the ')' after an expression, or on the last character of a variable. To
>   simplify the display, a count is not shown if it is equal to the count of an earlier
>   expression on the same line.

The character '=' following the count for an expression says that the expression has returned the same value each time it was evaluated. In other words, it is not yet covered for coverage testing purposes.

To clear the frequency count and coverage data for a definition, simply reinstrument it with `eval-defun`.

For example, after evaluating (fac 5) with a source breakpoint, and setting `edebug-test-coverage` to t, when the breakpoint is reached, the frequency data looks like this:

```
(defun fac (n)
  (if (= n 0) (edebug))
;#6              1       = =5
  (if (< 0 n)
;#5       =
      (* n (fac (1- n)))
;#    5                0
    1))
;#  0
```

The comment lines show that `fac` was called 6 times. The first `if` statement returned 5 times with the same result each time; the same is true of the condition on the second `if`. The recursive call of `fac` did not return at all.

17.2.14 The Outside Context

Edebug tries to be transparent to the program you are debugging, but it does not succeed completely. Edebug also tries to be transparent when you evaluate expressions with e or with the evaluation list buffer, by temporarily restoring the outside context. This section explains precisely what context Edebug restores, and how Edebug fails to be completely transparent.

17.2.14.1 Checking Whether to Stop

Whenever Edebug is entered, it needs to save and restore certain data before even deciding whether to make trace information or stop the program.

- `max-lisp-eval-depth` and `max-specpdl-size` are both increased to reduce Edebug's impact on the stack. You could, however, still run out of stack space when using Edebug.

- The state of keyboard macro execution is saved and restored. While Edebug is active, `executing-kbd-macro` is bound to `nil` unless `edebug-continue-kbd-macro` is non-nil.

17.2.14.2 Edebug Display Update

When Edebug needs to display something (e.g., in trace mode), it saves the current window configuration from outside Edebug (see Section 27.25 [Window Configurations], page 623). When you exit Edebug, it restores the previous window configuration.

Emacs redisplays only when it pauses. Usually, when you continue execution, the program re-enters Edebug at a breakpoint or after stepping, without pausing or reading input in between. In such cases, Emacs never gets a chance to redisplay the outside configuration. Consequently, what you see is the same window configuration as the last time Edebug was active, with no interruption.

Entry to Edebug for displaying something also saves and restores the following data (though some of them are deliberately not restored if an error or quit signal occurs).

- Which buffer is current, and the positions of point and the mark in the current buffer, are saved and restored.

- The outside window configuration is saved and restored if `edebug-save-windows` is non-`nil` (see Section 17.2.16 [Edebug Options], page 297).

  The window configuration is not restored on error or quit, but the outside selected window *is* reselected even on error or quit in case a `save-excursion` is active. If the value of `edebug-save-windows` is a list, only the listed windows are saved and restored.

  The window start and horizontal scrolling of the source code buffer are not restored, however, so that the display remains coherent within Edebug.

- The value of point in each displayed buffer is saved and restored if `edebug-save-displayed-buffer-points` is non-`nil`.

- The variables `overlay-arrow-position` and `overlay-arrow-string` are saved and restored, so you can safely invoke Edebug from the recursive edit elsewhere in the same buffer.

- `cursor-in-echo-area` is locally bound to `nil` so that the cursor shows up in the window.

17.2.14.3 Edebug Recursive Edit

When Edebug is entered and actually reads commands from the user, it saves (and later restores) these additional data:

- The current match data. See Section 33.6 [Match Data], page 807.

- The variables `last-command`, `this-command`, `last-command-event`, `last-input-event`, `last-event-frame`, `last-nonmenu-event`, and `track-mouse`. Commands in Edebug do not affect these variables outside of Edebug.

  Executing commands within Edebug can change the key sequence that would be returned by `this-command-keys`, and there is no way to reset the key sequence from Lisp.

  Edebug cannot save and restore the value of `unread-command-events`. Entering Edebug while this variable has a nontrivial value can interfere with execution of the program you are debugging.

- Complex commands executed while in Edebug are added to the variable `command-history`. In rare cases this can alter execution.

- Within Edebug, the recursion depth appears one deeper than the recursion depth outside Edebug. This is not true of the automatically updated evaluation list window.

- `standard-output` and `standard-input` are bound to `nil` by the `recursive-edit`, but Edebug temporarily restores them during evaluations.

- The state of keyboard macro definition is saved and restored. While Edebug is active, `defining-kbd-macro` is bound to `edebug-continue-kbd-macro`.

17.2.15 Edebug and Macros

To make Edebug properly instrument expressions that call macros, some extra care is needed. This subsection explains the details.

17.2.15.1 Instrumenting Macro Calls

When Edebug instruments an expression that calls a Lisp macro, it needs additional information about the macro to do the job properly. This is because there is no a-priori way to tell which subexpressions of the macro call are forms to be evaluated. (Evaluation may occur explicitly in the macro body, or when the resulting expansion is evaluated, or any time later.)

Therefore, you must define an Edebug specification for each macro that Edebug will encounter, to explain the format of calls to that macro. To do this, add a `debug` declaration to the macro definition. Here is a simple example that shows the specification for the `for` example macro (see Section 13.5.2 [Argument Evaluation], page 220).

```
(defmacro for (var from init to final do &rest body)
  "Execute a simple \"for\" loop.
For example, (for i from 1 to 10 do (print i))."
  (declare (debug (symbolp "from" form "to" form "do" &rest form)))
  ...)
```

The Edebug specification says which parts of a call to the macro are forms to be evaluated. For simple macros, the specification often looks very similar to the formal argument list of the macro definition, but specifications are much more general than macro arguments. See Section 13.4 [Defining Macros], page 219, for more explanation of the `declare` form.

Take care to ensure that the specifications are known to Edebug when you instrument code. If you are instrumenting a function from a file that uses `eval-when-compile` to require another file containing macro definitions, you may need to explicitly load that file.

You can also define an edebug specification for a macro separately from the macro definition with `def-edebug-spec`. Adding `debug` declarations is preferred, and more convenient, for macro definitions in Lisp, but `def-edebug-spec` makes it possible to define Edebug specifications for special forms implemented in C.

`def-edebug-spec` *macro specification*   [Macro]

>Specify which expressions of a call to macro *macro* are forms to be evaluated. *specification* should be the edebug specification. Neither argument is evaluated.
>
>The *macro* argument can actually be any symbol, not just a macro name.

Here is a table of the possibilities for *specification* and how each directs processing of arguments.

t   All arguments are instrumented for evaluation.

0   None of the arguments is instrumented.

a symbol The symbol must have an Edebug specification, which is used instead. This indirection is repeated until another kind of specification is found. This allows you to inherit the specification from another macro.

a list   The elements of the list describe the types of the arguments of a calling form. The possible elements of a specification list are described in the following sections.

If a macro has no Edebug specification, neither through a `debug` declaration nor through a `def-edebug-spec` call, the variable `edebug-eval-macro-args` comes into play.

`edebug-eval-macro-args`   [User Option]

> This controls the way Edebug treats macro arguments with no explicit Edebug specification. If it is `nil` (the default), none of the arguments is instrumented for evaluation. Otherwise, all arguments are instrumented.

17.2.15.2 Specification List

A *specification list* is required for an Edebug specification if some arguments of a macro call are evaluated while others are not. Some elements in a specification list match one or more arguments, but others modify the processing of all following elements. The latter, called *specification keywords*, are symbols beginning with '&' (such as `&optional`).

A specification list may contain sublists, which match arguments that are themselves lists, or it may contain vectors used for grouping. Sublists and groups thus subdivide the specification list into a hierarchy of levels. Specification keywords apply only to the remainder of the sublist or group they are contained in.

When a specification list involves alternatives or repetition, matching it against an actual macro call may require backtracking. For more details, see Section 17.2.15.3 [Backtracking], page 295.

Edebug specifications provide the power of regular expression matching, plus some context-free grammar constructs: the matching of sublists with balanced parentheses, recursive processing of forms, and recursion via indirect specifications.

Here's a table of the possible elements of a specification list, with their meanings (see Section 17.2.15.4 [Specification Examples], page 296, for the referenced examples):

`sexp`   A single unevaluated Lisp object, which is not instrumented.

`form`   A single evaluated expression, which is instrumented.

`place`   A generalized variable. See Section 11.15 [Generalized Variables], page 183.

`body`   Short for `&rest form`. See `&rest` below.

`function-form`

> A function form: either a quoted function symbol, a quoted lambda expression, or a form (that should evaluate to a function symbol or lambda expression). This is useful when an argument that's a lambda expression might be quoted with `quote` rather than `function`, since it instruments the body of the lambda expression either way.

`lambda-expr`

> A lambda expression with no quoting.

`&optional`

> All following elements in the specification list are optional; as soon as one does not match, Edebug stops matching at this level.
>
> To make just a few elements optional, followed by non-optional elements, use `[&optional specs...]`. To specify that several elements must all match or none, use `&optional [specs...]`. See the `defun` example.

&rest   All following elements in the specification list are repeated zero or more times.
           In the last repetition, however, it is not a problem if the expression runs out
           before matching all of the elements of the specification list.

           To repeat only a few elements, use [&rest *specs*...]. To specify several ele-
           ments that must all match on every repetition, use &rest [*specs*...].

&or   Each of the following elements in the specification list is an alternative. One of
           the alternatives must match, or the &or specification fails.

           Each list element following &or is a single alternative. To group two or more
           list elements as a single alternative, enclose them in [...].

&not   Each of the following elements is matched as alternatives as if by using &or, but
           if any of them match, the specification fails. If none of them match, nothing is
           matched, but the &not specification succeeds.

&define   Indicates that the specification is for a defining form. The defining form itself
           is not instrumented (that is, Edebug does not stop before and after the defining
           form), but forms inside it typically will be instrumented. The &define keyword
           should be the first element in a list specification.

nil   This is successful when there are no more arguments to match at the current ar-
           gument list level; otherwise it fails. See sublist specifications and the backquote
           example.

gate   No argument is matched but backtracking through the gate is disabled while
           matching the remainder of the specifications at this level. This is primarily
           used to generate more specific syntax error messages. See Section 17.2.15.3
           [Backtracking], page 295, for more details. Also see the let example.

other-symbol

           Any other symbol in a specification list may be a predicate or an indirect
           specification.

           If the symbol has an Edebug specification, this *indirect specification* should
           be either a list specification that is used in place of the symbol, or a function
           that is called to process the arguments. The specification may be defined with
           def-edebug-spec just as for macros. See the defun example.

           Otherwise, the symbol should be a predicate. The predicate is called with
           the argument, and if the predicate returns nil, the specification fails and the
           argument is not instrumented.

           Some suitable predicates include symbolp, integerp, stringp, vectorp, and
           atom.

[*elements*...]

           A vector of elements groups the elements into a single *group specification*. Its
           meaning has nothing to do with vectors.

"*string*"   The argument should be a symbol named *string*. This specification is equivalent
           to the quoted symbol, '*symbol*, where the name of *symbol* is the *string*, but
           the string form is preferred.

`(vector elements...)`
> The argument should be a vector whose elements must match the *elements* in the specification. See the backquote example.

`(elements...)`
> Any other list is a *sublist specification* and the argument must be a list whose elements match the specification *elements*.
>
> A sublist specification may be a dotted list and the corresponding list argument may then be a dotted list. Alternatively, the last CDR of a dotted list specification may be another sublist specification (via a grouping or an indirect specification, e.g., `(spec . [(more specs...)])`) whose elements match the non-dotted list arguments. This is useful in recursive specifications such as in the backquote example. Also see the description of a `nil` specification above for terminating such recursion.
>
> Note that a sublist specification written as `(specs . nil)` is equivalent to `(specs)`, and `(specs . (sublist-elements...))` is equivalent to `(specs sublist-elements...)`.

Here is a list of additional specifications that may appear only after `&define`. See the `defun` example.

`name`
> The argument, a symbol, is the name of the defining form.
>
> A defining form is not required to have a name field; and it may have multiple name fields.

`:name`
> This construct does not actually match an argument. The element following `:name` should be a symbol; it is used as an additional name component for the definition. You can use this to add a unique, static component to the name of the definition. It may be used more than once.

`arg`
> The argument, a symbol, is the name of an argument of the defining form. However, lambda-list keywords (symbols starting with '&') are not allowed.

`lambda-list`
> This matches a lambda list—the argument list of a lambda expression.

`def-body`
> The argument is the body of code in a definition. This is like `body`, described above, but a definition body must be instrumented with a different Edebug call that looks up information associated with the definition. Use `def-body` for the highest level list of forms within the definition.

`def-form`
> The argument is a single, highest-level form in a definition. This is like `def-body`, except it is used to match a single form rather than a list of forms. As a special case, `def-form` also means that tracing information is not output when the form is executed. See the `interactive` example.

17.2.15.3 Backtracking in Specifications

If a specification fails to match at some point, this does not necessarily mean a syntax error will be signaled; instead, *backtracking* will take place until all alternatives have been exhausted. Eventually every element of the argument list must be matched by some element in the specification, and every required element in the specification must match some argument.

When a syntax error is detected, it might not be reported until much later, after higher-level alternatives have been exhausted, and with the point positioned further from the real error. But if backtracking is disabled when an error occurs, it can be reported immediately. Note that backtracking is also reenabled automatically in several situations; when a new alternative is established by &optional, &rest, or &or, or at the start of processing a sublist, group, or indirect specification. The effect of enabling or disabling backtracking is limited to the remainder of the level currently being processed and lower levels.

Backtracking is disabled while matching any of the form specifications (that is, form, body, def-form, and def-body). These specifications will match any form so any error must be in the form itself rather than at a higher level.

Backtracking is also disabled after successfully matching a quoted symbol or string specification, since this usually indicates a recognized construct. But if you have a set of alternative constructs that all begin with the same symbol, you can usually work around this constraint by factoring the symbol out of the alternatives, e.g., ["foo" &or [first case] [second case] ...].

Most needs are satisfied by these two ways that backtracking is automatically disabled, but occasionally it is useful to explicitly disable backtracking by using the gate specification. This is useful when you know that no higher alternatives could apply. See the example of the let specification.

17.2.15.4 Specification Examples

It may be easier to understand Edebug specifications by studying the examples provided here.

A let special form has a sequence of bindings and a body. Each of the bindings is either a symbol or a sublist with a symbol and optional expression. In the specification below, notice the gate inside of the sublist to prevent backtracking once a sublist is found.

```
(def-edebug-spec let
  ((&rest
    &or symbolp (gate symbolp &optional form))
   body))
```

Edebug uses the following specifications for defun and the associated argument list and interactive specifications. It is necessary to handle interactive forms specially since an expression argument is actually evaluated outside of the function body. (The specification for defmacro is very similar to that for defun, but allows for the declare statement.)

```
(def-edebug-spec defun
  (&define name lambda-list
           [&optional stringp]     ; Match the doc string, if present.
           [&optional ("interactive" interactive)]
           def-body))

(def-edebug-spec lambda-list
  (([&rest arg]
    [&optional ["&optional" arg &rest arg]]
    &optional ["&rest" arg]
```

```
        )))

    (def-edebug-spec interactive
      (&optional &or stringp def-form))     ; Notice: def-form
```

The specification for backquote below illustrates how to match dotted lists and use `nil` to terminate recursion. It also illustrates how components of a vector may be matched. (The actual specification defined by Edebug is a little different, and does not support dotted lists because doing so causes very deep recursion that could fail.)

```
    (def-edebug-spec \` (backquote-form))     ; Alias just for clarity.

    (def-edebug-spec backquote-form
      (&or ([&or "," ",@"] &or ("quote" backquote-form) form)
           (backquote-form . [&or nil backquote-form])
           (vector &rest backquote-form)
           sexp))
```

17.2.16 Edebug Options

These options affect the behavior of Edebug:

edebug-setup-hook   [User Option]

> Functions to call before Edebug is used. Each time it is set to a new value, Edebug will call those functions once and then reset `edebug-setup-hook` to `nil`. You could use this to load up Edebug specifications associated with a package you are using, but only when you also use Edebug. See Section 17.2.2 [Instrumenting], page 280.

edebug-all-defs   [User Option]

> If this is non-`nil`, normal evaluation of defining forms such as `defun` and `defmacro` instruments them for Edebug. This applies to `eval-defun`, `eval-region`, `eval-buffer`, and `eval-current-buffer`.
>
> Use the command *M-x edebug-all-defs* to toggle the value of this option. See Section 17.2.2 [Instrumenting], page 280.

edebug-all-forms   [User Option]

> If this is non-`nil`, the commands `eval-defun`, `eval-region`, `eval-buffer`, and `eval-current-buffer` instrument all forms, even those that don't define anything. This doesn't apply to loading or evaluations in the minibuffer.
>
> Use the command *M-x edebug-all-forms* to toggle the value of this option. See Section 17.2.2 [Instrumenting], page 280.

edebug-save-windows   [User Option]

> If this is non-`nil`, Edebug saves and restores the window configuration. That takes some time, so if your program does not care what happens to the window configurations, it is better to set this variable to `nil`.
>
> If the value is a list, only the listed windows are saved and restored.
>
> You can use the *W* command in Edebug to change this variable interactively. See Section 17.2.14.2 [Edebug Display Update], page 290.

edebug-save-displayed-buffer-points   [User Option]

> If this is non-`nil`, Edebug saves and restores point in all displayed buffers.

Saving and restoring point in other buffers is necessary if you are debugging code that
changes the point of a buffer that is displayed in a non-selected window. If Edebug
or the user then selects the window, point in that buffer will move to the window's
value of point.

Saving and restoring point in all buffers is expensive, since it requires selecting each
window twice, so enable this only if you need it. See Section 17.2.14.2 [Edebug Display
Update], page 290.

edebug-initial-mode   [User Option]

If this variable is non-nil, it specifies the initial execution mode for Edebug when it is
first activated. Possible values are step, next, go, Go-nonstop, trace, Trace-fast,
continue, and Continue-fast.

The default value is step. This variable can be set interactively with C-x C-a
C-m (edebug-set-initial-mode). See Section 17.2.3 [Edebug Execution Modes],
page 281.

edebug-trace   [User Option]

If this is non-nil, trace each function entry and exit. Tracing output is displayed in
a buffer named *edebug-trace*, one function entry or exit per line, indented by the
recursion level.

Also see edebug-tracing, in Section 17.2.12 [Trace Buffer], page 288.

edebug-test-coverage   [User Option]

If non-nil, Edebug tests coverage of all expressions debugged. See Section 17.2.13
[Coverage Testing], page 289.

edebug-continue-kbd-macro   [User Option]

If non-nil, continue defining or executing any keyboard macro that is executing
outside of Edebug. Use this with caution since it is not debugged. See Section 17.2.3
[Edebug Execution Modes], page 281.

edebug-unwrap-results   [User Option]

If non-nil, Edebug tries to remove any of its own instrumentation when showing the
results of expressions. This is relevant when debugging macros where the results of
expressions are themselves instrumented expressions. As a very artificial example,
suppose that the example function fac has been instrumented, and consider a macro
of the form:

```
(defmacro test () "Edebug example."
  (if (symbol-function 'fac)
      ...))
```

If you instrument the test macro and step through it, then by default the result of
the symbol-function call has numerous edebug-after and edebug-before forms,
which can make it difficult to see the actual result. If edebug-unwrap-results is
non-nil, Edebug tries to remove these forms from the result.

edebug-on-error   [User Option]

Edebug binds debug-on-error to this value, if debug-on-error was previously nil.
See Section 17.2.7 [Trapping Errors], page 285.

edebug-on-quit   [User Option]
>   Edebug binds `debug-on-quit` to this value, if `debug-on-quit` was previously `nil`.
>   See Section 17.2.7 [Trapping Errors], page 285.

If you change the values of `edebug-on-error` or `edebug-on-quit` while Edebug is active,
their values won't be used until the *next* time Edebug is invoked via a new command.

edebug-global-break-condition   [User Option]
>   If non-`nil`, an expression to test for at every stop point. If the result is non-`nil`, then
>   break. Errors are ignored. See Section 17.2.6.2 [Global Break Condition], page 284.

17.3 Debugging Invalid Lisp Syntax

The Lisp reader reports invalid syntax, but cannot say where the real problem is. For
example, the error 'End of file during parsing' in evaluating an expression indicates an
excess of open parentheses (or square brackets). The reader detects this imbalance at
the end of the file, but it cannot figure out where the close parenthesis should have been.
Likewise, 'Invalid read syntax: ")"' indicates an excess close parenthesis or missing open
parenthesis, but does not say where the missing parenthesis belongs. How, then, to find
what to change?

If the problem is not simply an imbalance of parentheses, a useful technique is to try
`C-M-e` at the beginning of each defun, and see if it goes to the place where that defun
appears to end. If it does not, there is a problem in that defun.

However, unmatched parentheses are the most common syntax errors in Lisp, and we
can give further advice for those cases. (In addition, just moving point through the code
with Show Paren mode enabled might find the mismatch.)

17.3.1 Excess Open Parentheses

The first step is to find the defun that is unbalanced. If there is an excess open parenthesis,
the way to do this is to go to the end of the file and type `C-u C-M-u`. This will move you to
the beginning of the first defun that is unbalanced.

The next step is to determine precisely what is wrong. There is no way to be sure of this
except by studying the program, but often the existing indentation is a clue to where the
parentheses should have been. The easiest way to use this clue is to reindent with `C-M-q`
and see what moves. **But don't do this yet!** Keep reading, first.

Before you do this, make sure the defun has enough close parentheses. Otherwise, `C-M-q`
will get an error, or will reindent all the rest of the file until the end. So move to the end of
the defun and insert a close parenthesis there. Don't use `C-M-e` to move there, since that
too will fail to work until the defun is balanced.

Now you can go to the beginning of the defun and type `C-M-q`. Usually all the lines from
a certain point to the end of the function will shift to the right. There is probably a missing
close parenthesis, or a superfluous open parenthesis, near that point. (However, don't
assume this is true; study the code to make sure.) Once you have found the discrepancy,
undo the `C-M-q` with `C-_`, since the old indentation is probably appropriate to the intended
parentheses.

After you think you have fixed the problem, use *C-M-q* again. If the old indentation actually fit the intended nesting of parentheses, and you have put back those parentheses, *C-M-q* should not change anything.

17.3.2 Excess Close Parentheses

To deal with an excess close parenthesis, first go to the beginning of the file, then type *C-u -1 C-M-u* to find the end of the first unbalanced defun.

Then find the actual matching close parenthesis by typing *C-M-f* at the beginning of that defun. This will leave you somewhere short of the place where the defun ought to end. It is possible that you will find a spurious close parenthesis in that vicinity.

If you don't see a problem at that point, the next thing to do is to type *C-M-q* at the beginning of the defun. A range of lines will probably shift left; if so, the missing open parenthesis or spurious close parenthesis is probably near the first of those lines. (However, don't assume this is true; study the code to make sure.) Once you have found the discrepancy, undo the *C-M-q* with *C-_*, since the old indentation is probably appropriate to the intended parentheses.

After you think you have fixed the problem, use *C-M-q* again. If the old indentation actually fits the intended nesting of parentheses, and you have put back those parentheses, *C-M-q* should not change anything.

17.4 Test Coverage

You can do coverage testing for a file of Lisp code by loading the **testcover** library and using the command *M-x testcover-start RET file RET* to instrument the code. Then test your code by calling it one or more times. Then use the command *M-x testcover-mark-all* to display colored highlights on the code to show where coverage is insufficient. The command *M-x testcover-next-mark* will move point forward to the next highlighted spot.

Normally, a red highlight indicates the form was never completely evaluated; a brown highlight means it always evaluated to the same value (meaning there has been little testing of what is done with the result). However, the red highlight is skipped for forms that can't possibly complete their evaluation, such as **error**. The brown highlight is skipped for forms that are expected to always evaluate to the same value, such as (**setq x 14**).

For difficult cases, you can add do-nothing macros to your code to give advice to the test coverage tool.

1value *form*   [Macro]
    Evaluate *form* and return its value, but inform coverage testing that *form*'s value should always be the same.

noreturn *form*   [Macro]
    Evaluate *form*, informing coverage testing that *form* should never return. If it ever does return, you get a run-time error.

Edebug also has a coverage testing feature (see Section 17.2.13 [Coverage Testing], page 289). These features partly duplicate each other, and it would be cleaner to combine them.

17.5 Profiling

If your program is working correctly, but you want to make it run more quickly or efficiently, the first thing to do is *profile* your code so that you know how it is using resources. If you find that one particular function is responsible for a significant portion of the runtime, you can start looking for ways to optimize that piece.

Emacs has built-in support for this. To begin profiling, type *M-x profiler-start*. You can choose to profile by processor usage, memory usage, or both. After doing some work, type *M-x profiler-report* to display a summary buffer for each resource that you chose to profile. The names of the report buffers include the times at which the reports were generated, so you can generate another report later on without erasing previous results. When you have finished profiling, type *M-x profiler-stop* (there is a small overhead associated with profiling).

The profiler report buffer shows, on each line, a function that was called, followed by how much resource (processor or memory) it used in absolute and percentage times since profiling started. If a given line has a '+' symbol at the left-hand side, you can expand that line by typing RET, in order to see the function(s) called by the higher-level function. Use a prefix argument (C-u RET) to see the whole call tree below a function. Pressing RET again will collapse back to the original state.

Press *j* or *mouse-2* to jump to the definition of a function. Press *d* to view a function's documentation. You can save a profile to a file using *C-x C-w*. You can compare two profiles using *=*.

The `elp` library offers an alternative approach. See the file `elp.el` for instructions.

You can check the speed of individual Emacs Lisp forms using the **benchmark** library. See the functions **benchmark-run** and **benchmark-run-compiled** in **benchmark.el**.

18 Reading and Printing Lisp Objects

Printing and *reading* are the operations of converting Lisp objects to textual form and vice versa. They use the printed representations and read syntax described in Chapter 2 [Lisp Data Types], page 8.

This chapter describes the Lisp functions for reading and printing. It also describes *streams*, which specify where to get the text (if reading) or where to put it (if printing).

18.1 Introduction to Reading and Printing

Reading a Lisp object means parsing a Lisp expression in textual form and producing a corresponding Lisp object. This is how Lisp programs get into Lisp from files of Lisp code. We call the text the *read syntax* of the object. For example, the text '(a . 5)' is the read syntax for a cons cell whose CAR is a and whose CDR is the number 5.

Printing a Lisp object means producing text that represents that object—converting the object to its *printed representation* (see Section 2.1 [Printed Representation], page 8). Printing the cons cell described above produces the text '(a . 5)'.

Reading and printing are more or less inverse operations: printing the object that results from reading a given piece of text often produces the same text, and reading the text that results from printing an object usually produces a similar-looking object. For example, printing the symbol foo produces the text 'foo', and reading that text returns the symbol foo. Printing a list whose elements are a and b produces the text '(a b)', and reading that text produces a list (but not the same list) with elements a and b.

However, these two operations are not precisely inverse to each other. There are three kinds of exceptions:

- Printing can produce text that cannot be read. For example, buffers, windows, frames, subprocesses and markers print as text that starts with '#'; if you try to read this text, you get an error. There is no way to read those data types.

- One object can have multiple textual representations. For example, '1' and '01' represent the same integer, and '(a b)' and '(a . (b))' represent the same list. Reading will accept any of the alternatives, but printing must choose one of them.

- Comments can appear at certain points in the middle of an object's read sequence without affecting the result of reading it.

18.2 Input Streams

Most of the Lisp functions for reading text take an *input stream* as an argument. The input stream specifies where or how to get the characters of the text to be read. Here are the possible types of input stream:

buffer   The input characters are read from *buffer*, starting with the character directly after point. Point advances as characters are read.

marker   The input characters are read from the buffer that *marker* is in, starting with the character directly after the marker. The marker position advances as characters are read. The value of point in the buffer has no effect when the stream is a marker.

string   The input characters are taken from *string*, starting at the first character in the string and using as many characters as required.

function   The input characters are generated by *function*, which must support two kinds of calls:

- When it is called with no arguments, it should return the next character.
- When it is called with one argument (always a character), *function* should save the argument and arrange to return it on the next call. This is called *unreading* the character; it happens when the Lisp reader reads one character too many and wants to put it back where it came from. In this case, it makes no difference what value *function* returns.

t   t used as a stream means that the input is read from the minibuffer. In fact, the minibuffer is invoked once and the text given by the user is made into a string that is then used as the input stream. If Emacs is running in batch mode, standard input is used instead of the minibuffer. For example,

```
(message "%s" (read t))
```

will read a Lisp expression from standard input and print the result to standard output.

nil   nil supplied as an input stream means to use the value of **standard-input** instead; that value is the *default input stream*, and must be a non-**nil** input stream.

symbol   A symbol as input stream is equivalent to the symbol's function definition (if any).

Here is an example of reading from a stream that is a buffer, showing where point is located before and after:

```
---------- Buffer: foo ----------
This* is the contents of foo.
---------- Buffer: foo ----------

(read (get-buffer "foo"))
     ⇒ is
(read (get-buffer "foo"))
     ⇒ the

---------- Buffer: foo ----------
This is the* contents of foo.
---------- Buffer: foo ----------
```

Note that the first read skips a space. Reading skips any amount of whitespace preceding the significant text.

Here is an example of reading from a stream that is a marker, initially positioned at the beginning of the buffer shown. The value read is the symbol This.

```
---------- Buffer: foo ----------
This is the contents of foo.
---------- Buffer: foo ----------
```

```
(setq m (set-marker (make-marker) 1 (get-buffer "foo")))
    ⇒ #<marker at 1 in foo>
(read m)
    ⇒ This
m
    ⇒ #<marker at 5 in foo>    ;; Before the first space.
```

Here we read from the contents of a string:

```
(read "(When in) the course")
    ⇒ (When in)
```

The following example reads from the minibuffer. The prompt is: 'Lisp expression: '. (That is always the prompt used when you read from the stream t.) The user's input is shown following the prompt.

```
(read t)
    ⇒ 23
---------- Buffer: Minibuffer ----------
Lisp expression: 23 RET
---------- Buffer: Minibuffer ----------
```

Finally, here is an example of a stream that is a function, named useless-stream. Before we use the stream, we initialize the variable useless-list to a list of characters. Then each call to the function useless-stream obtains the next character in the list or unreads a character by adding it to the front of the list.

```
(setq useless-list (append "XY()" nil))
    ⇒ (88 89 40 41)

(defun useless-stream (&optional unread)
  (if unread
      (setq useless-list (cons unread useless-list))
    (prog1 (car useless-list)
           (setq useless-list (cdr useless-list)))))
    ⇒ useless-stream
```

Now we read using the stream thus constructed:

```
(read 'useless-stream)
    ⇒ XY

useless-list
    ⇒ (40 41)
```

Note that the open and close parentheses remain in the list. The Lisp reader encountered the open parenthesis, decided that it ended the input, and unread it. Another attempt to read from the stream at this point would read '()' and return nil.

18.3 Input Functions

This section describes the Lisp functions and variables that pertain to reading.

In the functions below, *stream* stands for an input stream (see the previous section). If *stream* is `nil` or omitted, it defaults to the value of `standard-input`.

An `end-of-file` error is signaled if reading encounters an unterminated list, vector, or string.

read &optional *stream*   [Function]

> This function reads one textual Lisp expression from *stream*, returning it as a Lisp object. This is the basic Lisp input function.

read-from-string *string* &optional *start end*   [Function]

> This function reads the first textual Lisp expression from the text in *string*. It returns a cons cell whose CAR is that expression, and whose CDR is an integer giving the position of the next remaining character in the string (i.e., the first one not read).
>
> If *start* is supplied, then reading begins at index *start* in the string (where the first character is at index 0). If you specify *end*, then reading is forced to stop just before that index, as if the rest of the string were not there.
>
> For example:
>
> ```
> (read-from-string "(setq x 55) (setq y 5)")
>      ⇒ ((setq x 55) . 11)
> (read-from-string "\"A short string\"")
>      ⇒ ("A short string" . 16)
>
>
> ;; Read starting at the first character.
> (read-from-string "(list 112)" 0)
>      ⇒ ((list 112) . 10)
> ;; Read starting at the second character.
> (read-from-string "(list 112)" 1)
>      ⇒ (list . 5)
> ;; Read starting at the seventh character,
> ;;    and stopping at the ninth.
> (read-from-string "(list 112)" 6 8)
>      ⇒ (11 . 8)
> ```

standard-input   [Variable]

> This variable holds the default input stream—the stream that `read` uses when the *stream* argument is `nil`. The default is `t`, meaning use the minibuffer.

read-circle   [Variable]

> If non-`nil`, this variable enables the reading of circular and shared structures. See Section 2.5 [Circular Objects], page 27. Its default value is `t`.

When reading or writing from the standard input/output streams of the Emacs process in batch mode, it is sometimes required to make sure any arbitrary binary data will be read/written verbatim, and/or that no translation of newlines to or from CR-LF pairs is performed. This issue does not exist on Posix hosts, only on MS-Windows and MS-DOS. The following function allows you to control the I/O mode of any standard stream of the Emacs process.

set-binary-mode *stream mode*   [Function]

 Switch *stream* into binary or text I/O mode. If *mode* is non-**nil**, switch to binary mode, otherwise switch to text mode. The value of *stream* can be one of **stdin**, **stdout**, or **stderr**. This function flushes any pending output data of *stream* as a side effect, and returns the previous value of I/O mode for *stream*. On Posix hosts, it always returns a non-**nil** value and does nothing except flushing pending output.

18.4 Output Streams

An output stream specifies what to do with the characters produced by printing. Most print functions accept an output stream as an optional argument. Here are the possible types of output stream:

buffer   The output characters are inserted into *buffer* at point. Point advances as characters are inserted.

marker   The output characters are inserted into the buffer that *marker* points into, at the marker position. The marker position advances as characters are inserted. The value of point in the buffer has no effect on printing when the stream is a marker, and this kind of printing does not move point (except that if the marker points at or before the position of point, point advances with the surrounding text, as usual).

function   The output characters are passed to *function*, which is responsible for storing them away. It is called with a single character as argument, as many times as there are characters to be output, and is responsible for storing the characters wherever you want to put them.

t   The output characters are displayed in the echo area.

nil   **nil** specified as an output stream means to use the value of **standard-output** instead; that value is the *default output stream*, and must not be **nil**.

symbol   A symbol as output stream is equivalent to the symbol's function definition (if any).

 Many of the valid output streams are also valid as input streams. The difference between input and output streams is therefore more a matter of how you use a Lisp object, than of different types of object.

 Here is an example of a buffer used as an output stream. Point is initially located as shown immediately before the 'h' in 'the'. At the end, point is located directly before that same 'h'.

```
---------- Buffer: foo ----------
This is t⋆he contents of foo.
---------- Buffer: foo ----------

(print "This is the output" (get-buffer "foo"))
     ⇒ "This is the output"
```

```
---------- Buffer: foo ----------
This is t
"This is the output"
*he contents of foo.
---------- Buffer: foo ----------
```

Now we show a use of a marker as an output stream. Initially, the marker is in buffer foo, between the 't' and the 'h' in the word 'the'. At the end, the marker has advanced over the inserted text so that it remains positioned before the same 'h'. Note that the location of point, shown in the usual fashion, has no effect.

```
---------- Buffer: foo ----------
This is the *output
---------- Buffer: foo ----------

(setq m (copy-marker 10))
     ⇒ #<marker at 10 in foo>

(print "More output for foo." m)
     ⇒ "More output for foo."

---------- Buffer: foo ----------
This is t
"More output for foo."
he *output
---------- Buffer: foo ----------

m
     ⇒ #<marker at 34 in foo>
```

The following example shows output to the echo area:

```
(print "Echo Area output" t)
     ⇒ "Echo Area output"
---------- Echo Area ----------
"Echo Area output"
---------- Echo Area ----------
```

Finally, we show the use of a function as an output stream. The function eat-output takes each character that it is given and conses it onto the front of the list last-output (see Section 5.4 [Building Lists], page 71). At the end, the list contains all the characters output, but in reverse order.

```
(setq last-output nil)
     ⇒ nil

(defun eat-output (c)
  (setq last-output (cons c last-output)))
     ⇒ eat-output

(print "This is the output" 'eat-output)
     ⇒ "This is the output"
```

```
last-output
    ⇒ (10 34 116 117 112 116 117 111 32 101 104
116 32 115 105 32 115 105 104 84 34 10)
```

Now we can put the output in the proper order by reversing the list:

```
(concat (nreverse last-output))
    ⇒ "
\"This is the output\"
"
```

Calling `concat` converts the list to a string so you can see its contents more clearly.

18.5 Output Functions

This section describes the Lisp functions for printing Lisp objects—converting objects into their printed representation.

Some of the Emacs printing functions add quoting characters to the output when necessary so that it can be read properly. The quoting characters used are '"' and '\'; they distinguish strings from symbols, and prevent punctuation characters in strings and symbols from being taken as delimiters when reading. See Section 2.1 [Printed Representation], page 8, for full details. You specify quoting or no quoting by the choice of printing function.

If the text is to be read back into Lisp, then you should print with quoting characters to avoid ambiguity. Likewise, if the purpose is to describe a Lisp object clearly for a Lisp programmer. However, if the purpose of the output is to look nice for humans, then it is usually better to print without quoting.

Lisp objects can refer to themselves. Printing a self-referential object in the normal way would require an infinite amount of text, and the attempt could cause infinite recursion. Emacs detects such recursion and prints '#level' instead of recursively printing an object already being printed. For example, here '#0' indicates a recursive reference to the object at level 0 of the current print operation:

```
(setq foo (list nil))
    ⇒ (nil)
(setcar foo foo)
    ⇒ (#0)
```

In the functions below, *stream* stands for an output stream. (See the previous section for a description of output streams.) If *stream* is `nil` or omitted, it defaults to the value of `standard-output`.

print *object* **&optional** *stream*   [Function]
> The `print` function is a convenient way of printing. It outputs the printed representation of *object* to *stream*, printing in addition one newline before *object* and another after it. Quoting characters are used. `print` returns *object*. For example:

```
(progn (print 'The\ cat\ in)
       (print "the hat")
       (print " came back"))
    ⊣
    ⊣ The\ cat\ in
    ⊣
    ⊣ "the hat"
    ⊣
    ⊣ " came back"
    ⇒ " came back"
```

prin1 *object* **&optional** *stream*   [Function]

This function outputs the printed representation of *object* to *stream*. It does not print newlines to separate output as **print** does, but it does use quoting characters just like **print**. It returns *object*.

```
(progn (prin1 'The\ cat\ in)
       (prin1 "the hat")
       (prin1 " came back"))
    ⊣ The\ cat\ in"the hat"" came back"
    ⇒ " came back"
```

princ *object* **&optional** *stream*   [Function]

This function outputs the printed representation of *object* to *stream*. It returns *object*.

This function is intended to produce output that is readable by people, not by **read**, so it doesn't insert quoting characters and doesn't put double-quotes around the contents of strings. It does not add any spacing between calls.

```
(progn
  (princ 'The\ cat)
  (princ " in the \"hat\""))
    ⊣ The cat in the "hat"
    ⇒ " in the \"hat\""
```

terpri **&optional** *stream ensure*   [Function]

This function outputs a newline to *stream*. The name stands for "terminate print". If *ensure* is non-nil no newline is printed if *stream* is already at the beginning of a line. Note in this case *stream* can not be a function and an error is signalled if it is. This function returns **t** if a newline is printed.

write-char *character* **&optional** *stream*   [Function]

This function outputs *character* to *stream*. It returns *character*.

prin1-to-string *object* **&optional** *noescape*   [Function]

This function returns a string containing the text that **prin1** would have printed for the same argument.

```
(prin1-to-string 'foo)
    ⇒ "foo"
```

```
(prin1-to-string (mark-marker))
     ⇒ "#<marker at 2773 in strings.texi>"
```

If *noescape* is non-nil, that inhibits use of quoting characters in the output. (This argument is supported in Emacs versions 19 and later.)

```
(prin1-to-string "foo")
     ⇒ "\"foo\""
(prin1-to-string "foo" t)
     ⇒ "foo"
```

See `format`, in Section 4.7 [Formatting Strings], page 59, for other ways to obtain the printed representation of a Lisp object as a string.

with-output-to-string *body...*   [Macro]

This macro executes the *body* forms with `standard-output` set up to feed output into a string. Then it returns that string.

For example, if the current buffer name is 'foo',

```
(with-output-to-string
  (princ "The buffer is ")
  (princ (buffer-name)))
```

returns `"The buffer is foo"`.

pp *object* **&optional** *stream*   [Function]

This function outputs *object* to *stream*, just like `prin1`, but does it in a prettier way. That is, it'll indent and fill the object to make it more readable for humans.

If you need to use binary I/O in batch mode, e.g., use the functions described in this section to write out arbitrary binary data or avoid conversion of newlines on non-Posix hosts, see Section 18.3 [Input Functions], page 304.

18.6 Variables Affecting Output

standard-output   [Variable]

The value of this variable is the default output stream—the stream that print functions use when the *stream* argument is `nil`. The default is `t`, meaning display in the echo area.

print-quoted   [Variable]

If this is non-nil, that means to print quoted forms using abbreviated reader syntax, e.g., (quote foo) prints as 'foo, and (function foo) as #'foo.

print-escape-newlines   [Variable]

If this variable is non-nil, then newline characters in strings are printed as '\n' and formfeeds are printed as '\f'. Normally these characters are printed as actual newlines and formfeeds.

This variable affects the print functions `prin1` and `print` that print with quoting. It does not affect `princ`. Here is an example using `prin1`:

```
(prin1 "a\nb")
     ⊣ "a
     ⊣  b"
     ⇒ "a
b"

(let ((print-escape-newlines t))
  (prin1 "a\nb"))
     ⊣ "a\nb"
     ⇒ "a
b"
```

In the second expression, the local binding of **print-escape-newlines** is in effect during the call to **prin1**, but not during the printing of the result.

print-escape-nonascii   [Variable]

> If this variable is non-**nil**, then unibyte non-ASCII characters in strings are unconditionally printed as backslash sequences by the print functions **prin1** and **print** that print with quoting.
>
> Those functions also use backslash sequences for unibyte non-ASCII characters, regardless of the value of this variable, when the output stream is a multibyte buffer or a marker pointing into one.

print-escape-multibyte   [Variable]

> If this variable is non-**nil**, then multibyte non-ASCII characters in strings are unconditionally printed as backslash sequences by the print functions **prin1** and **print** that print with quoting.
>
> Those functions also use backslash sequences for multibyte non-ASCII characters, regardless of the value of this variable, when the output stream is a unibyte buffer or a marker pointing into one.

print-length   [Variable]

> The value of this variable is the maximum number of elements to print in any list, vector or bool-vector. If an object being printed has more than this many elements, it is abbreviated with an ellipsis.
>
> If the value is **nil** (the default), then there is no limit.

```
(setq print-length 2)
     ⇒ 2
(print '(1 2 3 4 5))
     ⊣ (1 2 ...)
     ⇒ (1 2 ...)
```

print-level   [Variable]

> The value of this variable is the maximum depth of nesting of parentheses and brackets when printed. Any list or vector at a depth exceeding this limit is abbreviated with an ellipsis. A value of **nil** (which is the default) means no limit.

`eval-expression-print-length`   [User Option]

`eval-expression-print-level`   [User Option]

> These are the values for `print-length` and `print-level` used by `eval-expression`, and thus, indirectly, by many interactive evaluation commands (see Section "Evaluating Emacs-Lisp Expressions" in *The GNU Emacs Manual*).

These variables are used for detecting and reporting circular and shared structure:

`print-circle`   [Variable]

> If non-`nil`, this variable enables detection of circular and shared structure in printing. See Section 2.5 [Circular Objects], page 27.

`print-gensym`   [Variable]

> If non-`nil`, this variable enables detection of uninterned symbols (see Section 8.3 [Creating Symbols], page 117) in printing. When this is enabled, uninterned symbols print with the prefix '`#:`', which tells the Lisp reader to produce an uninterned symbol.

`print-continuous-numbering`   [Variable]

> If non-`nil`, that means number continuously across print calls. This affects the numbers printed for '`#n=`' labels and '`#m#`' references. Don't set this variable with `setq`; you should only bind it temporarily to `t` with `let`. When you do that, you should also bind `print-number-table` to `nil`.

`print-number-table`   [Variable]

> This variable holds a vector used internally by printing to implement the `print-circle` feature. You should not use it except to bind it to `nil` when you bind `print-continuous-numbering`.

`float-output-format`   [Variable]

> This variable specifies how to print floating-point numbers. The default is `nil`, meaning use the shortest output that represents the number without losing information.
>
> To control output format more precisely, you can put a string in this variable. The string should hold a '`%`'-specification to be used in the C function `sprintf`. For further restrictions on what you can use, see the variable's documentation string.

19 Minibuffers

A *minibuffer* is a special buffer that Emacs commands use to read arguments more complicated than the single numeric prefix argument. These arguments include file names, buffer names, and command names (as in `M-x`). The minibuffer is displayed on the bottom line of the frame, in the same place as the echo area (see Section 37.4 [The Echo Area], page 888), but only while it is in use for reading an argument.

19.1 Introduction to Minibuffers

In most ways, a minibuffer is a normal Emacs buffer. Most operations *within* a buffer, such as editing commands, work normally in a minibuffer. However, many operations for managing buffers do not apply to minibuffers. The name of a minibuffer always has the form ' `*Minibuf-number*`', and it cannot be changed. Minibuffers are displayed only in special windows used only for minibuffers; these windows always appear at the bottom of a frame. (Sometimes frames have no minibuffer window, and sometimes a special kind of frame contains nothing but a minibuffer window; see Section 28.9 [Minibuffers and Frames], page 656.)

The text in the minibuffer always starts with the *prompt string*, the text that was specified by the program that is using the minibuffer to tell the user what sort of input to type. This text is marked read-only so you won't accidentally delete or change it. It is also marked as a field (see Section 31.19.9 [Fields], page 748), so that certain motion functions, including `beginning-of-line`, `forward-word`, `forward-sentence`, and `forward-paragraph`, stop at the boundary between the prompt and the actual text.

The minibuffer's window is normally a single line; it grows automatically if the contents require more space. Whilst it is active, you can explicitly resize it temporarily with the window sizing commands; it reverts to its normal size when the minibuffer is exited. When the minibuffer is not active, you can resize it permanently by using the window sizing commands in the frame's other window, or dragging the mode line with the mouse. (Due to details of the current implementation, for this to work `resize-mini-windows` must be `nil`.) If the frame contains just a minibuffer, you can change the minibuffer's size by changing the frame's size.

Use of the minibuffer reads input events, and that alters the values of variables such as `this-command` and `last-command` (see Section 20.5 [Command Loop Info], page 355). Your program should bind them around the code that uses the minibuffer, if you do not want that to change them.

Under some circumstances, a command can use a minibuffer even if there is an active minibuffer; such a minibuffer is called a *recursive minibuffer*. The first minibuffer is named ' `*Minibuf-1*`'. Recursive minibuffers are named by incrementing the number at the end of the name. (The names begin with a space so that they won't show up in normal buffer lists.) Of several recursive minibuffers, the innermost (or most recently entered) is the active minibuffer. We usually call this *the* minibuffer. You can permit or forbid recursive minibuffers by setting the variable `enable-recursive-minibuffers`, or by putting properties of that name on command symbols (See Section 19.13 [Recursive Mini], page 343.)

Like other buffers, a minibuffer uses a local keymap (see Chapter 21 [Keymaps], page 391) to specify special key bindings. The function that invokes the minibuffer also sets up its local map according to the job to be done. See Section 19.2 [Text from Minibuffer], page 314, for the non-completion minibuffer local maps. See Section 19.6.3 [Completion Commands], page 326, for the minibuffer local maps for completion.

When a minibuffer is inactive, its major mode is `minibuffer-inactive-mode`, with keymap `minibuffer-inactive-mode-map`. This is only really useful if the minibuffer is in a separate frame. See Section 28.9 [Minibuffers and Frames], page 656.

When Emacs is running in batch mode, any request to read from the minibuffer actually reads a line from the standard input descriptor that was supplied when Emacs was started. This supports only basic input: none of the special minibuffer features (history, completion, etc.) are available in batch mode.

19.2 Reading Text Strings with the Minibuffer

The most basic primitive for minibuffer input is `read-from-minibuffer`, which can be used to read either a string or a Lisp object in textual form. The function `read-regexp` is used for reading regular expressions (see Section 33.3 [Regular Expressions], page 793), which are a special kind of string. There are also specialized functions for reading commands, variables, file names, etc. (see Section 19.6 [Completion], page 321).

In most cases, you should not call minibuffer input functions in the middle of a Lisp function. Instead, do all minibuffer input as part of reading the arguments for a command, in the `interactive` specification. See Section 20.2 [Defining Commands], page 346.

`read-from-minibuffer` *prompt* **&optional** *initial keymap read*   [Function]
        history default inherit-input-method

> This function is the most general way to get input from the minibuffer. By default, it accepts arbitrary text and returns it as a string; however, if *read* is non-`nil`, then it uses `read` to convert the text into a Lisp object (see Section 18.3 [Input Functions], page 304).
>
> The first thing this function does is to activate a minibuffer and display it with *prompt* (which must be a string) as the prompt. Then the user can edit text in the minibuffer.
>
> When the user types a command to exit the minibuffer, `read-from-minibuffer` constructs the return value from the text in the minibuffer. Normally it returns a string containing that text. However, if *read* is non-`nil`, `read-from-minibuffer` reads the text and returns the resulting Lisp object, unevaluated. (See Section 18.3 [Input Functions], page 304, for information about reading.)
>
> The argument *default* specifies default values to make available through the history commands. It should be a string, a list of strings, or `nil`. The string or strings become the minibuffer's "future history", available to the user with `M-n`.
>
> If *read* is non-`nil`, then *default* is also used as the input to `read`, if the user enters empty input. If *default* is a list of strings, the first string is used as the input. If *default* is `nil`, empty input results in an `end-of-file` error. However, in the usual case (where *read* is `nil`), `read-from-minibuffer` ignores *default* when the user enters empty input and returns an empty string, `""`. In this respect, it differs from all the other minibuffer input functions in this chapter.
>
> If *keymap* is non-`nil`, that keymap is the local keymap to use in the minibuffer. If *keymap* is omitted or `nil`, the value of `minibuffer-local-map` is used as the

keymap. Specifying a keymap is the most important way to customize the minibuffer for various applications such as completion.

The argument *history* specifies a history list variable to use for saving the input and for history commands used in the minibuffer. It defaults to `minibuffer-history`. You can optionally specify a starting position in the history list as well. See Section 19.4 [Minibuffer History], page 318.

If the variable `minibuffer-allow-text-properties` is non-`nil`, then the string that is returned includes whatever text properties were present in the minibuffer. Otherwise all the text properties are stripped when the value is returned.

If the argument *inherit-input-method* is non-`nil`, then the minibuffer inherits the current input method (see Section 32.11 [Input Methods], page 787) and the setting of `enable-multibyte-characters` (see Section 32.1 [Text Representations], page 761) from whichever buffer was current before entering the minibuffer.

Use of *initial* is mostly deprecated; we recommend using a non-`nil` value only in conjunction with specifying a cons cell for *history*. See Section 19.5 [Initial Input], page 320.

read-string *prompt* **&optional** *initial history default*   [Function]
      inherit-input-method

> This function reads a string from the minibuffer and returns it. The arguments *prompt*, *initial*, *history* and *inherit-input-method* are used as in `read-from-minibuffer`. The keymap used is `minibuffer-local-map`.
>
> The optional argument *default* is used as in `read-from-minibuffer`, except that, if non-`nil`, it also specifies a default value to return if the user enters null input. As in `read-from-minibuffer` it should be a string, a list of strings, or `nil`, which is equivalent to an empty string. When *default* is a string, that string is the default value. When it is a list of strings, the first string is the default value. (All these strings are available to the user in the "future minibuffer history".)
>
> This function works by calling the `read-from-minibuffer` function:
>
> ```
> (read-string prompt initial history default inherit)
> ≡
> (let ((value
>        (read-from-minibuffer prompt initial nil nil
>                              history default inherit)))
>   (if (and (equal value "") default)
>       (if (consp default) (car default) default)
>     value))
> ```

read-regexp *prompt* **&optional** *defaults history*   [Function]

> This function reads a regular expression as a string from the minibuffer and returns it. If the minibuffer prompt string *prompt* does not end in ':' (followed by optional whitespace), the function adds ': ' to the end, preceded by the default return value (see below), if that is non-empty.
>
> The optional argument *defaults* controls the default value to return if the user enters null input, and should be one of: a string; `nil`, which is equivalent to an empty string; a list of strings; or a symbol.

If *defaults* is a symbol, `read-regexp` consults the value of the variable `read-regexp-defaults-function` (see below), and if that is non-`nil` uses it in preference to *defaults*. The value in this case should be either:

— `regexp-history-last`, which means to use the first element of the appropriate minibuffer history list (see below).

— A function of no arguments, whose return value (which should be `nil`, a string, or a list of strings) becomes the value of *defaults*.

`read-regexp` now ensures that the result of processing *defaults* is a list (i.e., if the value is `nil` or a string, it converts it to a list of one element). To this list, `read-regexp` then appends a few potentially useful candidates for input. These are:

— The word or symbol at point.

— The last regexp used in an incremental search.

— The last string used in an incremental search.

— The last string or pattern used in query-replace commands.

The function now has a list of regular expressions that it passes to `read-from-minibuffer` to obtain the user's input. The first element of the list is the default result in case of empty input. All elements of the list are available to the user as the "future minibuffer history" list (see Section "Minibuffer History" in *The GNU Emacs Manual*).

The optional argument *history*, if non-`nil`, is a symbol specifying a minibuffer history list to use (see Section 19.4 [Minibuffer History], page 318). If it is omitted or `nil`, the history list defaults to `regexp-history`.

`read-regexp-defaults-function`   [User Option]
The function `read-regexp` may use the value of this variable to determine its list of default regular expressions. If non-`nil`, the value of this variable should be either:

— The symbol `regexp-history-last`.

— A function of no arguments that returns either `nil`, a string, or a list of strings.

See `read-regexp` above for details of how these values are used.

`minibuffer-allow-text-properties`   [Variable]
If this variable is `nil`, then `read-from-minibuffer` and `read-string` strip all text properties from the minibuffer input before returning it. However, `read-no-blanks-input` (see below), as well as `read-minibuffer` and related functions (see Section 19.3 [Reading Lisp Objects With the Minibuffer], page 317), and all functions that do minibuffer input with completion, discard text properties unconditionally, regardless of the value of this variable.

`minibuffer-local-map`   [Variable]
This is the default local keymap for reading from the minibuffer. By default, it makes the following bindings:

`C-j`   `exit-minibuffer`

`RET`   `exit-minibuffer`

C-g	`abort-recursive-edit`
M-n	
`DOWN`	`next-history-element`
M-p	
`UP`	`previous-history-element`
M-s	`next-matching-history-element`
M-r	`previous-matching-history-element`

`read-no-blanks-input` *prompt* **&optional** *initial*   [Function]
        inherit-input-method

This function reads a string from the minibuffer, but does not allow whitespace characters as part of the input: instead, those characters terminate the input. The arguments *prompt*, *initial*, and *inherit-input-method* are used as in `read-from-minibuffer`.

This is a simplified interface to the `read-from-minibuffer` function, and passes the value of the `minibuffer-local-ns-map` keymap as the *keymap* argument for that function. Since the keymap `minibuffer-local-ns-map` does not rebind *C-q*, it *is* possible to put a space into the string, by quoting it.

This function discards text properties, regardless of the value of `minibuffer-allow-text-properties`.

```
(read-no-blanks-input prompt initial)
≡
(let (minibuffer-allow-text-properties)
  (read-from-minibuffer prompt initial minibuffer-local-ns-map))
```

`minibuffer-local-ns-map`   [Variable]

This built-in variable is the keymap used as the minibuffer local keymap in the function `read-no-blanks-input`. By default, it makes the following bindings, in addition to those of `minibuffer-local-map`:

`SPC`	`exit-minibuffer`
`TAB`	`exit-minibuffer`
`?`	`self-insert-and-exit`

19.3 Reading Lisp Objects with the Minibuffer

This section describes functions for reading Lisp objects with the minibuffer.

`read-minibuffer` *prompt* **&optional** *initial*   [Function]

This function reads a Lisp object using the minibuffer, and returns it without evaluating it. The arguments *prompt* and *initial* are used as in `read-from-minibuffer`.

This is a simplified interface to the `read-from-minibuffer` function:

```
(read-minibuffer prompt initial)
≡
(let (minibuffer-allow-text-properties)
  (read-from-minibuffer prompt initial nil t))
```

Here is an example in which we supply the string `"(testing)"` as initial input:

```
(read-minibuffer
 "Enter an expression: " (format "%s" '(testing)))

;; Here is how the minibuffer is displayed:

---------- Buffer: Minibuffer ----------
Enter an expression: (testing)*
---------- Buffer: Minibuffer ----------
```

The user can type RET immediately to use the initial input as a default, or can edit the input.

eval-minibuffer *prompt* **&optional** *initial*   [Function]
This function reads a Lisp expression using the minibuffer, evaluates it, then returns the result. The arguments *prompt* and *initial* are used as in `read-from-minibuffer`.

This function simply evaluates the result of a call to `read-minibuffer`:

```
(eval-minibuffer prompt initial)
    ≡
(eval (read-minibuffer prompt initial))
```

edit-and-eval-command *prompt form*   [Function]
This function reads a Lisp expression in the minibuffer, evaluates it, then returns the result. The difference between this command and `eval-minibuffer` is that here the initial *form* is not optional and it is treated as a Lisp object to be converted to printed representation rather than as a string of text. It is printed with `prin1`, so if it is a string, double-quote characters (`'"'`) appear in the initial text. See Section 18.5 [Output Functions], page 308.

In the following example, we offer the user an expression with initial text that is already a valid form:

```
(edit-and-eval-command "Please edit: " '(forward-word 1))

;; After evaluation of the preceding expression,
;;    the following appears in the minibuffer:

---------- Buffer: Minibuffer ----------
Please edit: (forward-word 1)*
---------- Buffer: Minibuffer ----------
```

Typing RET right away would exit the minibuffer and evaluate the expression, thus moving point forward one word.

19.4 Minibuffer History

A *minibuffer history list* records previous minibuffer inputs so the user can reuse them conveniently. It is a variable whose value is a list of strings (previous inputs), most recent first.

There are many separate minibuffer history lists, used for different kinds of inputs. It's the Lisp programmer's job to specify the right history list for each use of the minibuffer.

You specify a minibuffer history list with the optional *history* argument to `read-from-minibuffer` or `completing-read`. Here are the possible values for it:

variable   Use *variable* (a symbol) as the history list.

(*variable* . *startpos*)

> Use *variable* (a symbol) as the history list, and assume that the initial history position is *startpos* (a nonnegative integer).
>
> Specifying 0 for *startpos* is equivalent to just specifying the symbol *variable*. `previous-history-element` will display the most recent element of the history list in the minibuffer. If you specify a positive *startpos*, the minibuffer history functions behave as if (`elt` *variable* (`1-` *startpos*)) were the history element currently shown in the minibuffer.
>
> For consistency, you should also specify that element of the history as the initial minibuffer contents, using the *initial* argument to the minibuffer input function (see Section 19.5 [Initial Input], page 320).

If you don't specify *history*, then the default history list `minibuffer-history` is used. For other standard history lists, see below. You can also create your own history list variable; just initialize it to `nil` before the first use.

Both `read-from-minibuffer` and `completing-read` add new elements to the history list automatically, and provide commands to allow the user to reuse items on the list. The only thing your program needs to do to use a history list is to initialize it and to pass its name to the input functions when you wish. But it is safe to modify the list by hand when the minibuffer input functions are not using it.

Emacs functions that add a new element to a history list can also delete old elements if the list gets too long. The variable `history-length` specifies the maximum length for most history lists. To specify a different maximum length for a particular history list, put the length in the `history-length` property of the history list symbol. The variable `history-delete-duplicates` specifies whether to delete duplicates in history.

add-to-history *history-var newelt* **&optional** *maxelt keep-all*   [Function]

> This function adds a new element *newelt*, if it isn't the empty string, to the history list stored in the variable *history-var*, and returns the updated history list. It limits the list length to the value of *maxelt* (if non-`nil`) or `history-length` (described below). The possible values of *maxelt* have the same meaning as the values of `history-length`.
>
> Normally, **add-to-history** removes duplicate members from the history list if `history-delete-duplicates` is non-`nil`. However, if *keep-all* is non-`nil`, that says not to remove duplicates, and to add *newelt* to the list even if it is empty.

history-add-new-input   [Variable]

> If the value of this variable is `nil`, standard functions that read from the minibuffer don't add new elements to the history list. This lets Lisp programs explicitly manage input history by using **add-to-history**. The default value is `t`.

history-length   [User Option]

> The value of this variable specifies the maximum length for all history lists that don't specify their own maximum lengths. If the value is `t`, that means there is no maximum (don't delete old elements). If a history list variable's symbol has a non-`nil` `history-length` property, it overrides this variable for that particular history list.

history-delete-duplicates   [User Option]

> If the value of this variable is `t`, that means when adding a new history element, all previous identical elements are deleted.

Here are some of the standard minibuffer history list variables:

`minibuffer-history` [Variable]
> The default history list for minibuffer history input.

`query-replace-history` [Variable]
> A history list for arguments to `query-replace` (and similar arguments to other commands).

`file-name-history` [Variable]
> A history list for file-name arguments.

`buffer-name-history` [Variable]
> A history list for buffer-name arguments.

`regexp-history` [Variable]
> A history list for regular expression arguments.

`extended-command-history` [Variable]
> A history list for arguments that are names of extended commands.

`shell-command-history` [Variable]
> A history list for arguments that are shell commands.

`read-expression-history` [Variable]
> A history list for arguments that are Lisp expressions to evaluate.

`face-name-history` [Variable]
> A history list for arguments that are faces.

19.5 Initial Input

Several of the functions for minibuffer input have an argument called *initial*. This is a mostly-deprecated feature for specifying that the minibuffer should start out with certain text, instead of empty as usual.

If *initial* is a string, the minibuffer starts out containing the text of the string, with point at the end, when the user starts to edit the text. If the user simply types RET to exit the minibuffer, it will use the initial input string to determine the value to return.

We discourage use of a non-`nil` value for *initial*, because initial input is an intrusive interface. History lists and default values provide a much more convenient method to offer useful default inputs to the user.

There is just one situation where you should specify a string for an *initial* argument. This is when you specify a cons cell for the *history* argument. See Section 19.4 [Minibuffer History], page 318.

initial can also be a cons cell of the form (*string . position*). This means to insert *string* in the minibuffer but put point at *position* within the string's text.

As a historical accident, *position* was implemented inconsistently in different functions. In `completing-read`, *position*'s value is interpreted as origin-zero; that is, a value of 0 means the beginning of the string, 1 means after the first character, etc. In `read-minibuffer`, and the other non-completion minibuffer input functions that support this argument, 1 means the beginning of the string, 2 means after the first character, etc.

Use of a cons cell as the value for *initial* arguments is deprecated.

19.6 Completion

Completion is a feature that fills in the rest of a name starting from an abbreviation for it. Completion works by comparing the user's input against a list of valid names and determining how much of the name is determined uniquely by what the user has typed. For example, when you type `C-x b` (`switch-to-buffer`) and then type the first few letters of the name of the buffer to which you wish to switch, and then type `TAB` (`minibuffer-complete`), Emacs extends the name as far as it can.

Standard Emacs commands offer completion for names of symbols, files, buffers, and processes; with the functions in this section, you can implement completion for other kinds of names.

The `try-completion` function is the basic primitive for completion: it returns the longest determined completion of a given initial string, with a given set of strings to match against.

The function `completing-read` provides a higher-level interface for completion. A call to `completing-read` specifies how to determine the list of valid names. The function then activates the minibuffer with a local keymap that binds a few keys to commands useful for completion. Other functions provide convenient simple interfaces for reading certain kinds of names with completion.

19.6.1 Basic Completion Functions

The following completion functions have nothing in themselves to do with minibuffers. We describe them here to keep them near the higher-level completion features that do use the minibuffer.

`try-completion` *string collection* **&optional** *predicate*   [Function]

This function returns the longest common substring of all possible completions of *string* in *collection*.

collection is called the *completion table*. Its value must be a list of strings or cons cells, an obarray, a hash table, or a completion function.

`try-completion` compares *string* against each of the permissible completions specified by the completion table. If no permissible completions match, it returns **nil**. If there is just one matching completion, and the match is exact, it returns **t**. Otherwise, it returns the longest initial sequence common to all possible matching completions.

If *collection* is a list, the permissible completions are specified by the elements of the list, each of which should be either a string, or a cons cell whose CAR is either a string or a symbol (a symbol is converted to a string using `symbol-name`). If the list contains elements of any other type, those are ignored.

If *collection* is an obarray (see Section 8.3 [Creating Symbols], page 117), the names of all symbols in the obarray form the set of permissible completions.

If *collection* is a hash table, then the keys that are strings or symbols are the possible completions. Other keys are ignored.

You can also use a function as *collection*. Then the function is solely responsible for performing completion; `try-completion` returns whatever this function returns. The function is called with three arguments: *string*, *predicate* and `nil` (the third argument is so that the same function can be used in `all-completions` and do the appropriate thing in either case). See Section 19.6.7 [Programmed Completion], page 334.

If the argument *predicate* is non-`nil`, then it must be a function of one argument, unless *collection* is a hash table, in which case it should be a function of two arguments. It is used to test each possible match, and the match is accepted only if *predicate* returns non-`nil`. The argument given to *predicate* is either a string or a cons cell (the CAR of which is a string) from the alist, or a symbol (*not* a symbol name) from the obarray. If *collection* is a hash table, *predicate* is called with two arguments, the string key and the associated value.

In addition, to be acceptable, a completion must also match all the regular expressions in `completion-regexp-list`. (Unless *collection* is a function, in which case that function has to handle `completion-regexp-list` itself.)

In the first of the following examples, the string 'foo' is matched by three of the alist CARs. All of the matches begin with the characters 'fooba', so that is the result. In the second example, there is only one possible match, and it is exact, so the return value is `t`.

```
(try-completion
 "foo"
 '(("foobar1" 1) ("barfoo" 2) ("foobaz" 3) ("foobar2" 4)))
     ⇒ "fooba"

(try-completion "foo" '(("barfoo" 2) ("foo" 3)))
     ⇒ t
```

In the following example, numerous symbols begin with the characters 'forw', and all of them begin with the word 'forward'. In most of the symbols, this is followed with a '-', but not in all, so no more than 'forward' can be completed.

```
(try-completion "forw" obarray)
     ⇒ "forward"
```

Finally, in the following example, only two of the three possible matches pass the predicate `test` (the string 'foobaz' is too short). Both of those begin with the string 'foobar'.

```
(defun test (s)
  (> (length (car s)) 6))
     ⇒ test
(try-completion
 "foo"
 '(("foobar1" 1) ("barfoo" 2) ("foobaz" 3) ("foobar2" 4))
 'test)
     ⇒ "foobar"
```

all-completions *string collection* **&optional** *predicate*   [Function]
  This function returns a list of all possible completions of *string*. The arguments to this function are the same as those of `try-completion`, and it uses `completion-regexp-list` in the same way that `try-completion` does.

If *collection* is a function, it is called with three arguments: *string*, *predicate* and
t; then `all-completions` returns whatever the function returns. See Section 19.6.7
[Programmed Completion], page 334.

Here is an example, using the function `test` shown in the example for
`try-completion`:

```
(defun test (s)
  (> (length (car s)) 6))
     ⇒ test

(all-completions
 "foo"
 '(("foobar1" 1) ("barfoo" 2) ("foobaz" 3) ("foobar2" 4))
 'test)
     ⇒ ("foobar1" "foobar2")
```

`test-completion` *string collection* **&optional** *predicate*   [Function]

This function returns non-`nil` if *string* is a valid completion alternative specified by
collection and *predicate*. The arguments are the same as in `try-completion`. For
instance, if *collection* is a list of strings, this is true if *string* appears in the list and
predicate is satisfied.

This function uses `completion-regexp-list` in the same way that `try-completion`
does.

If *predicate* is non-`nil` and if *collection* contains several strings that are equal to each
other, as determined by `compare-strings` according to `completion-ignore-case`,
then *predicate* should accept either all or none of them. Otherwise, the return value
of `test-completion` is essentially unpredictable.

If *collection* is a function, it is called with three arguments, the values *string*, *predicate*
and `lambda`; whatever it returns, `test-completion` returns in turn.

`completion-boundaries` *string collection predicate suffix*   [Function]

This function returns the boundaries of the field on which *collection* will operate,
assuming that *string* holds the text before point and *suffix* holds the text after point.

Normally completion operates on the whole string, so for all normal collections,
this will always return (0 . (length *suffix*)). But more complex completion
such as completion on files is done one field at a time. For example, completion
of "/usr/sh" will include "/usr/share/" but not "/usr/share/doc" even if
"/usr/share/doc" exists. Also `all-completions` on "/usr/sh" will not include
"/usr/share/" but only "share/". So if *string* is "/usr/sh" and *suffix* is "e/doc",
`completion-boundaries` will return (5 . 1) which tells us that the *collection* will
only return completion information that pertains to the area after "/usr/" and
before "/doc".

If you store a completion alist in a variable, you should mark the variable as risky
by giving it a non-`nil` `risky-local-variable` property. See Section 11.11 [File Local
Variables], page 177.

`completion-ignore-case`   [Variable]

If the value of this variable is non-`nil`, case is not considered significant in
completion. Within `read-file-name`, this variable is overridden by `read-file-name-completion-ignore-case` (see Section 19.6.5 [Reading File Names], page 330);

within `read-buffer`, it is overridden by `read-buffer-completion-ignore-case` (see Section 19.6.4 [High-Level Completion], page 328).

`completion-regexp-list`   [Variable]

This is a list of regular expressions. The completion functions only consider a completion acceptable if it matches all regular expressions in this list, with `case-fold-search` (see Section 33.2 [Searching and Case], page 792) bound to the value of `completion-ignore-case`.

`lazy-completion-table` *var fun*   [Macro]

This macro provides a way to initialize the variable *var* as a collection for completion in a lazy way, not computing its actual contents until they are first needed. You use this macro to produce a value that you store in *var*. The actual computation of the proper value is done the first time you do completion using *var*. It is done by calling *fun* with no arguments. The value *fun* returns becomes the permanent value of *var*.

Here is an example:

```
(defvar foo (lazy-completion-table foo make-my-alist))
```

There are several functions that take an existing completion table and return a modified version. `completion-table-case-fold` returns a case-insensitive table. `completion-table-in-turn` and `completion-table-merge` combine multiple input tables in different ways. `completion-table-subvert` alters a table to use a different initial prefix. `completion-table-with-quoting` returns a table suitable for operating on quoted text. `completion-table-with-predicate` filters a table with a predicate function. `completion-table-with-terminator` adds a terminating string.

19.6.2 Completion and the Minibuffer

This section describes the basic interface for reading from the minibuffer with completion.

`completing-read` *prompt collection* **&optional** *predicate*   [Function]
　　　require-match initial history default inherit-input-method

This function reads a string in the minibuffer, assisting the user by providing completion. It activates the minibuffer with prompt *prompt*, which must be a string.

The actual completion is done by passing the completion table *collection* and the completion predicate *predicate* to the function `try-completion` (see Section 19.6.1 [Basic Completion], page 321). This happens in certain commands bound in the local keymaps used for completion. Some of these commands also call `test-completion`. Thus, if *predicate* is non-`nil`, it should be compatible with *collection* and `completion-ignore-case`. See [Definition of test-completion], page 323.

See Section 19.6.7 [Programmed Completion], page 334, for detailed requirements when *collection* is a function.

The value of the optional argument *require-match* determines how the user may exit the minibuffer:

- If `nil`, the usual minibuffer exit commands work regardless of the input in the minibuffer.

- If `t`, the usual minibuffer exit commands won't exit unless the input completes to an element of *collection*.

- If `confirm`, the user can exit with any input, but is asked for confirmation if the input is not an element of *collection*.

- If `confirm-after-completion`, the user can exit with any input, but is asked for confirmation if the preceding command was a completion command (i.e., one of the commands in `minibuffer-confirm-exit-commands`) and the resulting input is not an element of *collection*. See Section 19.6.3 [Completion Commands], page 326.

- Any other value of *require-match* behaves like `t`, except that the exit commands won't exit if it performs completion.

However, empty input is always permitted, regardless of the value of *require-match*; in that case, `completing-read` returns the first element of *default*, if it is a list; `""`, if *default* is `nil`; or *default*. The string or strings in *default* are also available to the user through the history commands.

The function `completing-read` uses `minibuffer-local-completion-map` as the keymap if *require-match* is `nil`, and uses `minibuffer-local-must-match-map` if *require-match* is non-`nil`. See Section 19.6.3 [Completion Commands], page 326.

The argument *history* specifies which history list variable to use for saving the input and for minibuffer history commands. It defaults to `minibuffer-history`. See Section 19.4 [Minibuffer History], page 318.

The argument *initial* is mostly deprecated; we recommend using a non-`nil` value only in conjunction with specifying a cons cell for *history*. See Section 19.5 [Initial Input], page 320. For default input, use *default* instead.

If the argument *inherit-input-method* is non-`nil`, then the minibuffer inherits the current input method (see Section 32.11 [Input Methods], page 787) and the setting of `enable-multibyte-characters` (see Section 32.1 [Text Representations], page 761) from whichever buffer was current before entering the minibuffer.

If the variable `completion-ignore-case` is non-`nil`, completion ignores case when comparing the input against the possible matches. See Section 19.6.1 [Basic Completion], page 321. In this mode of operation, *predicate* must also ignore case, or you will get surprising results.

Here's an example of using `completing-read`:

```
(completing-read
 "Complete a foo: "
 '(("foobar1" 1) ("barfoo" 2) ("foobaz" 3) ("foobar2" 4))
 nil t "fo")

;; After evaluation of the preceding expression,
;;    the following appears in the minibuffer:

---------- Buffer: Minibuffer ----------
Complete a foo: fo⋆
---------- Buffer: Minibuffer ----------
```

If the user then types *DEL DEL b RET*, `completing-read` returns `barfoo`.

The `completing-read` function binds variables to pass information to the commands that actually do completion. They are described in the following section.

`completing-read-function` [Variable]

> The value of this variable must be a function, which is called by `completing-read` to actually do its work. It should accept the same arguments as `completing-read`. This can be bound to a different function to completely override the normal behavior of `completing-read`.

19.6.3 Minibuffer Commands that Do Completion

This section describes the keymaps, commands and user options used in the minibuffer to do completion.

`minibuffer-completion-table` [Variable]

> The value of this variable is the completion table used for completion in the minibuffer. This is the global variable that contains what `completing-read` passes to `try-completion`. It is used by minibuffer completion commands such as `minibuffer-complete-word`.

`minibuffer-completion-predicate` [Variable]

> This variable's value is the predicate that `completing-read` passes to `try-completion`. The variable is also used by the other minibuffer completion functions.

`minibuffer-completion-confirm` [Variable]

> This variable determines whether Emacs asks for confirmation before exiting the minibuffer; `completing-read` binds this variable, and the function `minibuffer-complete-and-exit` checks the value before exiting. If the value is `nil`, confirmation is not required. If the value is `confirm`, the user may exit with an input that is not a valid completion alternative, but Emacs asks for confirmation. If the value is `confirm-after-completion`, the user may exit with an input that is not a valid completion alternative, but Emacs asks for confirmation if the user submitted the input right after any of the completion commands in `minibuffer-confirm-exit-commands`.

`minibuffer-confirm-exit-commands` [Variable]

> This variable holds a list of commands that cause Emacs to ask for confirmation before exiting the minibuffer, if the *require-match* argument to `completing-read` is `confirm-after-completion`. The confirmation is requested if the user attempts to exit the minibuffer immediately after calling any command in this list.

`minibuffer-complete-word` [Command]

> This function completes the minibuffer contents by at most a single word. Even if the minibuffer contents have only one completion, `minibuffer-complete-word` does not add any characters beyond the first character that is not a word constituent. See Chapter 34 [Syntax Tables], page 816.

`minibuffer-complete` [Command]

> This function completes the minibuffer contents as far as possible.

`minibuffer-complete-and-exit` [Command]

> This function completes the minibuffer contents, and exits if confirmation is not required, i.e., if `minibuffer-completion-confirm` is `nil`. If confirmation *is* required,

it is given by repeating this command immediately—the command is programmed to work without confirmation when run twice in succession.

`minibuffer-completion-help` [Command]

> This function creates a list of the possible completions of the current minibuffer contents. It works by calling `all-completions` using the value of the variable `minibuffer-completion-table` as the *collection* argument, and the value of `minibuffer-completion-predicate` as the *predicate* argument. The list of completions is displayed as text in a buffer named *Completions*.

`display-completion-list` *completions* [Function]

> This function displays *completions* to the stream in `standard-output`, usually a buffer. (See Chapter 18 [Read and Print], page 302, for more information about streams.) The argument *completions* is normally a list of completions just returned by `all-completions`, but it does not have to be. Each element may be a symbol or a string, either of which is simply printed. It can also be a list of two strings, which is printed as if the strings were concatenated. The first of the two strings is the actual completion, the second string serves as annotation.
>
> This function is called by `minibuffer-completion-help`. A common way to use it is together with `with-output-to-temp-buffer`, like this:
>
> ```
> (with-output-to-temp-buffer "*Completions*"
>   (display-completion-list
>     (all-completions (buffer-string) my-alist)))
> ```

`completion-auto-help` [User Option]

> If this variable is non-`nil`, the completion commands automatically display a list of possible completions whenever nothing can be completed because the next character is not uniquely determined.

`minibuffer-local-completion-map` [Variable]

> `completing-read` uses this value as the local keymap when an exact match of one of the completions is not required. By default, this keymap makes the following bindings:
>
> | `?` | `minibuffer-completion-help` |
> | `SPC` | `minibuffer-complete-word` |
> | `TAB` | `minibuffer-complete` |
>
> and uses `minibuffer-local-map` as its parent keymap (see [Definition of minibuffer-local-map], page 316).

`minibuffer-local-must-match-map` [Variable]

> `completing-read` uses this value as the local keymap when an exact match of one of the completions is required. Therefore, no keys are bound to `exit-minibuffer`, the command that exits the minibuffer unconditionally. By default, this keymap makes the following bindings:
>
> | `C-j` | `minibuffer-complete-and-exit` |
> | `RET` | `minibuffer-complete-and-exit` |

and uses `minibuffer-local-completion-map` as its parent keymap.

`minibuffer-local-filename-completion-map`   [Variable]

> This is a sparse keymap that simply unbinds SPC; because filenames can contain spaces. The function `read-file-name` combines this keymap with either `minibuffer-local-completion-map` or `minibuffer-local-must-match-map`.

19.6.4 High-Level Completion Functions

This section describes the higher-level convenience functions for reading certain sorts of names with completion.

In most cases, you should not call these functions in the middle of a Lisp function. When possible, do all minibuffer input as part of reading the arguments for a command, in the `interactive` specification. See Section 20.2 [Defining Commands], page 346.

`read-buffer` *prompt* **&optional** *default require-match predicate*   [Function]

> This function reads the name of a buffer and returns it as a string. It prompts with *prompt*. The argument *default* is the default name to use, the value to return if the user exits with an empty minibuffer. If non-`nil`, it should be a string, a list of strings, or a buffer. If it is a list, the default value is the first element of this list. It is mentioned in the prompt, but is not inserted in the minibuffer as initial input.
>
> The argument *prompt* should be a string ending with a colon and a space. If *default* is non-`nil`, the function inserts it in *prompt* before the colon to follow the convention for reading from the minibuffer with a default value (see Section D.3 [Programming Tips], page 1056).
>
> The optional argument *require-match* has the same meaning as in `completing-read`. See Section 19.6.2 [Minibuffer Completion], page 324.
>
> The optional argument *predicate*, if non-`nil`, specifies a function to filter the buffers that should be considered: the function will be called with every potential candidate as its argument, and should return `nil` to reject the candidate, non-`nil` to accept it.
>
> In the following example, the user enters 'minibuffer.t', and then types RET. The argument *require-match* is `t`, and the only buffer name starting with the given input is 'minibuffer.texi', so that name is the value.

```
(read-buffer "Buffer name: " "foo" t)
;; After evaluation of the preceding expression,
;;    the following prompt appears,
;;    with an empty minibuffer:

---------- Buffer: Minibuffer ----------
Buffer name (default foo): *
---------- Buffer: Minibuffer ----------

;; The user types minibuffer.t RET.
     ⇒ "minibuffer.texi"
```

read-buffer-function   [User Option]

>   This variable, if non-nil, specifies a function for reading buffer names. `read-buffer` calls this function instead of doing its usual work, with the same arguments passed to `read-buffer`.

read-buffer-completion-ignore-case   [User Option]

>   If this variable is non-`nil`, `read-buffer` ignores case when performing completion while reading the buffer name.

read-command *prompt* **&optional** *default*   [Function]

>   This function reads the name of a command and returns it as a Lisp symbol. The argument *prompt* is used as in `read-from-minibuffer`. Recall that a command is anything for which `commandp` returns `t`, and a command name is a symbol for which `commandp` returns `t`. See Section 20.3 [Interactive Call], page 352.
>
>   The argument *default* specifies what to return if the user enters null input. It can be a symbol, a string or a list of strings. If it is a string, `read-command` interns it before returning it. If it is a list, `read-command` interns the first element of this list. If *default* is `nil`, that means no default has been specified; then if the user enters null input, the return value is (`intern ""`), that is, a symbol whose name is an empty string.
>
> ```
>     (read-command "Command name? ")
>
>     ;; After evaluation of the preceding expression,
>     ;;     the following prompt appears with an empty minibuffer:
>
>     ---------- Buffer: Minibuffer ----------
>     Command name?
>     ---------- Buffer: Minibuffer ----------
> ```
>
>   If the user types *forward-c RET*, then this function returns `forward-char`.
>
>   The `read-command` function is a simplified interface to `completing-read`. It uses the variable `obarray` so as to complete in the set of extant Lisp symbols, and it uses the `commandp` predicate so as to accept only command names:
>
> ```
>     (read-command prompt)
>     ≡
>     (intern (completing-read prompt obarray
>                              'commandp t nil))
> ```

read-variable *prompt* **&optional** *default*   [Function]

>   This function reads the name of a customizable variable and returns it as a symbol. Its arguments have the same form as those of `read-command`. It behaves just like `read-command`, except that it uses the predicate `custom-variable-p` instead of `commandp`.

read-color **&optional** *prompt convert allow-empty display*   [Command]

>   This function reads a string that is a color specification, either the color's name or an RGB hex value such as `#RRRGGGBBB`. It prompts with *prompt* (default: `"Color (name or #RGB triplet):"`) and provides completion for color names, but not for hex RGB

values. In addition to names of standard colors, completion candidates include the foreground and background colors at point.

Valid RGB values are described in Section 28.21 [Color Names], page 666.

The function's return value is the string typed by the user in the minibuffer. However, when called interactively or if the optional argument *convert* is non-`nil`, it converts any input color name into the corresponding RGB value string and instead returns that. This function requires a valid color specification to be input. Empty color names are allowed when *allow-empty* is non-`nil` and the user enters null input.

Interactively, or when *display* is non-`nil`, the return value is also displayed in the echo area.

See also the functions `read-coding-system` and `read-non-nil-coding-system`, in Section 32.10.4 [User-Chosen Coding Systems], page 779, and `read-input-method-name`, in Section 32.11 [Input Methods], page 787.

19.6.5 Reading File Names

The high-level completion functions `read-file-name`, `read-directory-name`, and `read-shell-command` are designed to read file names, directory names, and shell commands, respectively. They provide special features, including automatic insertion of the default directory.

read-file-name *prompt* **&optional** *directory default require-match*   [Function]
       initial predicate
   This function reads a file name, prompting with *prompt* and providing completion.

   As an exception, this function reads a file name using a graphical file dialog instead of the minibuffer, if all of the following are true:

   1. It is invoked via a mouse command.
   2. The selected frame is on a graphical display supporting such dialogs.
   3. The variable `use-dialog-box` is non-`nil`. See Section "Dialog Boxes" in *The GNU Emacs Manual*.
   4. The *directory* argument, described below, does not specify a remote file. See Section "Remote Files" in *The GNU Emacs Manual*.

   The exact behavior when using a graphical file dialog is platform-dependent. Here, we simply document the behavior when using the minibuffer.

   `read-file-name` does not automatically expand the returned file name. You must call `expand-file-name` yourself if an absolute file name is required.

   The optional argument *require-match* has the same meaning as in `completing-read`. See Section 19.6.2 [Minibuffer Completion], page 324.

   The argument *directory* specifies the directory to use for completing relative file names. It should be an absolute directory name. If the variable `insert-default-directory` is non-`nil`, *directory* is also inserted in the minibuffer as initial input. It defaults to the current buffer's value of `default-directory`.

   If you specify *initial*, that is an initial file name to insert in the buffer (after *directory*, if that is inserted). In this case, point goes at the beginning of *initial*. The default for *initial* is `nil`—don't insert any file name. To see what *initial* does, try the command `C-x C-v` in a buffer visiting a file. **Please note:** we recommend using *default* rather than *initial* in most cases.

If *default* is non-`nil`, then the function returns *default* if the user exits the minibuffer with the same non-empty contents that `read-file-name` inserted initially. The initial minibuffer contents are always non-empty if `insert-default-directory` is non-`nil`, as it is by default. *default* is not checked for validity, regardless of the value of *require-match*. However, if *require-match* is non-`nil`, the initial minibuffer contents should be a valid file (or directory) name. Otherwise `read-file-name` attempts completion if the user exits without any editing, and does not return *default*. *default* is also available through the history commands.

If *default* is `nil`, `read-file-name` tries to find a substitute default to use in its place, which it treats in exactly the same way as if it had been specified explicitly. If *default* is `nil`, but *initial* is non-`nil`, then the default is the absolute file name obtained from *directory* and *initial*. If both *default* and *initial* are `nil` and the buffer is visiting a file, `read-file-name` uses the absolute file name of that file as default. If the buffer is not visiting a file, then there is no default. In that case, if the user types `RET` without any editing, `read-file-name` simply returns the pre-inserted contents of the minibuffer.

If the user types `RET` in an empty minibuffer, this function returns an empty string, regardless of the value of *require-match*. This is, for instance, how the user can make the current buffer visit no file using `M-x set-visited-file-name`.

If *predicate* is non-`nil`, it specifies a function of one argument that decides which file names are acceptable completion alternatives. A file name is an acceptable value if *predicate* returns non-`nil` for it.

Here is an example of using `read-file-name`:

```
(read-file-name "The file is ")

;; After evaluation of the preceding expression,
;;    the following appears in the minibuffer:

---------- Buffer: Minibuffer ----------
The file is /gp/gnu/elisp/*
---------- Buffer: Minibuffer ----------
```

Typing *manual* `TAB` results in the following:

```
---------- Buffer: Minibuffer ----------
The file is /gp/gnu/elisp/manual.texi*
---------- Buffer: Minibuffer ----------
```

If the user types `RET`, `read-file-name` returns the file name as the string `"/gp/gnu/elisp/manual.texi"`.

`read-file-name-function`   [Variable]

If non-`nil`, this should be a function that accepts the same arguments as `read-file-name`. When `read-file-name` is called, it calls this function with the supplied arguments instead of doing its usual work.

`read-file-name-completion-ignore-case`   [User Option]
> If this variable is non-`nil`, `read-file-name` ignores case when performing completion.

`read-directory-name` *prompt* **&optional** *directory default* [Function]
> *require-match initial*
>
> This function is like `read-file-name` but allows only directory names as completion alternatives.
>
> If *default* is `nil` and *initial* is non-`nil`, `read-directory-name` constructs a substitute default by combining *directory* (or the current buffer's default directory if *directory* is `nil`) and *initial*. If both *default* and *initial* are `nil`, this function uses *directory* as substitute default, or the current buffer's default directory if *directory* is `nil`.

`insert-default-directory`   [User Option]
> This variable is used by `read-file-name`, and thus, indirectly, by most commands reading file names. (This includes all commands that use the code letters 'f' or 'F' in their interactive form. See Section 20.2.2 [Code Characters for interactive], page 348.) Its value controls whether `read-file-name` starts by placing the name of the default directory in the minibuffer, plus the initial file name, if any. If the value of this variable is `nil`, then `read-file-name` does not place any initial input in the minibuffer (unless you specify initial input with the *initial* argument). In that case, the default directory is still used for completion of relative file names, but is not displayed.
>
> If this variable is `nil` and the initial minibuffer contents are empty, the user may have to explicitly fetch the next history element to access a default value. If the variable is non-`nil`, the initial minibuffer contents are always non-empty and the user can always request a default value by immediately typing `RET` in an unedited minibuffer. (See above.)
>
> For example:
>
> ```
> ;; Here the minibuffer starts out with the default directory.
> (let ((insert-default-directory t))
>   (read-file-name "The file is "))
>
>
> ---------- Buffer: Minibuffer ----------
> The file is ~lewis/manual/*
> ---------- Buffer: Minibuffer ----------
>
>
> ;; Here the minibuffer is empty and only the prompt
> ;;    appears on its line.
> (let ((insert-default-directory nil))
>   (read-file-name "The file is "))
>
>
> ---------- Buffer: Minibuffer ----------
> The file is *
> ---------- Buffer: Minibuffer ----------
> ```

`read-shell-command` *prompt* **&optional** *initial history* **&rest** *args* [Function]
> This function reads a shell command from the minibuffer, prompting with *prompt* and providing intelligent completion. It completes the first word of the command using

candidates that are appropriate for command names, and the rest of the command words as file names.

This function uses `minibuffer-local-shell-command-map` as the keymap for minibuffer input. The *history* argument specifies the history list to use; if is omitted or `nil`, it defaults to `shell-command-history` (see Section 19.4 [Minibuffer History], page 318). The optional argument *initial* specifies the initial content of the minibuffer (see Section 19.5 [Initial Input], page 320). The rest of *args*, if present, are used as the *default* and *inherit-input-method* arguments in `read-from-minibuffer` (see Section 19.2 [Text from Minibuffer], page 314).

`minibuffer-local-shell-command-map`   [Variable]

> This keymap is used by `read-shell-command` for completing command and file names that are part of a shell command. It uses `minibuffer-local-map` as its parent keymap, and binds `TAB` to `completion-at-point`.

19.6.6 Completion Variables

Here are some variables that can be used to alter the default completion behavior.

`completion-styles`   [User Option]

> The value of this variable is a list of completion style (symbols) to use for performing completion. A *completion style* is a set of rules for generating completions. Each symbol occurring this list must have a corresponding entry in `completion-styles-alist`.

`completion-styles-alist`   [Variable]

> This variable stores a list of available completion styles. Each element in the list has the form
>
> > (*style try-completion all-completions doc*)
>
> Here, *style* is the name of the completion style (a symbol), which may be used in the `completion-styles` variable to refer to this style; *try-completion* is the function that does the completion; *all-completions* is the function that lists the completions; and *doc* is a string describing the completion style.
>
> The *try-completion* and *all-completions* functions should each accept four arguments: *string*, *collection*, *predicate*, and *point*. The *string*, *collection*, and *predicate* arguments have the same meanings as in `try-completion` (see Section 19.6.1 [Basic Completion], page 321), and the *point* argument is the position of point within *string*. Each function should return a non-`nil` value if it performed its job, and `nil` if it did not (e.g., if there is no way to complete *string* according to the completion style).
>
> When the user calls a completion command like `minibuffer-complete` (see Section 19.6.3 [Completion Commands], page 326), Emacs looks for the first style listed in `completion-styles` and calls its *try-completion* function. If this function returns `nil`, Emacs moves to the next listed completion style and calls its *try-completion* function, and so on until one of the *try-completion* functions successfully performs completion and returns a non-`nil` value. A similar procedure is used for listing completions, via the *all-completions* functions.
>
> See Section "Completion Styles" in *The GNU Emacs Manual*, for a description of the available completion styles.

`completion-category-overrides`   [User Option]

> This variable specifies special completion styles and other completion behaviors to use when completing certain types of text. Its value should be an alist with elements of the form (*category* . *alist*). *category* is a symbol describing what is being completed; currently, the `buffer`, `file`, and `unicode-name` categories are defined, but others can be defined via specialized completion functions (see Section 19.6.7 [Programmed Completion], page 334). *alist* is an association list describing how completion should behave for the corresponding category. The following alist keys are supported:
>
> styles   The value should be a list of completion styles (symbols).
>
> cycle   The value should be a value for `completion-cycle-threshold` (see Section "Completion Options" in *The GNU Emacs Manual*) for this category.
>
> Additional alist entries may be defined in the future.

`completion-extra-properties`   [Variable]

> This variable is used to specify extra properties of the current completion command. It is intended to be let-bound by specialized completion commands. Its value should be a list of property and value pairs. The following properties are supported:
>
> :annotation-function
>
> > The value should be a function to add annotations in the completions buffer. This function must accept one argument, a completion, and should either return `nil` or a string to be displayed next to the completion.
>
> :exit-function
>
> > The value should be a function to run after performing completion. The function should accept two arguments, *string* and *status*, where *string* is the text to which the field was completed, and *status* indicates what kind of operation happened: `finished` if text is now complete, `sole` if the text cannot be further completed but completion is not finished, or `exact` if the text is a valid completion but may be further completed.

19.6.7 Programmed Completion

Sometimes it is not possible or convenient to create an alist or an obarray containing all the intended possible completions ahead of time. In such a case, you can supply your own function to compute the completion of a given string. This is called *programmed completion*. Emacs uses programmed completion when completing file names (see Section 24.8.6 [File Name Completion], page 525), among many other cases.

To use this feature, pass a function as the *collection* argument to `completing-read`. The function `completing-read` arranges to pass your completion function along to `try-completion`, `all-completions`, and other basic completion functions, which will then let your function do all the work.

The completion function should accept three arguments:

- The string to be completed.

- A predicate function with which to filter possible matches, or `nil` if none. The function should call the predicate for each possible match, and ignore the match if the predicate returns `nil`.

- A flag specifying the type of completion operation to perform. This flag may be one of the following values.

nil
: This specifies a `try-completion` operation. The function should return `t` if the specified string is a unique and exact match; if there is more than one match, it should return the common substring of all matches (if the string is an exact match for one completion alternative but also matches other longer alternatives, the return value is the string); if there are no matches, it should return `nil`.

t
: This specifies an `all-completions` operation. The function should return a list of all possible completions of the specified string.

lambda
: This specifies a `test-completion` operation. The function should return `t` if the specified string is an exact match for some completion alternative; `nil` otherwise.

(boundaries . *suffix*)
: This specifies a `completion-boundaries` operation. The function should return (`boundaries` *start* . *end*), where *start* is the position of the beginning boundary in the specified string, and *end* is the position of the end boundary in *suffix*.

metadata
: This specifies a request for information about the state of the current completion. The return value should have the form (`metadata` . *alist*), where *alist* is an alist whose elements are described below.

If the flag has any other value, the completion function should return `nil`.

The following is a list of metadata entries that a completion function may return in response to a `metadata` flag argument:

category
: The value should be a symbol describing what kind of text the completion function is trying to complete. If the symbol matches one of the keys in `completion-category-overrides`, the usual completion behavior is overridden. See Section 19.6.6 [Completion Variables], page 333.

annotation-function
: The value should be a function for *annotating* completions. The function should take one argument, *string*, which is a possible completion. It should return a string, which is displayed after the completion *string* in the `*Completions*` buffer.

display-sort-function
: The value should be a function for sorting completions. The function should take one argument, a list of completion strings, and return a sorted list of completion strings. It is allowed to alter the input list destructively.

cycle-sort-function
: The value should be a function for sorting completions, when `completion-cycle-threshold` is non-`nil` and the user is cycling through completion alternatives. See Section "Completion Options" in *The GNU Emacs Manual*. Its argument list and return value are the same as for `display-sort-function`.

`completion-table-dynamic` *function* **&optional** *switch-buffer*   [Function]

> This function is a convenient way to write a function that can act as a programmed completion function. The argument *function* should be a function that takes one argument, a string, and returns an alist of possible completions of it. It is allowed to ignore the argument and return a full list of all possible completions. You can think of `completion-table-dynamic` as a transducer between that interface and the interface for programmed completion functions.
>
> If the optional argument *switch-buffer* is non-`nil`, and completion is performed in the minibuffer, *function* will be called with current buffer set to the buffer from which the minibuffer was entered.

`completion-table-with-cache` *function* **&optional** *ignore-case*   [Function]

> This is a wrapper for `completion-table-dynamic` that saves the last argument-result pair. This means that multiple lookups with the same argument only need to call *function* once. This can be useful when a slow operation is involved, such as calling an external process.

19.6.8 Completion in Ordinary Buffers

Although completion is usually done in the minibuffer, the completion facility can also be used on the text in ordinary Emacs buffers. In many major modes, in-buffer completion is performed by the *C-M-i* or *M-TAB* command, bound to `completion-at-point`. See Section "Symbol Completion" in *The GNU Emacs Manual*. This command uses the abnormal hook variable `completion-at-point-functions`:

`completion-at-point-functions`   [Variable]

> The value of this abnormal hook should be a list of functions, which are used to compute a completion table for completing the text at point. It can be used by major modes to provide mode-specific completion tables (see Section 22.2.1 [Major Mode Conventions], page 432).
>
> When the command `completion-at-point` runs, it calls the functions in the list one by one, without any argument. Each function should return `nil` if it is unable to produce a completion table for the text at point. Otherwise it should return a list of the form
>
>   (start end collection . props)
>
> *start* and *end* delimit the text to complete (which should enclose point). *collection* is a completion table for completing that text, in a form suitable for passing as the second argument to `try-completion` (see Section 19.6.1 [Basic Completion], page 321); completion alternatives will be generated from this completion table in the usual way, via the completion styles defined in `completion-styles` (see Section 19.6.6 [Completion Variables], page 333). *props* is a property list for additional information; any of the properties in `completion-extra-properties` are recognized (see Section 19.6.6 [Completion Variables], page 333), as well as the following additional ones:

`:predicate`

> The value should be a predicate that completion candidates need to satisfy.

`:exclusive`

> If the value is `no`, then if the completion table fails to match the text at point, `completion-at-point` moves on to the next function in `completion-at-point-functions` instead of reporting a completion failure.

Supplying a function for *collection* is strongly recommended if generating the list of completions is an expensive operation. Emacs may internally call functions in `completion-at-point-functions` many times, but care about the value of *collection* for only some of these calls. By supplying a function for *collection*, Emacs can defer generating completions until necessary. You can use *completion-table-dynamic* to create a wrapper function:

```
;; Avoid this pattern.
(let ((beg ...) (end ...) (my-completions (my-make-completions)))
  (list beg end my-completions))

;; Use this instead.
(let ((beg ...) (end ...))
  (list beg
        end
        (completion-table-dynamic
          (lambda (_)
            (my-make-completions)))))
```

A function in `completion-at-point-functions` may also return a function instead of a list as described above. In that case, that returned function is called, with no argument, and it is entirely responsible for performing the completion. We discourage this usage; it is intended to help convert old code to using `completion-at-point`.

The first function in `completion-at-point-functions` to return a non-`nil` value is used by `completion-at-point`. The remaining functions are not called. The exception to this is when there is an `:exclusive` specification, as described above.

The following function provides a convenient way to perform completion on an arbitrary stretch of text in an Emacs buffer:

`completion-in-region` *start end collection* **&optional** *predicate*   [Function]

> This function completes the text in the current buffer between the positions *start* and *end*, using *collection*. The argument *collection* has the same meaning as in `try-completion` (see Section 19.6.1 [Basic Completion], page 321).
>
> This function inserts the completion text directly into the current buffer. Unlike `completing-read` (see Section 19.6.2 [Minibuffer Completion], page 324), it does not activate the minibuffer.
>
> For this function to work, point must be somewhere between *start* and *end*.

19.7 Yes-or-No Queries

This section describes functions used to ask the user a yes-or-no question. The function `y-or-n-p` can be answered with a single character; it is useful for questions where an inadvertent wrong answer will not have serious consequences. `yes-or-no-p` is suitable for more momentous questions, since it requires three or four characters to answer.

If either of these functions is called in a command that was invoked using the mouse— more precisely, if `last-nonmenu-event` (see Section 20.5 [Command Loop Info], page 355) is either `nil` or a list—then it uses a dialog box or pop-up menu to ask the question. Otherwise, it uses keyboard input. You can force use either of the mouse or of keyboard input by binding `last-nonmenu-event` to a suitable value around the call.

Strictly speaking, `yes-or-no-p` uses the minibuffer and `y-or-n-p` does not; but it seems best to describe them together.

`y-or-n-p` *prompt*   [Function]
> This function asks the user a question, expecting input in the echo area. It returns `t` if the user types `y`, `nil` if the user types `n`. This function also accepts SPC to mean yes and DEL to mean no. It accepts `C-]` to quit, like `C-g`, because the question might look like a minibuffer and for that reason the user might try to use `C-]` to get out. The answer is a single character, with no RET needed to terminate it. Upper and lower case are equivalent.
>
> "Asking the question" means printing *prompt* in the echo area, followed by the string '`(y or n) `'. If the input is not one of the expected answers (`y`, `n`, SPC, DEL, or something that quits), the function responds '`Please answer y or n.`', and repeats the request.
>
> This function does not actually use the minibuffer, since it does not allow editing of the answer. It actually uses the echo area (see Section 37.4 [The Echo Area], page 888), which uses the same screen space as the minibuffer. The cursor moves to the echo area while the question is being asked.
>
> The answers and their meanings, even '`y`' and '`n`', are not hardwired, and are specified by the keymap `query-replace-map` (see Section 33.7 [Search and Replace], page 812). In particular, if the user enters the special responses `recenter`, `scroll-up`, `scroll-down`, `scroll-other-window`, or `scroll-other-window-down` (respectively bound to `C-l`, `C-v`, `M-v`, `C-M-v` and `C-M-S-v` in `query-replace-map`), this function performs the specified window recentering or scrolling operation, and poses the question again.
>
> We show successive lines of echo area messages, but only one actually appears on the screen at a time.

`y-or-n-p-with-timeout` *prompt seconds default*   [Function]
> Like `y-or-n-p`, except that if the user fails to answer within *seconds* seconds, this function stops waiting and returns *default*. It works by setting up a timer; see Section 38.11 [Timers], page 1006. The argument *seconds* should be a number.

`yes-or-no-p` *prompt*   [Function]
> This function asks the user a question, expecting input in the minibuffer. It returns `t` if the user enters '`yes`', `nil` if the user types '`no`'. The user must type RET to finalize the response. Upper and lower case are equivalent.
>
> `yes-or-no-p` starts by displaying *prompt* in the echo area, followed by '`(yes or no) `'. The user must type one of the expected responses; otherwise, the function responds '`Please answer yes or no.`', waits about two seconds and repeats the request.
>
> `yes-or-no-p` requires more work from the user than `y-or-n-p` and is appropriate for more crucial decisions.

Here is an example:

```
(yes-or-no-p "Do you really want to remove everything? ")

;; After evaluation of the preceding expression,
;;    the following prompt appears,
;;    with an empty minibuffer:

---------- Buffer: minibuffer ----------
Do you really want to remove everything? (yes or no)
---------- Buffer: minibuffer ----------
```

If the user first types *y RET*, which is invalid because this function demands the entire word '`yes`', it responds by displaying these prompts, with a brief pause between them:

```
---------- Buffer: minibuffer ----------
Please answer yes or no.
Do you really want to remove everything? (yes or no)
---------- Buffer: minibuffer ----------
```

19.8 Asking Multiple Y-or-N Questions

When you have a series of similar questions to ask, such as "Do you want to save this buffer?" for each buffer in turn, you should use `map-y-or-n-p` to ask the collection of questions, rather than asking each question individually. This gives the user certain convenient facilities such as the ability to answer the whole series at once.

`map-y-or-n-p` *prompter actor list* **&optional** *help action-alist*   [Function]
      no-cursor-in-echo-area

    This function asks the user a series of questions, reading a single-character answer in the echo area for each one.

    The value of *list* specifies the objects to ask questions about. It should be either a list of objects or a generator function. If it is a function, it should expect no arguments, and should return either the next object to ask about, or `nil`, meaning to stop asking questions.

    The argument *prompter* specifies how to ask each question. If *prompter* is a string, the question text is computed like this:

        `(format prompter object)`

    where *object* is the next object to ask about (as obtained from *list*).

    If not a string, *prompter* should be a function of one argument (the next object to ask about) and should return the question text. If the value is a string, that is the question to ask the user. The function can also return `t`, meaning do act on this object (and don't ask the user), or `nil`, meaning ignore this object (and don't ask the user).

    The argument *actor* says how to act on the answers that the user gives. It should be a function of one argument, and it is called with each object that the user says yes for. Its argument is always an object obtained from *list*.

    If the argument *help* is given, it should be a list of this form:

        `(singular plural action)`

where *singular* is a string containing a singular noun that describes the objects conceptually being acted on, *plural* is the corresponding plural noun, and *action* is a transitive verb describing what *actor* does.

If you don't specify *help*, the default is (`"object"` `"objects"` `"act on"`).

Each time a question is asked, the user may enter *y*, *Y*, or SPC to act on that object; *n*, *N*, or DEL to skip that object; *!* to act on all following objects; ESC or *q* to exit (skip all following objects); . (period) to act on the current object and then exit; or *C-h* to get help. These are the same answers that `query-replace` accepts. The keymap `query-replace-map` defines their meaning for `map-y-or-n-p` as well as for `query-replace`; see Section 33.7 [Search and Replace], page 812.

You can use *action-alist* to specify additional possible answers and what they mean. It is an alist of elements of the form (`char function help`), each of which defines one additional answer. In this element, *char* is a character (the answer); *function* is a function of one argument (an object from *list*); *help* is a string.

When the user responds with *char*, `map-y-or-n-p` calls *function*. If it returns non-`nil`, the object is considered acted upon, and `map-y-or-n-p` advances to the next object in *list*. If it returns `nil`, the prompt is repeated for the same object.

Normally, `map-y-or-n-p` binds `cursor-in-echo-area` while prompting. But if *no-cursor-in-echo-area* is non-`nil`, it does not do that.

If `map-y-or-n-p` is called in a command that was invoked using the mouse—more precisely, if `last-nonmenu-event` (see Section 20.5 [Command Loop Info], page 355) is either `nil` or a list—then it uses a dialog box or pop-up menu to ask the question. In this case, it does not use keyboard input or the echo area. You can force use either of the mouse or of keyboard input by binding `last-nonmenu-event` to a suitable value around the call.

The return value of `map-y-or-n-p` is the number of objects acted on.

19.9 Reading a Password

To read a password to pass to another program, you can use the function `read-passwd`.

`read-passwd` *prompt* **&optional** *confirm default*   [Function]
> This function reads a password, prompting with *prompt*. It does not echo the password as the user types it; instead, it echoes '.' for each character in the password. If you want to apply another character to hide the password, let-bind the variable `read-hide-char` with that character.
>
> The optional argument *confirm*, if non-`nil`, says to read the password twice and insist it must be the same both times. If it isn't the same, the user has to type it over and over until the last two times match.
>
> The optional argument *default* specifies the default password to return if the user enters empty input. If *default* is `nil`, then `read-passwd` returns the null string in that case.

19.10 Minibuffer Commands

This section describes some commands meant for use in the minibuffer.

`exit-minibuffer` [Command]

> This command exits the active minibuffer. It is normally bound to keys in minibuffer local keymaps.

`self-insert-and-exit` [Command]

> This command exits the active minibuffer after inserting the last character typed on the keyboard (found in `last-command-event`; see Section 20.5 [Command Loop Info], page 355).

`previous-history-element` *n* [Command]

> This command replaces the minibuffer contents with the value of the *n*th previous (older) history element.

`next-history-element` *n* [Command]

> This command replaces the minibuffer contents with the value of the *n*th more recent history element.

`previous-matching-history-element` *pattern n* [Command]

> This command replaces the minibuffer contents with the value of the *n*th previous (older) history element that matches *pattern* (a regular expression).

`next-matching-history-element` *pattern n* [Command]

> This command replaces the minibuffer contents with the value of the *n*th next (newer) history element that matches *pattern* (a regular expression).

`previous-complete-history-element` *n* [Command]

> This command replaces the minibuffer contents with the value of the *n*th previous (older) history element that completes the current contents of the minibuffer before the point.

`next-complete-history-element` *n* [Command]

> This command replaces the minibuffer contents with the value of the *n*th next (newer) history element that completes the current contents of the minibuffer before the point.

19.11 Minibuffer Windows

These functions access and select minibuffer windows, test whether they are active and control how they get resized.

`active-minibuffer-window` [Function]

> This function returns the currently active minibuffer window, or `nil` if there is none.

`minibuffer-window` &optional *frame* [Function]

> This function returns the minibuffer window used for frame *frame*. If *frame* is `nil`, that stands for the current frame. Note that the minibuffer window used by a frame need not be part of that frame—a frame that has no minibuffer of its own necessarily uses some other frame's minibuffer window.

`set-minibuffer-window` *window*   [Function]
> This function specifies *window* as the minibuffer window to use. This affects where
> the minibuffer is displayed if you put text in it without invoking the usual minibuffer
> commands. It has no effect on the usual minibuffer input functions because they all
> start by choosing the minibuffer window according to the current frame.

`window-minibuffer-p` **&optional** *window*   [Function]
> This function returns non-`nil` if *window* is a minibuffer window. *window* defaults to
> the selected window.

It is not correct to determine whether a given window is a minibuffer by comparing it
with the result of (`minibuffer-window`), because there can be more than one minibuffer
window if there is more than one frame.

`minibuffer-window-active-p` *window*   [Function]
> This function returns non-`nil` if *window* is the currently active minibuffer window.

The following two options control whether minibuffer windows are resized automatically
and how large they can get in the process.

`resize-mini-windows`   [User Option]
> This option specifies whether minibuffer windows are resized automatically. The
> default value is `grow-only`, which means that a minibuffer window by default expands
> automatically to accommodate the text it displays and shrinks back to one line as
> soon as the minibuffer gets empty. If the value is `t`, Emacs will always try to fit the
> height of a minibuffer window to the text it displays (with a minimum of one line). If
> the value is `nil`, a minibuffer window never changes size automatically. In that case
> the window resizing commands (see Section 27.4 [Resizing Windows], page 576) can
> be used to adjust its height.

`max-mini-window-height`   [User Option]
> This option provides a maximum height for resizing minibuffer windows automatically.
> A floating-point number specifies a fraction of the frame's height; an integer specifies
> the maximum number of lines. The default value is 0.25.

19.12 Minibuffer Contents

These functions access the minibuffer prompt and contents.

`minibuffer-prompt`   [Function]
> This function returns the prompt string of the currently active minibuffer. If no
> minibuffer is active, it returns `nil`.

`minibuffer-prompt-end`   [Function]
> This function returns the current position of the end of the minibuffer prompt, if a
> minibuffer is current. Otherwise, it returns the minimum valid buffer position.

`minibuffer-prompt-width`   [Function]
> This function returns the current display-width of the minibuffer prompt, if a mini-
> buffer is current. Otherwise, it returns zero.

`minibuffer-contents`   [Function]

> This function returns the editable contents of the minibuffer (that is, everything
> except the prompt) as a string, if a minibuffer is current. Otherwise, it returns the
> entire contents of the current buffer.

`minibuffer-contents-no-properties`   [Function]

> This is like `minibuffer-contents`, except that it does not copy text properties, just
> the characters themselves. See Section 31.19 [Text Properties], page 732.

`delete-minibuffer-contents`   [Command]

> This command erases the editable contents of the minibuffer (that is, everything
> except the prompt), if a minibuffer is current. Otherwise, it erases the entire current
> buffer.

19.13 Recursive Minibuffers

These functions and variables deal with recursive minibuffers (see Section 20.13 [Recursive
Editing], page 386):

`minibuffer-depth`   [Function]

> This function returns the current depth of activations of the minibuffer, a nonnegative
> integer. If no minibuffers are active, it returns zero.

`enable-recursive-minibuffers`   [User Option]

> If this variable is non-`nil`, you can invoke commands (such as `find-file`) that use
> minibuffers even while the minibuffer window is active. Such invocation produces a
> recursive editing level for a new minibuffer. The outer-level minibuffer is invisible
> while you are editing the inner one.
>
> If this variable is `nil`, you cannot invoke minibuffer commands when the minibuffer
> window is active, not even if you switch to another window to do it.

If a command name has a property `enable-recursive-minibuffers` that is non-`nil`,
then the command can use the minibuffer to read arguments even if it is invoked from the
minibuffer. A command can also achieve this by binding `enable-recursive-minibuffers`
to `t` in the interactive declaration (see Section 20.2.1 [Using Interactive], page 346). The
minibuffer command `next-matching-history-element` (normally *M-s* in the minibuffer)
does the latter.

19.14 Minibuffer Miscellany

`minibufferp` **&optional** *buffer-or-name*   [Function]

> This function returns non-`nil` if *buffer-or-name* is a minibuffer. If *buffer-or-name* is
> omitted, it tests the current buffer.

`minibuffer-setup-hook`   [Variable]

> This is a normal hook that is run whenever the minibuffer is entered. See Section 22.1
> [Hooks], page 429.

`minibuffer-exit-hook`   [Variable]

> This is a normal hook that is run whenever the minibuffer is exited. See Section 22.1 [Hooks], page 429.

`minibuffer-help-form`   [Variable]

> The current value of this variable is used to rebind `help-form` locally inside the minibuffer (see Section 23.5 [Help Functions], page 491).

`minibuffer-scroll-window`   [Variable]

> If the value of this variable is non-`nil`, it should be a window object. When the function `scroll-other-window` is called in the minibuffer, it scrolls this window.

`minibuffer-selected-window`   [Function]

> This function returns the window that was selected when the minibuffer was entered. If selected window is not a minibuffer window, it returns `nil`.

`max-mini-window-height`   [User Option]

> This variable specifies the maximum height for resizing minibuffer windows. If a float, it specifies a fraction of the height of the frame. If an integer, it specifies a number of lines.

`minibuffer-message` *string* **&rest** *args*   [Function]

> This function displays *string* temporarily at the end of the minibuffer text, for a few seconds, or until the next input event arrives, whichever comes first. The variable `minibuffer-message-timeout` specifies the number of seconds to wait in the absence of input. It defaults to 2. If *args* is non-`nil`, the actual message is obtained by passing *string* and *args* through `format-message`. See Section 4.7 [Formatting Strings], page 59.

`minibuffer-inactive-mode`   [Command]

> This is the major mode used in inactive minibuffers. It uses keymap `minibuffer-inactive-mode-map`. This can be useful if the minibuffer is in a separate frame. See Section 28.9 [Minibuffers and Frames], page 656.

20 Command Loop

When you run Emacs, it enters the *editor command loop* almost immediately. This loop reads key sequences, executes their definitions, and displays the results. In this chapter, we describe how these things are done, and the subroutines that allow Lisp programs to do them.

20.1 Command Loop Overview

The first thing the command loop must do is read a key sequence, which is a sequence of input events that translates into a command. It does this by calling the function `read-key-sequence`. Lisp programs can also call this function (see Section 20.8.1 [Key Sequence Input], page 373). They can also read input at a lower level with `read-key` or `read-event` (see Section 20.8.2 [Reading One Event], page 375), or discard pending input with `discard-input` (see Section 20.8.6 [Event Input Misc], page 380).

The key sequence is translated into a command through the currently active keymaps. See Section 21.10 [Key Lookup], page 403, for information on how this is done. The result should be a keyboard macro or an interactively callable function. If the key is `M-x`, then it reads the name of another command, which it then calls. This is done by the command `execute-extended-command` (see Section 20.3 [Interactive Call], page 352).

Prior to executing the command, Emacs runs `undo-boundary` to create an undo boundary. See Section 31.10 [Maintaining Undo], page 714.

To execute a command, Emacs first reads its arguments by calling `command-execute` (see Section 20.3 [Interactive Call], page 352). For commands written in Lisp, the `interactive` specification says how to read the arguments. This may use the prefix argument (see Section 20.12 [Prefix Command Arguments], page 384) or may read with prompting in the minibuffer (see Chapter 19 [Minibuffers], page 313). For example, the command `find-file` has an `interactive` specification which says to read a file name using the minibuffer. The function body of `find-file` does not use the minibuffer, so if you call `find-file` as a function from Lisp code, you must supply the file name string as an ordinary Lisp function argument.

If the command is a keyboard macro (i.e., a string or vector), Emacs executes it using `execute-kbd-macro` (see Section 20.16 [Keyboard Macros], page 389).

`pre-command-hook` [Variable]
> This normal hook is run by the editor command loop before it executes each command. At that time, `this-command` contains the command that is about to run, and `last-command` describes the previous command. See Section 20.5 [Command Loop Info], page 355.

`post-command-hook` [Variable]
> This normal hook is run by the editor command loop after it executes each command (including commands terminated prematurely by quitting or by errors). At that time, `this-command` refers to the command that just ran, and `last-command` refers to the command before that.
>
> This hook is also run when Emacs first enters the command loop (at which point `this-command` and `last-command` are both `nil`).

Quitting is suppressed while running `pre-command-hook` and `post-command-hook`. If an error happens while executing one of these hooks, it does not terminate execution of the hook; instead the error is silenced and the function in which the error occurred is removed from the hook.

A request coming into the Emacs server (see Section "Emacs Server" in *The GNU Emacs Manual*) runs these two hooks just as a keyboard command does.

20.2 Defining Commands

The special form `interactive` turns a Lisp function into a command. The `interactive` form must be located at top-level in the function body, usually as the first form in the body; this applies to both lambda expressions (see Section 12.2 [Lambda Expressions], page 188) and `defun` forms (see Section 12.4 [Defining Functions], page 192). This form does nothing during the actual execution of the function; its presence serves as a flag, telling the Emacs command loop that the function can be called interactively. The argument of the `interactive` form specifies how the arguments for an interactive call should be read.

Alternatively, an `interactive` form may be specified in a function symbol's `interactive-form` property. A non-`nil` value for this property takes precedence over any `interactive` form in the function body itself. This feature is seldom used.

Sometimes, a function is only intended to be called interactively, never directly from Lisp. In that case, give the function a non-`nil` `interactive-only` property, either directly or via `declare` (see Section 12.14 [Declare Form], page 212). This causes the byte compiler to warn if the command is called from Lisp. The output of `describe-function` will include similar information. The value of the property can be: a string, which the byte-compiler will use directly in its warning (it should end with a period, and not start with a capital, e.g., `"use (system-name) instead."`); `t`; any other symbol, which should be an alternative function to use in Lisp code.

20.2.1 Using `interactive`

This section describes how to write the `interactive` form that makes a Lisp function an interactively-callable command, and how to examine a command's `interactive` form.

interactive *arg-descriptor*   [Special Form]

This special form declares that a function is a command, and that it may therefore be called interactively (via `M-x` or by entering a key sequence bound to it). The argument *arg-descriptor* declares how to compute the arguments to the command when the command is called interactively.

A command may be called from Lisp programs like any other function, but then the caller supplies the arguments and *arg-descriptor* has no effect.

The `interactive` form must be located at top-level in the function body, or in the function symbol's `interactive-form` property (see Section 8.4 [Symbol Properties], page 119). It has its effect because the command loop looks for it before calling the function (see Section 20.3 [Interactive Call], page 352). Once the function is called, all its body forms are executed; at this time, if the `interactive` form occurs within the body, the form simply returns `nil` without even evaluating its argument.

By convention, you should put the `interactive` form in the function body, as the first top-level form. If there is an `interactive` form in both the `interactive-form` symbol property and the function body, the former takes precedence. The `interactive-form` symbol property can be used to add an interactive form to an existing function, or change how its arguments are processed interactively, without redefining the function.

There are three possibilities for the argument *arg-descriptor*:

- It may be omitted or `nil`; then the command is called with no arguments. This leads quickly to an error if the command requires one or more arguments.

- It may be a string; its contents are a sequence of elements separated by newlines, one for each argument[1]. Each element consists of a code character (see Section 20.2.2 [Interactive Codes], page 348) optionally followed by a prompt (which some code characters use and some ignore). Here is an example:

  ```
  (interactive "P\nbFrobnicate buffer: ")
  ```

  The code letter 'P' sets the command's first argument to the raw command prefix (see Section 20.12 [Prefix Command Arguments], page 384). 'bFrobnicate buffer: ' prompts the user with 'Frobnicate buffer: ' to enter the name of an existing buffer, which becomes the second and final argument.

  The prompt string can use '%' to include previous argument values (starting with the first argument) in the prompt. This is done using `format-message` (see Section 4.7 [Formatting Strings], page 59). For example, here is how you could read the name of an existing buffer followed by a new name to give to that buffer:

  ```
  (interactive "bBuffer to rename: \nsRename buffer %s to: ")
  ```

  If '*' appears at the beginning of the string, then an error is signaled if the buffer is read-only.

  If '@' appears at the beginning of the string, and if the key sequence used to invoke the command includes any mouse events, then the window associated with the first of those events is selected before the command is run.

  If '^' appears at the beginning of the string, and if the command was invoked through *shift-translation*, set the mark and activate the region temporarily, or extend an already active region, before the command is run. If the command was invoked without shift-translation, and the region is temporarily active, deactivate the region before the command is run. Shift-translation is controlled on the user level by `shift-select-mode`; see Section "Shift Selection" in *The GNU Emacs Manual*.

  You can use '*', '@', and ^ together; the order does not matter. Actual reading of arguments is controlled by the rest of the prompt string (starting with the first character that is not '*', '@', or '^').

- It may be a Lisp expression that is not a string; then it should be a form that is evaluated to get a list of arguments to pass to the command. Usually this form will call various functions to read input from the user, most often through the minibuffer (see Chapter 19 [Minibuffers], page 313) or directly from the keyboard (see Section 20.8 [Reading Input], page 373).

  Providing point or the mark as an argument value is also common, but if you do this *and* read input (whether using the minibuffer or not), be sure to get the integer values

---

[1] Some elements actually supply two arguments.

of point or the mark after reading. The current buffer may be receiving subprocess output; if subprocess output arrives while the command is waiting for input, it could relocate point and the mark.

Here's an example of what *not* to do:

```
(interactive
 (list (region-beginning) (region-end)
       (read-string "Foo: " nil 'my-history)))
```

Here's how to avoid the problem, by examining point and the mark after reading the keyboard input:

```
(interactive
 (let ((string (read-string "Foo: " nil 'my-history)))
   (list (region-beginning) (region-end) string)))
```

Warning: the argument values should not include any data types that can't be printed and then read. Some facilities save `command-history` in a file to be read in the subsequent sessions; if a command's arguments contain a data type that prints using '#<...>' syntax, those facilities won't work.

There are, however, a few exceptions: it is ok to use a limited set of expressions such as `(point)`, `(mark)`, `(region-beginning)`, and `(region-end)`, because Emacs recognizes them specially and puts the expression (rather than its value) into the command history. To see whether the expression you wrote is one of these exceptions, run the command, then examine `(car command-history)`.

`interactive-form` *function*   [Function]

> This function returns the `interactive` form of *function*. If *function* is an interactively callable function (see Section 20.3 [Interactive Call], page 352), the value is the command's `interactive` form (`interactive` *spec*), which specifies how to compute its arguments. Otherwise, the value is `nil`. If *function* is a symbol, its function definition is used.

20.2.2 Code Characters for `interactive`

The code character descriptions below contain a number of key words, defined here as follows:

Completion

> Provide completion. `TAB`, `SPC`, and `RET` perform name completion because the argument is read using `completing-read` (see Section 19.6 [Completion], page 321). `?` displays a list of possible completions.

Existing   Require the name of an existing object. An invalid name is not accepted; the commands to exit the minibuffer do not exit if the current input is not valid.

Default   A default value of some sort is used if the user enters no text in the minibuffer. The default depends on the code character.

No I/O   This code letter computes an argument without reading any input. Therefore, it does not use a prompt string, and any prompt string you supply is ignored.

> Even though the code letter doesn't use a prompt string, you must follow it with a newline if it is not the last code character in the string.

Prompt   A prompt immediately follows the code character. The prompt ends either with the end of the string or with a newline.

Special   This code character is meaningful only at the beginning of the interactive string, and it does not look for a prompt or a newline. It is a single, isolated character.

Here are the code character descriptions for use with `interactive`:

'*'   Signal an error if the current buffer is read-only. Special.

'@'   Select the window mentioned in the first mouse event in the key sequence that invoked this command. Special.

'^'   If the command was invoked through shift-translation, set the mark and activate the region temporarily, or extend an already active region, before the command is run. If the command was invoked without shift-translation, and the region is temporarily active, deactivate the region before the command is run. Special.

'a'   A function name (i.e., a symbol satisfying `fboundp`). Existing, Completion, Prompt.

'b'   The name of an existing buffer. By default, uses the name of the current buffer (see Chapter 26 [Buffers], page 550). Existing, Completion, Default, Prompt.

'B'   A buffer name. The buffer need not exist. By default, uses the name of a recently used buffer other than the current buffer. Completion, Default, Prompt.

'c'   A character. The cursor does not move into the echo area. Prompt.

'C'   A command name (i.e., a symbol satisfying `commandp`). Existing, Completion, Prompt.

'd'   The position of point, as an integer (see Section 29.1 [Point], page 673). No I/O.

'D'   A directory name. The default is the current default directory of the current buffer, `default-directory` (see Section 24.8.4 [File Name Expansion], page 522). Existing, Completion, Default, Prompt.

'e'   The first or next non-keyboard event in the key sequence that invoked the command. More precisely, 'e' gets events that are lists, so you can look at the data in the lists. See Section 20.7 [Input Events], page 358. No I/O.

           You use 'e' for mouse events and for special system events (see Section 20.7.10 [Misc Events], page 365). The event list that the command receives depends on the event. See Section 20.7 [Input Events], page 358, which describes the forms of the list for each event in the corresponding subsections.

           You can use 'e' more than once in a single command's interactive specification. If the key sequence that invoked the command has n events that are lists, the nth 'e' provides the nth such event. Events that are not lists, such as function keys and ASCII characters, do not count where 'e' is concerned.

'f'   A file name of an existing file (see Section 24.8 [File Names], page 517). The default directory is `default-directory`. Existing, Completion, Default, Prompt.

'F'   A file name. The file need not exist. Completion, Default, Prompt.

‘G’   A file name. The file need not exist. If the user enters just a directory name, then the value is just that directory name, with no file name within the directory added. Completion, Default, Prompt.

‘i’   An irrelevant argument. This code always supplies `nil` as the argument's value. No I/O.

‘k’   A key sequence (see Section 21.1 [Key Sequences], page 391). This keeps reading events until a command (or undefined command) is found in the current key maps. The key sequence argument is represented as a string or vector. The cursor does not move into the echo area. Prompt.

             If ‘k’ reads a key sequence that ends with a down-event, it also reads and discards the following up-event. You can get access to that up-event with the ‘U’ code character.

             This kind of input is used by commands such as `describe-key` and `global-set-key`.

‘K’   A key sequence, whose definition you intend to change. This works like ‘k’, except that it suppresses, for the last input event in the key sequence, the conversions that are normally used (when necessary) to convert an undefined key into a defined one.

‘m’   The position of the mark, as an integer. No I/O.

‘M’   Arbitrary text, read in the minibuffer using the current buffer's input method, and returned as a string (see Section "Input Methods" in *The GNU Emacs Manual*). Prompt.

‘n’   A number, read with the minibuffer. If the input is not a number, the user has to try again. ‘n’ never uses the prefix argument. Prompt.

‘N’   The numeric prefix argument; but if there is no prefix argument, read a number as with **n**. The value is always a number. See Section 20.12 [Prefix Command Arguments], page 384. Prompt.

‘p’   The numeric prefix argument. (Note that this ‘p’ is lower case.) No I/O.

‘P’   The raw prefix argument. (Note that this ‘P’ is upper case.) No I/O.

‘r’   Point and the mark, as two numeric arguments, smallest first. This is the only code letter that specifies two successive arguments rather than one. This will signal an error if the mark is not set in the buffer which is current when the command is invoked. No I/O.

‘s’   Arbitrary text, read in the minibuffer and returned as a string (see Section 19.2 [Text from Minibuffer], page 314). Terminate the input with either *C-j* or RET. (*C-q* may be used to include either of these characters in the input.) Prompt.

‘S’   An interned symbol whose name is read in the minibuffer. Terminate the input with either *C-j* or RET. Other characters that normally terminate a symbol (e.g., whitespace, parentheses and brackets) do not do so here. Prompt.

‘U’   A key sequence or `nil`. Can be used after a ‘k’ or ‘K’ argument to get the up-event that was discarded (if any) after ‘k’ or ‘K’ read a down-event. If no up-event has been discarded, ‘U’ provides `nil` as the argument. No I/O.

‘v’   A variable declared to be a user option (i.e., satisfying the predicate `custom-variable-p`). This reads the variable using `read-variable`. See [Definition of read-variable], page 329. Existing, Completion, Prompt.

‘x’   A Lisp object, specified with its read syntax, terminated with a *C-j* or RET. The object is not evaluated. See Section 19.3 [Object from Minibuffer], page 317. Prompt.

‘X’   A Lisp form's value. ‘X’ reads as ‘x’ does, then evaluates the form so that its value becomes the argument for the command. Prompt.

‘z’   A coding system name (a symbol). If the user enters null input, the argument value is `nil`. See Section 32.10 [Coding Systems], page 773. Completion, Existing, Prompt.

‘Z’   A coding system name (a symbol)—but only if this command has a prefix argument. With no prefix argument, ‘Z’ provides `nil` as the argument value. Completion, Existing, Prompt.

20.2.3 Examples of Using `interactive`

Here are some examples of `interactive`:

```
(defun foo1 ()           ; foo1 takes no arguments,
    (interactive)        ;    just moves forward two words.
    (forward-word 2))
    ⇒ foo1

(defun foo2 (n)          ; foo2 takes one argument,
    (interactive "^p")   ;    which is the numeric prefix.
                         ; under shift-select-mode,
                         ;    will activate or extend region.
    (forward-word (* 2 n)))
    ⇒ foo2

(defun foo3 (n)              ; foo3 takes one argument,
    (interactive "nCount:")  ;    which is read with the Minibuffer.
    (forward-word (* 2 n)))
    ⇒ foo3

(defun three-b (b1 b2 b3)
  "Select three existing buffers.
Put them into three windows, selecting the last one."
    (interactive "bBuffer1:\nbBuffer2:\nbBuffer3:")
    (delete-other-windows)
    (split-window (selected-window) 8)
    (switch-to-buffer b1)
    (other-window 1)
    (split-window (selected-window) 8)
    (switch-to-buffer b2)
    (other-window 1)
```

```
    (switch-to-buffer b3))
      ⇒ three-b
(three-b "*scratch*" "declarations.texi" "*mail*")
      ⇒ nil
```

20.2.4 Select among Command Alternatives

The macro `define-alternatives` can be used to define *generic commands*. These are interactive functions whose implementation can be selected from several alternatives, as a matter of user preference.

define-alternatives *command* **&rest** *customizations*   [Macro]
> Define the new command *command*, a symbol.
>
> When a user runs *M-x command RET* for the first time, Emacs prompts for which real form of the command to use, and records the selection by way of a custom variable. Using a prefix argument repeats this process of choosing an alternative.
>
> The variable *command*-`alternatives` should contain an alist with alternative implementations of *command*. Until this variable is set, `define-alternatives` has no effect.
>
> If *customizations* is non-`nil`, it should consist of alternating `defcustom` keywords (typically `:group` and `:version`) and values to add to the declaration of *command*-`alternatives`.

20.3 Interactive Call

After the command loop has translated a key sequence into a command, it invokes that command using the function `command-execute`. If the command is a function, `command-execute` calls `call-interactively`, which reads the arguments and calls the command. You can also call these functions yourself.

Note that the term "command", in this context, refers to an interactively callable function (or function-like object), or a keyboard macro. It does not refer to the key sequence used to invoke a command (see Chapter 21 [Keymaps], page 391).

commandp *object* **&optional** *for-call-interactively*   [Function]
> This function returns `t` if *object* is a command. Otherwise, it returns `nil`.
>
> Commands include strings and vectors (which are treated as keyboard macros), lambda expressions that contain a top-level `interactive` form (see Section 20.2.1 [Using Interactive], page 346), byte-code function objects made from such lambda expressions, autoload objects that are declared as interactive (non-`nil` fourth argument to `autoload`), and some primitive functions. Also, a symbol is considered a command if it has a non-`nil` `interactive-form` property, or if its function definition satisfies `commandp`.
>
> If *for-call-interactively* is non-`nil`, then `commandp` returns `t` only for objects that `call-interactively` could call—thus, not for keyboard macros.
>
> See `documentation` in Section 23.2 [Accessing Documentation], page 486, for a realistic example of using `commandp`.

call-interactively *command* **&optional** *record-flag keys*   [Function]

> This function calls the interactively callable function *command*, providing arguments according to its interactive calling specifications. It returns whatever *command* returns.
>
> If, for instance, you have a function with the following signature:
>
> ```
> (defun foo (begin end)
>   (interactive "r")
>   ...)
> ```
>
> then saying
>
> ```
> (call-interactively 'foo)
> ```
>
> will call `foo` with the region (`point` and `mark`) as the arguments.
>
> An error is signaled if *command* is not a function or if it cannot be called interactively (i.e., is not a command). Note that keyboard macros (strings and vectors) are not accepted, even though they are considered commands, because they are not functions. If *command* is a symbol, then `call-interactively` uses its function definition.
>
> If *record-flag* is non-`nil`, then this command and its arguments are unconditionally added to the list `command-history`. Otherwise, the command is added only if it uses the minibuffer to read an argument. See Section 20.15 [Command History], page 389.
>
> The argument *keys*, if given, should be a vector which specifies the sequence of events to supply if the command inquires which events were used to invoke it. If *keys* is omitted or `nil`, the default is the return value of `this-command-keys-vector`. See [Definition of this-command-keys-vector], page 356.

funcall-interactively *function* **&rest** *arguments*   [Function]

> This function works like `funcall` (see Section 12.5 [Calling Functions], page 194), but it makes the call look like an interactive invocation: a call to `called-interactively-p` inside *function* will return `t`. If *function* is not a command, it is called without signaling an error.

command-execute *command* **&optional** *record-flag keys special*   [Function]

> This function executes *command*. The argument *command* must satisfy the `commandp` predicate; i.e., it must be an interactively callable function or a keyboard macro.
>
> A string or vector as *command* is executed with `execute-kbd-macro`. A function is passed to `call-interactively` (see above), along with the *record-flag* and *keys* arguments.
>
> If *command* is a symbol, its function definition is used in its place. A symbol with an `autoload` definition counts as a command if it was declared to stand for an interactively callable function. Such a definition is handled by loading the specified library and then rechecking the definition of the symbol.
>
> The argument *special*, if given, means to ignore the prefix argument and not clear it. This is used for executing special events (see Section 20.9 [Special Events], page 381).

execute-extended-command *prefix-argument*   [Command]

> This function reads a command name from the minibuffer using `completing-read` (see Section 19.6 [Completion], page 321). Then it uses `command-execute` to call

the specified command. Whatever that command returns becomes the value of `execute-extended-command`.

If the command asks for a prefix argument, it receives the value *prefix-argument*. If `execute-extended-command` is called interactively, the current raw prefix argument is used for *prefix-argument*, and thus passed on to whatever command is run.

`execute-extended-command` is the normal definition of *M-x*, so it uses the string '`M-x `' as a prompt. (It would be better to take the prompt from the events used to invoke `execute-extended-command`, but that is painful to implement.) A description of the value of the prefix argument, if any, also becomes part of the prompt.

```
(execute-extended-command 3)
---------- Buffer: Minibuffer ----------
3 M-x forward-word RET
---------- Buffer: Minibuffer ----------
     ⇒ t
```

20.4 Distinguish Interactive Calls

Sometimes a command should display additional visual feedback (such as an informative message in the echo area) for interactive calls only. There are three ways to do this. The recommended way to test whether the function was called using `call-interactively` is to give it an optional argument `print-message` and use the `interactive` spec to make it non-`nil` in interactive calls. Here's an example:

```
(defun foo (&optional print-message)
  (interactive "p")
  (when print-message
    (message "foo")))
```

We use `"p"` because the numeric prefix argument is never `nil`. Defined in this way, the function does display the message when called from a keyboard macro.

The above method with the additional argument is usually best, because it allows callers to say "treat this call as interactive". But you can also do the job by testing `called-interactively-p`.

called-interactively-p *kind*   [Function]
> This function returns `t` when the calling function was called using `call-interactively`.
>
> The argument *kind* should be either the symbol `interactive` or the symbol `any`. If it is `interactive`, then `called-interactively-p` returns `t` only if the call was made directly by the user—e.g., if the user typed a key sequence bound to the calling function, but *not* if the user ran a keyboard macro that called the function (see Section 20.16 [Keyboard Macros], page 389). If *kind* is `any`, `called-interactively-p` returns `t` for any kind of interactive call, including keyboard macros.
>
> If in doubt, use `any`; the only known proper use of `interactive` is if you need to decide whether to display a helpful message while a function is running.
>
> A function is never considered to be called interactively if it was called via Lisp evaluation (or with `apply` or `funcall`).

Here is an example of using `called-interactively-p`:

```
(defun foo ()
  (interactive)
  (when (called-interactively-p 'any)
    (message "Interactive!")
    'foo-called-interactively))

;; Type M-x foo.
     ⊣ Interactive!

(foo)
     ⇒ nil
```

Here is another example that contrasts direct and indirect calls to `called-interactively-p`.

```
(defun bar ()
  (interactive)
  (message "%s" (list (foo) (called-interactively-p 'any))))

;; Type M-x bar.
     ⊣ (nil t)
```

20.5 Information from the Command Loop

The editor command loop sets several Lisp variables to keep status records for itself and for commands that are run. With the exception of `this-command` and `last-command` it's generally a bad idea to change any of these variables in a Lisp program.

`last-command`   [Variable]

> This variable records the name of the previous command executed by the command loop (the one before the current command). Normally the value is a symbol with a function definition, but this is not guaranteed.
>
> The value is copied from `this-command` when a command returns to the command loop, except when the command has specified a prefix argument for the following command.
>
> This variable is always local to the current terminal and cannot be buffer-local. See Section 28.2 [Multiple Terminals], page 631.

`real-last-command`   [Variable]

> This variable is set up by Emacs just like `last-command`, but never altered by Lisp programs.

`last-repeatable-command`   [Variable]

> This variable stores the most recently executed command that was not part of an input event. This is the command `repeat` will try to repeat, See Section "Repeating" in *The GNU Emacs Manual*.

this-command   [Variable]

This variable records the name of the command now being executed by the editor command loop. Like `last-command`, it is normally a symbol with a function definition.

The command loop sets this variable just before running a command, and copies its value into `last-command` when the command finishes (unless the command specified a prefix argument for the following command).

Some commands set this variable during their execution, as a flag for whatever command runs next. In particular, the functions for killing text set `this-command` to `kill-region` so that any kill commands immediately following will know to append the killed text to the previous kill.

If you do not want a particular command to be recognized as the previous command in the case where it got an error, you must code that command to prevent this. One way is to set `this-command` to `t` at the beginning of the command, and set `this-command` back to its proper value at the end, like this:

```
(defun foo (args...)
  (interactive ...)
  (let ((old-this-command this-command))
    (setq this-command t)
    ...do the work...
    (setq this-command old-this-command)))
```

We do not bind `this-command` with `let` because that would restore the old value in case of error—a feature of `let` which in this case does precisely what we want to avoid.

this-original-command   [Variable]

This has the same value as `this-command` except when command remapping occurs (see Section 21.13 [Remapping Commands], page 409). In that case, `this-command` gives the command actually run (the result of remapping), and `this-original-command` gives the command that was specified to run but remapped into another command.

this-command-keys   [Function]

This function returns a string or vector containing the key sequence that invoked the present command, plus any previous commands that generated the prefix argument for this command. Any events read by the command using `read-event` without a timeout get tacked on to the end.

However, if the command has called `read-key-sequence`, it returns the last read key sequence. See Section 20.8.1 [Key Sequence Input], page 373. The value is a string if all events in the sequence were characters that fit in a string. See Section 20.7 [Input Events], page 358.

```
(this-command-keys)
;; Now use C-u C-x C-e to evaluate that.
     ⇒ "^U^X^E"
```

this-command-keys-vector   [Function]

Like `this-command-keys`, except that it always returns the events in a vector, so you don't need to deal with the complexities of storing input events in a string (see Section 20.7.15 [Strings of Events], page 372).

clear-this-command-keys &optional *keep-record*   [Function]

> This function empties out the table of events for **this-command-keys** to return. Unless *keep-record* is non-**nil**, it also empties the records that the function **recent-keys** (see Section 38.13.2 [Recording Input], page 1011) will subsequently return. This is useful after reading a password, to prevent the password from echoing inadvertently as part of the next command in certain cases.

last-nonmenu-event   [Variable]

> This variable holds the last input event read as part of a key sequence, not counting events resulting from mouse menus.
>
> One use of this variable is for telling **x-popup-menu** where to pop up a menu. It is also used internally by **y-or-n-p** (see Section 19.7 [Yes-or-No Queries], page 337).

last-command-event   [Variable]

> This variable is set to the last input event that was read by the command loop as part of a command. The principal use of this variable is in **self-insert-command**, which uses it to decide which character to insert.
>
>   last-command-event
>   ;; Now use *C-u C-x C-e* to evaluate that.
>   ⇒ 5
>
> The value is 5 because that is the ASCII code for *C-e*.

last-event-frame   [Variable]

> This variable records which frame the last input event was directed to. Usually this is the frame that was selected when the event was generated, but if that frame has redirected input focus to another frame, the value is the frame to which the event was redirected. See Section 28.10 [Input Focus], page 656.
>
> If the last event came from a keyboard macro, the value is **macro**.

20.6 Adjusting Point After Commands

It is not easy to display a value of point in the middle of a sequence of text that has the **display**, **composition** or is invisible. Therefore, after a command finishes and returns to the command loop, if point is within such a sequence, the command loop normally moves point to the edge of the sequence.

A command can inhibit this feature by setting the variable **disable-point-adjustment**:

disable-point-adjustment   [Variable]

> If this variable is non-**nil** when a command returns to the command loop, then the command loop does not check for those text properties, and does not move point out of sequences that have them.
>
> The command loop sets this variable to **nil** before each command, so if a command sets it, the effect applies only to that command.

global-disable-point-adjustment   [Variable]

> If you set this variable to a non-**nil** value, the feature of moving point out of these sequences is completely turned off.

20.7 Input Events

The Emacs command loop reads a sequence of *input events* that represent keyboard or mouse activity, or system events sent to Emacs. The events for keyboard activity are characters or symbols; other events are always lists. This section describes the representation and meaning of input events in detail.

eventp *object*   [Function]
> This function returns non-`nil` if *object* is an input event or event type.
>
> Note that any symbol might be used as an event or an event type. `eventp` cannot distinguish whether a symbol is intended by Lisp code to be used as an event. Instead, it distinguishes whether the symbol has actually been used in an event that has been read as input in the current Emacs session. If a symbol has not yet been so used, `eventp` returns `nil`.

20.7.1 Keyboard Events

There are two kinds of input you can get from the keyboard: ordinary keys, and function keys. Ordinary keys correspond to characters; the events they generate are represented in Lisp as characters. The event type of a character event is the character itself (an integer); see Section 20.7.12 [Classifying Events], page 367.

An input character event consists of a *basic code* between 0 and 524287, plus any or all of these *modifier bits*:

meta
> The 2^{27} bit in the character code indicates a character typed with the meta key held down.

control
> The 2^{26} bit in the character code indicates a non-ASCII control character.
>
> ASCII control characters such as `C-a` have special basic codes of their own, so Emacs needs no special bit to indicate them. Thus, the code for `C-a` is just 1.
>
> But if you type a control combination not in ASCII, such as % with the control key, the numeric value you get is the code for % plus 2^{26} (assuming the terminal supports non-ASCII control characters).

shift
> The 2^{25} bit in the character code indicates an ASCII control character typed with the shift key held down.
>
> For letters, the basic code itself indicates upper versus lower case; for digits and punctuation, the shift key selects an entirely different character with a different basic code. In order to keep within the ASCII character set whenever possible, Emacs avoids using the 2^{25} bit for those characters.
>
> However, ASCII provides no way to distinguish `C-A` from `C-a`, so Emacs uses the 2^{25} bit in `C-A` and not in `C-a`.

hyper
> The 2^{24} bit in the character code indicates a character typed with the hyper key held down.

super
> The 2^{23} bit in the character code indicates a character typed with the super key held down.

alt
> The 2^{22} bit in the character code indicates a character typed with the alt key held down. (The key labeled `Alt` on most keyboards is actually treated as the meta key, not this.)

It is best to avoid mentioning specific bit numbers in your program. To test the modifier bits of a character, use the function `event-modifiers` (see Section 20.7.12 [Classifying Events], page 367). When making key bindings, you can use the read syntax for characters with modifier bits ('\C-', '\M-', and so on). For making key bindings with `define-key`, you can use lists such as `(control hyper ?x)` to specify the characters (see Section 21.12 [Changing Key Bindings], page 406). The function `event-convert-list` converts such a list into an event type (see Section 20.7.12 [Classifying Events], page 367).

20.7.2 Function Keys

Most keyboards also have *function keys*—keys that have names or symbols that are not characters. Function keys are represented in Emacs Lisp as symbols; the symbol's name is the function key's label, in lower case. For example, pressing a key labeled F1 generates an input event represented by the symbol `f1`.

The event type of a function key event is the event symbol itself. See Section 20.7.12 [Classifying Events], page 367.

Here are a few special cases in the symbol-naming convention for function keys:

`backspace`, `tab`, `newline`, `return`, `delete`
> These keys correspond to common ASCII control characters that have special keys on most keyboards.
>
> In ASCII, *C-i* and TAB are the same character. If the terminal can distinguish between them, Emacs conveys the distinction to Lisp programs by representing the former as the integer 9, and the latter as the symbol `tab`.
>
> Most of the time, it's not useful to distinguish the two. So normally `local-function-key-map` (see Section 21.14 [Translation Keymaps], page 410) is set up to map `tab` into 9. Thus, a key binding for character code 9 (the character *C-i*) also applies to `tab`. Likewise for the other symbols in this group. The function `read-char` likewise converts these events into characters.
>
> In ASCII, BS is really *C-h*. But `backspace` converts into the character code 127 (DEL), not into code 8 (BS). This is what most users prefer.

`left`, `up`, `right`, `down`
> Cursor arrow keys

`kp-add`, `kp-decimal`, `kp-divide`, . . .
> Keypad keys (to the right of the regular keyboard).

`kp-0`, `kp-1`, . . .
> Keypad keys with digits.

`kp-f1`, `kp-f2`, `kp-f3`, `kp-f4`
> Keypad PF keys.

`kp-home`, `kp-left`, `kp-up`, `kp-right`, `kp-down`
> Keypad arrow keys. Emacs normally translates these into the corresponding non-keypad keys `home`, `left`, . . .

`kp-prior`, `kp-next`, `kp-end`, `kp-begin`, `kp-insert`, `kp-delete`
> Additional keypad duplicates of keys ordinarily found elsewhere. Emacs normally translates these into the like-named non-keypad keys.

You can use the modifier keys ALT, CTRL, HYPER, META, SHIFT, and SUPER with function keys. The way to represent them is with prefixes in the symbol name:

'A-'   The alt modifier.

'C-'   The control modifier.

'H-'   The hyper modifier.

'M-'   The meta modifier.

'S-'   The shift modifier.

's-'   The super modifier.

Thus, the symbol for the key F3 with META held down is M-f3. When you use more than one prefix, we recommend you write them in alphabetical order; but the order does not matter in arguments to the key-binding lookup and modification functions.

20.7.3 Mouse Events

Emacs supports four kinds of mouse events: click events, drag events, button-down events, and motion events. All mouse events are represented as lists. The CAR of the list is the event type; this says which mouse button was involved, and which modifier keys were used with it. The event type can also distinguish double or triple button presses (see Section 20.7.7 [Repeat Events], page 363). The rest of the list elements give position and time information.

For key lookup, only the event type matters: two events of the same type necessarily run the same command. The command can access the full values of these events using the 'e' interactive code. See Section 20.2.2 [Interactive Codes], page 348.

A key sequence that starts with a mouse event is read using the keymaps of the buffer in the window that the mouse was in, not the current buffer. This does not imply that clicking in a window selects that window or its buffer—that is entirely under the control of the command binding of the key sequence.

20.7.4 Click Events

When the user presses a mouse button and releases it at the same location, that generates a *click* event. All mouse click event share the same format:

> (*event-type position click-count*)

event-type   This is a symbol that indicates which mouse button was used. It is one of the symbols mouse-1, mouse-2, . . ., where the buttons are numbered left to right.

You can also use prefixes 'A-', 'C-', 'H-', 'M-', 'S-' and 's-' for modifiers alt, control, hyper, meta, shift and super, just as you would with function keys.

This symbol also serves as the event type of the event. Key bindings describe events by their types; thus, if there is a key binding for mouse-1, that binding would apply to all events whose *event-type* is mouse-1.

position   This is a *mouse position list* specifying where the mouse click occurred; see below for details.

click-count

This is the number of rapid repeated presses so far of the same mouse button. See Section 20.7.7 [Repeat Events], page 363.

To access the contents of a mouse position list in the *position* slot of a click event, you should typically use the functions documented in Section 20.7.13 [Accessing Mouse], page 369. The explicit format of the list depends on where the click occurred. For clicks in the text area, mode line, header line, or in the fringe or marginal areas, the mouse position list has the form

```
(window pos-or-area (x . y) timestamp
 object text-pos (col . row)
 image (dx . dy) (width . height))
```

The meanings of these list elements are as follows:

window   The window in which the click occurred.

pos-or-area

> The buffer position of the character clicked on in the text area; or, if the click was outside the text area, the window area where it occurred. It is one of the symbols `mode-line`, `header-line`, `vertical-line`, `left-margin`, `right-margin`, `left-fringe`, or `right-fringe`.
>
> In one special case, *pos-or-area* is a list containing a symbol (one of the symbols listed above) instead of just the symbol. This happens after the imaginary prefix keys for the event are registered by Emacs. See Section 20.8.1 [Key Sequence Input], page 373.

x, y   The relative pixel coordinates of the click. For clicks in the text area of a window, the coordinate origin (0 . 0) is taken to be the top left corner of the text area. See Section 27.3 [Window Sizes], page 572. For clicks in a mode line or header line, the coordinate origin is the top left corner of the window itself. For fringes, margins, and the vertical border, *x* does not have meaningful data. For fringes and margins, *y* is relative to the bottom edge of the header line. In all cases, the *x* and *y* coordinates increase rightward and downward respectively.

timestamp

> The time at which the event occurred, as an integer number of milliseconds since a system-dependent initial time.

object   Either `nil` if there is no string-type text property at the click position, or a cons cell of the form (*string* . *string-pos*) if there is one:

> *string*   The string which was clicked on, including any properties.
>
> *string-pos* The position in the string where the click occurred.

text-pos For clicks on a marginal area or on a fringe, this is the buffer position of the first visible character in the corresponding line in the window. For clicks on the mode line or the header line, this is `nil`. For other events, it is the buffer position closest to the click.

col, row These are the actual column and row coordinate numbers of the glyph under the *x, y* position. If *x* lies beyond the last column of actual text on its line, *col* is reported by adding fictional extra columns that have the default character width. Row 0 is taken to be the header line if the window has one, or the topmost row of the text area otherwise. Column 0 is taken to be the leftmost column of the text area for clicks on a window text area, or the leftmost mode line or header line column for clicks there. For clicks on fringes or vertical borders, these have no meaningful data. For clicks on margins, *col* is measured from the left edge of the margin area and *row* is measured from the top of the margin area.

image
This is the image object on which the click occurred. It is either `nil` if there is no image at the position clicked on, or it is an image object as returned by `find-image` if click was in an image.

dx, *dy*
These are the pixel coordinates of the click, relative to the top left corner of *object*, which is (0 . 0). If *object* is `nil`, the coordinates are relative to the top left corner of the character glyph clicked on.

width, *height*
These are the pixel width and height of *object* or, if this is `nil`, those of the character glyph clicked on.

For clicks on a scroll bar, *position* has this form:

```
(window area (portion . whole) timestamp part)
```

window
The window whose scroll bar was clicked on.

area
This is the symbol `vertical-scroll-bar`.

portion
The number of pixels from the top of the scroll bar to the click position. On some toolkits, including GTK+, Emacs cannot extract this data, so the value is always 0.

whole
The total length, in pixels, of the scroll bar. On some toolkits, including GTK+, Emacs cannot extract this data, so the value is always 0.

timestamp
The time at which the event occurred, in milliseconds. On some toolkits, including GTK+, Emacs cannot extract this data, so the value is always 0.

part
The part of the scroll bar on which the click occurred. It is one of the symbols `handle` (the scroll bar handle), `above-handle` (the area above the handle), `below-handle` (the area below the handle), `up` (the up arrow at one end of the scroll bar), or `down` (the down arrow at one end of the scroll bar).

20.7.5 Drag Events

With Emacs, you can have a drag event without even changing your clothes. A *drag event* happens every time the user presses a mouse button and then moves the mouse to a different character position before releasing the button. Like all mouse events, drag events are represented in Lisp as lists. The lists record both the starting mouse position and the final position, like this:

```
(event-type
 (window1 START-POSITION)
 (window2 END-POSITION))
```

For a drag event, the name of the symbol *event-type* contains the prefix 'drag-'. For example, dragging the mouse with button 2 held down generates a drag-mouse-2 event. The second and third elements of the event give the starting and ending position of the drag, as mouse position lists (see Section 20.7.4 [Click Events], page 360). You can access the second element of any mouse event in the same way. However, the drag event may end outside the boundaries of the frame that was initially selected. In that case, the third element's position list contains that frame in place of a window.

The 'drag-' prefix follows the modifier key prefixes such as 'C-' and 'M-'.

If read-key-sequence receives a drag event that has no key binding, and the corresponding click event does have a binding, it changes the drag event into a click event at the drag's starting position. This means that you don't have to distinguish between click and drag events unless you want to.

20.7.6 Button-Down Events

Click and drag events happen when the user releases a mouse button. They cannot happen earlier, because there is no way to distinguish a click from a drag until the button is released.

If you want to take action as soon as a button is pressed, you need to handle *button-down* events.[2] These occur as soon as a button is pressed. They are represented by lists that look exactly like click events (see Section 20.7.4 [Click Events], page 360), except that the *event-type* symbol name contains the prefix 'down-'. The 'down-' prefix follows modifier key prefixes such as 'C-' and 'M-'.

The function read-key-sequence ignores any button-down events that don't have command bindings; therefore, the Emacs command loop ignores them too. This means that you need not worry about defining button-down events unless you want them to do something. The usual reason to define a button-down event is so that you can track mouse motion (by reading motion events) until the button is released. See Section 20.7.8 [Motion Events], page 364.

20.7.7 Repeat Events

If you press the same mouse button more than once in quick succession without moving the mouse, Emacs generates special *repeat* mouse events for the second and subsequent presses.

The most common repeat events are *double-click* events. Emacs generates a double-click event when you click a button twice; the event happens when you release the button (as is normal for all click events).

The event type of a double-click event contains the prefix 'double-'. Thus, a double click on the second mouse button with meta held down comes to the Lisp program as M-double-mouse-2. If a double-click event has no binding, the binding of the corresponding ordinary click event is used to execute it. Thus, you need not pay attention to the double click feature unless you really want to.

When the user performs a double click, Emacs generates first an ordinary click event, and then a double-click event. Therefore, you must design the command binding of the double click event to assume that the single-click command has already run. It must produce the desired results of a double click, starting from the results of a single click.

---

[2] Button-down is the conservative antithesis of drag.

This is convenient, if the meaning of a double click somehow builds on the meaning of a single click—which is recommended user interface design practice for double clicks.

If you click a button, then press it down again and start moving the mouse with the button held down, then you get a *double-drag* event when you ultimately release the button. Its event type contains 'double-drag' instead of just 'drag'. If a double-drag event has no binding, Emacs looks for an alternate binding as if the event were an ordinary drag.

Before the double-click or double-drag event, Emacs generates a *double-down* event when the user presses the button down for the second time. Its event type contains 'double-down' instead of just 'down'. If a double-down event has no binding, Emacs looks for an alternate binding as if the event were an ordinary button-down event. If it finds no binding that way either, the double-down event is ignored.

To summarize, when you click a button and then press it again right away, Emacs generates a down event and a click event for the first click, a double-down event when you press the button again, and finally either a double-click or a double-drag event.

If you click a button twice and then press it again, all in quick succession, Emacs generates a *triple-down* event, followed by either a *triple-click* or a *triple-drag*. The event types of these events contain 'triple' instead of 'double'. If any triple event has no binding, Emacs uses the binding that it would use for the corresponding double event.

If you click a button three or more times and then press it again, the events for the presses beyond the third are all triple events. Emacs does not have separate event types for quadruple, quintuple, etc. events. However, you can look at the event list to find out precisely how many times the button was pressed.

event-click-count *event*   [Function]
> This function returns the number of consecutive button presses that led up to *event*. If *event* is a double-down, double-click or double-drag event, the value is 2. If *event* is a triple event, the value is 3 or greater. If *event* is an ordinary mouse event (not a repeat event), the value is 1.

double-click-fuzz   [User Option]
> To generate repeat events, successive mouse button presses must be at approximately the same screen position. The value of double-click-fuzz specifies the maximum number of pixels the mouse may be moved (horizontally or vertically) between two successive clicks to make a double-click.
>
> This variable is also the threshold for motion of the mouse to count as a drag.

double-click-time   [User Option]
> To generate repeat events, the number of milliseconds between successive button presses must be less than the value of double-click-time. Setting double-click-time to nil disables multi-click detection entirely. Setting it to t removes the time limit; Emacs then detects multi-clicks by position only.

20.7.8 Motion Events

Emacs sometimes generates *mouse motion* events to describe motion of the mouse without any button activity. Mouse motion events are represented by lists that look like this:

```
(mouse-movement POSITION)
```

position is a mouse position list (see Section 20.7.4 [Click Events], page 360), specifying the current position of the mouse cursor. As with the end-position of a drag event, this position list may represent a location outside the boundaries of the initially selected frame, in which case the list contains that frame in place of a window.

The special form `track-mouse` enables generation of motion events within its body. Outside of `track-mouse` forms, Emacs does not generate events for mere motion of the mouse, and these events do not appear. See Section 28.14 [Mouse Tracking], page 660.

20.7.9 Focus Events

Window systems provide general ways for the user to control which window gets keyboard input. This choice of window is called the *focus*. When the user does something to switch between Emacs frames, that generates a *focus event*. The normal definition of a focus event, in the global keymap, is to select a new frame within Emacs, as the user would expect. See Section 28.10 [Input Focus], page 656, which also describes hooks related to focus events.

Focus events are represented in Lisp as lists that look like this:

```
(switch-frame new-frame)
```

where *new-frame* is the frame switched to.

Some X window managers are set up so that just moving the mouse into a window is enough to set the focus there. Usually, there is no need for a Lisp program to know about the focus change until some other kind of input arrives. Emacs generates a focus event only when the user actually types a keyboard key or presses a mouse button in the new frame; just moving the mouse between frames does not generate a focus event.

A focus event in the middle of a key sequence would garble the sequence. So Emacs never generates a focus event in the middle of a key sequence. If the user changes focus in the middle of a key sequence—that is, after a prefix key—then Emacs reorders the events so that the focus event comes either before or after the multi-event key sequence, and not within it.

20.7.10 Miscellaneous System Events

A few other event types represent occurrences within the system.

`(delete-frame (frame))`

>   This kind of event indicates that the user gave the window manager a command to delete a particular window, which happens to be an Emacs frame.

>   The standard definition of the `delete-frame` event is to delete *frame*.

`(iconify-frame (frame))`

>   This kind of event indicates that the user iconified *frame* using the window manager. Its standard definition is `ignore`; since the frame has already been iconified, Emacs has no work to do. The purpose of this event type is so that you can keep track of such events if you want to.

`(make-frame-visible (frame))`

>   This kind of event indicates that the user deiconified *frame* using the window manager. Its standard definition is `ignore`; since the frame has already been made visible, Emacs has no work to do.

(wheel-up *position*)
(wheel-down *position*)

These kinds of event are generated by moving a mouse wheel. The *position* element is a mouse position list (see Section 20.7.4 [Click Events], page 360), specifying the position of the mouse cursor when the event occurred.

This kind of event is generated only on some kinds of systems. On some systems, `mouse-4` and `mouse-5` are used instead. For portable code, use the variables `mouse-wheel-up-event` and `mouse-wheel-down-event` defined in `mwheel.el` to determine what event types to expect for the mouse wheel.

(drag-n-drop *position files*)

This kind of event is generated when a group of files is selected in an application outside of Emacs, and then dragged and dropped onto an Emacs frame.

The element *position* is a list describing the position of the event, in the same format as used in a mouse-click event (see Section 20.7.4 [Click Events], page 360), and *files* is the list of file names that were dragged and dropped. The usual way to handle this event is by visiting these files.

This kind of event is generated, at present, only on some kinds of systems.

help-echo

This kind of event is generated when a mouse pointer moves onto a portion of buffer text which has a `help-echo` text property. The generated event has this form:

(help-echo *frame help window object pos*)

The precise meaning of the event parameters and the way these parameters are used to display the help-echo text are described in [Text help-echo], page 739.

sigusr1
sigusr2   These events are generated when the Emacs process receives the signals `SIGUSR1` and `SIGUSR2`. They contain no additional data because signals do not carry additional information. They can be useful for debugging (see Section 17.1.1 [Error Debugging], page 270).

To catch a user signal, bind the corresponding event to an interactive command in the `special-event-map` (see Section 21.7 [Active Keymaps], page 398). The command is called with no arguments, and the specific signal event is available in `last-input-event`. For example:

```
(defun sigusr-handler ()
  (interactive)
  (message "Caught signal %S" last-input-event))

(define-key special-event-map [sigusr1] 'sigusr-handler)
```

To test the signal handler, you can make Emacs send a signal to itself:

```
(signal-process (emacs-pid) 'sigusr1)
```

language-change

This kind of event is generated on MS-Windows when the input language has changed. This typically means that the keyboard keys will send to Emacs characters from a different language. The generated event has this form:

(language-change *frame codepage language-id*)

Here *frame* is the frame which was current when the input language changed; *codepage* is the new codepage number; and *language-id* is the numerical ID of the new input language. The coding-system (see Section 32.10 [Coding Systems], page 773) that corresponds to *codepage* is `cp`*codepage* or `windows-`*codepage*. To convert *language-id* to a string (e.g., to use it for various language-dependent features, such as `set-language-environment`), use the `w32-get-locale-info` function, like this:

```
;; Get the abbreviated language name, such as "ENU" for English
(w32-get-locale-info language-id)
;; Get the full English name of the language,
;; such as "English (United States)"
(w32-get-locale-info language-id 4097)
;; Get the full localized name of the language
(w32-get-locale-info language-id t)
```

If one of these events arrives in the middle of a key sequence—that is, after a prefix key—then Emacs reorders the events so that this event comes either before or after the multi-event key sequence, not within it.

20.7.11 Event Examples

If the user presses and releases the left mouse button over the same location, that generates a sequence of events like this:

```
(down-mouse-1 (#<window 18 on NEWS> 2613 (0 . 38) -864320))
(mouse-1      (#<window 18 on NEWS> 2613 (0 . 38) -864180))
```

While holding the control key down, the user might hold down the second mouse button, and drag the mouse from one line to the next. That produces two events, as shown here:

```
(C-down-mouse-2 (#<window 18 on NEWS> 3440 (0 . 27) -731219))
(C-drag-mouse-2 (#<window 18 on NEWS> 3440 (0 . 27) -731219)
                (#<window 18 on NEWS> 3510 (0 . 28) -729648))
```

While holding down the meta and shift keys, the user might press the second mouse button on the window's mode line, and then drag the mouse into another window. That produces a pair of events like these:

```
(M-S-down-mouse-2 (#<window 18 on NEWS> mode-line (33 . 31) -457844))
(M-S-drag-mouse-2 (#<window 18 on NEWS> mode-line (33 . 31) -457844)
                  (#<window 20 on carlton-sanskrit.tex> 161 (33 . 3)
                  -453816))
```

The frame with input focus might not take up the entire screen, and the user might move the mouse outside the scope of the frame. Inside the `track-mouse` special form, that produces an event like this:

```
(mouse-movement (#<frame *ielm* 0x102849a30> nil (563 . 205) 532301936))
```

To handle a SIGUSR1 signal, define an interactive function, and bind it to the `signal usr1` event sequence:

```
(defun usr1-handler ()
  (interactive)
  (message "Got USR1 signal"))
(global-set-key [signal usr1] 'usr1-handler)
```

20.7.12 Classifying Events

Every event has an *event type*, which classifies the event for key binding purposes. For a keyboard event, the event type equals the event value; thus, the event type for a character is the character, and the event type for a function key symbol is the symbol itself. For events that are lists, the event type is the symbol in the CAR of the list. Thus, the event type is always a symbol or a character.

Two events of the same type are equivalent where key bindings are concerned; thus, they always run the same command. That does not necessarily mean they do the same things, however, as some commands look at the whole event to decide what to do. For example, some commands use the location of a mouse event to decide where in the buffer to act.

Sometimes broader classifications of events are useful. For example, you might want to ask whether an event involved the META key, regardless of which other key or mouse button was used.

The functions `event-modifiers` and `event-basic-type` are provided to get such information conveniently.

event-modifiers *event*   [Function]
> This function returns a list of the modifiers that *event* has. The modifiers are symbols; they include `shift`, `control`, `meta`, `alt`, `hyper` and `super`. In addition, the modifiers list of a mouse event symbol always contains one of `click`, `drag`, and `down`. For double or triple events, it also contains `double` or `triple`.
>
> The argument *event* may be an entire event object, or just an event type. If *event* is a symbol that has never been used in an event that has been read as input in the current Emacs session, then `event-modifiers` can return `nil`, even when *event* actually has modifiers.
>
> Here are some examples:
>
> ```
> (event-modifiers ?a)
>      ⇒ nil
> (event-modifiers ?A)
>      ⇒ (shift)
> (event-modifiers ?\C-a)
>      ⇒ (control)
> (event-modifiers ?\C-%)
>      ⇒ (control)
> (event-modifiers ?\C-\S-a)
>      ⇒ (control shift)
> (event-modifiers 'f5)
>      ⇒ nil
> (event-modifiers 's-f5)
>      ⇒ (super)
> (event-modifiers 'M-S-f5)
>      ⇒ (meta shift)
> (event-modifiers 'mouse-1)
>      ⇒ (click)
> (event-modifiers 'down-mouse-1)
>      ⇒ (down)
> ```
>
> The modifiers list for a click event explicitly contains `click`, but the event symbol name itself does not contain 'click'.

event-basic-type *event*   [Function]

> This function returns the key or mouse button that *event* describes, with all modifiers removed. The *event* argument is as in **event-modifiers**. For example:

```
(event-basic-type ?a)
    ⇒ 97
(event-basic-type ?A)
    ⇒ 97
(event-basic-type ?\C-a)
    ⇒ 97
(event-basic-type ?\C-\S-a)
    ⇒ 97
(event-basic-type 'f5)
    ⇒ f5
(event-basic-type 's-f5)
    ⇒ f5
(event-basic-type 'M-S-f5)
    ⇒ f5
(event-basic-type 'down-mouse-1)
    ⇒ mouse-1
```

mouse-movement-p *object*   [Function]

> This function returns non-**nil** if *object* is a mouse movement event. See Section 20.7.8 [Motion Events], page 364.

event-convert-list *list*   [Function]

> This function converts a list of modifier names and a basic event type to an event type which specifies all of them. The basic event type must be the last element of the list. For example,

```
(event-convert-list '(control ?a))
    ⇒ 1
(event-convert-list '(control meta ?a))
    ⇒ -134217727
(event-convert-list '(control super f1))
    ⇒ C-s-f1
```

20.7.13 Accessing Mouse Events

This section describes convenient functions for accessing the data in a mouse button or motion event. Keyboard event data can be accessed using the same functions, but data elements that aren't applicable to keyboard events are zero or **nil**.

The following two functions return a mouse position list (see Section 20.7.4 [Click Events], page 360), specifying the position of a mouse event.

event-start *event*   [Function]

> This returns the starting position of *event*.
>
> If *event* is a click or button-down event, this returns the location of the event. If *event* is a drag event, this returns the drag's starting position.

event-end *event*   [Function]

This returns the ending position of *event*.

If *event* is a drag event, this returns the position where the user released the mouse button. If *event* is a click or button-down event, the value is actually the starting position, which is the only position such events have.

posnp *object*   [Function]

This function returns non-**nil** if *object* is a mouse position list, in either of the formats documented in Section 20.7.4 [Click Events], page 360); and **nil** otherwise.

These functions take a mouse position list as argument, and return various parts of it:

posn-window *position*   [Function]

Return the window that *position* is in. If *position* represents a location outside the frame where the event was initiated, return that frame instead.

posn-area *position*   [Function]

Return the window area recorded in *position*. It returns **nil** when the event occurred in the text area of the window; otherwise, it is a symbol identifying the area in which the event occurred.

posn-point *position*   [Function]

Return the buffer position in *position*. When the event occurred in the text area of the window, in a marginal area, or on a fringe, this is an integer specifying a buffer position. Otherwise, the value is undefined.

posn-x-y *position*   [Function]

Return the pixel-based x and y coordinates in *position*, as a cons cell (*x* . *y*). These coordinates are relative to the window given by **posn-window**.

This example shows how to convert the window-relative coordinates in the text area of a window into frame-relative coordinates:

```
(defun frame-relative-coordinates (position)
  "Return frame-relative coordinates from POSITION.
POSITION is assumed to lie in a window text area."
  (let* ((x-y (posn-x-y position))
         (window (posn-window position))
         (edges (window-inside-pixel-edges window)))
    (cons (+ (car x-y) (car edges))
          (+ (cdr x-y) (cadr edges)))))
```

posn-col-row *position*   [Function]

This function returns a cons cell (*col* . *row*), containing the estimated column and row corresponding to buffer position in *position*. The return value is given in units of the frame's default character width and default line height (including spacing), as computed from the x and y values corresponding to *position*. (So, if the actual characters have non-default sizes, the actual row and column may differ from these computed values.)

Note that *row* is counted from the top of the text area. If the window given by *position* possesses a header line (see Section 22.4.7 [Header Lines], page 458), it is *not* included in the *row* count.

posn-actual-col-row *position*   [Function]
> Return the actual row and column in *position*, as a cons cell (*col . row*). The values are the actual row and column numbers in the window given by *position*. See Section 20.7.4 [Click Events], page 360, for details. The function returns **nil** if *position* does not include actual position values; in that case **posn-col-row** can be used to get approximate values.
>
> Note that this function doesn't account for the visual width of characters on display, like the number of visual columns taken by a tab character or an image. If you need the coordinates in canonical character units, use **posn-col-row** instead.

posn-string *position*   [Function]
> Return the string object in *position*, either **nil**, or a cons cell (*string . string-pos*).

posn-image *position*   [Function]
> Return the image object in *position*, either **nil**, or an image (**image** ...).

posn-object *position*   [Function]
> Return the image or string object in *position*, either **nil**, an image (**image** ...), or a cons cell (*string . string-pos*).

posn-object-x-y *position*   [Function]
> Return the pixel-based x and y coordinates relative to the upper left corner of the object in *position* as a cons cell (*dx . dy*). If the *position* is on buffer text, return the relative position of the buffer-text character closest to that position.

posn-object-width-height *position*   [Function]
> Return the pixel width and height of the object in *position* as a cons cell (*width . height*). If the *position* is a buffer position, return the size of the character at that position.

posn-timestamp *position*   [Function]
> Return the timestamp in *position*. This is the time at which the event occurred, in milliseconds.

These functions compute a position list given particular buffer position or screen position. You can access the data in this position list with the functions described above.

posn-at-point **&optional** *pos window*   [Function]
> This function returns a position list for position *pos* in *window*. *pos* defaults to point in *window*; *window* defaults to the selected window.
>
> **posn-at-point** returns **nil** if *pos* is not visible in *window*.

posn-at-x-y *x y* **&optional** *frame-or-window whole*   [Function]
> This function returns position information corresponding to pixel coordinates *x* and *y* in a specified frame or window, *frame-or-window*, which defaults to the selected window. The coordinates *x* and *y* are relative to the frame or window used. If *whole* is **nil**, the coordinates are relative to the window text area, otherwise they are relative to the entire window area including scroll bars, margins and fringes.

20.7.14 Accessing Scroll Bar Events

These functions are useful for decoding scroll bar events.

scroll-bar-event-ratio *event*   [Function]

>   This function returns the fractional vertical position of a scroll bar event within the
>   scroll bar. The value is a cons cell (*portion . whole*) containing two integers whose
>   ratio is the fractional position.

scroll-bar-scale *ratio total*   [Function]

>   This function multiplies (in effect) *ratio* by *total*, rounding the result to an integer.
>   The argument *ratio* is not a number, but rather a pair (*num . denom*)—typically a
>   value returned by **scroll-bar-event-ratio**.
>
>   This function is handy for scaling a position on a scroll bar into a buffer position.
>   Here's how to do that:
>
> ```
> (+ (point-min)
>    (scroll-bar-scale
>       (posn-x-y (event-start event))
>       (- (point-max) (point-min))))
> ```
>
>   Recall that scroll bar events have two integers forming a ratio, in place of a pair of x
>   and y coordinates.

20.7.15 Putting Keyboard Events in Strings

In most of the places where strings are used, we conceptualize the string as containing
text characters—the same kind of characters found in buffers or files. Occasionally Lisp
programs use strings that conceptually contain keyboard characters; for example, they may
be key sequences or keyboard macro definitions. However, storing keyboard characters in
a string is a complex matter, for reasons of historical compatibility, and it is not always
possible.

We recommend that new programs avoid dealing with these complexities by not storing
keyboard events in strings. Here is how to do that:

- Use vectors instead of strings for key sequences, when you plan to use them for anything other than as arguments to **lookup-key** and **define-key**. For example, you can
  use **read-key-sequence-vector** instead of **read-key-sequence**, and **this-command-
  keys-vector** instead of **this-command-keys**.

- Use vectors to write key sequence constants containing meta characters, even when
  passing them directly to **define-key**.

- When you have to look at the contents of a key sequence that might be a string,
  use **listify-key-sequence** (see Section 20.8.6 [Event Input Misc], page 380) first, to
  convert it to a list.

The complexities stem from the modifier bits that keyboard input characters can include.
Aside from the Meta modifier, none of these modifier bits can be included in a string, and
the Meta modifier is allowed only in special cases.

The earliest GNU Emacs versions represented meta characters as codes in the range of
128 to 255. At that time, the basic character codes ranged from 0 to 127, so all keyboard
character codes did fit in a string. Many Lisp programs used '\M-' in string constants to

stand for meta characters, especially in arguments to `define-key` and similar functions, and key sequences and sequences of events were always represented as strings.

When we added support for larger basic character codes beyond 127, and additional modifier bits, we had to change the representation of meta characters. Now the flag that represents the Meta modifier in a character is 2^{27} and such numbers cannot be included in a string.

To support programs with '\M-' in string constants, there are special rules for including certain meta characters in a string. Here are the rules for interpreting a string as a sequence of input characters:

- If the keyboard character value is in the range of 0 to 127, it can go in the string unchanged.

- The meta variants of those characters, with codes in the range of 2^{27} to $2^{27} + 127$, can also go in the string, but you must change their numeric values. You must set the 2^7 bit instead of the 2^{27} bit, resulting in a value between 128 and 255. Only a unibyte string can include these codes.

- Non-ASCII characters above 256 can be included in a multibyte string.

- Other keyboard character events cannot fit in a string. This includes keyboard events in the range of 128 to 255.

Functions such as `read-key-sequence` that construct strings of keyboard input characters follow these rules: they construct vectors instead of strings, when the events won't fit in a string.

When you use the read syntax '\M-' in a string, it produces a code in the range of 128 to 255—the same code that you get if you modify the corresponding keyboard event to put it in the string. Thus, meta events in strings work consistently regardless of how they get into the strings.

However, most programs would do well to avoid these issues by following the recommendations at the beginning of this section.

20.8 Reading Input

The editor command loop reads key sequences using the function `read-key-sequence`, which uses `read-event`. These and other functions for event input are also available for use in Lisp programs. See also `momentary-string-display` in Section 37.8 [Temporary Displays], page 900, and `sit-for` in Section 20.10 [Waiting], page 382. See Section 38.13 [Terminal Input], page 1010, for functions and variables for controlling terminal input modes and debugging terminal input.

For higher-level input facilities, see Chapter 19 [Minibuffers], page 313.

20.8.1 Key Sequence Input

The command loop reads input a key sequence at a time, by calling `read-key-sequence`. Lisp programs can also call this function; for example, `describe-key` uses it to read the key to describe.

`read-key-sequence` *prompt* **&optional** *continue-echo*   [Function]
    dont-downcase-last switch-frame-ok command-loop

> This function reads a key sequence and returns it as a string or vector. It keeps reading events until it has accumulated a complete key sequence; that is, enough to specify a non-prefix command using the currently active keymaps. (Remember that a key sequence that starts with a mouse event is read using the keymaps of the buffer in the window that the mouse was in, not the current buffer.)
>
> If the events are all characters and all can fit in a string, then `read-key-sequence` returns a string (see Section 20.7.15 [Strings of Events], page 372). Otherwise, it returns a vector, since a vector can hold all kinds of events—characters, symbols, and lists. The elements of the string or vector are the events in the key sequence.
>
> Reading a key sequence includes translating the events in various ways. See Section 21.14 [Translation Keymaps], page 410.
>
> The argument *prompt* is either a string to be displayed in the echo area as a prompt, or `nil`, meaning not to display a prompt. The argument *continue-echo*, if non-`nil`, means to echo this key as a continuation of the previous key.
>
> Normally any upper case event is converted to lower case if the original event is undefined and the lower case equivalent is defined. The argument *dont-downcase-last*, if non-`nil`, means do not convert the last event to lower case. This is appropriate for reading a key sequence to be defined.
>
> The argument *switch-frame-ok*, if non-`nil`, means that this function should process a `switch-frame` event if the user switches frames before typing anything. If the user switches frames in the middle of a key sequence, or at the start of the sequence but *switch-frame-ok* is `nil`, then the event will be put off until after the current key sequence.
>
> The argument *command-loop*, if non-`nil`, means that this key sequence is being read by something that will read commands one after another. It should be `nil` if the caller will read just one key sequence.
>
> In the following example, Emacs displays the prompt '?' in the echo area, and then the user types *C-x C-f*.
>
> ```
> (read-key-sequence "?")
>
> ---------- Echo Area ----------
> ?C-x C-f
> ---------- Echo Area ----------
>
>     ⇒ "^X^F"
> ```
>
> The function `read-key-sequence` suppresses quitting: *C-g* typed while reading with this function works like any other character, and does not set `quit-flag`. See Section 20.11 [Quitting], page 382.

`read-key-sequence-vector` *prompt* **&optional** *continue-echo*   [Function]
    dont-downcase-last switch-frame-ok command-loop

> This is like `read-key-sequence` except that it always returns the key sequence as a vector, never as a string. See Section 20.7.15 [Strings of Events], page 372.

If an input character is upper-case (or has the shift modifier) and has no key binding, but its lower-case equivalent has one, then `read-key-sequence` converts the character to lower case. Note that `lookup-key` does not perform case conversion in this way.

When reading input results in such a *shift-translation*, Emacs sets the variable `this-command-keys-shift-translated` to a non-`nil` value. Lisp programs can examine this variable if they need to modify their behavior when invoked by shift-translated keys. For example, the function `handle-shift-selection` examines the value of this variable to determine how to activate or deactivate the region (see Section 30.7 [The Mark], page 691).

The function `read-key-sequence` also transforms some mouse events. It converts unbound drag events into click events, and discards unbound button-down events entirely. It also reshuffles focus events and miscellaneous window events so that they never appear in a key sequence with any other events.

When mouse events occur in special parts of a window, such as a mode line or a scroll bar, the event type shows nothing special—it is the same symbol that would normally represent that combination of mouse button and modifier keys. The information about the window part is kept elsewhere in the event—in the coordinates. But `read-key-sequence` translates this information into imaginary prefix keys, all of which are symbols: `header-line`, `horizontal-scroll-bar`, `menu-bar`, `mode-line`, `vertical-line`, and `vertical-scroll-bar`. You can define meanings for mouse clicks in special window parts by defining key sequences using these imaginary prefix keys.

For example, if you call `read-key-sequence` and then click the mouse on the window's mode line, you get two events, like this:

```
(read-key-sequence "Click on the mode line: ")
    ⇒ [mode-line
        (mouse-1
         (#<window 6 on NEWS> mode-line
          (40 . 63) 5959987))]
```

`num-input-keys`   [Variable]
> This variable's value is the number of key sequences processed so far in this Emacs session. This includes key sequences read from the terminal and key sequences read from keyboard macros being executed.

20.8.2 Reading One Event

The lowest level functions for command input are `read-event`, `read-char`, and `read-char-exclusive`.

`read-event` &optional *prompt inherit-input-method seconds*   [Function]
> This function reads and returns the next event of command input, waiting if necessary until an event is available.
>
> The returned event may come directly from the user, or from a keyboard macro. It is not decoded by the keyboard's input coding system (see Section 32.10.8 [Terminal I/O Encoding], page 786).
>
> If the optional argument *prompt* is non-`nil`, it should be a string to display in the echo area as a prompt. Otherwise, `read-event` does not display any message to indicate it is waiting for input; instead, it prompts by echoing: it displays descriptions of the

events that led to or were read by the current command. See Section 37.4 [The Echo Area], page 888.

If *inherit-input-method* is non-`nil`, then the current input method (if any) is employed to make it possible to enter a non-ASCII character. Otherwise, input method handling is disabled for reading this event.

If `cursor-in-echo-area` is non-`nil`, then `read-event` moves the cursor temporarily to the echo area, to the end of any message displayed there. Otherwise `read-event` does not move the cursor.

If *seconds* is non-`nil`, it should be a number specifying the maximum time to wait for input, in seconds. If no input arrives within that time, `read-event` stops waiting and returns `nil`. A floating point *seconds* means to wait for a fractional number of seconds. Some systems support only a whole number of seconds; on these systems, *seconds* is rounded down. If *seconds* is `nil`, `read-event` waits as long as necessary for input to arrive.

If *seconds* is `nil`, Emacs is considered idle while waiting for user input to arrive. Idle timers—those created with `run-with-idle-timer` (see Section 38.12 [Idle Timers], page 1008)—can run during this period. However, if *seconds* is non-`nil`, the state of idleness remains unchanged. If Emacs is non-idle when `read-event` is called, it remains non-idle throughout the operation of `read-event`; if Emacs is idle (which can happen if the call happens inside an idle timer), it remains idle.

If `read-event` gets an event that is defined as a help character, then in some cases `read-event` processes the event directly without returning. See Section 23.5 [Help Functions], page 491. Certain other events, called *special events*, are also processed directly within `read-event` (see Section 20.9 [Special Events], page 381).

Here is what happens if you call `read-event` and then press the right-arrow function key:

```
(read-event)
     ⇒ right
```

read-char **&optional** *prompt inherit-input-method seconds*   [Function]
  This function reads and returns a character of command input. If the user generates an event which is not a character (i.e., a mouse click or function key event), `read-char` signals an error. The arguments work as in `read-event`.

  In the first example, the user types the character *1* (ASCII code 49). The second example shows a keyboard macro definition that calls `read-char` from the minibuffer using `eval-expression`. `read-char` reads the keyboard macro's very next character, which is *1*. Then `eval-expression` displays its return value in the echo area.

```
(read-char)
     ⇒ 49


;; We assume here you use M-: to evaluate this.
(symbol-function 'foo)
     ⇒ "^[:(read-char)^M1"
(execute-kbd-macro 'foo)
     ⊣ 49
     ⇒ nil
```

read-char-exclusive **&optional** *prompt inherit-input-method*   [Function]
    seconds
    This function reads and returns a character of command input. If the user generates
    an event which is not a character, `read-char-exclusive` ignores it and reads another
    event, until it gets a character. The arguments work as in `read-event`.

None of the above functions suppress quitting.

num-nonmacro-input-events   [Variable]
    This variable holds the total number of input events received so far from the
    terminal—not counting those generated by keyboard macros.

We emphasize that, unlike `read-key-sequence`, the functions `read-event`, `read-char`,
and `read-char-exclusive` do not perform the translations described in Section 21.14
[Translation Keymaps], page 410. If you wish to read a single key taking these translations into account, use the function `read-key`:

read-key **&optional** *prompt*   [Function]
    This function reads a single key. It is intermediate between `read-key-sequence` and
    `read-event`. Unlike the former, it reads a single key, not a key sequence. Unlike
    the latter, it does not return a raw event, but decodes and translates the user input
    according to `input-decode-map`, `local-function-key-map`, and `key-translation-
    map` (see Section 21.14 [Translation Keymaps], page 410).

    The argument *prompt* is either a string to be displayed in the echo area as a prompt,
    or `nil`, meaning not to display a prompt.

read-char-choice *prompt chars* **&optional** *inhibit-quit*   [Function]
    This function uses `read-key` to read and return a single character. It ignores any
    input that is not a member of *chars*, a list of accepted characters. Optionally, it
    will also ignore keyboard-quit events while it is waiting for valid input. If you bind
    `help-form` (see Section 23.5 [Help Functions], page 491) to a non-`nil` value while
    calling `read-char-choice`, then pressing `help-char` causes it to evaluate `help-form`
    and display the result. It then continues to wait for a valid input character, or
    keyboard-quit.

20.8.3 Modifying and Translating Input Events

Emacs modifies every event it reads according to `extra-keyboard-modifiers`, then
translates it through `keyboard-translate-table` (if applicable), before returning it from
`read-event`.

extra-keyboard-modifiers   [Variable]
    This variable lets Lisp programs "press" the modifier keys on the keyboard. The
    value is a character. Only the modifiers of the character matter. Each time the user
    types a keyboard key, it is altered as if those modifier keys were held down. For
    instance, if you bind `extra-keyboard-modifiers` to `?\C-\M-a`, then all keyboard
    input characters typed during the scope of the binding will have the control and meta
    modifiers applied to them. The character `?\C-@`, equivalent to the integer 0, does not
    count as a control character for this purpose, but as a character with no modifiers.
    Thus, setting `extra-keyboard-modifiers` to zero cancels any modification.

When using a window system, the program can press any of the modifier keys in this way. Otherwise, only the `CTL` and `META` keys can be virtually pressed.

Note that this variable applies only to events that really come from the keyboard, and has no effect on mouse events or any other events.

`keyboard-translate-table`   [Variable]

This terminal-local variable is the translate table for keyboard characters. It lets you reshuffle the keys on the keyboard without changing any command bindings. Its value is normally a char-table, or else `nil`. (It can also be a string or vector, but this is considered obsolete.)

If `keyboard-translate-table` is a char-table (see Section 6.6 [Char-Tables], page 104), then each character read from the keyboard is looked up in this char-table. If the value found there is non-`nil`, then it is used instead of the actual input character.

Note that this translation is the first thing that happens to a character after it is read from the terminal. Record-keeping features such as `recent-keys` and dribble files record the characters after translation.

Note also that this translation is done before the characters are supplied to input methods (see Section 32.11 [Input Methods], page 787). Use `translation-table-for-input` (see Section 32.9 [Translation of Characters], page 772), if you want to translate characters after input methods operate.

`keyboard-translate` *from to*   [Function]

This function modifies `keyboard-translate-table` to translate character code *from* into character code *to*. It creates the keyboard translate table if necessary.

Here's an example of using the `keyboard-translate-table` to make *C-x*, *C-c* and *C-v* perform the cut, copy and paste operations:

```
(keyboard-translate ?\C-x 'control-x)
(keyboard-translate ?\C-c 'control-c)
(keyboard-translate ?\C-v 'control-v)
(global-set-key [control-x] 'kill-region)
(global-set-key [control-c] 'kill-ring-save)
(global-set-key [control-v] 'yank)
```

On a graphical terminal that supports extended ASCII input, you can still get the standard Emacs meanings of one of those characters by typing it with the shift key. That makes it a different character as far as keyboard translation is concerned, but it has the same usual meaning.

See Section 21.14 [Translation Keymaps], page 410, for mechanisms that translate event sequences at the level of `read-key-sequence`.

20.8.4 Invoking the Input Method

The event-reading functions invoke the current input method, if any (see Section 32.11 [Input Methods], page 787). If the value of `input-method-function` is non-`nil`, it should be a function; when `read-event` reads a printing character (including `SPC`) with no modifier bits, it calls that function, passing the character as an argument.

`input-method-function`   [Variable]
>   If this is non-`nil`, its value specifies the current input method function.
>
>   **Warning:** don't bind this variable with `let`. It is often buffer-local, and if you bind
>   it around reading input (which is exactly when you *would* bind it), switching buffers
>   asynchronously while Emacs is waiting will cause the value to be restored in the wrong
>   buffer.

The input method function should return a list of events which should be used as input. (If the list is `nil`, that means there is no input, so `read-event` waits for another event.) These events are processed before the events in `unread-command-events` (see Section 20.8.6 [Event Input Misc], page 380). Events returned by the input method function are not passed to the input method function again, even if they are printing characters with no modifier bits.

If the input method function calls `read-event` or `read-key-sequence`, it should bind `input-method-function` to `nil` first, to prevent recursion.

The input method function is not called when reading the second and subsequent events of a key sequence. Thus, these characters are not subject to input method processing. The input method function should test the values of `overriding-local-map` and `overriding-terminal-local-map`; if either of these variables is non-`nil`, the input method should put its argument into a list and return that list with no further processing.

20.8.5 Quoted Character Input

You can use the function `read-quoted-char` to ask the user to specify a character, and allow the user to specify a control or meta character conveniently, either literally or as an octal character code. The command `quoted-insert` uses this function.

`read-quoted-char` &optional *prompt*   [Function]
>   This function is like `read-char`, except that if the first character read is an octal
>   digit (0–7), it reads any number of octal digits (but stopping if a non-octal digit is
>   found), and returns the character represented by that numeric character code. If the
>   character that terminates the sequence of octal digits is `RET`, it is discarded. Any
>   other terminating character is used as input after this function returns.
>
>   Quitting is suppressed when the first character is read, so that the user can enter a
>   *C-g*. See Section 20.11 [Quitting], page 382.
>
>   If *prompt* is supplied, it specifies a string for prompting the user. The prompt string
>   is always displayed in the echo area, followed by a single '-'.
>
>   In the following example, the user types in the octal number 177 (which is 127 in
>   decimal).
>
>   (read-quoted-char "What character")
>
>
>   ---------- Echo Area ----------
>   What character 1 7 7-
>   ---------- Echo Area ----------

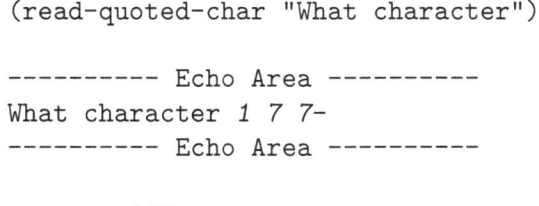

            ⇒ 127

20.8.6 Miscellaneous Event Input Features

This section describes how to peek ahead at events without using them up, how to check for pending input, and how to discard pending input. See also the function **read-passwd** (see Section 19.9 [Reading a Password], page 340).

unread-command-events   [Variable]
> This variable holds a list of events waiting to be read as command input. The events are used in the order they appear in the list, and removed one by one as they are used.
>
> The variable is needed because in some cases a function reads an event and then decides not to use it. Storing the event in this variable causes it to be processed normally, by the command loop or by the functions to read command input.
>
> For example, the function that implements numeric prefix arguments reads any number of digits. When it finds a non-digit event, it must unread the event so that it can be read normally by the command loop. Likewise, incremental search uses this feature to unread events with no special meaning in a search, because these events should exit the search and then execute normally.
>
> The reliable and easy way to extract events from a key sequence so as to put them in **unread-command-events** is to use **listify-key-sequence** (see below).
>
> Normally you add events to the front of this list, so that the events most recently unread will be reread first.
>
> Events read from this list are not normally added to the current command's key sequence (as returned by, e.g., **this-command-keys**), as the events will already have been added once as they were read for the first time. An element of the form (**t . event**) forces *event* to be added to the current command's key sequence.

listify-key-sequence *key*   [Function]
> This function converts the string or vector *key* to a list of individual events, which you can put in **unread-command-events**.

input-pending-p &optional *check-timers*   [Function]
> This function determines whether any command input is currently available to be read. It returns immediately, with value **t** if there is available input, **nil** otherwise. On rare occasions it may return **t** when no input is available.
>
> If the optional argument *check-timers* is non-**nil**, then if no input is available, Emacs runs any timers which are ready. See Section 38.11 [Timers], page 1006.

last-input-event   [Variable]
> This variable records the last terminal input event read, whether as part of a command or explicitly by a Lisp program.
>
> In the example below, the Lisp program reads the character *1*, ASCII code 49. It becomes the value of **last-input-event**, while *C-e* (we assume *C-x C-e* command is used to evaluate this expression) remains the value of **last-command-event**.

```
(progn (print (read-char))
       (print last-command-event)
       last-input-event)
     ⊣ 49
     ⊣ 5
     ⇒ 49
```

while-no-input *body...*   [Macro]

This construct runs the *body* forms and returns the value of the last one—but only if no input arrives. If any input arrives during the execution of the *body* forms, it aborts them (working much like a quit). The `while-no-input` form returns `nil` if aborted by a real quit, and returns `t` if aborted by arrival of other input.

If a part of *body* binds `inhibit-quit` to non-`nil`, arrival of input during those parts won't cause an abort until the end of that part.

If you want to be able to distinguish all possible values computed by *body* from both kinds of abort conditions, write the code like this:

```
(while-no-input
  (list
    (progn . body)))
```

discard-input   [Function]

This function discards the contents of the terminal input buffer and cancels any keyboard macro that might be in the process of definition. It returns `nil`.

In the following example, the user may type a number of characters right after starting the evaluation of the form. After the `sleep-for` finishes sleeping, `discard-input` discards any characters typed during the sleep.

```
(progn (sleep-for 2)
       (discard-input))
     ⇒ nil
```

20.9 Special Events

Certain *special events* are handled at a very low level—as soon as they are read. The `read-event` function processes these events itself, and never returns them. Instead, it keeps waiting for the first event that is not special and returns that one.

Special events do not echo, they are never grouped into key sequences, and they never appear in the value of `last-command-event` or (`this-command-keys`). They do not discard a numeric argument, they cannot be unread with `unread-command-events`, they may not appear in a keyboard macro, and they are not recorded in a keyboard macro while you are defining one.

Special events do, however, appear in `last-input-event` immediately after they are read, and this is the way for the event's definition to find the actual event.

The events types `iconify-frame`, `make-frame-visible`, `delete-frame`, `drag-n-drop`, `language-change`, and user signals like `sigusr1` are normally handled in this way. The keymap which defines how to handle special events—and which events are special—is in the variable `special-event-map` (see Section 21.7 [Active Keymaps], page 398).

20.10 Waiting for Elapsed Time or Input

The wait functions are designed to wait for a certain amount of time to pass or until there is input. For example, you may wish to pause in the middle of a computation to allow the user time to view the display. `sit-for` pauses and updates the screen, and returns immediately if input comes in, while `sleep-for` pauses without updating the screen.

`sit-for` *seconds* **&optional** *nodisp*   [Function]

> This function performs redisplay (provided there is no pending input from the user), then waits *seconds* seconds, or until input is available. The usual purpose of `sit-for` is to give the user time to read text that you display. The value is `t` if `sit-for` waited the full time with no input arriving (see Section 20.8.6 [Event Input Misc], page 380). Otherwise, the value is `nil`.
>
> The argument *seconds* need not be an integer. If it is floating point, `sit-for` waits for a fractional number of seconds. Some systems support only a whole number of seconds; on these systems, *seconds* is rounded down.
>
> The expression (`sit-for 0`) is equivalent to (`redisplay`), i.e., it requests a redisplay, without any delay, if there is no pending input. See Section 37.2 [Forcing Redisplay], page 886.
>
> If *nodisp* is non-`nil`, then `sit-for` does not redisplay, but it still returns as soon as input is available (or when the timeout elapses).
>
> In batch mode (see Section 38.17 [Batch Mode], page 1014), `sit-for` cannot be interrupted, even by input from the standard input descriptor. It is thus equivalent to `sleep-for`, which is described below.
>
> It is also possible to call `sit-for` with three arguments, as (`sit-for` *seconds millisec nodisp*), but that is considered obsolete.

`sleep-for` *seconds* **&optional** *millisec*   [Function]

> This function simply pauses for *seconds* seconds without updating the display. It pays no attention to available input. It returns `nil`.
>
> The argument *seconds* need not be an integer. If it is floating point, `sleep-for` waits for a fractional number of seconds. Some systems support only a whole number of seconds; on these systems, *seconds* is rounded down.
>
> The optional argument *millisec* specifies an additional waiting period measured in milliseconds. This adds to the period specified by *seconds*. If the system doesn't support waiting fractions of a second, you get an error if you specify nonzero *millisec*.
>
> Use `sleep-for` when you wish to guarantee a delay.

See Section 38.5 [Time of Day], page 999, for functions to get the current time.

20.11 Quitting

Typing *C-g* while a Lisp function is running causes Emacs to *quit* whatever it is doing. This means that control returns to the innermost active command loop.

Typing *C-g* while the command loop is waiting for keyboard input does not cause a quit; it acts as an ordinary input character. In the simplest case, you cannot tell the difference, because *C-g* normally runs the command `keyboard-quit`, whose effect is to quit. However, when *C-g* follows a prefix key, they combine to form an undefined key. The effect is to cancel the prefix key as well as any prefix argument.

In the minibuffer, *C-g* has a different definition: it aborts out of the minibuffer. This means, in effect, that it exits the minibuffer and then quits. (Simply quitting would return to the command loop *within* the minibuffer.) The reason why *C-g* does not quit directly when the command reader is reading input is so that its meaning can be redefined in the minibuffer in this way. *C-g* following a prefix key is not redefined in the minibuffer, and it has its normal effect of canceling the prefix key and prefix argument. This too would not be possible if *C-g* always quit directly.

When *C-g* does directly quit, it does so by setting the variable `quit-flag` to t. Emacs checks this variable at appropriate times and quits if it is not `nil`. Setting `quit-flag` non-`nil` in any way thus causes a quit.

At the level of C code, quitting cannot happen just anywhere; only at the special places that check `quit-flag`. The reason for this is that quitting at other places might leave an inconsistency in Emacs's internal state. Because quitting is delayed until a safe place, quitting cannot make Emacs crash.

Certain functions such as `read-key-sequence` or `read-quoted-char` prevent quitting entirely even though they wait for input. Instead of quitting, *C-g* serves as the requested input. In the case of `read-key-sequence`, this serves to bring about the special behavior of *C-g* in the command loop. In the case of `read-quoted-char`, this is so that *C-q* can be used to quote a *C-g*.

You can prevent quitting for a portion of a Lisp function by binding the variable `inhibit-quit` to a non-`nil` value. Then, although *C-g* still sets `quit-flag` to t as usual, the usual result of this—a quit—is prevented. Eventually, `inhibit-quit` will become `nil` again, such as when its binding is unwound at the end of a `let` form. At that time, if `quit-flag` is still non-`nil`, the requested quit happens immediately. This behavior is ideal when you wish to make sure that quitting does not happen within a critical section of the program.

In some functions (such as `read-quoted-char`), *C-g* is handled in a special way that does not involve quitting. This is done by reading the input with `inhibit-quit` bound to t, and setting `quit-flag` to `nil` before `inhibit-quit` becomes `nil` again. This excerpt from the definition of `read-quoted-char` shows how this is done; it also shows that normal quitting is permitted after the first character of input.

```
(defun read-quoted-char (&optional prompt)
  "...documentation..."
  (let ((message-log-max nil) done (first t) (code 0) char)
    (while (not done)
      (let ((inhibit-quit first)
            ...)
        (and prompt (message "%s-" prompt))
        (setq char (read-event))
        (if inhibit-quit (setq quit-flag nil)))
      ...set the variable code...)
    code))
```

`quit-flag`   [Variable]
> If this variable is non-`nil`, then Emacs quits immediately, unless `inhibit-quit` is non-`nil`. Typing *C-g* ordinarily sets `quit-flag` non-`nil`, regardless of `inhibit-quit`.

`inhibit-quit`   [Variable]
> This variable determines whether Emacs should quit when `quit-flag` is set to a value other than `nil`. If `inhibit-quit` is non-`nil`, then `quit-flag` has no special effect.

`with-local-quit` *body*...   [Macro]
> This macro executes *body* forms in sequence, but allows quitting, at least locally, within *body* even if `inhibit-quit` was non-`nil` outside this construct. It returns the value of the last form in *body*, unless exited by quitting, in which case it returns `nil`.
>
> If `inhibit-quit` is `nil` on entry to `with-local-quit`, it only executes the *body*, and setting `quit-flag` causes a normal quit. However, if `inhibit-quit` is non-`nil` so that ordinary quitting is delayed, a non-`nil` `quit-flag` triggers a special kind of local quit. This ends the execution of *body* and exits the `with-local-quit` body with `quit-flag` still non-`nil`, so that another (ordinary) quit will happen as soon as that is allowed. If `quit-flag` is already non-`nil` at the beginning of *body*, the local quit happens immediately and the body doesn't execute at all.
>
> This macro is mainly useful in functions that can be called from timers, process filters, process sentinels, `pre-command-hook`, `post-command-hook`, and other places where `inhibit-quit` is normally bound to `t`.

`keyboard-quit`   [Command]
> This function signals the `quit` condition with (`signal 'quit nil`). This is the same thing that quitting does. (See `signal` in Section 10.6.3 [Errors], page 148.)

You can specify a character other than *C-g* to use for quitting. See the function `set-input-mode` in Section 38.13.1 [Input Modes], page 1010.

20.12 Prefix Command Arguments

Most Emacs commands can use a *prefix argument*, a number specified before the command itself. (Don't confuse prefix arguments with prefix keys.) The prefix argument is at all times represented by a value, which may be `nil`, meaning there is currently no prefix argument. Each command may use the prefix argument or ignore it.

There are two representations of the prefix argument: *raw* and *numeric*. The editor command loop uses the raw representation internally, and so do the Lisp variables that store the information, but commands can request either representation.

Here are the possible values of a raw prefix argument:

- `nil`, meaning there is no prefix argument. Its numeric value is 1, but numerous commands make a distinction between `nil` and the integer 1.

- An integer, which stands for itself.

- A list of one element, which is an integer. This form of prefix argument results from one or a succession of *C-u*s with no digits. The numeric value is the integer in the list, but some commands make a distinction between such a list and an integer alone.

- The symbol -. This indicates that `M--` or `C-u` - was typed, without following digits. The equivalent numeric value is −1, but some commands make a distinction between the integer −1 and the symbol -.

We illustrate these possibilities by calling the following function with various prefixes:

```
(defun display-prefix (arg)
  "Display the value of the raw prefix arg."
  (interactive "P")
  (message "%s" arg))
```

Here are the results of calling `display-prefix` with various raw prefix arguments:

```
            M-x display-prefix   ⊣ nil

C-u     M-x display-prefix   ⊣ (4)

C-u C-u M-x display-prefix   ⊣ (16)

C-u 3   M-x display-prefix   ⊣ 3

M-3     M-x display-prefix   ⊣ 3        ; (Same as C-u 3.)

C-u -   M-x display-prefix   ⊣ -

M--     M-x display-prefix   ⊣ -        ; (Same as C-u -.)

C-u - 7 M-x display-prefix   ⊣ -7

M-- 7   M-x display-prefix   ⊣ -7       ; (Same as C-u -7.)
```

Emacs uses two variables to store the prefix argument: `prefix-arg` and `current-prefix-arg`. Commands such as `universal-argument` that set up prefix arguments for other commands store them in `prefix-arg`. In contrast, `current-prefix-arg` conveys the prefix argument to the current command, so setting it has no effect on the prefix arguments for future commands.

Normally, commands specify which representation to use for the prefix argument, either numeric or raw, in the `interactive` specification. (See Section 20.2.1 [Using Interactive], page 346.) Alternatively, functions may look at the value of the prefix argument directly in the variable `current-prefix-arg`, but this is less clean.

`prefix-numeric-value` *arg*   [Function]

> This function returns the numeric meaning of a valid raw prefix argument value, *arg*. The argument may be a symbol, a number, or a list. If it is `nil`, the value 1 is returned; if it is -, the value −1 is returned; if it is a number, that number is returned; if it is a list, the CAR of that list (which should be a number) is returned.

`current-prefix-arg`   [Variable]

> This variable holds the raw prefix argument for the *current* command. Commands may examine it directly, but the usual method for accessing it is with (`interactive` "P").

`prefix-arg`   [Variable]
>   The value of this variable is the raw prefix argument for the *next* editing command.
>   Commands such as `universal-argument` that specify prefix arguments for the fol-
>   lowing command work by setting this variable.

`last-prefix-arg`   [Variable]
>   The raw prefix argument value used by the previous command.

The following commands exist to set up prefix arguments for the following command.
Do not call them for any other reason.

`universal-argument`   [Command]
>   This command reads input and specifies a prefix argument for the following command.
>   Don't call this command yourself unless you know what you are doing.

`digit-argument` *arg*   [Command]
>   This command adds to the prefix argument for the following command. The argument
>   *arg* is the raw prefix argument as it was before this command; it is used to compute
>   the updated prefix argument. Don't call this command yourself unless you know what
>   you are doing.

`negative-argument` *arg*   [Command]
>   This command adds to the numeric argument for the next command. The argument
>   *arg* is the raw prefix argument as it was before this command; its value is negated
>   to form the new prefix argument. Don't call this command yourself unless you know
>   what you are doing.

20.13 Recursive Editing

The Emacs command loop is entered automatically when Emacs starts up. This top-level
invocation of the command loop never exits; it keeps running as long as Emacs does. Lisp
programs can also invoke the command loop. Since this makes more than one activation of
the command loop, we call it *recursive editing*. A recursive editing level has the effect of
suspending whatever command invoked it and permitting the user to do arbitrary editing
before resuming that command.

The commands available during recursive editing are the same ones available in the
top-level editing loop and defined in the keymaps. Only a few special commands exit
the recursive editing level; the others return to the recursive editing level when they finish.
(The special commands for exiting are always available, but they do nothing when recursive
editing is not in progress.)

All command loops, including recursive ones, set up all-purpose error handlers so that
an error in a command run from the command loop will not exit the loop.

Minibuffer input is a special kind of recursive editing. It has a few special wrinkles, such
as enabling display of the minibuffer and the minibuffer window, but fewer than you might
suppose. Certain keys behave differently in the minibuffer, but that is only because of the
minibuffer's local map; if you switch windows, you get the usual Emacs commands.

To invoke a recursive editing level, call the function `recursive-edit`. This function
contains the command loop; it also contains a call to `catch` with tag `exit`, which makes it

possible to exit the recursive editing level by throwing to `exit` (see Section 10.6.1 [Catch and Throw], page 145). If you throw a value other than `t`, then `recursive-edit` returns normally to the function that called it. The command `C-M-c` (`exit-recursive-edit`) does this. Throwing a `t` value causes `recursive-edit` to quit, so that control returns to the command loop one level up. This is called *aborting*, and is done by `C-]` (`abort-recursive-edit`).

Most applications should not use recursive editing, except as part of using the minibuffer. Usually it is more convenient for the user if you change the major mode of the current buffer temporarily to a special major mode, which should have a command to go back to the previous mode. (The `e` command in Rmail uses this technique.) Or, if you wish to give the user different text to edit recursively, create and select a new buffer in a special mode. In this mode, define a command to complete the processing and go back to the previous buffer. (The `m` command in Rmail does this.)

Recursive edits are useful in debugging. You can insert a call to `debug` into a function definition as a sort of breakpoint, so that you can look around when the function gets there. `debug` invokes a recursive edit but also provides the other features of the debugger.

Recursive editing levels are also used when you type `C-r` in `query-replace` or use `C-x q` (`kbd-macro-query`).

`recursive-edit`   [Command]

> This function invokes the editor command loop. It is called automatically by the initialization of Emacs, to let the user begin editing. When called from a Lisp program, it enters a recursive editing level.
>
> If the current buffer is not the same as the selected window's buffer, `recursive-edit` saves and restores the current buffer. Otherwise, if you switch buffers, the buffer you switched to is current after `recursive-edit` returns.
>
> In the following example, the function `simple-rec` first advances point one word, then enters a recursive edit, printing out a message in the echo area. The user can then do any editing desired, and then type `C-M-c` to exit and continue executing `simple-rec`.

```
(defun simple-rec ()
  (forward-word 1)
  (message "Recursive edit in progress")
  (recursive-edit)
  (forward-word 1))
     ⇒ simple-rec
(simple-rec)
     ⇒ nil
```

`exit-recursive-edit`   [Command]

> This function exits from the innermost recursive edit (including minibuffer input). Its definition is effectively (`throw 'exit nil`).

`abort-recursive-edit`   [Command]

> This function aborts the command that requested the innermost recursive edit (including minibuffer input), by signaling `quit` after exiting the recursive edit. Its definition is effectively (`throw 'exit t`). See Section 20.11 [Quitting], page 382.

`top-level`   [Command]

> This function exits all recursive editing levels; it does not return a value, as it jumps completely out of any computation directly back to the main command loop.

`recursion-depth`   [Function]

> This function returns the current depth of recursive edits. When no recursive edit is active, it returns 0.

20.14 Disabling Commands

Disabling a command marks the command as requiring user confirmation before it can be executed. Disabling is used for commands which might be confusing to beginning users, to prevent them from using the commands by accident.

The low-level mechanism for disabling a command is to put a non-`nil` `disabled` property on the Lisp symbol for the command. These properties are normally set up by the user's init file (see Section 38.1.2 [Init File], page 988) with Lisp expressions such as this:

```
(put 'upcase-region 'disabled t)
```

For a few commands, these properties are present by default (you can remove them in your init file if you wish).

If the value of the `disabled` property is a string, the message saying the command is disabled includes that string. For example:

```
(put 'delete-region 'disabled
    "Text deleted this way cannot be yanked back!\n")
```

See Section "Disabling" in *The GNU Emacs Manual*, for the details on what happens when a disabled command is invoked interactively. Disabling a command has no effect on calling it as a function from Lisp programs.

`enable-command` *command*   [Command]

> Allow *command* (a symbol) to be executed without special confirmation from now on, and alter the user's init file (see Section 38.1.2 [Init File], page 988) so that this will apply to future sessions.

`disable-command` *command*   [Command]

> Require special confirmation to execute *command* from now on, and alter the user's init file so that this will apply to future sessions.

`disabled-command-function`   [Variable]

> The value of this variable should be a function. When the user invokes a disabled command interactively, this function is called instead of the disabled command. It can use `this-command-keys` to determine what the user typed to run the command, and thus find the command itself.

> The value may also be `nil`. Then all commands work normally, even disabled ones.

> By default, the value is a function that asks the user whether to proceed.

20.15 Command History

The command loop keeps a history of the complex commands that have been executed, to make it convenient to repeat these commands. A *complex command* is one for which the interactive argument reading uses the minibuffer. This includes any `M-x` command, any `M-:` command, and any command whose `interactive` specification reads an argument from the minibuffer. Explicit use of the minibuffer during the execution of the command itself does not cause the command to be considered complex.

`command-history`   [Variable]

> This variable's value is a list of recent complex commands, each represented as a form to evaluate. It continues to accumulate all complex commands for the duration of the editing session, but when it reaches the maximum size (see Section 19.4 [Minibuffer History], page 318), the oldest elements are deleted as new ones are added.

```
command-history
⇒ ((switch-to-buffer "chistory.texi")
    (describe-key "^X^[")
    (visit-tags-table "~/emacs/src/")
    (find-tag "repeat-complex-command"))
```

> This history list is actually a special case of minibuffer history (see Section 19.4 [Minibuffer History], page 318), with one special twist: the elements are expressions rather than strings.

> There are a number of commands devoted to the editing and recall of previous commands. The commands `repeat-complex-command`, and `list-command-history` are described in the user manual (see Section "Repetition" in *The GNU Emacs Manual*). Within the minibuffer, the usual minibuffer history commands are available.

20.16 Keyboard Macros

A *keyboard macro* is a canned sequence of input events that can be considered a command and made the definition of a key. The Lisp representation of a keyboard macro is a string or vector containing the events. Don't confuse keyboard macros with Lisp macros (see Chapter 13 [Macros], page 217).

`execute-kbd-macro` *kbdmacro* **&optional** *count loopfunc*   [Function]

> This function executes *kbdmacro* as a sequence of events. If *kbdmacro* is a string or vector, then the events in it are executed exactly as if they had been input by the user. The sequence is *not* expected to be a single key sequence; normally a keyboard macro definition consists of several key sequences concatenated.

> If *kbdmacro* is a symbol, then its function definition is used in place of *kbdmacro*. If that is another symbol, this process repeats. Eventually the result should be a string or vector. If the result is not a symbol, string, or vector, an error is signaled.

> The argument *count* is a repeat count; *kbdmacro* is executed that many times. If *count* is omitted or `nil`, *kbdmacro* is executed once. If it is 0, *kbdmacro* is executed over and over until it encounters an error or a failing search.

If *loopfunc* is non-`nil`, it is a function that is called, without arguments, prior to each iteration of the macro. If *loopfunc* returns `nil`, then this stops execution of the macro.

See Section 20.8.2 [Reading One Event], page 375, for an example of using `execute-kbd-macro`.

`executing-kbd-macro`   [Variable]

This variable contains the string or vector that defines the keyboard macro that is currently executing. It is `nil` if no macro is currently executing. A command can test this variable so as to behave differently when run from an executing macro. Do not set this variable yourself.

`defining-kbd-macro`   [Variable]

This variable is non-`nil` if and only if a keyboard macro is being defined. A command can test this variable so as to behave differently while a macro is being defined. The value is `append` while appending to the definition of an existing macro. The commands `start-kbd-macro`, `kmacro-start-macro` and `end-kbd-macro` set this variable—do not set it yourself.

The variable is always local to the current terminal and cannot be buffer-local. See Section 28.2 [Multiple Terminals], page 631.

`last-kbd-macro`   [Variable]

This variable is the definition of the most recently defined keyboard macro. Its value is a string or vector, or `nil`.

The variable is always local to the current terminal and cannot be buffer-local. See Section 28.2 [Multiple Terminals], page 631.

`kbd-macro-termination-hook`   [Variable]

This normal hook is run when a keyboard macro terminates, regardless of what caused it to terminate (reaching the macro end or an error which ended the macro prematurely).

21 Keymaps

The command bindings of input events are recorded in data structures called *keymaps*. Each entry in a keymap associates (or *binds*) an individual event type, either to another keymap or to a command. When an event type is bound to a keymap, that keymap is used to look up the next input event; this continues until a command is found. The whole process is called *key lookup*.

21.1 Key Sequences

A *key sequence*, or *key* for short, is a sequence of one or more input events that form a unit. Input events include characters, function keys, mouse actions, or system events external to Emacs, such as `iconify-frame` (see Section 20.7 [Input Events], page 358). The Emacs Lisp representation for a key sequence is a string or vector. Unless otherwise stated, any Emacs Lisp function that accepts a key sequence as an argument can handle both representations.

In the string representation, alphanumeric characters ordinarily stand for themselves; for example, `"a"` represents *a* and `"2"` represents *2*. Control character events are prefixed by the substring `"\C-"`, and meta characters by `"\M-"`; for example, `"\C-x"` represents the key *C-x*. In addition, the TAB, RET, ESC, and DEL events are represented by `"\t"`, `"\r"`, `"\e"`, and `"\d"` respectively. The string representation of a complete key sequence is the concatenation of the string representations of the constituent events; thus, `"\C-xl"` represents the key sequence *C-x l*.

Key sequences containing function keys, mouse button events, system events, or non-ASCII characters such as *C-=* or *H-a* cannot be represented as strings; they have to be represented as vectors.

In the vector representation, each element of the vector represents an input event, in its Lisp form. See Section 20.7 [Input Events], page 358. For example, the vector `[?\C-x ?l]` represents the key sequence *C-x l*.

For examples of key sequences written in string and vector representations, Section "Init Rebinding" in *The GNU Emacs Manual*.

kbd *keyseq-text*   [Function]

This function converts the text *keyseq-text* (a string constant) into a key sequence (a string or vector constant). The contents of *keyseq-text* should use the same syntax as in the buffer invoked by the *C-x C-k RET* (`kmacro-edit-macro`) command; in particular, you must surround function key names with '`<...>`'. See Section "Edit Keyboard Macro" in *The GNU Emacs Manual*.

```
(kbd "C-x")  ⇒  "\C-x"
(kbd "C-x C-f")  ⇒  "\C-x\C-f"
(kbd "C-x 4 C-f")  ⇒  "\C-x4\C-f"
(kbd "X")  ⇒  "X"
(kbd "RET")  ⇒  "\^M"
(kbd "C-c SPC")  ⇒  "\C-c "
(kbd "<f1> SPC")  ⇒  [f1 32]
(kbd "C-M-<down>")  ⇒  [C-M-down]
```

21.2 Keymap Basics

A keymap is a Lisp data structure that specifies *key bindings* for various key sequences.

A single keymap directly specifies definitions for individual events. When a key sequence consists of a single event, its binding in a keymap is the keymap's definition for that event. The binding of a longer key sequence is found by an iterative process: first find the definition of the first event (which must itself be a keymap); then find the second event's definition in that keymap, and so on until all the events in the key sequence have been processed.

If the binding of a key sequence is a keymap, we call the key sequence a *prefix key*. Otherwise, we call it a *complete key* (because no more events can be added to it). If the binding is **nil**, we call the key *undefined*. Examples of prefix keys are *C-c*, *C-x*, and *C-x 4*. Examples of defined complete keys are *X*, RET, and *C-x 4 C-f*. Examples of undefined complete keys are *C-x C-g*, and *C-c 3*. See Section 21.6 [Prefix Keys], page 396, for more details.

The rule for finding the binding of a key sequence assumes that the intermediate bindings (found for the events before the last) are all keymaps; if this is not so, the sequence of events does not form a unit—it is not really one key sequence. In other words, removing one or more events from the end of any valid key sequence must always yield a prefix key. For example, *C-f C-n* is not a key sequence; *C-f* is not a prefix key, so a longer sequence starting with *C-f* cannot be a key sequence.

The set of possible multi-event key sequences depends on the bindings for prefix keys; therefore, it can be different for different keymaps, and can change when bindings are changed. However, a one-event sequence is always a key sequence, because it does not depend on any prefix keys for its well-formedness.

At any time, several primary keymaps are *active*—that is, in use for finding key bindings. These are the *global map*, which is shared by all buffers; the *local keymap*, which is usually associated with a specific major mode; and zero or more *minor mode keymaps*, which belong to currently enabled minor modes. (Not all minor modes have keymaps.) The local keymap bindings shadow (i.e., take precedence over) the corresponding global bindings. The minor mode keymaps shadow both local and global keymaps. See Section 21.7 [Active Keymaps], page 398, for details.

21.3 Format of Keymaps

Each keymap is a list whose CAR is the symbol **keymap**. The remaining elements of the list define the key bindings of the keymap. A symbol whose function definition is a keymap is also a keymap. Use the function **keymapp** (see below) to test whether an object is a keymap.

Several kinds of elements may appear in a keymap, after the symbol **keymap** that begins it:

(*type* . *binding*)

> This specifies one binding, for events of type *type*. Each ordinary binding applies to events of a particular *event type*, which is always a character or a symbol. See Section 20.7.12 [Classifying Events], page 367. In this kind of binding, *binding* is a command.

(*type* *item-name* . *binding*)

> This specifies a binding which is also a simple menu item that displays as *item-name* in the menu. See Section 21.17.1.1 [Simple Menu Items], page 416.

(*type* *item-name* *help-string* . *binding*)

> This is a simple menu item with help string *help-string*.

(*type* menu-item . *details*)

> This specifies a binding which is also an extended menu item. This allows use of other features. See Section 21.17.1.2 [Extended Menu Items], page 417.

(t . *binding*)

> This specifies a *default key binding*; any event not bound by other elements of the keymap is given *binding* as its binding. Default bindings allow a keymap to bind all possible event types without having to enumerate all of them. A keymap that has a default binding completely masks any lower-precedence keymap, except for events explicitly bound to nil (see below).

char-table

> If an element of a keymap is a char-table, it counts as holding bindings for all character events with no modifier bits (see [modifier bits], page 13): the element whose index is *c* is the binding for the character *c*. This is a compact way to record lots of bindings. A keymap with such a char-table is called a *full keymap*. Other keymaps are called *sparse keymaps*.

vector

> This kind of element is similar to a char-table: the element whose index is *c* is the binding for the character *c*. Since the range of characters that can be bound this way is limited by the vector size, and vector creation allocates space for all character codes from 0 up, this format should not be used except for creating menu keymaps (see Section 21.17 [Menu Keymaps], page 415), where the bindings themselves don't matter.

string

> Aside from elements that specify bindings for keys, a keymap can also have a string as an element. This is called the *overall prompt string* and makes it possible to use the keymap as a menu. See Section 21.17.1 [Defining Menus], page 415.

(keymap ...)

> If an element of a keymap is itself a keymap, it counts as if this inner keymap were inlined in the outer keymap. This is used for multiple-inheritance, such as in make-composed-keymap.

When the binding is nil, it doesn't constitute a definition but it does take precedence over a default binding or a binding in the parent keymap. On the other hand, a binding of nil does *not* override lower-precedence keymaps; thus, if the local map gives a binding of nil, Emacs uses the binding from the global map.

Keymaps do not directly record bindings for the meta characters. Instead, meta characters are regarded for purposes of key lookup as sequences of two characters, the first of which is ESC (or whatever is currently the value of meta-prefix-char). Thus, the key M-a is internally represented as *ESC* a, and its global binding is found at the slot for a in esc-map (see Section 21.6 [Prefix Keys], page 396).

This conversion applies only to characters, not to function keys or other input events; thus, *M-end* has nothing to do with *ESC end*.

Here as an example is the local keymap for Lisp mode, a sparse keymap. It defines bindings for DEL, *C-c C-z*, *C-M-q*, and *C-M-x* (the actual value also contains a menu binding, which is omitted here for the sake of brevity).

```
lisp-mode-map
⇒
(keymap
 (3 keymap
    ;; C-c C-z
    (26 . run-lisp))
 (27 keymap
     ;; C-M-x, treated as ESC C-x
     (24 . lisp-send-defun))
 ;; This part is inherited from lisp-mode-shared-map.
 keymap
 ;; DEL
 (127 . backward-delete-char-untabify)
 (27 keymap
     ;; C-M-q, treated as ESC C-q
     (17 . indent-sexp)))
```

keymapp *object*   [Function]

> This function returns **t** if *object* is a keymap, **nil** otherwise. More precisely, this function tests for a list whose CAR is **keymap**, or for a symbol whose function definition satisfies **keymapp**.
>
> ```
> (keymapp '(keymap))
>     ⇒ t
> (fset 'foo '(keymap))
> (keymapp 'foo)
>     ⇒ t
> (keymapp (current-global-map))
>     ⇒ t
> ```

21.4 Creating Keymaps

Here we describe the functions for creating keymaps.

make-sparse-keymap &optional *prompt*   [Function]

> This function creates and returns a new sparse keymap with no entries. (A sparse keymap is the kind of keymap you usually want.) The new keymap does not contain a char-table, unlike **make-keymap**, and does not bind any events.
>
> ```
> (make-sparse-keymap)
>     ⇒ (keymap)
> ```
>
> If you specify *prompt*, that becomes the overall prompt string for the keymap. You should specify this only for menu keymaps (see Section 21.17.1 [Defining Menus], page 415). A keymap with an overall prompt string will always present a mouse

menu or a keyboard menu if it is active for looking up the next input event. Don't specify an overall prompt string for the main map of a major or minor mode, because that would cause the command loop to present a keyboard menu every time.

make-keymap &optional *prompt* [Function]

This function creates and returns a new full keymap. That keymap contains a char-table (see Section 6.6 [Char-Tables], page 104) with slots for all characters without modifiers. The new keymap initially binds all these characters to `nil`, and does not bind any other kind of event. The argument *prompt* specifies a prompt string, as in `make-sparse-keymap`.

```
(make-keymap)
    ⇒ (keymap #^[nil nil keymap nil nil nil ...])
```

A full keymap is more efficient than a sparse keymap when it holds lots of bindings; for just a few, the sparse keymap is better.

copy-keymap *keymap* [Function]

This function returns a copy of *keymap*. Any keymaps that appear directly as bindings in *keymap* are also copied recursively, and so on to any number of levels. However, recursive copying does not take place when the definition of a character is a symbol whose function definition is a keymap; the same symbol appears in the new copy.

```
(setq map (copy-keymap (current-local-map)))
⇒ (keymap
      ;; (This implements meta characters.)
      (27 keymap
          (83 . center-paragraph)
          (115 . center-line))
      (9 . tab-to-tab-stop))

(eq map (current-local-map))
    ⇒ nil
(equal map (current-local-map))
    ⇒ t
```

21.5 Inheritance and Keymaps

A keymap can inherit the bindings of another keymap, which we call the *parent keymap*. Such a keymap looks like this:

```
(keymap elements... . parent-keymap)
```

The effect is that this keymap inherits all the bindings of *parent-keymap*, whatever they may be at the time a key is looked up, but can add to them or override them with *elements*.

If you change the bindings in *parent-keymap* using `define-key` or other key-binding functions, these changed bindings are visible in the inheriting keymap, unless shadowed by the bindings made by *elements*. The converse is not true: if you use `define-key` to change bindings in the inheriting keymap, these changes are recorded in *elements*, but have no effect on *parent-keymap*.

The proper way to construct a keymap with a parent is to use `set-keymap-parent`; if you have code that directly constructs a keymap with a parent, please convert the program to use `set-keymap-parent` instead.

`keymap-parent` *keymap*   [Function]

> This returns the parent keymap of *keymap*. If *keymap* has no parent, `keymap-parent` returns `nil`.

`set-keymap-parent` *keymap parent*   [Function]

> This sets the parent keymap of *keymap* to *parent*, and returns *parent*. If *parent* is `nil`, this function gives *keymap* no parent at all.
>
> If *keymap* has submaps (bindings for prefix keys), they too receive new parent keymaps that reflect what *parent* specifies for those prefix keys.

Here is an example showing how to make a keymap that inherits from `text-mode-map`:

```
(let ((map (make-sparse-keymap)))
  (set-keymap-parent map text-mode-map)
  map)
```

A non-sparse keymap can have a parent too, but this is not very useful. A non-sparse keymap always specifies something as the binding for every numeric character code without modifier bits, even if it is `nil`, so these character's bindings are never inherited from the parent keymap.

Sometimes you want to make a keymap that inherits from more than one map. You can use the function `make-composed-keymap` for this.

`make-composed-keymap` *maps* **&optional** *parent*   [Function]

> This function returns a new keymap composed of the existing keymap(s) *maps*, and optionally inheriting from a parent keymap *parent*. *maps* can be a single keymap or a list of more than one. When looking up a key in the resulting new map, Emacs searches in each of the *maps* in turn, and then in *parent*, stopping at the first match. A `nil` binding in any one of *maps* overrides any binding in *parent*, but it does not override any non-`nil` binding in any other of the *maps*.

For example, here is how Emacs sets the parent of `help-mode-map`, such that it inherits from both `button-buffer-map` and `special-mode-map`:

```
(defvar help-mode-map
  (let ((map (make-sparse-keymap)))
    (set-keymap-parent map
      (make-composed-keymap button-buffer-map special-mode-map))
    ... map) ... )
```

21.6 Prefix Keys

A *prefix key* is a key sequence whose binding is a keymap. The keymap defines what to do with key sequences that extend the prefix key. For example, `C-x` is a prefix key, and it uses a keymap that is also stored in the variable `ctl-x-map`. This keymap defines bindings for key sequences starting with `C-x`.

Some of the standard Emacs prefix keys use keymaps that are also found in Lisp variables:

- `esc-map` is the global keymap for the `ESC` prefix key. Thus, the global definitions of all meta characters are actually found here. This map is also the function definition of `ESC-prefix`.

- `help-map` is the global keymap for the *C-h* prefix key.

- `mode-specific-map` is the global keymap for the prefix key *C-c*. This map is actually global, not mode-specific, but its name provides useful information about *C-c* in the output of *C-h b* (`display-bindings`), since the main use of this prefix key is for mode-specific bindings.

- `ctl-x-map` is the global keymap used for the *C-x* prefix key. This map is found via the function cell of the symbol `Control-X-prefix`.

- `mule-keymap` is the global keymap used for the *C-x RET* prefix key.

- `ctl-x-4-map` is the global keymap used for the *C-x 4* prefix key.

- `ctl-x-5-map` is the global keymap used for the *C-x 5* prefix key.

- `2C-mode-map` is the global keymap used for the *C-x 6* prefix key.

- `vc-prefix-map` is the global keymap used for the *C-x v* prefix key.

- `goto-map` is the global keymap used for the *M-g* prefix key.

- `search-map` is the global keymap used for the *M-s* prefix key.

- `facemenu-keymap` is the global keymap used for the *M-o* prefix key.

- The other Emacs prefix keys are *C-x @*, *C-x a i*, *C-x ESC* and *ESC ESC*. They use keymaps that have no special names.

The keymap binding of a prefix key is used for looking up the event that follows the prefix key. (It may instead be a symbol whose function definition is a keymap. The effect is the same, but the symbol serves as a name for the prefix key.) Thus, the binding of *C-x* is the symbol `Control-X-prefix`, whose function cell holds the keymap for *C-x* commands. (The same keymap is also the value of `ctl-x-map`.)

Prefix key definitions can appear in any active keymap. The definitions of *C-c*, *C-x*, *C-h* and `ESC` as prefix keys appear in the global map, so these prefix keys are always available. Major and minor modes can redefine a key as a prefix by putting a prefix key definition for it in the local map or the minor mode's map. See Section 21.7 [Active Keymaps], page 398.

If a key is defined as a prefix in more than one active map, then its various definitions are in effect merged: the commands defined in the minor mode keymaps come first, followed by those in the local map's prefix definition, and then by those from the global map.

In the following example, we make *C-p* a prefix key in the local keymap, in such a way that *C-p* is identical to *C-x*. Then the binding for *C-p C-f* is the function `find-file`, just like *C-x C-f*. The key sequence *C-p 6* is not found in any active keymap.

```
(use-local-map (make-sparse-keymap))
    ⇒ nil
(local-set-key "\C-p" ctl-x-map)
    ⇒ nil
(key-binding "\C-p\C-f")
    ⇒ find-file
```

```
(key-binding "\C-p6")
    ⇒ nil
```

define-prefix-command *symbol* **&optional** *mapvar prompt*   [Function]

> This function prepares *symbol* for use as a prefix key's binding: it creates a sparse keymap and stores it as *symbol*'s function definition. Subsequently binding a key sequence to *symbol* will make that key sequence into a prefix key. The return value is `symbol`.

> This function also sets *symbol* as a variable, with the keymap as its value. But if *mapvar* is non-`nil`, it sets *mapvar* as a variable instead.

> If *prompt* is non-`nil`, that becomes the overall prompt string for the keymap. The prompt string should be given for menu keymaps (see Section 21.17.1 [Defining Menus], page 415).

21.7 Active Keymaps

Emacs contains many keymaps, but at any time only a few keymaps are *active*. When Emacs receives user input, it translates the input event (see Section 21.14 [Translation Keymaps], page 410), and looks for a key binding in the active keymaps.

Usually, the active keymaps are: (i) the keymap specified by the `keymap` property, (ii) the keymaps of enabled minor modes, (iii) the current buffer's local keymap, and (iv) the global keymap, in that order. Emacs searches for each input key sequence in all these keymaps.

Of these usual keymaps, the highest-precedence one is specified by the `keymap` text or overlay property at point, if any. (For a mouse input event, Emacs uses the event position instead of point; see the next section for details.)

Next in precedence are keymaps specified by enabled minor modes. These keymaps, if any, are specified by the variables `emulation-mode-map-alists`, `minor-mode-overriding-map-alist`, and `minor-mode-map-alist`. See Section 21.9 [Controlling Active Maps], page 400.

Next in precedence is the buffer's *local keymap*, containing key bindings specific to the buffer. The minibuffer also has a local keymap (see Section 19.1 [Intro to Minibuffers], page 313). If there is a `local-map` text or overlay property at point, that specifies the local keymap to use, in place of the buffer's default local keymap.

The local keymap is normally set by the buffer's major mode, and every buffer with the same major mode shares the same local keymap. Hence, if you call `local-set-key` (see Section 21.15 [Key Binding Commands], page 412) to change the local keymap in one buffer, that also affects the local keymaps in other buffers with the same major mode.

Finally, the *global keymap* contains key bindings that are defined regardless of the current buffer, such as *C-f*. It is always active, and is bound to the variable `global-map`.

Apart from the above usual keymaps, Emacs provides special ways for programs to make other keymaps active. Firstly, the variable `overriding-local-map` specifies a keymap that replaces the usual active keymaps, except for the global keymap. Secondly, the terminal-local variable `overriding-terminal-local-map` specifies a keymap that takes precedence over *all* other keymaps (including `overriding-local-map`); this is normally used for modal/transient keybindings (the function `set-transient-map` provides a convenient interface for this). See Section 21.9 [Controlling Active Maps], page 400, for details.

Making keymaps active is not the only way to use them. Keymaps are also used in other ways, such as for translating events within `read-key-sequence`. See Section 21.14 [Translation Keymaps], page 410.

See Appendix G [Standard Keymaps], page 1095, for a list of some standard keymaps.

`current-active-maps` &optional *olp position*   [Function]

> This returns the list of active keymaps that would be used by the command loop in the current circumstances to look up a key sequence. Normally it ignores `overriding-local-map` and `overriding-terminal-local-map`, but if *olp* is non-`nil` then it pays attention to them. *position* can optionally be either an event position as returned by `event-start` or a buffer position, and may change the keymaps as described for `key-binding`.

`key-binding` *key* &optional *accept-defaults no-remap position*   [Function]

> This function returns the binding for *key* according to the current active keymaps. The result is `nil` if *key* is undefined in the keymaps.
>
> The argument *accept-defaults* controls checking for default bindings, as in `lookup-key` (see Section 21.11 [Functions for Key Lookup], page 404).
>
> When commands are remapped (see Section 21.13 [Remapping Commands], page 409), `key-binding` normally processes command remappings so as to return the remapped command that will actually be executed. However, if *no-remap* is non-`nil`, `key-binding` ignores remappings and returns the binding directly specified for *key*.
>
> If *key* starts with a mouse event (perhaps following a prefix event), the maps to be consulted are determined based on the event's position. Otherwise, they are determined based on the value of point. However, you can override either of them by specifying *position*. If *position* is non-`nil`, it should be either a buffer position or an event position like the value of `event-start`. Then the maps consulted are determined based on *position*.
>
> Emacs signals an error if *key* is not a string or a vector.
>
> ```
> (key-binding "\C-x\C-f")
>     ⇒ find-file
> ```

21.8 Searching the Active Keymaps

Here is a pseudo-Lisp summary of how Emacs searches the active keymaps:

```
(or (if overriding-terminal-local-map
        (find-in overriding-terminal-local-map))
    (if overriding-local-map
        (find-in overriding-local-map)
      (or (find-in (get-char-property (point) 'keymap))
          (find-in-any emulation-mode-map-alists)
          (find-in-any minor-mode-overriding-map-alist)
          (find-in-any minor-mode-map-alist)
```

```
          (if (get-text-property (point) 'local-map)
              (find-in (get-char-property (point) 'local-map))
            (find-in (current-local-map)))))
      (find-in (current-global-map)))
```

Here, *find-in* and *find-in-any* are pseudo functions that search in one keymap and in an alist of keymaps, respectively. Note that the **set-transient-map** function works by setting **overriding-terminal-local-map** (see Section 21.9 [Controlling Active Maps], page 400).

In the above pseudo-code, if a key sequence starts with a mouse event (see Section 20.7.3 [Mouse Events], page 360), that event's position is used instead of point, and the event's buffer is used instead of the current buffer. In particular, this affects how the **keymap** and **local-map** properties are looked up. If a mouse event occurs on a string embedded with a **display**, **before-string**, or **after-string** property (see Section 31.19.4 [Special Properties], page 738), and the string has a non-**nil** **keymap** or **local-map** property, that overrides the corresponding property in the underlying buffer text (i.e., the property specified by the underlying text is ignored).

When a key binding is found in one of the active keymaps, and that binding is a command, the search is over—the command is executed. However, if the binding is a symbol with a value or a string, Emacs replaces the input key sequences with the variable's value or the string, and restarts the search of the active keymaps. See Section 21.10 [Key Lookup], page 403.

The command which is finally found might also be remapped. See Section 21.13 [Remapping Commands], page 409.

21.9 Controlling the Active Keymaps

global-map   [Variable]
> This variable contains the default global keymap that maps Emacs keyboard input to commands. The global keymap is normally this keymap. The default global keymap is a full keymap that binds **self-insert-command** to all of the printing characters.
>
> It is normal practice to change the bindings in the global keymap, but you should not assign this variable any value other than the keymap it starts out with.

current-global-map   [Function]
> This function returns the current global keymap. This is the same as the value of **global-map** unless you change one or the other. The return value is a reference, not a copy; if you use **define-key** or other functions on it you will alter global bindings.
>
> ```
> (current-global-map)
> ⇒ (keymap [set-mark-command beginning-of-line ...
>            delete-backward-char])
> ```

current-local-map   [Function]
> This function returns the current buffer's local keymap, or **nil** if it has none. In the following example, the keymap for the ***scratch*** buffer (using Lisp Interaction mode) is a sparse keymap in which the entry for **ESC**, ASCII code 27, is another sparse keymap.

```
(current-local-map)
⇒ (keymap
      (10 . eval-print-last-sexp)
      (9 . lisp-indent-line)
      (127 . backward-delete-char-untabify)
      (27 keymap
          (24 . eval-defun)
          (17 . indent-sexp)))
```

current-local-map returns a reference to the local keymap, not a copy of it; if you use define-key or other functions on it you will alter local bindings.

current-minor-mode-maps   [Function]
    This function returns a list of the keymaps of currently enabled minor modes.

use-global-map *keymap*   [Function]
    This function makes *keymap* the new current global keymap. It returns nil.

    It is very unusual to change the global keymap.

use-local-map *keymap*   [Function]
    This function makes *keymap* the new local keymap of the current buffer. If *keymap* is nil, then the buffer has no local keymap. use-local-map returns nil. Most major mode commands use this function.

minor-mode-map-alist   [Variable]
    This variable is an alist describing keymaps that may or may not be active according to the values of certain variables. Its elements look like this:

        (*variable* . *keymap*)

    The keymap *keymap* is active whenever *variable* has a non-nil value. Typically *variable* is the variable that enables or disables a minor mode. See Section 22.3.2 [Keymaps and Minor Modes], page 448.

    Note that elements of minor-mode-map-alist do not have the same structure as elements of minor-mode-alist. The map must be the CDR of the element; a list with the map as the second element will not do. The CDR can be either a keymap (a list) or a symbol whose function definition is a keymap.

    When more than one minor mode keymap is active, the earlier one in minor-mode-map-alist takes priority. But you should design minor modes so that they don't interfere with each other. If you do this properly, the order will not matter.

    See Section 22.3.2 [Keymaps and Minor Modes], page 448, for more information about minor modes. See also minor-mode-key-binding (see Section 21.11 [Functions for Key Lookup], page 404).

minor-mode-overriding-map-alist   [Variable]
    This variable allows major modes to override the key bindings for particular minor modes. The elements of this alist look like the elements of minor-mode-map-alist: (*variable* . *keymap*).

If a variable appears as an element of `minor-mode-overriding-map-alist`, the map specified by that element totally replaces any map specified for the same variable in `minor-mode-map-alist`.

`minor-mode-overriding-map-alist` is automatically buffer-local in all buffers.

`overriding-local-map`   [Variable]

    If non-`nil`, this variable holds a keymap to use instead of the buffer's local keymap, any text property or overlay keymaps, and any minor mode keymaps. This keymap, if specified, overrides all other maps that would have been active, except for the current global map.

`overriding-terminal-local-map`   [Variable]

    If non-`nil`, this variable holds a keymap to use instead of `overriding-local-map`, the buffer's local keymap, text property or overlay keymaps, and all the minor mode keymaps.

    This variable is always local to the current terminal and cannot be buffer-local. See Section 28.2 [Multiple Terminals], page 631. It is used to implement incremental search mode.

`overriding-local-map-menu-flag`   [Variable]

    If this variable is non-`nil`, the value of `overriding-local-map` or `overriding-terminal-local-map` can affect the display of the menu bar. The default value is `nil`, so those map variables have no effect on the menu bar.

    Note that these two map variables do affect the execution of key sequences entered using the menu bar, even if they do not affect the menu bar display. So if a menu bar key sequence comes in, you should clear the variables before looking up and executing that key sequence. Modes that use the variables would typically do this anyway; normally they respond to events that they do not handle by "unreading" them and exiting.

`special-event-map`   [Variable]

    This variable holds a keymap for special events. If an event type has a binding in this keymap, then it is special, and the binding for the event is run directly by `read-event`. See Section 20.9 [Special Events], page 381.

`emulation-mode-map-alists`   [Variable]

    This variable holds a list of keymap alists to use for emulation modes. It is intended for modes or packages using multiple minor-mode keymaps. Each element is a keymap alist which has the same format and meaning as `minor-mode-map-alist`, or a symbol with a variable binding which is such an alist. The active keymaps in each alist are used before `minor-mode-map-alist` and `minor-mode-overriding-map-alist`.

`set-transient-map` *keymap* **&optional** *keep-pred on-exit*   [Function]

    This function adds *keymap* as a *transient* keymap, which takes precedence over other keymaps for one (or more) subsequent keys.

    Normally, *keymap* is used just once, to look up the very next key. If the optional argument *keep-pred* is `t`, the map stays active as long as the user types keys defined in *keymap*; when the user types a key that is not in *keymap*, the transient keymap is deactivated and normal key lookup continues for that key.

The *keep-pred* argument can also be a function. In that case, the function is called with no arguments, prior to running each command, while *keymap* is active; it should return non-`nil` if *keymap* should stay active.

The optional argument *on-exit*, if non-nil, specifies a function that is called, with no arguments, after *keymap* is deactivated.

This function works by adding and removing *keymap* from the variable `overriding-terminal-local-map`, which takes precedence over all other active keymaps (see Section 21.8 [Searching Keymaps], page 399).

21.10 Key Lookup

Key lookup is the process of finding the binding of a key sequence from a given keymap. The execution or use of the binding is not part of key lookup.

Key lookup uses just the event type of each event in the key sequence; the rest of the event is ignored. In fact, a key sequence used for key lookup may designate a mouse event with just its types (a symbol) instead of the entire event (a list). See Section 20.7 [Input Events], page 358. Such a key sequence is insufficient for `command-execute` to run, but it is sufficient for looking up or rebinding a key.

When the key sequence consists of multiple events, key lookup processes the events sequentially: the binding of the first event is found, and must be a keymap; then the second event's binding is found in that keymap, and so on until all the events in the key sequence are used up. (The binding thus found for the last event may or may not be a keymap.) Thus, the process of key lookup is defined in terms of a simpler process for looking up a single event in a keymap. How that is done depends on the type of object associated with the event in that keymap.

Let's use the term *keymap entry* to describe the value found by looking up an event type in a keymap. (This doesn't include the item string and other extra elements in a keymap element for a menu item, because `lookup-key` and other key lookup functions don't include them in the returned value.) While any Lisp object may be stored in a keymap as a keymap entry, not all make sense for key lookup. Here is a table of the meaningful types of keymap entries:

`nil`   `nil` means that the events used so far in the lookup form an undefined key. When a keymap fails to mention an event type at all, and has no default binding, that is equivalent to a binding of `nil` for that event type.

command   The events used so far in the lookup form a complete key, and *command* is its binding. See Section 12.1 [What Is a Function], page 186.

array   The array (either a string or a vector) is a keyboard macro. The events used so far in the lookup form a complete key, and the array is its binding. See Section 20.16 [Keyboard Macros], page 389, for more information.

keymap   The events used so far in the lookup form a prefix key. The next event of the key sequence is looked up in *keymap*.

list   The meaning of a list depends on what it contains:

- If the CAR of *list* is the symbol `keymap`, then the list is a keymap, and is treated as a keymap (see above).

- If the CAR of *list* is `lambda`, then the list is a lambda expression. This is presumed to be a function, and is treated as such (see above). In order to execute properly as a key binding, this function must be a command— it must have an `interactive` specification. See Section 20.2 [Defining Commands], page 346.

symbol   The function definition of *symbol* is used in place of *symbol*. If that too is a symbol, then this process is repeated, any number of times. Ultimately this should lead to an object that is a keymap, a command, or a keyboard macro.

Note that keymaps and keyboard macros (strings and vectors) are not valid functions, so a symbol with a keymap, string, or vector as its function definition is invalid as a function. It is, however, valid as a key binding. If the definition is a keyboard macro, then the symbol is also valid as an argument to `command-execute` (see Section 20.3 [Interactive Call], page 352).

The symbol `undefined` is worth special mention: it means to treat the key as undefined. Strictly speaking, the key is defined, and its binding is the command `undefined`; but that command does the same thing that is done automatically for an undefined key: it rings the bell (by calling `ding`) but does not signal an error.

`undefined` is used in local keymaps to override a global key binding and make the key undefined locally. A local binding of `nil` would fail to do this because it would not override the global binding.

anything else

        If any other type of object is found, the events used so far in the lookup form a complete key, and the object is its binding, but the binding is not executable as a command.

In short, a keymap entry may be a keymap, a command, a keyboard macro, a symbol that leads to one of them, or `nil`.

21.11 Functions for Key Lookup

Here are the functions and variables pertaining to key lookup.

`lookup-key` *keymap key* **&optional** *accept-defaults*   [Function]
    This function returns the definition of *key* in *keymap*. All the other functions described in this chapter that look up keys use `lookup-key`. Here are examples:

```
(lookup-key (current-global-map) "\C-x\C-f")
     ⇒ find-file
(lookup-key (current-global-map) (kbd "C-x C-f"))
     ⇒ find-file
(lookup-key (current-global-map) "\C-x\C-f12345")
     ⇒ 2
```

If the string or vector *key* is not a valid key sequence according to the prefix keys specified in *keymap*, it must be too long and have extra events at the end that do not fit into a single key sequence. Then the value is a number, the number of events at the front of *key* that compose a complete key.

If *accept-defaults* is non-`nil`, then `lookup-key` considers default bindings as well as bindings for the specific events in *key*. Otherwise, `lookup-key` reports only bindings for the specific sequence *key*, ignoring default bindings except when you explicitly ask about them. (To do this, supply `t` as an element of *key*; see Section 21.3 [Format of Keymaps], page 392.)

If *key* contains a meta character (not a function key), that character is implicitly replaced by a two-character sequence: the value of `meta-prefix-char`, followed by the corresponding non-meta character. Thus, the first example below is handled by conversion into the second example.

```
(lookup-key (current-global-map) "\M-f")
    ⇒ forward-word
(lookup-key (current-global-map) "\ef")
    ⇒ forward-word
```

Unlike `read-key-sequence`, this function does not modify the specified events in ways that discard information (see Section 20.8.1 [Key Sequence Input], page 373). In particular, it does not convert letters to lower case and it does not change drag events to clicks.

`undefined` [Command]

Used in keymaps to undefine keys. It calls `ding`, but does not cause an error.

`local-key-binding` *key* &optional *accept-defaults* [Function]

This function returns the binding for *key* in the current local keymap, or `nil` if it is undefined there.

The argument *accept-defaults* controls checking for default bindings, as in `lookup-key` (above).

`global-key-binding` *key* &optional *accept-defaults* [Function]

This function returns the binding for command *key* in the current global keymap, or `nil` if it is undefined there.

The argument *accept-defaults* controls checking for default bindings, as in `lookup-key` (above).

`minor-mode-key-binding` *key* &optional *accept-defaults* [Function]

This function returns a list of all the active minor mode bindings of *key*. More precisely, it returns an alist of pairs (`modename . binding`), where *modename* is the variable that enables the minor mode, and *binding* is *key*'s binding in that mode. If *key* has no minor-mode bindings, the value is `nil`.

If the first binding found is not a prefix definition (a keymap or a symbol defined as a keymap), all subsequent bindings from other minor modes are omitted, since they would be completely shadowed. Similarly, the list omits non-prefix bindings that follow prefix bindings.

The argument *accept-defaults* controls checking for default bindings, as in `lookup-key` (above).

`meta-prefix-char`   [User Option]

    This variable is the meta-prefix character code. It is used for translating a meta character to a two-character sequence so it can be looked up in a keymap. For useful results, the value should be a prefix event (see Section 21.6 [Prefix Keys], page 396). The default value is 27, which is the ASCII code for `ESC`.

    As long as the value of `meta-prefix-char` remains 27, key lookup translates *M-b* into *ESC b*, which is normally defined as the `backward-word` command. However, if you were to set `meta-prefix-char` to 24, the code for *C-x*, then Emacs will translate *M-b* into *C-x b*, whose standard binding is the `switch-to-buffer` command. (Don't actually do this!) Here is an illustration of what would happen:

```
meta-prefix-char                 ; The default value.
     ⇒ 27
(key-binding "\M-b")
     ⇒ backward-word
?\C-x                            ; The print representation
     ⇒ 24                       ;   of a character.
(setq meta-prefix-char 24)
     ⇒ 24
(key-binding "\M-b")
     ⇒ switch-to-buffer          ; Now, typing M-b is
                                 ;   like typing C-x b.

(setq meta-prefix-char 27)       ; Avoid confusion!
     ⇒ 27                       ; Restore the default value!
```

    This translation of one event into two happens only for characters, not for other kinds of input events. Thus, *M-F1*, a function key, is not converted into *ESC F1*.

21.12 Changing Key Bindings

The way to rebind a key is to change its entry in a keymap. If you change a binding in the global keymap, the change is effective in all buffers (though it has no direct effect in buffers that shadow the global binding with a local one). If you change the current buffer's local map, that usually affects all buffers using the same major mode. The `global-set-key` and `local-set-key` functions are convenient interfaces for these operations (see Section 21.15 [Key Binding Commands], page 412). You can also use `define-key`, a more general function; then you must explicitly specify the map to change.

    When choosing the key sequences for Lisp programs to rebind, please follow the Emacs conventions for use of various keys (see Section D.2 [Key Binding Conventions], page 1056).

    In writing the key sequence to rebind, it is good to use the special escape sequences for control and meta characters (see Section 2.3.8 [String Type], page 18). The syntax '\C-' means that the following character is a control character and '\M-' means that the following character is a meta character. Thus, the string `"\M-x"` is read as containing a single *M-x*, `"\C-f"` is read as containing a single *C-f*, and `"\M-\C-x"` and `"\C-\M-x"` are both read as containing a single *C-M-x*. You can also use this escape syntax in vectors, as well as others that aren't allowed in strings; one example is '[?\C-\H-x home]'. See Section 2.3.3 [Character Type], page 10.

The key definition and lookup functions accept an alternate syntax for event types in a key sequence that is a vector: you can use a list containing modifier names plus one base event (a character or function key name). For example, (control ?a) is equivalent to ?\C-a and (hyper control left) is equivalent to C-H-left. One advantage of such lists is that the precise numeric codes for the modifier bits don't appear in compiled files.

The functions below signal an error if *keymap* is not a keymap, or if *key* is not a string or vector representing a key sequence. You can use event types (symbols) as shorthand for events that are lists. The kbd function (see Section 21.1 [Key Sequences], page 391) is a convenient way to specify the key sequence.

define-key *keymap key binding* [Function]

> This function sets the binding for *key* in *keymap*. (If *key* is more than one event long, the change is actually made in another keymap reached from *keymap*.) The argument *binding* can be any Lisp object, but only certain types are meaningful. (For a list of meaningful types, see Section 21.10 [Key Lookup], page 403.) The value returned by define-key is *binding*.
>
> If *key* is [t], this sets the default binding in *keymap*. When an event has no binding of its own, the Emacs command loop uses the keymap's default binding, if there is one.
>
> Every prefix of *key* must be a prefix key (i.e., bound to a keymap) or undefined; otherwise an error is signaled. If some prefix of *key* is undefined, then define-key defines it as a prefix key so that the rest of *key* can be defined as specified.
>
> If there was previously no binding for *key* in *keymap*, the new binding is added at the beginning of *keymap*. The order of bindings in a keymap makes no difference for keyboard input, but it does matter for menu keymaps (see Section 21.17 [Menu Keymaps], page 415).

This example creates a sparse keymap and makes a number of bindings in it:

```
(setq map (make-sparse-keymap))
    ⇒ (keymap)
(define-key map "\C-f" 'forward-char)
    ⇒ forward-char
map
    ⇒ (keymap (6 . forward-char))

;; Build sparse submap for C-x and bind f in that.
(define-key map (kbd "C-x f") 'forward-word)
    ⇒ forward-word
map
⇒ (keymap
    (24 keymap                  ; C-x
        (102 . forward-word)) ;      f
    (6 . forward-char))       ; C-f

;; Bind C-p to the ctl-x-map.
(define-key map (kbd "C-p") ctl-x-map)
;; ctl-x-map
⇒ [nil ... find-file ... backward-kill-sentence]

;; Bind C-f to foo in the ctl-x-map.
(define-key map (kbd "C-p C-f") 'foo)
⇒ 'foo
```

```
map
⇒ (keymap      ; Note foo in ctl-x-map.
    (16 keymap [nil ... foo ... backward-kill-sentence])
    (24 keymap
        (102 . forward-word))
    (6 . forward-char))
```

Note that storing a new binding for *C-p C-f* actually works by changing an entry in `ctl-x-map`, and this has the effect of changing the bindings of both *C-p C-f* and *C-x C-f* in the default global map.

The function `substitute-key-definition` scans a keymap for keys that have a certain binding and rebinds them with a different binding. Another feature which is cleaner and can often produce the same results is to remap one command into another (see Section 21.13 [Remapping Commands], page 409).

`substitute-key-definition` *olddef newdef keymap* **&optional**   [Function]
      oldmap

This function replaces *olddef* with *newdef* for any keys in *keymap* that were bound to *olddef*. In other words, *olddef* is replaced with *newdef* wherever it appears. The function returns `nil`.

For example, this redefines *C-x C-f*, if you do it in an Emacs with standard bindings:

```
(substitute-key-definition
   'find-file 'find-file-read-only (current-global-map))
```

If *oldmap* is non-`nil`, that changes the behavior of `substitute-key-definition`: the bindings in *oldmap* determine which keys to rebind. The rebindings still happen in *keymap*, not in *oldmap*. Thus, you can change one map under the control of the bindings in another. For example,

```
(substitute-key-definition
   'delete-backward-char 'my-funny-delete
   my-map global-map)
```

puts the special deletion command in `my-map` for whichever keys are globally bound to the standard deletion command.

Here is an example showing a keymap before and after substitution:

```
(setq map '(keymap
              (?1 . olddef-1)
              (?2 . olddef-2)
              (?3 . olddef-1)))
⇒ (keymap (49 . olddef-1) (50 . olddef-2) (51 . olddef-1))

(substitute-key-definition 'olddef-1 'newdef map)
⇒ nil
map
⇒ (keymap (49 . newdef) (50 . olddef-2) (51 . newdef))
```

`suppress-keymap` *keymap* **&optional** *nodigits*   [Function]

This function changes the contents of the full keymap *keymap* by remapping `self-insert-command` to the command `undefined` (see Section 21.13 [Remapping Commands], page 409). This has the effect of undefining all printing characters, thus making ordinary insertion of text impossible. `suppress-keymap` returns `nil`.

If *nodigits* is `nil`, then `suppress-keymap` defines digits to run `digit-argument`, and `-` to run `negative-argument`. Otherwise it makes them undefined like the rest of the printing characters.

The `suppress-keymap` function does not make it impossible to modify a buffer, as it does not suppress commands such as `yank` and `quoted-insert`. To prevent any modification of a buffer, make it read-only (see Section 26.7 [Read Only Buffers], page 558).

Since this function modifies *keymap*, you would normally use it on a newly created keymap. Operating on an existing keymap that is used for some other purpose is likely to cause trouble; for example, suppressing `global-map` would make it impossible to use most of Emacs.

This function can be used to initialize the local keymap of a major mode for which insertion of text is not desirable. But usually such a mode should be derived from `special-mode` (see Section 22.2.5 [Basic Major Modes], page 440); then its keymap will automatically inherit from `special-mode-map`, which is already suppressed. Here is how `special-mode-map` is defined:

```
(defvar special-mode-map
  (let ((map (make-sparse-keymap)))
    (suppress-keymap map)
    (define-key map "q" 'quit-window)
    ...
    map))
```

21.13 Remapping Commands

A special kind of key binding can be used to *remap* one command to another, without having to refer to the key sequence(s) bound to the original command. To use this feature, make a key binding for a key sequence that starts with the dummy event `remap`, followed by the command name you want to remap; for the binding, specify the new definition (usually a command name, but possibly any other valid definition for a key binding).

For example, suppose My mode provides a special command `my-kill-line`, which should be invoked instead of `kill-line`. To establish this, its mode keymap should contain the following remapping:

```
(define-key my-mode-map [remap kill-line] 'my-kill-line)
```

Then, whenever `my-mode-map` is active, if the user types `C-k` (the default global key sequence for `kill-line`) Emacs will instead run `my-kill-line`.

Note that remapping only takes place through active keymaps; for example, putting a remapping in a prefix keymap like `ctl-x-map` typically has no effect, as such keymaps are not themselves active. In addition, remapping only works through a single level; in the following example,

```
(define-key my-mode-map [remap kill-line] 'my-kill-line)
(define-key my-mode-map [remap my-kill-line] 'my-other-kill-line)
```

`kill-line` is *not* remapped to `my-other-kill-line`. Instead, if an ordinary key binding specifies `kill-line`, it is remapped to `my-kill-line`; if an ordinary binding specifies `my-kill-line`, it is remapped to `my-other-kill-line`.

To undo the remapping of a command, remap it to `nil`; e.g.,

```
(define-key my-mode-map [remap kill-line] nil)
```

`command-remapping` *command* **&optional** *position keymaps* [Function]
> This function returns the remapping for *command* (a symbol), given the current active keymaps. If *command* is not remapped (which is the usual situation), or not a symbol, the function returns `nil`. `position` can optionally specify a buffer position or an event position to determine the keymaps to use, as in `key-binding`.
>
> If the optional argument `keymaps` is non-`nil`, it specifies a list of keymaps to search in. This argument is ignored if `position` is non-`nil`.

21.14 Keymaps for Translating Sequences of Events

When the `read-key-sequence` function reads a key sequence (see Section 20.8.1 [Key Sequence Input], page 373), it uses *translation keymaps* to translate certain event sequences into others. The translation keymaps are `input-decode-map`, `local-function-key-map`, and `key-translation-map` (in order of priority).

Translation keymaps have the same structure as other keymaps, but are used differently: they specify translations to make while reading key sequences, rather than bindings for complete key sequences. As each key sequence is read, it is checked against each translation keymap. If one of the translation keymaps binds *k* to a vector *v*, then whenever *k* appears as a sub-sequence *anywhere* in a key sequence, that sub-sequence is replaced with the events in *v*.

For example, VT100 terminals send *ESC O P* when the keypad key PF1 is pressed. On such terminals, Emacs must translate that sequence of events into a single event `pf1`. This is done by binding *ESC O P* to `[pf1]` in `input-decode-map`. Thus, when you type *C-c PF1* on the terminal, the terminal emits the character sequence *C-c ESC O P*, and `read-key-sequence` translates this back into *C-c PF1* and returns it as the vector `[?\C-c pf1]`.

Translation keymaps take effect only after Emacs has decoded the keyboard input (via the input coding system specified by `keyboard-coding-system`). See Section 32.10.8 [Terminal I/O Encoding], page 786.

`input-decode-map` [Variable]
> This variable holds a keymap that describes the character sequences sent by function keys on an ordinary character terminal.
>
> The value of `input-decode-map` is usually set up automatically according to the terminal's Terminfo or Termcap entry, but sometimes those need help from terminal-specific Lisp files. Emacs comes with terminal-specific files for many common terminals; their main purpose is to make entries in `input-decode-map` beyond those that can be deduced from Termcap and Terminfo. See Section 38.1.3 [Terminal-Specific], page 989.

`local-function-key-map` [Variable]
> This variable holds a keymap similar to `input-decode-map` except that it describes key sequences which should be translated to alternative interpretations that are usually preferred. It applies after `input-decode-map` and before `key-translation-map`.
>
> Entries in `local-function-key-map` are ignored if they conflict with bindings made in the minor mode, local, or global keymaps. I.e., the remapping only applies if the original key sequence would otherwise not have any binding.

local-function-key-map inherits from function-key-map, but the latter should not be used directly.

key-translation-map   [Variable]
> This variable is another keymap used just like input-decode-map to translate input events into other events. It differs from input-decode-map in that it goes to work after local-function-key-map is finished rather than before; it receives the results of translation by local-function-key-map.
>
> Just like input-decode-map, but unlike local-function-key-map, this keymap is applied regardless of whether the input key-sequence has a normal binding. Note however that actual key bindings can have an effect on key-translation-map, even though they are overridden by it. Indeed, actual key bindings override local-function-key-map and thus may alter the key sequence that key-translation-map receives. Clearly, it is better to avoid this type of situation.
>
> The intent of key-translation-map is for users to map one character set to another, including ordinary characters normally bound to self-insert-command.

You can use input-decode-map, local-function-key-map, and key-translation-map for more than simple aliases, by using a function, instead of a key sequence, as the translation of a key. Then this function is called to compute the translation of that key.

The key translation function receives one argument, which is the prompt that was specified in read-key-sequence—or nil if the key sequence is being read by the editor command loop. In most cases you can ignore the prompt value.

If the function reads input itself, it can have the effect of altering the event that follows. For example, here's how to define C-c h to turn the character that follows into a Hyper character:

```
(defun hyperify (prompt)
  (let ((e (read-event)))
    (vector (if (numberp e)
                (logior (lsh 1 24) e)
              (if (memq 'hyper (event-modifiers e))
                  e
                (add-event-modifier "H-" e)))))))

(defun add-event-modifier (string e)
  (let ((symbol (if (symbolp e) e (car e))))
    (setq symbol (intern (concat string
                                 (symbol-name symbol))))
    (if (symbolp e)
        symbol
      (cons symbol (cdr e)))))

(define-key local-function-key-map "\C-ch" 'hyperify)
```

21.14.1 Interaction with normal keymaps

The end of a key sequence is detected when that key sequence either is bound to a command, or when Emacs determines that no additional event can lead to a sequence that is bound to a command.

This means that, while `input-decode-map` and `key-translation-map` apply regardless of whether the original key sequence would have a binding, the presence of such a binding can still prevent translation from taking place. For example, let us return to our VT100 example above and add a binding for *C-c ESC* to the global map; now when the user hits *C-c PF1* Emacs will fail to decode *C-c ESC O P* into *C-c PF1* because it will stop reading keys right after *C-x ESC*, leaving *O P* for later. This is in case the user really hit *C-c ESC*, in which case Emacs should not sit there waiting for the next key to decide whether the user really pressed ESC or PF1.

For that reason, it is better to avoid binding commands to key sequences where the end of the key sequence is a prefix of a key translation. The main such problematic suffixes/prefixes are ESC, *M-O* (which is really *ESC O*) and *M-[* (which is really *ESC [*).

21.15 Commands for Binding Keys

This section describes some convenient interactive interfaces for changing key bindings. They work by calling **define-key**.

People often use `global-set-key` in their init files (see Section 38.1.2 [Init File], page 988) for simple customization. For example,

    (global-set-key (kbd "C-x C-\\") 'next-line)

or

    (global-set-key [?\C-x ?\C-\\] 'next-line)

or

    (global-set-key [(control ?x) (control ?\\)] 'next-line)

redefines *C-x C-* to move down a line.

    (global-set-key [M-mouse-1] 'mouse-set-point)

redefines the first (leftmost) mouse button, entered with the Meta key, to set point where you click.

Be careful when using non-ASCII text characters in Lisp specifications of keys to bind. If these are read as multibyte text, as they usually will be in a Lisp file (see Section 15.4 [Loading Non-ASCII], page 249), you must type the keys as multibyte too. For instance, if you use this:

    (global-set-key "ö" 'my-function) ; bind o-umlaut

or

    (global-set-key ?ö 'my-function) ; bind o-umlaut

and your language environment is multibyte Latin-1, these commands actually bind the multibyte character with code 246, not the byte code 246 (*M-v*) sent by a Latin-1 terminal. In order to use this binding, you need to teach Emacs how to decode the keyboard by using an appropriate input method (see Section "Input Methods" in *The GNU Emacs Manual*).

global-set-key *key binding*   [Command]

> This function sets the binding of *key* in the current global map to *binding*.
>
>   (global-set-key key binding)
>   ≡
>   (define-key (current-global-map) key binding)

global-unset-key *key*   [Command]

> This function removes the binding of *key* from the current global map.
>
> One use of this function is in preparation for defining a longer key that uses *key* as a prefix—which would not be allowed if *key* has a non-prefix binding. For example:
>
>   (global-unset-key "\C-l")
>   ⇒ nil
>   (global-set-key "\C-l\C-l" 'redraw-display)
>   ⇒ nil
>
> This function is equivalent to using **define-key** as follows:
>
>   (global-unset-key key)
>   ≡
>   (define-key (current-global-map) key nil)

local-set-key *key binding*   [Command]

> This function sets the binding of *key* in the current local keymap to *binding*.
>
>   (local-set-key key binding)
>   ≡
>   (define-key (current-local-map) key binding)

local-unset-key *key*   [Command]

> This function removes the binding of *key* from the current local map.
>
>   (local-unset-key key)
>   ≡
>   (define-key (current-local-map) key nil)

21.16 Scanning Keymaps

This section describes functions used to scan all the current keymaps for the sake of printing help information.

accessible-keymaps *keymap* &optional *prefix*   [Function]

> This function returns a list of all the keymaps that can be reached (via zero or more prefix keys) from *keymap*. The value is an association list with elements of the form (*key . map*), where *key* is a prefix key whose definition in *keymap* is *map*.
>
> The elements of the alist are ordered so that the *key* increases in length. The first element is always ([] . *keymap*), because the specified keymap is accessible from itself with a prefix of no events.
>
> If *prefix* is given, it should be a prefix key sequence; then **accessible-keymaps** includes only the submaps whose prefixes start with *prefix*. These elements look just as they do in the value of (**accessible-keymaps**); the only difference is that some elements are omitted.
>
> In the example below, the returned alist indicates that the key **ESC**, which is displayed as '^['', is a prefix key whose definition is the sparse keymap (**keymap (83 . center-paragraph) (115 . foo)**).

```
(accessible-keymaps (current-local-map))
⇒(([] keymap
    (27 keymap     ; Note this keymap for ESC is repeated below.
        (83 . center-paragraph)
        (115 . center-line))
    (9 . tab-to-tab-stop))

  ("^[" keymap
   (83 . center-paragraph)
   (115 . foo)))
```

In the following example, *C-h* is a prefix key that uses a sparse keymap starting with
`(keymap (118 . describe-variable)...)`. Another prefix, *C-x 4*, uses a keymap
which is also the value of the variable `ctl-x-4-map`. The event `mode-line` is one of
several dummy events used as prefixes for mouse actions in special parts of a window.

```
(accessible-keymaps (current-global-map))
⇒ (([] keymap [set-mark-command beginning-of-line ...
                    delete-backward-char])
   ("^H" keymap (118 . describe-variable) ...
    (8 . help-for-help))
   ("^X" keymap [x-flush-mouse-queue ...
    backward-kill-sentence])
   ("^[" keymap [mark-sexp backward-sexp ...
    backward-kill-word])
   ("^X4" keymap (15 . display-buffer) ...)
   ([mode-line] keymap
    (S-mouse-2 . mouse-split-window-horizontally) ...))
```

These are not all the keymaps you would see in actuality.

map-keymap *function keymap*   [Function]

The function **map-keymap** calls *function* once for each binding in *keymap*. It passes
two arguments, the event type and the value of the binding. If *keymap* has a parent,
the parent's bindings are included as well. This works recursively: if the parent has
itself a parent, then the grandparent's bindings are also included and so on.

This function is the cleanest way to examine all the bindings in a keymap.

where-is-internal *command* **&optional** *keymap firstonly noindirect*   [Function]
        no-remap

This function is a subroutine used by the **where-is** command (see Section "Help" in
The GNU Emacs Manual). It returns a list of all key sequences (of any length) that
are bound to *command* in a set of keymaps.

The argument *command* can be any object; it is compared with all keymap entries
using **eq**.

If *keymap* is **nil**, then the maps used are the current active keymaps, disregarding
overriding-local-map (that is, pretending its value is **nil**). If *keymap* is a keymap,
then the maps searched are *keymap* and the global keymap. If *keymap* is a list of
keymaps, only those keymaps are searched.

Usually it's best to use **overriding-local-map** as the expression for *keymap*. Then
where-is-internal searches precisely the keymaps that are active. To search only
the global map, pass the value **(keymap)** (an empty keymap) as *keymap*.

If *firstonly* is `non-ascii`, then the value is a single vector representing the first key sequence found, rather than a list of all possible key sequences. If *firstonly* is `t`, then the value is the first key sequence, except that key sequences consisting entirely of ASCII characters (or meta variants of ASCII characters) are preferred to all other key sequences and that the return value can never be a menu binding.

If *noindirect* is non-`nil`, `where-is-internal` doesn't look inside menu-items to find their commands. This makes it possible to search for a menu-item itself.

The fifth argument, *no-remap*, determines how this function treats command remappings (see Section 21.13 [Remapping Commands], page 409). There are two cases of interest:

If a command *other-command* is remapped to *command*:

> If *no-remap* is `nil`, find the bindings for *other-command* and treat them as though they are also bindings for *command*. If *no-remap* is non-`nil`, include the vector [`remap` *other-command*] in the list of possible key sequences, instead of finding those bindings.

If *command* is remapped to *other-command*:

> If *no-remap* is `nil`, return the bindings for *other-command* rather than *command*. If *no-remap* is non-`nil`, return the bindings for *command*, ignoring the fact that it is remapped.

`describe-bindings` &optional *prefix buffer-or-name*   [Command]
> This function creates a listing of all current key bindings, and displays it in a buffer named `*Help*`. The text is grouped by modes—minor modes first, then the major mode, then global bindings.
>
> If *prefix* is non-`nil`, it should be a prefix key; then the listing includes only keys that start with *prefix*.
>
> When several characters with consecutive ASCII codes have the same definition, they are shown together, as '`firstchar..lastchar`'. In this instance, you need to know the ASCII codes to understand which characters this means. For example, in the default global map, the characters '`SPC .. ~`' are described by a single line. `SPC` is ASCII 32, `~` is ASCII 126, and the characters between them include all the normal printing characters, (e.g., letters, digits, punctuation, etc.); all these characters are bound to `self-insert-command`.
>
> If *buffer-or-name* is non-`nil`, it should be a buffer or a buffer name. Then `describe-bindings` lists that buffer's bindings, instead of the current buffer's.

21.17 Menu Keymaps

A keymap can operate as a menu as well as defining bindings for keyboard keys and mouse buttons. Menus are usually actuated with the mouse, but they can function with the keyboard also. If a menu keymap is active for the next input event, that activates the keyboard menu feature.

21.17.1 Defining Menus

A keymap acts as a menu if it has an *overall prompt string*, which is a string that appears as an element of the keymap. (See Section 21.3 [Format of Keymaps], page 392.) The string should describe the purpose of the menu's commands. Emacs displays the overall prompt string as the menu title in some cases, depending on the toolkit (if any) used for displaying menus.[1] Keyboard menus also display the overall prompt string.

The easiest way to construct a keymap with a prompt string is to specify the string as an argument when you call `make-keymap`, `make-sparse-keymap` (see Section 21.4 [Creating Keymaps], page 394), or `define-prefix-command` (see [Definition of define-prefix-command], page 398). If you do not want the keymap to operate as a menu, don't specify a prompt string for it.

`keymap-prompt` *keymap*   [Function]
> This function returns the overall prompt string of *keymap*, or `nil` if it has none.

The menu's items are the bindings in the keymap. Each binding associates an event type to a definition, but the event types have no significance for the menu appearance. (Usually we use pseudo-events, symbols that the keyboard cannot generate, as the event types for menu item bindings.) The menu is generated entirely from the bindings that correspond in the keymap to these events.

The order of items in the menu is the same as the order of bindings in the keymap. Since `define-key` puts new bindings at the front, you should define the menu items starting at the bottom of the menu and moving to the top, if you care about the order. When you add an item to an existing menu, you can specify its position in the menu using `define-key-after` (see Section 21.17.7 [Modifying Menus], page 426).

21.17.1.1 Simple Menu Items

The simpler (and original) way to define a menu item is to bind some event type (it doesn't matter what event type) to a binding like this:

> `(item-string . real-binding)`

The CAR, *item-string*, is the string to be displayed in the menu. It should be short— preferably one to three words. It should describe the action of the command it corresponds to. Note that not all graphical toolkits can display non-ASCII text in menus (it will work for keyboard menus and will work to a large extent with the GTK+ toolkit).

You can also supply a second string, called the help string, as follows:

> `(item-string help . real-binding)`

help specifies a help-echo string to display while the mouse is on that item in the same way as `help-echo` text properties (see [Help display], page 743).

As far as `define-key` is concerned, *item-string* and *help-string* are part of the event's binding. However, `lookup-key` returns just *real-binding*, and only *real-binding* is used for executing the key.

If *real-binding* is `nil`, then *item-string* appears in the menu but cannot be selected.

If *real-binding* is a symbol and has a non-`nil` `menu-enable` property, that property is an expression that controls whether the menu item is enabled. Every time the keymap is used to display a menu, Emacs evaluates the expression, and it enables the menu item only if the expression's value is non-`nil`. When a menu item is disabled, it is displayed in a fuzzy fashion, and cannot be selected.

---

[1] It is required for menus which do not use a toolkit, e.g., on a text terminal.

The menu bar does not recalculate which items are enabled every time you look at a menu. This is because the X toolkit requires the whole tree of menus in advance. To force recalculation of the menu bar, call `force-mode-line-update` (see Section 22.4 [Mode Line Format], page 451).

21.17.1.2 Extended Menu Items

An extended-format menu item is a more flexible and also cleaner alternative to the simple format. You define an event type with a binding that's a list starting with the symbol `menu-item`. For a non-selectable string, the binding looks like this:

```
(menu-item item-name)
```

A string starting with two or more dashes specifies a separator line; see Section 21.17.1.3 [Menu Separators], page 418.

To define a real menu item which can be selected, the extended format binding looks like this:

```
(menu-item item-name real-binding
    . item-property-list)
```

Here, *item-name* is an expression which evaluates to the menu item string. Thus, the string need not be a constant. The third element, *real-binding*, is the command to execute. The tail of the list, *item-property-list*, has the form of a property list which contains other information.

Here is a table of the properties that are supported:

`:enable` *form*

> The result of evaluating *form* determines whether the item is enabled (non-`nil` means yes). If the item is not enabled, you can't really click on it.

`:visible` *form*

> The result of evaluating *form* determines whether the item should actually appear in the menu (non-`nil` means yes). If the item does not appear, then the menu is displayed as if this item were not defined at all.

`:help` *help*

> The value of this property, *help*, specifies a help-echo string to display while the mouse is on that item. This is displayed in the same way as `help-echo` text properties (see [Help display], page 743). Note that this must be a constant string, unlike the `help-echo` property for text and overlays.

`:button` (*type* . *selected*)

> This property provides a way to define radio buttons and toggle buttons. The CAR, *type*, says which: it should be `:toggle` or `:radio`. The CDR, *selected*, should be a form; the result of evaluating it says whether this button is currently selected.
>
> A *toggle* is a menu item which is labeled as either on or off according to the value of *selected*. The command itself should toggle *selected*, setting it to `t` if it is `nil`, and to `nil` if it is `t`. Here is how the menu item to toggle the `debug-on-error` flag is defined:
>
> ```
> (menu-item "Debug on Error" toggle-debug-on-error
> ```

```
                        :button (:toggle
                                 . (and (boundp 'debug-on-error)
                                        debug-on-error)))
```

This works because `toggle-debug-on-error` is defined as a command which toggles the variable `debug-on-error`.

Radio buttons are a group of menu items, in which at any time one and only one is selected. There should be a variable whose value says which one is selected at any time. The *selected* form for each radio button in the group should check whether the variable has the right value for selecting that button. Clicking on the button should set the variable so that the button you clicked on becomes selected.

`:key-sequence` *key-sequence*

This property specifies which key sequence is likely to be bound to the same command invoked by this menu item. If you specify the right key sequence, that makes preparing the menu for display run much faster.

If you specify the wrong key sequence, it has no effect; before Emacs displays *key-sequence* in the menu, it verifies that *key-sequence* is really equivalent to this menu item.

`:key-sequence nil`

This property indicates that there is normally no key binding which is equivalent to this menu item. Using this property saves time in preparing the menu for display, because Emacs does not need to search the keymaps for a keyboard equivalent for this menu item.

However, if the user has rebound this item's definition to a key sequence, Emacs ignores the `:keys` property and finds the keyboard equivalent anyway.

`:keys` *string*

This property specifies that *string* is the string to display as the keyboard equivalent for this menu item. You can use the '`\\[...]`' documentation construct in *string*.

`:filter` *filter-fn*

This property provides a way to compute the menu item dynamically. The property value *filter-fn* should be a function of one argument; when it is called, its argument will be *real-binding*. The function should return the binding to use instead.

Emacs can call this function at any time that it does redisplay or operates on menu data structures, so you should write it so it can safely be called at any time.

21.17.1.3 Menu Separators

A menu separator is a kind of menu item that doesn't display any text—instead, it divides the menu into subparts with a horizontal line. A separator looks like this in the menu keymap:

```
(menu-item separator-type)
```

where *separator-type* is a string starting with two or more dashes.

In the simplest case, *separator-type* consists of only dashes. That specifies the default kind of separator. (For compatibility, `""` and `-` also count as separators.)

Certain other values of *separator-type* specify a different style of separator. Here is a table of them:

`"--no-line"`

`"--space"`
> An extra vertical space, with no actual line.

`"--single-line"`
> A single line in the menu's foreground color.

`"--double-line"`
> A double line in the menu's foreground color.

`"--single-dashed-line"`
> A single dashed line in the menu's foreground color.

`"--double-dashed-line"`
> A double dashed line in the menu's foreground color.

`"--shadow-etched-in"`
> A single line with a 3D sunken appearance. This is the default, used separators consisting of dashes only.

`"--shadow-etched-out"`
> A single line with a 3D raised appearance.

`"--shadow-etched-in-dash"`
> A single dashed line with a 3D sunken appearance.

`"--shadow-etched-out-dash"`
> A single dashed line with a 3D raised appearance.

`"--shadow-double-etched-in"`
> Two lines with a 3D sunken appearance.

`"--shadow-double-etched-out"`
> Two lines with a 3D raised appearance.

`"--shadow-double-etched-in-dash"`
> Two dashed lines with a 3D sunken appearance.

`"--shadow-double-etched-out-dash"`
> Two dashed lines with a 3D raised appearance.

You can also give these names in another style, adding a colon after the double-dash and replacing each single dash with capitalization of the following word. Thus, `"--:singleLine"`, is equivalent to `"--single-line"`.

You can use a longer form to specify keywords such as `:enable` and `:visible` for a menu separator:

> `(menu-item` *separator-type* `nil . ` *item-property-list*`)`

For example:

> `(menu-item "--" nil :visible (boundp 'foo))`

Some systems and display toolkits don't really handle all of these separator types. If you use a type that isn't supported, the menu displays a similar kind of separator that is supported.

21.17.1.4 Alias Menu Items

Sometimes it is useful to make menu items that use the same command but with different enable conditions. The best way to do this in Emacs now is with extended menu items; before that feature existed, it could be done by defining alias commands and using them in menu items. Here's an example that makes two aliases for `read-only-mode` and gives them different enable conditions:

```
(defalias 'make-read-only 'read-only-mode)
(put 'make-read-only 'menu-enable '(not buffer-read-only))
(defalias 'make-writable 'read-only-mode)
(put 'make-writable 'menu-enable 'buffer-read-only)
```

When using aliases in menus, often it is useful to display the equivalent key bindings for the real command name, not the aliases (which typically don't have any key bindings except for the menu itself). To request this, give the alias symbol a non-`nil` `menu-alias` property. Thus,

```
(put 'make-read-only 'menu-alias t)
(put 'make-writable 'menu-alias t)
```

causes menu items for `make-read-only` and `make-writable` to show the keyboard bindings for `read-only-mode`.

21.17.2 Menus and the Mouse

The usual way to make a menu keymap produce a menu is to make it the definition of a prefix key. (A Lisp program can explicitly pop up a menu and receive the user's choice—see Section 28.16 [Pop-Up Menus], page 662.)

If the prefix key ends with a mouse event, Emacs handles the menu keymap by popping up a visible menu, so that the user can select a choice with the mouse. When the user clicks on a menu item, the event generated is whatever character or symbol has the binding that brought about that menu item. (A menu item may generate a series of events if the menu has multiple levels or comes from the menu bar.)

It's often best to use a button-down event to trigger the menu. Then the user can select a menu item by releasing the button.

If the menu keymap contains a binding to a nested keymap, the nested keymap specifies a *submenu*. There will be a menu item, labeled by the nested keymap's item string, and clicking on this item automatically pops up the specified submenu. As a special exception, if the menu keymap contains a single nested keymap and no other menu items, the menu shows the contents of the nested keymap directly, not as a submenu.

However, if Emacs is compiled without X toolkit support, or on text terminals, submenus are not supported. Each nested keymap is shown as a menu item, but clicking on it does not automatically pop up the submenu. If you wish to imitate the effect of submenus, you can do that by giving a nested keymap an item string which starts with '@'. This causes Emacs to display the nested keymap using a separate *menu pane*; the rest of the item string after the '@' is the pane label. If Emacs is compiled without X toolkit support, or if a menu

is displayed on a text terminal, menu panes are not used; in that case, a '@' at the beginning
of an item string is omitted when the menu label is displayed, and has no other effect.

21.17.3 Menus and the Keyboard

When a prefix key ending with a keyboard event (a character or function key) has a definition
that is a menu keymap, the keymap operates as a keyboard menu; the user specifies the
next event by choosing a menu item with the keyboard.

Emacs displays the keyboard menu with the map's overall prompt string, followed by
the alternatives (the item strings of the map's bindings), in the echo area. If the bindings
don't all fit at once, the user can type SPC to see the next line of alternatives. Successive
uses of SPC eventually get to the end of the menu and then cycle around to the beginning.
(The variable `menu-prompt-more-char` specifies which character is used for this; SPC is the
default.)

When the user has found the desired alternative from the menu, he or she should type
the corresponding character—the one whose binding is that alternative.

`menu-prompt-more-char`   [Variable]

> This variable specifies the character to use to ask to see the next line of a menu. Its
> initial value is 32, the code for SPC.

21.17.4 Menu Example

Here is a complete example of defining a menu keymap. It is the definition of the 'Replace'
submenu in the 'Edit' menu in the menu bar, and it uses the extended menu item format
(see Section 21.17.1.2 [Extended Menu Items], page 417). First we create the keymap, and
give it a name:

```
(defvar menu-bar-replace-menu (make-sparse-keymap "Replace"))
```

Next we define the menu items:

```
(define-key menu-bar-replace-menu [tags-repl-continue]
  '(menu-item "Continue Replace" tags-loop-continue
          :help "Continue last tags replace operation"))
(define-key menu-bar-replace-menu [tags-repl]
  '(menu-item "Replace in tagged files" tags-query-replace
          :help "Interactively replace a regexp in all tagged files"))
(define-key menu-bar-replace-menu [separator-replace-tags]
  '(menu-item "--"))
;; ...
```

Note the symbols which the bindings are made for; these appear inside square brackets, in
the key sequence being defined. In some cases, this symbol is the same as the command
name; sometimes it is different. These symbols are treated as function keys, but they are
not real function keys on the keyboard. They do not affect the functioning of the menu
itself, but they are echoed in the echo area when the user selects from the menu, and they
appear in the output of `where-is` and `apropos`.

The menu in this example is intended for use with the mouse. If a menu is intended
for use with the keyboard, that is, if it is bound to a key sequence ending with a keyboard
event, then the menu items should be bound to characters or real function keys, that can
be typed with the keyboard.

The binding whose definition is ("--") is a separator line. Like a real menu item, the separator has a key symbol, in this case `separator-replace-tags`. If one menu has two separators, they must have two different key symbols.

Here is how we make this menu appear as an item in the parent menu:

```
(define-key menu-bar-edit-menu [replace]
  (list 'menu-item "Replace" menu-bar-replace-menu))
```

Note that this incorporates the submenu keymap, which is the value of the variable `menu-bar-replace-menu`, rather than the symbol `menu-bar-replace-menu` itself. Using that symbol in the parent menu item would be meaningless because `menu-bar-replace-menu` is not a command.

If you wanted to attach the same replace menu to a mouse click, you can do it this way:

```
(define-key global-map [C-S-down-mouse-1]
  menu-bar-replace-menu)
```

21.17.5 The Menu Bar

Emacs usually shows a *menu bar* at the top of each frame. See Section "Menu Bars" in *The GNU Emacs Manual*. Menu bar items are subcommands of the fake function key `menu-bar`, as defined in the active keymaps.

To add an item to the menu bar, invent a fake function key of your own (let's call it *key*), and make a binding for the key sequence [`menu-bar` *key*]. Most often, the binding is a menu keymap, so that pressing a button on the menu bar item leads to another menu.

When more than one active keymap defines the same function key for the menu bar, the item appears just once. If the user clicks on that menu bar item, it brings up a single, combined menu containing all the subcommands of that item—the global subcommands, the local subcommands, and the minor mode subcommands.

The variable `overriding-local-map` is normally ignored when determining the menu bar contents. That is, the menu bar is computed from the keymaps that would be active if `overriding-local-map` were `nil`. See Section 21.7 [Active Keymaps], page 398.

Here's an example of setting up a menu bar item:

```
;; Make a menu keymap (with a prompt string)
;; and make it the menu bar itemfls definition.
(define-key global-map [menu-bar words]
  (cons "Words" (make-sparse-keymap "Words")))

;; Define specific subcommands in this menu.
(define-key global-map
  [menu-bar words forward]
  '("Forward word" . forward-word))
(define-key global-map
  [menu-bar words backward]
  '("Backward word" . backward-word))
```

A local keymap can cancel a menu bar item made by the global keymap by rebinding the same fake function key with `undefined` as the binding. For example, this is how Dired suppresses the 'Edit' menu bar item:

```
(define-key dired-mode-map [menu-bar edit] 'undefined)
```

Here, `edit` is the fake function key used by the global map for the 'Edit' menu bar item. The main reason to suppress a global menu bar item is to regain space for mode-specific items.

`menu-bar-final-items` [Variable]
> Normally the menu bar shows global items followed by items defined by the local maps.
>
> This variable holds a list of fake function keys for items to display at the end of the menu bar rather than in normal sequence. The default value is (`help-menu`); thus, the 'Help' menu item normally appears at the end of the menu bar, following local menu items.

`menu-bar-update-hook` [Variable]
> This normal hook is run by redisplay to update the menu bar contents, before redisplaying the menu bar. You can use it to update menus whose contents should vary. Since this hook is run frequently, we advise you to ensure that the functions it calls do not take much time in the usual case.

Next to every menu bar item, Emacs displays a key binding that runs the same command (if such a key binding exists). This serves as a convenient hint for users who do not know the key binding. If a command has multiple bindings, Emacs normally displays the first one it finds. You can specify one particular key binding by assigning an `:advertised-binding` symbol property to the command. See Section 23.3 [Keys in Documentation], page 488.

21.17.6 Tool bars

A *tool bar* is a row of clickable icons at the top of a frame, just below the menu bar. See Section "Tool Bars" in *The GNU Emacs Manual*. Emacs normally shows a tool bar on graphical displays.

On each frame, the frame parameter `tool-bar-lines` controls how many lines' worth of height to reserve for the tool bar. A zero value suppresses the tool bar. If the value is nonzero, and `auto-resize-tool-bars` is non-`nil`, the tool bar expands and contracts automatically as needed to hold the specified contents. If the value is `grow-only`, the tool bar expands automatically, but does not contract automatically.

The tool bar contents are controlled by a menu keymap attached to a fake function key called `tool-bar` (much like the way the menu bar is controlled). So you define a tool bar item using `define-key`, like this:

```
(define-key global-map [tool-bar key] item)
```

where *key* is a fake function key to distinguish this item from other items, and *item* is a menu item key binding (see Section 21.17.1.2 [Extended Menu Items], page 417), which says how to display this item and how it behaves.

The usual menu keymap item properties, `:visible`, `:enable`, `:button`, and `:filter`, are useful in tool bar bindings and have their normal meanings. The *real-binding* in the item must be a command, not a keymap; in other words, it does not work to define a tool bar icon as a prefix key.

The `:help` property specifies a help-echo string to display while the mouse is on that item. This is displayed in the same way as `help-echo` text properties (see [Help display], page 743).

In addition, you should use the :image property; this is how you specify the image to display in the tool bar:

:image *image*

> *image* is either a single image specification (see Section 37.17 [Images], page 950) or a vector of four image specifications. If you use a vector of four, one of them is used, depending on circumstances:
>
> item 0   Used when the item is enabled and selected.
>
> item 1   Used when the item is enabled and deselected.
>
> item 2   Used when the item is disabled and selected.
>
> item 3   Used when the item is disabled and deselected.

The GTK+ and NS versions of Emacs ignores items 1 to 3, because disabled and/or deselected images are autocomputed from item 0.

If *image* is a single image specification, Emacs draws the tool bar button in disabled state by applying an edge-detection algorithm to the image.

The :rtl property specifies an alternative image to use for right-to-left languages. Only the GTK+ version of Emacs supports this at present.

Like the menu bar, the tool bar can display separators (see Section 21.17.1.3 [Menu Separators], page 418). Tool bar separators are vertical rather than horizontal, though, and only a single style is supported. They are represented in the tool bar keymap by (menu-item "--") entries; properties like :visible are not supported for tool bar separators. Separators are rendered natively in GTK+ and Nextstep tool bars; in the other cases, they are rendered using an image of a vertical line.

The default tool bar is defined so that items specific to editing do not appear for major modes whose command symbol has a mode-class property of special (see Section 22.2.1 [Major Mode Conventions], page 432). Major modes may add items to the global bar by binding [tool-bar *foo*] in their local map. It makes sense for some major modes to replace the default tool bar items completely, since not many can be accommodated conveniently, and the default bindings make this easy by using an indirection through tool-bar-map.

tool-bar-map   [Variable]

> By default, the global map binds [tool-bar] as follows:
>
>   (global-set-key [tool-bar]
>   `(menu-item ,(purecopy "tool bar") ignore
>   :filter tool-bar-make-keymap))

The function tool-bar-make-keymap, in turn, derives the actual tool bar map dynamically from the value of the variable tool-bar-map. Hence, you should normally adjust the default (global) tool bar by changing that map. Some major modes, such as Info mode, completely replace the global tool bar by making tool-bar-map buffer-local and setting it to a different keymap.

There are two convenience functions for defining tool bar items, as follows.

tool-bar-add-item *icon def key* **&rest** *props*   [Function]

> This function adds an item to the tool bar by modifying `tool-bar-map`. The image
> to use is defined by *icon*, which is the base name of an XPM, XBM or PBM image file
> to be located by `find-image`. Given a value '`"exit"`', say, `exit.xpm`, `exit.pbm` and
> `exit.xbm` would be searched for in that order on a color display. On a monochrome
> display, the search order is '.pbm', '.xbm' and '.xpm'. The binding to use is the
> command *def*, and *key* is the fake function key symbol in the prefix keymap. The
> remaining arguments *props* are additional property list elements to add to the menu
> item specification.

> To define items in some local map, bind `tool-bar-map` with `let` around calls of this
> function:

```
(defvar foo-tool-bar-map
  (let ((tool-bar-map (make-sparse-keymap)))
    (tool-bar-add-item ...)
    ...
    tool-bar-map))
```

tool-bar-add-item-from-menu *command icon* **&optional** *map* **&rest**   [Function]
          props

> This function is a convenience for defining tool bar items which are consistent with
> existing menu bar bindings. The binding of *command* is looked up in the menu bar
> in *map* (default `global-map`) and modified to add an image specification for *icon*,
> which is found in the same way as by `tool-bar-add-item`. The resulting binding is
> then placed in `tool-bar-map`, so use this function only for global tool bar items.

> *map* must contain an appropriate keymap bound to [menu-bar]. The remaining
> arguments *props* are additional property list elements to add to the menu item spec-
> ification.

tool-bar-local-item-from-menu *command icon in-map* **&optional**   [Function]
          from-map **&rest** *props*

> This function is used for making non-global tool bar items. Use it like `tool-bar-add-`
> `item-from-menu` except that *in-map* specifies the local map to make the definition
> in. The argument *from-map* is like the *map* argument of `tool-bar-add-item-from-`
> `menu`.

auto-resize-tool-bars   [Variable]

> If this variable is non-`nil`, the tool bar automatically resizes to show all defined tool
> bar items—but not larger than a quarter of the frame's height.

> If the value is `grow-only`, the tool bar expands automatically, but does not contract
> automatically. To contract the tool bar, the user has to redraw the frame by entering
> `C-l`.

> If Emacs is built with GTK or Nextstep, the tool bar can only show one line, so this
> variable has no effect.

auto-raise-tool-bar-buttons   [Variable]

> If this variable is non-`nil`, tool bar items display in raised form when the mouse
> moves over them.

`tool-bar-button-margin`   [Variable]
> This variable specifies an extra margin to add around tool bar items. The value is an integer, a number of pixels. The default is 4.

`tool-bar-button-relief`   [Variable]
> This variable specifies the shadow width for tool bar items. The value is an integer, a number of pixels. The default is 1.

`tool-bar-border`   [Variable]
> This variable specifies the height of the border drawn below the tool bar area. An integer specifies height as a number of pixels. If the value is one of `internal-border-width` (the default) or `border-width`, the tool bar border height corresponds to the corresponding frame parameter.

You can define a special meaning for clicking on a tool bar item with the shift, control, meta, etc., modifiers. You do this by setting up additional items that relate to the original item through the fake function keys. Specifically, the additional items should use the modified versions of the same fake function key used to name the original item.

Thus, if the original item was defined this way,

```
(define-key global-map [tool-bar shell]
  '(menu-item "Shell" shell
              :image (image :type xpm :file "shell.xpm")))
```

then here is how you can define clicking on the same tool bar image with the shift modifier:

```
(define-key global-map [tool-bar S-shell] 'some-command)
```

See Section 20.7.2 [Function Keys], page 359, for more information about how to add modifiers to function keys.

21.17.7 Modifying Menus

When you insert a new item in an existing menu, you probably want to put it in a particular place among the menu's existing items. If you use `define-key` to add the item, it normally goes at the front of the menu. To put it elsewhere in the menu, use `define-key-after`:

`define-key-after` *map key binding* **&optional** *after*   [Function]
> Define a binding in *map* for *key*, with value *binding*, just like `define-key`, but position the binding in *map* after the binding for the event *after*. The argument *key* should be of length one—a vector or string with just one element. But *after* should be a single event type—a symbol or a character, not a sequence. The new binding goes after the binding for *after*. If *after* is `t` or is omitted, then the new binding goes last, at the end of the keymap. However, new bindings are added before any inherited keymap.
>
> Here is an example:
>
> ```
> (define-key-after my-menu [drink]
>   '("Drink" . drink-command) 'eat)
> ```
>
> makes a binding for the fake function key `DRINK` and puts it right after the binding for `EAT`.
>
> Here is how to insert an item called 'Work' in the 'Signals' menu of Shell mode, after the item `break`:
>
> ```
> (define-key-after
> ```

```
(lookup-key shell-mode-map [menu-bar signals])
[work] '("Work" . work-command) 'break)
```

21.17.8 Easy Menu

The following macro provides a convenient way to define pop-up menus and/or menu bar menus.

easy-menu-define *symbol maps doc menu*   [Macro]

> This macro defines a pop-up menu and/or menu bar submenu, whose contents are given by *menu*.

> If *symbol* is non-**nil**, it should be a symbol; then this macro defines *symbol* as a function for popping up the menu (see Section 28.16 [Pop-Up Menus], page 662), with *doc* as its documentation string. *symbol* should not be quoted.

> Regardless of the value of *symbol*, if *maps* is a keymap, the menu is added to that keymap, as a top-level menu for the menu bar (see Section 21.17.5 [Menu Bar], page 422). It can also be a list of keymaps, in which case the menu is added separately to each of those keymaps.

> The first element of *menu* must be a string, which serves as the menu label. It may be followed by any number of the following keyword-argument pairs:

> **:filter** *function*
> > *function* must be a function which, if called with one argument—the list of the other menu items—returns the actual items to be displayed in the menu.

> **:visible** *include*
> > *include* is an expression; if it evaluates to **nil**, the menu is made invisible. **:included** is an alias for **:visible**.

> **:active** *enable*
> > *enable* is an expression; if it evaluates to **nil**, the menu is not selectable. **:enable** is an alias for **:active**.

> The remaining elements in *menu* are menu items.

> A menu item can be a vector of three elements, [*name callback enable*]. *name* is the menu item name (a string). *callback* is a command to run, or an expression to evaluate, when the item is chosen. *enable* is an expression; if it evaluates to **nil**, the item is disabled for selection.

> Alternatively, a menu item may have the form:

> > [*name callback* [*keyword arg*]...]

> where *name* and *callback* have the same meanings as above, and each optional *keyword* and *arg* pair should be one of the following:

> **:keys** *keys*
> > *keys* is a keyboard equivalent to the menu item (a string). This is normally not needed, as keyboard equivalents are computed automatically. *keys* is expanded with **substitute-command-keys** before it is displayed (see Section 23.3 [Keys in Documentation], page 488).

`:key-sequence` *keys*

> *keys* is a hint for speeding up Emacs's first display of the menu. It should be `nil` if you know that the menu item has no keyboard equivalent; otherwise it should be a string or vector specifying a keyboard equivalent for the menu item.

`:active` *enable*

> *enable* is an expression; if it evaluates to `nil`, the item is make unselectable.. `:enable` is an alias for `:active`.

`:visible` *include*

> *include* is an expression; if it evaluates to `nil`, the item is made invisible. `:included` is an alias for `:visible`.

`:label` *form*

> *form* is an expression that is evaluated to obtain a value which serves as the menu item's label (the default is *name*).

`:suffix` *form*

> *form* is an expression that is dynamically evaluated and whose value is concatenated with the menu entry's label.

`:style` *style*

> *style* is a symbol describing the type of menu item; it should be `toggle` (a checkbox), or `radio` (a radio button), or anything else (meaning an ordinary menu item).

`:selected` *selected*

> *selected* is an expression; the checkbox or radio button is selected whenever the expression's value is non-`nil`.

`:help` *help*

> *help* is a string describing the menu item.

Alternatively, a menu item can be a string. Then that string appears in the menu as unselectable text. A string consisting of dashes is displayed as a separator (see Section 21.17.1.3 [Menu Separators], page 418).

Alternatively, a menu item can be a list with the same format as *menu*. This is a submenu.

Here is an example of using `easy-menu-define` to define a menu similar to the one defined in the example in Section 21.17.5 [Menu Bar], page 422:

```
(easy-menu-define words-menu global-map
  "Menu for word navigation commands."
  '("Words"
    ["Forward word" forward-word]
    ["Backward word" backward-word]))
```

22 Major and Minor Modes

A *mode* is a set of definitions that customize Emacs behavior in useful ways. There are two varieties of modes: *minor modes*, which provide features that users can turn on and off while editing; and *major modes*, which are used for editing or interacting with a particular kind of text. Each buffer has exactly one *major mode* at a time.

This chapter describes how to write both major and minor modes, how to indicate them in the mode line, and how they run hooks supplied by the user. For related topics such as keymaps and syntax tables, see Chapter 21 [Keymaps], page 391, and Chapter 34 [Syntax Tables], page 816.

22.1 Hooks

A *hook* is a variable where you can store a function or functions to be called on a particular occasion by an existing program. Emacs provides hooks for the sake of customization. Most often, hooks are set up in the init file (see Section 38.1.2 [Init File], page 988), but Lisp programs can set them also. See Appendix H [Standard Hooks], page 1098, for a list of some standard hook variables.

Most of the hooks in Emacs are *normal hooks*. These variables contain lists of functions to be called with no arguments. By convention, whenever the hook name ends in '-hook', that tells you it is normal. We try to make all hooks normal, as much as possible, so that you can use them in a uniform way.

Every major mode command is supposed to run a normal hook called the *mode hook* as one of the last steps of initialization. This makes it easy for a user to customize the behavior of the mode, by overriding the buffer-local variable assignments already made by the mode. Most minor mode functions also run a mode hook at the end. But hooks are used in other contexts too. For example, the hook **suspend-hook** runs just before Emacs suspends itself (see Section 38.2.2 [Suspending Emacs], page 993).

The recommended way to add a hook function to a hook is by calling **add-hook** (see Section 22.1.2 [Setting Hooks], page 430). The hook functions may be any of the valid kinds of functions that **funcall** accepts (see Section 12.1 [What Is a Function], page 186). Most normal hook variables are initially void; **add-hook** knows how to deal with this. You can add hooks either globally or buffer-locally with **add-hook**.

If the hook variable's name does not end with '-hook', that indicates it is probably an *abnormal hook*. That means the hook functions are called with arguments, or their return values are used in some way. The hook's documentation says how the functions are called. You can use **add-hook** to add a function to an abnormal hook, but you must write the function to follow the hook's calling convention. By convention, abnormal hook names end in '-functions'.

If the variable's name ends in '-function', then its value is just a single function, not a list of functions. **add-hook** cannot be used to modify such a *single function hook*, and you have to use **add-function** instead (see Section 12.11 [Advising Functions], page 204).

22.1.1 Running Hooks

In this section, we document the **run-hooks** function, which is used to run a normal hook. We also document the functions for running various kinds of abnormal hooks.

run-hooks &rest *hookvars*   [Function]

> This function takes one or more normal hook variable names as arguments, and runs each hook in turn. Each argument should be a symbol that is a normal hook variable. These arguments are processed in the order specified.
>
> If a hook variable has a non-**nil** value, that value should be a list of functions. **run-hooks** calls all the functions, one by one, with no arguments.
>
> The hook variable's value can also be a single function—either a lambda expression or a symbol with a function definition—which **run-hooks** calls. But this usage is obsolete.
>
> If the hook variable is buffer-local, the buffer-local variable will be used instead of the global variable. However, if the buffer-local variable contains the element **t**, the global hook variable will be run as well.

run-hook-with-args *hook* **&rest** *args*   [Function]

> This function runs an abnormal hook by calling all the hook functions in *hook*, passing each one the arguments *args*.

run-hook-with-args-until-failure *hook* **&rest** *args*   [Function]

> This function runs an abnormal hook by calling each hook function in turn, stopping if one of them fails by returning **nil**. Each hook function is passed the arguments *args*. If this function stops because one of the hook functions fails, it returns **nil**; otherwise it returns a non-**nil** value.

run-hook-with-args-until-success *hook* **&rest** *args*   [Function]

> This function runs an abnormal hook by calling each hook function, stopping if one of them succeeds by returning a non-**nil** value. Each hook function is passed the arguments *args*. If this function stops because one of the hook functions returns a non-**nil** value, it returns that value; otherwise it returns **nil**.

22.1.2 Setting Hooks

Here's an example that uses a mode hook to turn on Auto Fill mode when in Lisp Interaction mode:

```
(add-hook 'lisp-interaction-mode-hook 'auto-fill-mode)
```

add-hook *hook function* **&optional** *append local*   [Function]

> This function is the handy way to add function *function* to hook variable *hook*. You can use it for abnormal hooks as well as for normal hooks. *function* can be any Lisp function that can accept the proper number of arguments for *hook*. For example,
>
> ```
> (add-hook 'text-mode-hook 'my-text-hook-function)
> ```
>
> adds **my-text-hook-function** to the hook called **text-mode-hook**.
>
> If *function* is already present in *hook* (comparing using **equal**), then **add-hook** does not add it a second time.
>
> If *function* has a non-**nil** property **permanent-local-hook**, then **kill-all-local-variables** (or changing major modes) won't delete it from the hook variable's local value.

For a normal hook, hook functions should be designed so that the order in which they are executed does not matter. Any dependence on the order is asking for trouble. However, the order is predictable: normally, *function* goes at the front of the hook list, so it is executed first (barring another `add-hook` call). If the optional argument *append* is non-`nil`, the new hook function goes at the end of the hook list and is executed last.

`add-hook` can handle the cases where *hook* is void or its value is a single function; it sets or changes the value to a list of functions.

If *local* is non-`nil`, that says to add *function* to the buffer-local hook list instead of to the global hook list. This makes the hook buffer-local and adds `t` to the buffer-local value. The latter acts as a flag to run the hook functions in the default value as well as in the local value.

remove-hook *hook function* **&optional** *local*   [Function]
This function removes *function* from the hook variable *hook*. It compares *function* with elements of *hook* using `equal`, so it works for both symbols and lambda expressions.

If *local* is non-`nil`, that says to remove *function* from the buffer-local hook list instead of from the global hook list.

22.2 Major Modes

Major modes specialize Emacs for editing or interacting with particular kinds of text. Each buffer has exactly one major mode at a time. Every major mode is associated with a *major mode command*, whose name should end in '`-mode`'. This command takes care of switching to that mode in the current buffer, by setting various buffer-local variables such as a local keymap. See Section 22.2.1 [Major Mode Conventions], page 432. Note that unlike minor modes there is no way to "turn off" a major mode, instead the buffer must be switched to a different one.

The least specialized major mode is called *Fundamental mode*, which has no mode-specific definitions or variable settings.

fundamental-mode   [Command]
This is the major mode command for Fundamental mode. Unlike other mode commands, it does *not* run any mode hooks (see Section 22.2.1 [Major Mode Conventions], page 432), since you are not supposed to customize this mode.

The easiest way to write a major mode is to use the macro `define-derived-mode`, which sets up the new mode as a variant of an existing major mode. See Section 22.2.4 [Derived Modes], page 438. We recommend using `define-derived-mode` even if the new mode is not an obvious derivative of another mode, as it automatically enforces many coding conventions for you. See Section 22.2.5 [Basic Major Modes], page 440, for common modes to derive from.

The standard GNU Emacs Lisp directory tree contains the code for several major modes, in files such as `text-mode.el`, `texinfo.el`, `lisp-mode.el`, and `rmail.el`. You can study these libraries to see how modes are written.

`major-mode`   [User Option]

    The buffer-local value of this variable holds the symbol for the current major mode. Its default value holds the default major mode for new buffers. The standard default value is `fundamental-mode`.

    If the default value is `nil`, then whenever Emacs creates a new buffer via a command such as *C-x b* (`switch-to-buffer`), the new buffer is put in the major mode of the previously current buffer. As an exception, if the major mode of the previous buffer has a `mode-class` symbol property with value `special`, the new buffer is put in Fundamental mode (see Section 22.2.1 [Major Mode Conventions], page 432).

22.2.1 Major Mode Conventions

The code for every major mode should follow various coding conventions, including conventions for local keymap and syntax table initialization, function and variable names, and hooks.

    If you use the `define-derived-mode` macro, it will take care of many of these conventions automatically. See Section 22.2.4 [Derived Modes], page 438. Note also that Fundamental mode is an exception to many of these conventions, because it represents the default state of Emacs.

    The following list of conventions is only partial. Each major mode should aim for consistency in general with other Emacs major modes, as this makes Emacs as a whole more coherent. It is impossible to list here all the possible points where this issue might come up; if the Emacs developers point out an area where your major mode deviates from the usual conventions, please make it compatible.

- Define a major mode command whose name ends in '`-mode`'. When called with no arguments, this command should switch to the new mode in the current buffer by setting up the keymap, syntax table, and buffer-local variables in an existing buffer. It should not change the buffer's contents.

- Write a documentation string for this command that describes the special commands available in this mode. See Section 22.2.3 [Mode Help], page 438.

  The documentation string may include the special documentation substrings, '`\[command]`', '`\{keymap}`', and '`\<keymap>`', which allow the help display to adapt automatically to the user's own key bindings. See Section 23.3 [Keys in Documentation], page 488.

- The major mode command should start by calling `kill-all-local-variables`. This runs the normal hook `change-major-mode-hook`, then gets rid of the buffer-local variables of the major mode previously in effect. See Section 11.10.2 [Creating Buffer-Local], page 172.

- The major mode command should set the variable `major-mode` to the major mode command symbol. This is how `describe-mode` discovers which documentation to print.

- The major mode command should set the variable `mode-name` to the "pretty" name of the mode, usually a string (but see Section 22.4.2 [Mode Line Data], page 452, for other possible forms). The name of the mode appears in the mode line.

- Since all global names are in the same name space, all the global variables, constants, and functions that are part of the mode should have names that start with the major mode name (or with an abbreviation of it if the name is long). See Section D.1 [Coding Conventions], page 1053.

- In a major mode for editing some kind of structured text, such as a programming language, indentation of text according to structure is probably useful. So the mode should set `indent-line-function` to a suitable function, and probably customize other variables for indentation. See Section 22.7 [Auto-Indentation], page 474.

- The major mode should usually have its own keymap, which is used as the local keymap in all buffers in that mode. The major mode command should call `use-local-map` to install this local map. See Section 21.7 [Active Keymaps], page 398, for more information.

  This keymap should be stored permanently in a global variable named *modename*-mode-map. Normally the library that defines the mode sets this variable.

  See Section 11.6 [Tips for Defining], page 163, for advice about how to write the code to set up the mode's keymap variable.

- The key sequences bound in a major mode keymap should usually start with *C-c*, followed by a control character, a digit, or *{*, *}*, *<*, *>*, *:* or *;*. The other punctuation characters are reserved for minor modes, and ordinary letters are reserved for users.

  A major mode can also rebind the keys *M-n*, *M-p* and *M-s*. The bindings for *M-n* and *M-p* should normally be some kind of moving forward and backward, but this does not necessarily mean cursor motion.

  It is legitimate for a major mode to rebind a standard key sequence if it provides a command that does the same job in a way better suited to the text this mode is used for. For example, a major mode for editing a programming language might redefine *C-M-a* to move to the beginning of a function in a way that works better for that language.

  It is also legitimate for a major mode to rebind a standard key sequence whose standard meaning is rarely useful in that mode. For instance, minibuffer modes rebind *M-r*, whose standard meaning is rarely of any use in the minibuffer. Major modes such as Dired or Rmail that do not allow self-insertion of text can reasonably redefine letters and other printing characters as special commands.

- Major modes for editing text should not define `RET` to do anything other than insert a newline. However, it is ok for specialized modes for text that users don't directly edit, such as Dired and Info modes, to redefine `RET` to do something entirely different.

- Major modes should not alter options that are primarily a matter of user preference, such as whether Auto-Fill mode is enabled. Leave this to each user to decide. However, a major mode should customize other variables so that Auto-Fill mode will work usefully *if* the user decides to use it.

- The mode may have its own syntax table or may share one with other related modes. If it has its own syntax table, it should store this in a variable named *modename*-mode-syntax-table. See Chapter 34 [Syntax Tables], page 816.

- If the mode handles a language that has a syntax for comments, it should set the variables that define the comment syntax. See Section "Options Controlling Comments" in *The GNU Emacs Manual*.

- The mode may have its own abbrev table or may share one with other related modes. If it has its own abbrev table, it should store this in a variable named *modename*-mode-

`abbrev-table`. If the major mode command defines any abbrevs itself, it should pass `t` for the *system-flag* argument to `define-abbrev`. See Section 35.2 [Defining Abbrevs], page 833.

- The mode should specify how to do highlighting for Font Lock mode, by setting up a buffer-local value for the variable `font-lock-defaults` (see Section 22.6 [Font Lock Mode], page 462).

- Each face that the mode defines should, if possible, inherit from an existing Emacs face. See Section 37.12.8 [Basic Faces], page 927, and Section 22.6.7 [Faces for Font Lock], page 470.

- The mode should specify how Imenu should find the definitions or sections of a buffer, by setting up a buffer-local value for the variable `imenu-generic-expression`, for the two variables `imenu-prev-index-position-function` and `imenu-extract-index-name-function`, or for the variable `imenu-create-index-function` (see Section 22.5 [Imenu], page 459).

- The mode can specify a local value for `eldoc-documentation-function` to tell ElDoc mode how to handle this mode.

- The mode can specify how to complete various keywords by adding one or more buffer-local entries to the special hook `completion-at-point-functions`. See Section 19.6.8 [Completion in Buffers], page 336.

- To make a buffer-local binding for an Emacs customization variable, use `make-local-variable` in the major mode command, not `make-variable-buffer-local`. The latter function would make the variable local to every buffer in which it is subsequently set, which would affect buffers that do not use this mode. It is undesirable for a mode to have such global effects. See Section 11.10 [Buffer-Local Variables], page 171.

  With rare exceptions, the only reasonable way to use `make-variable-buffer-local` in a Lisp package is for a variable which is used only within that package. Using it on a variable used by other packages would interfere with them.

- Each major mode should have a normal *mode hook* named *modename*-mode-hook. The very last thing the major mode command should do is to call `run-mode-hooks`. This runs the normal hook `change-major-mode-after-body-hook`, the mode hook, and then the normal hook `after-change-major-mode-hook`. See Section 22.2.6 [Mode Hooks], page 440.

- The major mode command may start by calling some other major mode command (called the *parent mode*) and then alter some of its settings. A mode that does this is called a *derived mode*. The recommended way to define one is to use the `define-derived-mode` macro, but this is not required. Such a mode should call the parent mode command inside a `delay-mode-hooks` form. (Using `define-derived-mode` does this automatically.) See Section 22.2.4 [Derived Modes], page 438, and Section 22.2.6 [Mode Hooks], page 440.

- If something special should be done if the user switches a buffer from this mode to any other major mode, this mode can set up a buffer-local value for `change-major-mode-hook` (see Section 11.10.2 [Creating Buffer-Local], page 172).

- If this mode is appropriate only for specially-prepared text produced by the mode itself (rather than by the user typing at the keyboard or by an external file), then the

major mode command symbol should have a property named `mode-class` with value
`special`, put on as follows:

```
(put 'funny-mode 'mode-class 'special)
```

This tells Emacs that new buffers created while the current buffer is in Funny mode
should not be put in Funny mode, even though the default value of `major-mode` is `nil`.
By default, the value of `nil` for `major-mode` means to use the current buffer's major
mode when creating new buffers (see Section 22.2.2 [Auto Major Mode], page 435), but
with such `special` modes, Fundamental mode is used instead. Modes such as Dired,
Rmail, and Buffer List use this feature.

The function `view-buffer` does not enable View mode in buffers whose mode-class is
special, because such modes usually provide their own View-like bindings.

The `define-derived-mode` macro automatically marks the derived mode as special
if the parent mode is special. Special mode is a convenient parent for such modes to
inherit from; See Section 22.2.5 [Basic Major Modes], page 440.

- If you want to make the new mode the default for files with certain recognizable names,
  add an element to `auto-mode-alist` to select the mode for those file names (see
  Section 22.2.2 [Auto Major Mode], page 435). If you define the mode command to
  autoload, you should add this element in the same file that calls `autoload`. If you use
  an autoload cookie for the mode command, you can also use an autoload cookie for the
  form that adds the element (see [autoload cookie], page 251). If you do not autoload
  the mode command, it is sufficient to add the element in the file that contains the mode
  definition.

- The top-level forms in the file defining the mode should be written so that they may
  be evaluated more than once without adverse consequences. For instance, use `defvar`
  or `defcustom` to set mode-related variables, so that they are not reinitialized if they
  already have a value (see Section 11.5 [Defining Variables], page 161).

22.2.2 How Emacs Chooses a Major Mode

When Emacs visits a file, it automatically selects a major mode for the buffer based on
information in the file name or in the file itself. It also processes local variables specified in
the file text.

`normal-mode` &optional *find-file*   [Command]

    This function establishes the proper major mode and buffer-local variable bindings for
    the current buffer. First it calls `set-auto-mode` (see below), then it runs `hack-local-`
    `variables` to parse, and bind or evaluate as appropriate, the file's local variables (see
    Section 11.11 [File Local Variables], page 177).

    If the *find-file* argument to `normal-mode` is non-`nil`, `normal-mode` assumes that the
    `find-file` function is calling it. In this case, it may process local variables in the
    '-*-' line or at the end of the file. The variable `enable-local-variables` controls
    whether to do so. See Section "Local Variables in Files" in *The GNU Emacs Manual*,
    for the syntax of the local variables section of a file.

    If you run `normal-mode` interactively, the argument *find-file* is normally `nil`. In this
    case, `normal-mode` unconditionally processes any file local variables.

The function calls `set-auto-mode` to choose a major mode. If this does not specify a mode, the buffer stays in the major mode determined by the default value of `major-mode` (see below).

`normal-mode` uses `condition-case` around the call to the major mode command, so errors are caught and reported as a 'File mode specification error', followed by the original error message.

`set-auto-mode &optional` *keep-mode-if-same*   [Function]

> This function selects the major mode that is appropriate for the current buffer. It bases its decision (in order of precedence) on the '-*-' line, on any 'mode:' local variable near the end of a file, on the '#!' line (using `interpreter-mode-alist`), on the text at the beginning of the buffer (using `magic-mode-alist`), and finally on the visited file name (using `auto-mode-alist`). See Section "How Major Modes are Chosen" in *The GNU Emacs Manual*. If `enable-local-variables` is nil, `set-auto-mode` does not check the '-*-' line, or near the end of the file, for any mode tag.
>
> There are some file types where it is not appropriate to scan the file contents for a mode specifier. For example, a tar archive may happen to contain, near the end of the file, a member file that has a local variables section specifying a mode for that particular file. This should not be applied to the containing tar file. Similarly, a tiff image file might just happen to contain a first line that seems to match the '-*-' pattern. For these reasons, both these file extensions are members of the list `inhibit-local-variables-regexps`. Add patterns to this list to prevent Emacs searching them for local variables of any kind (not just mode specifiers).
>
> If *keep-mode-if-same* is non-`nil`, this function does not call the mode command if the buffer is already in the proper major mode. For instance, `set-visited-file-name` sets this to `t` to avoid killing buffer local variables that the user may have set.

`set-buffer-major-mode` *buffer*   [Function]

> This function sets the major mode of *buffer* to the default value of `major-mode`; if that is `nil`, it uses the current buffer's major mode (if that is suitable). As an exception, if *buffer*'s name is `*scratch*`, it sets the mode to `initial-major-mode`.
>
> The low-level primitives for creating buffers do not use this function, but medium-level commands such as `switch-to-buffer` and `find-file-noselect` use it whenever they create buffers.

`initial-major-mode`   [User Option]

> The value of this variable determines the major mode of the initial `*scratch*` buffer. The value should be a symbol that is a major mode command. The default value is `lisp-interaction-mode`.

`interpreter-mode-alist`   [Variable]

> This variable specifies major modes to use for scripts that specify a command interpreter in a '#!' line. Its value is an alist with elements of the form (*regexp* . *mode*); this says to use mode *mode* if the file specifies an interpreter which matches \\`*regexp*\\'. For example, one of the default elements is `("python[0-9.]*" . python-mode)`.

`magic-mode-alist`   [Variable]

> This variable's value is an alist with elements of the form (*regexp . function*), where *regexp* is a regular expression and *function* is a function or `nil`. After visiting a file, `set-auto-mode` calls *function* if the text at the beginning of the buffer matches *regexp* and *function* is non-`nil`; if *function* is `nil`, `auto-mode-alist` gets to decide the mode.

`magic-fallback-mode-alist`   [Variable]

> This works like `magic-mode-alist`, except that it is handled only if `auto-mode-alist` does not specify a mode for this file.

`auto-mode-alist`   [Variable]

> This variable contains an association list of file name patterns (regular expressions) and corresponding major mode commands. Usually, the file name patterns test for suffixes, such as '.el' and '.c', but this need not be the case. An ordinary element of the alist looks like (*regexp . mode-function*).

> For example,

```
(("\\`/tmp/fol/" . text-mode)
 ("\\.texinfo\\'" . texinfo-mode)
 ("\\.texi\\'" . texinfo-mode)
 ("\\.el\\'" . emacs-lisp-mode)
 ("\\.c\\'" . c-mode)
 ("\\.h\\'" . c-mode)
 ...)
```

> When you visit a file whose expanded file name (see Section 24.8.4 [File Name Expansion], page 522), with version numbers and backup suffixes removed using `file-name-sans-versions` (see Section 24.8.1 [File Name Components], page 518), matches a *regexp*, `set-auto-mode` calls the corresponding *mode-function*. This feature enables Emacs to select the proper major mode for most files.

> If an element of `auto-mode-alist` has the form (*regexp function* t), then after calling *function*, Emacs searches `auto-mode-alist` again for a match against the portion of the file name that did not match before. This feature is useful for uncompression packages: an entry of the form ("\\.gz\\'" *function* t) can uncompress the file and then put the uncompressed file in the proper mode according to the name sans '.gz'.

> Here is an example of how to prepend several pattern pairs to `auto-mode-alist`. (You might use this sort of expression in your init file.)

```
(setq auto-mode-alist
  (append
   ;; File name (within directory) starts with a dot.
   '(("/\\.[^/]*\\'" . fundamental-mode)
     ;; File name has no dot.
     ("/[^\\./]*\\'" . fundamental-mode)
     ;; File name ends in '.C'.
     ("\\.C\\'" . c++-mode))
   auto-mode-alist))
```

22.2.3 Getting Help about a Major Mode

The `describe-mode` function provides information about major modes. It is normally bound to `C-h m`. It uses the value of the variable `major-mode` (see Section 22.2 [Major Modes], page 431), which is why every major mode command needs to set that variable.

`describe-mode &optional` *buffer* [Command]

> This command displays the documentation of the current buffer's major mode and minor modes. It uses the `documentation` function to retrieve the documentation strings of the major and minor mode commands (see Section 23.2 [Accessing Documentation], page 486).
>
> If called from Lisp with a non-`nil` *buffer* argument, this function displays the documentation for that buffer's major and minor modes, rather than those of the current buffer.

22.2.4 Defining Derived Modes

The recommended way to define a new major mode is to derive it from an existing one using `define-derived-mode`. If there is no closely related mode, you should inherit from either `text-mode`, `special-mode`, or `prog-mode`. See Section 22.2.5 [Basic Major Modes], page 440. If none of these are suitable, you can inherit from `fundamental-mode` (see Section 22.2 [Major Modes], page 431).

`define-derived-mode` *variant parent name docstring keyword-args. . .* [Macro]
> *body. . .*

> This macro defines *variant* as a major mode command, using *name* as the string form of the mode name. *variant* and *parent* should be unquoted symbols.
>
> The new command *variant* is defined to call the function *parent*, then override certain aspects of that parent mode:
>
> - The new mode has its own sparse keymap, named *variant*`-map`. `define-derived-mode` makes the parent mode's keymap the parent of the new map, unless *variant*`-map` is already set and already has a parent.
>
> - The new mode has its own syntax table, kept in the variable *variant*`-syntax-table`, unless you override this using the `:syntax-table` keyword (see below). `define-derived-mode` makes the parent mode's syntax-table the parent of *variant*`-syntax-table`, unless the latter is already set and already has a parent different from the standard syntax table.
>
> - The new mode has its own abbrev table, kept in the variable *variant*`-abbrev-table`, unless you override this using the `:abbrev-table` keyword (see below).
>
> - The new mode has its own mode hook, *variant*`-hook`. It runs this hook, after running the hooks of its ancestor modes, with `run-mode-hooks`, as the last thing it does. See Section 22.2.6 [Mode Hooks], page 440.
>
> In addition, you can specify how to override other aspects of *parent* with *body*. The command *variant* evaluates the forms in *body* after setting up all its usual overrides, just before running the mode hooks.
>
> If *parent* has a non-`nil` `mode-class` symbol property, then `define-derived-mode` sets the `mode-class` property of *variant* to the same value. This ensures, for example,

that if *parent* is a special mode, then *variant* is also a special mode (see Section 22.2.1 [Major Mode Conventions], page 432).

You can also specify `nil` for *parent*. This gives the new mode no parent. Then `define-derived-mode` behaves as described above, but, of course, omits all actions connected with *parent*.

The argument *docstring* specifies the documentation string for the new mode. `define-derived-mode` adds some general information about the mode's hook, followed by the mode's keymap, at the end of this documentation string. If you omit *docstring*, `define-derived-mode` generates a documentation string.

The *keyword-args* are pairs of keywords and values. The values are evaluated. The following keywords are currently supported:

`:syntax-table`
> You can use this to explicitly specify a syntax table for the new mode. If you specify a `nil` value, the new mode uses the same syntax table as *parent*, or the standard syntax table if *parent* is `nil`. (Note that this does *not* follow the convention used for non-keyword arguments that a `nil` value is equivalent with not specifying the argument.)

`:abbrev-table`
> You can use this to explicitly specify an abbrev table for the new mode. If you specify a `nil` value, the new mode uses the same abbrev table as *parent*, or `fundamental-mode-abbrev-table` if *parent* is `nil`. (Again, a `nil` value is *not* equivalent to not specifying this keyword.)

`:group`   If this is specified, the value should be the customization group for this mode. (Not all major modes have one.) The command `customize-mode` uses this. `define-derived-mode` does *not* automatically define the specified customization group.

Here is a hypothetical example:

```
(defvar hypertext-mode-map
  (let ((map (make-sparse-keymap)))
    (define-key map [down-mouse-3] 'do-hyper-link)
    map))

(define-derived-mode hypertext-mode
  text-mode "Hypertext"
  "Major mode for hypertext."
  (setq-local case-fold-search nil))
```

Do not write an `interactive` spec in the definition; `define-derived-mode` does that automatically.

derived-mode-p &rest *modes*   [Function]
> This function returns non-`nil` if the current major mode is derived from any of the major modes given by the symbols *modes*.

22.2.5 Basic Major Modes

Apart from Fundamental mode, there are three major modes that other major modes commonly derive from: Text mode, Prog mode, and Special mode. While Text mode is useful in its own right (e.g., for editing files ending in `.txt`), Prog mode and Special mode exist mainly to let other modes derive from them.

As far as possible, new major modes should be derived, either directly or indirectly, from one of these three modes. One reason is that this allows users to customize a single mode hook (e.g., `prog-mode-hook`) for an entire family of relevant modes (e.g., all programming language modes).

`text-mode`   [Command]
> Text mode is a major mode for editing human languages. It defines the '"' and '\' characters as having punctuation syntax (see Section 34.2.1 [Syntax Class Table], page 817), and binds *M-TAB* to `ispell-complete-word` (see Section "Spelling" in *The GNU Emacs Manual*).
>
> An example of a major mode derived from Text mode is HTML mode. See Section "SGML and HTML Modes" in *The GNU Emacs Manual*.

`prog-mode`   [Command]
> Prog mode is a basic major mode for buffers containing programming language source code. Most of the programming language major modes built into Emacs are derived from it.
>
> Prog mode binds `parse-sexp-ignore-comments` to `t` (see Section 34.6.1 [Motion via Parsing], page 825) and `bidi-paragraph-direction` to `left-to-right` (see Section 37.26 [Bidirectional Display], page 981).

`special-mode`   [Command]
> Special mode is a basic major mode for buffers containing text that is produced specially by Emacs, rather than directly from a file. Major modes derived from Special mode are given a `mode-class` property of `special` (see Section 22.2.1 [Major Mode Conventions], page 432).
>
> Special mode sets the buffer to read-only. Its keymap defines several common bindings, including *q* for `quit-window` and *g* for `revert-buffer` (see Section 25.3 [Reverting], page 547).
>
> An example of a major mode derived from Special mode is Buffer Menu mode, which is used by the `*Buffer List*` buffer. See Section "Listing Existing Buffers" in *The GNU Emacs Manual*.

In addition, modes for buffers of tabulated data can inherit from Tabulated List mode, which is in turn derived from Special mode. See Section 22.2.7 [Tabulated List Mode], page 441.

22.2.6 Mode Hooks

Every major mode command should finish by running the mode-independent normal hook `change-major-mode-after-body-hook`, its mode hook, and the normal hook `after-change-major-mode-hook`. It does this by calling `run-mode-hooks`. If the major mode is a derived mode, that is if it calls another major mode (the parent mode) in its body, it should do this inside `delay-mode-hooks` so that the parent won't run these hooks itself. Instead, the derived mode's call to `run-mode-hooks` runs the parent's mode hook too. See Section 22.2.1 [Major Mode Conventions], page 432.

Emacs versions before Emacs 22 did not have `delay-mode-hooks`. Versions before 24 did not have `change-major-mode-after-body-hook`. When user-implemented major modes do not use `run-mode-hooks` and have not been updated to use these newer features, they won't entirely follow these conventions: they may run the parent's mode hook too early, or fail to run `after-change-major-mode-hook`. If you encounter such a major mode, please correct it to follow these conventions.

When you define a major mode using `define-derived-mode`, it automatically makes sure these conventions are followed. If you define a major mode "by hand", not using `define-derived-mode`, use the following functions to handle these conventions automatically.

run-mode-hooks &rest *hookvars*   [Function]

    Major modes should run their mode hook using this function. It is similar to `run-hooks` (see Section 22.1 [Hooks], page 429), but it also runs `change-major-mode-after-body-hook` and `after-change-major-mode-hook`.

    When this function is called during the execution of a `delay-mode-hooks` form, it does not run the hooks immediately. Instead, it arranges for the next call to `run-mode-hooks` to run them.

delay-mode-hooks *body...*   [Macro]

    When one major mode command calls another, it should do so inside of `delay-mode-hooks`.

    This macro executes *body*, but tells all `run-mode-hooks` calls during the execution of *body* to delay running their hooks. The hooks will actually run during the next call to `run-mode-hooks` after the end of the `delay-mode-hooks` construct.

change-major-mode-after-body-hook   [Variable]

    This is a normal hook run by `run-mode-hooks`. It is run before the mode hooks.

after-change-major-mode-hook   [Variable]

    This is a normal hook run by `run-mode-hooks`. It is run at the very end of every properly-written major mode command.

22.2.7 Tabulated List mode

Tabulated List mode is a major mode for displaying tabulated data, i.e., data consisting of *entries*, each entry occupying one row of text with its contents divided into columns. Tabulated List mode provides facilities for pretty-printing rows and columns, and sorting the rows according to the values in each column. It is derived from Special mode (see Section 22.2.5 [Basic Major Modes], page 440).

Tabulated List mode is intended to be used as a parent mode by a more specialized major mode. Examples include Process Menu mode (see Section 36.6 [Process Information], page 851) and Package Menu mode (see Section "Package Menu" in *The GNU Emacs Manual*).

Such a derived mode should use `define-derived-mode` in the usual way, specifying `tabulated-list-mode` as the second argument (see Section 22.2.4 [Derived Modes], page 438). The body of the `define-derived-mode` form should specify the format of the tabulated data, by assigning values to the variables documented below; optionally, it can then call the function `tabulated-list-init-header`, which will populate a header with the names of the columns.

The derived mode should also define a *listing command*. This, not the mode command, is what the user calls (e.g., `M-x list-processes`). The listing command should create or switch to a buffer, turn on the derived mode, specify the tabulated data, and finally call `tabulated-list-print` to populate the buffer.

`tabulated-list-format`   [Variable]

> This buffer-local variable specifies the format of the Tabulated List data. Its value should be a vector. Each element of the vector represents a data column, and should be a list (`name width sort`), where
>
> - *name* is the column's name (a string).
> - *width* is the width to reserve for the column (an integer). This is meaningless for the last column, which runs to the end of each line.
> - *sort* specifies how to sort entries by the column. If `nil`, the column cannot be used for sorting. If `t`, the column is sorted by comparing string values. Otherwise, this should be a predicate function for `sort` (see Section 5.6.3 [Rearrangement], page 79), which accepts two arguments with the same form as the elements of `tabulated-list-entries` (see below).

`tabulated-list-entries`   [Variable]

> This buffer-local variable specifies the entries displayed in the Tabulated List buffer. Its value should be either a list, or a function.
>
> If the value is a list, each list element corresponds to one entry, and should have the form (`id contents`), where
>
> - *id* is either `nil`, or a Lisp object that identifies the entry. If the latter, the cursor stays on the same entry when re-sorting entries. Comparison is done with `equal`.
> - *contents* is a vector with the same number of elements as `tabulated-list-format`. Each vector element is either a string, which is inserted into the buffer as-is, or a list (`label . properties`), which means to insert a text button by calling `insert-text-button` with *label* and *properties* as arguments (see Section 37.19.3 [Making Buttons], page 965).
>
>   There should be no newlines in any of these strings.
>
> Otherwise, the value should be a function which returns a list of the above form when called with no arguments.

`tabulated-list-revert-hook`   [Variable]

> This normal hook is run prior to reverting a Tabulated List buffer. A derived mode can add a function to this hook to recompute `tabulated-list-entries`.

`tabulated-list-printer`   [Variable]

> The value of this variable is the function called to insert an entry at point, including its terminating newline. The function should accept two arguments, *id* and *contents*,

having the same meanings as in `tabulated-list-entries`. The default value is a function which inserts an entry in a straightforward way; a mode which uses Tabulated List mode in a more complex way can specify another function.

`tabulated-list-sort-key`   [Variable]

> The value of this variable specifies the current sort key for the Tabulated List buffer. If it is `nil`, no sorting is done. Otherwise, it should have the form (*name . flip*), where *name* is a string matching one of the column names in `tabulated-list-format`, and *flip*, if non-`nil`, means to invert the sort order.

`tabulated-list-init-header`   [Function]

> This function computes and sets `header-line-format` for the Tabulated List buffer (see Section 22.4.7 [Header Lines], page 458), and assigns a keymap to the header line to allow sorting entries by clicking on column headers.
>
> Modes derived from Tabulated List mode should call this after setting the above variables (in particular, only after setting `tabulated-list-format`).

`tabulated-list-print` **&optional** *remember-pos update*   [Function]

> This function populates the current buffer with entries. It should be called by the listing command. It erases the buffer, sorts the entries specified by `tabulated-list-entries` according to `tabulated-list-sort-key`, then calls the function specified by `tabulated-list-printer` to insert each entry.
>
> If the optional argument *remember-pos* is non-`nil`, this function looks for the *id* element on the current line, if any, and tries to move to that entry after all the entries are (re)inserted.
>
> If the optional argument *update* is non-`nil`, this function will only erase or add entries that have changed since the last print. This is several times faster if most entries haven't changed since the last time this function was called. The only difference in outcome is that tags placed via `tabulated-list-put-tag` will not be removed from entries that haven't changed (normally all tags are removed).

22.2.8 Generic Modes

Generic modes are simple major modes with basic support for comment syntax and Font Lock mode. To define a generic mode, use the macro `define-generic-mode`. See the file `generic-x.el` for some examples of the use of `define-generic-mode`.

`define-generic-mode` *mode comment-list keyword-list font-lock-list*   [Macro]
    auto-mode-list function-list **&optional** *docstring*

> This macro defines a generic mode command named *mode* (a symbol, not quoted). The optional argument *docstring* is the documentation for the mode command. If you do not supply it, `define-generic-mode` generates one by default.
>
> The argument *comment-list* is a list in which each element is either a character, a string of one or two characters, or a cons cell. A character or a string is set up in the mode's syntax table as a comment starter. If the entry is a cons cell, the CAR is set up as a comment starter and the CDR as a comment ender. (Use `nil` for the latter if you want comments to end at the end of the line.) Note that the syntax table mechanism has limitations about what comment starters and enders are actually possible. See Chapter 34 [Syntax Tables], page 816.

The argument *keyword-list* is a list of keywords to highlight with `font-lock-keyword-face`. Each keyword should be a string. Meanwhile, *font-lock-list* is a list of additional expressions to highlight. Each element of this list should have the same form as an element of `font-lock-keywords`. See Section 22.6.2 [Search-based Fontification], page 464.

The argument *auto-mode-list* is a list of regular expressions to add to the variable `auto-mode-alist`. They are added by the execution of the `define-generic-mode` form, not by expanding the macro call.

Finally, *function-list* is a list of functions for the mode command to call for additional setup. It calls these functions just before it runs the mode hook variable *mode-hook*.

22.2.9 Major Mode Examples

Text mode is perhaps the simplest mode besides Fundamental mode. Here are excerpts from `text-mode.el` that illustrate many of the conventions listed above:

```
;; Create the syntax table for this mode.
(defvar text-mode-syntax-table
  (let ((st (make-syntax-table)))
    (modify-syntax-entry ?\" ".    " st)
    (modify-syntax-entry ?\\ ".    " st)
    ;; Add 'p' so M-c on 'hello' leads to 'Hello', not 'hello'.
    (modify-syntax-entry ?' "w p" st)
    st)
  "Syntax table used while in `text-mode'.")

;; Create the keymap for this mode.
(defvar text-mode-map
  (let ((map (make-sparse-keymap)))
    (define-key map "\e\t" 'ispell-complete-word)
    map)
  "Keymap for `text-mode'.
Many other modes, such as `mail-mode', `outline-mode' and
`indented-text-mode', inherit all the commands defined in this map.")
```

Here is how the actual mode command is defined now:

```
(define-derived-mode text-mode nil "Text"
  "Major mode for editing text written for humans to read.
In this mode, paragraphs are delimited only by blank or white lines.
You can thus get the full benefit of adaptive filling
 (see the variable `adaptive-fill-mode').
\\{text-mode-map}
Turning on Text mode runs the normal hook `text-mode-hook'."
  (set (make-local-variable 'text-mode-variant) t)
  (set (make-local-variable 'require-final-newline)
       mode-require-final-newline)
  (set (make-local-variable 'indent-line-function) 'indent-relative))
```

(The last line is redundant nowadays, since `indent-relative` is the default value, and we'll delete it in a future version.)

The three Lisp modes (Lisp mode, Emacs Lisp mode, and Lisp Interaction mode) have more features than Text mode and the code is correspondingly more complicated. Here are excerpts from `lisp-mode.el` that illustrate how these modes are written.

Here is how the Lisp mode syntax and abbrev tables are defined:

```
;; Create mode-specific table variables.
(defvar lisp-mode-abbrev-table nil)
(define-abbrev-table 'lisp-mode-abbrev-table ())

(defvar lisp-mode-syntax-table
  (let ((table (copy-syntax-table emacs-lisp-mode-syntax-table)))
    (modify-syntax-entry ?\[ "_    " table)
    (modify-syntax-entry ?\] "_    " table)
    (modify-syntax-entry ?# "' 14" table)
    (modify-syntax-entry ?| "\" 23bn" table)
    table)
  "Syntax table used in `lisp-mode'.")
```

The three modes for Lisp share much of their code. For instance, each calls the following function to set various variables:

```
(defun lisp-mode-variables (&optional syntax keywords-case-insensitive)
  (when syntax
    (set-syntax-table lisp-mode-syntax-table))
  (setq local-abbrev-table lisp-mode-abbrev-table)
  ...
```

Amongst other things, this function sets up the **comment-start** variable to handle Lisp comments:

```
(make-local-variable 'comment-start)
(setq comment-start ";")
  ...
```

Each of the different Lisp modes has a slightly different keymap. For example, Lisp mode binds *C-c C-z* to **run-lisp**, but the other Lisp modes do not. However, all Lisp modes have some commands in common. The following code sets up the common commands:

```
(defvar lisp-mode-shared-map
  (let ((map (make-sparse-keymap)))
    (define-key map "\e\C-q" 'indent-sexp)
    (define-key map "\177" 'backward-delete-char-untabify)
    map)
  "Keymap for commands shared by all sorts of Lisp modes.")
```

And here is the code to set up the keymap for Lisp mode:

```
(defvar lisp-mode-map
  (let ((map (make-sparse-keymap))
(menu-map (make-sparse-keymap "Lisp")))
    (set-keymap-parent map lisp-mode-shared-map)
    (define-key map "\e\C-x" 'lisp-eval-defun)
    (define-key map "\C-c\C-z" 'run-lisp)
    ...
    map)
  "Keymap for ordinary Lisp mode.
All commands in `lisp-mode-shared-map' are inherited by this map.")
```

Finally, here is the major mode command for Lisp mode:

```
(define-derived-mode lisp-mode prog-mode "Lisp"
  "Major mode for editing Lisp code for Lisps other than GNU Emacs Lisp.
Commands:
Delete converts tabs to spaces as it moves back.
Blank lines separate paragraphs.  Semicolons start comments.

\\{lisp-mode-map}
Note that `run-lisp' may be used either to start an inferior Lisp job
or to switch back to an existing one.
```

```
Entry to this mode calls the value of `lisp-mode-hook'
if that value is non-nil."
  (lisp-mode-variables nil t)
  (set (make-local-variable 'find-tag-default-function)
       'lisp-find-tag-default)
  (set (make-local-variable 'comment-start-skip)
       "\\(\\(^\\|[^\\\\\n]\\)\\(\\\\\\\\\\\\)*\\)\\(;+\\|#|\\) *")
  (setq imenu-case-fold-search t))
```

22.3 Minor Modes

A *minor mode* provides optional features that users may enable or disable independently of the choice of major mode. Minor modes can be enabled individually or in combination.

Most minor modes implement features that are independent of the major mode, and can thus be used with most major modes. For example, Auto Fill mode works with any major mode that permits text insertion. A few minor modes, however, are specific to a particular major mode. For example, Diff Auto Refine mode is a minor mode that is intended to be used only with Diff mode.

Ideally, a minor mode should have its desired effect regardless of the other minor modes in effect. It should be possible to activate and deactivate minor modes in any order.

`minor-mode-list`   [Variable]

   The value of this variable is a list of all minor mode commands.

22.3.1 Conventions for Writing Minor Modes

There are conventions for writing minor modes just as there are for major modes. These conventions are described below. The easiest way to follow them is to use the macro `define-minor-mode`. See Section 22.3.3 [Defining Minor Modes], page 448.

- Define a variable whose name ends in '-mode'. We call this the *mode variable*. The minor mode command should set this variable. The value will be `nil` if the mode is disabled, and non-`nil` if the mode is enabled. The variable should be buffer-local if the minor mode is buffer-local.

  This variable is used in conjunction with the `minor-mode-alist` to display the minor mode name in the mode line. It also determines whether the minor mode keymap is active, via `minor-mode-map-alist` (see Section 21.9 [Controlling Active Maps], page 400). Individual commands or hooks can also check its value.

- Define a command, called the *mode command*, whose name is the same as the mode variable. Its job is to set the value of the mode variable, plus anything else that needs to be done to actually enable or disable the mode's features.

  The mode command should accept one optional argument. If called interactively with no prefix argument, it should toggle the mode (i.e., enable if it is disabled, and disable if it is enabled). If called interactively with a prefix argument, it should enable the mode if the argument is positive and disable it otherwise.

  If the mode command is called from Lisp (i.e., non-interactively), it should enable the mode if the argument is omitted or `nil`; it should toggle the mode if the argument is the symbol `toggle`; otherwise it should treat the argument in the same way as for an interactive call with a numeric prefix argument, as described above.

The following example shows how to implement this behavior (it is similar to the code generated by the `define-minor-mode` macro):

```
(interactive (list (or current-prefix-arg 'toggle)))
(let ((enable (if (eq arg 'toggle)
                  (not foo-mode) ; this modefls mode variable
                (> (prefix-numeric-value arg) 0))))
  (if enable
      do-enable
    do-disable))
```

The reason for this somewhat complex behavior is that it lets users easily toggle the minor mode interactively, and also lets the minor mode be easily enabled in a mode hook, like this:

```
(add-hook 'text-mode-hook 'foo-mode)
```

This behaves correctly whether or not `foo-mode` was already enabled, since the `foo-mode` mode command unconditionally enables the minor mode when it is called from Lisp with no argument. Disabling a minor mode in a mode hook is a little uglier:

```
(add-hook 'text-mode-hook (lambda () (foo-mode -1)))
```

However, this is not very commonly done.

- Add an element to `minor-mode-alist` for each minor mode (see [Definition of minor-mode-alist], page 456), if you want to indicate the minor mode in the mode line. This element should be a list of the following form:

```
(mode-variable string)
```

Here *mode-variable* is the variable that controls enabling of the minor mode, and *string* is a short string, starting with a space, to represent the mode in the mode line. These strings must be short so that there is room for several of them at once.

When you add an element to `minor-mode-alist`, use `assq` to check for an existing element, to avoid duplication. For example:

```
(unless (assq 'leif-mode minor-mode-alist)
  (push '(leif-mode " Leif") minor-mode-alist))
```

or like this, using `add-to-list` (see Section 5.5 [List Variables], page 74):

```
(add-to-list 'minor-mode-alist '(leif-mode " Leif"))
```

In addition, several major mode conventions apply to minor modes as well: those regarding the names of global symbols, the use of a hook at the end of the initialization function, and the use of keymaps and other tables.

The minor mode should, if possible, support enabling and disabling via Custom (see Chapter 14 [Customization], page 225). To do this, the mode variable should be defined with `defcustom`, usually with `:type 'boolean`. If just setting the variable is not sufficient to enable the mode, you should also specify a `:set` method which enables the mode by invoking the mode command. Note in the variable's documentation string that setting the variable other than via Custom may not take effect. Also, mark the definition with an autoload cookie (see [autoload cookie], page 251), and specify a `:require` so that customizing the variable will load the library that defines the mode. For example:

```
;;;###autoload
(defcustom msb-mode nil
  "Toggle msb-mode.
Setting this variable directly does not take effect;
use either \\[customize] or the function `msb-mode'."
  :set 'custom-set-minor-mode
  :initialize 'custom-initialize-default
  :version "20.4"
  :type    'boolean
  :group   'msb
  :require 'msb)
```

22.3.2 Keymaps and Minor Modes

Each minor mode can have its own keymap, which is active when the mode is enabled. To set up a keymap for a minor mode, add an element to the alist `minor-mode-map-alist`. See [Definition of minor-mode-map-alist], page 401.

One use of minor mode keymaps is to modify the behavior of certain self-inserting characters so that they do something else as well as self-insert. (Another way to customize `self-insert-command` is through `post-self-insert-hook`. Apart from this, the facilities for customizing `self-insert-command` are limited to special cases, designed for abbrevs and Auto Fill mode. Do not try substituting your own definition of `self-insert-command` for the standard one. The editor command loop handles this function specially.)

Minor modes may bind commands to key sequences consisting of `C-c` followed by a punctuation character. However, sequences consisting of `C-c` followed by one of `{}<>:;`, or a control character or digit, are reserved for major modes. Also, `C-c letter` is reserved for users. See Section D.2 [Key Binding Conventions], page 1056.

22.3.3 Defining Minor Modes

The macro `define-minor-mode` offers a convenient way of implementing a mode in one self-contained definition.

define-minor-mode *mode doc* [*init-value* [*lighter* [*keymap*]]]   [Macro]
        keyword-args. . . body. . .

> This macro defines a new minor mode whose name is *mode* (a symbol). It defines a command named *mode* to toggle the minor mode, with *doc* as its documentation string.

> The toggle command takes one optional (prefix) argument. If called interactively with no argument it toggles the mode on or off. A positive prefix argument enables the mode, any other prefix argument disables it. From Lisp, an argument of `toggle` toggles the mode, whereas an omitted or `nil` argument enables the mode. This makes it easy to enable the minor mode in a major mode hook, for example. If *doc* is `nil`, the macro supplies a default documentation string explaining the above.

> By default, it also defines a variable named *mode*, which is set to `t` or `nil` by enabling or disabling the mode. The variable is initialized to *init-value*. Except in unusual circumstances (see below), this value must be `nil`.

> The string *lighter* says what to display in the mode line when the mode is enabled; if it is `nil`, the mode is not displayed in the mode line.

The optional argument *keymap* specifies the keymap for the minor mode. If non-`nil`, it should be a variable name (whose value is a keymap), a keymap, or an alist of the form

    (key-sequence . definition)

where each *key-sequence* and *definition* are arguments suitable for passing to `define-key` (see Section 21.12 [Changing Key Bindings], page 406). If *keymap* is a keymap or an alist, this also defines the variable *mode*-`map`.

The above three arguments *init-value*, *lighter*, and *keymap* can be (partially) omitted when *keyword-args* are used. The *keyword-args* consist of keywords followed by corresponding values. A few keywords have special meanings:

`:group` *group*

> Custom group name to use in all generated `defcustom` forms. Defaults to *mode* without the possible trailing '`-mode`'. **Warning:** don't use this default group name unless you have written a `defgroup` to define that group properly. See Section 14.2 [Group Definitions], page 227.

`:global` *global*

> If non-`nil`, this specifies that the minor mode should be global rather than buffer-local. It defaults to `nil`.
>
> One of the effects of making a minor mode global is that the *mode* variable becomes a customization variable. Toggling it through the Customize interface turns the mode on and off, and its value can be saved for future Emacs sessions (see Section "Saving Customizations" in *The GNU Emacs Manual*. For the saved variable to work, you should ensure that the `define-minor-mode` form is evaluated each time Emacs starts; for packages that are not part of Emacs, the easiest way to do this is to specify a `:require` keyword.

`:init-value` *init-value*

> This is equivalent to specifying *init-value* positionally.

`:lighter` *lighter*

> This is equivalent to specifying *lighter* positionally.

`:keymap` *keymap*

> This is equivalent to specifying *keymap* positionally.

`:variable` *place*

> This replaces the default variable *mode*, used to store the state of the mode. If you specify this, the *mode* variable is not defined, and any *init-value* argument is unused. *place* can be a different named variable (which you must define yourself), or anything that can be used with the `setf` function (see Section 11.15 [Generalized Variables], page 183). *place* can also be a cons (*get* . *set*), where *get* is an expression that returns the current state, and *set* is a function of one argument (a state) that sets it.

`:after-hook` *after-hook*

> This defines a single Lisp form which is evaluated after the mode hooks have run. It should not be quoted.

Any other keyword arguments are passed directly to the `defcustom` generated for the variable *mode*.

The command named *mode* first performs the standard actions such as setting the variable named *mode* and then executes the *body* forms, if any. It then runs the mode hook variable *mode*-hook and finishes by evaluating any form in `:after-hook`.

The initial value must be `nil` except in cases where (1) the mode is preloaded in Emacs, or (2) it is painless for loading to enable the mode even though the user did not request it. For instance, if the mode has no effect unless something else is enabled, and will always be loaded by that time, enabling it by default is harmless. But these are unusual circumstances. Normally, the initial value must be `nil`.

The name `easy-mmode-define-minor-mode` is an alias for this macro.

Here is an example of using `define-minor-mode`:

```
(define-minor-mode hungry-mode
  "Toggle Hungry mode.
Interactively with no argument, this command toggles the mode.
A positive prefix argument enables the mode, any other prefix
argument disables it.  From Lisp, argument omitted or nil enables
the mode, `toggle' toggles the state.

When Hungry mode is enabled, the control delete key
gobbles all preceding whitespace except the last.
See the command \\[hungry-electric-delete]."
 ;; The initial value.
 nil
 ;; The indicator for the mode line.
 " Hungry"
 ;; The minor mode bindings.
 '(([C-backspace] . hungry-electric-delete))
 :group 'hunger)
```

This defines a minor mode named "Hungry mode", a command named `hungry-mode` to toggle it, a variable named `hungry-mode` which indicates whether the mode is enabled, and a variable named `hungry-mode-map` which holds the keymap that is active when the mode is enabled. It initializes the keymap with a key binding for *C-DEL*. It puts the variable `hungry-mode` into custom group `hunger`. There are no *body* forms—many minor modes don't need any.

Here's an equivalent way to write it:

```
(define-minor-mode hungry-mode
  "Toggle Hungry mode.
...rest of documentation as before..."
 ;; The initial value.
 :init-value nil
 ;; The indicator for the mode line.
 :lighter " Hungry"
 ;; The minor mode bindings.
 :keymap
 '(([C-backspace] . hungry-electric-delete)
   ([C-M-backspace]
    . (lambda ()
        (interactive)
        (hungry-electric-delete t))))
 :group 'hunger)
```

define-globalized-minor-mode *global-mode mode turn-on*   [Macro]
      keyword-args. . .

      This defines a global toggle named *global-mode* whose meaning is to enable or disable the buffer-local minor mode *mode* in all buffers. To turn on the minor mode in a buffer, it uses the function *turn-on*; to turn off the minor mode, it calls *mode* with −1 as argument.

      Globally enabling the mode also affects buffers subsequently created by visiting files, and buffers that use a major mode other than Fundamental mode; but it does not detect the creation of a new buffer in Fundamental mode.

      This defines the customization option *global-mode* (see Chapter 14 [Customization], page 225), which can be toggled in the Customize interface to turn the minor mode on and off. As with `define-minor-mode`, you should ensure that the `define-globalized-minor-mode` form is evaluated each time Emacs starts, for example by providing a `:require` keyword.

      Use `:group` *group* in *keyword-args* to specify the custom group for the mode variable of the global minor mode.

      Generally speaking, when you define a globalized minor mode, you should also define a non-globalized version, so that people can use (or disable) it in individual buffers. This also allows them to disable a globally enabled minor mode in a specific major mode, by using that mode's hook.

22.4 Mode Line Format

Each Emacs window (aside from minibuffer windows) typically has a mode line at the bottom, which displays status information about the buffer displayed in the window. The mode line contains information about the buffer, such as its name, associated file, depth of recursive editing, and major and minor modes. A window can also have a *header line*, which is much like the mode line but appears at the top of the window.

    This section describes how to control the contents of the mode line and header line. We include it in this chapter because much of the information displayed in the mode line relates to the enabled major and minor modes.

22.4.1 Mode Line Basics

The contents of each mode line are specified by the buffer-local variable `mode-line-format` (see Section 22.4.3 [Mode Line Top], page 453). This variable holds a *mode line construct*: a template that controls what is displayed on the buffer's mode line. The value of `header-line-format` specifies the buffer's header line in the same way. All windows for the same buffer use the same `mode-line-format` and `header-line-format`.

    For efficiency, Emacs does not continuously recompute each window's mode line and header line. It does so when circumstances appear to call for it—for instance, if you change the window configuration, switch buffers, narrow or widen the buffer, scroll, or modify the buffer. If you alter any of the variables referenced by `mode-line-format` or `header-line-format` (see Section 22.4.4 [Mode Line Variables], page 454), or any other data structures that affect how text is displayed (see Chapter 37 [Display], page 886), you should use the function `force-mode-line-update` to update the display.

`force-mode-line-update` &optional *all*   [Function]
>   This function forces Emacs to update the current buffer's mode line and header line, based on the latest values of all relevant variables, during its next redisplay cycle. If the optional argument *all* is non-`nil`, it forces an update for all mode lines and header lines.
>
>   This function also forces an update of the menu bar and frame title.

The selected window's mode line is usually displayed in a different color using the face `mode-line`. Other windows' mode lines appear in the face `mode-line-inactive` instead. See Section 37.12 [Faces], page 915.

22.4.2 The Data Structure of the Mode Line

The mode line contents are controlled by a data structure called a *mode line construct*, made up of lists, strings, symbols, and numbers kept in buffer-local variables. Each data type has a specific meaning for the mode line appearance, as described below. The same data structure is used for constructing frame titles (see Section 28.6 [Frame Titles], page 654) and header lines (see Section 22.4.7 [Header Lines], page 458).

A mode line construct may be as simple as a fixed string of text, but it usually specifies how to combine fixed strings with variables' values to construct the text. Many of these variables are themselves defined to have mode line constructs as their values.

Here are the meanings of various data types as mode line constructs:

string   A string as a mode line construct appears verbatim except for %-*constructs* in it. These stand for substitution of other data; see Section 22.4.5 [%-Constructs], page 457.

>   If parts of the string have `face` properties, they control display of the text just as they would text in the buffer. Any characters which have no `face` properties are displayed, by default, in the face `mode-line` or `mode-line-inactive` (see Section "Standard Faces" in *The GNU Emacs Manual*). The `help-echo` and `keymap` properties in *string* have special meanings. See Section 22.4.6 [Properties in Mode], page 458.

symbol   A symbol as a mode line construct stands for its value. The value of *symbol* is used as a mode line construct, in place of *symbol*. However, the symbols `t` and `nil` are ignored, as is any symbol whose value is void.

>   There is one exception: if the value of *symbol* is a string, it is displayed verbatim: the %-constructs are not recognized.

>   Unless *symbol* is marked as risky (i.e., it has a non-`nil` `risky-local-variable` property), all text properties specified in *symbol*'s value are ignored. This includes the text properties of strings in *symbol*'s value, as well as all `:eval` and `:propertize` forms in it. (The reason for this is security: non-risky variables could be set automatically from file variables without prompting the user.)

(*string rest*...)
(*list rest*...)

>   A list whose first element is a string or list means to process all the elements recursively and concatenate the results. This is the most common form of mode line construct.

(`:eval` *form*)

> A list whose first element is the symbol `:eval` says to evaluate *form*, and use the result as a string to display. Make sure this evaluation cannot load any files, as doing so could cause infinite recursion.

(`:propertize` *elt props...*)

> A list whose first element is the symbol `:propertize` says to process the mode line construct *elt* recursively, then add the text properties specified by *props* to the result. The argument *props* should consist of zero or more pairs *text-property value*.

(*symbol then else*)

> A list whose first element is a symbol that is not a keyword specifies a conditional. Its meaning depends on the value of *symbol*. If *symbol* has a non-`nil` value, the second element, *then*, is processed recursively as a mode line construct. Otherwise, the third element, *else*, is processed recursively. You may omit *else*; then the mode line construct displays nothing if the value of *symbol* is `nil` or void.

(*width rest...*)

> A list whose first element is an integer specifies truncation or padding of the results of *rest*. The remaining elements *rest* are processed recursively as mode line constructs and concatenated together. When *width* is positive, the result is space filled on the right if its width is less than *width*. When *width* is negative, the result is truncated on the right to $-width$ columns if its width exceeds $-width$.

> For example, the usual way to show what percentage of a buffer is above the top of the window is to use a list like this: (`-3 "%p"`).

22.4.3 The Top Level of Mode Line Control

The variable in overall control of the mode line is `mode-line-format`.

`mode-line-format`   [User Option]

> The value of this variable is a mode line construct that controls the contents of the mode-line. It is always buffer-local in all buffers.

> If you set this variable to `nil` in a buffer, that buffer does not have a mode line. (A window that is just one line tall also does not display a mode line.)

The default value of `mode-line-format` is designed to use the values of other variables such as `mode-line-position` and `mode-line-modes` (which in turn incorporates the values of the variables `mode-name` and `minor-mode-alist`). Very few modes need to alter `mode-line-format` itself. For most purposes, it is sufficient to alter some of the variables that `mode-line-format` either directly or indirectly refers to.

If you do alter `mode-line-format` itself, the new value should use the same variables that appear in the default value (see Section 22.4.4 [Mode Line Variables], page 454), rather than duplicating their contents or displaying the information in another fashion. This way, customizations made by the user or by Lisp programs (such as `display-time` and major modes) via changes to those variables remain effective.

Here is a hypothetical example of a `mode-line-format` that might be useful for Shell mode (in reality, Shell mode does not set `mode-line-format`):

```
(setq mode-line-format
  (list "-"
   'mode-line-mule-info
   'mode-line-modified
   'mode-line-frame-identification
   "%b--"
   ;; Note that this is evaluated while making the list.
   ;; It makes a mode line construct which is just a string.
   (getenv "HOST")
   ":"
   'default-directory
   "   "
   'global-mode-string
   "   %[("
   '(:eval (mode-line-mode-name))
   'mode-line-process
   'minor-mode-alist
   "%n"
   ")%]--"
   '(which-func-mode ("" which-func-format "--"))
   '(line-number-mode "L%l--")
   '(column-number-mode "C%c--")
   '(-3 "%p")))
```

(The variables `line-number-mode`, `column-number-mode` and `which-func-mode` enable particular minor modes; as usual, these variable names are also the minor mode command names.)

22.4.4 Variables Used in the Mode Line

This section describes variables incorporated by the standard value of `mode-line-format` into the text of the mode line. There is nothing inherently special about these variables; any other variables could have the same effects on the mode line if the value of `mode-line-format` is changed to use them. However, various parts of Emacs set these variables on the understanding that they will control parts of the mode line; therefore, practically speaking, it is essential for the mode line to use them. Also see Section "Optional Mode Line" in *The GNU Emacs Manual*.

`mode-line-mule-info`   [Variable]
    This variable holds the value of the mode line construct that displays information about the language environment, buffer coding system, and current input method. See Chapter 32 [Non-ASCII Characters], page 761.

`mode-line-modified`   [Variable]
    This variable holds the value of the mode line construct that displays whether the current buffer is modified. Its default value displays '`**`' if the buffer is modified, '`--`'

if the buffer is not modified, '%%' if the buffer is read only, and '%*' if the buffer is read only and modified.

Changing this variable does not force an update of the mode line.

mode-line-frame-identification   [Variable]
This variable identifies the current frame. Its default value displays " " if you are using a window system which can show multiple frames, or "-%F " on an ordinary terminal which shows only one frame at a time.

mode-line-buffer-identification   [Variable]
This variable identifies the buffer being displayed in the window. Its default value displays the buffer name, padded with spaces to at least 12 columns.

mode-line-position   [Variable]
This variable indicates the position in the buffer. Its default value displays the buffer percentage and, optionally, the buffer size, the line number and the column number.

vc-mode   [Variable]
The variable **vc-mode**, buffer-local in each buffer, records whether the buffer's visited file is maintained with version control, and, if so, which kind. Its value is a string that appears in the mode line, or **nil** for no version control.

mode-line-modes   [Variable]
This variable displays the buffer's major and minor modes. Its default value also displays the recursive editing level, information on the process status, and whether narrowing is in effect.

mode-line-remote   [Variable]
This variable is used to show whether **default-directory** for the current buffer is remote.

mode-line-client   [Variable]
This variable is used to identify **emacsclient** frames.

The following three variables are used in **mode-line-modes**:

mode-name   [Variable]
This buffer-local variable holds the "pretty" name of the current buffer's major mode. Each major mode should set this variable so that the mode name will appear in the mode line. The value does not have to be a string, but can use any of the data types valid in a mode-line construct (see Section 22.4.2 [Mode Line Data], page 452). To compute the string that will identify the mode name in the mode line, use **format-mode-line** (see Section 22.4.8 [Emulating Mode Line], page 459).

mode-line-process   [Variable]
This buffer-local variable contains the mode line information on process status in modes used for communicating with subprocesses. It is displayed immediately following the major mode name, with no intervening space. For example, its value in the *shell* buffer is (":%s"), which allows the shell to display its status along with the major mode as: '(Shell:run)'. Normally this variable is **nil**.

mode-line-front-space   [Variable]

> This variable is displayed at the front of the mode line. By default, this construct is displayed right at the beginning of the mode line, except that if there is a memory-full message, it is displayed first.

mode-line-end-spaces   [Variable]

> This variable is displayed at the end of the mode line.

mode-line-misc-info   [Variable]

> Mode line construct for miscellaneous information. By default, this shows the information specified by `global-mode-string`.

minor-mode-alist   [Variable]

> This variable holds an association list whose elements specify how the mode line should indicate that a minor mode is active. Each element of the `minor-mode-alist` should be a two-element list:
>
> > (*minor-mode-variable mode-line-string*)
>
> More generally, *mode-line-string* can be any mode line construct. It appears in the mode line when the value of *minor-mode-variable* is non-`nil`, and not otherwise. These strings should begin with spaces so that they don't run together. Conventionally, the *minor-mode-variable* for a specific mode is set to a non-`nil` value when that minor mode is activated.
>
> `minor-mode-alist` itself is not buffer-local. Each variable mentioned in the alist should be buffer-local if its minor mode can be enabled separately in each buffer.

global-mode-string   [Variable]

> This variable holds a mode line construct that, by default, appears in the mode line just after the `which-func-mode` minor mode if set, else after `mode-line-modes`. The command `display-time` sets `global-mode-string` to refer to the variable `display-time-string`, which holds a string containing the time and load information.
>
> The '%M' construct substitutes the value of `global-mode-string`, but that is obsolete, since the variable is included in the mode line from `mode-line-format`.

Here is a simplified version of the default value of `mode-line-format`. The real default value also specifies addition of text properties.

```
("-"
 mode-line-mule-info
 mode-line-modified
 mode-line-frame-identification
 mode-line-buffer-identification
 "   "
 mode-line-position
 (vc-mode vc-mode)
 "  "
 mode-line-modes
 (which-func-mode ("" which-func-format "--"))
 (global-mode-string ("--" global-mode-string))
 "-%-")
```

22.4.5 %-Constructs in the Mode Line

Strings used as mode line constructs can use certain %-constructs to substitute various kinds of data. The following is a list of the defined %-constructs, and what they mean.

In any construct except '%%', you can add a decimal integer after the '%' to specify a minimum field width. If the width is less, the field is padded to that width. Purely numeric constructs ('c', 'i', 'I', and 'l') are padded by inserting spaces to the left, and others are padded by inserting spaces to the right.

%b   The current buffer name, obtained with the `buffer-name` function. See Section 26.3 [Buffer Names], page 553.

%c   The current column number of point.

%e   When Emacs is nearly out of memory for Lisp objects, a brief message saying so. Otherwise, this is empty.

%f   The visited file name, obtained with the `buffer-file-name` function. See Section 26.4 [Buffer File Name], page 554.

%F   The title (only on a window system) or the name of the selected frame. See Section 28.4.3.1 [Basic Parameters], page 645.

%i   The size of the accessible part of the current buffer; basically (- (point-max) (point-min)).

%I   Like '%i', but the size is printed in a more readable way by using 'k' for 10^3, 'M' for 10^6, 'G' for 10^9, etc., to abbreviate.

%l   The current line number of point, counting within the accessible portion of the buffer.

%n   'Narrow' when narrowing is in effect; nothing otherwise (see `narrow-to-region` in Section 29.4 [Narrowing], page 684).

%p   The percentage of the buffer text above the **top** of window, or 'Top', 'Bottom' or 'All'. Note that the default mode line construct truncates this to three characters.

%P   The percentage of the buffer text that is above the **bottom** of the window (which includes the text visible in the window, as well as the text above the top), plus 'Top' if the top of the buffer is visible on screen; or 'Bottom' or 'All'.

%s   The status of the subprocess belonging to the current buffer, obtained with `process-status`. See Section 36.6 [Process Information], page 851.

%z   The mnemonics of keyboard, terminal, and buffer coding systems.

%Z   Like '%z', but including the end-of-line format.

%*   '%' if the buffer is read only (see `buffer-read-only`);
            '*' if the buffer is modified (see `buffer-modified-p`);
            '-' otherwise. See Section 26.5 [Buffer Modification], page 556.

%+   '*' if the buffer is modified (see `buffer-modified-p`);
            '%' if the buffer is read only (see `buffer-read-only`);
            '-' otherwise. This differs from '%*' only for a modified read-only buffer. See Section 26.5 [Buffer Modification], page 556.

%&	'*' if the buffer is modified, and '-' otherwise.
%[	An indication of the depth of recursive editing levels (not counting minibuffer levels): one '[' for each editing level. See Section 20.13 [Recursive Editing], page 386.
%]	One ']' for each recursive editing level (not counting minibuffer levels).
%-	Dashes sufficient to fill the remainder of the mode line.
%%	The character '%'—this is how to include a literal '%' in a string in which %-constructs are allowed.

The following two %-constructs are still supported, but they are obsolete, since you can get the same results with the variables `mode-name` and `global-mode-string`.

%m	The value of `mode-name`.
%M	The value of `global-mode-string`.

22.4.6 Properties in the Mode Line

Certain text properties are meaningful in the mode line. The `face` property affects the appearance of text; the `help-echo` property associates help strings with the text, and `keymap` can make the text mouse-sensitive.

There are four ways to specify text properties for text in the mode line:

1. Put a string with a text property directly into the mode line data structure.
2. Put a text property on a mode line %-construct such as '%12b'; then the expansion of the %-construct will have that same text property.
3. Use a (`:propertize` *elt props*...) construct to give *elt* a text property specified by *props*.
4. Use a list containing `:eval` *form* in the mode line data structure, and make *form* evaluate to a string that has a text property.

You can use the `keymap` property to specify a keymap. This keymap only takes real effect for mouse clicks; binding character keys and function keys to it has no effect, since it is impossible to move point into the mode line.

When the mode line refers to a variable which does not have a non-`nil` `risky-local-variable` property, any text properties given or specified within that variable's values are ignored. This is because such properties could otherwise specify functions to be called, and those functions could come from file local variables.

22.4.7 Window Header Lines

A window can have a *header line* at the top, just as it can have a mode line at the bottom. The header line feature works just like the mode line feature, except that it's controlled by `header-line-format`:

`header-line-format`   [Variable]
> This variable, local in every buffer, specifies how to display the header line, for windows displaying the buffer. The format of the value is the same as for `mode-line-format` (see Section 22.4.2 [Mode Line Data], page 452). It is normally `nil`, so that ordinary buffers have no header line.

`window-header-line-height` &optional *window* [Function]
> This function returns the height in pixels of *window*'s header line. *window* must be a live window, and defaults to the selected window.

A window that is just one line tall never displays a header line. A window that is two lines tall cannot display both a mode line and a header line at once; if it has a mode line, then it does not display a header line.

22.4.8 Emulating Mode Line Formatting

You can use the function `format-mode-line` to compute the text that would appear in a mode line or header line based on a certain mode line construct.

`format-mode-line` *format* **&optional** *face window buffer* [Function]
> This function formats a line of text according to *format* as if it were generating the mode line for *window*, but it also returns the text as a string. The argument *window* defaults to the selected window. If *buffer* is non-`nil`, all the information used is taken from *buffer*; by default, it comes from *window*'s buffer.
>
> The value string normally has text properties that correspond to the faces, keymaps, etc., that the mode line would have. Any character for which no `face` property is specified by *format* gets a default value determined by *face*. If *face* is `t`, that stands for either `mode-line` if *window* is selected, otherwise `mode-line-inactive`. If *face* is `nil` or omitted, that stands for the default face. If *face* is an integer, the value returned by this function will have no text properties.
>
> You can also specify other valid faces as the value of *face*. If specified, that face provides the `face` property for characters whose face is not specified by *format*.
>
> Note that using `mode-line`, `mode-line-inactive`, or `header-line` as *face* will actually redisplay the mode line or the header line, respectively, using the current definitions of the corresponding face, in addition to returning the formatted string. (Other faces do not cause redisplay.)
>
> For example, `(format-mode-line header-line-format)` returns the text that would appear in the selected window's header line (`""` if it has no header line). `(format-mode-line header-line-format 'header-line)` returns the same text, with each character carrying the face that it will have in the header line itself, and also redraws the header line.

22.5 Imenu

Imenu is a feature that lets users select a definition or section in the buffer, from a menu which lists all of them, to go directly to that location in the buffer. Imenu works by constructing a buffer index which lists the names and buffer positions of the definitions, or other named portions of the buffer; then the user can choose one of them and move point to it. Major modes can add a menu bar item to use Imenu using `imenu-add-to-menubar`.

`imenu-add-to-menubar` *name* [Command]
> This function defines a local menu bar item named *name* to run Imenu.

The user-level commands for using Imenu are described in the Emacs Manual (see Section "Imenu" in *the Emacs Manual*). This section explains how to customize Imenu's method of finding definitions or buffer portions for a particular major mode.

The usual and simplest way is to set the variable `imenu-generic-expression`:

`imenu-generic-expression`   [Variable]

> This variable, if non-`nil`, is a list that specifies regular expressions for finding definitions for Imenu. Simple elements of `imenu-generic-expression` look like this:
>
> > (*menu-title regexp index*)
>
> Here, if *menu-title* is non-`nil`, it says that the matches for this element should go in a submenu of the buffer index; *menu-title* itself specifies the name for the submenu. If *menu-title* is `nil`, the matches for this element go directly in the top level of the buffer index.
>
> The second item in the list, *regexp*, is a regular expression (see Section 33.3 [Regular Expressions], page 793); anything in the buffer that it matches is considered a definition, something to mention in the buffer index. The third item, *index*, is a nonnegative integer that indicates which subexpression in *regexp* matches the definition's name.
>
> An element can also look like this:
>
> > (*menu-title regexp index function arguments...*)
>
> Each match for this element creates an index item, and when the index item is selected by the user, it calls *function* with arguments consisting of the item name, the buffer position, and *arguments*.
>
> For Emacs Lisp mode, `imenu-generic-expression` could look like this:
>
> ```
>     ((nil "^\\s-*(def\\(un\\|subst\\|macro\\|advice\\)\
>     \\s-+\\([-A-Za-z0-9+]+\\)" 2)
>      ("*Vars*" "^\\s-*(def\\(var\\|const\\)\
>     \\s-+\\([-A-Za-z0-9+]+\\)" 2)
>      ("*Types*"
>       "^\\s-*\
>     (def\\(type\\|struct\\|class\\|ine-condition\\)\
>     \\s-+\\([-A-Za-z0-9+]+\\)" 2))
> ```
>
> Setting this variable makes it buffer-local in the current buffer.

`imenu-case-fold-search`   [Variable]

> This variable controls whether matching against the regular expressions in the value of `imenu-generic-expression` is case-sensitive: `t`, the default, means matching should ignore case.
>
> Setting this variable makes it buffer-local in the current buffer.

`imenu-syntax-alist`   [Variable]

> This variable is an alist of syntax table modifiers to use while processing `imenu-generic-expression`, to override the syntax table of the current buffer. Each element should have this form:
>
> > (*characters . syntax-description*)

The CAR, *characters*, can be either a character or a string. The element says to give that character or characters the syntax specified by *syntax-description*, which is passed to `modify-syntax-entry` (see Section 34.3 [Syntax Table Functions], page 821).

This feature is typically used to give word syntax to characters which normally have symbol syntax, and thus to simplify `imenu-generic-expression` and speed up matching. For example, Fortran mode uses it this way:

```
(setq imenu-syntax-alist '(("_$" . "w")))
```

The `imenu-generic-expression` regular expressions can then use '\\sw+' instead of '\\(\\sw\\|\\s_\\)+'. Note that this technique may be inconvenient when the mode needs to limit the initial character of a name to a smaller set of characters than are allowed in the rest of a name.

Setting this variable makes it buffer-local in the current buffer.

Another way to customize Imenu for a major mode is to set the variables `imenu-prev-index-position-function` and `imenu-extract-index-name-function`:

imenu-prev-index-position-function   [Variable]
>   If this variable is non-`nil`, its value should be a function that finds the next definition to put in the buffer index, scanning backward in the buffer from point. It should return `nil` if it doesn't find another definition before point. Otherwise it should leave point at the place it finds a definition and return any non-`nil` value.
>
>   Setting this variable makes it buffer-local in the current buffer.

imenu-extract-index-name-function   [Variable]
>   If this variable is non-`nil`, its value should be a function to return the name for a definition, assuming point is in that definition as the `imenu-prev-index-position-function` function would leave it.
>
>   Setting this variable makes it buffer-local in the current buffer.

The last way to customize Imenu for a major mode is to set the variable `imenu-create-index-function`:

imenu-create-index-function   [Variable]
>   This variable specifies the function to use for creating a buffer index. The function should take no arguments, and return an index alist for the current buffer. It is called within `save-excursion`, so where it leaves point makes no difference.
>
>   The index alist can have three types of elements. Simple elements look like this:
>
>      ```
>      (index-name . index-position)
>      ```
>
>   Selecting a simple element has the effect of moving to position *index-position* in the buffer. Special elements look like this:
>
>      ```
>      (index-name index-position function arguments...)
>      ```
>
>   Selecting a special element performs:
>
>      ```
>      (funcall function
>               index-name index-position arguments...)
>      ```

A nested sub-alist element looks like this:

```
(menu-title . sub-alist)
```

It creates the submenu *menu-title* specified by *sub-alist*.

The default value of `imenu-create-index-function` is `imenu-default-create-index-function`. This function calls the value of `imenu-prev-index-position-function` and the value of `imenu-extract-index-name-function` to produce the index alist. However, if either of these two variables is `nil`, the default function uses `imenu-generic-expression` instead.

Setting this variable makes it buffer-local in the current buffer.

22.6 Font Lock Mode

Font Lock mode is a buffer-local minor mode that automatically attaches `face` properties to certain parts of the buffer based on their syntactic role. How it parses the buffer depends on the major mode; most major modes define syntactic criteria for which faces to use in which contexts. This section explains how to customize Font Lock for a particular major mode.

Font Lock mode finds text to highlight in two ways: through syntactic parsing based on the syntax table, and through searching (usually for regular expressions). Syntactic fontification happens first; it finds comments and string constants and highlights them. Search-based fontification happens second.

22.6.1 Font Lock Basics

The Font Lock functionality is based on several basic functions. Each of these calls the function specified by the corresponding variable. This indirection allows major and minor modes to modify the way fontification works in the buffers of that mode, and even use the Font Lock mechanisms for features that have nothing to do with fontification. (This is why the description below says "should" when it describes what the functions do: the mode can customize the values of the corresponding variables to do something entirely different.) The variables mentioned below are described in Section 22.6.4 [Other Font Lock Variables], page 468.

`font-lock-fontify-buffer`
>   This function should fontify the current buffer's accessible portion, by calling the function specified by `font-lock-fontify-buffer-function`.

`font-lock-unfontify-buffer`
>   Used when turning Font Lock off to remove the fontification. Calls the function specified by `font-lock-unfontify-buffer-function`.

`font-lock-fontify-region beg end &optional loudly`
>   Should fontify the region between *beg* and *end*. If *loudly* is non-`nil`, should display status messages while fontifying. Calls the function specified by `font-lock-fontify-region-function`.

`font-lock-unfontify-region beg end`
>   Should remove fontification from the region between *beg* and *end*. Calls the function specified by `font-lock-unfontify-region-function`.

`font-lock-flush &optional beg end`

> This function should mark the fontification of the region between *beg* and *end* as outdated. If not specified or `nil`, *beg* and *end* default to the beginning and end of the buffer's accessible portion. Calls the function specified by `font-lock-flush-function`.

`font-lock-ensure &optional beg end`

> This function should make sure the region between *beg* and *end* has been fontified. The optional arguments *beg* and *end* default to the beginning and the end of the buffer's accessible portion. Calls the function specified by `font-lock-ensure-function`.

There are several variables that control how Font Lock mode highlights text. But major modes should not set any of these variables directly. Instead, they should set `font-lock-defaults` as a buffer-local variable. The value assigned to this variable is used, if and when Font Lock mode is enabled, to set all the other variables.

`font-lock-defaults` [Variable]

> This variable is set by modes to specify how to fontify text in that mode. It automatically becomes buffer-local when set. If its value is `nil`, Font Lock mode does no highlighting, and you can use the 'Faces' menu (under 'Edit' and then 'Text Properties' in the menu bar) to assign faces explicitly to text in the buffer.
>
> If non-`nil`, the value should look like this:
>
> ```
> (keywords [keywords-only [case-fold
> [syntax-alist other-vars...]]])
> ```
>
> The first element, *keywords*, indirectly specifies the value of `font-lock-keywords` which directs search-based fontification. It can be a symbol, a variable or a function whose value is the list to use for `font-lock-keywords`. It can also be a list of several such symbols, one for each possible level of fontification. The first symbol specifies the 'mode default' level of fontification, the next symbol level 1 fontification, the next level 2, and so on. The 'mode default' level is normally the same as level 1. It is used when `font-lock-maximum-decoration` has a `nil` value. See Section 22.6.5 [Levels of Font Lock], page 469.
>
> The second element, *keywords-only*, specifies the value of the variable `font-lock-keywords-only`. If this is omitted or `nil`, syntactic fontification (of strings and comments) is also performed. If this is non-`nil`, syntactic fontification is not performed. See Section 22.6.8 [Syntactic Font Lock], page 471.
>
> The third element, *case-fold*, specifies the value of `font-lock-keywords-case-fold-search`. If it is non-`nil`, Font Lock mode ignores case during search-based fontification.
>
> If the fourth element, *syntax-alist*, is non-`nil`, it should be a list of cons cells of the form (*char-or-string* . *string*). These are used to set up a syntax table for syntactic fontification; the resulting syntax table is stored in `font-lock-syntax-table`. If *syntax-alist* is omitted or `nil`, syntactic fontification uses the syntax table returned by the `syntax-table` function. See Section 34.3 [Syntax Table Functions], page 821.

All the remaining elements (if any) are collectively called *other-vars*. Each of these elements should have the form (`variable . value`)—which means, make *variable* buffer-local and then set it to *value*. You can use these *other-vars* to set other variables that affect fontification, aside from those you can control with the first five elements. See Section 22.6.4 [Other Font Lock Variables], page 468.

If your mode fontifies text explicitly by adding `font-lock-face` properties, it can specify (`nil t`) for `font-lock-defaults` to turn off all automatic fontification. However, this is not required; it is possible to fontify some things using `font-lock-face` properties and set up automatic fontification for other parts of the text.

22.6.2 Search-based Fontification

The variable which directly controls search-based fontification is `font-lock-keywords`, which is typically specified via the *keywords* element in `font-lock-defaults`.

`font-lock-keywords`   [Variable]

> The value of this variable is a list of the keywords to highlight. Lisp programs should not set this variable directly. Normally, the value is automatically set by Font Lock mode, using the *keywords* element in `font-lock-defaults`. The value can also be altered using the functions `font-lock-add-keywords` and `font-lock-remove-keywords` (see Section 22.6.3 [Customizing Keywords], page 467).

Each element of `font-lock-keywords` specifies how to find certain cases of text, and how to highlight those cases. Font Lock mode processes the elements of `font-lock-keywords` one by one, and for each element, it finds and handles all matches. Ordinarily, once part of the text has been fontified already, this cannot be overridden by a subsequent match in the same text; but you can specify different behavior using the *override* element of a *subexp-highlighter*.

Each element of `font-lock-keywords` should have one of these forms:

regexp   Highlight all matches for *regexp* using `font-lock-keyword-face`. For example,

> ; ; Highlight occurrences of the word 'foo'
> ; ; using `font-lock-keyword-face`.
> `"\\<foo\\>"`

Be careful when composing these regular expressions; a poorly written pattern can dramatically slow things down! The function `regexp-opt` (see Section 33.3.3 [Regexp Functions], page 802) is useful for calculating optimal regular expressions to match several keywords.

function Find text by calling *function*, and highlight the matches it finds using `font-lock-keyword-face`.

> When *function* is called, it receives one argument, the limit of the search; it should begin searching at point, and not search beyond the limit. It should return non-`nil` if it succeeds, and set the match data to describe the match that was found. Returning `nil` indicates failure of the search.

> Fontification will call *function* repeatedly with the same limit, and with point where the previous invocation left it, until *function* fails. On failure, *function* need not reset point in any particular way.

`(matcher . subexp)`

> In this kind of element, *matcher* is either a regular expression or a function, as described above. The CDR, *subexp*, specifies which subexpression of *matcher* should be highlighted (instead of the entire text that *matcher* matched).
>
> ```
> ;; Highlight the 'bar' in each occurrence of 'fubar',
> ;; using font-lock-keyword-face.
> ("fu\\(bar\\)" . 1)
> ```
>
> If you use `regexp-opt` to produce the regular expression *matcher*, you can use `regexp-opt-depth` (see Section 33.3.3 [Regexp Functions], page 802) to calculate the value for *subexp*.

`(matcher . facespec)`

> In this kind of element, *facespec* is an expression whose value specifies the face to use for highlighting. In the simplest case, *facespec* is a Lisp variable (a symbol) whose value is a face name.
>
> ```
> ;; Highlight occurrences of 'fubar',
> ;; using the face which is the value of fubar-face.
> ("fubar" . fubar-face)
> ```
>
> However, *facespec* can also evaluate to a list of this form:
>
> ```
> (face face prop1 val1 prop2 val2...)
> ```
>
> to specify the face *face* and various additional text properties to put on the text that matches. If you do this, be sure to add the other text property names that you set in this way to the value of `font-lock-extra-managed-props` so that the properties will also be cleared out when they are no longer appropriate. Alternatively, you can set the variable `font-lock-unfontify-region-function` to a function that clears these properties. See Section 22.6.4 [Other Font Lock Variables], page 468.

`(matcher . subexp-highlighter)`

> In this kind of element, *subexp-highlighter* is a list which specifies how to highlight matches found by *matcher*. It has the form:
>
> ```
> (subexp facespec [override [laxmatch]])
> ```
>
> The CAR, *subexp*, is an integer specifying which subexpression of the match to fontify (0 means the entire matching text). The second subelement, *facespec*, is an expression whose value specifies the face, as described above.
>
> The last two values in *subexp-highlighter*, *override* and *laxmatch*, are optional flags. If *override* is `t`, this element can override existing fontification made by previous elements of `font-lock-keywords`. If it is `keep`, then each character is fontified if it has not been fontified already by some other element. If it is `prepend`, the face specified by *facespec* is added to the beginning of the `font-lock-face` property. If it is `append`, the face is added to the end of the `font-lock-face` property.
>
> If *laxmatch* is non-`nil`, it means there should be no error if there is no subexpression numbered *subexp* in *matcher*. Obviously, fontification of the subexpression numbered *subexp* will not occur. However, fontification of other subexpressions

(and other regexps) will continue. If *laxmatch* is `nil`, and the specified subexpression is missing, then an error is signaled which terminates search-based fontification.

Here are some examples of elements of this kind, and what they do:

```
;; Highlight occurrences of either 'foo' or 'bar', using
;; foo-bar-face, even if they have already been highlighted.
;; foo-bar-face should be a variable whose value is a face.
("foo\\|bar" 0 foo-bar-face t)

;; Highlight the first subexpression within each occurrence
;; that the function fubar-match finds,
;; using the face which is the value of fubar-face.
(fubar-match 1 fubar-face)
```

`(matcher . anchored-highlighter)`

In this kind of element, *anchored-highlighter* specifies how to highlight text that follows a match found by *matcher*. So a match found by *matcher* acts as the anchor for further searches specified by *anchored-highlighter*. *anchored-highlighter* is a list of the following form:

```
(anchored-matcher pre-form post-form
                  subexp-highlighters...)
```

Here, *anchored-matcher*, like *matcher*, is either a regular expression or a function. After a match of *matcher* is found, point is at the end of the match. Now, Font Lock evaluates the form *pre-form*. Then it searches for matches of *anchored-matcher* and uses *subexp-highlighters* to highlight these. A *subexp-highlighter* is as described above. Finally, Font Lock evaluates *post-form*.

The forms *pre-form* and *post-form* can be used to initialize before, and cleanup after, *anchored-matcher* is used. Typically, *pre-form* is used to move point to some position relative to the match of *matcher*, before starting with *anchored-matcher*. *post-form* might be used to move back, before resuming with *matcher*.

After Font Lock evaluates *pre-form*, it does not search for *anchored-matcher* beyond the end of the line. However, if *pre-form* returns a buffer position that is greater than the position of point after *pre-form* is evaluated, then the position returned by *pre-form* is used as the limit of the search instead. It is generally a bad idea to return a position greater than the end of the line; in other words, the *anchored-matcher* search should not span lines.

For example,

```
;; Highlight occurrences of the word 'item' following
;; an occurrence of the word 'anchor' (on the same line)
;; in the value of item-face.
("\\<anchor\\>" "\\<item\\>" nil nil (0 item-face))
```

Here, *pre-form* and *post-form* are `nil`. Therefore searching for 'item' starts at the end of the match of 'anchor', and searching for subsequent instances of 'anchor' resumes from where searching for 'item' concluded.

`(matcher highlighters...)`

This sort of element specifies several *highlighter* lists for a single *matcher*. A *highlighter* list can be of the type *subexp-highlighter* or *anchored-highlighter* as described above.

For example,

```
;; Highlight occurrences of the word 'anchor' in the value
;; of anchor-face, and subsequent occurrences of the word
;; 'item' (on the same line) in the value of item-face.
("\\<anchor\\>" (0 anchor-face)
                        ("\\<item\\>" nil nil (0 item-face)))
```

`(eval . `*`form`*`)`
> Here *form* is an expression to be evaluated the first time this value of `font-lock-keywords` is used in a buffer. Its value should have one of the forms described in this table.

Warning: Do not design an element of `font-lock-keywords` to match text which spans lines; this does not work reliably. For details, see See Section 22.6.9 [Multiline Font Lock], page 472.

You can use *case-fold* in `font-lock-defaults` to specify the value of `font-lock-keywords-case-fold-search` which says whether search-based fontification should be case-insensitive.

`font-lock-keywords-case-fold-search` [Variable]
> Non-`nil` means that regular expression matching for the sake of `font-lock-keywords` should be case-insensitive.

22.6.3 Customizing Search-Based Fontification

You can use `font-lock-add-keywords` to add additional search-based fontification rules to a major mode, and `font-lock-remove-keywords` to remove rules.

`font-lock-add-keywords` *mode keywords* **&optional** *how* [Function]
> This function adds highlighting *keywords*, for the current buffer or for major mode *mode*. The argument *keywords* should be a list with the same format as the variable `font-lock-keywords`.
>
> If *mode* is a symbol which is a major mode command name, such as `c-mode`, the effect is that enabling Font Lock mode in *mode* will add *keywords* to `font-lock-keywords`. Calling with a non-`nil` value of *mode* is correct only in your `~/.emacs` file.
>
> If *mode* is `nil`, this function adds *keywords* to `font-lock-keywords` in the current buffer. This way of calling `font-lock-add-keywords` is usually used in mode hook functions.
>
> By default, *keywords* are added at the beginning of `font-lock-keywords`. If the optional argument *how* is `set`, they are used to replace the value of `font-lock-keywords`. If *how* is any other non-`nil` value, they are added at the end of `font-lock-keywords`.
>
> Some modes provide specialized support you can use in additional highlighting patterns. See the variables `c-font-lock-extra-types`, `c++-font-lock-extra-types`, and `java-font-lock-extra-types`, for example.
>
> **Warning:** Major mode commands must not call `font-lock-add-keywords` under any circumstances, either directly or indirectly, except through their mode hooks. (Doing so would lead to incorrect behavior for some minor modes.) They should set up their rules for search-based fontification by setting `font-lock-keywords`.

`font-lock-remove-keywords` *mode keywords*   [Function]

This function removes *keywords* from `font-lock-keywords` for the current buffer or for major mode *mode*. As in `font-lock-add-keywords`, *mode* should be a major mode command name or `nil`. All the caveats and requirements for `font-lock-add-keywords` apply here too. The argument *keywords* must exactly match the one used by the corresponding `font-lock-add-keywords`.

For example, the following code adds two fontification patterns for C mode: one to fontify the word 'FIXME', even in comments, and another to fontify the words 'and', 'or' and 'not' as keywords.

```
(font-lock-add-keywords 'c-mode
 '(("\\<\\(FIXME\\):" 1 font-lock-warning-face prepend)
   ("\\<\\(and\\|or\\|not\\)\\>" . font-lock-keyword-face)))
```

This example affects only C mode proper. To add the same patterns to C mode *and* all modes derived from it, do this instead:

```
(add-hook 'c-mode-hook
 (lambda ()
  (font-lock-add-keywords nil
   '(("\\<\\(FIXME\\):" 1 font-lock-warning-face prepend)
     ("\\<\\(and\\|or\\|not\\)\\>" .
      font-lock-keyword-face)))))
```

22.6.4 Other Font Lock Variables

This section describes additional variables that a major mode can set by means of *other-vars* in `font-lock-defaults` (see Section 22.6.1 [Font Lock Basics], page 462).

`font-lock-mark-block-function`   [Variable]

If this variable is non-`nil`, it should be a function that is called with no arguments, to choose an enclosing range of text for refontification for the command *M-o M-o* (`font-lock-fontify-block`).

The function should report its choice by placing the region around it. A good choice is a range of text large enough to give proper results, but not too large so that refontification becomes slow. Typical values are `mark-defun` for programming modes or `mark-paragraph` for textual modes.

`font-lock-extra-managed-props`   [Variable]

This variable specifies additional properties (other than `font-lock-face`) that are being managed by Font Lock mode. It is used by `font-lock-default-unfontify-region`, which normally only manages the `font-lock-face` property. If you want Font Lock to manage other properties as well, you must specify them in a *facespec* in `font-lock-keywords` as well as add them to this list. See Section 22.6.2 [Search-based Fontification], page 464.

`font-lock-fontify-buffer-function`   [Variable]

Function to use for fontifying the buffer. The default value is `font-lock-default-fontify-buffer`.

`font-lock-unfontify-buffer-function`   [Variable]

Function to use for unfontifying the buffer. This is used when turning off Font Lock mode. The default value is `font-lock-default-unfontify-buffer`.

`font-lock-fontify-region-function`   [Variable]
> Function to use for fontifying a region. It should take two arguments, the beginning
> and end of the region, and an optional third argument *verbose*. If *verbose* is non-`nil`,
> the function should print status messages. The default value is `font-lock-default-`
> `fontify-region`.

`font-lock-unfontify-region-function`   [Variable]
> Function to use for unfontifying a region. It should take two arguments, the beginning
> and end of the region. The default value is `font-lock-default-unfontify-region`.

`font-lock-flush-function`   [Variable]
> Function to use for declaring that a region's fontification is out of date. It takes two
> arguments, the beginning and end of the region. The default value of this variable is
> `font-lock-after-change-function`.

`font-lock-ensure-function`   [Variable]
> Function to use for making sure a region of the current buffer has been fontified. It
> is called with two arguments, the beginning and end of the region. The default value
> of this variable is a function that calls `font-lock-default-fontify-buffer` if the
> buffer is not fontified; the effect is to make sure the entire accessible portion of the
> buffer is fontified.

`jit-lock-register` *function* **&optional** *contextual*   [Function]
> This function tells Font Lock mode to run the Lisp function *function* any time it
> has to fontify or refontify part of the current buffer. It calls *function* before calling
> the default fontification functions, and gives it two arguments, *start* and *end*, which
> specify the region to be fontified or refontified.
>
> The optional argument *contextual*, if non-`nil`, forces Font Lock mode to always re-
> fontify a syntactically relevant part of the buffer, and not just the modified lines. This
> argument can usually be omitted.

`jit-lock-unregister` *function*   [Function]
> If *function* was previously registered as a fontification function using `jit-lock-`
> `register`, this function unregisters it.

22.6.5 Levels of Font Lock

Some major modes offer three different levels of fontification. You can define multiple levels
by using a list of symbols for *keywords* in `font-lock-defaults`. Each symbol specifies one
level of fontification; it is up to the user to choose one of these levels, normally by setting
`font-lock-maximum-decoration` (see Section "Font Lock" in *the GNU Emacs Manual*).
The chosen level's symbol value is used to initialize `font-lock-keywords`.

Here are the conventions for how to define the levels of fontification:

- Level 1: highlight function declarations, file directives (such as include or import directives), strings and comments. The idea is speed, so only the most important and
  top-level components are fontified.

- Level 2: in addition to level 1, highlight all language keywords, including type names
  that act like keywords, as well as named constant values. The idea is that all keywords
  (either syntactic or semantic) should be fontified appropriately.

- Level 3: in addition to level 2, highlight the symbols being defined in function and variable declarations, and all builtin function names, wherever they appear.

22.6.6 Precalculated Fontification

Some major modes such as `list-buffers` and `occur` construct the buffer text programmatically. The easiest way for them to support Font Lock mode is to specify the faces of text when they insert the text in the buffer.

The way to do this is to specify the faces in the text with the special text property `font-lock-face` (see Section 31.19.4 [Special Properties], page 738). When Font Lock mode is enabled, this property controls the display, just like the `face` property. When Font Lock mode is disabled, `font-lock-face` has no effect on the display.

It is ok for a mode to use `font-lock-face` for some text and also use the normal Font Lock machinery. But if the mode does not use the normal Font Lock machinery, it should not set the variable `font-lock-defaults`.

22.6.7 Faces for Font Lock

Font Lock mode can highlight using any face, but Emacs defines several faces specifically for Font Lock to use to highlight text. These *Font Lock faces* are listed below. They can also be used by major modes for syntactic highlighting outside of Font Lock mode (see Section 22.2.1 [Major Mode Conventions], page 432).

Each of these symbols is both a face name, and a variable whose default value is the symbol itself. Thus, the default value of `font-lock-comment-face` is `font-lock-comment-face`.

The faces are listed with descriptions of their typical usage, and in order of greater to lesser prominence. If a mode's syntactic categories do not fit well with the usage descriptions, the faces can be assigned using the ordering as a guide.

`font-lock-warning-face`
> for a construct that is peculiar, or that greatly changes the meaning of other text, like ';;;###autoload' in Emacs Lisp and '#error' in C.

`font-lock-function-name-face`
> for the name of a function being defined or declared.

`font-lock-variable-name-face`
> for the name of a variable being defined or declared.

`font-lock-keyword-face`
> for a keyword with special syntactic significance, like 'for' and 'if' in C.

`font-lock-comment-face`
> for comments.

`font-lock-comment-delimiter-face`
> for comments delimiters, like '/*' and '*/' in C. On most terminals, this inherits from `font-lock-comment-face`.

`font-lock-type-face`
> for the names of user-defined data types.

`font-lock-constant-face`
> for the names of constants, like 'NULL' in C.

`font-lock-builtin-face`
> for the names of built-in functions.

`font-lock-preprocessor-face`
> for preprocessor commands. This inherits, by default, from `font-lock-builtin-face`.

`font-lock-string-face`
> for string constants.

`font-lock-doc-face`
> for documentation strings in the code. This inherits, by default, from `font-lock-string-face`.

`font-lock-negation-char-face`
> for easily-overlooked negation characters.

22.6.8 Syntactic Font Lock

Syntactic fontification uses a syntax table (see Chapter 34 [Syntax Tables], page 816) to find and highlight syntactically relevant text. If enabled, it runs prior to search-based fontification. The variable `font-lock-syntactic-face-function`, documented below, determines which syntactic constructs to highlight. There are several variables that affect syntactic fontification; you should set them by means of `font-lock-defaults` (see Section 22.6.1 [Font Lock Basics], page 462).

Whenever Font Lock mode performs syntactic fontification on a stretch of text, it first calls the function specified by `syntax-propertize-function`. Major modes can use this to apply `syntax-table` text properties to override the buffer's syntax table in special cases. See Section 34.4 [Syntax Properties], page 823.

`font-lock-keywords-only`   [Variable]
> If the value of this variable is non-`nil`, Font Lock does not do syntactic fontification, only search-based fontification based on `font-lock-keywords`. It is normally set by Font Lock mode based on the *keywords-only* element in `font-lock-defaults`.

`font-lock-syntax-table`   [Variable]
> This variable holds the syntax table to use for fontification of comments and strings. It is normally set by Font Lock mode based on the *syntax-alist* element in `font-lock-defaults`. If this value is `nil`, syntactic fontification uses the buffer's syntax table (the value returned by the function `syntax-table`; see Section 34.3 [Syntax Table Functions], page 821).

`font-lock-syntactic-face-function`   [Variable]
> If this variable is non-`nil`, it should be a function to determine which face to use for a given syntactic element (a string or a comment). The value is normally set through an *other-vars* element in `font-lock-defaults`.

> The function is called with one argument, the parse state at point returned by `parse-partial-sexp`, and should return a face. The default value returns

`font-lock-comment-face` for comments and `font-lock-string-face` for strings (see Section 22.6.7 [Faces for Font Lock], page 470).

22.6.9 Multiline Font Lock Constructs

Normally, elements of `font-lock-keywords` should not match across multiple lines; that doesn't work reliably, because Font Lock usually scans just part of the buffer, and it can miss a multi-line construct that crosses the line boundary where the scan starts. (The scan normally starts at the beginning of a line.)

Making elements that match multiline constructs work properly has two aspects: correct *identification* and correct *rehighlighting*. The first means that Font Lock finds all multiline constructs. The second means that Font Lock will correctly rehighlight all the relevant text when a multiline construct is changed—for example, if some of the text that was previously part of a multiline construct ceases to be part of it. The two aspects are closely related, and often getting one of them to work will appear to make the other also work. However, for reliable results you must attend explicitly to both aspects.

There are three ways to ensure correct identification of multiline constructs:

- Add a function to `font-lock-extend-region-functions` that does the *identification* and extends the scan so that the scanned text never starts or ends in the middle of a multiline construct.

- Use the `font-lock-fontify-region-function` hook similarly to extend the scan so that the scanned text never starts or ends in the middle of a multiline construct.

- Somehow identify the multiline construct right when it gets inserted into the buffer (or at any point after that but before font-lock tries to highlight it), and mark it with a `font-lock-multiline` which will instruct font-lock not to start or end the scan in the middle of the construct.

There are three ways to do rehighlighting of multiline constructs:

- Place a `font-lock-multiline` property on the construct. This will rehighlight the whole construct if any part of it is changed. In some cases you can do this automatically by setting the `font-lock-multiline` variable, which see.

- Make sure `jit-lock-contextually` is set and rely on it doing its job. This will only rehighlight the part of the construct that follows the actual change, and will do it after a short delay. This only works if the highlighting of the various parts of your multiline construct never depends on text in subsequent lines. Since `jit-lock-contextually` is activated by default, this can be an attractive solution.

- Place a `jit-lock-defer-multiline` property on the construct. This works only if `jit-lock-contextually` is used, and with the same delay before rehighlighting, but like `font-lock-multiline`, it also handles the case where highlighting depends on subsequent lines.

22.6.9.1 Font Lock Multiline

One way to ensure reliable rehighlighting of multiline Font Lock constructs is to put on them the text property `font-lock-multiline`. It should be present and non-`nil` for text that is part of a multiline construct.

When Font Lock is about to highlight a range of text, it first extends the boundaries of the range as necessary so that they do not fall within text marked with the `font-lock-multiline` property. Then it removes any `font-lock-multiline` properties from the range, and highlights it. The highlighting specification (mostly `font-lock-keywords`) must reinstall this property each time, whenever it is appropriate.

Warning: don't use the `font-lock-multiline` property on large ranges of text, because that will make rehighlighting slow.

`font-lock-multiline`   [Variable]

> If the `font-lock-multiline` variable is set to `t`, Font Lock will try to add the `font-lock-multiline` property automatically on multiline constructs. This is not a universal solution, however, since it slows down Font Lock somewhat. It can miss some multiline constructs, or make the property larger or smaller than necessary.
>
> For elements whose *matcher* is a function, the function should ensure that submatch 0 covers the whole relevant multiline construct, even if only a small subpart will be highlighted. It is often just as easy to add the `font-lock-multiline` property by hand.

The `font-lock-multiline` property is meant to ensure proper refontification; it does not automatically identify new multiline constructs. Identifying the requires that Font Lock mode operate on large enough chunks at a time. This will happen by accident on many cases, which may give the impression that multiline constructs magically work. If you set the `font-lock-multiline` variable non-`nil`, this impression will be even stronger, since the highlighting of those constructs which are found will be properly updated from then on. But that does not work reliably.

To find multiline constructs reliably, you must either manually place the `font-lock-multiline` property on the text before Font Lock mode looks at it, or use `font-lock-fontify-region-function`.

22.6.9.2 Region to Fontify after a Buffer Change

When a buffer is changed, the region that Font Lock refontifies is by default the smallest sequence of whole lines that spans the change. While this works well most of the time, sometimes it doesn't—for example, when a change alters the syntactic meaning of text on an earlier line.

You can enlarge (or even reduce) the region to refontify by setting the following variable:

`font-lock-extend-after-change-region-function`   [Variable]

> This buffer-local variable is either `nil` or a function for Font Lock mode to call to determine the region to scan and fontify.
>
> The function is given three parameters, the standard *beg*, *end*, and *old-len* from `after-change-functions` (see Section 31.28 [Change Hooks], page 759). It should return either a cons of the beginning and end buffer positions (in that order) of the region to fontify, or `nil` (which means choose the region in the standard way). This function needs to preserve point, the match-data, and the current restriction. The region it returns may start or end in the middle of a line.
>
> Since this function is called after every buffer change, it should be reasonably fast.

22.7 Automatic Indentation of code

For programming languages, an important feature of a major mode is to provide automatic indentation. There are two parts: one is to decide what is the right indentation of a line, and the other is to decide when to reindent a line. By default, Emacs reindents a line whenever you type a character in `electric-indent-chars`, which by default only includes Newline. Major modes can add chars to `electric-indent-chars` according to the syntax of the language.

Deciding what is the right indentation is controlled in Emacs by `indent-line-function` (see Section 31.17.2 [Mode-Specific Indent], page 727). For some modes, the *right* indentation cannot be known reliably, typically because indentation is significant so several indentations are valid but with different meanings. In that case, the mode should set `electric-indent-inhibit` to make sure the line is not constantly re-indented against the user's wishes.

Writing a good indentation function can be difficult and to a large extent it is still a black art. Many major mode authors will start by writing a simple indentation function that works for simple cases, for example by comparing with the indentation of the previous text line. For most programming languages that are not really line-based, this tends to scale very poorly: improving such a function to let it handle more diverse situations tends to become more and more difficult, resulting in the end with a large, complex, unmaintainable indentation function which nobody dares to touch.

A good indentation function will usually need to actually parse the text, according to the syntax of the language. Luckily, it is not necessary to parse the text in as much detail as would be needed for a compiler, but on the other hand, the parser embedded in the indentation code will want to be somewhat friendly to syntactically incorrect code.

Good maintainable indentation functions usually fall into two categories: either parsing forward from some safe starting point until the position of interest, or parsing backward from the position of interest. Neither of the two is a clearly better choice than the other: parsing backward is often more difficult than parsing forward because programming languages are designed to be parsed forward, but for the purpose of indentation it has the advantage of not needing to guess a safe starting point, and it generally enjoys the property that only a minimum of text will be analyzed to decide the indentation of a line, so indentation will tend to be less affected by syntax errors in some earlier unrelated piece of code. Parsing forward on the other hand is usually easier and has the advantage of making it possible to reindent efficiently a whole region at a time, with a single parse.

Rather than write your own indentation function from scratch, it is often preferable to try and reuse some existing ones or to rely on a generic indentation engine. There are sadly few such engines. The CC-mode indentation code (used with C, C++, Java, Awk and a few other such modes) has been made more generic over the years, so if your language seems somewhat similar to one of those languages, you might try to use that engine. Another one is SMIE which takes an approach in the spirit of Lisp sexps and adapts it to non-Lisp languages.

22.7.1 Simple Minded Indentation Engine

SMIE is a package that provides a generic navigation and indentation engine. Based on a very simple parser using an operator precedence grammar, it lets major modes extend the sexp-based navigation of Lisp to non-Lisp languages as well as provide a simple to use but reliable auto-indentation.

Operator precedence grammar is a very primitive technology for parsing compared to some of the more common techniques used in compilers. It has the following characteristics: its parsing power is very limited, and it is largely unable to detect syntax errors, but it has the advantage of being algorithmically efficient and able to parse forward just as well as backward. In practice that means that SMIE can use it for indentation based on backward parsing, that it can provide both `forward-sexp` and `backward-sexp` functionality, and that it will naturally work on syntactically incorrect code without any extra effort. The downside is that it also means that most programming languages cannot be parsed correctly using SMIE, at least not without resorting to some special tricks (see Section 22.7.1.5 [SMIE Tricks], page 478).

22.7.1.1 SMIE Setup and Features

SMIE is meant to be a one-stop shop for structural navigation and various other features which rely on the syntactic structure of code, in particular automatic indentation. The main entry point is `smie-setup` which is a function typically called while setting up a major mode.

`smie-setup` *grammar rules-function* **&rest** *keywords*　　　　　　　　[Function]

> Setup SMIE navigation and indentation. *grammar* is a grammar table generated by `smie-prec2->grammar`. *rules-function* is a set of indentation rules for use on `smie-rules-function`. *keywords* are additional arguments, which can include the following keywords:
>
> - `:forward-token` *fun*: Specify the forward lexer to use.
> - `:backward-token` *fun*: Specify the backward lexer to use.

Calling this function is sufficient to make commands such as `forward-sexp`, `backward-sexp`, and `transpose-sexps` be able to properly handle structural elements other than just the paired parentheses already handled by syntax tables. For example, if the provided grammar is precise enough, `transpose-sexps` can correctly transpose the two arguments of a + operator, taking into account the precedence rules of the language.

Calling `smie-setup` is also sufficient to make TAB indentation work in the expected way, extends `blink-matching-paren` to apply to elements like `begin...end`, and provides some commands that you can bind in the major mode keymap.

`smie-close-block`　　　　　　　　　　　　　　　　　　　　　　[Command]

> This command closes the most recently opened (and not yet closed) block.

`smie-down-list` **&optional** *arg*　　　　　　　　　　　　　　　[Command]

> This command is like `down-list` but it also pays attention to nesting of tokens other than parentheses, such as `begin...end`.

22.7.1.2 Operator Precedence Grammars

SMIE's precedence grammars simply give to each token a pair of precedences: the left-precedence and the right-precedence. We say `T1` < `T2` if the right-precedence of token `T1` is less than the left-precedence of token `T2`. A good way to read this < is as a kind of parenthesis: if we find ... T1 `something` T2 ... then that should be parsed as ... T1 (`something` T2 ... rather than as ... T1 `something`) T2 .... The latter interpretation would be the case if we had T1 > T2. If we have T1 = T2, it means that token T2 follows token T1 in the same syntactic construction, so typically we have `"begin"` = `"end"`. Such pairs of precedences are sufficient to express left-associativity or right-associativity of infix operators, nesting of tokens like parentheses and many other cases.

`smie-prec2->grammar` *table*   [Function]
> This function takes a *prec2* grammar *table* and returns an alist suitable for use in `smie-setup`. The *prec2 table* is itself meant to be built by one of the functions below.

`smie-merge-prec2s` **&rest** *tables*   [Function]
> This function takes several *prec2 tables* and merges them into a new *prec2* table.

`smie-precs->prec2` *precs*   [Function]
> This function builds a *prec2* table from a table of precedences *precs*. *precs* should be a list, sorted by precedence (for example `"+"` will come before `"*"`), of elements of the form (*assoc op ...*), where each *op* is a token that acts as an operator; *assoc* is their associativity, which can be either `left`, `right`, `assoc`, or `nonassoc`. All operators in a given element share the same precedence level and associativity.

`smie-bnf->prec2` *bnf* **&rest** *resolvers*   [Function]
> This function lets you specify the grammar using a BNF notation. It accepts a *bnf* description of the grammar along with a set of conflict resolution rules *resolvers*, and returns a *prec2* table.
>
> *bnf* is a list of nonterminal definitions of the form (*nonterm rhs1 rhs2 ...*) where each *rhs* is a (non-empty) list of terminals (aka tokens) or non-terminals.
>
> Not all grammars are accepted:
>
> - An *rhs* cannot be an empty list (an empty list is never needed, since SMIE allows all non-terminals to match the empty string anyway).
>
> - An *rhs* cannot have 2 consecutive non-terminals: each pair of non-terminals needs to be separated by a terminal (aka token). This is a fundamental limitation of operator precedence grammars.
>
> Additionally, conflicts can occur:
>
> - The returned *prec2* table holds constraints between pairs of tokens, and for any given pair only one constraint can be present: T1 < T2, T1 = T2, or T1 > T2.
>
> - A token can be an `opener` (something similar to an open-paren), a `closer` (like a close-paren), or `neither` of the two (e.g., an infix operator, or an inner token like `"else"`).
>
> Precedence conflicts can be resolved via *resolvers*, which is a list of *precs* tables (see `smie-precs->prec2`): for each precedence conflict, if those `precs` tables specify a particular constraint, then the conflict is resolved by using this constraint instead, else a conflict is reported and one of the conflicting constraints is picked arbitrarily and the others are simply ignored.

22.7.1.3 Defining the Grammar of a Language

The usual way to define the SMIE grammar of a language is by defining a new global variable that holds the precedence table by giving a set of BNF rules. For example, the grammar definition for a small Pascal-like language could look like:

```
(require 'smie)
(defvar sample-smie-grammar
  (smie-prec2->grammar
   (smie-bnf->prec2
    '((id)
      (inst ("begin" insts "end")
            ("if" exp "then" inst "else" inst)
            (id ":=" exp)
            (exp))
      (insts (insts ";" insts) (inst))
      (exp (exp "+" exp)
           (exp "*" exp)
           ("(" exps ")"))
      (exps (exps "," exps) (exp)))
    '((assoc ";"))
    '((assoc ","))
    '((assoc "+") (assoc "*")))))
```

A few things to note:

- The above grammar does not explicitly mention the syntax of function calls: SMIE will automatically allow any sequence of sexps, such as identifiers, balanced parentheses, or **begin ... end** blocks to appear anywhere anyway.

- The grammar category **id** has no right hand side: this does not mean that it can match only the empty string, since as mentioned any sequence of sexps can appear anywhere anyway.

- Because non terminals cannot appear consecutively in the BNF grammar, it is difficult to correctly handle tokens that act as terminators, so the above grammar treats ";" as a statement *separator* instead, which SMIE can handle very well.

- Separators used in sequences (such as "," and ";" above) are best defined with BNF rules such as (foo (foo "separator" foo) ...) which generate precedence conflicts which are then resolved by giving them an explicit (assoc "separator").

- The ("(" exps ")") rule was not needed to pair up parens, since SMIE will pair up any characters that are marked as having paren syntax in the syntax table. What this rule does instead (together with the definition of **exps**) is to make it clear that "," should not appear outside of parentheses.

- Rather than have a single *precs* table to resolve conflicts, it is preferable to have several tables, so as to let the BNF part of the grammar specify relative precedences where possible.

- Unless there is a very good reason to prefer **left** or **right**, it is usually preferable to mark operators as associative, using **assoc**. For that reason "+" and "*" are defined above as **assoc**, although the language defines them formally as left associative.

22.7.1.4 Defining Tokens

SMIE comes with a predefined lexical analyzer which uses syntax tables in the following way: any sequence of characters that have word or symbol syntax is considered a token, and so is any sequence of characters that have punctuation syntax. This default lexer is often a good starting point but is rarely actually correct for any given language. For example, it will consider "2,+3" to be composed of 3 tokens: "2", ",+", and "3".

To describe the lexing rules of your language to SMIE, you need 2 functions, one to fetch the next token, and another to fetch the previous token. Those functions will usually first skip whitespace and comments and then look at the next chunk of text to see if it is a special token. If so it should skip the token and return a description of this token. Usually this is simply the string extracted from the buffer, but it can be anything you want. For example:

```
(defvar sample-keywords-regexp
  (regexp-opt '("+" "*" "," ";" ">" ">=" "<" "<=" ":=" "=")))
(defun sample-smie-forward-token ()
  (forward-comment (point-max))
  (cond
   ((looking-at sample-keywords-regexp)
    (goto-char (match-end 0))
    (match-string-no-properties 0))
   (t (buffer-substring-no-properties
        (point)
        (progn (skip-syntax-forward "w_")
               (point))))))
(defun sample-smie-backward-token ()
  (forward-comment (- (point)))
  (cond
   ((looking-back sample-keywords-regexp (- (point) 2) t)
    (goto-char (match-beginning 0))
    (match-string-no-properties 0))
   (t (buffer-substring-no-properties
        (point)
        (progn (skip-syntax-backward "w_")
               (point))))))
```

Notice how those lexers return the empty string when in front of parentheses. This is because SMIE automatically takes care of the parentheses defined in the syntax table. More specifically if the lexer returns **nil** or an empty string, SMIE tries to handle the corresponding text as a sexp according to syntax tables.

22.7.1.5 Living With a Weak Parser

The parsing technique used by SMIE does not allow tokens to behave differently in different contexts. For most programming languages, this manifests itself by precedence conflicts when converting the BNF grammar.

Sometimes, those conflicts can be worked around by expressing the grammar slightly differently. For example, for Modula-2 it might seem natural to have a BNF grammar that looks like this:

```
...
(inst ("IF" exp "THEN" insts "ELSE" insts "END")
      ("CASE" exp "OF" cases "END")
      ...)
(cases (cases "|" cases)
       (caselabel ":" insts)
       ("ELSE" insts))
...
```

But this will create conflicts for `"ELSE"`: on the one hand, the IF rule implies (among many other things) that `"ELSE"` = `"END"`; but on the other hand, since `"ELSE"` appears within `cases`, which appears left of `"END"`, we also have `"ELSE"` > `"END"`. We can solve the conflict either by using:

```
...
(inst ("IF" exp "THEN" insts "ELSE" insts "END")
      ("CASE" exp "OF" cases "END")
      ("CASE" exp "OF" cases "ELSE" insts "END")
      ...)
(cases (cases "|" cases) (caselabel ":" insts))
...
```

or

```
...
(inst ("IF" exp "THEN" else "END")
      ("CASE" exp "OF" cases "END")
      ...)
(else (insts "ELSE" insts))
(cases (cases "|" cases) (caselabel ":" insts) (else))
...
```

Reworking the grammar to try and solve conflicts has its downsides, tho, because SMIE assumes that the grammar reflects the logical structure of the code, so it is preferable to keep the BNF closer to the intended abstract syntax tree.

Other times, after careful consideration you may conclude that those conflicts are not serious and simply resolve them via the *resolvers* argument of `smie-bnf->prec2`. Usually this is because the grammar is simply ambiguous: the conflict does not affect the set of programs described by the grammar, but only the way those programs are parsed. This is typically the case for separators and associative infix operators, where you want to add a resolver like `'((assoc "|"))`. Another case where this can happen is for the classic *dangling else* problem, where you will use `'((assoc "else" "then"))`. It can also happen for cases where the conflict is real and cannot really be resolved, but it is unlikely to pose a problem in practice.

Finally, in many cases some conflicts will remain despite all efforts to restructure the grammar. Do not despair: while the parser cannot be made more clever, you can make the lexer as smart as you want. So, the solution is then to look at the tokens involved in the conflict and to split one of those tokens into 2 (or more) different tokens. E.g., if the grammar needs to distinguish between two incompatible uses of the token `"begin"`, make the lexer return different tokens (say `"begin-fun"` and `"begin-plain"`) depending on which kind of `"begin"` it finds. This pushes the work of distinguishing the different cases to the lexer, which will thus have to look at the surrounding text to find ad-hoc clues.

22.7.1.6 Specifying Indentation Rules

Based on the provided grammar, SMIE will be able to provide automatic indentation without any extra effort. But in practice, this default indentation style will probably not be good enough. You will want to tweak it in many different cases.

SMIE indentation is based on the idea that indentation rules should be as local as possible. To this end, it relies on the idea of *virtual* indentation, which is the indentation that a particular program point would have if it were at the beginning of a line. Of course, if that program point is indeed at the beginning of a line, its virtual indentation is its current indentation. But if not, then SMIE uses the indentation algorithm to compute the virtual indentation of that point. Now in practice, the virtual indentation of a program point does not have to be identical to the indentation it would have if we inserted a newline before it. To see how this works, the SMIE rule for indentation after a { in C does not care whether the { is standing on a line of its own or is at the end of the preceding line. Instead, these different cases are handled in the indentation rule that decides how to indent before a {.

Another important concept is the notion of *parent*: The *parent* of a token, is the head token of the nearest enclosing syntactic construct. For example, the parent of an `else` is the `if` to which it belongs, and the parent of an `if`, in turn, is the lead token of the surrounding construct. The command `backward-sexp` jumps from a token to its parent, but there are some caveats: for *openers* (tokens which start a construct, like `if`), you need to start with point before the token, while for others you need to start with point after the token. `backward-sexp` stops with point before the parent token if that is the *opener* of the token of interest, and otherwise it stops with point after the parent token.

SMIE indentation rules are specified using a function that takes two arguments *method* and *arg* where the meaning of *arg* and the expected return value depend on *method*.

method can be:

- `:after`, in which case *arg* is a token and the function should return the *offset* to use for indentation after *arg*.

- `:before`, in which case *arg* is a token and the function should return the *offset* to use to indent *arg* itself.

- `:elem`, in which case the function should return either the offset to use to indent function arguments (if *arg* is the symbol `arg`) or the basic indentation step (if *arg* is the symbol `basic`).

- `:list-intro`, in which case *arg* is a token and the function should return non-`nil` if the token is followed by a list of expressions (not separated by any token) rather than an expression.

When *arg* is a token, the function is called with point just before that token. A return value of `nil` always means to fallback on the default behavior, so the function should return `nil` for arguments it does not expect.

offset can be:

- `nil`: use the default indentation rule.

- `(column . column)`: indent to column *column*.

- *number*: offset by *number*, relative to a base token which is the current token for `:after` and its parent for `:before`.

22.7.1.7 Helper Functions for Indentation Rules

SMIE provides various functions designed specifically for use in the indentation rules function (several of those functions break if used in another context). These functions all start with the prefix `smie-rule-`.

`smie-rule-bolp`   [Function]
> Return non-`nil` if the current token is the first on the line.

`smie-rule-hanging-p`   [Function]
> Return non-`nil` if the current token is *hanging*. A token is *hanging* if it is the last token on the line and if it is preceded by other tokens: a lone token on a line is not hanging.

`smie-rule-next-p` &rest *tokens*   [Function]
> Return non-`nil` if the next token is among *tokens*.

`smie-rule-prev-p` &rest *tokens*   [Function]
> Return non-`nil` if the previous token is among *tokens*.

`smie-rule-parent-p` &rest *parents*   [Function]
> Return non-`nil` if the current token's parent is among *parents*.

`smie-rule-sibling-p`   [Function]
> Return non-`nil` if the current token's parent is actually a sibling. This is the case for example when the parent of a `","` is just the previous `","`.

`smie-rule-parent` &optional *offset*   [Function]
> Return the proper offset to align the current token with the parent. If non-`nil`, *offset* should be an integer giving an additional offset to apply.

`smie-rule-separator` *method*   [Function]
> Indent current token as a *separator*.
>
> By *separator*, we mean here a token whose sole purpose is to separate various elements within some enclosing syntactic construct, and which does not have any semantic significance in itself (i.e., it would typically not exist as a node in an abstract syntax tree).
>
> Such a token is expected to have an associative syntax and be closely tied to its syntactic parent. Typical examples are `","` in lists of arguments (enclosed inside parentheses), or `";"` in sequences of instructions (enclosed in a `{...}` or `begin...end` block).
>
> *method* should be the method name that was passed to `smie-rules-function`.

22.7.1.8 Sample Indentation Rules

Here is an example of an indentation function:

```
(defun sample-smie-rules (kind token)
  (pcase (cons kind token)
    (`(:elem . basic) sample-indent-basic)
    (`(,_ . ",") (smie-rule-separator kind))
    (`(:after . ":=") sample-indent-basic)
    (`(:before . ,(or `"begin" `"(" `"{"))
     (if (smie-rule-hanging-p) (smie-rule-parent)))
    (`(:before . "if")
     (and (not (smie-rule-bolp)) (smie-rule-prev-p "else")
          (smie-rule-parent)))))
```

A few things to note:

- The first case indicates the basic indentation increment to use. If `sample-indent-basic` is `nil`, then SMIE uses the global setting `smie-indent-basic`. The major mode could have set `smie-indent-basic` buffer-locally instead, but that is discouraged.

- The rule for the token `","` make SMIE try to be more clever when the comma separator is placed at the beginning of lines. It tries to outdent the separator so as to align the code after the comma; for example:

```
x = longfunctionname (
      arg1
    , arg2
    );
```

- The rule for indentation after `":="` exists because otherwise SMIE would treat `":="` as an infix operator and would align the right argument with the left one.

- The rule for indentation before `"begin"` is an example of the use of virtual indentation: This rule is used only when `"begin"` is hanging, which can happen only when `"begin"` is not at the beginning of a line. So this is not used when indenting `"begin"` itself but only when indenting something relative to this `"begin"`. Concretely, this rule changes the indentation from:

```
if x > 0 then begin
        dosomething(x);
      end
```

  to

```
if x > 0 then begin
      dosomething(x);
    end
```

- The rule for indentation before `"if"` is similar to the one for `"begin"`, but where the purpose is to treat `"else if"` as a single unit, so as to align a sequence of tests rather than indent each test further to the right. This function does this only in the case where the `"if"` is not placed on a separate line, hence the `smie-rule-bolp` test.

  If we know that the `"else"` is always aligned with its `"if"` and is always at the beginning of a line, we can use a more efficient rule:

```
((equal token "if")
```

```
(and (not (smie-rule-bolp))
     (smie-rule-prev-p "else")
     (save-excursion
       (sample-smie-backward-token)
       (cons 'column (current-column)))))))
```

The advantage of this formulation is that it reuses the indentation of the previous "else", rather than going all the way back to the first "if" of the sequence.

22.7.1.9 Customizing Indentation

If you are using a mode whose indentation is provided by SMIE, you can customize the indentation to suit your preferences. You can do this on a per-mode basis (using the option `smie-config`), or a per-file basis (using the function `smie-config-local` in a file-local variable specification).

`smie-config`   [User Option]

> This option lets you customize indentation on a per-mode basis. It is an alist with elements of the form (*mode . rules*). For the precise form of rules, see the variable's documentation; but you may find it easier to use the command `smie-config-guess`.

`smie-config-guess`   [Command]

> This command tries to work out appropriate settings to produce your preferred style of indentation. Simply call the command while visiting a file that is indented with your style.

`smie-config-save`   [Command]

> Call this command after using `smie-config-guess`, to save your settings for future sessions.

`smie-config-show-indent` **&optional** *move*   [Command]

> This command displays the rules that are used to indent the current line.

`smie-config-set-indent`   [Command]

> This command adds a local rule to adjust the indentation of the current line.

`smie-config-local` *rules*   [Function]

> This function adds *rules* as indentation rules for the current buffer. These add to any mode-specific rules defined by the `smie-config` option. To specify custom indentation rules for a specific file, add an entry to the file's local variables of the form: `eval:` (smie-config-local '(*rules*)).

22.8 Desktop Save Mode

Desktop Save Mode is a feature to save the state of Emacs from one session to another. The user-level commands for using Desktop Save Mode are described in the GNU Emacs Manual (see Section "Saving Emacs Sessions" in *the GNU Emacs Manual*). Modes whose buffers visit a file, don't have to do anything to use this feature.

For buffers not visiting a file to have their state saved, the major mode must bind the buffer local variable `desktop-save-buffer` to a non-`nil` value.

`desktop-save-buffer`   [Variable]

> If this buffer-local variable is non-`nil`, the buffer will have its state saved in the desktop file at desktop save. If the value is a function, it is called at desktop save with argument *desktop-dirname*, and its value is saved in the desktop file along with the state of the buffer for which it was called. When file names are returned as part of the auxiliary information, they should be formatted using the call
>
> > `(desktop-file-name file-name desktop-dirname)`

For buffers not visiting a file to be restored, the major mode must define a function to do the job, and that function must be listed in the alist `desktop-buffer-mode-handlers`.

`desktop-buffer-mode-handlers`   [Variable]

> Alist with elements
>
> > `(major-mode . restore-buffer-function)`
>
> The function *restore-buffer-function* will be called with argument list
>
> > `(buffer-file-name buffer-name desktop-buffer-misc)`
>
> and it should return the restored buffer. Here *desktop-buffer-misc* is the value returned by the function optionally bound to `desktop-save-buffer`.

23 Documentation

GNU Emacs has convenient built-in help facilities, most of which derive their information from documentation strings associated with functions and variables. This chapter describes how to access documentation strings in Lisp programs.

The contents of a documentation string should follow certain conventions. In particular, its first line should be a complete sentence (or two complete sentences) that briefly describes what the function or variable does. See Section D.6 [Documentation Tips], page 1059, for how to write good documentation strings.

Note that the documentation strings for Emacs are not the same thing as the Emacs manual. Manuals have their own source files, written in the Texinfo language; documentation strings are specified in the definitions of the functions and variables they apply to. A collection of documentation strings is not sufficient as a manual because a good manual is not organized in that fashion; it is organized in terms of topics of discussion.

For commands to display documentation strings, see Section "Help" in *The GNU Emacs Manual*.

23.1 Documentation Basics

A documentation string is written using the Lisp syntax for strings, with double-quote characters surrounding the text. It is, in fact, an actual Lisp string. When the string appears in the proper place in a function or variable definition, it serves as the function's or variable's documentation.

In a function definition (a `lambda` or `defun` form), the documentation string is specified after the argument list, and is normally stored directly in the function object. See Section 12.2.4 [Function Documentation], page 190. You can also put function documentation in the `function-documentation` property of a function name (see Section 23.2 [Accessing Documentation], page 486).

In a variable definition (a `defvar` form), the documentation string is specified after the initial value. See Section 11.5 [Defining Variables], page 161. The string is stored in the variable's `variable-documentation` property.

Sometimes, Emacs does not keep documentation strings in memory. There are two such circumstances. Firstly, to save memory, the documentation for preloaded functions and variables (including primitives) is kept in a file named `DOC`, in the directory specified by `doc-directory` (see Section 23.2 [Accessing Documentation], page 486). Secondly, when a function or variable is loaded from a byte-compiled file, Emacs avoids loading its documentation string (see Section 16.3 [Docs and Compilation], page 263). In both cases, Emacs looks up the documentation string from the file only when needed, such as when the user calls *C-h f* (`describe-function`) for a function.

Documentation strings can contain special *key substitution sequences*, referring to key bindings which are looked up only when the user views the documentation. This allows the help commands to display the correct keys even if a user rearranges the default key bindings. See Section 23.3 [Keys in Documentation], page 488.

In the documentation string of an autoloaded command (see Section 15.5 [Autoload], page 249), these key-substitution sequences have an additional special effect: they cause

`C-h f` on the command to trigger autoloading. (This is needed for correctly setting up the hyperlinks in the *Help* buffer.)

23.2 Access to Documentation Strings

documentation-property *symbol property* **&optional** *verbatim* [Function]
> This function returns the documentation string recorded in *symbol*'s property list under property *property*. It is most often used to look up the documentation strings of variables, for which *property* is `variable-documentation`. However, it can also be used to look up other kinds of documentation, such as for customization groups (but for function documentation, use the `documentation` function, below).
>
> If the property value refers to a documentation string stored in the `DOC` file or a byte-compiled file, this function looks up that string and returns it.
>
> If the property value isn't `nil`, isn't a string, and doesn't refer to text in a file, then it is evaluated as a Lisp expression to obtain a string.
>
> Finally, this function passes the string through `substitute-command-keys` to substitute key bindings (see Section 23.3 [Keys in Documentation], page 488). It skips this step if *verbatim* is non-`nil`.
>
> ```
> (documentation-property 'command-line-processed
>    'variable-documentation)
>      ⇒ "Non-nil once command line has been processed"
> (symbol-plist 'command-line-processed)
>      ⇒ (variable-documentation 188902)
> (documentation-property 'emacs 'group-documentation)
>      ⇒ "Customization of the One True Editor."
> ```

documentation *function* **&optional** *verbatim* [Function]
> This function returns the documentation string of *function*. It handles macros, named keyboard macros, and special forms, as well as ordinary functions.
>
> If *function* is a symbol, this function first looks for the `function-documentation` property of that symbol; if that has a non-`nil` value, the documentation comes from that value (if the value is not a string, it is evaluated).
>
> If *function* is not a symbol, or if it has no `function-documentation` property, then `documentation` extracts the documentation string from the actual function definition, reading it from a file if called for.
>
> Finally, unless *verbatim* is non-`nil`, this function calls `substitute-command-keys`. The result is the documentation string to return.
>
> The `documentation` function signals a `void-function` error if *function* has no function definition. However, it is OK if the function definition has no documentation string. In that case, `documentation` returns `nil`.

face-documentation *face* [Function]
> This function returns the documentation string of *face* as a face.

Here is an example of using the two functions, `documentation` and `documentation-property`, to display the documentation strings for several symbols in a *Help* buffer.

```
(defun describe-symbols (pattern)
  "Describe the Emacs Lisp symbols matching PATTERN.
All symbols that have PATTERN in their name are described
in the *Help* buffer."
  (interactive "sDescribe symbols matching: ")
  (let ((describe-func
         (function
          (lambda (s)
            ;; Print description of symbol.
            (if (fboundp s)                ; It is a function.
                (princ
                 (format "%s\t%s\n%s\n\n" s
                   (if (commandp s)
                       (let ((keys (where-is-internal s)))
                         (if keys
                             (concat
                              "Keys: "
                              (mapconcat 'key-description
                                         keys " "))
                           "Keys: none"))
                     "Function")
                   (or (documentation s)
                       "not documented"))))

            (if (boundp s)                 ; It is a variable.
                (princ
                 (format "%s\t%s\n%s\n\n" s
                   (if (custom-variable-p s)
                       "Option " "Variable")
                   (or (documentation-property
                        s 'variable-documentation)
                       "not documented")))))))
        sym-list)

    ;; Build a list of symbols that match pattern.
    (mapatoms (function
               (lambda (sym)
                 (if (string-match pattern (symbol-name sym))
                     (setq sym-list (cons sym sym-list))))))

    ;; Display the data.
    (help-setup-xref (list 'describe-symbols pattern) (interactive-p))
    (with-help-window (help-buffer)
      (mapcar describe-func (sort sym-list 'string<)))))
```

The `describe-symbols` function works like `apropos`, but provides more information.

```
(describe-symbols "goal")

---------- Buffer: *Help* ----------
goal-column     Option
Semipermanent goal column for vertical motion, as set by ...

minibuffer-temporary-goal-position      Variable
not documented

set-goal-column Keys: C-x C-n
Set the current horizontal position as a goal for C-n and C-p.
```

```
Those commands will move to this position in the line moved to
rather than trying to keep the same horizontal position.
With a non-nil argument ARG, clears out the goal column
so that C-n and C-p resume vertical motion.
The goal column is stored in the variable 'goal-column'.

(fn ARG)


temporary-goal-column    Variable
Current goal column for vertical motion.
It is the column where point was at the start of the current run
of vertical motion commands.

When moving by visual lines via the function 'line-move-visual', it is a cons
cell (COL . HSCROLL), where COL is the x-position, in pixels,
divided by the default column width, and HSCROLL is the number of
columns by which window is scrolled from left margin.

When the 'track-eol' feature is doing its job, the value is
'most-positive-fixnum'.
---------- Buffer: *Help* ----------
```

Snarf-documentation *filename*   [Function]

    This function is used when building Emacs, just before the runnable Emacs is dumped. It finds the positions of the documentation strings stored in the file *filename*, and records those positions into memory in the function definitions and variable property lists. See Section E.1 [Building Emacs], page 1067.

    Emacs reads the file *filename* from the `emacs/etc` directory. When the dumped Emacs is later executed, the same file will be looked for in the directory `doc-directory`. Usually *filename* is `"DOC"`.

doc-directory   [Variable]

    This variable holds the name of the directory which should contain the file `"DOC"` that contains documentation strings for built-in and preloaded functions and variables.

    In most cases, this is the same as `data-directory`. They may be different when you run Emacs from the directory where you built it, without actually installing it. See [Definition of data-directory], page 493.

23.3 Substituting Key Bindings in Documentation

When documentation strings refer to key sequences, they should use the current, actual key bindings. They can do so using certain special text sequences described below. Accessing documentation strings in the usual way substitutes current key binding information for these special sequences. This works by calling `substitute-command-keys`. You can also call that function yourself.

    Here is a list of the special sequences and what they mean:

`\[`*command*`]`

        stands for a key sequence that will invoke *command*, or 'M-x *command*' if *command* has no key bindings.

\\{*mapvar*\}

> stands for a summary of the keymap which is the value of the variable *mapvar*. The summary is made using `describe-bindings`.

\\<*mapvar*>

> stands for no text itself. It is used only for a side effect: it specifies *mapvar*'s value as the keymap for any following '\\[*command*]' sequences in this documentation string.

'

`

> (left single quotation mark and grave accent) both stand for a left quote. This generates a left single quotation mark, an apostrophe, or a grave accent depending on the value of `text-quoting-style`.

,

'

> (right single quotation mark and apostrophe) both stand for a right quote. This generates a right single quotation mark or an apostrophe depending on the value of `text-quoting-style`.

\\=

> quotes the following character and is discarded; thus, '\\=`' puts '`' into the output, '\\=\\[' puts '\\[' into the output, and '\\=\\=' puts '\\=' into the output.

> **Please note:** Each '\\' must be doubled when written in a string in Emacs Lisp.

`text-quoting-style`   [Variable]

> The value of this variable is a symbol that specifies the style Emacs should use for single quotes in the wording of help and messages. If the variable's value is `curve`, the style is 'like this' with curved single quotes. If the value is `straight`, the style is 'like this' with straight apostrophes. If the value is `grave`, the style is 'like this' with grave accent and apostrophe, the standard style before Emacs version 25. The default value `nil` acts like `curve` if curved single quotes are displayable, and like `grave` otherwise.

> This variable can be used by experts on platforms that have problems with curved quotes. As it is not intended for casual use, it is not a user option.

`substitute-command-keys` *string*   [Function]

> This function scans *string* for the above special sequences and replaces them by what they stand for, returning the result as a string. This permits display of documentation that refers accurately to the user's own customized key bindings.

> If a command has multiple bindings, this function normally uses the first one it finds. You can specify one particular key binding by assigning an `:advertised-binding` symbol property to the command, like this:

```
(put 'undo :advertised-binding [?\C-/])
```

> The `:advertised-binding` property also affects the binding shown in menu items (see Section 21.17.5 [Menu Bar], page 422). The property is ignored if it specifies a key binding that the command does not actually have.

> Here are examples of the special sequences:

```
(substitute-command-keys
   "To abort recursive edit, type `\\[abort-recursive-edit]'.")
⇒ "To abort recursive edit, type 'C-]'."
```

```
(substitute-command-keys
   "The keys that are defined for the minibuffer here are:
  \\{minibuffer-local-must-match-map}")
⇒ "The keys that are defined for the minibuffer here are:

?              minibuffer-completion-help
SPC            minibuffer-complete-word
TAB            minibuffer-complete
C-j            minibuffer-complete-and-exit
RET            minibuffer-complete-and-exit
C-g            abort-recursive-edit
"

(substitute-command-keys
   "To abort a recursive edit from the minibuffer, type \
`\\<minibuffer-local-must-match-map>\\[abort-recursive-edit]'.")
⇒ "To abort a recursive edit from the minibuffer, type `C-g'."
```

There are other special conventions for the text in documentation strings—for instance, you can refer to functions, variables, and sections of this manual. See Section D.6 [Documentation Tips], page 1059, for details.

23.4 Describing Characters for Help Messages

These functions convert events, key sequences, or characters to textual descriptions. These descriptions are useful for including arbitrary text characters or key sequences in messages, because they convert non-printing and whitespace characters to sequences of printing characters. The description of a non-whitespace printing character is the character itself.

key-description *sequence* **&optional** *prefix*   [Function]
> This function returns a string containing the Emacs standard notation for the input events in *sequence*. If *prefix* is non-**nil**, it is a sequence of input events leading up to *sequence* and is included in the return value. Both arguments may be strings, vectors or lists. See Section 20.7 [Input Events], page 358, for more information about valid events.
>
> ```
> (key-description [?\M-3 delete])
>     ⇒ "M-3 <delete>"
> (key-description [delete] "\M-3")
>     ⇒ "M-3 <delete>"
> ```
>
> See also the examples for **single-key-description**, below.

single-key-description *event* **&optional** *no-angles*   [Function]
> This function returns a string describing *event* in the standard Emacs notation for keyboard input. A normal printing character appears as itself, but a control character turns into a string starting with 'C-', a meta character turns into a string starting with 'M-', and space, tab, etc., appear as 'SPC', 'TAB', etc. A function key symbol appears inside angle brackets '<...>'. An event that is a list appears as the name of the symbol in the CAR of the list, inside angle brackets.
>
> If the optional argument *no-angles* is non-**nil**, the angle brackets around function keys and event symbols are omitted; this is for compatibility with old versions of Emacs which didn't use the brackets.

```
(single-key-description ?\C-x)
     ⇒ "C-x"
(key-description "\C-x \M-y \n \t \r \f123")
     ⇒ "C-x SPC M-y SPC C-j SPC TAB SPC RET SPC C-l 1 2 3"
(single-key-description 'delete)
     ⇒ "<delete>"
(single-key-description 'C-mouse-1)
     ⇒ "<C-mouse-1>"
(single-key-description 'C-mouse-1 t)
     ⇒ "C-mouse-1"
```

text-char-description *character*   [Function]

This function returns a string describing *character* in the standard Emacs notation for characters that appear in text—like **single-key-description**, except that control characters are represented with a leading caret (which is how control characters in Emacs buffers are usually displayed). Another difference is that **text-char-description** recognizes the 2**7 bit as the Meta character, whereas **single-key-description** uses the 2**27 bit for Meta.

```
(text-char-description ?\C-c)
     ⇒ "^C"
(text-char-description ?\M-m)
     ⇒ "\xed"
(text-char-description ?\C-\M-m)
     ⇒ "\x8d"
(text-char-description (+ 128 ?m))
     ⇒ "M-m"
(text-char-description (+ 128 ?\C-m))
     ⇒ "M-^M"
```

read-kbd-macro *string* **&optional** *need-vector*   [Command]

This function is used mainly for operating on keyboard macros, but it can also be used as a rough inverse for **key-description**. You call it with a string containing key descriptions, separated by spaces; it returns a string or vector containing the corresponding events. (This may or may not be a single valid key sequence, depending on what events you use; see Section 21.1 [Key Sequences], page 391.) If *need-vector* is non-**nil**, the return value is always a vector.

23.5 Help Functions

Emacs provides a variety of built-in help functions, all accessible to the user as subcommands of the prefix *C-h*. For more information about them, see Section "Help" in *The GNU Emacs Manual*. Here we describe some program-level interfaces to the same information.

apropos *pattern* **&optional** *do-all*   [Command]

This function finds all meaningful symbols whose names contain a match for the apropos pattern *pattern*. An apropos pattern is either a word to match, a space-separated list of words of which at least two must match, or a regular expression (if any special regular expression characters occur). A symbol is meaningful if it has a definition as a function, variable, or face, or has properties.

The function returns a list of elements that look like this:

```
(symbol score function-doc variable-doc
```

> *plist-doc widget-doc face-doc group-doc*)

Here, *score* is an integer measure of how important the symbol seems to be as a match. Each of the remaining elements is a documentation string, or `nil`, for *symbol* as a function, variable, etc.

It also displays the symbols in a buffer named `*Apropos*`, each with a one-line description taken from the beginning of its documentation string.

If *do-all* is non-`nil`, or if the user option `apropos-do-all` is non-`nil`, then `apropos` also shows key bindings for the functions that are found; it also shows *all* interned symbols, not just meaningful ones (and it lists them in the return value as well).

`help-map`   [Variable]

The value of this variable is a local keymap for characters following the Help key, *C-h*.

`help-command`   [Prefix Command]

This symbol is not a function; its function definition cell holds the keymap known as `help-map`. It is defined in `help.el` as follows:

```
(define-key global-map (string help-char) 'help-command)
(fset 'help-command help-map)
```

`help-char`   [User Option]

The value of this variable is the help character—the character that Emacs recognizes as meaning Help. By default, its value is 8, which stands for *C-h*. When Emacs reads this character, if `help-form` is a non-`nil` Lisp expression, it evaluates that expression, and displays the result in a window if it is a string.

Usually the value of `help-form` is `nil`. Then the help character has no special meaning at the level of command input, and it becomes part of a key sequence in the normal way. The standard key binding of *C-h* is a prefix key for several general-purpose help features.

The help character is special after prefix keys, too. If it has no binding as a subcommand of the prefix key, it runs `describe-prefix-bindings`, which displays a list of all the subcommands of the prefix key.

`help-event-list`   [User Option]

The value of this variable is a list of event types that serve as alternative help characters. These events are handled just like the event specified by `help-char`.

`help-form`   [Variable]

If this variable is non-`nil`, its value is a form to evaluate whenever the character `help-char` is read. If evaluating the form produces a string, that string is displayed.

A command that calls `read-event`, `read-char-choice`, or `read-char` probably should bind `help-form` to a non-`nil` expression while it does input. (The time when you should not do this is when *C-h* has some other meaning.) Evaluating this expression should result in a string that explains what the input is for and how to enter it properly.

Entry to the minibuffer binds this variable to the value of `minibuffer-help-form` (see [Definition of minibuffer-help-form], page 344).

`prefix-help-command`   [Variable]

> This variable holds a function to print help for a prefix key. The function is called when the user types a prefix key followed by the help character, and the help character has no binding after that prefix. The variable's default value is `describe-prefix-bindings`.

`describe-prefix-bindings`   [Command]

> This function calls `describe-bindings` to display a list of all the subcommands of the prefix key of the most recent key sequence. The prefix described consists of all but the last event of that key sequence. (The last event is, presumably, the help character.)

The following two functions are meant for modes that want to provide help without relinquishing control, such as the electric modes. Their names begin with 'Helper' to distinguish them from the ordinary help functions.

`Helper-describe-bindings`   [Command]

> This command pops up a window displaying a help buffer containing a listing of all of the key bindings from both the local and global keymaps. It works by calling `describe-bindings`.

`Helper-help`   [Command]

> This command provides help for the current mode. It prompts the user in the minibuffer with the message '`Help (Type ? for further options)`', and then provides assistance in finding out what the key bindings are, and what the mode is intended for. It returns `nil`.
>
> This can be customized by changing the map `Helper-help-map`.

`data-directory`   [Variable]

> This variable holds the name of the directory in which Emacs finds certain documentation and text files that come with Emacs.

`help-buffer`   [Function]

> This function returns the name of the help buffer, which is normally `*Help*`; if such a buffer does not exist, it is first created.

`with-help-window` *buffer-name body...*   [Macro]

> This macro evaluates *body* like `with-output-to-temp-buffer` (see Section 37.8 [Temporary Displays], page 900), inserting any output produced by its forms into a buffer named *buffer-name*. (Usually, *buffer-name* should be the value returned by the function `help-buffer`.) It also puts the specified buffer into Help mode and displays a message telling the user how to quit and scroll the help window. It selects the help window if the current value of the user option `help-window-select` has been set accordingly. It returns the last value in *body*.

`help-setup-xref` *item interactive-p*   [Function]

> This function updates the cross reference data in the `*Help*` buffer, which is used to regenerate the help information when the user clicks on the 'Back' or 'Forward' buttons. Most commands that use the `*Help*` buffer should invoke this function

before clearing the buffer. The *item* argument should have the form (`function` . `args`), where *function* is a function to call, with argument list *args*, to regenerate the help buffer. The *interactive-p* argument is non-`nil` if the calling command was invoked interactively; in that case, the stack of items for the `*Help*` buffer's 'Back' buttons is cleared.

See [describe-symbols example], page 486, for an example of using `help-buffer`, `with-help-window`, and `help-setup-xref`.

make-help-screen *fname help-line help-text help-map*   [Macro]
This macro defines a help command named *fname* that acts like a prefix key that shows a list of the subcommands it offers.

When invoked, *fname* displays *help-text* in a window, then reads and executes a key sequence according to *help-map*. The string *help-text* should describe the bindings available in *help-map*.

The command *fname* is defined to handle a few events itself, by scrolling the display of *help-text*. When *fname* reads one of those special events, it does the scrolling and then reads another event. When it reads an event that is not one of those few, and which has a binding in *help-map*, it executes that key's binding and then returns.

The argument *help-line* should be a single-line summary of the alternatives in *help-map*. In the current version of Emacs, this argument is used only if you set the option `three-step-help` to `t`.

This macro is used in the command `help-for-help` which is the binding of `C-h C-h`.

three-step-help   [User Option]
If this variable is non-`nil`, commands defined with `make-help-screen` display their *help-line* strings in the echo area at first, and display the longer *help-text* strings only if the user types the help character again.

24 Files

This chapter describes the Emacs Lisp functions and variables to find, create, view, save, and otherwise work with files and directories. A few other file-related functions are described in Chapter 26 [Buffers], page 550, and those related to backups and auto-saving are described in Chapter 25 [Backups and Auto-Saving], page 539.

Many of the file functions take one or more arguments that are file names. A file name is a string. Most of these functions expand file name arguments using the function `expand-file-name`, so that ~ is handled correctly, as are relative file names (including ../). See Section 24.8.4 [File Name Expansion], page 522.

In addition, certain *magic* file names are handled specially. For example, when a remote file name is specified, Emacs accesses the file over the network via an appropriate protocol. See Section "Remote Files" in *The GNU Emacs Manual*. This handling is done at a very low level, so you may assume that all the functions described in this chapter accept magic file names as file name arguments, except where noted. See Section 24.11 [Magic File Names], page 529, for details.

When file I/O functions signal Lisp errors, they usually use the condition `file-error` (see Section 10.6.3.3 [Handling Errors], page 150). The error message is in most cases obtained from the operating system, according to locale `system-messages-locale`, and decoded using coding system `locale-coding-system` (see Section 32.12 [Locales], page 788).

24.1 Visiting Files

Visiting a file means reading a file into a buffer. Once this is done, we say that the buffer is *visiting* that file, and call the file *the visited file* of the buffer.

A file and a buffer are two different things. A file is information recorded permanently in the computer (unless you delete it). A buffer, on the other hand, is information inside of Emacs that will vanish at the end of the editing session (or when you kill the buffer). When a buffer is visiting a file, it contains information copied from the file. The copy in the buffer is what you modify with editing commands. Changes to the buffer do not change the file; to make the changes permanent, you must *save* the buffer, which means copying the altered buffer contents back into the file.

Despite the distinction between files and buffers, people often refer to a file when they mean a buffer and vice-versa. Indeed, we say, "I am editing a file", rather than, "I am editing a buffer that I will soon save as a file of the same name". Humans do not usually need to make the distinction explicit. When dealing with a computer program, however, it is good to keep the distinction in mind.

24.1.1 Functions for Visiting Files

This section describes the functions normally used to visit files. For historical reasons, these functions have names starting with 'find-' rather than 'visit-'. See Section 26.4 [Buffer File Name], page 554, for functions and variables that access the visited file name of a buffer or that find an existing buffer by its visited file name.

In a Lisp program, if you want to look at the contents of a file but not alter it, the fastest way is to use `insert-file-contents` in a temporary buffer. Visiting the file is not necessary and takes longer. See Section 24.3 [Reading from Files], page 501.

`find-file` *filename* **&optional** *wildcards*   [Command]

This command selects a buffer visiting the file *filename*, using an existing buffer if there is one, and otherwise creating a new buffer and reading the file into it. It also returns that buffer.

Aside from some technical details, the body of the **`find-file`** function is basically equivalent to:

```
(switch-to-buffer (find-file-noselect filename nil nil wildcards))
```

(See **`switch-to-buffer`** in Section 27.12 [Switching Buffers], page 595.)

If *wildcards* is non-**`nil`**, which is always true in an interactive call, then **`find-file`** expands wildcard characters in *filename* and visits all the matching files.

When **`find-file`** is called interactively, it prompts for *filename* in the minibuffer.

`find-file-literally` *filename*   [Command]

This command visits *filename*, like **`find-file`** does, but it does not perform any format conversions (see Section 24.12 [Format Conversion], page 534), character code conversions (see Section 32.10 [Coding Systems], page 773), or end-of-line conversions (see Section 32.10.1 [Coding System Basics], page 774). The buffer visiting the file is made unibyte, and its major mode is Fundamental mode, regardless of the file name. File local variable specifications in the file (see Section 11.11 [File Local Variables], page 177) are ignored, and automatic decompression and adding a newline at the end of the file due to **`require-final-newline`** (see Section 24.2 [Saving Buffers], page 499) are also disabled.

Note that if Emacs already has a buffer visiting the same file non-literally, it will not visit the same file literally, but instead just switch to the existing buffer. If you want to be sure of accessing a file's contents literally, you should create a temporary buffer and then read the file contents into it using **`insert-file-contents-literally`** (see Section 24.3 [Reading from Files], page 501).

`find-file-noselect` *filename* **&optional** *nowarn rawfile wildcards*   [Function]

This function is the guts of all the file-visiting functions. It returns a buffer visiting the file *filename*. You may make the buffer current or display it in a window if you wish, but this function does not do so.

The function returns an existing buffer if there is one; otherwise it creates a new buffer and reads the file into it. When **`find-file-noselect`** uses an existing buffer, it first verifies that the file has not changed since it was last visited or saved in that buffer. If the file has changed, this function asks the user whether to reread the changed file. If the user says '**`yes`**', any edits previously made in the buffer are lost.

Reading the file involves decoding the file's contents (see Section 32.10 [Coding Systems], page 773), including end-of-line conversion, and format conversion (see Section 24.12 [Format Conversion], page 534). If *wildcards* is non-**`nil`**, then **`find-file-noselect`** expands wildcard characters in *filename* and visits all the matching files.

This function displays warning or advisory messages in various peculiar cases, unless the optional argument *nowarn* is non-**`nil`**. For example, if it needs to create a buffer, and there is no file named *filename*, it displays the message '**`(New file)`**' in the echo area, and leaves the buffer empty.

The `find-file-noselect` function normally calls `after-find-file` after reading the file (see Section 24.1.2 [Subroutines of Visiting], page 498). That function sets the buffer major mode, parses local variables, warns the user if there exists an auto-save file more recent than the file just visited, and finishes by running the functions in `find-file-hook`.

If the optional argument *rawfile* is non-`nil`, then `after-find-file` is not called, and the `find-file-not-found-functions` are not run in case of failure. What's more, a non-`nil` *rawfile* value suppresses coding system conversion and format conversion.

The `find-file-noselect` function usually returns the buffer that is visiting the file *filename*. But, if wildcards are actually used and expanded, it returns a list of buffers that are visiting the various files.

```
(find-file-noselect "/etc/fstab")
     ⇒ #<buffer fstab>
```

find-file-other-window *filename* **&optional** *wildcards*   [Command]
> This command selects a buffer visiting the file *filename*, but does so in a window other than the selected window. It may use another existing window or split a window; see Section 27.12 [Switching Buffers], page 595.
>
> When this command is called interactively, it prompts for *filename*.

find-file-read-only *filename* **&optional** *wildcards*   [Command]
> This command selects a buffer visiting the file *filename*, like `find-file`, but it marks the buffer as read-only. See Section 26.7 [Read Only Buffers], page 558, for related functions and variables.
>
> When this command is called interactively, it prompts for *filename*.

find-file-wildcards   [User Option]
> If this variable is non-`nil`, then the various `find-file` commands check for wildcard characters and visit all the files that match them (when invoked interactively or when their *wildcards* argument is non-`nil`). If this option is `nil`, then the `find-file` commands ignore their *wildcards* argument and never treat wildcard characters specially.

find-file-hook   [User Option]
> The value of this variable is a list of functions to be called after a file is visited. The file's local-variables specification (if any) will have been processed before the hooks are run. The buffer visiting the file is current when the hook functions are run.
>
> This variable is a normal hook. See Section 22.1 [Hooks], page 429.

find-file-not-found-functions   [Variable]
> The value of this variable is a list of functions to be called when `find-file` or `find-file-noselect` is passed a nonexistent file name. `find-file-noselect` calls these functions as soon as it detects a nonexistent file. It calls them in the order of the list, until one of them returns non-`nil`. `buffer-file-name` is already set up.
>
> This is not a normal hook because the values of the functions are used, and in many cases only some of the functions are called.

`find-file-literally`   [Variable]

> This buffer-local variable, if set to a non-`nil` value, makes `save-buffer` behave as
> if the buffer were visiting its file literally, i.e., without conversions of any kind. The
> command `find-file-literally` sets this variable's local value, but other equivalent
> functions and commands can do that as well, e.g., to avoid automatic addition of a
> newline at the end of the file. This variable is permanent local, so it is unaffected by
> changes of major modes.

24.1.2 Subroutines of Visiting

The `find-file-noselect` function uses two important subroutines which are sometimes
useful in user Lisp code: `create-file-buffer` and `after-find-file`. This section explains
how to use them.

`create-file-buffer` *filename*   [Function]

> This function creates a suitably named buffer for visiting *filename*, and returns it. It
> uses *filename* (sans directory) as the name if that name is free; otherwise, it appends
> a string such as '`<2>`' to get an unused name. See also Section 26.9 [Creating Buffers],
> page 562. Note that the `uniquify` library affects the result of this function. See
> Section "Uniquify" in *The GNU Emacs Manual*.
>
> **Please note:** `create-file-buffer` does *not* associate the new buffer with a file and
> does not select the buffer. It also does not use the default major mode.
>
> ```
>       (create-file-buffer "foo")
>            ⇒ #<buffer foo>
>       (create-file-buffer "foo")
>            ⇒ #<buffer foo<2>>
>       (create-file-buffer "foo")
>            ⇒ #<buffer foo<3>>
> ```
>
> This function is used by `find-file-noselect`. It uses `generate-new-buffer` (see
> Section 26.9 [Creating Buffers], page 562).

`after-find-file` &optional *error warn noauto*   [Function]
   after-find-file-from-revert-buffer nomodes

> This function sets the buffer major mode, and parses local variables (see Section 22.2.2
> [Auto Major Mode], page 435). It is called by `find-file-noselect` and by the default
> revert function (see Section 25.3 [Reverting], page 547).
>
> If reading the file got an error because the file does not exist, but its directory does
> exist, the caller should pass a non-`nil` value for *error*. In that case, `after-find-file`
> issues a warning: '`(New file)`'. For more serious errors, the caller should usually not
> call `after-find-file`.
>
> If *warn* is non-`nil`, then this function issues a warning if an auto-save file exists and
> is more recent than the visited file.
>
> If *noauto* is non-`nil`, that says not to enable or disable Auto-Save mode. The mode
> remains enabled if it was enabled before.
>
> If *after-find-file-from-revert-buffer* is non-`nil`, that means this call was from
> `revert-buffer`. This has no direct effect, but some mode functions and hook
> functions check the value of this variable.

If *nomodes* is non-`nil`, that means don't alter the buffer's major mode, don't process local variables specifications in the file, and don't run `find-file-hook`. This feature is used by `revert-buffer` in some cases.

The last thing `after-find-file` does is call all the functions in the list `find-file-hook`.

24.2 Saving Buffers

When you edit a file in Emacs, you are actually working on a buffer that is visiting that file—that is, the contents of the file are copied into the buffer and the copy is what you edit. Changes to the buffer do not change the file until you *save* the buffer, which means copying the contents of the buffer into the file.

save-buffer &optional *backup-option*   [Command]
> This function saves the contents of the current buffer in its visited file if the buffer has been modified since it was last visited or saved. Otherwise it does nothing.
>
> `save-buffer` is responsible for making backup files. Normally, *backup-option* is `nil`, and `save-buffer` makes a backup file only if this is the first save since visiting the file. Other values for *backup-option* request the making of backup files in other circumstances:
>
> - With an argument of 4 or 64, reflecting 1 or 3 *C-u*'s, the `save-buffer` function marks this version of the file to be backed up when the buffer is next saved.
>
> - With an argument of 16 or 64, reflecting 2 or 3 *C-u*'s, the `save-buffer` function unconditionally backs up the previous version of the file before saving it.
>
> - With an argument of 0, unconditionally do *not* make any backup file.

save-some-buffers &optional *save-silently-p pred*   [Command]
> This command saves some modified file-visiting buffers. Normally it asks the user about each buffer. But if *save-silently-p* is non-`nil`, it saves all the file-visiting buffers without querying the user.
>
> The optional *pred* argument controls which buffers to ask about (or to save silently if *save-silently-p* is non-`nil`). If it is `nil`, that means to ask only about file-visiting buffers. If it is `t`, that means also offer to save certain other non-file buffers—those that have a non-`nil` buffer-local value of `buffer-offer-save` (see Section 26.10 [Killing Buffers], page 563). A user who says 'yes' to saving a non-file buffer is asked to specify the file name to use. The `save-buffers-kill-emacs` function passes the value `t` for *pred*.
>
> If *pred* is neither `t` nor `nil`, then it should be a function of no arguments. It will be called in each buffer to decide whether to offer to save that buffer. If it returns a non-`nil` value in a certain buffer, that means do offer to save that buffer.

write-file *filename* &optional *confirm*   [Command]
> This function writes the current buffer into file *filename*, makes the buffer visit that file, and marks it not modified. Then it renames the buffer based on *filename*, appending a string like '<2>' if necessary to make a unique buffer name. It does most of this work by calling `set-visited-file-name` (see Section 26.4 [Buffer File Name], page 554) and `save-buffer`.

If *confirm* is non-**nil**, that means to ask for confirmation before overwriting an existing file. Interactively, confirmation is required, unless the user supplies a prefix argument.

If *filename* is an existing directory, or a symbolic link to one, **write-file** uses the name of the visited file, in directory *filename*. If the buffer is not visiting a file, it uses the buffer name instead.

Saving a buffer runs several hooks. It also performs format conversion (see Section 24.12 [Format Conversion], page 534). Note that these hooks, described below, are only run by **save-buffer**, they are not run by other primitives and functions that write buffer text to files, and in particular auto-saving (see Section 25.2 [Auto-Saving], page 544) doesn't run these hooks.

write-file-functions   [Variable]

The value of this variable is a list of functions to be called before writing out a buffer to its visited file. If one of them returns non-**nil**, the file is considered already written and the rest of the functions are not called, nor is the usual code for writing the file executed.

If a function in **write-file-functions** returns non-**nil**, it is responsible for making a backup file (if that is appropriate). To do so, execute the following code:

```
(or buffer-backed-up (backup-buffer))
```

You might wish to save the file modes value returned by **backup-buffer** and use that (if non-**nil**) to set the mode bits of the file that you write. This is what **save-buffer** normally does. See Section 25.1.1 [Making Backup Files], page 539.

The hook functions in **write-file-functions** are also responsible for encoding the data (if desired): they must choose a suitable coding system and end-of-line conversion (see Section 32.10.3 [Lisp and Coding Systems], page 776), perform the encoding (see Section 32.10.7 [Explicit Encoding], page 784), and set **last-coding-system-used** to the coding system that was used (see Section 32.10.2 [Encoding and I/O], page 775).

If you set this hook locally in a buffer, it is assumed to be associated with the file or the way the contents of the buffer were obtained. Thus the variable is marked as a permanent local, so that changing the major mode does not alter a buffer-local value. On the other hand, calling **set-visited-file-name** will reset it. If this is not what you want, you might like to use **write-contents-functions** instead.

Even though this is not a normal hook, you can use **add-hook** and **remove-hook** to manipulate the list. See Section 22.1 [Hooks], page 429.

write-contents-functions   [Variable]

This works just like **write-file-functions**, but it is intended for hooks that pertain to the buffer's contents, not to the particular visited file or its location. Such hooks are usually set up by major modes, as buffer-local bindings for this variable. This variable automatically becomes buffer-local whenever it is set; switching to a new major mode always resets this variable, but calling **set-visited-file-name** does not.

If any of the functions in this hook returns non-**nil**, the file is considered already written and the rest are not called and neither are the functions in **write-file-functions**.

before-save-hook [User Option]

> This normal hook runs before a buffer is saved in its visited file, regardless of whether that is done normally or by one of the hooks described above. For instance, the `copyright.el` program uses this hook to make sure the file you are saving has the current year in its copyright notice.

after-save-hook [User Option]

> This normal hook runs after a buffer has been saved in its visited file. One use of this hook is in Fast Lock mode; it uses this hook to save the highlighting information in a cache file.

file-precious-flag [User Option]

> If this variable is non-`nil`, then `save-buffer` protects against I/O errors while saving by writing the new file to a temporary name instead of the name it is supposed to have, and then renaming it to the intended name after it is clear there are no errors. This procedure prevents problems such as a lack of disk space from resulting in an invalid file.
>
> As a side effect, backups are necessarily made by copying. See Section 25.1.2 [Rename or Copy], page 541. Yet, at the same time, saving a precious file always breaks all hard links between the file you save and other file names.
>
> Some modes give this variable a non-`nil` buffer-local value in particular buffers.

require-final-newline [User Option]

> This variable determines whether files may be written out that do *not* end with a newline. If the value of the variable is `t`, then `save-buffer` silently adds a newline at the end of the buffer whenever it does not already end in one. If the value is `visit`, Emacs adds a missing newline just after it visits the file. If the value is `visit-save`, Emacs adds a missing newline both on visiting and on saving. For any other non-`nil` value, `save-buffer` asks the user whether to add a newline each time the case arises.
>
> If the value of the variable is `nil`, then `save-buffer` doesn't add newlines at all. `nil` is the default value, but a few major modes set it to `t` in particular buffers.

See also the function `set-visited-file-name` (see Section 26.4 [Buffer File Name], page 554).

24.3 Reading from Files

To copy the contents of a file into a buffer, use the function `insert-file-contents`. (Don't use the command `insert-file` in a Lisp program, as that sets the mark.)

insert-file-contents *filename* **&optional** *visit beg end replace* [Function]

> This function inserts the contents of file *filename* into the current buffer after point. It returns a list of the absolute file name and the length of the data inserted. An error is signaled if *filename* is not the name of a file that can be read.
>
> This function checks the file contents against the defined file formats, and converts the file contents if appropriate and also calls the functions in the list `after-insert-file-functions`. See Section 24.12 [Format Conversion], page 534. Normally, one of the functions in the `after-insert-file-functions` list determines the coding

system (see Section 32.10 [Coding Systems], page 773) used for decoding the file's contents, including end-of-line conversion. However, if the file contains null bytes, it is by default visited without any code conversions. See Section 32.10.3 [Lisp and Coding Systems], page 776.

If *visit* is non-**nil**, this function additionally marks the buffer as unmodified and sets up various fields in the buffer so that it is visiting the file *filename*: these include the buffer's visited file name and its last save file modtime. This feature is used by **find-file-noselect** and you probably should not use it yourself.

If *beg* and *end* are non-**nil**, they should be numbers that are byte offsets specifying the portion of the file to insert. In this case, *visit* must be **nil**. For example,

```
(insert-file-contents filename nil 0 500)
```

inserts the first 500 characters of a file.

If the argument *replace* is non-**nil**, it means to replace the contents of the buffer (actually, just the accessible portion) with the contents of the file. This is better than simply deleting the buffer contents and inserting the whole file, because (1) it preserves some marker positions and (2) it puts less data in the undo list.

It is possible to read a special file (such as a FIFO or an I/O device) with **insert-file-contents**, as long as *replace* and *visit* are **nil**.

insert-file-contents-literally *filename* **&optional** *visit beg end*   [Function]
    replace

This function works like **insert-file-contents** except that it does not run **find-file-hook**, and does not do format decoding, character code conversion, automatic uncompression, and so on.

If you want to pass a file name to another process so that another program can read the file, use the function **file-local-copy**; see Section 24.11 [Magic File Names], page 529.

24.4 Writing to Files

You can write the contents of a buffer, or part of a buffer, directly to a file on disk using the **append-to-file** and **write-region** functions. Don't use these functions to write to files that are being visited; that could cause confusion in the mechanisms for visiting.

append-to-file *start end filename*   [Command]

This function appends the contents of the region delimited by *start* and *end* in the current buffer to the end of file *filename*. If that file does not exist, it is created. This function returns **nil**.

An error is signaled if *filename* specifies a nonwritable file, or a nonexistent file in a directory where files cannot be created.

When called from Lisp, this function is completely equivalent to:

```
(write-region start end filename t)
```

write-region *start end filename* **&optional** *append visit lockname*   [Command]
    mustbenew

This function writes the region delimited by *start* and *end* in the current buffer into the file specified by *filename*.

If *start* is `nil`, then the command writes the entire buffer contents (*not* just the accessible portion) to the file and ignores *end*.

If *start* is a string, then `write-region` writes or appends that string, rather than text from the buffer. *end* is ignored in this case.

If *append* is non-`nil`, then the specified text is appended to the existing file contents (if any). If *append* is a number, `write-region` seeks to that byte offset from the start of the file and writes the data from there.

If *mustbenew* is non-`nil`, then `write-region` asks for confirmation if *filename* names an existing file. If *mustbenew* is the symbol `excl`, then `write-region` does not ask for confirmation, but instead it signals an error `file-already-exists` if the file already exists.

The test for an existing file, when *mustbenew* is `excl`, uses a special system feature. At least for files on a local disk, there is no chance that some other program could create a file of the same name before Emacs does, without Emacs's noticing.

If *visit* is `t`, then Emacs establishes an association between the buffer and the file: the buffer is then visiting that file. It also sets the last file modification time for the current buffer to *filename*'s modtime, and marks the buffer as not modified. This feature is used by `save-buffer`, but you probably should not use it yourself.

If *visit* is a string, it specifies the file name to visit. This way, you can write the data to one file (*filename*) while recording the buffer as visiting another file (*visit*). The argument *visit* is used in the echo area message and also for file locking; *visit* is stored in `buffer-file-name`. This feature is used to implement `file-precious-flag`; don't use it yourself unless you really know what you're doing.

The optional argument *lockname*, if non-`nil`, specifies the file name to use for purposes of locking and unlocking, overriding *filename* and *visit* for that purpose.

The function `write-region` converts the data which it writes to the appropriate file formats specified by `buffer-file-format` and also calls the functions in the list `write-region-annotate-functions`. See Section 24.12 [Format Conversion], page 534.

Normally, `write-region` displays the message 'Wrote *filename*' in the echo area. This message is inhibited if *visit* is neither `t` nor `nil` nor a string, or if Emacs is operating in batch mode (see Section 38.17 [Batch Mode], page 1014). This feature is useful for programs that use files for internal purposes, files that the user does not need to know about.

with-temp-file *file body. . .*   [Macro]
The `with-temp-file` macro evaluates the *body* forms with a temporary buffer as the current buffer; then, at the end, it writes the buffer contents into file *file*. It kills the temporary buffer when finished, restoring the buffer that was current before the `with-temp-file` form. Then it returns the value of the last form in *body*.

The current buffer is restored even in case of an abnormal exit via `throw` or error (see Section 10.6 [Nonlocal Exits], page 145).

See also `with-temp-buffer` in [The Current Buffer], page 552.

24.5 File Locks

When two users edit the same file at the same time, they are likely to interfere with each other. Emacs tries to prevent this situation from arising by recording a *file lock* when a file is being modified. Emacs can then detect the first attempt to modify a buffer visiting a file that is locked by another Emacs job, and ask the user what to do. The file lock is really a file, a symbolic link with a special name, stored in the same directory as the file you are editing. (On file systems that do not support symbolic links, a regular file is used.)

When you access files using NFS, there may be a small probability that you and another user will both lock the same file simultaneously. If this happens, it is possible for the two users to make changes simultaneously, but Emacs will still warn the user who saves second. Also, the detection of modification of a buffer visiting a file changed on disk catches some cases of simultaneous editing; see Section 26.6 [Modification Time], page 557.

file-locked-p *filename*   [Function]

> This function returns **nil** if the file *filename* is not locked. It returns **t** if it is locked by this Emacs process, and it returns the name of the user who has locked it if it is locked by some other job.
>
> ```
> (file-locked-p "foo")
>      ⇒ nil
> ```

lock-buffer **&optional** *filename*   [Function]

> This function locks the file *filename*, if the current buffer is modified. The argument *filename* defaults to the current buffer's visited file. Nothing is done if the current buffer is not visiting a file, or is not modified, or if the option **create-lockfiles** is **nil**.

unlock-buffer   [Function]

> This function unlocks the file being visited in the current buffer, if the buffer is modified. If the buffer is not modified, then the file should not be locked, so this function does nothing. It also does nothing if the current buffer is not visiting a file, or is not locked.

create-lockfiles   [User Option]

> If this variable is **nil**, Emacs does not lock files.

ask-user-about-lock *file other-user*   [Function]

> This function is called when the user tries to modify *file*, but it is locked by another user named *other-user*. The default definition of this function asks the user to say what to do. The value this function returns determines what Emacs does next:
>
> - A value of **t** says to grab the lock on the file. Then this user may edit the file and *other-user* loses the lock.
>
> - A value of **nil** says to ignore the lock and let this user edit the file anyway.
>
> - This function may instead signal a **file-locked** error, in which case the change that the user was about to make does not take place.
>
>   The error message for this error looks like this:
>
>   error   **File is locked:** *file other-user*

where `file` is the name of the file and *other-user* is the name of the user who has locked the file.

If you wish, you can replace the `ask-user-about-lock` function with your own version that makes the decision in another way.

24.6 Information about Files

This section describes the functions for retrieving various types of information about files (or directories or symbolic links), such as whether a file is readable or writable, and its size. These functions all take arguments which are file names. Except where noted, these arguments need to specify existing files, or an error is signaled.

Be careful with file names that end in spaces. On some filesystems (notably, MS-Windows), trailing whitespace characters in file names are silently and automatically ignored.

24.6.1 Testing Accessibility

These functions test for permission to access a file for reading, writing, or execution. Unless explicitly stated otherwise, they recursively follow symbolic links for their file name arguments, at all levels (at the level of the file itself and at all levels of parent directories).

On some operating systems, more complex sets of access permissions can be specified, via mechanisms such as Access Control Lists (ACLs). See Section 24.6.5 [Extended Attributes], page 512, for how to query and set those permissions.

`file-exists-p` *filename*   [Function]
> This function returns `t` if a file named *filename* appears to exist. This does not mean you can necessarily read the file, only that you can find out its attributes. (On Unix and GNU/Linux, this is true if the file exists and you have execute permission on the containing directories, regardless of the permissions of the file itself.)
>
> If the file does not exist, or if access control policies prevent you from finding its attributes, this function returns `nil`.
>
> Directories are files, so `file-exists-p` returns `t` when given a directory name. However, symbolic links are treated specially; `file-exists-p` returns `t` for a symbolic link name only if the target file exists.

`file-readable-p` *filename*   [Function]
> This function returns `t` if a file named *filename* exists and you can read it. It returns `nil` otherwise.

`file-executable-p` *filename*   [Function]
> This function returns `t` if a file named *filename* exists and you can execute it. It returns `nil` otherwise. On Unix and GNU/Linux, if the file is a directory, execute permission means you can check the existence and attributes of files inside the directory, and open those files if their modes permit.

`file-writable-p` *filename*   [Function]
> This function returns `t` if the file *filename* can be written or created by you, and `nil` otherwise. A file is writable if the file exists and you can write it. It is creatable

if it does not exist, but the specified directory does exist and you can write in that directory.

In the example below, `foo` is not writable because the parent directory does not exist, even though the user could create such a directory.

```
(file-writable-p "~/no-such-dir/foo")
     ⇒ nil
```

`file-accessible-directory-p` *dirname*   [Function]

This function returns `t` if you have permission to open existing files in the directory whose name as a file is *dirname*; otherwise (or if there is no such directory), it returns `nil`. The value of *dirname* may be either a directory name (such as `/foo/`) or the file name of a file which is a directory (such as `/foo`, without the final slash).

For example, from the following we deduce that any attempt to read a file in `/foo/` will give an error:

```
(file-accessible-directory-p "/foo")
     ⇒ nil
```

`access-file` *filename string*   [Function]

This function opens file *filename* for reading, then closes it and returns `nil`. However, if the open fails, it signals an error using *string* as the error message text.

`file-ownership-preserved-p` *filename* **&optional** *group*   [Function]

This function returns `t` if deleting the file *filename* and then creating it anew would keep the file's owner unchanged. It also returns `t` for nonexistent files.

If the optional argument *group* is non-`nil`, this function also checks that the file's group would be unchanged.

If *filename* is a symbolic link, then, unlike the other functions discussed here, `file-ownership-preserved-p` does *not* replace *filename* with its target. However, it does recursively follow symbolic links at all levels of parent directories.

`file-modes` *filename*   [Function]

This function returns the *mode bits* of *filename*—an integer summarizing its read, write, and execution permissions. Symbolic links in *filename* are recursively followed at all levels. If the file does not exist, the return value is `nil`.

See Section "File permissions" in *The GNU Coreutils Manual*, for a description of mode bits. For example, if the low-order bit is 1, the file is executable by all users; if the second-lowest-order bit is 1, the file is writable by all users; etc. The highest possible value is 4095 (7777 octal), meaning that everyone has read, write, and execute permission, the SUID bit is set for both others and group, and the sticky bit is set.

See Section 24.7 [Changing Files], page 514, for the `set-file-modes` function, which can be used to set these permissions.

```
(file-modes "~/junk/diffs")
     ⇒ 492                        ; Decimal integer.
(format "%o" 492)
     ⇒ "754"                      ; Convert to octal.
```

```
(set-file-modes "~/junk/diffs" #o666)
     ⇒ nil

$ ls -l diffs
-rw-rw-rw- 1 lewis lewis 3063 Oct 30 16:00 diffs
```

MS-DOS note: On MS-DOS, there is no such thing as an executable file mode bit. So `file-modes` considers a file executable if its name ends in one of the standard executable extensions, such as `.com`, `.bat`, `.exe`, and some others. Files that begin with the Unix-standard '#!' signature, such as shell and Perl scripts, are also considered executable. Directories are also reported as executable, for compatibility with Unix. These conventions are also followed by `file-attributes` (see Section 24.6.4 [File Attributes], page 509).

24.6.2 Distinguishing Kinds of Files

This section describes how to distinguish various kinds of files, such as directories, symbolic links, and ordinary files.

`file-symlink-p` *filename*   [Function]

> If the file *filename* is a symbolic link, the `file-symlink-p` function returns its (non-recursive) link target as a string. (The link target string is not necessarily the full absolute file name of the target; determining the full file name that the link points to is nontrivial, see below.) If the leading directories of *filename* include symbolic links, this function recursively follows them.
>
> If the file *filename* is not a symbolic link, or does not exist, `file-symlink-p` returns `nil`.
>
> Here are a few examples of using this function:
>
> ```
> (file-symlink-p "not-a-symlink")
>      ⇒ nil
> (file-symlink-p "sym-link")
>      ⇒ "not-a-symlink"
> (file-symlink-p "sym-link2")
>      ⇒ "sym-link"
> (file-symlink-p "/bin")
>      ⇒ "/pub/bin"
> ```
>
> Note that in the third example, the function returned `sym-link`, but did not proceed to resolve it, although that file is itself a symbolic link. This is what we meant by "non-recursive" above—the process of following the symbolic links does not recurse if the link target is itself a link.
>
> The string that this function returns is what is recorded in the symbolic link; it may or may not include any leading directories. This function does *not* expand the link target to produce a fully-qualified file name, and in particular does not use the leading directories, if any, of the *filename* argument if the link target is not an absolute file name. Here's an example:
>
> ```
> (file-symlink-p "/foo/bar/baz")
>      ⇒ "some-file"
> ```

Here, although `/foo/bar/baz` was given as a fully-qualified file name, the result is not, and in fact does not have any leading directories at all. And since `some-file` might itself be a symbolic link, you cannot simply prepend leading directories to it, nor even naively use `expand-file-name` (see Section 24.8.4 [File Name Expansion], page 522) to produce its absolute file name.

For this reason, this function is seldom useful if you need to determine more than just the fact that a file is or isn't a symbolic link. If you actually need the file name of the link target, use `file-chase-links` or `file-truename`, described in Section 24.6.3 [Truenames], page 508.

The next two functions recursively follow symbolic links at all levels for *filename*.

`file-directory-p` *filename*   [Function]
> This function returns `t` if *filename* is the name of an existing directory, `nil` otherwise.
>
> ```
> (file-directory-p "~rms")
>      ⇒ t
> (file-directory-p "~rms/lewis/files.texi")
>      ⇒ nil
> (file-directory-p "~rms/lewis/no-such-file")
>      ⇒ nil
> (file-directory-p "$HOME")
>      ⇒ nil
> (file-directory-p
>  (substitute-in-file-name "$HOME"))
>      ⇒ t
> ```

`file-regular-p` *filename*   [Function]
> This function returns `t` if the file *filename* exists and is a regular file (not a directory, named pipe, terminal, or other I/O device).

24.6.3 Truenames

The *truename* of a file is the name that you get by following symbolic links at all levels until none remain, then simplifying away '.' and '..' appearing as name components. This results in a sort of canonical name for the file. A file does not always have a unique truename; the number of distinct truenames a file has is equal to the number of hard links to the file. However, truenames are useful because they eliminate symbolic links as a cause of name variation.

`file-truename` *filename*   [Function]
> This function returns the truename of the file *filename*. If the argument is not an absolute file name, this function first expands it against `default-directory`.
>
> This function does not expand environment variables. Only `substitute-in-file-name` does that. See [Definition of substitute-in-file-name], page 523.
>
> If you may need to follow symbolic links preceding '..' appearing as a name component, call `file-truename` without prior direct or indirect calls to `expand-file-name`. Otherwise, the file name component immediately preceding '..' will be simplified away before `file-truename` is called. To eliminate the need for a call to

expand-file-name, `file-truename` handles '~' in the same way that `expand-file-name` does. See Section 24.8.4 [Functions that Expand Filenames], page 522.

file-chase-links *filename* **&optional** *limit* [Function]

This function follows symbolic links, starting with *filename*, until it finds a file name which is not the name of a symbolic link. Then it returns that file name. This function does *not* follow symbolic links at the level of parent directories.

If you specify a number for *limit*, then after chasing through that many links, the function just returns what it has even if that is still a symbolic link.

To illustrate the difference between `file-chase-links` and `file-truename`, suppose that `/usr/foo` is a symbolic link to the directory `/home/foo`, and `/home/foo/hello` is an ordinary file (or at least, not a symbolic link) or nonexistent. Then we would have:

```
(file-chase-links "/usr/foo/hello")
     ;; This does not follow the links in the parent directories.
     ⇒ "/usr/foo/hello"
(file-truename "/usr/foo/hello")
     ;; Assuming that /home is not a symbolic link.
     ⇒ "/home/foo/hello"
```

file-equal-p *file1* *file2* [Function]

This function returns `t` if the files *file1* and *file2* name the same file. This is similar to comparing their truenames, except that remote file names are also handled in an appropriate manner. If *file1* or *file2* does not exist, the return value is unspecified.

file-in-directory-p *file* *dir* [Function]

This function returns `t` if *file* is a file in directory *dir*, or in a subdirectory of *dir*. It also returns `t` if *file* and *dir* are the same directory. It compares the truenames of the two directories. If *dir* does not name an existing directory, the return value is `nil`.

vc-responsible-backend *file* [Function]

This function determines the responsible VC backend of the given *file*. For example, if emacs.c is a file tracked by Git, (`vc-responsible-backend "emacs.c"`) returns 'Git'. Note that if *file* is a symbolic link, `vc-responsible-backend` will not resolve it—the backend of the symbolic link file itself is reported. To get the backend VC of the file to which *file* refers, wrap *file* with a symbolic link resolving function such as `file-chase-links`:

```
(vc-responsible-backend (file-chase-links "emacs.c"))
```

24.6.4 File Attributes

This section describes the functions for getting detailed information about a file, including the owner and group numbers, the number of names, the inode number, the size, and the times of access and modification.

file-newer-than-file-p *filename1* *filename2* [Function]

This function returns `t` if the file *filename1* is newer than file *filename2*. If *filename1* does not exist, it returns `nil`. If *filename1* does exist, but *filename2* does not, it returns `t`.

In the following example, assume that the file `aug-19` was written on the 19th, `aug-20` was written on the 20th, and the file `no-file` doesn't exist at all.

```
(file-newer-than-file-p "aug-19" "aug-20")
     ⇒ nil
(file-newer-than-file-p "aug-20" "aug-19")
     ⇒ t
(file-newer-than-file-p "aug-19" "no-file")
     ⇒ t
(file-newer-than-file-p "no-file" "aug-19")
     ⇒ nil
```

If the *filename* argument to the next two functions is a symbolic link, then these function do *not* replace it with its target. However, they both recursively follow symbolic links at all levels of parent directories.

file-attributes *filename* **&optional** *id-format*   [Function]
    This function returns a list of attributes of file *filename*. If the specified file cannot be opened, it returns `nil`. The optional parameter *id-format* specifies the preferred format of attributes UID and GID (see below)—the valid values are `'string` and `'integer`. The latter is the default, but we plan to change that, so you should specify a non-`nil` value for *id-format* if you use the returned UID or GID.

    The elements of the list, in order, are:

0. `t` for a directory, a string for a symbolic link (the name linked to), or `nil` for a text file.

1. The number of names the file has. Alternate names, also known as hard links, can be created by using the **add-name-to-file** function (see Section 24.7 [Changing Files], page 514).

2. The file's UID, normally as a string. However, if it does not correspond to a named user, the value is a number.

3. The file's GID, likewise.

4. The time of last access, as a list of four integers (*sec-high sec-low microsec picosec*). (This is similar to the value of `current-time`; see Section 38.5 [Time of Day], page 999.) Note that on some FAT-based filesystems, only the date of last access is recorded, so this time will always hold the midnight of the day of last access.

5. The time of last modification as a list of four integers (as above). This is the last time when the file's contents were modified.

6. The time of last status change as a list of four integers (as above). This is the time of the last change to the file's access mode bits, its owner and group, and other information recorded in the filesystem for the file, beyond the file's contents.

7. The size of the file in bytes. This is floating point if the size is too large to fit in a Lisp integer.

8. The file's modes, as a string of ten letters or dashes, as in '`ls -l`'.

9. An unspecified value, present for backward compatibility.

10. The file's inode number. If possible, this is an integer. If the inode number is too large to be represented as an integer in Emacs Lisp but dividing it by 2^{16} yields a representable integer, then the value has the form (*high* . *low*), where *low* holds the low 16 bits. If the inode number is too wide for even that, the value is of the form (*high middle* . *low*), where **high** holds the high bits, *middle* the middle 24 bits, and *low* the low 16 bits.

11. The filesystem number of the device that the file is on. Depending on the magnitude of the value, this can be either an integer or a cons cell, in the same manner as the inode number. This element and the file's inode number together give enough information to distinguish any two files on the system—no two files can have the same values for both of these numbers.

For example, here are the file attributes for `files.texi`:

```
(file-attributes "files.texi" 'string)
   ⇒  (nil 1 "lh" "users"
        (20614 64019 50040 152000)
        (20000 23 0 0)
        (20614 64555 902289 872000)
        122295 "-rw-rw-rw-"
        t (5888 2 . 43978)
        (15479 . 46724))
```

and here is how the result is interpreted:

`nil`   is neither a directory nor a symbolic link.

`1`   has only one name (the name `files.texi` in the current default directory).

`"lh"`   is owned by the user with name 'lh'.

`"users"`   is in the group with name 'users'.

(20614 64019 50040 152000)
               was last accessed on October 23, 2012, at 20:12:03.050040152 UTC.

(20000 23 0 0)
               was last modified on July 15, 2001, at 08:53:43 UTC.

(20614 64555 902289 872000)
               last had its status changed on October 23, 2012, at 20:20:59.902289872 UTC.

`122295`   is 122295 bytes long. (It may not contain 122295 characters, though, if some of the bytes belong to multibyte sequences, and also if the end-of-line format is CR-LF.)

`"-rw-rw-rw-"`
               has a mode of read and write access for the owner, group, and world.

`t`   is merely a placeholder; it carries no information.

(5888 2 . 43978)
               has an inode number of 6473924464520138.

```
(15479 . 46724)
```
            is on the file-system device whose number is 1014478468.

file-nlinks *filename*   [Function]

> This function returns the number of names (i.e., hard links) that file *filename* has. If
> the file does not exist, this function returns **nil**. Note that symbolic links have no
> effect on this function, because they are not considered to be names of the files they
> link to.
>
> ```
> $ ls -l foo*
> -rw-rw-rw- 2 rms rms 4 Aug 19 01:27 foo
> -rw-rw-rw- 2 rms rms 4 Aug 19 01:27 foo1
>
> (file-nlinks "foo")
>     ⇒ 2
> (file-nlinks "doesnt-exist")
>     ⇒ nil
> ```

24.6.5 Extended File Attributes

On some operating systems, each file can be associated with arbitrary *extended file attributes*. At present, Emacs supports querying and setting two specific sets of extended
file attributes: Access Control Lists (ACLs) and SELinux contexts. These extended file
attributes are used, on some systems, to impose more sophisticated file access controls than
the basic Unix-style permissions discussed in the previous sections.

A detailed explanation of ACLs and SELinux is beyond the scope of this manual. For
our purposes, each file can be associated with an *ACL*, which specifies its properties under
an ACL-based file control system, and/or an *SELinux context*, which specifies its properties
under the SELinux system.

file-acl *filename*   [Function]

> This function returns the ACL for the file *filename*. The exact Lisp representation of
> the ACL is unspecified (and may change in future Emacs versions), but it is the same
> as what **set-file-acl** takes for its *acl* argument (see Section 24.7 [Changing Files],
> page 514).
>
> The underlying ACL implementation is platform-specific; on GNU/Linux and BSD,
> Emacs uses the POSIX ACL interface, while on MS-Windows Emacs emulates the
> POSIX ACL interface with native file security APIs.
>
> If Emacs was not compiled with ACL support, or the file does not exist or is inacces-
> sible, or Emacs was unable to determine the ACL entries for any other reason, then
> the return value is **nil**.

file-selinux-context *filename*   [Function]

> This function returns the SELinux context of the file *filename*, as a list of the form
> (*user role type range*). The list elements are the context's user, role, type, and
> range respectively, as Lisp strings; see the SELinux documentation for details about
> what these actually mean. The return value has the same form as what **set-file-
> selinux-context** takes for its *context* argument (see Section 24.7 [Changing Files],
> page 514).

If Emacs was not compiled with SELinux support, or the file does not exist or is inaccessible, or if the system does not support SELinux, then the return value is (nil nil nil nil).

file-extended-attributes *filename* [Function]

This function returns an alist of the Emacs-recognized extended attributes of file *filename*. Currently, it serves as a convenient way to retrieve both the ACL and SELinux context; you can then call the function `set-file-extended-attributes`, with the returned alist as its second argument, to apply the same file access attributes to another file (see Section 24.7 [Changing Files], page 514).

One of the elements is (acl . *acl*), where *acl* has the same form returned by `file-acl`.

Another element is (selinux-context . *context*), where *context* is the SELinux context, in the same form returned by `file-selinux-context`.

24.6.6 Locating Files in Standard Places

This section explains how to search for a file in a list of directories (a *path*), or for an executable file in the standard list of executable file directories.

To search for a user-specific configuration file, See Section 24.8.7 [Standard File Names], page 526, for the `locate-user-emacs-file` function.

locate-file *filename path* **&optional** *suffixes predicate* [Function]

This function searches for a file whose name is *filename* in a list of directories given by *path*, trying the suffixes in *suffixes*. If it finds such a file, it returns the file's absolute file name (see Section 24.8.2 [Relative File Names], page 520); otherwise it returns nil.

The optional argument *suffixes* gives the list of file-name suffixes to append to *filename* when searching. `locate-file` tries each possible directory with each of these suffixes. If *suffixes* is nil, or (""), then there are no suffixes, and *filename* is used only as-is. Typical values of *suffixes* are `exec-suffixes` (see Section 36.1 [Subprocess Creation], page 839), `load-suffixes`, `load-file-rep-suffixes` and the return value of the function `get-load-suffixes` (see Section 15.2 [Load Suffixes], page 246).

Typical values for *path* are `exec-path` (see Section 36.1 [Subprocess Creation], page 839) when looking for executable programs, or `load-path` (see Section 15.3 [Library Search], page 247) when looking for Lisp files. If *filename* is absolute, *path* has no effect, but the suffixes in *suffixes* are still tried.

The optional argument *predicate*, if non-nil, specifies a predicate function for testing whether a candidate file is suitable. The predicate is passed the candidate file name as its single argument. If *predicate* is nil or omitted, `locate-file` uses `file-readable-p` as the predicate. See Section 24.6.2 [Kinds of Files], page 507, for other useful predicates, e.g., `file-executable-p` and `file-directory-p`.

For compatibility, *predicate* can also be one of the symbols `executable`, `readable`, `writable`, `exists`, or a list of one or more of these symbols.

executable-find *program* [Function]

This function searches for the executable file of the named *program* and returns the absolute file name of the executable, including its file-name extensions, if any. It

returns `nil` if the file is not found. The functions searches in all the directories in
`exec-path`, and tries all the file-name extensions in `exec-suffixes` (see Section 36.1
[Subprocess Creation], page 839).

24.7 Changing File Names and Attributes

The functions in this section rename, copy, delete, link, and set the modes (permissions) of
files. They all signal a `file-error` error if they fail to perform their function, reporting
the system-dependent error message that describes the reason for the failure.

In the functions that have an argument *newname*, if a file by the name of *newname*
already exists, the actions taken depend on the value of the argument *ok-if-already-exists*:

- Signal a `file-already-exists` error if *ok-if-already-exists* is `nil`.

- Request confirmation if *ok-if-already-exists* is a number.

- Replace the old file without confirmation if *ok-if-already-exists* is any other value.

The next four commands all recursively follow symbolic links at all levels of parent
directories for their first argument, but, if that argument is itself a symbolic link, then only
`copy-file` replaces it with its (recursive) target.

`add-name-to-file` *oldname newname* **&optional** *ok-if-already-exists*   [Command]
    This function gives the file named *oldname* the additional name *newname*. This
    means that *newname* becomes a new hard link to *oldname*.

    In the first part of the following example, we list two files, `foo` and `foo3`.

        $ ls -li fo*
        81908 -rw-rw-rw- 1 rms rms 29 Aug 18 20:32 foo
        84302 -rw-rw-rw- 1 rms rms 24 Aug 18 20:31 foo3

    Now we create a hard link, by calling `add-name-to-file`, then list the files again.
    This shows two names for one file, `foo` and `foo2`.

        (add-name-to-file "foo" "foo2")
             ⇒ nil

        $ ls -li fo*
        81908 -rw-rw-rw- 2 rms rms 29 Aug 18 20:32 foo
        81908 -rw-rw-rw- 2 rms rms 29 Aug 18 20:32 foo2
        84302 -rw-rw-rw- 1 rms rms 24 Aug 18 20:31 foo3

    Finally, we evaluate the following:

        (add-name-to-file "foo" "foo3" t)

    and list the files again. Now there are three names for one file: `foo`, `foo2`, and `foo3`.
    The old contents of `foo3` are lost.

        (add-name-to-file "foo1" "foo3")
             ⇒ nil

        $ ls -li fo*
        81908 -rw-rw-rw- 3 rms rms 29 Aug 18 20:32 foo
        81908 -rw-rw-rw- 3 rms rms 29 Aug 18 20:32 foo2
        81908 -rw-rw-rw- 3 rms rms 29 Aug 18 20:32 foo3

This function is meaningless on operating systems where multiple names for one file are not allowed. Some systems implement multiple names by copying the file instead.

See also `file-nlinks` in Section 24.6.4 [File Attributes], page 509.

rename-file *filename newname* **&optional** *ok-if-already-exists* [Command]
This command renames the file *filename* as *newname*.

If *filename* has additional names aside from *filename*, it continues to have those names. In fact, adding the name *newname* with `add-name-to-file` and then deleting *filename* has the same effect as renaming, aside from momentary intermediate states.

copy-file *oldname newname* **&optional** *ok-if-exists time* [Command]
 preserve-uid-gid preserve-extended-attributes
This command copies the file *oldname* to *newname*. An error is signaled if *oldname* does not exist. If *newname* names a directory, it copies *oldname* into that directory, preserving its final name component.

If *time* is non-`nil`, then this function gives the new file the same last-modified time that the old one has. (This works on only some operating systems.) If setting the time gets an error, `copy-file` signals a `file-date-error` error. In an interactive call, a prefix argument specifies a non-`nil` value for *time*.

If argument *preserve-uid-gid* is `nil`, we let the operating system decide the user and group ownership of the new file (this is usually set to the user running Emacs). If *preserve-uid-gid* is non-`nil`, we attempt to copy the user and group ownership of the file. This works only on some operating systems, and only if you have the correct permissions to do so.

If the optional argument *preserve-permissions* is non-`nil`, this function copies the file modes (or "permissions") of *oldname* to *newname*, as well as the Access Control List and SELinux context (if any). See Section 24.6 [Information about Files], page 505.

Otherwise, the file modes of *newname* are left unchanged if it is an existing file, and set to those of *oldname*, masked by the default file permissions (see `set-default-file-modes` below), if *newname* is to be newly created. The Access Control List or SELinux context are not copied over in either case.

make-symbolic-link *filename newname* **&optional** *ok-if-exists* [Command]
This command makes a symbolic link to *filename*, named *newname*. This is like the shell command '`ln -s filename newname`'.

This function is not available on systems that don't support symbolic links.

delete-file *filename* **&optional** *trash* [Command]
This command deletes the file *filename*. If the file has multiple names, it continues to exist under the other names. If *filename* is a symbolic link, `delete-file` deletes only the symbolic link and not its target (though it does follow symbolic links at all levels of parent directories).

A suitable kind of `file-error` error is signaled if the file does not exist, or is not deletable. (On Unix and GNU/Linux, a file is deletable if its directory is writable.)

If the optional argument *trash* is non-`nil` and the variable `delete-by-moving-to-trash` is non-`nil`, this command moves the file into the system Trash instead of

deleting it. See Section "Miscellaneous File Operations" in *The GNU Emacs Manual*.
When called interactively, *trash* is `t` if no prefix argument is given, and `nil` otherwise.

See also `delete-directory` in Section 24.10 [Create/Delete Dirs], page 529.

`set-file-modes` *filename mode*   [Command]
> This function sets the *file mode* (or *permissions*) of *filename* to *mode*. It recursively
> follows symbolic links at all levels for *filename*.
>
> If called non-interactively, *mode* must be an integer. Only the lowest 12 bits of the
> integer are used; on most systems, only the lowest 9 bits are meaningful. You can use
> the Lisp construct for octal numbers to enter *mode*. For example,
>
> > `(set-file-modes #o644)`
>
> specifies that the file should be readable and writable for its owner, readable for group
> members, and readable for all other users. See Section "File permissions" in *The* GNU
> Coreutils *Manual*, for a description of mode bit specifications.
>
> Interactively, *mode* is read from the minibuffer using `read-file-modes` (see below),
> which lets the user type in either an integer or a string representing the permissions
> symbolically.
>
> See Section 24.6.4 [File Attributes], page 509, for the function `file-modes`, which
> returns the permissions of a file.

`set-default-file-modes` *mode*   [Function]
> This function sets the default permissions for new files created by Emacs and its
> subprocesses. Every file created with Emacs initially has these permissions, or a
> subset of them (`write-region` will not grant execute permissions even if the default
> file permissions allow execution). On Unix and GNU/Linux, the default permissions
> are given by the bitwise complement of the 'umask' value.
>
> The argument *mode* should be an integer which specifies the permissions, similar to
> `set-file-modes` above. Only the lowest 9 bits are meaningful.
>
> The default file permissions have no effect when you save a modified version of an
> existing file; saving a file preserves its existing permissions.

`with-file-modes` *mode body...*   [Macro]
> This macro evaluates the *body* forms with the default permissions for new files tem-
> porarily set to *modes* (whose value is as for `set-file-modes` above). When finished,
> it restores the original default file permissions, and returns the value of the last form
> in *body*.
>
> This is useful for creating private files, for example.

`default-file-modes`   [Function]
> This function returns the default file permissions, as an integer.

`read-file-modes` **&optional** *prompt base-file*   [Function]
> This function reads a set of file mode bits from the minibuffer. The first optional
> argument *prompt* specifies a non-default prompt. Second second optional argument
> *base-file* is the name of a file on whose permissions to base the mode bits that this
> function returns, if what the user types specifies mode bits relative to permissions of
> an existing file.

If user input represents an octal number, this function returns that number. If it is a complete symbolic specification of mode bits, as in `"u=rwx"`, the function converts it to the equivalent numeric value using `file-modes-symbolic-to-number` and returns the result. If the specification is relative, as in `"o+g"`, then the permissions on which the specification is based are taken from the mode bits of *base-file*. If *base-file* is omitted or `nil`, the function uses 0 as the base mode bits. The complete and relative specifications can be combined, as in `"u+r,g+rx,o+r,g-w"`. See Section "File permissions" in *The* GNU `Coreutils` *Manual*, for a description of file mode specifications.

file-modes-symbolic-to-number *modes* **&optional** *base-modes*   [Function]
> This function converts a symbolic file mode specification in *modes* into the equivalent integer. If the symbolic specification is based on an existing file, that file's mode bits are taken from the optional argument *base-modes*; if that argument is omitted or `nil`, it defaults to 0, i.e., no access rights at all.

set-file-times *filename* **&optional** *time*   [Function]
> This function sets the access and modification times of *filename* to *time*. The return value is `t` if the times are successfully set, otherwise it is `nil`. *time* defaults to the current time and must be in the format returned by `current-time` (see Section 38.5 [Time of Day], page 999).

set-file-extended-attributes *filename* *attribute-alist*   [Function]
> This function sets the Emacs-recognized extended file attributes for `filename`. The second argument *attribute-alist* should be an alist of the same form returned by `file-extended-attributes`. The return value is `t` if the attributes are successfully set, otherwise it is `nil`. See Section 24.6.5 [Extended Attributes], page 512.

set-file-selinux-context *filename* *context*   [Function]
> This function sets the SELinux security context for *filename* to *context*. The *context* argument should be a list `(user role type range)`, where each element is a string. See Section 24.6.5 [Extended Attributes], page 512.
>
> The function returns `t` if it succeeds in setting the SELinux context of *filename*. It returns `nil` if the context was not set (e.g., if SELinux is disabled, or if Emacs was compiled without SELinux support).

set-file-acl *filename* *acl*   [Function]
> This function sets the Access Control List for *filename* to *acl*. The *acl* argument should have the same form returned by the function `file-acl`. See Section 24.6.5 [Extended Attributes], page 512.
>
> The function returns `t` if it successfully sets the ACL of *filename*, `nil` otherwise.

24.8 File Names

Files are generally referred to by their names, in Emacs as elsewhere. File names in Emacs are represented as strings. The functions that operate on a file all expect a file name argument.

In addition to operating on files themselves, Emacs Lisp programs often need to operate on file names; i.e., to take them apart and to use part of a name to construct related file names. This section describes how to manipulate file names.

The functions in this section do not actually access files, so they can operate on file names that do not refer to an existing file or directory.

On MS-DOS and MS-Windows, these functions (like the function that actually operate on files) accept MS-DOS or MS-Windows file-name syntax, where backslashes separate the components, as well as Unix syntax; but they always return Unix syntax. This enables Lisp programs to specify file names in Unix syntax and work properly on all systems without change.[1]

24.8.1 File Name Components

The operating system groups files into directories. To specify a file, you must specify the directory and the file's name within that directory. Therefore, Emacs considers a file name as having two main parts: the *directory name* part, and the *nondirectory* part (or *file name within the directory*). Either part may be empty. Concatenating these two parts reproduces the original file name.

On most systems, the directory part is everything up to and including the last slash (backslash is also allowed in input on MS-DOS or MS-Windows); the nondirectory part is the rest.

For some purposes, the nondirectory part is further subdivided into the name proper and the *version number*. On most systems, only backup files have version numbers in their names.

file-name-directory *filename*   [Function]
> This function returns the directory part of *filename*, as a directory name (see Section 24.8.3 [Directory Names], page 520), or `nil` if *filename* does not include a directory part.
>
> On GNU and Unix systems, a string returned by this function always ends in a slash. On MS-DOS it can also end in a colon.
>
>   (file-name-directory "lewis/foo")   ; Unix example
>   ⇒ "lewis/"
>   (file-name-directory "foo")   ; Unix example
>   ⇒ nil

file-name-nondirectory *filename*   [Function]
> This function returns the nondirectory part of *filename*.
>
>   (file-name-nondirectory "lewis/foo")
>   ⇒ "foo"
>   (file-name-nondirectory "foo")
>   ⇒ "foo"
>   (file-name-nondirectory "lewis/")
>   ⇒ ""

file-name-sans-versions *filename* **&optional** *keep-backup-version*   [Function]
> This function returns *filename* with any file version numbers, backup version numbers, or trailing tildes discarded.

---

[1] In MS-Windows versions of Emacs compiled for the Cygwin environment, you can use the functions `cygwin-convert-file-name-to-windows` and `cygwin-convert-file-name-from-windows` to convert between the two file-name syntaxes.

If *keep-backup-version* is non-`nil`, then true file version numbers understood as such by the file system are discarded from the return value, but backup version numbers are kept.

```
(file-name-sans-versions "~rms/foo.~1~")
     ⇒ "~rms/foo"
(file-name-sans-versions "~rms/foo~")
     ⇒ "~rms/foo"
(file-name-sans-versions "~rms/foo")
     ⇒ "~rms/foo"
```

file-name-extension *filename* &optional *period*   [Function]
This function returns *filename*'s final extension, if any, after applying `file-name-sans-versions` to remove any version/backup part. The extension, in a file name, is the part that follows the last '.' in the last name component (minus any version/backup part).

This function returns `nil` for extensionless file names such as `foo`. It returns `""` for null extensions, as in `foo..` If the last component of a file name begins with a '.', that '.' doesn't count as the beginning of an extension. Thus, `.emacs`'s extension is `nil`, not '.emacs'.

If *period* is non-`nil`, then the returned value includes the period that delimits the extension, and if *filename* has no extension, the value is `""`.

file-name-sans-extension *filename*   [Function]
This function returns *filename* minus its extension, if any. The version/backup part, if present, is only removed if the file has an extension. For example,

```
(file-name-sans-extension "foo.lose.c")
     ⇒ "foo.lose"
(file-name-sans-extension "big.hack/foo")
     ⇒ "big.hack/foo"
(file-name-sans-extension "/my/home/.emacs")
     ⇒ "/my/home/.emacs"
(file-name-sans-extension "/my/home/.emacs.el")
     ⇒ "/my/home/.emacs"
(file-name-sans-extension "~/foo.el.~3~")
     ⇒ "~/foo"
(file-name-sans-extension "~/foo.~3~")
     ⇒ "~/foo.~3~"
```

Note that the '.~3~' in the two last examples is the backup part, not an extension.

file-name-base &optional *filename*   [Function]
This function is the composition of `file-name-sans-extension` and `file-name-nondirectory`. For example,

```
(file-name-base "/my/home/foo.c")
     ⇒ "foo"
```

The *filename* argument defaults to `buffer-file-name`.

24.8.2 Absolute and Relative File Names

All the directories in the file system form a tree starting at the root directory. A file name can specify all the directory names starting from the root of the tree; then it is called an *absolute* file name. Or it can specify the position of the file in the tree relative to a default directory; then it is called a *relative* file name. On Unix and GNU/Linux, an absolute file name starts with a '/' or a '~' (see [abbreviate-file-name], page 521), and a relative one does not. On MS-DOS and MS-Windows, an absolute file name starts with a slash or a backslash, or with a drive specification 'x:/', where x is the *drive letter*.

`file-name-absolute-p` *filename*   [Function]
    This function returns t if file *filename* is an absolute file name, nil otherwise.

```
(file-name-absolute-p "~rms/foo")
    ⇒ t
(file-name-absolute-p "rms/foo")
    ⇒ nil
(file-name-absolute-p "/user/rms/foo")
    ⇒ t
```

Given a possibly relative file name, you can convert it to an absolute name using `expand-file-name` (see Section 24.8.4 [File Name Expansion], page 522). This function converts absolute file names to relative names:

`file-relative-name` *filename* **&optional** *directory*   [Function]
    This function tries to return a relative name that is equivalent to *filename*, assuming the result will be interpreted relative to *directory* (an absolute directory name or directory file name). If *directory* is omitted or nil, it defaults to the current buffer's default directory.

    On some operating systems, an absolute file name begins with a device name. On such systems, *filename* has no relative equivalent based on *directory* if they start with two different device names. In this case, `file-relative-name` returns *filename* in absolute form.

```
(file-relative-name "/foo/bar" "/foo/")
    ⇒ "bar"
(file-relative-name "/foo/bar" "/hack/")
    ⇒ "../foo/bar"
```

24.8.3 Directory Names

A *directory name* is the name of a directory. A directory is actually a kind of file, so it has a file name (called the *directory file name*, which is related to the directory name but not identical to it. (This is not quite the same as the usual Unix terminology.) These two different names for the same entity are related by a syntactic transformation. On GNU and Unix systems, this is simple: a directory name ends in a slash, whereas the directory file name lacks that slash. On MS-DOS the relationship is more complicated.

The difference between directory name and directory file name is subtle but crucial. When an Emacs variable or function argument is described as being a directory name, a directory file name is not acceptable. When `file-name-directory` returns a string, that is always a directory name.

The following two functions convert between directory names and directory file names. They do nothing special with environment variable substitutions such as '$HOME', and the constructs '~', '.' and '..'.

file-name-as-directory *filename* [Function]

> This function returns a string representing *filename* in a form that the operating system will interpret as the name of a directory (a directory name). On most systems, this means appending a slash to the string (if it does not already end in one).
>
> ```
> (file-name-as-directory "~rms/lewis")
>      ⇒ "~rms/lewis/"
> ```

directory-name-p *filename* [Function]

> This function returns non-**nil** if *filename* ends with a directory separator character. This is the forward slash '/' on Unix and GNU systems; MS-Windows and MS-DOS recognize both the forward slash and the backslash '\' as directory separators.

directory-file-name *dirname* [Function]

> This function returns a string representing *dirname* in a form that the operating system will interpret as the name of a file (a directory file name). On most systems, this means removing the final slash (or backslash) from the string.
>
> ```
> (directory-file-name "~lewis/")
>      ⇒ "~lewis"
> ```

Given a directory name, you can combine it with a relative file name using **concat**:

```
(concat dirname relfile)
```

Be sure to verify that the file name is relative before doing that. If you use an absolute file name, the results could be syntactically invalid or refer to the wrong file.

If you want to use a directory file name in making such a combination, you must first convert it to a directory name using **file-name-as-directory**:

```
(concat (file-name-as-directory dirfile) relfile)
```

Don't try concatenating a slash by hand, as in

```
;;; Wrong!
(concat dirfile "/" relfile)
```

because this is not portable. Always use **file-name-as-directory**.

To avoid the issues mentioned above, or if the *dirname* value might be nil (for example, from an element of **load-path**), use:

```
(expand-file-name relfile dirname)
```

To convert a directory name to its abbreviation, use this function:

abbreviate-file-name *filename* [Function]

> This function returns an abbreviated form of *filename*. It applies the abbreviations specified in **directory-abbrev-alist** (see Section "File Aliases" in *The GNU Emacs Manual*), then substitutes '~' for the user's home directory if the argument names a file in the home directory or one of its subdirectories. If the home directory is a root directory, it is not replaced with '~', because this does not make the result shorter on many systems.

You can use this function for directory names and for file names, because it recognizes abbreviations even as part of the name.

24.8.4 Functions that Expand Filenames

Expanding a file name means converting a relative file name to an absolute one. Since this is done relative to a default directory, you must specify the default directory name as well as the file name to be expanded. It also involves expanding abbreviations like ~/ and eliminating redundancies like ./ and *name*/../.

expand-file-name *filename* **&optional** *directory*   [Function]

This function converts *filename* to an absolute file name. If *directory* is supplied, it is the default directory to start with if *filename* is relative. (The value of *directory* should itself be an absolute directory name or directory file name; it may start with '~'.) Otherwise, the current buffer's value of `default-directory` is used. For example:

```
(expand-file-name "foo")
     ⇒ "/xcssun/users/rms/lewis/foo"
(expand-file-name "../foo")
     ⇒ "/xcssun/users/rms/foo"
(expand-file-name "foo" "/usr/spool/")
     ⇒ "/usr/spool/foo"
```

If the part of the combined file name before the first slash is '~', it expands to the value of the `HOME` environment variable (usually your home directory). If the part before the first slash is '~*user*' and if *user* is a valid login name, it expands to *user*'s home directory.

Filenames containing '.' or '..' are simplified to their canonical form:

```
(expand-file-name "bar/../foo")
     ⇒ "/xcssun/users/rms/lewis/foo"
```

In some cases, a leading '..' component can remain in the output:

```
(expand-file-name "../home" "/")
     ⇒ "/../home"
```

This is for the sake of filesystems that have the concept of a superroot above the root directory /. On other filesystems, /../ is interpreted exactly the same as /.

Note that `expand-file-name` does *not* expand environment variables; only `substitute-in-file-name` does that:

```
(expand-file-name "$HOME/foo")
     ⇒ "/xcssun/users/rms/lewis/$HOME/foo"
```

Note also that `expand-file-name` does not follow symbolic links at any level. This results in a difference between the way `file-truename` and `expand-file-name` treat '..'. Assuming that '/tmp/bar' is a symbolic link to the directory '/tmp/foo/bar' we get:

```
(file-truename "/tmp/bar/../myfile")
     ⇒ "/tmp/foo/myfile"
(expand-file-name "/tmp/bar/../myfile")
     ⇒ "/tmp/myfile"
```

If you may need to follow symbolic links preceding '..', you should make sure to call `file-truename` without prior direct or indirect calls to `expand-file-name`. See Section 24.6.3 [Truenames], page 508.

`default-directory`   [Variable]

> The value of this buffer-local variable is the default directory for the current buffer. It should be an absolute directory name; it may start with '~'. This variable is buffer-local in every buffer.
>
> `expand-file-name` uses the default directory when its second argument is `nil`.
>
> The value is always a string ending with a slash.
>
> ```
>     default-directory
>          ⇒ "/user/lewis/manual/"
> ```

`substitute-in-file-name` *filename*   [Function]

> This function replaces environment variable references in *filename* with the environment variable values. Following standard Unix shell syntax, '$' is the prefix to substitute an environment variable value. If the input contains '$$', that is converted to '$'; this gives the user a way to quote a '$'.
>
> The environment variable name is the series of alphanumeric characters (including underscores) that follow the '$'. If the character following the '$' is a '{', then the variable name is everything up to the matching '}'.
>
> Calling `substitute-in-file-name` on output produced by `substitute-in-file-name` tends to give incorrect results. For instance, use of '$$' to quote a single '$' won't work properly, and '$' in an environment variable's value could lead to repeated substitution. Therefore, programs that call this function and put the output where it will be passed to this function need to double all '$' characters to prevent subsequent incorrect results.
>
> Here we assume that the environment variable HOME, which holds the user's home directory name, has value '/xcssun/users/rms'.
>
> ```
>     (substitute-in-file-name "$HOME/foo")
>          ⇒ "/xcssun/users/rms/foo"
> ```
>
> After substitution, if a '~' or a '/' appears immediately after another '/', the function discards everything before it (up through the immediately preceding '/').
>
> ```
>     (substitute-in-file-name "bar/~/foo")
>          ⇒ "~/foo"
>     (substitute-in-file-name "/usr/local/$HOME/foo")
>          ⇒ "/xcssun/users/rms/foo"
>          ;; /usr/local/ has been discarded.
> ```

24.8.5 Generating Unique File Names

Some programs need to write temporary files. Here is the usual way to construct a name for such a file:

```
    (make-temp-file name-of-application)
```

The job of `make-temp-file` is to prevent two different users or two different jobs from trying to use the exact same file name.

`make-temp-file` *prefix* **&optional** *dir-flag suffix*   [Function]

> This function creates a temporary file and returns its name. Emacs creates the temporary file's name by adding to *prefix* some random characters that are different in each Emacs job. The result is guaranteed to be a newly created empty file. On MS-DOS, this function can truncate the *string* prefix to fit into the 8+3 file-name limits. If *prefix* is a relative file name, it is expanded against `temporary-file-directory`.
>
> ```
>       (make-temp-file "foo")
>           ⇒ "/tmp/foo232J6v"
> ```
>
> When `make-temp-file` returns, the file has been created and is empty. At that point, you should write the intended contents into the file.
>
> If *dir-flag* is non-`nil`, `make-temp-file` creates an empty directory instead of an empty file. It returns the file name, not the directory name, of that directory. See Section 24.8.3 [Directory Names], page 520.
>
> If *suffix* is non-`nil`, `make-temp-file` adds it at the end of the file name.
>
> To prevent conflicts among different libraries running in the same Emacs, each Lisp program that uses `make-temp-file` should have its own *prefix*. The number added to the end of *prefix* distinguishes between the same application running in different Emacs jobs. Additional added characters permit a large number of distinct names even in one Emacs job.

The default directory for temporary files is controlled by the variable `temporary-file-directory`. This variable gives the user a uniform way to specify the directory for all temporary files. Some programs use `small-temporary-file-directory` instead, if that is non-`nil`. To use it, you should expand the prefix against the proper directory before calling `make-temp-file`.

`temporary-file-directory`   [User Option]

> This variable specifies the directory name for creating temporary files. Its value should be a directory name (see Section 24.8.3 [Directory Names], page 520), but it is good for Lisp programs to cope if the value is a directory's file name instead. Using the value as the second argument to `expand-file-name` is a good way to achieve that.
>
> The default value is determined in a reasonable way for your operating system; it is based on the `TMPDIR`, `TMP` and `TEMP` environment variables, with a fall-back to a system-dependent name if none of these variables is defined.
>
> Even if you do not use `make-temp-file` to create the temporary file, you should still use this variable to decide which directory to put the file in. However, if you expect the file to be small, you should use `small-temporary-file-directory` first if that is non-`nil`.

`small-temporary-file-directory`   [User Option]

> This variable specifies the directory name for creating certain temporary files, which are likely to be small.
>
> If you want to write a temporary file which is likely to be small, you should compute the directory like this:
>
> ```
>       (make-temp-file
>         (expand-file-name prefix
> ```

```
              (or small-temporary-file-directory
                 temporary-file-directory)))
```

`make-temp-name` *base-name*   [Function]

This function generates a string that can be used as a unique file name. The name starts with *base-name*, and has several random characters appended to it, which are different in each Emacs job. It is like `make-temp-file` except that (i) it just constructs a name, and does not create a file, and (ii) *base-name* should be an absolute file name (on MS-DOS, this function can truncate *base-name* to fit into the 8+3 file-name limits).

Warning: In most cases, you should not use this function; use `make-temp-file` instead! This function is susceptible to a race condition, between the `make-temp-name` call and the creation of the file, which in some cases may cause a security hole.

24.8.6 File Name Completion

This section describes low-level subroutines for completing a file name. For higher level functions, see Section 19.6.5 [Reading File Names], page 330.

`file-name-all-completions` *partial-filename directory*   [Function]

This function returns a list of all possible completions for a file whose name starts with *partial-filename* in directory *directory*. The order of the completions is the order of the files in the directory, which is unpredictable and conveys no useful information.

The argument *partial-filename* must be a file name containing no directory part and no slash (or backslash on some systems). The current buffer's default directory is prepended to *directory*, if *directory* is not absolute.

In the following example, suppose that `~rms/lewis` is the current default directory, and has five files whose names begin with 'f': `foo`, `file~`, `file.c`, `file.c.~1~`, and `file.c.~2~`.

```
    (file-name-all-completions "f" "")
        ⇒ ("foo" "file~" "file.c.~2~"
                  "file.c.~1~" "file.c")


    (file-name-all-completions "fo" "")
        ⇒ ("foo")
```

`file-name-completion` *filename directory* **&optional** *predicate*   [Function]

This function completes the file name *filename* in directory *directory*. It returns the longest prefix common to all file names in directory *directory* that start with *filename*. If *predicate* is non-`nil` then it ignores possible completions that don't satisfy *predicate*, after calling that function with one argument, the expanded absolute file name.

If only one match exists and *filename* matches it exactly, the function returns `t`. The function returns `nil` if directory *directory* contains no name starting with *filename*.

In the following example, suppose that the current default directory has five files whose names begin with 'f': `foo`, `file~`, `file.c`, `file.c.~1~`, and `file.c.~2~`.

```
    (file-name-completion "fi" "")
        ⇒ "file"
```

```
(file-name-completion "file.c.~1" "")
     ⇒ "file.c.~1~"

(file-name-completion "file.c.~1~" "")
     ⇒ t

(file-name-completion "file.c.~3" "")
     ⇒ nil
```

completion-ignored-extensions   [User Option]
    file-name-completion usually ignores file names that end in any string in this list.
    It does not ignore them when all the possible completions end in one of these suffixes.
    This variable has no effect on file-name-all-completions.

    A typical value might look like this:

```
completion-ignored-extensions
     ⇒ (".o" ".elc" "~" ".dvi")
```

    If an element of completion-ignored-extensions ends in a slash '/', it signals a
    directory. The elements which do *not* end in a slash will never match a directory;
    thus, the above value will not filter out a directory named foo.elc.

24.8.7 Standard File Names

Sometimes, an Emacs Lisp program needs to specify a standard file name for a particular
use—typically, to hold configuration data specified by the current user. Usually, such files
should be located in the directory specified by user-emacs-directory, which is ~/.emacs.d
by default (see Section 38.1.2 [Init File], page 988). For example, abbrev definitions are
stored by default in ~/.emacs.d/abbrev_defs. The easiest way to specify such a file name
is to use the function locate-user-emacs-file.

locate-user-emacs-file *base-name* **&optional** *old-name*   [Function]
    This function returns an absolute file name for an Emacs-specific configuration or
    data file. The argument base-name should be a relative file name. The return value
    is the absolute name of a file in the directory specified by user-emacs-directory; if
    that directory does not exist, this function creates it.

    If the optional argument *old-name* is non-nil, it specifies a file in the user's home
    directory, ~/*old-name*. If such a file exists, the return value is the absolute name of
    that file, instead of the file specified by *base-name*. This argument is intended to be
    used by Emacs packages to provide backward compatibility. For instance, prior to the
    introduction of user-emacs-directory, the abbrev file was located in ~/.abbrev_
    defs. Here is the definition of abbrev-file-name:

```
(defcustom abbrev-file-name
  (locate-user-emacs-file "abbrev_defs" ".abbrev_defs")
  "Default name of file from which to read abbrevs."
  ...
  :type 'file)
```

A lower-level function for standardizing file names, which `locate-user-emacs-file` uses as a subroutine, is `convert-standard-filename`.

`convert-standard-filename` *filename* [Function]

> This function returns a file name based on *filename*, which fits the conventions of the current operating system.

> On GNU and Unix systems, this simply returns *filename*. On other operating systems, it may enforce system-specific file name conventions; for example, on MS-DOS this function performs a variety of changes to enforce MS-DOS file name limitations, including converting any leading '.' to '_' and truncating to three characters after the '.'.

> The recommended way to use this function is to specify a name which fits the conventions of GNU and Unix systems, and pass it to `convert-standard-filename`.

24.9 Contents of Directories

A directory is a kind of file that contains other files entered under various names. Directories are a feature of the file system.

Emacs can list the names of the files in a directory as a Lisp list, or display the names in a buffer using the `ls` shell command. In the latter case, it can optionally display information about each file, depending on the options passed to the `ls` command.

`directory-files` *directory* **&optional** *full-name match-regexp nosort* [Function]

> This function returns a list of the names of the files in the directory *directory*. By default, the list is in alphabetical order.

> If *full-name* is non-`nil`, the function returns the files' absolute file names. Otherwise, it returns the names relative to the specified directory.

> If *match-regexp* is non-`nil`, this function returns only those file names that contain a match for that regular expression—the other file names are excluded from the list. On case-insensitive filesystems, the regular expression matching is case-insensitive.

> If *nosort* is non-`nil`, `directory-files` does not sort the list, so you get the file names in no particular order. Use this if you want the utmost possible speed and don't care what order the files are processed in. If the order of processing is visible to the user, then the user will probably be happier if you do sort the names.

```
(directory-files "~lewis")
     ⇒ ("#foo#" "#foo.el#" "." ".."
        "dired-mods.el" "files.texi"
        "files.texi.~1~")
```

> An error is signaled if *directory* is not the name of a directory that can be read.

`directory-files-recursively` *directory regexp* **&optional** [Function]
      include-directories

> Return all files under *directory* whose names match *regexp*. This function searches the specified *directory* and its sub-directories, recursively, for files whose basenames (i.e., without the leading directories) match the specified *regexp*, and returns a list of the absolute file names of the matching files (see Section 24.8.2 [Relative File

Names], page 520). The file names are returned in depth-first order, meaning that files in some sub-directory are returned before the files in its parent directory. In addition, matching files found in each subdirectory are sorted alphabetically by their basenames. By default, directories whose names match *regexp* are omitted from the list, but if the optional argument *include-directories* is non-`nil`, they are included.

`directory-files-and-attributes` *directory* **&optional** *full-name*   [Function]
  match-regexp nosort id-format
  This is similar to `directory-files` in deciding which files to report on and how to report their names. However, instead of returning a list of file names, it returns for each file a list (`filename . attributes`), where *attributes* is what `file-attributes` would return for that file. The optional argument *id-format* has the same meaning as the corresponding argument to `file-attributes` (see [Definition of file-attributes], page 510).

`file-expand-wildcards` *pattern* **&optional** *full*   [Function]
  This function expands the wildcard pattern *pattern*, returning a list of file names that match it.

  If *pattern* is written as an absolute file name, the values are absolute also.

  If *pattern* is written as a relative file name, it is interpreted relative to the current default directory. The file names returned are normally also relative to the current default directory. However, if *full* is non-`nil`, they are absolute.

`insert-directory` *file switches* **&optional** *wildcard full-directory-p*   [Function]
  This function inserts (in the current buffer) a directory listing for directory *file*, formatted with `ls` according to *switches*. It leaves point after the inserted text. *switches* may be a string of options, or a list of strings representing individual options.

  The argument *file* may be either a directory name or a file specification including wildcard characters. If *wildcard* is non-`nil`, that means treat *file* as a file specification with wildcards.

  If *full-directory-p* is non-`nil`, that means the directory listing is expected to show the full contents of a directory. You should specify `t` when *file* is a directory and switches do not contain '`-d`'. (The '`-d`' option to `ls` says to describe a directory itself as a file, rather than showing its contents.)

  On most systems, this function works by running a directory listing program whose name is in the variable `insert-directory-program`. If *wildcard* is non-`nil`, it also runs the shell specified by `shell-file-name`, to expand the wildcards.

  MS-DOS and MS-Windows systems usually lack the standard Unix program `ls`, so this function emulates the standard Unix program `ls` with Lisp code.

  As a technical detail, when *switches* contains the long '`--dired`' option, `insert-directory` treats it specially, for the sake of dired. However, the normally equivalent short '`-D`' option is just passed on to `insert-directory-program`, as any other option.

`insert-directory-program`   [Variable]
  This variable's value is the program to run to generate a directory listing for the function `insert-directory`. It is ignored on systems which generate the listing with Lisp code.

24.10 Creating, Copying and Deleting Directories

Most Emacs Lisp file-manipulation functions get errors when used on files that are directories. For example, you cannot delete a directory with `delete-file`. These special functions exist to create and delete directories.

make-directory *dirname* **&optional** *parents*   [Command]

> This command creates a directory named *dirname*. If *parents* is non-`nil`, as is always the case in an interactive call, that means to create the parent directories first, if they don't already exist.
>
> `mkdir` is an alias for this.

copy-directory *dirname newname* **&optional** *keep-time parents*   [Command]
> *copy-contents*
>
> This command copies the directory named *dirname* to *newname*. If *newname* names an existing directory, *dirname* will be copied to a subdirectory there.
>
> It always sets the file modes of the copied files to match the corresponding original file.
>
> The third argument *keep-time* non-`nil` means to preserve the modification time of the copied files. A prefix arg makes *keep-time* non-`nil`.
>
> The fourth argument *parents* says whether to create parent directories if they don't exist. Interactively, this happens by default.
>
> The fifth argument *copy-contents*, if non-`nil`, means to copy the contents of *dirname* directly into *newname* if the latter is an existing directory, instead of copying *dirname* into it as a subdirectory.

delete-directory *dirname* **&optional** *recursive trash*   [Command]

> This command deletes the directory named *dirname*. The function `delete-file` does not work for files that are directories; you must use `delete-directory` for them. If *recursive* is `nil`, and the directory contains any files, `delete-directory` signals an error.
>
> `delete-directory` only follows symbolic links at the level of parent directories.
>
> If the optional argument *trash* is non-`nil` and the variable `delete-by-moving-to-trash` is non-`nil`, this command moves the file into the system Trash instead of deleting it. See Section "Miscellaneous File Operations" in *The GNU Emacs Manual*. When called interactively, *trash* is `t` if no prefix argument is given, and `nil` otherwise.

24.11 Making Certain File Names "Magic"

You can implement special handling for certain file names. This is called making those names *magic*. The principal use for this feature is in implementing access to remote files (see Section "Remote Files" in *The GNU Emacs Manual*).

To define a kind of magic file name, you must supply a regular expression to define the class of names (all those that match the regular expression), plus a handler that implements all the primitive Emacs file operations for file names that match.

The variable `file-name-handler-alist` holds a list of handlers, together with regular expressions that determine when to apply each handler. Each element has this form:

    (*regexp* . *handler*)

All the Emacs primitives for file access and file name transformation check the given file name against `file-name-handler-alist`. If the file name matches *regexp*, the primitives handle that file by calling *handler*.

The first argument given to *handler* is the name of the primitive, as a symbol; the remaining arguments are the arguments that were passed to that primitive. (The first of these arguments is most often the file name itself.) For example, if you do this:

    (file-exists-p *filename*)

and *filename* has handler *handler*, then *handler* is called like this:

    (funcall *handler* 'file-exists-p *filename*)

When a function takes two or more arguments that must be file names, it checks each of those names for a handler. For example, if you do this:

    (expand-file-name *filename* *dirname*)

then it checks for a handler for *filename* and then for a handler for *dirname*. In either case, the *handler* is called like this:

    (funcall *handler* 'expand-file-name *filename* *dirname*)

The *handler* then needs to figure out whether to handle *filename* or *dirname*.

If the specified file name matches more than one handler, the one whose match starts last in the file name gets precedence. This rule is chosen so that handlers for jobs such as uncompression are handled first, before handlers for jobs such as remote file access.

Here are the operations that a magic file name handler gets to handle:

access-file, add-name-to-file,
byte-compiler-base-file-name,
copy-directory, copy-file,
delete-directory, delete-file,
diff-latest-backup-file,
directory-file-name,
directory-files,
directory-files-and-attributes,
dired-compress-file, dired-uncache,
expand-file-name,
file-accessible-directory-p,
file-acl,
file-attributes,
file-directory-p,
file-equal-p,
file-executable-p, file-exists-p,
file-in-directory-p,
file-local-copy,
file-modes, file-name-all-completions,
file-name-as-directory,
file-name-completion,

```
file-name-directory,
file-name-nondirectory,
file-name-sans-versions, file-newer-than-file-p,
file-notify-add-watch, file-notify-rm-watch,
file-notify-valid-p,
file-ownership-preserved-p,
file-readable-p, file-regular-p,
file-remote-p, file-selinux-context,
file-symlink-p, file-truename, file-writable-p,
find-backup-file-name,
get-file-buffer,
insert-directory,
insert-file-contents,
load,
make-auto-save-file-name,
make-directory,
make-directory-internal,
make-symbolic-link,
process-file,
rename-file, set-file-acl, set-file-modes,
set-file-selinux-context, set-file-times,
set-visited-file-modtime, shell-command,
start-file-process,
substitute-in-file-name,
unhandled-file-name-directory,
vc-registered,
verify-visited-file-modtime,
write-region.
```

Handlers for `insert-file-contents` typically need to clear the buffer's modified flag, with (`set-buffer-modified-p nil`), if the *visit* argument is non-`nil`. This also has the effect of unlocking the buffer if it is locked.

The handler function must handle all of the above operations, and possibly others to be added in the future. It need not implement all these operations itself—when it has nothing special to do for a certain operation, it can reinvoke the primitive, to handle the operation in the usual way. It should always reinvoke the primitive for an operation it does not recognize. Here's one way to do this:

```
(defun my-file-handler (operation &rest args)
  ;; First check for the specific operations
  ;; that we have special handling for.
  (cond ((eq operation 'insert-file-contents) ...)
        ((eq operation 'write-region) ...)
        ...
        ;; Handle any operation we don{ft know about.
        (t (let ((inhibit-file-name-handlers
                  (cons 'my-file-handler
                        (and (eq inhibit-file-name-operation operation)
                             inhibit-file-name-handlers)))
                 (inhibit-file-name-operation operation))
             (apply operation args)))))
```

When a handler function decides to call the ordinary Emacs primitive for the operation at hand, it needs to prevent the primitive from calling the same handler once again, thus leading to an infinite recursion. The example above shows how to do this, with the variables `inhibit-file-name-handlers` and `inhibit-file-name-operation`. Be careful to use them exactly as shown above; the details are crucial for proper behavior in the case of multiple handlers, and for operations that have two file names that may each have handlers.

Handlers that don't really do anything special for actual access to the file—such as the ones that implement completion of host names for remote file names—should have a non-`nil` `safe-magic` property. For instance, Emacs normally protects directory names it finds in `PATH` from becoming magic, if they look like magic file names, by prefixing them with '/:'. But if the handler that would be used for them has a non-`nil` `safe-magic` property, the '/:' is not added.

A file name handler can have an `operations` property to declare which operations it handles in a nontrivial way. If this property has a non-`nil` value, it should be a list of operations; then only those operations will call the handler. This avoids inefficiency, but its main purpose is for autoloaded handler functions, so that they won't be loaded except when they have real work to do.

Simply deferring all operations to the usual primitives does not work. For instance, if the file name handler applies to `file-exists-p`, then it must handle `load` itself, because the usual `load` code won't work properly in that case. However, if the handler uses the `operations` property to say it doesn't handle `file-exists-p`, then it need not handle `load` nontrivially.

`inhibit-file-name-handlers`   [Variable]

> This variable holds a list of handlers whose use is presently inhibited for a certain operation.

`inhibit-file-name-operation`   [Variable]

> The operation for which certain handlers are presently inhibited.

`find-file-name-handler` *file operation*   [Function]

> This function returns the handler function for file name *file*, or `nil` if there is none. The argument *operation* should be the operation to be performed on the file—the value you will pass to the handler as its first argument when you call it. If *operation* equals `inhibit-file-name-operation`, or if it is not found in the `operations` property of the handler, this function returns `nil`.

`file-local-copy` *filename*   [Function]

> This function copies file *filename* to an ordinary non-magic file on the local machine, if it isn't on the local machine already. Magic file names should handle the `file-local-copy` operation if they refer to files on other machines. A magic file name that is used for other purposes than remote file access should not handle `file-local-copy`; then this function will treat the file as local.
>
> If *filename* is local, whether magic or not, this function does nothing and returns `nil`. Otherwise it returns the file name of the local copy file.

file-remote-p *filename* **&optional** *identification connected*   [Function]

This function tests whether *filename* is a remote file. If *filename* is local (not remote), the return value is `nil`. If *filename* is indeed remote, the return value is a string that identifies the remote system.

This identifier string can include a host name and a user name, as well as characters designating the method used to access the remote system. For example, the remote identifier string for the filename `/sudo::/some/file` is `/sudo:root@localhost:`.

If `file-remote-p` returns the same identifier for two different filenames, that means they are stored on the same file system and can be accessed locally with respect to each other. This means, for example, that it is possible to start a remote process accessing both files at the same time. Implementers of file handlers need to ensure this principle is valid.

identification specifies which part of the identifier shall be returned as string. *identification* can be the symbol `method`, `user` or `host`; any other value is handled like `nil` and means to return the complete identifier string. In the example above, the remote `user` identifier string would be `root`.

If *connected* is non-`nil`, this function returns `nil` even if *filename* is remote, if Emacs has no network connection to its host. This is useful when you want to avoid the delay of making connections when they don't exist.

unhandled-file-name-directory *filename*   [Function]

This function returns the name of a directory that is not magic. For a non-magic *filename* it returns the corresponding directory name (see Section 24.8.3 [Directory Names], page 520). For a magic *filename*, it invokes the file name handler, which therefore decides what value to return. If *filename* is not accessible from a local process, then the file name handler should indicate that by returning `nil`.

This is useful for running a subprocess; every subprocess must have a non-magic directory to serve as its current directory, and this function is a good way to come up with one.

remote-file-name-inhibit-cache   [User Option]

The attributes of remote files can be cached for better performance. If they are changed outside of Emacs's control, the cached values become invalid, and must be reread.

When this variable is set to `nil`, cached values are never expired. Use this setting with caution, only if you are sure nothing other than Emacs ever changes the remote files. If it is set to `t`, cached values are never used. This is the safest value, but could result in performance degradation.

A compromise is to set it to a positive number. This means that cached values are used for that amount of seconds since they were cached. If a remote file is checked regularly, it might be a good idea to let-bind this variable to a value less than the time period between consecutive checks. For example:

```
(defun display-time-file-nonempty-p (file)
  (let ((remote-file-name-inhibit-cache
         (- display-time-interval 5)))
    (and (file-exists-p file)
```

```
(< 0 (nth 7 (file-attributes
                  (file-chase-links file)))))))))
```

24.12 File Format Conversion

Emacs performs several steps to convert the data in a buffer (text, text properties, and possibly other information) to and from a representation suitable for storing into a file. This section describes the fundamental functions that perform this *format conversion*, namely `insert-file-contents` for reading a file into a buffer, and `write-region` for writing a buffer into a file.

24.12.1 Overview

The function `insert-file-contents`:

- initially, inserts bytes from the file into the buffer;
- decodes bytes to characters as appropriate;
- processes formats as defined by entries in `format-alist`; and
- calls functions in `after-insert-file-functions`.

The function `write-region`:

- initially, calls functions in `write-region-annotate-functions`;
- processes formats as defined by entries in `format-alist`;
- encodes characters to bytes as appropriate; and
- modifies the file with the bytes.

This shows the symmetry of the lowest-level operations; reading and writing handle things in opposite order. The rest of this section describes the two facilities surrounding the three variables named above, as well as some related functions. Section 32.10 [Coding Systems], page 773, for details on character encoding and decoding.

24.12.2 Round-Trip Specification

The most general of the two facilities is controlled by the variable `format-alist`, a list of *file format* specifications, which describe textual representations used in files for the data in an Emacs buffer. The descriptions for reading and writing are paired, which is why we call this "round-trip" specification (see Section 24.12.3 [Format Conversion Piecemeal], page 536, for non-paired specification).

`format-alist`   [Variable]
    This list contains one format definition for each defined file format. Each format definition is a list of this form:

         (*name doc-string regexp from-fn to-fn modify mode-fn preserve*)

    Here is what the elements in a format definition mean:

    name   The name of this format.

    doc-string A documentation string for the format.

    regexp   A regular expression which is used to recognize files represented in this format. If `nil`, the format is never applied automatically.

from-fn   A shell command or function to decode data in this format (to convert file data into the usual Emacs data representation).

A shell command is represented as a string; Emacs runs the command as a filter to perform the conversion.

If *from-fn* is a function, it is called with two arguments, *begin* and *end*, which specify the part of the buffer it should convert. It should convert the text by editing it in place. Since this can change the length of the text, *from-fn* should return the modified end position.

One responsibility of *from-fn* is to make sure that the beginning of the file no longer matches *regexp*. Otherwise it is likely to get called again.

to-fn   A shell command or function to encode data in this format—that is, to convert the usual Emacs data representation into this format.

If *to-fn* is a string, it is a shell command; Emacs runs the command as a filter to perform the conversion.

If *to-fn* is a function, it is called with three arguments: *begin* and *end*, which specify the part of the buffer it should convert, and *buffer*, which specifies which buffer. There are two ways it can do the conversion:

- By editing the buffer in place. In this case, *to-fn* should return the end-position of the range of text, as modified.

- By returning a list of annotations. This is a list of elements of the form (`position . string`), where *position* is an integer specifying the relative position in the text to be written, and *string* is the annotation to add there. The list must be sorted in order of position when *to-fn* returns it.

  When `write-region` actually writes the text from the buffer to the file, it intermixes the specified annotations at the corresponding positions. All this takes place without modifying the buffer.

modify   A flag, `t` if the encoding function modifies the buffer, and `nil` if it works by returning a list of annotations.

mode-fn   A minor-mode function to call after visiting a file converted from this format. The function is called with one argument, the integer 1; that tells a minor-mode function to enable the mode.

preserve   A flag, `t` if `format-write-file` should not remove this format from `buffer-file-format`.

The function `insert-file-contents` automatically recognizes file formats when it reads the specified file. It checks the text of the beginning of the file against the regular expressions of the format definitions, and if it finds a match, it calls the decoding function for that format. Then it checks all the known formats over again. It keeps checking them until none of them is applicable.

Visiting a file, with `find-file-noselect` or the commands that use it, performs conversion likewise (because it calls `insert-file-contents`); it also calls the mode function for each format that it decodes. It stores a list of the format names in the buffer-local variable `buffer-file-format`.

`buffer-file-format`   [Variable]

> This variable states the format of the visited file. More precisely, this is a list of the file format names that were decoded in the course of visiting the current buffer's file. It is always buffer-local in all buffers.

When `write-region` writes data into a file, it first calls the encoding functions for the formats listed in `buffer-file-format`, in the order of appearance in the list.

`format-write-file` *file format* &**optional** *confirm*   [Command]

> This command writes the current buffer contents into the file *file* in a format based on *format*, which is a list of format names. It constructs the actual format starting from *format*, then appending any elements from the value of `buffer-file-format` with a non-`nil` *preserve* flag (see above), if they are not already present in *format*. It then updates `buffer-file-format` with this format, making it the default for future saves. Except for the *format* argument, this command is similar to `write-file`. In particular, *confirm* has the same meaning and interactive treatment as the corresponding argument to `write-file`. See [Definition of write-file], page 499.

`format-find-file` *file format*   [Command]

> This command finds the file *file*, converting it according to format *format*. It also makes *format* the default if the buffer is saved later.

> The argument *format* is a list of format names. If *format* is `nil`, no conversion takes place. Interactively, typing just RET for *format* specifies `nil`.

`format-insert-file` *file format* &**optional** *beg end*   [Command]

> This command inserts the contents of file *file*, converting it according to format *format*. If *beg* and *end* are non-`nil`, they specify which part of the file to read, as in `insert-file-contents` (see Section 24.3 [Reading from Files], page 501).

> The return value is like what `insert-file-contents` returns: a list of the absolute file name and the length of the data inserted (after conversion).

> The argument *format* is a list of format names. If *format* is `nil`, no conversion takes place. Interactively, typing just RET for *format* specifies `nil`.

`buffer-auto-save-file-format`   [Variable]

> This variable specifies the format to use for auto-saving. Its value is a list of format names, just like the value of `buffer-file-format`; however, it is used instead of `buffer-file-format` for writing auto-save files. If the value is `t`, the default, auto-saving uses the same format as a regular save in the same buffer. This variable is always buffer-local in all buffers.

24.12.3 Piecemeal Specification

In contrast to the round-trip specification described in the previous subsection (see Section 24.12.2 [Format Conversion Round-Trip], page 534), you can use the variables `after-insert-file-functions` and `write-region-annotate-functions` to separately control the respective reading and writing conversions.

Conversion starts with one representation and produces another representation. When there is only one conversion to do, there is no conflict about what to start with. However, when there are multiple conversions involved, conflict may arise when two conversions need to start with the same data.

This situation is best understood in the context of converting text properties during `write-region`. For example, the character at position 42 in a buffer is 'X' with a text property `foo`. If the conversion for `foo` is done by inserting into the buffer, say, 'FOO:', then that changes the character at position 42 from 'X' to 'F'. The next conversion will start with the wrong data straight away.

To avoid conflict, cooperative conversions do not modify the buffer, but instead specify *annotations*, a list of elements of the form (*position . string*), sorted in order of increasing *position*.

If there is more than one conversion, `write-region` merges their annotations destructively into one sorted list. Later, when the text from the buffer is actually written to the file, it intermixes the specified annotations at the corresponding positions. All this takes place without modifying the buffer.

In contrast, when reading, the annotations intermixed with the text are handled immediately. `insert-file-contents` sets point to the beginning of some text to be converted, then calls the conversion functions with the length of that text. These functions should always return with point at the beginning of the inserted text. This approach makes sense for reading because annotations removed by the first converter can't be mistakenly processed by a later converter. Each conversion function should scan for the annotations it recognizes, remove the annotation, modify the buffer text (to set a text property, for example), and return the updated length of the text, as it stands after those changes. The value returned by one function becomes the argument to the next function.

`write-region-annotate-functions`   [Variable]
> A list of functions for `write-region` to call. Each function in the list is called with two arguments: the start and end of the region to be written. These functions should not alter the contents of the buffer. Instead, they should return annotations.
>
> As a special case, a function may return with a different buffer current. Emacs takes this to mean that the current buffer contains altered text to be output. It therefore changes the *start* and *end* arguments of the `write-region` call, giving them the values of `point-min` and `point-max` in the new buffer, respectively. It also discards all previous annotations, because they should have been dealt with by this function.

`write-region-post-annotation-function`   [Variable]
> The value of this variable, if non-`nil`, should be a function. This function is called, with no arguments, after `write-region` has completed.
>
> If any function in `write-region-annotate-functions` returns with a different buffer current, Emacs calls `write-region-post-annotation-function` more than once. Emacs calls it with the last buffer that was current, and again with the buffer before that, and so on back to the original buffer.
>
> Thus, a function in `write-region-annotate-functions` can create a buffer, give this variable the local value of `kill-buffer` in that buffer, set up the buffer with altered text, and make the buffer current. The buffer will be killed after `write-region` is done.

`after-insert-file-functions`   [Variable]

    Each function in this list is called by `insert-file-contents` with one argument, the number of characters inserted, and with point at the beginning of the inserted text. Each function should leave point unchanged, and return the new character count describing the inserted text as modified by the function.

We invite users to write Lisp programs to store and retrieve text properties in files, using these hooks, and thus to experiment with various data formats and find good ones. Eventually we hope users will produce good, general extensions we can install in Emacs.

We suggest not trying to handle arbitrary Lisp objects as text property names or values—because a program that general is probably difficult to write, and slow. Instead, choose a set of possible data types that are reasonably flexible, and not too hard to encode.

25 Backups and Auto-Saving

Backup files and auto-save files are two methods by which Emacs tries to protect the user from the consequences of crashes or of the user's own errors. Auto-saving preserves the text from earlier in the current editing session; backup files preserve file contents prior to the current session.

25.1 Backup Files

A *backup file* is a copy of the old contents of a file you are editing. Emacs makes a backup file the first time you save a buffer into its visited file. Thus, normally, the backup file contains the contents of the file as it was before the current editing session. The contents of the backup file normally remain unchanged once it exists.

Backups are usually made by renaming the visited file to a new name. Optionally, you can specify that backup files should be made by copying the visited file. This choice makes a difference for files with multiple names; it also can affect whether the edited file remains owned by the original owner or becomes owned by the user editing it.

By default, Emacs makes a single backup file for each file edited. You can alternatively request numbered backups; then each new backup file gets a new name. You can delete old numbered backups when you don't want them any more, or Emacs can delete them automatically.

25.1.1 Making Backup Files

`backup-buffer`   [Function]

This function makes a backup of the file visited by the current buffer, if appropriate. It is called by `save-buffer` before saving the buffer the first time.

If a backup was made by renaming, the return value is a cons cell of the form (*modes extra-alist backupname*), where *modes* are the mode bits of the original file, as returned by `file-modes` (see Section 24.6.1 [Testing Accessibility], page 505), *extra-alist* is an alist describing the original file's extended attributes, as returned by `file-extended-attributes` (see Section 24.6.5 [Extended Attributes], page 512), and *backupname* is the name of the backup.

In all other cases (i.e., if a backup was made by copying or if no backup was made), this function returns `nil`.

`buffer-backed-up`   [Variable]

This buffer-local variable says whether this buffer's file has been backed up on account of this buffer. If it is non-`nil`, the backup file has been written. Otherwise, the file should be backed up when it is next saved (if backups are enabled). This is a permanent local; `kill-all-local-variables` does not alter it.

`make-backup-files`   [User Option]

This variable determines whether or not to make backup files. If it is non-`nil`, then Emacs creates a backup of each file when it is saved for the first time—provided that `backup-inhibited` is `nil` (see below).

The following example shows how to change the `make-backup-files` variable only in the Rmail buffers and not elsewhere. Setting it `nil` stops Emacs from making backups of these files, which may save disk space. (You would put this code in your init file.)

```
(add-hook 'rmail-mode-hook
          (lambda () (setq-local make-backup-files nil)))
```

backup-enable-predicate   [Variable]

This variable's value is a function to be called on certain occasions to decide whether a file should have backup files. The function receives one argument, an absolute file name to consider. If the function returns `nil`, backups are disabled for that file. Otherwise, the other variables in this section say whether and how to make backups.

The default value is `normal-backup-enable-predicate`, which checks for files in `temporary-file-directory` and `small-temporary-file-directory`.

backup-inhibited   [Variable]

If this variable is non-`nil`, backups are inhibited. It records the result of testing `backup-enable-predicate` on the visited file name. It can also coherently be used by other mechanisms that inhibit backups based on which file is visited. For example, VC sets this variable non-`nil` to prevent making backups for files managed with a version control system.

This is a permanent local, so that changing the major mode does not lose its value. Major modes should not set this variable—they should set `make-backup-files` instead.

backup-directory-alist   [User Option]

This variable's value is an alist of filename patterns and backup directory names. Each element looks like

```
(regexp . directory)
```

Backups of files with names matching *regexp* will be made in *directory*. *directory* may be relative or absolute. If it is absolute, so that all matching files are backed up into the same directory, the file names in this directory will be the full name of the file backed up with all directory separators changed to '`!`' to prevent clashes. This will not work correctly if your filesystem truncates the resulting name.

For the common case of all backups going into one directory, the alist should contain a single element pairing '`"."`' with the appropriate directory name.

If this variable is `nil` (the default), or it fails to match a filename, the backup is made in the original file's directory.

On MS-DOS filesystems without long names this variable is always ignored.

make-backup-file-name-function   [User Option]

This variable's value is a function to use for making backup file names. The function `make-backup-file-name` calls it. See Section 25.1.4 [Naming Backup Files], page 542.

This could be buffer-local to do something special for specific files. If you change it, you may need to change `backup-file-name-p` and `file-name-sans-versions` too.

25.1.2 Backup by Renaming or by Copying?

There are two ways that Emacs can make a backup file:

- Emacs can rename the original file so that it becomes a backup file, and then write the buffer being saved into a new file. After this procedure, any other names (i.e., hard links) of the original file now refer to the backup file. The new file is owned by the user doing the editing, and its group is the default for new files written by the user in that directory.

- Emacs can copy the original file into a backup file, and then overwrite the original file with new contents. After this procedure, any other names (i.e., hard links) of the original file continue to refer to the current (updated) version of the file. The file's owner and group will be unchanged.

The first method, renaming, is the default.

The variable `backup-by-copying`, if non-`nil`, says to use the second method, which is to copy the original file and overwrite it with the new buffer contents. The variable `file-precious-flag`, if non-`nil`, also has this effect (as a sideline of its main significance). See Section 24.2 [Saving Buffers], page 499.

`backup-by-copying`   [User Option]

> If this variable is non-`nil`, Emacs always makes backup files by copying. The default is `nil`.

The following three variables, when non-`nil`, cause the second method to be used in certain special cases. They have no effect on the treatment of files that don't fall into the special cases.

`backup-by-copying-when-linked`   [User Option]

> If this variable is non-`nil`, Emacs makes backups by copying for files with multiple names (hard links). The default is `nil`.
>
> This variable is significant only if `backup-by-copying` is `nil`, since copying is always used when that variable is non-`nil`.

`backup-by-copying-when-mismatch`   [User Option]

> If this variable is non-`nil` (the default), Emacs makes backups by copying in cases where renaming would change either the owner or the group of the file.
>
> The value has no effect when renaming would not alter the owner or group of the file; that is, for files which are owned by the user and whose group matches the default for a new file created there by the user.
>
> This variable is significant only if `backup-by-copying` is `nil`, since copying is always used when that variable is non-`nil`.

`backup-by-copying-when-privileged-mismatch`   [User Option]

> This variable, if non-`nil`, specifies the same behavior as `backup-by-copying-when-mismatch`, but only for certain user-id values: namely, those less than or equal to a certain number. You set this variable to that number.
>
> Thus, if you set `backup-by-copying-when-privileged-mismatch` to 0, backup by copying is done for the superuser only, when necessary to prevent a change in the owner of the file.

The default is 200.

25.1.3 Making and Deleting Numbered Backup Files

If a file's name is `foo`, the names of its numbered backup versions are `foo.~v~`, for various integers *v*, like this: `foo.~1~`, `foo.~2~`, `foo.~3~`, `...`, `foo.~259~`, and so on.

`version-control`   [User Option]
> This variable controls whether to make a single non-numbered backup file or multiple numbered backups.
>
> `nil`   Make numbered backups if the visited file already has numbered backups; otherwise, do not. This is the default.
>
> `never`   Do not make numbered backups.
>
> *anything else*
>   Make numbered backups.

The use of numbered backups ultimately leads to a large number of backup versions, which must then be deleted. Emacs can do this automatically or it can ask the user whether to delete them.

`kept-new-versions`   [User Option]
> The value of this variable is the number of newest versions to keep when a new numbered backup is made. The newly made backup is included in the count. The default value is 2.

`kept-old-versions`   [User Option]
> The value of this variable is the number of oldest versions to keep when a new numbered backup is made. The default value is 2.

If there are backups numbered 1, 2, 3, 5, and 7, and both of these variables have the value 2, then the backups numbered 1 and 2 are kept as old versions and those numbered 5 and 7 are kept as new versions; backup version 3 is excess. The function `find-backup-file-name` (see Section 25.1.4 [Backup Names], page 542) is responsible for determining which backup versions to delete, but does not delete them itself.

`delete-old-versions`   [User Option]
> If this variable is `t`, then saving a file deletes excess backup versions silently. If it is `nil`, that means to ask for confirmation before deleting excess backups. Otherwise, they are not deleted at all.

`dired-kept-versions`   [User Option]
> This variable specifies how many of the newest backup versions to keep in the Dired command . (`dired-clean-directory`). That's the same thing `kept-new-versions` specifies when you make a new backup file. The default is 2.

25.1.4 Naming Backup Files

The functions in this section are documented mainly because you can customize the naming conventions for backup files by redefining them. If you change one, you probably need to change the rest.

backup-file-name-p *filename* [Function]

This function returns a non-`nil` value if *filename* is a possible name for a backup file. It just checks the name, not whether a file with the name *filename* exists.

```
(backup-file-name-p "foo")
     ⇒ nil
(backup-file-name-p "foo~")
     ⇒ 3
```

The standard definition of this function is as follows:

```
(defun backup-file-name-p (file)
  "Return non-nil if FILE is a backup file \
name (numeric or not)..."
  (string-match "~\\'" file))
```

Thus, the function returns a non-`nil` value if the file name ends with a '`~`'. (We use a backslash to split the documentation string's first line into two lines in the text, but produce just one line in the string itself.)

This simple expression is placed in a separate function to make it easy to redefine for customization.

make-backup-file-name *filename* [Function]

This function returns a string that is the name to use for a non-numbered backup file for file *filename*. On Unix, this is just *filename* with a tilde appended.

The standard definition of this function, on most operating systems, is as follows:

```
(defun make-backup-file-name (file)
  "Create the non-numeric backup file name for FILE..."
  (concat file "~"))
```

You can change the backup-file naming convention by redefining this function. The following example redefines `make-backup-file-name` to prepend a '`.`' in addition to appending a tilde:

```
(defun make-backup-file-name (filename)
  (expand-file-name
    (concat "." (file-name-nondirectory filename) "~")
    (file-name-directory filename)))

(make-backup-file-name "backups.texi")
     ⇒ ".backups.texi~"
```

Some parts of Emacs, including some Dired commands, assume that backup file names end with '`~`'. If you do not follow that convention, it will not cause serious problems, but these commands may give less-than-desirable results.

find-backup-file-name *filename* [Function]

This function computes the file name for a new backup file for *filename*. It may also propose certain existing backup files for deletion. `find-backup-file-name` returns a list whose CAR is the name for the new backup file and whose CDR is a list of backup files whose deletion is proposed. The value can also be `nil`, which means not to make a backup.

Two variables, `kept-old-versions` and `kept-new-versions`, determine which backup versions should be kept. This function keeps those versions by excluding them from the CDR of the value. See Section 25.1.3 [Numbered Backups], page 542.

In this example, the value says that `~rms/foo.~5~` is the name to use for the new backup file, and `~rms/foo.~3~` is an excess version that the caller should consider deleting now.

```
(find-backup-file-name "~rms/foo")
    ⇒ ("~rms/foo.~5~" "~rms/foo.~3~")
```

`file-newest-backup` *filename*   [Function]

>   This function returns the name of the most recent backup file for *filename*, or `nil` if that file has no backup files.

>   Some file comparison commands use this function so that they can automatically compare a file with its most recent backup.

25.2 Auto-Saving

Emacs periodically saves all files that you are visiting; this is called *auto-saving*. Auto-saving prevents you from losing more than a limited amount of work if the system crashes. By default, auto-saves happen every 300 keystrokes, or after around 30 seconds of idle time. See Section "Auto-Saving: Protection Against Disasters" in *The GNU Emacs Manual*, for information on auto-save for users. Here we describe the functions used to implement auto-saving and the variables that control them.

`buffer-auto-save-file-name`   [Variable]

>   This buffer-local variable is the name of the file used for auto-saving the current buffer. It is `nil` if the buffer should not be auto-saved.

```
buffer-auto-save-file-name
    ⇒ "/xcssun/users/rms/lewis/#backups.texi#"
```

`auto-save-mode` *arg*   [Command]

>   This is the mode command for Auto Save mode, a buffer-local minor mode. When Auto Save mode is enabled, auto-saving is enabled in the buffer. The calling convention is the same as for other minor mode commands (see Section 22.3.1 [Minor Mode Conventions], page 446).

>   Unlike most minor modes, there is no `auto-save-mode` variable. Auto Save mode is enabled if `buffer-auto-save-file-name` is non-`nil` and `buffer-saved-size` (see below) is non-zero.

`auto-save-file-name-p` *filename*   [Function]

>   This function returns a non-`nil` value if *filename* is a string that could be the name of an auto-save file. It assumes the usual naming convention for auto-save files: a name that begins and ends with hash marks ('#') is a possible auto-save file name. The argument *filename* should not contain a directory part.

```
(make-auto-save-file-name)
    ⇒ "/xcssun/users/rms/lewis/#backups.texi#"
(auto-save-file-name-p "#backups.texi#")
    ⇒ 0
(auto-save-file-name-p "backups.texi")
    ⇒ nil
```

The standard definition of this function is as follows:

```
(defun auto-save-file-name-p (filename)
  "Return non-nil if FILENAME can be yielded by..."
  (string-match "^#.*#$" filename))
```

This function exists so that you can customize it if you wish to change the naming convention for auto-save files. If you redefine it, be sure to redefine the function `make-auto-save-file-name` correspondingly.

`make-auto-save-file-name`   [Function]

This function returns the file name to use for auto-saving the current buffer. This is just the file name with hash marks ('#') prepended and appended to it. This function does not look at the variable `auto-save-visited-file-name` (described below); callers of this function should check that variable first.

```
(make-auto-save-file-name)
     ⇒ "/xcssun/users/rms/lewis/#backups.texi#"
```

Here is a simplified version of the standard definition of this function:

```
(defun make-auto-save-file-name ()
  "Return file name to use for auto-saves \
of current buffer.."
  (if buffer-file-name
      (concat
        (file-name-directory buffer-file-name)
        "#"
        (file-name-nondirectory buffer-file-name)
        "#")
    (expand-file-name
      (concat "#%" (buffer-name) "#"))))
```

This exists as a separate function so that you can redefine it to customize the naming convention for auto-save files. Be sure to change `auto-save-file-name-p` in a corresponding way.

`auto-save-visited-file-name`   [User Option]

If this variable is non-`nil`, Emacs auto-saves buffers in the files they are visiting. That is, the auto-save is done in the same file that you are editing. Normally, this variable is `nil`, so auto-save files have distinct names that are created by `make-auto-save-file-name`.

When you change the value of this variable, the new value does not take effect in an existing buffer until the next time auto-save mode is reenabled in it. If auto-save mode is already enabled, auto-saves continue to go in the same file name until `auto-save-mode` is called again.

Note that setting this variable to a non-`nil` value does not change the fact that auto-saving is different from saving the buffer; e.g., the hooks described in Section 24.2 [Saving Buffers], page 499, are *not* run when a buffer is auto-saved.

`recent-auto-save-p`   [Function]

This function returns `t` if the current buffer has been auto-saved since the last time it was read in or saved.

`set-buffer-auto-saved`   [Function]
> This function marks the current buffer as auto-saved. The buffer will not be auto-saved again until the buffer text is changed again. The function returns `nil`.

`auto-save-interval`   [User Option]
> The value of this variable specifies how often to do auto-saving, in terms of number of input events. Each time this many additional input events are read, Emacs does auto-saving for all buffers in which that is enabled. Setting this to zero disables autosaving based on the number of characters typed.

`auto-save-timeout`   [User Option]
> The value of this variable is the number of seconds of idle time that should cause auto-saving. Each time the user pauses for this long, Emacs does auto-saving for all buffers in which that is enabled. (If the current buffer is large, the specified timeout is multiplied by a factor that increases as the size increases; for a million-byte buffer, the factor is almost 4.)
>
> If the value is zero or `nil`, then auto-saving is not done as a result of idleness, only after a certain number of input events as specified by `auto-save-interval`.

`auto-save-hook`   [Variable]
> This normal hook is run whenever an auto-save is about to happen.

`auto-save-default`   [User Option]
> If this variable is non-`nil`, buffers that are visiting files have auto-saving enabled by default. Otherwise, they do not.

`do-auto-save` **&optional** *no-message current-only*   [Command]
> This function auto-saves all buffers that need to be auto-saved. It saves all buffers for which auto-saving is enabled and that have been changed since the previous auto-save.
>
> If any buffers are auto-saved, `do-auto-save` normally displays a message saying 'Auto-saving...' in the echo area while auto-saving is going on. However, if *no-message* is non-`nil`, the message is inhibited.
>
> If *current-only* is non-`nil`, only the current buffer is auto-saved.

`delete-auto-save-file-if-necessary` **&optional** *force*   [Function]
> This function deletes the current buffer's auto-save file if `delete-auto-save-files` is non-`nil`. It is called every time a buffer is saved.
>
> Unless *force* is non-`nil`, this function only deletes the file if it was written by the current Emacs session since the last true save.

`delete-auto-save-files`   [User Option]
> This variable is used by the function `delete-auto-save-file-if-necessary`. If it is non-`nil`, Emacs deletes auto-save files when a true save is done (in the visited file). This saves disk space and unclutters your directory.

`rename-auto-save-file`   [Function]
> This function adjusts the current buffer's auto-save file name if the visited file name has changed. It also renames an existing auto-save file, if it was made in the current Emacs session. If the visited file name has not changed, this function does nothing.

`buffer-saved-size`   [Variable]

> The value of this buffer-local variable is the length of the current buffer, when it was
> last read in, saved, or auto-saved. This is used to detect a substantial decrease in
> size, and turn off auto-saving in response.
>
> If it is −1, that means auto-saving is temporarily shut off in this buffer due to a
> substantial decrease in size. Explicitly saving the buffer stores a positive value in this
> variable, thus reenabling auto-saving. Turning auto-save mode off or on also updates
> this variable, so that the substantial decrease in size is forgotten.
>
> If it is −2, that means this buffer should disregard changes in buffer size; in particular,
> it should not shut off auto-saving temporarily due to changes in buffer size.

`auto-save-list-file-name`   [Variable]

> This variable (if non-`nil`) specifies a file for recording the names of all the auto-save
> files. Each time Emacs does auto-saving, it writes two lines into this file for each
> buffer that has auto-saving enabled. The first line gives the name of the visited file
> (it's empty if the buffer has none), and the second gives the name of the auto-save
> file.
>
> When Emacs exits normally, it deletes this file; if Emacs crashes, you can look in the
> file to find all the auto-save files that might contain work that was otherwise lost.
> The `recover-session` command uses this file to find them.
>
> The default name for this file specifies your home directory and starts with '`.saves-`'.
> It also contains the Emacs process ID and the host name.

`auto-save-list-file-prefix`   [User Option]

> After Emacs reads your init file, it initializes `auto-save-list-file-name` (if you
> have not already set it non-`nil`) based on this prefix, adding the host name and
> process ID. If you set this to `nil` in your init file, then Emacs does not initialize
> `auto-save-list-file-name`.

25.3 Reverting

If you have made extensive changes to a file and then change your mind about them, you
can get rid of them by reading in the previous version of the file with the `revert-buffer`
command. See Section "Reverting a Buffer" in *The GNU Emacs Manual*.

`revert-buffer` **&optional** *ignore-auto noconfirm preserve-modes*   [Command]

> This command replaces the buffer text with the text of the visited file on disk. This
> action undoes all changes since the file was visited or saved.
>
> By default, if the latest auto-save file is more recent than the visited file, and the
> argument *ignore-auto* is `nil`, `revert-buffer` asks the user whether to use that auto-
> save instead. When you invoke this command interactively, *ignore-auto* is `t` if there is
> no numeric prefix argument; thus, the interactive default is not to check the auto-save
> file.
>
> Normally, `revert-buffer` asks for confirmation before it changes the buffer; but if
> the argument *noconfirm* is non-`nil`, `revert-buffer` does not ask for confirmation.
>
> Normally, this command reinitializes the buffer's major and minor modes using
> `normal-mode`. But if *preserve-modes* is non-`nil`, the modes remain unchanged.

Reverting tries to preserve marker positions in the buffer by using the replacement feature of `insert-file-contents`. If the buffer contents and the file contents are identical before the revert operation, reverting preserves all the markers. If they are not identical, reverting does change the buffer; in that case, it preserves the markers in the unchanged text (if any) at the beginning and end of the buffer. Preserving any additional markers would be problematical.

`revert-buffer-in-progress-p`   [Variable]
 `revert-buffer` binds this variable to a non-`nil` value while it is working.

You can customize how `revert-buffer` does its work by setting the variables described in the rest of this section.

`revert-without-query`   [User Option]
 This variable holds a list of files that should be reverted without query. The value is a list of regular expressions. If the visited file name matches one of these regular expressions, and the file has changed on disk but the buffer is not modified, then `revert-buffer` reverts the file without asking the user for confirmation.

Some major modes customize `revert-buffer` by making buffer-local bindings for these variables:

`revert-buffer-function`   [Variable]
 The value of this variable is the function to use to revert this buffer. It should be a function with two optional arguments to do the work of reverting. The two optional arguments, *ignore-auto* and *noconfirm*, are the arguments that `revert-buffer` received.

 Modes such as Dired mode, in which the text being edited does not consist of a file's contents but can be regenerated in some other fashion, can give this variable a buffer-local value that is a special function to regenerate the contents.

`revert-buffer-insert-file-contents-function`   [Variable]
 The value of this variable specifies the function to use to insert the updated contents when reverting this buffer. The function receives two arguments: first the file name to use; second, `t` if the user has asked to read the auto-save file.

 The reason for a mode to change this variable instead of `revert-buffer-function` is to avoid duplicating or replacing the rest of what `revert-buffer` does: asking for confirmation, clearing the undo list, deciding the proper major mode, and running the hooks listed below.

`before-revert-hook`   [Variable]
 This normal hook is run by the default `revert-buffer-function` before inserting the modified contents. A custom `revert-buffer-function` may or may not run this hook.

`after-revert-hook`   [Variable]
 This normal hook is run by the default `revert-buffer-function` after inserting the modified contents. A custom `revert-buffer-function` may or may not run this hook.

`buffer-stale-function` [Variable]

    The value of this variable specifies a function to call to check whether a buffer needs reverting. The default value only handles buffers that are visiting files, by checking their modification time. Buffers that are not visiting files require a custom function (see Section "Supporting additional buffers" in *Specialized Emacs Features*).

26 Buffers

A *buffer* is a Lisp object containing text to be edited. Buffers are used to hold the contents of files that are being visited; there may also be buffers that are not visiting files. While several buffers may exist at one time, only one buffer is designated the *current buffer* at any time. Most editing commands act on the contents of the current buffer. Each buffer, including the current buffer, may or may not be displayed in any windows.

26.1 Buffer Basics

Buffers in Emacs editing are objects that have distinct names and hold text that can be edited. Buffers appear to Lisp programs as a special data type. You can think of the contents of a buffer as a string that you can extend; insertions and deletions may occur in any part of the buffer. See Chapter 31 [Text], page 696.

A Lisp buffer object contains numerous pieces of information. Some of this information is directly accessible to the programmer through variables, while other information is accessible only through special-purpose functions. For example, the visited file name is directly accessible through a variable, while the value of point is accessible only through a primitive function.

Buffer-specific information that is directly accessible is stored in *buffer-local* variable bindings, which are variable values that are effective only in a particular buffer. This feature allows each buffer to override the values of certain variables. Most major modes override variables such as `fill-column` or `comment-column` in this way. For more information about buffer-local variables and functions related to them, see Section 11.10 [Buffer-Local Variables], page 171.

For functions and variables related to visiting files in buffers, see Section 24.1 [Visiting Files], page 495, and Section 24.2 [Saving Buffers], page 499. For functions and variables related to the display of buffers in windows, see Section 27.11 [Buffers and Windows], page 594.

`bufferp` *object*   [Function]
> This function returns `t` if *object* is a buffer, `nil` otherwise.

26.2 The Current Buffer

There are, in general, many buffers in an Emacs session. At any time, one of them is designated the *current buffer*—the buffer in which most editing takes place. Most of the primitives for examining or changing text operate implicitly on the current buffer (see Chapter 31 [Text], page 696).

Normally, the buffer displayed in the selected window is the current buffer, but this is not always so: a Lisp program can temporarily designate any buffer as current in order to operate on its contents, without changing what is displayed on the screen. The most basic function for designating a current buffer is `set-buffer`.

`current-buffer`   [Function]
> This function returns the current buffer.
>
>   (current-buffer)
>   ⇒ #<buffer buffers.texi>

`set-buffer` *buffer-or-name*   [Function]
> This function makes *buffer-or-name* the current buffer. *buffer-or-name* must be an existing buffer or the name of an existing buffer. The return value is the buffer made current.
>
> This function does not display the buffer in any window, so the user cannot necessarily see the buffer. But Lisp programs will now operate on it.

When an editing command returns to the editor command loop, Emacs automatically calls `set-buffer` on the buffer shown in the selected window. This is to prevent confusion: it ensures that the buffer that the cursor is in, when Emacs reads a command, is the buffer to which that command applies (see Chapter 20 [Command Loop], page 345). Thus, you should not use `set-buffer` to switch visibly to a different buffer; for that, use the functions described in Section 27.12 [Switching Buffers], page 595.

When writing a Lisp function, do *not* rely on this behavior of the command loop to restore the current buffer after an operation. Editing commands can also be called as Lisp functions by other programs, not just from the command loop; it is convenient for the caller if the subroutine does not change which buffer is current (unless, of course, that is the subroutine's purpose).

To operate temporarily on another buffer, put the `set-buffer` within a `save-current-buffer` form. Here, as an example, is a simplified version of the command `append-to-buffer`:

```
(defun append-to-buffer (buffer start end)
  "Append the text of the region to BUFFER."
  (interactive "BAppend to buffer: \nr")
  (let ((oldbuf (current-buffer)))
    (save-current-buffer
      (set-buffer (get-buffer-create buffer))
      (insert-buffer-substring oldbuf start end))))
```

Here, we bind a local variable to record the current buffer, and then `save-current-buffer` arranges to make it current again later. Next, `set-buffer` makes the specified buffer current, and `insert-buffer-substring` copies the string from the original buffer to the specified (and now current) buffer.

Alternatively, we can use the `with-current-buffer` macro:

```
(defun append-to-buffer (buffer start end)
  "Append the text of the region to BUFFER."
  (interactive "BAppend to buffer: \nr")
  (let ((oldbuf (current-buffer)))
    (with-current-buffer (get-buffer-create buffer)
      (insert-buffer-substring oldbuf start end))))
```

In either case, if the buffer appended to happens to be displayed in some window, the next redisplay will show how its text has changed. If it is not displayed in any window, you will not see the change immediately on the screen. The command causes the buffer to become current temporarily, but does not cause it to be displayed.

If you make local bindings (with `let` or function arguments) for a variable that may also have buffer-local bindings, make sure that the same buffer is current at the beginning and at the end of the local binding's scope. Otherwise you might bind it in one buffer and unbind it in another!

Do not rely on using `set-buffer` to change the current buffer back, because that won't do the job if a quit happens while the wrong buffer is current. For instance, in the previous example, it would have been wrong to do this:

```
(let ((oldbuf (current-buffer)))
  (set-buffer (get-buffer-create buffer))
  (insert-buffer-substring oldbuf start end)
  (set-buffer oldbuf))
```

Using `save-current-buffer` or `with-current-buffer`, as we did, correctly handles quitting, errors, and `throw`, as well as ordinary evaluation.

---

save-current-buffer *body*...   [Special Form]

  The `save-current-buffer` special form saves the identity of the current buffer, evaluates the *body* forms, and finally restores that buffer as current. The return value is the value of the last form in *body*. The current buffer is restored even in case of an abnormal exit via `throw` or error (see Section 10.6 [Nonlocal Exits], page 145).

  If the buffer that used to be current has been killed by the time of exit from `save-current-buffer`, then it is not made current again, of course. Instead, whichever buffer was current just before exit remains current.

---

with-current-buffer *buffer-or-name body*...   [Macro]

  The `with-current-buffer` macro saves the identity of the current buffer, makes *buffer-or-name* current, evaluates the *body* forms, and finally restores the current buffer. *buffer-or-name* must specify an existing buffer or the name of an existing buffer.

  The return value is the value of the last form in *body*. The current buffer is restored even in case of an abnormal exit via `throw` or error (see Section 10.6 [Nonlocal Exits], page 145).

---

with-temp-buffer *body*...   [Macro]

  The `with-temp-buffer` macro evaluates the *body* forms with a temporary buffer as the current buffer. It saves the identity of the current buffer, creates a temporary buffer and makes it current, evaluates the *body* forms, and finally restores the previous current buffer while killing the temporary buffer. By default, undo information (see Section 31.9 [Undo], page 712) is not recorded in the buffer created by this macro (but *body* can enable that, if needed).

  The return value is the value of the last form in *body*. You can return the contents of the temporary buffer by using `(buffer-string)` as the last form.

  The current buffer is restored even in case of an abnormal exit via `throw` or error (see Section 10.6 [Nonlocal Exits], page 145).

  See also `with-temp-file` in [Writing to Files], page 503.

26.3 Buffer Names

Each buffer has a unique name, which is a string. Many of the functions that work on buffers accept either a buffer or a buffer name as an argument. Any argument called *buffer-or-name* is of this sort, and an error is signaled if it is neither a string nor a buffer. Any argument called *buffer* must be an actual buffer object, not a name.

Buffers that are ephemeral and generally uninteresting to the user have names starting with a space, so that the `list-buffers` and `buffer-menu` commands don't mention them (but if such a buffer visits a file, it **is** mentioned). A name starting with space also initially disables recording undo information; see Section 31.9 [Undo], page 712.

`buffer-name` &optional *buffer*   [Function]

> This function returns the name of *buffer* as a string. *buffer* defaults to the current buffer.
>
> If `buffer-name` returns `nil`, it means that *buffer* has been killed. See Section 26.10 [Killing Buffers], page 563.
>
> ```
> (buffer-name)
>      ⇒ "buffers.texi"
>
>
> (setq foo (get-buffer "temp"))
>      ⇒ #<buffer temp>
> (kill-buffer foo)
>      ⇒ nil
> (buffer-name foo)
>      ⇒ nil
> foo
>      ⇒ #<killed buffer>
> ```

`rename-buffer` *newname* &optional *unique*   [Command]

> This function renames the current buffer to *newname*. An error is signaled if *newname* is not a string.
>
> Ordinarily, `rename-buffer` signals an error if *newname* is already in use. However, if *unique* is non-`nil`, it modifies *newname* to make a name that is not in use. Interactively, you can make *unique* non-`nil` with a numeric prefix argument. (This is how the command `rename-uniquely` is implemented.)
>
> This function returns the name actually given to the buffer.

`get-buffer` *buffer-or-name*   [Function]

> This function returns the buffer specified by *buffer-or-name*. If *buffer-or-name* is a string and there is no buffer with that name, the value is `nil`. If *buffer-or-name* is a buffer, it is returned as given; that is not very useful, so the argument is usually a name. For example:
>
> ```
> (setq b (get-buffer "lewis"))
>      ⇒ #<buffer lewis>
> (get-buffer b)
>      ⇒ #<buffer lewis>
> (get-buffer "Frazzle-nots")
>      ⇒ nil
> ```

See also the function `get-buffer-create` in Section 26.9 [Creating Buffers], page 562.

`generate-new-buffer-name` *starting-name* **&optional** *ignore*   [Function]

> This function returns a name that would be unique for a new buffer—but does not create the buffer. It starts with *starting-name*, and produces a name not currently in use for any buffer by appending a number inside of '`<...>`'. It starts at 2 and keeps incrementing the number until it is not the name of an existing buffer.
>
> If the optional second argument *ignore* is non-`nil`, it should be a string, a potential buffer name. It means to consider that potential buffer acceptable, if it is tried, even it is the name of an existing buffer (which would normally be rejected). Thus, if buffers named '`foo`', '`foo<2>`', '`foo<3>`' and '`foo<4>`' exist,
>
> ```
> (generate-new-buffer-name "foo")
>     ⇒ "foo<5>"
> (generate-new-buffer-name "foo" "foo<3>")
>     ⇒ "foo<3>"
> (generate-new-buffer-name "foo" "foo<6>")
>     ⇒ "foo<5>"
> ```
>
> See the related function `generate-new-buffer` in Section 26.9 [Creating Buffers], page 562.

26.4 Buffer File Name

The *buffer file name* is the name of the file that is visited in that buffer. When a buffer is not visiting a file, its buffer file name is `nil`. Most of the time, the buffer name is the same as the nondirectory part of the buffer file name, but the buffer file name and the buffer name are distinct and can be set independently. See Section 24.1 [Visiting Files], page 495.

`buffer-file-name` **&optional** *buffer*   [Function]

> This function returns the absolute file name of the file that *buffer* is visiting. If *buffer* is not visiting any file, `buffer-file-name` returns `nil`. If *buffer* is not supplied, it defaults to the current buffer.
>
> ```
> (buffer-file-name (other-buffer))
>     ⇒ "/usr/user/lewis/manual/files.texi"
> ```

`buffer-file-name`   [Variable]

> This buffer-local variable contains the name of the file being visited in the current buffer, or `nil` if it is not visiting a file. It is a permanent local variable, unaffected by `kill-all-local-variables`.
>
> ```
> buffer-file-name
>     ⇒ "/usr/user/lewis/manual/buffers.texi"
> ```
>
> It is risky to change this variable's value without doing various other things. Normally it is better to use `set-visited-file-name` (see below); some of the things done there, such as changing the buffer name, are not strictly necessary, but others are essential to avoid confusing Emacs.

`buffer-file-truename`   [Variable]

> This buffer-local variable holds the abbreviated truename of the file visited in the current buffer, or `nil` if no file is visited. It is a permanent local, unaffected by `kill-all-`

`local-variables`. See Section 24.6.3 [Truenames], page 508, and [abbreviate-file-name], page 521.

`buffer-file-number` [Variable]

This buffer-local variable holds the file number and directory device number of the file visited in the current buffer, or `nil` if no file or a nonexistent file is visited. It is a permanent local, unaffected by `kill-all-local-variables`.

The value is normally a list of the form (*filenum devnum*). This pair of numbers uniquely identifies the file among all files accessible on the system. See the function `file-attributes`, in Section 24.6.4 [File Attributes], page 509, for more information about them.

If `buffer-file-name` is the name of a symbolic link, then both numbers refer to the recursive target.

`get-file-buffer` *filename* [Function]

This function returns the buffer visiting file *filename*. If there is no such buffer, it returns `nil`. The argument *filename*, which must be a string, is expanded (see Section 24.8.4 [File Name Expansion], page 522), then compared against the visited file names of all live buffers. Note that the buffer's `buffer-file-name` must match the expansion of *filename* exactly. This function will not recognize other names for the same file.

```
(get-file-buffer "buffers.texi")
    ⇒ #<buffer buffers.texi>
```

In unusual circumstances, there can be more than one buffer visiting the same file name. In such cases, this function returns the first such buffer in the buffer list.

`find-buffer-visiting` *filename* **&optional** *predicate* [Function]

This is like `get-file-buffer`, except that it can return any buffer visiting the file *possibly under a different name*. That is, the buffer's `buffer-file-name` does not need to match the expansion of *filename* exactly, it only needs to refer to the same file. If *predicate* is non-`nil`, it should be a function of one argument, a buffer visiting *filename*. The buffer is only considered a suitable return value if *predicate* returns non-`nil`. If it can not find a suitable buffer to return, `find-buffer-visiting` returns `nil`.

`set-visited-file-name` *filename* **&optional** *no-query* [Command]
    along-with-file

If *filename* is a non-empty string, this function changes the name of the file visited in the current buffer to *filename*. (If the buffer had no visited file, this gives it one.) The *next time* the buffer is saved it will go in the newly-specified file.

This command marks the buffer as modified, since it does not (as far as Emacs knows) match the contents of *filename*, even if it matched the former visited file. It also renames the buffer to correspond to the new file name, unless the new name is already in use.

If *filename* is `nil` or the empty string, that stands for "no visited file". In this case, `set-visited-file-name` marks the buffer as having no visited file, without changing the buffer's modified flag.

Normally, this function asks the user for confirmation if there already is a buffer visiting *filename*. If *no-query* is non-`nil`, that prevents asking this question. If there already is a buffer visiting *filename*, and the user confirms or *no-query* is non-`nil`, this function makes the new buffer name unique by appending a number inside of '`<...>`' to *filename*.

If *along-with-file* is non-`nil`, that means to assume that the former visited file has been renamed to *filename*. In this case, the command does not change the buffer's modified flag, nor the buffer's recorded last file modification time as reported by `visited-file-modtime` (see Section 26.6 [Modification Time], page 557). If *along-with-file* is `nil`, this function clears the recorded last file modification time, after which `visited-file-modtime` returns zero.

When the function `set-visited-file-name` is called interactively, it prompts for *filename* in the minibuffer.

`list-buffers-directory`   [Variable]

This buffer-local variable specifies a string to display in a buffer listing where the visited file name would go, for buffers that don't have a visited file name. Dired buffers use this variable.

26.5 Buffer Modification

Emacs keeps a flag called the *modified flag* for each buffer, to record whether you have changed the text of the buffer. This flag is set to `t` whenever you alter the contents of the buffer, and cleared to `nil` when you save it. Thus, the flag shows whether there are unsaved changes. The flag value is normally shown in the mode line (see Section 22.4.4 [Mode Line Variables], page 454), and controls saving (see Section 24.2 [Saving Buffers], page 499) and auto-saving (see Section 25.2 [Auto-Saving], page 544).

Some Lisp programs set the flag explicitly. For example, the function `set-visited-file-name` sets the flag to `t`, because the text does not match the newly-visited file, even if it is unchanged from the file formerly visited.

The functions that modify the contents of buffers are described in Chapter 31 [Text], page 696.

`buffer-modified-p` &optional *buffer*   [Function]

This function returns `t` if the buffer *buffer* has been modified since it was last read in from a file or saved, or `nil` otherwise. If *buffer* is not supplied, the current buffer is tested.

`set-buffer-modified-p` *flag*   [Function]

This function marks the current buffer as modified if *flag* is non-`nil`, or as unmodified if the flag is `nil`.

Another effect of calling this function is to cause unconditional redisplay of the mode line for the current buffer. In fact, the function `force-mode-line-update` works by doing this:

```
(set-buffer-modtied-p (buffer-modified-p))
```

`restore-buffer-modified-p` *flag*   [Function]

Like `set-buffer-modified-p`, but does not force redisplay of mode lines.

`not-modified` **&optional** *arg*   [Command]

> This command marks the current buffer as unmodified, and not needing to be saved. If *arg* is non-`nil`, it marks the buffer as modified, so that it will be saved at the next suitable occasion. Interactively, *arg* is the prefix argument.
>
> Don't use this function in programs, since it prints a message in the echo area; use `set-buffer-modified-p` (above) instead.

`buffer-modified-tick` **&optional** *buffer*   [Function]

> This function returns *buffer*'s modification-count. This is a counter that increments every time the buffer is modified. If *buffer* is `nil` (or omitted), the current buffer is used. The counter can wrap around occasionally.

`buffer-chars-modified-tick` **&optional** *buffer*   [Function]

> This function returns *buffer*'s character-change modification-count. Changes to text properties leave this counter unchanged; however, each time text is inserted or removed from the buffer, the counter is reset to the value that would be returned by `buffer-modified-tick`. By comparing the values returned by two `buffer-chars-modified-tick` calls, you can tell whether a character change occurred in that buffer in between the calls. If *buffer* is `nil` (or omitted), the current buffer is used.

26.6 Buffer Modification Time

Suppose that you visit a file and make changes in its buffer, and meanwhile the file itself is changed on disk. At this point, saving the buffer would overwrite the changes in the file. Occasionally this may be what you want, but usually it would lose valuable information. Emacs therefore checks the file's modification time using the functions described below before saving the file. (See Section 24.6.4 [File Attributes], page 509, for how to examine a file's modification time.)

`verify-visited-file-modtime` **&optional** *buffer*   [Function]

> This function compares what *buffer* (by default, the current-buffer) has recorded for the modification time of its visited file against the actual modification time of the file as recorded by the operating system. The two should be the same unless some other process has written the file since Emacs visited or saved it.
>
> The function returns `t` if the last actual modification time and Emacs's recorded modification time are the same, `nil` otherwise. It also returns `t` if the buffer has no recorded last modification time, that is if `visited-file-modtime` would return zero.
>
> It always returns `t` for buffers that are not visiting a file, even if `visited-file-modtime` returns a non-zero value. For instance, it always returns `t` for dired buffers. It returns `t` for buffers that are visiting a file that does not exist and never existed, but `nil` for file-visiting buffers whose file has been deleted.

`clear-visited-file-modtime`   [Function]

> This function clears out the record of the last modification time of the file being visited by the current buffer. As a result, the next attempt to save this buffer will not complain of a discrepancy in file modification times.
>
> This function is called in `set-visited-file-name` and other exceptional places where the usual test to avoid overwriting a changed file should not be done.

`visited-file-modtime`   [Function]

> This function returns the current buffer's recorded last file modification time, as a list of the form (*high low microsec picosec*). (This is the same format that `file-attributes` uses to return time values; see Section 24.6.4 [File Attributes], page 509.)
>
> If the buffer has no recorded last modification time, this function returns zero. This case occurs, for instance, if the buffer is not visiting a file or if the time has been explicitly cleared by `clear-visited-file-modtime`. Note, however, that `visited-file-modtime` returns a list for some non-file buffers too. For instance, in a Dired buffer listing a directory, it returns the last modification time of that directory, as recorded by Dired.
>
> If the buffer is not visiting a file, this function returns -1.

`set-visited-file-modtime` &optional *time*   [Function]

> This function updates the buffer's record of the last modification time of the visited file, to the value specified by *time* if *time* is not `nil`, and otherwise to the last modification time of the visited file.
>
> If *time* is neither `nil` nor zero, it should have the form (*high low microsec picosec*), the format used by `current-time` (see Section 38.5 [Time of Day], page 999).
>
> This function is useful if the buffer was not read from the file normally, or if the file itself has been changed for some known benign reason.

`ask-user-about-supersession-threat` *filename*   [Function]

> This function is used to ask a user how to proceed after an attempt to modify an buffer visiting file *filename* when the file is newer than the buffer text. Emacs detects this because the modification time of the file on disk is newer than the last save-time of the buffer. This means some other program has probably altered the file.
>
> Depending on the user's answer, the function may return normally, in which case the modification of the buffer proceeds, or it may signal a `file-supersession` error with data (*filename*), in which case the proposed buffer modification is not allowed.
>
> This function is called automatically by Emacs on the proper occasions. It exists so you can customize Emacs by redefining it. See the file `userlock.el` for the standard definition.
>
> See also the file locking mechanism in Section 24.5 [File Locks], page 504.

26.7 Read-Only Buffers

If a buffer is *read-only*, then you cannot change its contents, although you may change your view of the contents by scrolling and narrowing.

Read-only buffers are used in two kinds of situations:

- A buffer visiting a write-protected file is normally read-only.

  Here, the purpose is to inform the user that editing the buffer with the aim of saving it in the file may be futile or undesirable. The user who wants to change the buffer text despite this can do so after clearing the read-only flag with `C-x C-q`.

- Modes such as Dired and Rmail make buffers read-only when altering the contents with the usual editing commands would probably be a mistake.

  The special commands of these modes bind `buffer-read-only` to `nil` (with `let`) or bind `inhibit-read-only` to `t` around the places where they themselves change the text.

`buffer-read-only` [Variable]

> This buffer-local variable specifies whether the buffer is read-only. The buffer is read-only if this variable is non-`nil`. However, characters that have the `inhibit-read-only` text property can still be modified. See Section 31.19.4 [Special Properties], page 738.

`inhibit-read-only` [Variable]

> If this variable is non-`nil`, then read-only buffers and, depending on the actual value, some or all read-only characters may be modified. Read-only characters in a buffer are those that have a non-`nil` `read-only` text property. See Section 31.19.4 [Special Properties], page 738, for more information about text properties.
>
> If `inhibit-read-only` is `t`, all `read-only` character properties have no effect. If `inhibit-read-only` is a list, then `read-only` character properties have no effect if they are members of the list (comparison is done with `eq`).

`read-only-mode` **&optional** *arg* [Command]

> This is the mode command for Read Only minor mode, a buffer-local minor mode. When the mode is enabled, `buffer-read-only` is non-`nil` in the buffer; when disabled, `buffer-read-only` is `nil` in the buffer. The calling convention is the same as for other minor mode commands (see Section 22.3.1 [Minor Mode Conventions], page 446).
>
> This minor mode mainly serves as a wrapper for `buffer-read-only`; unlike most minor modes, there is no separate `read-only-mode` variable. Even when Read Only mode is disabled, characters with non-`nil` `read-only` text properties remain read-only. To temporarily ignore all read-only states, bind `inhibit-read-only`, as described above.
>
> When enabling Read Only mode, this mode command also enables View mode if the option `view-read-only` is non-`nil`. See Section "Miscellaneous Buffer Operations" in *The GNU Emacs Manual*. When disabling Read Only mode, it disables View mode if View mode was enabled.

`barf-if-buffer-read-only` **&optional** *position* [Function]

> This function signals a `buffer-read-only` error if the current buffer is read-only. If the text at *position* (which defaults to point) has the `inhibit-read-only` text property set, the error will not be raised.
>
> See Section 20.2.1 [Using Interactive], page 346, for another way to signal an error if the current buffer is read-only.

26.8 The Buffer List

The *buffer list* is a list of all live buffers. The order of the buffers in this list is based primarily on how recently each buffer has been displayed in a window. Several functions, notably `other-buffer`, use this ordering. A buffer list displayed for the user also follows this order.

Creating a buffer adds it to the end of the buffer list, and killing a buffer removes it from that list. A buffer moves to the front of this list whenever it is chosen for display in a window (see Section 27.12 [Switching Buffers], page 595) or a window displaying it is selected (see Section 27.9 [Selecting Windows], page 590). A buffer moves to the end of the list when it is buried (see `bury-buffer`, below). There are no functions available to the Lisp programmer which directly manipulate the buffer list.

In addition to the fundamental buffer list just described, Emacs maintains a local buffer list for each frame, in which the buffers that have been displayed (or had their windows selected) in that frame come first. (This order is recorded in the frame's `buffer-list` frame parameter; see Section 28.4.3.5 [Buffer Parameters], page 649.) Buffers never displayed in that frame come afterward, ordered according to the fundamental buffer list.

`buffer-list &optional` *frame*   [Function]
>   This function returns the buffer list, including all buffers, even those whose names begin with a space. The elements are actual buffers, not their names.
>
>   If *frame* is a frame, this returns *frame*'s local buffer list. If *frame* is `nil` or omitted, the fundamental buffer list is used: the buffers appear in order of most recent display or selection, regardless of which frames they were displayed on.
>
> ```
> (buffer-list)
>     ⇒ (#<buffer buffers.texi>
>        #<buffer  *Minibuf-1*> #<buffer buffer.c>
>        #<buffer *Help*> #<buffer TAGS>)
>
> ;; Note that the name of the minibuffer
> ;;    begins with a space!
> (mapcar (function buffer-name) (buffer-list))
>     ⇒ ("buffers.texi" " *Minibuf-1*"
>        "buffer.c" "*Help*" "TAGS")
> ```

The list returned by `buffer-list` is constructed specifically; it is not an internal Emacs data structure, and modifying it has no effect on the order of buffers. If you want to change the order of buffers in the fundamental buffer list, here is an easy way:

```
(defun reorder-buffer-list (new-list)
  (while new-list
    (bury-buffer (car new-list))
    (setq new-list (cdr new-list))))
```

With this method, you can specify any order for the list, but there is no danger of losing a buffer or adding something that is not a valid live buffer.

To change the order or value of a specific frame's buffer list, set that frame's `buffer-list` parameter with `modify-frame-parameters` (see Section 28.4.1 [Parameter Access], page 643).

`other-buffer` **&optional** *buffer visible-ok frame* [Function]

This function returns the first buffer in the buffer list other than *buffer*. Usually, this is the buffer appearing in the most recently selected window (in frame *frame* or else the selected frame, see Section 28.10 [Input Focus], page 656), aside from *buffer*. Buffers whose names start with a space are not considered at all.

If *buffer* is not supplied (or if it is not a live buffer), then `other-buffer` returns the first buffer in the selected frame's local buffer list. (If *frame* is non-`nil`, it returns the first buffer in *frame*'s local buffer list instead.)

If *frame* has a non-`nil` `buffer-predicate` parameter, then `other-buffer` uses that predicate to decide which buffers to consider. It calls the predicate once for each buffer, and if the value is `nil`, that buffer is ignored. See Section 28.4.3.5 [Buffer Parameters], page 649.

If *visible-ok* is `nil`, `other-buffer` avoids returning a buffer visible in any window on any visible frame, except as a last resort. If *visible-ok* is non-`nil`, then it does not matter whether a buffer is displayed somewhere or not.

If no suitable buffer exists, the buffer `*scratch*` is returned (and created, if necessary).

`last-buffer` **&optional** *buffer visible-ok frame* [Function]

This function returns the last buffer in *frame*'s buffer list other than *buffer*. If *frame* is omitted or `nil`, it uses the selected frame's buffer list.

The argument *visible-ok* is handled as with `other-buffer`, see above. If no suitable buffer can be found, the buffer `*scratch*` is returned.

`bury-buffer` **&optional** *buffer-or-name* [Command]

This command puts *buffer-or-name* at the end of the buffer list, without changing the order of any of the other buffers on the list. This buffer therefore becomes the least desirable candidate for `other-buffer` to return. The argument can be either a buffer itself or the name of one.

This function operates on each frame's `buffer-list` parameter as well as the fundamental buffer list; therefore, the buffer that you bury will come last in the value of (`buffer-list` *frame*) and in the value of (`buffer-list`). In addition, it also puts the buffer at the end of the list of buffer of the selected window (see Section 27.16 [Window History], page 605) provided it is shown in that window.

If *buffer-or-name* is `nil` or omitted, this means to bury the current buffer. In addition, if the current buffer is displayed in the selected window, this makes sure that the window is either deleted or another buffer is shown in it. More precisely, if the selected window is dedicated (see Section 27.17 [Dedicated Windows], page 606) and there are other windows on its frame, the window is deleted. If it is the only window on its frame and that frame is not the only frame on its terminal, the frame is dismissed by calling the function specified by `frame-auto-hide-function` (see Section 27.18 [Quitting Windows], page 607). Otherwise, it calls `switch-to-prev-buffer` (see Section 27.16 [Window History], page 605) to show another buffer in that window. If *buffer-or-name* is displayed in some other window, it remains displayed there.

To replace a buffer in all the windows that display it, use `replace-buffer-in-windows`, See Section 27.11 [Buffers and Windows], page 594.

unbury-buffer   [Command]
> This command switches to the last buffer in the local buffer list of the selected frame.
> More precisely, it calls the function `switch-to-buffer` (see Section 27.12 [Switching
> Buffers], page 595), to display the buffer returned by `last-buffer` (see above), in the
> selected window.

buffer-list-update-hook   [Variable]
> This is a normal hook run whenever the buffer list changes. Functions (implicitly)
> running this hook are `get-buffer-create` (see Section 26.9 [Creating Buffers],
> page 562), `rename-buffer` (see Section 26.3 [Buffer Names], page 553), `kill-buffer`
> (see Section 26.10 [Killing Buffers], page 563), `bury-buffer` (see above) and
> `select-window` (see Section 27.9 [Selecting Windows], page 590).

26.9 Creating Buffers

This section describes the two primitives for creating buffers. `get-buffer-create` creates
a buffer if it finds no existing buffer with the specified name; `generate-new-buffer` always
creates a new buffer and gives it a unique name.

Other functions you can use to create buffers include `with-output-to-temp-buffer` (see
Section 37.8 [Temporary Displays], page 900) and `create-file-buffer` (see Section 24.1
[Visiting Files], page 495). Starting a subprocess can also create a buffer (see Chapter 36
[Processes], page 839).

get-buffer-create *buffer-or-name*   [Function]
> This function returns a buffer named *buffer-or-name*. The buffer returned does not
> become the current buffer—this function does not change which buffer is current.
>
> *buffer-or-name* must be either a string or an existing buffer. If it is a string and a
> live buffer with that name already exists, `get-buffer-create` returns that buffer. If
> no such buffer exists, it creates a new buffer. If *buffer-or-name* is a buffer instead of
> a string, it is returned as given, even if it is dead.
>
> ```
> (get-buffer-create "foo")
>      ⇒ #<buffer foo>
> ```
>
> The major mode for a newly created buffer is set to Fundamental mode. (The default
> value of the variable `major-mode` is handled at a higher level; see Section 22.2.2 [Auto
> Major Mode], page 435.) If the name begins with a space, the buffer initially disables
> undo information recording (see Section 31.9 [Undo], page 712).

generate-new-buffer *name*   [Function]
> This function returns a newly created, empty buffer, but does not make it current.
> The name of the buffer is generated by passing *name* to the function `generate-new-`
> `buffer-name` (see Section 26.3 [Buffer Names], page 553). Thus, if there is no buffer
> named *name*, then that is the name of the new buffer; if that name is in use, a suffix
> of the form '`<n>`', where *n* is an integer, is appended to *name*.
>
> An error is signaled if *name* is not a string.
>
> ```
> (generate-new-buffer "bar")
>      ⇒ #<buffer bar>
> (generate-new-buffer "bar")
>      ⇒ #<buffer bar<2>>
> ```

```
(generate-new-buffer "bar")
    ⇒ #<buffer bar<3>>
```

The major mode for the new buffer is set to Fundamental mode. The default value of the variable `major-mode` is handled at a higher level. See Section 22.2.2 [Auto Major Mode], page 435.

26.10 Killing Buffers

Killing a buffer makes its name unknown to Emacs and makes the memory space it occupied available for other use.

The buffer object for the buffer that has been killed remains in existence as long as anything refers to it, but it is specially marked so that you cannot make it current or display it. Killed buffers retain their identity, however; if you kill two distinct buffers, they remain distinct according to `eq` although both are dead.

If you kill a buffer that is current or displayed in a window, Emacs automatically selects or displays some other buffer instead. This means that killing a buffer can change the current buffer. Therefore, when you kill a buffer, you should also take the precautions associated with changing the current buffer (unless you happen to know that the buffer being killed isn't current). See Section 26.2 [Current Buffer], page 550.

If you kill a buffer that is the base buffer of one or more indirect buffers, the indirect buffers are automatically killed as well.

The `buffer-name` of a buffer is `nil` if, and only if, the buffer is killed. A buffer that has not been killed is called a *live* buffer. To test whether a buffer is live or killed, use the function `buffer-live-p` (see below).

kill-buffer &optional *buffer-or-name*   [Command]
> This function kills the buffer *buffer-or-name*, freeing all its memory for other uses or to be returned to the operating system. If *buffer-or-name* is `nil` or omitted, it kills the current buffer.

> Any processes that have this buffer as the `process-buffer` are sent the `SIGHUP` (hangup) signal, which normally causes them to terminate. See Section 36.8 [Signals to Processes], page 855.

> If the buffer is visiting a file and contains unsaved changes, `kill-buffer` asks the user to confirm before the buffer is killed. It does this even if not called interactively. To prevent the request for confirmation, clear the modified flag before calling `kill-buffer`. See Section 26.5 [Buffer Modification], page 556.

> This function calls `replace-buffer-in-windows` for cleaning up all windows currently displaying the buffer to be killed.

> Killing a buffer that is already dead has no effect.

> This function returns `t` if it actually killed the buffer. It returns `nil` if the user refuses to confirm or if *buffer-or-name* was already dead.

> ```
> (kill-buffer "foo.unchanged")
>     ⇒ t
> (kill-buffer "foo.changed")
> 
> ---------- Buffer: Minibuffer ----------
> ```

```
Buffer foo.changed modified; kill anyway? (yes or no) yes
---------- Buffer: Minibuffer ----------
```

⇒ t

kill-buffer-query-functions   [Variable]

Before confirming unsaved changes, `kill-buffer` calls the functions in the list `kill-buffer-query-functions`, in order of appearance, with no arguments. The buffer being killed is the current buffer when they are called. The idea of this feature is that these functions will ask for confirmation from the user. If any of them returns `nil`, `kill-buffer` spares the buffer's life.

kill-buffer-hook   [Variable]

This is a normal hook run by `kill-buffer` after asking all the questions it is going to ask, just before actually killing the buffer. The buffer to be killed is current when the hook functions run. See Section 22.1 [Hooks], page 429. This variable is a permanent local, so its local binding is not cleared by changing major modes.

buffer-offer-save   [User Option]

This variable, if non-`nil` in a particular buffer, tells `save-buffers-kill-emacs` and `save-some-buffers` (if the second optional argument to that function is `t`) to offer to save that buffer, just as they offer to save file-visiting buffers. See [Definition of save-some-buffers], page 499. The variable `buffer-offer-save` automatically becomes buffer-local when set for any reason. See Section 11.10 [Buffer-Local Variables], page 171.

buffer-save-without-query   [Variable]

This variable, if non-`nil` in a particular buffer, tells `save-buffers-kill-emacs` and `save-some-buffers` to save this buffer (if it's modified) without asking the user. The variable automatically becomes buffer-local when set for any reason.

buffer-live-p *object*   [Function]

This function returns `t` if *object* is a live buffer (a buffer which has not been killed), `nil` otherwise.

26.11 Indirect Buffers

An *indirect buffer* shares the text of some other buffer, which is called the *base buffer* of the indirect buffer. In some ways it is the analogue, for buffers, of a symbolic link among files. The base buffer may not itself be an indirect buffer.

The text of the indirect buffer is always identical to the text of its base buffer; changes made by editing either one are visible immediately in the other. This includes the text properties as well as the characters themselves.

In all other respects, the indirect buffer and its base buffer are completely separate. They have different names, independent values of point, independent narrowing, independent markers and overlays (though inserting or deleting text in either buffer relocates the markers and overlays for both), independent major modes, and independent buffer-local variable bindings.

An indirect buffer cannot visit a file, but its base buffer can. If you try to save the indirect buffer, that actually saves the base buffer.

Killing an indirect buffer has no effect on its base buffer. Killing the base buffer effectively kills the indirect buffer in that it cannot ever again be the current buffer.

make-indirect-buffer *base-buffer name* **&optional** *clone*   [Command]
> This creates and returns an indirect buffer named *name* whose base buffer is *base-buffer*. The argument *base-buffer* may be a live buffer or the name (a string) of an existing buffer. If *name* is the name of an existing buffer, an error is signaled.
>
> If *clone* is non-**nil**, then the indirect buffer originally shares the state of *base-buffer* such as major mode, minor modes, buffer local variables and so on. If *clone* is omitted or **nil** the indirect buffer's state is set to the default state for new buffers.
>
> If *base-buffer* is an indirect buffer, its base buffer is used as the base for the new buffer. If, in addition, *clone* is non-**nil**, the initial state is copied from the actual base buffer, not from *base-buffer*.

clone-indirect-buffer *newname display-flag* **&optional** *norecord*   [Command]
> This function creates and returns a new indirect buffer that shares the current buffer's base buffer and copies the rest of the current buffer's attributes. (If the current buffer is not indirect, it is used as the base buffer.)
>
> If *display-flag* is non-**nil**, that means to display the new buffer by calling **pop-to-buffer**. If *norecord* is non-**nil**, that means not to put the new buffer to the front of the buffer list.

buffer-base-buffer **&optional** *buffer*   [Function]
> This function returns the base buffer of *buffer*, which defaults to the current buffer. If *buffer* is not indirect, the value is **nil**. Otherwise, the value is another buffer, which is never an indirect buffer.

26.12 Swapping Text Between Two Buffers

Specialized modes sometimes need to let the user access from the same buffer several vastly different types of text. For example, you may need to display a summary of the buffer text, in addition to letting the user access the text itself.

This could be implemented with multiple buffers (kept in sync when the user edits the text), or with narrowing (see Section 29.4 [Narrowing], page 684). But these alternatives might sometimes become tedious or prohibitively expensive, especially if each type of text requires expensive buffer-global operations in order to provide correct display and editing commands.

Emacs provides another facility for such modes: you can quickly swap buffer text between two buffers with **buffer-swap-text**. This function is very fast because it doesn't move any text, it only changes the internal data structures of the buffer object to point to a different chunk of text. Using it, you can pretend that a group of two or more buffers are actually a single virtual buffer that holds the contents of all the individual buffers together.

`buffer-swap-text` *buffer*   [Function]

> This function swaps the text of the current buffer and that of its argument *buffer*. It signals an error if one of the two buffers is an indirect buffer (see Section 26.11 [Indirect Buffers], page 564) or is a base buffer of an indirect buffer.
>
> All the buffer properties that are related to the buffer text are swapped as well: the positions of point and mark, all the markers, the overlays, the text properties, the undo list, the value of the `enable-multibyte-characters` flag (see Section 32.1 [Text Representations], page 761), etc.
>
> **Warning:** If this function is called from within a `save-excursion` form, the current buffer will be set to *buffer* upon leaving the form, since the marker used by `save-excursion` to save the position and buffer will be swapped as well.

If you use `buffer-swap-text` on a file-visiting buffer, you should set up a hook to save the buffer's original text rather than what it was swapped with. `write-region-annotate-functions` works for this purpose. You should probably set `buffer-saved-size` to -2 in the buffer, so that changes in the text it is swapped with will not interfere with auto-saving.

26.13 The Buffer Gap

Emacs buffers are implemented using an invisible *gap* to make insertion and deletion faster. Insertion works by filling in part of the gap, and deletion adds to the gap. Of course, this means that the gap must first be moved to the locus of the insertion or deletion. Emacs moves the gap only when you try to insert or delete. This is why your first editing command in one part of a large buffer, after previously editing in another far-away part, sometimes involves a noticeable delay.

This mechanism works invisibly, and Lisp code should never be affected by the gap's current location, but these functions are available for getting information about the gap status.

`gap-position`   [Function]

> This function returns the current gap position in the current buffer.

`gap-size`   [Function]

> This function returns the current gap size of the current buffer.

27 Windows

This chapter describes the functions and variables related to Emacs windows. See Chapter 28 [Frames], page 630, for how windows are assigned an area of screen available for Emacs to use. See Chapter 37 [Display], page 886, for information on how text is displayed in windows.

27.1 Basic Concepts of Emacs Windows

A *window* is an area of the screen that is used to display a buffer (see Chapter 26 [Buffers], page 550). In Emacs Lisp, windows are represented by a special Lisp object type.

Windows are grouped into frames (see Chapter 28 [Frames], page 630). Each frame contains at least one window; the user can subdivide it into multiple, non-overlapping windows to view several buffers at once. Lisp programs can use multiple windows for a variety of purposes. In Rmail, for example, you can view a summary of message titles in one window, and the contents of the selected message in another window.

Emacs uses the word "window" with a different meaning than in graphical desktop environments and window systems, such as the X Window System. When Emacs is run on X, each of its graphical X windows is an Emacs frame (containing one or more Emacs windows). When Emacs is run on a text terminal, the frame fills the entire terminal screen.

Unlike X windows, Emacs windows are *tiled*; they never overlap within the area of the frame. When a window is created, resized, or deleted, the change in window space is taken from or given to the adjacent windows, so that the total area of the frame is unchanged.

windowp *object*   [Function]
> This function returns t if *object* is a window (whether or not it displays a buffer). Otherwise, it returns nil.

A *live window* is one that is actually displaying a buffer in a frame.

window-live-p *object*   [Function]
> This function returns t if *object* is a live window and nil otherwise. A live window is one that displays a buffer.

The windows in each frame are organized into a *window tree*. See Section 27.2 [Windows and Frames], page 568. The leaf nodes of each window tree are live windows—the ones actually displaying buffers. The internal nodes of the window tree are *internal windows*, which are not live.

A *valid window* is one that is either live or internal. A valid window can be *deleted*, i.e., removed from its frame (see Section 27.7 [Deleting Windows], page 584); then it is no longer valid, but the Lisp object representing it might be still referenced from other Lisp objects. A deleted window may be made valid again by restoring a saved window configuration (see Section 27.25 [Window Configurations], page 623).

You can distinguish valid windows from deleted windows with **window-valid-p**.

window-valid-p *object*   [Function]
> This function returns t if *object* is a live window, or an internal window in a window tree. Otherwise, it returns nil, including for the case where *object* is a deleted window.

In each frame, at any time, exactly one Emacs window is designated as *selected within the frame*. For the selected frame, that window is called the *selected window*—the one in which most editing takes place, and in which the cursor for selected windows appears (see Section 28.4.3.7 [Cursor Parameters], page 650). The selected window's buffer is usually also the current buffer, except when `set-buffer` has been used (see Section 26.2 [Current Buffer], page 550). As for non-selected frames, the window selected within the frame becomes the selected window if the frame is ever selected. See Section 27.9 [Selecting Windows], page 590.

`selected-window`   [Function]
> This function returns the selected window (which is always a live window).

Sometimes several windows collectively and cooperatively display a buffer, for example, under the management of Follow Mode (see Section "Follow Mode" in `emacs`), where the windows together display a bigger portion of the buffer than one window could alone. It is often useful to consider such a *window group* as a single entity. Several functions such as `window-group-start` (see Section 27.20 [Window Start and End], page 610) allow you to do this by supplying, as an argument, one of the windows as a stand in for the whole group.

`selected-window-group`   [Function]
> When the selected window is a member of a group of windows, this function returns a list of the windows in the group, ordered such that the first window in the list is displaying the earliest part of the buffer, and so on. Otherwise the function returns a list containing just the selected window.
>
> The selected window is considered part of a group when the buffer local variable `selected-window-group-function` is set to a function. In this case, `selected-window-group` calls it with no arguments and returns its result (which should be the list of windows in the group).

27.2 Windows and Frames

Each window belongs to exactly one frame (see Chapter 28 [Frames], page 630).

`window-frame &optional` *window*   [Function]
> This function returns the frame that the window *window* belongs to. If *window* is `nil`, it defaults to the selected window.

`window-list &optional` *frame minibuffer window*   [Function]
> This function returns a list of live windows belonging to the frame *frame*. If *frame* is omitted or `nil`, it defaults to the selected frame.
>
> The optional argument *minibuffer* specifies whether to include the minibuffer window in the returned list. If *minibuffer* is `t`, the minibuffer window is included. If *minibuffer* is `nil` or omitted, the minibuffer window is included only if it is active. If *minibuffer* is neither `nil` nor `t`, the minibuffer window is never included.
>
> The optional argument *window*, if non-`nil`, should be a live window on the specified frame; then *window* will be the first element in the returned list. If *window* is omitted or `nil`, the window selected within the frame is the first element.

Windows in the same frame are organized into a *window tree*, whose leaf nodes are the live windows. The internal nodes of a window tree are not live; they exist for the purpose of organizing the relationships between live windows. The root node of a window tree is called the *root window*. It can be either a live window (if the frame has just one window), or an internal window.

A minibuffer window (see Section 19.11 [Minibuffer Windows], page 341) is not part of its frame's window tree unless the frame is a minibuffer-only frame. Nonetheless, most of the functions in this section accept the minibuffer window as an argument. Also, the function `window-tree` described at the end of this section lists the minibuffer window alongside the actual window tree.

`frame-root-window` &optional *frame-or-window*   [Function]

> This function returns the root window for *frame-or-window*. The argument *frame-or-window* should be either a window or a frame; if omitted or `nil`, it defaults to the selected frame. If *frame-or-window* is a window, the return value is the root window of that window's frame.

When a window is split, there are two live windows where previously there was one. One of these is represented by the same Lisp window object as the original window, and the other is represented by a newly-created Lisp window object. Both of these live windows become leaf nodes of the window tree, as *child windows* of a single internal window. If necessary, Emacs automatically creates this internal window, which is also called the *parent window*, and assigns it to the appropriate position in the window tree. A set of windows that share the same parent are called *siblings*.

`window-parent` &optional *window*   [Function]

> This function returns the parent window of *window*. If *window* is omitted or `nil`, it defaults to the selected window. The return value is `nil` if *window* has no parent (i.e., it is a minibuffer window or the root window of its frame).

Each internal window always has at least two child windows. If this number falls to one as a result of window deletion, Emacs automatically deletes the internal window, and its sole remaining child window takes its place in the window tree.

Each child window can be either a live window, or an internal window (which in turn would have its own child windows). Therefore, each internal window can be thought of as occupying a certain rectangular *screen area*—the union of the areas occupied by the live windows that are ultimately descended from it.

For each internal window, the screen areas of the immediate children are arranged either vertically or horizontally (never both). If the child windows are arranged one above the other, they are said to form a *vertical combination*; if they are arranged side by side, they are said to form a *horizontal combination*. Consider the following example:

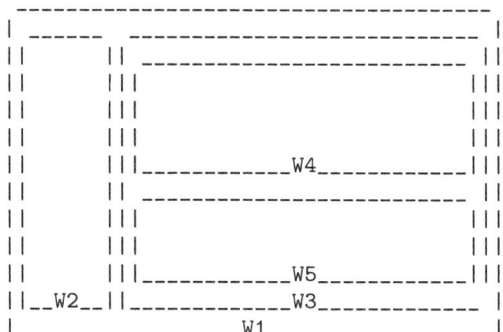

The root window of this frame is an internal window, *W1*. Its child windows form a horizontal combination, consisting of the live window *W2* and the internal window *W3*. The child windows of *W3* form a vertical combination, consisting of the live windows *W4* and *W5*. Hence, the live windows in this window tree are *W2*, *W4*, and *W5*.

The following functions can be used to retrieve a child window of an internal window, and the siblings of a child window.

window-top-child **&optional** *window*   [Function]
> This function returns the topmost child window of *window*, if *window* is an internal window whose children form a vertical combination. For any other type of window, the return value is `nil`.

window-left-child **&optional** *window*   [Function]
> This function returns the leftmost child window of *window*, if *window* is an internal window whose children form a horizontal combination. For any other type of window, the return value is `nil`.

window-child *window*   [Function]
> This function returns the first child window of the internal window *window*—the topmost child window for a vertical combination, or the leftmost child window for a horizontal combination. If *window* is a live window, the return value is `nil`.

window-combined-p **&optional** *window horizontal*   [Function]
> This function returns a non-`nil` value if and only if *window* is part of a vertical combination. If *window* is omitted or `nil`, it defaults to the selected one.
>
> If the optional argument *horizontal* is non-`nil`, this means to return non-`nil` if and only if *window* is part of a horizontal combination.

window-next-sibling **&optional** *window*   [Function]
> This function returns the next sibling of the window *window*. If omitted or `nil`, *window* defaults to the selected window. The return value is `nil` if *window* is the last child of its parent.

window-prev-sibling **&optional** *window*   [Function]
> This function returns the previous sibling of the window *window*. If omitted or `nil`, *window* defaults to the selected window. The return value is `nil` if *window* is the first child of its parent.

The functions `window-next-sibling` and `window-prev-sibling` should not be confused with the functions `next-window` and `previous-window`, which return the next and previous window, respectively, in the cyclic ordering of windows (see Section 27.10 [Cyclic Window Ordering], page 591).

You can use the following functions to find the first live window on a frame and the window nearest to a given window.

`frame-first-window` &optional *frame-or-window*   [Function]
> This function returns the live window at the upper left corner of the frame specified by *frame-or-window*. The argument *frame-or-window* must denote a window or a live frame and defaults to the selected frame. If *frame-or-window* specifies a window, this function returns the first window on that window's frame. Under the assumption that the frame from our canonical example is selected (`frame-first-window`) returns *W2*.

`window-in-direction` *direction* &optional *window ignore sign wrap*   [Function]
>   *mini*
> This function returns the nearest live window in direction *direction* as seen from the position of `window-point` in window *window*. The argument *direction* must be one of `above`, `below`, `left` or `right`. The optional argument *window* must denote a live window and defaults to the selected one.
>
> This function does not return a window whose `no-other-window` parameter is non-`nil` (see Section 27.26 [Window Parameters], page 625). If the nearest window's `no-other-window` parameter is non-`nil`, this function tries to find another window in the indicated direction whose `no-other-window` parameter is `nil`. If the optional argument *ignore* is non-`nil`, a window may be returned even if its `no-other-window` parameter is non-`nil`.
>
> If the optional argument *sign* is a negative number, it means to use the right or bottom edge of *window* as reference position instead of `window-point`. If *sign* is a positive number, it means to use the left or top edge of *window* as reference position.
>
> If the optional argument *wrap* is non-`nil`, this means to wrap *direction* around frame borders. For example, if *window* is at the top of the frame and *direction* is `above`, then this function usually returns the frame's minibuffer window if it's active and a window at the bottom of the frame otherwise.
>
> If the optional argument *mini* is `nil`, this means to return the minibuffer window if and only if it is currently active. If *mini* is non-`nil`, this function may return the minibuffer window even when it's not active. However, if *wrap* is non-`nil`, it always acts as if *mini* were `nil`.
>
> If it doesn't find a suitable window, this function returns `nil`.

The following function allows the entire window tree of a frame to be retrieved:

`window-tree` &optional *frame*   [Function]
> This function returns a list representing the window tree for frame *frame*. If *frame* is omitted or `nil`, it defaults to the selected frame.
>
> The return value is a list of the form (`root mini`), where *root* represents the window tree of the frame's root window, and *mini* is the frame's minibuffer window.

If the root window is live, *root* is that window itself. Otherwise, *root* is a list (`dir edges w1 w2 ...`) where *dir* is `nil` for a horizontal combination and `t` for a vertical combination, *edges* gives the size and position of the combination, and the remaining elements are the child windows. Each child window may again be a window object (for a live window) or a list with the same format as above (for an internal window). The *edges* element is a list (`left top right bottom`), similar to the value returned by `window-edges` (see Section 27.24 [Coordinates and Windows], page 620).

27.3 Window Sizes

The following schematic shows the structure of a live window:

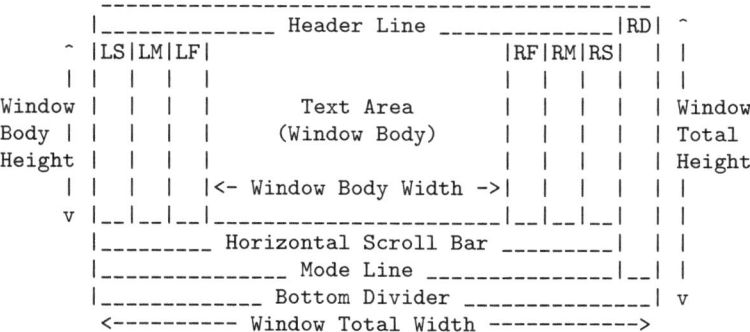

```
                ------------------------------------------------
                |_____ Header Line _____|RD| ^
            ^   |LS|LM|LF|                     |RF|RM|RS|  | |
            |   | |  |  |                      |  |  |  |  | |
    Window  |   | |  |  |      Text Area       |  |  |  |  | Window
    Body    |   | |  |  |    (Window Body)     |  |  |  |  | Total
    Height  |   | |  |  |                      |  |  |  |  | Height
            |   | |  |  | |<- Window Body Width ->|  |  |  |  | |
            v   |__|__|__|_____|__|__|__|  | |
                |_____ Horizontal Scroll Bar _____|  | |
                |_____ Mode Line _____|__| |
                |_____ Bottom Divider _____| v
                <---------- Window Total Width ----------->
```

At the center of the window is the *text area*, or *body*, where the buffer text is displayed. The text area can be surrounded by a series of optional areas. On the left and right, from innermost to outermost, these are the left and right fringes, denoted by LF and RF (see Section 37.13 [Fringes], page 937); the left and right margins, denoted by LM and RM in the schematic (see Section 37.16.5 [Display Margins], page 949); the left or right vertical scroll bar, only one of which is present at any time, denoted by LS and RS (see Section 37.14 [Scroll Bars], page 942); and the right divider, denoted by RD (see Section 37.15 [Window Dividers], page 944). At the top of the window is the header line (see Section 22.4.7 [Header Lines], page 458). At the bottom of the window are the horizontal scroll bar (see Section 37.14 [Scroll Bars], page 942); the mode line (see Section 22.4 [Mode Line Format], page 451); and the bottom divider (see Section 37.15 [Window Dividers], page 944).

Emacs provides miscellaneous functions for finding the height and width of a window. The return value of many of these functions can be specified either in units of pixels or in units of lines and columns. On a graphical display, the latter actually correspond to the height and width of a default character specified by the frame's default font as returned by `frame-char-height` and `frame-char-width` (see Section 28.3.2 [Frame Font], page 639). Thus, if a window is displaying text with a different font or size, the reported line height and column width for that window may differ from the actual number of text lines or columns displayed within it.

The *total height* of a window is the number of lines comprising the window's body, the header line, the horizontal scroll bar, the mode line and the bottom divider (if any).

window-total-height &optional *window round*   [Function]
>   This function returns the total height, in lines, of the window *window*. If *window* is omitted or `nil`, it defaults to the selected window. If *window* is an internal window, the return value is the total height occupied by its descendant windows.
>
>   If a window's pixel height is not an integral multiple of its frame's default character height, the number of lines occupied by the window is rounded internally. This is done in a way such that, if the window is a parent window, the sum of the total heights of all its child windows internally equals the total height of their parent. This means that although two windows have the same pixel height, their internal total heights may differ by one line. This means also, that if window is vertically combined and has a next sibling, the topmost row of that sibling can be calculated as the sum of this window's topmost row and total height (see Section 27.24 [Coordinates and Windows], page 620)
>
>   If the optional argument *round* is `ceiling`, this function returns the smallest integer larger than *window*'s pixel height divided by the character height of its frame; if it is `floor`, it returns the largest integer smaller than said value; with any other *round* it returns the internal value of *windows*'s total height.

The *total width* of a window is the number of lines comprising the window's body, its margins, fringes, scroll bars and a right divider (if any).

window-total-width &optional *window round*   [Function]
>   This function returns the total width, in columns, of the window *window*. If *window* is omitted or `nil`, it defaults to the selected window. If *window* is internal, the return value is the total width occupied by its descendant windows.
>
>   If a window's pixel width is not an integral multiple of its frame's character width, the number of lines occupied by the window is rounded internally. This is done in a way such that, if the window is a parent window, the sum of the total widths of all its children internally equals the total width of their parent. This means that although two windows have the same pixel width, their internal total widths may differ by one column. This means also, that if this window is horizontally combined and has a next sibling, the leftmost column of that sibling can be calculated as the sum of this window's leftmost column and total width (see Section 27.24 [Coordinates and Windows], page 620). The optional argument *round* behaves as it does for `window-total-height`.

window-total-size &optional *window horizontal round*   [Function]
>   This function returns either the total height in lines or the total width in columns of the window *window*. If *horizontal* is omitted or `nil`, this is equivalent to calling `window-total-height` for *window*; otherwise it is equivalent to calling `window-total-width` for *window*. The optional argument *round* behaves as it does for `window-total-height`.

The following two functions can be used to return the total size of a window in units of pixels.

window-pixel-height &optional *window*   [Function]
>   This function returns the total height of window *window* in pixels. *window* must be a valid window and defaults to the selected one.

The return value includes mode and header line, a horizontal scroll bar and a bottom
divider, if any. If *window* is an internal window, its pixel height is the pixel height of
the screen areas spanned by its children.

window-pixel-width **&optional** *window*   [Function]

This function returns the width of window *window* in pixels. *window* must be a valid
window and defaults to the selected one.

The return value includes the fringes and margins of *window* as well as any vertical
dividers or scroll bars belonging to *window*. If *window* is an internal window, its pixel
width is the width of the screen areas spanned by its children.

The following functions can be used to determine whether a given window has any
adjacent windows.

window-full-height-p **&optional** *window*   [Function]

This function returns non-`nil` if *window* has no other window above or below it in
its frame. More precisely, this means that the total height of *window* equals the total
height of the root window on that frame. The minibuffer window does not count in
this regard. If *window* is omitted or `nil`, it defaults to the selected window.

window-full-width-p **&optional** *window*   [Function]

This function returns non-`nil` if *window* has no other window to the left or right in
its frame, i.e., its total width equals that of the root window on that frame. If *window*
is omitted or `nil`, it defaults to the selected window.

The *body height* of a window is the height of its text area, which does not include a
mode or header line, a horizontal scroll bar, or a bottom divider.

window-body-height **&optional** *window pixelwise*   [Function]

This function returns the height, in lines, of the body of window *window*. If *window*
is omitted or `nil`, it defaults to the selected window; otherwise it must be a live
window.

If the optional argument *pixelwise* is non-`nil`, this function returns the body height
of *window* counted in pixels.

If *pixelwise* is `nil`, the return value is rounded down to the nearest integer, if necessary. This means that if a line at the bottom of the text area is only partially visible,
that line is not counted. It also means that the height of a window's body can never
exceed its total height as returned by `window-total-height`.

The *body width* of a window is the width of its text area, which does not include the
scroll bar, fringes, margins or a right divider. Note that when one or both fringes are
removed (by setting their width to zero), the display engine reserves two character cells,
one on each side of the window, for displaying the continuation and truncation glyphs,
which leaves 2 columns less for text display. (The function `window-max-chars-per-line`,
described below, takes this peculiarity into account.)

window-body-width **&optional** *window pixelwise*   [Function]

This function returns the width, in columns, of the body of window *window*. If
window is omitted or `nil`, it defaults to the selected window; otherwise it must be a
live window.

If the optional argument *pixelwise* is non-`nil`, this function returns the body width of *window* in units of pixels.

If *pixelwise* is `nil`, the return value is rounded down to the nearest integer, if necessary. This means that if a column on the right of the text area is only partially visible, that column is not counted. It also means that the width of a window's body can never exceed its total width as returned by `window-total-width`.

`window-body-size` &optional *window horizontal pixelwise*   [Function]
This function returns the body height or body width of *window*. If *horizontal* is omitted or `nil`, it is equivalent to calling `window-body-height` for *window*; otherwise it is equivalent to calling `window-body-width`. In either case, the optional argument *pixelwise* is passed to the function called.

For compatibility with previous versions of Emacs, `window-height` is an alias for `window-total-height`, and `window-width` is an alias for `window-body-width`. These aliases are considered obsolete and will be removed in the future.

The pixel heights of a window's mode and header line can be retrieved with the functions given below. Their return value is usually accurate unless the window has not been displayed before: In that case, the return value is based on an estimate of the font used for the window's frame.

`window-mode-line-height` &optional *window*   [Function]
This function returns the height in pixels of *window*'s mode line. *window* must be a live window and defaults to the selected one. If *window* has no mode line, the return value is zero.

`window-header-line-height` &optional *window*   [Function]
This function returns the height in pixels of *window*'s header line. *window* must be a live window and defaults to the selected one. If *window* has no header line, the return value is zero.

Functions for retrieving the height and/or width of window dividers (see Section 37.15 [Window Dividers], page 944), fringes (see Section 37.13 [Fringes], page 937), scroll bars (see Section 37.14 [Scroll Bars], page 942), and display margins (see Section 37.16.5 [Display Margins], page 949) are described in the corresponding sections.

If your Lisp program needs to make layout decisions, you will find the following function useful:

`window-max-chars-per-line` &optional *window face*   [Function]
This function returns the number of characters displayed in the specified face *face* in the specified window *window* (which must be a live window). If *face* was remapped (see Section 37.12.5 [Face Remapping], page 924), the information is returned for the remapped face. If omitted or `nil`, *face* defaults to the default face, and *window* defaults to the selected window.

Unlike `window-body-width`, this function accounts for the actual size of *face*'s font, instead of working in units of the canonical character width of *window*'s frame (see Section 28.3.2 [Frame Font], page 639). It also accounts for space used by the continuation glyph, if *window* lacks one or both of its fringes.

Commands that change the size of windows (see Section 27.4 [Resizing Windows], page 576), or split them (see Section 27.6 [Splitting Windows], page 581), obey the variables `window-min-height` and `window-min-width`, which specify the smallest allowable window height and width. They also obey the variable `window-size-fixed`, with which a window can be *fixed* in size (see Section 27.5 [Preserving Window Sizes], page 580).

`window-min-height` [User Option]
> This option specifies the minimum total height, in lines, of any window. Its value has to accommodate at least one text line as well as a mode and header line, a horizontal scroll bar and a bottom divider, if present.

`window-min-width` [User Option]
> This option specifies the minimum total width, in columns, of any window. Its value has to accommodate two text columns as well as margins, fringes, a scroll bar and a right divider, if present.

The following function tells how small a specific window can get taking into account the sizes of its areas and the values of `window-min-height`, `window-min-width` and `window-size-fixed` (see Section 27.5 [Preserving Window Sizes], page 580).

`window-min-size` &optional *window horizontal ignore pixelwise* [Function]
> This function returns the minimum size of *window*. *window* must be a valid window and defaults to the selected one. The optional argument *horizontal* non-`nil` means to return the minimum number of columns of *window*; otherwise return the minimum number of *window*'s lines.
>
> The return value makes sure that all components of *window* remain fully visible if *window*'s size were actually set to it. With *horizontal* `nil` it includes the mode and header line, the horizontal scroll bar and the bottom divider, if present. With *horizontal* non-`nil` it includes the margins and fringes, the vertical scroll bar and the right divider, if present.
>
> The optional argument *ignore*, if non-`nil`, means ignore restrictions imposed by fixed size windows, `window-min-height` or `window-min-width` settings. If *ignore* equals `safe`, live windows may get as small as `window-safe-min-height` lines and `window-safe-min-width` columns. If *ignore* is a window, ignore restrictions for that window only. Any other non-`nil` value means ignore all of the above restrictions for all windows.
>
> The optional argument *pixelwise* non-`nil` means to return the minimum size of *window* counted in pixels.

27.4 Resizing Windows

This section describes functions for resizing a window without changing the size of its frame. Because live windows do not overlap, these functions are meaningful only on frames that contain two or more windows: resizing a window also changes the size of a neighboring window. If there is just one window on a frame, its size cannot be changed except by resizing the frame (see Section 28.3.3 [Size and Position], page 639).

Except where noted, these functions also accept internal windows as arguments. Resizing an internal window causes its child windows to be resized to fit the same space.

window-resizable *window delta* **&optional** *horizontal ignore*   [Function]
     pixelwise
     This function returns *delta* if the size of *window* can be changed vertically by *delta*
     lines. If the optional argument *horizontal* is non-`nil`, it instead returns *delta* if
     window can be resized horizontally by *delta* columns. It does not actually change the
     window size.

     If *window* is `nil`, it defaults to the selected window.

     A positive value of *delta* means to check whether the window can be enlarged by that
     number of lines or columns; a negative value of *delta* means to check whether the
     window can be shrunk by that many lines or columns. If *delta* is non-zero, a return
     value of 0 means that the window cannot be resized.

     Normally, the variables `window-min-height` and `window-min-width` specify the
     smallest allowable window size (see Section 27.3 [Window Sizes], page 572). However,
     if the optional argument *ignore* is non-`nil`, this function ignores `window-min-height`
     and `window-min-width`, as well as `window-size-fixed`. Instead, it considers
     the minimum-height window to be one consisting of a header and a mode line, a
     horizontal scrollbar and a bottom divider (if any), plus a text area one line tall; and
     a minimum-width window as one consisting of fringes, margins, a scroll bar and a
     right divider (if any), plus a text area two columns wide.

     If the optional argument *pixelwise* is non-`nil`, *delta* is interpreted as pixels.

window-resize *window delta* **&optional** *horizontal ignore pixelwise*   [Function]
     This function resizes *window* by *delta* increments. If *horizontal* is `nil`, it changes the
     height by *delta* lines; otherwise, it changes the width by *delta* columns. A positive
     delta means to enlarge the window, and a negative *delta* means to shrink it.

     If *window* is `nil`, it defaults to the selected window. If the window cannot be resized
     as demanded, an error is signaled.

     The optional argument *ignore* has the same meaning as for the function
     `window-resizable` above.

     If the optional argument *pixelwise* is non-`nil`, *delta* will be interpreted as pixels.

     The choice of which window edges this function alters depends on the values of the
     option `window-combination-resize` and the combination limits of the involved win-
     dows; in some cases, it may alter both edges. See Section 27.8 [Recombining Win-
     dows], page 585. To resize by moving only the bottom or right edge of a window, use
     the function `adjust-window-trailing-edge`.

adjust-window-trailing-edge *window delta* **&optional** *horizontal*   [Function]
     pixelwise
     This function moves *window*'s bottom edge by *delta* lines. If optional argument
     horizontal is non-`nil`, it instead moves the right edge by *delta* columns. If *window* is
     `nil`, it defaults to the selected window.

     If the optional argument *pixelwise* is non-`nil`, *delta* is interpreted as pixels.

     A positive *delta* moves the edge downwards or to the right; a negative *delta* moves it
     upwards or to the left. If the edge cannot be moved as far as specified by *delta*, this
     function moves it as far as possible but does not signal a error.

This function tries to resize windows adjacent to the edge that is moved. If this is not possible for some reason (e.g., if that adjacent window is fixed-size), it may resize other windows.

`window-resize-pixelwise`   [User Option]

If the value of this option is non-`nil`, Emacs resizes windows in units of pixels. This currently affects functions like `split-window` (see Section 27.6 [Splitting Windows], page 581), `maximize-window`, `minimize-window`, `fit-window-to-buffer`, `fit-frame-to-buffer` and `shrink-window-if-larger-than-buffer` (all listed below).

Note that when a frame's pixel size is not a multiple of its character size, at least one window may get resized pixelwise even if this option is `nil`. The default value is `nil`.

The following commands resize windows in more specific ways. When called interactively, they act on the selected window.

`fit-window-to-buffer` &optional *window max-height min-height*   [Command]
    max-width min-width preserve-size

This command adjusts the height or width of *window* to fit the text in it. It returns non-`nil` if it was able to resize *window*, and `nil` otherwise. If *window* is omitted or `nil`, it defaults to the selected window. Otherwise, it should be a live window.

If *window* is part of a vertical combination, this function adjusts *window*'s height. The new height is calculated from the actual height of the accessible portion of its buffer. The optional argument *max-height*, if non-`nil`, specifies the maximum total height that this function can give *window*. The optional argument *min-height*, if non-`nil`, specifies the minimum total height that it can give, which overrides the variable `window-min-height`. Both *max-height* and *min-height* are specified in lines and include mode and header line and a bottom divider, if any.

If *window* is part of a horizontal combination and the value of the option `fit-window-to-buffer-horizontally` (see below) is non-`nil`, this function adjusts *window*'s height. The new width of *window* is calculated from the maximum length of its buffer's lines that follow the current start position of *window*. The optional argument *max-width* specifies a maximum width and defaults to the width of *window*'s frame. The optional argument *min-width* specifies a minimum width and defaults to `window-min-width`. Both *max-width* and *min-width* are specified in columns and include fringes, margins and scrollbars, if any.

The optional argument *preserve-size*, if non-`nil`, will install a parameter to preserve the size of *window* during future resize operations (see Section 27.5 [Preserving Window Sizes], page 580).

If the option `fit-frame-to-buffer` (see below) is non-`nil`, this function will try to resize the frame of *window* to fit its contents by calling `fit-frame-to-buffer` (see below).

`fit-window-to-buffer-horizontally`   [User Option]

If this is non-`nil`, `fit-window-to-buffer` can resize windows horizontally. If this is `nil` (the default) `fit-window-to-buffer` never resizes windows horizontally. If this is `only`, it can resize windows horizontally only. Any other value means `fit-window-to-buffer` can resize windows in both dimensions.

`fit-frame-to-buffer`   [User Option]

> If this option is non-`nil`, `fit-window-to-buffer` can fit a frame to its buffer. A
> frame is fit if and only if its root window is a live window and this option is non-`nil`.
> If this is `horizontally`, frames are fit horizontally only. If this is `vertically`, frames
> are fit vertically only. Any other non-`nil` value means frames can be resized in both
> dimensions.

If you have a frame that displays only one window, you can fit that frame to its buffer
using the command `fit-frame-to-buffer`.

`fit-frame-to-buffer` **&optional** *frame max-height min-height*   [Command]
      max-width min-width only

> This command adjusts the size of *frame* to display the contents of its buffer exactly.
> *frame* can be any live frame and defaults to the selected one. Fitting is done only if
> *frame*'s root window is live. The arguments *max-height*, *min-height*, *max-width* and
> *min-width* specify bounds on the new total size of *frame*'s root window. *min-height*
> and *min-width* default to the values of `window-min-height` and `window-min-width`
> respectively.

> If the optional argument *only* is `vertically`, this function may resize the frame
> vertically only. If *only* is `horizontally`, it may resize the frame horizontally only.

The behavior of `fit-frame-to-buffer` can be controlled with the help of the two options
listed next.

`fit-frame-to-buffer-margins`   [User Option]

> This option can be used to specify margins around frames to be fit by `fit-frame-to-`
> `buffer`. Such margins can be useful to avoid, for example, that such frames overlap
> the taskbar.

> It specifies the numbers of pixels to be left free on the left, above, the right, and
> below a frame that shall be fit. The default specifies `nil` for each which means to use
> no margins. The value specified here can be overridden for a specific frame by that
> frame's `fit-frame-to-buffer-margins` parameter, if present.

`fit-frame-to-buffer-sizes`   [User Option]

> This option specifies size boundaries for `fit-frame-to-buffer`. It specifies the total
> maximum and minimum lines and maximum and minimum columns of the root win-
> dow of any frame that shall be fit to its buffer. If any of these values is non-`nil`, it
> overrides the corresponding argument of `fit-frame-to-buffer`.

`shrink-window-if-larger-than-buffer` **&optional** *window*   [Command]

> This command attempts to reduce *window*'s height as much as possible while still
> showing its full buffer, but no less than `window-min-height` lines. The return value
> is non-`nil` if the window was resized, and `nil` otherwise. If *window* is omitted or
> `nil`, it defaults to the selected window. Otherwise, it should be a live window.

> This command does nothing if the window is already too short to display all of its
> buffer, or if any of the buffer is scrolled off-screen, or if the window is the only live
> window in its frame.

> This command calls `fit-window-to-buffer` (see above) to do its work.

`balance-windows` &optional *window-or-frame* [Command]

> This function balances windows in a way that gives more space to full-width and/or full-height windows. If *window-or-frame* specifies a frame, it balances all windows on that frame. If *window-or-frame* specifies a window, it balances only that window and its siblings (see Section 27.2 [Windows and Frames], page 568).

`balance-windows-area` [Command]

> This function attempts to give all windows on the selected frame approximately the same share of the screen area. Full-width or full-height windows are not given more space than other windows.

`maximize-window` &optional *window* [Command]

> This function attempts to make *window* as large as possible, in both dimensions, without resizing its frame or deleting other windows. If *window* is omitted or `nil`, it defaults to the selected window.

`minimize-window` &optional *window* [Command]

> This function attempts to make *window* as small as possible, in both dimensions, without deleting it or resizing its frame. If *window* is omitted or `nil`, it defaults to the selected window.

27.5 Preserving Window Sizes

A window can get resized explicitly by using one of the functions from the preceding section or implicitly, for example, when resizing an adjacent window, when splitting or deleting a window (see Section 27.6 [Splitting Windows], page 581, see Section 27.7 [Deleting Windows], page 584) or when resizing the window's frame (see Section 28.3.3 [Size and Position], page 639).

It is possible to avoid implicit resizing of a specific window when there are one or more other resizable windows on the same frame. For this purpose, Emacs must be advised to *preserve* the size of that window. There are two basic ways to do that.

`window-size-fixed` [Variable]

> If this buffer-local variable is non-`nil`, the size of any window displaying the buffer cannot normally be changed. Deleting a window or changing the frame's size may still change the window's size, if there is no choice.

> If the value is `height`, then only the window's height is fixed; if the value is `width`, then only the window's width is fixed. Any other non-`nil` value fixes both the width and the height.

> If this variable is `nil`, this does not necessarily mean that any window showing the buffer can be resized in the desired direction. To determine that, use the function `window-resizable`. See Section 27.4 [Resizing Windows], page 576.

Often `window-size-fixed` is overly aggressive because it inhibits any attempt to explicitly resize or split an affected window as well. This may even happen after the window has been resized implicitly, for example, when deleting an adjacent window or resizing the window's frame. The following function tries hard to never disallow resizing such a window explicitly:

window-preserve-size **&optional** *window horizontal preserve*   [Function]
This function (un-)marks the height of window *window* as preserved for future resize operations. *window* must be a live window and defaults to the selected one. If the optional argument *horizontal* is non-**nil**, it (un-)marks the width of *window* as preserved.

If the optional argument *preserve* is **t**, this means to preserve the current height/width of *window*'s body. The height/width of *window* will change only if Emacs has no better choice. Resizing a window whose height/width is preserved by this function never throws an error.

If *preserve* is **nil**, this means to stop preserving the height/width of *window*, lifting any respective restraint induced by a previous call of this function for *window*. Calling **enlarge-window**, **shrink-window** or **fit-window-to-buffer** with *window* as argument may also remove the respective restraint.

window-preserve-size is currently invoked by the following functions:

fit-window-to-buffer
If the optional argument *preserve-size* of that function (see Section 27.4 [Resizing Windows], page 576) is non-**nil**, the size established by that function is preserved.

display-buffer
If the *alist* argument of that function (see Section 27.13 [Choosing Window], page 598) contains a **preserve-size** entry, the size of the window produced by that function is preserved.

window-preserve-size installs a window parameter (see Section 27.26 [Window Parameters], page 625) called **preserved-size** which is consulted by the window resizing functions. This parameter will not prevent resizing the window when the window shows another buffer than the one when **window-preserve-size** was invoked or if its size has changed since then.

The following function can be used to check whether the height of a particular window is preserved:

window-preserved-size **&optional** *window horizontal*   [Function]
This function returns the preserved height of window *window* in pixels. *window* must be a live window and defaults to the selected one. If the optional argument *horizontal* is non-**nil**, it returns the preserved width of *window*. It returns **nil** if the size of *window* is not preserved.

27.6 Splitting Windows

This section describes functions for creating a new window by *splitting* an existing one.

split-window **&optional** *window size side pixelwise*   [Function]
This function creates a new live window next to the window *window*. If *window* is omitted or **nil**, it defaults to the selected window. That window is split, and reduced in size. The space is taken up by the new window, which is returned.

The optional second argument *size* determines the sizes of *window* and/or the new window. If it is omitted or `nil`, both windows are given equal sizes; if there is an odd line, it is allocated to the new window. If *size* is a positive number, *window* is given *size* lines (or columns, depending on the value of *side*). If *size* is a negative number, the new window is given −*size* lines (or columns).

If *size* is `nil`, this function obeys the variables `window-min-height` and `window-min-width` (see Section 27.3 [Window Sizes], page 572). Thus, it signals an error if splitting would result in making a window smaller than those variables specify. However, a non-`nil` value for *size* causes those variables to be ignored; in that case, the smallest allowable window is considered to be one that has space for a text area one line tall and/or two columns wide.

Hence, if *size* is specified, it's the caller's responsibility to check whether the emanating windows are large enough to encompass all areas like a mode line or a scroll bar. The function `window-min-size` (see Section 27.3 [Window Sizes], page 572) can be used to determine the minimum requirements of *window* in this regard. Since the new window usually inherits areas like the mode line or the scroll bar from *window*, that function is also a good guess for the minimum size of the new window. The caller should specify a smaller size only if it correspondingly removes an inherited area before the next redisplay.

The optional third argument *side* determines the position of the new window relative to *window*. If it is `nil` or `below`, the new window is placed below *window*. If it is `above`, the new window is placed above *window*. In both these cases, *size* specifies a total window height, in lines.

If *side* is `t` or `right`, the new window is placed on the right of *window*. If *side* is `left`, the new window is placed on the left of *window*. In both these cases, *size* specifies a total window width, in columns.

The optional fourth argument *pixelwise*, if non-`nil`, means to interpret *size* in units of pixels, instead of lines and columns.

If *window* is a live window, the new window inherits various properties from it, including margins and scroll bars. If *window* is an internal window, the new window inherits the properties of the window selected within *window*'s frame.

The behavior of this function may be altered by the window parameters of *window*, so long as the variable `ignore-window-parameters` is `nil`. If the value of the `split-window` window parameter is `t`, this function ignores all other window parameters. Otherwise, if the value of the `split-window` window parameter is a function, that function is called with the arguments *window*, *size*, and *side*, in lieu of the usual action of `split-window`. Otherwise, this function obeys the `window-atom` or `window-side` window parameter, if any. See Section 27.26 [Window Parameters], page 625.

As an example, here is a sequence of `split-window` calls that yields the window configuration discussed in Section 27.2 [Windows and Frames], page 568. This example demonstrates splitting a live window as well as splitting an internal window. We begin with a frame containing a single window (a live root window), which we denote by *W4*. Calling (`split-window W4`) yields this window configuration:

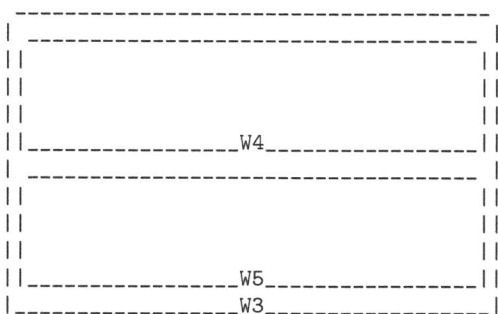

The `split-window` call has created a new live window, denoted by *W5*. It has also created a new internal window, denoted by *W3*, which becomes the root window and the parent of both *W4* and *W5*.

Next, we call (`split-window W3 nil 'left`), passing the internal window *W3* as the argument. The result:

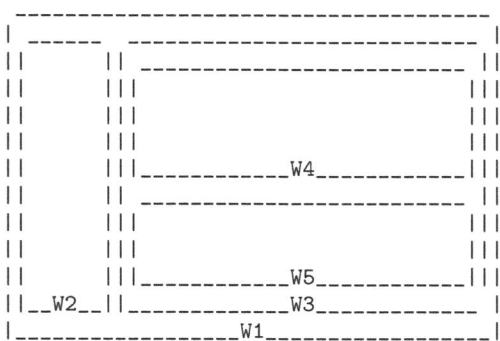

A new live window *W2* is created, to the left of the internal window *W3*. A new internal window *W1* is created, becoming the new root window.

For interactive use, Emacs provides two commands which always split the selected window. These call `split-window` internally.

split-window-right **&optional** *size*   [Command]

> This function splits the selected window into two side-by-side windows, putting the selected window on the left. If *size* is positive, the left window gets *size* columns; if *size* is negative, the right window gets −*size* columns.

split-window-below **&optional** *size*   [Command]

> This function splits the selected window into two windows, one above the other, leaving the upper window selected. If *size* is positive, the upper window gets *size* lines; if *size* is negative, the lower window gets −*size* lines.

split-window-keep-point   [User Option]

> If the value of this variable is non-`nil` (the default), `split-window-below` behaves as described above.
>
> If it is `nil`, `split-window-below` adjusts point in each of the two windows to minimize redisplay. (This is useful on slow terminals.) It selects whichever window contains the

screen line that point was previously on. Note that this only affects `split-window-below`, not the lower-level `split-window` function.

27.7 Deleting Windows

Deleting a window removes it from the frame's window tree. If the window is a live window, it disappears from the screen. If the window is an internal window, its child windows are deleted too.

Even after a window is deleted, it continues to exist as a Lisp object, until there are no more references to it. Window deletion can be reversed, by restoring a saved window configuration (see Section 27.25 [Window Configurations], page 623).

delete-window &optional *window* [Command]

> This function removes *window* from display and returns `nil`. If *window* is omitted or `nil`, it defaults to the selected window. If deleting the window would leave no more windows in the window tree (e.g., if it is the only live window in the frame), an error is signaled.
>
> By default, the space taken up by *window* is given to one of its adjacent sibling windows, if any. However, if the variable `window-combination-resize` is non-`nil`, the space is proportionally distributed among any remaining windows in the same window combination. See Section 27.8 [Recombining Windows], page 585.
>
> The behavior of this function may be altered by the window parameters of *window*, so long as the variable `ignore-window-parameters` is `nil`. If the value of the `delete-window` window parameter is `t`, this function ignores all other window parameters. Otherwise, if the value of the `delete-window` window parameter is a function, that function is called with the argument *window*, in lieu of the usual action of `delete-window`. Otherwise, this function obeys the `window-atom` or `window-side` window parameter, if any. See Section 27.26 [Window Parameters], page 625.

delete-other-windows &optional *window* [Command]

> This function makes *window* fill its frame, by deleting other windows as necessary. If *window* is omitted or `nil`, it defaults to the selected window. The return value is `nil`.
>
> The behavior of this function may be altered by the window parameters of *window*, so long as the variable `ignore-window-parameters` is `nil`. If the value of the `delete-other-windows` window parameter is `t`, this function ignores all other window parameters. Otherwise, if the value of the `delete-other-windows` window parameter is a function, that function is called with the argument *window*, in lieu of the usual action of `delete-other-windows`. Otherwise, this function obeys the `window-atom` or `window-side` window parameter, if any. See Section 27.26 [Window Parameters], page 625.

delete-windows-on &optional *buffer-or-name frame* [Command]

> This function deletes all windows showing *buffer-or-name*, by calling `delete-window` on those windows. *buffer-or-name* should be a buffer, or the name of a buffer; if omitted or `nil`, it defaults to the current buffer. If there are no windows showing the specified buffer, this function does nothing. If the specified buffer is a minibuffer, an error is signaled.

If there is a dedicated window showing the buffer, and that window is the only one on its frame, this function also deletes that frame if it is not the only frame on the terminal.

The optional argument *frame* specifies which frames to operate on:

- `nil` means operate on all frames.
- `t` means operate on the selected frame.
- `visible` means operate on all visible frames.
- `0` means operate on all visible or iconified frames.
- A frame means operate on that frame.

Note that this argument does not have the same meaning as in other functions which scan all live windows (see Section 27.10 [Cyclic Window Ordering], page 591). Specifically, the meanings of `t` and `nil` here are the opposite of what they are in those other functions.

27.8 Recombining Windows

When deleting the last sibling of a window *W*, its parent window is deleted too, with *W* replacing it in the window tree. This means that *W* must be recombined with its parent's siblings to form a new window combination (see Section 27.2 [Windows and Frames], page 568). In some occasions, deleting a live window may even entail the deletion of two internal windows.

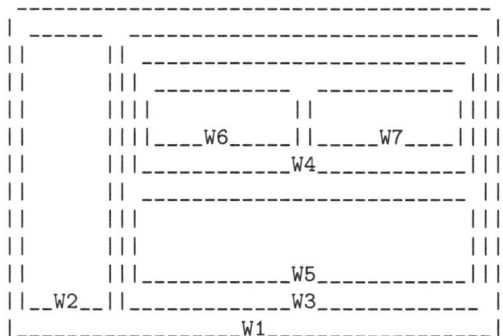

Deleting *W5* in this configuration normally causes the deletion of *W3* and *W4*. The remaining live windows *W2*, *W6* and *W7* are recombined to form a new horizontal combination with parent *W1*.

Sometimes, however, it makes sense to not delete a parent window like *W4*. In particular, a parent window should not be removed when it was used to preserve a combination embedded in a combination of the same type. Such embeddings make sense to assure that when you split a window and subsequently delete the new window, Emacs reestablishes the layout of the associated frame as it existed before the splitting.

Consider a scenario starting with two live windows *W2* and *W3* and their parent *W1*.

Split *W2* to make a new window *W4* as follows.

Now, when enlarging a window vertically, Emacs tries to obtain the corresponding space from its lower sibling, provided such a window exists. In our scenario, enlarging *W4* will steal space from *W3*.

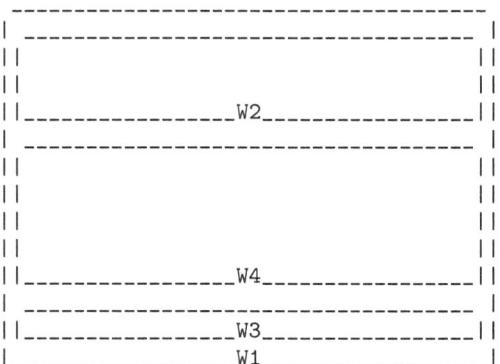

Deleting *W4* will now give its entire space to *W2*, including the space earlier stolen from *W3*.

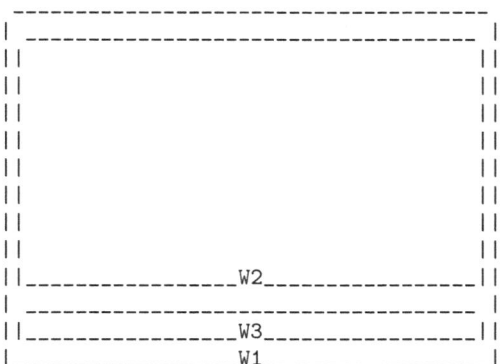

This can be counterintuitive, in particular if *W4* were used for displaying a buffer only temporarily (see Section 37.8 [Temporary Displays], page 900), and you want to continue working with the initial layout.

The behavior can be fixed by making a new parent window when splitting *W2*. The variable described next allows that to be done.

`window-combination-limit`   [User Option]

> This variable controls whether splitting a window shall make a new parent window. The following values are recognized:

> `nil`
>> This means that the new live window is allowed to share the existing parent window, if one exists, provided the split occurs in the same direction as the existing window combination (otherwise, a new internal window is created anyway).

> `window-size`
>> In this case `display-buffer` makes a new parent window if it is passed a `window-height` or `window-width` entry in the *alist* argument (see Section 27.14 [Display Action Functions], page 599).

> `temp-buffer`
>> This value causes the creation of a new parent window when a window is split for showing a temporary buffer (see Section 37.8 [Temporary Displays], page 900) only.

> `display-buffer`
>> This means that when `display-buffer` (see Section 27.13 [Choosing Window], page 598) splits a window it always makes a new parent window.

> `t`
>> In this case a new parent window is always created when splitting a window. Thus, if the value of this variable is at all times `t`, then at all times every window tree is a binary tree (a tree where each window except the root window has exactly one sibling).

> The default is `nil`. Other values are reserved for future use.

> If, as a consequence of this variable's setting, `split-window` makes a new parent window, it also calls `set-window-combination-limit` (see below) on the newly-created

internal window. This affects how the window tree is rearranged when the child windows are deleted (see below).

If `window-combination-limit` is `t`, splitting *W2* in the initial configuration of our scenario would have produced this:

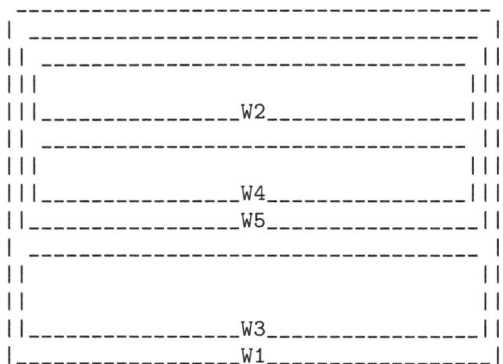

A new internal window *W5* has been created; its children are *W2* and the new live window *W4*. Now, *W2* is the only sibling of *W4*, so enlarging *W4* will try to shrink *W2*, leaving *W3* unaffected. Observe that *W5* represents a vertical combination of two windows embedded in the vertical combination *W1*.

set-window-combination-limit *window limit*   [Function]
> This function sets the *combination limit* of the window *window* to *limit*. This value can be retrieved via the function `window-combination-limit`. See below for its effects; note that it is only meaningful for internal windows. The `split-window` function automatically calls this function, passing it `t` as *limit*, provided the value of the variable `window-combination-limit` is `t` when it is called.

window-combination-limit *window*   [Function]
> This function returns the combination limit for *window*.
>
> The combination limit is meaningful only for an internal window. If it is `nil`, then Emacs is allowed to automatically delete *window*, in response to a window deletion, in order to group the child windows of *window* with its sibling windows to form a new window combination. If the combination limit is `t`, the child windows of *window* are never automatically recombined with its siblings.
>
> If, in the configuration shown at the beginning of this section, the combination limit of *W4* (the parent window of *W6* and *W7*) is `t`, deleting *W5* will not implicitly delete *W4* too.

Alternatively, the problems sketched above can be avoided by always resizing all windows in the same combination whenever one of its windows is split or deleted. This also permits splitting windows that would be otherwise too small for such an operation.

window-combination-resize   [User Option]
> If this variable is `nil`, `split-window` can only split a window (denoted by *window*) if *window*'s screen area is large enough to accommodate both itself and the new window.

If this variable is `t`, `split-window` tries to resize all windows that are part of the same combination as *window*, in order to accommodate the new window. In particular, this may allow `split-window` to succeed even if *window* is a fixed-size window or too small to ordinarily split. Furthermore, subsequently resizing or deleting *window* may resize all other windows in its combination.

The default is `nil`. Other values are reserved for future use. A specific split operation may ignore the value of this variable if it is affected by a non-`nil` value of `window-combination-limit`.

To illustrate the effect of `window-combination-resize`, consider the following frame layout.

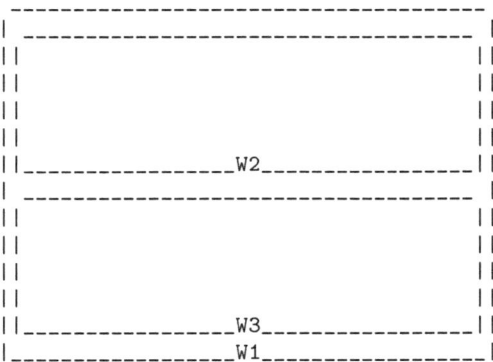

If `window-combination-resize` is `nil`, splitting window *W3* leaves the size of *W2* unchanged:

If `window-combination-resize` is `t`, splitting *W3* instead leaves all three live windows with approximately the same height:

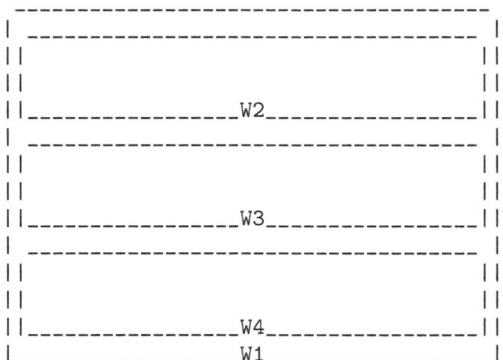

Deleting any of the live windows *W2*, *W3* or *W4* will distribute its space proportionally among the two remaining live windows.

27.9 Selecting Windows

`select-window` *window* **&optional** *norecord*   [Function]

> This function makes *window* the selected window and the window selected within its frame (see Section 27.1 [Basic Windows], page 567) and selects that frame. It also makes *window*'s buffer (see Section 27.11 [Buffers and Windows], page 594) current and sets that buffer's value of `point` to the value of `window-point` (see Section 27.19 [Window Point], page 609) in *window*. *window* must be a live window. The return value is *window*.

> By default, this function also moves *window*'s buffer to the front of the buffer list (see Section 26.8 [Buffer List], page 560), and makes *window* the most recently selected window. However, if the optional argument *norecord* is non-`nil`, these additional actions are omitted.

> This function runs `buffer-list-update-hook` (see Section 26.8 [Buffer List], page 560) unless *norecord* is non-`nil`. Note that applications and internal routines often temporarily select a window in order to simplify coding. As a rule, such selections (including those made by the macros `save-selected-window` and `with-selected-window` below) are not recorded thus avoiding to pollute `buffer-list-update-hook`. Selections that really count are those causing a visible change in the next redisplay of *window*'s frame and should be always recorded. This also means that to run a function each time a window gets selected, putting it on `buffer-list-update-hook` should be the right choice.

The sequence of calls to `select-window` with a non-`nil` *norecord* argument determines an ordering of windows by their selection time. The function `get-lru-window` can be used to retrieve the least recently selected live window (see Section 27.10 [Cyclic Window Ordering], page 591).

`save-selected-window` *forms*...   [Macro]

> This macro records the selected frame, as well as the selected window of each frame, executes *forms* in sequence, then restores the earlier selected frame and windows. It

also saves and restores the current buffer. It returns the value of the last form in *forms*.

This macro does not save or restore anything about the sizes, arrangement or contents of windows; therefore, if *forms* change them, the change persists. If the previously selected window of some frame is no longer live at the time of exit from *forms*, that frame's selected window is left alone. If the previously selected window is no longer live, then whatever window is selected at the end of *forms* remains selected. The current buffer is restored if and only if it is still live when exiting *forms*.

This macro changes neither the ordering of recently selected windows nor the buffer list.

with-selected-window *window forms...*   [Macro]

This macro selects *window*, executes *forms* in sequence, then restores the previously selected window and current buffer. The ordering of recently selected windows and the buffer list remain unchanged unless you deliberately change them within *forms*; for example, by calling `select-window` with argument *norecord* `nil`.

This macro does not change the order of recently selected windows or the buffer list.

frame-selected-window **&optional** *frame*   [Function]

This function returns the window on *frame* that is selected within that frame. *frame* should be a live frame; if omitted or `nil`, it defaults to the selected frame.

set-frame-selected-window *frame window* **&optional** *norecord*   [Function]

This function makes *window* the window selected within the frame *frame*. *frame* should be a live frame; if `nil`, it defaults to the selected frame. *window* should be a live window; if `nil`, it defaults to the selected window.

If *frame* is the selected frame, this makes *window* the selected window.

If the optional argument *norecord* is non-`nil`, this function does not alter the list of most recently selected windows, nor the buffer list.

window-use-time **&optional** *window*   [Function]

This functions returns the use time of window *window*. *window* must be a live window and defaults to the selected one.

The *use time* of a window is not really a time value, but an integer that does increase monotonically with each call of `select-window` with a `nil` *norecord* argument. The window with the lowest use time is usually called the least recently used window while the window with the highest use time is called the most recently used one (see Section 27.10 [Cyclic Window Ordering], page 591).

27.10 Cyclic Ordering of Windows

When you use the command `C-x o` (`other-window`) to select some other window, it moves through live windows in a specific order. For any given configuration of windows, this order never varies. It is called the *cyclic ordering of windows*.

The ordering is determined by a depth-first traversal of each frame's window tree, retrieving the live windows which are the leaf nodes of the tree (see Section 27.2 [Windows and Frames], page 568). If the minibuffer is active, the minibuffer window is included too. The ordering is cyclic, so the last window in the sequence is followed by the first one.

next-window **&optional** *window minibuf all-frames*   [Function]

This function returns a live window, the one following *window* in the cyclic ordering of windows. *window* should be a live window; if omitted or **nil**, it defaults to the selected window.

The optional argument *minibuf* specifies whether minibuffer windows should be included in the cyclic ordering. Normally, when *minibuf* is **nil**, a minibuffer window is included only if it is currently active; this matches the behavior of *C-x o*. (Note that a minibuffer window is active as long as its minibuffer is in use; see Chapter 19 [Minibuffers], page 313).

If *minibuf* is **t**, the cyclic ordering includes all minibuffer windows. If *minibuf* is neither **t** nor **nil**, minibuffer windows are not included even if they are active.

The optional argument *all-frames* specifies which frames to consider:

- **nil** means to consider windows on *window*'s frame. If the minibuffer window is considered (as specified by the *minibuf* argument), then frames that share the minibuffer window are considered too.

- **t** means to consider windows on all existing frames.

- **visible** means to consider windows on all visible frames.

- 0 means to consider windows on all visible or iconified frames.

- A frame means to consider windows on that specific frame.

- Anything else means to consider windows on *window*'s frame, and no others.

If more than one frame is considered, the cyclic ordering is obtained by appending the orderings for those frames, in the same order as the list of all live frames (see Section 28.8 [Finding All Frames], page 655).

previous-window **&optional** *window minibuf all-frames*   [Function]

This function returns a live window, the one preceding *window* in the cyclic ordering of windows. The other arguments are handled like in **next-window**.

other-window *count* **&optional** *all-frames*   [Command]

This function selects a live window, one *count* places from the selected window in the cyclic ordering of windows. If *count* is a positive number, it skips *count* windows forwards; if *count* is negative, it skips −*count* windows backwards; if *count* is zero, that simply re-selects the selected window. When called interactively, *count* is the numeric prefix argument.

The optional argument *all-frames* has the same meaning as in **next-window**, like a **nil** *minibuf* argument to **next-window**.

This function does not select a window that has a non-**nil** **no-other-window** window parameter (see Section 27.26 [Window Parameters], page 625).

walk-windows *fun* **&optional** *minibuf all-frames*   [Function]

This function calls the function *fun* once for each live window, with the window as the argument.

It follows the cyclic ordering of windows. The optional arguments *minibuf* and *all-frames* specify the set of windows included; these have the same arguments as in **next-window**. If *all-frames* specifies a frame, the first window walked is the first window on that frame (the one returned by `frame-first-window`), not necessarily the selected window.

If *fun* changes the window configuration by splitting or deleting windows, that does not alter the set of windows walked, which is determined prior to calling *fun* for the first time.

`one-window-p` **&optional** *no-mini all-frames* [Function]

This function returns `t` if the selected window is the only live window, and `nil` otherwise.

If the minibuffer window is active, it is normally considered (so that this function returns `nil`). However, if the optional argument *no-mini* is non-`nil`, the minibuffer window is ignored even if active. The optional argument *all-frames* has the same meaning as for `next-window`.

The following functions return a window which satisfies some criterion, without selecting it:

`get-lru-window` **&optional** *all-frames dedicated not-selected* [Function]

This function returns a live window which is heuristically the least recently used. The optional argument *all-frames* has the same meaning as in `next-window`.

If any full-width windows are present, only those windows are considered. A minibuffer window is never a candidate. A dedicated window (see Section 27.17 [Dedicated Windows], page 606) is never a candidate unless the optional argument *dedicated* is non-`nil`. The selected window is never returned, unless it is the only candidate. However, if the optional argument *not-selected* is non-`nil`, this function returns `nil` in that case.

`get-mru-window` **&optional** *all-frames dedicated not-selected* [Function]

This function is like `get-lru-window`, but it returns the most recently used window instead. The meaning of the arguments is the same as described for `get-lru-window`.

`get-largest-window` **&optional** *all-frames dedicated not-selected* [Function]

This function returns the window with the largest area (height times width). The optional argument *all-frames* specifies the windows to search, and has the same meaning as in `next-window`.

A minibuffer window is never a candidate. A dedicated window (see Section 27.17 [Dedicated Windows], page 606) is never a candidate unless the optional argument *dedicated* is non-`nil`. The selected window is not a candidate if the optional argument *not-selected* is non-`nil`. If the optional argument *not-selected* is non-`nil` and the selected window is the only candidate, this function returns `nil`.

If there are two candidate windows of the same size, this function prefers the one that comes first in the cyclic ordering of windows, starting from the selected window.

`get-window-with-predicate` *predicate* **&optional** *minibuf all-frames* [Function]
    default

This function calls the function *predicate* for each of the windows in the cyclic order of windows in turn, passing it the window as an argument. If the predicate returns non-`nil` for any window, this function stops and returns that window. If no such window is found, the return value is *default* (which defaults to `nil`).

The optional arguments *minibuf* and *all-frames* specify the windows to search, and have the same meanings as in `next-window`.

27.11 Buffers and Windows

This section describes low-level functions for examining and setting the contents of windows. See Section 27.12 [Switching Buffers], page 595, for higher-level functions for displaying a specific buffer in a window.

`window-buffer` **&optional** *window*   [Function]
> This function returns the buffer that *window* is displaying. If *window* is omitted or `nil` it defaults to the selected window. If *window* is an internal window, this function returns `nil`.

`set-window-buffer` *window buffer-or-name* **&optional** *keep-margins*   [Function]
> This function makes *window* display *buffer-or-name*. *window* should be a live window; if `nil`, it defaults to the selected window. *buffer-or-name* should be a buffer, or the name of an existing buffer. This function does not change which window is selected, nor does it directly change which buffer is current (see Section 26.2 [Current Buffer], page 550). Its return value is `nil`.
>
> If *window* is *strongly dedicated* to a buffer and *buffer-or-name* does not specify that buffer, this function signals an error. See Section 27.17 [Dedicated Windows], page 606.
>
> By default, this function resets *window*'s position, display margins, fringe widths, and scroll bar settings, based on the local variables in the specified buffer. However, if the optional argument *keep-margins* is non-`nil`, it leaves the display margins and fringe widths unchanged.
>
> When writing an application, you should normally use the higher-level functions described in Section 27.12 [Switching Buffers], page 595, instead of calling `set-window-buffer` directly.
>
> This runs `window-scroll-functions`, followed by `window-configuration-change-hook`. See Section 27.27 [Window Hooks], page 628.

`buffer-display-count`   [Variable]
> This buffer-local variable records the number of times a buffer has been displayed in a window. It is incremented each time `set-window-buffer` is called for the buffer.

`buffer-display-time`   [Variable]
> This buffer-local variable records the time at which a buffer was last displayed in a window. The value is `nil` if the buffer has never been displayed. It is updated each time `set-window-buffer` is called for the buffer, with the value returned by `current-time` (see Section 38.5 [Time of Day], page 999).

`get-buffer-window` **&optional** *buffer-or-name all-frames*   [Function]
> This function returns the first window displaying *buffer-or-name* in the cyclic ordering of windows, starting from the selected window (see Section 27.10 [Cyclic Window Ordering], page 591). If no such window exists, the return value is `nil`.

buffer-or-name should be a buffer or the name of a buffer; if omitted or `nil`, it defaults to the current buffer. The optional argument *all-frames* specifies which windows to consider:

- `t` means consider windows on all existing frames.

- `visible` means consider windows on all visible frames.

- 0 means consider windows on all visible or iconified frames.

- A frame means consider windows on that frame only.

- Any other value means consider windows on the selected frame.

Note that these meanings differ slightly from those of the *all-frames* argument to `next-window` (see Section 27.10 [Cyclic Window Ordering], page 591). This function may be changed in a future version of Emacs to eliminate this discrepancy.

`get-buffer-window-list` **&optional** *buffer-or-name minibuf*   [Function]
   all-frames
  This function returns a list of all windows currently displaying *buffer-or-name*. *buffer-or-name* should be a buffer or the name of an existing buffer. If omitted or `nil`, it defaults to the current buffer. If the currently selected window displays *buffer-or-name*, it will be the first in the list returned by this function.

  The arguments *minibuf* and *all-frames* have the same meanings as in the function `next-window` (see Section 27.10 [Cyclic Window Ordering], page 591). Note that the *all-frames* argument does *not* behave exactly like in `get-buffer-window`.

`replace-buffer-in-windows` **&optional** *buffer-or-name*   [Command]
  This command replaces *buffer-or-name* with some other buffer, in all windows displaying it. *buffer-or-name* should be a buffer, or the name of an existing buffer; if omitted or `nil`, it defaults to the current buffer.

  The replacement buffer in each window is chosen via `switch-to-prev-buffer` (see Section 27.16 [Window History], page 605). Any dedicated window displaying *buffer-or-name* is deleted if possible (see Section 27.17 [Dedicated Windows], page 606). If such a window is the only window on its frame and there are other frames on the same terminal, the frame is deleted as well. If the dedicated window is the only window on the only frame on its terminal, the buffer is replaced anyway.

27.12 Switching to a Buffer in a Window

This section describes high-level functions for switching to a specified buffer in some window. In general, "switching to a buffer" means to (1) show the buffer in some window, (2) make that window the selected window (and its frame the selected frame), and (3) make the buffer the current buffer.

 Do *not* use these functions to make a buffer temporarily current just so a Lisp program can access or modify it. They have side-effects, such as changing window histories (see Section 27.16 [Window History], page 605), which will surprise the user if used that way. If you want to make a buffer current to modify it in Lisp, use `with-current-buffer`, `save-current-buffer`, or `set-buffer`. See Section 26.2 [Current Buffer], page 550.

`switch-to-buffer` *buffer-or-name* **&optional** *norecord*   [Command]
      force-same-window

> This command attempts to display *buffer-or-name* in the selected window and make it the current buffer. It is often used interactively (as the binding of `C-x b`), as well as in Lisp programs. The return value is the buffer switched to.
>
> If *buffer-or-name* is `nil`, it defaults to the buffer returned by `other-buffer` (see Section 26.8 [Buffer List], page 560). If *buffer-or-name* is a string that is not the name of any existing buffer, this function creates a new buffer with that name; the new buffer's major mode is determined by the variable `major-mode` (see Section 22.2 [Major Modes], page 431).
>
> Normally, the specified buffer is put at the front of the buffer list—both the global buffer list and the selected frame's buffer list (see Section 26.8 [Buffer List], page 560). However, this is not done if the optional argument *norecord* is non-`nil`.
>
> Sometimes, the selected window may not be suitable for displaying the buffer. This happens if the selected window is a minibuffer window, or if the selected window is strongly dedicated to its buffer (see Section 27.17 [Dedicated Windows], page 606). In such cases, the command normally tries to display the buffer in some other window, by invoking `pop-to-buffer` (see below).
>
> If the optional argument *force-same-window* is non-`nil` and the selected window is not suitable for displaying the buffer, this function always signals an error when called non-interactively. In interactive use, if the selected window is a minibuffer window, this function will try to use some other window instead. If the selected window is strongly dedicated to its buffer, the option `switch-to-buffer-in-dedicated-window` described next can be used to proceed.

`switch-to-buffer-in-dedicated-window`   [User Option]

> This option, if non-`nil`, allows `switch-to-buffer` to proceed when called interactively and the selected window is strongly dedicated to its buffer.
>
> The following values are respected:

> `nil`   Disallows switching and signals an error as in non-interactive use.
>
> `prompt`   Prompts the user whether to allow switching.
>
> `pop`   Invokes `pop-to-buffer` to proceed.
>
> `t`   Marks the selected window as non-dedicated and proceeds.

> This option does not affect non-interactive calls of `switch-to-buffer`.

By default, `switch-to-buffer` shows the buffer at its position of `point`. This behavior can be tuned using the following option.

`switch-to-buffer-preserve-window-point`   [User Option]

> If this variable is `nil`, `switch-to-buffer` displays the buffer specified by *buffer-or-name* at the position of that buffer's `point`. If this variable is `already-displayed`, it tries to display the buffer at its previous position in the selected window, provided the buffer is currently displayed in some other window on any visible or iconified frame. If this variable is `t`, `switch-to-buffer` unconditionally tries to display the buffer at its previous position in the selected window.

This variable is ignored if the buffer is already displayed in the selected window or never appeared in it before, or if `switch-to-buffer` calls `pop-to-buffer` to display the buffer.

The next two commands are similar to `switch-to-buffer`, except for the described features.

`switch-to-buffer-other-window` *buffer-or-name* **&optional**   [Command]
    norecord

This function displays the buffer specified by *buffer-or-name* in some window other than the selected window. It uses the function `pop-to-buffer` internally (see below).

If the selected window already displays the specified buffer, it continues to do so, but another window is nonetheless found to display it as well.

The *buffer-or-name* and *norecord* arguments have the same meanings as in `switch-to-buffer`.

`switch-to-buffer-other-frame` *buffer-or-name* **&optional**   [Command]
    norecord

This function displays the buffer specified by *buffer-or-name* in a new frame. It uses the function `pop-to-buffer` internally (see below).

If the specified buffer is already displayed in another window, in any frame on the current terminal, this switches to that window instead of creating a new frame. However, the selected window is never used for this.

The *buffer-or-name* and *norecord* arguments have the same meanings as in `switch-to-buffer`.

The above commands use the function `pop-to-buffer`, which flexibly displays a buffer in some window and selects that window for editing. In turn, `pop-to-buffer` uses `display-buffer` for displaying the buffer. Hence, all the variables affecting `display-buffer` will affect it as well. See Section 27.13 [Choosing Window], page 598, for the documentation of `display-buffer`.

`pop-to-buffer` *buffer-or-name* **&optional** *action norecord*   [Command]

This function makes *buffer-or-name* the current buffer and displays it in some window, preferably not the window currently selected. It then selects the displaying window. If that window is on a different graphical frame, that frame is given input focus if possible (see Section 28.10 [Input Focus], page 656). The return value is the buffer that was switched to.

If *buffer-or-name* is `nil`, it defaults to the buffer returned by `other-buffer` (see Section 26.8 [Buffer List], page 560). If *buffer-or-name* is a string that is not the name of any existing buffer, this function creates a new buffer with that name; the new buffer's major mode is determined by the variable `major-mode` (see Section 22.2 [Major Modes], page 431).

If *action* is non-`nil`, it should be a display action to pass to `display-buffer` (see Section 27.13 [Choosing Window], page 598). Alternatively, a non-`nil`, non-list value means to pop to a window other than the selected one—even if the buffer is already displayed in the selected window.

Like `switch-to-buffer`, this function updates the buffer list unless *norecord* is non-nil.

27.13 Choosing a Window for Display

The command `display-buffer` flexibly chooses a window for display, and displays a specified buffer in that window. It can be called interactively, via the key binding *C-x 4 C-o*. It is also used as a subroutine by many functions and commands, including `switch-to-buffer` and `pop-to-buffer` (see Section 27.12 [Switching Buffers], page 595).

This command performs several complex steps to find a window to display in. These steps are described by means of *display actions*, which have the form (`function . alist`). Here, *function* is either a function or a list of functions, which we refer to as *action functions*; *alist* is an association list, which we refer to as an *action alist*.

An action function accepts two arguments: the buffer to display and an action alist. It attempts to display the buffer in some window, picking or creating a window according to its own criteria. If successful, it returns the window; otherwise, it returns `nil`. See Section 27.14 [Display Action Functions], page 599, for a list of predefined action functions.

`display-buffer` works by combining display actions from several sources, and calling the action functions in turn, until one of them manages to display the buffer and returns a non-`nil` value.

`display-buffer` *buffer-or-name* **&optional** *action frame*   [Command]

> This command makes *buffer-or-name* appear in some window, without selecting the window or making the buffer current. The argument *buffer-or-name* must be a buffer or the name of an existing buffer. The return value is the window chosen to display the buffer.
>
> The optional argument *action*, if non-`nil`, should normally be a display action (described above). `display-buffer` builds a list of action functions and an action alist, by consolidating display actions from the following sources (in order):
>
> - The variable `display-buffer-overriding-action`.
> - The user option `display-buffer-alist`.
> - The *action* argument.
> - The user option `display-buffer-base-action`.
> - The constant `display-buffer-fallback-action`.
>
> Each action function is called in turn, passing the buffer as the first argument and the combined action alist as the second argument, until one of the functions returns non-`nil`. The caller can pass (`allow-no-window . t`) as an element of the action alist to indicate its readiness to handle the case of not displaying the buffer in a window.
>
> The argument *action* can also have a non-`nil`, non-list value. This has the special meaning that the buffer should be displayed in a window other than the selected one, even if the selected window is already displaying it. If called interactively with a prefix argument, *action* is `t`.
>
> The optional argument *frame*, if non-`nil`, specifies which frames to check when deciding whether the buffer is already displayed. It is equivalent to adding an element (`reusable-frames . frame`) to the action alist of *action*. See Section 27.14 [Display Action Functions], page 599.

display-buffer-overriding-action   [Variable]

The value of this variable should be a display action, which is treated with the highest priority by `display-buffer`. The default value is empty, i.e., `(nil . nil)`.

display-buffer-alist   [User Option]

The value of this option is an alist mapping conditions to display actions. Each condition may be either a regular expression matching a buffer name or a function that takes two arguments: a buffer name and the *action* argument passed to `display-buffer`. If the name of the buffer passed to `display-buffer` either matches a regular expression in this alist or the function specified by a condition returns non-`nil`, then `display-buffer` uses the corresponding display action to display the buffer.

display-buffer-base-action   [User Option]

The value of this option should be a display action. This option can be used to define a standard display action for calls to `display-buffer`.

display-buffer-fallback-action   [Constant]

This display action specifies the fallback behavior for `display-buffer` if no other display actions are given.

27.14 Action Functions for `display-buffer`

The following basic action functions are defined in Emacs. Each of these functions takes two arguments: *buffer*, the buffer to display, and *alist*, an action alist. Each action function returns the window if it succeeds, and `nil` if it fails.

display-buffer-same-window *buffer alist*   [Function]

This function tries to display *buffer* in the selected window. It fails if the selected window is a minibuffer window or is dedicated to another buffer (see Section 27.17 [Dedicated Windows], page 606). It also fails if *alist* has a non-`nil` `inhibit-same-window` entry.

display-buffer-reuse-window *buffer alist*   [Function]

This function tries to display *buffer* by finding a window that is already displaying it.

If *alist* has a non-`nil` `inhibit-same-window` entry, the selected window is not eligible for reuse. If *alist* contains a `reusable-frames` entry, its value determines which frames to search for a reusable window:

- `nil` means consider windows on the selected frame. (Actually, the last non-minibuffer frame.)
- `t` means consider windows on all frames.
- `visible` means consider windows on all visible frames.
- `0` means consider windows on all visible or iconified frames.
- A frame means consider windows on that frame only.

Note that these meanings differ slightly from those of the *all-frames* argument to `next-window` (see Section 27.10 [Cyclic Window Ordering], page 591).

If *alist* contains no `reusable-frames` entry, this function normally searches just the selected frame; however, if the variable `pop-up-frames` is non-`nil`, it searches all frames on the current terminal. See Section 27.15 [Choosing Window Options], page 603.

If this function chooses a window on another frame, it makes that frame visible and, unless *alist* contains an `inhibit-switch-frame` entry (see Section 27.15 [Choosing Window Options], page 603), raises that frame if necessary.

`display-buffer-pop-up-frame` *buffer alist*   [Function]
This function creates a new frame, and displays the buffer in that frame's window. It actually performs the frame creation by calling the function specified in `pop-up-frame-function` (see Section 27.15 [Choosing Window Options], page 603). If *alist* contains a `pop-up-frame-parameters` entry, the associated value is added to the newly created frame's parameters.

`display-buffer-use-some-frame` *buffer alist*   [Function]
This function tries to display *buffer* by trying to find a frame that meets a predicate (by default any frame other than the current frame).

If this function chooses a window on another frame, it makes that frame visible and, unless *alist* contains an `inhibit-switch-frame` entry (see Section 27.15 [Choosing Window Options], page 603), raises that frame if necessary.

If *alist* has a non-`nil` `frame-predicate` entry, its value is a function taking one argument (a frame), returning non-`nil` if the frame is a candidate; this function replaces the default predicate.

If *alist* has a non-`nil` `inhibit-same-window` entry, the selected window is used; thus if the selected frame has a single window, it is not used.

`display-buffer-pop-up-window` *buffer alist*   [Function]
This function tries to display *buffer* by splitting the largest or least recently-used window (typically one on the selected frame). It actually performs the split by calling the function specified in `split-window-preferred-function` (see Section 27.15 [Choosing Window Options], page 603).

The size of the new window can be adjusted by supplying `window-height` and `window-width` entries in *alist*. To adjust the window's height, use an entry whose CAR is `window-height` and whose CDR is one of:

- `nil` means to leave the height of the new window alone.
- A number specifies the desired height of the new window. An integer specifies the number of lines of the window. A floating-point number gives the fraction of the window's height with respect to the height of the frame's root window.
- If the CDR specifies a function, that function is called with one argument: the new window. The function is supposed to adjust the height of the window; its return value is ignored. Suitable functions are `shrink-window-if-larger-than-buffer` and `fit-window-to-buffer`, see Section 27.4 [Resizing Windows], page 576.

To adjust the window's width, use an entry whose CAR is `window-width` and whose CDR is one of:

- `nil` means to leave the width of the new window alone.

- A number specifies the desired width of the new window. An integer specifies the number of columns of the window. A floating-point number gives the fraction of the window's width with respect to the width of the frame's root window.

- If the CDR specifies a function, that function is called with one argument: the new window. The function is supposed to adjust the width of the window; its return value is ignored.

If *alist* contains a `preserve-size` entry, Emacs will try to preserve the size of the new window during future resize operations (see Section 27.5 [Preserving Window Sizes], page 580). The CDR of that entry must be a cons cell whose CAR, if non-`nil`, means to preserve the width of the window and whose CDR, if non-`nil`, means to preserve the height of the window.

This function can fail if no window splitting can be performed for some reason (e.g., if the selected frame has an `unsplittable` frame parameter; see Section 28.4.3.5 [Buffer Parameters], page 649).

`display-buffer-below-selected` *buffer alist*   [Function]
  This function tries to display *buffer* in a window below the selected window. This means to either split the selected window or use the window below the selected one. If it does create a new window, it will also adjust its size provided *alist* contains a suitable `window-height` or `window-width` entry, see above.

`display-buffer-in-previous-window` *buffer alist*   [Function]
  This function tries to display *buffer* in a window previously showing it. If *alist* has a non-`nil` `inhibit-same-window` entry, the selected window is not eligible for reuse. If *alist* contains a `reusable-frames` entry, its value determines which frames to search for a suitable window as with `display-buffer-reuse-window`.

  If *alist* has a `previous-window` entry, the window specified by that entry will override any other window found by the methods above, even if that window never showed *buffer* before.

`display-buffer-at-bottom` *buffer alist*   [Function]
  This function tries to display *buffer* in a window at the bottom of the selected frame.

  This either splits the window at the bottom of the frame or the frame's root window, or reuses an existing window at the bottom of the selected frame.

`display-buffer-use-some-window` *buffer alist*   [Function]
  This function tries to display *buffer* by choosing an existing window and displaying the buffer in that window. It can fail if all windows are dedicated to another buffer (see Section 27.17 [Dedicated Windows], page 606).

`display-buffer-no-window` *buffer alist*   [Function]
  If *alist* has a non-`nil` `allow-no-window` entry, then this function does not display `buffer`. This allows you to override the default action and avoid displaying the buffer. It is assumed that when the caller specifies a non-`nil` `allow-no-window` value it can handle a `nil` value returned from `display-buffer` in this case.

To illustrate the use of action functions, consider the following example.

```
(display-buffer
 (get-buffer-create "*foo*")
 '((display-buffer-reuse-window
    display-buffer-pop-up-window
    display-buffer-pop-up-frame)
   (reusable-frames . 0)
   (window-height . 10) (window-width . 40)))
```

Evaluating the form above will cause `display-buffer` to proceed as follows: If a buffer called *foo* already appears on a visible or iconified frame, it will reuse its window. Otherwise, it will try to pop up a new window or, if that is impossible, a new frame and show the buffer there. If all these steps fail, it will proceed using whatever `display-buffer-base-action` and `display-buffer-fallback-action` prescribe.

Furthermore, `display-buffer` will try to adjust a reused window (provided *foo* was put by `display-buffer` there before) or a popped-up window as follows: If the window is part of a vertical combination, it will set its height to ten lines. Note that if, instead of the number 10, we specified the function `fit-window-to-buffer`, `display-buffer` would come up with a one-line window to fit the empty buffer. If the window is part of a horizontal combination, it sets its width to 40 columns. Whether a new window is vertically or horizontally combined depends on the shape of the window split and the values of `split-window-preferred-function`, `split-height-threshold` and `split-width-threshold` (see Section 27.15 [Choosing Window Options], page 603).

Now suppose we combine this call with a preexisting setup for `display-buffer-alist` as follows.

```
(let ((display-buffer-alist
       (cons
        '("\\*foo\\*"
          (display-buffer-reuse-window display-buffer-below-selected)
          (reusable-frames)
          (window-height . 5))
        display-buffer-alist)))
  (display-buffer
   (get-buffer-create "*foo*")
   '((display-buffer-reuse-window
      display-buffer-pop-up-window
      display-buffer-pop-up-frame)
     (reusable-frames . 0)
     (window-height . 10) (window-width . 40))))
```

This form will have `display-buffer` first try reusing a window that shows *foo* on the selected frame. If there's no such window, it will try to split the selected window or, if that is impossible, use the window below the selected window.

If there's no window below the selected one, or the window below the selected one is dedicated to its buffer, `display-buffer` will proceed as described in the previous example. Note, however, that when it tries to adjust the height of any reused or popped-up window, it will in any case try to set its number of lines to 5 since that value overrides the corresponding specification in the *action* argument of `display-buffer`.

27.15 Additional Options for Displaying Buffers

The behavior of the standard display actions of `display-buffer` (see Section 27.13 [Choosing Window], page 598) can be modified by a variety of user options.

`pop-up-windows`   [User Option]

> If the value of this variable is non-`nil`, `display-buffer` is allowed to split an existing window to make a new window for displaying in. This is the default.
>
> This variable is provided mainly for backward compatibility. It is obeyed by `display-buffer` via a special mechanism in `display-buffer-fallback-action`, which only calls the action function `display-buffer-pop-up-window` (see Section 27.14 [Display Action Functions], page 599) when the value is `nil`. It is not consulted by `display-buffer-pop-up-window` itself, which the user may specify directly in `display-buffer-alist` etc.

`split-window-preferred-function`   [User Option]

> This variable specifies a function for splitting a window, in order to make a new window for displaying a buffer. It is used by the `display-buffer-pop-up-window` action function to actually split the window (see Section 27.14 [Display Action Functions], page 599).
>
> The default value is `split-window-sensibly`, which is documented below. The value must be a function that takes one argument, a window, and return either a new window (which will be used to display the desired buffer) or `nil` (which means the splitting failed).

`split-window-sensibly` **&optional** *window*   [Function]

> This function tries to split *window*, and return the newly created window. If *window* cannot be split, it returns `nil`. If *window* is omitted or `nil`, it defaults to the selected window.
>
> This function obeys the usual rules that determine when a window may be split (see Section 27.6 [Splitting Windows], page 581). It first tries to split by placing the new window below, subject to the restriction imposed by `split-height-threshold` (see below), in addition to any other restrictions. If that fails, it tries to split by placing the new window to the right, subject to `split-width-threshold` (see below). If that fails, and the window is the only window on its frame, this function again tries to split and place the new window below, disregarding `split-height-threshold`. If this fails as well, this function gives up and returns `nil`.

`split-height-threshold`   [User Option]

> This variable, used by `split-window-sensibly`, specifies whether to split the window placing the new window below. If it is an integer, that means to split only if the original window has at least that many lines. If it is `nil`, that means not to split this way.

split-width-threshold   [User Option]

    This variable, used by `split-window-sensibly`, specifies whether to split the window placing the new window to the right. If the value is an integer, that means to split only if the original window has at least that many columns. If the value is `nil`, that means not to split this way.

even-window-sizes   [User Option]

    This variable, if non-`nil`, causes `display-buffer` to even window sizes whenever it reuses an existing window and that window is adjacent to the selected one.

    If its value is `width-only`, sizes are evened only if the reused window is on the left or right of the selected one and the selected window is wider than the reused one. If its value is `height-only` sizes are evened only if the reused window is above or beneath the selected window and the selected window is higher than the reused one. Any other non-`nil` value means to even sizes in any of these cases provided the selected window is larger than the reused one in the sense of their combination.

pop-up-frames   [User Option]

    If the value of this variable is non-`nil`, that means `display-buffer` may display buffers by making new frames. The default is `nil`.

    A non-`nil` value also means that when `display-buffer` is looking for a window already displaying *buffer-or-name*, it can search any visible or iconified frame, not just the selected frame.

    This variable is provided mainly for backward compatibility. It is obeyed by `display-buffer` via a special mechanism in `display-buffer-fallback-action`, which calls the action function `display-buffer-pop-up-frame` (see Section 27.14 [Display Action Functions], page 599) if the value is non-`nil`. (This is done before attempting to split a window.) This variable is not consulted by `display-buffer-pop-up-frame` itself, which the user may specify directly in `display-buffer-alist` etc.

pop-up-frame-function   [User Option]

    This variable specifies a function for creating a new frame, in order to make a new window for displaying a buffer. It is used by the `display-buffer-pop-up-frame` action function (see Section 27.14 [Display Action Functions], page 599).

    The value should be a function that takes no arguments and returns a frame, or `nil` if no frame could be created. The default value is a function that creates a frame using the parameters specified by `pop-up-frame-alist` (see below).

pop-up-frame-alist   [User Option]

    This variable holds an alist of frame parameters (see Section 28.4 [Frame Parameters], page 642), which is used by the default function in `pop-up-frame-function` to make a new frame. The default is `nil`.

same-window-buffer-names   [User Option]

    A list of buffer names for buffers that should be displayed in the selected window. If a buffer's name is in this list, `display-buffer` handles the buffer by showing it in the selected window.

`same-window-regexps`   [User Option]

> A list of regular expressions that specify buffers that should be displayed in the selected window. If the buffer's name matches any of the regular expressions in this list, `display-buffer` handles the buffer by showing it in the selected window.

`same-window-p` *buffer-name*   [Function]

> This function returns `t` if displaying a buffer named *buffer-name* with `display-buffer` would put it in the selected window.

27.16 Window History

Each window remembers in a list the buffers it has previously displayed, and the order in which these buffers were removed from it. This history is used, for example, by `replace-buffer-in-windows` (see Section 27.11 [Buffers and Windows], page 594), and when quitting windows (see Section 27.18 [Quitting Windows], page 607). The list is automatically maintained by Emacs, but you can use the following functions to explicitly inspect or alter it:

`window-prev-buffers` **&optional** *window*   [Function]

> This function returns a list specifying the previous contents of *window*. The optional argument *window* should be a live window and defaults to the selected one.
>
> Each list element has the form (`buffer window-start window-pos`), where *buffer* is a buffer previously shown in the window, *window-start* is the window start position (see Section 27.20 [Window Start and End], page 610) when that buffer was last shown, and *window-pos* is the point position (see Section 27.19 [Window Point], page 609) when that buffer was last shown in *window*.
>
> The list is ordered so that earlier elements correspond to more recently-shown buffers, and the first element usually corresponds to the buffer most recently removed from the window.

`set-window-prev-buffers` *window prev-buffers*   [Function]

> This function sets *window*'s previous buffers to the value of *prev-buffers*. The argument *window* must be a live window and defaults to the selected one. The argument *prev-buffers* should be a list of the same form as that returned by `window-prev-buffers`.

In addition, each buffer maintains a list of *next buffers*, which is a list of buffers re-shown by `switch-to-prev-buffer` (see below). This list is mainly used by `switch-to-prev-buffer` and `switch-to-next-buffer` for choosing buffers to switch to.

`window-next-buffers` **&optional** *window*   [Function]

> This function returns the list of buffers recently re-shown in *window* via `switch-to-prev-buffer`. The *window* argument must denote a live window or `nil` (meaning the selected window).

`set-window-next-buffers` *window next-buffers*   [Function]

> This function sets the next buffer list of *window* to *next-buffers*. The *window* argument should be a live window or `nil` (meaning the selected window). The argument *next-buffers* should be a list of buffers.

The following commands can be used to cycle through the global buffer list, much like `bury-buffer` and `unbury-buffer`. However, they cycle according to the specified window's history list, rather than the global buffer list. In addition, they restore window-specific window start and point positions, and may show a buffer even if it is already shown in another window. The `switch-to-prev-buffer` command, in particular, is used by `replace-buffer-in-windows`, `bury-buffer` and `quit-window` to find a replacement buffer for a window.

`switch-to-prev-buffer` **&optional** *window bury-or-kill*   [Command]

> This command displays the previous buffer in *window*. The argument *window* should be a live window or `nil` (meaning the selected window). If the optional argument *bury-or-kill* is non-`nil`, this means that the buffer currently shown in *window* is about to be buried or killed and consequently should not be switched to in future invocations of this command.
>
> The previous buffer is usually the buffer shown before the buffer currently shown in *window*. However, a buffer that has been buried or killed, or has been already shown by a recent invocation of `switch-to-prev-buffer`, does not qualify as previous buffer.
>
> If repeated invocations of this command have already shown all buffers previously shown in *window*, further invocations will show buffers from the buffer list of the frame *window* appears on (see Section 26.8 [Buffer List], page 560), trying to skip buffers that are already shown in another window on that frame.

`switch-to-next-buffer` **&optional** *window*   [Command]

> This command switches to the next buffer in *window*, thus undoing the effect of the last `switch-to-prev-buffer` command in *window*. The argument *window* must be a live window and defaults to the selected one.
>
> If there is no recent invocation of `switch-to-prev-buffer` that can be undone, this function tries to show a buffer from the buffer list of the frame *window* appears on (see Section 26.8 [Buffer List], page 560).

By default `switch-to-prev-buffer` and `switch-to-next-buffer` can switch to a buffer that is already shown in another window on the same frame. The following option can be used to override this behavior.

`switch-to-visible-buffer`   [User Option]

> If this variable is non-`nil`, `switch-to-prev-buffer` and `switch-to-next-buffer` may switch to a buffer that is already visible on the same frame, provided the buffer was shown in the relevant window before. If it is `nil`, `switch-to-prev-buffer` and `switch-to-next-buffer` always try to avoid switching to a buffer that is already visible in another window on the same frame. The default is `t`.

27.17 Dedicated Windows

Functions for displaying a buffer can be told to not use specific windows by marking these windows as *dedicated* to their buffers. `display-buffer` (see Section 27.13 [Choosing Window], page 598) never uses a dedicated window for displaying another buffer in it. `get-lru-window` and `get-largest-window` (see Section 27.10 [Cyclic Window Ordering], page 591) do not consider dedicated windows as candidates when their *dedicated* argument is non-`nil`. The behavior of `set-window-buffer` (see Section 27.11 [Buffers and Windows], page 594) with respect to dedicated windows is slightly different, see below.

Functions supposed to remove a buffer from a window or a window from a frame can behave specially when a window they operate on is dedicated. We will distinguish three basic cases, namely where (1) the window is not the only window on its frame, (2) the window is the only window on its frame but there are other frames on the same terminal left, and (3) the window is the only window on the only frame on the same terminal.

In particular, `delete-windows-on` (see Section 27.7 [Deleting Windows], page 584) handles case (2) by deleting the associated frame and case (3) by showing another buffer in that frame's only window. The function `replace-buffer-in-windows` (see Section 27.11 [Buffers and Windows], page 594) which is called when a buffer gets killed, deletes the window in case (1) and behaves like `delete-windows-on` otherwise.

When `bury-buffer` (see Section 26.8 [Buffer List], page 560) operates on the selected window (which shows the buffer that shall be buried), it handles case (2) by calling `frame-auto-hide-function` (see Section 27.18 [Quitting Windows], page 607) to deal with the selected frame. The other two cases are handled as with `replace-buffer-in-windows`.

`window-dedicated-p` **&optional** *window*   [Function]
> This function returns non-`nil` if *window* is dedicated to its buffer and `nil` otherwise. More precisely, the return value is the value assigned by the last call of `set-window-dedicated-p` for *window*, or `nil` if that function was never called with *window* as its argument. The default for *window* is the selected window.

`set-window-dedicated-p` *window flag*   [Function]
> This function marks *window* as dedicated to its buffer if *flag* is non-`nil`, and non-dedicated otherwise.
>
> As a special case, if *flag* is `t`, *window* becomes *strongly* dedicated to its buffer. `set-window-buffer` signals an error when the window it acts upon is strongly dedicated to its buffer and does not already display the buffer it is asked to display. Other functions do not treat `t` differently from any non-`nil` value.

27.18 Quitting Windows

When you want to get rid of a window used for displaying a buffer, you can call `delete-window` or `delete-windows-on` (see Section 27.7 [Deleting Windows], page 584) to remove that window from its frame. If the buffer is shown on a separate frame, you might want to call `delete-frame` (see Section 28.7 [Deleting Frames], page 655) instead. If, on the other hand, a window has been reused for displaying the buffer, you might prefer showing the buffer previously shown in that window, by calling the function `switch-to-prev-buffer` (see Section 27.16 [Window History], page 605). Finally, you might want to either bury (see Section 26.8 [Buffer List], page 560) or kill (see Section 26.10 [Killing Buffers], page 563) the window's buffer.

The following command uses information on how the window for displaying the buffer was obtained in the first place, thus attempting to automate the above decisions for you.

`quit-window` **&optional** *kill window* [Command]

> This command quits *window* and buries its buffer. The argument *window* must be a live window and defaults to the selected one. With prefix argument *kill* non-`nil`, it kills the buffer instead of burying it. It calls the function `quit-restore-window` described next to deal with the window and its buffer.

`quit-restore-window` **&optional** *window bury-or-kill* [Function]

> This function handles *window* and its buffer after quitting. The optional argument *window* must be a live window and defaults to the selected one. The function's behavior is determined by the four elements of the `quit-restore` window parameter (see Section 27.26 [Window Parameters], page 625), which is set to nil afterwards.
>
> The window is deleted entirely if: 1) the first element of the `quit-restore` parameter is one of 'window or 'frame, 2) the window has no history of previously-displayed buffers, and 3) the displayed buffer matches the one in the fourth element of the `quit-restore` parameter. If *window* is the only window on its frame and there are other frames on the frame's terminal, the value of the optional argument *bury-or-kill* determines how to proceed with the window. If *bury-or-kill* equals `kill`, the frame is deleted unconditionally. Otherwise, the fate of the frame is determined by calling `frame-auto-hide-function` (see below) with that frame as sole argument.
>
> If the third element of the `quit-restore` parameter is a list of buffer, window start (see Section 27.20 [Window Start and End], page 610), and point (see Section 27.19 [Window Point], page 609), and that buffer is still live, the buffer will be displayed, and start and point set accordingly. If, in addition, *window*'s buffer was temporarily resized, this function will also try to restore the original height of *window*.
>
> Otherwise, if *window* was previously used for displaying other buffers (see Section 27.16 [Window History], page 605), the most recent buffer in that history will be displayed.
>
> The optional argument *bury-or-kill* specifies how to deal with *window*'s buffer. The following values are handled:
>
> `nil` This means to not deal with the buffer in any particular way. As a consequence, if *window* is not deleted, invoking `switch-to-prev-buffer` will usually show the buffer again.
>
> `append` This means that if *window* is not deleted, its buffer is moved to the end of *window*'s list of previous buffers, so it's less likely that a future invocation of `switch-to-prev-buffer` will switch to it. Also, it moves the buffer to the end of the frame's buffer list.
>
> `bury` This means that if *window* is not deleted, its buffer is removed from *window*'s list of previous buffers. Also, it moves the buffer to the end of the frame's buffer list. This value provides the most reliable remedy to not have `switch-to-prev-buffer` switch to this buffer again without killing the buffer.
>
> `kill` This means to kill *window*'s buffer.
>
> Typically, the display routines run by `display-buffer` will set the `quit-restore` window parameter correctly. It's also possible to set it manually, using the following code for displaying *buffer* in *window*:

```
(display-buffer-record-window type window buffer)
```

```
(set-window-buffer window buffer)
```

```
(set-window-prev-buffers window nil)
```

Setting the window history to nil ensures that a future call to `quit-window` can delete the window altogether.

The following option specifies how to deal with a frame containing just one window that should be either quit, or whose buffer should be buried.

`frame-auto-hide-function`   [User Option]

The function specified by this option is called to automatically hide frames. This function is called with one argument—a frame.

The function specified here is called by `bury-buffer` (see Section 26.8 [Buffer List], page 560) when the selected window is dedicated and shows the buffer to bury. It is also called by `quit-restore-window` (see above) when the frame of the window to quit has been specially created for displaying that window's buffer and the buffer is not killed.

The default is to call `iconify-frame` (see Section 28.11 [Visibility of Frames], page 658). Alternatively, you may specify either `delete-frame` (see Section 28.7 [Deleting Frames], page 655) to remove the frame from its display, `ignore` to leave the frame unchanged, or any other function that can take a frame as its sole argument.

Note that the function specified by this option is called only if the specified frame contains just one live window and there is at least one other frame on the same terminal.

27.19 Windows and Point

Each window has its own value of point (see Section 29.1 [Point], page 673), independent of the value of point in other windows displaying the same buffer. This makes it useful to have multiple windows showing one buffer.

- The window point is established when a window is first created; it is initialized from the buffer's point, or from the window point of another window opened on the buffer if such a window exists.

- Selecting a window sets the value of point in its buffer from the window's value of point. Conversely, deselecting a window sets the window's value of point from that of the buffer. Thus, when you switch between windows that display a given buffer, the point value for the selected window is in effect in the buffer, while the point values for the other windows are stored in those windows.

- As long as the selected window displays the current buffer, the window's point and the buffer's point always move together; they remain equal.

Emacs displays the cursor, by default as a rectangular block, in each window at the position of that window's point. When the user switches to another buffer in a window, Emacs moves that window's cursor to where point is in that buffer. If the exact position of point is hidden behind some display element, such as a display string or an image, Emacs displays the cursor immediately before or after that display element.

`window-point` &optional *window*   [Function]

> This function returns the current position of point in *window*. For a nonselected window, this is the value point would have (in that window's buffer) if that window were selected. The default for *window* is the selected window.
>
> When *window* is the selected window, the value returned is the value of point in that window's buffer. Strictly speaking, it would be more correct to return the top-level value of point, outside of any `save-excursion` forms. But that value is hard to find.

`set-window-point` *window position*   [Function]

> This function positions point in *window* at position *position* in *window*'s buffer. It returns *position*.
>
> If *window* is selected, this simply does `goto-char` in *window*'s buffer.

`window-point-insertion-type`   [Variable]

> This variable specifies the marker insertion type (see Section 30.5 [Marker Insertion Types], page 690) of `window-point`. The default is `nil`, so `window-point` will stay behind text inserted there.

27.20 The Window Start and End Positions

Each window maintains a marker used to keep track of a buffer position that specifies where in the buffer display should start. This position is called the *display-start* position of the window (or just the *start*). The character after this position is the one that appears at the upper left corner of the window. It is usually, but not inevitably, at the beginning of a text line.

After switching windows or buffers, and in some other cases, if the window start is in the middle of a line, Emacs adjusts the window start to the start of a line. This prevents certain operations from leaving the window start at a meaningless point within a line. This feature may interfere with testing some Lisp code by executing it using the commands of Lisp mode, because they trigger this readjustment. To test such code, put it into a command and bind the command to a key.

`window-start` &optional *window*   [Function]

> This function returns the display-start position of window *window*. If *window* is `nil`, the selected window is used.
>
> When you create a window, or display a different buffer in it, the display-start position is set to a display-start position recently used for the same buffer, or to `point-min` if the buffer doesn't have any.
>
> Redisplay updates the window-start position (if you have not specified it explicitly since the previous redisplay)—to make sure point appears on the screen. Nothing except redisplay automatically changes the window-start position; if you move point, do not expect the window-start position to change in response until after the next redisplay.

window-group-start &optional *window*   [Function]

This function is like `window-start`, except that when *window* is a part of a group of windows (see [Window Group], page 568), `window-group-start` returns the start position of the entire group. This condition holds when the buffer local variable `window-group-start-function` is set to a function. In this case, `window-group-start` calls the function with the single argument *window*, then returns its result.

window-end &optional *window update*   [Function]

This function returns the position where display of its buffer ends in *window*. The default for *window* is the selected window.

Simply changing the buffer text or moving point does not update the value that `window-end` returns. The value is updated only when Emacs redisplays and redisplay completes without being preempted.

If the last redisplay of *window* was preempted, and did not finish, Emacs does not know the position of the end of display in that window. In that case, this function returns `nil`.

If *update* is non-`nil`, `window-end` always returns an up-to-date value for where display ends, based on the current `window-start` value. If a previously saved value of that position is still valid, `window-end` returns that value; otherwise it computes the correct value by scanning the buffer text.

Even if *update* is non-`nil`, `window-end` does not attempt to scroll the display if point has moved off the screen, the way real redisplay would do. It does not alter the `window-start` value. In effect, it reports where the displayed text will end if scrolling is not required.

window-group-end &optional *window update*   [Function]

This function is like `window-end`, except that when *window* is a part of a group of windows (see [Window Group], page 568), `window-group-end` returns the end position of the entire group. This condition holds when the buffer local variable `window-group-end-function` is set to a function. In this case, `window-group-end` calls the function with the two arguments *window* and *update*, then returns its result. The argument *update* has the same meaning as in `window-end`.

set-window-start *window position* **&optional** *noforce*   [Function]

This function sets the display-start position of *window* to *position* in *window*'s buffer. It returns *position*.

The display routines insist that the position of point be visible when a buffer is displayed. Normally, they change the display-start position (that is, scroll the window) whenever necessary to make point visible. However, if you specify the start position with this function using `nil` for *noforce*, it means you want display to start at *position* even if that would put the location of point off the screen. If this does place point off screen, the display routines move point to the left margin on the middle line in the window.

For example, if point is 1 and you set the start of the window to 37, the start of the next line, point will be above the top of the window. The display routines will automatically move point if it is still 1 when redisplay occurs. Here is an example:

```
;; Here is what 'foo' looks like before executing
;;   the set-window-start expression.

---------- Buffer: foo ----------
*This is the contents of buffer foo.
2
3
4
5
6
---------- Buffer: foo ----------

(set-window-start
 (selected-window)
 (save-excursion
   (goto-char 1)
   (forward-line 1)
   (point)))
⇒ 37

;; Here is what 'foo' looks like after executing
;;   the set-window-start expression.
---------- Buffer: foo ----------
2
3
*4
5
6
---------- Buffer: foo ----------
```

If *noforce* is non-`nil`, and *position* would place point off screen at the next redisplay, then redisplay computes a new window-start position that works well with point, and thus *position* is not used.

set-window-group-start *window position* **&optional** *noforce*   [Function]
This function is like `set-window-start`, except that when *window* is a part of a group of windows (see [Window Group], page 568), `set-window-group-start` sets the start position of the entire group. This condition holds when the buffer local variable `set-window-group-start-function` is set to a function. In this case, `set-window-group-start` calls the function with the three arguments *window*, *position*, and *noforce*, then returns its result. The arguments *position* and *noforce* in this function have the same meaning as in `set-window-start`.

pos-visible-in-window-p **&optional** *position window partially*   [Function]
This function returns non-`nil` if *position* is within the range of text currently visible on the screen in *window*. It returns `nil` if *position* is scrolled vertically out of view. Locations that are partially obscured are not considered visible unless *partially* is non-`nil`. The argument *position* defaults to the current position of point in *window*;

window defaults to the selected window. If *position* is **t**, that means to check either the first visible position of the last screen line in *window*, or the end-of-buffer position, whichever comes first.

This function considers only vertical scrolling. If *position* is out of view only because *window* has been scrolled horizontally, **pos-visible-in-window-p** returns non-**nil** anyway. See Section 27.23 [Horizontal Scrolling], page 618.

If *position* is visible, **pos-visible-in-window-p** returns **t** if *partially* is **nil**; if *partially* is non-**nil**, and the character following *position* is fully visible, it returns a list of the form (*x y*), where *x* and *y* are the pixel coordinates relative to the top left corner of the window; otherwise it returns an extended list of the form (*x y rtop rbot rowh vpos*), where *rtop* and *rbot* specify the number of off-window pixels at the top and bottom of the row at *position*, *rowh* specifies the visible height of that row, and *vpos* specifies the vertical position (zero-based row number) of that row.

Here is an example:

```
;; If point is off the screen now, recenter it now.
(or (pos-visible-in-window-p
       (point) (selected-window))
    (recenter 0))
```

pos-visible-in-window-group-p &optional *position window*   [Function]
       partially

This function is like **pos-visible-in-window-p**, except that when *window* is a part of a group of windows (see [Window Group], page 568), **pos-visible-in-window-group-p** tests the visibility of *pos* in the entire group, not just in the single *window*. This condition holds when the buffer local variable **pos-visible-in-window-group-p-function** is set to a function. In this case **pos-visible-in-window-group-p** calls the function with the three arguments *position*, *window*, and *partially*, then returns its result. The arguments *position* and *partially* have the same meaning as in **pos-visible-in-window-p**.

window-line-height &optional *line window*   [Function]

This function returns the height of text line *line* in *window*. If *line* is one of **header-line** or **mode-line**, **window-line-height** returns information about the corresponding line of the window. Otherwise, *line* is a text line number starting from 0. A negative number counts from the end of the window. The default for *line* is the current line in *window*; the default for *window* is the selected window.

If the display is not up to date, **window-line-height** returns **nil**. In that case, **pos-visible-in-window-p** may be used to obtain related information.

If there is no line corresponding to the specified *line*, **window-line-height** returns **nil**. Otherwise, it returns a list (*height vpos ypos offbot*), where *height* is the height in pixels of the visible part of the line, *vpos* and *ypos* are the vertical position in lines and pixels of the line relative to the top of the first text line, and *offbot* is the number of off-window pixels at the bottom of the text line. If there are off-window pixels at the top of the (first) text line, *ypos* is negative.

27.21 Textual Scrolling

Textual scrolling means moving the text up or down through a window. It works by changing the window's display-start location. It may also change the value of `window-point` to keep point on the screen (see Section 27.19 [Window Point], page 609).

The basic textual scrolling functions are `scroll-up` (which scrolls forward) and `scroll-down` (which scrolls backward). In these function names, "up" and "down" refer to the direction of motion of the buffer text relative to the window. Imagine that the text is written on a long roll of paper and that the scrolling commands move the paper up and down. Thus, if you are looking at the middle of a buffer and repeatedly call `scroll-down`, you will eventually see the beginning of the buffer.

Unfortunately, this sometimes causes confusion, because some people tend to think in terms of the opposite convention: they imagine the window moving over text that remains in place, so that "down" commands take you to the end of the buffer. This convention is consistent with fact that such a command is bound to a key named `PageDown` on modern keyboards.

Textual scrolling functions (aside from `scroll-other-window`) have unpredictable results if the current buffer is not the one displayed in the selected window. See Section 26.2 [Current Buffer], page 550.

If the window contains a row taller than the height of the window (for example in the presence of a large image), the scroll functions will adjust the window's vertical scroll position to scroll the partially visible row. Lisp callers can disable this feature by binding the variable `auto-window-vscroll` to `nil` (see Section 27.22 [Vertical Scrolling], page 617).

`scroll-up` **&optional** *count*   [Command]
> This function scrolls forward by *count* lines in the selected window.
>
> If *count* is negative, it scrolls backward instead. If *count* is `nil` (or omitted), the distance scrolled is `next-screen-context-lines` lines less than the height of the window's text area.
>
> If the selected window cannot be scrolled any further, this function signals an error. Otherwise, it returns `nil`.

`scroll-down` **&optional** *count*   [Command]
> This function scrolls backward by *count* lines in the selected window.
>
> If *count* is negative, it scrolls forward instead. In other respects, it behaves the same way as `scroll-up` does.

`scroll-up-command` **&optional** *count*   [Command]
> This behaves like `scroll-up`, except that if the selected window cannot be scrolled any further and the value of the variable `scroll-error-top-bottom` is `t`, it tries to move to the end of the buffer instead. If point is already there, it signals an error.

`scroll-down-command` **&optional** *count*   [Command]
> This behaves like `scroll-down`, except that if the selected window cannot be scrolled any further and the value of the variable `scroll-error-top-bottom` is `t`, it tries to move to the beginning of the buffer instead. If point is already there, it signals an error.

`scroll-other-window` **&optional** *count* [Command]

This function scrolls the text in another window upward *count* lines. Negative values of *count*, or `nil`, are handled as in `scroll-up`.

You can specify which buffer to scroll by setting the variable `other-window-scroll-buffer` to a buffer. If that buffer isn't already displayed, `scroll-other-window` displays it in some window.

When the selected window is the minibuffer, the next window is normally the leftmost one immediately above it. You can specify a different window to scroll, when the minibuffer is selected, by setting the variable `minibuffer-scroll-window`. This variable has no effect when any other window is selected. When it is non-`nil` and the minibuffer is selected, it takes precedence over `other-window-scroll-buffer`. See [Definition of minibuffer-scroll-window], page 344.

When the minibuffer is active, it is the next window if the selected window is the one at the bottom right corner. In this case, `scroll-other-window` attempts to scroll the minibuffer. If the minibuffer contains just one line, it has nowhere to scroll to, so the line reappears after the echo area momentarily displays the message 'End of buffer'.

`other-window-scroll-buffer` [Variable]

If this variable is non-`nil`, it tells `scroll-other-window` which buffer's window to scroll.

`scroll-margin` [User Option]

This option specifies the size of the scroll margin—a minimum number of lines between point and the top or bottom of a window. Whenever point gets within this many lines of the top or bottom of the window, redisplay scrolls the text automatically (if possible) to move point out of the margin, closer to the center of the window.

`scroll-conservatively` [User Option]

This variable controls how scrolling is done automatically when point moves off the screen (or into the scroll margin). If the value is a positive integer n, then redisplay scrolls the text up to n lines in either direction, if that will bring point back into proper view. This behavior is called *conservative scrolling*. Otherwise, scrolling happens in the usual way, under the control of other variables such as `scroll-up-aggressively` and `scroll-down-aggressively`.

The default value is zero, which means that conservative scrolling never happens.

`scroll-down-aggressively` [User Option]

The value of this variable should be either `nil` or a fraction f between 0 and 1. If it is a fraction, that specifies where on the screen to put point when scrolling down. More precisely, when a window scrolls down because point is above the window start, the new start position is chosen to put point f part of the window height from the top. The larger f, the more aggressive the scrolling.

A value of `nil` is equivalent to .5, since its effect is to center point. This variable automatically becomes buffer-local when set in any fashion.

scroll-up-aggressively   [User Option]

Likewise, for scrolling up. The value, *f*, specifies how far point should be placed from the bottom of the window; thus, as with `scroll-up-aggressively`, a larger value scrolls more aggressively.

scroll-step   [User Option]

This variable is an older variant of `scroll-conservatively`. The difference is that if its value is *n*, that permits scrolling only by precisely *n* lines, not a smaller number. This feature does not work with `scroll-margin`. The default value is zero.

scroll-preserve-screen-position   [User Option]

If this option is `t`, whenever a scrolling command moves point off-window, Emacs tries to adjust point to keep the cursor at its old vertical position in the window, rather than the window edge.

If the value is non-`nil` and not `t`, Emacs adjusts point to keep the cursor at the same vertical position, even if the scrolling command didn't move point off-window.

This option affects all scroll commands that have a non-`nil` `scroll-command` symbol property.

next-screen-context-lines   [User Option]

The value of this variable is the number of lines of continuity to retain when scrolling by full screens. For example, `scroll-up` with an argument of `nil` scrolls so that this many lines at the bottom of the window appear instead at the top. The default value is 2.

scroll-error-top-bottom   [User Option]

If this option is `nil` (the default), `scroll-up-command` and `scroll-down-command` simply signal an error when no more scrolling is possible.

If the value is `t`, these commands instead move point to the beginning or end of the buffer (depending on scrolling direction); only if point is already on that position do they signal an error.

recenter &optional *count*   [Command]

This function scrolls the text in the selected window so that point is displayed at a specified vertical position within the window. It does not move point with respect to the text.

If *count* is a non-negative number, that puts the line containing point *count* lines down from the top of the window. If *count* is a negative number, then it counts upward from the bottom of the window, so that −1 stands for the last usable line in the window.

If *count* is `nil` (or a non-`nil` list), `recenter` puts the line containing point in the middle of the window. If *count* is `nil`, this function may redraw the frame, according to the value of `recenter-redisplay`.

When `recenter` is called interactively, *count* is the raw prefix argument. Thus, typing *C-u* as the prefix sets the *count* to a non-`nil` list, while typing *C-u 4* sets *count* to 4, which positions the current line four lines from the top.

With an argument of zero, `recenter` positions the current line at the top of the window. The command `recenter-top-bottom` offers a more convenient way to achieve this.

`recenter-window-group` **&optional** *count*   [Function]

This function is like `recenter`, except that when the selected window is part of a group of windows (see [Window Group], page 568), `recenter-window-group` scrolls the entire group. This condition holds when the buffer local variable `recenter-window-group-function` is set to a function. In this case, `recenter-window-group` calls the function with the argument *count*, then returns its result. The argument *count* has the same meaning as in `recenter`, but with respect to the entire window group.

`recenter-redisplay`   [User Option]

If this variable is non-`nil`, calling `recenter` with a `nil` argument redraws the frame. The default value is `tty`, which means only redraw the frame if it is a tty frame.

`recenter-top-bottom` **&optional** *count*   [Command]

This command, which is the default binding for `C-l`, acts like `recenter`, except if called with no argument. In that case, successive calls place point according to the cycling order defined by the variable `recenter-positions`.

`recenter-positions`   [User Option]

This variable controls how `recenter-top-bottom` behaves when called with no argument. The default value is (`middle top bottom`), which means that successive calls of `recenter-top-bottom` with no argument cycle between placing point at the middle, top, and bottom of the window.

27.22 Vertical Fractional Scrolling

Vertical fractional scrolling means shifting text in a window up or down by a specified multiple or fraction of a line. Each window has a *vertical scroll position*, which is a number, never less than zero. It specifies how far to raise the contents of the window. Raising the window contents generally makes all or part of some lines disappear off the top, and all or part of some other lines appear at the bottom. The usual value is zero.

The vertical scroll position is measured in units of the normal line height, which is the height of the default font. Thus, if the value is .5, that means the window contents are scrolled up half the normal line height. If it is 3.3, that means the window contents are scrolled up somewhat over three times the normal line height.

What fraction of a line the vertical scrolling covers, or how many lines, depends on what the lines contain. A value of .5 could scroll a line whose height is very short off the screen, while a value of 3.3 could scroll just part of the way through a tall line or an image.

`window-vscroll` **&optional** *window pixels-p*   [Function]

This function returns the current vertical scroll position of *window*. The default for *window* is the selected window. If *pixels-p* is non-`nil`, the return value is measured in pixels, rather than in units of the normal line height.

```
(window-vscroll)
    ⇒ 0
```

`set-window-vscroll` *window lines* **&optional** *pixels-p*   [Function]

> This function sets *window*'s vertical scroll position to *lines*. If *window* is `nil`, the selected window is used. The argument *lines* should be zero or positive; if not, it is taken as zero.
>
> The actual vertical scroll position must always correspond to an integral number of pixels, so the value you specify is rounded accordingly.
>
> The return value is the result of this rounding.
>
> ```
> (set-window-vscroll (selected-window) 1.2)
>      ⇒ 1.13
> ```
>
> If *pixels-p* is non-`nil`, *lines* specifies a number of pixels. In this case, the return value is *lines*.

`auto-window-vscroll`   [Variable]

> If this variable is non-`nil`, the `line-move`, `scroll-up`, and `scroll-down` functions will automatically modify the vertical scroll position to scroll through display rows that are taller than the height of the window, for example in the presence of large images.

27.23 Horizontal Scrolling

Horizontal scrolling means shifting the image in the window left or right by a specified multiple of the normal character width. Each window has a *horizontal scroll position*, which is a number, never less than zero. It specifies how far to shift the contents left. Shifting the window contents left generally makes all or part of some characters disappear off the left, and all or part of some other characters appear at the right. The usual value is zero.

The horizontal scroll position is measured in units of the normal character width, which is the width of space in the default font. Thus, if the value is 5, that means the window contents are scrolled left by 5 times the normal character width. How many characters actually disappear off to the left depends on their width, and could vary from line to line.

Because we read from side to side in the inner loop, and from top to bottom in the outer loop, the effect of horizontal scrolling is not like that of textual or vertical scrolling. Textual scrolling involves selection of a portion of text to display, and vertical scrolling moves the window contents contiguously; but horizontal scrolling causes part of *each line* to go off screen.

Usually, no horizontal scrolling is in effect; then the leftmost column is at the left edge of the window. In this state, scrolling to the right is meaningless, since there is no data to the left of the edge to be revealed by it; so this is not allowed. Scrolling to the left is allowed; it scrolls the first columns of text off the edge of the window and can reveal additional columns on the right that were truncated before. Once a window has a nonzero amount of leftward horizontal scrolling, you can scroll it back to the right, but only so far as to reduce the net horizontal scroll to zero. There is no limit to how far left you can scroll, but eventually all the text will disappear off the left edge.

If `auto-hscroll-mode` is set, redisplay automatically alters the horizontal scrolling of a window as necessary to ensure that point is always visible. However, you can still set the horizontal scrolling value explicitly. The value you specify serves as a lower bound for automatic scrolling, i.e., automatic scrolling will not scroll a window to a column less than the specified one.

scroll-left &optional *count set-minimum*   [Command]

> This function scrolls the selected window *count* columns to the left (or to the right if *count* is negative). The default for *count* is the window width, minus 2.
>
> The return value is the total amount of leftward horizontal scrolling in effect after the change—just like the value returned by `window-hscroll` (below).
>
> Note that text in paragraphs whose base direction is right-to-left (see Section 37.26 [Bidirectional Display], page 981) moves in the opposite direction: e.g., it moves to the right when `scroll-left` is invoked with a positive value of *count*.
>
> Once you scroll a window as far right as it can go, back to its normal position where the total leftward scrolling is zero, attempts to scroll any farther right have no effect.
>
> If *set-minimum* is non-`nil`, the new scroll amount becomes the lower bound for automatic scrolling; that is, automatic scrolling will not scroll a window to a column less than the value returned by this function. Interactive calls pass non-`nil` for *set-minimum*.

scroll-right &optional *count set-minimum*   [Command]

> This function scrolls the selected window *count* columns to the right (or to the left if *count* is negative). The default for *count* is the window width, minus 2. Aside from the direction of scrolling, this works just like `scroll-left`.

window-hscroll &optional *window*   [Function]

> This function returns the total leftward horizontal scrolling of *window*—the number of columns by which the text in *window* is scrolled left past the left margin. (In right-to-left paragraphs, the value is the total amount of the rightward scrolling instead.) The default for *window* is the selected window.
>
> The return value is never negative. It is zero when no horizontal scrolling has been done in *window* (which is usually the case).

```
(window-hscroll)
     ⇒ 0
(scroll-left 5)
     ⇒ 5
(window-hscroll)
     ⇒ 5
```

set-window-hscroll *window columns*   [Function]

> This function sets horizontal scrolling of *window*. The value of *columns* specifies the amount of scrolling, in terms of columns from the left margin (right margin in right-to-left paragraphs). The argument *columns* should be zero or positive; if not, it is taken as zero. Fractional values of *columns* are not supported at present.
>
> Note that `set-window-hscroll` may appear not to work if you test it by evaluating a call with `M-:` in a simple way. What happens is that the function sets the horizontal scroll value and returns, but then redisplay adjusts the horizontal scrolling to make point visible, and this overrides what the function did. You can observe the function's

effect if you call it while point is sufficiently far from the left margin that it will remain visible.

The value returned is *columns*.

```
(set-window-hscroll (selected-window) 10)
    ⇒ 10
```

Here is how you can determine whether a given position *position* is off the screen due to horizontal scrolling:

```
(defun hscroll-on-screen (window position)
  (save-excursion
    (goto-char position)
    (and
      (>= (- (current-column) (window-hscroll window)) 0)
      (< (- (current-column) (window-hscroll window))
        (window-width window)))))
```

27.24 Coordinates and Windows

This section describes functions that report the position of a window. Most of these functions report positions relative to an origin at the native position of the window's frame (see Section 28.3 [Frame Geometry], page 635). Some functions report positions relative to the origin of the display of the window's frame. In any case, the origin has the coordinates (0, 0) and X and Y coordinates increase rightward and downward respectively.

For the following functions, X and Y coordinates are reported in integer character units, i.e., numbers of lines and columns respectively. On a graphical display, each "line" and "column" corresponds to the height and width of the default character specified by the frame's default font (see Section 28.3.2 [Frame Font], page 639).

window-edges &optional *window body absolute pixelwise*   [Function]
   This function returns a list of the edge coordinates of *window*. If *window* is omitted or **nil**, it defaults to the selected window.

   The return value has the form (*left top right bottom*). These list elements are, respectively, the X coordinate of the leftmost column occupied by the window, the Y coordinate of the topmost row, the X coordinate one column to the right of the rightmost column, and the Y coordinate one row down from the bottommost row.

   Note that these are the actual outer edges of the window, including any header line, mode line, scroll bar, fringes, window divider and display margins. On a text terminal, if the window has a neighbor on its right, its right edge includes the separator line between the window and its neighbor.

   If the optional argument *body* is **nil**, this means to return the edges corresponding to the total size of *window*. *body* non-**nil** means to return the edges of *window*'s body (aka text area). If *body* is non-**nil**, *window* must specify a live window.

   If the optional argument *absolute* is **nil**, this means to return edges relative to the native position of *window*'s frame. *absolute* non-**nil** means to return coordinates relative to the origin (0, 0) of *window*'s display. On non-graphical systems this argument has no effect.

If the optional argument *pixelwise* is `nil`, this means to return the coordinates in terms of the default character width and height of *window*'s frame (see Section 28.3.2 [Frame Font], page 639), rounded if necessary. *pixelwise* non-`nil` means to return the coordinates in pixels. Note that the pixel specified by *right* and *bottom* is immediately outside of these edges. If *absolute* is non-`nil`, *pixelwise* is implicitly non-`nil` too.

window-body-edges &optional *window*   [Function]
This function returns the edges of *window*'s body (see Section 27.3 [Window Sizes], page 572). Calling (`window-body-edges window`) is equivalent to calling (`window-edges window t`), see above.

The following functions can be used to relate a set of frame-relative coordinates to a window:

window-at *x y* &optional *frame*   [Function]
This function returns the live window at the coordinates *x* and *y* given in default character sizes (see Section 28.3.2 [Frame Font], page 639) relative to the native position of *frame* (see Section 28.3 [Frame Geometry], page 635).

If there is no window at that position, the return value is `nil`. If *frame* is omitted or `nil`, it defaults to the selected frame.

coordinates-in-window-p *coordinates window*   [Function]
This function checks whether a window *window* occupies the frame relative coordinates *coordinates*, and if so, which part of the window that is. *window* should be a live window.

coordinates should be a cons cell of the form (*x . y*), where *x* and *y* are given in default character sizes (see Section 28.3.2 [Frame Font], page 639) relative to the native position of *window*'s frame (see Section 28.3 [Frame Geometry], page 635).

If there is no window at the specified position, the return value is `nil` . Otherwise, the return value is one of the following:

(*relx . rely*)
> The coordinates are inside *window*. The numbers *relx* and *rely* are the equivalent window-relative coordinates for the specified position, counting from 0 at the top left corner of the window.

`mode-line`
> The coordinates are in the mode line of *window*.

`header-line`
> The coordinates are in the header line of *window*.

`right-divider`
> The coordinates are in the divider separating *window* from a window on the right.

`bottom-divider`
> The coordinates are in the divider separating *window* from a window beneath.

`vertical-line`
>   The coordinates are in the vertical line between *window* and its neighbor to the right. This value occurs only if the window doesn't have a scroll bar; positions in a scroll bar are considered outside the window for these purposes.

`left-fringe`
`right-fringe`
>   The coordinates are in the left or right fringe of the window.

`left-margin`
`right-margin`
>   The coordinates are in the left or right margin of the window.

`nil`   The coordinates are not in any part of *window*.

The function `coordinates-in-window-p` does not require a frame as argument because it always uses the frame that *window* is on.

The following functions return window positions in pixels, rather than character units. Though mostly useful on graphical displays, they can also be called on text terminals, where the screen area of each text character is taken to be one pixel.

`window-pixel-edges` **&optional** *window*   [Function]
>   This function returns a list of pixel coordinates for the edges of *window*. Calling (`window-pixel-edges` *window*) is equivalent to calling (`window-edges` *window* `nil nil t`), see above.

`window-body-pixel-edges` **&optional** *window*   [Function]
>   This function returns the pixel edges of *window*'s body. Calling (`window-body-pixel-edges` *window*) is equivalent to calling (`window-edges` *window* `t nil t`), see above.

The following functions return window positions in pixels, relative to the origin of the display screen rather than that of the frame:

`window-absolute-pixel-edges` **&optional** *window*   [Function]
>   This function returns the pixel coordinates of *window* relative to an origin at (0, 0) of the display of *window*'s frame. Calling (`window-absolute-pixel-edges`) is equivalent to calling (`window-edges` *window* `nil t t`), see above.

`window-absolute-body-pixel-edges` **&optional** *window*   [Function]
>   This function returns the pixel coordinates of *window*'s body relative to an origin at (0, 0) of the display of *window*'s frame. Calling (`window-absolute-body-pixel-edges` *window*) is equivalent to calling (`window-edges` *window* `t t t`), see above.
>
>   Combined with `set-mouse-absolute-pixel-position`, this function can be used to move the mouse pointer to an arbitrary buffer position visible in some window:
>
>   ```
>   (let ((edges (window-absolute-body-pixel-edges))
>         (position (pos-visible-in-window-p nil nil t)))
>     (set-mouse-absolute-pixel-position
>      (+ (nth 0 edges) (nth 0 position))
>      (+ (nth 1 edges) (nth 1 position))))
>   ```

On a graphical terminal this form "warps" the mouse cursor to the upper left corner of the glyph at the selected window's point. A position calculated this way can be also used to show a tooltip window there.

The following function returns the screen coordinates of a buffer position visible in a window:

window-absolute-pixel-position **&optional** *position window*   [Function]

If the buffer position *position* is visible in window *window*, this function returns the display coordinates of the upper/left corner of the glyph at *position*. The return value is a cons of the X- and Y-coordinates of that corner, relative to an origin at (0, 0) of *window*'s display. It returns `nil` if *position* is not visible in *window*.

window must be a live window and defaults to the selected window. *position* defaults to the value of `window-point` of *window*.

This means that in order to move the mouse pointer to the position of point in the selected window, it's sufficient to write:

```
(let ((position (window-absolute-pixel-position)))
  (set-mouse-absolute-pixel-position
   (car position) (cdr position)))
```

27.25 Window Configurations

A *window configuration* records the entire layout of one frame—all windows, their sizes, which buffers they contain, how those buffers are scrolled, and their value of point; also their fringes, margins, and scroll bar settings. It also includes the value of `minibuffer-scroll-window`. As a special exception, the window configuration does not record the value of point in the selected window for the current buffer.

You can bring back an entire frame layout by restoring a previously saved window configuration. If you want to record the layout of all frames instead of just one, use a frame configuration instead of a window configuration. See Section 28.13 [Frame Configurations], page 660.

current-window-configuration **&optional** *frame*   [Function]

This function returns a new object representing *frame*'s current window configuration. The default for *frame* is the selected frame. The variable `window-persistent-parameters` specifies which window parameters (if any) are saved by this function. See Section 27.26 [Window Parameters], page 625.

set-window-configuration *configuration*   [Function]

This function restores the configuration of windows and buffers as specified by *configuration*, for the frame that *configuration* was created for.

The argument *configuration* must be a value that was previously returned by `current-window-configuration`. The configuration is restored in the frame from which *configuration* was made, whether that frame is selected or not. This always counts as a window size change and triggers execution of the `window-size-change-functions` (see Section 27.27 [Window Hooks], page 628), because `set-window-configuration` doesn't know how to tell whether the new configuration actually differs from the old one.

If the frame from which *configuration* was saved is dead, all this function does is restore the three variables `window-min-height`, `window-min-width` and `minibuffer-scroll-window`. In this case, the function returns `nil`. Otherwise, it returns `t`.

Here is a way of using this function to get the same effect as `save-window-excursion`:

```
(let ((config (current-window-configuration)))
  (unwind-protect
      (progn (split-window-below nil)
             ...)
    (set-window-configuration config)))
```

`save-window-excursion` *forms...*   [Macro]

This macro records the window configuration of the selected frame, executes *forms* in sequence, then restores the earlier window configuration. The return value is the value of the final form in *forms*.

Most Lisp code should not use this macro; `save-selected-window` is typically sufficient. In particular, this macro cannot reliably prevent the code in *forms* from opening new windows, because new windows might be opened in other frames (see Section 27.13 [Choosing Window], page 598), and `save-window-excursion` only saves and restores the window configuration on the current frame.

Do not use this macro in `window-size-change-functions`; exiting the macro triggers execution of `window-size-change-functions`, leading to an endless loop.

`window-configuration-p` *object*   [Function]

This function returns `t` if *object* is a window configuration.

`compare-window-configurations` *config1 config2*   [Function]

This function compares two window configurations as regards the structure of windows, but ignores the values of point and the saved scrolling positions—it can return `t` even if those aspects differ.

The function `equal` can also compare two window configurations; it regards configurations as unequal if they differ in any respect, even a saved point.

`window-configuration-frame` *config*   [Function]

This function returns the frame for which the window configuration *config* was made.

Other primitives to look inside of window configurations would make sense, but are not implemented because we did not need them. See the file `winner.el` for some more operations on windows configurations.

The objects returned by `current-window-configuration` die together with the Emacs process. In order to store a window configuration on disk and read it back in another Emacs session, you can use the functions described next. These functions are also useful to clone the state of a frame into an arbitrary live window (`set-window-configuration` effectively clones the windows of a frame into the root window of that very frame only).

`window-state-get` **&optional** *window writable*   [Function]

This function returns the state of *window* as a Lisp object. The argument *window* must be a valid window and defaults to the root window of the selected frame.

If the optional argument *writable* is non-`nil`, this means to not use markers for sampling positions like `window-point` or `window-start`. This argument should be non-`nil` when the state will be written to disk and read back in another session.

Together, the argument *writable* and the variable `window-persistent-parameters` specify which window parameters are saved by this function. See Section 27.26 [Window Parameters], page 625.

The value returned by `window-state-get` can be used in the same session to make a clone of a window in another window. It can be also written to disk and read back in another session. In either case, use the following function to restore the state of the window.

`window-state-put` *state* **&optional** *window ignore* [Function]
> This function puts the window state *state* into *window*. The argument *state* should be the state of a window returned by an earlier invocation of `window-state-get`, see above. The optional argument *window* can be either a live window or an internal window (see Section 27.2 [Windows and Frames], page 568) and defaults to the selected one. If *window* is not live, it is replaced by a live window before putting *state* into it.
>
> If the optional argument *ignore* is non-`nil`, it means to ignore minimum window sizes and fixed-size restrictions. If *ignore* is `safe`, this means windows can get as small as one line and/or two columns.

27.26 Window Parameters

This section describes how window parameters can be used to associate additional information with windows.

`window-parameter` *window parameter* [Function]
> This function returns *window*'s value for *parameter*. The default for *window* is the selected window. If *window* has no setting for *parameter*, this function returns `nil`.

`window-parameters` **&optional** *window* [Function]
> This function returns all parameters of *window* and their values. The default for *window* is the selected window. The return value is either `nil`, or an association list whose elements have the form (**parameter** . **value**).

`set-window-parameter` *window parameter value* [Function]
> This function sets *window*'s value of *parameter* to *value* and returns *value*. The default for *window* is the selected window.

By default, the functions that save and restore window configurations or the states of windows (see Section 27.25 [Window Configurations], page 623) do not care about window parameters. This means that when you change the value of a parameter within the body of a `save-window-excursion`, the previous value is not restored when that macro exits. It also means that when you restore via `window-state-put` a window state saved earlier by `window-state-get`, all cloned windows have their parameters reset to `nil`. The following variable allows you to override the standard behavior:

window-persistent-parameters [Variable]

This variable is an alist specifying which parameters get saved by `current-window-configuration` and `window-state-get`, and subsequently restored by `set-window-configuration` and `window-state-put`. See Section 27.25 [Window Configurations], page 623.

The CAR of each entry of this alist is a symbol specifying the parameter. The CDR should be one of the following:

nil   This value means the parameter is saved neither by `window-state-get` nor by `current-window-configuration`.

t   This value specifies that the parameter is saved by `current-window-configuration` and (provided its *writable* argument is `nil`) by `window-state-get`.

writable   This means that the parameter is saved unconditionally by both `current-window-configuration` and `window-state-get`. This value should not be used for parameters whose values do not have a read syntax. Otherwise, invoking `window-state-put` in another session may fail with an `invalid-read-syntax` error.

Some functions (notably `delete-window`, `delete-other-windows` and `split-window`), may behave specially when their *window* argument has a parameter set. You can override such special behavior by binding the following variable to a non-`nil` value:

ignore-window-parameters [Variable]

If this variable is non-`nil`, some standard functions do not process window parameters. The functions currently affected by this are `split-window`, `delete-window`, `delete-other-windows`, and `other-window`.

An application can bind this variable to a non-`nil` value around calls to these functions. If it does so, the application is fully responsible for correctly assigning the parameters of all involved windows when exiting that function.

The following parameters are currently used by the window management code:

delete-window
        This parameter affects the execution of `delete-window` (see Section 27.7 [Deleting Windows], page 584).

delete-other-windows
        This parameter affects the execution of `delete-other-windows` (see Section 27.7 [Deleting Windows], page 584).

split-window
        This parameter affects the execution of `split-window` (see Section 27.6 [Splitting Windows], page 581).

other-window
        This parameter affects the execution of `other-window` (see Section 27.10 [Cyclic Window Ordering], page 591).

no-other-window

> This parameter marks the window as not selectable by other-window (see Section 27.10 [Cyclic Window Ordering], page 591).

clone-of   This parameter specifies the window that this one has been cloned from. It is installed by window-state-get (see Section 27.25 [Window Configurations], page 623).

preserved-size

> This parameter specifies a buffer, a direction where nil means vertical and t horizontal, and a size in pixels. If this window displays the specified buffer and its size in the indicated direction equals the size specified by this parameter, then Emacs will try to preserve the size of this window in the indicated direction. This parameter is installed and updated by the function window-preserve-size (see Section 27.5 [Preserving Window Sizes], page 580).

quit-restore

> This parameter is installed by the buffer display functions (see Section 27.13 [Choosing Window], page 598) and consulted by quit-restore-window (see Section 27.18 [Quitting Windows], page 607). It contains four elements:

> The first element is one of the symbols window, meaning that the window has been specially created by display-buffer; frame, a separate frame has been created; same, the window has only ever displayed this buffer; or other, the window showed another buffer before. frame and window affect how the window is quit, while same and other affect the redisplay of buffers previously shown in this window.

> The second element is either one of the symbols window or frame, or a list whose elements are the buffer shown in the window before, that buffer's window start and window point positions, and the window's height at that time. If that buffer is still live when the window is quit, then the function quit-restore-window reuses the window to display the buffer.

> The third element is the window selected at the time the parameter was created. If quit-restore-window deletes the window passed to it as argument, it then tries to reselect this window.

> The fourth element is the buffer whose display caused the creation of this parameter. quit-restore-window deletes the specified window only if it still shows that buffer.

min-margins

> The value of this parameter is a cons cell whose CAR and CDR, if non-nil, specify the minimum values (in columns) for the left and right margin of this window. When present, Emacs will use these values instead of the actual margin widths for determining whether a window can be split or shrunk horizontally.

> Emacs never auto-adjusts the margins of any window after splitting or resizing it. It is the sole responsibility of any application setting this parameter to adjust the margins of this window as well as those of any new window that inherits this window's margins due to a split. Both window-configuration-change-hook and window-size-change-functions (see Section 27.27 [Window Hooks], page 628) should be employed for this purpose.

> This parameter was introduced in Emacs version 25.1 to support applications that use large margins to center buffer text within a window and should be used, with due care, exclusively by those applications. It might be replaced by an improved solution in future versions of Emacs.

There are additional parameters `window-atom` and `window-side`; these are reserved and should not be used by applications.

27.27 Hooks for Window Scrolling and Changes

This section describes how a Lisp program can take action whenever a window displays a different part of its buffer or a different buffer. There are three actions that can change this: scrolling the window, switching buffers in the window, and changing the size of the window. The first two actions run `window-scroll-functions`; the last runs `window-size-change-functions`.

`window-scroll-functions`   [Variable]

> This variable holds a list of functions that Emacs should call before redisplaying a window with scrolling. Displaying a different buffer in the window also runs these functions.
>
> This variable is not a normal hook, because each function is called with two arguments: the window, and its new display-start position.
>
> These functions must take care when using `window-end` (see Section 27.20 [Window Start and End], page 610); if you need an up-to-date value, you must use the *update* argument to ensure you get it.
>
> **Warning:** don't use this feature to alter the way the window is scrolled. It's not designed for that, and such use probably won't work.

`window-size-change-functions`   [Variable]

> This variable holds a list of functions to be called if the size of any window changes for any reason. The functions are called at the beginning of a redisplay cycle, and just once for each frame on which size changes have occurred.
>
> Each function receives the frame as its sole argument. There is no direct way to find out which windows on that frame have changed size, or precisely how. However, if a size-change function records, at each call, the existing windows and their sizes, it can also compare the present sizes and the previous sizes.
>
> Creating or deleting windows counts as a size change, and therefore causes these functions to be called. Changing the frame size also counts, because it changes the sizes of the existing windows.
>
> You may use `save-selected-window` in these functions (see Section 27.9 [Selecting Windows], page 590). However, do not use `save-window-excursion` (see Section 27.25 [Window Configurations], page 623); exiting that macro counts as a size change, which would cause these functions to be called over and over.

`window-configuration-change-hook`   [Variable]

> A normal hook that is run every time you change the window configuration of an existing frame. This includes splitting or deleting windows, changing the sizes of windows, or displaying a different buffer in a window.

The buffer-local part of this hook is run once for each window on the affected frame, with the relevant window selected and its buffer current. The global part is run once for the modified frame, with that frame selected.

In addition, you can use `jit-lock-register` to register a Font Lock fontification function, which will be called whenever parts of a buffer are (re)fontified because a window was scrolled or its size changed. See Section 22.6.4 [Other Font Lock Variables], page 468.

28 Frames

A *frame* is a screen object that contains one or more Emacs windows (see Chapter 27 [Windows], page 567). It is the kind of object called a "window" in the terminology of graphical environments; but we can't call it a "window" here, because Emacs uses that word in a different way. In Emacs Lisp, a *frame object* is a Lisp object that represents a frame on the screen. See Section 2.4.4 [Frame Type], page 25.

A frame initially contains a single main window and/or a minibuffer window; you can subdivide the main window vertically or horizontally into smaller windows. See Section 27.6 [Splitting Windows], page 581.

A *terminal* is a display device capable of displaying one or more Emacs frames. In Emacs Lisp, a *terminal object* is a Lisp object that represents a terminal. See Section 2.4.5 [Terminal Type], page 25.

There are two classes of terminals: *text terminals* and *graphical terminals*. Text terminals are non-graphics-capable displays, including `xterm` and other terminal emulators. On a text terminal, each Emacs frame occupies the terminal's entire screen; although you can create additional frames and switch between them, the terminal only shows one frame at a time. Graphical terminals, on the other hand, are managed by graphical display systems such as the X Window System, which allow Emacs to show multiple frames simultaneously on the same display.

On GNU and Unix systems, you can create additional frames on any available terminal, within a single Emacs session, regardless of whether Emacs was started on a text or graphical terminal. Emacs can display on both graphical and text terminals simultaneously. This comes in handy, for instance, when you connect to the same session from several remote locations. See Section 28.2 [Multiple Terminals], page 631.

`framep` *object*   [Function]

This predicate returns a non-`nil` value if *object* is a frame, and `nil` otherwise. For a frame, the value indicates which kind of display the frame uses:

`t`   The frame is displayed on a text terminal.

`x`   The frame is displayed on an X graphical terminal.

`w32`   The frame is displayed on a MS-Windows graphical terminal.

`ns`   The frame is displayed on a GNUstep or Macintosh Cocoa graphical terminal.

`pc`   The frame is displayed on an MS-DOS terminal.

`frame-terminal` **&optional** *frame*   [Function]

This function returns the terminal object that displays *frame*. If *frame* is `nil` or unspecified, it defaults to the selected frame.

`terminal-live-p` *object*   [Function]

This predicate returns a non-`nil` value if *object* is a terminal that is live (i.e., not deleted), and `nil` otherwise. For live terminals, the return value indicates what kind of frames are displayed on that terminal; the list of possible values is the same as for `framep` above.

28.1 Creating Frames

To create a new frame, call the function `make-frame`.

`make-frame &optional alist`   [Command]

> This function creates and returns a new frame, displaying the current buffer.
>
> The *alist* argument is an alist that specifies frame parameters for the new frame. See Section 28.4 [Frame Parameters], page 642. If you specify the `terminal` parameter in *alist*, the new frame is created on that terminal. Otherwise, if you specify the `window-system` frame parameter in *alist*, that determines whether the frame should be displayed on a text terminal or a graphical terminal. See Section 37.24 [Window Systems], page 979. If neither is specified, the new frame is created in the same terminal as the selected frame.
>
> Any parameters not mentioned in *alist* default to the values in the alist `default-frame-alist` (see Section 28.4.2 [Initial Parameters], page 644); parameters not specified there default from the X resources or its equivalent on your operating system (see Section "X Resources" in *The GNU Emacs Manual*). After the frame is created, Emacs applies any parameters listed in `frame-inherited-parameters` (see below) and not present in the argument, taking the values from the frame that was selected when `make-frame` was called.
>
> Note that on multi-monitor displays (see Section 28.2 [Multiple Terminals], page 631), the window manager might position the frame differently than specified by the positional parameters in *alist* (see Section 28.4.3.2 [Position Parameters], page 645). For example, some window managers have a policy of displaying the frame on the monitor that contains the largest part of the window (a.k.a. the *dominating* monitor).
>
> This function itself does not make the new frame the selected frame. See Section 28.10 [Input Focus], page 656. The previously selected frame remains selected. On graphical terminals, however, the windowing system may select the new frame for its own reasons.

`before-make-frame-hook`   [Variable]

> A normal hook run by `make-frame` before it creates the frame.

`after-make-frame-functions`   [Variable]

> An abnormal hook run by `make-frame` after it creates the frame. Each function in `after-make-frame-functions` receives one argument, the frame just created.

`frame-inherited-parameters`   [Variable]

> This variable specifies the list of frame parameters that a newly created frame inherits from the currently selected frame. For each parameter (a symbol) that is an element in the list and is not present in the argument to `make-frame`, the function sets the value of that parameter in the created frame to its value in the selected frame.

28.2 Multiple Terminals

Emacs represents each terminal as a *terminal object* data type (see Section 2.4.5 [Terminal Type], page 25). On GNU and Unix systems, Emacs can use multiple terminals simultaneously in each session. On other systems, it can only use a single terminal. Each terminal object has the following attributes:

- The name of the device used by the terminal (e.g., ':0.0' or /dev/tty).

- The terminal and keyboard coding systems used on the terminal. See Section 32.10.8 [Terminal I/O Encoding], page 786.

- The kind of display associated with the terminal. This is the symbol returned by the function `terminal-live-p` (i.e., `x`, `t`, `w32`, `ns`, or `pc`). See Chapter 28 [Frames], page 630.

- A list of terminal parameters. See Section 28.5 [Terminal Parameters], page 653.

There is no primitive for creating terminal objects. Emacs creates them as needed, such as when you call `make-frame-on-display` (described below).

`terminal-name &optional terminal`   [Function]
> This function returns the file name of the device used by *terminal*. If *terminal* is omitted or `nil`, it defaults to the selected frame's terminal. *terminal* can also be a frame, meaning that frame's terminal.

`terminal-list`   [Function]
> This function returns a list of all live terminal objects.

`get-device-terminal device`   [Function]
> This function returns a terminal whose device name is given by *device*. If *device* is a string, it can be either the file name of a terminal device, or the name of an X display of the form '*host:server.screen*'. If *device* is a frame, this function returns that frame's terminal; `nil` means the selected frame. Finally, if *device* is a terminal object that represents a live terminal, that terminal is returned. The function signals an error if its argument is none of the above.

`delete-terminal &optional terminal force`   [Function]
> This function deletes all frames on *terminal* and frees the resources used by it. It runs the abnormal hook `delete-terminal-functions`, passing *terminal* as the argument to each function.
>
> If *terminal* is omitted or `nil`, it defaults to the selected frame's terminal. *terminal* can also be a frame, meaning that frame's terminal.
>
> Normally, this function signals an error if you attempt to delete the sole active terminal, but if *force* is non-`nil`, you are allowed to do so. Emacs automatically calls this function when the last frame on a terminal is deleted (see Section 28.7 [Deleting Frames], page 655).

`delete-terminal-functions`   [Variable]
> An abnormal hook run by `delete-terminal`. Each function receives one argument, the *terminal* argument passed to `delete-terminal`. Due to technical details, the functions may be called either just before the terminal is deleted, or just afterwards.

A few Lisp variables are *terminal-local*; that is, they have a separate binding for each terminal. The binding in effect at any time is the one for the terminal that the currently selected frame belongs to. These variables include `default-minibuffer-frame`, `defining-kbd-macro`, `last-kbd-macro`, and `system-key-alist`. They are always terminal-local, and can never be buffer-local (see Section 11.10 [Buffer-Local Variables], page 171).

On GNU and Unix systems, each X display is a separate graphical terminal. When Emacs is started from within the X window system, it uses the X display specified by the `DISPLAY` environment variable, or by the '`--display`' option (see Section "Initial Options" in *The GNU Emacs Manual*). Emacs can connect to other X displays via the command `make-frame-on-display`. Each X display has its own selected frame and its own minibuffer windows; however, only one of those frames is *the* selected frame at any given moment (see Section 28.10 [Input Focus], page 656). Emacs can even connect to other text terminals, by interacting with the `emacsclient` program. See Section "Emacs Server" in *The GNU Emacs Manual*.

A single X server can handle more than one display. Each X display has a three-part name, '`hostname:displaynumber.screennumber`'. The first part, *hostname*, specifies the name of the machine to which the display is physically connected. The second part, *displaynumber*, is a zero-based number that identifies one or more monitors connected to that machine that share a common keyboard and pointing device (mouse, tablet, etc.). The third part, *screennumber*, identifies a zero-based screen number (a separate monitor) that is part of a single monitor collection on that X server. When you use two or more screens belonging to one server, Emacs knows by the similarity in their names that they share a single keyboard.

Systems that don't use the X window system, such as MS-Windows, don't support the notion of X displays, and have only one display on each host. The display name on these systems doesn't follow the above 3-part format; for example, the display name on MS-Windows systems is a constant string '`w32`', and exists for compatibility, so that you could pass it to functions that expect a display name.

make-frame-on-display *display* **&optional** *parameters* [Command]

This function creates and returns a new frame on *display*, taking the other frame parameters from the alist *parameters*. *display* should be the name of an X display (a string).

Before creating the frame, this function ensures that Emacs is set up to display graphics. For instance, if Emacs has not processed X resources (e.g., if it was started on a text terminal), it does so at this time. In all other respects, this function behaves like `make-frame` (see Section 28.1 [Creating Frames], page 631).

x-display-list [Function]

This function returns a list that indicates which X displays Emacs has a connection to. The elements of the list are strings, and each one is a display name.

x-open-connection *display* **&optional** *xrm-string must-succeed* [Function]

This function opens a connection to the X display *display*, without creating a frame on that display. Normally, Emacs Lisp programs need not call this function, as `make-frame-on-display` calls it automatically. The only reason for calling it is to check whether communication can be established with a given X display.

The optional argument *xrm-string*, if not `nil`, is a string of resource names and values, in the same format used in the `.Xresources` file. See Section "X Resources" in *The GNU Emacs Manual*. These values apply to all Emacs frames created on this display, overriding the resource values recorded in the X server. Here's an example of what this string might look like:

```
    "*BorderWidth: 3\n*InternalBorder: 2\n"
```

If *must-succeed* is non-nil, failure to open the connection terminates Emacs. Otherwise, it is an ordinary Lisp error.

x-close-connection *display*   [Function]

This function closes the connection to display *display*. Before you can do this, you must first delete all the frames that were open on that display (see Section 28.7 [Deleting Frames], page 655).

On some multi-monitor setups, a single X display outputs to more than one physical monitor. You can use the functions `display-monitor-attributes-list` and `frame-monitor-attributes` to obtain information about such setups.

display-monitor-attributes-list &optional *display*   [Function]

This function returns a list of physical monitor attributes on *display*, which can be a display name (a string), a terminal, or a frame; if omitted or `nil`, it defaults to the selected frame's display. Each element of the list is an association list, representing the attributes of a physical monitor. The first element corresponds to the primary monitor. The attribute keys and values are:

'geometry'

> Position of the top-left corner of the monitor's screen and its size, in pixels, as '(*x y width height*)'. Note that, if the monitor is not the primary monitor, some of the coordinates might be negative.

'workarea'

> Position of the top-left corner and size of the work area (usable space) in pixels as '(*x y width height*)'. This may be different from 'geometry' in that space occupied by various window manager features (docks, taskbars, etc.) may be excluded from the work area. Whether or not such features actually subtract from the work area depends on the platform and environment. Again, if the monitor is not the primary monitor, some of the coordinates might be negative.

'mm-size' Width and height in millimeters as '(*width height*)'

'frames'   List of frames that this physical monitor dominates (see below).

'name'   Name of the physical monitor as *string*.

'source'   Source of the multi-monitor information as *string*; e.g., 'XRandr' or 'Xinerama'.

x, *y*, *width*, and *height* are integers. 'name' and 'source' may be absent.

A frame is *dominated* by a physical monitor when either the largest area of the frame resides in that monitor, or (if the frame does not intersect any physical monitors) that monitor is the closest to the frame. Every (non-tooltip) frame (whether visible or not) in a graphical display is dominated by exactly one physical monitor at a time, though the frame can span multiple (or no) physical monitors.

Here's an example of the data produced by this function on a 2-monitor display:

```
    (display-monitor-attributes-list)
```

```
⇒
(((geometry 0 0 1920 1080)  ;; Left-hand, primary monitor
  (workarea 0 0 1920 1050)  ;; A taskbar occupies some of the height
  (mm-size 677 381)
  (name . "DISPLAY1")
  (frames #<frame emacs@host *Messages* 0x11578c0>
          #<frame emacs@host *scratch* 0x114b838>))
 ((geometry 1920 0 1680 1050)  ;; Right-hand monitor
  (workarea 1920 0 1680 1050)  ;; Whole screen can be used
  (mm-size 593 370)
  (name . "DISPLAY2")
  (frames)))
```

`frame-monitor-attributes` **&optional** *frame*   [Function]

   This function returns the attributes of the physical monitor dominating (see above) *frame*, which defaults to the selected frame.

28.3 Frame Geometry

The geometry of a frame depends on the toolkit that was used to build this instance of Emacs and the terminal that displays the frame. This chapter describes these dependencies and some of the functions to deal with them. Note that the *frame* argument of all of these functions has to specify a live frame (see Section 28.7 [Deleting Frames], page 655). If omitted or `nil`, it specifies the selected frame (see Section 28.10 [Input Focus], page 656).

28.3.1 Frame Layout

The drawing below sketches the layout of a frame on a graphical terminal:

```
             <----------- Outer Frame Width ----------->

             -----------------------------------------------
         ^(0)  _____ External Border _____    |
         | |  |_____ Title Bar _____|   |
         | | (1)_____ Menu Bar _____|   |  ^
         | | (2)_____ Tool Bar _____|   |  ^
         | | (3) _____ Internal Border _____   |  |  ^
         | |  | |   ^                             | |  | |  |
         | |  | |   |                             | |  | |  |
  Outer  | |  | | Inner                           | |  | Native
  Frame  | |  | | Frame                           | |  | Frame
  Height | |  | | Height                          | |  | Height
         | |  | |   |                             | |  | |  |
         | |  | |<--+--- Inner Frame Width ------>| |  | |  |
         | |  | |   |                             | |  | |  |
         | |  | |___v_____| |  | |  |
         | |  |_____ Internal Border _____|  | v
         v |_____ External Border _____|
             <-------- Native Frame Width -------->
```

   In practice not all of the areas shown in the drawing will or may be present. The meaning of these areas is:

'Outer Frame'

> The *outer frame* is a rectangle comprising all areas shown in the drawing. The edges of that rectangle are called the *outer edges* of the frame. The *outer width* and *outer height* of the frame specify the size of that rectangle.
>
> The upper left corner of the outer frame (indicated by '(0)' in the drawing above) is the *outer position* or the frame. It is specified by and settable via the `left` and `top` frame parameters (see Section 28.4.3.2 [Position Parameters], page 645) as well as the functions `frame-position` and `set-frame-position` (see Section 28.3.3 [Size and Position], page 639).

'External Border'

> The *external border* is part of the decorations supplied by the window manager. It's typically used for resizing the frame with the mouse. The external border is normally not shown on "fullboth" and maximized frames (see Section 28.4.3.3 [Size Parameters], page 647) and doesn't exist for text terminal frames.
>
> The external border should not be confused with the *outer border* specified by the `border-width` frame parameter (see Section 28.4.3.4 [Layout Parameters], page 648). Since the outer border is usually ignored on most platforms it is not covered here.

'Title Bar'

> The *title bar* is also part of the window manager's decorations and typically displays the title of the frame (see Section 28.6 [Frame Titles], page 654) as well as buttons for minimizing, maximizing and deleting the frame. The title bar is usually not displayed on fullboth (see Section 28.4.3.3 [Size Parameters], page 647) or tooltip frames. Title bars don't exist for text terminal frames.

'Menu Bar' The menu bar (see Section 21.17.5 [Menu Bar], page 422) can be either internal (drawn by Emacs itself) or external (drawn by a toolkit). Most builds (GTK+, Lucid, Motif and Windows) rely on an external menu bar. NS also uses an external menu bar which, however, is not part of the outer frame. Non-toolkit builds can provide an internal menu bar. On text terminal frames, the menu bar is part of the frame's root window (see Section 27.2 [Windows and Frames], page 568).

'Tool Bar' Like the menu bar, the tool bar (see Section 21.17.6 [Tool Bar], page 423) can be either internal (drawn by Emacs itself) or external (drawn by a toolkit). The GTK+ and NS builds have the tool bar drawn by the toolkit. The remaining builds use internal tool bars. With GTK+ the tool bar can be located on either side of the frame, immediately outside the internal border, see below.

'Native Frame'

> The *native frame* is a rectangle located entirely within the outer frame. It excludes the areas occupied by the external border, the title bar and any external menu or external tool bar. The area enclosed by the native frame is sometimes also referred to as the *display area* of the frame. The edges of the native frame are called the *native edges* of the frame. The *native width* and *native height* of the frame specify the size of the rectangle.
>
> The top left corner of the native frame specifies the *native position* of the frame. (1)–(3) in the drawing above indicate that position for the various builds:

(1) non-toolkit and terminal frames

(2) Lucid, Motif and Windows frames

(3) GTK+ and NS frames

Accordingly, the native height of a frame includes the height of the tool bar but not that of the menu bar (Lucid, Motif, Windows) or those of the menu bar and the tool bar (non-toolkit and text terminal frames).

The native position of a frame is the reference position of functions that set or return the current position of the mouse (see Section 28.15 [Mouse Position], page 661) and for functions dealing with the position of windows like `window-edges`, `window-at` or `coordinates-in-window-p` (see Section 27.24 [Coordinates and Windows], page 620).

'`Internal Border`'

The internal border (see Section 28.4.3.4 [Layout Parameters], page 648) is a border drawn by Emacs around the inner frame (see below).

'`Inner Frame`'

The *inner frame* is the rectangle reserved for the frame's windows. It's enclosed by the internal border which, however, is not part of the inner frame. Its edges are called the *inner edges* of the frame. The *inner width* and *inner height* specify the size of the rectangle.

As a rule, the inner frame is subdivided into the frame's root window (see Section 27.2 [Windows and Frames], page 568) and the frame's minibuffer window (see Section 19.11 [Minibuffer Windows], page 341). There are two notable exceptions to this rule: A *minibuffer-less frame* contains a root window only and does not contain a minibuffer window. A *minibuffer-only frame* contains only a minibuffer window which also serves as that frame's root window. See Section 28.4.2 [Initial Parameters], page 644, for how to create such frame configurations.

'`Text Area`'

The *text area* of a frame is a somewhat fictitious area located entirely within the native frame. It can be obtained by removing from the native frame any internal borders, one vertical and one horizontal scroll bar, and one left and one right fringe as specified for this frame, see Section 28.4.3.4 [Layout Parameters], page 648.

The *absolute position* of a frame or its edges is usually given in terms of pixels counted from an origin at position (0, 0) of the frame's display. Note that with multiple monitors the origin does not necessarily coincide with the top left corner of the entire usable display area. Hence the absolute outer position of a frame or the absolute positions of the edges of the outer, native or inner frame can be negative in such an environment even when that frame is completely visible.

For a frame on a graphical terminal the following function returns the sizes of the areas described above:

frame-geometry &optional *frame*   [Function]

This function returns geometric attributes of *frame*. The return value is an association list of the attributes listed below. All coordinate, height and width values are integers counting pixels.

outer-position

    A cons of the absolute X- and Y-coordinates of the outer position of *frame*, relative to the origin at position (0, 0) of *frame*'s display.

outer-size

    A cons of the outer width and height of *frame*.

external-border-size

    A cons of the horizontal and vertical width of *frame*'s external borders as supplied by the window manager. If the window manager doesn't supply these values, Emacs will try to guess them from the coordinates of the outer and inner frame.

title-bar-size

    A cons of the width and height of the title bar of *frame* as supplied by the window manager or operating system. If both of them are zero, the frame has no title bar. If only the width is zero, Emacs was not able to retrieve the width information.

menu-bar-external

    If non-**nil**, this means the menu bar is external (not part of the native frame of *frame*).

menu-bar-size

    A cons of the width and height of the menu bar of *frame*.

tool-bar-external

    If non-**nil**, this means the tool bar is external (not part of the native frame of *frame*).

tool-bar-position

    This tells on which side the tool bar on *frame* is and can be one of **left**, **top**, **right** or **bottom**. The only toolkit that currently supports a value other than **top** is GTK+.

tool-bar-size

    A cons of the width and height of the tool bar of *frame*.

internal-border-width

    The width of the internal border of *frame*.

The following function can be used to retrieve the edges of the outer, native and inner frame.

frame-edges &optional *frame type*   [Function]

This function returns the edges of the outer, native or inner frame of *frame*. *frame* must be a live frame and defaults to the selected one. The list returned has the form (*left top right bottom*) where all values are in pixels relative to the position (0, 0) of *frame*'s display. For terminal frames *left* and *top* are both zero.

Optional argument *type* specifies the type of the edges to return: *type* `outer-edges` means to return the outer edges of *frame*, `native-edges` (or `nil`) means to return its native edges and `inner-edges` means to return its inner edges.

Notice that the pixels at the positions *bottom* and *right* lie immediately outside the corresponding frame. This means that if you have, for example, two side-by-side frames positioned such that the right outer edge of the frame on the left equals the left outer edge of the frame on the right, the pixels representing that edge are part of the frame on the right.

28.3.2 Frame Font

Each frame has a *default font* which specifies the default character size for that frame. This size is meant when retrieving or changing the size of a frame in terms of columns or lines (see Section 28.4.3.3 [Size Parameters], page 647). It is also used when resizing (see Section 27.3 [Window Sizes], page 572) or splitting (see Section 27.6 [Splitting Windows], page 581) windows.

The terms *line height* and *canonical character height* are sometimes used instead of "default character height". Similarly, the terms *column width* and *canonical character width* are used instead of "default character width".

`frame-char-height` &optional *frame*   [Function]
`frame-char-width` &optional *frame*   [Function]

> These functions return the default height and width of a character in *frame*, measured in pixels. Together, these values establish the size of the default font on *frame*. The values depend on the choice of font for *frame*, see Section 28.4.3.8 [Font and Color Parameters], page 651.

The default font can be also set directly with the following function:

`set-frame-font` *font* &optional *keep-size frames*   [Command]

> This sets the default font to *font*. When called interactively, it prompts for the name of a font, and uses that font on the selected frame. When called from Lisp, *font* should be a font name (a string), a font object, font entity, or a font spec.
>
> If the optional argument *keep-size* is `nil`, this keeps the number of frame lines and columns fixed. (If non-`nil`, the option `frame-inhibit-implied-resize` described in the next section will override this.) If *keep-size* is non-`nil` (or with a prefix argument), it tries to keep the size of the display area of the current frame fixed by adjusting the number of lines and columns.
>
> If the optional argument *frames* is `nil`, this applies the font to the selected frame only. If *frames* is non-`nil`, it should be a list of frames to act upon, or `t` meaning all existing and all future graphical frames.

28.3.3 Size and Position

You can read or change the position of a frame using the frame parameters `left` and `top` (see Section 28.4.3.2 [Position Parameters], page 645) and its size using the `height` and `width` parameters (see Section 28.4.3.3 [Size Parameters], page 647). Here are some special features for working with sizes and positions. For all of these functions the argument *frame* must denote a live frame and defaults to the selected frame.

frame-position **&optional** *frame*   [Function]

 This function returns the outer position (see Section 28.3.1 [Frame Layout], page 635) of *frame* in pixels. The value is a cons giving the coordinates of the top left corner of the outer frame of *frame* relative to an origin at the position (0, 0) of the frame's display. On a text terminal frame both values are zero.

set-frame-position *frame x y*   [Function]

 This function sets the outer frame position of *frame* to *x* and *y*. The latter arguments specify pixels and normally count from an origin at the position (0, 0) of *frame*'s display.

 A negative parameter value positions the right edge of the outer frame by -*x* pixels left from the right edge of the screen or the bottom edge by -*y* pixels up from the bottom edge of the screen.

 This function has no effect on text terminal frames.

frame-pixel-height **&optional** *frame*   [Function]
frame-pixel-width **&optional** *frame*   [Function]

 These functions return the inner height and width (the height and width of the display area, see Section 28.3.1 [Frame Layout], page 635) of *frame* in pixels. For a text terminal, the results are in characters rather than pixels.

frame-text-height **&optional** *frame*   [Function]
frame-text-width **&optional** *frame*   [Function]

 These functions return the height and width of the text area of *frame* (see Section 28.3.1 [Frame Layout], page 635), measured in pixels. For a text terminal, the results are in characters rather than pixels.

 The value returned by **frame-text-height** differs from that returned by **frame-pixel-height** by not including the heights of any internal tool bar or menu bar, the height of one horizontal scroll bar and the widths of the internal border.

 The value returned by **frame-text-width** differs from that returned by **frame-pixel-width** by not including the width of one vertical scroll bar, the widths of one left and one right fringe and the widths of the internal border.

frame-height **&optional** *frame*   [Function]
frame-width **&optional** *frame*   [Function]

 These functions return the height and width of the text area of *frame*, measured in units of the default font height and width of *frame* (see Section 28.3.2 [Frame Font], page 639). These functions are plain shorthands for writing (`frame-parameter frame 'height`) and (`frame-parameter frame 'width`).

 If the text area of *frame* measured in pixels is not a multiple of its default font size, the values returned by these functions are rounded down to the number of characters of the default font that fully fit into the text area.

frame-resize-pixelwise   [User Option]

 If this option is **nil**, a frame's size is usually rounded to a multiple of the current values of that frame's **frame-char-height** and **frame-char-width** whenever the frame is resized. If this is non-**nil**, no rounding occurs, hence frame sizes can increase/decrease by one pixel.

Setting this variable usually causes the next resize operation to pass the corresponding size hints to the window manager. This means that this variable should be set only in a user's initial file; applications should never bind it temporarily.

The precise meaning of a value of `nil` for this option depends on the toolkit used. Dragging the external border with the mouse is done character-wise provided the window manager is willing to process the corresponding size hints. Calling `set-frame-size` (see below) with arguments that do not specify the frame size as an integer multiple of its character size, however, may: be ignored, cause a rounding (GTK+), or be accepted (Lucid, Motif, MS-Windows).

With some window managers you may have to set this to non-`nil` in order to make a frame appear truly maximized or full-screen.

`set-frame-size` *frame width height* **&optional** *pixelwise*   [Function]
This function sets the size of the text area of *frame*, measured in terms of the canonical height and width of a character on *frame* (see Section 28.3.2 [Frame Font], page 639).

The optional argument *pixelwise* non-`nil` means to measure the new width and height in units of pixels instead. Note that if `frame-resize-pixelwise` is `nil`, some toolkits may refuse to fully honor the request if it does not increase/decrease the frame size to a multiple of its character size.

`set-frame-height` *frame height* **&optional** *pretend pixelwise*   [Function]
This function resizes the text area of *frame* to a height of *height* lines. The sizes of existing windows in *frame* are altered proportionally to fit.

If *pretend* is non-`nil`, then Emacs displays *height* lines of output in *frame*, but does not change its value for the actual height of the frame. This is only useful on text terminals. Using a smaller height than the terminal actually implements may be useful to reproduce behavior observed on a smaller screen, or if the terminal malfunctions when using its whole screen. Setting the frame height directly does not always work, because knowing the correct actual size may be necessary for correct cursor positioning on text terminals.

The optional fourth argument *pixelwise* non-`nil` means that *frame* should be *height* pixels high. Note that if `frame-resize-pixelwise` is `nil`, some toolkits may refuse to fully honor the request if it does not increase/decrease the frame height to a multiple of its character height.

`set-frame-width` *frame width* **&optional** *pretend pixelwise*   [Function]
This function sets the width of the text area of *frame*, measured in characters. The argument *pretend* has the same meaning as in `set-frame-height`.

The optional fourth argument *pixelwise* non-`nil` means that *frame* should be *width* pixels wide. Note that if `frame-resize-pixelwise` is `nil`, some toolkits may refuse to fully honor the request if it does not increase/decrease the frame width to a multiple of its character width.

None of these three functions will make a frame smaller than needed to display all of its windows together with their scroll bars, fringes, margins, dividers, mode and header lines. This contrasts with requests by the window manager triggered, for example, by dragging the external border of a frame with the mouse. Such requests are always honored by clipping, if necessary, portions that cannot be displayed at the right, bottom corner of the frame.

28.3.4 Implied Frame Resizing

By default, Emacs tries to keep the number of lines and columns of a frame's text area unaltered when, for example, adding or removing the menu bar, changing the default font or setting the width of the frame's scroll bars. This means, however, that in such case Emacs must ask the window manager to resize the outer frame in order to accommodate the size change. Note that wrapping a menu or tool bar usually does not resize the frame's outer size, hence this will alter the number of displayed lines.

Occasionally, such *implied frame resizing* may be unwanted, for example, when the frame is maximized or made full-screen (where it's turned off by default). In other cases you can disable implied resizing with the following option:

frame-inhibit-implied-resize   [User Option]

> If this option is `nil`, changing font, menu bar, tool bar, internal borders, fringes or scroll bars of a specific frame may implicitly resize the frame's display area in order to preserve the number of columns or lines the frame displays. If this option is non-`nil`, no implied resizing is done.
>
> The value of this option can be also be a list of frame parameters. In that case, implied resizing is inhibited when changing a parameter that appears in this list. The frame parameters currently handled by this option are: `font`, `font-backend`, `internal-border-width`, `menu-bar-lines` and `tool-bar-lines`.
>
> Changing any of the `scroll-bar-width`, `scroll-bar-height`, `vertical-scroll-bars`, `horizontal-scroll-bars`, `left-fringe` and `right-fringe` frame parameters is handled as if the frame contained just one live window. This means, for example, that removing vertical scroll bars on a frame containing several side by side windows will shrink the outer frame width by the width of one scroll bar provided this option is `nil` and keep it unchanged if this option is either `t` or a list containing `vertical-scroll-bars`.
>
> The default value is `'(tool-bar-lines)` for Lucid, Motif and Windows (which means that adding/removing a tool bar there does not change the outer frame height), `nil` on all other window systems including GTK+ (which means that changing any of the parameters listed above may change the size of the outer frame), and `t` otherwise (which means the outer frame size never changes implicitly when there's no window system support).
>
> Note that when a frame is not large enough to accommodate a change of any of the parameters listed above, Emacs may try to enlarge the frame even if this option is non-`nil`.

28.4 Frame Parameters

A frame has many parameters that control its appearance and behavior. Just what parameters a frame has depends on what display mechanism it uses.

Frame parameters exist mostly for the sake of graphical displays. Most frame parameters have no effect when applied to a frame on a text terminal; only the `height`, `width`, `name`, `title`, `menu-bar-lines`, `buffer-list` and `buffer-predicate` parameters do something special. If the terminal supports colors, the parameters `foreground-color`, `background-color`, `background-mode` and `display-type` are also meaningful. If the terminal supports frame transparency, the parameter `alpha` is also meaningful.

28.4.1 Access to Frame Parameters

These functions let you read and change the parameter values of a frame.

`frame-parameter` *frame parameter*   [Function]

> This function returns the value of the parameter *parameter* (a symbol) of *frame*. If *frame* is `nil`, it returns the selected frame's parameter. If *frame* has no setting for *parameter*, this function returns `nil`.

`frame-parameters` **&optional** *frame*   [Function]

> The function `frame-parameters` returns an alist listing all the parameters of *frame* and their values. If *frame* is `nil` or omitted, this returns the selected frame's parameters

`modify-frame-parameters` *frame alist*   [Function]

> This function alters the frame *frame* based on the elements of *alist*. Each element of *alist* has the form (*parm . value*), where *parm* is a symbol naming a parameter. If you don't mention a parameter in *alist*, its value doesn't change. If *frame* is `nil`, it defaults to the selected frame.
>
> Some parameters are only meaningful for frames on certain kinds of display (see Chapter 28 [Frames], page 630). If *alist* includes parameters that are not meaningful for the *frame*'s display, this function will change its value in the frame's parameter list, but will otherwise ignore it.
>
> When *alist* specifies more than one parameter whose value can affect the new size of *frame*, the final size of the frame may differ according to the toolkit used. For example, specifying that a frame should from now on have a menu and/or tool bar instead of none and simultaneously specifying the new height of the frame will inevitably lead to a recalculation of the frame's height. Conceptually, in such case, this function will try to have the explicit height specification prevail. It cannot be excluded, however, that the addition (or removal) of the menu or tool bar, when eventually performed by the toolkit, will defeat this intention.
>
> Sometimes, binding `frame-inhibit-implied-resize` (see Section 28.3.4 [Implied Frame Resizing], page 642) to a non-`nil` value around calls to this function may fix the problem sketched here. Sometimes, however, exactly such binding may be hit by the problem.

`set-frame-parameter` *frame parm value*   [Function]

> This function sets the frame parameter *parm* to the specified *value*. If *frame* is `nil`, it defaults to the selected frame.

`modify-all-frames-parameters` *alist*   [Function]

> This function alters the frame parameters of all existing frames according to *alist*, then modifies `default-frame-alist` (and, if necessary, `initial-frame-alist`) to apply the same parameter values to frames that will be created henceforth.

28.4.2 Initial Frame Parameters

You can specify the parameters for the initial startup frame by setting `initial-frame-alist` in your init file (see Section 38.1.2 [Init File], page 988).

`initial-frame-alist`   [User Option]

> This variable's value is an alist of parameter values used when creating the initial frame. You can set this variable to specify the appearance of the initial frame without altering subsequent frames. Each element has the form:
>
> > `(parameter . value)`
>
> Emacs creates the initial frame before it reads your init file. After reading that file, Emacs checks `initial-frame-alist`, and applies the parameter settings in the altered value to the already created initial frame.
>
> If these settings affect the frame geometry and appearance, you'll see the frame appear with the wrong ones and then change to the specified ones. If that bothers you, you can specify the same geometry and appearance with X resources; those do take effect before the frame is created. See Section "X Resources" in *The GNU Emacs Manual*.
>
> X resource settings typically apply to all frames. If you want to specify some X resources solely for the sake of the initial frame, and you don't want them to apply to subsequent frames, here's how to achieve this. Specify parameters in `default-frame-alist` to override the X resources for subsequent frames; then, to prevent these from affecting the initial frame, specify the same parameters in `initial-frame-alist` with values that match the X resources.

If these parameters include `(minibuffer . nil)`, that indicates that the initial frame should have no minibuffer. In this case, Emacs creates a separate *minibuffer-only frame* as well.

`minibuffer-frame-alist`   [User Option]

> This variable's value is an alist of parameter values used when creating an initial minibuffer-only frame (i.e., the minibuffer-only frame that Emacs creates if `initial-frame-alist` specifies a frame with no minibuffer).

`default-frame-alist`   [User Option]

> This is an alist specifying default values of frame parameters for all Emacs frames—the first frame, and subsequent frames. When using the X Window System, you can get the same results by means of X resources in many cases.
>
> Setting this variable does not affect existing frames. Furthermore, functions that display a buffer in a separate frame may override the default parameters by supplying their own parameters.

If you invoke Emacs with command-line options that specify frame appearance, those options take effect by adding elements to either `initial-frame-alist` or `default-frame-alist`. Options which affect just the initial frame, such as '`--geometry`' and '`--maximized`', add to `initial-frame-alist`; the others add to `default-frame-alist`. see Section "Command Line Arguments for Emacs Invocation" in *The GNU Emacs Manual*.

28.4.3 Window Frame Parameters

Just what parameters a frame has depends on what display mechanism it uses. This section describes the parameters that have special meanings on some or all kinds of terminals. Of these, `name`, `title`, `height`, `width`, `buffer-list` and `buffer-predicate` provide meaningful information in terminal frames, and `tty-color-mode` is meaningful only for frames on text terminals.

28.4.3.1 Basic Parameters

These frame parameters give the most basic information about the frame. `title` and `name` are meaningful on all terminals.

display
: The display on which to open this frame. It should be a string of the form '*host*:*dpy*.*screen*', just like the `DISPLAY` environment variable. See Section 28.2 [Multiple Terminals], page 631, for more details about display names.

display-type
: This parameter describes the range of possible colors that can be used in this frame. Its value is `color`, `grayscale` or `mono`.

title
: If a frame has a non-`nil` title, it appears in the window system's title bar at the top of the frame, and also in the mode line of windows in that frame if `mode-line-frame-identification` uses '`%F`' (see Section 22.4.5 [%-Constructs], page 457). This is normally the case when Emacs is not using a window system, and can only display one frame at a time. See Section 28.6 [Frame Titles], page 654.

name
: The name of the frame. The frame name serves as a default for the frame title, if the `title` parameter is unspecified or `nil`. If you don't specify a name, Emacs sets the frame name automatically (see Section 28.6 [Frame Titles], page 654).

    If you specify the frame name explicitly when you create the frame, the name is also used (instead of the name of the Emacs executable) when looking up X resources for the frame.

explicit-name
: If the frame name was specified explicitly when the frame was created, this parameter will be that name. If the frame wasn't explicitly named, this parameter will be `nil`.

28.4.3.2 Position Parameters

Position parameters' values are measured in pixels. (Note that none of these parameters exist on TTY frames.)

left
: The position, in pixels, of the left (or right) edge of the frame with respect to the left (or right) edge of the screen. The value may be:

    an integer
    : A positive integer relates the left edge of the frame to the left edge of the screen. A negative integer relates the right frame edge to the right screen edge.

(+ *pos*)   This specifies the position of the left frame edge relative to the left
screen edge. The integer *pos* may be positive or negative; a negative
value specifies a position outside the screen or on a monitor other
than the primary one (for multi-monitor displays).

(- *pos*)   This specifies the position of the right frame edge relative to the
right screen edge. The integer *pos* may be positive or negative; a
negative value specifies a position outside the screen or on a monitor
other than the primary one (for multi-monitor displays).

Some window managers ignore program-specified positions. If you want to be
sure the position you specify is not ignored, specify a non-`nil` value for the
`user-position` parameter as well.

If the window manager refuses to align a frame at the left or top screen edge,
combining position notation and `user-position` as in

```
(modify-frame-parameters
    nil '((user-position . t) (left . (+ -4))))
```

may help to override that.

top   The screen position of the top (or bottom) edge, in pixels, with respect to the
top (or bottom) edge of the screen. It works just like `left`, except vertically
instead of horizontally.

icon-left

The screen position of the left edge of the frame's icon, in pixels, counting from
the left edge of the screen. This takes effect when the frame is iconified, if the
window manager supports this feature. If you specify a value for this parameter,
then you must also specify a value for `icon-top` and vice versa.

icon-top   The screen position of the top edge of the frame's icon, in pixels, counting from
the top edge of the screen. This takes effect when the frame is iconified, if the
window manager supports this feature.

user-position

When you create a frame and specify its screen position with the `left` and
`top` parameters, use this parameter to say whether the specified position was
user-specified (explicitly requested in some way by a human user) or merely
program-specified (chosen by a program). A non-`nil` value says the position
was user-specified.

Window managers generally heed user-specified positions, and some heed
program-specified positions too. But many ignore program-specified positions,
placing the window in a default fashion or letting the user place it with the
mouse. Some window managers, including `twm`, let the user specify whether to
obey program-specified positions or ignore them.

When you call `make-frame`, you should specify a non-`nil` value for this parameter if the values of the `left` and `top` parameters represent the user's stated
preference; otherwise, use `nil`.

28.4.3.3 Size Parameters

Frame parameters specify frame sizes in character units. On graphical displays, the `default` face determines the actual pixel sizes of these character units (see Section 37.12.1 [Face Attributes], page 915).

`height`   The height of the frame's text area (see Section 28.3 [Frame Geometry], page 635), in characters.

`width`   The width of the frame's text area (see Section 28.3 [Frame Geometry], page 635), in characters.

`user-size`

   This does for the size parameters `height` and `width` what the `user-position` parameter (see Section 28.4.3.2 [Position Parameters], page 645) does for the position parameters `top` and `left`.

`fullscreen`

   This parameter specifies whether to maximize the frame's width, height or both. Its value can be `fullwidth`, `fullheight`, `fullboth`, or `maximized`. A *fullwidth* frame is as wide as possible, a *fullheight* frame is as tall as possible, and a *fullboth* frame is both as wide and as tall as possible. A *maximized* frame is like a "fullboth" frame, except that it usually keeps its title bar and the buttons for resizing and closing the frame. Also, maximized frames typically avoid hiding any task bar or panels displayed on the desktop. A "fullboth" frame, on the other hand, usually omits the title bar and occupies the entire available screen space.

   Full-height and full-width frames are more similar to maximized frames in this regard. However, these typically display an external border which might be absent with maximized frames. Hence the heights of maximized and full-height frames and the widths of maximized and full-width frames often differ by a few pixels.

   With some window managers you may have to customize the variable `frame-resize-pixelwise` (see Section 28.3.3 [Size and Position], page 639) in order to make a frame truly appear maximized or full-screen. Moreover, some window managers might not support smooth transition between the various full-screen or maximization states. Customizing the variable `x-frame-normalize-before-maximize` can help to overcome that.

`fullscreen-restore`

   This parameter specifies the desired fullscreen state of the frame after invoking the `toggle-frame-fullscreen` command (see Section "Frame Commands" in *The GNU Emacs Manual*) in the "fullboth" state. Normally this parameter is installed automatically by that command when toggling the state to fullboth. If, however, you start Emacs in the "fullboth" state, you have to specify the desired behavior in your initial file as, for example

   ```
   (setq default-frame-alist
         '((fullscreen . fullboth) (fullscreen-restore . fullheight)))
   ```

   This will give a new frame full height after typing in it `F11` for the first time.

28.4.3.4 Layout Parameters

These frame parameters enable or disable various parts of the frame, or control their sizes.

`border-width`
> The width in pixels of the frame's border.

`internal-border-width`
> The distance in pixels between text (or fringe) and the frame's border.

`vertical-scroll-bars`
> Whether the frame has scroll bars for vertical scrolling, and which side of the frame they should be on. The possible values are `left`, `right`, and `nil` for no scroll bars.

`horizontal-scroll-bars`
> Whether the frame has scroll bars for horizontal scrolling (`t` and `bottom` mean yes, `nil` means no).

`scroll-bar-width`
> The width of vertical scroll bars, in pixels, or `nil` meaning to use the default width.

`scroll-bar-height`
> The height of horizontal scroll bars, in pixels, or `nil` meaning to use the default height.

`left-fringe`
`right-fringe`
> The default width of the left and right fringes of windows in this frame (see Section 37.13 [Fringes], page 937). If either of these is zero, that effectively removes the corresponding fringe.
>
> When you use `frame-parameter` to query the value of either of these two frame parameters, the return value is always an integer. When using `set-frame-parameter`, passing a `nil` value imposes an actual default value of 8 pixels.

`right-divider-width`
> The width (thickness) reserved for the right divider (see Section 37.15 [Window Dividers], page 944) of any window on the frame, in pixels. A value of zero means to not draw right dividers.

`bottom-divider-width`
> The width (thickness) reserved for the bottom divider (see Section 37.15 [Window Dividers], page 944) of any window on the frame, in pixels. A value of zero means to not draw bottom dividers.

`menu-bar-lines`
> The number of lines to allocate at the top of the frame for a menu bar. The default is 1 if Menu Bar mode is enabled, and 0 otherwise. See Section "Menu Bars" in *The GNU Emacs Manual*.

`tool-bar-lines`
> The number of lines to use for the tool bar. The default is 1 if Tool Bar mode is enabled, and 0 otherwise. See Section "Tool Bars" in *The GNU Emacs Manual*.

`tool-bar-position`
> The position of the tool bar. Currently only for the GTK tool bar. Value can be one of `top`, `bottom` `left`, `right`. The default is `top`.

`line-spacing`
> Additional space to leave below each text line, in pixels (a positive integer). See Section 37.11 [Line Height], page 913, for more information.

28.4.3.5 Buffer Parameters

These frame parameters, meaningful on all kinds of terminals, deal with which buffers have been, or should, be displayed in the frame.

`minibuffer`
> Whether this frame has its own minibuffer. The value `t` means yes, `nil` means no, `only` means this frame is just a minibuffer. If the value is a minibuffer window (in some other frame), the frame uses that minibuffer.
>
> This frame parameter takes effect when the frame is created, and can not be changed afterwards.

`buffer-predicate`
> The buffer-predicate function for this frame. The function `other-buffer` uses this predicate (from the selected frame) to decide which buffers it should consider, if the predicate is not `nil`. It calls the predicate with one argument, a buffer, once for each buffer; if the predicate returns a non-`nil` value, it considers that buffer.

`buffer-list`
> A list of buffers that have been selected in this frame, ordered most-recently-selected first.

`unsplittable`
> If non-`nil`, this frame's window is never split automatically.

28.4.3.6 Window Management Parameters

The following frame parameters control various aspects of the frame's interaction with the window manager. They have no effect on text terminals.

`visibility`
> The state of visibility of the frame. There are three possibilities: `nil` for invisible, `t` for visible, and `icon` for iconified. See Section 28.11 [Visibility of Frames], page 658.

`auto-raise`
> If non-`nil`, Emacs automatically raises the frame when it is selected. Some window managers do not allow this.

`auto-lower`
> If non-`nil`, Emacs automatically lowers the frame when it is deselected. Some window managers do not allow this.

icon-type

> The type of icon to use for this frame. If the value is a string, that specifies a file containing a bitmap to use; nil specifies no icon (in which case the window manager decides what to show); any other non-nil value specifies the default Emacs icon.

icon-name

> The name to use in the icon for this frame, when and if the icon appears. If this is nil, the frame's title is used.

window-id

> The ID number which the graphical display uses for this frame. Emacs assigns this parameter when the frame is created; changing the parameter has no effect on the actual ID number.

outer-window-id

> The ID number of the outermost window-system window in which the frame exists. As with window-id, changing this parameter has no actual effect.

wait-for-wm

> If non-nil, tell Xt to wait for the window manager to confirm geometry changes. Some window managers, including versions of Fvwm2 and KDE, fail to confirm, so Xt hangs. Set this to nil to prevent hanging with those window managers.

sticky

> If non-nil, the frame is visible on all virtual desktops on systems with virtual desktops.

28.4.3.7 Cursor Parameters

This frame parameter controls the way the cursor looks.

cursor-type

> How to display the cursor. Legitimate values are:
>
> box   Display a filled box. (This is the default.)
>
> hollow   Display a hollow box.
>
> nil   Don't display a cursor.
>
> bar   Display a vertical bar between characters.
>
> (bar . width)
> > Display a vertical bar width pixels wide between characters.
>
> hbar   Display a horizontal bar.
>
> (hbar . height)
> > Display a horizontal bar height pixels high.

The cursor-type frame parameter may be overridden by the variables cursor-type and cursor-in-non-selected-windows:

cursor-type   [Variable]

> This buffer-local variable controls how the cursor looks in a selected window showing the buffer. If its value is t, that means to use the cursor specified by the cursor-type frame parameter. Otherwise, the value should be one of the cursor types listed above, and it overrides the cursor-type frame parameter.

`cursor-in-non-selected-windows`   [User Option]

This buffer-local variable controls how the cursor looks in a window that is not selected. It supports the same values as the `cursor-type` frame parameter; also, `nil` means don't display a cursor in nonselected windows, and `t` (the default) means use a standard modification of the usual cursor type (solid box becomes hollow box, and bar becomes a narrower bar).

`x-stretch-cursor`   [User Option]

This variable controls the width of the block cursor displayed on extra-wide glyphs such as a tab or a stretch of white space. By default, the block cursor is only as wide as the font's default character, and will not cover all of the width of the glyph under it if that glyph is extra-wide. A non-`nil` value of this variable means draw the block cursor as wide as the glyph under it. The default value is `nil`.

This variable has no effect on text-mode frames, since the text-mode cursor is drawn by the terminal out of Emacs's control.

`blink-cursor-alist`   [User Option]

This variable specifies how to blink the cursor. Each element has the form (*on-state* . *off-state*). Whenever the cursor type equals *on-state* (comparing using `equal`), the corresponding *off-state* specifies what the cursor looks like when it blinks off. Both *on-state* and *off-state* should be suitable values for the `cursor-type` frame parameter.

There are various defaults for how to blink each type of cursor, if the type is not mentioned as an *on-state* here. Changes in this variable do not take effect immediately, only when you specify the `cursor-type` frame parameter.

28.4.3.8 Font and Color Parameters

These frame parameters control the use of fonts and colors.

`font-backend`

A list of symbols, specifying the *font backends* to use for drawing fonts in the frame, in order of priority. On X, there are currently two available font backends: `x` (the X core font driver) and `xft` (the Xft font driver). On MS-Windows, there are currently two available font backends: `gdi` and `uniscribe` (see Section "Windows Fonts" in *The GNU Emacs Manual*). On other systems, there is only one available font backend, so it does not make sense to modify this frame parameter.

`background-mode`

This parameter is either `dark` or `light`, according to whether the background color is a light one or a dark one.

`tty-color-mode`

This parameter overrides the terminal's color support as given by the system's terminal capabilities database in that this parameter's value specifies the color mode to use on a text terminal. The value can be either a symbol or a number. A number specifies the number of colors to use (and, indirectly, what commands to issue to produce each color). For example, (`tty-color-mode` . 8) specifies use of the ANSI escape sequences for 8 standard text colors. A value of -1 turns off color support.

If the parameter's value is a symbol, it specifies a number through the value of `tty-color-mode-alist`, and the associated number is used instead.

screen-gamma

If this is a number, Emacs performs gamma correction which adjusts the brightness of all colors. The value should be the screen gamma of your display.

Usual PC monitors have a screen gamma of 2.2, so color values in Emacs, and in X windows generally, are calibrated to display properly on a monitor with that gamma value. If you specify 2.2 for `screen-gamma`, that means no correction is needed. Other values request correction, designed to make the corrected colors appear on your screen the way they would have appeared without correction on an ordinary monitor with a gamma value of 2.2.

If your monitor displays colors too light, you should specify a `screen-gamma` value smaller than 2.2. This requests correction that makes colors darker. A screen gamma value of 1.5 may give good results for LCD color displays.

alpha

This parameter specifies the opacity of the frame, on graphical displays that support variable opacity. It should be an integer between 0 and 100, where 0 means completely transparent and 100 means completely opaque. It can also have a `nil` value, which tells Emacs not to set the frame opacity (leaving it to the window manager).

To prevent the frame from disappearing completely from view, the variable `frame-alpha-lower-limit` defines a lower opacity limit. If the value of the frame parameter is less than the value of this variable, Emacs uses the latter. By default, `frame-alpha-lower-limit` is 20.

The `alpha` frame parameter can also be a cons cell (*active* . *inactive*), where *active* is the opacity of the frame when it is selected, and *inactive* is the opacity when it is not selected.

The following frame parameters are semi-obsolete in that they are automatically equivalent to particular face attributes of particular faces (see Section "Standard Faces" in *The Emacs Manual*):

font

The name of the font for displaying text in the frame. This is a string, either a valid font name for your system or the name of an Emacs fontset (see Section 37.12.11 [Fontsets], page 930). It is equivalent to the `font` attribute of the `default` face.

foreground-color

The color to use for the image of a character. It is equivalent to the `:foreground` attribute of the `default` face.

background-color

The color to use for the background of characters. It is equivalent to the `:background` attribute of the `default` face.

mouse-color

The color for the mouse pointer. It is equivalent to the `:background` attribute of the `mouse` face.

cursor-color
>   The color for the cursor that shows point. It is equivalent to the :background
>   attribute of the cursor face.

border-color
>   The color for the border of the frame. It is equivalent to the :background
>   attribute of the border face.

scroll-bar-foreground
>   If non-nil, the color for the foreground of scroll bars. It is equivalent to the
>   :foreground attribute of the scroll-bar face.

scroll-bar-background
>   If non-nil, the color for the background of scroll bars. It is equivalent to the
>   :background attribute of the scroll-bar face.

28.4.4 Geometry

Here's how to examine the data in an X-style window geometry specification:

x-parse-geometry *geom*   [Function]
>   The function x-parse-geometry converts a standard X window geometry string to
>   an alist that you can use as part of the argument to make-frame.
>
>   The alist describes which parameters were specified in *geom*, and gives the values
>   specified for them. Each element looks like (*parameter . value*). The possible
>   *parameter* values are left, top, width, and height.
>
>   For the size parameters, the value must be an integer. The position parameter names
>   left and top are not totally accurate, because some values indicate the position of
>   the right or bottom edges instead. The *value* possibilities for the position parame-
>   ters are: an integer, a list (+ *pos*), or a list (- *pos*); as previously described (see
>   Section 28.4.3.2 [Position Parameters], page 645).
>
>   Here is an example:

```
(x-parse-geometry "35x70+0-0")
     ⇒ ((height . 70) (width . 35)
        (top - 0) (left . 0))
```

28.5 Terminal Parameters

Each terminal has a list of associated parameters. These *terminal parameters* are mostly a
convenient way of storage for terminal-local variables, but some terminal parameters have
a special meaning.

   This section describes functions to read and change the parameter values of a terminal.
They all accept as their argument either a terminal or a frame; the latter means use that
frame's terminal. An argument of nil means the selected frame's terminal.

terminal-parameters **&optional** *terminal*   [Function]
>   This function returns an alist listing all the parameters of *terminal* and their values.

terminal-parameter *terminal parameter*   [Function]
>   This function returns the value of the parameter *parameter* (a symbol) of *terminal*.
>   If *terminal* has no setting for *parameter*, this function returns nil.

set-terminal-parameter *terminal parameter value*   [Function]
>   This function sets the parameter *parameter* of *terminal* to the specified *value*, and
>   returns the previous value of that parameter.

Here's a list of a few terminal parameters that have a special meaning:

background-mode
>   The classification of the terminal's background color, either `light` or `dark`.

normal-erase-is-backspace
>   Value is either 1 or 0, depending on whether `normal-erase-is-backspace-mode` is turned on or off on this terminal. See Section "DEL Does Not Delete"
>   in *The Emacs Manual*.

terminal-initted
>   After the terminal is initialized, this is set to the terminal-specific initialization
>   function.

tty-mode-set-strings
>   When present, a list of strings containing escape sequences that Emacs will
>   output while configuring a tty for rendering. Emacs emits these strings only
>   when configuring a terminal: if you want to enable a mode on a terminal that
>   is already active (for example, while in `tty-setup-hook`), explicitly output
>   the necessary escape sequence using `send-string-to-terminal` in addition to
>   adding the sequence to `tty-mode-set-strings`.

tty-mode-reset-strings
>   When present, a list of strings that undo the effects of the strings in `tty-mode-set-strings`. Emacs emits these strings when exiting, deleting a terminal, or
>   suspending itself.

28.6 Frame Titles

Every frame has a `name` parameter; this serves as the default for the frame title which
window systems typically display at the top of the frame. You can specify a name explicitly
by setting the `name` frame property.

Normally you don't specify the name explicitly, and Emacs computes the frame name
automatically based on a template stored in the variable `frame-title-format`. Emacs
recomputes the name each time the frame is redisplayed.

frame-title-format   [Variable]
>   This variable specifies how to compute a name for a frame when you have not explicitly specified one. The variable's value is actually a mode line construct, just
>   like `mode-line-format`, except that the '%c' and '%l' constructs are ignored. See
>   Section 22.4.2 [Mode Line Data], page 452.

icon-title-format   [Variable]
>   This variable specifies how to compute the name for an iconified frame, when you
>   have not explicitly specified the frame title. This title appears in the icon itself.

multiple-frames   [Variable]

>   This variable is set automatically by Emacs. Its value is **t** when there are two or
>   more frames (not counting minibuffer-only frames or invisible frames). The default
>   value of **frame-title-format** uses **multiple-frames** so as to put the buffer name in
>   the frame title only when there is more than one frame.
>
>   The value of this variable is not guaranteed to be accurate except while processing
>   **frame-title-format** or **icon-title-format**.

28.7 Deleting Frames

A *live frame* is one that has not been deleted. When a frame is deleted, it is removed from
its terminal display, although it may continue to exist as a Lisp object until there are no
more references to it.

delete-frame &optional *frame force*   [Command]

>   This function deletes the frame *frame*. Unless *frame* is a tooltip, it first runs the hook
>   **delete-frame-functions** (each function gets one argument, *frame*). By default,
>   *frame* is the selected frame.
>
>   A frame cannot be deleted as long as its minibuffer serves as surrogate minibuffer for
>   another frame (see Section 28.9 [Minibuffers and Frames], page 656). Normally, you
>   cannot delete a frame if all other frames are invisible, but if *force* is non-**nil**, then
>   you are allowed to do so.

frame-live-p *frame*   [Function]

>   The function **frame-live-p** returns non-**nil** if the frame *frame* has not been deleted.
>   The possible non-**nil** return values are like those of **framep**. See Chapter 28 [Frames],
>   page 630.

Some window managers provide a command to delete a window. These work by sending
a special message to the program that operates the window. When Emacs gets one of these
commands, it generates a **delete-frame** event, whose normal definition is a command that
calls the function **delete-frame**. See Section 20.7.10 [Misc Events], page 365.

28.8 Finding All Frames

frame-list   [Function]

>   This function returns a list of all the live frames, i.e., those that have not been deleted.
>   It is analogous to **buffer-list** for buffers, and includes frames on all terminals. The
>   list that you get is newly created, so modifying the list doesn't have any effect on the
>   internals of Emacs.

visible-frame-list   [Function]

>   This function returns a list of just the currently visible frames. See Section 28.11
>   [Visibility of Frames], page 658. Frames on text terminals always count as visible,
>   even though only the selected one is actually displayed.

next-frame &optional *frame minibuf*   [Function]

>   This function lets you cycle conveniently through all the frames on the current display
>   from an arbitrary starting point. It returns the next frame after *frame* in the cycle.

If *frame* is omitted or `nil`, it defaults to the selected frame (see Section 28.10 [Input Focus], page 656).

The second argument, *minibuf*, says which frames to consider:

`nil`   Exclude minibuffer-only frames.

`visible`   Consider all visible frames.

0   Consider all visible or iconified frames.

a window   Consider only the frames using that particular window as their minibuffer.

anything else
            Consider all frames.

`previous-frame` **&optional** *frame minibuf*   [Function]
    Like `next-frame`, but cycles through all frames in the opposite direction.

See also `next-window` and `previous-window`, in Section 27.10 [Cyclic Window Ordering], page 591.

28.9 Minibuffers and Frames

Normally, each frame has its own minibuffer window at the bottom, which is used whenever that frame is selected. If the frame has a minibuffer, you can get it with `minibuffer-window` (see Section 19.11 [Minibuffer Windows], page 341).

However, you can also create a frame without a minibuffer. Such a frame must use the minibuffer window of some other frame. That other frame will serve as *surrogate minibuffer frame* for this frame and cannot be deleted via `delete-frame` (see Section 28.7 [Deleting Frames], page 655) as long as this frame is live.

When you create the frame, you can explicitly specify the minibuffer window to use (in some other frame). If you don't, then the minibuffer is found in the frame which is the value of the variable `default-minibuffer-frame`. Its value should be a frame that does have a minibuffer.

If you use a minibuffer-only frame, you might want that frame to raise when you enter the minibuffer. If so, set the variable `minibuffer-auto-raise` to `t`. See Section 28.12 [Raising and Lowering], page 659.

`default-minibuffer-frame`   [Variable]
    This variable specifies the frame to use for the minibuffer window, by default. It does not affect existing frames. It is always local to the current terminal and cannot be buffer-local. See Section 28.2 [Multiple Terminals], page 631.

28.10 Input Focus

At any time, one frame in Emacs is the *selected frame*. The selected window always resides on the selected frame.

When Emacs displays its frames on several terminals (see Section 28.2 [Multiple Terminals], page 631), each terminal has its own selected frame. But only one of these is *the* selected frame: it's the frame that belongs to the terminal from which the most recent input came. That is, when Emacs runs a command that came from a certain terminal, the selected frame is the one of that terminal. Since Emacs runs only a single command at any given time, it needs to consider only one selected frame at a time; this frame is what we call *the selected frame* in this manual. The display on which the selected frame is shown is the *selected frame's display*.

selected-frame   [Function]
    This function returns the selected frame.

Some window systems and window managers direct keyboard input to the window object that the mouse is in; others require explicit clicks or commands to *shift the focus* to various window objects. Either way, Emacs automatically keeps track of which frame has the focus. To explicitly switch to a different frame from a Lisp function, call **select-frame-set-input-focus**.

Lisp programs can also switch frames temporarily by calling the function **select-frame**. This does not alter the window system's concept of focus; rather, it escapes from the window manager's control until that control is somehow reasserted.

When using a text terminal, only one frame can be displayed at a time on the terminal, so after a call to **select-frame**, the next redisplay actually displays the newly selected frame. This frame remains selected until a subsequent call to **select-frame**. Each frame on a text terminal has a number which appears in the mode line before the buffer name (see Section 22.4.4 [Mode Line Variables], page 454).

select-frame-set-input-focus *frame* **&optional** *norecord*   [Function]
    This function selects *frame*, raises it (should it happen to be obscured by other frames) and tries to give it the X server's focus. On a text terminal, the next redisplay displays the new frame on the entire terminal screen. The optional argument *norecord* has the same meaning as for **select-frame** (see below). The return value of this function is not significant.

select-frame *frame* **&optional** *norecord*   [Command]
    This function selects frame *frame*, temporarily disregarding the focus of the X server if any. The selection of *frame* lasts until the next time the user does something to select a different frame, or until the next time this function is called. (If you are using a window system, the previously selected frame may be restored as the selected frame after return to the command loop, because it still may have the window system's input focus.)

    The specified *frame* becomes the selected frame, and its terminal becomes the selected terminal. This function then calls **select-window** as a subroutine, passing the window selected within *frame* as its first argument and *norecord* as its second argument (hence, if *norecord* is non-**nil**, this avoids changing the order of recently selected windows nor the buffer list). See Section 27.9 [Selecting Windows], page 590.

    This function returns *frame*, or **nil** if *frame* has been deleted.

    In general, you should never use **select-frame** in a way that could switch to a different terminal without switching back when you're done.

Emacs cooperates with the window system by arranging to select frames as the server and window manager request. It does so by generating a special kind of input event, called a *focus* event, when appropriate. The command loop handles a focus event by calling `handle-switch-frame`. See Section 20.7.9 [Focus Events], page 365.

`handle-switch-frame` *frame*   [Command]

> This function handles a focus event by selecting frame *frame*.
>
> Focus events normally do their job by invoking this command. Don't call it for any other reason.

`redirect-frame-focus` *frame* **&optional** *focus-frame*   [Function]

> This function redirects focus from *frame* to *focus-frame*. This means that *focus-frame* will receive subsequent keystrokes and events intended for *frame*. After such an event, the value of `last-event-frame` will be *focus-frame*. Also, switch-frame events specifying *frame* will instead select *focus-frame*.
>
> If *focus-frame* is omitted or `nil`, that cancels any existing redirection for *frame*, which therefore once again receives its own events.
>
> One use of focus redirection is for frames that don't have minibuffers. These frames use minibuffers on other frames. Activating a minibuffer on another frame redirects focus to that frame. This puts the focus on the minibuffer's frame, where it belongs, even though the mouse remains in the frame that activated the minibuffer.
>
> Selecting a frame can also change focus redirections. Selecting frame `bar`, when `foo` had been selected, changes any redirections pointing to `foo` so that they point to `bar` instead. This allows focus redirection to work properly when the user switches from one frame to another using `select-window`.
>
> This means that a frame whose focus is redirected to itself is treated differently from a frame whose focus is not redirected. `select-frame` affects the former but not the latter.
>
> The redirection lasts until `redirect-frame-focus` is called to change it.

`focus-in-hook`   [Variable]

> This is a normal hook run when an Emacs frame gains input focus.

`focus-out-hook`   [Variable]

> This is a normal hook run when an Emacs frame loses input focus.

`focus-follows-mouse`   [User Option]

> This option is how you inform Emacs whether the window manager transfers focus when the user moves the mouse. Non-`nil` says that it does. When this is so, the command `other-frame` moves the mouse to a position consistent with the new selected frame.

28.11 Visibility of Frames

A frame on a graphical display may be *visible*, *invisible*, or *iconified*. If it is visible, its contents are displayed in the usual manner. If it is iconified, its contents are not displayed, but there is a little icon somewhere to bring the frame back into view (some window managers refer to this state as *minimized* rather than *iconified*, but from Emacs' point of view they are the same thing). If a frame is invisible, it is not displayed at all.

Visibility is meaningless on text terminals, since only the selected one is actually displayed in any case.

frame-visible-p *frame* [Function]

> This function returns the visibility status of frame *frame*. The value is **t** if *frame* is visible, **nil** if it is invisible, and **icon** if it is iconified.
>
> On a text terminal, all frames are considered visible for the purposes of this function, even though only one frame is displayed. See Section 28.12 [Raising and Lowering], page 659.

iconify-frame **&optional** *frame* [Command]

> This function iconifies frame *frame*. If you omit *frame*, it iconifies the selected frame.

make-frame-visible **&optional** *frame* [Command]

> This function makes frame *frame* visible. If you omit *frame*, it makes the selected frame visible. This does not raise the frame, but you can do that with **raise-frame** if you wish (see Section 28.12 [Raising and Lowering], page 659).

make-frame-invisible **&optional** *frame force* [Command]

> This function makes frame *frame* invisible. If you omit *frame*, it makes the selected frame invisible.
>
> Unless *force* is non-**nil**, this function refuses to make *frame* invisible if all other frames are invisible..

The visibility status of a frame is also available as a frame parameter. You can read or change it as such. See Section 28.4.3.6 [Management Parameters], page 649. The user can also iconify and deiconify frames with the window manager. This happens below the level at which Emacs can exert any control, but Emacs does provide events that you can use to keep track of such changes. See Section 20.7.10 [Misc Events], page 365.

28.12 Raising and Lowering Frames

Most window systems use a desktop metaphor. Part of this metaphor is the idea that system-level windows (e.g., Emacs frames) are stacked in a notional third dimension perpendicular to the screen surface. Where two overlap, the one higher up covers the one underneath. You can *raise* or *lower* a frame using the functions **raise-frame** and **lower-frame**.

raise-frame **&optional** *frame* [Command]

> This function raises frame *frame* (default, the selected frame). If *frame* is invisible or iconified, this makes it visible.

lower-frame **&optional** *frame* [Command]

> This function lowers frame *frame* (default, the selected frame).

minibuffer-auto-raise [User Option]

> If this is non-**nil**, activation of the minibuffer raises the frame that the minibuffer window is in.

On window systems, you can also enable auto-raising (on frame selection) or auto-lowering (on frame deselection) using frame parameters. See Section 28.4.3.6 [Management Parameters], page 649.

The concept of raising and lowering frames also applies to text terminal frames. On each text terminal, only the top frame is displayed at any one time.

tty-top-frame &optional *terminal*   [Function]

> This function returns the top frame on *terminal*. *terminal* should be a terminal object, a frame (meaning that frame's terminal), or **nil** (meaning the selected frame's terminal). If it does not refer to a text terminal, the return value is **nil**.

28.13 Frame Configurations

A *frame configuration* records the current arrangement of frames, all their properties, and the window configuration of each one. (See Section 27.25 [Window Configurations], page 623.)

current-frame-configuration   [Function]

> This function returns a frame configuration list that describes the current arrangement of frames and their contents.

set-frame-configuration *configuration* **&optional** *nodelete*   [Function]

> This function restores the state of frames described in *configuration*. However, this function does not restore deleted frames.
>
> Ordinarily, this function deletes all existing frames not listed in *configuration*. But if *nodelete* is non-**nil**, the unwanted frames are iconified instead.

28.14 Mouse Tracking

Sometimes it is useful to *track* the mouse, which means to display something to indicate where the mouse is and move the indicator as the mouse moves. For efficient mouse tracking, you need a way to wait until the mouse actually moves.

The convenient way to track the mouse is to ask for events to represent mouse motion. Then you can wait for motion by waiting for an event. In addition, you can easily handle any other sorts of events that may occur. That is useful, because normally you don't want to track the mouse forever—only until some other event, such as the release of a button.

track-mouse *body. . .*   [Special Form]

> This special form executes *body*, with generation of mouse motion events enabled. Typically, *body* would use **read-event** to read the motion events and modify the display accordingly. See Section 20.7.8 [Motion Events], page 364, for the format of mouse motion events.
>
> The value of **track-mouse** is that of the last form in *body*. You should design *body* to return when it sees the up-event that indicates the release of the button, or whatever kind of event means it is time to stop tracking.
>
> The **track-mouse** form causes Emacs to generate mouse motion events by binding the variable **track-mouse** to a non-**nil** value. If that variable has the special value **dragging**, it additionally instructs the display engine to refrain from changing the shape of the mouse pointer. This is desirable in Lisp programs that require mouse dragging across large portions of Emacs display, which might otherwise cause the mouse pointer to change its shape according to the display portion it hovers on (see Section 28.18 [Pointer Shape], page 664). Therefore, Lisp programs that need the mouse pointer to retain its original shape during dragging should bind **track-mouse** to the value **dragging** at the beginning of their *body*.

The usual purpose of tracking mouse motion is to indicate on the screen the consequences of pushing or releasing a button at the current position.

In many cases, you can avoid the need to track the mouse by using the `mouse-face` text property (see Section 31.19.4 [Special Properties], page 738). That works at a much lower level and runs more smoothly than Lisp-level mouse tracking.

28.15 Mouse Position

The functions `mouse-position` and `set-mouse-position` give access to the current position of the mouse.

mouse-position [Function]

This function returns a description of the position of the mouse. The value looks like (*frame x . y*), where *x* and *y* are integers giving the (possibly rounded) position in multiples of the default character size of *frame* (see Section 28.3.2 [Frame Font], page 639) relative to the native position of *frame* (see Section 28.3 [Frame Geometry], page 635).

mouse-position-function [Variable]

If non-`nil`, the value of this variable is a function for `mouse-position` to call. `mouse-position` calls this function just before returning, with its normal return value as the sole argument, and it returns whatever this function returns to it.

This abnormal hook exists for the benefit of packages like `xt-mouse.el` that need to do mouse handling at the Lisp level.

set-mouse-position *frame x y* [Function]

This function *warps the mouse* to position *x, y* in frame *frame*. The arguments *x* and *y* are integers, giving the position in multiples of the default character size of *frame* (see Section 28.3.2 [Frame Font], page 639) relative to the native position of *frame* (see Section 28.3 [Frame Geometry], page 635).

The resulting mouse position is constrained to the native frame of *frame*. If *frame* is not visible, this function does nothing. The return value is not significant.

mouse-pixel-position [Function]

This function is like `mouse-position` except that it returns coordinates in units of pixels rather than units of characters.

set-mouse-pixel-position *frame x y* [Function]

This function warps the mouse like `set-mouse-position` except that *x* and *y* are in units of pixels rather than units of characters.

The resulting mouse position is not constrained to the native frame of *frame*. If *frame* is not visible, this function does nothing. The return value is not significant.

On a graphical terminal the following two functions allow the absolute position of the mouse cursor to be retrieved and set.

mouse-absolute-pixel-position [Function]

This function returns a cons cell (*x . y*) of the coordinates of the mouse cursor position in pixels, relative to a position (0, 0) of the selected frame's display.

set-mouse-absolute-pixel-position *x y*   [Function]
> This function moves the mouse cursor to the position (*x*, *y*). The coordinates *x* and *y* are interpreted in pixels relative to a position (0, 0) of the selected frame's display.

The following function can tell whether the mouse cursor is currently visible on a frame:

frame-pointer-visible-p **&optional** *frame*   [Function]
> This predicate function returns non-`nil` if the mouse pointer displayed on *frame* is visible; otherwise it returns `nil`. *frame* omitted or `nil` means the selected frame. This is useful when `make-pointer-invisible` is set to `t`: it allows you to know if the pointer has been hidden. See Section "Mouse Avoidance" in *The Emacs Manual*.

28.16 Pop-Up Menus

A Lisp program can pop up a menu so that the user can choose an alternative with the mouse. On a text terminal, if the mouse is not available, the user can choose an alternative using the keyboard motion keys—*C-n*, *C-p*, or up- and down-arrow keys.

x-popup-menu *position menu*   [Function]
> This function displays a pop-up menu and returns an indication of what selection the user makes.
>
> The argument *position* specifies where on the screen to put the top left corner of the menu. It can be either a mouse button event (which says to put the menu where the user actuated the button) or a list of this form:
>
> > (*(xoffset yoffset)* *window*)
>
> where *xoffset* and *yoffset* are coordinates, measured in pixels, counting from the top left corner of *window*. *window* may be a window or a frame.
>
> If *position* is `t`, it means to use the current mouse position (or the top-left corner of the frame if the mouse is not available on a text terminal). If *position* is `nil`, it means to precompute the key binding equivalents for the keymaps specified in *menu*, without actually displaying or popping up the menu.
>
> The argument *menu* says what to display in the menu. It can be a keymap or a list of keymaps (see Section 21.17 [Menu Keymaps], page 415). In this case, the return value is the list of events corresponding to the user's choice. This list has more than one element if the choice occurred in a submenu. (Note that `x-popup-menu` does not actually execute the command bound to that sequence of events.) On text terminals and toolkits that support menu titles, the title is taken from the prompt string of *menu* if *menu* is a keymap, or from the prompt string of the first keymap in *menu* if it is a list of keymaps (see Section 21.17.1 [Defining Menus], page 415).
>
> Alternatively, *menu* can have the following form:
>
> > (*title pane1 pane2...*)
>
> where each pane is a list of form
>
> > (*title item1 item2...*)
>
> Each *item* should be a cons cell, (*line . value*), where *line* is a string and *value* is the value to return if that *line* is chosen. Unlike in a menu keymap, a `nil` *value*

does not make the menu item non-selectable. Alternatively, each *item* can be a string rather than a cons cell; this makes a non-selectable menu item.

If the user gets rid of the menu without making a valid choice, for instance by clicking the mouse away from a valid choice or by typing `C-g`, then this normally results in a quit and `x-popup-menu` does not return. But if *position* is a mouse button event (indicating that the user invoked the menu with the mouse) then no quit occurs and `x-popup-menu` returns `nil`.

Usage note: Don't use `x-popup-menu` to display a menu if you could do the job with a prefix key defined with a menu keymap. If you use a menu keymap to implement a menu, `C-h c` and `C-h a` can see the individual items in that menu and provide help for them. If instead you implement the menu by defining a command that calls `x-popup-menu`, the help facilities cannot know what happens inside that command, so they cannot give any help for the menu's items.

The menu bar mechanism, which lets you switch between submenus by moving the mouse, cannot look within the definition of a command to see that it calls `x-popup-menu`. Therefore, if you try to implement a submenu using `x-popup-menu`, it cannot work with the menu bar in an integrated fashion. This is why all menu bar submenus are implemented with menu keymaps within the parent menu, and never with `x-popup-menu`. See Section 21.17.5 [Menu Bar], page 422.

If you want a menu bar submenu to have contents that vary, you should still use a menu keymap to implement it. To make the contents vary, add a hook function to `menu-bar-update-hook` to update the contents of the menu keymap as necessary.

28.17 Dialog Boxes

A dialog box is a variant of a pop-up menu—it looks a little different, it always appears in the center of a frame, and it has just one level and one or more buttons. The main use of dialog boxes is for asking questions that the user can answer with "yes", "no", and a few other alternatives. With a single button, they can also force the user to acknowledge important information. The functions `y-or-n-p` and `yes-or-no-p` use dialog boxes instead of the keyboard, when called from commands invoked by mouse clicks.

`x-popup-dialog` *position contents* **&optional** *header* [Function]

> This function displays a pop-up dialog box and returns an indication of what selection the user makes. The argument *contents* specifies the alternatives to offer; it has this format:
>
> ```
> (title (string . value)...)
> ```
>
> which looks like the list that specifies a single pane for `x-popup-menu`.
>
> The return value is *value* from the chosen alternative.
>
> As for `x-popup-menu`, an element of the list may be just a string instead of a cons cell (*string . value*). That makes a box that cannot be selected.
>
> If `nil` appears in the list, it separates the left-hand items from the right-hand items; items that precede the `nil` appear on the left, and items that follow the `nil` appear on the right. If you don't include a `nil` in the list, then approximately half the items appear on each side.

Dialog boxes always appear in the center of a frame; the argument *position* specifies which frame. The possible values are as in `x-popup-menu`, but the precise coordinates or the individual window don't matter; only the frame matters.

If *header* is non-`nil`, the frame title for the box is 'Information', otherwise it is 'Question'. The former is used for `message-box` (see [message-box], page 889). (On text terminals, the box title is not displayed.)

In some configurations, Emacs cannot display a real dialog box; so instead it displays the same items in a pop-up menu in the center of the frame.

If the user gets rid of the dialog box without making a valid choice, for instance using the window manager, then this produces a quit and `x-popup-dialog` does not return.

28.18 Pointer Shape

You can specify the mouse pointer style for particular text or images using the `pointer` text property, and for images with the `:pointer` and `:map` image properties. The values you can use in these properties are `text` (or `nil`), `arrow`, `hand`, `vdrag`, `hdrag`, `modeline`, and `hourglass`. `text` stands for the usual mouse pointer style used over text.

Over void parts of the window (parts that do not correspond to any of the buffer contents), the mouse pointer usually uses the `arrow` style, but you can specify a different style (one of those above) by setting `void-text-area-pointer`.

`void-text-area-pointer`   [User Option]
> This variable specifies the mouse pointer style for void text areas. These include the areas after the end of a line or below the last line in the buffer. The default is to use the `arrow` (non-text) pointer style.

When using X, you can specify what the `text` pointer style really looks like by setting the variable `x-pointer-shape`.

`x-pointer-shape`   [Variable]
> This variable specifies the pointer shape to use ordinarily in the Emacs frame, for the `text` pointer style.

`x-sensitive-text-pointer-shape`   [Variable]
> This variable specifies the pointer shape to use when the mouse is over mouse-sensitive text.

These variables affect newly created frames. They do not normally affect existing frames; however, if you set the mouse color of a frame, that also installs the current value of those two variables. See Section 28.4.3.8 [Font and Color Parameters], page 651.

The values you can use, to specify either of these pointer shapes, are defined in the file `lisp/term/x-win.el`. Use *M-x apropos RET x-pointer RET* to see a list of them.

28.19 Window System Selections

In window systems, such as X, data can be transferred between different applications by means of *selections*. X defines an arbitrary number of *selection types*, each of which can store its own data; however, only three are commonly used: the *clipboard*, *primary selection*, and *secondary selection*. Other window systems support only the clipboard. See Section "Cut and Paste" in *The GNU Emacs Manual*, for Emacs commands that make use of these selections. This section documents the low-level functions for reading and setting window-system selections.

gui-set-selection *type data*   [Command]

> This function sets a window-system selection. It takes two arguments: a selection type *type*, and the value to assign to it, *data*.
>
> *type* should be a symbol; it is usually one of `PRIMARY`, `SECONDARY` or `CLIPBOARD`. These are symbols with upper-case names, in accord with X Window System conventions. If *type* is `nil`, that stands for `PRIMARY`.
>
> If *data* is `nil`, it means to clear out the selection. Otherwise, *data* may be a string, a symbol, an integer (or a cons of two integers or list of two integers), an overlay, or a cons of two markers pointing to the same buffer. An overlay or a pair of markers stands for text in the overlay or between the markers. The argument *data* may also be a vector of valid non-vector selection values.
>
> This function returns *data*.

gui-get-selection **&optional** *type data-type*   [Function]

> This function accesses selections set up by Emacs or by other programs. It takes two optional arguments, *type* and *data-type*. The default for *type*, the selection type, is `PRIMARY`.
>
> The *data-type* argument specifies the form of data conversion to use, to convert the raw data obtained from another program into Lisp data. Meaningful values include `TEXT`, `STRING`, `UTF8_STRING`, `TARGETS`, `LENGTH`, `DELETE`, `FILE_NAME`, `CHARACTER_POSITION`, `NAME`, `LINE_NUMBER`, `COLUMN_NUMBER`, `OWNER_OS`, `HOST_NAME`, `USER`, `CLASS`, `ATOM`, and `INTEGER`. (These are symbols with upper-case names in accord with X conventions.) The default for *data-type* is `STRING`. Window systems other than X usually support only a small subset of these types, in addition to `STRING`.

selection-coding-system   [User Option]

> This variable specifies the coding system to use when reading and writing selections or the clipboard. See Section 32.10 [Coding Systems], page 773. The default is `compound-text-with-extensions`, which converts to the text representation that X11 normally uses.

When Emacs runs on MS-Windows, it does not implement X selections in general, but it does support the clipboard. `gui-get-selection` and `gui-set-selection` on MS-Windows support the text data type only; if the clipboard holds other types of data, Emacs treats the clipboard as empty. The supported data type is `STRING`.

For backward compatibility, there are obsolete aliases `x-get-selection` and `x-set-selection`, which were the names of `gui-get-selection` and `gui-set-selection` before Emacs 25.1.

28.20 Drag and Drop

When a user drags something from another application over Emacs, that other application expects Emacs to tell it if Emacs can handle the data that is dragged. The variable `x-dnd-test-function` is used by Emacs to determine what to reply. The default value is `x-dnd-default-test-function` which accepts drops if the type of the data to be dropped is present in `x-dnd-known-types`. You can customize `x-dnd-test-function` and/or `x-dnd-known-types` if you want Emacs to accept or reject drops based on some other criteria.

If you want to change the way Emacs handles drop of different types or add a new type, customize `x-dnd-types-alist`. This requires detailed knowledge of what types other applications use for drag and drop.

When an URL is dropped on Emacs it may be a file, but it may also be another URL type (ftp, http, etc.). Emacs first checks `dnd-protocol-alist` to determine what to do with the URL. If there is no match there and if `browse-url-browser-function` is an alist, Emacs looks for a match there. If no match is found the text for the URL is inserted. If you want to alter Emacs behavior, you can customize these variables.

28.21 Color Names

A color name is text (usually in a string) that specifies a color. Symbolic names such as 'black', 'white', 'red', etc., are allowed; use *M-x list-colors-display* to see a list of defined names. You can also specify colors numerically in forms such as '*#rgb*' and '*RGB:r/g/b*', where *r* specifies the red level, *g* specifies the green level, and *b* specifies the blue level. You can use either one, two, three, or four hex digits for *r*; then you must use the same number of hex digits for all *g* and *b* as well, making either 3, 6, 9 or 12 hex digits in all. (See the documentation of the X Window System for more details about numerical RGB specification of colors.)

These functions provide a way to determine which color names are valid, and what they look like. In some cases, the value depends on the *selected frame*, as described below; see Section 28.10 [Input Focus], page 656, for the meaning of the term "selected frame".

To read user input of color names with completion, use `read-color` (see Section 19.6.4 [High-Level Completion], page 328).

`color-defined-p` *color* **&optional** *frame*   [Function]
> This function reports whether a color name is meaningful. It returns `t` if so; otherwise, `nil`. The argument *frame* says which frame's display to ask about; if *frame* is omitted or `nil`, the selected frame is used.
>
> Note that this does not tell you whether the display you are using really supports that color. When using X, you can ask for any defined color on any kind of display, and you will get some result—typically, the closest it can do. To determine whether a frame can really display a certain color, use `color-supported-p` (see below).
>
> This function used to be called `x-color-defined-p`, and that name is still supported as an alias.

`defined-colors` **&optional** *frame*   [Function]
> This function returns a list of the color names that are defined and supported on frame *frame* (default, the selected frame). If *frame* does not support colors, the value is `nil`.

This function used to be called `x-defined-colors`, and that name is still supported as an alias.

`color-supported-p` *color* **&optional** *frame background-p*   [Function]

This returns `t` if *frame* can really display the color *color* (or at least something close to it). If *frame* is omitted or `nil`, the question applies to the selected frame.

Some terminals support a different set of colors for foreground and background. If *background-p* is non-`nil`, that means you are asking whether *color* can be used as a background; otherwise you are asking whether it can be used as a foreground.

The argument *color* must be a valid color name.

`color-gray-p` *color* **&optional** *frame*   [Function]

This returns `t` if *color* is a shade of gray, as defined on *frame*'s display. If *frame* is omitted or `nil`, the question applies to the selected frame. If *color* is not a valid color name, this function returns `nil`.

`color-values` *color* **&optional** *frame*   [Function]

This function returns a value that describes what *color* should ideally look like on *frame*. If *color* is defined, the value is a list of three integers, which give the amount of red, the amount of green, and the amount of blue. Each integer ranges in principle from 0 to 65535, but some displays may not use the full range. This three-element list is called the *rgb values* of the color.

If *color* is not defined, the value is `nil`.

```
(color-values "black")
     ⇒ (0 0 0)
(color-values "white")
     ⇒ (65280 65280 65280)
(color-values "red")
     ⇒ (65280 0 0)
(color-values "pink")
     ⇒ (65280 49152 51968)
(color-values "hungry")
     ⇒ nil
```

The color values are returned for *frame*'s display. If *frame* is omitted or `nil`, the information is returned for the selected frame's display. If the frame cannot display colors, the value is `nil`.

This function used to be called `x-color-values`, and that name is still supported as an alias.

28.22 Text Terminal Colors

Text terminals usually support only a small number of colors, and the computer uses small integers to select colors on the terminal. This means that the computer cannot reliably tell what the selected color looks like; instead, you have to inform your application which small integers correspond to which colors. However, Emacs does know the standard set of colors and will try to use them automatically.

The functions described in this section control how terminal colors are used by Emacs.

Several of these functions use or return *rgb values*, described in Section 28.21 [Color Names], page 666.

These functions accept a display (either a frame or the name of a terminal) as an optional argument. We hope in the future to make Emacs support different colors on different text terminals; then this argument will specify which terminal to operate on (the default being the selected frame's terminal; see Section 28.10 [Input Focus], page 656). At present, though, the *frame* argument has no effect.

`tty-color-define` *name number* **&optional** *rgb frame* [Function]
> This function associates the color name *name* with color number *number* on the terminal.
>
> The optional argument *rgb*, if specified, is an rgb value, a list of three numbers that specify what the color actually looks like. If you do not specify *rgb*, then this color cannot be used by `tty-color-approximate` to approximate other colors, because Emacs will not know what it looks like.

`tty-color-clear` **&optional** *frame* [Function]
> This function clears the table of defined colors for a text terminal.

`tty-color-alist` **&optional** *frame* [Function]
> This function returns an alist recording the known colors supported by a text terminal.
>
> Each element has the form (`name number . rgb`) or (`name number`). Here, *name* is the color name, *number* is the number used to specify it to the terminal. If present, *rgb* is a list of three color values (for red, green, and blue) that says what the color actually looks like.

`tty-color-approximate` *rgb* **&optional** *frame* [Function]
> This function finds the closest color, among the known colors supported for *display*, to that described by the rgb value *rgb* (a list of color values). The return value is an element of `tty-color-alist`.

`tty-color-translate` *color* **&optional** *frame* [Function]
> This function finds the closest color to *color* among the known colors supported for *display* and returns its index (an integer). If the name *color* is not defined, the value is `nil`.

28.23 X Resources

This section describes some of the functions and variables for querying and using X resources, or their equivalent on your operating system. See Section "X Resources" in *The GNU Emacs Manual*, for more information about X resources.

`x-get-resource` *attribute class* **&optional** *component subclass* [Function]
> The function `x-get-resource` retrieves a resource value from the X Window defaults database.
>
> Resources are indexed by a combination of a *key* and a *class*. This function searches using a key of the form '`instance.attribute`' (where *instance* is the name under which Emacs was invoked), and using '`Emacs.class`' as the class.

The optional arguments *component* and *subclass* add to the key and the class, respectively. You must specify both of them or neither. If you specify them, the key is '`instance.component.attribute`', and the class is '`Emacs.class.subclass`'.

x-resource-class   [Variable]

This variable specifies the application name that `x-get-resource` should look up. The default value is `"Emacs"`. You can examine X resources for other application names by binding this variable to some other string, around a call to `x-get-resource`.

x-resource-name   [Variable]

This variable specifies the instance name that `x-get-resource` should look up. The default value is the name Emacs was invoked with, or the value specified with the '`-name`' or '`-rn`' switches.

To illustrate some of the above, suppose that you have the line:

```
xterm.vt100.background: yellow
```

in your X resources file (whose name is usually `~/.Xdefaults` or `~/.Xresources`). Then:

```
(let ((x-resource-class "XTerm") (x-resource-name "xterm"))
  (x-get-resource "vt100.background" "VT100.Background"))
     ⇒ "yellow"
(let ((x-resource-class "XTerm") (x-resource-name "xterm"))
  (x-get-resource "background" "VT100" "vt100" "Background"))
     ⇒ "yellow"
```

inhibit-x-resources   [Variable]

If this variable is non-`nil`, Emacs does not look up X resources, and X resources do not have any effect when creating new frames.

28.24 Display Feature Testing

The functions in this section describe the basic capabilities of a particular display. Lisp programs can use them to adapt their behavior to what the display can do. For example, a program that ordinarily uses a popup menu could use the minibuffer if popup menus are not supported.

The optional argument *display* in these functions specifies which display to ask the question about. It can be a display name, a frame (which designates the display that frame is on), or `nil` (which refers to the selected frame's display, see Section 28.10 [Input Focus], page 656).

See Section 28.21 [Color Names], page 666, Section 28.22 [Text Terminal Colors], page 667, for other functions to obtain information about displays.

display-popup-menus-p &optional *display*   [Function]

This function returns `t` if popup menus are supported on *display*, `nil` if not. Support for popup menus requires that the mouse be available, since the menu is popped up by clicking the mouse on some portion of the Emacs display.

display-graphic-p &optional *display*   [Function]

This function returns `t` if *display* is a graphic display capable of displaying several frames and several different fonts at once. This is true for displays that use a window system such as X, and false for text terminals.

display-mouse-p &optional *display*   [Function]
> This function returns t if *display* has a mouse available, nil if not.

display-color-p &optional *display*   [Function]
> This function returns t if the screen is a color screen. It used to be called x-display-color-p, and that name is still supported as an alias.

display-grayscale-p &optional *display*   [Function]
> This function returns t if the screen can display shades of gray. (All color displays can do this.)

display-supports-face-attributes-p *attributes* **&optional** *display*   [Function]
> This function returns non-nil if all the face attributes in *attributes* are supported (see Section 37.12.1 [Face Attributes], page 915).
>
> The definition of "supported" is somewhat heuristic, but basically means that a face containing all the attributes in *attributes*, when merged with the default face for display, can be represented in a way that's
>
> 1. different in appearance than the default face, and
>
> 2. close in spirit to what the attributes specify, if not exact.
>
> Point (2) implies that a :weight black attribute will be satisfied by any display that can display bold, as will :foreground "yellow" as long as some yellowish color can be displayed, but :slant italic will *not* be satisfied by the tty display code's automatic substitution of a dim face for italic.

display-selections-p &optional *display*   [Function]
> This function returns t if *display* supports selections. Windowed displays normally support selections, but they may also be supported in some other cases.

display-images-p &optional *display*   [Function]
> This function returns t if *display* can display images. Windowed displays ought in principle to handle images, but some systems lack the support for that. On a display that does not support images, Emacs cannot display a tool bar.

display-screens &optional *display*   [Function]
> This function returns the number of screens associated with the display.

display-pixel-height &optional *display*   [Function]
> This function returns the height of the screen in pixels. On a character terminal, it gives the height in characters.
>
> For graphical terminals, note that on multi-monitor setups this refers to the pixel height for all physical monitors associated with *display*. See Section 28.2 [Multiple Terminals], page 631.

display-pixel-width &optional *display*   [Function]
> This function returns the width of the screen in pixels. On a character terminal, it gives the width in characters.
>
> For graphical terminals, note that on multi-monitor setups this refers to the pixel width for all physical monitors associated with *display*. See Section 28.2 [Multiple Terminals], page 631.

display-mm-height &optional *display*   [Function]
>   This function returns the height of the screen in millimeters, or `nil` if Emacs cannot get that information.
>
>   For graphical terminals, note that on multi-monitor setups this refers to the height for all physical monitors associated with *display*. See Section 28.2 [Multiple Terminals], page 631.

display-mm-width &optional *display*   [Function]
>   This function returns the width of the screen in millimeters, or `nil` if Emacs cannot get that information.
>
>   For graphical terminals, note that on multi-monitor setups this refers to the width for all physical monitors associated with *display*. See Section 28.2 [Multiple Terminals], page 631.

display-mm-dimensions-alist   [User Option]
>   This variable allows the user to specify the dimensions of graphical displays returned by `display-mm-height` and `display-mm-width` in case the system provides incorrect values.

display-backing-store &optional *display*   [Function]
>   This function returns the backing store capability of the display. Backing store means recording the pixels of windows (and parts of windows) that are not exposed, so that when exposed they can be displayed very quickly.
>
>   Values can be the symbols `always`, `when-mapped`, or `not-useful`. The function can also return `nil` when the question is inapplicable to a certain kind of display.

display-save-under &optional *display*   [Function]
>   This function returns non-`nil` if the display supports the SaveUnder feature. That feature is used by pop-up windows to save the pixels they obscure, so that they can pop down quickly.

display-planes &optional *display*   [Function]
>   This function returns the number of planes the display supports. This is typically the number of bits per pixel. For a tty display, it is log to base two of the number of colors supported.

display-visual-class &optional *display*   [Function]
>   This function returns the visual class for the screen. The value is one of the symbols `static-gray` (a limited, unchangeable number of grays), `gray-scale` (a full range of grays), `static-color` (a limited, unchangeable number of colors), `pseudo-color` (a limited number of colors), `true-color` (a full range of colors), and `direct-color` (a full range of colors).

display-color-cells &optional *display*   [Function]
>   This function returns the number of color cells the screen supports.

These functions obtain additional information about the window system in use where Emacs shows the specified *display*. (Their names begin with `x-` for historical reasons.)

`x-server-version` **&optional** *display*   [Function]

   This function returns the list of version numbers of the GUI window system running on *display*, such as the X server on GNU and Unix systems. The value is a list of three integers: the major and minor version numbers of the protocol, and the distributor-specific release number of the window system software itself. On GNU and Unix systems, these are normally the version of the X protocol and the distributor-specific release number of the X server software. On MS-Windows, this is the version of the Windows OS.

`x-server-vendor` **&optional** *display*   [Function]

   This function returns the vendor that provided the window system software (as a string). On GNU and Unix systems this really means whoever distributes the X server. On MS-Windows this is the vendor ID string of the Windows OS (Microsoft).

   When the developers of X labeled software distributors as "vendors", they showed their false assumption that no system could ever be developed and distributed non-commercially.

29 Positions

A *position* is the index of a character in the text of a buffer. More precisely, a position identifies the place between two characters (or before the first character, or after the last character), so we can speak of the character before or after a given position. However, we often speak of the character "at" a position, meaning the character after that position.

Positions are usually represented as integers starting from 1, but can also be represented as *markers*—special objects that relocate automatically when text is inserted or deleted so they stay with the surrounding characters. Functions that expect an argument to be a position (an integer), but accept a marker as a substitute, normally ignore which buffer the marker points into; they convert the marker to an integer, and use that integer, exactly as if you had passed the integer as the argument, even if the marker points to the wrong buffer. A marker that points nowhere cannot convert to an integer; using it instead of an integer causes an error. See Chapter 30 [Markers], page 687.

See also the field feature (see Section 31.19.9 [Fields], page 748), which provides functions that are used by many cursor-motion commands.

29.1 Point

Point is a special buffer position used by many editing commands, including the self-inserting typed characters and text insertion functions. Other commands move point through the text to allow editing and insertion at different places.

Like other positions, point designates a place between two characters (or before the first character, or after the last character), rather than a particular character. Usually terminals display the cursor over the character that immediately follows point; point is actually before the character on which the cursor sits.

The value of point is a number no less than 1, and no greater than the buffer size plus 1. If narrowing is in effect (see Section 29.4 [Narrowing], page 684), then point is constrained to fall within the accessible portion of the buffer (possibly at one end of it).

Each buffer has its own value of point, which is independent of the value of point in other buffers. Each window also has a value of point, which is independent of the value of point in other windows on the same buffer. This is why point can have different values in various windows that display the same buffer. When a buffer appears in only one window, the buffer's point and the window's point normally have the same value, so the distinction is rarely important. See Section 27.19 [Window Point], page 609, for more details.

point   [Function]
    This function returns the value of point in the current buffer, as an integer.

```
(point)
     ⇒ 175
```

point-min   [Function]
    This function returns the minimum accessible value of point in the current buffer. This is normally 1, but if narrowing is in effect, it is the position of the start of the region that you narrowed to. (See Section 29.4 [Narrowing], page 684.)

point-max   [Function]

This function returns the maximum accessible value of point in the current buffer. This is (`1+ (buffer-size)`), unless narrowing is in effect, in which case it is the position of the end of the region that you narrowed to. (See Section 29.4 [Narrowing], page 684.)

buffer-end *flag*   [Function]

This function returns (`point-max`) if *flag* is greater than 0, (`point-min`) otherwise. The argument *flag* must be a number.

buffer-size **&optional** *buffer*   [Function]

This function returns the total number of characters in the current buffer. In the absence of any narrowing (see Section 29.4 [Narrowing], page 684), `point-max` returns a value one larger than this.

If you specify a buffer, *buffer*, then the value is the size of *buffer*.

```
(buffer-size)
    ⇒ 35
(point-max)
    ⇒ 36
```

29.2 Motion

Motion functions change the value of point, either relative to the current value of point, relative to the beginning or end of the buffer, or relative to the edges of the selected window. See Section 29.1 [Point], page 673.

29.2.1 Motion by Characters

These functions move point based on a count of characters. `goto-char` is the fundamental primitive; the other functions use that.

goto-char *position*   [Command]

This function sets point in the current buffer to the value *position*.

If narrowing is in effect, *position* still counts from the beginning of the buffer, but point cannot go outside the accessible portion. If *position* is out of range, `goto-char` moves point to the beginning or the end of the accessible portion.

When this function is called interactively, *position* is the numeric prefix argument, if provided; otherwise it is read from the minibuffer.

`goto-char` returns *position*.

forward-char **&optional** *count*   [Command]

This function moves point *count* characters forward, towards the end of the buffer (or backward, towards the beginning of the buffer, if *count* is negative). If *count* is `nil`, the default is 1.

If this attempts to move past the beginning or end of the buffer (or the limits of the accessible portion, when narrowing is in effect), it signals an error with error symbol `beginning-of-buffer` or `end-of-buffer`.

In an interactive call, *count* is the numeric prefix argument.

`backward-char &optional` *count* [Command]

This is just like `forward-char` except that it moves in the opposite direction.

29.2.2 Motion by Words

The functions for parsing words described below use the syntax table and `char-script-table` to decide whether a given character is part of a word. See Chapter 34 [Syntax Tables], page 816, and see Section 32.6 [Character Properties], page 766.

`forward-word &optional` *count* [Command]

This function moves point forward *count* words (or backward if *count* is negative). If *count* is omitted or `nil`, it defaults to 1. In an interactive call, *count* is specified by the numeric prefix argument.

"Moving one word" means moving until point crosses a word-constituent character, which indicates the beginning of a word, and then continue moving until the word ends. By default, characters that begin and end words, known as *word boundaries*, are defined by the current buffer's syntax table (see Section 34.2.1 [Syntax Class Table], page 817), but modes can override that by setting up a suitable `find-word-boundary-function-table`, described below. Characters that belong to different scripts (as defined by `char-syntax-table`), also define a word boundary (see Section 32.6 [Character Properties], page 766). In any case, this function cannot move point past the boundary of the accessible portion of the buffer, or across a field boundary (see Section 31.19.9 [Fields], page 748). The most common case of a field boundary is the end of the prompt in the minibuffer.

If it is possible to move *count* words, without being stopped prematurely by the buffer boundary or a field boundary, the value is `t`. Otherwise, the return value is `nil` and point stops at the buffer boundary or field boundary.

If `inhibit-field-text-motion` is non-`nil`, this function ignores field boundaries.

`backward-word &optional` *count* [Command]

This function is just like `forward-word`, except that it moves backward until encountering the front of a word, rather than forward.

`words-include-escapes` [User Option]

This variable affects the behavior of `forward-word` and `backward-word`, and everything that uses them. If it is non-`nil`, then characters in the escape and character-quote syntax classes count as part of words. Otherwise, they do not.

`inhibit-field-text-motion` [Variable]

If this variable is non-`nil`, certain motion functions including `forward-word`, `forward-sentence`, and `forward-paragraph` ignore field boundaries.

`find-word-boundary-function-table` [Variable]

This variable affects the behavior of `forward-word` and `backward-word`, and everything that uses them. Its value is a char-table (see Section 6.6 [Char-Tables], page 104) of functions to search for word boundaries. If a character has a non-`nil` entry in this table, then when a word starts or ends with that character, the corresponding function will be called with 2 arguments: *pos* and *limit*. The function should return the position of the other word boundary. Specifically, if *pos* is smaller than *limit*, then *pos* is at the beginning of a word, and the function should return the position after the last character of the word; otherwise, *pos* is at the last character of a word, and the function should return the position of that word's first character.

forward-word-strictly &optional *count*   [Function]
This function is like `forward-word`, but it is not affected by `find-word-boundary-function-table`. Lisp programs that should not change behavior when word movement is modified by modes which set that table, such as `subword-mode`, should use this function instead of `forward-word`.

backward-word-strictly &optional *count*   [Function]
This function is like `backward-word`, but it is not affected by `find-word-boundary-function-table`. Like with `forward-word-strictly`, use this function instead of `backward-word` when movement by words should only consider syntax tables.

29.2.3 Motion to an End of the Buffer

To move point to the beginning of the buffer, write:

```
(goto-char (point-min))
```

Likewise, to move to the end of the buffer, use:

```
(goto-char (point-max))
```

Here are two commands that users use to do these things. They are documented here to warn you not to use them in Lisp programs, because they set the mark and display messages in the echo area.

beginning-of-buffer &optional *n*   [Command]
This function moves point to the beginning of the buffer (or the limits of the accessible portion, when narrowing is in effect), setting the mark at the previous position (except in Transient Mark mode, if the mark is already active, it does not set the mark.)

If *n* is non-`nil`, then it puts point *n* tenths of the way from the beginning of the accessible portion of the buffer. In an interactive call, *n* is the numeric prefix argument, if provided; otherwise *n* defaults to `nil`.

Warning: Don't use this function in Lisp programs!

end-of-buffer &optional *n*   [Command]
This function moves point to the end of the buffer (or the limits of the accessible portion, when narrowing is in effect), setting the mark at the previous position (except in Transient Mark mode when the mark is already active). If *n* is non-`nil`, then it puts point *n* tenths of the way from the end of the accessible portion of the buffer.

In an interactive call, *n* is the numeric prefix argument, if provided; otherwise *n* defaults to `nil`.

Warning: Don't use this function in Lisp programs!

29.2.4 Motion by Text Lines

Text lines are portions of the buffer delimited by newline characters, which are regarded as part of the previous line. The first text line begins at the beginning of the buffer, and the last text line ends at the end of the buffer whether or not the last character is a newline.

The division of the buffer into text lines is not affected by the width of the window, by line continuation in display, or by how tabs and control characters are displayed.

beginning-of-line &optional *count*   [Command]

> This function moves point to the beginning of the current line. With an argument *count* not `nil` or 1, it moves forward *count*−1 lines and then to the beginning of the line.
>
> This function does not move point across a field boundary (see Section 31.19.9 [Fields], page 748) unless doing so would move beyond there to a different line; therefore, if *count* is `nil` or 1, and point starts at a field boundary, point does not move. To ignore field boundaries, either bind `inhibit-field-text-motion` to `t`, or use the `forward-line` function instead. For instance, `(forward-line 0)` does the same thing as `(beginning-of-line)`, except that it ignores field boundaries.
>
> If this function reaches the end of the buffer (or of the accessible portion, if narrowing is in effect), it positions point there. No error is signaled.

line-beginning-position &optional *count*   [Function]

> Return the position that `(beginning-of-line count)` would move to.

end-of-line &optional *count*   [Command]

> This function moves point to the end of the current line. With an argument *count* not `nil` or 1, it moves forward *count*−1 lines and then to the end of the line.
>
> This function does not move point across a field boundary (see Section 31.19.9 [Fields], page 748) unless doing so would move beyond there to a different line; therefore, if *count* is `nil` or 1, and point starts at a field boundary, point does not move. To ignore field boundaries, bind `inhibit-field-text-motion` to `t`.
>
> If this function reaches the end of the buffer (or of the accessible portion, if narrowing is in effect), it positions point there. No error is signaled.

line-end-position &optional *count*   [Function]

> Return the position that `(end-of-line count)` would move to.

forward-line &optional *count*   [Command]

> This function moves point forward *count* lines, to the beginning of the line following that. If *count* is negative, it moves point −*count* lines backward, to the beginning of a line preceding that. If *count* is zero, it moves point to the beginning of the current line. If *count* is `nil`, that means 1.
>
> If `forward-line` encounters the beginning or end of the buffer (or of the accessible portion) before finding that many lines, it sets point there. No error is signaled.
>
> `forward-line` returns the difference between *count* and the number of lines actually moved. If you attempt to move down five lines from the beginning of a buffer that has only three lines, point stops at the end of the last line, and the value will be 2. As an explicit exception, if the last accessible line is non-empty, but has no newline (e.g., if the buffer ends without a newline), the function sets point to the end of that line, and the value returned by the function counts that line as one line successfully moved.
>
> In an interactive call, *count* is the numeric prefix argument.

`count-lines` *start end*   [Function]

> This function returns the number of lines between the positions *start* and *end* in the current buffer. If *start* and *end* are equal, then it returns 0. Otherwise it returns at least 1, even if *start* and *end* are on the same line. This is because the text between them, considered in isolation, must contain at least one line unless it is empty.

`count-words` *start end*   [Command]

> This function returns the number of words between the positions *start* and *end* in the current buffer.

> This function can also be called interactively. In that case, it prints a message reporting the number of lines, words, and characters in the buffer, or in the region if the region is active.

`line-number-at-pos` **&optional** *pos*   [Function]

> This function returns the line number in the current buffer corresponding to the buffer position *pos*. If *pos* is `nil` or omitted, the current buffer position is used.

Also see the functions `bolp` and `eolp` in Section 31.1 [Near Point], page 696. These functions do not move point, but test whether it is already at the beginning or end of a line.

29.2.5 Motion by Screen Lines

The line functions in the previous section count text lines, delimited only by newline characters. By contrast, these functions count screen lines, which are defined by the way the text appears on the screen. A text line is a single screen line if it is short enough to fit the width of the selected window, but otherwise it may occupy several screen lines.

In some cases, text lines are truncated on the screen rather than continued onto additional screen lines. In these cases, `vertical-motion` moves point much like `forward-line`. See Section 37.3 [Truncation], page 887.

Because the width of a given string depends on the flags that control the appearance of certain characters, `vertical-motion` behaves differently, for a given piece of text, depending on the buffer it is in, and even on the selected window (because the width, the truncation flag, and display table may vary between windows). See Section 37.22.1 [Usual Display], page 973.

These functions scan text to determine where screen lines break, and thus take time proportional to the distance scanned.

`vertical-motion` *count* **&optional** *window cur-col*   [Function]

> This function moves point to the start of the screen line *count* screen lines down from the screen line containing point. If *count* is negative, it moves up instead.

> The *count* argument can be a cons cell, (`cols . lines`), instead of an integer. Then the function moves by *lines* screen lines, and puts point *cols* columns from the visual start of that screen line. Note that *cols* are counted from the *visual* start of the line; if the window is scrolled horizontally (see Section 27.23 [Horizontal Scrolling], page 618), the column on which point will end is in addition to the number of columns by which the text is scrolled.

The return value is the number of screen lines over which point was moved. The value may be less in absolute value than *count* if the beginning or end of the buffer was reached.

The window *window* is used for obtaining parameters such as the width, the horizontal scrolling, and the display table. But `vertical-motion` always operates on the current buffer, even if *window* currently displays some other buffer.

The optional argument *cur-col* specifies the current column when the function is called. This is the window-relative horizontal coordinate of point, measured in units of font width of the frame's default face. Providing it speeds up the function, especially in very long lines, because it doesn't have to go back in the buffer in order to determine the current column. Note that *cur-col* is also counted from the visual start of the line.

`count-screen-lines` &optional *beg end count-final-newline window* [Function]
This function returns the number of screen lines in the text from *beg* to *end*. The number of screen lines may be different from the number of actual lines, due to line continuation, the display table, etc. If *beg* and *end* are `nil` or omitted, they default to the beginning and end of the accessible portion of the buffer.

If the region ends with a newline, that is ignored unless the optional third argument *count-final-newline* is non-`nil`.

The optional fourth argument *window* specifies the window for obtaining parameters such as width, horizontal scrolling, and so on. The default is to use the selected window's parameters.

Like `vertical-motion`, `count-screen-lines` always uses the current buffer, regardless of which buffer is displayed in *window*. This makes possible to use `count-screen-lines` in any buffer, whether or not it is currently displayed in some window.

`move-to-window-line` *count* [Command]
This function moves point with respect to the text currently displayed in the selected window. It moves point to the beginning of the screen line *count* screen lines from the top of the window. If *count* is negative, that specifies a position −*count* lines from the bottom (or the last line of the buffer, if the buffer ends above the specified screen position).

If *count* is `nil`, then point moves to the beginning of the line in the middle of the window. If the absolute value of *count* is greater than the size of the window, then point moves to the place that would appear on that screen line if the window were tall enough. This will probably cause the next redisplay to scroll to bring that location onto the screen.

In an interactive call, *count* is the numeric prefix argument.

The value returned is the window line number point has moved to, with the top line in the window numbered 0.

`move-to-window-group-line` *count* [Function]
This function is like `move-to-window-line`, except that when the selected window is a part of a group of windows (see [Window Group], page 568), `move-to-window-group-line` will move to a position with respect to the entire group, not just the single

window. This condition holds when the buffer local variable `move-to-window-group-line-function` is set to a function. In this case, `move-to-window-group-line` calls the function with the argument *count*, then returns its result.

`compute-motion` *from frompos to topos width offsets window* [Function]
This function scans the current buffer, calculating screen positions. It scans the buffer forward from position *from*, assuming that is at screen coordinates *frompos*, to position *to* or coordinates *topos*, whichever comes first. It returns the ending buffer position and screen coordinates.

The coordinate arguments *frompos* and *topos* are cons cells of the form (*hpos . vpos*).

The argument *width* is the number of columns available to display text; this affects handling of continuation lines. `nil` means the actual number of usable text columns in the window, which is equivalent to the value returned by (`window-width window`).

The argument *offsets* is either `nil` or a cons cell of the form (*hscroll . tab-offset*). Here *hscroll* is the number of columns not being displayed at the left margin; most callers get this by calling `window-hscroll`. Meanwhile, *tab-offset* is the offset between column numbers on the screen and column numbers in the buffer. This can be nonzero in a continuation line, when the previous screen lines' widths do not add up to a multiple of `tab-width`. It is always zero in a non-continuation line.

The window *window* serves only to specify which display table to use. `compute-motion` always operates on the current buffer, regardless of what buffer is displayed in *window*.

The return value is a list of five elements:

> (*pos hpos vpos prevhpos contin*)

Here *pos* is the buffer position where the scan stopped, *vpos* is the vertical screen position, and *hpos* is the horizontal screen position.

The result *prevhpos* is the horizontal position one character back from *pos*. The result *contin* is `t` if the last line was continued after (or within) the previous character.

For example, to find the buffer position of column *col* of screen line *line* of a certain window, pass the window's display start location as *from* and the window's upper-left coordinates as *frompos*. Pass the buffer's (`point-max`) as *to*, to limit the scan to the end of the accessible portion of the buffer, and pass *line* and *col* as *topos*. Here's a function that does this:

```
(defun coordinates-of-position (col line)
  (car (compute-motion (window-start)
                       '(0 . 0)
                       (point-max)
                       (cons col line)
                       (window-width)
                       (cons (window-hscroll) 0)
                       (selected-window))))
```

When you use `compute-motion` for the minibuffer, you need to use `minibuffer-prompt-width` to get the horizontal position of the beginning of the first screen line. See Section 19.12 [Minibuffer Contents], page 342.

29.2.6 Moving over Balanced Expressions

Here are several functions concerned with balanced-parenthesis expressions (also called *sexps* in connection with moving across them in Emacs). The syntax table controls how these functions interpret various characters; see Chapter 34 [Syntax Tables], page 816. See Section 34.6 [Parsing Expressions], page 824, for lower-level primitives for scanning sexps or parts of sexps. For user-level commands, see Section "Commands for Editing with Parentheses" in *The GNU Emacs Manual*.

`forward-list &optional` *arg*   [Command]

> This function moves forward across *arg* (default 1) balanced groups of parentheses. (Other syntactic entities such as words or paired string quotes are ignored.)

`backward-list &optional` *arg*   [Command]

> This function moves backward across *arg* (default 1) balanced groups of parentheses. (Other syntactic entities such as words or paired string quotes are ignored.)

`up-list &optional` *arg escape-strings no-syntax-crossing*   [Command]

> This function moves forward out of *arg* (default 1) levels of parentheses. A negative argument means move backward but still to a less deep spot. If *escape-strings* is non-`nil` (as it is interactively), move out of enclosing strings as well. If *no-syntax-crossing* is non-`nil` (as it is interactively), prefer to break out of any enclosing string instead of moving to the start of a list broken across multiple strings. On error, location of point is unspecified.

`backward-up-list &optional` *arg escape-strings no-syntax-crossing*   [Command]

> This function is just like `up-list`, but with a negated argument.

`down-list &optional` *arg*   [Command]

> This function moves forward into *arg* (default 1) levels of parentheses. A negative argument means move backward but still go deeper in parentheses (−*arg* levels).

`forward-sexp &optional` *arg*   [Command]

> This function moves forward across *arg* (default 1) balanced expressions. Balanced expressions include both those delimited by parentheses and other kinds, such as words and string constants. See Section 34.6 [Parsing Expressions], page 824. For example,

```
---------- Buffer: foo ----------
(concat⋆ "foo " (car x) y z)
---------- Buffer: foo ----------


(forward-sexp 3)
     ⇒ nil


---------- Buffer: foo ----------
(concat "foo " (car x) y⋆ z)
---------- Buffer: foo ----------
```

`backward-sexp &optional` *arg*   [Command]

> This function moves backward across *arg* (default 1) balanced expressions.

beginning-of-defun **&optional** *arg*   [Command]

>   This function moves back to the *arg*th beginning of a defun. If *arg* is negative, this
>   actually moves forward, but it still moves to the beginning of a defun, not to the end
>   of one. *arg* defaults to 1.

end-of-defun **&optional** *arg*   [Command]

>   This function moves forward to the *arg*th end of a defun. If *arg* is negative, this
>   actually moves backward, but it still moves to the end of a defun, not to the beginning
>   of one. *arg* defaults to 1.

defun-prompt-regexp   [User Option]

>   If non-`nil`, this buffer-local variable holds a regular expression that specifies what
>   text can appear before the open-parenthesis that starts a defun. That is to say, a
>   defun begins on a line that starts with a match for this regular expression, followed
>   by a character with open-parenthesis syntax.

open-paren-in-column-0-is-defun-start   [User Option]

>   If this variable's value is non-`nil`, an open parenthesis in column 0 is considered to
>   be the start of a defun. If it is `nil`, an open parenthesis in column 0 has no special
>   meaning. The default is `t`.

beginning-of-defun-function   [Variable]

>   If non-`nil`, this variable holds a function for finding the beginning of a defun. The
>   function `beginning-of-defun` calls this function instead of using its normal method,
>   passing it its optional argument. If the argument is non-`nil`, the function should
>   move back by that many functions, like `beginning-of-defun` does.

end-of-defun-function   [Variable]

>   If non-`nil`, this variable holds a function for finding the end of a defun. The function
>   `end-of-defun` calls this function instead of using its normal method.

29.2.7 Skipping Characters

The following two functions move point over a specified set of characters. For example,
they are often used to skip whitespace. For related functions, see Section 34.5 [Motion and
Syntax], page 824.

These functions convert the set string to multibyte if the buffer is multibyte, and they
convert it to unibyte if the buffer is unibyte, as the search functions do (see Chapter 33
[Searching and Matching], page 790).

skip-chars-forward *character-set* **&optional** *limit*   [Function]

>   This function moves point in the current buffer forward, skipping over a given set
>   of characters. It examines the character following point, then advances point if the
>   character matches *character-set*. This continues until it reaches a character that does
>   not match. The function returns the number of characters moved over.

>   The argument *character-set* is a string, like the inside of a '`[...]`' in a regular ex-
>   pression except that '`]`' does not terminate it, and '`\`' quotes '`^`', '`-`' or '`\`'. Thus,
>   `"a-zA-Z"` skips over all letters, stopping before the first nonletter, and `"^a-zA-Z"`

skips nonletters stopping before the first letter. See See Section 33.3 [Regular Expressions], page 793. Character classes can also be used, e.g., `"[:alnum:]"`. See see Section 33.3.1.2 [Char Classes], page 796.

If *limit* is supplied (it must be a number or a marker), it specifies the maximum position in the buffer that point can be skipped to. Point will stop at or before *limit*.

In the following example, point is initially located directly before the 'T'. After the form is evaluated, point is located at the end of that line (between the 't' of 'hat' and the newline). The function skips all letters and spaces, but not newlines.

```
---------- Buffer: foo ----------
I read "⋆The cat in the hat
comes back" twice.
---------- Buffer: foo ----------


(skip-chars-forward "a-zA-Z ")
     ⇒ 18


---------- Buffer: foo ----------
I read "The cat in the hat⋆
comes back" twice.
---------- Buffer: foo ----------
```

skip-chars-backward *character-set* **&optional** *limit*   [Function]
　　This function moves point backward, skipping characters that match *character-set*, until *limit*. It is just like **skip-chars-forward** except for the direction of motion.

　　The return value indicates the distance traveled. It is an integer that is zero or less.

29.3 Excursions

It is often useful to move point temporarily within a localized portion of the program. This is called an *excursion*, and it is done with the **save-excursion** special form. This construct remembers the initial identity of the current buffer, and its value of point, and restores them after the excursion completes. It is the standard way to move point within one part of a program and avoid affecting the rest of the program, and is used thousands of times in the Lisp sources of Emacs.

　　If you only need to save and restore the identity of the current buffer, use **save-current-buffer** or **with-current-buffer** instead (see Section 26.2 [Current Buffer], page 550). If you need to save or restore window configurations, see the forms described in Section 27.25 [Window Configurations], page 623, and in Section 28.13 [Frame Configurations], page 660.

save-excursion *body...*   [Special Form]
　　This special form saves the identity of the current buffer and the value of point in it, evaluates *body*, and finally restores the buffer and its saved value of point. Both saved values are restored even in case of an abnormal exit via **throw** or error (see Section 10.6 [Nonlocal Exits], page 145).

　　The value returned by **save-excursion** is the result of the last form in *body*, or **nil** if no body forms were given.

Because `save-excursion` only saves point for the buffer that was current at the start of the excursion, any changes made to point in other buffers, during the excursion, will remain in effect afterward. This frequently leads to unintended consequences, so the byte compiler warns if you call `set-buffer` during an excursion:

```
Warning: Use 'with-current-buffer' rather than
         save-excursion+set-buffer
```

To avoid such problems, you should call `save-excursion` only after setting the desired current buffer, as in the following example:

```
(defun append-string-to-buffer (string buffer)
  "Append STRING to the end of BUFFER."
  (with-current-buffer buffer
    (save-excursion
      (goto-char (point-max))
      (insert string))))
```

Likewise, `save-excursion` does not restore window-buffer correspondences altered by functions such as `switch-to-buffer`.

Warning: Ordinary insertion of text adjacent to the saved point value relocates the saved value, just as it relocates all markers. More precisely, the saved value is a marker with insertion type `nil`. See Section 30.5 [Marker Insertion Types], page 690. Therefore, when the saved point value is restored, it normally comes before the inserted text.

`save-mark-and-excursion` *body...*   [Macro]

> This macro is like `save-excursion`, but also saves and restores the mark location and `mark-active`. This macro does what `save-excursion` did before Emacs 25.1.

29.4 Narrowing

Narrowing means limiting the text addressable by Emacs editing commands to a limited range of characters in a buffer. The text that remains addressable is called the *accessible portion* of the buffer.

Narrowing is specified with two buffer positions, which become the beginning and end of the accessible portion. For most editing commands and primitives, these positions replace the values of the beginning and end of the buffer. While narrowing is in effect, no text outside the accessible portion is displayed, and point cannot move outside the accessible portion. Note that narrowing does not alter actual buffer positions (see Section 29.1 [Point], page 673); it only determines which positions are considered the accessible portion of the buffer. Most functions refuse to operate on text that is outside the accessible portion.

Commands for saving buffers are unaffected by narrowing; they save the entire buffer regardless of any narrowing.

If you need to display in a single buffer several very different types of text, consider using an alternative facility described in Section 26.12 [Swapping Text], page 565.

`narrow-to-region` *start end*   [Command]

> This function sets the accessible portion of the current buffer to start at *start* and end at *end*. Both arguments should be character positions.
>
> In an interactive call, *start* and *end* are set to the bounds of the current region (point and the mark, with the smallest first).

narrow-to-page &optional *move-count*   [Command]

> This function sets the accessible portion of the current buffer to include just the
> current page. An optional first argument *move-count* non-`nil` means to move for-
> ward or backward by *move-count* pages and then narrow to one page. The variable
> `page-delimiter` specifies where pages start and end (see Section 33.8 [Standard Reg-
> exps], page 814).
>
> In an interactive call, *move-count* is set to the numeric prefix argument.

widen   [Command]

> This function cancels any narrowing in the current buffer, so that the entire contents
> are accessible. This is called *widening*. It is equivalent to the following expression:
>
> ```
> (narrow-to-region 1 (1+ (buffer-size)))
> ```

buffer-narrowed-p   [Function]

> This function returns non-`nil` if the buffer is narrowed, and `nil` otherwise.

save-restriction *body...*   [Special Form]

> This special form saves the current bounds of the accessible portion, evaluates the
> *body* forms, and finally restores the saved bounds, thus restoring the same state of
> narrowing (or absence thereof) formerly in effect. The state of narrowing is restored
> even in the event of an abnormal exit via `throw` or error (see Section 10.6 [Nonlo-
> cal Exits], page 145). Therefore, this construct is a clean way to narrow a buffer
> temporarily.
>
> The value returned by `save-restriction` is that returned by the last form in *body*,
> or `nil` if no body forms were given.
>
> **Caution:** it is easy to make a mistake when using the `save-restriction` construct.
> Read the entire description here before you try it.
>
> If *body* changes the current buffer, `save-restriction` still restores the restrictions
> on the original buffer (the buffer whose restrictions it saved from), but it does not
> restore the identity of the current buffer.
>
> `save-restriction` does *not* restore point; use `save-excursion` for that. If you
> use both `save-restriction` and `save-excursion` together, `save-excursion` should
> come first (on the outside). Otherwise, the old point value would be restored with
> temporary narrowing still in effect. If the old point value were outside the limits of
> the temporary narrowing, this would fail to restore it accurately.
>
> Here is a simple example of correct use of `save-restriction`:
>
> ```
>          ---------- Buffer: foo ----------
>          This is the contents of foo
>          This is the contents of foo
>          This is the contents of foo⋆
>          ---------- Buffer: foo ----------
> ```

```
(save-excursion
  (save-restriction
    (goto-char 1)
    (forward-line 2)
    (narrow-to-region 1 (point))
    (goto-char (point-min))
    (replace-string "foo" "bar")))

---------- Buffer: foo ----------
This is the contents of bar
This is the contents of bar
This is the contents of foo⋆
---------- Buffer: foo ----------
```

30 Markers

A *marker* is a Lisp object used to specify a position in a buffer relative to the surrounding text. A marker changes its offset from the beginning of the buffer automatically whenever text is inserted or deleted, so that it stays with the two characters on either side of it.

30.1 Overview of Markers

A marker specifies a buffer and a position in that buffer. A marker can be used to represent a position in functions that require one, just as an integer could be used. In that case, the marker's buffer is normally ignored. Of course, a marker used in this way usually points to a position in the buffer that the function operates on, but that is entirely the programmer's responsibility. See Chapter 29 [Positions], page 673, for a complete description of positions.

A marker has three attributes: the marker position, the marker buffer, and the insertion type. The marker position is an integer that is equivalent (at a given time) to the marker as a position in that buffer. But the marker's position value can change during the life of the marker, and often does. Insertion and deletion of text in the buffer relocate the marker. The idea is that a marker positioned between two characters remains between those two characters despite insertion and deletion elsewhere in the buffer. Relocation changes the integer equivalent of the marker.

Deleting text around a marker's position leaves the marker between the characters immediately before and after the deleted text. Inserting text at the position of a marker normally leaves the marker either in front of or after the new text, depending on the marker's *insertion type* (see Section 30.5 [Marker Insertion Types], page 690)—unless the insertion is done with `insert-before-markers` (see Section 31.4 [Insertion], page 700).

Insertion and deletion in a buffer must check all the markers and relocate them if necessary. This slows processing in a buffer with a large number of markers. For this reason, it is a good idea to make a marker point nowhere if you are sure you don't need it any more. Markers that can no longer be accessed are eventually removed (see Section E.3 [Garbage Collection], page 1069).

Because it is common to perform arithmetic operations on a marker position, most of these operations (including + and -) accept markers as arguments. In such cases, the marker stands for its current position.

Here are examples of creating markers, setting markers, and moving point to markers:

```
;; Make a new marker that initially does not point anywhere:
(setq m1 (make-marker))
     ⇒ #<marker in no buffer>

;; Set m1 to point between the 99th and 100th characters
;;     in the current buffer:
(set-marker m1 100)
     ⇒ #<marker at 100 in markers.texi>
```

```
;; Now insert one character at the beginning of the buffer:
(goto-char (point-min))
     ⇒ 1
(insert "Q")
     ⇒ nil

;; m1 is updated appropriately.
m1
     ⇒ #<marker at 101 in markers.texi>

;; Two markers that point to the same position
;;    are not eq, but they are equal.
(setq m2 (copy-marker m1))
     ⇒ #<marker at 101 in markers.texi>
(eq m1 m2)
     ⇒ nil
(equal m1 m2)
     ⇒ t

;; When you are finished using a marker, make it point nowhere.
(set-marker m1 nil)
     ⇒ #<marker in no buffer>
```

30.2 Predicates on Markers

You can test an object to see whether it is a marker, or whether it is either an integer or a marker. The latter test is useful in connection with the arithmetic functions that work with both markers and integers.

markerp *object*   [Function]
> This function returns **t** if *object* is a marker, **nil** otherwise. Note that integers are not markers, even though many functions will accept either a marker or an integer.

integer-or-marker-p *object*   [Function]
> This function returns **t** if *object* is an integer or a marker, **nil** otherwise.

number-or-marker-p *object*   [Function]
> This function returns **t** if *object* is a number (either integer or floating point) or a marker, **nil** otherwise.

30.3 Functions that Create Markers

When you create a new marker, you can make it point nowhere, or point to the present position of point, or to the beginning or end of the accessible portion of the buffer, or to the same place as another given marker.

The next four functions all return markers with insertion type **nil**. See Section 30.5 [Marker Insertion Types], page 690.

make-marker   [Function]

> This function returns a newly created marker that does not point anywhere.
>
>   (make-marker)
>   ⇒ #<marker in no buffer>

point-marker   [Function]

> This function returns a new marker that points to the present position of point in the current buffer. See Section 29.1 [Point], page 673. For an example, see **copy-marker**, below.

point-min-marker   [Function]

> This function returns a new marker that points to the beginning of the accessible portion of the buffer. This will be the beginning of the buffer unless narrowing is in effect. See Section 29.4 [Narrowing], page 684.

point-max-marker   [Function]

> This function returns a new marker that points to the end of the accessible portion of the buffer. This will be the end of the buffer unless narrowing is in effect. See Section 29.4 [Narrowing], page 684.
>
> Here are examples of this function and **point-min-marker**, shown in a buffer containing a version of the source file for the text of this chapter.
>
>   (point-min-marker)
>   ⇒ #<marker at 1 in markers.texi>
>   (point-max-marker)
>   ⇒ #<marker at 24080 in markers.texi>
>
>   (narrow-to-region 100 200)
>   ⇒ nil
>   (point-min-marker)
>   ⇒ #<marker at 100 in markers.texi>
>   (point-max-marker)
>   ⇒ #<marker at 200 in markers.texi>

copy-marker &optional *marker-or-integer insertion-type*   [Function]

> If passed a marker as its argument, **copy-marker** returns a new marker that points to the same place and the same buffer as does *marker-or-integer*. If passed an integer as its argument, **copy-marker** returns a new marker that points to position *marker-or-integer* in the current buffer.
>
> The new marker's insertion type is specified by the argument *insertion-type*. See Section 30.5 [Marker Insertion Types], page 690.
>
>   (copy-marker 0)
>   ⇒ #<marker at 1 in markers.texi>
>
>   (copy-marker 90000)
>   ⇒ #<marker at 24080 in markers.texi>
>
> An error is signaled if *marker* is neither a marker nor an integer.

Two distinct markers are considered `equal` (even though not `eq`) to each other if they have the same position and buffer, or if they both point nowhere.

```
(setq p (point-marker))
     ⇒ #<marker at 2139 in markers.texi>

(setq q (copy-marker p))
     ⇒ #<marker at 2139 in markers.texi>

(eq p q)
     ⇒ nil

(equal p q)
     ⇒ t
```

30.4 Information from Markers

This section describes the functions for accessing the components of a marker object.

`marker-position` *marker*   [Function]
> This function returns the position that *marker* points to, or `nil` if it points nowhere.

`marker-buffer` *marker*   [Function]
> This function returns the buffer that *marker* points into, or `nil` if it points nowhere.
>
> ```
> (setq m (make-marker))
>      ⇒ #<marker in no buffer>
> (marker-position m)
>      ⇒ nil
> (marker-buffer m)
>      ⇒ nil
>
> (set-marker m 3770 (current-buffer))
>      ⇒ #<marker at 3770 in markers.texi>
> (marker-buffer m)
>      ⇒ #<buffer markers.texi>
> (marker-position m)
>      ⇒ 3770
> ```

30.5 Marker Insertion Types

When you insert text directly at the place where a marker points, there are two possible ways to relocate that marker: it can point before the inserted text, or point after it. You can specify which one a given marker should do by setting its *insertion type*. Note that use of `insert-before-markers` ignores markers' insertion types, always relocating a marker to point after the inserted text.

`set-marker-insertion-type` *marker type*   [Function]
> This function sets the insertion type of marker *marker* to *type*. If *type* is `t`, *marker* will advance when text is inserted at its position. If *type* is `nil`, *marker* does not advance when text is inserted there.

`marker-insertion-type` *marker*   [Function]
    This function reports the current insertion type of *marker*.

All functions that create markers without accepting an argument that specifies the insertion type, create them with insertion type `nil` (see Section 30.3 [Creating Markers], page 688). Also, the mark has, by default, insertion type `nil`.

30.6 Moving Marker Positions

This section describes how to change the position of an existing marker. When you do this, be sure you know whether the marker is used outside of your program, and, if so, what effects will result from moving it—otherwise, confusing things may happen in other parts of Emacs.

`set-marker` *marker position* **&optional** *buffer*   [Function]
    This function moves *marker* to *position* in *buffer*. If *buffer* is not provided, it defaults to the current buffer.

    If *position* is `nil` or a marker that points nowhere, then *marker* is set to point nowhere.

    The value returned is *marker*.

```
(setq m (point-marker))
     ⇒ #<marker at 4714 in markers.texi>
(set-marker m 55)
     ⇒ #<marker at 55 in markers.texi>
(setq b (get-buffer "foo"))
     ⇒ #<buffer foo>
(set-marker m 0 b)
     ⇒ #<marker at 1 in foo>
```

`move-marker` *marker position* **&optional** *buffer*   [Function]
    This is another name for `set-marker`.

30.7 The Mark

Each buffer has a special marker, which is designated *the mark*. When a buffer is newly created, this marker exists but does not point anywhere; this means that the mark doesn't exist in that buffer yet. Subsequent commands can set the mark.

The mark specifies a position to bound a range of text for many commands, such as `kill-region` and `indent-rigidly`. These commands typically act on the text between point and the mark, which is called the *region*. If you are writing a command that operates on the region, don't examine the mark directly; instead, use `interactive` with the 'r' specification. This provides the values of point and the mark as arguments to the command in an interactive call, but permits other Lisp programs to specify arguments explicitly. See Section 20.2.2 [Interactive Codes], page 348.

Some commands set the mark as a side-effect. Commands should do this only if it has a potential use to the user, and never for their own internal purposes. For example, the `replace-regexp` command sets the mark to the value of point before doing any replacements, because this enables the user to move back there conveniently after the replace is finished.

Once the mark exists in a buffer, it normally never ceases to exist. However, it may become *inactive*, if Transient Mark mode is enabled. The buffer-local variable `mark-active`, if non-`nil`, means that the mark is active. A command can call the function `deactivate-mark` to deactivate the mark directly, or it can request deactivation of the mark upon return to the editor command loop by setting the variable `deactivate-mark` to a non-`nil` value.

If Transient Mark mode is enabled, certain editing commands that normally apply to text near point, apply instead to the region when the mark is active. This is the main motivation for using Transient Mark mode. (Another is that this enables highlighting of the region when the mark is active. See Chapter 37 [Display], page 886.)

In addition to the mark, each buffer has a *mark ring* which is a list of markers containing previous values of the mark. When editing commands change the mark, they should normally save the old value of the mark on the mark ring. The variable `mark-ring-max` specifies the maximum number of entries in the mark ring; once the list becomes this long, adding a new element deletes the last element.

There is also a separate global mark ring, but that is used only in a few particular user-level commands, and is not relevant to Lisp programming. So we do not describe it here.

mark &optional *force*   [Function]

> This function returns the current buffer's mark position as an integer, or `nil` if no mark has ever been set in this buffer.
>
> If Transient Mark mode is enabled, and `mark-even-if-inactive` is `nil`, `mark` signals an error if the mark is inactive. However, if *force* is non-`nil`, then `mark` disregards inactivity of the mark, and returns the mark position (or `nil`) anyway.

mark-marker   [Function]

> This function returns the marker that represents the current buffer's mark. It is not a copy, it is the marker used internally. Therefore, changing this marker's position will directly affect the buffer's mark. Don't do that unless that is the effect you want.
>
> ```
> (setq m (mark-marker))
>      ⇒ #<marker at 3420 in markers.texi>
> (set-marker m 100)
>      ⇒ #<marker at 100 in markers.texi>
> (mark-marker)
>      ⇒ #<marker at 100 in markers.texi>
> ```
>
> Like any marker, this marker can be set to point at any buffer you like. If you make it point at any buffer other than the one of which it is the mark, it will yield perfectly consistent, but rather odd, results. We recommend that you not do it!

set-mark *position*   [Function]

> This function sets the mark to *position*, and activates the mark. The old value of the mark is *not* pushed onto the mark ring.
>
> **Please note:** Use this function only if you want the user to see that the mark has moved, and you want the previous mark position to be lost. Normally, when a new mark is set, the old one should go on the `mark-ring`. For this reason, most applications should use `push-mark` and `pop-mark`, not `set-mark`.

Novice Emacs Lisp programmers often try to use the mark for the wrong purposes. The mark saves a location for the user's convenience. An editing command should not alter the mark unless altering the mark is part of the user-level functionality of the command. (And, in that case, this effect should be documented.) To remember a location for internal use in the Lisp program, store it in a Lisp variable. For example:

```
(let ((beg (point)))
  (forward-line 1)
  (delete-region beg (point))).
```

push-mark &optional *position nomsg activate*   [Function]

This function sets the current buffer's mark to *position*, and pushes a copy of the previous mark onto `mark-ring`. If *position* is `nil`, then the value of point is used.

The function `push-mark` normally *does not* activate the mark. To do that, specify `t` for the argument *activate*.

A 'Mark set' message is displayed unless *nomsg* is non-`nil`.

pop-mark   [Function]

This function pops off the top element of `mark-ring` and makes that mark become the buffer's actual mark. This does not move point in the buffer, and it does nothing if `mark-ring` is empty. It deactivates the mark.

transient-mark-mode   [User Option]

This variable, if non-`nil`, enables Transient Mark mode. In Transient Mark mode, every buffer-modifying primitive sets `deactivate-mark`. As a consequence, most commands that modify the buffer also deactivate the mark.

When Transient Mark mode is enabled and the mark is active, many commands that normally apply to the text near point instead apply to the region. Such commands should use the function `use-region-p` to test whether they should operate on the region. See Section 30.8 [The Region], page 695.

Lisp programs can set `transient-mark-mode` to non-`nil`, non-`t` values to enable Transient Mark mode temporarily. If the value is `lambda`, Transient Mark mode is automatically turned off after any action, such as buffer modification, that would normally deactivate the mark. If the value is `(only . oldval)`, then `transient-mark-mode` is set to the value *oldval* after any subsequent command that moves point and is not shift-translated (see Section 20.8.1 [Key Sequence Input], page 373), or after any other action that would normally deactivate the mark.

mark-even-if-inactive   [User Option]

If this is non-`nil`, Lisp programs and the Emacs user can use the mark even when it is inactive. This option affects the behavior of Transient Mark mode. When the option is non-`nil`, deactivation of the mark turns off region highlighting, but commands that use the mark behave as if the mark were still active.

deactivate-mark   [Variable]

If an editor command sets this variable non-`nil`, then the editor command loop deactivates the mark after the command returns (if Transient Mark mode is enabled). All the primitives that change the buffer set `deactivate-mark`, to deactivate the mark when the command is finished. Setting this variable makes it buffer-local.

To write Lisp code that modifies the buffer without causing deactivation of the mark at the end of the command, bind `deactivate-mark` to `nil` around the code that does the modification. For example:

```
(let (deactivate-mark)
  (insert " "))
```

deactivate-mark &optional *force*   [Function]

If Transient Mark mode is enabled or *force* is non-`nil`, this function deactivates the mark and runs the normal hook `deactivate-mark-hook`. Otherwise, it does nothing.

mark-active   [Variable]

The mark is active when this variable is non-`nil`. This variable is always buffer-local in each buffer. Do *not* use the value of this variable to decide whether a command that normally operates on text near point should operate on the region instead. Use the function `use-region-p` for that (see Section 30.8 [The Region], page 695).

activate-mark-hook   [Variable]
deactivate-mark-hook   [Variable]

These normal hooks are run, respectively, when the mark becomes active and when it becomes inactive. The hook `activate-mark-hook` is also run at the end of the command loop if the mark is active and it is possible that the region may have changed.

handle-shift-selection   [Function]

This function implements the shift-selection behavior of point-motion commands. See Section "Shift Selection" in *The GNU Emacs Manual*. It is called automatically by the Emacs command loop whenever a command with a '^' character in its `interactive` spec is invoked, before the command itself is executed (see Section 20.2.2 [Interactive Codes], page 348).

If `shift-select-mode` is non-`nil` and the current command was invoked via shift translation (see Section 20.8.1 [Key Sequence Input], page 373), this function sets the mark and temporarily activates the region, unless the region was already temporarily activated in this way. Otherwise, if the region has been activated temporarily, it deactivates the mark and restores the variable `transient-mark-mode` to its earlier value.

mark-ring   [Variable]

The value of this buffer-local variable is the list of saved former marks of the current buffer, most recent first.

```
mark-ring
⇒ (#<marker at 11050 in markers.texi>
   #<marker at 10832 in markers.texi>
   ...)
```

mark-ring-max   [User Option]

The value of this variable is the maximum size of `mark-ring`. If more marks than this are pushed onto the `mark-ring`, `push-mark` discards an old mark when it adds a new one.

When Delete Selection mode (see Section "Using Region" in *The GNU Emacs Manual*) is enabled, commands that operate on the active region (a.k.a. "selection") behave slightly differently. This works by adding the function `delete-selection-pre-hook` to the `pre-command-hook` (see Section 20.1 [Command Overview], page 345). That function calls `delete-selection-helper` to delete the selection as appropriate for the command. If you want to adapt a command to Delete Selection mode, put the `delete-selection` property on the function's symbol (see Section 8.4.1 [Symbol Plists], page 120); commands that don't have this property on their symbol won't delete the selection. This property can have one of several values to tailor the behavior to what the command is supposed to do; see the doc strings of `delete-selection-pre-hook` and `delete-selection-helper` for the details.

30.8 The Region

The text between point and the mark is known as *the region*. Various functions operate on text delimited by point and the mark, but only those functions specifically related to the region itself are described here.

The next two functions signal an error if the mark does not point anywhere. If Transient Mark mode is enabled and `mark-even-if-inactive` is `nil`, they also signal an error if the mark is inactive.

`region-beginning` [Function]
> This function returns the position of the beginning of the region (as an integer). This is the position of either point or the mark, whichever is smaller.

`region-end` [Function]
> This function returns the position of the end of the region (as an integer). This is the position of either point or the mark, whichever is larger.

Instead of using `region-beginning` and `region-end`, a command designed to operate on a region should normally use `interactive` with the 'r' specification to find the beginning and end of the region. This lets other Lisp programs specify the bounds explicitly as arguments. See Section 20.2.2 [Interactive Codes], page 348.

`use-region-p` [Function]
> This function returns `t` if Transient Mark mode is enabled, the mark is active, and there is a valid region in the buffer. This function is intended to be used by commands that operate on the region, instead of on text near point, when the mark is active.
>
> A region is valid if it has a non-zero size, or if the user option `use-empty-active-region` is non-`nil` (by default, it is `nil`). The function `region-active-p` is similar to `use-region-p`, but considers all regions as valid. In most cases, you should not use `region-active-p`, since if the region is empty it is often more appropriate to operate on point.

31 Text

This chapter describes the functions that deal with the text in a buffer. Most examine, insert, or delete text in the current buffer, often operating at point or on text adjacent to point. Many are interactive. All the functions that change the text provide for undoing the changes (see Section 31.9 [Undo], page 712).

Many text-related functions operate on a region of text defined by two buffer positions passed in arguments named *start* and *end*. These arguments should be either markers (see Chapter 30 [Markers], page 687) or numeric character positions (see Chapter 29 [Positions], page 673). The order of these arguments does not matter; it is all right for *start* to be the end of the region and *end* the beginning. For example, (delete-region 1 10) and (delete-region 10 1) are equivalent. An args-out-of-range error is signaled if either *start* or *end* is outside the accessible portion of the buffer. In an interactive call, point and the mark are used for these arguments.

Throughout this chapter, "text" refers to the characters in the buffer, together with their properties (when relevant). Keep in mind that point is always between two characters, and the cursor appears on the character after point.

31.1 Examining Text Near Point

Many functions are provided to look at the characters around point. Several simple functions are described here. See also looking-at in Section 33.4 [Regexp Search], page 803.

In the following four functions, "beginning" or "end" of buffer refers to the beginning or end of the accessible portion.

char-after &optional *position*   [Function]
> This function returns the character in the current buffer at (i.e., immediately after) position *position*. If *position* is out of range for this purpose, either before the beginning of the buffer, or at or beyond the end, then the value is nil. The default for *position* is point.
>
> In the following example, assume that the first character in the buffer is '@':
>
>   (string (char-after 1))
>   ⇒ "@"

char-before &optional *position*   [Function]
> This function returns the character in the current buffer immediately before position *position*. If *position* is out of range for this purpose, either at or before the beginning of the buffer, or beyond the end, then the value is nil. The default for *position* is point.

following-char   [Function]
> This function returns the character following point in the current buffer. This is similar to (char-after (point)). However, if point is at the end of the buffer, then following-char returns 0.
>
> Remember that point is always between characters, and the cursor normally appears over the character following point. Therefore, the character returned by following-char is the character the cursor is over.

In this example, point is between the 'a' and the 'c'.

```
---------- Buffer: foo ----------
Gentlemen may cry ``Pea⋆ce! Peace!,''
but there is no peace.
---------- Buffer: foo ----------


(string (preceding-char))
     ⇒ "a"
(string (following-char))
     ⇒ "c"
```

preceding-char   [Function]

> This function returns the character preceding point in the current buffer. See above, under `following-char`, for an example. If point is at the beginning of the buffer, `preceding-char` returns 0.

bobp   [Function]

> This function returns `t` if point is at the beginning of the buffer. If narrowing is in effect, this means the beginning of the accessible portion of the text. See also `point-min` in Section 29.1 [Point], page 673.

eobp   [Function]

> This function returns `t` if point is at the end of the buffer. If narrowing is in effect, this means the end of accessible portion of the text. See also `point-max` in See Section 29.1 [Point], page 673.

bolp   [Function]

> This function returns `t` if point is at the beginning of a line. See Section 29.2.4 [Text Lines], page 676. The beginning of the buffer (or of its accessible portion) always counts as the beginning of a line.

eolp   [Function]

> This function returns `t` if point is at the end of a line. The end of the buffer (or of its accessible portion) is always considered the end of a line.

31.2 Examining Buffer Contents

This section describes functions that allow a Lisp program to convert any portion of the text in the buffer into a string.

buffer-substring *start end*   [Function]

> This function returns a string containing a copy of the text of the region defined by positions *start* and *end* in the current buffer. If the arguments are not positions in the accessible portion of the buffer, `buffer-substring` signals an `args-out-of-range` error.
>
> Here's an example which assumes Font-Lock mode is not enabled:
>
> ```
> ---------- Buffer: foo ----------
> This is the contents of buffer foo
>
>
> ---------- Buffer: foo ----------
> ```

```
(buffer-substring 1 10)
    ⇒ "This is t"
(buffer-substring (point-max) 10)
    ⇒ "he contents of buffer foo\n"
```

If the text being copied has any text properties, these are copied into the string along with the characters they belong to. See Section 31.19 [Text Properties], page 732. However, overlays (see Section 37.9 [Overlays], page 904) in the buffer and their properties are ignored, not copied.

For example, if Font-Lock mode is enabled, you might get results like these:

```
(buffer-substring 1 10)
    ⇒ #("This is t" 0 1 (fontified t) 1 9 (fontified t))
```

buffer-substring-no-properties *start end*   [Function]

    This is like `buffer-substring`, except that it does not copy text properties, just the characters themselves. See Section 31.19 [Text Properties], page 732.

buffer-string   [Function]

    This function returns the contents of the entire accessible portion of the current buffer, as a string.

If you need to make sure the resulting string, when copied to a different location, will not change its visual appearance due to reordering of bidirectional text, use the `buffer-substring-with-bidi-context` function (see Section 37.26 [Bidirectional Display], page 981).

filter-buffer-substring *start end* **&optional** *delete*   [Function]

    This function filters the buffer text between *start* and *end* using a function specified by the variable `filter-buffer-substring-function`, and returns the result.

    The default filter function consults the obsolete wrapper hook `filter-buffer-substring-functions` (see the documentation string of the macro `with-wrapper-hook` for the details about this obsolete facility), and the obsolete variable `buffer-substring-filters`. If both of these are `nil`, it returns the unaltered text from the buffer, i.e., what `buffer-substring` would return.

    If *delete* is non-`nil`, the function deletes the text between *start* and *end* after copying it, like `delete-and-extract-region`.

    Lisp code should use this function instead of `buffer-substring`, `buffer-substring-no-properties`, or `delete-and-extract-region` when copying into user-accessible data structures such as the kill-ring, X clipboard, and registers. Major and minor modes can modify `filter-buffer-substring-function` to alter such text as it is copied out of the buffer.

filter-buffer-substring-function   [Variable]

    The value of this variable is a function that `filter-buffer-substring` will call to do the actual work. The function receives three arguments, the same as those of `filter-buffer-substring`, which it should treat as per the documentation of that function. It should return the filtered text (and optionally delete the source text).

The following two variables are obsoleted by `filter-buffer-substring-function`, but are still supported for backward compatibility.

`filter-buffer-substring-functions` [Variable]

This obsolete variable is a wrapper hook, whose members should be functions that accept four arguments: *fun*, *start*, *end*, and *delete*. *fun* is a function that takes three arguments (*start*, *end*, and *delete*), and returns a string. In both cases, the *start*, *end*, and *delete* arguments are the same as those of `filter-buffer-substring`.

The first hook function is passed a *fun* that is equivalent to the default operation of `filter-buffer-substring`, i.e., it returns the buffer-substring between *start* and *end* (processed by any `buffer-substring-filters`) and optionally deletes the original text from the buffer. In most cases, the hook function will call *fun* once, and then do its own processing of the result. The next hook function receives a *fun* equivalent to this, and so on. The actual return value is the result of all the hook functions acting in sequence.

`buffer-substring-filters` [Variable]

The value of this obsolete variable should be a list of functions that accept a single string argument and return another string. The default `filter-buffer-substring` function passes the buffer substring to the first function in this list, and the return value of each function is passed to the next function. The return value of the last function is passed to `filter-buffer-substring-functions`.

`current-word` &optional *strict really-word* [Function]

This function returns the symbol (or word) at or near point, as a string. The return value includes no text properties.

If the optional argument *really-word* is non-`nil`, it finds a word; otherwise, it finds a symbol (which includes both word characters and symbol constituent characters).

If the optional argument *strict* is non-`nil`, then point must be in or next to the symbol or word—if no symbol or word is there, the function returns `nil`. Otherwise, a nearby symbol or word on the same line is acceptable.

`thing-at-point` *thing* &optional *no-properties* [Function]

Return the *thing* around or next to point, as a string.

The argument *thing* is a symbol which specifies a kind of syntactic entity. Possibilities include `symbol`, `list`, `sexp`, `defun`, `filename`, `url`, `word`, `sentence`, `whitespace`, `line`, `page`, and others.

When the optional argument *no-properties* is non-`nil`, this function strips text properties from the return value.

```
---------- Buffer: foo ----------
Gentlemen may cry ``Pea⋆ce! Peace!,''
but there is no peace.
---------- Buffer: foo ----------

(thing-at-point 'word)
     ⇒ "Peace"
(thing-at-point 'line)
```

```
                    ⇒ "Gentlemen may cry ``Peace! Peace!,''\n"
            (thing-at-point 'whitespace)
                    ⇒ nil
```

31.3 Comparing Text

This function lets you compare portions of the text in a buffer, without copying them into strings first.

compare-buffer-substrings *buffer1 start1 end1 buffer2 start2 end2*   [Function]
> This function lets you compare two substrings of the same buffer or two different buffers. The first three arguments specify one substring, giving a buffer (or a buffer name) and two positions within the buffer. The last three arguments specify the other substring in the same way. You can use **nil** for *buffer1*, *buffer2*, or both to stand for the current buffer.
>
> The value is negative if the first substring is less, positive if the first is greater, and zero if they are equal. The absolute value of the result is one plus the index of the first differing characters within the substrings.
>
> This function ignores case when comparing characters if **case-fold-search** is non-**nil**. It always ignores text properties.
>
> Suppose you have the text '**foobarbar haha!rara!**' in the current buffer; then in this example the two substrings are '**rbar** ' and '**rara!**'. The value is 2 because the first substring is greater at the second character.
>
> ```
> (compare-buffer-substrings nil 6 11 nil 16 21)
>         ⇒ 2
> ```

31.4 Inserting Text

Insertion means adding new text to a buffer. The inserted text goes at point—between the character before point and the character after point. Some insertion functions leave point before the inserted text, while other functions leave it after. We call the former insertion *after point* and the latter insertion *before point*.

Insertion moves markers located at positions after the insertion point, so that they stay with the surrounding text (see Chapter 30 [Markers], page 687). When a marker points at the place of insertion, insertion may or may not relocate the marker, depending on the marker's insertion type (see Section 30.5 [Marker Insertion Types], page 690). Certain special functions such as **insert-before-markers** relocate all such markers to point after the inserted text, regardless of the markers' insertion type.

Insertion functions signal an error if the current buffer is read-only (see Section 26.7 [Read Only Buffers], page 558) or if they insert within read-only text (see Section 31.19.4 [Special Properties], page 738).

These functions copy text characters from strings and buffers along with their properties. The inserted characters have exactly the same properties as the characters they were copied from. By contrast, characters specified as separate arguments, not part of a string or buffer, inherit their text properties from the neighboring text.

The insertion functions convert text from unibyte to multibyte in order to insert in a multibyte buffer, and vice versa—if the text comes from a string or from a buffer. However, they do not convert unibyte character codes 128 through 255 to multibyte characters, not even if the current buffer is a multibyte buffer. See Section 32.3 [Converting Representations], page 763.

insert **&rest** *args* [Function]

    This function inserts the strings and/or characters *args* into the current buffer, at point, moving point forward. In other words, it inserts the text before point. An error is signaled unless all *args* are either strings or characters. The value is `nil`.

insert-before-markers **&rest** *args* [Function]

    This function inserts the strings and/or characters *args* into the current buffer, at point, moving point forward. An error is signaled unless all *args* are either strings or characters. The value is `nil`.

    This function is unlike the other insertion functions in that it relocates markers initially pointing at the insertion point, to point after the inserted text. If an overlay begins at the insertion point, the inserted text falls outside the overlay; if a nonempty overlay ends at the insertion point, the inserted text falls inside that overlay.

insert-char *character* **&optional** *count inherit* [Command]

    This command inserts *count* instances of *character* into the current buffer before point. The argument *count* must be an integer, and *character* must be a character.

    If called interactively, this command prompts for *character* using its Unicode name or its code point. See Section "Inserting Text" in *The GNU Emacs Manual*.

    This function does not convert unibyte character codes 128 through 255 to multibyte characters, not even if the current buffer is a multibyte buffer. See Section 32.3 [Converting Representations], page 763.

    If *inherit* is non-`nil`, the inserted characters inherit sticky text properties from the two characters before and after the insertion point. See Section 31.19.6 [Sticky Properties], page 744.

insert-buffer-substring *from-buffer-or-name* **&optional** *start end* [Function]

    This function inserts a portion of buffer *from-buffer-or-name* into the current buffer before point. The text inserted is the region between *start* (inclusive) and *end* (exclusive). (These arguments default to the beginning and end of the accessible portion of that buffer.) This function returns `nil`.

    In this example, the form is executed with buffer 'bar' as the current buffer. We assume that buffer 'bar' is initially empty.

```
---------- Buffer: foo ----------
We hold these truths to be self-evident, that all
---------- Buffer: foo ----------

(insert-buffer-substring "foo" 1 20)
     ⇒ nil

---------- Buffer: bar ----------
We hold these truth★
---------- Buffer: bar ----------
```

insert-buffer-substring-no-properties *from-buffer-or-name* [Function]
&optional *start end*
> This is like **insert-buffer-substring** except that it does not copy any text properties.

See Section 31.19.6 [Sticky Properties], page 744, for other insertion functions that inherit text properties from the nearby text in addition to inserting it. Whitespace inserted by indentation functions also inherits text properties.

31.5 User-Level Insertion Commands

This section describes higher-level commands for inserting text, commands intended primarily for the user but useful also in Lisp programs.

insert-buffer *from-buffer-or-name* [Command]
> This command inserts the entire accessible contents of *from-buffer-or-name* (which must exist) into the current buffer after point. It leaves the mark after the inserted text. The value is **nil**.

self-insert-command *count* [Command]
> This command inserts the last character typed; it does so *count* times, before point, and returns **nil**. Most printing characters are bound to this command. In routine use, **self-insert-command** is the most frequently called function in Emacs, but programs rarely use it except to install it on a keymap.
>
> In an interactive call, *count* is the numeric prefix argument.
>
> Self-insertion translates the input character through **translation-table-for-input**. See Section 32.9 [Translation of Characters], page 772.
>
> This command calls **auto-fill-function** whenever that is non-**nil** and the character inserted is in the table **auto-fill-chars** (see Section 31.14 [Auto Filling], page 721).
>
> This command performs abbrev expansion if Abbrev mode is enabled and the inserted character does not have word-constituent syntax. (See Chapter 35 [Abbrevs], page 832, and Section 34.2.1 [Syntax Class Table], page 817.) It is also responsible for calling **blink-paren-function** when the inserted character has close parenthesis syntax (see Section 37.21 [Blinking], page 972).
>
> The final thing this command does is to run the hook **post-self-insert-hook**. You could use this to automatically reindent text as it is typed, for example.
>
> Do not try substituting your own definition of **self-insert-command** for the standard one. The editor command loop handles this function specially.

newline &optional *number-of-newlines* [Command]
> This command inserts newlines into the current buffer before point. If *number-of-newlines* is supplied, that many newline characters are inserted.
>
> This function calls **auto-fill-function** if the current column number is greater than the value of **fill-column** and *number-of-newlines* is **nil**. Typically what **auto-fill-function** does is insert a newline; thus, the overall result in this case is to insert two newlines at different places: one at point, and another earlier in the line. **newline** does not auto-fill if *number-of-newlines* is non-**nil**.

This command indents to the left margin if that is not zero. See Section 31.12 [Margins], page 718.

The value returned is `nil`. In an interactive call, *count* is the numeric prefix argument.

`overwrite-mode`   [Variable]

This variable controls whether overwrite mode is in effect. The value should be `overwrite-mode-textual`, `overwrite-mode-binary`, or `nil`. `overwrite-mode-textual` specifies textual overwrite mode (treats newlines and tabs specially), and `overwrite-mode-binary` specifies binary overwrite mode (treats newlines and tabs like any other characters).

31.6 Deleting Text

Deletion means removing part of the text in a buffer, without saving it in the kill ring (see Section 31.8 [The Kill Ring], page 706). Deleted text can't be yanked, but can be reinserted using the undo mechanism (see Section 31.9 [Undo], page 712). Some deletion functions do save text in the kill ring in some special cases.

All of the deletion functions operate on the current buffer.

`erase-buffer`   [Command]

This function deletes the entire text of the current buffer (*not* just the accessible portion), leaving it empty. If the buffer is read-only, it signals a `buffer-read-only` error; if some of the text in it is read-only, it signals a `text-read-only` error. Otherwise, it deletes the text without asking for any confirmation. It returns `nil`.

Normally, deleting a large amount of text from a buffer inhibits further auto-saving of that buffer because it has shrunk. However, `erase-buffer` does not do this, the idea being that the future text is not really related to the former text, and its size should not be compared with that of the former text.

`delete-region` *start end*   [Command]

This command deletes the text between positions *start* and *end* in the current buffer, and returns `nil`. If point was inside the deleted region, its value afterward is *start*. Otherwise, point relocates with the surrounding text, as markers do.

`delete-and-extract-region` *start end*   [Function]

This function deletes the text between positions *start* and *end* in the current buffer, and returns a string containing the text just deleted.

If point was inside the deleted region, its value afterward is *start*. Otherwise, point relocates with the surrounding text, as markers do.

`delete-char` *count* **&optional** *killp*   [Command]

This command deletes *count* characters directly after point, or before point if *count* is negative. If *killp* is non-`nil`, then it saves the deleted characters in the kill ring.

In an interactive call, *count* is the numeric prefix argument, and *killp* is the unprocessed prefix argument. Therefore, if a prefix argument is supplied, the text is saved in the kill ring. If no prefix argument is supplied, then one character is deleted, but not saved in the kill ring.

The value returned is always `nil`.

`delete-backward-char` *count* **&optional** *killp*   [Command]

> This command deletes *count* characters directly before point, or after point if *count* is negative. If *killp* is non-`nil`, then it saves the deleted characters in the kill ring.

> In an interactive call, *count* is the numeric prefix argument, and *killp* is the unprocessed prefix argument. Therefore, if a prefix argument is supplied, the text is saved in the kill ring. If no prefix argument is supplied, then one character is deleted, but not saved in the kill ring.

> The value returned is always `nil`.

`backward-delete-char-untabify` *count* **&optional** *killp*   [Command]

> This command deletes *count* characters backward, changing tabs into spaces. When the next character to be deleted is a tab, it is first replaced with the proper number of spaces to preserve alignment and then one of those spaces is deleted instead of the tab. If *killp* is non-`nil`, then the command saves the deleted characters in the kill ring.

> Conversion of tabs to spaces happens only if *count* is positive. If it is negative, exactly −*count* characters after point are deleted.

> In an interactive call, *count* is the numeric prefix argument, and *killp* is the unprocessed prefix argument. Therefore, if a prefix argument is supplied, the text is saved in the kill ring. If no prefix argument is supplied, then one character is deleted, but not saved in the kill ring.

> The value returned is always `nil`.

`backward-delete-char-untabify-method`   [User Option]

> This option specifies how `backward-delete-char-untabify` should deal with whitespace. Possible values include `untabify`, the default, meaning convert a tab to many spaces and delete one; `hungry`, meaning delete all tabs and spaces before point with one command; `all` meaning delete all tabs, spaces and newlines before point, and `nil`, meaning do nothing special for whitespace characters.

31.7 User-Level Deletion Commands

This section describes higher-level commands for deleting text, commands intended primarily for the user but useful also in Lisp programs.

`delete-horizontal-space` **&optional** *backward-only*   [Command]

> This function deletes all spaces and tabs around point. It returns `nil`.

> If *backward-only* is non-`nil`, the function deletes spaces and tabs before point, but not after point.

> In the following examples, we call `delete-horizontal-space` four times, once on each line, with point between the second and third characters on the line each time.

```
---------- Buffer: foo ----------
I ⋆thought
I ⋆      thought
We⋆ thought
Yo⋆u thought
---------- Buffer: foo ----------
```

```
(delete-horizontal-space)    ; Four times.
     ⇒ nil


---------- Buffer: foo ----------
Ithought
Ithought
Wethought
You thought
---------- Buffer: foo ----------
```

delete-indentation &optional *join-following-p* [Command]

This function joins the line point is on to the previous line, deleting any whitespace at the join and in some cases replacing it with one space. If *join-following-p* is non-nil, `delete-indentation` joins this line to the following line instead. The function returns `nil`.

If there is a fill prefix, and the second of the lines being joined starts with the prefix, then `delete-indentation` deletes the fill prefix before joining the lines. See Section 31.12 [Margins], page 718.

In the example below, point is located on the line starting '`events`', and it makes no difference if there are trailing spaces in the preceding line.

```
---------- Buffer: foo ----------
When in the course of human
⋆    events, it becomes necessary
---------- Buffer: foo ----------

(delete-indentation)
     ⇒ nil


---------- Buffer: foo ----------
When in the course of human⋆ events, it becomes necessary
---------- Buffer: foo ----------
```

After the lines are joined, the function `fixup-whitespace` is responsible for deciding whether to leave a space at the junction.

fixup-whitespace [Command]

This function replaces all the horizontal whitespace surrounding point with either one space or no space, according to the context. It returns `nil`.

At the beginning or end of a line, the appropriate amount of space is none. Before a character with close parenthesis syntax, or after a character with open parenthesis or expression-prefix syntax, no space is also appropriate. Otherwise, one space is appropriate. See Section 34.2.1 [Syntax Class Table], page 817.

In the example below, `fixup-whitespace` is called the first time with point before the word '`spaces`' in the first line. For the second invocation, point is directly after the '`(`'.

```
---------- Buffer: foo ----------
This has too many     ⋆spaces
This has too many spaces at the start of (⋆   this list)
---------- Buffer: foo ----------
```

```
(fixup-whitespace)
     ⇒ nil
(fixup-whitespace)
     ⇒ nil


---------- Buffer: foo ----------
This has too many spaces
This has too many spaces at the start of (this list)
---------- Buffer: foo ----------
```

`just-one-space` **&optional** *n*   [Command]

> This command replaces any spaces and tabs around point with a single space, or *n* spaces if *n* is specified. It returns `nil`.

`delete-blank-lines`   [Command]

> This function deletes blank lines surrounding point. If point is on a blank line with one or more blank lines before or after it, then all but one of them are deleted. If point is on an isolated blank line, then it is deleted. If point is on a nonblank line, the command deletes all blank lines immediately following it.
>
> A blank line is defined as a line containing only tabs and spaces.
>
> `delete-blank-lines` returns `nil`.

`delete-trailing-whitespace` **&optional** *start end*   [Command]

> Delete trailing whitespace in the region defined by *start* and *end*.
>
> This command deletes whitespace characters after the last non-whitespace character in each line in the region.
>
> If this command acts on the entire buffer (i.e., if called interactively with the mark inactive, or called from Lisp with *end* `nil`), it also deletes all trailing lines at the end of the buffer if the variable `delete-trailing-lines` is non-`nil`.

31.8 The Kill Ring

Kill functions delete text like the deletion functions, but save it so that the user can reinsert it by *yanking*. Most of these functions have 'kill-' in their name. By contrast, the functions whose names start with 'delete-' normally do not save text for yanking (though they can still be undone); these are deletion functions.

Most of the kill commands are primarily for interactive use, and are not described here. What we do describe are the functions provided for use in writing such commands. You can use these functions to write commands for killing text. When you need to delete text for internal purposes within a Lisp function, you should normally use deletion functions, so as not to disturb the kill ring contents. See Section 31.6 [Deletion], page 703.

Killed text is saved for later yanking in the *kill ring*. This is a list that holds a number of recent kills, not just the last text kill. We call this a "ring" because yanking treats it as having elements in a cyclic order. The list is kept in the variable `kill-ring`, and can be operated on with the usual functions for lists; there are also specialized functions, described in this section, that treat it as a ring.

Some people think this use of the word "kill" is unfortunate, since it refers to operations that specifically *do not* destroy the entities killed. This is in sharp contrast to ordinary life, in which death is permanent and killed entities do not come back to life. Therefore, other metaphors have been proposed. For example, the term "cut ring" makes sense to people who, in pre-computer days, used scissors and paste to cut up and rearrange manuscripts. However, it would be difficult to change the terminology now.

31.8.1 Kill Ring Concepts

The kill ring records killed text as strings in a list, most recent first. A short kill ring, for example, might look like this:

```
("some text" "a different piece of text" "even older text")
```

When the list reaches `kill-ring-max` entries in length, adding a new entry automatically deletes the last entry.

When kill commands are interwoven with other commands, each kill command makes a new entry in the kill ring. Multiple kill commands in succession build up a single kill ring entry, which would be yanked as a unit; the second and subsequent consecutive kill commands add text to the entry made by the first one.

For yanking, one entry in the kill ring is designated the front of the ring. Some yank commands rotate the ring by designating a different element as the front. But this virtual rotation doesn't change the list itself—the most recent entry always comes first in the list.

31.8.2 Functions for Killing

`kill-region` is the usual subroutine for killing text. Any command that calls this function is a kill command (and should probably have 'kill' in its name). `kill-region` puts the newly killed text in a new element at the beginning of the kill ring or adds it to the most recent element. It determines automatically (using `last-command`) whether the previous command was a kill command, and if so appends the killed text to the most recent entry.

The commands described below can filter the killed text before they save it in the kill ring. They call `filter-buffer-substring` (see Section 31.2 [Buffer Contents], page 697) to perform the filtering. By default, there's no filtering, but major and minor modes and hook functions can set up filtering, so that text saved in the kill ring is different from what was in the buffer.

`kill-region` *start end* **&optional** *region*   [Command]

> This function kills the stretch of text between *start* and *end*; but if the optional argument *region* is non-`nil`, it ignores *start* and *end*, and kills the text in the current region instead. The text is deleted but saved in the kill ring, along with its text properties. The value is always `nil`.
>
> In an interactive call, *start* and *end* are point and the mark, and *region* is always non-`nil`, so the command always kills the text in the current region.
>
> If the buffer or text is read-only, `kill-region` modifies the kill ring just the same, then signals an error without modifying the buffer. This is convenient because it lets the user use a series of kill commands to copy text from a read-only buffer into the kill ring.

`kill-read-only-ok`   [User Option]

> If this option is non-`nil`, `kill-region` does not signal an error if the buffer or text is read-only. Instead, it simply returns, updating the kill ring but not changing the buffer.

`copy-region-as-kill` *start end* **&optional** *region*   [Command]

> This function saves the stretch of text between *start* and *end* on the kill ring (including text properties), but does not delete the text from the buffer. However, if the optional argument *region* is non-`nil`, the function ignores *start* and *end*, and saves the current region instead. It always returns `nil`.
>
> In an interactive call, *start* and *end* are point and the mark, and *region* is always non-`nil`, so the command always saves the text in the current region.
>
> The command does not set `this-command` to `kill-region`, so a subsequent kill command does not append to the same kill ring entry.

31.8.3 Yanking

Yanking means inserting text from the kill ring, but it does not insert the text blindly. The `yank` command, and related commands, use `insert-for-yank` to perform special processing on the text before it is inserted.

`insert-for-yank` *string*   [Function]

> This function works like `insert`, except that it processes the text in *string* according to the `yank-handler` text property, as well as the variables `yank-handled-properties` and `yank-excluded-properties` (see below), before inserting the result into the current buffer.

`insert-buffer-substring-as-yank` *buf* **&optional** *start end*   [Function]

> This function resembles `insert-buffer-substring`, except that it processes the text according to `yank-handled-properties` and `yank-excluded-properties`. (It does not handle the `yank-handler` property, which does not normally occur in buffer text anyway.)

If you put a `yank-handler` text property on all or part of a string, that alters how `insert-for-yank` inserts the string. If different parts of the string have different `yank-handler` values (comparison being done with `eq`), each substring is handled separately. The property value must be a list of one to four elements, with the following format (where elements after the first may be omitted):

> `(function param noexclude undo)`

Here is what the elements do:

function
  When *function* is non-`nil`, it is called instead of `insert` to insert the string, with one argument—the string to insert.

param
  If *param* is present and non-`nil`, it replaces *string* (or the substring of *string* being processed) as the object passed to *function* (or `insert`). For example, if *function* is `yank-rectangle`, *param* should be a list of strings to insert as a rectangle.

noexclude
  If *noexclude* is present and non-`nil`, that disables the normal action of `yank-handled-properties` and `yank-excluded-properties` on the inserted string.

undo
  If *undo* is present and non-`nil`, it is a function that will be called by `yank-pop` to undo the insertion of the current object. It is called with two arguments,

the start and end of the current region. *function* can set `yank-undo-function` to override the *undo* value.

`yank-handled-properties` [User Option]

> This variable specifies special text property handling conditions for yanked text. It takes effect after the text has been inserted (either normally, or via the `yank-handler` property), and prior to `yank-excluded-properties` taking effect.

> The value should be an alist of elements (*prop . fun*). Each alist element is handled in order. The inserted text is scanned for stretches of text having text properties `eq` to *prop*; for each such stretch, *fun* is called with three arguments: the value of the property, and the start and end positions of the text.

`yank-excluded-properties` [User Option]

> The value of this variable is the list of properties to remove from inserted text. Its default value contains properties that might lead to annoying results, such as causing the text to respond to the mouse or specifying key bindings. It takes effect after `yank-handled-properties`.

31.8.4 Functions for Yanking

This section describes higher-level commands for yanking, which are intended primarily for the user but useful also in Lisp programs. Both `yank` and `yank-pop` honor the `yank-excluded-properties` variable and `yank-handler` text property (see Section 31.8.3 [Yanking], page 708).

`yank &optional` *arg* [Command]

> This command inserts before point the text at the front of the kill ring. It sets the mark at the beginning of that text, using `push-mark` (see Section 30.7 [The Mark], page 691), and puts point at the end.

> If *arg* is a non-`nil` list (which occurs interactively when the user types *C-u* with no digits), then `yank` inserts the text as described above, but puts point before the yanked text and sets the mark after it.

> If *arg* is a number, then `yank` inserts the *arg*th most recently killed text—the *arg*th element of the kill ring list, counted cyclically from the front, which is considered the first element for this purpose.

> `yank` does not alter the contents of the kill ring, unless it used text provided by another program, in which case it pushes that text onto the kill ring. However if *arg* is an integer different from one, it rotates the kill ring to place the yanked string at the front.

> `yank` returns `nil`.

`yank-pop &optional` *arg* [Command]

> This command replaces the just-yanked entry from the kill ring with a different entry from the kill ring.

> This is allowed only immediately after a `yank` or another `yank-pop`. At such a time, the region contains text that was just inserted by yanking. `yank-pop` deletes that text and inserts in its place a different piece of killed text. It does not add the deleted

text to the kill ring, since it is already in the kill ring somewhere. It does however rotate the kill ring to place the newly yanked string at the front.

If *arg* is **nil**, then the replacement text is the previous element of the kill ring. If *arg* is numeric, the replacement is the *arg*th previous kill. If *arg* is negative, a more recent kill is the replacement.

The sequence of kills in the kill ring wraps around, so that after the oldest one comes the newest one, and before the newest one goes the oldest.

The return value is always **nil**.

yank-undo-function   [Variable]

If this variable is non-**nil**, the function **yank-pop** uses its value instead of **delete-region** to delete the text inserted by the previous **yank** or **yank-pop** command. The value must be a function of two arguments, the start and end of the current region.

The function **insert-for-yank** automatically sets this variable according to the *undo* element of the **yank-handler** text property, if there is one.

31.8.5 Low-Level Kill Ring

These functions and variables provide access to the kill ring at a lower level, but are still convenient for use in Lisp programs, because they take care of interaction with window system selections (see Section 28.19 [Window System Selections], page 664).

current-kill *n* **&optional** *do-not-move*   [Function]

The function **current-kill** rotates the yanking pointer, which designates the front of the kill ring, by *n* places (from newer kills to older ones), and returns the text at that place in the ring.

If the optional second argument *do-not-move* is non-**nil**, then **current-kill** doesn't alter the yanking pointer; it just returns the *n*th kill, counting from the current yanking pointer.

If *n* is zero, indicating a request for the latest kill, **current-kill** calls the value of **interprogram-paste-function** (documented below) before consulting the kill ring. If that value is a function and calling it returns a string or a list of several string, **current-kill** pushes the strings onto the kill ring and returns the first string. It also sets the yanking pointer to point to the kill-ring entry of the first string returned by **interprogram-paste-function**, regardless of the value of *do-not-move*. Otherwise, **current-kill** does not treat a zero value for *n* specially: it returns the entry pointed at by the yanking pointer and does not move the yanking pointer.

kill-new *string* **&optional** *replace*   [Function]

This function pushes the text *string* onto the kill ring and makes the yanking pointer point to it. It discards the oldest entry if appropriate. It also invokes the value of **interprogram-cut-function** (see below).

If *replace* is non-**nil**, then **kill-new** replaces the first element of the kill ring with *string*, rather than pushing *string* onto the kill ring.

kill-append *string before-p*   [Function]

> This function appends the text *string* to the first entry in the kill ring and makes the
> yanking pointer point to the combined entry. Normally *string* goes at the end of the
> entry, but if *before-p* is non-`nil`, it goes at the beginning. This function also invokes
> the value of `interprogram-cut-function` (see below).

interprogram-paste-function   [Variable]

> This variable provides a way of transferring killed text from other programs, when
> you are using a window system. Its value should be `nil` or a function of no arguments.

> If the value is a function, `current-kill` calls it to get the most recent kill. If the
> function returns a non-`nil` value, then that value is used as the most recent kill. If it
> returns `nil`, then the front of the kill ring is used.

> To facilitate support for window systems that support multiple selections, this func-
> tion may also return a list of strings. In that case, the first string is used as the most
> recent kill, and all the other strings are pushed onto the kill ring, for easy access by
> `yank-pop`.

> The normal use of this function is to get the window system's clipboard as the most
> recent kill, even if the selection belongs to another application. See Section 28.19
> [Window System Selections], page 664. However, if the clipboard contents come from
> the current Emacs session, this function should return `nil`.

interprogram-cut-function   [Variable]

> This variable provides a way of communicating killed text to other programs, when
> you are using a window system. Its value should be `nil` or a function of one required
> argument.

> If the value is a function, `kill-new` and `kill-append` call it with the new first element
> of the kill ring as the argument.

> The normal use of this function is to put newly killed text in the window system's
> clipboard. See Section 28.19 [Window System Selections], page 664.

31.8.6 Internals of the Kill Ring

The variable `kill-ring` holds the kill ring contents, in the form of a list of strings. The
most recent kill is always at the front of the list.

The `kill-ring-yank-pointer` variable points to a link in the kill ring list, whose CAR is
the text to yank next. We say it identifies the front of the ring. Moving `kill-ring-yank-
pointer` to a different link is called *rotating the kill ring*. We call the kill ring a "ring"
because the functions that move the yank pointer wrap around from the end of the list to
the beginning, or vice-versa. Rotation of the kill ring is virtual; it does not change the value
of `kill-ring`.

Both `kill-ring` and `kill-ring-yank-pointer` are Lisp variables whose values are normally lists. The word "pointer" in the name of the `kill-ring-yank-pointer` indicates
that the variable's purpose is to identify one element of the list for use by the next yank
command.

The value of `kill-ring-yank-pointer` is always `eq` to one of the links in the kill ring
list. The element it identifies is the CAR of that link. Kill commands, which change the kill

ring, also set this variable to the value of `kill-ring`. The effect is to rotate the ring so that the newly killed text is at the front.

Here is a diagram that shows the variable `kill-ring-yank-pointer` pointing to the second entry in the kill ring (`"some text"` `"a different piece of text"` `"yet older text"`).

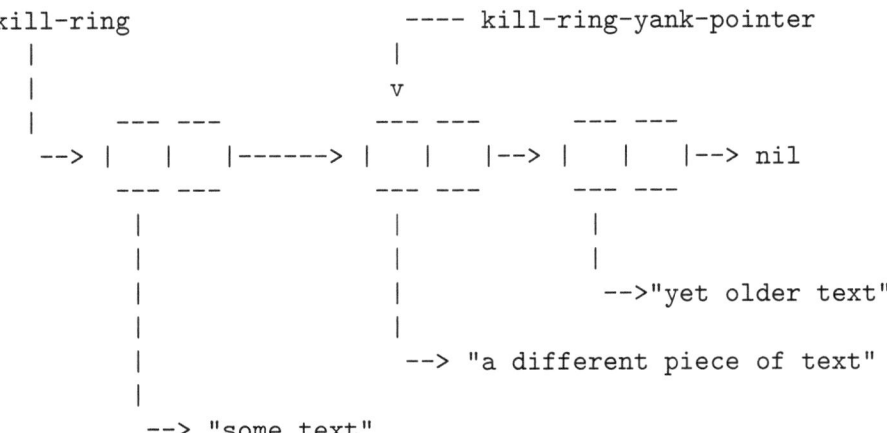

This state of affairs might occur after *C-y* (`yank`) immediately followed by *M-y* (`yank-pop`).

`kill-ring`   [Variable]

>   This variable holds the list of killed text sequences, most recently killed first.

`kill-ring-yank-pointer`   [Variable]

>   This variable's value indicates which element of the kill ring is at the front of the ring for yanking. More precisely, the value is a tail of the value of `kill-ring`, and its CAR is the kill string that *C-y* should yank.

`kill-ring-max`   [User Option]

>   The value of this variable is the maximum length to which the kill ring can grow, before elements are thrown away at the end. The default value for `kill-ring-max` is 60.

31.9 Undo

Most buffers have an *undo list*, which records all changes made to the buffer's text so that they can be undone. (The buffers that don't have one are usually special-purpose buffers for which Emacs assumes that undoing is not useful. In particular, any buffer whose name begins with a space has its undo recording off by default; see Section 26.3 [Buffer Names], page 553.) All the primitives that modify the text in the buffer automatically add elements to the front of the undo list, which is in the variable `buffer-undo-list`.

`buffer-undo-list`   [Variable]

>   This buffer-local variable's value is the undo list of the current buffer. A value of `t` disables the recording of undo information.

Here are the kinds of elements an undo list can have:

position   This kind of element records a previous value of point; undoing this element moves point to *position*. Ordinary cursor motion does not make any sort of undo record, but deletion operations use these entries to record where point was before the command.

`(beg . end)`

This kind of element indicates how to delete text that was inserted. Upon insertion, the text occupied the range *beg–end* in the buffer.

`(text . position)`

This kind of element indicates how to reinsert text that was deleted. The deleted text itself is the string *text*. The place to reinsert it is (`abs` *position*). If *position* is positive, point was at the beginning of the deleted text, otherwise it was at the end. Zero or more (*marker . adjustment*) elements follow immediately after this element.

`(t . time-flag)`

This kind of element indicates that an unmodified buffer became modified. A *time-flag* of the form (`sec-high sec-low microsec picosec`) represents the visited file's modification time as of when it was previously visited or saved, using the same format as `current-time`; see Section 38.5 [Time of Day], page 999. A *time-flag* of 0 means the buffer does not correspond to any file; −1 means the visited file previously did not exist. `primitive-undo` uses these values to determine whether to mark the buffer as unmodified once again; it does so only if the file's status matches that of *time-flag*.

`(nil property value beg . end)`

This kind of element records a change in a text property. Here's how you might undo the change:

> `(put-text-property beg end property value)`

`(marker . adjustment)`

This kind of element records the fact that the marker *marker* was relocated due to deletion of surrounding text, and that it moved *adjustment* character positions. If the marker's location is consistent with the (*text . position*) element preceding it in the undo list, then undoing this element moves *marker* − *adjustment* characters.

`(apply funname . args)`

This is an extensible undo item, which is undone by calling *funname* with arguments *args*.

`(apply delta beg end funname . args)`

This is an extensible undo item, which records a change limited to the range *beg* to *end*, which increased the size of the buffer by *delta* characters. It is undone by calling *funname* with arguments *args*.

This kind of element enables undo limited to a region to determine whether the element pertains to that region.

`nil`

This element is a boundary. The elements between two boundaries are called a *change group*; normally, each change group corresponds to one keyboard command, and undo commands normally undo an entire group as a unit.

undo-boundary   [Function]

> This function places a boundary element in the undo list. The undo command stops
> at such a boundary, and successive undo commands undo to earlier and earlier bound-
> aries. This function returns `nil`.
>
> Calling this function explicitly is useful for splitting the effects of a command into
> more than one unit. For example, `query-replace` calls `undo-boundary` after each
> replacement, so that the user can undo individual replacements one by one.
>
> Mostly, however, this function is called automatically at an appropriate time.

undo-auto-amalgamate   [Function]

> The editor command loop automatically calls `undo-boundary` just before executing
> each key sequence, so that each undo normally undoes the effects of one command. A
> few exceptional commands are *amalgamating*: these commands generally cause small
> changes to buffers, so with these a boundary is inserted only every 20th command, al-
> lowing the changes to be undone as a group. By default, the commands `self-insert-`
> `command`, which produces self-inserting input characters (see Section 31.5 [Commands
> for Insertion], page 702), and `delete-char`, which deletes characters (see Section 31.6
> [Deletion], page 703), are amalgamating. Where a command affects the contents of
> several buffers, as may happen, for example, when a function on the `post-command-`
> `hook` affects a buffer other than the `current-buffer`, then `undo-boundary` will be
> called in each of the affected buffers.

undo-auto-current-boundary-timer   [Variable]

> Some buffers, such as process buffers, can change even when no commands are exe-
> cuting. In these cases, `undo-boundary` is normally called periodically by the timer in
> this variable. Setting this variable to non-`nil` prevents this behavior.

undo-in-progress   [Variable]

> This variable is normally `nil`, but the undo commands bind it to `t`. This is so
> that various kinds of change hooks can tell when they're being called for the sake of
> undoing.

primitive-undo *count list*   [Function]

> This is the basic function for undoing elements of an undo list. It undoes the first
> *count* elements of *list*, returning the rest of *list*.
>
> `primitive-undo` adds elements to the buffer's undo list when it changes the buffer.
> Undo commands avoid confusion by saving the undo list value at the beginning of a
> sequence of undo operations. Then the undo operations use and update the saved
> value. The new elements added by undoing are not part of this saved value, so they
> don't interfere with continuing to undo.
>
> This function does not bind `undo-in-progress`.

31.10 Maintaining Undo Lists

This section describes how to enable and disable undo information for a given buffer. It
also explains how the undo list is truncated automatically so it doesn't get too big.

Recording of undo information in a newly created buffer is normally enabled to start
with; but if the buffer name starts with a space, the undo recording is initially disabled.

You can explicitly enable or disable undo recording with the following two functions, or by setting `buffer-undo-list` yourself.

`buffer-enable-undo` &optional *buffer-or-name* [Command]

> This command enables recording undo information for buffer *buffer-or-name*, so that subsequent changes can be undone. If no argument is supplied, then the current buffer is used. This function does nothing if undo recording is already enabled in the buffer. It returns `nil`.
>
> In an interactive call, *buffer-or-name* is the current buffer. You cannot specify any other buffer.

`buffer-disable-undo` &optional *buffer-or-name* [Command]

> This function discards the undo list of *buffer-or-name*, and disables further recording of undo information. As a result, it is no longer possible to undo either previous changes or any subsequent changes. If the undo list of *buffer-or-name* is already disabled, this function has no effect.
>
> In an interactive call, BUFFER-OR-NAME is the current buffer. You cannot specify any other buffer. This function returns `nil`.

As editing continues, undo lists get longer and longer. To prevent them from using up all available memory space, garbage collection trims them back to size limits you can set. (For this purpose, the size of an undo list measures the cons cells that make up the list, plus the strings of deleted text.) Three variables control the range of acceptable sizes: `undo-limit`, `undo-strong-limit` and `undo-outer-limit`. In these variables, size is counted as the number of bytes occupied, which includes both saved text and other data.

`undo-limit` [User Option]

> This is the soft limit for the acceptable size of an undo list. The change group at which this size is exceeded is the last one kept.

`undo-strong-limit` [User Option]

> This is the upper limit for the acceptable size of an undo list. The change group at which this size is exceeded is discarded itself (along with all older change groups). There is one exception: the very latest change group is only discarded if it exceeds `undo-outer-limit`.

`undo-outer-limit` [User Option]

> If at garbage collection time the undo info for the current command exceeds this limit, Emacs discards the info and displays a warning. This is a last ditch limit to prevent memory overflow.

`undo-ask-before-discard` [User Option]

> If this variable is non-`nil`, when the undo info exceeds `undo-outer-limit`, Emacs asks in the echo area whether to discard the info. The default value is `nil`, which means to discard it automatically.
>
> This option is mainly intended for debugging. Garbage collection is inhibited while the question is asked, which means that Emacs might leak memory if the user waits too long before answering the question.

31.11 Filling

Filling means adjusting the lengths of lines (by moving the line breaks) so that they are nearly (but no greater than) a specified maximum width. Additionally, lines can be *justified*, which means inserting spaces to make the left and/or right margins line up precisely. The width is controlled by the variable `fill-column`. For ease of reading, lines should be no longer than 70 or so columns.

You can use Auto Fill mode (see Section 31.14 [Auto Filling], page 721) to fill text automatically as you insert it, but changes to existing text may leave it improperly filled. Then you must fill the text explicitly.

Most of the commands in this section return values that are not meaningful. All the functions that do filling take note of the current left margin, current right margin, and current justification style (see Section 31.12 [Margins], page 718). If the current justification style is `none`, the filling functions don't actually do anything.

Several of the filling functions have an argument *justify*. If it is non-`nil`, that requests some kind of justification. It can be `left`, `right`, `full`, or `center`, to request a specific style of justification. If it is `t`, that means to use the current justification style for this part of the text (see `current-justification`, below). Any other value is treated as `full`.

When you call the filling functions interactively, using a prefix argument implies the value `full` for *justify*.

fill-paragraph &optional *justify region*   [Command]
> This command fills the paragraph at or after point. If *justify* is non-`nil`, each line is justified as well. It uses the ordinary paragraph motion commands to find paragraph boundaries. See Section "Paragraphs" in *The GNU Emacs Manual*.
>
> When *region* is non-`nil`, then if Transient Mark mode is enabled and the mark is active, this command calls `fill-region` to fill all the paragraphs in the region, instead of filling only the current paragraph. When this command is called interactively, *region* is `t`.

fill-region *start end* **&optional** *justify nosqueeze to-eop*   [Command]
> This command fills each of the paragraphs in the region from *start* to *end*. It justifies as well if *justify* is non-`nil`.
>
> If *nosqueeze* is non-`nil`, that means to leave whitespace other than line breaks untouched. If *to-eop* is non-`nil`, that means to keep filling to the end of the paragraph— or the next hard newline, if `use-hard-newlines` is enabled (see below).
>
> The variable `paragraph-separate` controls how to distinguish paragraphs. See Section 33.8 [Standard Regexps], page 814.

fill-individual-paragraphs *start end* **&optional** *justify*   [Command]
> *citation-regexp*
> This command fills each paragraph in the region according to its individual fill prefix. Thus, if the lines of a paragraph were indented with spaces, the filled paragraph will remain indented in the same fashion.
>
> The first two arguments, *start* and *end*, are the beginning and end of the region to be filled. The third and fourth arguments, *justify* and *citation-regexp*, are optional. If *justify* is non-`nil`, the paragraphs are justified as well as filled. If *citation-regexp* is

non-**nil**, it means the function is operating on a mail message and therefore should not fill the header lines. If *citation-regexp* is a string, it is used as a regular expression; if it matches the beginning of a line, that line is treated as a citation marker.

Ordinarily, **fill-individual-paragraphs** regards each change in indentation as starting a new paragraph. If **fill-individual-varying-indent** is non-**nil**, then only separator lines separate paragraphs. That mode can handle indented paragraphs with additional indentation on the first line.

fill-individual-varying-indent   [User Option]
  This variable alters the action of **fill-individual-paragraphs** as described above.

fill-region-as-paragraph *start end* **&optional** *justify nosqueeze*   [Command]
      squeeze-after
  This command considers a region of text as a single paragraph and fills it. If the region was made up of many paragraphs, the blank lines between paragraphs are removed. This function justifies as well as filling when *justify* is non-**nil**.

  If *nosqueeze* is non-**nil**, that means to leave whitespace other than line breaks untouched. If *squeeze-after* is non-**nil**, it specifies a position in the region, and means don't canonicalize spaces before that position.

  In Adaptive Fill mode, this command calls **fill-context-prefix** to choose a fill prefix by default. See Section 31.13 [Adaptive Fill], page 720.

justify-current-line **&optional** *how eop nosqueeze*   [Command]
  This command inserts spaces between the words of the current line so that the line ends exactly at **fill-column**. It returns **nil**.

  The argument *how*, if non-**nil** specifies explicitly the style of justification. It can be **left**, **right**, **full**, **center**, or **none**. If it is **t**, that means to do follow specified justification style (see **current-justification**, below). **nil** means to do full justification.

  If *eop* is non-**nil**, that means do only left-justification if **current-justification** specifies full justification. This is used for the last line of a paragraph; even if the paragraph as a whole is fully justified, the last line should not be.

  If *nosqueeze* is non-**nil**, that means do not change interior whitespace.

default-justification   [User Option]
  This variable's value specifies the style of justification to use for text that doesn't specify a style with a text property. The possible values are **left**, **right**, **full**, **center**, or **none**. The default value is **left**.

current-justification   [Function]
  This function returns the proper justification style to use for filling the text around point.

  This returns the value of the **justification** text property at point, or the variable *default-justification* if there is no such text property. However, it returns **nil** rather than **none** to mean "don't justify".

`sentence-end-double-space`   [User Option]

> If this variable is non-`nil`, a period followed by just one space does not count as the end of a sentence, and the filling functions avoid breaking the line at such a place.

`sentence-end-without-period`   [User Option]

> If this variable is non-`nil`, a sentence can end without a period. This is used for languages like Thai, where sentences end with a double space but without a period.

`sentence-end-without-space`   [User Option]

> If this variable is non-`nil`, it should be a string of characters that can end a sentence without following spaces.

`fill-paragraph-function`   [Variable]

> This variable provides a way to override the filling of paragraphs. If its value is non-`nil`, `fill-paragraph` calls this function to do the work. If the function returns a non-`nil` value, `fill-paragraph` assumes the job is done, and immediately returns that value.
>
> The usual use of this feature is to fill comments in programming language modes. If the function needs to fill a paragraph in the usual way, it can do so as follows:

```
(let ((fill-paragraph-function nil))
  (fill-paragraph arg))
```

`fill-forward-paragraph-function`   [Variable]

> This variable provides a way to override how the filling functions, such as `fill-region` and `fill-paragraph`, move forward to the next paragraph. Its value should be a function, which is called with a single argument n, the number of paragraphs to move, and should return the difference between n and the number of paragraphs actually moved. The default value of this variable is `forward-paragraph`. See Section "Paragraphs" in *The GNU Emacs Manual*.

`use-hard-newlines`   [Variable]

> If this variable is non-`nil`, the filling functions do not delete newlines that have the `hard` text property. These hard newlines act as paragraph separators. See Section "Hard and Soft Newlines" in *The GNU Emacs Manual*.

31.12 Margins for Filling

`fill-prefix`   [User Option]

> This buffer-local variable, if non-`nil`, specifies a string of text that appears at the beginning of normal text lines and should be disregarded when filling them. Any line that fails to start with the fill prefix is considered the start of a paragraph; so is any line that starts with the fill prefix followed by additional whitespace. Lines that start with the fill prefix but no additional whitespace are ordinary text lines that can be filled together. The resulting filled lines also start with the fill prefix.
>
> The fill prefix follows the left margin whitespace, if any.

`fill-column`   [User Option]

> This buffer-local variable specifies the maximum width of filled lines. Its value should be an integer, which is a number of columns. All the filling, justification, and centering

commands are affected by this variable, including Auto Fill mode (see Section 31.14 [Auto Filling], page 721).

As a practical matter, if you are writing text for other people to read, you should set `fill-column` to no more than 70. Otherwise the line will be too long for people to read comfortably, and this can make the text seem clumsy.

The default value for `fill-column` is 70.

`set-left-margin` *from to margin*   [Command]

> This sets the `left-margin` property on the text from *from* to *to* to the value *margin*. If Auto Fill mode is enabled, this command also refills the region to fit the new margin.

`set-right-margin` *from to margin*   [Command]

> This sets the `right-margin` property on the text from *from* to *to* to the value *margin*. If Auto Fill mode is enabled, this command also refills the region to fit the new margin.

`current-left-margin`   [Function]

> This function returns the proper left margin value to use for filling the text around point. The value is the sum of the `left-margin` property of the character at the start of the current line (or zero if none), and the value of the variable `left-margin`.

`current-fill-column`   [Function]

> This function returns the proper fill column value to use for filling the text around point. The value is the value of the `fill-column` variable, minus the value of the `right-margin` property of the character after point.

`move-to-left-margin` **&optional** *n force*   [Command]

> This function moves point to the left margin of the current line. The column moved to is determined by calling the function `current-left-margin`. If the argument *n* is non-`nil`, `move-to-left-margin` moves forward $n-1$ lines first.
>
> If *force* is non-`nil`, that says to fix the line's indentation if that doesn't match the left margin value.

`delete-to-left-margin` **&optional** *from to*   [Function]

> This function removes left margin indentation from the text between *from* and *to*. The amount of indentation to delete is determined by calling `current-left-margin`. In no case does this function delete non-whitespace. If *from* and *to* are omitted, they default to the whole buffer.

`indent-to-left-margin`   [Function]

> This function adjusts the indentation at the beginning of the current line to the value specified by the variable `left-margin`. (That may involve either inserting or deleting whitespace.) This function is value of `indent-line-function` in Paragraph-Indent Text mode.

`left-margin`   [User Option]

> This variable specifies the base left margin column. In Fundamental mode, `RET` indents to this column. This variable automatically becomes buffer-local when set in any fashion.

`fill-nobreak-predicate`												[User Option]

> This variable gives major modes a way to specify not to break a line at certain places. Its value should be a list of functions. Whenever filling considers breaking the line at a certain place in the buffer, it calls each of these functions with no arguments and with point located at that place. If any of the functions returns non-`nil`, then the line won't be broken there.

31.13 Adaptive Fill Mode

When *Adaptive Fill Mode* is enabled, Emacs determines the fill prefix automatically from the text in each paragraph being filled rather than using a predetermined value. During filling, this fill prefix gets inserted at the start of the second and subsequent lines of the paragraph as described in Section 31.11 [Filling], page 716, and in Section 31.14 [Auto Filling], page 721.

`adaptive-fill-mode`												[User Option]

> Adaptive Fill mode is enabled when this variable is non-`nil`. It is `t` by default.

`fill-context-prefix` *from to*												[Function]

> This function implements the heart of Adaptive Fill mode; it chooses a fill prefix based on the text between *from* and *to*, typically the start and end of a paragraph. It does this by looking at the first two lines of the paragraph, based on the variables described below.
>
> Usually, this function returns the fill prefix, a string. However, before doing this, the function makes a final check (not specially mentioned in the following) that a line starting with this prefix wouldn't look like the start of a paragraph. Should this happen, the function signals the anomaly by returning `nil` instead.
>
> In detail, `fill-context-prefix` does this:
>
> 1. It takes a candidate for the fill prefix from the first line—it tries first the function in `adaptive-fill-function` (if any), then the regular expression `adaptive-fill-regexp` (see below). The first non-`nil` result of these, or the empty string if they're both `nil`, becomes the first line's candidate.
>
> 2. If the paragraph has as yet only one line, the function tests the validity of the prefix candidate just found. The function then returns the candidate if it's valid, or a string of spaces otherwise. (see the description of `adaptive-fill-first-line-regexp` below).
>
> 3. When the paragraph already has two lines, the function next looks for a prefix candidate on the second line, in just the same way it did for the first line. If it doesn't find one, it returns `nil`.
>
> 4. The function now compares the two candidate prefixes heuristically: if the non-whitespace characters in the line 2 candidate occur in the same order in the line 1 candidate, the function returns the line 2 candidate. Otherwise, it returns the largest initial substring which is common to both candidates (which might be the empty string).

`adaptive-fill-regexp`   [User Option]

> Adaptive Fill mode matches this regular expression against the text starting after
> the left margin whitespace (if any) on a line; the characters it matches are that line's
> candidate for the fill prefix.
>
> The default value matches whitespace with certain punctuation characters intermin-
> gled.

`adaptive-fill-first-line-regexp`   [User Option]

> Used only in one-line paragraphs, this regular expression acts as an additional check
> of the validity of the one available candidate fill prefix: the candidate must match
> this regular expression, or match `comment-start-skip`. If it doesn't, `fill-context-`
> `prefix` replaces the candidate with a string of spaces of the same width as it.
>
> The default value of this variable is `"\\`[\t]*\\'"`, which matches only a string
> of whitespace. The effect of this default is to force the fill prefixes found in one-line
> paragraphs always to be pure whitespace.

`adaptive-fill-function`   [User Option]

> You can specify more complex ways of choosing a fill prefix automatically by setting
> this variable to a function. The function is called with point after the left margin (if
> any) of a line, and it must preserve point. It should return either that line's fill prefix
> or `nil`, meaning it has failed to determine a prefix.

31.14 Auto Filling

Auto Fill mode is a minor mode that fills lines automatically as text is inserted. This section
describes the hook used by Auto Fill mode. For a description of functions that you can call
explicitly to fill and justify existing text, see Section 31.11 [Filling], page 716.

Auto Fill mode also enables the functions that change the margins and justification style
to refill portions of the text. See Section 31.12 [Margins], page 718.

`auto-fill-function`   [Variable]

> The value of this buffer-local variable should be a function (of no arguments) to be
> called after self-inserting a character from the table `auto-fill-chars`. It may be
> `nil`, in which case nothing special is done in that case.
>
> The value of `auto-fill-function` is `do-auto-fill` when Auto-Fill mode is enabled.
> That is a function whose sole purpose is to implement the usual strategy for breaking
> a line.

`normal-auto-fill-function`   [Variable]

> This variable specifies the function to use for `auto-fill-function`, if and when Auto
> Fill is turned on. Major modes can set buffer-local values for this variable to alter
> how Auto Fill works.

`auto-fill-chars`   [Variable]

> A char table of characters which invoke `auto-fill-function` when self-inserted—
> space and newline in most language environments. They have an entry `t` in the
> table.

31.15 Sorting Text

The sorting functions described in this section all rearrange text in a buffer. This is in contrast to the function `sort`, which rearranges the order of the elements of a list (see Section 5.6.3 [Rearrangement], page 79). The values returned by these functions are not meaningful.

`sort-subr` *reverse nextrecfun endrecfun* **&optional** *startkeyfun*   [Function]
            endkeyfun predicate

> This function is the general text-sorting routine that subdivides a buffer into records and then sorts them. Most of the commands in this section use this function.

> To understand how `sort-subr` works, consider the whole accessible portion of the buffer as being divided into disjoint pieces called *sort records*. The records may or may not be contiguous, but they must not overlap. A portion of each sort record (perhaps all of it) is designated as the sort key. Sorting rearranges the records in order by their sort keys.

> Usually, the records are rearranged in order of ascending sort key. If the first argument to the `sort-subr` function, *reverse*, is non-`nil`, the sort records are rearranged in order of descending sort key.

> The next four arguments to `sort-subr` are functions that are called to move point across a sort record. They are called many times from within `sort-subr`.

> 1. *nextrecfun* is called with point at the end of a record. This function moves point to the start of the next record. The first record is assumed to start at the position of point when `sort-subr` is called. Therefore, you should usually move point to the beginning of the buffer before calling `sort-subr`.

>   This function can indicate there are no more sort records by leaving point at the end of the buffer.

> 2. *endrecfun* is called with point within a record. It moves point to the end of the record.

> 3. *startkeyfun* is called to move point from the start of a record to the start of the sort key. This argument is optional; if it is omitted, the whole record is the sort key. If supplied, the function should either return a non-`nil` value to be used as the sort key, or return `nil` to indicate that the sort key is in the buffer starting at point. In the latter case, *endkeyfun* is called to find the end of the sort key.

> 4. *endkeyfun* is called to move point from the start of the sort key to the end of the sort key. This argument is optional. If *startkeyfun* returns `nil` and this argument is omitted (or `nil`), then the sort key extends to the end of the record. There is no need for *endkeyfun* if *startkeyfun* returns a non-`nil` value.

> The argument *predicate* is the function to use to compare keys. If keys are numbers, it defaults to `<`; otherwise it defaults to `string<`.

> As an example of `sort-subr`, here is the complete function definition for `sort-lines`:

```
;; Note that the first two lines of doc string
;;  are effectively one line when viewed by a user.
(defun sort-lines (reverse beg end)
  "Sort lines in region alphabetically;\
 argument means descending order.
Called from a program, there are three arguments:
REVERSE (non-nil means reverse order),\
 BEG and END (region to sort).
The variable `sort-fold-case' determines\
 whether alphabetic case affects
the sort order."
  (interactive "P\nr")
  (save-excursion
    (save-restriction
      (narrow-to-region beg end)
      (goto-char (point-min))
      (let ((inhibit-field-text-motion t))
        (sort-subr reverse 'forward-line 'end-of-line)))))
```

Here **forward-line** moves point to the start of the next record, and **end-of-line** moves point to the end of record. We do not pass the arguments *startkeyfun* and *endkeyfun*, because the entire record is used as the sort key.

The **sort-paragraphs** function is very much the same, except that its **sort-subr** call looks like this:

```
(sort-subr reverse
           (function
            (lambda ()
              (while (and (not (eobp))
                          (looking-at paragraph-separate))
                (forward-line 1))))
           'forward-paragraph)
```

Markers pointing into any sort records are left with no useful position after **sort-subr** returns.

sort-fold-case   [User Option]

    If this variable is non-**nil**, **sort-subr** and the other buffer sorting functions ignore case when comparing strings.

sort-regexp-fields *reverse record-regexp key-regexp start end*   [Command]

    This command sorts the region between *start* and *end* alphabetically as specified by *record-regexp* and *key-regexp*. If *reverse* is a negative integer, then sorting is in reverse order.

    Alphabetical sorting means that two sort keys are compared by comparing the first characters of each, the second characters of each, and so on. If a mismatch is found, it means that the sort keys are unequal; the sort key whose character is less at the point of first mismatch is the lesser sort key. The individual characters are compared according to their numerical character codes in the Emacs character set.

The value of the *record-regexp* argument specifies how to divide the buffer into sort records. At the end of each record, a search is done for this regular expression, and the text that matches it is taken as the next record. For example, the regular expression '^.+$', which matches lines with at least one character besides a newline, would make each such line into a sort record. See Section 33.3 [Regular Expressions], page 793, for a description of the syntax and meaning of regular expressions.

The value of the *key-regexp* argument specifies what part of each record is the sort key. The *key-regexp* could match the whole record, or only a part. In the latter case, the rest of the record has no effect on the sorted order of records, but it is carried along when the record moves to its new position.

The *key-regexp* argument can refer to the text matched by a subexpression of *record-regexp*, or it can be a regular expression on its own.

If *key-regexp* is:

'*digit*'   then the text matched by the *digit*th '\(...\)' parenthesis grouping in *record-regexp* is the sort key.

'\&'   then the whole record is the sort key.

a regular expression

then `sort-regexp-fields` searches for a match for the regular expression within the record. If such a match is found, it is the sort key. If there is no match for *key-regexp* within a record then that record is ignored, which means its position in the buffer is not changed. (The other records may move around it.)

For example, if you plan to sort all the lines in the region by the first word on each line starting with the letter 'f', you should set *record-regexp* to '^.*$' and set *key-regexp* to '\<f\w*\>'. The resulting expression looks like this:

```
(sort-regexp-fields nil "^.*$" "\\<f\\w*\\>"
                    (region-beginning)
                    (region-end))
```

If you call `sort-regexp-fields` interactively, it prompts for *record-regexp* and *key-regexp* in the minibuffer.

sort-lines *reverse start end*   [Command]
This command alphabetically sorts lines in the region between *start* and *end*. If *reverse* is non-**nil**, the sort is in reverse order.

sort-paragraphs *reverse start end*   [Command]
This command alphabetically sorts paragraphs in the region between *start* and *end*. If *reverse* is non-**nil**, the sort is in reverse order.

sort-pages *reverse start end*   [Command]
This command alphabetically sorts pages in the region between *start* and *end*. If *reverse* is non-**nil**, the sort is in reverse order.

sort-fields *field start end*   [Command]
This command sorts lines in the region between *start* and *end*, comparing them alphabetically by the *field*th field of each line. Fields are separated by whitespace

and numbered starting from 1. If *field* is negative, sorting is by the −*field*th field from the end of the line. This command is useful for sorting tables.

sort-numeric-fields *field start end*   [Command]

This command sorts lines in the region between *start* and *end*, comparing them numerically by the *field*th field of each line. Fields are separated by whitespace and numbered starting from 1. The specified field must contain a number in each line of the region. Numbers starting with 0 are treated as octal, and numbers starting with '0x' are treated as hexadecimal.

If *field* is negative, sorting is by the −*field*th field from the end of the line. This command is useful for sorting tables.

sort-numeric-base   [User Option]

This variable specifies the default radix for **sort-numeric-fields** to parse numbers.

sort-columns *reverse* **&optional** *beg end*   [Command]

This command sorts the lines in the region between *beg* and *end*, comparing them alphabetically by a certain range of columns. The column positions of *beg* and *end* bound the range of columns to sort on.

If *reverse* is non-**nil**, the sort is in reverse order.

One unusual thing about this command is that the entire line containing position *beg*, and the entire line containing position *end*, are included in the region sorted.

Note that **sort-columns** rejects text that contains tabs, because tabs could be split across the specified columns. Use *M-x* **untabify** to convert tabs to spaces before sorting.

When possible, this command actually works by calling the **sort** utility program.

31.16 Counting Columns

The column functions convert between a character position (counting characters from the beginning of the buffer) and a column position (counting screen characters from the beginning of a line).

These functions count each character according to the number of columns it occupies on the screen. This means control characters count as occupying 2 or 4 columns, depending upon the value of **ctl-arrow**, and tabs count as occupying a number of columns that depends on the value of **tab-width** and on the column where the tab begins. See Section 37.22.1 [Usual Display], page 973.

Column number computations ignore the width of the window and the amount of horizontal scrolling. Consequently, a column value can be arbitrarily high. The first (or leftmost) column is numbered 0. They also ignore overlays and text properties, aside from invisibility.

current-column   [Function]

This function returns the horizontal position of point, measured in columns, counting from 0 at the left margin. The column position is the sum of the widths of all the displayed representations of the characters between the start of the current line and point.

move-to-column *column* **&optional** *force*   [Command]

> This function moves point to *column* in the current line. The calculation of *column* takes into account the widths of the displayed representations of the characters between the start of the line and point.
>
> When called interactively, *column* is the value of prefix numeric argument. If *column* is not an integer, an error is signaled.
>
> If it is impossible to move to column *column* because that is in the middle of a multi-column character such as a tab, point moves to the end of that character. However, if *force* is non-`nil`, and *column* is in the middle of a tab, then `move-to-column` converts the tab into spaces so that it can move precisely to column *column*. Other multi-column characters can cause anomalies despite *force*, since there is no way to split them.
>
> The argument *force* also has an effect if the line isn't long enough to reach column *column*; if it is `t`, that means to add whitespace at the end of the line to reach that column.
>
> The return value is the column number actually moved to.

31.17 Indentation

The indentation functions are used to examine, move to, and change whitespace that is at the beginning of a line. Some of the functions can also change whitespace elsewhere on a line. Columns and indentation count from zero at the left margin.

31.17.1 Indentation Primitives

This section describes the primitive functions used to count and insert indentation. The functions in the following sections use these primitives. See Section 37.10 [Size of Displayed Text], page 912, for related functions.

current-indentation   [Function]

> This function returns the indentation of the current line, which is the horizontal position of the first nonblank character. If the contents are entirely blank, then this is the horizontal position of the end of the line.

indent-to *column* **&optional** *minimum*   [Command]

> This function indents from point with tabs and spaces until *column* is reached. If *minimum* is specified and non-`nil`, then at least that many spaces are inserted even if this requires going beyond *column*. Otherwise the function does nothing if point is already beyond *column*. The value is the column at which the inserted indentation ends.
>
> The inserted whitespace characters inherit text properties from the surrounding text (usually, from the preceding text only). See Section 31.19.6 [Sticky Properties], page 744.

indent-tabs-mode   [User Option]

> If this variable is non-`nil`, indentation functions can insert tabs as well as spaces. Otherwise, they insert only spaces. Setting this variable automatically makes it buffer-local in the current buffer.

31.17.2 Indentation Controlled by Major Mode

An important function of each major mode is to customize the `TAB` key to indent properly for the language being edited. This section describes the mechanism of the `TAB` key and how to control it. The functions in this section return unpredictable values.

`indent-for-tab-command &optional` *rigid*   [Command]

> This is the command bound to `TAB` in most editing modes. Its usual action is to indent the current line, but it can alternatively insert a tab character or indent a region.
>
> Here is what it does:
>
> - First, it checks whether Transient Mark mode is enabled and the region is active. If so, it called `indent-region` to indent all the text in the region (see Section 31.17.3 [Region Indent], page 728).
>
> - Otherwise, if the indentation function in `indent-line-function` is `indent-to-left-margin` (a trivial command that inserts a tab character), or if the variable `tab-always-indent` specifies that a tab character ought to be inserted (see below), then it inserts a tab character.
>
> - Otherwise, it indents the current line; this is done by calling the function in `indent-line-function`. If the line is already indented, and the value of `tab-always-indent` is `complete` (see below), it tries completing the text at point.
>
> If *rigid* is non-`nil` (interactively, with a prefix argument), then after this command indents a line or inserts a tab, it also rigidly indents the entire balanced expression which starts at the beginning of the current line, in order to reflect the new indentation. This argument is ignored if the command indents the region.

`indent-line-function`   [Variable]

> This variable's value is the function to be used by `indent-for-tab-command`, and various other indentation commands, to indent the current line. It is usually assigned by the major mode; for instance, Lisp mode sets it to `lisp-indent-line`, C mode sets it to `c-indent-line`, and so on. The default value is `indent-relative`. See Section 22.7 [Auto-Indentation], page 474.

`indent-according-to-mode`   [Command]

> This command calls the function in `indent-line-function` to indent the current line in a way appropriate for the current major mode.

`newline-and-indent`   [Command]

> This function inserts a newline, then indents the new line (the one following the newline just inserted) according to the major mode. It does indentation by calling `indent-according-to-mode`.

`reindent-then-newline-and-indent`   [Command]

> This command reindents the current line, inserts a newline at point, and then indents the new line (the one following the newline just inserted). It does indentation on both lines by calling `indent-according-to-mode`.

`tab-always-indent`   [User Option]

> This variable can be used to customize the behavior of the **TAB** (`indent-for-tab-command`) command. If the value is **t** (the default), the command normally just indents the current line. If the value is **nil**, the command indents the current line only if point is at the left margin or in the line's indentation; otherwise, it inserts a tab character. If the value is **complete**, the command first tries to indent the current line, and if the line was already indented, it calls `completion-at-point` to complete the text at point (see Section 19.6.8 [Completion in Buffers], page 336).

31.17.3 Indenting an Entire Region

This section describes commands that indent all the lines in the region. They return unpredictable values.

`indent-region` *start end* **&optional** *to-column*   [Command]

> This command indents each nonblank line starting between *start* (inclusive) and *end* (exclusive). If *to-column* is **nil**, `indent-region` indents each nonblank line by calling the current mode's indentation function, the value of `indent-line-function`.

> If *to-column* is non-nil, it should be an integer specifying the number of columns of indentation; then this function gives each line exactly that much indentation, by either adding or deleting whitespace.

> If there is a fill prefix, `indent-region` indents each line by making it start with the fill prefix.

`indent-region-function`   [Variable]

> The value of this variable is a function that can be used by `indent-region` as a short cut. It should take two arguments, the start and end of the region. You should design the function so that it will produce the same results as indenting the lines of the region one by one, but presumably faster.

> If the value is **nil**, there is no short cut, and `indent-region` actually works line by line.

> A short-cut function is useful in modes such as C mode and Lisp mode, where the `indent-line-function` must scan from the beginning of the function definition: applying it to each line would be quadratic in time. The short cut can update the scan information as it moves through the lines indenting them; this takes linear time. In a mode where indenting a line individually is fast, there is no need for a short cut.

> `indent-region` with a non-**nil** argument *to-column* has a different meaning and does not use this variable.

`indent-rigidly` *start end count*   [Command]

> This function indents all lines starting between *start* (inclusive) and *end* (exclusive) sideways by *count* columns. This preserves the shape of the affected region, moving it as a rigid unit.

> This is useful not only for indenting regions of unindented text, but also for indenting regions of formatted code. For example, if *count* is 3, this command adds 3 columns of indentation to every line that begins in the specified region.

If called interactively with no prefix argument, this command invokes a transient mode for adjusting indentation rigidly. See Section "Indentation Commands" in *The GNU Emacs Manual*.

indent-code-rigidly *start end columns* **&optional**   [Command]
      nochange-regexp

This is like `indent-rigidly`, except that it doesn't alter lines that start within strings or comments.

In addition, it doesn't alter a line if *nochange-regexp* matches at the beginning of the line (if *nochange-regexp* is non-`nil`).

31.17.4 Indentation Relative to Previous Lines

This section describes two commands that indent the current line based on the contents of previous lines.

indent-relative **&optional** *unindented-ok*   [Command]

This command inserts whitespace at point, extending to the same column as the next *indent point* of the previous nonblank line. An indent point is a non-whitespace character following whitespace. The next indent point is the first one at a column greater than the current column of point. For example, if point is underneath and to the left of the first non-blank character of a line of text, it moves to that column by inserting whitespace.

If the previous nonblank line has no next indent point (i.e., none at a great enough column position), `indent-relative` either does nothing (if *unindented-ok* is non-`nil`) or calls `tab-to-tab-stop`. Thus, if point is underneath and to the right of the last column of a short line of text, this command ordinarily moves point to the next tab stop by inserting whitespace.

The return value of `indent-relative` is unpredictable.

In the following example, point is at the beginning of the second line:

```
            This line is indented twelve spaces.
    ★The quick brown fox jumped.
```

Evaluation of the expression `(indent-relative nil)` produces the following:

```
            This line is indented twelve spaces.
            ★The quick brown fox jumped.
```

In this next example, point is between the 'm' and 'p' of 'jumped':

```
            This line is indented twelve spaces.
    The quick brown fox jum★ped.
```

Evaluation of the expression `(indent-relative nil)` produces the following:

```
            This line is indented twelve spaces.
    The quick brown fox jum  ★ped.
```

indent-relative-maybe   [Command]

This command indents the current line like the previous nonblank line, by calling `indent-relative` with `t` as the *unindented-ok* argument. The return value is unpredictable.

If the previous nonblank line has no indent points beyond the current column, this command does nothing.

31.17.5 Adjustable Tab Stops

This section explains the mechanism for user-specified tab stops and the mechanisms that use and set them. The name "tab stops" is used because the feature is similar to that of the tab stops on a typewriter. The feature works by inserting an appropriate number of spaces and tab characters to reach the next tab stop column; it does not affect the display of tab characters in the buffer (see Section 37.22.1 [Usual Display], page 973). Note that the `TAB` character as input uses this tab stop feature only in a few major modes, such as Text mode. See Section "Tab Stops" in *The GNU Emacs Manual*.

`tab-to-tab-stop`   [Command]

> This command inserts spaces or tabs before point, up to the next tab stop column defined by `tab-stop-list`.

`tab-stop-list`   [User Option]

> This variable defines the tab stop columns used by `tab-to-tab-stop`. It should be either `nil`, or a list of increasing integers, which need not be evenly spaced. The list is implicitly extended to infinity through repetition of the interval between the last and penultimate elements (or `tab-width` if the list has fewer than two elements). A value of `nil` means a tab stop every `tab-width` columns.
>
> Use *M-x edit-tab-stops* to edit the location of tab stops interactively.

31.17.6 Indentation-Based Motion Commands

These commands, primarily for interactive use, act based on the indentation in the text.

`back-to-indentation`   [Command]

> This command moves point to the first non-whitespace character in the current line (which is the line in which point is located). It returns `nil`.

`backward-to-indentation &optional` *arg*   [Command]

> This command moves point backward *arg* lines and then to the first nonblank character on that line. It returns `nil`. If *arg* is omitted or `nil`, it defaults to 1.

`forward-to-indentation &optional` *arg*   [Command]

> This command moves point forward *arg* lines and then to the first nonblank character on that line. It returns `nil`. If *arg* is omitted or `nil`, it defaults to 1.

31.18 Case Changes

The case change commands described here work on text in the current buffer. See Section 4.8 [Case Conversion], page 62, for case conversion functions that work on strings and characters. See Section 4.9 [Case Tables], page 64, for how to customize which characters are upper or lower case and how to convert them.

`capitalize-region` *start end*   [Command]

> This function capitalizes all words in the region defined by *start* and *end*. To capitalize means to convert each word's first character to upper case and convert the rest of each word to lower case. The function returns `nil`.

If one end of the region is in the middle of a word, the part of the word within the region is treated as an entire word.

When `capitalize-region` is called interactively, *start* and *end* are point and the mark, with the smallest first.

```
---------- Buffer: foo ----------
This is the contents of the 5th foo.
---------- Buffer: foo ----------


(capitalize-region 1 37)
⇒ nil


---------- Buffer: foo ----------
This Is The Contents Of The 5th Foo.
---------- Buffer: foo ----------
```

downcase-region *start end*   [Command]

This function converts all of the letters in the region defined by *start* and *end* to lower case. The function returns `nil`.

When `downcase-region` is called interactively, *start* and *end* are point and the mark, with the smallest first.

upcase-region *start end*   [Command]

This function converts all of the letters in the region defined by *start* and *end* to upper case. The function returns `nil`.

When `upcase-region` is called interactively, *start* and *end* are point and the mark, with the smallest first.

capitalize-word *count*   [Command]

This function capitalizes *count* words after point, moving point over as it does. To capitalize means to convert each word's first character to upper case and convert the rest of each word to lower case. If *count* is negative, the function capitalizes the −*count* previous words but does not move point. The value is `nil`.

If point is in the middle of a word, the part of the word before point is ignored when moving forward. The rest is treated as an entire word.

When `capitalize-word` is called interactively, *count* is set to the numeric prefix argument.

downcase-word *count*   [Command]

This function converts the *count* words after point to all lower case, moving point over as it does. If *count* is negative, it converts the −*count* previous words but does not move point. The value is `nil`.

When `downcase-word` is called interactively, *count* is set to the numeric prefix argument.

upcase-word *count*   [Command]

This function converts the *count* words after point to all upper case, moving point over as it does. If *count* is negative, it converts the −*count* previous words but does not move point. The value is `nil`.

When `upcase-word` is called interactively, *count* is set to the numeric prefix argument.

31.19 Text Properties

Each character position in a buffer or a string can have a *text property list*, much like the property list of a symbol (see Section 5.9 [Property Lists], page 87). The properties belong to a particular character at a particular place, such as, the letter 'T' at the beginning of this sentence or the first 'o' in 'foo'—if the same character occurs in two different places, the two occurrences in general have different properties.

Each property has a name and a value. Both of these can be any Lisp object, but the name is normally a symbol. Typically each property name symbol is used for a particular purpose; for instance, the text property `face` specifies the faces for displaying the character (see Section 31.19.4 [Special Properties], page 738). The usual way to access the property list is to specify a name and ask what value corresponds to it.

If a character has a `category` property, we call it the *property category* of the character. It should be a symbol. The properties of the symbol serve as defaults for the properties of the character.

Copying text between strings and buffers preserves the properties along with the characters; this includes such diverse functions as `substring`, `insert`, and `buffer-substring`.

31.19.1 Examining Text Properties

The simplest way to examine text properties is to ask for the value of a particular property of a particular character. For that, use `get-text-property`. Use `text-properties-at` to get the entire property list of a character. See Section 31.19.3 [Property Search], page 736, for functions to examine the properties of a number of characters at once.

These functions handle both strings and buffers. Keep in mind that positions in a string start from 0, whereas positions in a buffer start from 1.

`get-text-property` *pos prop* **&optional** *object*   [Function]
> This function returns the value of the *prop* property of the character after position *pos* in *object* (a buffer or string). The argument *object* is optional and defaults to the current buffer.
>
> If there is no *prop* property strictly speaking, but the character has a property category that is a symbol, then `get-text-property` returns the *prop* property of that symbol.

`get-char-property` *position prop* **&optional** *object*   [Function]
> This function is like `get-text-property`, except that it checks overlays first and then text properties. See Section 37.9 [Overlays], page 904.
>
> The argument *object* may be a string, a buffer, or a window. If it is a window, then the buffer displayed in that window is used for text properties and overlays, but only the overlays active for that window are considered. If *object* is a buffer, then overlays in that buffer are considered first, in order of decreasing priority, followed by the text properties. If *object* is a string, only text properties are considered, since strings never have overlays.

get-pos-property *position prop* **&optional** *object*   [Function]

> This function is like `get-char-property`, except that it pays attention to properties' stickiness and overlays' advancement settings instead of the property of the character at (i.e., right after) *position*.

get-char-property-and-overlay *position prop* **&optional** *object*   [Function]

> This is like `get-char-property`, but gives extra information about the overlay that the property value comes from.
>
> Its value is a cons cell whose CAR is the property value, the same value `get-char-property` would return with the same arguments. Its CDR is the overlay in which the property was found, or `nil`, if it was found as a text property or not found at all.
>
> If *position* is at the end of *object*, both the CAR and the CDR of the value are `nil`.

char-property-alias-alist   [Variable]

> This variable holds an alist which maps property names to a list of alternative property names. If a character does not specify a direct value for a property, the alternative property names are consulted in order; the first non-`nil` value is used. This variable takes precedence over `default-text-properties`, and `category` properties take precedence over this variable.

text-properties-at *position* **&optional** *object*   [Function]

> This function returns the entire property list of the character at *position* in the string or buffer *object*. If *object* is `nil`, it defaults to the current buffer.

default-text-properties   [Variable]

> This variable holds a property list giving default values for text properties. Whenever a character does not specify a value for a property, neither directly, through a category symbol, or through `char-property-alias-alist`, the value stored in this list is used instead. Here is an example:
>
> ```
> (setq default-text-properties '(foo 69)
>       char-property-alias-alist nil)
> ;; Make sure character 1 has no properties of its own.
> (set-text-properties 1 2 nil)
> ;; What we get, when we ask, is the default value.
> (get-text-property 1 'foo)
>      ⇒ 69
> ```

31.19.2 Changing Text Properties

The primitives for changing properties apply to a specified range of text in a buffer or string. The function `set-text-properties` (see end of section) sets the entire property list of the text in that range; more often, it is useful to add, change, or delete just certain properties specified by name.

Since text properties are considered part of the contents of the buffer (or string), and can affect how a buffer looks on the screen, any change in buffer text properties marks the buffer as modified. Buffer text property changes are undoable also (see Section 31.9 [Undo], page 712). Positions in a string start from 0, whereas positions in a buffer start from 1.

`put-text-property` *start end prop value* **&optional** *object*   [Function]
> This function sets the *prop* property to *value* for the text between *start* and *end* in the string or buffer *object*. If *object* is `nil`, it defaults to the current buffer.

`add-text-properties` *start end props* **&optional** *object*   [Function]
> This function adds or overrides text properties for the text between *start* and *end* in the string or buffer *object*. If *object* is `nil`, it defaults to the current buffer.
>
> The argument *props* specifies which properties to add. It should have the form of a property list (see Section 5.9 [Property Lists], page 87): a list whose elements include the property names followed alternately by the corresponding values.
>
> The return value is `t` if the function actually changed some property's value; `nil` otherwise (if *props* is `nil` or its values agree with those in the text).
>
> For example, here is how to set the `comment` and `face` properties of a range of text:
> ```
> (add-text-properties start end
>                      '(comment t face highlight))
> ```

`remove-text-properties` *start end props* **&optional** *object*   [Function]
> This function deletes specified text properties from the text between *start* and *end* in the string or buffer *object*. If *object* is `nil`, it defaults to the current buffer.
>
> The argument *props* specifies which properties to delete. It should have the form of a property list (see Section 5.9 [Property Lists], page 87): a list whose elements are property names alternating with corresponding values. But only the names matter—the values that accompany them are ignored. For example, here's how to remove the `face` property.
> ```
> (remove-text-properties start end '(face nil))
> ```
> The return value is `t` if the function actually changed some property's value; `nil` otherwise (if *props* is `nil` or if no character in the specified text had any of those properties).
>
> To remove all text properties from certain text, use `set-text-properties` and specify `nil` for the new property list.

`remove-list-of-text-properties` *start end list-of-properties*   [Function]
>   **&optional** *object*
> Like `remove-text-properties` except that *list-of-properties* is a list of property names only, not an alternating list of property names and values.

`set-text-properties` *start end props* **&optional** *object*   [Function]
> This function completely replaces the text property list for the text between *start* and *end* in the string or buffer *object*. If *object* is `nil`, it defaults to the current buffer.
>
> The argument *props* is the new property list. It should be a list whose elements are property names alternating with corresponding values.
>
> After `set-text-properties` returns, all the characters in the specified range have identical properties.
>
> If *props* is `nil`, the effect is to get rid of all properties from the specified range of text. Here's an example:
> ```
> (set-text-properties start end nil)
> ```
> Do not rely on the return value of this function.

`add-face-text-property` *start end face* **&optional** *appendp object*   [Function]

> This function acts on the text between *start* and *end*, adding the face *face* to the `face` text property. *face* should be a valid value for the `face` property (see Section 31.19.4 [Special Properties], page 738), such as a face name or an anonymous face (see Section 37.12 [Faces], page 915).
>
> If any text in the region already has a non-`nil` `face` property, those face(s) are retained. This function sets the `face` property to a list of faces, with *face* as the first element (by default) and the pre-existing faces as the remaining elements. If the optional argument *append* is non-`nil`, *face* is appended to the end of the list instead. Note that in a face list, the first occurring value for each attribute takes precedence.
>
> For example, the following code would assign a italicized green face to the text between *start* and *end*:
>
> ```
> (add-face-text-property start end 'italic)
> (add-face-text-property start end '(:foreground "red"))
> (add-face-text-property start end '(:foreground "green"))
> ```
>
> The optional argument *object*, if non-`nil`, specifies a buffer or string to act on, rather than the current buffer. If *object* is a string, then *start* and *end* are zero-based indices into the string.

The easiest way to make a string with text properties is with `propertize`:

`propertize` *string* **&rest** *properties*   [Function]

> This function returns a copy of *string* with the text properties *properties* added. These properties apply to all the characters in the string that is returned. Here is an example that constructs a string with a `face` property and a `mouse-face` property:
>
> ```
> (propertize "foo" 'face 'italic
>             'mouse-face 'bold-italic)
>      ⇒ #("foo" 0 3 (mouse-face bold-italic face italic))
> ```
>
> To put different properties on various parts of a string, you can construct each part with `propertize` and then combine them with `concat`:
>
> ```
> (concat
>  (propertize "foo" 'face 'italic
>              'mouse-face 'bold-italic)
>  " and "
>  (propertize "bar" 'face 'italic
>              'mouse-face 'bold-italic))
>      ⇒ #("foo and bar"
>              0 3 (face italic mouse-face bold-italic)
>              3 8 nil
>              8 11 (face italic mouse-face bold-italic))
> ```

See Section 31.2 [Buffer Contents], page 697, for the function `buffer-substring-no-properties`, which copies text from the buffer but does not copy its properties.

If you wish to add or remove text properties to a buffer without marking the buffer as modified, you can wrap the calls above in the `with-silent-modifications` macro.

31.19.3 Text Property Search Functions

In typical use of text properties, most of the time several or many consecutive characters have the same value for a property. Rather than writing your programs to examine characters one by one, it is much faster to process chunks of text that have the same property value.

Here are functions you can use to do this. They use `eq` for comparing property values. In all cases, *object* defaults to the current buffer.

For good performance, it's very important to use the *limit* argument to these functions, especially the ones that search for a single property—otherwise, they may spend a long time scanning to the end of the buffer, if the property you are interested in does not change.

These functions do not move point; instead, they return a position (or `nil`). Remember that a position is always between two characters; the position returned by these functions is between two characters with different properties.

next-property-change *pos* **&optional** *object limit*   [Function]
> The function scans the text forward from position *pos* in the string or buffer *object* until it finds a change in some text property, then returns the position of the change. In other words, it returns the position of the first character beyond *pos* whose properties are not identical to those of the character just after *pos*.
>
> If *limit* is non-`nil`, then the scan ends at position *limit*. If there is no property change before that point, this function returns *limit*.
>
> The value is `nil` if the properties remain unchanged all the way to the end of *object* and *limit* is `nil`. If the value is non-`nil`, it is a position greater than or equal to *pos*. The value equals *pos* only when *limit* equals *pos*.
>
> Here is an example of how to scan the buffer by chunks of text within which all properties are constant:
>
> ```
> (while (not (eobp))
>   (let ((plist (text-properties-at (point)))
>         (next-change
>          (or (next-property-change (point) (current-buffer))
>              (point-max))))
>     Process text from point to next-change...
>     (goto-char next-change)))
> ```

previous-property-change *pos* **&optional** *object limit*   [Function]
> This is like **next-property-change**, but scans back from *pos* instead of forward. If the value is non-`nil`, it is a position less than or equal to *pos*; it equals *pos* only if *limit* equals *pos*.

next-single-property-change *pos prop* **&optional** *object limit*   [Function]
> The function scans text for a change in the *prop* property, then returns the position of the change. The scan goes forward from position *pos* in the string or buffer *object*. In other words, this function returns the position of the first character beyond *pos* whose *prop* property differs from that of the character just after *pos*.
>
> If *limit* is non-`nil`, then the scan ends at position *limit*. If there is no property change before that point, **next-single-property-change** returns *limit*.

The value is `nil` if the property remains unchanged all the way to the end of *object* and *limit* is `nil`. If the value is non-`nil`, it is a position greater than or equal to *pos*; it equals *pos* only if *limit* equals *pos*.

previous-single-property-change *pos prop* **&optional** *object limit*   [Function]
This is like **next-single-property-change**, but scans back from *pos* instead of forward. If the value is non-`nil`, it is a position less than or equal to *pos*; it equals *pos* only if *limit* equals *pos*.

next-char-property-change *pos* **&optional** *limit*   [Function]
This is like **next-property-change** except that it considers overlay properties as well as text properties, and if no change is found before the end of the buffer, it returns the maximum buffer position rather than `nil` (in this sense, it resembles the corresponding overlay function **next-overlay-change**, rather than **next-property-change**). There is no *object* operand because this function operates only on the current buffer. It returns the next address at which either kind of property changes.

previous-char-property-change *pos* **&optional** *limit*   [Function]
This is like **next-char-property-change**, but scans back from *pos* instead of forward, and returns the minimum buffer position if no change is found.

next-single-char-property-change *pos prop* **&optional** *object limit*   [Function]
This is like **next-single-property-change** except that it considers overlay properties as well as text properties, and if no change is found before the end of the *object*, it returns the maximum valid position in *object* rather than `nil`. Unlike **next-char-property-change**, this function *does* have an *object* operand; if *object* is not a buffer, only text-properties are considered.

previous-single-char-property-change *pos prop* **&optional** *object limit*   [Function]
This is like **next-single-char-property-change**, but scans back from *pos* instead of forward, and returns the minimum valid position in *object* if no change is found.

text-property-any *start end prop value* **&optional** *object*   [Function]
This function returns non-`nil` if at least one character between *start* and *end* has a property *prop* whose value is *value*. More precisely, it returns the position of the first such character. Otherwise, it returns `nil`.

The optional fifth argument, *object*, specifies the string or buffer to scan. Positions are relative to *object*. The default for *object* is the current buffer.

text-property-not-all *start end prop value* **&optional** *object*   [Function]
This function returns non-`nil` if at least one character between *start* and *end* does not have a property *prop* with value *value*. More precisely, it returns the position of the first such character. Otherwise, it returns `nil`.

The optional fifth argument, *object*, specifies the string or buffer to scan. Positions are relative to *object*. The default for *object* is the current buffer.

31.19.4 Properties with Special Meanings

Here is a table of text property names that have special built-in meanings. The following sections list a few additional special property names that control filling and property inheritance. All other names have no standard meaning, and you can use them as you like.

Note: the properties `composition`, `display`, `invisible` and `intangible` can also cause point to move to an acceptable place, after each Emacs command. See Section 20.6 [Adjusting Point], page 357.

category   If a character has a `category` property, we call it the *property category* of the character. It should be a symbol. The properties of this symbol serve as defaults for the properties of the character.

face   The `face` property controls the appearance of the character (see Section 37.12 [Faces], page 915). The value of the property can be the following:

- A face name (a symbol or string).

- An anonymous face: a property list of the form (*keyword value* ...), where each *keyword* is a face attribute name and *value* is a value for that attribute.

- A list of faces. Each list element should be either a face name or an anonymous face. This specifies a face which is an aggregate of the attributes of each of the listed faces. Faces occurring earlier in the list have higher priority.

- A cons cell of the form (`foreground-color` . *color-name*) or (`background-color` . *color-name*). This specifies the foreground or background color, similar to (`:foreground` *color-name*) or (`:background` *color-name*). This form is supported for backward compatibility only, and should be avoided.

    Font Lock mode (see Section 22.6 [Font Lock Mode], page 462) works in most buffers by dynamically updating the `face` property of characters based on the context.

    The `add-face-text-property` function provides a convenient way to set this text property. See Section 31.19.2 [Changing Properties], page 733.

font-lock-face
            This property specifies a value for the `face` property that Font Lock mode should apply to the underlying text. It is one of the fontification methods used by Font Lock mode, and is useful for special modes that implement their own highlighting. See Section 22.6.6 [Precalculated Fontification], page 470. When Font Lock mode is disabled, `font-lock-face` has no effect.

mouse-face
            This property is used instead of `face` when the mouse is on or near the character. For this purpose, "near" means that all text between the character and where the mouse is have the same `mouse-face` property value.

            Emacs ignores all face attributes from the `mouse-face` property that alter the text size (e.g., `:height`, `:weight`, and `:slant`). Those attributes are always the same as for the unhighlighted text.

fontified

> This property says whether the text is ready for display. If `nil`, Emacs's redisplay routine calls the functions in `fontification-functions` (see Section 37.12.7 [Auto Faces], page 926) to prepare this part of the buffer before it is displayed. It is used internally by the just-in-time font locking code.

display

> This property activates various features that change the way text is displayed. For example, it can make text appear taller or shorter, higher or lower, wider or narrow, or replaced with an image. See Section 37.16 [Display Property], page 945.

help-echo

> If text has a string as its `help-echo` property, then when you move the mouse onto that text, Emacs displays that string in the echo area, or in the tooltip window (see Section 37.25 [Tooltips], page 979).
>
> If the value of the `help-echo` property is a function, that function is called with three arguments, *window*, *object* and *pos* and should return a help string or `nil` for none. The first argument, *window* is the window in which the help was found. The second, *object*, is the buffer, overlay or string which had the `help-echo` property. The *pos* argument is as follows:
>
> - If *object* is a buffer, *pos* is the position in the buffer.
> - If *object* is an overlay, that overlay has a `help-echo` property, and *pos* is the position in the overlay's buffer.
> - If *object* is a string (an overlay string or a string displayed with the `display` property), *pos* is the position in that string.
>
> If the value of the `help-echo` property is neither a function nor a string, it is evaluated to obtain a help string.
>
> You can alter the way help text is displayed by setting the variable `show-help-function` (see [Help display], page 743).
>
> This feature is used in the mode line and for other active text.

keymap

> The `keymap` property specifies an additional keymap for commands. When this keymap applies, it is used for key lookup before the minor mode keymaps and before the buffer's local map. See Section 21.7 [Active Keymaps], page 398. If the property value is a symbol, the symbol's function definition is used as the keymap.
>
> The property's value for the character before point applies if it is non-`nil` and rear-sticky, and the property's value for the character after point applies if it is non-`nil` and front-sticky. (For mouse clicks, the position of the click is used instead of the position of point.)

local-map

> This property works like `keymap` except that it specifies a keymap to use *instead of* the buffer's local map. For most purposes (perhaps all purposes), it is better to use the `keymap` property.

syntax-table

> The `syntax-table` property overrides what the syntax table says about this particular character. See Section 34.4 [Syntax Properties], page 823.

`read-only`

> If a character has the property `read-only`, then modifying that character is not allowed. Any command that would do so gets an error, `text-read-only`. If the property value is a string, that string is used as the error message.
>
> Insertion next to a read-only character is an error if inserting ordinary text there would inherit the `read-only` property due to stickiness. Thus, you can control permission to insert next to read-only text by controlling the stickiness. See Section 31.19.6 [Sticky Properties], page 744.
>
> Since changing properties counts as modifying the buffer, it is not possible to remove a `read-only` property unless you know the special trick: bind `inhibit-read-only` to a non-nil value and then remove the property. See Section 26.7 [Read Only Buffers], page 558.

`inhibit-read-only`

> Characters that have the property `inhibit-read-only` can be edited even in read-only buffers. See Section 26.7 [Read Only Buffers], page 558.

`invisible`

> A non-nil `invisible` property can make a character invisible on the screen. See Section 37.6 [Invisible Text], page 896, for details.

`intangible`

> If a group of consecutive characters have equal and non-nil `intangible` properties, then you cannot place point between them. If you try to move point forward into the group, point actually moves to the end of the group. If you try to move point backward into the group, point actually moves to the start of the group.
>
> If consecutive characters have unequal non-nil `intangible` properties, they belong to separate groups; each group is separately treated as described above.
>
> When the variable `inhibit-point-motion-hooks` is non-nil (as it is by default), the `intangible` property is ignored.
>
> Beware: this property operates at a very low level, and affects a lot of code in unexpected ways. So use it with extreme caution. A common misuse is to put an intangible property on invisible text, which is actually unnecessary since the command loop will move point outside of the invisible text at the end of each command anyway. See Section 20.6 [Adjusting Point], page 357. For these reasons, this property is obsolete; use the `cursor-intangible` property instead.

`cursor-intangible`

> When the minor mode `cursor-intangible-mode` is turned on, point is moved away of any position that has a non-nil `cursor-intangible` property, just before redisplay happens.

`field`   Consecutive characters with the same `field` property constitute a *field*. Some motion functions including `forward-word` and `beginning-of-line` stop moving at a field boundary. See Section 31.19.9 [Fields], page 748.

`cursor`   Normally, the cursor is displayed at the beginning or the end of any overlay and text property strings present at the current buffer position. You can place the

cursor on any desired character of these strings by giving that character a non-
`nil` `cursor` text property. In addition, if the value of the `cursor` property is an
integer, it specifies the number of buffer's character positions, starting with the
position where the overlay or the `display` property begins, for which the cursor
should be displayed on that character. Specifically, if the value of the `cursor`
property of a character is the number *n*, the cursor will be displayed on this
character for any buffer position in the range `[`*ovpos*`..`*ovpos+n*`)`, where *ovpos*
is the overlay's starting position given by `overlay-start` (see Section 37.9.1
[Managing Overlays], page 904), or the position where the `display` text property begins in the buffer.

In other words, the string character with the `cursor` property of any non-`nil`
value is the character where to display the cursor. The value of the property
says for which buffer positions to display the cursor there. If the value is an
integer *n*, the cursor is displayed there when point is anywhere between the
beginning of the overlay or `display` property and *n* positions after that. If
the value is anything else and non-`nil`, the cursor is displayed there only when
point is at the beginning of the `display` property or at `overlay-start`.

When the buffer has many overlay strings (e.g., see Section 37.9.2 [Overlay
Properties], page 907) that conceal some of the buffer text or `display` properties
that are strings, it is a good idea to use the `cursor` property on these strings to
cue the Emacs display about the places where to put the cursor while traversing
these strings. This directly communicates to the display engine where the Lisp
program wants to put the cursor, or where the user would expect the cursor,
when point is located on some buffer position that is "covered" by the display
or overlay string.

`pointer`   This specifies a specific pointer shape when the mouse pointer is over this text
              or image. See Section 28.18 [Pointer Shape], page 664, for possible pointer
              shapes.

`line-spacing`
              A newline can have a `line-spacing` text or overlay property that controls the
              height of the display line ending with that newline. The property value overrides
              the default frame line spacing and the buffer local `line-spacing` variable. See
              Section 37.11 [Line Height], page 913.

`line-height`
              A newline can have a `line-height` text or overlay property that controls the
              total height of the display line ending in that newline. See Section 37.11 [Line
              Height], page 913.

`wrap-prefix`
              If text has a `wrap-prefix` property, the prefix it defines will be added at display
              time to the beginning of every continuation line due to text wrapping (so if lines
              are truncated, the wrap-prefix is never used). It may be a string or an image (see
              Section 37.16.4 [Other Display Specs], page 948), or a stretch of whitespace such
              as specified by the `:width` or `:align-to` display properties (see Section 37.16.2
              [Specified Space], page 946).

A wrap-prefix may also be specified for an entire buffer using the `wrap-prefix` buffer-local variable (however, a `wrap-prefix` text-property takes precedence over the value of the `wrap-prefix` variable). See Section 37.3 [Truncation], page 887.

`line-prefix`

> If text has a `line-prefix` property, the prefix it defines will be added at display time to the beginning of every non-continuation line. It may be a string or an image (see Section 37.16.4 [Other Display Specs], page 948), or a stretch of whitespace such as specified by the `:width` or `:align-to` display properties (see Section 37.16.2 [Specified Space], page 946).
>
> A line-prefix may also be specified for an entire buffer using the `line-prefix` buffer-local variable (however, a `line-prefix` text-property takes precedence over the value of the `line-prefix` variable). See Section 37.3 [Truncation], page 887.

`modification-hooks`

> If a character has the property `modification-hooks`, then its value should be a list of functions; modifying that character calls all of those functions before the actual modification. Each function receives two arguments: the beginning and end of the part of the buffer being modified. Note that if a particular modification hook function appears on several characters being modified by a single primitive, you can't predict how many times the function will be called. Furthermore, insertion will not modify any existing character, so this hook will only be run when removing some characters, replacing them with others, or changing their text-properties.
>
> If these functions modify the buffer, they should bind `inhibit-modification-hooks` to `t` around doing so, to avoid confusing the internal mechanism that calls these hooks.
>
> Overlays also support the `modification-hooks` property, but the details are somewhat different (see Section 37.9.2 [Overlay Properties], page 907).

`insert-in-front-hooks`
`insert-behind-hooks`

> The operation of inserting text in a buffer also calls the functions listed in the `insert-in-front-hooks` property of the following character and in the `insert-behind-hooks` property of the preceding character. These functions receive two arguments, the beginning and end of the inserted text. The functions are called *after* the actual insertion takes place.
>
> See also Section 31.28 [Change Hooks], page 759, for other hooks that are called when you change text in a buffer.

`point-entered`
`point-left`

> The special properties `point-entered` and `point-left` record hook functions that report motion of point. Each time point moves, Emacs compares these two property values:
>
> - the `point-left` property of the character after the old location, and

- the `point-entered` property of the character after the new location.

If these two values differ, each of them is called (if not `nil`) with two arguments: the old value of point, and the new one.

The same comparison is made for the characters before the old and new locations. The result may be to execute two `point-left` functions (which may be the same function) and/or two `point-entered` functions (which may be the same function). In any case, all the `point-left` functions are called first, followed by all the `point-entered` functions.

It is possible to use `char-after` to examine characters at various buffer positions without moving point to those positions. Only an actual change in the value of point runs these hook functions.

The variable `inhibit-point-motion-hooks` by default inhibits running the `point-left` and `point-entered` hooks, see [Inhibit point motion hooks], page 743.

These properties are obsolete; please use `cursor-sensor-functions` instead.

`cursor-sensor-functions`

This special property records a list of functions that react to cursor motion. Each function in the list is called, just before redisplay, with 3 arguments: the affected window, the previous known position of the cursor, and one of the symbols `entered` or `left`, depending on whether the cursor is entering the text that has this property or leaving it. The functions are called only when the minor mode `cursor-sensor-mode` is turned on.

`composition`

This text property is used to display a sequence of characters as a single glyph composed from components. But the value of the property itself is completely internal to Emacs and should not be manipulated directly by, for instance, `put-text-property`.

`inhibit-point-motion-hooks`   [Variable]

When this obsolete variable is non-`nil`, `point-left` and `point-entered` hooks are not run, and the `intangible` property has no effect. Do not set this variable globally; bind it with `let`. Since the affected properties are obsolete, this variable's default value is `t`, to effectively disable them.

`show-help-function`   [Variable]

If this variable is non-`nil`, it specifies a function called to display help strings. These may be `help-echo` properties, menu help strings (see Section 21.17.1.1 [Simple Menu Items], page 416, see Section 21.17.1.2 [Extended Menu Items], page 417), or tool bar help strings (see Section 21.17.6 [Tool Bar], page 423). The specified function is called with one argument, the help string to display, which is passed through `substitute-command-keys` before being given to the function; see Section 23.3 [Keys in Documentation], page 488. Tooltip mode (see Section "Tooltips" in *The GNU Emacs Manual*) provides an example.

31.19.5 Formatted Text Properties

These text properties affect the behavior of the fill commands. They are used for representing formatted text. See Section 31.11 [Filling], page 716, and Section 31.12 [Margins], page 718.

hard   If a newline character has this property, it is a "hard" newline. The fill commands do not alter hard newlines and do not move words across them. However, this property takes effect only if the `use-hard-newlines` minor mode is enabled. See Section "Hard and Soft Newlines" in *The GNU Emacs Manual.*

right-margin
              This property specifies an extra right margin for filling this part of the text.

left-margin
              This property specifies an extra left margin for filling this part of the text.

justification
              This property specifies the style of justification for filling this part of the text.

31.19.6 Stickiness of Text Properties

Self-inserting characters, the ones that get inserted into a buffer when the user types them (see Section 31.5 [Commands for Insertion], page 702), normally take on the same properties as the preceding character. This is called *inheritance* of properties.

By contrast, a Lisp program can do insertion with inheritance or without, depending on the choice of insertion primitive. The ordinary text insertion functions, such as `insert`, do not inherit any properties. They insert text with precisely the properties of the string being inserted, and no others. This is correct for programs that copy text from one context to another—for example, into or out of the kill ring. To insert with inheritance, use the special primitives described in this section. Self-inserting characters inherit properties because they work using these primitives.

When you do insertion with inheritance, *which* properties are inherited, and from where, depends on which properties are *sticky*. Insertion after a character inherits those of its properties that are *rear-sticky*. Insertion before a character inherits those of its properties that are *front-sticky*. When both sides offer different sticky values for the same property, the previous character's value takes precedence.

By default, a text property is rear-sticky but not front-sticky; thus, the default is to inherit all the properties of the preceding character, and nothing from the following character.

You can control the stickiness of various text properties with two specific text properties, `front-sticky` and `rear-nonsticky`, and with the variable `text-property-default-nonsticky`. You can use the variable to specify a different default for a given property. You can use those two text properties to make any specific properties sticky or nonsticky in any particular part of the text.

If a character's `front-sticky` property is `t`, then all its properties are front-sticky. If the `front-sticky` property is a list, then the sticky properties of the character are those whose names are in the list. For example, if a character has a `front-sticky` property whose value is (`face read-only`), then insertion before the character can inherit its `face` property and its `read-only` property, but no others.

The `rear-nonsticky` property works the opposite way. Most properties are rear-sticky by default, so the `rear-nonsticky` property says which properties are *not* rear-sticky. If a character's `rear-nonsticky` property is `t`, then none of its properties are rear-sticky. If the `rear-nonsticky` property is a list, properties are rear-sticky *unless* their names are in the list.

`text-property-default-nonsticky`   [Variable]
> This variable holds an alist which defines the default rear-stickiness of various text properties. Each element has the form (*property . nonstickiness*), and it defines the stickiness of a particular text property, *property*.
>
> If *nonstickiness* is non-`nil`, this means that the property *property* is rear-nonsticky by default. Since all properties are front-nonsticky by default, this makes *property* nonsticky in both directions by default.
>
> The text properties `front-sticky` and `rear-nonsticky`, when used, take precedence over the default *nonstickiness* specified in `text-property-default-nonsticky`.

Here are the functions that insert text with inheritance of properties:

`insert-and-inherit &rest` *strings*   [Function]
> Insert the strings *strings*, just like the function `insert`, but inherit any sticky properties from the adjoining text.

`insert-before-markers-and-inherit &rest` *strings*   [Function]
> Insert the strings *strings*, just like the function `insert-before-markers`, but inherit any sticky properties from the adjoining text.

See Section 31.4 [Insertion], page 700, for the ordinary insertion functions which do not inherit.

31.19.7 Lazy Computation of Text Properties

Instead of computing text properties for all the text in the buffer, you can arrange to compute the text properties for parts of the text when and if something depends on them.

The primitive that extracts text from the buffer along with its properties is `buffer-substring`. Before examining the properties, this function runs the abnormal hook `buffer-access-fontify-functions`.

`buffer-access-fontify-functions`   [Variable]
> This variable holds a list of functions for computing text properties. Before `buffer-substring` copies the text and text properties for a portion of the buffer, it calls all the functions in this list. Each of the functions receives two arguments that specify the range of the buffer being accessed. (The buffer itself is always the current buffer.)

The function `buffer-substring-no-properties` does not call these functions, since it ignores text properties anyway.

In order to prevent the hook functions from being called more than once for the same part of the buffer, you can use the variable `buffer-access-fontified-property`.

buffer-access-fontified-property   [Variable]

> If this variable's value is non-nil, it is a symbol which is used as a text property name. A non-nil value for that text property means the other text properties for this character have already been computed.
>
> If all the characters in the range specified for `buffer-substring` have a non-nil value for this property, `buffer-substring` does not call the `buffer-access-fontify-functions` functions. It assumes these characters already have the right text properties, and just copies the properties they already have.
>
> The normal way to use this feature is that the `buffer-access-fontify-functions` functions add this property, as well as others, to the characters they operate on. That way, they avoid being called over and over for the same text.

31.19.8 Defining Clickable Text

Clickable text is text that can be clicked, with either the mouse or via a keyboard command, to produce some result. Many major modes use clickable text to implement textual hyperlinks, or *links* for short.

The easiest way to insert and manipulate links is to use the `button` package. See Section 37.19 [Buttons], page 963. In this section, we will explain how to manually set up clickable text in a buffer, using text properties. For simplicity, we will refer to the clickable text as a *link*.

Implementing a link involves three separate steps: (1) indicating clickability when the mouse moves over the link; (2) making `RET` or *mouse-2* on that link do something; and (3) setting up a `follow-link` condition so that the link obeys `mouse-1-click-follows-link`.

To indicate clickability, add the `mouse-face` text property to the text of the link; then Emacs will highlight the link when the mouse moves over it. In addition, you should define a tooltip or echo area message, using the `help-echo` text property. See Section 31.19.4 [Special Properties], page 738. For instance, here is how Dired indicates that file names are clickable:

```
(if (dired-move-to-filename)
    (add-text-properties
      (point)
      (save-excursion
        (dired-move-to-end-of-filename)
        (point))
      '(mouse-face highlight
        help-echo "mouse-2: visit this file in other window")))
```

To make the link clickable, bind `RET` and *mouse-2* to commands that perform the desired action. Each command should check to see whether it was called on a link, and act accordingly. For instance, Dired's major mode keymap binds *mouse-2* to the following command:

```
(defun dired-mouse-find-file-other-window (event)
  "In Dired, visit the file or directory name you click on."
  (interactive "e")
  (let ((window (posn-window (event-end event)))
        (pos (posn-point (event-end event)))
        file)
    (if (not (windowp window))
        (error "No file chosen"))
```

```
(with-current-buffer (window-buffer window)
  (goto-char pos)
  (setq file (dired-get-file-for-visit)))
(if (file-directory-p file)
    (or (and (cdr dired-subdir-alist)
             (dired-goto-subdir file))
        (progn
          (select-window window)
          (dired-other-window file)))
  (select-window window)
  (find-file-other-window (file-name-sans-versions file t)))))
```

This command uses the functions `posn-window` and `posn-point` to determine where the click occurred, and `dired-get-file-for-visit` to determine which file to visit.

Instead of binding the mouse command in a major mode keymap, you can bind it within the link text, using the `keymap` text property (see Section 31.19.4 [Special Properties], page 738). For instance:

```
(let ((map (make-sparse-keymap)))
  (define-key map [mouse-2] 'operate-this-button)
  (put-text-property link-start link-end 'keymap map))
```

With this method, you can easily define different commands for different links. Furthermore, the global definition of `RET` and *mouse-2* remain available for the rest of the text in the buffer.

The basic Emacs command for clicking on links is *mouse-2*. However, for compatibility with other graphical applications, Emacs also recognizes *mouse-1* clicks on links, provided the user clicks on the link quickly without moving the mouse. This behavior is controlled by the user option `mouse-1-click-follows-link`. See Section "Mouse References" in *The GNU Emacs Manual*.

To set up the link so that it obeys `mouse-1-click-follows-link`, you must either (1) apply a `follow-link` text or overlay property to the link text, or (2) bind the `follow-link` event to a keymap (which can be a major mode keymap or a local keymap specified via the `keymap` text property). The value of the `follow-link` property, or the binding for the `follow-link` event, acts as a condition for the link action. This condition tells Emacs two things: the circumstances under which a *mouse-1* click should be regarded as occurring inside the link, and how to compute an action code that says what to translate the *mouse-1* click into. The link action condition can be one of the following:

`mouse-face`

If the condition is the symbol `mouse-face`, a position is inside a link if there is a non-`nil` `mouse-face` property at that position. The action code is always `t`.

For example, here is how Info mode handles *mouse-1*:

```
(define-key Info-mode-map [follow-link] 'mouse-face)
```

a function   If the condition is a function, *func*, then a position *pos* is inside a link if (*func pos*) evaluates to non-`nil`. The value returned by *func* serves as the action code.

For example, here is how pcvs enables *mouse-1* to follow links on file names only:

```
(define-key map [follow-link]
```

```
(lambda (pos)
  (eq (get-char-property pos 'face) 'cvs-filename-face)))
```

anything else

> If the condition value is anything else, then the position is inside a link and the condition itself is the action code. Clearly, you should specify this kind of condition only when applying the condition via a text or property overlay on the link text (so that it does not apply to the entire buffer).

The action code tells *mouse-1* how to follow the link:

a string or vector

> If the action code is a string or vector, the *mouse-1* event is translated into the first element of the string or vector; i.e., the action of the *mouse-1* click is the local or global binding of that character or symbol. Thus, if the action code is `"foo"`, *mouse-1* translates into *f*. If it is `[foo]`, *mouse-1* translates into `foo`.

anything else

> For any other non-`nil` action code, the *mouse-1* event is translated into a *mouse-2* event at the same position.

To define *mouse-1* to activate a button defined with `define-button-type`, give the button a `follow-link` property. The property value should be a link action condition, as described above. See Section 37.19 [Buttons], page 963. For example, here is how Help mode handles *mouse-1*:

```
(define-button-type 'help-xref
  'follow-link t
  'action #'help-button-action)
```

To define *mouse-1* on a widget defined with `define-widget`, give the widget a `:follow-link` property. The property value should be a link action condition, as described above. For example, here is how the `link` widget specifies that a `mouse-1` click shall be translated to RET:

```
(define-widget 'link 'item
  "An embedded link."
  :button-prefix 'widget-link-prefix
  :button-suffix 'widget-link-suffix
  :follow-link "\C-m"
  :help-echo "Follow the link."
  :format "%[%t%]")
```

`mouse-on-link-p` *pos*   [Function]
> This function returns non-`nil` if position *pos* in the current buffer is on a link. *pos* can also be a mouse event location, as returned by `event-start` (see Section 20.7.13 [Accessing Mouse], page 369).

31.19.9 Defining and Using Fields

A field is a range of consecutive characters in the buffer that are identified by having the same value (comparing with `eq`) of the `field` property (either a text-property or an overlay property). This section describes special functions that are available for operating on fields.

You specify a field with a buffer position, *pos*. We think of each field as containing a range of buffer positions, so the position you specify stands for the field containing that position.

When the characters before and after *pos* are part of the same field, there is no doubt which field contains *pos*: the one those characters both belong to. When *pos* is at a boundary between fields, which field it belongs to depends on the stickiness of the `field` properties of the two surrounding characters (see Section 31.19.6 [Sticky Properties], page 744). The field whose property would be inherited by text inserted at *pos* is the field that contains *pos*.

There is an anomalous case where newly inserted text at *pos* would not inherit the `field` property from either side. This happens if the previous character's `field` property is not rear-sticky, and the following character's `field` property is not front-sticky. In this case, *pos* belongs to neither the preceding field nor the following field; the field functions treat it as belonging to an empty field whose beginning and end are both at *pos*.

In all of these functions, if *pos* is omitted or `nil`, the value of point is used by default. If narrowing is in effect, then *pos* should fall within the accessible portion. See Section 29.4 [Narrowing], page 684.

`field-beginning` **&optional** *pos escape-from-edge limit*   [Function]
    This function returns the beginning of the field specified by *pos*.

    If *pos* is at the beginning of its field, and *escape-from-edge* is non-`nil`, then the return value is always the beginning of the preceding field that *ends* at *pos*, regardless of the stickiness of the `field` properties around *pos*.

    If *limit* is non-`nil`, it is a buffer position; if the beginning of the field is before *limit*, then *limit* will be returned instead.

`field-end` **&optional** *pos escape-from-edge limit*   [Function]
    This function returns the end of the field specified by *pos*.

    If *pos* is at the end of its field, and *escape-from-edge* is non-`nil`, then the return value is always the end of the following field that *begins* at *pos*, regardless of the stickiness of the `field` properties around *pos*.

    If *limit* is non-`nil`, it is a buffer position; if the end of the field is after *limit*, then *limit* will be returned instead.

`field-string` **&optional** *pos*   [Function]
    This function returns the contents of the field specified by *pos*, as a string.

`field-string-no-properties` **&optional** *pos*   [Function]
    This function returns the contents of the field specified by *pos*, as a string, discarding text properties.

`delete-field` **&optional** *pos*   [Function]
    This function deletes the text of the field specified by *pos*.

`constrain-to-field` *new-pos old-pos* **&optional** *escape-from-edge*   [Function]
        only-in-line inhibit-capture-property
    This function constrains *new-pos* to the field that *old-pos* belongs to—in other words, it returns the position closest to *new-pos* that is in the same field as *old-pos*.

    If *new-pos* is `nil`, then `constrain-to-field` uses the value of point instead, and moves point to the resulting position in addition to returning that position.

If *old-pos* is at the boundary of two fields, then the acceptable final positions depend on the argument *escape-from-edge*. If *escape-from-edge* is `nil`, then *new-pos* must be in the field whose `field` property equals what new characters inserted at *old-pos* would inherit. (This depends on the stickiness of the `field` property for the characters before and after *old-pos*.) If *escape-from-edge* is non-`nil`, *new-pos* can be anywhere in the two adjacent fields. Additionally, if two fields are separated by another field with the special value `boundary`, then any point within this special field is also considered to be on the boundary.

Commands like `C-a` with no argument, that normally move backward to a specific kind of location and stay there once there, probably should specify `nil` for *escape-from-edge*. Other motion commands that check fields should probably pass `t`.

If the optional argument *only-in-line* is non-`nil`, and constraining *new-pos* in the usual way would move it to a different line, *new-pos* is returned unconstrained. This used in commands that move by line, such as `next-line` and `beginning-of-line`, so that they respect field boundaries only in the case where they can still move to the right line.

If the optional argument *inhibit-capture-property* is non-`nil`, and *old-pos* has a non-`nil` property of that name, then any field boundaries are ignored.

You can cause `constrain-to-field` to ignore all field boundaries (and so never constrain anything) by binding the variable `inhibit-field-text-motion` to a non-`nil` value.

31.19.10 Why Text Properties are not Intervals

Some editors that support adding attributes to text in the buffer do so by letting the user specify intervals within the text, and adding the properties to the intervals. Those editors permit the user or the programmer to determine where individual intervals start and end. We deliberately provided a different sort of interface in Emacs Lisp to avoid certain paradoxical behavior associated with text modification.

If the actual subdivision into intervals is meaningful, that means you can distinguish between a buffer that is just one interval with a certain property, and a buffer containing the same text subdivided into two intervals, both of which have that property.

Suppose you take the buffer with just one interval and kill part of the text. The text remaining in the buffer is one interval, and the copy in the kill ring (and the undo list) becomes a separate interval. Then if you yank back the killed text, you get two intervals with the same properties. Thus, editing does not preserve the distinction between one interval and two.

Suppose we attempt to fix this problem by coalescing the two intervals when the text is inserted. That works fine if the buffer originally was a single interval. But suppose instead that we have two adjacent intervals with the same properties, and we kill the text of one interval and yank it back. The same interval-coalescence feature that rescues the other case causes trouble in this one: after yanking, we have just one interval. Once again, editing does not preserve the distinction between one interval and two.

Insertion of text at the border between intervals also raises questions that have no satisfactory answer.

However, it is easy to arrange for editing to behave consistently for questions of the form, "What are the properties of text at this buffer or string position?" So we have decided these are the only questions that make sense; we have not implemented asking questions about where intervals start or end.

In practice, you can usually use the text property search functions in place of explicit interval boundaries. You can think of them as finding the boundaries of intervals, assuming that intervals are always coalesced whenever possible. See Section 31.19.3 [Property Search], page 736.

Emacs also provides explicit intervals as a presentation feature; see Section 37.9 [Overlays], page 904.

31.20 Substituting for a Character Code

The following functions replace characters within a specified region based on their character codes.

subst-char-in-region *start end old-char new-char* **&optional**   [Function]
      noundo

    This function replaces all occurrences of the character *old-char* with the character *new-char* in the region of the current buffer defined by *start* and *end*.

    If *noundo* is non-nil, then **subst-char-in-region** does not record the change for undo and does not mark the buffer as modified. This was useful for controlling the old selective display feature (see Section 37.7 [Selective Display], page 899).

    subst-char-in-region does not move point and returns **nil**.

```
---------- Buffer: foo ----------
This is the contents of the buffer before.
---------- Buffer: foo ----------

(subst-char-in-region 1 20 ?i ?X)
     ⇒ nil

---------- Buffer: foo ----------
ThXs Xs the contents of the buffer before.
---------- Buffer: foo ----------
```

translate-region *start end table*   [Command]
    This function applies a translation table to the characters in the buffer between positions *start* and *end*.

    The translation table *table* is a string or a char-table; (**aref table ochar**) gives the translated character corresponding to *ochar*. If *table* is a string, any characters with codes larger than the length of *table* are not altered by the translation.

    The return value of **translate-region** is the number of characters that were actually changed by the translation. This does not count characters that were mapped into themselves in the translation table.

31.21 Registers

A register is a sort of variable used in Emacs editing that can hold a variety of different kinds of values. Each register is named by a single character. All ASCII characters and their meta variants (but with the exception of *C-g*) can be used to name registers. Thus, there are 255 possible registers. A register is designated in Emacs Lisp by the character that is its name.

register-alist   [Variable]

> This variable is an alist of elements of the form (*name . contents*). Normally, there is one element for each Emacs register that has been used.
>
> The object *name* is a character (an integer) identifying the register.

The *contents* of a register can have several possible types:

a number A number stands for itself. If **insert-register** finds a number in the register, it converts the number to decimal.

a marker A marker represents a buffer position to jump to.

a string A string is text saved in the register.

a rectangle
> A rectangle is represented by a list of strings.

(*window-configuration position*)
> This represents a window configuration to restore in one frame, and a position to jump to in the current buffer.

(*frame-configuration position*)
> This represents a frame configuration to restore, and a position to jump to in the current buffer.

(file *filename*)
> This represents a file to visit; jumping to this value visits file *filename*.

(file-query *filename position*)
> This represents a file to visit and a position in it; jumping to this value visits file *filename* and goes to buffer position *position*. Restoring this type of position asks the user for confirmation first.

The functions in this section return unpredictable values unless otherwise stated.

get-register *reg*   [Function]

> This function returns the contents of the register *reg*, or **nil** if it has no contents.

set-register *reg value*   [Function]

> This function sets the contents of register *reg* to *value*. A register can be set to any value, but the other register functions expect only certain data types. The return value is *value*.

view-register *reg*   [Command]

> This command displays what is contained in register *reg*.

insert-register *reg* **&optional** *beforep*   [Command]

> This command inserts contents of register *reg* into the current buffer.
>
> Normally, this command puts point before the inserted text, and the mark after it. However, if the optional second argument *beforep* is non-**nil**, it puts the mark before and point after.
>
> When called interactively, the command defaults to putting point after text, and a prefix argument inverts this behavior.
>
> If the register contains a rectangle, then the rectangle is inserted with its upper left corner at point. This means that text is inserted in the current line and underneath it on successive lines.
>
> If the register contains something other than saved text (a string) or a rectangle (a list), currently useless things happen. This may be changed in the future.

register-read-with-preview *prompt*   [Function]

> This function reads and returns a register name, prompting with *prompt* and possibly showing a preview of the existing registers and their contents. The preview is shown in a temporary window, after the delay specified by the user option **register-preview-delay**, if its value and **register-alist** are both non-**nil**. The preview is also shown if the user requests help (e.g., by typing the help character). We recommend that all interactive commands which read register names use this function.

31.22 Transposition of Text

This function can be used to transpose stretches of text:

transpose-regions *start1 end1 start2 end2* **&optional** *leave-markers*   [Function]

> This function exchanges two nonoverlapping portions of the buffer. Arguments *start1* and *end1* specify the bounds of one portion and arguments *start2* and *end2* specify the bounds of the other portion.
>
> Normally, **transpose-regions** relocates markers with the transposed text; a marker previously positioned within one of the two transposed portions moves along with that portion, thus remaining between the same two characters in their new position. However, if *leave-markers* is non-**nil**, **transpose-regions** does not do this—it leaves all markers unrelocated.

31.23 Dealing With Compressed Data

When **auto-compression-mode** is enabled, Emacs automatically uncompresses compressed files when you visit them, and automatically recompresses them if you alter and save them. See Section "Compressed Files" in *The GNU Emacs Manual*.

The above feature works by calling an external executable (e.g., **gzip**). Emacs can also be compiled with support for built-in decompression using the zlib library, which is faster than calling an external program.

zlib-available-p   [Function]

> This function returns non-**nil** if built-in zlib decompression is available.

`zlib-decompress-region` *start end*   [Function]

> This function decompresses the region between *start* and *end*, using built-in zlib decompression. The region should contain data that were compressed with gzip or zlib. On success, the function replaces the contents of the region with the decompressed data. On failure, the function leaves the region unchanged and returns `nil`. This function can be called only in unibyte buffers.

31.24 Base 64 Encoding

Base 64 code is used in email to encode a sequence of 8-bit bytes as a longer sequence of ASCII graphic characters. It is defined in Internet RFC[1]2045. This section describes the functions for converting to and from this code.

`base64-encode-region` *beg end* **&optional** *no-line-break*   [Command]

> This function converts the region from *beg* to *end* into base 64 code. It returns the length of the encoded text. An error is signaled if a character in the region is multibyte, i.e., in a multibyte buffer the region must contain only characters from the charsets `ascii`, `eight-bit-control` and `eight-bit-graphic`.
>
> Normally, this function inserts newline characters into the encoded text, to avoid overlong lines. However, if the optional argument *no-line-break* is non-`nil`, these newlines are not added, so the output is just one long line.

`base64-encode-string` *string* **&optional** *no-line-break*   [Function]

> This function converts the string *string* into base 64 code. It returns a string containing the encoded text. As for `base64-encode-region`, an error is signaled if a character in the string is multibyte.
>
> Normally, this function inserts newline characters into the encoded text, to avoid overlong lines. However, if the optional argument *no-line-break* is non-`nil`, these newlines are not added, so the result string is just one long line.

`base64-decode-region` *beg end*   [Command]

> This function converts the region from *beg* to *end* from base 64 code into the corresponding decoded text. It returns the length of the decoded text.
>
> The decoding functions ignore newline characters in the encoded text.

`base64-decode-string` *string*   [Function]

> This function converts the string *string* from base 64 code into the corresponding decoded text. It returns a unibyte string containing the decoded text.
>
> The decoding functions ignore newline characters in the encoded text.

31.25 Checksum/Hash

Emacs has built-in support for computing *cryptographic hashes*. A cryptographic hash, or *checksum*, is a digital fingerprint of a piece of data (e.g., a block of text) which can be used to check that you have an unaltered copy of that data.

---

[1] An RFC, an acronym for *Request for Comments*, is a numbered Internet informational document describing a standard. RFCs are usually written by technical experts acting on their own initiative, and are traditionally written in a pragmatic, experience-driven manner.

Emacs supports several common cryptographic hash algorithms: MD5, SHA-1, SHA-2, SHA-224, SHA-256, SHA-384 and SHA-512. MD5 is the oldest of these algorithms, and is commonly used in *message digests* to check the integrity of messages transmitted over a network. MD5 is not collision resistant (i.e., it is possible to deliberately design different pieces of data which have the same MD5 hash), so you should not used it for anything security-related. A similar theoretical weakness also exists in SHA-1. Therefore, for security-related applications you should use the other hash types, such as SHA-2.

secure-hash *algorithm object* **&optional** *start end binary* [Function]

> This function returns a hash for *object*. The argument *algorithm* is a symbol stating which hash to compute: one of **md5**, **sha1**, **sha224**, **sha256**, **sha384** or **sha512**. The argument *object* should be a buffer or a string.

> The optional arguments *start* and *end* are character positions specifying the portion of *object* to compute the message digest for. If they are **nil** or omitted, the hash is computed for the whole of *object*.

> If the argument *binary* is omitted or **nil**, the function returns the *text form* of the hash, as an ordinary Lisp string. If *binary* is non-**nil**, it returns the hash in *binary form*, as a sequence of bytes stored in a unibyte string.

> This function does not compute the hash directly from the internal representation of *object*'s text (see Section 32.1 [Text Representations], page 761). Instead, it encodes the text using a coding system (see Section 32.10 [Coding Systems], page 773), and computes the hash from that encoded text. If *object* is a buffer, the coding system used is the one which would be chosen by default for writing the text into a file. If *object* is a string, the user's preferred coding system is used (see Section "Recognize Coding" in *GNU Emacs Manual*).

md5 *object* **&optional** *start end coding-system noerror* [Function]

> This function returns an MD5 hash. It is semi-obsolete, since for most purposes it is equivalent to calling **secure-hash** with **md5** as the *algorithm* argument. The *object*, *start* and *end* arguments have the same meanings as in **secure-hash**.

> If *coding-system* is non-**nil**, it specifies a coding system to use to encode the text; if omitted or **nil**, the default coding system is used, like in **secure-hash**.

> Normally, **md5** signals an error if the text can't be encoded using the specified or chosen coding system. However, if *noerror* is non-**nil**, it silently uses **raw-text** coding instead.

31.26 Parsing HTML and XML

When Emacs is compiled with libxml2 support, the following functions are available to parse HTML or XML text into Lisp object trees.

libxml-parse-html-region *start end* **&optional** *base-url* [Function]
discard-comments

> This function parses the text between *start* and *end* as HTML, and returns a list representing the HTML *parse tree*. It attempts to handle real-world HTML by robustly coping with syntax mistakes.

The optional argument *base-url*, if non-`nil`, should be a string specifying the base URL for relative URLs occurring in links.

If the optional argument *discard-comments* is non-`nil`, then the parse tree is created without any comments.

In the parse tree, each HTML node is represented by a list in which the first element is a symbol representing the node name, the second element is an alist of node attributes, and the remaining elements are the subnodes.

The following example demonstrates this. Given this (malformed) HTML document:

```
<html><head></head><body width=101><div class=thing>Foo<div>Yes
```

A call to `libxml-parse-html-region` returns this DOM (document object model):

```
(html nil
 (head nil)
 (body ((width . "101"))
  (div ((class . "thing"))
   "Foo"
   (div nil
    "Yes"))))
```

`shr-insert-document` *dom*   [Function]
> This function renders the parsed HTML in *dom* into the current buffer. The argument *dom* should be a list as generated by `libxml-parse-html-region`. This function is, e.g., used by *The Emacs Web Wowser Manual*.

`libxml-parse-xml-region` *start end* **&optional** *base-url*   [Function]
> *discard-comments*
> This function is the same as `libxml-parse-html-region`, except that it parses the text as XML rather than HTML (so it is stricter about syntax).

31.26.1 Document Object Model

The DOM returned by `libxml-parse-html-region` (and the other XML parsing functions) is a tree structure where each node has a node name (called a *tag*), and optional key/value *attribute* list, and then a list of *child nodes*. The child nodes are either strings or DOM objects.

```
(body ((width . "101"))
 (div ((class . "thing"))
  "Foo"
  (div nil
   "Yes")))
```

`dom-node` *tag* **&optional** *attributes* **&rest** *children*   [Function]
> This function creates a DOM node of type *tag*. If given, *attributes* should be a key/value pair list. If given, *children* should be DOM nodes.

The following functions can be used to work with this structure. Each function takes a DOM node, or a list of nodes. In the latter case, only the first node in the list is used.

Simple accessors:

dom-tag *node*

    Return the *tag* (also called "node name") of the node.

dom-attr *node attribute*

    Return the value of *attribute* in the node. A common usage would be:

```
(dom-attr img 'href)
=> "http://fsf.org/logo.png"
```

dom-children *node*

    Return all the children of the node.

dom-non-text-children *node*

    Return all the non-string children of the node.

dom-attributes *node*

    Return the key/value pair list of attributes of the node.

dom-text *node*

    Return all the textual elements of the node as a concatenated string.

dom-texts *node*

    Return all the textual elements of the node, as well as the textual elements of all the children of the node, recursively, as a concatenated string. This function also takes an optional separator to be inserted between the textual elements.

dom-parent *dom node*

    Return the parent of *node* in *dom*.

The following are functions for altering the DOM.

dom-set-attribute *node attribute value*

    Set the *attribute* of the node to *value*.

dom-append-child *node child*

    Append *child* as the last child of *node*.

dom-add-child-before *node child before*

    Add *child* to *node*'s child list before the *before* node. If *before* is **nil**, make *child* the first child.

dom-set-attributes *node attributes*

    Replace all the attributes of the node with a new key/value list.

The following are functions for searching for elements in the DOM. They all return lists of matching nodes.

dom-by-tag *dom tag*

    Return all nodes in *dom* that are of type *tag*. A typical use would be:

```
(dom-by-tag dom 'td)
=> '((td ...) (td ...) (td ...))
```

dom-by-class *dom match*

    Return all nodes in *dom* that have class names that match *match*, which is a regular expression.

`dom-by-style` *dom* *style*

> Return all nodes in *dom* that have styles that match *match*, which is a regular expression.

`dom-by-id` *dom* *style*

> Return all nodes in *dom* that have IDs that match *match*, which is a regular expression.

`dom-strings` *dom*

> Return all strings in *dom*.

Utility functions:

`dom-pp` *dom* &optional *remove-empty*

> Pretty-print *dom* at point. If *remove-empty*, don't print textual nodes that just contain white-space.

31.27 Atomic Change Groups

In database terminology, an *atomic* change is an indivisible change—it can succeed entirely or it can fail entirely, but it cannot partly succeed. A Lisp program can make a series of changes to one or several buffers as an *atomic change group*, meaning that either the entire series of changes will be installed in their buffers or, in case of an error, none of them will be.

To do this for one buffer, the one already current, simply write a call to `atomic-change-group` around the code that makes the changes, like this:

```
(atomic-change-group
  (insert foo)
  (delete-region x y))
```

If an error (or other nonlocal exit) occurs inside the body of `atomic-change-group`, it unmakes all the changes in that buffer that were during the execution of the body. This kind of change group has no effect on any other buffers—any such changes remain.

If you need something more sophisticated, such as to make changes in various buffers constitute one atomic group, you must directly call lower-level functions that `atomic-change-group` uses.

`prepare-change-group` &optional *buffer*   [Function]

> This function sets up a change group for buffer *buffer*, which defaults to the current buffer. It returns a handle that represents the change group. You must use this handle to activate the change group and subsequently to finish it.

To use the change group, you must *activate* it. You must do this before making any changes in the text of *buffer*.

`activate-change-group` *handle*   [Function]

> This function activates the change group that *handle* designates.

After you activate the change group, any changes you make in that buffer become part of it. Once you have made all the desired changes in the buffer, you must *finish* the change group. There are two ways to do this: you can either accept (and finalize) all the changes, or cancel them all.

accept-change-group *handle* [Function]

This function accepts all the changes in the change group specified by *handle*, making them final.

cancel-change-group *handle* [Function]

This function cancels and undoes all the changes in the change group specified by *handle*.

Your code should use `unwind-protect` to make sure the group is always finished. The call to `activate-change-group` should be inside the `unwind-protect`, in case the user types *C-g* just after it runs. (This is one reason why `prepare-change-group` and `activate-change-group` are separate functions, because normally you would call `prepare-change-group` before the start of that `unwind-protect`.) Once you finish the group, don't use the handle again—in particular, don't try to finish the same group twice.

To make a multibuffer change group, call `prepare-change-group` once for each buffer you want to cover, then use `nconc` to combine the returned values, like this:

```
(nconc (prepare-change-group buffer-1)
       (prepare-change-group buffer-2))
```

You can then activate the multibuffer change group with a single call to `activate-change-group`, and finish it with a single call to `accept-change-group` or `cancel-change-group`.

Nested use of several change groups for the same buffer works as you would expect. Non-nested use of change groups for the same buffer will get Emacs confused, so don't let it happen; the first change group you start for any given buffer should be the last one finished.

31.28 Change Hooks

These hook variables let you arrange to take notice of changes in buffers (or in a particular buffer, if you make them buffer-local). See also Section 31.19.4 [Special Properties], page 738, for how to detect changes to specific parts of the text.

The functions you use in these hooks should save and restore the match data if they do anything that uses regular expressions; otherwise, they will interfere in bizarre ways with the editing operations that call them.

before-change-functions [Variable]

This variable holds a list of functions to call when Emacs is about to modify a buffer. Each function gets two arguments, the beginning and end of the region that is about to change, represented as integers. The buffer that is about to change is always the current buffer when the function is called.

after-change-functions [Variable]

This variable holds a list of functions to call after Emacs modifies a buffer. Each function receives three arguments: the beginning and end of the region just changed, and the length of the text that existed before the change. All three arguments are integers. The buffer that has been changed is always the current buffer when the function is called.

The length of the old text is the difference between the buffer positions before and after that text as it was before the change. As for the changed text, its length is simply the difference between the first two arguments.

Output of messages into the `*Messages*` buffer does not call these functions, and neither do certain internal buffer changes, such as changes in buffers created by Emacs internally for certain jobs, that should not be visible to Lisp programs.

Do *not* expect the before-change hooks and the after-change hooks be called in balanced pairs around each buffer change. Also don't expect the before-change hooks to be called for every chunk of text Emacs is about to delete. These hooks are provided on the assumption that Lisp programs will use either before- or the after-change hooks, but not both, and the boundaries of the region where the changes happen might include more than just the actual changed text, or even lump together several changes done piecemeal.

`combine-after-change-calls` *body...*   [Macro]
> The macro executes *body* normally, but arranges to call the after-change functions just once for a series of several changes—if that seems safe.
>
> If a program makes several text changes in the same area of the buffer, using the macro `combine-after-change-calls` around that part of the program can make it run considerably faster when after-change hooks are in use. When the after-change hooks are ultimately called, the arguments specify a portion of the buffer including all of the changes made within the `combine-after-change-calls` body.
>
> **Warning:** You must not alter the values of `after-change-functions` within the body of a `combine-after-change-calls` form.
>
> **Warning:** if the changes you combine occur in widely scattered parts of the buffer, this will still work, but it is not advisable, because it may lead to inefficient behavior for some change hook functions.

`first-change-hook`   [Variable]
> This variable is a normal hook that is run whenever a buffer is changed that was previously in the unmodified state.

`inhibit-modification-hooks`   [Variable]
> If this variable is non-`nil`, all of the change hooks are disabled; none of them run. This affects all the hook variables described above in this section, as well as the hooks attached to certain special text properties (see Section 31.19.4 [Special Properties], page 738) and overlay properties (see Section 37.9.2 [Overlay Properties], page 907).
>
> Also, this variable is bound to non-`nil` while running those same hook variables, so that by default modifying the buffer from a modification hook does not cause other modification hooks to be run. If you do want modification hooks to be run in a particular piece of code that is itself run from a modification hook, then rebind locally `inhibit-modification-hooks` to `nil`.

32 Non-ASCII Characters

This chapter covers the special issues relating to characters and how they are stored in strings and buffers.

32.1 Text Representations

Emacs buffers and strings support a large repertoire of characters from many different scripts, allowing users to type and display text in almost any known written language.

To support this multitude of characters and scripts, Emacs closely follows the *Unicode Standard*. The Unicode Standard assigns a unique number, called a *codepoint*, to each and every character. The range of codepoints defined by Unicode, or the Unicode *codespace*, is `0..#x10FFFF` (in hexadecimal notation), inclusive. Emacs extends this range with codepoints in the range `#x110000..#x3FFFFF`, which it uses for representing characters that are not unified with Unicode and *raw 8-bit bytes* that cannot be interpreted as characters. Thus, a character codepoint in Emacs is a 22-bit integer.

To conserve memory, Emacs does not hold fixed-length 22-bit numbers that are codepoints of text characters within buffers and strings. Rather, Emacs uses a variable-length internal representation of characters, that stores each character as a sequence of 1 to 5 8-bit bytes, depending on the magnitude of its codepoint[1]. For example, any ASCII character takes up only 1 byte, a Latin-1 character takes up 2 bytes, etc. We call this representation of text *multibyte*.

Outside Emacs, characters can be represented in many different encodings, such as ISO-8859-1, GB-2312, Big-5, etc. Emacs converts between these external encodings and its internal representation, as appropriate, when it reads text into a buffer or a string, or when it writes text to a disk file or passes it to some other process.

Occasionally, Emacs needs to hold and manipulate encoded text or binary non-text data in its buffers or strings. For example, when Emacs visits a file, it first reads the file's text verbatim into a buffer, and only then converts it to the internal representation. Before the conversion, the buffer holds encoded text.

Encoded text is not really text, as far as Emacs is concerned, but rather a sequence of raw 8-bit bytes. We call buffers and strings that hold encoded text *unibyte* buffers and strings, because Emacs treats them as a sequence of individual bytes. Usually, Emacs displays unibyte buffers and strings as octal codes such as `\237`. We recommend that you never use unibyte buffers and strings except for manipulating encoded text or binary non-text data.

In a buffer, the buffer-local value of the variable `enable-multibyte-characters` specifies the representation used. The representation for a string is determined and recorded in the string when the string is constructed.

`enable-multibyte-characters`   [Variable]
> This variable specifies the current buffer's text representation. If it is non-`nil`, the buffer contains multibyte text; otherwise, it contains unibyte encoded text or binary non-text data.

---

[1] This internal representation is based on one of the encodings defined by the Unicode Standard, called *UTF-8*, for representing any Unicode codepoint, but Emacs extends UTF-8 to represent the additional codepoints it uses for raw 8-bit bytes and characters not unified with Unicode.

You cannot set this variable directly; instead, use the function `set-buffer-multibyte` to change a buffer's representation.

`position-bytes` *position*   [Function]

Buffer positions are measured in character units. This function returns the byte-position corresponding to buffer position *position* in the current buffer. This is 1 at the start of the buffer, and counts upward in bytes. If *position* is out of range, the value is `nil`.

`byte-to-position` *byte-position*   [Function]

Return the buffer position, in character units, corresponding to given *byte-position* in the current buffer. If *byte-position* is out of range, the value is `nil`. In a multibyte buffer, an arbitrary value of *byte-position* can be not at character boundary, but inside a multibyte sequence representing a single character; in this case, this function returns the buffer position of the character whose multibyte sequence includes *byte-position*. In other words, the value does not change for all byte positions that belong to the same character.

The following two functions are useful when a Lisp program needs to map buffer positions to byte offsets in a file visited by the buffer.

`bufferpos-to-filepos` *position* **&optional** *quality coding-system*   [Function]

This function is similar to `position-bytes`, but instead of byte position in the current buffer it returns the offset from the beginning of the current buffer's file of the byte that corresponds to the given character *position* in the buffer. The conversion requires to know how the text is encoded in the buffer's file; this is what the *coding-system* argument is for, defaulting to the value of `buffer-file-coding-system`. The optional argument *quality* specifies how accurate the result should be; it should be one of the following:

`exact`   The result must be accurate. The function may need to encode and decode a large part of the buffer, which is expensive and can be slow.

`approximate`
          The value can be an approximation. The function may avoid expensive processing and return an inexact result.

`nil`   If the exact result needs expensive processing, the function will return `nil` rather than an approximation. This is the default if the argument is omitted.

`filepos-to-bufferpos` *byte* **&optional** *quality coding-system*   [Function]

This function returns the buffer position corresponding to a file position specified by *byte*, a zero-base byte offset from the file's beginning. The function performs the conversion opposite to what `bufferpos-to-filepos` does. Optional arguments *quality* and *coding-system* have the same meaning and values as for `bufferpos-to-filepos`.

`multibyte-string-p` *string*   [Function]

Return `t` if *string* is a multibyte string, `nil` otherwise. This function also returns `nil` if *string* is some object other than a string.

string-bytes *string*   [Function]

> This function returns the number of bytes in *string*. If *string* is a multibyte string, this can be greater than (`length string`).

unibyte-string &rest *bytes*   [Function]

> This function concatenates all its argument *bytes* and makes the result a unibyte string.

32.2 Disabling Multibyte Characters

By default, Emacs starts in multibyte mode: it stores the contents of buffers and strings using an internal encoding that represents non-ASCII characters using multi-byte sequences. Multibyte mode allows you to use all the supported languages and scripts without limitations.

Under very special circumstances, you may want to disable multibyte character support, for a specific buffer. When multibyte characters are disabled in a buffer, we call that *unibyte mode*. In unibyte mode, each character in the buffer has a character code ranging from 0 through 255 (0377 octal); 0 through 127 (0177 octal) represent ASCII characters, and 128 (0200 octal) through 255 (0377 octal) represent non-ASCII characters.

To edit a particular file in unibyte representation, visit it using `find-file-literally`. See Section 24.1.1 [Visiting Functions], page 495. You can convert a multibyte buffer to unibyte by saving it to a file, killing the buffer, and visiting the file again with `find-file-literally`. Alternatively, you can use *C-x RET c* (`universal-coding-system-argument`) and specify 'raw-text' as the coding system with which to visit or save a file. See Section "Specifying a Coding System for File Text" in *GNU Emacs Manual*. Unlike `find-file-literally`, finding a file as 'raw-text' doesn't disable format conversion, uncompression, or auto mode selection.

The buffer-local variable `enable-multibyte-characters` is non-`nil` in multibyte buffers, and `nil` in unibyte ones. The mode line also indicates whether a buffer is multibyte or not. With a graphical display, in a multibyte buffer, the portion of the mode line that indicates the character set has a tooltip that (amongst other things) says that the buffer is multibyte. In a unibyte buffer, the character set indicator is absent. Thus, in a unibyte buffer (when using a graphical display) there is normally nothing before the indication of the visited file's end-of-line convention (colon, backslash, etc.), unless you are using an input method.

You can turn off multibyte support in a specific buffer by invoking the command `toggle-enable-multibyte-characters` in that buffer.

32.3 Converting Text Representations

Emacs can convert unibyte text to multibyte; it can also convert multibyte text to unibyte, provided that the multibyte text contains only ASCII and 8-bit raw bytes. In general, these conversions happen when inserting text into a buffer, or when putting text from several strings together in one string. You can also explicitly convert a string's contents to either representation.

Emacs chooses the representation for a string based on the text from which it is constructed. The general rule is to convert unibyte text to multibyte text when combining it with other multibyte text, because the multibyte representation is more general and can hold whatever characters the unibyte text has.

When inserting text into a buffer, Emacs converts the text to the buffer's representation, as specified by `enable-multibyte-characters` in that buffer. In particular, when you insert multibyte text into a unibyte buffer, Emacs converts the text to unibyte, even though this conversion cannot in general preserve all the characters that might be in the multibyte text. The other natural alternative, to convert the buffer contents to multibyte, is not acceptable because the buffer's representation is a choice made by the user that cannot be overridden automatically.

Converting unibyte text to multibyte text leaves ASCII characters unchanged, and converts bytes with codes 128 through 255 to the multibyte representation of raw eight-bit bytes.

Converting multibyte text to unibyte converts all ASCII and eight-bit characters to their single-byte form, but loses information for non-ASCII characters by discarding all but the low 8 bits of each character's codepoint. Converting unibyte text to multibyte and back to unibyte reproduces the original unibyte text.

The next two functions either return the argument *string*, or a newly created string with no text properties.

`string-to-multibyte` *string*   [Function]
> This function returns a multibyte string containing the same sequence of characters as *string*. If *string* is a multibyte string, it is returned unchanged. The function assumes that *string* includes only ASCII characters and raw 8-bit bytes; the latter are converted to their multibyte representation corresponding to the codepoints `#x3FFF80` through `#x3FFFFF`, inclusive (see Section 32.1 [Text Representations], page 761).

`string-to-unibyte` *string*   [Function]
> This function returns a unibyte string containing the same sequence of characters as *string*. It signals an error if *string* contains a non-ASCII character. If *string* is a unibyte string, it is returned unchanged. Use this function for *string* arguments that contain only ASCII and eight-bit characters.

`byte-to-string` *byte*   [Function]
> This function returns a unibyte string containing a single byte of character data, *character*. It signals an error if *character* is not an integer between 0 and 255.

`multibyte-char-to-unibyte` *char*   [Function]
> This converts the multibyte character *char* to a unibyte character, and returns that character. If *char* is neither ASCII nor eight-bit, the function returns −1.

`unibyte-char-to-multibyte` *char*   [Function]
> This convert the unibyte character *char* to a multibyte character, assuming *char* is either ASCII or raw 8-bit byte.

32.4 Selecting a Representation

Sometimes it is useful to examine an existing buffer or string as multibyte when it was unibyte, or vice versa.

`set-buffer-multibyte` *multibyte*   [Function]

Set the representation type of the current buffer. If *multibyte* is non-`nil`, the buffer becomes multibyte. If *multibyte* is `nil`, the buffer becomes unibyte.

This function leaves the buffer contents unchanged when viewed as a sequence of bytes. As a consequence, it can change the contents viewed as characters; for instance, a sequence of three bytes which is treated as one character in multibyte representation will count as three characters in unibyte representation. Eight-bit characters representing raw bytes are an exception. They are represented by one byte in a unibyte buffer, but when the buffer is set to multibyte, they are converted to two-byte sequences, and vice versa.

This function sets `enable-multibyte-characters` to record which representation is in use. It also adjusts various data in the buffer (including overlays, text properties and markers) so that they cover the same text as they did before.

This function signals an error if the buffer is narrowed, since the narrowing might have occurred in the middle of multibyte character sequences.

This function also signals an error if the buffer is an indirect buffer. An indirect buffer always inherits the representation of its base buffer.

`string-as-unibyte` *string*   [Function]

If *string* is already a unibyte string, this function returns *string* itself. Otherwise, it returns a new string with the same bytes as *string*, but treating each byte as a separate character (so that the value may have more characters than *string*); as an exception, each eight-bit character representing a raw byte is converted into a single byte. The newly-created string contains no text properties.

`string-as-multibyte` *string*   [Function]

If *string* is a multibyte string, this function returns *string* itself. Otherwise, it returns a new string with the same bytes as *string*, but treating each multibyte sequence as one character. This means that the value may have fewer characters than *string* has. If a byte sequence in *string* is invalid as a multibyte representation of a single character, each byte in the sequence is treated as a raw 8-bit byte. The newly-created string contains no text properties.

32.5 Character Codes

The unibyte and multibyte text representations use different character codes. The valid character codes for unibyte representation range from 0 to `#xFF` (255)—the values that can fit in one byte. The valid character codes for multibyte representation range from 0 to `#x3FFFFF`. In this code space, values 0 through `#x7F` (127) are for ASCII characters, and values `#x80` (128) through `#x3FFF7F` (4194175) are for non-ASCII characters.

Emacs character codes are a superset of the Unicode standard. Values 0 through `#x10FFFF` (1114111) correspond to Unicode characters of the same codepoint; values `#x110000` (1114112) through `#x3FFF7F` (4194175) represent characters that are not unified with Unicode; and values `#x3FFF80` (4194176) through `#x3FFFFF` (4194303) represent eight-bit raw bytes.

characterp *charcode*   [Function]

This returns **t** if *charcode* is a valid character, and **nil** otherwise.

```
(characterp 65)
    ⇒ t
(characterp 4194303)
    ⇒ t
(characterp 4194304)
    ⇒ nil
```

max-char   [Function]

This function returns the largest value that a valid character codepoint can have.

```
(characterp (max-char))
    ⇒ t
(characterp (1+ (max-char)))
    ⇒ nil
```

get-byte **&optional** *pos string*   [Function]

This function returns the byte at character position *pos* in the current buffer. If the current buffer is unibyte, this is literally the byte at that position. If the buffer is multibyte, byte values of ASCII characters are the same as character codepoints, whereas eight-bit raw bytes are converted to their 8-bit codes. The function signals an error if the character at *pos* is non-ASCII.

The optional argument *string* means to get a byte value from that string instead of the current buffer.

32.6 Character Properties

A *character property* is a named attribute of a character that specifies how the character behaves and how it should be handled during text processing and display. Thus, character properties are an important part of specifying the character's semantics.

On the whole, Emacs follows the Unicode Standard in its implementation of character properties. In particular, Emacs supports the Unicode Character Property Model (`http://www.unicode.org/reports/tr23/`), and the Emacs character property database is derived from the Unicode Character Database (UCD). See the Character Properties chapter of the Unicode Standard (`http://www.unicode.org/versions/Unicode6.2.0/ch04.pdf`), for a detailed description of Unicode character properties and their meaning. This section assumes you are already familiar with that chapter of the Unicode Standard, and want to apply that knowledge to Emacs Lisp programs.

In Emacs, each property has a name, which is a symbol, and a set of possible values, whose types depend on the property; if a character does not have a certain property, the value is **nil**. As a general rule, the names of character properties in Emacs are produced from the corresponding Unicode properties by downcasing them and replacing each '_' character with a dash '-'. For example, `Canonical_Combining_Class` becomes `canonical-combining-class`. However, sometimes we shorten the names to make their use easier.

Some codepoints are left *unassigned* by the UCD—they don't correspond to any character. The Unicode Standard defines default values of properties for such codepoints; they are mentioned below for each property.

Here is the full list of value types for all the character properties that Emacs knows about:

`name`
Corresponds to the `Name` Unicode property. The value is a string consisting of upper-case Latin letters A to Z, digits, spaces, and hyphen '-' characters. For unassigned codepoints, the value is `nil`.

`general-category`
Corresponds to the `General_Category` Unicode property. The value is a symbol whose name is a 2-letter abbreviation of the character's classification. For unassigned codepoints, the value is `Cn`.

`canonical-combining-class`
Corresponds to the `Canonical_Combining_Class` Unicode property. The value is an integer. For unassigned codepoints, the value is zero.

`bidi-class`
Corresponds to the Unicode `Bidi_Class` property. The value is a symbol whose name is the Unicode *directional type* of the character. Emacs uses this property when it reorders bidirectional text for display (see Section 37.26 [Bidirectional Display], page 981). For unassigned codepoints, the value depends on the code blocks to which the codepoint belongs: most unassigned codepoints get the value of `L` (strong L), but some get values of `AL` (Arabic letter) or `R` (strong R).

`decomposition`
Corresponds to the Unicode properties `Decomposition_Type` and `Decomposition_Value`. The value is a list, whose first element may be a symbol representing a compatibility formatting tag, such as `small`[2]; the other elements are characters that give the compatibility decomposition sequence of this character. For characters that don't have decomposition sequences, and for unassigned codepoints, the value is a list with a single member, the character itself.

`decimal-digit-value`
Corresponds to the Unicode `Numeric_Value` property for characters whose `Numeric_Type` is 'Decimal'. The value is an integer, or `nil` if the character has no decimal digit value. For unassigned codepoints, the value is `nil`, which means NaN, or "not a number".

`digit-value`
Corresponds to the Unicode `Numeric_Value` property for characters whose `Numeric_Type` is 'Digit'. The value is an integer. Examples of such characters include compatibility subscript and superscript digits, for which the value is the corresponding number. For characters that don't have any numeric value, and for unassigned codepoints, the value is `nil`, which means NaN.

---

[2] The Unicode specification writes these tag names inside '<..>' brackets, but the tag names in Emacs do not include the brackets; e.g., Unicode specifies '<small>' where Emacs uses 'small'.

numeric-value

Corresponds to the Unicode `Numeric_Value` property for characters whose `Numeric_Type` is 'Numeric'. The value of this property is a number. Examples of characters that have this property include fractions, subscripts, superscripts, Roman numerals, currency numerators, and encircled numbers. For example, the value of this property for the character U+2155 (VULGAR FRACTION ONE FIFTH) is `0.2`. For characters that don't have any numeric value, and for unassigned codepoints, the value is `nil`, which means NaN.

mirrored   Corresponds to the Unicode `Bidi_Mirrored` property. The value of this property is a symbol, either `Y` or `N`. For unassigned codepoints, the value is `N`.

mirroring

Corresponds to the Unicode `Bidi_Mirroring_Glyph` property. The value of this property is a character whose glyph represents the mirror image of the character's glyph, or `nil` if there's no defined mirroring glyph. All the characters whose `mirrored` property is `N` have `nil` as their `mirroring` property; however, some characters whose `mirrored` property is `Y` also have `nil` for `mirroring`, because no appropriate characters exist with mirrored glyphs. Emacs uses this property to display mirror images of characters when appropriate (see Section 37.26 [Bidirectional Display], page 981). For unassigned codepoints, the value is `nil`.

paired-bracket

Corresponds to the Unicode `Bidi_Paired_Bracket` property. The value of this property is the codepoint of a character's *paired bracket*, or `nil` if the character is not a bracket character. This establishes a mapping between characters that are treated as bracket pairs by the Unicode Bidirectional Algorithm; Emacs uses this property when it decides how to reorder for display parentheses, braces, and other similar characters (see Section 37.26 [Bidirectional Display], page 981).

bracket-type

Corresponds to the Unicode `Bidi_Paired_Bracket_Type` property. For characters whose `paired-bracket` property is non-`nil`, the value of this property is a symbol, either `o` (for opening bracket characters) or `c` (for closing bracket characters). For characters whose `paired-bracket` property is `nil`, the value is the symbol `n` (None). Like `paired-bracket`, this property is used for bidirectional display.

old-name   Corresponds to the Unicode `Unicode_1_Name` property. The value is a string. For unassigned codepoints, and characters that have no value for this property, the value is `nil`.

iso-10646-comment

Corresponds to the Unicode `ISO_Comment` property. The value is either a string or `nil`. For unassigned codepoints, the value is `nil`.

uppercase

Corresponds to the Unicode `Simple_Uppercase_Mapping` property. The value of this property is a single character. For unassigned codepoints, the value is `nil`, which means the character itself.

lowercase

> Corresponds to the Unicode `Simple_Lowercase_Mapping` property. The value of this property is a single character. For unassigned codepoints, the value is `nil`, which means the character itself.

titlecase

> Corresponds to the Unicode `Simple_Titlecase_Mapping` property. *Title case* is a special form of a character used when the first character of a word needs to be capitalized. The value of this property is a single character. For unassigned codepoints, the value is `nil`, which means the character itself.

`get-char-code-property` *char propname*   [Function]

> This function returns the value of *char*'s *propname* property.

```
(get-char-code-property ?\s 'general-category)
     ⇒ Zs
(get-char-code-property ?1 'general-category)
     ⇒ Nd
;; U+2084 SUBSCRIPT FOUR
(get-char-code-property ?\u2084 'digit-value)
     ⇒ 4
;; U+2155 VULGAR FRACTION ONE FIFTH
(get-char-code-property ?\u2155 'numeric-value)
     ⇒ 0.2
;; U+2163 ROMAN NUMERAL FOUR
(get-char-code-property ?\u2163 'numeric-value)
     ⇒ 4
(get-char-code-property ?\( 'paired-bracket)
     ⇒ 41   ;; closing parenthesis
(get-char-code-property ?\) 'bracket-type)
     ⇒ c
```

`char-code-property-description` *prop value*   [Function]

> This function returns the description string of property *prop*'s *value*, or `nil` if *value* has no description.

```
(char-code-property-description 'general-category 'Zs)
     ⇒ "Separator, Space"
(char-code-property-description 'general-category 'Nd)
     ⇒ "Number, Decimal Digit"
(char-code-property-description 'numeric-value '1/5)
     ⇒ nil
```

`put-char-code-property` *char propname value*   [Function]

> This function stores *value* as the value of the property *propname* for the character *char*.

`unicode-category-table`   [Variable]

> The value of this variable is a char-table (see Section 6.6 [Char-Tables], page 104) that specifies, for each character, its Unicode `General_Category` property as a symbol.

char-script-table [Variable]

The value of this variable is a char-table that specifies, for each character, a symbol whose name is the script to which the character belongs, according to the Unicode Standard classification of the Unicode code space into script-specific blocks. This char-table has a single extra slot whose value is the list of all script symbols.

char-width-table [Variable]

The value of this variable is a char-table that specifies the width of each character in columns that it will occupy on the screen.

printable-chars [Variable]

The value of this variable is a char-table that specifies, for each character, whether it is printable or not. That is, if evaluating (aref printable-chars char) results in t, the character is printable, and if it results in nil, it is not.

32.7 Character Sets

An Emacs *character set*, or *charset*, is a set of characters in which each character is assigned a numeric code point. (The Unicode Standard calls this a *coded character set*.) Each Emacs charset has a name which is a symbol. A single character can belong to any number of different character sets, but it will generally have a different code point in each charset. Examples of character sets include ascii, iso-8859-1, greek-iso8859-7, and windows-1255. The code point assigned to a character in a charset is usually different from its code point used in Emacs buffers and strings.

Emacs defines several special character sets. The character set unicode includes all the characters whose Emacs code points are in the range 0..#x10FFFF. The character set emacs includes all ASCII and non-ASCII characters. Finally, the eight-bit charset includes the 8-bit raw bytes; Emacs uses it to represent raw bytes encountered in text.

charsetp *object* [Function]

Returns t if *object* is a symbol that names a character set, nil otherwise.

charset-list [Variable]

The value is a list of all defined character set names.

charset-priority-list &optional *highestp* [Function]

This function returns a list of all defined character sets ordered by their priority. If *highestp* is non-nil, the function returns a single character set of the highest priority.

set-charset-priority &rest *charsets* [Function]

This function makes *charsets* the highest priority character sets.

char-charset *character* &optional *restriction* [Function]

This function returns the name of the character set of highest priority that *character* belongs to. ASCII characters are an exception: for them, this function always returns ascii.

If *restriction* is non-nil, it should be a list of charsets to search. Alternatively, it can be a coding system, in which case the returned charset must be supported by that coding system (see Section 32.10 [Coding Systems], page 773).

charset-plist *charset* [Function]

> This function returns the property list of the character set *charset*. Although *charset* is a symbol, this is not the same as the property list of that symbol. Charset properties include important information about the charset, such as its documentation string, short name, etc.

put-charset-property *charset propname value* [Function]

> This function sets the *propname* property of *charset* to the given *value*.

get-charset-property *charset propname* [Function]

> This function returns the value of *charset*s property *propname*.

list-charset-chars *charset* [Command]

> This command displays a list of characters in the character set *charset*.

Emacs can convert between its internal representation of a character and the character's codepoint in a specific charset. The following two functions support these conversions.

decode-char *charset code-point* [Function]

> This function decodes a character that is assigned a *code-point* in *charset*, to the corresponding Emacs character, and returns it. If *charset* doesn't contain a character of that code point, the value is **nil**. If *code-point* doesn't fit in a Lisp integer (see Section 3.1 [Integer Basics], page 34), it can be specified as a cons cell (**high . low**), where *low* are the lower 16 bits of the value and *high* are the high 16 bits.

encode-char *char charset* [Function]

> This function returns the code point assigned to the character *char* in *charset*. If the result does not fit in a Lisp integer, it is returned as a cons cell (**high . low**) that fits the second argument of **decode-char** above. If *charset* doesn't have a codepoint for *char*, the value is **nil**.

The following function comes in handy for applying a certain function to all or part of the characters in a charset:

map-charset-chars *function charset* **&optional** *arg from-code* [Function]
> *to-code*
>
> Call *function* for characters in *charset*. *function* is called with two arguments. The first one is a cons cell (**from . to**), where *from* and *to* indicate a range of characters contained in charset. The second argument passed to *function* is *arg*.
>
> By default, the range of codepoints passed to *function* includes all the characters in *charset*, but optional arguments *from-code* and *to-code* limit that to the range of characters between these two codepoints of *charset*. If either of them is **nil**, it defaults to the first or last codepoint of *charset*, respectively.

32.8 Scanning for Character Sets

Sometimes it is useful to find out which character set a particular character belongs to. One use for this is in determining which coding systems (see Section 32.10 [Coding Systems], page 773) are capable of representing all of the text in question; another is to determine the font(s) for displaying that text.

charset-after &optional *pos*   [Function]

> This function returns the charset of highest priority containing the character at position *pos* in the current buffer. If *pos* is omitted or `nil`, it defaults to the current value of point. If *pos* is out of range, the value is `nil`.

find-charset-region *beg end* **&optional** *translation*   [Function]

> This function returns a list of the character sets of highest priority that contain characters in the current buffer between positions *beg* and *end*.

> The optional argument *translation* specifies a translation table to use for scanning the text (see Section 32.9 [Translation of Characters], page 772). If it is non-`nil`, then each character in the region is translated through this table, and the value returned describes the translated characters instead of the characters actually in the buffer.

find-charset-string *string* **&optional** *translation*   [Function]

> This function returns a list of character sets of highest priority that contain characters in *string*. It is just like `find-charset-region`, except that it applies to the contents of *string* instead of part of the current buffer.

32.9 Translation of Characters

A *translation table* is a char-table (see Section 6.6 [Char-Tables], page 104) that specifies a mapping of characters into characters. These tables are used in encoding and decoding, and for other purposes. Some coding systems specify their own particular translation tables; there are also default translation tables which apply to all other coding systems.

A translation table has two extra slots. The first is either `nil` or a translation table that performs the reverse translation; the second is the maximum number of characters to look up for translating sequences of characters (see the description of `make-translation-table-from-alist` below).

make-translation-table &rest *translations*   [Function]

> This function returns a translation table based on the argument *translations*. Each element of *translations* should be a list of elements of the form (*from* . *to*); this says to translate the character *from* into *to*.

> The arguments and the forms in each argument are processed in order, and if a previous form already translates *to* to some other character, say *to-alt*, *from* is also translated to *to-alt*.

During decoding, the translation table's translations are applied to the characters that result from ordinary decoding. If a coding system has the property `:decode-translation-table`, that specifies the translation table to use, or a list of translation tables to apply in sequence. (This is a property of the coding system, as returned by `coding-system-get`, not a property of the symbol that is the coding system's name. See Section 32.10.1 [Basic Concepts of Coding Systems], page 774.) Finally, if `standard-translation-table-for-decode` is non-`nil`, the resulting characters are translated by that table.

During encoding, the translation table's translations are applied to the characters in the buffer, and the result of translation is actually encoded. If a coding system has property `:encode-translation-table`, that specifies the translation table to use, or a list of translation tables to apply in sequence. In addition, if the variable `standard-translation-table-for-encode` is non-`nil`, it specifies the translation table to use for translating the result.

`standard-translation-table-for-decode`   [Variable]

> This is the default translation table for decoding. If a coding systems specifies its own translation tables, the table that is the value of this variable, if non-`nil`, is applied after them.

`standard-translation-table-for-encode`   [Variable]

> This is the default translation table for encoding. If a coding systems specifies its own translation tables, the table that is the value of this variable, if non-`nil`, is applied after them.

`translation-table-for-input`   [Variable]

> Self-inserting characters are translated through this translation table before they are inserted. Search commands also translate their input through this table, so they can compare more reliably with what's in the buffer.

> This variable automatically becomes buffer-local when set.

`make-translation-table-from-vector` *vec*   [Function]

> This function returns a translation table made from *vec* that is an array of 256 elements to map bytes (values 0 through #xFF) to characters. Elements may be `nil` for untranslated bytes. The returned table has a translation table for reverse mapping in the first extra slot, and the value `1` in the second extra slot.

> This function provides an easy way to make a private coding system that maps each byte to a specific character. You can specify the returned table and the reverse translation table using the properties `:decode-translation-table` and `:encode-translation-table` respectively in the *props* argument to `define-coding-system`.

`make-translation-table-from-alist` *alist*   [Function]

> This function is similar to `make-translation-table` but returns a complex translation table rather than a simple one-to-one mapping. Each element of *alist* is of the form (*from . to*), where *from* and *to* are either characters or vectors specifying a sequence of characters. If *from* is a character, that character is translated to *to* (i.e., to a character or a character sequence). If *from* is a vector of characters, that sequence is translated to *to*. The returned table has a translation table for reverse mapping in the first extra slot, and the maximum length of all the *from* character sequences in the second extra slot.

32.10 Coding Systems

When Emacs reads or writes a file, and when Emacs sends text to a subprocess or receives text from a subprocess, it normally performs character code conversion and end-of-line conversion as specified by a particular *coding system*.

How to define a coding system is an arcane matter, and is not documented here.

32.10.1 Basic Concepts of Coding Systems

Character code conversion involves conversion between the internal representation of characters used inside Emacs and some other encoding. Emacs supports many different encodings, in that it can convert to and from them. For example, it can convert text to or from encodings such as Latin 1, Latin 2, Latin 3, Latin 4, Latin 5, and several variants of ISO 2022. In some cases, Emacs supports several alternative encodings for the same characters; for example, there are three coding systems for the Cyrillic (Russian) alphabet: ISO, Alternativnyj, and KOI8.

Every coding system specifies a particular set of character code conversions, but the coding system `undecided` is special: it leaves the choice unspecified, to be chosen heuristically for each file, based on the file's data. The coding system `prefer-utf-8` is like `undecided`, but it prefers to choose `utf-8` when possible.

In general, a coding system doesn't guarantee roundtrip identity: decoding a byte sequence using coding system, then encoding the resulting text in the same coding system, can produce a different byte sequence. But some coding systems do guarantee that the byte sequence will be the same as what you originally decoded. Here are a few examples:

> iso-8859-1, utf-8, big5, shift_jis, euc-jp

Encoding buffer text and then decoding the result can also fail to reproduce the original text. For instance, if you encode a character with a coding system which does not support that character, the result is unpredictable, and thus decoding it using the same coding system may produce a different text. Currently, Emacs can't report errors that result from encoding unsupported characters.

End of line conversion handles three different conventions used on various systems for representing end of line in files. The Unix convention, used on GNU and Unix systems, is to use the linefeed character (also called newline). The DOS convention, used on MS-Windows and MS-DOS systems, is to use a carriage-return and a linefeed at the end of a line. The Mac convention is to use just carriage-return. (This was the convention used in Classic Mac OS.)

Base coding systems such as `latin-1` leave the end-of-line conversion unspecified, to be chosen based on the data. *Variant coding systems* such as `latin-1-unix`, `latin-1-dos` and `latin-1-mac` specify the end-of-line conversion explicitly as well. Most base coding systems have three corresponding variants whose names are formed by adding '`-unix`', '`-dos`' and '`-mac`'.

The coding system `raw-text` is special in that it prevents character code conversion, and causes the buffer visited with this coding system to be a unibyte buffer. For historical reasons, you can save both unibyte and multibyte text with this coding system. When you use `raw-text` to encode multibyte text, it does perform one character code conversion: it converts eight-bit characters to their single-byte external representation. `raw-text` does not specify the end-of-line conversion, allowing that to be determined as usual by the data, and has the usual three variants which specify the end-of-line conversion.

`no-conversion` (and its alias `binary`) is equivalent to `raw-text-unix`: it specifies no conversion of either character codes or end-of-line.

The coding system `utf-8-emacs` specifies that the data is represented in the internal Emacs encoding (see Section 32.1 [Text Representations], page 761). This is like `raw-text` in that no code conversion happens, but different in that the result is multibyte data. The name `emacs-internal` is an alias for `utf-8-emacs`.

`coding-system-get` *coding-system property*   [Function]
> This function returns the specified property of the coding system *coding-system*. Most coding system properties exist for internal purposes, but one that you might find useful is `:mime-charset`. That property's value is the name used in MIME for the character coding which this coding system can read and write. Examples:
>
> > ```
> > (coding-system-get 'iso-latin-1 :mime-charset)
> >      ⇒ iso-8859-1
> > (coding-system-get 'iso-2022-cn :mime-charset)
> >      ⇒ iso-2022-cn
> > (coding-system-get 'cyrillic-koi8 :mime-charset)
> >      ⇒ koi8-r
> > ```
>
> The value of the `:mime-charset` property is also defined as an alias for the coding system.

`coding-system-aliases` *coding-system*   [Function]
> This function returns the list of aliases of *coding-system*.

32.10.2 Encoding and I/O

The principal purpose of coding systems is for use in reading and writing files. The function `insert-file-contents` uses a coding system to decode the file data, and `write-region` uses one to encode the buffer contents.

You can specify the coding system to use either explicitly (see Section 32.10.6 [Specifying Coding Systems], page 783), or implicitly using a default mechanism (see Section 32.10.5 [Default Coding Systems], page 780). But these methods may not completely specify what to do. For example, they may choose a coding system such as `undecided` which leaves the character code conversion to be determined from the data. In these cases, the I/O operation finishes the job of choosing a coding system. Very often you will want to find out afterwards which coding system was chosen.

`buffer-file-coding-system`   [Variable]
> This buffer-local variable records the coding system used for saving the buffer and for writing part of the buffer with `write-region`. If the text to be written cannot be safely encoded using the coding system specified by this variable, these operations select an alternative encoding by calling the function `select-safe-coding-system` (see Section 32.10.4 [User-Chosen Coding Systems], page 779). If selecting a different encoding requires to ask the user to specify a coding system, `buffer-file-coding-system` is updated to the newly selected coding system.
>
> `buffer-file-coding-system` does *not* affect sending text to a subprocess.

`save-buffer-coding-system`   [Variable]
> This variable specifies the coding system for saving the buffer (by overriding `buffer-file-coding-system`). Note that it is not used for `write-region`.
>
> When a command to save the buffer starts out to use `buffer-file-coding-system` (or `save-buffer-coding-system`), and that coding system cannot handle the actual text in the buffer, the command asks the user to choose another coding system

(by calling `select-safe-coding-system`). After that happens, the command also updates `buffer-file-coding-system` to represent the coding system that the user specified.

`last-coding-system-used`   [Variable]

I/O operations for files and subprocesses set this variable to the coding system name that was used. The explicit encoding and decoding functions (see Section 32.10.7 [Explicit Encoding], page 784) set it too.

Warning: Since receiving subprocess output sets this variable, it can change whenever Emacs waits; therefore, you should copy the value shortly after the function call that stores the value you are interested in.

The variable `selection-coding-system` specifies how to encode selections for the window system. See Section 28.19 [Window System Selections], page 664.

`file-name-coding-system`   [Variable]

The variable `file-name-coding-system` specifies the coding system to use for encoding file names. Emacs encodes file names using that coding system for all file operations. If `file-name-coding-system` is `nil`, Emacs uses a default coding system determined by the selected language environment. In the default language environment, any non-ASCII characters in file names are not encoded specially; they appear in the file system using the internal Emacs representation.

Warning: if you change `file-name-coding-system` (or the language environment) in the middle of an Emacs session, problems can result if you have already visited files whose names were encoded using the earlier coding system and are handled differently under the new coding system. If you try to save one of these buffers under the visited file name, saving may use the wrong file name, or it may get an error. If such a problem happens, use `C-x C-w` to specify a new file name for that buffer.

On Windows 2000 and later, Emacs by default uses Unicode APIs to pass file names to the OS, so the value of `file-name-coding-system` is largely ignored. Lisp applications that need to encode or decode file names on the Lisp level should use `utf-8` coding-system when `system-type` is `windows-nt`; the conversion of UTF-8 encoded file names to the encoding appropriate for communicating with the OS is performed internally by Emacs.

32.10.3 Coding Systems in Lisp

Here are the Lisp facilities for working with coding systems:

`coding-system-list` &optional *base-only*   [Function]

This function returns a list of all coding system names (symbols). If *base-only* is non-`nil`, the value includes only the base coding systems. Otherwise, it includes alias and variant coding systems as well.

`coding-system-p` *object*   [Function]

This function returns `t` if *object* is a coding system name or `nil`.

`check-coding-system` *coding-system*   [Function]

This function checks the validity of *coding-system*. If that is valid, it returns *coding-system*. If *coding-system* is `nil`, the function return `nil`. For any other values, it signals an error whose `error-symbol` is `coding-system-error` (see Section 10.6.3.1 [Signaling Errors], page 148).

`coding-system-eol-type` *coding-system* [Function]

> This function returns the type of end-of-line (a.k.a. *eol*) conversion used by *coding-system*. If *coding-system* specifies a certain eol conversion, the return value is an integer 0, 1, or 2, standing for `unix`, `dos`, and `mac`, respectively. If *coding-system* doesn't specify eol conversion explicitly, the return value is a vector of coding systems, each one with one of the possible eol conversion types, like this:
>
> > `(coding-system-eol-type 'latin-1)`
> > ⇒ `[latin-1-unix latin-1-dos latin-1-mac]`
>
> If this function returns a vector, Emacs will decide, as part of the text encoding or decoding process, what eol conversion to use. For decoding, the end-of-line format of the text is auto-detected, and the eol conversion is set to match it (e.g., DOS-style CRLF format will imply `dos` eol conversion). For encoding, the eol conversion is taken from the appropriate default coding system (e.g., default value of `buffer-file-coding-system` for `buffer-file-coding-system`), or from the default eol conversion appropriate for the underlying platform.

`coding-system-change-eol-conversion` *coding-system eol-type* [Function]

> This function returns a coding system which is like *coding-system* except for its eol conversion, which is specified by `eol-type`. *eol-type* should be `unix`, `dos`, `mac`, or `nil`. If it is `nil`, the returned coding system determines the end-of-line conversion from the data.
>
> *eol-type* may also be 0, 1 or 2, standing for `unix`, `dos` and `mac`, respectively.

`coding-system-change-text-conversion` *eol-coding text-coding* [Function]

> This function returns a coding system which uses the end-of-line conversion of *eol-coding*, and the text conversion of *text-coding*. If *text-coding* is `nil`, it returns `undecided`, or one of its variants according to *eol-coding*.

`find-coding-systems-region` *from to* [Function]

> This function returns a list of coding systems that could be used to encode a text between *from* and *to*. All coding systems in the list can safely encode any multibyte characters in that portion of the text.
>
> If the text contains no multibyte characters, the function returns the list (`undecided`).

`find-coding-systems-string` *string* [Function]

> This function returns a list of coding systems that could be used to encode the text of *string*. All coding systems in the list can safely encode any multibyte characters in *string*. If the text contains no multibyte characters, this returns the list (`undecided`).

`find-coding-systems-for-charsets` *charsets* [Function]

> This function returns a list of coding systems that could be used to encode all the character sets in the list *charsets*.

`check-coding-systems-region` *start end coding-system-list* [Function]

> This function checks whether coding systems in the list `coding-system-list` can encode all the characters in the region between *start* and *end*. If all of the coding systems in the list can encode the specified text, the function returns `nil`. If some coding

systems cannot encode some of the characters, the value is an alist, each element of which has the form (`coding-system1 pos1 pos2 ...`), meaning that *coding-system1* cannot encode characters at buffer positions *pos1*, *pos2*, ...

start may be a string, in which case *end* is ignored and the returned value references string indices instead of buffer positions.

`detect-coding-region` *start end* **&optional** *highest*   [Function]

> This function chooses a plausible coding system for decoding the text from *start* to *end*. This text should be a byte sequence, i.e., unibyte text or multibyte text with only ASCII and eight-bit characters (see Section 32.10.7 [Explicit Encoding], page 784).
>
> Normally this function returns a list of coding systems that could handle decoding the text that was scanned. They are listed in order of decreasing priority. But if *highest* is non-`nil`, then the return value is just one coding system, the one that is highest in priority.
>
> If the region contains only ASCII characters except for such ISO-2022 control characters ISO-2022 as `ESC`, the value is `undecided` or (`undecided`), or a variant specifying end-of-line conversion, if that can be deduced from the text.
>
> If the region contains null bytes, the value is `no-conversion`, even if the region contains text encoded in some coding system.

`detect-coding-string` *string* **&optional** *highest*   [Function]

> This function is like `detect-coding-region` except that it operates on the contents of *string* instead of bytes in the buffer.

`inhibit-null-byte-detection`   [Variable]

> If this variable has a non-`nil` value, null bytes are ignored when detecting the encoding of a region or a string. This allows the encoding of text that contains null bytes to be correctly detected, such as Info files with Index nodes.

`inhibit-iso-escape-detection`   [Variable]

> If this variable has a non-`nil` value, ISO-2022 escape sequences are ignored when detecting the encoding of a region or a string. The result is that no text is ever detected as encoded in some ISO-2022 encoding, and all escape sequences become visible in a buffer. **Warning:** *Use this variable with extreme caution, because many files in the Emacs distribution use ISO-2022 encoding.*

`coding-system-charset-list` *coding-system*   [Function]

> This function returns the list of character sets (see Section 32.7 [Character Sets], page 770) supported by *coding-system*. Some coding systems that support too many character sets to list them all yield special values:
>
> - If *coding-system* supports all Emacs characters, the value is (`emacs`).
> - If *coding-system* supports all Unicode characters, the value is (`unicode`).
> - If *coding-system* supports all ISO-2022 charsets, the value is `iso-2022`.
> - If *coding-system* supports all the characters in the internal coding system used by Emacs version 21 (prior to the implementation of internal Unicode support), the value is `emacs-mule`.

See [Process Information], page 854, in particular the description of the functions `process-coding-system` and `set-process-coding-system`, for how to examine or set the coding systems used for I/O to a subprocess.

32.10.4 User-Chosen Coding Systems

`select-safe-coding-system` *from to* **&optional** [Function]
        default-coding-system accept-default-p file

This function selects a coding system for encoding specified text, asking the user to choose if necessary. Normally the specified text is the text in the current buffer between *from* and *to*. If *from* is a string, the string specifies the text to encode, and *to* is ignored.

If the specified text includes raw bytes (see Section 32.1 [Text Representations], page 761), `select-safe-coding-system` suggests `raw-text` for its encoding.

If *default-coding-system* is non-`nil`, that is the first coding system to try; if that can handle the text, `select-safe-coding-system` returns that coding system. It can also be a list of coding systems; then the function tries each of them one by one. After trying all of them, it next tries the current buffer's value of `buffer-file-coding-system` (if it is not `undecided`), then the default value of `buffer-file-coding-system` and finally the user's most preferred coding system, which the user can set using the command `prefer-coding-system` (see Section "Recognizing Coding Systems" in *The GNU Emacs Manual*).

If one of those coding systems can safely encode all the specified text, `select-safe-coding-system` chooses it and returns it. Otherwise, it asks the user to choose from a list of coding systems which can encode all the text, and returns the user's choice.

default-coding-system can also be a list whose first element is `t` and whose other elements are coding systems. Then, if no coding system in the list can handle the text, `select-safe-coding-system` queries the user immediately, without trying any of the three alternatives described above. This is handy for checking only the coding systems in the list.

The optional argument *accept-default-p* determines whether a coding system selected without user interaction is acceptable. If it's omitted or `nil`, such a silent selection is always acceptable. If it is non-`nil`, it should be a function; `select-safe-coding-system` calls this function with one argument, the base coding system of the selected coding system. If the function returns `nil`, `select-safe-coding-system` rejects the silently selected coding system, and asks the user to select a coding system from a list of possible candidates.

If the variable `select-safe-coding-system-accept-default-p` is non-`nil`, it should be a function taking a single argument. It is used in place of *accept-default-p*, overriding any value supplied for this argument.

As a final step, before returning the chosen coding system, `select-safe-coding-system` checks whether that coding system is consistent with what would be selected if the contents of the region were read from a file. (If not, this could lead to data corruption in a file subsequently re-visited and edited.) Normally, `select-safe-coding-system` uses `buffer-file-name` as the file for this purpose, but if *file* is non-`nil`, it uses that file instead (this can be relevant for `write-region` and similar functions). If it detects an apparent inconsistency, `select-safe-coding-system` queries the user before selecting the coding system.

`select-safe-coding-system-function`   [Variable]

> This variable names the function to be called to request the user to select a proper coding system for encoding text when the default coding system for an output operation cannot safely encode that text. The default value of this variable is `select-safe-coding-system`. Emacs primitives that write text to files, such as `write-region`, or send text to other processes, such as `process-send-region`, normally call the value of this variable, unless `coding-system-for-write` is bound to a non-`nil` value (see Section 32.10.6 [Specifying Coding Systems], page 783).

Here are two functions you can use to let the user specify a coding system, with completion. See Section 19.6 [Completion], page 321.

`read-coding-system` *prompt* **&optional** *default*   [Function]

> This function reads a coding system using the minibuffer, prompting with string *prompt*, and returns the coding system name as a symbol. If the user enters null input, *default* specifies which coding system to return. It should be a symbol or a string.

`read-non-nil-coding-system` *prompt*   [Function]

> This function reads a coding system using the minibuffer, prompting with string *prompt*, and returns the coding system name as a symbol. If the user tries to enter null input, it asks the user to try again. See Section 32.10 [Coding Systems], page 773.

32.10.5 Default Coding Systems

This section describes variables that specify the default coding system for certain files or when running certain subprograms, and the function that I/O operations use to access them.

The idea of these variables is that you set them once and for all to the defaults you want, and then do not change them again. To specify a particular coding system for a particular operation in a Lisp program, don't change these variables; instead, override them using `coding-system-for-read` and `coding-system-for-write` (see Section 32.10.6 [Specifying Coding Systems], page 783).

`auto-coding-regexp-alist`   [User Option]

> This variable is an alist of text patterns and corresponding coding systems. Each element has the form (*regexp* . *coding-system*); a file whose first few kilobytes match *regexp* is decoded with *coding-system* when its contents are read into a buffer. The settings in this alist take priority over `coding:` tags in the files and the contents of `file-coding-system-alist` (see below). The default value is set so that Emacs automatically recognizes mail files in Babyl format and reads them with no code conversions.

`file-coding-system-alist`   [User Option]

> This variable is an alist that specifies the coding systems to use for reading and writing particular files. Each element has the form (*pattern* . *coding*), where *pattern* is a

regular expression that matches certain file names. The element applies to file names that match *pattern*.

The CDR of the element, *coding*, should be either a coding system, a cons cell containing two coding systems, or a function name (a symbol with a function definition). If *coding* is a coding system, that coding system is used for both reading the file and writing it. If *coding* is a cons cell containing two coding systems, its CAR specifies the coding system for decoding, and its CDR specifies the coding system for encoding.

If *coding* is a function name, the function should take one argument, a list of all arguments passed to `find-operation-coding-system`. It must return a coding system or a cons cell containing two coding systems. This value has the same meaning as described above.

If *coding* (or what returned by the above function) is **undecided**, the normal code-detection is performed.

`auto-coding-alist`   [User Option]
> This variable is an alist that specifies the coding systems to use for reading and writing particular files. Its form is like that of `file-coding-system-alist`, but, unlike the latter, this variable takes priority over any `coding:` tags in the file.

`process-coding-system-alist`   [Variable]
> This variable is an alist specifying which coding systems to use for a subprocess, depending on which program is running in the subprocess. It works like `file-coding-system-alist`, except that *pattern* is matched against the program name used to start the subprocess. The coding system or systems specified in this alist are used to initialize the coding systems used for I/O to the subprocess, but you can specify other coding systems later using `set-process-coding-system`.

Warning: Coding systems such as **undecided**, which determine the coding system from the data, do not work entirely reliably with asynchronous subprocess output. This is because Emacs handles asynchronous subprocess output in batches, as it arrives. If the coding system leaves the character code conversion unspecified, or leaves the end-of-line conversion unspecified, Emacs must try to detect the proper conversion from one batch at a time, and this does not always work.

Therefore, with an asynchronous subprocess, if at all possible, use a coding system which determines both the character code conversion and the end of line conversion—that is, one like `latin-1-unix`, rather than **undecided** or `latin-1`.

`network-coding-system-alist`   [Variable]
> This variable is an alist that specifies the coding system to use for network streams. It works much like `file-coding-system-alist`, with the difference that the *pattern* in an element may be either a port number or a regular expression. If it is a regular expression, it is matched against the network service name used to open the network stream.

`default-process-coding-system`   [Variable]
> This variable specifies the coding systems to use for subprocess (and network stream) input and output, when nothing else specifies what to do.

The value should be a cons cell of the form (*input-coding* . *output-coding*). Here *input-coding* applies to input from the subprocess, and *output-coding* applies to output to it.

auto-coding-functions   [User Option]

This variable holds a list of functions that try to determine a coding system for a file based on its undecoded contents.

Each function in this list should be written to look at text in the current buffer, but should not modify it in any way. The buffer will contain undecoded text of parts of the file. Each function should take one argument, *size*, which tells it how many characters to look at, starting from point. If the function succeeds in determining a coding system for the file, it should return that coding system. Otherwise, it should return **nil**.

If a file has a 'coding:' tag, that takes precedence, so these functions won't be called.

find-auto-coding *filename size*   [Function]

This function tries to determine a suitable coding system for *filename*. It examines the buffer visiting the named file, using the variables documented above in sequence, until it finds a match for one of the rules specified by these variables. It then returns a cons cell of the form (*coding* . *source*), where *coding* is the coding system to use and *source* is a symbol, one of **auto-coding-alist**, **auto-coding-regexp-alist**, **:coding**, or **auto-coding-functions**, indicating which one supplied the matching rule. The value **:coding** means the coding system was specified by the **coding:** tag in the file (see Section "coding tag" in *The GNU Emacs Manual*). The order of looking for a matching rule is **auto-coding-alist** first, then **auto-coding-regexp-alist**, then the **coding:** tag, and lastly **auto-coding-functions**. If no matching rule was found, the function returns **nil**.

The second argument *size* is the size of text, in characters, following point. The function examines text only within *size* characters after point. Normally, the buffer should be positioned at the beginning when this function is called, because one of the places for the **coding:** tag is the first one or two lines of the file; in that case, *size* should be the size of the buffer.

set-auto-coding *filename size*   [Function]

This function returns a suitable coding system for file *filename*. It uses **find-auto-coding** to find the coding system. If no coding system could be determined, the function returns **nil**. The meaning of the argument *size* is like in **find-auto-coding**.

find-operation-coding-system *operation* **&rest** *arguments*   [Function]

This function returns the coding system to use (by default) for performing *operation* with *arguments*. The value has this form:

> (*decoding-system* . *encoding-system*)

The first element, *decoding-system*, is the coding system to use for decoding (in case *operation* does decoding), and *encoding-system* is the coding system for encoding (in case *operation* does encoding).

The argument *operation* is a symbol; it should be one of **write-region**, **start-process**, **call-process**, **call-process-region**, **insert-file-contents**, or `open-network-stream`. These are the names of the Emacs I/O primitives that can do character code and eol conversion.

The remaining arguments should be the same arguments that might be given to the corresponding I/O primitive. Depending on the primitive, one of those arguments is selected as the *target*. For example, if *operation* does file I/O, whichever argument specifies the file name is the target. For subprocess primitives, the process name is the target. For `open-network-stream`, the target is the service name or port number.

Depending on *operation*, this function looks up the target in `file-coding-system-alist`, `process-coding-system-alist`, or `network-coding-system-alist`. If the target is found in the alist, `find-operation-coding-system` returns its association in the alist; otherwise it returns `nil`.

If *operation* is `insert-file-contents`, the argument corresponding to the target may be a cons cell of the form (*filename* . *buffer*). In that case, *filename* is a file name to look up in `file-coding-system-alist`, and *buffer* is a buffer that contains the file's contents (not yet decoded). If `file-coding-system-alist` specifies a function to call for this file, and that function needs to examine the file's contents (as it usually does), it should examine the contents of *buffer* instead of reading the file.

32.10.6 Specifying a Coding System for One Operation

You can specify the coding system for a specific operation by binding the variables `coding-system-for-read` and/or `coding-system-for-write`.

`coding-system-for-read`   [Variable]

>   If this variable is non-`nil`, it specifies the coding system to use for reading a file, or for input from a synchronous subprocess.
>
>   It also applies to any asynchronous subprocess or network stream, but in a different way: the value of `coding-system-for-read` when you start the subprocess or open the network stream specifies the input decoding method for that subprocess or network stream. It remains in use for that subprocess or network stream unless and until overridden.
>
>   The right way to use this variable is to bind it with `let` for a specific I/O operation. Its global value is normally `nil`, and you should not globally set it to any other value. Here is an example of the right way to use the variable:
>
> ```
>       ;; Read the file with no character code conversion.
>       (let ((coding-system-for-read 'no-conversion))
>         (insert-file-contents filename))
> ```
>
>   When its value is non-`nil`, this variable takes precedence over all other methods of specifying a coding system to use for input, including `file-coding-system-alist`, `process-coding-system-alist` and `network-coding-system-alist`.

`coding-system-for-write`   [Variable]

>   This works much like `coding-system-for-read`, except that it applies to output rather than input. It affects writing to files, as well as sending output to subprocesses and net connections. It also applies to encoding command-line arguments with which Emacs invokes subprocesses.

When a single operation does both input and output, as do `call-process-region` and `start-process`, both `coding-system-for-read` and `coding-system-for-write` affect it.

`coding-system-require-warning`   [Variable]

> Binding `coding-system-for-write` to a non-`nil` value prevents output primitives from calling the function specified by `select-safe-coding-system-function` (see Section 32.10.4 [User-Chosen Coding Systems], page 779). This is because `C-x RET c` (`universal-coding-system-argument`) works by binding `coding-system-for-write`, and Emacs should obey user selection. If a Lisp program binds `coding-system-for-write` to a value that might not be safe for encoding the text to be written, it can also bind `coding-system-require-warning` to a non-`nil` value, which will force the output primitives to check the encoding by calling the value of `select-safe-coding-system-function` even though `coding-system-for-write` is non-`nil`. Alternatively, call `select-safe-coding-system` explicitly before using the specified encoding.

`inhibit-eol-conversion`   [User Option]

> When this variable is non-`nil`, no end-of-line conversion is done, no matter which coding system is specified. This applies to all the Emacs I/O and subprocess primitives, and to the explicit encoding and decoding functions (see Section 32.10.7 [Explicit Encoding], page 784).

Sometimes, you need to prefer several coding systems for some operation, rather than fix a single one. Emacs lets you specify a priority order for using coding systems. This ordering affects the sorting of lists of coding systems returned by functions such as `find-coding-systems-region` (see Section 32.10.3 [Lisp and Coding Systems], page 776).

`coding-system-priority-list` &optional *highestp*   [Function]

> This function returns the list of coding systems in the order of their current priorities. Optional argument *highestp*, if non-`nil`, means return only the highest priority coding system.

`set-coding-system-priority` &rest *coding-systems*   [Function]

> This function puts *coding-systems* at the beginning of the priority list for coding systems, thus making their priority higher than all the rest.

`with-coding-priority` *coding-systems* &rest *body*...   [Macro]

> This macro execute *body*, like `progn` does (see Section 10.1 [Sequencing], page 135), with *coding-systems* at the front of the priority list for coding systems. *coding-systems* should be a list of coding systems to prefer during execution of *body*.

32.10.7 Explicit Encoding and Decoding

All the operations that transfer text in and out of Emacs have the ability to use a coding system to encode or decode the text. You can also explicitly encode and decode text using the functions in this section.

The result of encoding, and the input to decoding, are not ordinary text. They logically consist of a series of byte values; that is, a series of ASCII and eight-bit characters. In unibyte buffers and strings, these characters have codes in the range 0 through #xFF (255). In a multibyte buffer or string, eight-bit characters have character codes higher than #xFF (see Section 32.1 [Text Representations], page 761), but Emacs transparently converts them to their single-byte values when you encode or decode such text.

The usual way to read a file into a buffer as a sequence of bytes, so you can decode the contents explicitly, is with `insert-file-contents-literally` (see Section 24.3 [Reading from Files], page 501); alternatively, specify a non-`nil` *rawfile* argument when visiting a file with `find-file-noselect`. These methods result in a unibyte buffer.

The usual way to use the byte sequence that results from explicitly encoding text is to copy it to a file or process—for example, to write it with `write-region` (see Section 24.4 [Writing to Files], page 502), and suppress encoding by binding `coding-system-for-write` to `no-conversion`.

Here are the functions to perform explicit encoding or decoding. The encoding functions produce sequences of bytes; the decoding functions are meant to operate on sequences of bytes. All of these functions discard text properties. They also set `last-coding-system-used` to the precise coding system they used.

`encode-coding-region` *start end coding-system* **&optional**   [Command]
   destination

  This command encodes the text from *start* to *end* according to coding system *coding-system*. Normally, the encoded text replaces the original text in the buffer, but the optional argument *destination* can change that. If *destination* is a buffer, the encoded text is inserted in that buffer after point (point does not move); if it is `t`, the command returns the encoded text as a unibyte string without inserting it.

  If encoded text is inserted in some buffer, this command returns the length of the encoded text.

  The result of encoding is logically a sequence of bytes, but the buffer remains multibyte if it was multibyte before, and any 8-bit bytes are converted to their multibyte representation (see Section 32.1 [Text Representations], page 761).

  Do *not* use `undecided` for *coding-system* when encoding text, since that may lead to unexpected results. Instead, use `select-safe-coding-system` (see Section 32.10.4 [User-Chosen Coding Systems], page 779) to suggest a suitable encoding, if there's no obvious pertinent value for *coding-system*.

`encode-coding-string` *string coding-system* **&optional** *nocopy*   [Function]
   buffer

  This function encodes the text in *string* according to coding system *coding-system*. It returns a new string containing the encoded text, except when *nocopy* is non-`nil`, in which case the function may return *string* itself if the encoding operation is trivial. The result of encoding is a unibyte string.

`decode-coding-region` *start end coding-system* **&optional**   [Command]
   destination

  This command decodes the text from *start* to *end* according to coding system *coding-system*. To make explicit decoding useful, the text before decoding ought to be a sequence of byte values, but both multibyte and unibyte buffers are acceptable (in the multibyte case, the raw byte values should be represented as eight-bit characters). Normally, the decoded text replaces the original text in the buffer, but the optional argument *destination* can change that. If *destination* is a buffer, the decoded text is inserted in that buffer after point (point does not move); if it is **t**, the command returns the decoded text as a multibyte string without inserting it.

If decoded text is inserted in some buffer, this command returns the length of the decoded text.

This command puts a **charset** text property on the decoded text. The value of the property states the character set used to decode the original text.

decode-coding-string *string coding-system* **&optional** *nocopy*   [Function]
          buffer
This function decodes the text in *string* according to *coding-system*. It returns a new string containing the decoded text, except when *nocopy* is non-**nil**, in which case the function may return *string* itself if the decoding operation is trivial. To make explicit decoding useful, the contents of *string* ought to be a unibyte string with a sequence of byte values, but a multibyte string is also acceptable (assuming it contains 8-bit bytes in their multibyte form).

If optional argument *buffer* specifies a buffer, the decoded text is inserted in that buffer after point (point does not move). In this case, the return value is the length of the decoded text.

This function puts a **charset** text property on the decoded text. The value of the property states the character set used to decode the original text:

```
(decode-coding-string "Gr\374ss Gott" 'latin-1)
     ⇒ #("Grüss Gott" 0 9 (charset iso-8859-1))
```

decode-coding-inserted-region *from to filename* **&optional** *visit*   [Function]
          beg end replace
This function decodes the text from *from* to *to* as if it were being read from file *filename* using **insert-file-contents** using the rest of the arguments provided.

The normal way to use this function is after reading text from a file without decoding, if you decide you would rather have decoded it. Instead of deleting the text and reading it again, this time with decoding, you can call this function.

32.10.8 Terminal I/O Encoding

Emacs can use coding systems to decode keyboard input and encode terminal output. This is useful for terminals that transmit or display text using a particular encoding, such as Latin-1. Emacs does not set **last-coding-system-used** when encoding or decoding terminal I/O.

keyboard-coding-system **&optional** *terminal*   [Function]
This function returns the coding system used for decoding keyboard input from *terminal*. A value of **no-conversion** means no decoding is done. If *terminal* is omitted or **nil**, it means the selected frame's terminal. See Section 28.2 [Multiple Terminals], page 631.

set-keyboard-coding-system *coding-system* **&optional** *terminal*   [Command]

> This command specifies *coding-system* as the coding system to use for decoding keyboard input from *terminal*. If *coding-system* is `nil`, that means not to decode keyboard input. If *terminal* is a frame, it means that frame's terminal; if it is `nil`, that means the currently selected frame's terminal. See Section 28.2 [Multiple Terminals], page 631.

terminal-coding-system **&optional** *terminal*   [Function]

> This function returns the coding system that is in use for encoding terminal output from *terminal*. A value of `no-conversion` means no encoding is done. If *terminal* is a frame, it means that frame's terminal; if it is `nil`, that means the currently selected frame's terminal.

set-terminal-coding-system *coding-system* **&optional** *terminal*   [Command]

> This command specifies *coding-system* as the coding system to use for encoding terminal output from *terminal*. If *coding-system* is `nil`, that means not to encode terminal output. If *terminal* is a frame, it means that frame's terminal; if it is `nil`, that means the currently selected frame's terminal.

32.11 Input Methods

Input methods provide convenient ways of entering non-ASCII characters from the keyboard. Unlike coding systems, which translate non-ASCII characters to and from encodings meant to be read by programs, input methods provide human-friendly commands. (See Section "Input Methods" in *The GNU Emacs Manual*, for information on how users use input methods to enter text.) How to define input methods is not yet documented in this manual, but here we describe how to use them.

Each input method has a name, which is currently a string; in the future, symbols may also be usable as input method names.

current-input-method   [Variable]

> This variable holds the name of the input method now active in the current buffer. (It automatically becomes local in each buffer when set in any fashion.) It is `nil` if no input method is active in the buffer now.

default-input-method   [User Option]

> This variable holds the default input method for commands that choose an input method. Unlike `current-input-method`, this variable is normally global.

set-input-method *input-method*   [Command]

> This command activates input method *input-method* for the current buffer. It also sets `default-input-method` to *input-method*. If *input-method* is `nil`, this command deactivates any input method for the current buffer.

read-input-method-name *prompt* **&optional** *default inhibit-null*   [Function]

> This function reads an input method name with the minibuffer, prompting with *prompt*. If *default* is non-`nil`, that is returned by default, if the user enters empty input. However, if *inhibit-null* is non-`nil`, empty input signals an error.
>
> The returned value is a string.

`input-method-alist`   [Variable]

This variable defines all the supported input methods. Each element defines one input method, and should have the form:

```
(input-method language-env activate-func
  title description args...)
```

Here *input-method* is the input method name, a string; *language-env* is another string, the name of the language environment this input method is recommended for. (That serves only for documentation purposes.)

activate-func is a function to call to activate this method. The *args*, if any, are passed as arguments to *activate-func*. All told, the arguments to *activate-func* are *input-method* and the *args*.

title is a string to display in the mode line while this method is active. *description* is a string describing this method and what it is good for.

The fundamental interface to input methods is through the variable `input-method-function`. See Section 20.8.2 [Reading One Event], page 375, and Section 20.8.4 [Invoking the Input Method], page 378.

32.12 Locales

In POSIX, locales control which language to use in language-related features. These Emacs variables control how Emacs interacts with these features.

`locale-coding-system`   [Variable]

This variable specifies the coding system to use for decoding system error messages and—on X Window system only—keyboard input, for sending batch output to the standard output and error streams, for encoding the format argument to `format-time-string`, and for decoding the return value of `format-time-string`.

`system-messages-locale`   [Variable]

This variable specifies the locale to use for generating system error messages. Changing the locale can cause messages to come out in a different language or in a different orthography. If the variable is `nil`, the locale is specified by environment variables in the usual POSIX fashion.

`system-time-locale`   [Variable]

This variable specifies the locale to use for formatting time values. Changing the locale can cause messages to appear according to the conventions of a different language. If the variable is `nil`, the locale is specified by environment variables in the usual POSIX fashion.

`locale-info` *item*   [Function]

This function returns locale data *item* for the current POSIX locale, if available. *item* should be one of these symbols:

codeset   Return the character set as a string (locale item `CODESET`).

days   Return a 7-element vector of day names (locale items `DAY_1` through `DAY_7`);

months   Return a 12-element vector of month names (locale items `MON_1` through `MON_12`).

paper   Return a list (*width height*) for the default paper size measured in millimeters (locale items `PAPER_WIDTH` and `PAPER_HEIGHT`).

If the system can't provide the requested information, or if *item* is not one of those symbols, the value is `nil`. All strings in the return value are decoded using `locale-coding-system`. See Section "Locales" in *The GNU Libc Manual*, for more information about locales and locale items.

33 Searching and Matching

GNU Emacs provides two ways to search through a buffer for specified text: exact string searches and regular expression searches. After a regular expression search, you can examine the *match data* to determine which text matched the whole regular expression or various portions of it.

The 'skip-chars...' functions also perform a kind of searching. See Section 29.2.7 [Skipping Characters], page 682. To search for changes in character properties, see Section 31.19.3 [Property Search], page 736.

33.1 Searching for Strings

These are the primitive functions for searching through the text in a buffer. They are meant for use in programs, but you may call them interactively. If you do so, they prompt for the search string; the arguments *limit* and *noerror* are `nil`, and *repeat* is 1. For more details on interactive searching, see Section "Searching and Replacement" in *The GNU Emacs Manual*.

These search functions convert the search string to multibyte if the buffer is multibyte; they convert the search string to unibyte if the buffer is unibyte. See Section 32.1 [Text Representations], page 761.

`search-forward` *string* &optional *limit noerror count*   [Command]
> This function searches forward from point for an exact match for *string*. If successful, it sets point to the end of the occurrence found, and returns the new value of point. If no match is found, the value and side effects depend on *noerror* (see below).
>
> In the following example, point is initially at the beginning of the line. Then `(search-forward "fox")` moves point after the last letter of 'fox':
>
> ```
>        ---------- Buffer: foo ----------
>        *The quick brown fox jumped over the lazy dog.
>        ---------- Buffer: foo ----------
>
>        (search-forward "fox")
>             ⇒ 20
>
>        ---------- Buffer: foo ----------
>        The quick brown fox* jumped over the lazy dog.
>        ---------- Buffer: foo ----------
> ```
>
> The argument *limit* specifies the bound to the search, and should be a position in the current buffer. No match extending after that position is accepted. If *limit* is omitted or `nil`, it defaults to the end of the accessible portion of the buffer.
>
> What happens when the search fails depends on the value of *noerror*. If *noerror* is `nil`, a `search-failed` error is signaled. If *noerror* is `t`, `search-forward` returns `nil` and does nothing. If *noerror* is neither `nil` nor `t`, then `search-forward` moves point to the upper bound and returns `nil`.
>
> The argument *noerror* only affects valid searches which fail to find a match. Invalid arguments cause errors regardless of *noerror*.

If *count* is a positive number *n*, the search is done *n* times; each successive search starts at the end of the previous match. If all these successive searches succeed, the function call succeeds, moving point and returning its new value. Otherwise the function call fails, with results depending on the value of *noerror*, as described above. If *count* is a negative number *-n*, the search is done *n* times in the opposite (backward) direction.

search-backward *string* **&optional** *limit noerror count*   [Command]
> This function searches backward from point for *string*. It is like `search-forward`, except that it searches backwards rather than forwards. Backward searches leave point at the beginning of the match.

word-search-forward *string* **&optional** *limit noerror count*   [Command]
> This function searches forward from point for a word match for *string*. If it finds a match, it sets point to the end of the match found, and returns the new value of point.
>
> Word matching regards *string* as a sequence of words, disregarding punctuation that separates them. It searches the buffer for the same sequence of words. Each word must be distinct in the buffer (searching for the word 'ball' does not match the word 'balls'), but the details of punctuation and spacing are ignored (searching for 'ball boy' does match 'ball. Boy!').
>
> In this example, point is initially at the beginning of the buffer; the search leaves it between the 'y' and the '!'.
>
> ```
> ---------- Buffer: foo ----------
> *He said "Please!  Find
> the ball boy!"
> ---------- Buffer: foo ----------
>
>
> (word-search-forward "Please find the ball, boy.")
>      ⇒ 39
>
>
> ---------- Buffer: foo ----------
> He said "Please!  Find
> the ball boy*!"
> ---------- Buffer: foo ----------
> ```
>
> If *limit* is non-`nil`, it must be a position in the current buffer; it specifies the upper bound to the search. The match found must not extend after that position.
>
> If *noerror* is `nil`, then `word-search-forward` signals an error if the search fails. If *noerror* is `t`, then it returns `nil` instead of signaling an error. If *noerror* is neither `nil` nor `t`, it moves point to *limit* (or the end of the accessible portion of the buffer) and returns `nil`.
>
> If *count* is a positive number, it specifies how many successive occurrences to search for. Point is positioned at the end of the last match. If *count* is a negative number, the search is backward and point is positioned at the beginning of the last match.
>
> Internally, `word-search-forward` and related functions use the function `word-search-regexp` to convert *string* to a regular expression that ignores punctuation.

word-search-forward-lax *string* **&optional** *limit noerror count*   [Command]

> This command is identical to `word-search-forward`, except that the beginning or the end of *string* need not match a word boundary, unless *string* begins or ends in whitespace. For instance, searching for 'ball boy' matches 'ball boyee', but does not match 'balls boy'.

word-search-backward *string* **&optional** *limit noerror count*   [Command]

> This function searches backward from point for a word match to *string*. This function is just like `word-search-forward` except that it searches backward and normally leaves point at the beginning of the match.

word-search-backward-lax *string* **&optional** *limit noerror count*   [Command]

> This command is identical to `word-search-backward`, except that the beginning or the end of *string* need not match a word boundary, unless *string* begins or ends in whitespace.

33.2 Searching and Case

By default, searches in Emacs ignore the case of the text they are searching through; if you specify searching for 'FOO', then 'Foo' or 'foo' is also considered a match. This applies to regular expressions, too; thus, '[aB]' would match 'a' or 'A' or 'b' or 'B'.

If you do not want this feature, set the variable `case-fold-search` to `nil`. Then all letters must match exactly, including case. This is a buffer-local variable; altering the variable affects only the current buffer. (See Section 11.10.1 [Intro to Buffer-Local], page 171.) Alternatively, you may change the default value. In Lisp code, you will more typically use `let` to bind `case-fold-search` to the desired value.

Note that the user-level incremental search feature handles case distinctions differently. When the search string contains only lower case letters, the search ignores case, but when the search string contains one or more upper case letters, the search becomes case-sensitive. But this has nothing to do with the searching functions used in Lisp code. See Section "Incremental Search" in *The GNU Emacs Manual*.

case-fold-search   [User Option]

> This buffer-local variable determines whether searches should ignore case. If the variable is `nil` they do not ignore case; otherwise (and by default) they do ignore case.

case-replace   [User Option]

> This variable determines whether the higher-level replacement functions should preserve case. If the variable is `nil`, that means to use the replacement text verbatim. A non-`nil` value means to convert the case of the replacement text according to the text being replaced.

> This variable is used by passing it as an argument to the function `replace-match`. See Section 33.6.1 [Replacing Match], page 807.

33.3 Regular Expressions

A *regular expression*, or *regexp* for short, is a pattern that denotes a (possibly infinite) set of strings. Searching for matches for a regexp is a very powerful operation. This section explains how to write regexps; the following section says how to search for them.

For interactive development of regular expressions, you can use the *M-x re-builder* command. It provides a convenient interface for creating regular expressions, by giving immediate visual feedback in a separate buffer. As you edit the regexp, all its matches in the target buffer are highlighted. Each parenthesized sub-expression of the regexp is shown in a distinct face, which makes it easier to verify even very complex regexps.

33.3.1 Syntax of Regular Expressions

Regular expressions have a syntax in which a few characters are special constructs and the rest are *ordinary*. An ordinary character is a simple regular expression that matches that character and nothing else. The special characters are '.', '*', '+', '?', '[', '^', '$', and '\'; no new special characters will be defined in the future. The character ']' is special if it ends a character alternative (see later). The character '-' is special inside a character alternative. A '[:' and balancing ':]' enclose a character class inside a character alternative. Any other character appearing in a regular expression is ordinary, unless a '\' precedes it.

For example, 'f' is not a special character, so it is ordinary, and therefore 'f' is a regular expression that matches the string 'f' and no other string. (It does *not* match the string 'fg', but it does match a *part* of that string.) Likewise, 'o' is a regular expression that matches only 'o'.

Any two regular expressions *a* and *b* can be concatenated. The result is a regular expression that matches a string if *a* matches some amount of the beginning of that string and *b* matches the rest of the string.

As a simple example, we can concatenate the regular expressions 'f' and 'o' to get the regular expression 'fo', which matches only the string 'fo'. Still trivial. To do something more powerful, you need to use one of the special regular expression constructs.

33.3.1.1 Special Characters in Regular Expressions

Here is a list of the characters that are special in a regular expression.

'.' (Period)
> is a special character that matches any single character except a newline. Using concatenation, we can make regular expressions like 'a.b', which matches any three-character string that begins with 'a' and ends with 'b'.

'*'
> is not a construct by itself; it is a postfix operator that means to match the preceding regular expression repetitively as many times as possible. Thus, 'o*' matches any number of 'o's (including no 'o's).
>
> '*' always applies to the *smallest* possible preceding expression. Thus, 'fo*' has a repeating 'o', not a repeating 'fo'. It matches 'f', 'fo', 'foo', and so on.
>
> The matcher processes a '*' construct by matching, immediately, as many repetitions as can be found. Then it continues with the rest of the pattern. If that fails, backtracking occurs, discarding some of the matches of the '*'-modified construct in the hope that that will make it possible to match the rest of the

pattern. For example, in matching 'ca*ar' against the string 'caaar', the 'a*' first tries to match all three 'a's; but the rest of the pattern is 'ar' and there is only 'r' left to match, so this try fails. The next alternative is for 'a*' to match only two 'a's. With this choice, the rest of the regexp matches successfully.

Warning: Nested repetition operators can run for an indefinitely long time, if they lead to ambiguous matching. For example, trying to match the regular expression '\(x+y*\)*a' against the string 'xxxxxxxxxxxxxxxxxxxxxxxxxxxxxxxxxxxxxxz' could take hours before it ultimately fails. Emacs must try each way of grouping the 'x's before concluding that none of them can work. Even worse, '\(x*\)*' can match the null string in infinitely many ways, so it causes an infinite loop. To avoid these problems, check nested repetitions carefully, to make sure that they do not cause combinatorial explosions in backtracking.

'+'   is a postfix operator, similar to '*' except that it must match the preceding expression at least once. So, for example, 'ca+r' matches the strings 'car' and 'caaar' but not the string 'cr', whereas 'ca*r' matches all three strings.

'?'   is a postfix operator, similar to '*' except that it must match the preceding expression either once or not at all. For example, 'ca?r' matches 'car' or 'cr'; nothing else.

'*?', '+?', '??'

These are *non-greedy* variants of the operators '*', '+' and '?'. Where those operators match the largest possible substring (consistent with matching the entire containing expression), the non-greedy variants match the smallest possible substring (consistent with matching the entire containing expression).

For example, the regular expression 'c[ad]*a' when applied to the string 'cdaaada' matches the whole string; but the regular expression 'c[ad]*?a', applied to that same string, matches just 'cda'. (The smallest possible match here for '[ad]*?' that permits the whole expression to match is 'd'.)

'[...]'   is a *character alternative*, which begins with '[' and is terminated by ']'. In the simplest case, the characters between the two brackets are what this character alternative can match.

Thus, '[ad]' matches either one 'a' or one 'd', and '[ad]*' matches any string composed of just 'a's and 'd's (including the empty string). It follows that 'c[ad]*r' matches 'cr', 'car', 'cdr', 'caddaar', etc.

You can also include character ranges in a character alternative, by writing the starting and ending characters with a '-' between them. Thus, '[a-z]' matches any lower-case ASCII letter. Ranges may be intermixed freely with individual characters, as in '[a-z$%.]', which matches any lower case ASCII letter or '$', '%' or period.

If `case-fold-search` is non-`nil`, '[a-z]' also matches upper-case letters. Note that a range like '[a-z]' is not affected by the locale's collation sequence, it always represents a sequence in ASCII order.

Note also that the usual regexp special characters are not special inside a character alternative. A completely different set of characters is special inside character alternatives: '`]`', '`-`' and '`^`'.

To include a '`]`' in a character alternative, you must make it the first character. For example, '`[]a]`' matches '`]`' or '`a`'. To include a '`-`', write '`-`' as the first or last character of the character alternative, or put it after a range. Thus, '`[]-]`' matches both '`]`' and '`-`'. (As explained below, you cannot use '`\]`' to include a '`]`' inside a character alternative, since '`\`' is not special there.)

To include '`^`' in a character alternative, put it anywhere but at the beginning.

If a range starts with a unibyte character c and ends with a multibyte character $c2$, the range is divided into two parts: one spans the unibyte characters '`c..?\377`', the other the multibyte characters '`c1..c2`', where $c1$ is the first character of the charset to which $c2$ belongs.

A character alternative can also specify named character classes (see Section 33.3.1.2 [Char Classes], page 796). This is a POSIX feature. For example, '`[[:ascii:]]`' matches any ASCII character. Using a character class is equivalent to mentioning each of the characters in that class; but the latter is not feasible in practice, since some classes include thousands of different characters.

'`[^ ... ]`'   '`[^`' begins a *complemented character alternative*. This matches any character except the ones specified. Thus, '`[^a-z0-9A-Z]`' matches all characters *except* letters and digits.

'`^`' is not special in a character alternative unless it is the first character. The character following the '`^`' is treated as if it were first (in other words, '`-`' and '`]`' are not special there).

A complemented character alternative can match a newline, unless newline is mentioned as one of the characters not to match. This is in contrast to the handling of regexps in programs such as `grep`.

You can specify named character classes, just like in character alternatives. For instance, '`[^[:ascii:]]`' matches any non-ASCII character. See Section 33.3.1.2 [Char Classes], page 796.

'`^`'   When matching a buffer, '`^`' matches the empty string, but only at the beginning of a line in the text being matched (or the beginning of the accessible portion of the buffer). Otherwise it fails to match anything. Thus, '`^foo`' matches a '`foo`' that occurs at the beginning of a line.

When matching a string instead of a buffer, '`^`' matches at the beginning of the string or after a newline character.

For historical compatibility reasons, '`^`' can be used only at the beginning of the regular expression, or after '`\(`', '`\(?:`' or '`\|`'.

'`$`'   is similar to '`^`' but matches only at the end of a line (or the end of the accessible portion of the buffer). Thus, '`x+$`' matches a string of one '`x`' or more at the end of a line.

When matching a string instead of a buffer, '`$`' matches at the end of the string or before a newline character.

For historical compatibility reasons, '$' can be used only at the end of the regular expression, or before '\)' or '\|'.

'\' has two functions: it quotes the special characters (including '\'), and it introduces additional special constructs.

Because '\' quotes special characters, '\$' is a regular expression that matches only '$', and '\[' is a regular expression that matches only '[', and so on.

Note that '\' also has special meaning in the read syntax of Lisp strings (see Section 2.3.8 [String Type], page 18), and must be quoted with '\'. For example, the regular expression that matches the '\' character is '\\'. To write a Lisp string that contains the characters '\\', Lisp syntax requires you to quote each '\' with another '\'. Therefore, the read syntax for a regular expression matching '\' is "\\\\".

Please note: For historical compatibility, special characters are treated as ordinary ones if they are in contexts where their special meanings make no sense. For example, '*foo' treats '*' as ordinary since there is no preceding expression on which the '*' can act. It is poor practice to depend on this behavior; quote the special character anyway, regardless of where it appears.

As a '\' is not special inside a character alternative, it can never remove the special meaning of '-' or ']'. So you should not quote these characters when they have no special meaning either. This would not clarify anything, since backslashes can legitimately precede these characters where they *have* special meaning, as in '[^\]' ("[^\\]" for Lisp string syntax), which matches any single character except a backslash.

In practice, most ']' that occur in regular expressions close a character alternative and hence are special. However, occasionally a regular expression may try to match a complex pattern of literal '[' and ']'. In such situations, it sometimes may be necessary to carefully parse the regexp from the start to determine which square brackets enclose a character alternative. For example, '[^][]]' consists of the complemented character alternative '[^][]' (which matches any single character that is not a square bracket), followed by a literal ']'.

The exact rules are that at the beginning of a regexp, '[' is special and ']' not. This lasts until the first unquoted '[', after which we are in a character alternative; '[' is no longer special (except when it starts a character class) but ']' is special, unless it immediately follows the special '[' or that '[' followed by a '^'. This lasts until the next special ']' that does not end a character class. This ends the character alternative and restores the ordinary syntax of regular expressions; an unquoted '[' is special again and a ']' not.

33.3.1.2 Character Classes

Here is a table of the classes you can use in a character alternative, and what they mean:

'[:ascii:]'

This matches any ASCII character (codes 0–127).

'[:alnum:]'

This matches any letter or digit. For multibyte characters, it matches characters whose Unicode 'general-category' property (see Section 32.6 [Character Properties], page 766) indicates they are alphabetic or decimal number characters.

'[:alpha:]'
> This matches any letter. For multibyte characters, it matches characters whose Unicode 'general-category' property (see Section 32.6 [Character Properties], page 766) indicates they are alphabetic characters.

'[:blank:]'
> This matches space and tab only.

'[:cntrl:]'
> This matches any ASCII control character.

'[:digit:]'
> This matches '0' through '9'. Thus, '[-+[:digit:]]' matches any digit, as well as '+' and '-'.

'[:graph:]'
> This matches graphic characters—everything except whitespace, ASCII and non-ASCII control characters, surrogates, and codepoints unassigned by Unicode, as indicated by the Unicode 'general-category' property (see Section 32.6 [Character Properties], page 766).

'[:lower:]'
> This matches any lower-case letter, as determined by the current case table (see Section 4.9 [Case Tables], page 64). If case-fold-search is non-nil, this also matches any upper-case letter.

'[:multibyte:]'
> This matches any multibyte character (see Section 32.1 [Text Representations], page 761).

'[:nonascii:]'
> This matches any non-ASCII character.

'[:print:]'
> This matches any printing character—either whitespace, or a graphic character matched by '[:graph:]'.

'[:punct:]'
> This matches any punctuation character. (At present, for multibyte characters, it matches anything that has non-word syntax.)

'[:space:]'
> This matches any character that has whitespace syntax (see Section 34.2.1 [Syntax Class Table], page 817).

'[:unibyte:]'
> This matches any unibyte character (see Section 32.1 [Text Representations], page 761).

'[:upper:]'
> This matches any upper-case letter, as determined by the current case table (see Section 4.9 [Case Tables], page 64). If case-fold-search is non-nil, this also matches any lower-case letter.

'[:word:]'
> This matches any character that has word syntax (see Section 34.2.1 [Syntax Class Table], page 817).

'[:xdigit:]'
> This matches the hexadecimal digits: '0' through '9', 'a' through 'f' and 'A' through 'F'.

33.3.1.3 Backslash Constructs in Regular Expressions

For the most part, '\' followed by any character matches only that character. However, there are several exceptions: certain sequences starting with '\' that have special meanings. Here is a table of the special '\' constructs.

'\|'
> specifies an alternative. Two regular expressions a and b with '\|' in between form an expression that matches anything that either a or b matches.
>
> Thus, 'foo\|bar' matches either 'foo' or 'bar' but no other string.
>
> '\|' applies to the largest possible surrounding expressions. Only a surrounding '\(... \)' grouping can limit the grouping power of '\|'.
>
> If you need full backtracking capability to handle multiple uses of '\|', use the POSIX regular expression functions (see Section 33.5 [POSIX Regexps], page 806).

'\{m\}'
> is a postfix operator that repeats the previous pattern exactly m times. Thus, 'x\{5\}' matches the string 'xxxxx' and nothing else. 'c[ad]\{3\}r' matches string such as 'caaar', 'cdddr', 'cadar', and so on.

'\{m,n\}'
> is a more general postfix operator that specifies repetition with a minimum of m repeats and a maximum of n repeats. If m is omitted, the minimum is 0; if n is omitted, there is no maximum.
>
> For example, 'c[ad]\{1,2\}r' matches the strings 'car', 'cdr', 'caar', 'cadr', 'cdar', and 'cddr', and nothing else.
> '\{0,1\}' or '\{,1\}' is equivalent to '?'.
> '\{0,\}' or '\{,\}' is equivalent to '*'.
> '\{1,\}' is equivalent to '+'.

'\(... \)'
> is a grouping construct that serves three purposes:
>
> 1. To enclose a set of '\|' alternatives for other operations. Thus, the regular expression '\(foo\|bar\)x' matches either 'foox' or 'barx'.
>
> 2. To enclose a complicated expression for the postfix operators '*', '+' and '?' to operate on. Thus, 'ba\(na\)*' matches 'ba', 'bana', 'banana', 'bananana', etc., with any number (zero or more) of 'na' strings.
>
> 3. To record a matched substring for future reference with '\digit' (see below).
>
> This last application is not a consequence of the idea of a parenthetical grouping; it is a separate feature that was assigned as a second meaning to the same '\(... \)' construct because, in practice, there was usually no conflict between

the two meanings. But occasionally there is a conflict, and that led to the introduction of shy groups.

'\(?: ... \)'

> is the *shy group* construct. A shy group serves the first two purposes of an ordinary group (controlling the nesting of other operators), but it does not get a number, so you cannot refer back to its value with '*digit*'. Shy groups are particularly useful for mechanically-constructed regular expressions, because they can be added automatically without altering the numbering of ordinary, non-shy groups.
>
> Shy groups are also called *non-capturing* or *unnumbered groups*.

'\(?*num*: ... \)'

> is the *explicitly numbered group* construct. Normal groups get their number implicitly, based on their position, which can be inconvenient. This construct allows you to force a particular group number. There is no particular restriction on the numbering, e.g., you can have several groups with the same number in which case the last one to match (i.e., the rightmost match) will win. Implicitly numbered groups always get the smallest integer larger than the one of any previous group.

'*digit*'

matches the same text that matched the *digit*th occurrence of a grouping ('\(... \)') construct.

> In other words, after the end of a group, the matcher remembers the beginning and end of the text matched by that group. Later on in the regular expression you can use '\' followed by *digit* to match that same text, whatever it may have been.
>
> The strings matching the first nine grouping constructs appearing in the entire regular expression passed to a search or matching function are assigned numbers 1 through 9 in the order that the open parentheses appear in the regular expression. So you can use '\1' through '\9' to refer to the text matched by the corresponding grouping constructs.
>
> For example, '\(.*\)\1' matches any newline-free string that is composed of two identical halves. The '\(.*\)' matches the first half, which may be anything, but the '\1' that follows must match the same exact text.
>
> If a '\(... \)' construct matches more than once (which can happen, for instance, if it is followed by '*'), only the last match is recorded.
>
> If a particular grouping construct in the regular expression was never matched—for instance, if it appears inside of an alternative that wasn't used, or inside of a repetition that repeated zero times—then the corresponding '*digit*' construct never matches anything. To use an artificial example, '\(foo\(b*\)\|lose\)\2' cannot match 'lose': the second alternative inside the larger group matches it, but then '\2' is undefined and can't match anything. But it can match 'foobb', because the first alternative matches 'foob' and '\2' matches 'b'.

'\w'

matches any word-constituent character. The editor syntax table determines which characters these are. See Chapter 34 [Syntax Tables], page 816.

'\W'   matches any character that is not a word constituent.

'\s*code*' matches any character whose syntax is *code*. Here *code* is a character that
            represents a syntax code: thus, 'w' for word constituent, '-' for whitespace, '('
            for open parenthesis, etc. To represent whitespace syntax, use either '-' or a
            space character. See Section 34.2.1 [Syntax Class Table], page 817, for a list of
            syntax codes and the characters that stand for them.

'\S*code*' matches any character whose syntax is not *code*.

'\c*c*'   matches any character whose category is *c*. Here *c* is a character that repre-
            sents a category: thus, 'c' for Chinese characters or 'g' for Greek characters in
            the standard category table. You can see the list of all the currently defined
            categories with *M-x describe-categories RET*. You can also define your own
            categories in addition to the standard ones using the **define-category** function
            (see Section 34.8 [Categories], page 829).

'\C*c*'   matches any character whose category is not *c*.

The following regular expression constructs match the empty string—that is, they don't
use up any characters—but whether they match depends on the context. For all, the
beginning and end of the accessible portion of the buffer are treated as if they were the
actual beginning and end of the buffer.

'\`'   matches the empty string, but only at the beginning of the buffer or string
            being matched against.

'\''   matches the empty string, but only at the end of the buffer or string being
            matched against.

'\='   matches the empty string, but only at point. (This construct is not defined
            when matching against a string.)

'\b'   matches the empty string, but only at the beginning or end of a word. Thus,
            '\bfoo\b' matches any occurrence of 'foo' as a separate word. '\bballs?\b'
            matches 'ball' or 'balls' as a separate word.

            '\b' matches at the beginning or end of the buffer (or string) regardless of what
            text appears next to it.

'\B'   matches the empty string, but *not* at the beginning or end of a word, nor at
            the beginning or end of the buffer (or string).

'\<'   matches the empty string, but only at the beginning of a word. '\<' matches
            at the beginning of the buffer (or string) only if a word-constituent character
            follows.

'\>'   matches the empty string, but only at the end of a word. '\>' matches at the
            end of the buffer (or string) only if the contents end with a word-constituent
            character.

'_<'   matches the empty string, but only at the beginning of a symbol. A symbol is a
            sequence of one or more word or symbol constituent characters. '_<' matches
            at the beginning of the buffer (or string) only if a symbol-constituent character
            follows.

'_>'   matches the empty string, but only at the end of a symbol. '_>' matches at the end of the buffer (or string) only if the contents end with a symbol-constituent character.

Not every string is a valid regular expression. For example, a string that ends inside a character alternative without a terminating ']' is invalid, and so is a string that ends with a single '\'. If an invalid regular expression is passed to any of the search functions, an `invalid-regexp` error is signaled.

33.3.2 Complex Regexp Example

Here is a complicated regexp which was formerly used by Emacs to recognize the end of a sentence together with any whitespace that follows. (Nowadays Emacs uses a similar but more complex default regexp constructed by the function **sentence-end**. See Section 33.8 [Standard Regexps], page 814.)

Below, we show first the regexp as a string in Lisp syntax (to distinguish spaces from tab characters), and then the result of evaluating it. The string constant begins and ends with a double-quote. '\"' stands for a double-quote as part of the string, '\\' for a backslash as part of the string, '\t' for a tab and '\n' for a newline.

```
"[.?!][]\"')}]*\\($\\| $\\|\t\\|  \\)[ \t\n]*"
    ⇒ "[.?!][]\"')}]*\\($\\| $\\|  \\|  \\)[
]*"
```

In the output, tab and newline appear as themselves.

This regular expression contains four parts in succession and can be deciphered as follows:

[.?!]   The first part of the pattern is a character alternative that matches any one of three characters: period, question mark, and exclamation mark. The match must begin with one of these three characters. (This is one point where the new default regexp used by Emacs differs from the old. The new value also allows some non-ASCII characters that end a sentence without any following whitespace.)

[]\"')}]*

The second part of the pattern matches any closing braces and quotation marks, zero or more of them, that may follow the period, question mark or exclamation mark. The \" is Lisp syntax for a double-quote in a string. The '*' at the end indicates that the immediately preceding regular expression (a character alternative, in this case) may be repeated zero or more times.

\\($\\| $\\|\t\\| \\)

The third part of the pattern matches the whitespace that follows the end of a sentence: the end of a line (optionally with a space), or a tab, or two spaces. The double backslashes mark the parentheses and vertical bars as regular expression syntax; the parentheses delimit a group and the vertical bars separate alternatives. The dollar sign is used to match the end of a line.

[\t\n]*   Finally, the last part of the pattern matches any additional whitespace beyond the minimum needed to end a sentence.

33.3.3 Regular Expression Functions

These functions operate on regular expressions.

regexp-quote *string* [Function]

>   This function returns a regular expression whose only exact match is *string*. Using this regular expression in `looking-at` will succeed only if the next characters in the buffer are *string*; using it in a search function will succeed if the text being searched contains *string*. See Section 33.4 [Regexp Search], page 803.

>   This allows you to request an exact string match or search when calling a function that wants a regular expression.

```
(regexp-quote "^The cat$")
    ⇒ "\\^The cat\\$"
```

>   One use of `regexp-quote` is to combine an exact string match with context described as a regular expression. For example, this searches for the string that is the value of *string*, surrounded by whitespace:

```
(re-search-forward
 (concat "\\s-" (regexp-quote string) "\\s-"))
```

regexp-opt *strings* **&optional** *paren* [Function]

>   This function returns an efficient regular expression that will match any of the strings in the list *strings*. This is useful when you need to make matching or searching as fast as possible—for example, for Font Lock mode[1].

>   The optional argument *paren* can be any of the following:

> a string
>> The resulting regexp is preceded by *paren* and followed by '\)', e.g. use '"\\(?1:"' to produce an explicitly numbered group.

> words
>> The resulting regexp is surrounded by '\<\(' and '\)\>'.

> symbols
>> The resulting regexp is surrounded by '_<\(' and '\)_>' (this is often appropriate when matching programming-language keywords and the like).

> non-nil
>> The resulting regexp is surrounded by '\(' and '\)'.

> nil
>> The resulting regexp is surrounded by '\(?:' and '\)', if it is necessary to ensure that a postfix operator appended to it will apply to the whole expression.

>   The resulting regexp of `regexp-opt` is equivalent to but usually more efficient than that of a simplified version:

```
(defun simplified-regexp-opt (strings &optional paren)
  (let ((parens
         (cond
          ((stringp paren)      (cons paren "\\)"))
          ((eq paren 'words)    '("\\<\\(" . "\\)\\>"))
```

---

[1] Note that `regexp-opt` does not guarantee that its result is absolutely the most efficient form possible. A hand-tuned regular expression can sometimes be slightly more efficient, but is almost never worth the effort.

```
                 ((eq paren 'symbols) '("\\_<\\(" . "\\)\\_>"))
                 ((null paren)          '("\\(?:" . "\\)"))
                 (t                       '("\\(" . "\\)")))))
        (concat (car paren)
                (mapconcat 'regexp-quote strings "\\|")
                (cdr paren)))))
```

regexp-opt-depth *regexp*   [Function]

This function returns the total number of grouping constructs (parenthesized expressions) in *regexp*. This does not include shy groups (see Section 33.3.1.3 [Regexp Backslash], page 798).

regexp-opt-charset *chars*   [Function]

This function returns a regular expression matching a character in the list of characters *chars*.

```
        (regexp-opt-charset '(?a ?b ?c ?d ?e))
            ⇒ "[a-e]"
```

33.4 Regular Expression Searching

In GNU Emacs, you can search for the next match for a regular expression (see Section 33.3.1 [Syntax of Regexps], page 793) either incrementally or not. For incremental search commands, see Section "Regular Expression Search" in *The GNU Emacs Manual*. Here we describe only the search functions useful in programs. The principal one is `re-search-forward`.

These search functions convert the regular expression to multibyte if the buffer is multibyte; they convert the regular expression to unibyte if the buffer is unibyte. See Section 32.1 [Text Representations], page 761.

re-search-forward *regexp* **&optional** *limit noerror count*   [Command]

This function searches forward in the current buffer for a string of text that is matched by the regular expression *regexp*. The function skips over any amount of text that is not matched by *regexp*, and leaves point at the end of the first match found. It returns the new value of point.

If *limit* is non-`nil`, it must be a position in the current buffer. It specifies the upper bound to the search. No match extending after that position is accepted. If *limit* is omitted or `nil`, it defaults to the end of the accessible portion of the buffer.

What `re-search-forward` does when the search fails depends on the value of *noerror*:

nil   Signal a `search-failed` error.

t   Do nothing and return `nil`.

anything else

           Move point to *limit* (or the end of the accessible portion of the buffer) and return `nil`.

The argument *noerror* only affects valid searches which fail to find a match. Invalid arguments cause errors regardless of *noerror*.

If *count* is a positive number *n*, the search is done *n* times; each successive search starts at the end of the previous match. If all these successive searches succeed, the function call succeeds, moving point and returning its new value. Otherwise the function call fails, with results depending on the value of *noerror*, as described above. If *count* is a negative number *-n*, the search is done *n* times in the opposite (backward) direction.

In the following example, point is initially before the 'T'. Evaluating the search call moves point to the end of that line (between the 't' of 'hat' and the newline).

```
---------- Buffer: foo ----------
I read "*The cat in the hat
comes back" twice.
---------- Buffer: foo ----------


(re-search-forward "[a-z]+" nil t 5)
     ⇒ 27


---------- Buffer: foo ----------
I read "The cat in the hat*
comes back" twice.
---------- Buffer: foo ----------
```

re-search-backward *regexp* **&optional** *limit noerror count*   [Command]

This function searches backward in the current buffer for a string of text that is matched by the regular expression *regexp*, leaving point at the beginning of the first text found.

This function is analogous to **re-search-forward**, but they are not simple mirror images. **re-search-forward** finds the match whose beginning is as close as possible to the starting point. If **re-search-backward** were a perfect mirror image, it would find the match whose end is as close as possible. However, in fact it finds the match whose beginning is as close as possible (and yet ends before the starting point). The reason for this is that matching a regular expression at a given spot always works from beginning to end, and starts at a specified beginning position.

A true mirror-image of **re-search-forward** would require a special feature for matching regular expressions from end to beginning. It's not worth the trouble of implementing that.

string-match *regexp string* **&optional** *start*   [Function]

This function returns the index of the start of the first match for the regular expression *regexp* in *string*, or **nil** if there is no match. If *start* is non-**nil**, the search starts at that index in *string*.

For example,

```
(string-match
 "quick" "The quick brown fox jumped quickly.")
     ⇒ 4
(string-match
 "quick" "The quick brown fox jumped quickly." 8)
     ⇒ 27
```

The index of the first character of the string is 0, the index of the second character is 1, and so on.

If this function finds a match, the index of the first character beyond the match is available as (match-end 0). See Section 33.6 [Match Data], page 807.

```
(string-match
 "quick" "The quick brown fox jumped quickly." 8)
    ⇒ 27

(match-end 0)
    ⇒ 32
```

string-match-p *regexp string* **&optional** *start*   [Function]
    This predicate function does what string-match does, but it avoids modifying the match data.

looking-at *regexp*   [Function]
    This function determines whether the text in the current buffer directly following point matches the regular expression *regexp*. "Directly following" means precisely that: the search is "anchored" and it can succeed only starting with the first character following point. The result is t if so, nil otherwise.

    This function does not move point, but it does update the match data. See Section 33.6 [Match Data], page 807. If you need to test for a match without modifying the match data, use looking-at-p, described below.

    In this example, point is located directly before the 'T'. If it were anywhere else, the result would be nil.

```
---------- Buffer: foo ----------
I read "*The cat in the hat
comes back" twice.
---------- Buffer: foo ----------

(looking-at "The cat in the hat$")
    ⇒ t
```

looking-back *regexp limit* **&optional** *greedy*   [Function]
    This function returns t if *regexp* matches the text immediately before point (i.e., ending at point), and nil otherwise.

    Because regular expression matching works only going forward, this is implemented by searching backwards from point for a match that ends at point. That can be quite slow if it has to search a long distance. You can bound the time required by specifying a non-nil value for *limit*, which says not to search before *limit*. In this case, the match that is found must begin at or after *limit*. Here's an example:

```
---------- Buffer: foo ----------
I read "*The cat in the hat
comes back" twice.
---------- Buffer: foo ----------

(looking-back "read \"" 3)
     ⇒ t
(looking-back "read \"" 4)
     ⇒ nil
```

If *greedy* is non-**nil**, this function extends the match backwards as far as possible, stopping when a single additional previous character cannot be part of a match for *regexp*. When the match is extended, its starting position is allowed to occur before *limit*.

As a general recommendation, try to avoid using **looking-back** wherever possible, since it is slow. For this reason, there are no plans to add a **looking-back-p** function.

looking-at-p *regexp*   [Function]
   This predicate function works like **looking-at**, but without updating the match data.

search-spaces-regexp   [Variable]
   If this variable is non-**nil**, it should be a regular expression that says how to search for whitespace. In that case, any group of spaces in a regular expression being searched for stands for use of this regular expression. However, spaces inside of constructs such as '[...]' and '*', '+', '?' are not affected by **search-spaces-regexp**.

   Since this variable affects all regular expression search and match constructs, you should bind it temporarily for as small as possible a part of the code.

33.5 POSIX Regular Expression Searching

The usual regular expression functions do backtracking when necessary to handle the '\|' and repetition constructs, but they continue this only until they find *some* match. Then they succeed and report the first match found.

   This section describes alternative search functions which perform the full backtracking specified by the POSIX standard for regular expression matching. They continue backtracking until they have tried all possibilities and found all matches, so they can report the longest match, as required by POSIX. This is much slower, so use these functions only when you really need the longest match.

   The POSIX search and match functions do not properly support the non-greedy repetition operators (see Section 33.3.1.1 [Regexp Special], page 793). This is because POSIX backtracking conflicts with the semantics of non-greedy repetition.

posix-search-forward *regexp* **&optional** *limit noerror count*   [Command]
   This is like **re-search-forward** except that it performs the full backtracking specified by the POSIX standard for regular expression matching.

posix-search-backward *regexp* **&optional** *limit noerror count*   [Command]
   This is like **re-search-backward** except that it performs the full backtracking specified by the POSIX standard for regular expression matching.

posix-looking-at *regexp* [Function]

> This is like `looking-at` except that it performs the full backtracking specified by the POSIX standard for regular expression matching.

posix-string-match *regexp string* **&optional** *start* [Function]

> This is like `string-match` except that it performs the full backtracking specified by the POSIX standard for regular expression matching.

33.6 The Match Data

Emacs keeps track of the start and end positions of the segments of text found during a search; this is called the *match data*. Thanks to the match data, you can search for a complex pattern, such as a date in a mail message, and then extract parts of the match under control of the pattern.

Because the match data normally describe the most recent search only, you must be careful not to do another search inadvertently between the search you wish to refer back to and the use of the match data. If you can't avoid another intervening search, you must save and restore the match data around it, to prevent it from being overwritten.

Notice that all functions are allowed to overwrite the match data unless they're explicitly documented not to do so. A consequence is that functions that are run implicitly in the background (see Section 38.11 [Timers], page 1006, and Section 38.12 [Idle Timers], page 1008) should likely save and restore the match data explicitly.

33.6.1 Replacing the Text that Matched

This function replaces all or part of the text matched by the last search. It works by means of the match data.

replace-match *replacement* **&optional** *fixedcase literal string subexp* [Function]

> This function performs a replacement operation on a buffer or string.
>
> If you did the last search in a buffer, you should omit the *string* argument or specify `nil` for it, and make sure that the current buffer is the one in which you performed the last search. Then this function edits the buffer, replacing the matched text with *replacement*. It leaves point at the end of the replacement text.
>
> If you performed the last search on a string, pass the same string as *string*. Then this function returns a new string, in which the matched text is replaced by *replacement*.
>
> If *fixedcase* is non-`nil`, then `replace-match` uses the replacement text without case conversion; otherwise, it converts the replacement text depending upon the capitalization of the text to be replaced. If the original text is all upper case, this converts the replacement text to upper case. If all words of the original text are capitalized, this capitalizes all the words of the replacement text. If all the words are one-letter and they are all upper case, they are treated as capitalized words rather than all-upper-case words.
>
> If *literal* is non-`nil`, then *replacement* is inserted exactly as it is, the only alterations being case changes as needed. If it is `nil` (the default), then the character '\' is treated specially. If a '\' appears in *replacement*, then it must be part of one of the following sequences:
>
> '\&'   This stands for the entire text being replaced.

'\n', where n is a digit

> This stands for the text that matched the nth subexpression in the original regexp. Subexpressions are those expressions grouped inside '\(...\)'. If the nth subexpression never matched, an empty string is substituted.

'\\'   This stands for a single '\' in the replacement text.

'\?'   This stands for itself (for compatibility with `replace-regexp` and related commands; see Section "Regexp Replace" in *The GNU Emacs Manual*).

Any other character following '\' signals an error.

The substitutions performed by '\&' and '\n' occur after case conversion, if any. Therefore, the strings they substitute are never case-converted.

If *subexp* is non-`nil`, that says to replace just subexpression number *subexp* of the regexp that was matched, not the entire match. For example, after matching 'foo \(ba*r\)', calling `replace-match` with 1 as *subexp* means to replace just the text that matched '\(ba*r\)'.

`match-substitute-replacement` *replacement* &**optional** *fixedcase*   [Function]
    literal string subexp

> This function returns the text that would be inserted into the buffer by `replace-match`, but without modifying the buffer. It is useful if you want to present the user with actual replacement result, with constructs like '\n' or '\&' substituted with matched groups. Arguments *replacement* and optional *fixedcase*, *literal*, *string* and *subexp* have the same meaning as for `replace-match`.

33.6.2 Simple Match Data Access

This section explains how to use the match data to find out what was matched by the last search or match operation, if it succeeded.

You can ask about the entire matching text, or about a particular parenthetical subexpression of a regular expression. The *count* argument in the functions below specifies which. If *count* is zero, you are asking about the entire match. If *count* is positive, it specifies which subexpression you want.

Recall that the subexpressions of a regular expression are those expressions grouped with escaped parentheses, '\(...\)'. The *count*th subexpression is found by counting occurrences of '\(' from the beginning of the whole regular expression. The first subexpression is numbered 1, the second 2, and so on. Only regular expressions can have subexpressions—after a simple string search, the only information available is about the entire match.

Every successful search sets the match data. Therefore, you should query the match data immediately after searching, before calling any other function that might perform another search. Alternatively, you may save and restore the match data (see Section 33.6.4 [Saving Match Data], page 811) around the call to functions that could perform another search. Or use the functions that explicitly do not modify the match data; e.g., `string-match-p`.

A search which fails may or may not alter the match data. In the current implementation, it does not, but we may change it in the future. Don't try to rely on the value of the match data after a failing search.

match-string *count* **&optional** *in-string*   [Function]
> This function returns, as a string, the text matched in the last search or match operation. It returns the entire text if *count* is zero, or just the portion corresponding to the *count*th parenthetical subexpression, if *count* is positive.
>
> If the last such operation was done against a string with **string-match**, then you should pass the same string as the argument *in-string*. After a buffer search or match, you should omit *in-string* or pass **nil** for it; but you should make sure that the current buffer when you call **match-string** is the one in which you did the searching or matching. Failure to follow this advice will lead to incorrect results.
>
> The value is **nil** if *count* is out of range, or for a subexpression inside a '\|' alternative that wasn't used or a repetition that repeated zero times.

match-string-no-properties *count* **&optional** *in-string*   [Function]
> This function is like **match-string** except that the result has no text properties.

match-beginning *count*   [Function]
> If the last regular expression search found a match, this function returns the position of the start of the matching text or of a subexpression of it.
>
> If *count* is zero, then the value is the position of the start of the entire match. Otherwise, *count* specifies a subexpression in the regular expression, and the value of the function is the starting position of the match for that subexpression.
>
> The value is **nil** for a subexpression inside a '\|' alternative that wasn't used or a repetition that repeated zero times.

match-end *count*   [Function]
> This function is like **match-beginning** except that it returns the position of the end of the match, rather than the position of the beginning.

Here is an example of using the match data, with a comment showing the positions within the text:

```
(string-match "\\(qu\\)\\(ick\\)"
              "The quick fox jumped quickly.")
              ;0123456789
     ⇒ 4

(match-string 0 "The quick fox jumped quickly.")
     ⇒ "quick"
(match-string 1 "The quick fox jumped quickly.")
     ⇒ "qu"
(match-string 2 "The quick fox jumped quickly.")
     ⇒ "ick"

(match-beginning 1)        ; The beginning of the match
     ⇒ 4                   ;    with 'qu' is at index 4.

(match-beginning 2)        ; The beginning of the match
     ⇒ 6                   ;    with 'ick' is at index 6.
```

```
(match-end 1)                    ; The end of the match
    ⇒ 6                          ;    with 'qu' is at index 6.

(match-end 2)                    ; The end of the match
    ⇒ 9                          ;    with 'ick' is at index 9.
```

Here is another example. Point is initially located at the beginning of the line. Searching moves point to between the space and the word 'in'. The beginning of the entire match is at the 9th character of the buffer ('T'), and the beginning of the match for the first subexpression is at the 13th character ('c').

```
(list
  (re-search-forward "The \\(cat \\)")
  (match-beginning 0)
  (match-beginning 1))
    ⇒ (17 9 13)


---------- Buffer: foo ----------
I read "The cat *in the hat comes back" twice.
         ^   ^
         9  13
---------- Buffer: foo ----------
```

(In this case, the index returned is a buffer position; the first character of the buffer counts as 1.)

33.6.3 Accessing the Entire Match Data

The functions match-data and set-match-data read or write the entire match data, all at once.

---

match-data &optional *integers reuse reseat*   [Function]

This function returns a list of positions (markers or integers) that record all the information on the text that the last search matched. Element zero is the position of the beginning of the match for the whole expression; element one is the position of the end of the match for the expression. The next two elements are the positions of the beginning and end of the match for the first subexpression, and so on. In general, element number $2n$ corresponds to (match-beginning n); and element number $2n+1$ corresponds to (match-end n).

Normally all the elements are markers or nil, but if *integers* is non-nil, that means to use integers instead of markers. (In that case, the buffer itself is appended as an additional element at the end of the list, to facilitate complete restoration of the match data.) If the last match was done on a string with string-match, then integers are always used, since markers can't point into a string.

If *reuse* is non-nil, it should be a list. In that case, match-data stores the match data in *reuse*. That is, *reuse* is destructively modified. *reuse* does not need to have the right length. If it is not long enough to contain the match data, it is extended. If it is too long, the length of *reuse* stays the same, but the elements that were not used are set to `nil`. The purpose of this feature is to reduce the need for garbage collection.

If *reseat* is non-`nil`, all markers on the *reuse* list are reseated to point to nowhere.

As always, there must be no possibility of intervening searches between the call to a search function and the call to `match-data` that is intended to access the match data for that search.

```
(match-data)
     ⇒ (#<marker at 9 in foo>
        #<marker at 17 in foo>
        #<marker at 13 in foo>
        #<marker at 17 in foo>)
```

`set-match-data` *match-list* **&optional** *reseat*   [Function]
 This function sets the match data from the elements of *match-list*, which should be a list that was the value of a previous call to `match-data`. (More precisely, anything that has the same format will work.)

 If *match-list* refers to a buffer that doesn't exist, you don't get an error; that sets the match data in a meaningless but harmless way.

 If *reseat* is non-`nil`, all markers on the *match-list* list are reseated to point to nowhere.

 `store-match-data` is a semi-obsolete alias for `set-match-data`.

33.6.4 Saving and Restoring the Match Data

When you call a function that may search, you may need to save and restore the match data around that call, if you want to preserve the match data from an earlier search for later use. Here is an example that shows the problem that arises if you fail to save the match data:

```
(re-search-forward "The \\(cat \\)")
     ⇒ 48
(foo)                          ; foo does more searching.
(match-end 0)
     ⇒ 61                      ; Unexpected result—not 48!
```

You can save and restore the match data with `save-match-data`:

`save-match-data` *body*...   [Macro]
 This macro executes *body*, saving and restoring the match data around it. The return value is the value of the last form in *body*.

You could use `set-match-data` together with `match-data` to imitate the effect of the special form `save-match-data`. Here is how:

```
(let ((data (match-data)))
  (unwind-protect
      ...    ; Ok to change the original match data.
    (set-match-data data)))
```

Emacs automatically saves and restores the match data when it runs process filter functions (see Section 36.9.2 [Filter Functions], page 859) and process sentinels (see Section 36.10 [Sentinels], page 862).

33.7 Search and Replace

If you want to find all matches for a regexp in part of the buffer, and replace them, the best way is to write an explicit loop using `re-search-forward` and `replace-match`, like this:

```
(while (re-search-forward "foo[ \t]+bar" nil t)
  (replace-match "foobar"))
```

See Section 33.6.1 [Replacing the Text that Matched], page 807, for a description of `replace-match`.

However, replacing matches in a string is more complex, especially if you want to do it efficiently. So Emacs provides a function to do this.

`replace-regexp-in-string` *regexp rep string* **&optional** *fixedcase*   [Function]
     literal subexp start

> This function copies *string* and searches it for matches for *regexp*, and replaces them with *rep*. It returns the modified copy. If *start* is non-`nil`, the search for matches starts at that index in *string*, so matches starting before that index are not changed.

> This function uses `replace-match` to do the replacement, and it passes the optional arguments *fixedcase*, *literal* and *subexp* along to `replace-match`.

> Instead of a string, *rep* can be a function. In that case, `replace-regexp-in-string` calls *rep* for each match, passing the text of the match as its sole argument. It collects the value *rep* returns and passes that to `replace-match` as the replacement string. The match data at this point are the result of matching *regexp* against a substring of *string*.

If you want to write a command along the lines of `query-replace`, you can use `perform-replace` to do the work.

`perform-replace` *from-string replacements query-flag regexp-flag*   [Function]
     delimited-flag **&optional** *repeat-count map start end*

> This function is the guts of `query-replace` and related commands. It searches for occurrences of *from-string* in the text between positions *start* and *end* and replaces some or all of them. If *start* is `nil` (or omitted), point is used instead, and the end of the buffer's accessible portion is used for *end*.

> If *query-flag* is `nil`, it replaces all occurrences; otherwise, it asks the user what to do about each one.

> If *regexp-flag* is non-`nil`, then *from-string* is considered a regular expression; otherwise, it must match literally. If *delimited-flag* is non-`nil`, then only replacements surrounded by word boundaries are considered.

> The argument *replacements* specifies what to replace occurrences with. If it is a string, that string is used. It can also be a list of strings, to be used in cyclic order.

> If *replacements* is a cons cell, (`function` . `data`), this means to call *function* after each match to get the replacement text. This function is called with two arguments: *data*, and the number of replacements already made.

> If *repeat-count* is non-`nil`, it should be an integer. Then it specifies how many times to use each of the strings in the *replacements* list before advancing cyclically to the next one.

If *from-string* contains upper-case letters, then `perform-replace` binds `case-fold-search` to `nil`, and it uses the *replacements* without altering their case.

Normally, the keymap `query-replace-map` defines the possible user responses for queries. The argument *map*, if non-`nil`, specifies a keymap to use instead of `query-replace-map`.

This function uses one of two functions to search for the next occurrence of *from-string*. These functions are specified by the values of two variables: `replace-re-search-function` and `replace-search-function`. The former is called when the argument *regexp-flag* is non-`nil`, the latter when it is `nil`.

`query-replace-map`   [Variable]

This variable holds a special keymap that defines the valid user responses for `perform-replace` and the commands that use it, as well as `y-or-n-p` and `map-y-or-n-p`. This map is unusual in two ways:

- The key bindings are not commands, just symbols that are meaningful to the functions that use this map.

- Prefix keys are not supported; each key binding must be for a single-event key sequence. This is because the functions don't use `read-key-sequence` to get the input; instead, they read a single event and look it up "by hand".

Here are the meaningful bindings for `query-replace-map`. Several of them are meaningful only for `query-replace` and friends.

`act`   Do take the action being considered—in other words, "yes".

`skip`   Do not take action for this question—in other words, "no".

`exit`   Answer this question "no", and give up on the entire series of questions, assuming that the answers will be "no".

`exit-prefix`
               Like `exit`, but add the key that was pressed to `unread-command-events` (see Section 20.8.6 [Event Input Misc], page 380).

`act-and-exit`
               Answer this question "yes", and give up on the entire series of questions, assuming that subsequent answers will be "no".

`act-and-show`
               Answer this question "yes", but show the results—don't advance yet to the next question.

`automatic`
               Answer this question and all subsequent questions in the series with "yes", without further user interaction.

`backup`   Move back to the previous place that a question was asked about.

`edit`   Enter a recursive edit to deal with this question—instead of any other action that would normally be taken.

`edit-replacement`
               Edit the replacement for this question in the minibuffer.

`delete-and-edit`
>   Delete the text being considered, then enter a recursive edit to replace it.

`recenter`
`scroll-up`
`scroll-down`
`scroll-other-window`
`scroll-other-window-down`
>   Perform the specified window scroll operation, then ask the same question again.
>   Only `y-or-n-p` and related functions use this answer.

`quit`   Perform a quit right away. Only `y-or-n-p` and related functions use this answer.

`help`   Display some help, then ask again.

`multi-query-replace-map`   [Variable]
>   This variable holds a keymap that extends `query-replace-map` by providing additional keybindings that are useful in multi-buffer replacements. The additional bindings are:

> `automatic-all`
> >   Answer this question and all subsequent questions in the series with "yes", without further user interaction, for all remaining buffers.

> `exit-current`
> >   Answer this question "no", and give up on the entire series of questions for the current buffer. Continue to the next buffer in the sequence.

`replace-search-function`   [Variable]
>   This variable specifies a function that `perform-replace` calls to search for the next string to replace. Its default value is `search-forward`. Any other value should name a function of 3 arguments: the first 3 arguments of `search-forward` (see Section 33.1 [String Search], page 790).

`replace-re-search-function`   [Variable]
>   This variable specifies a function that `perform-replace` calls to search for the next regexp to replace. Its default value is `re-search-forward`. Any other value should name a function of 3 arguments: the first 3 arguments of `re-search-forward` (see Section 33.4 [Regexp Search], page 803).

33.8 Standard Regular Expressions Used in Editing

This section describes some variables that hold regular expressions used for certain purposes in editing:

`page-delimiter`   [User Option]
>   This is the regular expression describing line-beginnings that separate pages. The default value is `"^\014"` (i.e., `"^^L"` or `"^\C-l"`); this matches a line that starts with a formfeed character.

The following two regular expressions should *not* assume the match always starts at the beginning of a line; they should not use '^' to anchor the match. Most often, the paragraph commands do check for a match only at the beginning of a line, which means that '^' would be superfluous. When there is a nonzero left margin, they accept matches that start after the left margin. In that case, a '^' would be incorrect. However, a '^' is harmless in modes where a left margin is never used.

paragraph-separate   [User Option]

This is the regular expression for recognizing the beginning of a line that separates paragraphs. (If you change this, you may have to change `paragraph-start` also.) The default value is `"[ \t\f]*$"`, which matches a line that consists entirely of spaces, tabs, and form feeds (after its left margin).

paragraph-start   [User Option]

This is the regular expression for recognizing the beginning of a line that starts *or* separates paragraphs. The default value is `"\f\\|[ \t]*$"`, which matches a line containing only whitespace or starting with a form feed (after its left margin).

sentence-end   [User Option]

If non-`nil`, the value should be a regular expression describing the end of a sentence, including the whitespace following the sentence. (All paragraph boundaries also end sentences, regardless.)

If the value is `nil`, as it is by default, then the function `sentence-end` constructs the regexp. That is why you should always call the function `sentence-end` to obtain the regexp to be used to recognize the end of a sentence.

sentence-end   [Function]

This function returns the value of the variable `sentence-end`, if non-`nil`. Otherwise it returns a default value based on the values of the variables `sentence-end-double-space` (see [Definition of sentence-end-double-space], page 718), `sentence-end-without-period`, and `sentence-end-without-space`.

34 Syntax Tables

A *syntax table* specifies the syntactic role of each character in a buffer. It can be used to determine where words, symbols, and other syntactic constructs begin and end. This information is used by many Emacs facilities, including Font Lock mode (see Section 22.6 [Font Lock Mode], page 462) and the various complex movement commands (see Section 29.2 [Motion], page 674).

34.1 Syntax Table Concepts

A syntax table is a data structure which can be used to look up the *syntax class* and other syntactic properties of each character. Syntax tables are used by Lisp programs for scanning and moving across text.

Internally, a syntax table is a char-table (see Section 6.6 [Char-Tables], page 104). The element at index *c* describes the character with code *c*; its value is a cons cell which specifies the syntax of the character in question. See Section 34.7 [Syntax Table Internals], page 828, for details. However, instead of using `aset` and `aref` to modify and inspect syntax table contents, you should usually use the higher-level functions `char-syntax` and `modify-syntax-entry`, which are described in Section 34.3 [Syntax Table Functions], page 821.

`syntax-table-p` *object*   [Function]
    This function returns `t` if *object* is a syntax table.

Each buffer has its own major mode, and each major mode has its own idea of the syntax class of various characters. For example, in Lisp mode, the character ';' begins a comment, but in C mode, it terminates a statement. To support these variations, the syntax table is local to each buffer. Typically, each major mode has its own syntax table, which it installs in all buffers that use that mode. For example, the variable `emacs-lisp-mode-syntax-table` holds the syntax table used by Emacs Lisp mode, and `c-mode-syntax-table` holds the syntax table used by C mode. Changing a major mode's syntax table alters the syntax in all of that mode's buffers, as well as in any buffers subsequently put in that mode. Occasionally, several similar modes share one syntax table. See Section 22.2.9 [Example Major Modes], page 444, for an example of how to set up a syntax table.

A syntax table can *inherit* from another syntax table, which is called its *parent syntax table*. A syntax table can leave the syntax class of some characters unspecified, by giving them the "inherit" syntax class; such a character then acquires the syntax class specified by the parent syntax table (see Section 34.2.1 [Syntax Class Table], page 817). Emacs defines a *standard syntax table*, which is the default parent syntax table, and is also the syntax table used by Fundamental mode.

`standard-syntax-table`   [Function]
    This function returns the standard syntax table, which is the syntax table used in Fundamental mode.

Syntax tables are not used by the Emacs Lisp reader, which has its own built-in syntactic rules which cannot be changed. (Some Lisp systems provide ways to redefine the read syntax, but we decided to leave this feature out of Emacs Lisp for simplicity.)

34.2 Syntax Descriptors

The *syntax class* of a character describes its syntactic role. Each syntax table specifies the syntax class of each character. There is no necessary relationship between the class of a character in one syntax table and its class in any other table.

Each syntax class is designated by a mnemonic character, which serves as the name of the class when you need to specify a class. Usually, this designator character is one that is often assigned that class; however, its meaning as a designator is unvarying and independent of what syntax that character currently has. Thus, '\' as a designator character always stands for escape character syntax, regardless of whether the '\' character actually has that syntax in the current syntax table.

A *syntax descriptor* is a Lisp string that describes the syntax class and other syntactic properties of a character. When you want to modify the syntax of a character, that is done by calling the function `modify-syntax-entry` and passing a syntax descriptor as one of its arguments (see Section 34.3 [Syntax Table Functions], page 821).

The first character in a syntax descriptor must be a syntax class designator character. The second character, if present, specifies a matching character (e.g., in Lisp, the matching character for '(' is ')'); a space specifies that there is no matching character. Then come characters specifying additional syntax properties (see Section 34.2.2 [Syntax Flags], page 820).

If no matching character or flags are needed, only one character (specifying the syntax class) is sufficient.

For example, the syntax descriptor for the character '*' in C mode is ". 23" (i.e., punctuation, matching character slot unused, second character of a comment-starter, first character of a comment-ender), and the entry for '/' is '. 14' (i.e., punctuation, matching character slot unused, first character of a comment-starter, second character of a comment-ender).

Emacs also defines *raw syntax descriptors*, which are used to describe syntax classes at a lower level. See Section 34.7 [Syntax Table Internals], page 828.

34.2.1 Table of Syntax Classes

Here is a table of syntax classes, the characters that designate them, their meanings, and examples of their use.

Whitespace characters: ' ' or '–'

> Characters that separate symbols and words from each other. Typically, whitespace characters have no other syntactic significance, and multiple whitespace characters are syntactically equivalent to a single one. Space, tab, and formfeed are classified as whitespace in almost all major modes.

> This syntax class can be designated by either ' ' or '–'. Both designators are equivalent.

Word constituents: 'w'

> Parts of words in human languages. These are typically used in variable and command names in programs. All upper- and lower-case letters, and the digits, are typically word constituents.

Symbol constituents: '_'

> Extra characters used in variable and command names along with word constituents. Examples include the characters '$&*+-_<>' in Lisp mode, which may be part of a symbol name even though they are not part of English words. In standard C, the only non-word-constituent character that is valid in symbols is underscore ('_').

Punctuation characters: '.'

> Characters used as punctuation in a human language, or used in a programming language to separate symbols from one another. Some programming language modes, such as Emacs Lisp mode, have no characters in this class since the few characters that are not symbol or word constituents all have other uses. Other programming language modes, such as C mode, use punctuation syntax for operators.

Open parenthesis characters: '('
Close parenthesis characters: ')'

> Characters used in dissimilar pairs to surround sentences or expressions. Such a grouping is begun with an open parenthesis character and terminated with a close. Each open parenthesis character matches a particular close parenthesis character, and vice versa. Normally, Emacs indicates momentarily the matching open parenthesis when you insert a close parenthesis. See Section 37.21 [Blinking], page 972.

> In human languages, and in C code, the parenthesis pairs are '()', '[]', and '{}'. In Emacs Lisp, the delimiters for lists and vectors ('()' and '[]') are classified as parenthesis characters.

String quotes: '"'

> Characters used to delimit string constants. The same string quote character appears at the beginning and the end of a string. Such quoted strings do not nest.

> The parsing facilities of Emacs consider a string as a single token. The usual syntactic meanings of the characters in the string are suppressed.

> The Lisp modes have two string quote characters: double-quote ('"') and vertical bar ('|'). '|' is not used in Emacs Lisp, but it is used in Common Lisp. C also has two string quote characters: double-quote for strings, and apostrophe (''') for character constants.

> Human text has no string quote characters. We do not want quotation marks to turn off the usual syntactic properties of other characters in the quotation.

Escape-syntax characters: '\'

> Characters that start an escape sequence, such as is used in string and character constants. The character '\' belongs to this class in both C and Lisp. (In C, it is used thus only inside strings, but it turns out to cause no trouble to treat it this way throughout C code.)

> Characters in this class count as part of words if `words-include-escapes` is non-`nil`. See Section 29.2.2 [Word Motion], page 675.

Character quotes: '/'

> Characters used to quote the following character so that it loses its normal syntactic meaning. This differs from an escape character in that only the character immediately following is ever affected.
>
> Characters in this class count as part of words if `words-include-escapes` is non-`nil`. See Section 29.2.2 [Word Motion], page 675.
>
> This class is used for backslash in TEX mode.

Paired delimiters: '$'

> Similar to string quote characters, except that the syntactic properties of the characters between the delimiters are not suppressed. Only TEX mode uses a paired delimiter presently—the '$' that both enters and leaves math mode.

Expression prefixes: '''

> Characters used for syntactic operators that are considered as part of an expression if they appear next to one. In Lisp modes, these characters include the apostrophe, ''' (used for quoting), the comma, ',' (used in macros), and '#' (used in the read syntax for certain data types).

Comment starters: '<'
Comment enders: '>'

> Characters used in various languages to delimit comments. Human text has no comment characters. In Lisp, the semicolon (';') starts a comment and a newline or formfeed ends one.

Inherit standard syntax: '@'

> This syntax class does not specify a particular syntax. It says to look in the standard syntax table to find the syntax of this character.

Generic comment delimiters: '!'

> Characters that start or end a special kind of comment. *Any* generic comment delimiter matches *any* generic comment delimiter, but they cannot match a comment starter or comment ender; generic comment delimiters can only match each other.
>
> This syntax class is primarily meant for use with the `syntax-table` text property (see Section 34.4 [Syntax Properties], page 823). You can mark any range of characters as forming a comment, by giving the first and last characters of the range `syntax-table` properties identifying them as generic comment delimiters.

Generic string delimiters: '|'

> Characters that start or end a string. This class differs from the string quote class in that *any* generic string delimiter can match any other generic string delimiter; but they do not match ordinary string quote characters.
>
> This syntax class is primarily meant for use with the `syntax-table` text property (see Section 34.4 [Syntax Properties], page 823). You can mark any range of characters as forming a string constant, by giving the first and last characters of the range `syntax-table` properties identifying them as generic string delimiters.

34.2.2 Syntax Flags

In addition to the classes, entries for characters in a syntax table can specify flags. There are eight possible flags, represented by the characters '1', '2', '3', '4', 'b', 'c', 'n', and 'p'.

All the flags except 'p' are used to describe comment delimiters. The digit flags are used for comment delimiters made up of 2 characters. They indicate that a character can *also* be part of a comment sequence, in addition to the syntactic properties associated with its character class. The flags are independent of the class and each other for the sake of characters such as '*' in C mode, which is a punctuation character, *and* the second character of a start-of-comment sequence ('/*'), *and* the first character of an end-of-comment sequence ('*/'). The flags 'b', 'c', and 'n' are used to qualify the corresponding comment delimiter.

Here is a table of the possible flags for a character c, and what they mean:

- '1' means c is the start of a two-character comment-start sequence.
- '2' means c is the second character of such a sequence.
- '3' means c is the start of a two-character comment-end sequence.
- '4' means c is the second character of such a sequence.
- 'b' means that c as a comment delimiter belongs to the alternative "b" comment style. For a two-character comment starter, this flag is only significant on the second char, and for a 2-character comment ender it is only significant on the first char.
- 'c' means that c as a comment delimiter belongs to the alternative "c" comment style. For a two-character comment delimiter, 'c' on either character makes it of style "c".
- 'n' on a comment delimiter character specifies that this kind of comment can be nested. For a two-character comment delimiter, 'n' on either character makes it nestable.

Emacs supports several comment styles simultaneously in any one syntax table. A comment style is a set of flags 'b', 'c', and 'n', so there can be up to 8 different comment styles. Each comment delimiter has a style and only matches comment delimiters of the same style. Thus if a comment starts with the comment-start sequence of style "bn", it will extend until the next matching comment-end sequence of style "bn".

The appropriate comment syntax settings for C++ can be as follows:

'/'   '124'

'*'   '23b'

newline   '>'

This defines four comment-delimiting sequences:

'/*'   This is a comment-start sequence for "b" style because the second charac-
               ter, '*', has the 'b' flag.

'//'   This is a comment-start sequence for "a" style because the second charac-
               ter, '/', does not have the 'b' flag.

'*/'   This is a comment-end sequence for "b" style because the first character,
               '*', has the 'b' flag.

newline   This is a comment-end sequence for "a" style, because the newline character
               does not have the 'b' flag.

- 'p' identifies an additional prefix character for Lisp syntax. These characters are treated as whitespace when they appear between expressions. When they appear within an expression, they are handled according to their usual syntax classes.

  The function `backward-prefix-chars` moves back over these characters, as well as over characters whose primary syntax class is prefix ('`'). See Section 34.5 [Motion and Syntax], page 824.

34.3 Syntax Table Functions

In this section we describe functions for creating, accessing and altering syntax tables.

`make-syntax-table &optional` *table*   [Function]

This function creates a new syntax table. If *table* is non-`nil`, the parent of the new syntax table is *table*; otherwise, the parent is the standard syntax table.

In the new syntax table, all characters are initially given the "inherit" ('@') syntax class, i.e., their syntax is inherited from the parent table (see Section 34.2.1 [Syntax Class Table], page 817).

`copy-syntax-table &optional` *table*   [Function]

This function constructs a copy of *table* and returns it. If *table* is omitted or `nil`, it returns a copy of the standard syntax table. Otherwise, an error is signaled if *table* is not a syntax table.

`modify-syntax-entry` *char syntax-descriptor* `&optional` *table*   [Command]

This function sets the syntax entry for *char* according to *syntax-descriptor*. *char* must be a character, or a cons cell of the form (*min . max*); in the latter case, the function sets the syntax entries for all characters in the range between *min* and *max*, inclusive.

The syntax is changed only for *table*, which defaults to the current buffer's syntax table, and not in any other syntax table.

The argument *syntax-descriptor* is a syntax descriptor, i.e., a string whose first character is a syntax class designator and whose second and subsequent characters optionally specify a matching character and syntax flags. See Section 34.2 [Syntax Descriptors], page 817. An error is signaled if *syntax-descriptor* is not a valid syntax descriptor.

This function always returns `nil`. The old syntax information in the table for this character is discarded.

Examples:

```
;; Put the space character in class whitespace.
(modify-syntax-entry ?\s " ")
     ⇒ nil

;; Make '$' an open parenthesis character,
;;    with '^' as its matching close.
(modify-syntax-entry ?$ "(^")
     ⇒ nil
```

```
;; Make '^' a close parenthesis character,
;;    with '$' as its matching open.
(modify-syntax-entry ?^ ")$")
       ⇒ nil
```

```
;; Make '/' a punctuation character,
;;    the first character of a start-comment sequence,
;;    and the second character of an end-comment sequence.
;;    This is used in C mode.
(modify-syntax-entry ?/ ". 14")
       ⇒ nil
```

char-syntax *character*   [Function]

  This function returns the syntax class of *character*, represented by its designator
  character (see Section 34.2.1 [Syntax Class Table], page 817). This returns *only* the
  class, not its matching character or syntax flags.

  The following examples apply to C mode. (We use **string** to make it easier to see
  the character returned by **char-syntax**.)

```
;; Space characters have whitespace syntax class.
(string (char-syntax ?\s))
       ⇒ " "
```

```
;; Forward slash characters have punctuation syntax.
;; Note that this char-syntax call does not reveal
;; that it is also part of comment-start and -end sequences.
(string (char-syntax ?/))
       ⇒ "."
```

```
;; Open parenthesis characters have open parenthesis syntax.
;; Note that this char-syntax call does not reveal that
;; it has a matching character, ')'.
(string (char-syntax ?\())
       ⇒ "("
```

set-syntax-table *table*   [Function]

  This function makes *table* the syntax table for the current buffer. It returns *table*.

syntax-table   [Function]

  This function returns the current syntax table, which is the table for the current
  buffer.

describe-syntax **&optional** *buffer*   [Command]

  This command displays the contents of the syntax table of *buffer* (by default, the
  current buffer) in a help buffer.

with-syntax-table *table body*...   [Macro]

  This macro executes *body* using *table* as the current syntax table. It returns the
  value of the last form in *body*, after restoring the old current syntax table.

Since each buffer has its own current syntax table, we should make that more precise: `with-syntax-table` temporarily alters the current syntax table of whichever buffer is current at the time the macro execution starts. Other buffers are not affected.

34.4 Syntax Properties

When the syntax table is not flexible enough to specify the syntax of a language, you can override the syntax table for specific character occurrences in the buffer, by applying a `syntax-table` text property. See Section 31.19 [Text Properties], page 732, for how to apply text properties.

The valid values of `syntax-table` text property are:

syntax-table

> If the property value is a syntax table, that table is used instead of the current buffer's syntax table to determine the syntax for the underlying text character.

(syntax-code . matching-char)

> A cons cell of this format is a raw syntax descriptor (see Section 34.7 [Syntax Table Internals], page 828), which directly specifies a syntax class for the underlying text character.

`nil`

> If the property is `nil`, the character's syntax is determined from the current syntax table in the usual way.

`parse-sexp-lookup-properties`   [Variable]

> If this is non-`nil`, the syntax scanning functions, like `forward-sexp`, pay attention to syntax text properties. Otherwise they use only the current syntax table.

`syntax-propertize-function`   [Variable]

> This variable, if non-`nil`, should store a function for applying `syntax-table` properties to a specified stretch of text. It is intended to be used by major modes to install a function which applies `syntax-table` properties in some mode-appropriate way.
>
> The function is called by `syntax-ppss` (see Section 34.6.2 [Position Parse], page 825), and by Font Lock mode during syntactic fontification (see Section 22.6.8 [Syntactic Font Lock], page 471). It is called with two arguments, *start* and *end*, which are the starting and ending positions of the text on which it should act. It is allowed to call `syntax-ppss` on any position before *end*. However, it should not call `syntax-ppss-flush-cache`; so, it is not allowed to call `syntax-ppss` on some position and later modify the buffer at an earlier position.

`syntax-propertize-extend-region-functions`   [Variable]

> This abnormal hook is run by the syntax parsing code prior to calling `syntax-propertize-function`. Its role is to help locate safe starting and ending buffer positions for passing to `syntax-propertize-function`. For example, a major mode can add a function to this hook to identify multi-line syntactic constructs, and ensure that the boundaries do not fall in the middle of one.
>
> Each function in this hook should accept two arguments, *start* and *end*. It should return either a cons cell of two adjusted buffer positions, *(new-start . new-end)*, or `nil` if no adjustment is necessary. The hook functions are run in turn, repeatedly, until they all return `nil`.

34.5 Motion and Syntax

This section describes functions for moving across characters that have certain syntax classes.

skip-syntax-forward *syntaxes* **&optional** *limit*   [Function]

> This function moves point forward across characters having syntax classes mentioned in *syntaxes* (a string of syntax class characters). It stops when it encounters the end of the buffer, or position *limit* (if specified), or a character it is not supposed to skip.
>
> If *syntaxes* starts with '^', then the function skips characters whose syntax is *not* in *syntaxes*.
>
> The return value is the distance traveled, which is a nonnegative integer.

skip-syntax-backward *syntaxes* **&optional** *limit*   [Function]

> This function moves point backward across characters whose syntax classes are mentioned in *syntaxes*. It stops when it encounters the beginning of the buffer, or position *limit* (if specified), or a character it is not supposed to skip.
>
> If *syntaxes* starts with '^', then the function skips characters whose syntax is *not* in *syntaxes*.
>
> The return value indicates the distance traveled. It is an integer that is zero or less.

backward-prefix-chars   [Function]

> This function moves point backward over any number of characters with expression prefix syntax. This includes both characters in the expression prefix syntax class, and characters with the 'p' flag.

34.6 Parsing Expressions

This section describes functions for parsing and scanning balanced expressions. We will refer to such expressions as *sexps*, following the terminology of Lisp, even though these functions can act on languages other than Lisp. Basically, a sexp is either a balanced parenthetical grouping, a string, or a symbol (i.e., a sequence of characters whose syntax is either word constituent or symbol constituent). However, characters in the expression prefix syntax class (see Section 34.2.1 [Syntax Class Table], page 817) are treated as part of the sexp if they appear next to it.

The syntax table controls the interpretation of characters, so these functions can be used for Lisp expressions when in Lisp mode and for C expressions when in C mode. See Section 29.2.6 [List Motion], page 681, for convenient higher-level functions for moving over balanced expressions.

A character's syntax controls how it changes the state of the parser, rather than describing the state itself. For example, a string delimiter character toggles the parser state between in-string and in-code, but the syntax of characters does not directly say whether they are inside a string. For example (note that 15 is the syntax code for generic string delimiters),

```
(put-text-property 1 9 'syntax-table '(15 . nil))
```

does not tell Emacs that the first eight chars of the current buffer are a string, but rather that they are all string delimiters. As a result, Emacs treats them as four consecutive empty string constants.

34.6.1 Motion Commands Based on Parsing

This section describes simple point-motion functions that operate based on parsing expressions.

`scan-lists` *from count depth*   [Function]

>   This function scans forward *count* balanced parenthetical groupings from position *from*. It returns the position where the scan stops. If *count* is negative, the scan moves backwards.
>
>   If *depth* is nonzero, treat the starting position as being *depth* parentheses deep. The scanner moves forward or backward through the buffer until the depth changes to zero *count* times. Hence, a positive value for *depth* has the effect of moving out *depth* levels of parenthesis from the starting position, while a negative *depth* has the effect of moving deeper by -*depth* levels of parenthesis.
>
>   Scanning ignores comments if `parse-sexp-ignore-comments` is non-`nil`.
>
>   If the scan reaches the beginning or end of the accessible part of the buffer before it has scanned over *count* parenthetical groupings, the return value is `nil` if the depth at that point is zero; if the depth is non-zero, a `scan-error` error is signaled.

`scan-sexps` *from count*   [Function]

>   This function scans forward *count* sexps from position *from*. It returns the position where the scan stops. If *count* is negative, the scan moves backwards.
>
>   Scanning ignores comments if `parse-sexp-ignore-comments` is non-`nil`.
>
>   If the scan reaches the beginning or end of (the accessible part of) the buffer while in the middle of a parenthetical grouping, an error is signaled. If it reaches the beginning or end between groupings but before count is used up, `nil` is returned.

`forward-comment` *count*   [Function]

>   This function moves point forward across *count* complete comments (that is, including the starting delimiter and the terminating delimiter if any), plus any whitespace encountered on the way. It moves backward if *count* is negative. If it encounters anything other than a comment or whitespace, it stops, leaving point at the place where it stopped. This includes (for instance) finding the end of a comment when moving forward and expecting the beginning of one. The function also stops immediately after moving over the specified number of complete comments. If *count* comments are found as expected, with nothing except whitespace between them, it returns `t`; otherwise it returns `nil`.
>
>   This function cannot tell whether the comments it traverses are embedded within a string. If they look like comments, it treats them as comments.
>
>   To move forward over all comments and whitespace following point, use `(forward-comment (buffer-size))`. `(buffer-size)` is a good argument to use, because the number of comments in the buffer cannot exceed that many.

34.6.2 Finding the Parse State for a Position

For syntactic analysis, such as in indentation, often the useful thing is to compute the syntactic state corresponding to a given buffer position. This function does that conveniently.

syntax-ppss &optional *pos*   [Function]
> This function returns the parser state that the parser would reach at position *pos* starting from the beginning of the buffer. See the next section for for a description of the parser state.
>
> The return value is the same as if you call the low-level parsing function **parse-partial-sexp** to parse from the beginning of the buffer to *pos* (see Section 34.6.4 [Low-Level Parsing], page 827). However, **syntax-ppss** uses a cache to speed up the computation. Due to this optimization, the second value (previous complete subexpression) and sixth value (minimum parenthesis depth) in the returned parser state are not meaningful.
>
> This function has a side effect: it adds a buffer-local entry to **before-change-functions** (see Section 31.28 [Change Hooks], page 759) for **syntax-ppss-flush-cache** (see below). This entry keeps the cache consistent as the buffer is modified. However, the cache might not be updated if **syntax-ppss** is called while **before-change-functions** is temporarily let-bound, or if the buffer is modified without running the hook, such as when using **inhibit-modification-hooks**. In those cases, it is necessary to call **syntax-ppss-flush-cache** explicitly.

syntax-ppss-flush-cache *beg* **&rest** *ignored-args*   [Function]
> This function flushes the cache used by **syntax-ppss**, starting at position *beg*. The remaining arguments, *ignored-args*, are ignored; this function accepts them so that it can be directly used on hooks such as **before-change-functions** (see Section 31.28 [Change Hooks], page 759).

34.6.3 Parser State

A *parser state* is a list of ten elements describing the state of the syntactic parser, after it parses the text between a specified starting point and a specified end point in the buffer. Parsing functions such as **syntax-ppss** return a parser state as the value. Some parsing functions accept a parser state as an argument, for resuming parsing.

Here are the meanings of the elements of the parser state:

0. The depth in parentheses, counting from 0. **Warning:** this can be negative if there are more close parens than open parens between the parser's starting point and end point.

1. The character position of the start of the innermost parenthetical grouping containing the stopping point; **nil** if none.

2. The character position of the start of the last complete subexpression terminated; **nil** if none.

3. Non-**nil** if inside a string. More precisely, this is the character that will terminate the string, or **t** if a generic string delimiter character should terminate it.

4. **t** if inside a non-nestable comment (of any comment style; see Section 34.2.2 [Syntax Flags], page 820); or the comment nesting level if inside a comment that can be nested.

5. **t** if the end point is just after a quote character.

6. The minimum parenthesis depth encountered during this scan.

7. What kind of comment is active: **nil** if not in a comment or in a comment of style 'a'; 1 for a comment of style 'b'; 2 for a comment of style 'c'; and **syntax-table** for a comment that should be ended by a generic comment delimiter character.

8. The string or comment start position. While inside a comment, this is the position where the comment began; while inside a string, this is the position where the string began. When outside of strings and comments, this element is `nil`.

9. Internal data for continuing the parsing. The meaning of this data is subject to change; it is used if you pass this list as the *state* argument to another call.

Elements 1, 2, and 6 are ignored in a state which you pass as an argument to continue parsing, and elements 8 and 9 are used only in trivial cases. Those elements are mainly used internally by the parser code.

One additional piece of useful information is available from a parser state using this function:

`syntax-ppss-toplevel-pos` *state*   [Function]
> This function extracts, from parser state *state*, the last position scanned in the parse which was at top level in grammatical structure. "At top level" means outside of any parentheses, comments, or strings.
>
> The value is `nil` if *state* represents a parse which has arrived at a top level position.

34.6.4 Low-Level Parsing

The most basic way to use the expression parser is to tell it to start at a given position with a certain state, and parse up to a specified end position.

`parse-partial-sexp` *start limit* **&optional** *target-depth stop-before*   [Function]
> *state stop-comment*
>
> This function parses a sexp in the current buffer starting at *start*, not scanning past *limit*. It stops at position *limit* or when certain criteria described below are met, and sets point to the location where parsing stops. It returns a parser state describing the status of the parse at the point where it stops.
>
> If the third argument *target-depth* is non-`nil`, parsing stops if the depth in parentheses becomes equal to *target-depth*. The depth starts at 0, or at whatever is given in *state*.
>
> If the fourth argument *stop-before* is non-`nil`, parsing stops when it comes to any character that starts a sexp. If *stop-comment* is non-`nil`, parsing stops when it comes to the start of a comment. If *stop-comment* is the symbol `syntax-table`, parsing stops after the start of a comment or a string, or the end of a comment or a string, whichever comes first.
>
> If *state* is `nil`, *start* is assumed to be at the top level of parenthesis structure, such as the beginning of a function definition. Alternatively, you might wish to resume parsing in the middle of the structure. To do this, you must provide a *state* argument that describes the initial status of parsing. The value returned by a previous call to `parse-partial-sexp` will do nicely.

34.6.5 Parameters to Control Parsing

`multibyte-syntax-as-symbol`   [Variable]
> If this variable is non-`nil`, `scan-sexps` treats all non-ASCII characters as symbol constituents regardless of what the syntax table says about them. (However, text properties can still override the syntax.)

`parse-sexp-ignore-comments`   [User Option]
> If the value is non-`nil`, then comments are treated as whitespace by the functions in
> this section and by `forward-sexp`, `scan-lists` and `scan-sexps`.

The behavior of `parse-partial-sexp` is also affected by `parse-sexp-lookup-properties` (see Section 34.4 [Syntax Properties], page 823).

`comment-end-can-be-escaped`   [Variable]
> If this buffer local variable is non-`nil`, a single character which usually terminates a
> comment doesn't do so when that character is escaped. This is used in C and C++
> Modes, where line comments starting with '`//`' can be continued onto the next line
> by escaping the newline with '`\`'.

You can use `forward-comment` to move forward or backward over one comment or several comments.

34.7 Syntax Table Internals

Syntax tables are implemented as char-tables (see Section 6.6 [Char-Tables], page 104), but most Lisp programs don't work directly with their elements. Syntax tables do not store syntax data as syntax descriptors (see Section 34.2 [Syntax Descriptors], page 817); they use an internal format, which is documented in this section. This internal format can also be assigned as syntax properties (see Section 34.4 [Syntax Properties], page 823).

Each entry in a syntax table is a *raw syntax descriptor*: a cons cell of the form (*syntax-code . matching-char*). *syntax-code* is an integer which encodes the syntax class and syntax flags, according to the table below. *matching-char*, if non-`nil`, specifies a matching character (similar to the second character in a syntax descriptor).

Here are the syntax codes corresponding to the various syntax classes:

Code	Class	Code	Class
0	whitespace	8	paired delimiter
1	punctuation	9	escape
2	word	10	character quote
3	symbol	11	comment-start
4	open parenthesis	12	comment-end
5	close parenthesis	13	inherit
6	expression prefix	14	generic comment
7	string quote	15	generic string

For example, in the standard syntax table, the entry for '`(`' is (4 . 41). 41 is the character code for '`)`'.

Syntax flags are encoded in higher order bits, starting 16 bits from the least significant bit. This table gives the power of two which corresponds to each syntax flag.

Prefix	Flag	Prefix	Flag
'1'	(lsh 1 16)	'p'	(lsh 1 20)
'2'	(lsh 1 17)	'b'	(lsh 1 21)
'3'	(lsh 1 18)	'n'	(lsh 1 22)
'4'	(lsh 1 19)		

string-to-syntax *desc*   [Function]

> Given a syntax descriptor *desc* (a string), this function returns the corresponding raw syntax descriptor.

syntax-after *pos*   [Function]

> This function returns the raw syntax descriptor for the character in the buffer after position *pos*, taking account of syntax properties as well as the syntax table. If *pos* is outside the buffer's accessible portion (see Section 29.4 [Narrowing], page 684), the return value is `nil`.

syntax-class *syntax*   [Function]

> This function returns the syntax code for the raw syntax descriptor *syntax*. More precisely, it takes the raw syntax descriptor's *syntax-code* component, masks off the high 16 bits which record the syntax flags, and returns the resulting integer.
>
> If *syntax* is `nil`, the return value is returns `nil`. This is so that the expression
>
> > (syntax-class (syntax-after pos))
>
> evaluates to `nil` if *pos* is outside the buffer's accessible portion, without throwing errors or returning an incorrect code.

34.8 Categories

Categories provide an alternate way of classifying characters syntactically. You can define several categories as needed, then independently assign each character to one or more categories. Unlike syntax classes, categories are not mutually exclusive; it is normal for one character to belong to several categories.

Each buffer has a *category table* which records which categories are defined and also which characters belong to each category. Each category table defines its own categories, but normally these are initialized by copying from the standard categories table, so that the standard categories are available in all modes.

Each category has a name, which is an ASCII printing character in the range ' ' to '~'. You specify the name of a category when you define it with `define-category`.

The category table is actually a char-table (see Section 6.6 [Char-Tables], page 104). The element of the category table at index *c* is a *category set*—a bool-vector—that indicates which categories character *c* belongs to. In this category set, if the element at index *cat* is `t`, that means category *cat* is a member of the set, and that character *c* belongs to category *cat*.

For the next three functions, the optional argument *table* defaults to the current buffer's category table.

define-category *char docstring* **&optional** *table*   [Function]

> This function defines a new category, with name *char* and documentation *docstring*, for the category table *table*.
>
> Here's an example of defining a new category for characters that have strong right-to-left directionality (see Section 37.26 [Bidirectional Display], page 981) and using it in a special category table. To obtain the information about the directionality of characters, the example code uses the '`bidi-class`' Unicode property (see Section 32.6 [Character Properties], page 766).

```
(defvar special-category-table-for-bidi
  ;;      Make an empty category-table.
  (let ((category-table (make-category-table))
        ;; Create a char-table which gives the 'bidi-class' Unicode
        ;; property for each character.
        (uniprop-table (unicode-property-table-internal 'bidi-class)))
    (define-category ?R "Characters of bidi-class R, AL, or RLO"
                     category-table)
    ;; Modify the category entry of each character whose 'bidi-class'
    ;; Unicode property is R, AL, or RLO -- these have a
    ;; right-to-left directionality.
    (map-char-table
     #'(lambda (key val)
         (if (memq val '(R AL RLO))
             (modify-category-entry key ?R category-table)))
     uniprop-table)
    category-table))
```

category-docstring *category* **&optional** *table*   [Function]

This function returns the documentation string of category *category* in category table *table*.

```
(category-docstring ?a)
    ⇒ "ASCII"
(category-docstring ?l)
    ⇒ "Latin"
```

get-unused-category **&optional** *table*   [Function]

This function returns a category name (a character) which is not currently defined in *table*. If all possible categories are in use in *table*, it returns nil.

category-table   [Function]

This function returns the current buffer's category table.

category-table-p *object*   [Function]

This function returns t if *object* is a category table, otherwise nil.

standard-category-table   [Function]

This function returns the standard category table.

copy-category-table **&optional** *table*   [Function]

This function constructs a copy of *table* and returns it. If *table* is not supplied (or is nil), it returns a copy of the standard category table. Otherwise, an error is signaled if *table* is not a category table.

set-category-table *table*   [Function]

This function makes *table* the category table for the current buffer. It returns *table*.

make-category-table   [Function]

This creates and returns an empty category table. In an empty category table, no categories have been allocated, and no characters belong to any categories.

make-category-set *categories* [Function]

This function returns a new category set—a bool-vector—whose initial contents are the categories listed in the string *categories*. The elements of *categories* should be category names; the new category set has **t** for each of those categories, and **nil** for all other categories.

```
(make-category-set "al")
    ⇒ #&128"\0\0\0\0\0\0\0\0\0\0\0\0\2\20\0\0"
```

char-category-set *char* [Function]

This function returns the category set for character *char* in the current buffer's category table. This is the bool-vector which records which categories the character *char* belongs to. The function **char-category-set** does not allocate storage, because it returns the same bool-vector that exists in the category table.

```
(char-category-set ?a)
    ⇒ #&128"\0\0\0\0\0\0\0\0\0\0\0\0\2\20\0\0"
```

category-set-mnemonics *category-set* [Function]

This function converts the category set *category-set* into a string containing the characters that designate the categories that are members of the set.

```
(category-set-mnemonics (char-category-set ?a))
    ⇒ "al"
```

modify-category-entry *char category* **&optional** *table reset* [Function]

This function modifies the category set of *char* in category table *table* (which defaults to the current buffer's category table). *char* can be a character, or a cons cell of the form (*min . max*); in the latter case, the function modifies the category sets of all characters in the range between *min* and *max*, inclusive.

Normally, it modifies a category set by adding *category* to it. But if *reset* is non-**nil**, then it deletes *category* instead.

describe-categories **&optional** *buffer-or-name* [Command]

This function describes the category specifications in the current category table. It inserts the descriptions in a buffer, and then displays that buffer. If *buffer-or-name* is non-**nil**, it describes the category table of that buffer instead.

35 Abbrevs and Abbrev Expansion

An abbreviation or *abbrev* is a string of characters that may be expanded to a longer string. The user can insert the abbrev string and find it replaced automatically with the expansion of the abbrev. This saves typing.

The set of abbrevs currently in effect is recorded in an *abbrev table*. Each buffer has a local abbrev table, but normally all buffers in the same major mode share one abbrev table. There is also a global abbrev table. Normally both are used.

An abbrev table is represented as an obarray. See Section 8.3 [Creating Symbols], page 117, for information about obarrays. Each abbreviation is represented by a symbol in the obarray. The symbol's name is the abbreviation; its value is the expansion; its function definition is the hook function for performing the expansion (see Section 35.2 [Defining Abbrevs], page 833); and its property list cell contains various additional properties, including the use count and the number of times the abbreviation has been expanded (see Section 35.6 [Abbrev Properties], page 837).

Certain abbrevs, called *system abbrevs*, are defined by a major mode instead of the user. A system abbrev is identified by its non-`nil` `:system` property (see Section 35.6 [Abbrev Properties], page 837). When abbrevs are saved to an abbrev file, system abbrevs are omitted. See Section 35.3 [Abbrev Files], page 834.

Because the symbols used for abbrevs are not interned in the usual obarray, they will never appear as the result of reading a Lisp expression; in fact, normally they are never used except by the code that handles abbrevs. Therefore, it is safe to use them in a nonstandard way.

If the minor mode Abbrev mode is enabled, the buffer-local variable `abbrev-mode` is non-`nil`, and abbrevs are automatically expanded in the buffer. For the user-level commands for abbrevs, see Section "Abbrev Mode" in *The GNU Emacs Manual*.

35.1 Abbrev Tables

This section describes how to create and manipulate abbrev tables.

`make-abbrev-table &optional` *props*   [Function]
> This function creates and returns a new, empty abbrev table—an obarray containing no symbols. It is a vector filled with zeros. *props* is a property list that is applied to the new table (see Section 35.7 [Abbrev Table Properties], page 838).

`abbrev-table-p` *object*   [Function]
> This function returns a non-`nil` value if *object* is an abbrev table.

`clear-abbrev-table` *abbrev-table*   [Function]
> This function undefines all the abbrevs in *abbrev-table*, leaving it empty.

`copy-abbrev-table` *abbrev-table*   [Function]
> This function returns a copy of *abbrev-table*—a new abbrev table containing the same abbrev definitions. It does *not* copy any property lists; only the names, values, and functions.

define-abbrev-table *tabname definitions* **&optional** *docstring*   [Function]
      &rest *props*

> This function defines *tabname* (a symbol) as an abbrev table name, i.e., as a variable whose value is an abbrev table. It defines abbrevs in the table according to *definitions*, a list of elements of the form (`abbrevname expansion [hook] [props...]`). These elements are passed as arguments to `define-abbrev`.
>
> The optional string *docstring* is the documentation string of the variable *tabname*. The property list *props* is applied to the abbrev table (see Section 35.7 [Abbrev Table Properties], page 838).
>
> If this function is called more than once for the same *tabname*, subsequent calls add the definitions in *definitions* to *tabname*, rather than overwriting the entire original contents. (A subsequent call only overrides abbrevs explicitly redefined or undefined in *definitions*.)

abbrev-table-name-list   [Variable]

> This is a list of symbols whose values are abbrev tables. `define-abbrev-table` adds the new abbrev table name to this list.

insert-abbrev-table-description *name* **&optional** *human*   [Function]

> This function inserts before point a description of the abbrev table named *name*. The argument *name* is a symbol whose value is an abbrev table.
>
> If *human* is non-`nil`, the description is human-oriented. System abbrevs are listed and identified as such. Otherwise the description is a Lisp expression—a call to `define-abbrev-table` that would define *name* as it is currently defined, but without the system abbrevs. (The mode or package using *name* is supposed to add these to *name* separately.)

35.2 Defining Abbrevs

`define-abbrev` is the low-level basic function for defining an abbrev in an abbrev table.

When a major mode defines a system abbrev, it should call `define-abbrev` and specify `t` for the `:system` property. Be aware that any saved non-system abbrevs are restored at startup, i.e., before some major modes are loaded. Therefore, major modes should not assume that their abbrev tables are empty when they are first loaded.

define-abbrev *abbrev-table name expansion* **&optional** *hook* **&rest**   [Function]
      props

> This function defines an abbrev named *name*, in *abbrev-table*, to expand to *expansion* and call *hook*, with properties *props* (see Section 35.6 [Abbrev Properties], page 837). The return value is *name*. The `:system` property in *props* is treated specially here: if it has the value `force`, then it will overwrite an existing definition even for a non-system abbrev of the same name.
>
> *name* should be a string. The argument *expansion* is normally the desired expansion (a string), or `nil` to undefine the abbrev. If it is anything but a string or `nil`, then the abbreviation expands solely by running *hook*.
>
> The argument *hook* is a function or `nil`. If *hook* is non-`nil`, then it is called with no arguments after the abbrev is replaced with *expansion*; point is located at the end of *expansion* when *hook* is called.

If *hook* is a non-`nil` symbol whose `no-self-insert` property is non-`nil`, *hook* can explicitly control whether to insert the self-inserting input character that triggered the expansion. If *hook* returns non-`nil` in this case, that inhibits insertion of the character. By contrast, if *hook* returns `nil`, `expand-abbrev` (or `abbrev-insert`) also returns `nil`, as if expansion had not really occurred.

Normally, `define-abbrev` sets the variable `abbrevs-changed` to `t`, if it actually changes the abbrev. This is so that some commands will offer to save the abbrevs. It does not do this for a system abbrev, since those aren't saved anyway.

`only-global-abbrevs`   [User Option]

> If this variable is non-`nil`, it means that the user plans to use global abbrevs only. This tells the commands that define mode-specific abbrevs to define global ones instead. This variable does not alter the behavior of the functions in this section; it is examined by their callers.

35.3 Saving Abbrevs in Files

A file of saved abbrev definitions is actually a file of Lisp code. The abbrevs are saved in the form of a Lisp program to define the same abbrev tables with the same contents. Therefore, you can load the file with `load` (see Section 15.1 [How Programs Do Loading], page 244). However, the function `quietly-read-abbrev-file` is provided as a more convenient interface. Emacs automatically calls this function at startup.

User-level facilities such as `save-some-buffers` can save abbrevs in a file automatically, under the control of variables described here.

`abbrev-file-name`   [User Option]

> This is the default file name for reading and saving abbrevs. By default, Emacs will look for `~/.emacs.d/abbrev_defs`, and, if not found, for `~/.abbrev_defs`; if neither file exists, Emacs will create `~/.emacs.d/abbrev_defs`.

`quietly-read-abbrev-file` **&optional** *filename*   [Function]

> This function reads abbrev definitions from a file named *filename*, previously written with `write-abbrev-file`. If *filename* is omitted or `nil`, the file specified in `abbrev-file-name` is used.

> As the name implies, this function does not display any messages.

`save-abbrevs`   [User Option]

> A non-`nil` value for `save-abbrevs` means that Emacs should offer to save abbrevs (if any have changed) when files are saved. If the value is `silently`, Emacs saves the abbrevs without asking the user. `abbrev-file-name` specifies the file to save the abbrevs in. The default value is `t`.

`abbrevs-changed`   [Variable]

> This variable is set non-`nil` by defining or altering any abbrevs (except system abbrevs). This serves as a flag for various Emacs commands to offer to save your abbrevs.

write-abbrev-file &optional *filename* [Command]

> Save all abbrev definitions (except system abbrevs), for all abbrev tables listed in `abbrev-table-name-list`, in the file *filename*, in the form of a Lisp program that when loaded will define the same abbrevs. If *filename* is `nil` or omitted, `abbrev-file-name` is used. This function returns `nil`.

35.4 Looking Up and Expanding Abbreviations

Abbrevs are usually expanded by certain interactive commands, including `self-insert-command`. This section describes the subroutines used in writing such commands, as well as the variables they use for communication.

abbrev-symbol *abbrev* **&optional** *table* [Function]

> This function returns the symbol representing the abbrev named *abbrev*. It returns `nil` if that abbrev is not defined. The optional second argument *table* is the abbrev table in which to look it up. If *table* is `nil`, this function tries first the current buffer's local abbrev table, and second the global abbrev table.

abbrev-expansion *abbrev* **&optional** *table* [Function]

> This function returns the string that *abbrev* would expand into (as defined by the abbrev tables used for the current buffer). It returns `nil` if *abbrev* is not a valid abbrev. The optional argument *table* specifies the abbrev table to use, as in `abbrev-symbol`.

expand-abbrev [Command]

> This command expands the abbrev before point, if any. If point does not follow an abbrev, this command does nothing. To do the expansion, it calls the function that is the value of the `abbrev-expand-function` variable, with no arguments, and returns whatever that function does.

> The default expansion function returns the abbrev symbol if it did expansion, and `nil` otherwise. If the abbrev symbol has a hook function that is a symbol whose `no-self-insert` property is non-`nil`, and if the hook function returns `nil` as its value, then the default expansion function returns `nil`, even though expansion did occur.

abbrev-insert *abbrev* **&optional** *name start end* [Function]

> This function inserts the abbrev expansion of *abbrev*, replacing the text between `start` and `end`. If `start` is omitted, it defaults to point. `name`, if non-`nil`, should be the name by which this abbrev was found (a string); it is used to figure out whether to adjust the capitalization of the expansion. The function returns `abbrev` if the abbrev was successfully inserted, otherwise it returns `nil`.

abbrev-prefix-mark &optional *arg* [Command]

> This command marks the current location of point as the beginning of an abbrev. The next call to `expand-abbrev` will use the text from here to point (where it is then) as the abbrev to expand, rather than using the previous word as usual.

> First, this command expands any abbrev before point, unless *arg* is non-`nil`. (Interactively, *arg* is the prefix argument.) Then it inserts a hyphen before point, to indicate the start of the next abbrev to be expanded. The actual expansion removes the hyphen.

`abbrev-all-caps`   [User Option]

> When this is set non-`nil`, an abbrev entered entirely in upper case is expanded using
> all upper case. Otherwise, an abbrev entered entirely in upper case is expanded by
> capitalizing each word of the expansion.

`abbrev-start-location`   [Variable]

> The value of this variable is a buffer position (an integer or a marker) for
> `expand-abbrev` to use as the start of the next abbrev to be expanded. The
> value can also be `nil`, which means to use the word before point instead.
> `abbrev-start-location` is set to `nil` each time `expand-abbrev` is called. This
> variable is also set by `abbrev-prefix-mark`.

`abbrev-start-location-buffer`   [Variable]

> The value of this variable is the buffer for which `abbrev-start-location` has been
> set. Trying to expand an abbrev in any other buffer clears `abbrev-start-location`.
> This variable is set by `abbrev-prefix-mark`.

`last-abbrev`   [Variable]

> This is the `abbrev-symbol` of the most recent abbrev expanded. This information is
> left by `expand-abbrev` for the sake of the `unexpand-abbrev` command (see Section
> "Expanding Abbrevs" in *The GNU Emacs Manual*).

`last-abbrev-location`   [Variable]

> This is the location of the most recent abbrev expanded. This contains information
> left by `expand-abbrev` for the sake of the `unexpand-abbrev` command.

`last-abbrev-text`   [Variable]

> This is the exact expansion text of the most recent abbrev expanded, after case
> conversion (if any). Its value is `nil` if the abbrev has already been unexpanded. This
> contains information left by `expand-abbrev` for the sake of the `unexpand-abbrev`
> command.

`abbrev-expand-function`   [Variable]

> The value of this variable is a function that `expand-abbrev` will call with no argu-
> ments to do the expansion. The function can do anything it wants before and after
> performing the expansion. It should return the abbrev symbol if expansion took place.

The following sample code shows a simple use of `abbrev-expand-function`. It assumes
that `foo-mode` is a mode for editing certain files in which lines that start with '#' are comments. You want to use Text mode abbrevs for those lines. The regular local abbrev table,
`foo-mode-abbrev-table` is appropriate for all other lines. See Section 35.5 [Standard Abbrev Tables], page 837, for the definitions of `local-abbrev-table` and `text-mode-abbrev-
table`. See Section 12.11 [Advising Functions], page 204, for details of `add-function`.

```
(defun foo-mode-abbrev-expand-function (expand)
  (if (not (save-excursion (forward-line 0) (eq (char-after) ?#)))
      ;; Performs normal expansion.
      (funcall expand)
    ;; We're inside a comment: use the text-mode abbrevs.
    (let ((local-abbrev-table text-mode-abbrev-table))
      (funcall expand))))
```

```
(add-hook 'foo-mode-hook
          #'(lambda ()
              (add-function :around (local 'abbrev-expand-function)
                            #'foo-mode-abbrev-expand-function)))
```

35.5 Standard Abbrev Tables

Here we list the variables that hold the abbrev tables for the preloaded major modes of Emacs.

global-abbrev-table   [Variable]
> This is the abbrev table for mode-independent abbrevs. The abbrevs defined in it apply to all buffers. Each buffer may also have a local abbrev table, whose abbrev definitions take precedence over those in the global table.

local-abbrev-table   [Variable]
> The value of this buffer-local variable is the (mode-specific) abbreviation table of the current buffer. It can also be a list of such tables.

abbrev-minor-mode-table-alist   [Variable]
> The value of this variable is a list of elements of the form (*mode . abbrev-table*) where *mode* is the name of a variable: if the variable is bound to a non-nil value, then the *abbrev-table* is active, otherwise it is ignored. *abbrev-table* can also be a list of abbrev tables.

fundamental-mode-abbrev-table   [Variable]
> This is the local abbrev table used in Fundamental mode; in other words, it is the local abbrev table in all buffers in Fundamental mode.

text-mode-abbrev-table   [Variable]
> This is the local abbrev table used in Text mode.

lisp-mode-abbrev-table   [Variable]
> This is the local abbrev table used in Lisp mode. It is the parent of the local abbrev table used in Emacs Lisp mode. See Section 35.7 [Abbrev Table Properties], page 838.

35.6 Abbrev Properties

Abbrevs have properties, some of which influence the way they work. You can provide them as arguments to **define-abbrev**, and manipulate them with the following functions:

abbrev-put *abbrev prop val*   [Function]
> Set the property *prop* of *abbrev* to value *val*.

abbrev-get *abbrev prop*   [Function]
> Return the property *prop* of *abbrev*, or nil if the abbrev has no such property.

The following properties have special meanings:

:count
> This property counts the number of times the abbrev has been expanded. If not explicitly set, it is initialized to 0 by **define-abbrev**.

:system   If non-**nil**, this property marks the abbrev as a system abbrev. Such abbrevs
           are not saved (see Section 35.3 [Abbrev Files], page 834).

:enable-function
           If non-**nil**, this property should be a function of no arguments which returns
           nil if the abbrev should not be used and **t** otherwise.

:case-fixed
           If non-**nil**, this property indicates that the case of the abbrev's name is signif-
           icant and should only match a text with the same pattern of capitalization. It
           also disables the code that modifies the capitalization of the expansion.

35.7 Abbrev Table Properties

Like abbrevs, abbrev tables have properties, some of which influence the way they work.
You can provide them as arguments to **define-abbrev-table**, and manipulate them with
the functions:

abbrev-table-put *table prop val*   [Function]
       Set the property *prop* of abbrev table *table* to value *val*.

abbrev-table-get *table prop*   [Function]
       Return the property *prop* of abbrev table *table*, or **nil** if the abbrev has no such
       property.

   The following properties have special meaning:

:enable-function
           This is like the :enable-function abbrev property except that it applies to
           all abbrevs in the table. It is used before even trying to find the abbrev before
           point, so it can dynamically modify the abbrev table.

:case-fixed
           This is like the :case-fixed abbrev property except that it applies to all ab-
           brevs in the table.

:regexp   If non-**nil**, this property is a regular expression that indicates how to extract
           the name of the abbrev before point, before looking it up in the table. When
           the regular expression matches before point, the abbrev name is expected to
           be in submatch 1. If this property is **nil**, the default is to use **backward-word**
           and **forward-word** to find the name. This property allows the use of abbrevs
           whose name contains characters of non-word syntax.

:parents   This property holds a list of tables from which to inherit other abbrevs.

:abbrev-table-modiff
           This property holds a counter incremented each time a new abbrev is added to
           the table.

36 Processes

In the terminology of operating systems, a *process* is a space in which a program can execute. Emacs runs in a process. Emacs Lisp programs can invoke other programs in processes of their own. These are called *subprocesses* or *child processes* of the Emacs process, which is their *parent process*.

A subprocess of Emacs may be *synchronous* or *asynchronous*, depending on how it is created. When you create a synchronous subprocess, the Lisp program waits for the subprocess to terminate before continuing execution. When you create an asynchronous subprocess, it can run in parallel with the Lisp program. This kind of subprocess is represented within Emacs by a Lisp object which is also called a "process". Lisp programs can use this object to communicate with the subprocess or to control it. For example, you can send signals, obtain status information, receive output from the process, or send input to it.

In addition to processes that run programs, Lisp programs can open connections of several types to devices or processes running on the same machine or on other machines. The supported connection types are: TCP and UDP network connections, serial port connections, and pipe connections. Each such connection is also represented by a process object.

processp *object* [Function]
> This function returns **t** if *object* represents an Emacs process object, **nil** otherwise. The process object can represent a subprocess running a program or a connection of any supported type.

In addition to subprocesses of the current Emacs session, you can also access other processes running on your machine. See Section 36.12 [System Processes], page 865.

36.1 Functions that Create Subprocesses

There are three primitives that create a new subprocess in which to run a program. One of them, **make-process**, creates an asynchronous process and returns a process object (see Section 36.4 [Asynchronous Processes], page 846). The other two, **call-process** and **call-process-region**, create a synchronous process and do not return a process object (see Section 36.3 [Synchronous Processes], page 842). There are various higher-level functions that make use of these primitives to run particular types of process.

Synchronous and asynchronous processes are explained in the following sections. Since the three functions are all called in a similar fashion, their common arguments are described here.

In all cases, the functions specify the program to be run. An error is signaled if the file is not found or cannot be executed. If the file name is relative, the variable **exec-path** contains a list of directories to search. Emacs initializes **exec-path** when it starts up, based on the value of the environment variable PATH. The standard file name constructs, '~', '.', and '..', are interpreted as usual in **exec-path**, but environment variable substitutions ('$HOME', etc.) are not recognized; use **substitute-in-file-name** to perform them (see Section 24.8.4 [File Name Expansion], page 522). **nil** in this list refers to **default-directory**.

Executing a program can also try adding suffixes to the specified name:

exec-suffixes   [User Option]

> This variable is a list of suffixes (strings) to try adding to the specified program file name. The list should include "" if you want the name to be tried exactly as specified. The default value is system-dependent.

Please note: The argument *program* contains only the name of the program file; it may not contain any command-line arguments. You must use a separate argument, *args*, to provide those, as described below.

Each of the subprocess-creating functions has a *buffer-or-name* argument that specifies where the output from the program will go. It should be a buffer or a buffer name; if it is a buffer name, that will create the buffer if it does not already exist. It can also be `nil`, which says to discard the output, unless a custom filter function handles it. (See Section 36.9.2 [Filter Functions], page 859, and Chapter 18 [Read and Print], page 302.) Normally, you should avoid having multiple processes send output to the same buffer because their output would be intermixed randomly. For synchronous processes, you can send the output to a file instead of a buffer (and the corresponding argument is therefore more appropriately called *destination*). By default, both standard output and standard error streams go to the same destination, but all the 3 primitives allow optionally to direct the standard error stream to a different destination.

All three of the subprocess-creating functions allow to specify command-line arguments for the process to run. For `call-process` and `call-process-region`, these come in the form of a `&rest` argument, *args*. For `make-process`, both the program to run and its command-line arguments are specified as a list of strings. The command-line arguments must all be strings, and they are supplied to the program as separate argument strings. Wildcard characters and other shell constructs have no special meanings in these strings, since the strings are passed directly to the specified program.

The subprocess inherits its environment from Emacs, but you can specify overrides for it with `process-environment`. See Section 38.3 [System Environment], page 994. The subprocess gets its current directory from the value of `default-directory`.

exec-directory   [Variable]

> The value of this variable is a string, the name of a directory that contains programs that come with GNU Emacs and are intended for Emacs to invoke. The program `movemail` is an example of such a program; Rmail uses it to fetch new mail from an inbox.

exec-path   [User Option]

> The value of this variable is a list of directories to search for programs to run in subprocesses. Each element is either the name of a directory (i.e., a string), or `nil`, which stands for the default directory (which is the value of `default-directory`). See Section 24.6.6 [Locating Files], page 513, for the details of this search.
>
> The value of `exec-path` is used by `call-process` and `start-process` when the *program* argument is not an absolute file name.
>
> Generally, you should not modify `exec-path` directly. Instead, ensure that your `PATH` environment variable is set appropriately before starting Emacs. Trying to modify `exec-path` independently of `PATH` can lead to confusing results.

36.2 Shell Arguments

Lisp programs sometimes need to run a shell and give it a command that contains file names that were specified by the user. These programs ought to be able to support any valid file name. But the shell gives special treatment to certain characters, and if these characters occur in the file name, they will confuse the shell. To handle these characters, use the function `shell-quote-argument`:

`shell-quote-argument` *argument*   [Function]
>   This function returns a string that represents, in shell syntax, an argument whose actual contents are *argument*. It should work reliably to concatenate the return value into a shell command and then pass it to a shell for execution.
>
>   Precisely what this function does depends on your operating system. The function is designed to work with the syntax of your system's standard shell; if you use an unusual shell, you will need to redefine this function. See Section 38.22 [Security Considerations], page 1023.
>
> ```
>         ;; This example shows the behavior on GNU and Unix systems.
> (shell-quote-argument "foo > bar")
>         ⇒ "foo\\ \\>\\ bar"
>
>         ;; This example shows the behavior on MS-DOS and MS-Windows.
> (shell-quote-argument "foo > bar")
>         ⇒ "\"foo > bar\""
> ```
>
>   Here's an example of using `shell-quote-argument` to construct a shell command:
>
> ```
> (concat "diff -u "
>         (shell-quote-argument oldfile)
>         " "
>         (shell-quote-argument newfile))
> ```

The following two functions are useful for combining a list of individual command-line argument strings into a single string, and taking a string apart into a list of individual command-line arguments. These functions are mainly intended for converting user input in the minibuffer, a Lisp string, into a list of string arguments to be passed to `make-process`, `call-process` or `start-process`, or for converting such lists of arguments into a single Lisp string to be presented in the minibuffer or echo area. Note that if a shell is involved (e.g., if using `call-process-shell-command`), arguments should still be protected by `shell-quote-argument`; `combine-and-quote-strings` is *not* intended to protect special characters from shell evaluation.

`split-string-and-unquote` *string* **&optional** *separators*   [Function]
>   This function splits *string* into substrings at matches for the regular expression *separators*, like `split-string` does (see Section 4.3 [Creating Strings], page 50); in addition, it removes quoting from the substrings. It then makes a list of the substrings and returns it.
>
>   If *separators* is omitted or `nil`, it defaults to `"\\s-+"`, which is a regular expression that matches one or more characters with whitespace syntax (see Section 34.2.1 [Syntax Class Table], page 817).

This function supports two types of quoting: enclosing a whole string in double quotes
"...", and quoting individual characters with a backslash escape '\'. The latter is
also used in Lisp strings, so this function can handle those as well.

combine-and-quote-strings *list-of-strings* **&optional** *separator*   [Function]
> This function concatenates *list-of-strings* into a single string, quoting each string as
> necessary. It also sticks the *separator* string between each pair of strings; if *separator*
> is omitted or **nil**, it defaults to " ". The return value is the resulting string.
>
> The strings in *list-of-strings* that need quoting are those that include *separator* as
> their substring. Quoting a string encloses it in double quotes "...". In the simplest
> case, if you are consing a command from the individual command-line arguments,
> every argument that includes embedded blanks will be quoted.

36.3 Creating a Synchronous Process

After a *synchronous process* is created, Emacs waits for the process to terminate before
continuing. Starting Dired on GNU or Unix[1] is an example of this: it runs **ls** in a synchronous process, then modifies the output slightly. Because the process is synchronous,
the entire directory listing arrives in the buffer before Emacs tries to do anything with it.

While Emacs waits for the synchronous subprocess to terminate, the user can quit by
typing *C-g*. The first *C-g* tries to kill the subprocess with a **SIGINT** signal; but it waits
until the subprocess actually terminates before quitting. If during that time the user types
another *C-g*, that kills the subprocess instantly with **SIGKILL** and quits immediately (except
on MS-DOS, where killing other processes doesn't work). See Section 20.11 [Quitting],
page 382.

The synchronous subprocess functions return an indication of how the process terminated.

The output from a synchronous subprocess is generally decoded using a coding system,
much like text read from a file. The input sent to a subprocess by **call-process-region** is
encoded using a coding system, much like text written into a file. See Section 32.10 [Coding
Systems], page 773.

call-process *program* **&optional** *infile destination display* **&rest**   [Function]
> **args**
> This function calls *program* and waits for it to finish.
>
> The current working directory of the subprocess is set to the current buffer's value
> of **default-directory** if that is local (as determined by **unhandled-file-name-
> directory**), or "~" otherwise. If you want to run a process in a remote directory use
> **process-file**.
>
> The standard input for the new process comes from file *infile* if *infile* is not **nil**,
> and from the null device otherwise. The argument *destination* says where to put the
> process output. Here are the possibilities:
>
> a buffer   Insert the output in that buffer, before point. This includes both the
>   standard output stream and the standard error stream of the process.

---

[1] On other systems, Emacs uses a Lisp emulation of **ls**; see Section 24.9 [Contents of Directories], page 527.

a buffer name (a string)
> Insert the output in a buffer with that name, before point.

t
> Insert the output in the current buffer, before point.

nil
> Discard the output.

0
> Discard the output, and return `nil` immediately without waiting for the subprocess to finish.
>
> In this case, the process is not truly synchronous, since it can run in parallel with Emacs; but you can think of it as synchronous in that Emacs is essentially finished with the subprocess as soon as this function returns.
>
> MS-DOS doesn't support asynchronous subprocesses, so this option doesn't work there.

`(:file file-name)`
> Send the output to the file name specified, overwriting it if it already exists.

`(real-destination error-destination)`
> Keep the standard output stream separate from the standard error stream; deal with the ordinary output as specified by *real-destination*, and dispose of the error output according to *error-destination*. If *error-destination* is `nil`, that means to discard the error output, `t` means mix it with the ordinary output, and a string specifies a file name to redirect error output into.
>
> You can't directly specify a buffer to put the error output in; that is too difficult to implement. But you can achieve this result by sending the error output to a temporary file and then inserting the file into a buffer when the subprocess finishes.

If *display* is non-`nil`, then `call-process` redisplays the buffer as output is inserted. (However, if the coding system chosen for decoding output is `undecided`, meaning deduce the encoding from the actual data, then redisplay sometimes cannot continue once non-ASCII characters are encountered. There are fundamental reasons why it is hard to fix this; see Section 36.9 [Output from Processes], page 857.)

Otherwise the function `call-process` does no redisplay, and the results become visible on the screen only when Emacs redisplays that buffer in the normal course of events.

The remaining arguments, *args*, are strings that specify command line arguments for the program. Each string is passed to *program* as a separate argument.

The value returned by `call-process` (unless you told it not to wait) indicates the reason for process termination. A number gives the exit status of the subprocess; 0 means success, and any other value means failure. If the process terminated with a signal, `call-process` returns a string describing the signal. If you told `call-process` not to wait, it returns `nil`.

In the examples below, the buffer 'foo' is current.

```
(call-process "pwd" nil t)
    ⇒ 0

---------- Buffer: foo ----------
/home/lewis/manual
---------- Buffer: foo ----------

(call-process "grep" nil "bar" nil "lewis" "/etc/passwd")
    ⇒ 0

---------- Buffer: bar ----------
lewis:x:1001:1001:Bil Lewis,,,,:/home/lewis:/bin/bash

---------- Buffer: bar ----------
```

Here is an example of the use of `call-process`, as used to be found in the definition of the `insert-directory` function:

```
(call-process insert-directory-program nil t nil switches
              (if full-directory-p
                  (concat (file-name-as-directory file) ".")
                file))
```

process-file *program* **&optional** *infile buffer display* **&rest** *args*   [Function]
This function processes files synchronously in a separate process. It is similar to `call-process`, but may invoke a file handler based on the value of the variable `default-directory`, which specifies the current working directory of the subprocess.

The arguments are handled in almost the same way as for `call-process`, with the following differences:

Some file handlers may not support all combinations and forms of the arguments *infile*, *buffer*, and *display*. For example, some file handlers might behave as if *display* were `nil`, regardless of the value actually passed. As another example, some file handlers might not support separating standard output and error output by way of the *buffer* argument.

If a file handler is invoked, it determines the program to run based on the first argument *program*. For instance, suppose that a handler for remote files is invoked. Then the path that is used for searching for the program might be different from `exec-path`.

The second argument *infile* may invoke a file handler. The file handler could be different from the handler chosen for the `process-file` function itself. (For example, `default-directory` could be on one remote host, and *infile* on a different remote host. Or `default-directory` could be non-special, whereas *infile* is on a remote host.)

If *buffer* is a list of the form (`real-destination error-destination`), and *error-destination* names a file, then the same remarks as for *infile* apply.

The remaining arguments (*args*) will be passed to the process verbatim. Emacs is not involved in processing file names that are present in *args*. To avoid confusion, it may be best to avoid absolute file names in *args*, but rather to specify all file names as relative to `default-directory`. The function `file-relative-name` is useful for constructing such relative file names.

`process-file-side-effects`   [Variable]

>   This variable indicates whether a call of `process-file` changes remote files.

>   By default, this variable is always set to `t`, meaning that a call of `process-file` could potentially change any file on a remote host. When set to `nil`, a file handler could optimize its behavior with respect to remote file attribute caching.

>   You should only ever change this variable with a let-binding; never with `setq`.

`call-process-region` *start end program* **&optional** *delete*   [Function]
>   *destination display* **&rest** *args*
>   This function sends the text from *start* to *end* as standard input to a process running *program*. It deletes the text sent if *delete* is non-`nil`; this is useful when *destination* is `t`, to insert the output in the current buffer in place of the input.

>   The arguments *destination* and *display* control what to do with the output from the subprocess, and whether to update the display as it comes in. For details, see the description of `call-process`, above. If *destination* is the integer 0, `call-process-region` discards the output and returns `nil` immediately, without waiting for the subprocess to finish (this only works if asynchronous subprocesses are supported; i.e., not on MS-DOS).

>   The remaining arguments, *args*, are strings that specify command line arguments for the program.

>   The return value of `call-process-region` is just like that of `call-process`: `nil` if you told it to return without waiting; otherwise, a number or string which indicates how the subprocess terminated.

>   In the following example, we use `call-process-region` to run the `cat` utility, with standard input being the first five characters in buffer 'foo' (the word 'input'). `cat` copies its standard input into its standard output. Since the argument *destination* is `t`, this output is inserted in the current buffer.

```
---------- Buffer: foo ----------
input⋆
---------- Buffer: foo ----------

(call-process-region 1 6 "cat" nil t)
     ⇒ 0

---------- Buffer: foo ----------
inputinput⋆
---------- Buffer: foo ----------
```

>   For example, the `shell-command-on-region` command uses `call-process-region` in a manner similar to this:

```
(call-process-region
 start end
 shell-file-name        ; name of program
 nil                    ; do not delete region
 buffer                 ; send output to buffer
 nil                    ; no redisplay during output
 "-c" command)          ; arguments for the shell
```

`call-process-shell-command` *command* **&optional** *infile destination*   [Function]
    display

    This function executes the shell command *command* synchronously. The other arguments are handled as in `call-process`. An old calling convention allowed passing any number of additional arguments after *display*, which were concatenated to *command*; this is still supported, but strongly discouraged.

`process-file-shell-command` *command* **&optional** *infile destination*   [Function]
    display

    This function is like `call-process-shell-command`, but uses `process-file` internally. Depending on `default-directory`, *command* can be executed also on remote hosts. An old calling convention allowed passing any number of additional arguments after *display*, which were concatenated to *command*; this is still supported, but strongly discouraged.

`shell-command-to-string` *command*   [Function]

    This function executes *command* (a string) as a shell command, then returns the command's output as a string.

`process-lines` *program* **&rest** *args*   [Function]

    This function runs *program*, waits for it to finish, and returns its output as a list of strings. Each string in the list holds a single line of text output by the program; the end-of-line characters are stripped from each line. The arguments beyond *program*, *args*, are strings that specify command-line arguments with which to run the program.

    If *program* exits with a non-zero exit status, this function signals an error.

    This function works by calling `call-process`, so program output is decoded in the same way as for `call-process`.

36.4 Creating an Asynchronous Process

In this section, we describe how to create an *asynchronous process*. After an asynchronous process is created, it runs in parallel with Emacs, and Emacs can communicate with it using the functions described in the following sections (see Section 36.7 [Input to Processes], page 854, and see Section 36.9 [Output from Processes], page 857). Note that process communication is only partially asynchronous: Emacs sends data to the process only when certain functions are called, and Emacs accepts data from the process only while waiting for input or for a time delay.

    An asynchronous process is controlled either via a *pty* (pseudo-terminal) or a *pipe*. The choice of pty or pipe is made when creating the process, by default based on the value of the variable `process-connection-type` (see below). If available, ptys are usually preferable for processes visible to the user, as in Shell mode, because they allow for job control (*C-c*, *C-z*, etc.) between the process and its children, and because interactive programs treat ptys as terminal devices, whereas pipes don't support these features. However, for subprocesses used by Lisp programs for internal purposes, it is often better to use a pipe, because pipes are more efficient, and because they are immune to stray character injections that ptys introduce for large (around 500 byte) messages. Also, the total number of ptys is limited on many systems and it is good not to waste them.

make-process **&rest** *args* [Function]

This function is the basic low-level primitive for starting asynchronous subprocesses. It returns a process object representing the subprocess. Compared to the more high-level **start-process**, described below, it takes keyword arguments, is more flexible, and allows to specify process filters and sentinels in a single call.

The arguments *args* are a list of keyword/argument pairs. Omitting a keyword is always equivalent to specifying it with value **nil**. Here are the meaningful keywords:

:name *name*

Use the string *name* as the process name; if a process with this name already exists, then *name* is modified (by appending '<1>', etc.) to be unique.

:buffer *buffer*

Use *buffer* as the process buffer. If the value is **nil**, the subprocess is not associated with any buffer.

:command *command*

Use *command* as the command line of the process. The value should be a list starting with the program's executable file name, followed by strings to give to the program as its arguments. If the first element of the list is **nil**, Emacs opens a new pseudoterminal (pty) and associates its input and output with *buffer*, without actually running any program; the rest of the list elements are ignored in that case.

:coding *coding*

If *coding* is a symbol, it specifies the coding system to be used for both reading and writing of data from and to the connection. If *coding* is a cons cell (*decoding . encoding*), then *decoding* will be used for reading and *encoding* for writing. The coding system used for encoding the data written to the program is also used for encoding the command-line arguments (but not the program itself, whose file name is encoded as any other file name; see Section 32.10.2 [Encoding and I/O], page 775).

If *coding* is **nil**, the default rules for finding the coding system will apply. See Section 32.10.5 [Default Coding Systems], page 780.

:connection-type *type*

Initialize the type of device used to communicate with the subprocess. Possible values are **pty** to use a pty, **pipe** to use a pipe, or **nil** to use the default derived from the value of the **process-connection-type** variable. This parameter and the value of **process-connection-type** are ignored if a non-**nil** value is specified for the **:stderr** parameter; in that case, the type will always be **pipe**.

:noquery *query-flag*

Initialize the process query flag to *query-flag*. See Section 36.11 [Query Before Exit], page 864.

:stop *stopped*

If *stopped* is non-**nil**, start the process in the stopped state.

:filter *filter*

> Initialize the process filter to *filter*. If not specified, a default filter will be provided, which can be overridden later. See Section 36.9.2 [Filter Functions], page 859 .

:sentinel *sentinel*

> Initialize the process sentinel to *sentinel*. If not specified, a default sentinel will be used, which can be overridden later. See Section 36.10 [Sentinels], page 862.

:stderr *stderr*

> Associate *stderr* with the standard error of the process. A non-`nil` value should be either a buffer or a pipe process created with `make-pipe-process`, described below.

The original argument list, modified with the actual connection information, is available via the `process-contact` function.

The current working directory of the subprocess is set to the current buffer's value of `default-directory` if that is local (as determined by 'unhandled-file-name-directory'), or `"~"` otherwise. If you want to run a process in a remote direcotry use `start-file-process`.

make-pipe-process &rest *args*   [Function]

> This function creates a bidirectional pipe which can be attached to a child process. This is useful with the `:stderr` keyword of `make-process`. The function returns a process object.

The arguments *args* are a list of keyword/argument pairs. Omitting a keyword is always equivalent to specifying it with value `nil`.

Here are the meaningful keywords:

:name *name*

> Use the string *name* as the process name. As with `make-process`, it is modified if necessary to make it unique.

:buffer *buffer*

> Use *buffer* as the process buffer.

:coding *coding*

> If *coding* is a symbol, it specifies the coding system to be used for both reading and writing of data from and to the connection. If *coding* is a cons cell (`decoding . encoding`), then *decoding* will be used for reading and *encoding* for writing.
>
> If *coding* is `nil`, the default rules for finding the coding system will apply. See Section 32.10.5 [Default Coding Systems], page 780.

:noquery *query-flag*

> Initialize the process query flag to *query-flag*. See Section 36.11 [Query Before Exit], page 864.

:stop *stopped*

> If *stopped* is non-`nil`, start the process in the stopped state.

:filter *filter*

> Initialize the process filter to *filter*. If not specified, a default filter will be provided, which can be changed later. See Section 36.9.2 [Filter Functions], page 859.

:sentinel *sentinel*

> Initialize the process sentinel to *sentinel*. If not specified, a default sentinel will be used, which can be changed later. See Section 36.10 [Sentinels], page 862.

The original argument list, modified with the actual connection information, is available via the `process-contact` function.

`start-process` *name buffer-or-name program* **&rest** *args*   [Function]

> This function is a higher-level wrapper around `make-process`, exposing an interface that is similar to `call-process`. It creates a new asynchronous subprocess and starts the specified *program* running in it. It returns a process object that stands for the new subprocess in Lisp. The argument *name* specifies the name for the process object; as with `make-process`, it is modified if necessary to make it unique. The buffer *buffer-or-name* is the buffer to associate with the process.
>
> If *program* is `nil`, Emacs opens a new pseudoterminal (pty) and associates its input and output with *buffer-or-name*, without creating a subprocess. In that case, the remaining arguments *args* are ignored.
>
> The rest of *args* are strings that specify command line arguments for the subprocess.
>
> In the example below, the first process is started and runs (rather, sleeps) for 100 seconds (the output buffer 'foo' is created immediately). Meanwhile, the second process is started, and given the name 'my-process<1>' for the sake of uniqueness. It inserts the directory listing at the end of the buffer 'foo', before the first process finishes. Then it finishes, and a message to that effect is inserted in the buffer. Much later, the first process finishes, and another message is inserted in the buffer for it.
>
> ```
> (start-process "my-process" "foo" "sleep" "100")
>      ⇒ #<process my-process>
>
> (start-process "my-process" "foo" "ls" "-l" "/bin")
>      ⇒ #<process my-process<1>>
>
> ---------- Buffer: foo ----------
> total 8336
> -rwxr-xr-x 1 root root 971384 Mar 30 10:14 bash
> -rwxr-xr-x 1 root root 146920 Jul  5  2011 bsd-csh
> ...
> -rwxr-xr-x 1 root root 696880 Feb 28 15:55 zsh4
>
> Process my-process<1> finished
>
> Process my-process finished
> ---------- Buffer: foo ----------
> ```

`start-file-process` *name buffer-or-name program* **&rest** *args*   [Function]

> Like `start-process`, this function starts a new asynchronous subprocess running *program* in it, and returns its process object.

The difference from `start-process` is that this function may invoke a file handler based on the value of `default-directory`. This handler ought to run *program*, perhaps on the local host, perhaps on a remote host that corresponds to `default-directory`. In the latter case, the local part of `default-directory` becomes the working directory of the process.

This function does not try to invoke file name handlers for *program* or for the rest of *args*.

Depending on the implementation of the file handler, it might not be possible to apply `process-filter` or `process-sentinel` to the resulting process object. See Section 36.9.2 [Filter Functions], page 859, and Section 36.10 [Sentinels], page 862.

Some file handlers may not support `start-file-process` (for example the function `ange-ftp-hook-function`). In such cases, this function does nothing and returns `nil`.

`start-process-shell-command` *name buffer-or-name command*   [Function]
This function is like `start-process`, except that it uses a shell to execute the specified *command*. The argument *command* is a shell command string. The variable `shell-file-name` specifies which shell to use.

The point of running a program through the shell, rather than directly with `make-process` or `start-process`, is so that you can employ shell features such as wildcards in the arguments. It follows that if you include any arbitrary user-specified arguments in the command, you should quote them with `shell-quote-argument` first, so that any special shell characters do *not* have their special shell meanings. See Section 36.2 [Shell Arguments], page 841. Of course, when executing commands based on user input you should also consider the security implications.

`start-file-process-shell-command` *name buffer-or-name*   [Function]
    command
This function is like `start-process-shell-command`, but uses `start-file-process` internally. Because of this, *command* can also be executed on remote hosts, depending on `default-directory`.

`process-connection-type`   [Variable]
This variable controls the type of device used to communicate with asynchronous subprocesses. If it is non-`nil`, then ptys are used, when available. Otherwise, pipes are used.

The value of `process-connection-type` takes effect when `make-process` or `start-process` is called. So you can specify how to communicate with one subprocess by binding the variable around the call to these functions.

Note that the value of this variable is ignored when `make-process` is called with a non-`nil` value of the `:stderr` parameter; in that case, Emacs will communicate with the process using pipes.

```
(let ((process-connection-type nil))  ; use a pipe
  (start-process ...))
```

To determine whether a given subprocess actually got a pipe or a pty, use the function `process-tty-name` (see Section 36.6 [Process Information], page 851).

36.5 Deleting Processes

Deleting a process disconnects Emacs immediately from the subprocess. Processes are deleted automatically after they terminate, but not necessarily right away. You can delete a process explicitly at any time. If you explicitly delete a terminated process before it is deleted automatically, no harm results. Deleting a running process sends a signal to terminate it (and its child processes, if any), and calls the process sentinel. See Section 36.10 [Sentinels], page 862.

When a process is deleted, the process object itself continues to exist as long as other Lisp objects point to it. All the Lisp primitives that work on process objects accept deleted processes, but those that do I/O or send signals will report an error. The process mark continues to point to the same place as before, usually into a buffer where output from the process was being inserted.

delete-exited-processes   [User Option]
>   This variable controls automatic deletion of processes that have terminated (due to calling `exit` or to a signal). If it is `nil`, then they continue to exist until the user runs `list-processes`. Otherwise, they are deleted immediately after they exit.

delete-process *process*   [Function]
>   This function deletes a process, killing it with a `SIGKILL` signal if the process was running a program. The argument may be a process, the name of a process, a buffer, or the name of a buffer. (A buffer or buffer-name stands for the process that `get-buffer-process` returns.) Calling `delete-process` on a running process terminates it, updates the process status, and runs the sentinel immediately. If the process has already terminated, calling `delete-process` has no effect on its status, or on the running of its sentinel (which will happen sooner or later).
>
>   If the process object represents a network, serial, or pipe connection, its status changes to `closed`; otherwise, it changes to `signal`, unless the process already exited. See Section 36.6 [Process Information], page 851.
>
> ```
> (delete-process "*shell*")
>      ⇒ nil
> ```

36.6 Process Information

Several functions return information about processes.

list-processes &optional *query-only buffer*   [Command]
>   This command displays a listing of all living processes. In addition, it finally deletes any process whose status was 'Exited' or 'Signaled'. It returns `nil`.
>
>   The processes are shown in a buffer named `*Process List*` (unless you specify otherwise using the optional argument *buffer*), whose major mode is Process Menu mode.
>
>   If *query-only* is non-`nil`, it only lists processes whose query flag is non-`nil`. See Section 36.11 [Query Before Exit], page 864.

process-list   [Function]
>   This function returns a list of all processes that have not been deleted.
>
> ```
> (process-list)
>      ⇒ (#<process display-time> #<process shell>)
> ```

get-process *name*   [Function]

    This function returns the process named *name* (a string), or `nil` if there is none. The argument *name* can also be a process object, in which case it is returned.

```
(get-process "shell")
     ⇒ #<process shell>
```

process-command *process*   [Function]

    This function returns the command that was executed to start *process*. This is a list of strings, the first string being the program executed and the rest of the strings being the arguments that were given to the program. For a network, serial, or pipe connection, this is either `nil`, which means the process is running or `t` (process is stopped).

```
(process-command (get-process "shell"))
     ⇒ ("bash" "-i")
```

process-contact *process* **&optional** *key*   [Function]

    This function returns information about how a network, a serial, or a pipe connection was set up. When *key* is `nil`, it returns (*hostname service*) for a network connection, (*port speed*) for a serial connection, and `t` for a pipe connection. For an ordinary child process, this function always returns `t` when called with a `nil` *key*.

    If *key* is `t`, the value is the complete status information for the connection, server, serial port, or pipe; that is, the list of keywords and values specified in `make-network-process`, `make-serial-process`, or `make-pipe-process`, except that some of the values represent the current status instead of what you specified.

    For a network process, the values include (see `make-network-process` for a complete list):

  `:buffer`   The associated value is the process buffer.

  `:filter`   The associated value is the process filter function. See Section 36.9.2 [Filter Functions], page 859.

  `:sentinel`

        The associated value is the process sentinel function. See Section 36.10 [Sentinels], page 862.

  `:remote`   In a connection, the address in internal format of the remote peer.

  `:local`   The local address, in internal format.

  `:service` In a server, if you specified `t` for *service*, this value is the actual port number.

    `:local` and `:remote` are included even if they were not specified explicitly in `make-network-process`.

    For a serial connection, see `make-serial-process` and `serial-process-configure` for the list of keys. For a pipe connection, see `make-pipe-process` for the list of keys.

    If *key* is a keyword, the function returns the value corresponding to that keyword.

process-id *process*   [Function]

    This function returns the PID of *process*. This is an integral number that distinguishes the process *process* from all other processes running on the same computer at the current time. The PID of a process is chosen by the operating system kernel when the process is started and remains constant as long as the process exists. For network, serial, and pipe connections, this function returns `nil`.

process-name *process*   [Function]
    This function returns the name of *process*, as a string.

process-status *process-name*   [Function]
    This function returns the status of *process-name* as a symbol. The argument *process-name* must be a process, a buffer, or a process name (a string).

    The possible values for an actual subprocess are:

`run`	for a process that is running.
`stop`	for a process that is stopped but continuable.
`exit`	for a process that has exited.
`signal`	for a process that has received a fatal signal.
`open`	for a network, serial, or pipe connection that is open.
`closed`	for a network, serial, or pipe connection that is closed. Once a connection is closed, you cannot reopen it, though you might be able to open a new connection to the same place.
`connect`	for a non-blocking connection that is waiting to complete.
`failed`	for a non-blocking connection that has failed to complete.
`listen`	for a network server that is listening.
`nil`	if *process-name* is not the name of an existing process.

        `(process-status (get-buffer "*shell*"))`
            ⇒ `run`

For a network, serial, or pipe connection, `process-status` returns one of the symbols `open`, `stop`, or `closed`. The latter means that the other side closed the connection, or Emacs did `delete-process`. The value `stop` means that `stop-process` was called on the connection.

process-live-p *process*   [Function]
    This function returns non-`nil` if *process* is alive. A process is considered alive if its status is `run`, `open`, `listen`, `connect` or `stop`.

process-type *process*   [Function]
    This function returns the symbol `network` for a network connection or server, `serial` for a serial port connection, `pipe` for a pipe connection, or `real` for a subprocess created for running a program.

process-exit-status *process*   [Function]
    This function returns the exit status of *process* or the signal number that killed it. (Use the result of `process-status` to determine which of those it is.) If *process* has not yet terminated, the value is 0. For network, serial, and pipe connections that are already closed, the value is either 0 or 256, depending on whether the connection was closed normally or abnormally.

process-tty-name *process*   [Function]
> This function returns the terminal name that *process* is using for its communication
> with Emacs—or **nil** if it is using pipes instead of a pty (see **process-connection-type** in Section 36.4 [Asynchronous Processes], page 846). If *process* represents a
> program running on a remote host, the terminal name used by that program on the
> remote host is provided as process property **remote-tty**. If *process* represents a
> network, serial, or pipe connection, the value is **nil**.

process-coding-system *process*   [Function]
> This function returns a cons cell (*decode . encode*), describing the coding systems
> in use for decoding output from, and encoding input to, *process* (see Section 32.10
> [Coding Systems], page 773).

set-process-coding-system *process* **&optional** *decoding-system*   [Function]
>   *encoding-system*
> This function specifies the coding systems to use for subsequent output from and input
> to *process*. It will use *decoding-system* to decode subprocess output, and *encoding-system* to encode subprocess input.

Every process also has a property list that you can use to store miscellaneous values
associated with the process.

process-get *process propname*   [Function]
> This function returns the value of the *propname* property of *process*.

process-put *process propname value*   [Function]
> This function sets the value of the *propname* property of *process* to *value*.

process-plist *process*   [Function]
> This function returns the process plist of *process*.

set-process-plist *process plist*   [Function]
> This function sets the process plist of *process* to *plist*.

36.7 Sending Input to Processes

Asynchronous subprocesses receive input when it is sent to them by Emacs, which is done
with the functions in this section. You must specify the process to send input to, and the
input data to send. If the subprocess runs a program, the data appears on the standard
input of that program; for connections, the data is sent to the connected device or program.

Some operating systems have limited space for buffered input in a pty. On these systems,
Emacs sends an EOF periodically amidst the other characters, to force them through. For
most programs, these EOFs do no harm.

Subprocess input is normally encoded using a coding system before the subprocess receives it, much like text written into a file. You can use **set-process-coding-system** to
specify which coding system to use (see Section 36.6 [Process Information], page 851). Otherwise, the coding system comes from **coding-system-for-write**, if that is non-**nil**; or else
from the defaulting mechanism (see Section 32.10.5 [Default Coding Systems], page 780).

Sometimes the system is unable to accept input for that process, because the input buffer is full. When this happens, the send functions wait a short while, accepting output from subprocesses, and then try again. This gives the subprocess a chance to read more of its pending input and make space in the buffer. It also allows filters, sentinels and timers to run—so take account of that in writing your code.

In these functions, the *process* argument can be a process or the name of a process, or a buffer or buffer name (which stands for a process via `get-buffer-process`). `nil` means the current buffer's process.

`process-send-string` *process string* [Function]

This function sends *process* the contents of *string* as standard input. It returns `nil`.

For example, to make a Shell buffer list files:

```
(process-send-string "shell<1>" "ls\n")
     ⇒ nil
```

`process-send-region` *process start end* [Function]

This function sends the text in the region defined by *start* and *end* as standard input to *process*.

An error is signaled unless both *start* and *end* are integers or markers that indicate positions in the current buffer. (It is unimportant which number is larger.)

`process-send-eof` **&optional** *process* [Function]

This function makes *process* see an end-of-file in its input. The EOF comes after any text already sent to it. The function returns *process*.

```
(process-send-eof "shell")
     ⇒ "shell"
```

`process-running-child-p` **&optional** *process* [Function]

This function will tell you whether a *process*, which must not be a connection but a real subprocess, has given control of its terminal to a child process of its own. If this is true, the function returns the numeric ID of the foreground process group of *process*; it returns `nil` if Emacs can be certain that this is not so. The value is `t` if Emacs cannot tell whether this is true. This function signals an error if *process* is a network, serial, or pipe connection, or is the subprocess is not active.

36.8 Sending Signals to Processes

Sending a signal to a subprocess is a way of interrupting its activities. There are several different signals, each with its own meaning. The set of signals and their names is defined by the operating system. For example, the signal `SIGINT` means that the user has typed `C-c`, or that some analogous thing has happened.

Each signal has a standard effect on the subprocess. Most signals kill the subprocess, but some stop (or resume) execution instead. Most signals can optionally be handled by programs; if the program handles the signal, then we can say nothing in general about its effects.

You can send signals explicitly by calling the functions in this section. Emacs also sends signals automatically at certain times: killing a buffer sends a `SIGHUP` signal to all its associated processes; killing Emacs sends a `SIGHUP` signal to all remaining processes. (`SIGHUP` is a signal that usually indicates that the user "hung up the phone", i.e., disconnected.)

Each of the signal-sending functions takes two optional arguments: *process* and *current-group*.

The argument *process* must be either a process, a process name, a buffer, a buffer name, or `nil`. A buffer or buffer name stands for a process through `get-buffer-process`. `nil` stands for the process associated with the current buffer. Except with `stop-process` and `continue-process`, an error is signaled if *process* does not identify an active process, or if it represents a network, serial, or pipe connection.

The argument *current-group* is a flag that makes a difference when you are running a job-control shell as an Emacs subprocess. If it is non-`nil`, then the signal is sent to the current process-group of the terminal that Emacs uses to communicate with the subprocess. If the process is a job-control shell, this means the shell's current subjob. If *current-group* is `nil`, the signal is sent to the process group of the immediate subprocess of Emacs. If the subprocess is a job-control shell, this is the shell itself. If *current-group* is `lambda`, the signal is sent to the process-group that owns the terminal, but only if it is not the shell itself.

The flag *current-group* has no effect when a pipe is used to communicate with the subprocess, because the operating system does not support the distinction in the case of pipes. For the same reason, job-control shells won't work when a pipe is used. See `process-connection-type` in Section 36.4 [Asynchronous Processes], page 846.

`interrupt-process` &optional *process current-group*   [Function]
> This function interrupts the process *process* by sending the signal `SIGINT`. Outside of Emacs, typing the interrupt character (normally `C-c` on some systems, and `DEL` on others) sends this signal. When the argument *current-group* is non-`nil`, you can think of this function as typing `C-c` on the terminal by which Emacs talks to the subprocess.

`kill-process` &optional *process current-group*   [Function]
> This function kills the process *process* by sending the signal `SIGKILL`. This signal kills the subprocess immediately, and cannot be handled by the subprocess.

`quit-process` &optional *process current-group*   [Function]
> This function sends the signal `SIGQUIT` to the process *process*. This signal is the one sent by the quit character (usually `C-\`) when you are not inside Emacs.

`stop-process` &optional *process current-group*   [Function]
> This function stops the specified *process*. If it is a real subprocess running a program, it sends the signal `SIGTSTP` to that subprocess. If *process* represents a network, serial, or pipe connection, this function inhibits handling of the incoming data from the connection; for a network server, this means not accepting new connections. Use `continue-process` to resume normal execution.
>
> Outside of Emacs, on systems with job control, the stop character (usually `C-z`) normally sends the `SIGTSTP` signal to a subprocess. When *current-group* is non-`nil`, you can think of this function as typing `C-z` on the terminal Emacs uses to communicate with the subprocess.

`continue-process` &optional *process current-group*   [Function]
> This function resumes execution of the process *process*. If it is a real subprocess running a program, it sends the signal `SIGCONT` to that subprocess; this presumes

that *process* was stopped previously. If *process* represents a network, serial, or pipe connection, this function resumes handling of the incoming data from the connection. For serial connections, data that arrived during the time the process was stopped might be lost.

signal-process *process signal*   [Command]

>   This function sends a signal to process *process*. The argument *signal* specifies which signal to send; it should be an integer, or a symbol whose name is a signal.

>   The *process* argument can be a system process ID (an integer); that allows you to send signals to processes that are not children of Emacs. See Section 36.12 [System Processes], page 865.

36.9 Receiving Output from Processes

The output that an asynchronous subprocess writes to its standard output stream is passed to a function called the *filter function*. The default filter function simply inserts the output into a buffer, which is called the associated buffer of the process (see Section 36.9.1 [Process Buffers], page 858). If the process has no buffer then the default filter discards the output.

If the subprocess writes to its standard error stream, by default the error output is also passed to the process filter function. If Emacs uses a pseudo-TTY (pty) for communication with the subprocess, then it is impossible to separate the standard output and standard error streams of the subprocess, because a pseudo-TTY has only one output channel. In that case, if you want to keep the output to those streams separate, you should redirect one of them to a file—for example, by using an appropriate shell command via **start-process-shell-command** or a similar function.

Alternatively, you could use the **:stderr** parameter with a non-**nil** value in a call to **make-process** (see Section 36.4 [Asynchronous Processes], page 846) to make the destination of the error output separate from the standard output; in that case, Emacs will use pipes for communicating with the subprocess.

When a subprocess terminates, Emacs reads any pending output, then stops reading output from that subprocess. Therefore, if the subprocess has children that are still live and still producing output, Emacs won't receive that output.

Output from a subprocess can arrive only while Emacs is waiting: when reading terminal input (see the function **waiting-for-user-input-p**), in **sit-for** and **sleep-for** (see Section 20.10 [Waiting], page 382), and in **accept-process-output** (see Section 36.9.4 [Accepting Output], page 862). This minimizes the problem of timing errors that usually plague parallel programming. For example, you can safely create a process and only then specify its buffer or filter function; no output can arrive before you finish, if the code in between does not call any primitive that waits.

process-adaptive-read-buffering   [Variable]

>   On some systems, when Emacs reads the output from a subprocess, the output data is read in very small blocks, potentially resulting in very poor performance. This behavior can be remedied to some extent by setting the variable **process-adaptive-read-buffering** to a non-**nil** value (the default), as it will automatically delay reading from such processes, thus allowing them to produce more output before Emacs tries to read it.

36.9.1 Process Buffers

A process can (and usually does) have an *associated buffer*, which is an ordinary Emacs buffer that is used for two purposes: storing the output from the process, and deciding when to kill the process. You can also use the buffer to identify a process to operate on, since in normal practice only one process is associated with any given buffer. Many applications of processes also use the buffer for editing input to be sent to the process, but this is not built into Emacs Lisp.

By default, process output is inserted in the associated buffer. (You can change this by defining a custom filter function, see Section 36.9.2 [Filter Functions], page 859.) The position to insert the output is determined by the `process-mark`, which is then updated to point to the end of the text just inserted. Usually, but not always, the `process-mark` is at the end of the buffer.

Killing the associated buffer of a process also kills the process. Emacs asks for confirmation first, if the process's `process-query-on-exit-flag` is non-`nil` (see Section 36.11 [Query Before Exit], page 864). This confirmation is done by the function `process-kill-buffer-query-function`, which is run from `kill-buffer-query-functions` (see Section 26.10 [Killing Buffers], page 563).

`process-buffer` *process*   [Function]
>   This function returns the associated buffer of the specified *process*.
>
>   (process-buffer (get-process "shell"))
>   ⇒ #<buffer *shell*>

`process-mark` *process*   [Function]
>   This function returns the process marker for *process*, which is the marker that says where to insert output from the process.
>
>   If *process* does not have a buffer, `process-mark` returns a marker that points nowhere.
>
>   The default filter function uses this marker to decide where to insert process output, and updates it to point after the inserted text. That is why successive batches of output are inserted consecutively.
>
>   Custom filter functions normally should use this marker in the same fashion. For an example of a filter function that uses `process-mark`, see [Process Filter Example], page 860.
>
>   When the user is expected to enter input in the process buffer for transmission to the process, the process marker separates the new input from previous output.

`set-process-buffer` *process buffer*   [Function]
>   This function sets the buffer associated with *process* to *buffer*. If *buffer* is `nil`, the process becomes associated with no buffer.

`get-buffer-process` *buffer-or-name*   [Function]
>   This function returns a nondeleted process associated with the buffer specified by *buffer-or-name*. If there are several processes associated with it, this function chooses one (currently, the one most recently created, but don't count on that). Deletion of a process (see `delete-process`) makes it ineligible for this function to return.
>
>   It is usually a bad idea to have more than one process associated with the same buffer.
>
>   (get-buffer-process "*shell*")
>   ⇒ #<process shell>

Killing the process's buffer deletes the process, which kills the subprocess with a SIGHUP signal (see Section 36.8 [Signals to Processes], page 855).

If the process's buffer is displayed in a window, your Lisp program may wish to tell the process the dimensions of that window, so that the process could adapt its output to those dimensions, much as it adapts to the screen dimensions. The following functions allow communicating this kind of information to processes; however, not all systems support the underlying functionality, so it is best to provide fallbacks, e.g., via command-line arguments or environment variables.

set-process-window-size *process height width*   [Function]

Tell *process* that its logical window size has dimensions *width* by *height*, in character units. If this function succeeds in communicating this information to the process, it returns t; otherwise it returns nil.

When windows that display buffers associated with process change their dimensions, the affected processes should be told about these changes. By default, when the window configuration changes, Emacs will automatically call set-process-window-size on behalf of every process whose buffer is displayed in a window, passing it the smallest dimensions of all the windows displaying the process's buffer. This works via window-configuration-change-hook (see Section 27.27 [Window Hooks], page 628), which is told to invoke the function that is the value of the variable window-adjust-process-window-size-function for each process whose buffer is displayed in at least one window. You can customize this behavior by setting the value of that variable.

window-adjust-process-window-size-function   [User Option]

The value of this variable should be a function of two arguments: a process and the list of windows displaying the process's buffer. When the function is called, the process's buffer is the current buffer. The function should return a cons cell (*width . height*) that describes the dimensions of the logical process window to be passed via a call to set-process-window-size. The function can also return nil, in which case Emacs will not call set-process-window-size for this process.

Emacs supplies two predefined values for this variable: window-adjust-process-window-size-smallest, which returns the smallest of all the dimensions of the windows that display a process's buffer; and window-adjust-process-window-size-largest, which returns the largest dimensions. For more complex strategies, write your own function.

This variable can be buffer-local.

If the process has the adjust-window-size-function property (see Section 36.6 [Process Information], page 851), its value overrides the global and buffer-local values of window-adjust-process-window-size-function.

36.9.2 Process Filter Functions

A process *filter function* is a function that receives the standard output from the associated process. *All* output from that process is passed to the filter. The default filter simply outputs directly to the process buffer.

By default, the error output from the process, if any, is also passed to the filter function, unless the destination for the standard error stream of the process was separated from the standard output when the process was created (see Section 36.9 [Output from Processes], page 857).

The filter function can only be called when Emacs is waiting for something, because process output arrives only at such times. Emacs waits when reading terminal input (see the function `waiting-for-user-input-p`), in `sit-for` and `sleep-for` (see Section 20.10 [Waiting], page 382), and in `accept-process-output` (see Section 36.9.4 [Accepting Output], page 862).

A filter function must accept two arguments: the associated process and a string, which is output just received from it. The function is then free to do whatever it chooses with the output.

Quitting is normally inhibited within a filter function—otherwise, the effect of typing *C-g* at command level or to quit a user command would be unpredictable. If you want to permit quitting inside a filter function, bind `inhibit-quit` to `nil`. In most cases, the right way to do this is with the macro `with-local-quit`. See Section 20.11 [Quitting], page 382.

If an error happens during execution of a filter function, it is caught automatically, so that it doesn't stop the execution of whatever program was running when the filter function was started. However, if `debug-on-error` is non-`nil`, errors are not caught. This makes it possible to use the Lisp debugger to debug filter functions. See Section 17.1 [Debugger], page 270.

Many filter functions sometimes (or always) insert the output in the process's buffer, mimicking the actions of the default filter. Such filter functions need to make sure that they save the current buffer, select the correct buffer (if different) before inserting output, and then restore the original buffer. They should also check whether the buffer is still alive, update the process marker, and in some cases update the value of point. Here is how to do these things:

```
(defun ordinary-insertion-filter (proc string)
  (when (buffer-live-p (process-buffer proc))
    (with-current-buffer (process-buffer proc)
      (let ((moving (= (point) (process-mark proc))))
        (save-excursion
          ;; Insert the text, advancing the process marker.
          (goto-char (process-mark proc))
          (insert string)
          (set-marker (process-mark proc) (point)))
        (if moving (goto-char (process-mark proc)))))))
```

To make the filter force the process buffer to be visible whenever new text arrives, you could insert a line like the following just before the `with-current-buffer` construct:

```
(display-buffer (process-buffer proc))
```

To force point to the end of the new output, no matter where it was previously, eliminate the variable `moving` from the example and call `goto-char` unconditionally.

Note that Emacs automatically saves and restores the match data while executing filter functions. See Section 33.6 [Match Data], page 807.

The output to the filter may come in chunks of any size. A program that produces the same output twice in a row may send it as one batch of 200 characters one time, and five batches of 40 characters the next. If the filter looks for certain text strings in the subprocess output, make sure to handle the case where one of these strings is split across two or more batches of output; one way to do this is to insert the received text into a temporary buffer, which can then be searched.

set-process-filter *process filter*   [Function]
> This function gives *process* the filter function *filter*. If *filter* is `nil`, it gives the process the default filter, which inserts the process output into the process buffer.

process-filter *process*   [Function]
> This function returns the filter function of *process*.

In case the process's output needs to be passed to several filters, you can use `add-function` to combine an existing filter with a new one. See Section 12.11 [Advising Functions], page 204.

> Here is an example of the use of a filter function:

```
(defun keep-output (process output)
  (setq kept (cons output kept)))
     ⇒ keep-output
(setq kept nil)
     ⇒ nil
(set-process-filter (get-process "shell") 'keep-output)
     ⇒ keep-output
(process-send-string "shell" "ls ~/other\n")
     ⇒ nil
kept
     ⇒ ("lewis@slug:$ "
"FINAL-W87-SHORT.MSS     backup.otl          kolstad.mss~
address.txt             backup.psf          kolstad.psf
backup.bib~             david.mss           resume-Dec-86.mss~
backup.err              david.psf           resume-Dec.psf
backup.mss              dland               syllabus.mss
"
"#backups.mss#          backup.mss~         kolstad.mss
")
```

36.9.3 Decoding Process Output

When Emacs writes process output directly into a multibyte buffer, it decodes the output according to the process output coding system. If the coding system is `raw-text` or `no-conversion`, Emacs converts the unibyte output to multibyte using `string-to-multibyte`, and inserts the resulting multibyte text.

You can use `set-process-coding-system` to specify which coding system to use (see Section 36.6 [Process Information], page 851). Otherwise, the coding system comes from `coding-system-for-read`, if that is non-`nil`; or else from the defaulting mechanism (see Section 32.10.5 [Default Coding Systems], page 780). If the text output by a process contains null bytes, Emacs by default uses `no-conversion` for it; see Section 32.10.3 [Lisp and Coding Systems], page 776, for how to control this behavior.

Warning: Coding systems such as `undecided`, which determine the coding system from the data, do not work entirely reliably with asynchronous subprocess output. This is because Emacs has to process asynchronous subprocess output in batches, as it arrives. Emacs must try to detect the proper coding system from one batch at a time, and this does not always work. Therefore, if at all possible, specify a coding system that determines both the character code conversion and the end of line conversion—that is, one like `latin-1-unix`, rather than `undecided` or `latin-1`.

When Emacs calls a process filter function, it provides the process output as a multi-byte string or as a unibyte string according to the process's filter coding system. Emacs decodes the output according to the process output coding system, which usually produces a multibyte string, except for coding systems such as `binary` and `raw-text`.

36.9.4 Accepting Output from Processes

Output from asynchronous subprocesses normally arrives only while Emacs is waiting for some sort of external event, such as elapsed time or terminal input. Occasionally it is useful in a Lisp program to explicitly permit output to arrive at a specific point, or even to wait until output arrives from a process.

`accept-process-output` &optional *process seconds millisec*   [Function]
    just-this-one

> This function allows Emacs to read pending output from processes. The output is given to their filter functions. If *process* is non-`nil` then this function does not return until some output has been received from *process*.
>
> The arguments *seconds* and *millisec* let you specify timeout periods. The former specifies a period measured in seconds and the latter specifies one measured in milliseconds. The two time periods thus specified are added together, and `accept-process-output` returns after that much time, even if there is no subprocess output.
>
> The argument *millisec* is obsolete (and should not be used), because *seconds* can be floating point to specify waiting a fractional number of seconds. If *seconds* is 0, the function accepts whatever output is pending but does not wait.
>
> If *process* is a process, and the argument *just-this-one* is non-`nil`, only output from that process is handled, suspending output from other processes until some output has been received from that process or the timeout expires. If *just-this-one* is an integer, also inhibit running timers. This feature is generally not recommended, but may be necessary for specific applications, such as speech synthesis.
>
> The function `accept-process-output` returns non-`nil` if it got output from *process*, or from any process if *process* is `nil`. It returns `nil` if the timeout expired before output arrived.

36.10 Sentinels: Detecting Process Status Changes

A *process sentinel* is a function that is called whenever the associated process changes status for any reason, including signals (whether sent by Emacs or caused by the process's own actions) that terminate, stop, or continue the process. The process sentinel is also called if the process exits. The sentinel receives two arguments: the process for which the event occurred, and a string describing the type of event.

If no sentinel function was specified for a process, it will use the default sentinel function, which inserts a message in the process's buffer with the process name and the string describing the event.

The string describing the event looks like one of the following:

- `"finished\n"`.

- `"deleted\n"`.

- `"exited abnormally with code exitcode (core dumped)\n"`. The "core dumped" part is optional, and only appears if the process dumped core.

- `"failed with code fail-code\n"`.

- `"signal-description (core dumped)\n"`. The *signal-description* is a system-dependent textual description of a signal, e.g., `"killed"` for `SIGKILL`. The "core dumped" part is optional, and only appears if the process dumped core.

- `"open from host-name\n"`.

- `"open\n"`.

- `"connection broken by remote peer\n"`.

A sentinel runs only while Emacs is waiting (e.g., for terminal input, or for time to elapse, or for process output). This avoids the timing errors that could result from running sentinels at random places in the middle of other Lisp programs. A program can wait, so that sentinels will run, by calling `sit-for` or `sleep-for` (see Section 20.10 [Waiting], page 382), or `accept-process-output` (see Section 36.9.4 [Accepting Output], page 862). Emacs also allows sentinels to run when the command loop is reading input. `delete-process` calls the sentinel when it terminates a running process.

Emacs does not keep a queue of multiple reasons to call the sentinel of one process; it records just the current status and the fact that there has been a change. Therefore two changes in status, coming in quick succession, can call the sentinel just once. However, process termination will always run the sentinel exactly once. This is because the process status can't change again after termination.

Emacs explicitly checks for output from the process before running the process sentinel. Once the sentinel runs due to process termination, no further output can arrive from the process.

A sentinel that writes the output into the buffer of the process should check whether the buffer is still alive. If it tries to insert into a dead buffer, it will get an error. If the buffer is dead, `(buffer-name (process-buffer process))` returns `nil`.

Quitting is normally inhibited within a sentinel—otherwise, the effect of typing *C-g* at command level or to quit a user command would be unpredictable. If you want to permit quitting inside a sentinel, bind `inhibit-quit` to `nil`. In most cases, the right way to do this is with the macro `with-local-quit`. See Section 20.11 [Quitting], page 382.

If an error happens during execution of a sentinel, it is caught automatically, so that it doesn't stop the execution of whatever programs was running when the sentinel was started. However, if `debug-on-error` is non-`nil`, errors are not caught. This makes it possible to use the Lisp debugger to debug the sentinel. See Section 17.1 [Debugger], page 270.

While a sentinel is running, the process sentinel is temporarily set to `nil` so that the sentinel won't run recursively. For this reason it is not possible for a sentinel to specify a new sentinel.

Note that Emacs automatically saves and restores the match data while executing sentinels. See Section 33.6 [Match Data], page 807.

set-process-sentinel *process sentinel*   [Function]

> This function associates *sentinel* with *process*. If *sentinel* is `nil`, then the process will
> have the default sentinel, which inserts a message in the process's buffer when the
> process status changes.
>
> Changes in process sentinels take effect immediately—if the sentinel is slated to be
> run but has not been called yet, and you specify a new sentinel, the eventual call to
> the sentinel will use the new one.

```
(defun msg-me (process event)
  (princ
    (format "Process: %s had the event '%s'" process event)))
(set-process-sentinel (get-process "shell") 'msg-me)
    ⇒ msg-me
(kill-process (get-process "shell"))
    ⊣ Process: #<process shell> had the event 'killed'
    ⇒ #<process shell>
```

process-sentinel *process*   [Function]

> This function returns the sentinel of *process*.

In case a process status changes need to be passed to several sentinels, you can use
`add-function` to combine an existing sentinel with a new one. See Section 12.11 [Advising
Functions], page 204.

waiting-for-user-input-p   [Function]

> While a sentinel or filter function is running, this function returns non-`nil` if Emacs
> was waiting for keyboard input from the user at the time the sentinel or filter function
> was called, or `nil` if it was not.

36.11 Querying Before Exit

When Emacs exits, it terminates all its subprocesses. For subprocesses that run a program,
it sends them the `SIGHUP` signal; connections are simply closed. Because subprocesses may
be doing valuable work, Emacs normally asks the user to confirm that it is ok to terminate
them. Each process has a query flag, which, if non-`nil`, says that Emacs should ask for
confirmation before exiting and thus killing that process. The default for the query flag is
`t`, meaning *do* query.

process-query-on-exit-flag *process*   [Function]

> This returns the query flag of *process*.

set-process-query-on-exit-flag *process flag*   [Function]

> This function sets the query flag of *process* to *flag*. It returns *flag*.
>
> Here is an example of using `set-process-query-on-exit-flag` on a shell process to
> avoid querying:

```
(set-process-query-on-exit-flag (get-process "shell") nil)
    ⇒ nil
```

36.12 Accessing Other Processes

In addition to accessing and manipulating processes that are subprocesses of the current Emacs session, Emacs Lisp programs can also access other processes running on the same machine. We call these *system processes*, to distinguish them from Emacs subprocesses.

Emacs provides several primitives for accessing system processes. Not all platforms support these primitives; on those which don't, these primitives return `nil`.

`list-system-processes`   [Function]

> This function returns a list of all the processes running on the system. Each process is identified by its PID, a numerical process ID that is assigned by the OS and distinguishes the process from all the other processes running on the same machine at the same time.

`process-attributes` *pid*   [Function]

> This function returns an alist of attributes for the process specified by its process ID *pid*. Each association in the alist is of the form (*key* . *value*), where *key* designates the attribute and *value* is the value of that attribute. The various attribute *keys* that this function can return are listed below. Not all platforms support all of these attributes; if an attribute is not supported, its association will not appear in the returned alist. Values that are numbers can be either integer or floating point, depending on the magnitude of the value.

> | | |
> |---|---|
> | euid | The effective user ID of the user who invoked the process. The corresponding *value* is a number. If the process was invoked by the same user who runs the current Emacs session, the value is identical to what `user-uid` returns (see Section 38.4 [User Identification], page 998). |
> | user | User name corresponding to the process's effective user ID, a string. |
> | egid | The group ID of the effective user ID, a number. |
> | group | Group name corresponding to the effective user's group ID, a string. |
> | comm | The name of the command that runs in the process. This is a string that usually specifies the name of the executable file of the process, without the leading directories. However, some special system processes can report strings that do not correspond to an executable file of a program. |
> | state | The state code of the process. This is a short string that encodes the scheduling state of the process. Here's a list of the most frequently seen codes: |

> > | | |
> > |---|---|
> > | "D" | uninterruptible sleep (usually I/O) |
> > | "R" | running |
> > | "S" | interruptible sleep (waiting for some event) |
> > | "T" | stopped, e.g., by a job control signal |
> > | "Z" | zombie: a process that terminated, but was not reaped by its parent |

For the full list of the possible states, see the manual page of the `ps` command.

`ppid`
: The process ID of the parent process, a number.

`pgrp`
: The process group ID of the process, a number.

`sess`
: The session ID of the process. This is a number that is the process ID of the process's *session leader*.

`ttname`
: A string that is the name of the process's controlling terminal. On Unix and GNU systems, this is normally the file name of the corresponding terminal device, such as `/dev/pts65`.

`tpgid`
: The numerical process group ID of the foreground process group that uses the process's terminal.

`minflt`
: The number of minor page faults caused by the process since its beginning. (Minor page faults are those that don't involve reading from disk.)

`majflt`
: The number of major page faults caused by the process since its beginning. (Major page faults require a disk to be read, and are thus more expensive than minor page faults.)

`cminflt`
`cmajflt`
: Like `minflt` and `majflt`, but include the number of page faults for all the child processes of the given process.

`utime`
: Time spent by the process in the user context, for running the application's code. The corresponding *value* is in the (`high low microsec picosec`) format, the same format used by functions `current-time` (see Section 38.5 [Time of Day], page 999) and `file-attributes` (see Section 24.6.4 [File Attributes], page 509).

`stime`
: Time spent by the process in the system (kernel) context, for processing system calls. The corresponding *value* is in the same format as for `utime`.

`time`
: The sum of `utime` and `stime`. The corresponding *value* is in the same format as for `utime`.

`cutime`
`cstime`
`ctime`
: Like `utime`, `stime`, and `time`, but include the times of all the child processes of the given process.

`pri`
: The numerical priority of the process.

`nice`
: The *nice value* of the process, a number. (Processes with smaller nice values get scheduled more favorably.)

`thcount`
: The number of threads in the process.

`start`
: The time when the process was started, in the same (`high low microsec picosec`) format used by `file-attributes` and `current-time`.

`etime`
: The time elapsed since the process started, in the format (`high low microsec picosec`).

vsize	The virtual memory size of the process, measured in kilobytes.
rss	The size of the process's *resident set*, the number of kilobytes occupied by the process in the machine's physical memory.
pcpu	The percentage of the CPU time used by the process since it started. The corresponding *value* is a floating-point number between 0 and 100.
pmem	The percentage of the total physical memory installed on the machine used by the process's resident set. The value is a floating-point number between 0 and 100.
args	The command-line with which the process was invoked. This is a string in which individual command-line arguments are separated by blanks; whitespace characters that are embedded in the arguments are quoted as appropriate for the system's shell: escaped by backslash characters on GNU and Unix, and enclosed in double quote characters on Windows. Thus, this command-line string can be directly used in primitives such as shell-command.

36.13 Transaction Queues

You can use a *transaction queue* to communicate with a subprocess using transactions. First use tq-create to create a transaction queue communicating with a specified process. Then you can call tq-enqueue to send a transaction.

tq-create *process*   [Function]

> This function creates and returns a transaction queue communicating with *process*. The argument *process* should be a subprocess capable of sending and receiving streams of bytes. It may be a child process, or it may be a TCP connection to a server, possibly on another machine.

tq-enqueue *queue question regexp closure fn* **&optional**   [Function]
>   *delay-question*

> This function sends a transaction to queue *queue*. Specifying the queue has the effect of specifying the subprocess to talk to.

> The argument *question* is the outgoing message that starts the transaction. The argument *fn* is the function to call when the corresponding answer comes back; it is called with two arguments: *closure*, and the answer received.

> The argument *regexp* is a regular expression that should match text at the end of the entire answer, but nothing before; that's how tq-enqueue determines where the answer ends.

> If the argument *delay-question* is non-nil, delay sending this question until the process has finished replying to any previous questions. This produces more reliable results with some processes.

tq-close *queue*   [Function]

> Shut down transaction queue *queue*, waiting for all pending transactions to complete, and then terminate the connection or child process.

Transaction queues are implemented by means of a filter function. See Section 36.9.2 [Filter Functions], page 859.

36.14 Network Connections

Emacs Lisp programs can open stream (TCP) and datagram (UDP) network connections (see Section 36.16 [Datagrams], page 871) to other processes on the same machine or other machines. A network connection is handled by Lisp much like a subprocess, and is represented by a process object. However, the process you are communicating with is not a child of the Emacs process, has no process ID, and you can't kill it or send it signals. All you can do is send and receive data. `delete-process` closes the connection, but does not kill the program at the other end; that program must decide what to do about closure of the connection.

Lisp programs can listen for connections by creating network servers. A network server is also represented by a kind of process object, but unlike a network connection, the network server never transfers data itself. When it receives a connection request, it creates a new network connection to represent the connection just made. (The network connection inherits certain information, including the process plist, from the server.) The network server then goes back to listening for more connection requests.

Network connections and servers are created by calling `make-network-process` with an argument list consisting of keyword/argument pairs, for example `:server t` to create a server process, or `:type 'datagram` to create a datagram connection. See Section 36.17 [Low-Level Network], page 871, for details. You can also use the `open-network-stream` function described below.

To distinguish the different types of processes, the `process-type` function returns the symbol `network` for a network connection or server, `serial` for a serial port connection, `pipe` for a pipe connection, or `real` for a real subprocess.

The `process-status` function returns `open`, `closed`, `connect`, `stop`, or `failed` for network connections. For a network server, the status is always `listen`. Except for `stop`, none of those values is possible for a real subprocess. See Section 36.6 [Process Information], page 851.

You can stop and resume operation of a network process by calling `stop-process` and `continue-process`. For a server process, being stopped means not accepting new connections. (Up to 5 connection requests will be queued for when you resume the server; you can increase this limit, unless it is imposed by the operating system—see the `:server` keyword of `make-network-process`, Section 36.17.1 [Network Processes], page 871.) For a network stream connection, being stopped means not processing input (any arriving input waits until you resume the connection). For a datagram connection, some number of packets may be queued but input may be lost. You can use the function `process-command` to determine whether a network connection or server is stopped; a non-`nil` value means yes.

Emacs can create encrypted network connections, using either built-in or external support. The built-in support uses the GnuTLS Transport Layer Security Library; see the GnuTLS project page (http://www.gnu.org/software/gnutls/). If your Emacs was compiled with GnuTLS support, the function `gnutls-available-p` is defined and returns non-`nil`. For more details, see Section "Overview" in *The Emacs-GnuTLS manual*. The external support uses the `starttls.el` library, which requires a helper utility such as `gnutls-cli` to be installed on the system. The `open-network-stream` function can transparently handle the details of creating encrypted connections for you, using whatever support is available.

open-network-stream *name buffer host service* **&rest** *parameters*   [Function]
 This function opens a TCP connection, with optional encryption, and returns a process object that represents the connection.

The *name* argument specifies the name for the process object. It is modified as necessary to make it unique.

The *buffer* argument is the buffer to associate with the connection. Output from the connection is inserted in the buffer, unless you specify your own filter function to handle the output. If *buffer* is `nil`, it means that the connection is not associated with any buffer.

The arguments *host* and *service* specify where to connect to; *host* is the host name (a string), and *service* is the name of a defined network service (a string) or a port number (an integer).

The remaining arguments *parameters* are keyword/argument pairs that are mainly relevant to encrypted connections:

`:nowait` *boolean*
> If non-`nil`, try to make an asynchronous connection.

`:type` *type*
> The type of connection. Options are:
>
> | | |
> |---|---|
> | `plain` | An ordinary, unencrypted connection. |
> | `tls` `ssl` | A TLS (Transport Layer Security) connection. |
> | `nil` `network` | Start with a plain connection, and if parameters ':`success`' and ':`capability-command`' are supplied, try to upgrade to an encrypted connection via STARTTLS. If that fails, retain the unencrypted connection. |
> | `starttls` | As for `nil`, but if STARTTLS fails drop the connection. |
> | `shell` | A shell connection. |

`:always-query-capabilities` *boolean*
> If non-`nil`, always ask for the server's capabilities, even when doing a 'plain' connection.

`:capability-command` *capability-command*
> Command string to query the host capabilities.

`:end-of-command` *regexp*
`:end-of-capability` *regexp*
> Regular expression matching the end of a command, or the end of the command *capability-command*. The latter defaults to the former.

`:starttls-function` *function*
> Function of one argument (the response to *capability-command*), which returns either `nil`, or the command to activate STARTTLS if supported.

:success *regexp*

> Regular expression matching a successful STARTTLS negotiation.

:use-starttls-if-possible *boolean*

> If non-nil, do opportunistic STARTTLS upgrades even if Emacs doesn't have built-in TLS support.

:warn-unless-encrypted *boolean*

> If non-nil, and :return-value is also non-nil, Emacs will warn if the connection isn't encrypted. This is useful for protocols like IMAP and the like, where most users would expect the network traffic to be encrypted.

:client-certificate *list-or-t*

> Either a list of the form (*key-file cert-file*), naming the certificate key file and certificate file itself, or t, meaning to query auth-source for this information (see Section "Overview" in *The Auth-Source Manual*). Only used for TLS or STARTTLS.

:return-list *cons-or-nil*

> The return value of this function. If omitted or nil, return a process object. Otherwise, a cons of the form (*process-object . plist*), where *plist* has keywords:
>
> :greeting *string-or-nil*
>
> > If non-nil, the greeting string returned by the host.
>
> :capabilities *string-or-nil*
>
> > If non-nil, the host's capability string.
>
> :type *symbol*
>
> > The connection type: 'plain' or 'tls'.

36.15 Network Servers

You create a server by calling make-network-process (see Section 36.17.1 [Network Processes], page 871) with :server t. The server will listen for connection requests from clients. When it accepts a client connection request, that creates a new network connection, itself a process object, with the following parameters:

- The connection's process name is constructed by concatenating the server process's *name* with a client identification string. The client identification string for an IPv4 connection looks like '<*a.b.c.d:p*>', which represents an address and port number. Otherwise, it is a unique number in brackets, as in '<*nnn*>'. The number is unique for each connection in the Emacs session.

- If the server has a non-default filter, the connection process does not get a separate process buffer; otherwise, Emacs creates a new buffer for the purpose. The buffer name is the server's buffer name or process name, concatenated with the client identification string.

The server's process buffer value is never used directly, but the log function can retrieve it and use it to log connections by inserting text there.

- The communication type and the process filter and sentinel are inherited from those of the server. The server never directly uses its filter and sentinel; their sole purpose is to initialize connections made to the server.

- The connection's process contact information is set according to the client's addressing information (typically an IP address and a port number). This information is associated with the `process-contact` keywords :host, :service, :remote.

- The connection's local address is set up according to the port number used for the connection.

- The client process's plist is initialized from the server's plist.

36.16 Datagrams

A *datagram* connection communicates with individual packets rather than streams of data. Each call to `process-send` sends one datagram packet (see Section 36.7 [Input to Processes], page 854), and each datagram received results in one call to the filter function.

The datagram connection doesn't have to talk with the same remote peer all the time. It has a *remote peer address* which specifies where to send datagrams to. Each time an incoming datagram is passed to the filter function, the peer address is set to the address that datagram came from; that way, if the filter function sends a datagram, it will go back to that place. You can specify the remote peer address when you create the datagram connection using the :remote keyword. You can change it later on by calling `set-process-datagram-address`.

process-datagram-address *process*   [Function]
> If *process* is a datagram connection or server, this function returns its remote peer address.

set-process-datagram-address *process address*   [Function]
> If *process* is a datagram connection or server, this function sets its remote peer address to *address*.

36.17 Low-Level Network Access

You can also create network connections by operating at a lower level than that of `open-network-stream`, using `make-network-process`.

36.17.1 make-network-process

The basic function for creating network connections and network servers is `make-network-process`. It can do either of those jobs, depending on the arguments you give it.

make-network-process &rest *args*   [Function]
> This function creates a network connection or server and returns the process object that represents it. The arguments *args* are a list of keyword/argument pairs. Omitting a keyword is always equivalent to specifying it with value **nil**, except for :coding, :filter-multibyte, and :reuseaddr. Here are the meaningful keywords (those corresponding to network options are listed in the following section):

:name *name*

>   Use the string *name* as the process name. It is modified if necessary to make it unique.

:type *type*   Specify the communication type. A value of `nil` specifies a stream connection (the default); `datagram` specifies a datagram connection; `seqpacket` specifies a sequenced packet stream connection. Both connections and servers can be of these types.

:server *server-flag*

>   If *server-flag* is non-`nil`, create a server. Otherwise, create a connection. For a stream type server, *server-flag* may be an integer, which then specifies the length of the queue of pending connections to the server. The default queue length is 5.

:host *host*   Specify the host to connect to. *host* should be a host name or Internet address, as a string, or the symbol `local` to specify the local host. If you specify *host* for a server, it must specify a valid address for the local host, and only clients connecting to that address will be accepted.

:service *service*

>   *service* specifies a port number to connect to; or, for a server, the port number to listen on. It should be a service name that translates to a port number, or an integer specifying the port number directly. For a server, it can also be `t`, which means to let the system select an unused port number.

:family *family*

>   *family* specifies the address (and protocol) family for communication. `nil` means determine the proper address family automatically for the given *host* and *service*. `local` specifies a Unix socket, in which case *host* is ignored. `ipv4` and `ipv6` specify to use IPv4 and IPv6, respectively.

:local *local-address*

>   For a server process, *local-address* is the address to listen on. It overrides *family*, *host* and *service*, so you might as well not specify them.

:remote *remote-address*

>   For a connection, *remote-address* is the address to connect to. It overrides *family*, *host* and *service*, so you might as well not specify them.
>
>   For a datagram server, *remote-address* specifies the initial setting of the remote datagram address.
>
>   The format of *local-address* or *remote-address* depends on the address family:
>
>   - An IPv4 address is represented as a five-element vector of four 8-bit integers and one 16-bit integer [a b c d p] corresponding to numeric IPv4 address *a.b.c.d* and port number *p*.
>   - An IPv6 address is represented as a nine-element vector of 16-bit integers [a b c d e f g h p] corresponding to numeric IPv6 address *a:b:c:d:e:f:g:h* and port number *p*.

> - A local address is represented as a string, which specifies the address in the local address space.
>
> - An unsupported-family address is represented by a cons (`f . av`), where *f* is the family number and *av* is a vector specifying the socket address using one element per address data byte. Do not rely on this format in portable code, as it may depend on implementation defined constants, data sizes, and data structure alignment.

:nowait *bool*

> If *bool* is non-`nil` for a stream connection, return without waiting for the connection to complete. When the connection succeeds or fails, Emacs will call the sentinel function, with a second argument matching `"open"` (if successful) or `"failed"`. The default is to block, so that `make-network-process` does not return until the connection has succeeded or failed.

:stop *stopped*

> If *stopped* is non-`nil`, start the network connection or server in the stopped state.

:buffer *buffer*

> Use *buffer* as the process buffer.

:coding *coding*

> Use *coding* as the coding system for this process. To specify different coding systems for decoding data from the connection and for encoding data sent to it, specify (`decoding . encoding`) for *coding*.
>
> If you don't specify this keyword at all, the default is to determine the coding systems from the data.

:noquery *query-flag*

> Initialize the process query flag to *query-flag*. See Section 36.11 [Query Before Exit], page 864.

:filter *filter*

> Initialize the process filter to *filter*.

:filter-multibyte *multibyte*

> If *multibyte* is non-`nil`, strings given to the process filter are multibyte, otherwise they are unibyte. The default is the default value of `enable-multibyte-characters`.

:sentinel *sentinel*

> Initialize the process sentinel to *sentinel*.

:log *log*   Initialize the log function of a server process to *log*. The log function is called each time the server accepts a network connection from a client. The arguments passed to the log function are *server*, *connection*, and *message*; where *server* is the server process, *connection* is the new process for the connection, and *message* is a string describing what has happened.

:plist *plist*   Initialize the process plist to *plist*.

The original argument list, modified with the actual connection information, is available via the `process-contact` function.

36.17.2 Network Options

The following network options can be specified when you create a network process. Except for `:reuseaddr`, you can also set or modify these options later, using `set-network-process-option`.

For a server process, the options specified with `make-network-process` are not inherited by the client connections, so you will need to set the necessary options for each child connection as it is created.

:bindtodevice *device-name*

> If *device-name* is a non-empty string identifying a network interface name (see `network-interface-list`), only handle packets received on that interface. If *device-name* is `nil` (the default), handle packets received on any interface.
>
> Using this option may require special privileges on some systems.

:broadcast *broadcast-flag*

> If *broadcast-flag* is non-`nil` for a datagram process, the process will receive datagram packet sent to a broadcast address, and be able to send packets to a broadcast address. This is ignored for a stream connection.

:dontroute *dontroute-flag*

> If *dontroute-flag* is non-`nil`, the process can only send to hosts on the same network as the local host.

:keepalive *keepalive-flag*

> If *keepalive-flag* is non-`nil` for a stream connection, enable exchange of low-level keep-alive messages.

:linger *linger-arg*

> If *linger-arg* is non-`nil`, wait for successful transmission of all queued packets on the connection before it is deleted (see `delete-process`). If *linger-arg* is an integer, it specifies the maximum time in seconds to wait for queued packets to be sent before closing the connection. The default is `nil`, which means to discard unsent queued packets when the process is deleted.

:oobinline *oobinline-flag*

> If *oobinline-flag* is non-`nil` for a stream connection, receive out-of-band data in the normal data stream. Otherwise, ignore out-of-band data.

:priority *priority*

> Set the priority for packets sent on this connection to the integer *priority*. The interpretation of this number is protocol specific; such as setting the TOS (type of service) field on IP packets sent on this connection. It may also have system dependent effects, such as selecting a specific output queue on the network interface.

:reuseaddr *reuseaddr-flag*

> If *reuseaddr-flag* is non-`nil` (the default) for a stream server process, allow this server to reuse a specific port number (see `:service`), unless another process

on this host is already listening on that port. If *reuseaddr-flag* is `nil`, there may be a period of time after the last use of that port (by any process on the host) where it is not possible to make a new server on that port.

set-network-process-option *process option value* **&optional**   [Function]
        no-error

> This function sets or modifies a network option for network process *process*. The accepted options and values are as for `make-network-process`. If *no-error* is non-`nil`, this function returns `nil` instead of signaling an error if *option* is not a supported option. If the function successfully completes, it returns `t`.
>
> The current setting of an option is available via the `process-contact` function.

36.17.3 Testing Availability of Network Features

To test for the availability of a given network feature, use `featurep` like this:

        (featurep 'make-network-process '(*keyword value*))

The result of this form is `t` if it works to specify *keyword* with value *value* in `make-network-process`. Here are some of the *keyword—value* pairs you can test in this way.

`(:nowait t)`
> Non-`nil` if non-blocking connect is supported.

`(:type datagram)`
> Non-`nil` if datagrams are supported.

`(:family local)`
> Non-`nil` if local (a.k.a. "UNIX domain") sockets are supported.

`(:family ipv6)`
> Non-`nil` if IPv6 is supported.

`(:service t)`
> Non-`nil` if the system can select the port for a server.

To test for the availability of a given network option, use `featurep` like this:

        (featurep 'make-network-process '*keyword*)

The accepted *keyword* values are `:bindtodevice`, etc. For the complete list, see Section 36.17.2 [Network Options], page 874. This form returns non-`nil` if that particular network option is supported by `make-network-process` (or `set-network-process-option`).

36.18 Misc Network Facilities

These additional functions are useful for creating and operating on network connections. Note that they are supported only on some systems.

network-interface-list   [Function]
> This function returns a list describing the network interfaces of the machine you are using. The value is an alist whose elements have the form (*name . address*). *address* has the same form as the *local-address* and *remote-address* arguments to `make-network-process`.

network-interface-info *ifname*   [Function]

> This function returns information about the network interface named *ifname*. The value is a list of the form (`addr bcast netmask hwaddr flags`).
>
> *addr*   The Internet protocol address.
>
> *bcast*   The broadcast address.
>
> *netmask*   The network mask.
>
> *hwaddr*   The layer 2 address (Ethernet MAC address, for instance).
>
> *flags*   The current flags of the interface.

format-network-address *address* **&optional** *omit-port*   [Function]

> This function converts the Lisp representation of a network address to a string.
>
> A five-element vector [`a b c d p`] represents an IPv4 address *a.b.c.d* and port number *p*. `format-network-address` converts that to the string `"a.b.c.d:p"`.
>
> A nine-element vector [`a b c d e f g h p`] represents an IPv6 address along with a port number. `format-network-address` converts that to the string `"[a:b:c:d:e:f:g:h]:p"`.
>
> If the vector does not include the port number, *p*, or if *omit-port* is non-**nil**, the result does not include the `:p` suffix.

36.19 Communicating with Serial Ports

Emacs can communicate with serial ports. For interactive use, *M-x serial-term* opens a terminal window. In a Lisp program, `make-serial-process` creates a process object.

The serial port can be configured at run-time, without having to close and re-open it. The function `serial-process-configure` lets you change the speed, bytesize, and other parameters. In a terminal window created by `serial-term`, you can click on the mode line for configuration.

A serial connection is represented by a process object, which can be used in a similar way to a subprocess or network process. You can send and receive data, and configure the serial port. A serial process object has no process ID, however, and you can't send signals to it, and the status codes are different from other types of processes. `delete-process` on the process object or `kill-buffer` on the process buffer close the connection, but this does not affect the device connected to the serial port.

The function `process-type` returns the symbol `serial` for a process object representing a serial port connection.

Serial ports are available on GNU/Linux, Unix, and MS Windows systems.

serial-term *port speed*   [Command]

> Start a terminal-emulator for a serial port in a new buffer. *port* is the name of the serial port to connect to. For example, this could be `/dev/ttyS0` on Unix. On MS Windows, this could be `COM1`, or `\\.\COM10` (double the backslashes in Lisp strings).
>
> *speed* is the speed of the serial port in bits per second. 9600 is a common value. The buffer is in Term mode; see Section "Term Mode" in *The GNU Emacs Manual*, for the commands to use in that buffer. You can change the speed and the configuration in the mode line menu.

make-serial-process &rest *args*   [Function]

This function creates a process and a buffer. Arguments are specified as keyword/argument pairs. Here's the list of the meaningful keywords, with the first two (*port* and *speed*) being mandatory:

:port *port*

> This is the name of the serial port. On Unix and GNU systems, this is a file name such as /dev/ttyS0. On Windows, this could be COM1, or \\.\COM10 for ports higher than COM9 (double the backslashes in Lisp strings).

:speed *speed*

> The speed of the serial port in bits per second. This function calls **serial-process-configure** to handle the speed; see the following documentation of that function for more details.

:name *name*

> The name of the process. If *name* is not given, *port* will serve as the process name as well.

:buffer *buffer*

> The buffer to associate with the process. The value can be either a buffer or a string that names a buffer. Process output goes at the end of that buffer, unless you specify an output stream or filter function to handle the output. If *buffer* is not given, the process buffer's name is taken from the value of the :name keyword.

:coding *coding*

> If *coding* is a symbol, it specifies the coding system used for both reading and writing for this process. If *coding* is a cons (*decoding . encoding*), *decoding* is used for reading, and *encoding* is used for writing. If not specified, the default is to determine the coding systems from the data itself.

:noquery *query-flag*

> Initialize the process query flag to *query-flag*. See Section 36.11 [Query Before Exit], page 864. The flags defaults to **nil** if unspecified.

:stop *bool*

> Start process in the stopped state if *bool* is non-nil. In the stopped state, a serial process does not accept incoming data, but you can send outgoing data. The stopped state is cleared by **continue-process** and set by **stop-process**.

:filter *filter*

> Install *filter* as the process filter.

:sentinel *sentinel*

> Install *sentinel* as the process sentinel.

:plist *plist*

> Install *plist* as the initial plist of the process.

```
:bytesize
:parity
:stopbits
:flowcontrol
```
> These are handled by `serial-process-configure`, which is called by `make-serial-process`.

The original argument list, possibly modified by later configuration, is available via the function `process-contact`.

Here is an example:

```
(make-serial-process :port "/dev/ttyS0" :speed 9600)
```

serial-process-configure &rest *args*   [Function]
> This function configures a serial port connection. Arguments are specified as keyword/argument pairs. Attributes that are not given are re-initialized from the process's current configuration (available via the function `process-contact`), or set to reasonable default values. The following arguments are defined:

```
:process process
:name name
:buffer buffer
:port port
```
> Any of these arguments can be given to identify the process that is to be configured. If none of these arguments is given, the current buffer's process is used.

```
:speed speed
```
> The speed of the serial port in bits per second, a.k.a. *baud rate*. The value can be any number, but most serial ports work only at a few defined values between 1200 and 115200, with 9600 being the most common value. If *speed* is `nil`, the function ignores all other arguments and does not configure the port. This may be useful for special serial ports such as Bluetooth-to-serial converters, which can only be configured through 'AT' commands sent through the connection. The value of `nil` for *speed* is valid only for connections that were already opened by a previous call to `make-serial-process` or `serial-term`.

```
:bytesize bytesize
```
> The number of bits per byte, which can be 7 or 8. If *bytesize* is not given or `nil`, it defaults to 8.

```
:parity parity
```
> The value can be `nil` (don't use parity), the symbol `odd` (use odd parity), or the symbol `even` (use even parity). If *parity* is not given, it defaults to no parity.

```
:stopbits stopbits
```
> The number of stopbits used to terminate a transmission of each byte. *stopbits* can be 1 or 2. If *stopbits* is not given or `nil`, it defaults to 1.

```
:flowcontrol flowcontrol
```
> The type of flow control to use for this connection, which is either `nil` (don't use flow control), the symbol `hw` (use RTS/CTS hardware flow control), or the symbol `sw` (use XON/XOFF software flow control). If *flowcontrol* is not given, it defaults to no flow control.

Internally, `make-serial-process` calls `serial-process-configure` for the initial configuration of the serial port.

36.20 Packing and Unpacking Byte Arrays

This section describes how to pack and unpack arrays of bytes, usually for binary network protocols. These functions convert byte arrays to alists, and vice versa. The byte array can be represented as a unibyte string or as a vector of integers, while the alist associates symbols either with fixed-size objects or with recursive sub-alists. To use the functions referred to in this section, load the `bindat` library.

Conversion from byte arrays to nested alists is also known as *deserializing* or *unpacking*, while going in the opposite direction is also known as *serializing* or *packing*.

36.20.1 Describing Data Layout

To control unpacking and packing, you write a *data layout specification*, a special nested list describing named and typed *fields*. This specification controls the length of each field to be processed, and how to pack or unpack it. We normally keep bindat specs in variables whose names end in '`-bindat-spec`'; that kind of name is automatically recognized as risky.

A field's *type* describes the size (in bytes) of the object that the field represents and, in the case of multibyte fields, how the bytes are ordered within the field. The two possible orderings are *big endian* (also known as "network byte ordering") and *little endian*. For instance, the number `#x23cd` (decimal 9165) in big endian would be the two bytes `#x23` `#xcd`; and in little endian, `#xcd` `#x23`. Here are the possible type values:

`u8` `byte`	Unsigned byte, with length 1.

`u16`
`word`
`short`
	Unsigned integer in network byte order, with length 2.

`u24`	Unsigned integer in network byte order, with length 3.

`u32`
`dword`
`long`
	Unsigned integer in network byte order, with length 4. Note: These values may be limited by Emacs's integer implementation limits.

`u16r`
`u24r`
`u32r`
	Unsigned integer in little endian order, with length 2, 3 and 4, respectively.

`str` *len*	String of length *len*.
`strz` *len*	Zero-terminated string, in a fixed-size field with length *len*.

vec `len` **[**`type`**]**

> Vector of *len* elements of type *type*, defaulting to bytes. The *type* is any of the simple types above, or another vector specified as a list of the form (**vec** `len` **[**`type`**]**).

ip   Four-byte vector representing an Internet address. For example: **[127 0 0 1]** for localhost.

bits `len`   List of set bits in *len* bytes. The bytes are taken in big endian order and the bits are numbered starting with **8 * `len` − 1** and ending with zero. For example: **bits 2** unpacks **#x28 #x1c** to (**2 3 4 11 13**) and **#x1c #x28** to (**3 5 10 11 12**).

(eval `form`**)**

> *form* is a Lisp expression evaluated at the moment the field is unpacked or packed. The result of the evaluation should be one of the above-listed type specifications.

For a fixed-size field, the length *len* is given as an integer specifying the number of bytes in the field.

When the length of a field is not fixed, it typically depends on the value of a preceding field. In this case, the length *len* can be given either as a list (**`name` ...**) identifying a *field name* in the format specified for **bindat-get-field** below, or by an expression (**eval** `form`) where *form* should evaluate to an integer, specifying the field length.

A field specification generally has the form (**[`name`]** `handler`), where *name* is optional. Don't use names that are symbols meaningful as type specifications (above) or handler specifications (below), since that would be ambiguous. *name* can be a symbol or an expression (**eval** `form`), in which case *form* should evaluate to a symbol.

handler describes how to unpack or pack the field and can be one of the following:

`type`   Unpack/pack this field according to the type specification *type*.

eval `form`   Evaluate *form*, a Lisp expression, for side-effect only. If the field name is specified, the value is bound to that field name.

fill `len`   Skip *len* bytes. In packing, this leaves them unchanged, which normally means they remain zero. In unpacking, this means they are ignored.

align `len` Skip to the next multiple of *len* bytes.

struct `spec-name`

> Process *spec-name* as a sub-specification. This describes a structure nested within another structure.

union `form` **(**`tag` `spec`**)**...

> Evaluate *form*, a Lisp expression, find the first *tag* that matches it, and process its associated data layout specification *spec*. Matching can occur in one of three ways:
>
> - If a *tag* has the form (**eval** `expr`), evaluate *expr* with the variable **tag** dynamically bound to the value of *form*. A non-**nil** result indicates a match.
> - *tag* matches if it is **equal** to the value of *form*.

- *tag* matches unconditionally if it is **t**.

repeat *count field-specs*...

> Process the *field-specs* recursively, in order, then repeat starting from the first one, processing all the specifications *count* times overall. The *count* is given using the same formats as a field length—if an **eval** form is used, it is evaluated just once. For correct operation, each specification in *field-specs* must include a name.

For the (**eval** *form*) forms used in a bindat specification, the *form* can access and update these dynamically bound variables during evaluation:

last   Value of the last field processed.

bindat-raw

> The data as a byte array.

bindat-idx

> Current index (within **bindat-raw**) for unpacking or packing.

struct   The alist containing the structured data that have been unpacked so far, or the entire structure being packed. You can use **bindat-get-field** to access specific fields of this structure.

count
index   Inside a **repeat** block, these contain the maximum number of repetitions (as specified by the *count* parameter), and the current repetition number (counting from 0). Setting **count** to zero will terminate the inner-most repeat block after the current repetition has completed.

36.20.2 Functions to Unpack and Pack Bytes

In the following documentation, *spec* refers to a data layout specification, **bindat-raw** to a byte array, and *struct* to an alist representing unpacked field data.

bindat-unpack *spec bindat-raw* **&optional** *bindat-idx*   [Function]

> This function unpacks data from the unibyte string or byte array **bindat-raw** according to *spec*. Normally, this starts unpacking at the beginning of the byte array, but if *bindat-idx* is non-**nil**, it specifies a zero-based starting position to use instead.
>
> The value is an alist or nested alist in which each element describes one unpacked field.

bindat-get-field *struct* **&rest** *name*   [Function]

> This function selects a field's data from the nested alist *struct*. Usually *struct* was returned by **bindat-unpack**. If *name* corresponds to just one argument, that means to extract a top-level field value. Multiple *name* arguments specify repeated lookup of sub-structures. An integer name acts as an array index.
>
> For example, if *name* is (**a b 2 c**), that means to find field **c** in the third element of subfield **b** of field **a**. (This corresponds to **struct.a.b[2].c** in C.)

Although packing and unpacking operations change the organization of data (in memory), they preserve the data's *total length*, which is the sum of all the fields' lengths, in bytes. This value is not generally inherent in either the specification or alist alone; instead, both pieces of information contribute to its calculation. Likewise, the length of a string or array being unpacked may be longer than the data's total length as described by the specification.

bindat-length *spec struct*   [Function]
> This function returns the total length of the data in *struct*, according to *spec*.

bindat-pack *spec struct* **&optional** *bindat-raw bindat-idx*   [Function]
> This function returns a byte array packed according to *spec* from the data in the alist *struct*. It normally creates and fills a new byte array starting at the beginning. However, if *bindat-raw* is non-`nil`, it specifies a pre-allocated unibyte string or vector to pack into. If *bindat-idx* is non-`nil`, it specifies the starting offset for packing into `bindat-raw`.
>
> When pre-allocating, you should make sure (`length` `bindat-raw`) meets or exceeds the total length to avoid an out-of-range error.

bindat-ip-to-string *ip*   [Function]
> Convert the Internet address vector *ip* to a string in the usual dotted notation.
>
> ```
> (bindat-ip-to-string [127 0 0 1])
>      ⇒ "127.0.0.1"
> ```

36.20.3 Examples of Byte Unpacking and Packing

Here is a complete example of byte unpacking and packing:

```
(require 'bindat)

(defvar fcookie-index-spec
  '((:version  u32)
    (:count    u32)
    (:longest  u32)
    (:shortest u32)
    (:flags    u32)
    (:delim    u8)
    (:ignored  fill 3)
    (:offset   repeat (:count) (:foo u32)))
  "Description of a fortune cookie index file's contents.")

(defun fcookie (cookies &optional index)
  "Display a random fortune cookie from file COOKIES.
Optional second arg INDEX specifies the associated index
filename, by default \"COOKIES.dat\".  Display cookie text
in buffer \"*Fortune Cookie: BASENAME*\", where BASENAME
is COOKIES without the directory part."
  (interactive "fCookies file: ")
  (let* ((info (with-temp-buffer
                 (insert-file-contents-literally
                  (or index (concat cookies ".dat")))
```

```
                          (bindat-unpack fcookie-index-spec
                                       (buffer-string))))
            (sel (random (bindat-get-field info :count)))
            (beg (cdar (bindat-get-field info :offset sel)))
            (end (or (cdar (bindat-get-field info
                                             :offset (1+ sel)))
                     (nth 7 (file-attributes cookies)))))
        (switch-to-buffer
         (get-buffer-create
          (format "*Fortune Cookie: %s*"
                  (file-name-nondirectory cookies))))
        (erase-buffer)
        (insert-file-contents-literally
         cookies nil beg (- end 3)))))

(defun fcookie-create-index (cookies &optional index delim)
  "Scan file COOKIES, and write out its index file.
Optional arg INDEX specifies the index filename, which by
default is \"COOKIES.dat\".  Optional arg DELIM specifies the
unibyte character that, when found on a line of its own in
COOKIES, indicates the border between entries."
  (interactive "fCookies file: ")
  (setq delim (or delim ?%))
  (let ((delim-line (format "\n%c\n" delim))
        (count 0)
        (max 0)
        min p q len offsets)
    (unless (= 3 (string-bytes delim-line))
      (error "Delimiter cannot be represented in one byte"))
    (with-temp-buffer
      (insert-file-contents-literally cookies)
      (while (and (setq p (point))
                  (search-forward delim-line (point-max) t)
                  (setq len (- (point) 3 p)))
        (setq count (1+ count)
              max (max max len)
              min (min (or min max) len)
              offsets (cons (1- p) offsets))))
    (with-temp-buffer
      (set-buffer-multibyte nil)
      (insert
       (bindat-pack
        fcookie-index-spec
        `((:version . 2)
          (:count . ,count)
          (:longest . ,max)
          (:shortest . ,min)
```

```
                        (:flags . 0)
                        (:delim . ,delim)
                        (:offset . ,(mapcar (lambda (o)
                                               (list (cons :foo o)))
                                            (nreverse offsets)))))))
                 (let ((coding-system-for-write 'raw-text-unix))
                   (write-file (or index (concat cookies ".dat")))))))))
```

The following is an example of defining and unpacking a complex structure. Consider the following C structures:

```
struct header {
    unsigned long    dest_ip;
    unsigned long    src_ip;
    unsigned short   dest_port;
    unsigned short   src_port;
};

struct data {
    unsigned char    type;
    unsigned char    opcode;
    unsigned short   length;  /* in network byte order  */
    unsigned char    id[8];   /* null-terminated string  */
    unsigned char    data[/* (length + 3) & ~3 */];
};

struct packet {
    struct header    header;
    unsigned long    counters[2];  /* in little endian order  */
    unsigned char    items;
    unsigned char    filler[3];
    struct data      item[/* items */];

};
```

The corresponding data layout specification is:

```
(setq header-spec
      '((dest-ip   ip)
        (src-ip    ip)
        (dest-port u16)
        (src-port  u16)))

(setq data-spec
      '((type      u8)
        (opcode    u8)
        (length    u16)  ; network byte order
        (id        strz 8)
        (data      vec (length))
        (align     4)))
```

```
(setq packet-spec
      '((header    struct header-spec)
        (counters  vec 2 u32r)   ; little endian order
        (items     u8)
        (fill      3)
        (item      repeat (items)
                   (struct data-spec))))
```

A binary data representation is:

```
(setq binary-data
      [ 192 168 1 100 192 168 1 101 01 28 21 32
        160 134 1 0 5 1 0 0 2 0 0 0
        2 3 0 5 ?A ?B ?C ?D ?E ?F 0 0 1 2 3 4 5 0 0 0
        1 4 0 7 ?B ?C ?D ?E ?F ?G 0 0 6 7 8 9 10 11 12 0 ])
```

The corresponding decoded structure is:

```
(setq decoded (bindat-unpack packet-spec binary-data))
    ⇒
((header
  (dest-ip    . [192 168 1 100])
  (src-ip     . [192 168 1 101])
  (dest-port . 284)
  (src-port  . 5408))
 (counters . [100000 261])
 (items . 2)
 (item ((data . [1 2 3 4 5])
        (id . "ABCDEF")
        (length . 5)
        (opcode . 3)
        (type . 2))
       ((data . [6 7 8 9 10 11 12])
        (id . "BCDEFG")
        (length . 7)
        (opcode . 4)
        (type . 1))))
```

An example of fetching data from this structure:

```
(bindat-get-field decoded 'item 1 'id)
    ⇒ "BCDEFG"
```

37 Emacs Display

This chapter describes a number of features related to the display that Emacs presents to the user.

37.1 Refreshing the Screen

The function `redraw-frame` clears and redisplays the entire contents of a given frame (see Chapter 28 [Frames], page 630). This is useful if the screen is corrupted.

redraw-frame &optional *frame*　　　　　　　　　　　　　　　　[Function]
> This function clears and redisplays frame *frame*. If *frame* is omitted or nil, it redraws the selected frame.

Even more powerful is `redraw-display`:

redraw-display　　　　　　　　　　　　　　　　　　　　　　[Command]
> This function clears and redisplays all visible frames.

In Emacs, processing user input takes priority over redisplay. If you call these functions when input is available, they don't redisplay immediately, but the requested redisplay does happen eventually—after all the input has been processed.

On text terminals, suspending and resuming Emacs normally also refreshes the screen. Some terminal emulators record separate contents for display-oriented programs such as Emacs and for ordinary sequential display. If you are using such a terminal, you might want to inhibit the redisplay on resumption.

no-redraw-on-reenter　　　　　　　　　　　　　　　　　　[User Option]
> This variable controls whether Emacs redraws the entire screen after it has been suspended and resumed. Non-`nil` means there is no need to redraw, `nil` means redrawing is needed. The default is `nil`.

37.2 Forcing Redisplay

Emacs normally tries to redisplay the screen whenever it waits for input. With the following function, you can request an immediate attempt to redisplay, in the middle of Lisp code, without actually waiting for input.

redisplay &optional *force*　　　　　　　　　　　　　　　　[Function]
> This function tries immediately to redisplay. The optional argument *force*, if non-`nil`, forces the redisplay to be performed, instead of being preempted if input is pending.
>
> The function returns `t` if it actually tried to redisplay, and `nil` otherwise. A value of `t` does not mean that redisplay proceeded to completion; it could have been preempted by newly arriving input.

Although `redisplay` tries immediately to redisplay, it does not change how Emacs decides which parts of its frame(s) to redisplay. By contrast, the following function adds certain windows to the pending redisplay work (as if their contents had completely changed), but does not immediately try to perform redisplay.

force-window-update &optional *object*   [Function]

>   This function forces some or all windows to be updated the next time Emacs does a redisplay. If *object* is a window, that window is to be updated. If *object* is a buffer or buffer name, all windows displaying that buffer are to be updated. If *object* is `nil` (or omitted), all windows are to be updated.

>   This function does not do a redisplay immediately; Emacs does that as it waits for input, or when the function `redisplay` is called.

pre-redisplay-function   [Variable]

>   A function run just before redisplay. It is called with one argument, the set of windows to be redisplayed. The set can be `nil`, meaning only the selected window, or `t`, meaning all the windows.

pre-redisplay-functions   [Variable]

>   This hook is run just before redisplay. It is called once in each window that is about to be redisplayed, with `current-buffer` set to the buffer displayed in that window.

37.3 Truncation

When a line of text extends beyond the right edge of a window, Emacs can *continue* the line (make it wrap to the next screen line), or *truncate* the line (limit it to one screen line). The additional screen lines used to display a long text line are called *continuation* lines. Continuation is not the same as filling; continuation happens on the screen only, not in the buffer contents, and it breaks a line precisely at the right margin, not at a word boundary. See Section 31.11 [Filling], page 716.

   On a graphical display, tiny arrow images in the window fringes indicate truncated and continued lines (see Section 37.13 [Fringes], page 937). On a text terminal, a '$' in the rightmost column of the window indicates truncation; a '\' on the rightmost column indicates a line that wraps. (The display table can specify alternate characters to use for this; see Section 37.22.2 [Display Tables], page 974).

truncate-lines   [User Option]

>   If this buffer-local variable is non-`nil`, lines that extend beyond the right edge of the window are truncated; otherwise, they are continued. As a special exception, the variable `truncate-partial-width-windows` takes precedence in *partial-width* windows (i.e., windows that do not occupy the entire frame width).

truncate-partial-width-windows   [User Option]

>   This variable controls line truncation in *partial-width* windows. A partial-width window is one that does not occupy the entire frame width (see Section 27.6 [Splitting Windows], page 581). If the value is `nil`, line truncation is determined by the variable `truncate-lines` (see above). If the value is an integer *n*, lines are truncated if the partial-width window has fewer than *n* columns, regardless of the value of `truncate-lines`; if the partial-width window has *n* or more columns, line truncation is determined by `truncate-lines`. For any other non-`nil` value, lines are truncated in every partial-width window, regardless of the value of `truncate-lines`.

   When horizontal scrolling (see Section 27.23 [Horizontal Scrolling], page 618) is in use in a window, that forces truncation.

`wrap-prefix`   [Variable]

> If this buffer-local variable is non-`nil`, it defines a *wrap prefix* which Emacs displays at the start of every continuation line. (If lines are truncated, `wrap-prefix` is never used.) Its value may be a string or an image (see Section 37.16.4 [Other Display Specs], page 948), or a stretch of whitespace such as specified by the `:width` or `:align-to` display properties (see Section 37.16.2 [Specified Space], page 946). The value is interpreted in the same way as a `display` text property. See Section 37.16 [Display Property], page 945.

> A wrap prefix may also be specified for regions of text, using the `wrap-prefix` text or overlay property. This takes precedence over the `wrap-prefix` variable. See Section 31.19.4 [Special Properties], page 738.

`line-prefix`   [Variable]

> If this buffer-local variable is non-`nil`, it defines a *line prefix* which Emacs displays at the start of every non-continuation line. Its value may be a string or an image (see Section 37.16.4 [Other Display Specs], page 948), or a stretch of whitespace such as specified by the `:width` or `:align-to` display properties (see Section 37.16.2 [Specified Space], page 946). The value is interpreted in the same way as a `display` text property. See Section 37.16 [Display Property], page 945.

> A line prefix may also be specified for regions of text using the `line-prefix` text or overlay property. This takes precedence over the `line-prefix` variable. See Section 31.19.4 [Special Properties], page 738.

37.4 The Echo Area

The *echo area* is used for displaying error messages (see Section 10.6.3 [Errors], page 148), for messages made with the `message` primitive, and for echoing keystrokes. It is not the same as the minibuffer, despite the fact that the minibuffer appears (when active) in the same place on the screen as the echo area. See Section "The Minibuffer" in *The GNU Emacs Manual*.

Apart from the functions documented in this section, you can print Lisp objects to the echo area by specifying `t` as the output stream. See Section 18.4 [Output Streams], page 306.

37.4.1 Displaying Messages in the Echo Area

This section describes the standard functions for displaying messages in the echo area.

`message` *format-string* **&rest** *arguments*   [Function]

> This function displays a message in the echo area. *format-string* is a format string, and *arguments* are the objects for its format specifications, like in the `format-message` function (see Section 4.7 [Formatting Strings], page 59). The resulting formatted string is displayed in the echo area; if it contains `face` text properties, it is displayed with the specified faces (see Section 37.12 [Faces], page 915). The string is also added to the `*Messages*` buffer, but without text properties (see Section 37.4.3 [Logging Messages], page 892).

> The `text-quoting-style` variable controls what quotes are generated; See Section 23.3 [Keys in Documentation], page 488. A call using a format like `"Missing '%s'"` with grave accents and apostrophes typically generates a message like

"Missing 'foo'" with matching curved quotes. In contrast, a call using a format like "Missing '%s'" with only apostrophes typically generates a message like "Missing 'foo'" with only closing curved quotes, an unusual style in English.

In batch mode, the message is printed to the standard error stream, followed by a newline.

When `inhibit-message` is non-`nil`, no message will be displayed in the echo area, it will only be logged to '*Messages*'.

If *format-string* is `nil` or the empty string, `message` clears the echo area; if the echo area has been expanded automatically, this brings it back to its normal size. If the minibuffer is active, this brings the minibuffer contents back onto the screen immediately.

```
(message "Reverting `%s'..." (buffer-name))
    ⊣ Reverting 'subr.el'...
    ⇒ "Reverting 'subr.el'..."


---------- Echo Area ----------
Reverting 'subr.el'...
---------- Echo Area ----------
```

To automatically display a message in the echo area or in a pop-buffer, depending on its size, use `display-message-or-buffer` (see below).

Warning: If you want to use your own string as a message verbatim, don't just write (message *string*). If *string* contains '%', '`', or ''' it may be reformatted, with undesirable results. Instead, use (message "%s" *string*).

`inhibit-message`   [Variable]
> When this variable is non-`nil`, `message` and related functions will not use the Echo Area to display messages.

`with-temp-message` *message* **&rest** *body*   [Macro]
> This construct displays a message in the echo area temporarily, during the execution of *body*. It displays *message*, executes *body*, then returns the value of the last body form while restoring the previous echo area contents.

`message-or-box` *format-string* **&rest** *arguments*   [Function]
> This function displays a message like `message`, but may display it in a dialog box instead of the echo area. If this function is called in a command that was invoked using the mouse—more precisely, if `last-nonmenu-event` (see Section 20.5 [Command Loop Info], page 355) is either `nil` or a list—then it uses a dialog box or pop-up menu to display the message. Otherwise, it uses the echo area. (This is the same criterion that `y-or-n-p` uses to make a similar decision; see Section 19.7 [Yes-or-No Queries], page 337.)
>
> You can force use of the mouse or of the echo area by binding `last-nonmenu-event` to a suitable value around the call.

`message-box` *format-string* **&rest** *arguments*   [Function]
> This function displays a message like `message`, but uses a dialog box (or a pop-up menu) whenever that is possible. If it is impossible to use a dialog box or pop-up

menu, because the terminal does not support them, then `message-box` uses the echo area, like `message`.

`display-message-or-buffer` *message* **&optional** *buffer-name action* [Function]
> *frame*
>
> This function displays the message *message*, which may be either a string or a buffer. If it is shorter than the maximum height of the echo area, as defined by `max-mini-window-height`, it is displayed in the echo area, using `message`. Otherwise, `display-buffer` is used to show it in a pop-up buffer.
>
> Returns either the string shown in the echo area, or when a pop-up buffer is used, the window used to display it.
>
> If *message* is a string, then the optional argument *buffer-name* is the name of the buffer used to display it when a pop-up buffer is used, defaulting to `*Message*`. In the case where *message* is a string and displayed in the echo area, it is not specified whether the contents are inserted into the buffer anyway.
>
> The optional arguments *action* and *frame* are as for `display-buffer`, and only used if a buffer is displayed.

`current-message` [Function]
> This function returns the message currently being displayed in the echo area, or `nil` if there is none.

37.4.2 Reporting Operation Progress

When an operation can take a while to finish, you should inform the user about the progress it makes. This way the user can estimate remaining time and clearly see that Emacs is busy working, not hung. A convenient way to do this is to use a *progress reporter*.

Here is a working example that does nothing useful:

```
(let ((progress-reporter
       (make-progress-reporter "Collecting mana for Emacs..."
                               0  500)))
    (dotimes (k 500)
      (sit-for 0.01)
      (progress-reporter-update progress-reporter k))
    (progress-reporter-done progress-reporter))
```

`make-progress-reporter` *message* **&optional** *min-value max-value* [Function]
> *current-value min-change min-time*
>
> This function creates and returns a progress reporter object, which you will use as an argument for the other functions listed below. The idea is to precompute as much data as possible to make progress reporting very fast.
>
> When this progress reporter is subsequently used, it will display *message* in the echo area, followed by progress percentage. *message* is treated as a simple string. If you need it to depend on a filename, for instance, use `format-message` before calling this function.
>
> The arguments *min-value* and *max-value* should be numbers standing for the starting and final states of the operation. For instance, an operation that scans a buffer should set these to the results of `point-min` and `point-max` correspondingly. *max-value* should be greater than *min-value*.

Alternatively, you can set *min-value* and *max-value* to `nil`. In that case, the progress reporter does not report process percentages; it instead displays a "spinner" that rotates a notch each time you update the progress reporter.

If *min-value* and *max-value* are numbers, you can give the argument *current-value* a numerical value specifying the initial progress; if omitted, this defaults to *min-value*.

The remaining arguments control the rate of echo area updates. The progress reporter will wait for at least *min-change* more percents of the operation to be completed before printing next message; the default is one percent. *min-time* specifies the minimum time in seconds to pass between successive prints; the default is 0.2 seconds. (On some operating systems, the progress reporter may handle fractions of seconds with varying precision).

This function calls `progress-reporter-update`, so the first message is printed immediately.

`progress-reporter-update` *reporter* **&optional** *value* [Function]

This function does the main work of reporting progress of your operation. It displays the message of *reporter*, followed by progress percentage determined by *value*. If percentage is zero, or close enough according to the *min-change* and *min-time* arguments, then it is omitted from the output.

reporter must be the result of a call to `make-progress-reporter`. *value* specifies the current state of your operation and must be between *min-value* and *max-value* (inclusive) as passed to `make-progress-reporter`. For instance, if you scan a buffer, then *value* should be the result of a call to `point`.

This function respects *min-change* and *min-time* as passed to `make-progress-reporter` and so does not output new messages on every invocation. It is thus very fast and normally you should not try to reduce the number of calls to it: resulting overhead will most likely negate your effort.

`progress-reporter-force-update` *reporter* **&optional** *value* [Function]
      new-message

This function is similar to `progress-reporter-update` except that it prints a message in the echo area unconditionally.

The first two arguments have the same meaning as for `progress-reporter-update`. Optional *new-message* allows you to change the message of the *reporter*. Since this function always updates the echo area, such a change will be immediately presented to the user.

`progress-reporter-done` *reporter* [Function]

This function should be called when the operation is finished. It prints the message of *reporter* followed by word 'done' in the echo area.

You should always call this function and not hope for `progress-reporter-update` to print '100%'. Firstly, it may never print it, there are many good reasons for this not to happen. Secondly, 'done' is more explicit.

dotimes-with-progress-reporter (*var count* [*result*]) *message*   [Macro]
      body...

> This is a convenience macro that works the same way as **dotimes** does, but also reports loop progress using the functions described above. It allows you to save some typing.

> You can rewrite the example in the beginning of this node using this macro this way:

```
(dotimes-with-progress-reporter
    (k 500)
    "Collecting some mana for Emacs..."
  (sit-for 0.01))
```

37.4.3 Logging Messages in *Messages*

Almost all the messages displayed in the echo area are also recorded in the *Messages* buffer so that the user can refer back to them. This includes all the messages that are output with **message**. By default, this buffer is read-only and uses the major mode **messages-buffer-mode**. Nothing prevents the user from killing the *Messages* buffer, but the next display of a message recreates it. Any Lisp code that needs to access the *Messages* buffer directly and wants to ensure that it exists should use the function **messages-buffer**.

messages-buffer   [Function]

> This function returns the *Messages* buffer. If it does not exist, it creates it, and switches it to **messages-buffer-mode**.

message-log-max   [User Option]

> This variable specifies how many lines to keep in the *Messages* buffer. The value **t** means there is no limit on how many lines to keep. The value **nil** disables message logging entirely. Here's how to display a message and prevent it from being logged:

```
(let (message-log-max)
  (message ...))
```

To make *Messages* more convenient for the user, the logging facility combines successive identical messages. It also combines successive related messages for the sake of two cases: question followed by answer, and a series of progress messages.

A question followed by an answer has two messages like the ones produced by **y-or-n-p**: the first is '*question*', and the second is '*question...answer*'. The first message conveys no additional information beyond what's in the second, so logging the second message discards the first from the log.

A series of progress messages has successive messages like those produced by **make-progress-reporter**. They have the form '*base...how-far*', where *base* is the same each time, while *how-far* varies. Logging each message in the series discards the previous one, provided they are consecutive.

The functions **make-progress-reporter** and **y-or-n-p** don't have to do anything special to activate the message log combination feature. It operates whenever two consecutive messages are logged that share a common prefix ending in '...'.

37.4.4 Echo Area Customization

These variables control details of how the echo area works.

cursor-in-echo-area   [Variable]

> This variable controls where the cursor appears when a message is displayed in the echo area. If it is non-nil, then the cursor appears at the end of the message. Otherwise, the cursor appears at point—not in the echo area at all.
>
> The value is normally nil; Lisp programs bind it to t for brief periods of time.

echo-area-clear-hook   [Variable]

> This normal hook is run whenever the echo area is cleared—either by (message nil) or for any other reason.

echo-keystrokes   [User Option]

> This variable determines how much time should elapse before command characters echo. Its value must be a number, and specifies the number of seconds to wait before echoing. If the user types a prefix key (such as C-x) and then delays this many seconds before continuing, the prefix key is echoed in the echo area. (Once echoing begins in a key sequence, all subsequent characters in the same key sequence are echoed immediately.)
>
> If the value is zero, then command input is not echoed.

message-truncate-lines   [Variable]

> Normally, displaying a long message resizes the echo area to display the entire message. But if the variable message-truncate-lines is non-nil, the echo area does not resize, and the message is truncated to fit it.

The variable max-mini-window-height, which specifies the maximum height for resizing minibuffer windows, also applies to the echo area (which is really a special use of the minibuffer window; see Section 19.14 [Minibuffer Misc], page 343).

37.5 Reporting Warnings

Warnings are a facility for a program to inform the user of a possible problem, but continue running.

37.5.1 Warning Basics

Every warning has a textual message, which explains the problem for the user, and a *severity level* which is a symbol. Here are the possible severity levels, in order of decreasing severity, and their meanings:

:emergency

> A problem that will seriously impair Emacs operation soon if you do not attend to it promptly.

:error   A report of data or circumstances that are inherently wrong.

:warning   A report of data or circumstances that are not inherently wrong, but raise suspicion of a possible problem.

`:debug`   A report of information that may be useful if you are debugging.

When your program encounters invalid input data, it can either signal a Lisp error by calling `error` or `signal` or report a warning with severity `:error`. Signaling a Lisp error is the easiest thing to do, but it means the program cannot continue processing. If you want to take the trouble to implement a way to continue processing despite the bad data, then reporting a warning of severity `:error` is the right way to inform the user of the problem. For instance, the Emacs Lisp byte compiler can report an error that way and continue compiling other functions. (If the program signals a Lisp error and then handles it with `condition-case`, the user won't see the error message; it could show the message to the user by reporting it as a warning.)

Each warning has a *warning type* to classify it. The type is a list of symbols. The first symbol should be the custom group that you use for the program's user options. For example, byte compiler warnings use the warning type (`bytecomp`). You can also subcategorize the warnings, if you wish, by using more symbols in the list.

`display-warning` *type message* **&optional** *level buffer-name*   [Function]
> This function reports a warning, using *message* as the message and *type* as the warning type. *level* should be the severity level, with `:warning` being the default.
>
> *buffer-name*, if non-`nil`, specifies the name of the buffer for logging the warning. By default, it is `*Warnings*`.

`lwarn` *type level message* **&rest** *args*   [Function]
> This function reports a warning using the value of (`format-message` *message args...`) as the message in the `*Warnings*` buffer. In other respects it is equivalent to `display-warning`.

`warn` *message* **&rest** *args*   [Function]
> This function reports a warning using the value of (`format-message` *message args...`) as the message, (`emacs`) as the type, and `:warning` as the severity level. It exists for compatibility only; we recommend not using it, because you should specify a specific warning type.

37.5.2 Warning Variables

Programs can customize how their warnings appear by binding the variables described in this section.

`warning-levels`   [Variable]
> This list defines the meaning and severity order of the warning severity levels. Each element defines one severity level, and they are arranged in order of decreasing severity.
>
> Each element has the form (`level string function`), where *level* is the severity level it defines. *string* specifies the textual description of this level. *string* should use '`%s`' to specify where to put the warning type information, or it can omit the '`%s`' so as not to include that information.
>
> The optional *function*, if non-`nil`, is a function to call with no arguments, to get the user's attention.
>
> Normally you should not change the value of this variable.

`warning-prefix-function`   [Variable]

> If non-`nil`, the value is a function to generate prefix text for warnings. Programs can bind the variable to a suitable function. `display-warning` calls this function with the warnings buffer current, and the function can insert text in it. That text becomes the beginning of the warning message.
>
> The function is called with two arguments, the severity level and its entry in `warning-levels`. It should return a list to use as the entry (this value need not be an actual member of `warning-levels`). By constructing this value, the function can change the severity of the warning, or specify different handling for a given severity level.
>
> If the variable's value is `nil` then there is no function to call.

`warning-series`   [Variable]

> Programs can bind this variable to `t` to say that the next warning should begin a series. When several warnings form a series, that means to leave point on the first warning of the series, rather than keep moving it for each warning so that it appears on the last one. The series ends when the local binding is unbound and `warning-series` becomes `nil` again.
>
> The value can also be a symbol with a function definition. That is equivalent to `t`, except that the next warning will also call the function with no arguments with the warnings buffer current. The function can insert text which will serve as a header for the series of warnings.
>
> Once a series has begun, the value is a marker which points to the buffer position in the warnings buffer of the start of the series.
>
> The variable's normal value is `nil`, which means to handle each warning separately.

`warning-fill-prefix`   [Variable]

> When this variable is non-`nil`, it specifies a fill prefix to use for filling each warning's text.

`warning-type-format`   [Variable]

> This variable specifies the format for displaying the warning type in the warning message. The result of formatting the type this way gets included in the message under the control of the string in the entry in `warning-levels`. The default value is `" (%s)"`. If you bind it to `""` then the warning type won't appear at all.

37.5.3 Warning Options

These variables are used by users to control what happens when a Lisp program reports a warning.

`warning-minimum-level`   [User Option]

> This user option specifies the minimum severity level that should be shown immediately to the user. The default is `:warning`, which means to immediately display all warnings except `:debug` warnings.

`warning-minimum-log-level` [User Option]

> This user option specifies the minimum severity level that should be logged in the warnings buffer. The default is `:warning`, which means to log all warnings except `:debug` warnings.

`warning-suppress-types` [User Option]

> This list specifies which warning types should not be displayed immediately for the user. Each element of the list should be a list of symbols. If its elements match the first elements in a warning type, then that warning is not displayed immediately.

`warning-suppress-log-types` [User Option]

> This list specifies which warning types should not be logged in the warnings buffer. Each element of the list should be a list of symbols. If it matches the first few elements in a warning type, then that warning is not logged.

37.5.4 Delayed Warnings

Sometimes, you may wish to avoid showing a warning while a command is running, and only show it only after the end of the command. You can use the variable `delayed-warnings-list` for this.

`delayed-warnings-list` [Variable]

> The value of this variable is a list of warnings to be displayed after the current command has finished. Each element must be a list
>
> > (`type message [level [buffer-name]]`)
>
> with the same form, and the same meanings, as the argument list of `display-warning` (see Section 37.5.1 [Warning Basics], page 893). Immediately after running `post-command-hook` (see Section 20.1 [Command Overview], page 345), the Emacs command loop displays all the warnings specified by this variable, then resets it to `nil`.

Programs which need to further customize the delayed warnings mechanism can change the variable `delayed-warnings-hook`:

`delayed-warnings-hook` [Variable]

> This is a normal hook which is run by the Emacs command loop, after `post-command-hook`, in order to to process and display delayed warnings.
>
> Its default value is a list of two functions:
>
> > (`collapse-delayed-warnings display-delayed-warnings`)
>
> The function `collapse-delayed-warnings` removes repeated entries from `delayed-warnings-list`. The function `display-delayed-warnings` calls `display-warning` on each of the entries in `delayed-warnings-list`, in turn, and then sets `delayed-warnings-list` to `nil`.

37.6 Invisible Text

You can make characters *invisible*, so that they do not appear on the screen, with the `invisible` property. This can be either a text property (see Section 31.19 [Text Properties], page 732) or an overlay property (see Section 37.9 [Overlays], page 904). Cursor motion also partly ignores these characters; if the command loop finds that point is inside a range of invisible text after a command, it relocates point to the other side of the text.

In the simplest case, any non-`nil` `invisible` property makes a character invisible. This is the default case—if you don't alter the default value of `buffer-invisibility-spec`, this is how the `invisible` property works. You should normally use `t` as the value of the `invisible` property if you don't plan to set `buffer-invisibility-spec` yourself.

More generally, you can use the variable `buffer-invisibility-spec` to control which values of the `invisible` property make text invisible. This permits you to classify the text into different subsets in advance, by giving them different `invisible` values, and subsequently make various subsets visible or invisible by changing the value of `buffer-invisibility-spec`.

Controlling visibility with `buffer-invisibility-spec` is especially useful in a program to display the list of entries in a database. It permits the implementation of convenient filtering commands to view just a part of the entries in the database. Setting this variable is very fast, much faster than scanning all the text in the buffer looking for properties to change.

`buffer-invisibility-spec`   [Variable]
> This variable specifies which kinds of `invisible` properties actually make a character invisible. Setting this variable makes it buffer-local.
>
> `t`   A character is invisible if its `invisible` property is non-`nil`. This is the default.
>
> a list   Each element of the list specifies a criterion for invisibility; if a character's `invisible` property fits any one of these criteria, the character is invisible. The list can have two kinds of elements:
>
>> `atom`   A character is invisible if its `invisible` property value is *atom* or if it is a list with *atom* as a member; comparison is done with `eq`.
>>
>> `(atom . t)`
>>   A character is invisible if its `invisible` property value is *atom* or if it is a list with *atom* as a member; comparison is done with `eq`. Moreover, a sequence of such characters displays as an ellipsis.

Two functions are specifically provided for adding elements to `buffer-invisibility-spec` and removing elements from it.

`add-to-invisibility-spec` *element*   [Function]
> This function adds the element *element* to `buffer-invisibility-spec`. If `buffer-invisibility-spec` was `t`, it changes to a list, `(t)`, so that text whose `invisible` property is `t` remains invisible.

`remove-from-invisibility-spec` *element*   [Function]
> This removes the element *element* from `buffer-invisibility-spec`. This does nothing if *element* is not in the list.

A convention for use of `buffer-invisibility-spec` is that a major mode should use the mode's own name as an element of `buffer-invisibility-spec` and as the value of the `invisible` property:

```
;; If you want to display an ellipsis:
(add-to-invisibility-spec '(my-symbol . t))
;; If you donflt want ellipsis:
(add-to-invisibility-spec 'my-symbol)

(overlay-put (make-overlay beginning end)
             'invisible 'my-symbol)

;; When done with the invisibility:
(remove-from-invisibility-spec '(my-symbol . t))
;; Or respectively:
(remove-from-invisibility-spec 'my-symbol)
```

You can check for invisibility using the following function:

`invisible-p` *pos-or-prop*   [Function]

> If *pos-or-prop* is a marker or number, this function returns a non-`nil` value if the text at that position is invisible.

> If *pos-or-prop* is any other kind of Lisp object, that is taken to mean a possible value of the `invisible` text or overlay property. In that case, this function returns a non-`nil` value if that value would cause text to become invisible, based on the current value of `buffer-invisibility-spec`.

Ordinarily, functions that operate on text or move point do not care whether the text is invisible, they process invisible characters and visible characters alike. The user-level line motion commands, such as `next-line`, `previous-line`, ignore invisible newlines if `line-move-ignore-invisible` is non-`nil` (the default), i.e., behave like these invisible newlines didn't exist in the buffer, but only because they are explicitly programmed to do so.

If a command ends with point inside or at the boundary of invisible text, the main editing loop relocates point to one of the two ends of the invisible text. Emacs chooses the direction of relocation so that it is the same as the overall movement direction of the command; if in doubt, it prefers a position where an inserted char would not inherit the `invisible` property. Additionally, if the text is not replaced by an ellipsis and the command only moved within the invisible text, then point is moved one extra character so as to try and reflect the command's movement by a visible movement of the cursor.

Thus, if the command moved point back to an invisible range (with the usual stickiness), Emacs moves point back to the beginning of that range. If the command moved point forward into an invisible range, Emacs moves point forward to the first visible character that follows the invisible text and then forward one more character.

These *adjustments* of point that ended up in the middle of invisible text can be disabled by setting `disable-point-adjustment` to a non-`nil` value. See Section 20.6 [Adjusting Point], page 357.

Incremental search can make invisible overlays visible temporarily and/or permanently when a match includes invisible text. To enable this, the overlay should have a non-**nil** **isearch-open-invisible** property. The property value should be a function to be called with the overlay as an argument. This function should make the overlay visible permanently; it is used when the match overlaps the overlay on exit from the search.

During the search, such overlays are made temporarily visible by temporarily modifying their invisible and intangible properties. If you want this to be done differently for a certain overlay, give it an **isearch-open-invisible-temporary** property which is a function. The function is called with two arguments: the first is the overlay, and the second is **nil** to make the overlay visible, or **t** to make it invisible again.

37.7 Selective Display

Selective display refers to a pair of related features for hiding certain lines on the screen.

The first variant, explicit selective display, was designed for use in a Lisp program: it controls which lines are hidden by altering the text. This kind of hiding is now obsolete; instead you can get the same effect with the **invisible** property (see Section 37.6 [Invisible Text], page 896).

In the second variant, the choice of lines to hide is made automatically based on indentation. This variant is designed to be a user-level feature.

The way you control explicit selective display is by replacing a newline (control-j) with a carriage return (control-m). The text that was formerly a line following that newline is now hidden. Strictly speaking, it is temporarily no longer a line at all, since only newlines can separate lines; it is now part of the previous line.

Selective display does not directly affect editing commands. For example, *C-f* (**forward-char**) moves point unhesitatingly into hidden text. However, the replacement of newline characters with carriage return characters affects some editing commands. For example, **next-line** skips hidden lines, since it searches only for newlines. Modes that use selective display can also define commands that take account of the newlines, or that control which parts of the text are hidden.

When you write a selectively displayed buffer into a file, all the control-m's are output as newlines. This means that when you next read in the file, it looks OK, with nothing hidden. The selective display effect is seen only within Emacs.

selective-display   [Variable]

    This buffer-local variable enables selective display. This means that lines, or portions of lines, may be made hidden.

- If the value of **selective-display** is **t**, then the character control-m marks the start of hidden text; the control-m, and the rest of the line following it, are not displayed. This is explicit selective display.

- If the value of **selective-display** is a positive integer, then lines that start with more than that many columns of indentation are not displayed.

    When some portion of a buffer is hidden, the vertical movement commands operate as if that portion did not exist, allowing a single **next-line** command to skip any number of hidden lines. However, character movement commands (such as **forward-char**) do not skip the hidden portion, and it is possible (if tricky) to insert or delete text in an hidden portion.

In the examples below, we show the *display appearance* of the buffer `foo`, which changes with the value of `selective-display`. The *contents* of the buffer do not change.

```
(setq selective-display nil)
     ⇒ nil


---------- Buffer: foo ----------
1 on this column
 2on this column
  3n this column
  3n this column
 2on this column
1 on this column
---------- Buffer: foo ----------


(setq selective-display 2)
     ⇒ 2


---------- Buffer: foo ----------
1 on this column
 2on this column
 2on this column
1 on this column
---------- Buffer: foo ----------
```

`selective-display-ellipses`   [User Option]

If this buffer-local variable is non-`nil`, then Emacs displays '...' at the end of a line that is followed by hidden text. This example is a continuation of the previous one.

```
(setq selective-display-ellipses t)
     ⇒ t


---------- Buffer: foo ----------
1 on this column
 2on this column ...
 2on this column
1 on this column
---------- Buffer: foo ----------
```

You can use a display table to substitute other text for the ellipsis ('...'). See Section 37.22.2 [Display Tables], page 974.

37.8 Temporary Displays

Temporary displays are used by Lisp programs to put output into a buffer and then present it to the user for perusal rather than for editing. Many help commands use this feature.

with-output-to-temp-buffer *buffer-name body...*   [Macro]

    This function executes the forms in *body* while arranging to insert any output they print into the buffer named *buffer-name*, which is first created if necessary, and put into Help mode. (See the similar form `with-temp-buffer-window` below.) Finally, the buffer is displayed in some window, but that window is not selected.

    If the forms in *body* do not change the major mode in the output buffer, so that it is still Help mode at the end of their execution, then `with-output-to-temp-buffer` makes this buffer read-only at the end, and also scans it for function and variable names to make them into clickable cross-references. See [Tips for Documentation Strings], page 1060, in particular the item on hyperlinks in documentation strings, for more details.

    The string *buffer-name* specifies the temporary buffer, which need not already exist. The argument must be a string, not a buffer. The buffer is erased initially (with no questions asked), and it is marked as unmodified after `with-output-to-temp-buffer` exits.

    `with-output-to-temp-buffer` binds `standard-output` to the temporary buffer, then it evaluates the forms in *body*. Output using the Lisp output functions within *body* goes by default to that buffer (but screen display and messages in the echo area, although they are "output" in the general sense of the word, are not affected). See Section 18.5 [Output Functions], page 308.

    Several hooks are available for customizing the behavior of this construct; they are listed below.

    The value of the last form in *body* is returned.

```
---------- Buffer: foo ----------
 This is the contents of foo.
---------- Buffer: foo ----------

(with-output-to-temp-buffer "foo"
    (print 20)
    (print standard-output))
⇒ #<buffer foo>

---------- Buffer: foo ----------

20

#<buffer foo>

---------- Buffer: foo ----------
```

temp-buffer-show-function   [User Option]

    If this variable is non-`nil`, `with-output-to-temp-buffer` calls it as a function to do the job of displaying a help buffer. The function gets one argument, which is the buffer it should display.

It is a good idea for this function to run `temp-buffer-show-hook` just as `with-output-to-temp-buffer` normally would, inside of `save-selected-window` and with the chosen window and buffer selected.

`temp-buffer-setup-hook`   [Variable]

> This normal hook is run by `with-output-to-temp-buffer` before evaluating *body*. When the hook runs, the temporary buffer is current. This hook is normally set up with a function to put the buffer in Help mode.

`temp-buffer-show-hook`   [Variable]

> This normal hook is run by `with-output-to-temp-buffer` after displaying the temporary buffer. When the hook runs, the temporary buffer is current, and the window it was displayed in is selected.

`with-temp-buffer-window` *buffer-or-name action quit-function*   [Macro]
>   *body...*
> This macro is similar to `with-output-to-temp-buffer`. Like that construct, it executes *body* while arranging to insert any output it prints into the buffer named *buffer-or-name* and displays that buffer in some window. Unlike `with-output-to-temp-buffer`, however, it does not automatically switch that buffer to Help mode.
>
> The argument *buffer-or-name* specifies the temporary buffer. It can be either a buffer, which must already exist, or a string, in which case a buffer of that name is created, if necessary. The buffer is marked as unmodified and read-only when `with-temp-buffer-window` exits.
>
> This macro does not call `temp-buffer-show-function`. Rather, it passes the *action* argument to `display-buffer` (see Section 27.13 [Choosing Window], page 598) in order to display the buffer.
>
> The value of the last form in *body* is returned, unless the argument *quit-function* is specified. In that case, it is called with two arguments: the window showing the buffer and the result of *body*. The final return value is then whatever *quit-function* returns.
>
> This macro uses the normal hooks `temp-buffer-window-setup-hook` and `temp-buffer-window-show-hook` in place of the analogous hooks run by `with-output-to-temp-buffer`.

The two constructs described next are mostly identical to `with-temp-buffer-window` but differ from it as specified:

`with-current-buffer-window` *buffer-or-name action quit-function*   [Macro]
>   **&rest** *body*
> This macro is like `with-temp-buffer-window` but unlike that makes the buffer specified by *buffer-or-name* current for running *body*.

`with-displayed-buffer-window` *buffer-or-name action quit-function*   [Macro]
>   **&rest** *body*
> This macro is like `with-current-buffer-window` but unlike that displays the buffer specified by *buffer-or-name* *before* running *body*.

A window showing a temporary buffer can be fit to the size of that buffer using the following mode:

`temp-buffer-resize-mode`   [User Option]

    When this minor mode is enabled, windows showing a temporary buffer are automatically resized to fit their buffer's contents.

    A window is resized if and only if it has been specially created for the buffer. In particular, windows that have shown another buffer before are not resized. By default, this mode uses `fit-window-to-buffer` (see Section 27.4 [Resizing Windows], page 576) for resizing. You can specify a different function by customizing the options `temp-buffer-max-height` and `temp-buffer-max-width` below.

`temp-buffer-max-height`   [User Option]

    This option specifies the maximum height (in lines) of a window displaying a temporary buffer when `temp-buffer-resize-mode` is enabled. It can also be a function to be called to choose the height for such a buffer. It gets one argument, the buffer, and should return a positive integer. At the time the function is called, the window to be resized is selected.

`temp-buffer-max-width`   [User Option]

    This option specifies the maximum width of a window (in columns) displaying a temporary buffer when `temp-buffer-resize-mode` is enabled. It can also be a function to be called to choose the width for such a buffer. It gets one argument, the buffer, and should return a positive integer. At the time the function is called, the window to be resized is selected.

The following function uses the current buffer for temporal display:

`momentary-string-display` *string position* **&optional** *char message*   [Function]

    This function momentarily displays *string* in the current buffer at *position*. It has no effect on the undo list or on the buffer's modification status.

    The momentary display remains until the next input event. If the next input event is *char*, `momentary-string-display` ignores it and returns. Otherwise, that event remains buffered for subsequent use as input. Thus, typing *char* will simply remove the string from the display, while typing (say) `C-f` will remove the string from the display and later (presumably) move point forward. The argument *char* is a space by default.

    The return value of `momentary-string-display` is not meaningful.

    If the string *string* does not contain control characters, you can do the same job in a more general way by creating (and then subsequently deleting) an overlay with a `before-string` property. See Section 37.9.2 [Overlay Properties], page 907.

    If *message* is non-`nil`, it is displayed in the echo area while *string* is displayed in the buffer. If it is `nil`, a default message says to type *char* to continue.

    In this example, point is initially located at the beginning of the second line:

```
---------- Buffer: foo ----------
This is the contents of foo.
*Second line.
---------- Buffer: foo ----------
```

```
(momentary-string-display
  "**** Important Message! ****"
  (point) ?\r
  "Type RET when done reading")
⇒ t


---------- Buffer: foo ----------
This is the contents of foo.
**** Important Message! ****Second line.
---------- Buffer: foo ----------


---------- Echo Area ----------
Type RET when done reading
---------- Echo Area ----------
```

37.9 Overlays

You can use *overlays* to alter the appearance of a buffer's text on the screen, for the sake of presentation features. An overlay is an object that belongs to a particular buffer, and has a specified beginning and end. It also has properties that you can examine and set; these affect the display of the text within the overlay.

The visual effect of an overlay is the same as of the corresponding text property (see Section 31.19 [Text Properties], page 732). However, due to a different implementation, overlays generally don't scale well (many operations take a time that is proportional to the number of overlays in the buffer). If you need to affect the visual appearance of many portions in the buffer, we recommend using text properties.

An overlay uses markers to record its beginning and end; thus, editing the text of the buffer adjusts the beginning and end of each overlay so that it stays with the text. When you create the overlay, you can specify whether text inserted at the beginning should be inside the overlay or outside, and likewise for the end of the overlay.

37.9.1 Managing Overlays

This section describes the functions to create, delete and move overlays, and to examine their contents. Overlay changes are not recorded in the buffer's undo list, since the overlays are not part of the buffer's contents.

overlayp *object*   [Function]
> This function returns t if *object* is an overlay.

make-overlay *start end* **&optional** *buffer front-advance rear-advance*   [Function]
> This function creates and returns an overlay that belongs to *buffer* and ranges from *start* to *end*. Both *start* and *end* must specify buffer positions; they may be integers or markers. If *buffer* is omitted, the overlay is created in the current buffer.
>
> An overlay whose *start* and *end* specify the same buffer position is known as *empty*. A non-empty overlay can become empty if the text between its *start* and *end* is deleted. When that happens, the overlay is by default not deleted, but you can cause it to be

deleted by giving it the 'evaporate' property (see Section 37.9.2 [Overlay Properties], page 907).

The arguments *front-advance* and *rear-advance* specify the marker insertion type for the start of the overlay and for the end of the overlay, respectively. See Section 30.5 [Marker Insertion Types], page 690. If they are both nil, the default, then the overlay extends to include any text inserted at the beginning, but not text inserted at the end. If *front-advance* is non-nil, text inserted at the beginning of the overlay is excluded from the overlay. If *rear-advance* is non-nil, text inserted at the end of the overlay is included in the overlay.

overlay-start *overlay*   [Function]
 This function returns the position at which *overlay* starts, as an integer.

overlay-end *overlay*   [Function]
 This function returns the position at which *overlay* ends, as an integer.

overlay-buffer *overlay*   [Function]
 This function returns the buffer that *overlay* belongs to. It returns nil if *overlay* has been deleted.

delete-overlay *overlay*   [Function]
 This function deletes *overlay*. The overlay continues to exist as a Lisp object, and its property list is unchanged, but it ceases to be attached to the buffer it belonged to, and ceases to have any effect on display.

 A deleted overlay is not permanently disconnected. You can give it a position in a buffer again by calling move-overlay.

move-overlay *overlay start end* &optional *buffer*   [Function]
 This function moves *overlay* to *buffer*, and places its bounds at *start* and *end*. Both arguments *start* and *end* must specify buffer positions; they may be integers or markers.

 If *buffer* is omitted, *overlay* stays in the same buffer it was already associated with; if *overlay* was deleted, it goes into the current buffer.

 The return value is *overlay*.

 This is the only valid way to change the endpoints of an overlay. Do not try modifying the markers in the overlay by hand, as that fails to update other vital data structures and can cause some overlays to be lost.

remove-overlays &optional *start end name value*   [Function]
 This function removes all the overlays between *start* and *end* whose property *name* has the value *value*. It can move the endpoints of the overlays in the region, or split them.

 If *name* is omitted or nil, it means to delete all overlays in the specified region. If *start* and/or *end* are omitted or nil, that means the beginning and end of the buffer respectively. Therefore, (remove-overlays) removes all the overlays in the current buffer.

copy-overlay *overlay*   [Function]

    This function returns a copy of *overlay*. The copy has the same endpoints and prop-
erties as *overlay*. However, the marker insertion type for the start of the overlay and
for the end of the overlay are set to their default values (see Section 30.5 [Marker
Insertion Types], page 690).

Here are some examples:

```
;; Create an overlay.
(setq foo (make-overlay 1 10))
     ⇒ #<overlay from 1 to 10 in display.texi>
(overlay-start foo)
     ⇒ 1
(overlay-end foo)
     ⇒ 10
(overlay-buffer foo)
     ⇒ #<buffer display.texi>
;; Give it a property we can check later.
(overlay-put foo 'happy t)
     ⇒ t
;; Verify the property is present.
(overlay-get foo 'happy)
     ⇒ t
;; Move the overlay.
(move-overlay foo 5 20)
     ⇒ #<overlay from 5 to 20 in display.texi>
(overlay-start foo)
     ⇒ 5
(overlay-end foo)
     ⇒ 20
;; Delete the overlay.
(delete-overlay foo)
     ⇒ nil
;; Verify it is deleted.
foo
     ⇒ #<overlay in no buffer>
;; A deleted overlay has no position.
(overlay-start foo)
     ⇒ nil
(overlay-end foo)
     ⇒ nil
(overlay-buffer foo)
     ⇒ nil
;; Undelete the overlay.
(move-overlay foo 1 20)
     ⇒ #<overlay from 1 to 20 in display.texi>
;; Verify the results.
(overlay-start foo)
```

```
        ⇒ 1
(overlay-end foo)
        ⇒ 20
(overlay-buffer foo)
        ⇒ #<buffer display.texi>
;; Moving and deleting the overlay does not change its properties.
(overlay-get foo 'happy)
        ⇒ t
```

Emacs stores the overlays of each buffer in two lists, divided around an arbitrary center position. One list extends backwards through the buffer from that center position, and the other extends forwards from that center position. The center position can be anywhere in the buffer.

overlay-recenter *pos*   [Function]
> This function recenters the overlays of the current buffer around position *pos*. That makes overlay lookup faster for positions near *pos*, but slower for positions far away from *pos*.

A loop that scans the buffer forwards, creating overlays, can run faster if you do `(overlay-recenter (point-max))` first.

37.9.2 Overlay Properties

Overlay properties are like text properties in that the properties that alter how a character is displayed can come from either source. But in most respects they are different. See Section 31.19 [Text Properties], page 732, for comparison.

Text properties are considered a part of the text; overlays and their properties are specifically considered not to be part of the text. Thus, copying text between various buffers and strings preserves text properties, but does not try to preserve overlays. Changing a buffer's text properties marks the buffer as modified, while moving an overlay or changing its properties does not. Unlike text property changes, overlay property changes are not recorded in the buffer's undo list.

Since more than one overlay can specify a property value for the same character, Emacs lets you specify a priority value of each overlay. The priority value is used to decide which of the overlapping overlays will "win".

These functions read and set the properties of an overlay:

overlay-get *overlay prop*   [Function]
> This function returns the value of property *prop* recorded in *overlay*, if any. If *overlay* does not record any value for that property, but it does have a **category** property which is a symbol, that symbol's *prop* property is used. Otherwise, the value is **nil**.

overlay-put *overlay prop value*   [Function]
> This function sets the value of property *prop* recorded in *overlay* to *value*. It returns *value*.

overlay-properties *overlay*   [Function]
> This returns a copy of the property list of *overlay*.

See also the function `get-char-property` which checks both overlay properties and text properties for a given character. See Section 31.19.1 [Examining Properties], page 732.

Many overlay properties have special meanings; here is a table of them:

priority   This property's value determines the priority of the overlay. If you want to specify a priority value, use either `nil` (or zero), or a positive integer. Any other value has undefined behavior.

The priority matters when two or more overlays cover the same character and both specify the same property; the one whose `priority` value is larger overrides the other. (For the `face` property, the higher priority overlay's value does not completely override the other value; instead, its face attributes override the face attributes of the lower priority `face` property.) If two overlays have the same priority value, and one is nested in the other, then the inner one will prevail over the outer one. If neither is nested in the other then you should not make assumptions about which overlay will prevail.

Currently, all overlays take priority over text properties.

Note that Emacs sometimes uses non-numeric priority values for some of its internal overlays, so do not try to do arithmetic on the priority of an overlay (unless it is one that you created). In particular, the overlay used for showing the region uses a priority value of the form (*primary . secondary*), where the *primary* value is used as described above, and *secondary* is the fallback value used when *primary* and the nesting considerations fail to resolve the precedence between overlays. However, you are advised not to design Lisp programs based on this implementation detail; if you need to put overlays in priority order, use the *sorted* argument of `overlays-at`. See Section 37.9.3 [Finding Overlays], page 911.

window   If the `window` property is non-`nil`, then the overlay applies only on that window.

category   If an overlay has a `category` property, we call it the *category* of the overlay. It should be a symbol. The properties of the symbol serve as defaults for the properties of the overlay.

face   This property controls the appearance of the text (see Section 37.12 [Faces], page 915). The value of the property can be the following:

• A face name (a symbol or string).

• An anonymous face: a property list of the form (*keyword value* ...), where each *keyword* is a face attribute name and *value* is a value for that attribute.

• A list of faces. Each list element should be either a face name or an anonymous face. This specifies a face which is an aggregate of the attributes of each of the listed faces. Faces occurring earlier in the list have higher priority.

• A cons cell of the form (`foreground-color` . *color-name*) or (`background-color` . *color-name*). This specifies the foreground or background color, similar to (`:foreground` *color-name*) or (`:background` *color-name*). This form is supported for backward compatibility only, and should be avoided.

mouse-face
: This property is used instead of `face` when the mouse is within the range of the overlay. However, Emacs ignores all face attributes from this property that alter the text size (e.g., `:height`, `:weight`, and `:slant`). Those attributes are always the same as in the unhighlighted text.

display
: This property activates various features that change the way text is displayed. For example, it can make text appear taller or shorter, higher or lower, wider or narrower, or replaced with an image. See Section 37.16 [Display Property], page 945.

help-echo
: If an overlay has a `help-echo` property, then when you move the mouse onto the text in the overlay, Emacs displays a help string in the echo area, or in the tooltip window. For details see [Text help-echo], page 739.

field
: Consecutive characters with the same `field` property constitute a *field*. Some motion functions including `forward-word` and `beginning-of-line` stop moving at a field boundary. See Section 31.19.9 [Fields], page 748.

modification-hooks
: This property's value is a list of functions to be called if any character within the overlay is changed or if text is inserted strictly within the overlay.

    The hook functions are called both before and after each change. If the functions save the information they receive, and compare notes between calls, they can determine exactly what change has been made in the buffer text.

    When called before a change, each function receives four arguments: the overlay, `nil`, and the beginning and end of the text range to be modified.

    When called after a change, each function receives five arguments: the overlay, `t`, the beginning and end of the text range just modified, and the length of the pre-change text replaced by that range. (For an insertion, the pre-change length is zero; for a deletion, that length is the number of characters deleted, and the post-change beginning and end are equal.)

    If these functions modify the buffer, they should bind `inhibit-modification-hooks` to `t` around doing so, to avoid confusing the internal mechanism that calls these hooks.

    Text properties also support the `modification-hooks` property, but the details are somewhat different (see Section 31.19.4 [Special Properties], page 738).

insert-in-front-hooks
: This property's value is a list of functions to be called before and after inserting text right at the beginning of the overlay. The calling conventions are the same as for the `modification-hooks` functions.

insert-behind-hooks
: This property's value is a list of functions to be called before and after inserting text right at the end of the overlay. The calling conventions are the same as for the `modification-hooks` functions.

`invisible`

> The `invisible` property can make the text in the overlay invisible, which means that it does not appear on the screen. See Section 37.6 [Invisible Text], page 896, for details.

`intangible`

> The `intangible` property on an overlay works just like the `intangible` text property. It is obsolete. See Section 31.19.4 [Special Properties], page 738, for details.

`isearch-open-invisible`

> This property tells incremental search how to make an invisible overlay visible, permanently, if the final match overlaps it. See Section 37.6 [Invisible Text], page 896.

`isearch-open-invisible-temporary`

> This property tells incremental search how to make an invisible overlay visible, temporarily, during the search. See Section 37.6 [Invisible Text], page 896.

`before-string`

> This property's value is a string to add to the display at the beginning of the overlay. The string does not appear in the buffer in any sense—only on the screen.

`after-string`

> This property's value is a string to add to the display at the end of the overlay. The string does not appear in the buffer in any sense—only on the screen.

`line-prefix`

> This property specifies a display spec to prepend to each non-continuation line at display-time. See Section 37.3 [Truncation], page 887.

`wrap-prefix`

> This property specifies a display spec to prepend to each continuation line at display-time. See Section 37.3 [Truncation], page 887.

`evaporate`

> If this property is non-`nil`, the overlay is deleted automatically if it becomes empty (i.e., if its length becomes zero). If you give an empty overlay (see Section 37.9.1 [Managing Overlays], page 904) a non-`nil` `evaporate` property, that deletes it immediately. Note that, unless an overlay has this property, it will not be deleted when the text between its starting and ending positions is deleted from the buffer.

`keymap`

> If this property is non-`nil`, it specifies a keymap for a portion of the text. This keymap is used when the character after point is within the overlay, and takes precedence over most other keymaps. See Section 21.7 [Active Keymaps], page 398.

`local-map`

> The `local-map` property is similar to `keymap` but replaces the buffer's local map rather than augmenting existing keymaps. This also means it has lower precedence than minor mode keymaps.

The `keymap` and `local-map` properties do not affect a string displayed by the `before-string`, `after-string`, or `display` properties. This is only relevant for mouse clicks and other mouse events that fall on the string, since point is never on the string. To bind special mouse events for the string, assign it a `keymap` or `local-map` text property. See Section 31.19.4 [Special Properties], page 738.

37.9.3 Searching for Overlays

overlays-at *pos* **&optional** *sorted*   [Function]

This function returns a list of all the overlays that cover the character at position *pos* in the current buffer. If *sorted* is non-`nil`, the list is in decreasing order of priority, otherwise it is in no particular order. An overlay contains position *pos* if it begins at or before *pos*, and ends after *pos*.

To illustrate usage, here is a Lisp function that returns a list of the overlays that specify property *prop* for the character at point:

```
(defun find-overlays-specifying (prop)
  (let ((overlays (overlays-at (point)))
        found)
    (while overlays
      (let ((overlay (car overlays)))
        (if (overlay-get overlay prop)
            (setq found (cons overlay found))))
      (setq overlays (cdr overlays)))
    found))
```

overlays-in *beg end*   [Function]

This function returns a list of the overlays that overlap the region *beg* through *end*. An overlay overlaps with a region if it contains one or more characters in the region; empty overlays (see Section 37.9.1 [Managing Overlays], page 904) overlap if they are at *beg*, strictly between *beg* and *end*, or at *end* when *end* denotes the position at the end of the buffer.

next-overlay-change *pos*   [Function]

This function returns the buffer position of the next beginning or end of an overlay, after *pos*. If there is none, it returns (`point-max`).

previous-overlay-change *pos*   [Function]

This function returns the buffer position of the previous beginning or end of an overlay, before *pos*. If there is none, it returns (`point-min`).

As an example, here's a simplified (and inefficient) version of the primitive function `next-single-char-property-change` (see Section 31.19.3 [Property Search], page 736). It searches forward from position *pos* for the next position where the value of a given property `prop`, as obtained from either overlays or text properties, changes.

```
(defun next-single-char-property-change (position prop)
  (save-excursion
    (goto-char position)
    (let ((propval (get-char-property (point) prop)))
      (while (and (not (eobp))
                  (eq (get-char-property (point) prop) propval))
        (goto-char (min (next-overlay-change (point))
                        (next-single-property-change (point) prop)))))
    (point)))
```

37.10 Size of Displayed Text

Since not all characters have the same width, these functions let you check the width of a character. See Section 31.17.1 [Primitive Indent], page 726, and Section 29.2.5 [Screen Lines], page 678, for related functions.

char-width *char*   [Function]
> This function returns the width in columns of the character *char*, if it were displayed in the current buffer (i.e., taking into account the buffer's display table, if any; see Section 37.22.2 [Display Tables], page 974). The width of a tab character is usually `tab-width` (see Section 37.22.1 [Usual Display], page 973).

string-width *string*   [Function]
> This function returns the width in columns of the string *string*, if it were displayed in the current buffer and the selected window.

truncate-string-to-width *string width* **&optional** *start-column*   [Function]
> *padding ellipsis*
>
> This function returns the part of *string* that fits within *width* columns, as a new string.
>
> If *string* does not reach *width*, then the result ends where *string* ends. If one multi-column character in *string* extends across the column *width*, that character is not included in the result. Thus, the result can fall short of *width* but cannot go beyond it.
>
> The optional argument *start-column* specifies the starting column. If this is non-`nil`, then the first *start-column* columns of the string are omitted from the value. If one multi-column character in *string* extends across the column *start-column*, that character is not included.
>
> The optional argument *padding*, if non-`nil`, is a padding character added at the beginning and end of the result string, to extend it to exactly *width* columns. The padding character is used at the end of the result if it falls short of *width*. It is also used at the beginning of the result if one multi-column character in *string* extends across the column *start-column*.
>
> If *ellipsis* is non-`nil`, it should be a string which will replace the end of *string* (including any padding) if it extends beyond *width*, unless the display width of *string* is equal to or less than the display width of *ellipsis*. If *ellipsis* is non-`nil` and not a string, it stands for the value of the variable `truncate-string-ellipsis`.
>
> ```
> (truncate-string-to-width "\tab\t" 12 4)
>      ⇒ "ab"
> (truncate-string-to-width "\tab\t" 12 4 ?\s)
>      ⇒ "    ab  "
> ```

The following function returns the size in pixels of text as if it were displayed in a given window. This function is used by `fit-window-to-buffer` and `fit-frame-to-buffer` (see Section 27.4 [Resizing Windows], page 576) to make a window exactly as large as the text it contains.

window-text-pixel-size &optional *window from to x-limit y-limit*   [Function]
   mode-and-header-line
>   This function returns the size of the text of *window*'s buffer in pixels. *window* must
>   be a live window and defaults to the selected one. The return value is a cons of the
>   maximum pixel-width of any text line and the maximum pixel-height of all text lines.
>
>   The optional argument *from*, if non-**nil**, specifies the first text position to consider
>   and defaults to the minimum accessible position of the buffer. If *from* is **t**, it uses the
>   minimum accessible position that is not a newline character. The optional argument
>   *to*, if non-**nil**, specifies the last text position to consider and defaults to the maximum
>   accessible position of the buffer. If *to* is **t**, it uses the maximum accessible position
>   that is not a newline character.
>
>   The optional argument *x-limit*, if non-**nil**, specifies the maximum pixel-width that
>   can be returned. *x-limit* **nil** or omitted, means to use the pixel-width of *window*'s
>   body (see Section 27.3 [Window Sizes], page 572); this is useful when the caller does
>   not intend to change the width of *window*. Otherwise, the caller should specify here
>   the maximum width *window*'s body may assume. Text whose x-coordinate is beyond
>   *x-limit* is ignored. Since calculating the width of long lines can take some time, it's
>   always a good idea to make this argument as small as needed; in particular, if the
>   buffer might contain long lines that will be truncated anyway.
>
>   The optional argument *y-limit*, if non-**nil**, specifies the maximum pixel-height that
>   can be returned. Text lines whose y-coordinate is beyond *y-limit* are ignored. Since
>   calculating the pixel-height of a large buffer can take some time, it makes sense to
>   specify this argument; in particular, if the caller does not know the size of the buffer.
>
>   The optional argument *mode-and-header-line* **nil** or omitted means to not include
>   the height of the mode- or header-line of *window* in the return value. If it is either the
>   symbol **mode-line** or **header-line**, include only the height of that line, if present, in
>   the return value. If it is **t**, include the height of both, if present, in the return value.

line-pixel-height   [Function]
>   This function returns the height in pixels of the line at point in the selected win-
>   dow. The value includes the line spacing of the line (see Section 37.11 [Line Height],
>   page 913).

37.11 Line Height

The total height of each display line consists of the height of the contents of the line, plus
optional additional vertical line spacing above or below the display line.

   The height of the line contents is the maximum height of any character or image on that
display line, including the final newline if there is one. (A display line that is continued
doesn't include a final newline.) That is the default line height, if you do nothing to specify
a greater height. (In the most common case, this equals the height of the corresponding
frame's default font, see Section 28.3.2 [Frame Font], page 639.)

   There are several ways to explicitly specify a larger line height, either by specifying an
absolute height for the display line, or by specifying vertical space. However, no matter
what you specify, the actual line height can never be less than the default.

A newline can have a `line-height` text or overlay property that controls the total height of the display line ending in that newline.

If the property value is `t`, the newline character has no effect on the displayed height of the line—the visible contents alone determine the height. The `line-spacing` property, described below, is also ignored in this case. This is useful for tiling small images (or image slices) without adding blank areas between the images.

If the property value is a list of the form (*height total*), that adds extra space *below* the display line. First Emacs uses *height* as a height spec to control extra space *above* the line; then it adds enough space *below* the line to bring the total line height up to *total*. In this case, any value of `line-spacing` property for the newline is ignored.

Any other kind of property value is a height spec, which translates into a number—the specified line height. There are several ways to write a height spec; here's how each of them translates into a number:

integer   If the height spec is a positive integer, the height value is that integer.

float   If the height spec is a float, *float*, the numeric height value is *float* times the frame's default line height.

(*face . ratio*)
            If the height spec is a cons of the format shown, the numeric height is *ratio* times the height of face *face*. *ratio* can be any type of number, or `nil` which means a ratio of 1. If *face* is `t`, it refers to the current face.

(*nil . ratio*)
            If the height spec is a cons of the format shown, the numeric height is *ratio* times the height of the contents of the line.

Thus, any valid height spec determines the height in pixels, one way or another. If the line contents' height is less than that, Emacs adds extra vertical space above the line to achieve the specified total height.

If you don't specify the `line-height` property, the line's height consists of the contents' height plus the line spacing. There are several ways to specify the line spacing for different parts of Emacs text.

On graphical terminals, you can specify the line spacing for all lines in a frame, using the `line-spacing` frame parameter (see Section 28.4.3.4 [Layout Parameters], page 648). However, if the default value of `line-spacing` is non-`nil`, it overrides the frame's `line-spacing` parameter. An integer specifies the number of pixels put below lines. A floating-point number specifies the spacing relative to the frame's default line height.

You can specify the line spacing for all lines in a buffer via the buffer-local `line-spacing` variable. An integer specifies the number of pixels put below lines. A floating-point number specifies the spacing relative to the default frame line height. This overrides line spacings specified for the frame.

Finally, a newline can have a `line-spacing` text or overlay property that can enlarge the default frame line spacing and the buffer local `line-spacing` variable: if its value is larger than the buffer or frame defaults, that larger value is used instead, for the display line ending in that newline.

One way or another, these mechanisms specify a Lisp value for the spacing of each line. The value is a height spec, and it translates into a Lisp value as described above. However, in this case the numeric height value specifies the line spacing, rather than the line height.

On text terminals, the line spacing cannot be altered.

37.12 Faces

A *face* is a collection of graphical attributes for displaying text: font, foreground color, background color, optional underlining, etc. Faces control how Emacs displays text in buffers, as well as other parts of the frame such as the mode line.

One way to represent a face is as a property list of attributes, like (:foreground "red" :weight bold). Such a list is called an *anonymous face*. For example, you can assign an anonymous face as the value of the `face` text property, and Emacs will display the underlying text with the specified attributes. See Section 31.19.4 [Special Properties], page 738.

More commonly, a face is referred to via a *face name*: a Lisp symbol associated with a set of face attributes[1]. Named faces are defined using the `defface` macro (see Section 37.12.2 [Defining Faces], page 918). Emacs comes with several standard named faces (see Section 37.12.8 [Basic Faces], page 927).

Many parts of Emacs required named faces, and do not accept anonymous faces. These include the functions documented in Section 37.12.3 [Attribute Functions], page 921, and the variable `font-lock-keywords` (see Section 22.6.2 [Search-based Fontification], page 464). Unless otherwise stated, we will use the term *face* to refer only to named faces.

`facep` *object*   [Function]
    This function returns a non-`nil` value if *object* is a named face: a Lisp symbol or string which serves as a face name. Otherwise, it returns `nil`.

37.12.1 Face Attributes

Face attributes determine the visual appearance of a face. The following table lists all the face attributes, their possible values, and their effects.

Apart from the values given below, each face attribute can have the value `unspecified`. This special value means that the face doesn't specify that attribute directly. An `unspecified` attribute tells Emacs to refer instead to a parent face (see the description `:inherit` attribute below); or, failing that, to an underlying face (see Section 37.12.4 [Displaying Faces], page 924). The `default` face must specify all attributes.

Some of these attributes are meaningful only on certain kinds of displays. If your display cannot handle a certain attribute, the attribute is ignored.

`:family`   Font family or fontset (a string). See Section "Fonts" in *The GNU Emacs Manual*, for more information about font families. The function `font-family-list` (see below) returns a list of available family names. See Section 37.12.11 [Fontsets], page 930, for information about fontsets.

`:foundry` The name of the *font foundry* for the font family specified by the `:family` attribute (a string). See Section "Fonts" in *The GNU Emacs Manual*.

---

[1] For backward compatibility, you can also use a string to specify a face name; that is equivalent to a Lisp symbol with the same name.

:width   Relative character width. This should be one of the symbols `ultra-condensed`, `extra-condensed`, `condensed`, `semi-condensed`, `normal`, `semi-expanded`, `expanded`, `extra-expanded`, or `ultra-expanded`.

:height   The height of the font. In the simplest case, this is an integer in units of 1/10 point.

The value can also be floating point or a function, which specifies the height relative to an *underlying face* (see Section 37.12.4 [Displaying Faces], page 924). A floating-point value specifies the amount by which to scale the height of the underlying face. A function value is called with one argument, the height of the underlying face, and returns the height of the new face. If the function is passed an integer argument, it must return an integer.

The height of the default face must be specified using an integer; floating point and function values are not allowed.

:weight   Font weight—one of the symbols (from densest to faintest) `ultra-bold`, `extra-bold`, `bold`, `semi-bold`, `normal`, `semi-light`, `light`, `extra-light`, or `ultra-light`. On text terminals which support variable-brightness text, any weight greater than normal is displayed as extra bright, and any weight less than normal is displayed as half-bright.

:slant   Font slant—one of the symbols `italic`, `oblique`, `normal`, `reverse-italic`, or `reverse-oblique`. On text terminals that support variable-brightness text, slanted text is displayed as half-bright.

:foreground
            Foreground color, a string. The value can be a system-defined color name, or a hexadecimal color specification. See Section 28.21 [Color Names], page 666. On black-and-white displays, certain shades of gray are implemented by stipple patterns.

:distant-foreground
            Alternative foreground color, a string. This is like `:foreground` but the color is only used as a foreground when the background color is near to the foreground that would have been used. This is useful for example when marking text (i.e., the region face). If the text has a foreground that is visible with the region face, that foreground is used. If the foreground is near the region face background, `:distant-foreground` is used instead so the text is readable.

:background
            Background color, a string. The value can be a system-defined color name, or a hexadecimal color specification. See Section 28.21 [Color Names], page 666.

:underline
            Whether or not characters should be underlined, and in what way. The possible values of the `:underline` attribute are:

            nil   Don't underline.

            t   Underline with the foreground color of the face.

            color   Underline in color *color*, a string specifying a color.

(:color *color* :style *style*)

> *color* is either a string, or the symbol `foreground-color`, meaning the foreground color of the face. Omitting the attribute `:color` means to use the foreground color of the face. *style* should be a symbol `line` or `wave`, meaning to use a straight or wavy line. Omitting the attribute `:style` means to use a straight line.

`:overline`
> Whether or not characters should be overlined, and in what color. If the value is `t`, overlining uses the foreground color of the face. If the value is a string, overlining uses that color. The value `nil` means do not overline.

`:strike-through`
> Whether or not characters should be strike-through, and in what color. The value is used like that of `:overline`.

`:box`
> Whether or not a box should be drawn around characters, its color, the width of the box lines, and 3D appearance. Here are the possible values of the `:box` attribute, and what they mean:

> `nil`   Don't draw a box.

> `t`   Draw a box with lines of width 1, in the foreground color.

> *color*   Draw a box with lines of width 1, in color *color*.

> (:line-width *width* :color *color* :style *style*)

>> This way you can explicitly specify all aspects of the box. The value *width* specifies the width of the lines to draw; it defaults to 1. A negative width *-n* means to draw a line of width *n* that occupies the space of the underlying text, thus avoiding any increase in the character height or width.

>> The value *color* specifies the color to draw with. The default is the foreground color of the face for simple boxes, and the background color of the face for 3D boxes.

>> The value *style* specifies whether to draw a 3D box. If it is `released-button`, the box looks like a 3D button that is not being pressed. If it is `pressed-button`, the box looks like a 3D button that is being pressed. If it is `nil` or omitted, a plain 2D box is used.

`:inverse-video`
> Whether or not characters should be displayed in inverse video. The value should be `t` (yes) or `nil` (no).

`:stipple`   The background stipple, a bitmap.

> The value can be a string; that should be the name of a file containing external-format X bitmap data. The file is found in the directories listed in the variable `x-bitmap-file-path`.

> Alternatively, the value can specify the bitmap directly, with a list of the form (*width height data*). Here, *width* and *height* specify the size in pixels, and

data is a string containing the raw bits of the bitmap, row by row. Each row occupies $(width+7)/8$ consecutive bytes in the string (which should be a unibyte string for best results). This means that each row always occupies at least one whole byte.

If the value is `nil`, that means use no stipple pattern.

Normally you do not need to set the stipple attribute, because it is used automatically to handle certain shades of gray.

`:font`   The font used to display the face. Its value should be a font object. See Section 37.12.12 [Low-Level Font], page 932, for information about font objects, font specs, and font entities.

When specifying this attribute using `set-face-attribute` (see Section 37.12.3 [Attribute Functions], page 921), you may also supply a font spec, a font entity, or a string. Emacs converts such values to an appropriate font object, and stores that font object as the actual attribute value. If you specify a string, the contents of the string should be a font name (see Section "Fonts" in *The GNU Emacs Manual*); if the font name is an XLFD containing wildcards, Emacs chooses the first font matching those wildcards. Specifying this attribute also changes the values of the `:family`, `:foundry`, `:width`, `:height`, `:weight`, and `:slant` attributes.

`:inherit`   The name of a face from which to inherit attributes, or a list of face names. Attributes from inherited faces are merged into the face like an underlying face would be, with higher priority than underlying faces (see Section 37.12.4 [Displaying Faces], page 924). If a list of faces is used, attributes from faces earlier in the list override those from later faces.

`font-family-list` **&optional** *frame*   [Function]
> This function returns a list of available font family names. The optional argument *frame* specifies the frame on which the text is to be displayed; if it is `nil`, the selected frame is used.

`underline-minimum-offset`   [User Option]
> This variable specifies the minimum distance between the baseline and the underline, in pixels, when displaying underlined text.

`x-bitmap-file-path`   [User Option]
> This variable specifies a list of directories for searching for bitmap files, for the `:stipple` attribute.

`bitmap-spec-p` *object*   [Function]
> This returns `t` if *object* is a valid bitmap specification, suitable for use with `:stipple` (see above). It returns `nil` otherwise.

37.12.2 Defining Faces

The usual way to define a face is through the `defface` macro. This macro associates a face name (a symbol) with a default *face spec*. A face spec is a construct which specifies what attributes a face should have on any given terminal; for example, a face spec might specify one foreground color on high-color terminals, and a different foreground color on low-color terminals.

People are sometimes tempted to create a variable whose value is a face name. In the vast majority of cases, this is not necessary; the usual procedure is to define a face with `defface`, and then use its name directly.

`defface` *face spec doc* [*keyword value*]. . .   [Macro]

This macro declares *face* as a named face whose default face spec is given by *spec*. You should not quote the symbol *face*, and it should not end in '`-face`' (that would be redundant). The argument *doc* is a documentation string for the face. The additional *keyword* arguments have the same meanings as in `defgroup` and `defcustom` (see Section 14.1 [Common Keywords], page 225).

If *face* already has a default face spec, this macro does nothing.

The default face spec determines *face*'s appearance when no customizations are in effect (see Chapter 14 [Customization], page 225). If *face* has already been customized (via Custom themes or via customizations read from the init file), its appearance is determined by the custom face spec(s), which override the default face spec *spec*. However, if the customizations are subsequently removed, the appearance of *face* will again be determined by its default face spec.

As an exception, if you evaluate a `defface` form with `C-M-x` in Emacs Lisp mode (`eval-defun`), a special feature of `eval-defun` overrides any custom face specs on the face, causing the face to reflect exactly what the `defface` says.

The *spec* argument is a *face spec*, which states how the face should appear on different kinds of terminals. It should be an alist whose elements each have the form

    `(display . plist)`

display specifies a class of terminals (see below). *plist* is a property list of face attributes and their values, specifying how the face appears on such terminals. For backward compatibility, you can also write an element as `(display plist)`.

The *display* part of an element of *spec* determines which terminals the element matches. If more than one element of *spec* matches a given terminal, the first element that matches is the one used for that terminal. There are three possibilities for *display*:

`default`   This element of *spec* doesn't match any terminal; instead, it specifies defaults that apply to all terminals. This element, if used, must be the first element of *spec*. Each of the following elements can override any or all of these defaults.

`t`   This element of *spec* matches all terminals. Therefore, any subsequent elements of *spec* are never used. Normally `t` is used in the last (or only) element of *spec*.

a list   If *display* is a list, each element should have the form (`characteristic value...`). Here *characteristic* specifies a way of classifying terminals, and the *values* are possible classifications which *display* should apply to. Here are the possible values of *characteristic*:

    `type`   The kind of window system the terminal uses—either `graphic` (any graphics-capable display), `x`, `pc` (for the

MS-DOS console), `w32` (for MS Windows 9X/NT/2K/XP), or `tty` (a non-graphics-capable display). See Section 37.24 [Window Systems], page 979.

class
: What kinds of colors the terminal supports—either `color`, `grayscale`, or `mono`.

background
: The kind of background—either `light` or `dark`.

min-colors
: An integer that represents the minimum number of colors the terminal should support. This matches a terminal if its `display-color-cells` value is at least the specified integer.

supports
: Whether or not the terminal can display the face attributes given in *value...* (see Section 37.12.1 [Face Attributes], page 915). See [Display Face Attribute Testing], page 670, for more information on exactly how this testing is done.

If an element of *display* specifies more than one *value* for a given *characteristic*, any of those values is acceptable. If *display* has more than one element, each element should specify a different *characteristic*; then *each* characteristic of the terminal must match one of the *values* specified for it in *display*.

For example, here's the definition of the standard face `highlight`:

```
(defface highlight
  '((((class color) (min-colors 88) (background light))
     :background "darkseagreen2")
    (((class color) (min-colors 88) (background dark))
     :background "darkolivegreen")
    (((class color) (min-colors 16) (background light))
     :background "darkseagreen2")
    (((class color) (min-colors 16) (background dark))
     :background "darkolivegreen")
    (((class color) (min-colors 8))
     :background "green" :foreground "black")
    (t :inverse-video t))
  "Basic face for highlighting."
  :group 'basic-faces)
```

Internally, Emacs stores each face's default spec in its `face-defface-spec` symbol property (see Section 8.4 [Symbol Properties], page 119). The `saved-face` property stores any face spec saved by the user using the customization buffer; the `customized-face` property stores the face spec customized for the current session, but not saved; and the `theme-face` property stores an alist associating the active customization settings and Custom themes with the face specs for that face. The face's documentation string is stored in the `face-documentation` property.

Normally, a face is declared just once, using `defface`, and any further changes to its appearance are applied using the Customize framework (e.g., via the Customize user interface or via the `custom-set-faces` function; see Section 14.5 [Applying Customizations], page 241), or by face remapping (see Section 37.12.5 [Face Remapping], page 924). In the rare event that you need to change a face spec directly from Lisp, you can use the `face-spec-set` function.

`face-spec-set` *face spec* **&optional** *spec-type*   [Function]

> This function applies *spec* as a face spec for `face`. *spec* should be a face spec, as described in the above documentation for `defface`.
>
> This function also defines *face* as a valid face name if it is not already one, and (re)calculates its attributes on existing frames.
>
> The argument *spec-type* determines which spec to set. If it is `nil` or `face-override-spec`, this function sets the *override spec*, which overrides over all other face specs on *face*. If it is `customized-face` or `saved-face`, this function sets the customized spec or the saved custom spec. If it is `face-defface-spec`, this function sets the default face spec (the same one set by `defface`). If it is `reset`, this function clears out all customization specs and override specs from *face* (in this case, the value of *spec* is ignored). Any other value of *spec-type* is reserved for internal use.

37.12.3 Face Attribute Functions

This section describes functions for directly accessing and modifying the attributes of a named face.

`face-attribute` *face attribute* **&optional** *frame inherit*   [Function]

> This function returns the value of the *attribute* attribute for *face* on *frame*.
>
> If *frame* is omitted or `nil`, that means the selected frame (see Section 28.10 [Input Focus], page 656). If *frame* is `t`, this function returns the value of the specified attribute for newly-created frames (this is normally `unspecified`, unless you have specified some value using `set-face-attribute`; see below).
>
> If *inherit* is `nil`, only attributes directly defined by *face* are considered, so the return value may be `unspecified`, or a relative value. If *inherit* is non-`nil`, *face*'s definition of *attribute* is merged with the faces specified by its `:inherit` attribute; however the return value may still be `unspecified` or relative. If *inherit* is a face or a list of faces, then the result is further merged with that face (or faces), until it becomes specified and absolute.
>
> To ensure that the return value is always specified and absolute, use a value of `default` for *inherit*; this will resolve any unspecified or relative values by merging with the `default` face (which is always completely specified).
>
> For example,
>
> ```
> (face-attribute 'bold :weight)
>      ⇒ bold
> ```

`face-attribute-relative-p` *attribute value*   [Function]

> This function returns non-`nil` if *value*, when used as the value of the face attribute *attribute*, is relative. This means it would modify, rather than completely override, any value that comes from a subsequent face in the face list or that is inherited from another face.

> unspecified is a relative value for all attributes. For :height, floating point and
> function values are also relative.
>
> For example:
>
>   (face-attribute-relative-p :height 2.0)
>   ⇒ t

face-all-attributes *face* &**optional** *frame*   [Function]

> This function returns an alist of attributes of *face*. The elements of the result are
> name-value pairs of the form (attr-name . attr-value). Optional argument *frame*
> specifies the frame whose definition of *face* to return; if omitted or nil, the returned
> value describes the default attributes of *face* for newly created frames.

merge-face-attribute *attribute value1 value2*   [Function]

> If *value1* is a relative value for the face attribute *attribute*, returns it merged with
> the underlying value *value2*; otherwise, if *value1* is an absolute value for the face
> attribute *attribute*, returns *value1* unchanged.

Normally, Emacs uses the face specs of each face to automatically calculate its attributes
on each frame (see Section 37.12.2 [Defining Faces], page 918). The function set-face-
attribute can override this calculation by directly assigning attributes to a face, either on
a specific frame or for all frames. This function is mostly intended for internal usage.

set-face-attribute *face frame* &**rest** *arguments*   [Function]

> This function sets one or more attributes of *face* for *frame*. The attributes specifies
> in this way override the face spec(s) belonging to *face*.
>
> The extra arguments *arguments* specify the attributes to set, and the values for them.
> They should consist of alternating attribute names (such as :family or :underline)
> and values. Thus,
>
>   (set-face-attribute 'foo nil :weight 'bold :slant 'italic)
>
> sets the attribute :weight to bold and the attribute :slant to italic.
>
> If *frame* is t, this function sets the default attributes for newly created frames. If
> *frame* is nil, this function sets the attributes for all existing frames, as well as for
> newly created frames.

The following commands and functions mostly provide compatibility with old versions
of Emacs. They work by calling set-face-attribute. Values of t and nil (or omitted)
for their *frame* argument are handled just like set-face-attribute and face-attribute.
The commands read their arguments using the minibuffer, if called interactively.

set-face-foreground *face color* &**optional** *frame*   [Command]
set-face-background *face color* &**optional** *frame*   [Command]

> These set the :foreground attribute (or :background attribute, respectively) of *face*
> to *color*.

set-face-stipple *face pattern* &**optional** *frame*   [Command]

> This sets the :stipple attribute of *face* to *pattern*.

set-face-font *face font* &**optional** *frame*   [Command]

> This sets the :font attribute of *face* to *font*.

set-face-bold *face bold-p* **&optional** *frame*   [Function]
> This sets the `:weight` attribute of *face* to *normal* if *bold-p* is `nil`, and to *bold* otherwise.

set-face-italic *face italic-p* **&optional** *frame*   [Function]
> This sets the `:slant` attribute of *face* to *normal* if *italic-p* is `nil`, and to *italic* otherwise.

set-face-underline *face underline* **&optional** *frame*   [Function]
> This sets the `:underline` attribute of *face* to *underline*.

set-face-inverse-video *face inverse-video-p* **&optional** *frame*   [Function]
> This sets the `:inverse-video` attribute of *face* to *inverse-video-p*.

invert-face *face* **&optional** *frame*   [Command]
> This swaps the foreground and background colors of face *face*.

The following functions examine the attributes of a face. They mostly provide compatibility with old versions of Emacs. If you don't specify *frame*, they refer to the selected frame; `t` refers to the default data for new frames. They return `unspecified` if the face doesn't define any value for that attribute. If *inherit* is `nil`, only an attribute directly defined by the face is returned. If *inherit* is non-`nil`, any faces specified by its `:inherit` attribute are considered as well, and if *inherit* is a face or a list of faces, then they are also considered, until a specified attribute is found. To ensure that the return value is always specified, use a value of `default` for *inherit*.

face-font *face* **&optional** *frame character*   [Function]
> This function returns the name of the font of face *face*.
>
> If the optional argument *frame* is specified, it returns the name of the font of *face* for that frame. If *frame* is omitted or `nil`, the selected frame is used. And, in this case, if the optional third argument *character* is supplied, it returns the font name used for *character*.

face-foreground *face* **&optional** *frame inherit*   [Function]
face-background *face* **&optional** *frame inherit*   [Function]
> These functions return the foreground color (or background color, respectively) of face *face*, as a string. If the color is unspecified, they return `nil`.

face-stipple *face* **&optional** *frame inherit*   [Function]
> This function returns the name of the background stipple pattern of face *face*, or `nil` if it doesn't have one.

face-bold-p *face* **&optional** *frame inherit*   [Function]
> This function returns a non-`nil` value if the `:weight` attribute of *face* is bolder than normal (i.e., one of `semi-bold`, `bold`, `extra-bold`, or `ultra-bold`). Otherwise, it returns `nil`.

face-italic-p *face* **&optional** *frame inherit*   [Function]
> This function returns a non-`nil` value if the `:slant` attribute of *face* is `italic` or `oblique`, and `nil` otherwise.

`face-underline-p` *face* **&optional** *frame inherit* [Function]
> This function returns non-`nil` if face *face* specifies a non-`nil` `:underline` attribute.

`face-inverse-video-p` *face* **&optional** *frame inherit* [Function]
> This function returns non-`nil` if face *face* specifies a non-`nil` `:inverse-video` attribute.

37.12.4 Displaying Faces

When Emacs displays a given piece of text, the visual appearance of the text may be determined by faces drawn from different sources. If these various sources together specify more than one face for a particular character, Emacs merges the attributes of the various faces. Here is the order in which Emacs merges the faces, from highest to lowest priority:

- If the text consists of a special glyph, the glyph can specify a particular face. See Section 37.22.4 [Glyphs], page 976.

- If the text lies within an active region, Emacs highlights it using the `region` face. See Section "Standard Faces" in *The GNU Emacs Manual.*

- If the text lies within an overlay with a non-`nil` `face` property, Emacs applies the face(s) specified by that property. If the overlay has a `mouse-face` property and the mouse is near enough to the overlay, Emacs applies the face or face attributes specified by the `mouse-face` property instead. See Section 37.9.2 [Overlay Properties], page 907.

  When multiple overlays cover one character, an overlay with higher priority overrides those with lower priority. See Section 37.9 [Overlays], page 904.

- If the text contains a `face` or `mouse-face` property, Emacs applies the specified faces and face attributes. See Section 31.19.4 [Special Properties], page 738. (This is how Font Lock mode faces are applied. See Section 22.6 [Font Lock Mode], page 462.)

- If the text lies within the mode line of the selected window, Emacs applies the `mode-line` face. For the mode line of a non-selected window, Emacs applies the `mode-line-inactive` face. For a header line, Emacs applies the `header-line` face.

- If any given attribute has not been specified during the preceding steps, Emacs applies the attribute of the `default` face.

At each stage, if a face has a valid `:inherit` attribute, Emacs treats any attribute with an `unspecified` value as having the corresponding value drawn from the parent face(s). see Section 37.12.1 [Face Attributes], page 915. Note that the parent face(s) may also leave the attribute unspecified; in that case, the attribute remains unspecified at the next level of face merging.

37.12.5 Face Remapping

The variable `face-remapping-alist` is used for buffer-local or global changes in the appearance of a face. For instance, it is used to implement the `text-scale-adjust` command (see Section "Text Scale" in *The GNU Emacs Manual*).

`face-remapping-alist` [Variable]
> The value of this variable is an alist whose elements have the form (*face* . *remapping*). This causes Emacs to display any text having the face *face* with *remapping*, rather than the ordinary definition of *face*.

remapping may be any face spec suitable for a `face` text property: either a face (i.e., a face name or a property list of attribute/value pairs), or a list of faces. For details, see the description of the `face` text property in Section 31.19.4 [Special Properties], page 738. *remapping* serves as the complete specification for the remapped face—it replaces the normal definition of *face*, instead of modifying it.

If `face-remapping-alist` is buffer-local, its local value takes effect only within that buffer.

Note: face remapping is non-recursive. If *remapping* references the same face name *face*, either directly or via the `:inherit` attribute of some other face in *remapping*, that reference uses the normal definition of *face*. For instance, if the `mode-line` face is remapped using this entry in `face-remapping-alist`:

        (mode-line italic mode-line)

then the new definition of the `mode-line` face inherits from the `italic` face, and the *normal* (non-remapped) definition of `mode-line` face.

The following functions implement a higher-level interface to `face-remapping-alist`. Most Lisp code should use these functions instead of setting `face-remapping-alist` directly, to avoid trampling on remappings applied elsewhere. These functions are intended for buffer-local remappings, so they all make `face-remapping-alist` buffer-local as a side-effect. They manage `face-remapping-alist` entries of the form

        (*face relative-spec-1 relative-spec-2 ... base-spec*)

where, as explained above, each of the *relative-spec-N* and *base-spec* is either a face name, or a property list of attribute/value pairs. Each of the *relative remapping* entries, *relative-spec-N*, is managed by the `face-remap-add-relative` and `face-remap-remove-relative` functions; these are intended for simple modifications like changing the text size. The *base remapping* entry, *base-spec*, has the lowest priority and is managed by the `face-remap-set-base` and `face-remap-reset-base` functions; it is intended for major modes to remap faces in the buffers they control.

`face-remap-add-relative` *face* **&rest** *specs*   [Function]
> This function adds the face spec in *specs* as relative remappings for face *face* in the current buffer. The remaining arguments, *specs*, should form either a list of face names, or a property list of attribute/value pairs.
>
> The return value is a Lisp object that serves as a cookie; you can pass this object as an argument to `face-remap-remove-relative` if you need to remove the remapping later.
>
> ```
>        ;; Remap the 'escape-glyph' face into a combination
>        ;; of the 'highlight' and 'italic' faces:
>        (face-remap-add-relative 'escape-glyph 'highlight 'italic)
>
>        ;; Increase the size of the 'default' face by 50%:
>        (face-remap-add-relative 'default :height 1.5)
> ```

`face-remap-remove-relative` *cookie*   [Function]
> This function removes a relative remapping previously added by `face-remap-add-relative`. *cookie* should be the Lisp object returned by `face-remap-add-relative` when the remapping was added.

face-remap-set-base *face* **&rest** *specs* [Function]

> This function sets the base remapping of *face* in the current buffer to *specs*. If *specs* is empty, the default base remapping is restored, similar to calling `face-remap-reset-base` (see below); note that this is different from *specs* containing a single value `nil`, which has the opposite result (the global definition of *face* is ignored).

> This overwrites the default *base-spec*, which inherits the global face definition, so it is up to the caller to add such inheritance if so desired.

face-remap-reset-base *face* [Function]

> This function sets the base remapping of *face* to its default value, which inherits from *face*'s global definition.

37.12.6 Functions for Working with Faces

Here are additional functions for creating and working with faces.

face-list [Function]

> This function returns a list of all defined face names.

face-id *face* [Function]

> This function returns the *face number* of face *face*. This is a number that uniquely identifies a face at low levels within Emacs. It is seldom necessary to refer to a face by its face number.

face-documentation *face* [Function]

> This function returns the documentation string of face *face*, or `nil` if none was specified for it.

face-equal *face1* *face2* **&optional** *frame* [Function]

> This returns `t` if the faces *face1* and *face2* have the same attributes for display.

face-differs-from-default-p *face* **&optional** *frame* [Function]

> This returns non-`nil` if the face *face* displays differently from the default face.

A *face alias* provides an equivalent name for a face. You can define a face alias by giving the alias symbol the `face-alias` property, with a value of the target face name. The following example makes `modeline` an alias for the `mode-line` face.

```
(put 'modeline 'face-alias 'mode-line)
```

define-obsolete-face-alias *obsolete-face current-face when* [Macro]

> This macro defines `obsolete-face` as an alias for *current-face*, and also marks it as obsolete, indicating that it may be removed in future. *when* should be a string indicating when `obsolete-face` was made obsolete (usually a version number string).

37.12.7 Automatic Face Assignment

This hook is used for automatically assigning faces to text in the buffer. It is part of the implementation of Jit-Lock mode, used by Font-Lock.

`fontification-functions`   *[Variable]*

> This variable holds a list of functions that are called by Emacs redisplay as needed, just before doing redisplay. They are called even when Font Lock Mode isn't enabled. When Font Lock Mode is enabled, this variable usually holds just one function, `jit-lock-function`.
>
> The functions are called in the order listed, with one argument, a buffer position *pos*. Collectively they should attempt to assign faces to the text in the current buffer starting at *pos*.
>
> The functions should record the faces they assign by setting the `face` property. They should also add a non-`nil` `fontified` property to all the text they have assigned faces to. That property tells redisplay that faces have been assigned to that text already.
>
> It is probably a good idea for the functions to do nothing if the character after *pos* already has a non-`nil` `fontified` property, but this is not required. If one function overrides the assignments made by a previous one, the properties after the last function finishes are the ones that really matter.
>
> For efficiency, we recommend writing these functions so that they usually assign faces to around 400 to 600 characters at each call.

37.12.8 Basic Faces

If your Emacs Lisp program needs to assign some faces to text, it is often a good idea to use certain existing faces or inherit from them, rather than defining entirely new faces. This way, if other users have customized the basic faces to give Emacs a certain look, your program will fit in without additional customization.

Some of the basic faces defined in Emacs are listed below. In addition to these, you might want to make use of the Font Lock faces for syntactic highlighting, if highlighting is not already handled by Font Lock mode, or if some Font Lock faces are not in use. See Section 22.6.7 [Faces for Font Lock], page 470.

`default`   The default face, whose attributes are all specified. All other faces implicitly inherit from it: any unspecified attribute defaults to the attribute on this face (see Section 37.12.1 [Face Attributes], page 915).

`bold`
`italic`
`bold-italic`
`underline`
`fixed-pitch`
`fixed-pitch-serif`
`variable-pitch`
            These have the attributes indicated by their names (e.g., `bold` has a bold `:weight` attribute), with all other attributes unspecified (and so given by `default`).

`shadow`   For dimmed-out text. For example, it is used for the ignored part of a filename in the minibuffer (see Section "Minibuffers for File Names" in *The GNU Emacs Manual*).

link
link-visited
> For clickable text buttons that send the user to a different buffer or location.

highlight
> For stretches of text that should temporarily stand out. For example, it is commonly assigned to the `mouse-face` property for cursor highlighting (see Section 31.19.4 [Special Properties], page 738).

match
isearch
lazy-highlight
> For text matching (respectively) permanent search matches, interactive search matches, and lazy highlighting other matches than the current interactive one.

error
warning
success
> For text concerning errors, warnings, or successes. For example, these are used for messages in `*Compilation*` buffers.

37.12.9 Font Selection

Before Emacs can draw a character on a graphical display, it must select a *font* for that character[2]. See Section "Fonts" in *The GNU Emacs Manual*. Normally, Emacs automatically chooses a font based on the faces assigned to that character—specifically, the face attributes `:family`, `:weight`, `:slant`, and `:width` (see Section 37.12.1 [Face Attributes], page 915). The choice of font also depends on the character to be displayed; some fonts can only display a limited set of characters. If no available font exactly fits the requirements, Emacs looks for the *closest matching font*. The variables in this section control how Emacs makes this selection.

`face-font-family-alternatives`   [User Option]
> If a given family is specified but does not exist, this variable specifies alternative font families to try. Each element should have this form:
>
>   (family alternate-families...)
>
> If *family* is specified but not available, Emacs will try the other families given in *alternate-families*, one by one, until it finds a family that does exist.

`face-font-selection-order`   [User Option]
> If there is no font that exactly matches all desired face attributes (`:width`, `:height`, `:weight`, and `:slant`), this variable specifies the order in which these attributes should be considered when selecting the closest matching font. The value should be a list containing those four attribute symbols, in order of decreasing importance. The default is (`:width :height :weight :slant`).
>
> Font selection first finds the best available matches for the first attribute in the list; then, among the fonts which are best in that way, it searches for the best matches in the second attribute, and so on.

---

[2] In this context, the term *font* has nothing to do with Font Lock (see Section 22.6 [Font Lock Mode], page 462).

The attributes `:weight` and `:width` have symbolic values in a range centered around `normal`. Matches that are more extreme (farther from `normal`) are somewhat preferred to matches that are less extreme (closer to `normal`); this is designed to ensure that non-normal faces contrast with normal ones, whenever possible.

One example of a case where this variable makes a difference is when the default font has no italic equivalent. With the default ordering, the `italic` face will use a non-italic font that is similar to the default one. But if you put `:slant` before `:height`, the `italic` face will use an italic font, even if its height is not quite right.

`face-font-registry-alternatives`   [User Option]

> This variable lets you specify alternative font registries to try, if a given registry is specified and doesn't exist. Each element should have this form:
>
> > (*registry* *alternate-registries*...)
>
> If *registry* is specified but not available, Emacs will try the other registries given in *alternate-registries*, one by one, until it finds a registry that does exist.

Emacs can make use of scalable fonts, but by default it does not use them.

`scalable-fonts-allowed`   [User Option]

> This variable controls which scalable fonts to use. A value of `nil`, the default, means do not use scalable fonts. `t` means to use any scalable font that seems appropriate for the text.
>
> Otherwise, the value must be a list of regular expressions. Then a scalable font is enabled for use if its name matches any regular expression in the list. For example,
>
> > `(setq scalable-fonts-allowed '("iso10646-1$"))`
>
> allows the use of scalable fonts with registry `iso10646-1`.

`face-font-rescale-alist`   [Variable]

> This variable specifies scaling for certain faces. Its value should be a list of elements of the form
>
> > (*fontname-regexp* . *scale-factor*)
>
> If *fontname-regexp* matches the font name that is about to be used, this says to choose a larger similar font according to the factor *scale-factor*. You would use this feature to normalize the font size if certain fonts are bigger or smaller than their nominal heights and widths would suggest.

37.12.10 Looking Up Fonts

`x-list-fonts` *name* **&optional** *reference-face frame maximum width*   [Function]

> This function returns a list of available font names that match *name*. *name* should be a string containing a font name in either the Fontconfig, GTK, or XLFD format (see Section "Fonts" in *The GNU Emacs Manual*). Within an XLFD string, wildcard characters may be used: the '`*`' character matches any substring, and the '`?`' character matches any single character. Case is ignored when matching font names.
>
> If the optional arguments *reference-face* and *frame* are specified, the returned list includes only fonts that are the same size as *reference-face* (a face name) currently is on the frame *frame*.

The optional argument *maximum* sets a limit on how many fonts to return. If it is non-`nil`, then the return value is truncated after the first *maximum* matching fonts. Specifying a small value for *maximum* can make this function much faster, in cases where many fonts match the pattern.

The optional argument *width* specifies a desired font width. If it is non-`nil`, the function only returns those fonts whose characters are (on average) *width* times as wide as *reference-face*.

x-family-fonts **&optional** *family frame*   [Function]

This function returns a list describing the available fonts for family *family* on *frame*. If *family* is omitted or `nil`, this list applies to all families, and therefore, it contains all available fonts. Otherwise, *family* must be a string; it may contain the wildcards '?' and '*'.

The list describes the display that *frame* is on; if *frame* is omitted or `nil`, it applies to the selected frame's display (see Section 28.10 [Input Focus], page 656).

Each element in the list is a vector of the following form:

```
[family width point-size weight slant
 fixed-p full registry-and-encoding]
```

The first five elements correspond to face attributes; if you specify these attributes for a face, it will use this font.

The last three elements give additional information about the font. *fixed-p* is non-`nil` if the font is fixed-pitch. *full* is the full name of the font, and *registry-and-encoding* is a string giving the registry and encoding of the font.

37.12.11 Fontsets

A *fontset* is a list of fonts, each assigned to a range of character codes. An individual font cannot display the whole range of characters that Emacs supports, but a fontset can. Fontsets have names, just as fonts do, and you can use a fontset name in place of a font name when you specify the font for a frame or a face. Here is information about defining a fontset under Lisp program control.

create-fontset-from-fontset-spec *fontset-spec* **&optional**   [Function]
        style-variant-p noerror

This function defines a new fontset according to the specification string *fontset-spec*. The string should have this format:

```
fontpattern, [charset:font]...
```

Whitespace characters before and after the commas are ignored.

The first part of the string, *fontpattern*, should have the form of a standard X font name, except that the last two fields should be '`fontset-alias`'.

The new fontset has two names, one long and one short. The long name is *fontpattern* in its entirety. The short name is '`fontset-alias`'. You can refer to the fontset by either name. If a fontset with the same name already exists, an error is signaled, unless *noerror* is non-`nil`, in which case this function does nothing.

If optional argument *style-variant-p* is non-`nil`, that says to create bold, italic and bold-italic variants of the fontset as well. These variant fontsets do not have a short name, only a long one, which is made by altering *fontpattern* to indicate the bold and/or italic status.

The specification string also says which fonts to use in the fontset. See below for the details.

The construct '`charset:font`' specifies which font to use (in this fontset) for one particular character set. Here, *charset* is the name of a character set, and *font* is the font to use for that character set. You can use this construct any number of times in the specification string.

For the remaining character sets, those that you don't specify explicitly, Emacs chooses a font based on *fontpattern*: it replaces '`fontset-alias`' with a value that names one character set. For the ASCII character set, '`fontset-alias`' is replaced with '`ISO8859-1`'.

In addition, when several consecutive fields are wildcards, Emacs collapses them into a single wildcard. This is to prevent use of auto-scaled fonts. Fonts made by scaling larger fonts are not usable for editing, and scaling a smaller font is not useful because it is better to use the smaller font in its own size, which Emacs does.

Thus if *fontpattern* is this,

```
-*-fixed-medium-r-normal-*-24-*-*-*-*-*-fontset-24
```

the font specification for ASCII characters would be this:

```
-*-fixed-medium-r-normal-*-24-*-ISO8859-1
```

and the font specification for Chinese GB2312 characters would be this:

```
-*-fixed-medium-r-normal-*-24-*-gb2312*-*
```

You may not have any Chinese font matching the above font specification. Most X distributions include only Chinese fonts that have '`song ti`' or '`fangsong ti`' in the *family* field. In such a case, '`Fontset-n`' can be specified as below:

```
Emacs.Fontset-0: -*-fixed-medium-r-normal-*-24-*-*-*-*-*-fontset-24,\
        chinese-gb2312:-*-*-medium-r-normal-*-24-*-gb2312*-*
```

Then, the font specifications for all but Chinese GB2312 characters have '`fixed`' in the *family* field, and the font specification for Chinese GB2312 characters has a wild card '`*`' in the *family* field.

`set-fontset-font` *name character font-spec* **&optional** *frame add*   [Function]
    This function modifies the existing fontset *name* to use the font matching with *font-spec* for the specified *character*.

    If *name* is `nil`, this function modifies the fontset of the selected frame or that of *frame* if *frame* is not `nil`.

    If *name* is `t`, this function modifies the default fontset, whose short name is '`fontset-default`'.

    In addition to specifying a single codepoint, *character* may be a cons (`from . to`), where *from* and *to* are character codepoints. In that case, use *font-spec* for all the characters in the range *from* and *to* (inclusive).

    character may be a charset. In that case, use *font-spec* for all character in the charsets.

    character may be a script name. In that case, use *font-spec* for all character in the charsets.

font-spec may be a font-spec object created by the function `font-spec` (see Section 37.12.12 [Low-Level Font], page 932).

font-spec may be a cons; (`family . registry`), where *family* is a family name of a font (possibly including a foundry name at the head), *registry* is a registry name of a font (possibly including an encoding name at the tail).

font-spec may be a font name string.

font-spec may be `nil`, which explicitly specifies that there's no font for the specified *character*. This is useful, for example, to avoid expensive system-wide search for fonts for characters that have no glyphs, like those from the Unicode Private Use Area (PUA).

The optional argument *add*, if non-`nil`, specifies how to add *font-spec* to the font specifications previously set. If it is `prepend`, *font-spec* is prepended. If it is `append`, *font-spec* is appended. By default, *font-spec* overrides the previous settings.

For instance, this changes the default fontset to use a font of which family name is 'Kochi Gothic' for all characters belonging to the charset `japanese-jisx0208`.

```
(set-fontset-font t 'japanese-jisx0208
                  (font-spec :family "Kochi Gothic"))
```

`char-displayable-p` *char*   [Function]
> This function returns `t` if Emacs ought to be able to display *char*. More precisely, if the selected frame's fontset has a font to display the character set that *char* belongs to.
>
> Fontsets can specify a font on a per-character basis; when the fontset does that, this function's value may not be accurate.

37.12.12 Low-Level Font Representation

Normally, it is not necessary to manipulate fonts directly. In case you need to do so, this section explains how.

In Emacs Lisp, fonts are represented using three different Lisp object types: *font objects*, *font specs*, and *font entities*.

`fontp` *object* **&optional** *type*   [Function]
> Return `t` if *object* is a font object, font spec, or font entity. Otherwise, return `nil`.
>
> The optional argument *type*, if non-`nil`, determines the exact type of Lisp object to check for. In that case, *type* should be one of `font-object`, `font-spec`, or `font-entity`.

A font object is a Lisp object that represents a font that Emacs has *opened*. Font objects cannot be modified in Lisp, but they can be inspected.

`font-at` *position* **&optional** *window string*   [Function]
> Return the font object that is being used to display the character at position *position* in the window *window*. If *window* is `nil`, it defaults to the selected window. If *string* is `nil`, *position* specifies a position in the current buffer; otherwise, *string* should be a string, and *position* specifies a position in that string.

A font spec is a Lisp object that contains a set of specifications that can be used to find a font. More than one font may match the specifications in a font spec.

font-spec &rest *arguments* [Function]

Return a new font spec using the specifications in *arguments*, which should come in `property-value` pairs. The possible specifications are as follows:

`:name`   The font name (a string), in either XLFD, Fontconfig, or GTK format. See Section "Fonts" in *The GNU Emacs Manual*.

`:family`
`:foundry`
`:weight`
`:slant`
`:width`   These have the same meanings as the face attributes of the same name. See Section 37.12.1 [Face Attributes], page 915.

`:size`   The font size—either a non-negative integer that specifies the pixel size, or a floating-point number that specifies the point size.

`:adstyle`   Additional typographic style information for the font, such as '`sans`'. The value should be a string or a symbol.

`:registry`
The charset registry and encoding of the font, such as '`iso8859-1`'. The value should be a string or a symbol.

`:script`   The script that the font must support (a symbol).

`:lang`   The language that the font should support. The value should be a symbol whose name is a two-letter ISO-639 language name. On X, the value is matched against the "Additional Style" field of the XLFD name of a font, if it is non-empty. On MS-Windows, fonts matching the spec are required to support codepages needed for the language. Currently, only a small set of CJK languages is supported with this property: '`ja`', '`ko`', and '`zh`'.

`:otf`   The font must be an OpenType font that supports these OpenType features, provided Emacs is compiled with a library, such as '`libotf`' on GNU/Linux, that supports complex text layout for scripts which need that. The value must be a list of the form

(*script-tag langsys-tag gsub gpos*)

where *script-tag* is the OpenType script tag symbol; *langsys-tag* is the OpenType language system tag symbol, or `nil` to use the default language system; `gsub` is a list of OpenType GSUB feature tag symbols, or `nil` if none is required; and `gpos` is a list of OpenType GPOS feature tag symbols, or `nil` if none is required. If `gsub` or `gpos` is a list, a `nil` element in that list means that the font must not match any of the remaining tag symbols. The `gpos` element may be omitted.

font-put *font-spec property value* [Function]

Set the font property *property* in the font-spec *font-spec* to *value*.

A font entity is a reference to a font that need not be open. Its properties are intermediate between a font object and a font spec: like a font object, and unlike a font spec, it refers to a single, specific font. Unlike a font object, creating a font entity does not load the contents of that font into computer memory. Emacs may open multiple font objects of different sizes from a single font entity referring to a scalable font.

find-font *font-spec* **&optional** *frame* [Function]

    This function returns a font entity that best matches the font spec *font-spec* on frame *frame*. If *frame* is `nil`, it defaults to the selected frame.

list-fonts *font-spec* **&optional** *frame num prefer* [Function]

    This function returns a list of all font entities that match the font spec *font-spec*.

    The optional argument *frame*, if non-`nil`, specifies the frame on which the fonts are to be displayed. The optional argument *num*, if non-`nil`, should be an integer that specifies the maximum length of the returned list. The optional argument *prefer*, if non-`nil`, should be another font spec, which is used to control the order of the returned list; the returned font entities are sorted in order of decreasing closeness to that font spec.

If you call `set-face-attribute` and pass a font spec, font entity, or font name string as the value of the `:font` attribute, Emacs opens the best matching font that is available for display. It then stores the corresponding font object as the actual value of the `:font` attribute for that face.

The following functions can be used to obtain information about a font. For these functions, the *font* argument can be a font object, a font entity, or a font spec.

font-get *font property* [Function]

    This function returns the value of the font property *property* for *font*.

    If *font* is a font spec and the font spec does not specify *property*, the return value is `nil`. If *font* is a font object or font entity, the value for the *:script* property may be a list of scripts supported by the font.

font-face-attributes *font* **&optional** *frame* [Function]

    This function returns a list of face attributes corresponding to *font*. The optional argument *frame* specifies the frame on which the font is to be displayed. If it is `nil`, the selected frame is used. The return value has the form

```
(:family family :height height :weight weight
  :slant slant :width width)
```

    where the values of *family*, *height*, *weight*, *slant*, and *width* are face attribute values. Some of these key-attribute pairs may be omitted from the list if they are not specified by *font*.

font-xlfd-name *font* **&optional** *fold-wildcards* [Function]

    This function returns the XLFD (X Logical Font Descriptor), a string, matching *font*. See Section "Fonts" in *The GNU Emacs Manual*, for information about XLFDs. If the name is too long for an XLFD (which can contain at most 255 characters), the function returns `nil`.

    If the optional argument *fold-wildcards* is non-`nil`, consecutive wildcards in the XLFD are folded into one.

The following two functions return important information about a font.

font-info *name* **&optional** *frame*   [Function]
>   This function returns information about a font specified by its *name*, a string, as it
>   is used on *frame*. If *frame* is omitted or `nil`, it defaults to the selected frame.
>
>   The value returned by the function is a vector of the form [`opened-name full-name`
>   `size height baseline-offset relative-compose default-ascent max-width`
>   `ascent descent space-width average-width filename capability`]. Here's the
>   description of each components of this vector:
>
>   *opened-name*
>   > The name used to open the font, a string.
>
>   *full-name* The full name of the font, a string.
>
>   *size*   The pixel size of the font.
>
>   *height*   The height of the font in pixels.
>
>   *baseline-offset*
>   > The offset in pixels from the ASCII baseline, positive upward.
>
>   *relative-compose*
>   *default-ascent*
>   > Numbers controlling how to compose characters.
>
>   *ascent*
>   *descent*   The ascent and descent of this font. The sum of these two numbers should
>   > be equal to the value of *height* above.
>
>   *space-width*
>   > The width, in pixels, of the font's space character.
>
>   *average-width*
>   > The average width of the font characters. If this is zero, Emacs uses the
>   > value of *space-width* instead, when it calculates text layout on display.
>
>   *filename*   The file name of the font as a string. This can be `nil` if the font back-end
>   > does not provide a way to find out the font's file name.
>
>   *capability* A list whose first element is a symbol representing the font type, one
>   > of `x`, `opentype`, `truetype`, `type1`, `pcf`, or `bdf`. For OpenType fonts,
>   > the list includes 2 additional elements describing the GSUB and GPOS
>   > features supported by the font. Each of these elements is a list of the form
>   > ((*script* (*langsys* *feature* ...) ...) ...), where *script* is a symbol
>   > representing an OpenType script tag, *langsys* is a symbol representing
>   > an OpenType langsys tag (or `nil`, which stands for the default langsys),
>   > and each *feature* is a symbol representing an OpenType feature tag.

query-font *font-object*   [Function]
>   This function returns information about a *font-object*. (This is in contrast to
>   `font-info`, which takes the font name, a string, as its argument.)

The value returned by the function is a vector of the form [`name filename pixel-size max-width ascent descent space-width average-width capability`]. Here's the description of each components of this vector:

name   The font name, a string.

filename   The file name of the font as a string. This can be `nil` if the font back-end does not provide a way to find out the font's file name.

pixel-size The pixel size of the font used to open the font.

max-width
              The maximum advance width of the font.

ascent
descent   The ascent and descent of this font. The sum of these two numbers gives the font height.

space-width
              The width, in pixels, of the font's space character.

average-width
              The average width of the font characters. If this is zero, Emacs uses the value of *space-width* instead, when it calculates text layout on display.

capability A list whose first element is a symbol representing the font type, one of `x`, `opentype`, `truetype`, `type1`, `pcf`, or `bdf`. For OpenType fonts, the list includes 2 additional elements describing the GSUB and GPOS features supported by the font. Each of these elements is a list of the form ((`script` (`langsys feature` ...) ...) ...), where *script* is a symbol representing an OpenType script tag, *langsys* is a symbol representing an OpenType langsys tag (or `nil`, which stands for the default langsys), and each *feature* is a symbol representing an OpenType feature tag.

The following four functions return size information about fonts used by various faces, allowing various layout considerations in Lisp programs. These functions take face remapping into consideration, returning information about the remapped face, if the face in question was remapped. See Section 37.12.5 [Face Remapping], page 924.

`default-font-width`   [Function]
    This function returns the average width in pixels of the font used by the current buffer's default face.

`default-font-height`   [Function]
    This function returns the height in pixels of the font used by the current buffer's default face.

`window-font-width` &optional *window face*   [Function]
    This function returns the average width in pixels for the font used by *face* in *window*. The specified *window* must be a live window. If `nil` or omitted, *window* defaults to the selected window, and *face* defaults to the default face in *window*.

window-font-height &optional *window face* [Function]

> This function returns the height in pixels for the font used by *face* in *window*. The specified *window* must be a live window. If `nil` or omitted, *window* defaults to the selected window, and *face* defaults to the default face in *window*.

37.13 Fringes

On graphical displays, Emacs draws *fringes* next to each window: thin vertical strips down the sides which can display bitmaps indicating truncation, continuation, horizontal scrolling, and so on.

37.13.1 Fringe Size and Position

The following buffer-local variables control the position and width of fringes in windows showing that buffer.

fringes-outside-margins [Variable]

> The fringes normally appear between the display margins and the window text. If the value is non-`nil`, they appear outside the display margins. See Section 37.16.5 [Display Margins], page 949.

left-fringe-width [Variable]

> This variable, if non-`nil`, specifies the width of the left fringe in pixels. A value of `nil` means to use the left fringe width from the window's frame.

right-fringe-width [Variable]

> This variable, if non-`nil`, specifies the width of the right fringe in pixels. A value of `nil` means to use the right fringe width from the window's frame.

Any buffer which does not specify values for these variables uses the values specified by the `left-fringe` and `right-fringe` frame parameters (see Section 28.4.3.4 [Layout Parameters], page 648).

The above variables actually take effect via the function `set-window-buffer` (see Section 27.11 [Buffers and Windows], page 594), which calls `set-window-fringes` as a subroutine. If you change one of these variables, the fringe display is not updated in existing windows showing the buffer, unless you call `set-window-buffer` again in each affected window. You can also use `set-window-fringes` to control the fringe display in individual windows.

set-window-fringes *window left* **&optional** *right outside-margins* [Function]

> This function sets the fringe widths of window *window*. If *window* is `nil`, the selected window is used.
>
> The argument *left* specifies the width in pixels of the left fringe, and likewise *right* for the right fringe. A value of `nil` for either one stands for the default width. If *outside-margins* is non-`nil`, that specifies that fringes should appear outside of the display margins.

window-fringes &optional *window* [Function]

> This function returns information about the fringes of a window *window*. If *window* is omitted or `nil`, the selected window is used. The value has the form (*left-width right-width outside-margins*).

37.13.2 Fringe Indicators

Fringe indicators are tiny icons displayed in the window fringe to indicate truncated or continued lines, buffer boundaries, etc.

`indicate-empty-lines`   [User Option]

> When this is non-`nil`, Emacs displays a special glyph in the fringe of each empty line at the end of the buffer, on graphical displays. See Section 37.13 [Fringes], page 937. This variable is automatically buffer-local in every buffer.

`indicate-buffer-boundaries`   [User Option]

> This buffer-local variable controls how the buffer boundaries and window scrolling are indicated in the window fringes.
>
> Emacs can indicate the buffer boundaries—that is, the first and last line in the buffer—with angle icons when they appear on the screen. In addition, Emacs can display an up-arrow in the fringe to show that there is text above the screen, and a down-arrow to show there is text below the screen.
>
> There are three kinds of basic values:
>
> | | |
> |---|---|
> | `nil` | Don't display any of these fringe icons. |
> | `left` | Display the angle icons and arrows in the left fringe. |
> | `right` | Display the angle icons and arrows in the right fringe. |
>
> any non-alist
>
> > Display the angle icons in the left fringe and don't display the arrows.
>
> Otherwise the value should be an alist that specifies which fringe indicators to display and where. Each element of the alist should have the form (*indicator . position*). Here, *indicator* is one of `top`, `bottom`, `up`, `down`, and `t` (which covers all the icons not yet specified), while *position* is one of `left`, `right` and `nil`.
>
> For example, `((top . left) (t . right))` places the top angle bitmap in left fringe, and the bottom angle bitmap as well as both arrow bitmaps in right fringe. To show the angle bitmaps in the left fringe, and no arrow bitmaps, use `((top . left) (bottom . left))`.

`fringe-indicator-alist`   [Variable]

> This buffer-local variable specifies the mapping from logical fringe indicators to the actual bitmaps displayed in the window fringes. The value is an alist of elements (*indicator . bitmaps*), where *indicator* specifies a logical indicator type and *bitmaps* specifies the fringe bitmaps to use for that indicator.
>
> Each *indicator* should be one of the following symbols:
>
> `truncation`, `continuation`.
>
> > Used for truncation and continuation lines.
>
> `up`, `down`, `top`, `bottom`, `top-bottom`
>
> > Used when `indicate-buffer-boundaries` is non-`nil`: `up` and `down` indicate a buffer boundary lying above or below the window edge; `top` and `bottom` indicate the topmost and bottommost buffer text line; and `top-bottom` indicates where there is just one line of text in the buffer.

`empty-line`
>   Used to indicate empty lines when `indicate-empty-lines` is non-`nil`.

`overlay-arrow`
>   Used for overlay arrows (see Section 37.13.6 [Overlay Arrow], page 941).

Each *bitmaps* value may be a list of symbols (`left right [left1 right1]`). The *left* and *right* symbols specify the bitmaps shown in the left and/or right fringe, for the specific indicator. *left1* and *right1* are specific to the `bottom` and `top-bottom` indicators, and are used to indicate that the last text line has no final newline. Alternatively, *bitmaps* may be a single symbol which is used in both left and right fringes.

See Section 37.13.4 [Fringe Bitmaps], page 940, for a list of standard bitmap symbols and how to define your own. In addition, `nil` represents the empty bitmap (i.e., an indicator that is not shown).

When `fringe-indicator-alist` has a buffer-local value, and there is no bitmap defined for a logical indicator, or the bitmap is `t`, the corresponding value from the default value of `fringe-indicator-alist` is used.

37.13.3 Fringe Cursors

When a line is exactly as wide as the window, Emacs displays the cursor in the right fringe instead of using two lines. Different bitmaps are used to represent the cursor in the fringe depending on the current buffer's cursor type.

`overflow-newline-into-fringe`   [User Option]
>   If this is non-`nil`, lines exactly as wide as the window (not counting the final newline character) are not continued. Instead, when point is at the end of the line, the cursor appears in the right fringe.

`fringe-cursor-alist`   [Variable]
>   This variable specifies the mapping from logical cursor type to the actual fringe bitmaps displayed in the right fringe. The value is an alist where each element has the form (`cursor-type . bitmap`), which means to use the fringe bitmap *bitmap* to display cursors of type *cursor-type*.

>   Each *cursor-type* should be one of `box`, `hollow`, `bar`, `hbar`, or `hollow-small`. The first four have the same meanings as in the `cursor-type` frame parameter (see Section 28.4.3.7 [Cursor Parameters], page 650). The `hollow-small` type is used instead of `hollow` when the normal `hollow-rectangle` bitmap is too tall to fit on a specific display line.

>   Each *bitmap* should be a symbol specifying the fringe bitmap to be displayed for that logical cursor type. See the next subsection for details.

>   When `fringe-cursor-alist` has a buffer-local value, and there is no bitmap defined for a cursor type, the corresponding value from the default value of `fringes-indicator-alist` is used.

37.13.4 Fringe Bitmaps

The *fringe bitmaps* are the actual bitmaps which represent the logical fringe indicators for truncated or continued lines, buffer boundaries, overlay arrows, etc. Each bitmap is represented by a symbol. These symbols are referred to by the variables `fringe-indicator-alist` and `fringe-cursor-alist`, described in the previous subsections.

Lisp programs can also directly display a bitmap in the left or right fringe, by using a `display` property for one of the characters appearing in the line (see Section 37.16.4 [Other Display Specs], page 948). Such a display specification has the form

> (*fringe bitmap* [*face*])

fringe is either the symbol `left-fringe` or `right-fringe`. *bitmap* is a symbol identifying the bitmap to display. The optional *face* names a face whose foreground color is used to display the bitmap; this face is automatically merged with the `fringe` face.

Here is a list of the standard fringe bitmaps defined in Emacs, and how they are currently used in Emacs (via `fringe-indicator-alist` and `fringe-cursor-alist`):

`left-arrow, right-arrow`
> Used to indicate truncated lines.

`left-curly-arrow, right-curly-arrow`
> Used to indicate continued lines.

`right-triangle, left-triangle`
> The former is used by overlay arrows. The latter is unused.

`up-arrow, down-arrow, top-left-angle top-right-angle`
`bottom-left-angle, bottom-right-angle`
`top-right-angle, top-left-angle`
`left-bracket, right-bracket, top-right-angle, top-left-angle`
> Used to indicate buffer boundaries.

`filled-rectangle, hollow-rectangle`
`filled-square, hollow-square`
`vertical-bar, horizontal-bar`
> Used for different types of fringe cursors.

`empty-line, exclamation-mark, question-mark, exclamation-mark`
> Not used by core Emacs features.

The next subsection describes how to define your own fringe bitmaps.

fringe-bitmaps-at-pos **&optional** *pos window*   [Function]
> This function returns the fringe bitmaps of the display line containing position *pos* in window *window*. The return value has the form (*left right ov*), where *left* is the symbol for the fringe bitmap in the left fringe (or `nil` if no bitmap), *right* is similar for the right fringe, and *ov* is non-`nil` if there is an overlay arrow in the left fringe.
>
> The value is `nil` if *pos* is not visible in *window*. If *window* is `nil`, that stands for the selected window. If *pos* is `nil`, that stands for the value of point in *window*.

37.13.5 Customizing Fringe Bitmaps

define-fringe-bitmap *bitmap bits* **&optional** *height width align*   [Function]
This function defines the symbol *bitmap* as a new fringe bitmap, or replaces an existing bitmap with that name.

The argument *bits* specifies the image to use. It should be either a string or a vector of integers, where each element (an integer) corresponds to one row of the bitmap. Each bit of an integer corresponds to one pixel of the bitmap, where the low bit corresponds to the rightmost pixel of the bitmap.

The height is normally the length of *bits*. However, you can specify a different height with non-`nil` *height*. The width is normally 8, but you can specify a different width with non-`nil` *width*. The width must be an integer between 1 and 16.

The argument *align* specifies the positioning of the bitmap relative to the range of rows where it is used; the default is to center the bitmap. The allowed values are `top`, `center`, or `bottom`.

The *align* argument may also be a list (`align periodic`) where *align* is interpreted as described above. If *periodic* is non-`nil`, it specifies that the rows in `bits` should be repeated enough times to reach the specified height.

destroy-fringe-bitmap *bitmap*   [Function]
This function destroy the fringe bitmap identified by *bitmap*. If *bitmap* identifies a standard fringe bitmap, it actually restores the standard definition of that bitmap, instead of eliminating it entirely.

set-fringe-bitmap-face *bitmap* **&optional** *face*   [Function]
This sets the face for the fringe bitmap *bitmap* to *face*. If *face* is `nil`, it selects the `fringe` face. The bitmap's face controls the color to draw it in.

face is merged with the `fringe` face, so normally *face* should specify only the foreground color.

37.13.6 The Overlay Arrow

The *overlay arrow* is useful for directing the user's attention to a particular line in a buffer. For example, in the modes used for interface to debuggers, the overlay arrow indicates the line of code about to be executed. This feature has nothing to do with *overlays* (see Section 37.9 [Overlays], page 904).

overlay-arrow-string   [Variable]
This variable holds the string to display to call attention to a particular line, or `nil` if the arrow feature is not in use. On a graphical display the contents of the string are ignored; instead a glyph is displayed in the fringe area to the left of the display area.

overlay-arrow-position   [Variable]
This variable holds a marker that indicates where to display the overlay arrow. It should point at the beginning of a line. On a non-graphical display the arrow text appears at the beginning of that line, overlaying any text that would otherwise appear. Since the arrow is usually short, and the line usually begins with indentation, normally nothing significant is overwritten.

The overlay-arrow string is displayed in any given buffer if the value of `overlay-arrow-position` in that buffer points into that buffer. Thus, it is possible to display multiple overlay arrow strings by creating buffer-local bindings of `overlay-arrow-position`. However, it is usually cleaner to use `overlay-arrow-variable-list` to achieve this result.

You can do a similar job by creating an overlay with a `before-string` property. See Section 37.9.2 [Overlay Properties], page 907.

You can define multiple overlay arrows via the variable `overlay-arrow-variable-list`.

`overlay-arrow-variable-list`   [Variable]
> This variable's value is a list of variables, each of which specifies the position of an overlay arrow. The variable `overlay-arrow-position` has its normal meaning because it is on this list.

Each variable on this list can have properties `overlay-arrow-string` and `overlay-arrow-bitmap` that specify an overlay arrow string (for text terminals) or fringe bitmap (for graphical terminals) to display at the corresponding overlay arrow position. If either property is not set, the default `overlay-arrow-string` or `overlay-arrow` fringe indicator is used.

37.14 Scroll Bars

Normally the frame parameter `vertical-scroll-bars` controls whether the windows in the frame have vertical scroll bars, and whether they are on the left or right. The frame parameter `scroll-bar-width` specifies how wide they are (`nil` meaning the default).

The frame parameter `horizontal-scroll-bars` controls whether the windows in the frame have horizontal scroll bars. The frame parameter `scroll-bar-height` specifies how high they are (`nil` meaning the default). See Section 28.4.3.4 [Layout Parameters], page 648.

Horizontal scroll bars are not available on all platforms. The function `horizontal-scroll-bars-available-p` which takes no argument returns non-`nil` if they are available on your system.

The following three functions take as argument a live frame which defaults to the selected one.

`frame-current-scroll-bars` &optional *frame*   [Function]
> This function reports the scroll bar types for frame *frame*. The value is a cons cell (*vertical-type* . *horizontal-type*), where *vertical-type* is either `left`, `right`, or `nil` (which means no vertical scroll bar.) *horizontal-type* is either `bottom` or `nil` (which means no horizontal scroll bar).

`frame-scroll-bar-width` &optional *frame*   [Function]
> This function returns the width of vertical scroll bars of *frame* in pixels.

`frame-scroll-bar-height` &optional *frame*   [Function]
> This function returns the height of horizontal scroll bars of *frame* in pixels.

You can override the frame specific settings for individual windows by using the following function:

set-window-scroll-bars *window* **&optional** *width vertical-type*　　　　[Function]
　　　　height horizontal-type

> This function sets the width and/or height and the types of scroll bars for window
> *window*.
>
> *width* specifies the width of the vertical scroll bar in pixels (`nil` means use the width
> specified for the frame). *vertical-type* specifies whether to have a vertical scroll bar
> and, if so, where. The possible values are `left`, `right`, `t`, which means to use the
> frame's default, and `nil` for no vertical scroll bar.
>
> *height* specifies the height of the horizontal scroll bar in pixels (`nil` means use the
> height specified for the frame). *horizontal-type* specifies whether to have a horizontal
> scroll bar. The possible values are `bottom`, `t`, which means to use the frame's default,
> and `nil` for no horizontal scroll bar.
>
> If *window* is `nil`, the selected window is used.

The following four functions take as argument a live window which defaults to the
selected one.

window-scroll-bars **&optional** *window*　　　　　　　　　　　　[Function]

> This function returns a list of the form (`width columns vertical-type height`
> `lines horizontal-type`).
>
> The value *width* is the value that was specified for the width of the vertical scroll bar
> (which may be `nil`); *columns* is the (possibly rounded) number of columns that the
> vertical scroll bar actually occupies.
>
> The value *height* is the value that was specified for the height of the horizontal scroll
> bar (which may be `nil`); *lines* is the (possibly rounded) number of lines that the
> horizontally scroll bar actually occupies.

window-current-scroll-bars **&optional** *window*　　　　　　　　[Function]

> This function reports the scroll bar type for window *window*. The value is a cons
> cell (`vertical-type . horizontal-type`). Unlike `window-scroll-bars`, this re-
> ports the scroll bar type actually used, once frame defaults and `scroll-bar-mode`
> are taken into account.

window-scroll-bar-width **&optional** *window*　　　　　　　　　　[Function]

> This function returns the width in pixels of *window*'s vertical scrollbar.

window-scroll-bar-height **&optional** *window*　　　　　　　　　[Function]

> This function returns the height in pixels of *window*'s horizontal scrollbar.

If you don't specify these values for a window with `set-window-scroll-bars`, the buffer-
local variables `vertical-scroll-bar`, `horizontal-scroll-bar`, `scroll-bar-width` and
`scroll-bar-height` in the buffer being displayed control the window's scroll bars. The
function `set-window-buffer` examines these variables. If you change them in a buffer that
is already visible in a window, you can make the window take note of the new values by
calling `set-window-buffer` specifying the same buffer that is already displayed.

You can control the appearance of scroll bars for a particular buffer by setting the
following variables which automatically become buffer-local when set.

`vertical-scroll-bar`   [Variable]

> This variable specifies the location of the vertical scroll bar. The possible values are `left`, `right`, `t`, which means to use the frame's default, and `nil` for no scroll bar.

`horizontal-scroll-bar`   [Variable]

> This variable specifies the location of the horizontal scroll bar. The possible values are `bottom`, `t`, which means to use the frame's default, and `nil` for no scroll bar.

`scroll-bar-width`   [Variable]

> This variable specifies the width of the buffer's vertical scroll bars, measured in pixels. A value of `nil` means to use the value specified by the frame.

`scroll-bar-height`   [Variable]

> This variable specifies the height of the buffer's horizontal scroll bar, measured in pixels. A value of `nil` means to use the value specified by the frame.

Finally you can toggle the display of scroll bars on all frames by customizing the variables `scroll-bar-mode` and `horizontal-scroll-bar-mode`.

`scroll-bar-mode`   [User Option]

> This variable controls whether and where to put vertical scroll bars in all frames. The possible values are `nil` for no scroll bars, `left` to put scroll bars on the left and `right` to put scroll bars on the right.

`horizontal-scroll-bar-mode`   [User Option]

> This variable controls whether to display horizontal scroll bars on all frames.

37.15 Window Dividers

Window dividers are bars drawn between a frame's windows. A right divider is drawn between a window and any adjacent windows on the right. Its width (thickness) is specified by the frame parameter `right-divider-width`. A bottom divider is drawn between a window and adjacent windows on the bottom or the echo area. Its width is specified by the frame parameter `bottom-divider-width`. In either case, specifying a width of zero means to not draw such dividers. See Section 28.4.3.4 [Layout Parameters], page 648.

Technically, a right divider belongs to the window on its left, which means that its width contributes to the total width of that window. A bottom divider belongs to the window above it, which means that its width contributes to the total height of that window. See Section 27.3 [Window Sizes], page 572. When a window has both, a right and a bottom divider, the bottom divider prevails. This means that a bottom divider is drawn over the full total width of its window while the right divider ends above the bottom divider.

Dividers can be dragged with the mouse and are therefore useful for adjusting the sizes of adjacent windows with the mouse. They also serve to visually set apart adjacent windows when no scroll bars or mode lines are present. The following three faces allow the customization of the appearance of dividers:

`window-divider`

> When a divider is less than three pixels wide, it is drawn solidly with the foreground of this face. For larger dividers this face is used for the inner part only, excluding the first and last pixel.

`window-divider-first-pixel`

> This is the face used for drawing the first pixel of a divider that is at least three pixels wide. To obtain a solid appearance, set this to the same value used for the `window-divider` face.

`window-divider-last-pixel`

> This is the face used for drawing the last pixel of a divider that is at least three pixels wide. To obtain a solid appearance, set this to the same value used for the `window-divider` face.

You can get the sizes of the dividers of a specific window with the following two functions.

`window-right-divider-width` **&optional** *window* [Function]

> Return the width (thickness) in pixels of *window*'s right divider. *window* must be a live window and defaults to the selected one. The return value is always zero for a rightmost window.

`window-bottom-divider-width` **&optional** *window* [Function]

> Return the width (thickness) in pixels of *window*'s bottom divider. *window* must be a live window and defaults to the selected one. The return value is zero for the minibuffer window or a bottommost window on a minibuffer-less frame.

37.16 The `display` Property

The `display` text property (or overlay property) is used to insert images into text, and to control other aspects of how text displays. The value of the `display` property should be a display specification, or a list or vector containing several display specifications. Display specifications in the same `display` property value generally apply in parallel to the text they cover.

If several sources (overlays and/or a text property) specify values for the `display` property, only one of the values takes effect, following the rules of `get-char-property`. See Section 31.19.1 [Examining Properties], page 732.

The rest of this section describes several kinds of display specifications and what they mean.

37.16.1 Display Specs That Replace The Text

Some kinds of display specifications specify something to display instead of the text that has the property. These are called *replacing* display specifications. Emacs does not allow the user to interactively move point into the middle of buffer text that is replaced in this way.

If a list of display specifications includes more than one replacing display specification, the first overrides the rest. Replacing display specifications make most other display specifications irrelevant, since those don't apply to the replacement.

For replacing display specifications, *the text that has the property* means all the consecutive characters that have the same Lisp object as their `display` property; these characters are replaced as a single unit. If two characters have different Lisp objects as their `display` properties (i.e., objects which are not `eq`), they are handled separately.

Here is an example which illustrates this point. A string serves as a replacing display specification, which replaces the text that has the property with the specified string (see Section 37.16.4 [Other Display Specs], page 948). Consider the following function:

```
(defun foo ()
  (dotimes (i 5)
    (let ((string (concat "A"))
          (start (+ i i (point-min))))
      (put-text-property start (1+ start) 'display string)
      (put-text-property start (+ 2 start) 'display string))))
```

This function gives each of the first ten characters in the buffer a `display` property which is a string `"A"`, but they don't all get the same string object. The first two characters get the same string object, so they are replaced with one 'A'; the fact that the display property was assigned in two separate calls to `put-text-property` is irrelevant. Similarly, the next two characters get a second string (`concat` creates a new string object), so they are replaced with one 'A'; and so on. Thus, the ten characters appear as five A's.

37.16.2 Specified Spaces

To display a space of specified width and/or height, use a display specification of the form (`space . props`), where *props* is a property list (a list of alternating properties and values). You can put this property on one or more consecutive characters; a space of the specified height and width is displayed in place of *all* of those characters. These are the properties you can use in *props* to specify the weight of the space:

`:width` *width*

> If *width* is a number, it specifies that the space width should be *width* times the normal character width. *width* can also be a *pixel width* specification (see Section 37.16.3 [Pixel Specification], page 947).

`:relative-width` *factor*

> Specifies that the width of the stretch should be computed from the first character in the group of consecutive characters that have the same `display` property. The space width is the pixel width of that character, multiplied by *factor*. (On text-mode terminals, the "pixel width" of a character is usually 1, but it could be more for TABs and double-width CJK characters.)

`:align-to` *hpos*

> Specifies that the space should be wide enough to reach *hpos*. If *hpos* is a number, it is measured in units of the normal character width. *hpos* can also be a *pixel width* specification (see Section 37.16.3 [Pixel Specification], page 947).

You should use one and only one of the above properties. You can also specify the height of the space, with these properties:

`:height` *height*

> Specifies the height of the space. If *height* is a number, it specifies that the space height should be *height* times the normal character height. The *height* may also be a *pixel height* specification (see Section 37.16.3 [Pixel Specification], page 947).

`:relative-height` *factor*

> Specifies the height of the space, multiplying the ordinary height of the text having this display specification by *factor*.

`:ascent` *ascent*

> If the value of *ascent* is a non-negative number no greater than 100, it specifies that *ascent* percent of the height of the space should be considered as the ascent of the space—that is, the part above the baseline. The ascent may also be specified in pixel units with a *pixel ascent* specification (see Section 37.16.3 [Pixel Specification], page 947).

Don't use both `:height` and `:relative-height` together.

The `:width` and `:align-to` properties are supported on non-graphic terminals, but the other space properties in this section are not.

Note that space properties are treated as paragraph separators for the purposes of re-ordering bidirectional text for display. See Section 37.26 [Bidirectional Display], page 981, for the details.

37.16.3 Pixel Specification for Spaces

The value of the `:width`, `:align-to`, `:height`, and `:ascent` properties can be a special kind of expression that is evaluated during redisplay. The result of the evaluation is used as an absolute number of pixels.

The following expressions are supported:

```
expr ::= num | (num) | unit | elem | pos | image | form
num  ::= integer | float | symbol
unit ::= in | mm | cm | width | height
elem ::= left-fringe | right-fringe | left-margin | right-margin
       | scroll-bar | text
pos  ::= left | center | right
form ::= (num . expr) | (op expr ...)
op   ::= + | -
```

The form *num* specifies a fraction of the default frame font height or width. The form `(num)` specifies an absolute number of pixels. If *num* is a symbol, *symbol*, its buffer-local variable binding is used.

The `in`, `mm`, and `cm` units specify the number of pixels per inch, millimeter, and centimeter, respectively. The `width` and `height` units correspond to the default width and height of the current face. An image specification `image` corresponds to the width or height of the image.

The elements `left-fringe`, `right-fringe`, `left-margin`, `right-margin`, `scroll-bar`, and `text` specify to the width of the corresponding area of the window.

The `left`, `center`, and `right` positions can be used with `:align-to` to specify a position relative to the left edge, center, or right edge of the text area.

Any of the above window elements (except `text`) can also be used with `:align-to` to specify that the position is relative to the left edge of the given area. Once the base offset for a relative position has been set (by the first occurrence of one of these symbols), further occurrences of these symbols are interpreted as the width of the specified area. For example, to align to the center of the left-margin, use

```
:align-to (+ left-margin (0.5 . left-margin))
```

If no specific base offset is set for alignment, it is always relative to the left edge of the text area. For example, ':`align-to` 0' in a header-line aligns with the first text column in the text area.

A value of the form (*num* . *expr*) stands for the product of the values of *num* and *expr*. For example, (2 . in) specifies a width of 2 inches, while (0.5 . *image*) specifies half the width (or height) of the specified image.

The form (+ *expr* ...) adds up the value of the expressions. The form (- *expr* ...) negates or subtracts the value of the expressions.

37.16.4 Other Display Specifications

Here are the other sorts of display specifications that you can use in the `display` text property.

string   Display *string* instead of the text that has this property.

Recursive display specifications are not supported—*string*'s `display` properties, if any, are not used.

(image . *image-props*)

This kind of display specification is an image descriptor (see Section 37.17 [Images], page 950). When used as a display specification, it means to display the image instead of the text that has the display specification.

(slice *x y width height*)

This specification together with `image` specifies a *slice* (a partial area) of the image to display. The elements *y* and *x* specify the top left corner of the slice, within the image; *width* and *height* specify the width and height of the slice. Integers are numbers of pixels. A floating-point number in the range 0.0–1.0 stands for that fraction of the width or height of the entire image.

((margin nil) *string*)

A display specification of this form means to display *string* instead of the text that has the display specification, at the same position as that text. It is equivalent to using just *string*, but it is done as a special case of marginal display (see Section 37.16.5 [Display Margins], page 949).

(left-fringe *bitmap* [*face*])
(right-fringe *bitmap* [*face*])

This display specification on any character of a line of text causes the specified *bitmap* be displayed in the left or right fringes for that line, instead of the characters that have the display specification. The optional *face* specifies the colors to be used for the bitmap. See Section 37.13.4 [Fringe Bitmaps], page 940, for the details.

(space-width *factor*)

This display specification affects all the space characters within the text that has the specification. It displays all of these spaces *factor* times as wide as normal. The element *factor* should be an integer or float. Characters other than spaces are not affected at all; in particular, this has no effect on tab characters.

(height *height*)

This display specification makes the text taller or shorter. Here are the possibilities for *height*:

(+ *n*)   This means to use a font that is *n* steps larger. A *step* is defined by the set of available fonts—specifically, those that match what was otherwise specified for this text, in all attributes except height. Each size for which a suitable font is available counts as another step. n should be an integer.

(- n)   This means to use a font that is n steps smaller.

a number, *factor*

A number, *factor*, means to use a font that is *factor* times as tall as the default font.

a symbol, *function*

A symbol is a function to compute the height. It is called with the current height as argument, and should return the new height to use.

anything else, *form*

If the *height* value doesn't fit the previous possibilities, it is a form. Emacs evaluates it to get the new height, with the symbol `height` bound to the current specified font height.

(raise *factor*)

This kind of display specification raises or lowers the text it applies to, relative to the baseline of the line. It is mainly meant to support display of subscripts and superscripts.

The *factor* must be a number, which is interpreted as a multiple of the height of the affected text. If it is positive, that means to display the characters raised. If it is negative, that means to display them lower down.

Note that if the text also has a `height` display specification, which was specified before (i.e. to the left of) `raise`, the latter will affect the amount of raising or lowering in pixels, because that is based on the height of the text being raised. Therefore, if you want to display a sub- or superscript that is smaller than the normal text height, consider specifying `raise` before `height`.

You can make any display specification conditional. To do that, package it in another list of the form (`when` *condition* . *spec*). Then the specification *spec* applies only when *condition* evaluates to a non-`nil` value. During the evaluation, `object` is bound to the string or buffer having the conditional `display` property. `position` and `buffer-position` are bound to the position within `object` and the buffer position where the `display` property was found, respectively. Both positions can be different when `object` is a string.

37.16.5 Displaying in the Margins

A buffer can have blank areas called *display margins* on the left and on the right. Ordinary text never appears in these areas, but you can put things into the display margins using the `display` property. There is currently no way to make text or images in the margin mouse-sensitive.

The way to display something in the margins is to specify it in a margin display specification in the `display` property of some text. This is a replacing display specification, meaning that the text you put it on does not get displayed; the margin display appears, but that text does not.

A margin display specification looks like `((margin right-margin) spec)` or `((margin left-margin) spec)`. Here, *spec* is another display specification that says what to display in the margin. Typically it is a string of text to display, or an image descriptor.

To display something in the margin *in association with* certain buffer text, without altering or preventing the display of that text, put a `before-string` property on the text and put the margin display specification on the contents of the before-string.

Before the display margins can display anything, you must give them a nonzero width. The usual way to do that is to set these variables:

`left-margin-width`   [Variable]
> This variable specifies the width of the left margin, in character cell (a.k.a. "column") units. It is buffer-local in all buffers. A value of `nil` means no left marginal area.

`right-margin-width`   [Variable]
> This variable specifies the width of the right margin, in character cell units. It is buffer-local in all buffers. A value of `nil` means no right marginal area.

Setting these variables does not immediately affect the window. These variables are checked when a new buffer is displayed in the window. Thus, you can make changes take effect by calling `set-window-buffer`.

You can also set the margin widths immediately.

`set-window-margins` *window left* **&optional** *right*   [Function]
> This function specifies the margin widths for window *window*, in character cell units. The argument *left* controls the left margin, and *right* controls the right margin (default `0`).

`window-margins` **&optional** *window*   [Function]
> This function returns the width of the left and right margins of *window* as a cons cell of the form (`left . right`). If one of the two marginal areas does not exist, its width is returned as `nil`; if neither of the two margins exist, the function returns (`nil`). If *window* is `nil`, the selected window is used.

37.17 Images

To display an image in an Emacs buffer, you must first create an image descriptor, then use it as a display specifier in the `display` property of text that is displayed (see Section 37.16 [Display Property], page 945).

Emacs is usually able to display images when it is run on a graphical terminal. Images cannot be displayed in a text terminal, on certain graphical terminals that lack the support for this, or if Emacs is compiled without image support. You can use the function `display-images-p` to determine if images can in principle be displayed (see Section 28.24 [Display Feature Testing], page 669).

37.17.1 Image Formats

Emacs can display a number of different image formats. Some of these image formats are supported only if particular support libraries are installed. On some platforms, Emacs can load support libraries on demand; if so, the variable `dynamic-library-alist` can be used to modify the set of known names for these dynamic libraries. See Section 38.21 [Dynamic Libraries], page 1022.

Supported image formats (and the required support libraries) include PBM and XBM (which do not depend on support libraries and are always available), XPM (`libXpm`), GIF (`libgif` or `libungif`), PostScript (`gs`), JPEG (`libjpeg`), TIFF (`libtiff`), PNG (`libpng`), and SVG (`librsvg`).

Each of these image formats is associated with an *image type symbol*. The symbols for the above formats are, respectively, `pbm`, `xbm`, `xpm`, `gif`, `postscript`, `jpeg`, `tiff`, `png`, and `svg`.

Furthermore, if you build Emacs with ImageMagick (`libMagickWand`) support, Emacs can display any image format that ImageMagick can. See Section 37.17.6 [ImageMagick Images], page 955. All images displayed via ImageMagick have type symbol `imagemagick`.

`image-types`   [Variable]
> This variable contains a list of type symbols for image formats which are potentially supported in the current configuration.
>
> "Potentially" means that Emacs knows about the image types, not necessarily that they can be used (for example, they could depend on unavailable dynamic libraries). To know which image types are really available, use `image-type-available-p`.

`image-type-available-p` *type*   [Function]
> This function returns non-`nil` if images of type *type* can be loaded and displayed. *type* must be an image type symbol.
>
> For image types whose support libraries are statically linked, this function always returns `t`. For image types whose support libraries are dynamically loaded, it returns `t` if the library could be loaded and `nil` otherwise.

37.17.2 Image Descriptors

An *image descriptor* is a list which specifies the underlying data for an image, and how to display it. It is typically used as the value of a `display` overlay or text property (see Section 37.16.4 [Other Display Specs], page 948); but See Section 37.17.9 [Showing Images], page 959, for convenient helper functions to insert images into buffers.

Each image descriptor has the form (`image . props`), where *props* is a property list of alternating keyword symbols and values, including at least the pair `:type` *type* that specifies the image type.

The following is a list of properties that are meaningful for all image types (there are also properties which are meaningful only for certain image types, as documented in the following subsections):

`:type` *type*
> The image type. Every image descriptor must include this property.

`:file` *file*
> This says to load the image from file *file*. If *file* is not an absolute file name, it is expanded in `data-directory`.

`:data data`

> This specifies the raw image data. Each image descriptor must have either `:data` or `:file`, but not both.
>
> For most image types, the value of a `:data` property should be a string containing the image data. Some image types do not support `:data`; for some others, `:data` alone is not enough, so you need to use other image properties along with `:data`. See the following subsections for details.

`:margin margin`

> This specifies how many pixels to add as an extra margin around the image. The value, *margin*, must be a non-negative number, or a pair (*x . y*) of such numbers. If it is a pair, *x* specifies how many pixels to add horizontally, and *y* specifies how many pixels to add vertically. If `:margin` is not specified, the default is zero.

`:ascent ascent`

> This specifies the amount of the image's height to use for its ascent—that is, the part above the baseline. The value, *ascent*, must be a number in the range 0 to 100, or the symbol `center`.
>
> If *ascent* is a number, that percentage of the image's height is used for its ascent.
>
> If *ascent* is `center`, the image is vertically centered around a centerline which would be the vertical centerline of text drawn at the position of the image, in the manner specified by the text properties and overlays that apply to the image.
>
> If this property is omitted, it defaults to 50.

`:relief relief`

> This adds a shadow rectangle around the image. The value, *relief*, specifies the width of the shadow lines, in pixels. If *relief* is negative, shadows are drawn so that the image appears as a pressed button; otherwise, it appears as an unpressed button.

`:conversion algorithm`

> This specifies a conversion algorithm that should be applied to the image before it is displayed; the value, *algorithm*, specifies which algorithm.
>
> `laplace`
> `emboss`   Specifies the Laplace edge detection algorithm, which blurs out small differences in color while highlighting larger differences. People sometimes consider this useful for displaying the image for a disabled button.
>
> `(edge-detection :matrix matrix :color-adjust adjust)`
> Specifies a general edge-detection algorithm. *matrix* must be either a nine-element list or a nine-element vector of numbers. A pixel at position x/y in the transformed image is computed from original pixels around that position. *matrix* specifies, for each pixel in the neighborhood of x/y, a factor with which that pixel will influence the transformed pixel; element 0 specifies the factor for the pixel

at $x - 1/y - 1$, element 1 the factor for the pixel at $x/y - 1$ etc., as shown below:

$$\begin{pmatrix} x - 1/y - 1 & x/y - 1 & x + 1/y - 1 \\ x - 1/y & x/y & x + 1/y \\ x - 1/y + 1 & x/y + 1 & x + 1/y + 1 \end{pmatrix}$$

The resulting pixel is computed from the color intensity of the color resulting from summing up the RGB values of surrounding pixels, multiplied by the specified factors, and dividing that sum by the sum of the factors' absolute values.

Laplace edge-detection currently uses a matrix of

$$\begin{pmatrix} 1 & 0 & 0 \\ 0 & 0 & 0 \\ 0 & 0 & -1 \end{pmatrix}$$

Emboss edge-detection uses a matrix of

$$\begin{pmatrix} 2 & -1 & 0 \\ -1 & 0 & 1 \\ 0 & 1 & -2 \end{pmatrix}$$

`disabled`   Specifies transforming the image so that it looks disabled.

`:mask` *mask*

If *mask* is `heuristic` or `(heuristic bg)`, build a clipping mask for the image, so that the background of a frame is visible behind the image. If *bg* is not specified, or if *bg* is `t`, determine the background color of the image by looking at the four corners of the image, assuming the most frequently occurring color from the corners is the background color of the image. Otherwise, *bg* must be a list `(red green blue)` specifying the color to assume for the background of the image.

If *mask* is `nil`, remove a mask from the image, if it has one. Images in some formats include a mask which can be removed by specifying `:mask nil`.

`:pointer` *shape*

This specifies the pointer shape when the mouse pointer is over this image. See Section 28.18 [Pointer Shape], page 664, for available pointer shapes.

`:map` *map*   This associates an image map of *hot spots* with this image.

An image map is an alist where each element has the format `(area id plist)`. An *area* is specified as either a rectangle, a circle, or a polygon.

A rectangle is a cons `(rect . ((x0 . y0) . (x1 . y1)))` which specifies the pixel coordinates of the upper left and bottom right corners of the rectangle area.

A circle is a cons `(circle . ((x0 . y0) . r))` which specifies the center and the radius of the circle; *r* may be a float or integer.

A polygon is a cons (`poly` . [*x0 y0 x1 y1* ...]) where each pair in the vector describes one corner in the polygon.

When the mouse pointer lies on a hot-spot area of an image, the *plist* of that hot-spot is consulted; if it contains a `help-echo` property, that defines a tool-tip for the hot-spot, and if it contains a `pointer` property, that defines the shape of the mouse cursor when it is on the hot-spot. See Section 28.18 [Pointer Shape], page 664, for available pointer shapes.

When you click the mouse when the mouse pointer is over a hot-spot, an event is composed by combining the *id* of the hot-spot with the mouse event; for instance, [`area4 mouse-1`] if the hot-spot's *id* is `area4`.

`image-mask-p` *spec* **&optional** *frame*   [Function]
> This function returns `t` if image *spec* has a mask bitmap. *frame* is the frame on which the image will be displayed. *frame* `nil` or omitted means to use the selected frame (see Section 28.10 [Input Focus], page 656).

37.17.3 XBM Images

To use XBM format, specify `xbm` as the image type. This image format doesn't require an external library, so images of this type are always supported.

Additional image properties supported for the `xbm` image type are:

`:foreground` *foreground*
> The value, *foreground*, should be a string specifying the image foreground color, or `nil` for the default color. This color is used for each pixel in the XBM that is 1. The default is the frame's foreground color.

`:background` *background*
> The value, *background*, should be a string specifying the image background color, or `nil` for the default color. This color is used for each pixel in the XBM that is 0. The default is the frame's background color.

If you specify an XBM image using data within Emacs instead of an external file, use the following three properties:

`:data` *data*
> The value, *data*, specifies the contents of the image. There are three formats you can use for *data*:
>
> - A vector of strings or bool-vectors, each specifying one line of the image. Do specify `:height` and `:width`.
>
> - A string containing the same byte sequence as an XBM file would contain. You must not specify `:height` and `:width` in this case, because omitting them is what indicates the data has the format of an XBM file. The file contents specify the height and width of the image.
>
> - A string or a bool-vector containing the bits of the image (plus perhaps some extra bits at the end that will not be used). It should contain at least *width* * `height` bits. In this case, you must specify `:height` and `:width`, both to indicate that the string contains just the bits rather than a whole XBM file, and to specify the size of the image.

`:width` *width*
> The value, *width*, specifies the width of the image, in pixels.

`:height` *height*
> The value, *height*, specifies the height of the image, in pixels.

37.17.4 XPM Images

To use XPM format, specify **xpm** as the image type. The additional image property `:color-symbols` is also meaningful with the **xpm** image type:

`:color-symbols` *symbols*
> The value, *symbols*, should be an alist whose elements have the form (**name** . **color**). In each element, *name* is the name of a color as it appears in the image file, and *color* specifies the actual color to use for displaying that name.

37.17.5 PostScript Images

To use PostScript for an image, specify image type **postscript**. This works only if you have Ghostscript installed. You must always use these three properties:

`:pt-width` *width*
> The value, *width*, specifies the width of the image measured in points (1/72 inch). *width* must be an integer.

`:pt-height` *height*
> The value, *height*, specifies the height of the image in points (1/72 inch). *height* must be an integer.

`:bounding-box` *box*
> The value, *box*, must be a list or vector of four integers, which specifying the bounding box of the PostScript image, analogous to the 'BoundingBox' comment found in PostScript files.
>
> `%%BoundingBox: 22 171 567 738`

37.17.6 ImageMagick Images

If you build Emacs with ImageMagick support, you can use the ImageMagick library to load many image formats (see Section "File Conveniences" in *The GNU Emacs Manual*). The image type symbol for images loaded via ImageMagick is **imagemagick**, regardless of the actual underlying image format.

To check for ImageMagick support, use the following:

```
(image-type-available-p 'imagemagick)
```

`imagemagick-types`   [Function]
> This function returns a list of image file extensions supported by the current ImageMagick installation. Each list element is a symbol representing an internal ImageMagick name for an image type, such as BMP for `.bmp` images.

`imagemagick-enabled-types`   [User Option]
> The value of this variable is a list of ImageMagick image types which Emacs may attempt to render using ImageMagick. Each list element should be one of the symbols

in the list returned by `imagemagick-types`, or an equivalent string. Alternatively, a value of `t` enables ImageMagick for all possible image types. Regardless of the value of this variable, `imagemagick-types-inhibit` (see below) takes precedence.

`imagemagick-types-inhibit`   [User Option]

> The value of this variable lists the ImageMagick image types which should never be rendered using ImageMagick, regardless of the value of `imagemagick-enabled-types`. A value of `t` disables ImageMagick entirely.

`image-format-suffixes`   [Variable]

> This variable is an alist mapping image types to file name extensions. Emacs uses this in conjunction with the `:format` image property (see below) to give a hint to the ImageMagick library as to the type of an image. Each element has the form (*type extension*), where *type* is a symbol specifying an image content-type, and *extension* is a string that specifies the associated file name extension.

Images loaded with ImageMagick support the following additional image descriptor properties:

`:background` *background*

> *background*, if non-`nil`, should be a string specifying a color, which is used as the image's background color if the image supports transparency. If the value is `nil`, it defaults to the frame's background color.

`:width` *width*, `:height` *height*

> The `:width` and `:height` keywords are used for scaling the image. If only one of them is specified, the other one will be calculated so as to preserve the aspect ratio. If both are specified, aspect ratio may not be preserved.

`:max-width` *max-width*, `:max-height` *max-height*

> The `:max-width` and `:max-height` keywords are used for scaling if the size of the image of the image exceeds these values. If `:width` is set it will have precedence over `max-width`, and if `:height` is set it will have precedence over `max-height`, but you can otherwise mix these keywords as you wish. `:max-width` and `:max-height` will always preserve the aspect ratio.

`:format` *type*

> The value, *type*, should be a symbol specifying the type of the image data, as found in `image-format-suffixes`. This is used when the image does not have an associated file name, to provide a hint to ImageMagick to help it detect the image type.

`:rotation` *angle*

> Specifies a rotation angle in degrees.

`:index` *frame*

> See Section 37.17.10 [Multi-Frame Images], page 960.

37.17.7 Other Image Types

For PBM images, specify image type `pbm`. Color, gray-scale and monochromatic images are supported. For mono PBM images, two additional image properties are supported.

`:foreground` *foreground*

> The value, *foreground*, should be a string specifying the image foreground color, or `nil` for the default color. This color is used for each pixel in the PBM that is 1. The default is the frame's foreground color.

`:background` *background*

> The value, *background*, should be a string specifying the image background color, or `nil` for the default color. This color is used for each pixel in the PBM that is 0. The default is the frame's background color.

The remaining image types that Emacs can support are:

GIF   Image type `gif`. Supports the `:index` property. See Section 37.17.10 [Multi-Frame Images], page 960.

JPEG   Image type `jpeg`.

PNG   Image type `png`.

SVG   Image type `svg`.

TIFF   Image type `tiff`. Supports the `:index` property. See Section 37.17.10 [Multi-Frame Images], page 960.

37.17.8 Defining Images

The functions `create-image`, `defimage` and `find-image` provide convenient ways to create image descriptors.

create-image *file-or-data* **&optional** *type data-p* **&rest** *props*   [Function]

> This function creates and returns an image descriptor which uses the data in *file-or-data*. *file-or-data* can be a file name or a string containing the image data; *data-p* should be `nil` for the former case, non-`nil` for the latter case.
>
> The optional argument *type* is a symbol specifying the image type. If *type* is omitted or `nil`, `create-image` tries to determine the image type from the file's first few bytes, or else from the file's name.
>
> The remaining arguments, *props*, specify additional image properties—for example,
>
> ```
> (create-image "foo.xpm" 'xpm nil :heuristic-mask t)
> ```
>
> The function returns `nil` if images of this type are not supported. Otherwise it returns an image descriptor.

defimage *symbol specs* **&optional** *doc*   [Macro]

> This macro defines *symbol* as an image name. The arguments *specs* is a list which specifies how to display the image. The third argument, *doc*, is an optional documentation string.
>
> Each argument in *specs* has the form of a property list, and each one should specify at least the `:type` property and either the `:file` or the `:data` property. The value of `:type` should be a symbol specifying the image type, the value of `:file` is the file to load the image from, and the value of `:data` is a string containing the actual image data. Here is an example:
>
> ```
> (defimage test-image
> ```

```
((:type xpm :file "~/test1.xpm")
 (:type xbm :file "~/test1.xbm")))
```

`defimage` tests each argument, one by one, to see if it is usable—that is, if the type is supported and the file exists. The first usable argument is used to make an image descriptor which is stored in *symbol*.

If none of the alternatives will work, then *symbol* is defined as `nil`.

`find-image` *specs*   [Function]

This function provides a convenient way to find an image satisfying one of a list of image specifications *specs*.

Each specification in *specs* is a property list with contents depending on image type. All specifications must at least contain the properties `:type` *type* and either `:file` *file* or `:data` *data*, where *type* is a symbol specifying the image type, e.g., `xbm`, *file* is the file to load the image from, and *data* is a string containing the actual image data. The first specification in the list whose *type* is supported, and *file* exists, is used to construct the image specification to be returned. If no specification is satisfied, `nil` is returned.

The image is looked for in `image-load-path`.

`image-load-path`   [User Option]

This variable's value is a list of locations in which to search for image files. If an element is a string or a variable symbol whose value is a string, the string is taken to be the name of a directory to search. If an element is a variable symbol whose value is a list, that is taken to be a list of directory names to search.

The default is to search in the `images` subdirectory of the directory specified by `data-directory`, then the directory specified by `data-directory`, and finally in the directories in `load-path`. Subdirectories are not automatically included in the search, so if you put an image file in a subdirectory, you have to supply the subdirectory name explicitly. For example, to find the image `images/foo/bar.xpm` within `data-directory`, you should specify the image as follows:

```
(defimage foo-image '((:type xpm :file "foo/bar.xpm")))
```

`image-load-path-for-library` *library image* **&optional** *path*   [Function]
        no-error

This function returns a suitable search path for images used by the Lisp package *library*.

The function searches for *image* first using `image-load-path`, excluding `data-directory/images`, and then in `load-path`, followed by a path suitable for *library*, which includes `../../etc/images` and `../etc/images` relative to the library file itself, and finally in `data-directory/images`.

Then this function returns a list of directories which contains first the directory in which *image* was found, followed by the value of `load-path`. If *path* is given, it is used instead of `load-path`.

If *no-error* is non-`nil` and a suitable path can't be found, don't signal an error. Instead, return a list of directories as before, except that `nil` appears in place of the image directory.

Here is an example of using `image-load-path-for-library`:

```
(defvar image-load-path) ; shush compiler
(let* ((load-path (image-load-path-for-library
                        "mh-e" "mh-logo.xpm"))
       (image-load-path (cons (car load-path)
                                   image-load-path)))
  (mh-tool-bar-folder-buttons-init))
```

37.17.9 Showing Images

You can use an image descriptor by setting up the `display` property yourself, but it is easier to use the functions in this section.

`insert-image` *image* &optional *string area slice*   [Function]

> This function inserts *image* in the current buffer at point. The value *image* should be an image descriptor; it could be a value returned by `create-image`, or the value of a symbol defined with `defimage`. The argument *string* specifies the text to put in the buffer to hold the image. If it is omitted or `nil`, `insert-image` uses " " by default.
>
> The argument *area* specifies whether to put the image in a margin. If it is `left-margin`, the image appears in the left margin; `right-margin` specifies the right margin. If *area* is `nil` or omitted, the image is displayed at point within the buffer's text.
>
> The argument *slice* specifies a slice of the image to insert. If *slice* is `nil` or omitted the whole image is inserted. Otherwise, *slice* is a list (*x y width height*) which specifies the *x* and *y* positions and *width* and *height* of the image area to insert. Integer values are in units of pixels. A floating-point number in the range 0.0–1.0 stands for that fraction of the width or height of the entire image.
>
> Internally, this function inserts *string* in the buffer, and gives it a `display` property which specifies *image*. See Section 37.16 [Display Property], page 945.

`insert-sliced-image` *image* &optional *string area rows cols*   [Function]

> This function inserts *image* in the current buffer at point, like `insert-image`, but splits the image into *rows*x*cols* equally sized slices.
>
> Emacs displays each slice as a separate image, and allows more intuitive scrolling up/down, instead of jumping up/down the entire image when paging through a buffer that displays (large) images.

`put-image` *image pos* &optional *string area*   [Function]

> This function puts image *image* in front of *pos* in the current buffer. The argument *pos* should be an integer or a marker. It specifies the buffer position where the image should appear. The argument *string* specifies the text that should hold the image as an alternative to the default.
>
> The argument *image* must be an image descriptor, perhaps returned by `create-image` or stored by `defimage`.
>
> The argument *area* specifies whether to put the image in a margin. If it is `left-margin`, the image appears in the left margin; `right-margin` specifies the

right margin. If *area* is `nil` or omitted, the image is displayed at point within the buffer's text.

Internally, this function creates an overlay, and gives it a `before-string` property containing text that has a `display` property whose value is the image. (Whew!)

`remove-images` *start end* **&optional** *buffer*   [Function]

This function removes images in *buffer* between positions *start* and *end*. If *buffer* is omitted or `nil`, images are removed from the current buffer.

This removes only images that were put into *buffer* the way `put-image` does it, not images that were inserted with `insert-image` or in other ways.

`image-size` *spec* **&optional** *pixels frame*   [Function]

This function returns the size of an image as a pair (`width . height`). *spec* is an image specification. *pixels* non-`nil` means return sizes measured in pixels, otherwise return sizes measured in the default character size of *frame* (see Section 28.3.2 [Frame Font], page 639). *frame* is the frame on which the image will be displayed. *frame* null or omitted means use the selected frame (see Section 28.10 [Input Focus], page 656).

`max-image-size`   [Variable]

This variable is used to define the maximum size of image that Emacs will load. Emacs will refuse to load (and display) any image that is larger than this limit.

If the value is an integer, it directly specifies the maximum image height and width, measured in pixels. If it is floating point, it specifies the maximum image height and width as a ratio to the frame height and width. If the value is non-numeric, there is no explicit limit on the size of images.

The purpose of this variable is to prevent unreasonably large images from accidentally being loaded into Emacs. It only takes effect the first time an image is loaded. Once an image is placed in the image cache, it can always be displayed, even if the value of `max-image-size` is subsequently changed (see Section 37.17.11 [Image Cache], page 961).

37.17.10 Multi-Frame Images

Some image files can contain more than one image. We say that there are multiple "frames" in the image. At present, Emacs supports multiple frames for GIF, TIFF, and certain ImageMagick formats such as DJVM.

The frames can be used either to represent multiple pages (this is usually the case with multi-frame TIFF files, for example), or to create animation (usually the case with multi-frame GIF files).

A multi-frame image has a property `:index`, whose value is an integer (counting from 0) that specifies which frame is being displayed.

`image-multi-frame-p` *image*   [Function]

This function returns non-`nil` if *image* contains more than one frame. The actual return value is a cons (`nimages . delay`), where *nimages* is the number of frames and *delay* is the delay in seconds between them, or `nil` if the image does not specify a delay. Images that are intended to be animated usually specify a frame delay, whereas ones that are intended to be treated as multiple pages do not.

`image-current-frame` *image*   [Function]
> This function returns the index of the current frame number for *image*, counting from 0.

`image-show-frame` *image n* **&optional** *nocheck*   [Function]
> This function switches *image* to frame number *n*. It replaces a frame number outside the valid range with that of the end of the range, unless *nocheck* is non-`nil`. If *image* does not contain a frame with the specified number, the image displays as a hollow box.

`image-animate` *image* **&optional** *index limit*   [Function]
> This function animates *image*. The optional integer *index* specifies the frame from which to start (default 0). The optional argument *limit* controls the length of the animation. If omitted or `nil`, the image animates once only; if `t` it loops forever; if a number animation stops after that many seconds.

Animation operates by means of a timer. Note that Emacs imposes a minimum frame delay of 0.01 (`image-minimum-frame-delay`) seconds. If the image itself does not specify a delay, Emacs uses `image-default-frame-delay`.

`image-animate-timer` *image*   [Function]
> This function returns the timer responsible for animating *image*, if there is one.

37.17.11 Image Cache

Emacs caches images so that it can display them again more efficiently. When Emacs displays an image, it searches the image cache for an existing image specification `equal` to the desired specification. If a match is found, the image is displayed from the cache. Otherwise, Emacs loads the image normally.

`image-flush` *spec* **&optional** *frame*   [Function]
> This function removes the image with specification *spec* from the image cache of frame *frame*. Image specifications are compared using `equal`. If *frame* is `nil`, it defaults to the selected frame. If *frame* is `t`, the image is flushed on all existing frames.
>
> In Emacs's current implementation, each graphical terminal possesses an image cache, which is shared by all the frames on that terminal (see Section 28.2 [Multiple Terminals], page 631). Thus, refreshing an image in one frame also refreshes it in all other frames on the same terminal.

One use for `image-flush` is to tell Emacs about a change in an image file. If an image specification contains a `:file` property, the image is cached based on the file's contents when the image is first displayed. Even if the file subsequently changes, Emacs continues displaying the old version of the image. Calling `image-flush` flushes the image from the cache, forcing Emacs to re-read the file the next time it needs to display that image.

Another use for `image-flush` is for memory conservation. If your Lisp program creates a large number of temporary images over a period much shorter than `image-cache-eviction-delay` (see below), you can opt to flush unused images yourself, instead of waiting for Emacs to do it automatically.

`clear-image-cache` **&optional** *filter* [Function]

> This function clears an image cache, removing all the images stored in it. If *filter* is omitted or `nil`, it clears the cache for the selected frame. If *filter* is a frame, it clears the cache for that frame. If *filter* is `t`, all image caches are cleared. Otherwise, *filter* is taken to be a file name, and all images associated with that file name are removed from all image caches.

If an image in the image cache has not been displayed for a specified period of time, Emacs removes it from the cache and frees the associated memory.

`image-cache-eviction-delay` [Variable]

> This variable specifies the number of seconds an image can remain in the cache without being displayed. When an image is not displayed for this length of time, Emacs removes it from the image cache.
>
> Under some circumstances, if the number of images in the cache grows too large, the actual eviction delay may be shorter than this.
>
> If the value is `nil`, Emacs does not remove images from the cache except when you explicitly clear it. This mode can be useful for debugging.

37.18 Embedded Native Widgets

Emacs is able to display native widgets, such as GTK WebKit widgets, in Emacs buffers when it was built with the necessary support libraries and is running on a graphical terminal. To test whether Emacs supports display of embedded widgets, check that the `xwidget-internal` feature is available (see Section 15.7 [Named Features], page 253).

To display an embedded widget in a buffer, you must first create an xwidget object, and then use that object as the display specifier in a `display` text or overlay property (see Section 37.16 [Display Property], page 945).

`make-xwidget` *type title width height arguments* **&optional** *buffer* [Function]

> This creates and returns an xwidget object. If *buffer* is omitted or `nil`, it defaults to the current buffer. If *buffer* names a buffer that doesn't exist, it will be created. The *type* identifies the type of the xwidget component, it can be one of the following:
>
> `webkit`   The WebKit component.
>
> The *width* and *height* arguments specify the widget size in pixels, and *title*, a string, specifies its title.

`xwidgetp` *object* [Function]

> This function returns `t` if *object* is an xwidget, `nil` otherwise.

`xwidget-plist` *xwidget* [Function]

> This function returns the property list of *xwidget*.

`set-xwidget-plist` *xwidget plist* [Function]

> This function replaces the property list of *xwidget* with a new property list given by *plist*.

`xwidget-buffer` *xwidget* [Function]

> This function returns the buffer of *xwidget*.

get-buffer-xwidgets *buffer*   [Function]

    This function returns a list of xwidget objects associated with the *buffer*, which can be specified as a buffer object or a name of an existing buffer, a string. The value is `nil` if *buffer* contains no xwidgets.

xwidget-webkit-goto-uri *xwidget uri*   [Function]

    This function browses the specified *uri* in the given *xwidget*. The *uri* is a string that specifies the name of a file or a URL.

xwidget-webkit-execute-script *xwidget script*   [Function]

    This function causes the browser widget specified by *xwidget* to execute the specified JavaScript `script`.

xwidget-webkit-execute-script-rv *xwidget script* **&optional**   [Function]
      default

    This function executes the specified *script* like `xwidget-webkit-execute-script` does, but it also returns the script's return value as a string. If *script* doesn't return a value, this function returns *default*, or `nil` if *default* was omitted.

xwidget-webkit-get-title *xwidget*   [Function]

    This function returns the title of *xwidget* as a string.

xwidget-resize *xwidget width height*   [Function]

    This function resizes the specified *xwidget* to the size *widthxheight* pixels.

xwidget-size-request *xwidget*   [Function]

    This function returns the desired size of *xwidget* as a list of the form (`width height`). The dimensions are in pixels.

xwidget-info *xwidget*   [Function]

    This function returns the attributes of *xwidget* as a vector of the form [`type title width height`]. The attributes are usually determined by `make-xwidget` when the xwidget is created.

set-xwidget-query-on-exit-flag *xwidget flag*   [Function]

    This function allows you to arrange that Emacs will ask the user for confirmation before exiting or before killing a buffer that has *xwidget* associated with it. If *flag* is non-`nil`, Emacs will query the user, otherwise it will not.

xwidget-query-on-exit-flag *xwidget*   [Function]

    This function returns the current setting of *xwidget*s query-on-exit flag, either `t` or `nil`.

37.19 Buttons

The Button package defines functions for inserting and manipulating *buttons* that can be activated with the mouse or via keyboard commands. These buttons are typically used for various kinds of hyperlinks.

    A button is essentially a set of text or overlay properties, attached to a stretch of text in a buffer. These properties are called *button properties*. One of these properties, the *action property*, specifies a function which is called when the user invokes the button using the keyboard or the mouse. The action function may examine the button and use its other properties as desired.

In some ways, the Button package duplicates the functionality in the Widget package. See Section "Introduction" in *The Emacs Widget Library*. The advantage of the Button package is that it is faster, smaller, and simpler to program. From the point of view of the user, the interfaces produced by the two packages are very similar.

37.19.1 Button Properties

Each button has an associated list of properties defining its appearance and behavior, and other arbitrary properties may be used for application specific purposes. The following properties have special meaning to the Button package:

action
: The function to call when the user invokes the button, which is passed the single argument *button*. By default this is `ignore`, which does nothing.

mouse-action
: This is similar to `action`, and when present, will be used instead of `action` for button invocations resulting from mouse-clicks (instead of the user hitting RET). If not present, mouse-clicks use `action` instead.

face
: This is an Emacs face controlling how buttons of this type are displayed; by default this is the `button` face.

mouse-face
: This is an additional face which controls appearance during mouse-overs (merged with the usual button face); by default this is the usual Emacs `highlight` face.

keymap
: The button's keymap, defining bindings active within the button region. By default this is the usual button region keymap, stored in the variable `button-map`, which defines RET and `mouse-2` to invoke the button.

type
: The button type. See Section 37.19.2 [Button Types], page 965.

help-echo
: A string displayed by the Emacs tool-tip help system; by default, `"mouse-2, RET: Push this button"`.

follow-link
: The follow-link property, defining how a `mouse-1` click behaves on this button, See Section 31.19.8 [Clickable Text], page 746.

button
: All buttons have a non-`nil` `button` property, which may be useful in finding regions of text that comprise buttons (which is what the standard button functions do).

There are other properties defined for the regions of text in a button, but these are not generally interesting for typical uses.

37.19.2 Button Types

Every button has a *button type*, which defines default values for the button's properties. Button types are arranged in a hierarchy, with specialized types inheriting from more general types, so that it's easy to define special-purpose types of buttons for specific tasks.

`define-button-type` *name* **&rest** *properties*   [Function]

> Define a button type called *name* (a symbol). The remaining arguments form a sequence of *property value* pairs, specifying default property values for buttons with this type (a button's type may be set by giving it a `type` property when creating the button, using the `:type` keyword argument).
>
> In addition, the keyword argument `:supertype` may be used to specify a button-type from which *name* inherits its default property values. Note that this inheritance happens only when *name* is defined; subsequent changes to a supertype are not reflected in its subtypes.

Using `define-button-type` to define default properties for buttons is not necessary—buttons without any specified type use the built-in button-type `button`—but it is encouraged, since doing so usually makes the resulting code clearer and more efficient.

37.19.3 Making Buttons

Buttons are associated with a region of text, using an overlay or text properties to hold button-specific information, all of which are initialized from the button's type (which defaults to the built-in button type `button`). Like all Emacs text, the appearance of the button is governed by the `face` property; by default (via the `face` property inherited from the `button` button-type) this is a simple underline, like a typical web-page link.

For convenience, there are two sorts of button-creation functions, those that add button properties to an existing region of a buffer, called `make-...button`, and those that also insert the button text, called `insert-...button`.

The button-creation functions all take the **&rest** argument *properties*, which should be a sequence of *property value* pairs, specifying properties to add to the button; see Section 37.19.1 [Button Properties], page 964. In addition, the keyword argument `:type` may be used to specify a button-type from which to inherit other properties; see Section 37.19.2 [Button Types], page 965. Any properties not explicitly specified during creation will be inherited from the button's type (if the type defines such a property).

The following functions add a button using an overlay (see Section 37.9 [Overlays], page 904) to hold the button properties:

`make-button` *beg end* **&rest** *properties*   [Function]

> This makes a button from *beg* to *end* in the current buffer, and returns it.

`insert-button` *label* **&rest** *properties*   [Function]

> This insert a button with the label *label* at point, and returns it.

The following functions are similar, but using text properties (see Section 31.19 [Text Properties], page 732) to hold the button properties. Such buttons do not add markers to the buffer, so editing in the buffer does not slow down if there is an extremely large numbers of buttons. However, if there is an existing face text property on the text (e.g., a face assigned by Font Lock mode), the button face may not be visible. Both of these functions return the starting position of the new button.

make-text-button *beg end* **&rest** *properties*   [Function]
>   This makes a button from *beg* to *end* in the current buffer, using text properties.

insert-text-button *label* **&rest** *properties*   [Function]
>   This inserts a button with the label *label* at point, using text properties.

37.19.4 Manipulating Buttons

These are functions for getting and setting properties of buttons. Often these are used by a button's invocation function to determine what to do.

Where a *button* parameter is specified, it means an object referring to a specific button, either an overlay (for overlay buttons), or a buffer-position or marker (for text property buttons). Such an object is passed as the first argument to a button's invocation function when it is invoked.

button-start *button*   [Function]
>   Return the position at which *button* starts.

button-end *button*   [Function]
>   Return the position at which *button* ends.

button-get *button prop*   [Function]
>   Get the property of button *button* named *prop*.

button-put *button prop val*   [Function]
>   Set *button*'s *prop* property to *val*.

button-activate *button* **&optional** *use-mouse-action*   [Function]
>   Call *button*'s `action` property (i.e., invoke the function that is the value of that property, passing it the single argument *button*). If *use-mouse-action* is non-`nil`, try to invoke the button's `mouse-action` property instead of `action`; if the button has no `mouse-action` property, use `action` as normal.

button-label *button*   [Function]
>   Return *button*'s text label.

button-type *button*   [Function]
>   Return *button*'s button-type.

button-has-type-p *button type*   [Function]
>   Return `t` if *button* has button-type *type*, or one of *type*'s subtypes.

button-at *pos*   [Function]
>   Return the button at position *pos* in the current buffer, or `nil`. If the button at *pos* is a text property button, the return value is a marker pointing to *pos*.

button-type-put *type prop val*   [Function]
>   Set the button-type *type*'s *prop* property to *val*.

`button-type-get` *type prop*   [Function]
> Get the property of button-type *type* named *prop*.

`button-type-subtype-p` *type supertype*   [Function]
> Return `t` if button-type *type* is a subtype of *supertype*.

37.19.5 Button Buffer Commands

These are commands and functions for locating and operating on buttons in an Emacs buffer.

`push-button` is the command that a user uses to actually push a button, and is bound by default in the button itself to `RET` and to `mouse-2` using a local keymap in the button's overlay or text properties. Commands that are useful outside the buttons itself, such as `forward-button` and `backward-button` are additionally available in the keymap stored in `button-buffer-map`; a mode which uses buttons may want to use `button-buffer-map` as a parent keymap for its keymap.

If the button has a non-`nil` `follow-link` property, and `mouse-1-click-follows-link` is set, a quick `mouse-1` click will also activate the `push-button` command. See Section 31.19.8 [Clickable Text], page 746.

`push-button` **&optional** *pos use-mouse-action*   [Command]
> Perform the action specified by a button at location *pos*. *pos* may be either a buffer position or a mouse-event. If *use-mouse-action* is non-`nil`, or *pos* is a mouse-event (see Section 20.7.3 [Mouse Events], page 360), try to invoke the button's `mouse-action` property instead of `action`; if the button has no `mouse-action` property, use `action` as normal. *pos* defaults to point, except when `push-button` is invoked interactively as the result of a mouse-event, in which case, the mouse event's position is used. If there's no button at *pos*, do nothing and return `nil`, otherwise return `t`.

`forward-button` *n* **&optional** *wrap display-message*   [Command]
> Move to the *n*th next button, or *n*th previous button if *n* is negative. If *n* is zero, move to the start of any button at point. If *wrap* is non-`nil`, moving past either end of the buffer continues from the other end. If *display-message* is non-`nil`, the button's help-echo string is displayed. Any button with a non-`nil` `skip` property is skipped over. Returns the button found.

`backward-button` *n* **&optional** *wrap display-message*   [Command]
> Move to the *n*th previous button, or *n*th next button if *n* is negative. If *n* is zero, move to the start of any button at point. If *wrap* is non-`nil`, moving past either end of the buffer continues from the other end. If *display-message* is non-`nil`, the button's help-echo string is displayed. Any button with a non-`nil` `skip` property is skipped over. Returns the button found.

`next-button` *pos* **&optional** *count-current*   [Function]
`previous-button` *pos* **&optional** *count-current*   [Function]
> Return the next button after (for `next-button`) or before (for `previous-button`) position *pos* in the current buffer. If *count-current* is non-`nil`, count any button at *pos* in the search, instead of starting at the next button.

37.20 Abstract Display

The Ewoc package constructs buffer text that represents a structure of Lisp objects, and updates the text to follow changes in that structure. This is like the "view" component in the "model–view–controller" design paradigm. Ewoc means "Emacs's Widget for Object Collections".

An *ewoc* is a structure that organizes information required to construct buffer text that represents certain Lisp data. The buffer text of the ewoc has three parts, in order: first, fixed *header* text; next, textual descriptions of a series of data elements (Lisp objects that you specify); and last, fixed *footer* text. Specifically, an ewoc contains information on:

- The buffer which its text is generated in.
- The text's start position in the buffer.
- The header and footer strings.
- A doubly-linked chain of *nodes*, each of which contains:
  - A *data element*, a single Lisp object.
  - Links to the preceding and following nodes in the chain.
- A *pretty-printer* function which is responsible for inserting the textual representation of a data element value into the current buffer.

Typically, you define an ewoc with `ewoc-create`, and then pass the resulting ewoc structure to other functions in the Ewoc package to build nodes within it, and display it in the buffer. Once it is displayed in the buffer, other functions determine the correspondence between buffer positions and nodes, move point from one node's textual representation to another, and so forth. See Section 37.20.1 [Abstract Display Functions], page 968.

A node *encapsulates* a data element much the way a variable holds a value. Normally, encapsulation occurs as a part of adding a node to the ewoc. You can retrieve the data element value and place a new value in its place, like so:

```
(ewoc-data node)
⇒ value
```

```
(ewoc-set-data node new-value)
⇒ new-value
```

You can also use, as the data element value, a Lisp object (list or vector) that is a container for the real value, or an index into some other structure. The example (see Section 37.20.2 [Abstract Display Example], page 970) uses the latter approach.

When the data changes, you will want to update the text in the buffer. You can update all nodes by calling `ewoc-refresh`, or just specific nodes using `ewoc-invalidate`, or all nodes satisfying a predicate using `ewoc-map`. Alternatively, you can delete invalid nodes using `ewoc-delete` or `ewoc-filter`, and add new nodes in their place. Deleting a node from an ewoc deletes its associated textual description from buffer, as well.

37.20.1 Abstract Display Functions

In this subsection, *ewoc* and *node* stand for the structures described above (see Section 37.20 [Abstract Display], page 968), while *data* stands for an arbitrary Lisp object used as a data element.

ewoc-create *pretty-printer* **&optional** *header footer nosep*   [Function]

> This constructs and returns a new ewoc, with no nodes (and thus no data elements). *pretty-printer* should be a function that takes one argument, a data element of the sort you plan to use in this ewoc, and inserts its textual description at point using `insert` (and never `insert-before-markers`, because that would interfere with the Ewoc package's internal mechanisms).
>
> Normally, a newline is automatically inserted after the header, the footer and every node's textual description. If *nosep* is non-`nil`, no newline is inserted. This may be useful for displaying an entire ewoc on a single line, for example, or for making nodes invisible by arranging for *pretty-printer* to do nothing for those nodes.
>
> An ewoc maintains its text in the buffer that is current when you create it, so switch to the intended buffer before calling `ewoc-create`.

ewoc-buffer *ewoc*   [Function]

> This returns the buffer where *ewoc* maintains its text.

ewoc-get-hf *ewoc*   [Function]

> This returns a cons cell (`header . footer`) made from *ewoc*'s header and footer.

ewoc-set-hf *ewoc header footer*   [Function]

> This sets the header and footer of *ewoc* to the strings *header* and *footer*, respectively.

ewoc-enter-first *ewoc data*   [Function]
ewoc-enter-last *ewoc data*   [Function]

> These add a new node encapsulating *data*, putting it, respectively, at the beginning or end of *ewoc*'s chain of nodes.

ewoc-enter-before *ewoc node data*   [Function]
ewoc-enter-after *ewoc node data*   [Function]

> These add a new node encapsulating *data*, adding it to *ewoc* before or after *node*, respectively.

ewoc-prev *ewoc node*   [Function]
ewoc-next *ewoc node*   [Function]

> These return, respectively, the previous node and the next node of *node* in *ewoc*.

ewoc-nth *ewoc n*   [Function]

> This returns the node in *ewoc* found at zero-based index *n*. A negative *n* means count from the end. `ewoc-nth` returns `nil` if *n* is out of range.

ewoc-data *node*   [Function]

> This extracts the data encapsulated by *node* and returns it.

ewoc-set-data *node data*   [Function]

> This sets the data encapsulated by *node* to *data*.

ewoc-locate *ewoc* **&optional** *pos guess*   [Function]

> This determines the node in *ewoc* which contains point (or *pos* if specified), and returns that node. If *ewoc* has no nodes, it returns `nil`. If *pos* is before the first node, it returns the first node; if *pos* is after the last node, it returns the last node. The optional third arg *guess* should be a node that is likely to be near *pos*; this doesn't alter the result, but makes the function run faster.

`ewoc-location` *node*   [Function]
> This returns the start position of *node*.

`ewoc-goto-prev` *ewoc arg*   [Function]
`ewoc-goto-next` *ewoc arg*   [Function]
> These move point to the previous or next, respectively, *arg*th node in *ewoc*.
> `ewoc-goto-prev` does not move if it is already at the first node or if *ewoc* is empty,
> whereas `ewoc-goto-next` moves past the last node, returning `nil`. Excepting this
> special case, these functions return the node moved to.

`ewoc-goto-node` *ewoc node*   [Function]
> This moves point to the start of *node* in *ewoc*.

`ewoc-refresh` *ewoc*   [Function]
> This function regenerates the text of *ewoc*. It works by deleting the text between the
> header and the footer, i.e., all the data elements' representations, and then calling
> the pretty-printer function for each node, one by one, in order.

`ewoc-invalidate` *ewoc* **&rest** *nodes*   [Function]
> This is similar to `ewoc-refresh`, except that only *nodes* in *ewoc* are updated instead
> of the entire set.

`ewoc-delete` *ewoc* **&rest** *nodes*   [Function]
> This deletes each node in *nodes* from *ewoc*.

`ewoc-filter` *ewoc predicate* **&rest** *args*   [Function]
> This calls *predicate* for each data element in *ewoc* and deletes those nodes for which
> *predicate* returns `nil`. Any *args* are passed to *predicate*.

`ewoc-collect` *ewoc predicate* **&rest** *args*   [Function]
> This calls *predicate* for each data element in *ewoc* and returns a list of those elements
> for which *predicate* returns non-`nil`. The elements in the list are ordered as in the
> buffer. Any *args* are passed to *predicate*.

`ewoc-map` *map-function ewoc* **&rest** *args*   [Function]
> This calls *map-function* for each data element in *ewoc* and updates those nodes for
> which *map-function* returns non-`nil`. Any *args* are passed to *map-function*.

37.20.2 Abstract Display Example

Here is a simple example using functions of the ewoc package to implement a *color components* display, an area in a buffer that represents a vector of three integers (itself representing
a 24-bit RGB value) in various ways.

```
(setq colorcomp-ewoc nil
      colorcomp-data nil
      colorcomp-mode-map nil
      colorcomp-labels ["Red" "Green" "Blue"])

(defun colorcomp-pp (data)
  (if data
```

```
            (let ((comp (aref colorcomp-data data)))
              (insert (aref colorcomp-labels data) "\t: #x"
                      (format "%02X" comp) " "
                      (make-string (ash comp -2) ?#) "\n"))
          (let ((cstr (format "#%02X%02X%02X"
                              (aref colorcomp-data 0)
                              (aref colorcomp-data 1)
                              (aref colorcomp-data 2)))
                (samp " (sample text) "))
            (insert "Color\t: "
                    (propertize samp 'face
                                `(foreground-color . ,cstr))
                    (propertize samp 'face
                                `(background-color . ,cstr))
                    "\n")))))

(defun colorcomp (color)
  "Allow fiddling with COLOR in a new buffer.
The buffer is in Color Components mode."
  (interactive "sColor (name or #RGB or #RRGGBB): ")
  (when (string= "" color)
    (setq color "green"))
  (unless (color-values color)
    (error "No such color: %S" color))
  (switch-to-buffer
   (generate-new-buffer (format "originally: %s" color)))
  (kill-all-local-variables)
  (setq major-mode 'colorcomp-mode
        mode-name "Color Components")
  (use-local-map colorcomp-mode-map)
  (erase-buffer)
  (buffer-disable-undo)
  (let ((data (apply 'vector (mapcar (lambda (n) (ash n -8))
                                     (color-values color))))
        (ewoc (ewoc-create 'colorcomp-pp
                           "\nColor Components\n\n"
                           (substitute-command-keys
                            "\n\\{colorcomp-mode-map}"))))
    (set (make-local-variable 'colorcomp-data) data)
    (set (make-local-variable 'colorcomp-ewoc) ewoc)
    (ewoc-enter-last ewoc 0)
    (ewoc-enter-last ewoc 1)
    (ewoc-enter-last ewoc 2)
    (ewoc-enter-last ewoc nil)))
```

This example can be extended to be a color selection widget (in other words, the "controller" part of the "model–view–controller" design paradigm) by defining commands to modify `colorcomp-data` and to finish the selection process, and a keymap to tie it all together conveniently.

```
(defun colorcomp-mod (index limit delta)
  (let ((cur (aref colorcomp-data index)))
    (unless (= limit cur)
      (aset colorcomp-data index (+ cur delta)))
    (ewoc-invalidate
     colorcomp-ewoc
     (ewoc-nth colorcomp-ewoc index)
     (ewoc-nth colorcomp-ewoc -1))))

(defun colorcomp-R-more () (interactive) (colorcomp-mod 0 255 1))
(defun colorcomp-G-more () (interactive) (colorcomp-mod 1 255 1))
(defun colorcomp-B-more () (interactive) (colorcomp-mod 2 255 1))
(defun colorcomp-R-less () (interactive) (colorcomp-mod 0 0 -1))
(defun colorcomp-G-less () (interactive) (colorcomp-mod 1 0 -1))
(defun colorcomp-B-less () (interactive) (colorcomp-mod 2 0 -1))

(defun colorcomp-copy-as-kill-and-exit ()
  "Copy the color components into the kill ring and kill the buffer.
The string is formatted #RRGGBB (hash followed by six hex digits)."
  (interactive)
  (kill-new (format "#%02X%02X%02X"
                    (aref colorcomp-data 0)
                    (aref colorcomp-data 1)
                    (aref colorcomp-data 2)))
  (kill-buffer nil))

(setq colorcomp-mode-map
      (let ((m (make-sparse-keymap)))
        (suppress-keymap m)
        (define-key m "i" 'colorcomp-R-less)
        (define-key m "o" 'colorcomp-R-more)
        (define-key m "k" 'colorcomp-G-less)
        (define-key m "l" 'colorcomp-G-more)
        (define-key m "," 'colorcomp-B-less)
        (define-key m "." 'colorcomp-B-more)
        (define-key m " " 'colorcomp-copy-as-kill-and-exit)
        m))
```

Note that we never modify the data in each node, which is fixed when the ewoc is created to be either `nil` or an index into the vector `colorcomp-data`, the actual color components.

37.21 Blinking Parentheses

This section describes the mechanism by which Emacs shows a matching open parenthesis when the user inserts a close parenthesis.

`blink-paren-function`   [Variable]

> The value of this variable should be a function (of no arguments) to be called whenever a character with close parenthesis syntax is inserted. The value of `blink-paren-function` may be `nil`, in which case nothing is done.

`blink-matching-paren`   [User Option]

> If this variable is `nil`, then `blink-matching-open` does nothing.

blink-matching-paren-distance   [User Option]

> This variable specifies the maximum distance to scan for a matching parenthesis before giving up.

blink-matching-delay   [User Option]

> This variable specifies the number of seconds to keep indicating the matching parenthesis. A fraction of a second often gives good results, but the default is 1, which works on all systems.

blink-matching-open   [Command]

> This function is the default value of `blink-paren-function`. It assumes that point follows a character with close parenthesis syntax and applies the appropriate effect momentarily to the matching opening character. If that character is not already on the screen, it displays the character's context in the echo area. To avoid long delays, this function does not search farther than `blink-matching-paren-distance` characters.
>
> Here is an example of calling this function explicitly.
>
> ```
> (defun interactive-blink-matching-open ()
>   "Indicate momentarily the start of parenthesized sexp before point."
>   (interactive)
>   (let ((blink-matching-paren-distance
>          (buffer-size))
>         (blink-matching-paren t))
>     (blink-matching-open)))
> ```

37.22 Character Display

This section describes how characters are actually displayed by Emacs. Typically, a character is displayed as a *glyph* (a graphical symbol which occupies one character position on the screen), whose appearance corresponds to the character itself. For example, the character 'a' (character code 97) is displayed as 'a'. Some characters, however, are displayed specially. For example, the formfeed character (character code 12) is usually displayed as a sequence of two glyphs, '^L', while the newline character (character code 10) starts a new screen line.

You can modify how each character is displayed by defining a *display table*, which maps each character code into a sequence of glyphs. See Section 37.22.2 [Display Tables], page 974.

37.22.1 Usual Display Conventions

Here are the conventions for displaying each character code (in the absence of a display table, which can override these conventions).

- The *printable ASCII characters*, character codes 32 through 126 (consisting of numerals, English letters, and symbols like '#') are displayed literally.

- The tab character (character code 9) displays as whitespace stretching up to the next tab stop column. See Section "Text Display" in *The GNU Emacs Manual*. The variable `tab-width` controls the number of spaces per tab stop (see below).

- The newline character (character code 10) has a special effect: it ends the preceding line and starts a new line.

- The non-printable *ASCII control characters*—character codes 0 through 31, as well as the DEL character (character code 127)—display in one of two ways according to the variable `ctl-arrow`. If this variable is non-`nil` (the default), these characters are displayed as sequences of two glyphs, where the first glyph is '^' (a display table can specify a glyph to use instead of '^'); e.g., the DEL character is displayed as '^?'.

If `ctl-arrow` is `nil`, these characters are displayed as octal escapes (see below).

This rule also applies to carriage return (character code 13), if that character appears in the buffer. But carriage returns usually do not appear in buffer text; they are eliminated as part of end-of-line conversion (see Section 32.10.1 [Coding System Basics], page 774).

- *Raw bytes* are non-ASCII characters with codes 128 through 255 (see Section 32.1 [Text Representations], page 761). These characters display as *octal escapes*: sequences of four glyphs, where the first glyph is the ASCII code for '\', and the others are digit characters representing the character code in octal. (A display table can specify a glyph to use instead of '\'.)

- Each non-ASCII character with code above 255 is displayed literally, if the terminal supports it. If the terminal does not support it, the character is said to be *glyphless*, and it is usually displayed using a placeholder glyph. For example, if a graphical terminal has no font for a character, Emacs usually displays a box containing the character code in hexadecimal. See Section 37.22.5 [Glyphless Chars], page 977.

The above display conventions apply even when there is a display table, for any character whose entry in the active display table is `nil`. Thus, when you set up a display table, you need only specify the characters for which you want special behavior.

The following variables affect how certain characters are displayed on the screen. Since they change the number of columns the characters occupy, they also affect the indentation functions. They also affect how the mode line is displayed; if you want to force redisplay of the mode line using the new values, call the function `force-mode-line-update` (see Section 22.4 [Mode Line Format], page 451).

`ctl-arrow`   [User Option]
> This buffer-local variable controls how control characters are displayed. If it is non-`nil`, they are displayed as a caret followed by the character: '^A'. If it is `nil`, they are displayed as octal escapes: a backslash followed by three octal digits, as in '\001'.

`tab-width`   [User Option]
> The value of this buffer-local variable is the spacing between tab stops used for displaying tab characters in Emacs buffers. The value is in units of columns, and the default is 8. Note that this feature is completely independent of the user-settable tab stops used by the command `tab-to-tab-stop`. See Section 31.17.5 [Indent Tabs], page 730.

37.22.2 Display Tables

A display table is a special-purpose char-table (see Section 6.6 [Char-Tables], page 104), with `display-table` as its subtype, which is used to override the usual character display conventions. This section describes how to make, inspect, and assign elements to a display table object.

`make-display-table`   [Function]
> This creates and returns a display table. The table initially has `nil` in all elements.

The ordinary elements of the display table are indexed by character codes; the element at index c says how to display the character code c. The value should be `nil` (which means to display the character c according to the usual display conventions; see Section 37.22.1 [Usual Display], page 973), or a vector of glyph codes (which means to display the character c as those glyphs; see Section 37.22.4 [Glyphs], page 976).

Warning: if you use the display table to change the display of newline characters, the whole buffer will be displayed as one long line.

The display table also has six *extra slots* which serve special purposes. Here is a table of their meanings; `nil` in any slot means to use the default for that slot, as stated below.

0   The glyph for the end of a truncated screen line (the default for this is '$'). See Section 37.22.4 [Glyphs], page 976. On graphical terminals, Emacs uses arrows in the fringes to indicate truncation, so the display table has no effect.

1   The glyph for the end of a continued line (the default is '\'). On graphical terminals, Emacs uses curved arrows in the fringes to indicate continuation, so the display table has no effect.

2   The glyph for indicating a character displayed as an octal character code (the default is '\').

3   The glyph for indicating a control character (the default is '^').

4   A vector of glyphs for indicating the presence of invisible lines (the default is '...'). See Section 37.7 [Selective Display], page 899.

5   The glyph used to draw the border between side-by-side windows (the default is '|'). See Section 27.6 [Splitting Windows], page 581. This takes effect only when there are no scroll bars; if scroll bars are supported and in use, a scroll bar separates the two windows.

For example, here is how to construct a display table that mimics the effect of setting `ctl-arrow` to a non-`nil` value (see Section 37.22.4 [Glyphs], page 976, for the function `make-glyph-code`):

```
(setq disptab (make-display-table))
(dotimes (i 32)
  (or (= i ?\t)
      (= i ?\n)
      (aset disptab i
            (vector (make-glyph-code ?^ 'escape-glyph)
                    (make-glyph-code (+ i 64) 'escape-glyph)))))
(aset disptab 127
      (vector (make-glyph-code ?^ 'escape-glyph)
              (make-glyph-code ?? 'escape-glyph)))))
```

`display-table-slot` *display-table slot*   [Function]
          This function returns the value of the extra slot *slot* of *display-table*. The argument *slot* may be a number from 0 to 5 inclusive, or a slot name (symbol). Valid symbols are `truncation`, `wrap`, `escape`, `control`, `selective-display`, and `vertical-border`.

set-display-table-slot *display-table slot value*   [Function]
>   This function stores *value* in the extra slot *slot* of *display-table*. The argument *slot*
>   may be a number from 0 to 5 inclusive, or a slot name (symbol). Valid symbols are
>   `truncation`, `wrap`, `escape`, `control`, `selective-display`, and `vertical-border`.

describe-display-table *display-table*   [Function]
>   This function displays a description of the display table *display-table* in a help buffer.

describe-current-display-table   [Command]
>   This command displays a description of the current display table in a help buffer.

37.22.3 Active Display Table

Each window can specify a display table, and so can each buffer. The window's display
table, if there is one, takes precedence over the buffer's display table. If neither exists,
Emacs tries to use the standard display table; if that is `nil`, Emacs uses the usual character
display conventions (see Section 37.22.1 [Usual Display], page 973).

Note that display tables affect how the mode line is displayed, so if you want to force
redisplay of the mode line using a new display table, call `force-mode-line-update` (see
Section 22.4 [Mode Line Format], page 451).

window-display-table **&optional** *window*   [Function]
>   This function returns *window*'s display table, or `nil` if there is none. The default for
>   *window* is the selected window.

set-window-display-table *window table*   [Function]
>   This function sets the display table of *window* to *table*. The argument *table* should
>   be either a display table or `nil`.

buffer-display-table   [Variable]
>   This variable is automatically buffer-local in all buffers; its value specifies the buffer's
>   display table. If it is `nil`, there is no buffer display table.

standard-display-table   [Variable]
>   The value of this variable is the standard display table, which is used when Emacs
>   is displaying a buffer in a window with neither a window display table nor a buffer
>   display table defined, or when Emacs is outputting text to the standard output or
>   error streams. Although its default is typically `nil`, in an interactive session if the
>   terminal cannot display curved quotes, its default maps curved quotes to ASCII ap-
>   proximations. See Section 23.3 [Keys in Documentation], page 488.

The `disp-table` library defines several functions for changing the standard display table.

37.22.4 Glyphs

A *glyph* is a graphical symbol which occupies a single character position on the screen. Each
glyph is represented in Lisp as a *glyph code*, which specifies a character and optionally a
face to display it in (see Section 37.12 [Faces], page 915). The main use of glyph codes is as
the entries of display tables (see Section 37.22.2 [Display Tables], page 974). The following
functions are used to manipulate glyph codes:

make-glyph-code *char* **&optional** *face*   [Function]
>   This function returns a glyph code representing char *char* with face *face*. If *face* is
>   omitted or **nil**, the glyph uses the default face; in that case, the glyph code is an
>   integer. If *face* is non-**nil**, the glyph code is not necessarily an integer object.

glyph-char *glyph*   [Function]
>   This function returns the character of glyph code *glyph*.

glyph-face *glyph*   [Function]
>   This function returns face of glyph code *glyph*, or **nil** if *glyph* uses the default face.

37.22.5 Glyphless Character Display

Glyphless characters are characters which are displayed in a special way, e.g., as a box
containing a hexadecimal code, instead of being displayed literally. These include characters
which are explicitly defined to be glyphless, as well as characters for which there is no
available font (on a graphical display), and characters which cannot be encoded by the
terminal's coding system (on a text terminal).

glyphless-char-display   [Variable]
>   The value of this variable is a char-table which defines glyphless characters and how
>   they are displayed. Each entry must be one of the following display methods:
>
>   **nil**   Display the character in the usual way.
>
>   **zero-width**
>   Don't display the character.
>
>   **thin-space**
>   Display a thin space, 1-pixel wide on graphical displays, or 1-character
>   wide on text terminals.
>
>   **empty-box**
>   Display an empty box.
>
>   **hex-code** Display a box containing the Unicode codepoint of the character, in hex-
>   adecimal notation.
>
>   an ASCII string
>   Display a box containing that string. The string should contain at most
>   6 ASCII characters.
>
>   a cons cell (*graphical . text*)
>   Display with *graphical* on graphical displays, and with *text* on text ter-
>   minals. Both *graphical* and *text* must be one of the display methods
>   described above.
>
>   The **thin-space**, **empty-box**, **hex-code**, and ASCII string display methods are drawn
>   with the **glyphless-char** face. On text terminals, a box is emulated by square
>   brackets, '**[]**'.
>
>   The char-table has one extra slot, which determines how to display any character
>   that cannot be displayed with any available font, or cannot be encoded by the ter-
>   minal's coding system. Its value should be one of the above display methods, except
>   **zero-width** or a cons cell.

If a character has a non-`nil` entry in an active display table, the display table takes effect; in this case, Emacs does not consult `glyphless-char-display` at all.

`glyphless-char-display-control`   [User Option]

> This user option provides a convenient way to set `glyphless-char-display` for groups of similar characters. Do not set its value directly from Lisp code; the value takes effect only via a custom `:set` function (see Section 14.3 [Variable Definitions], page 228), which updates `glyphless-char-display`.
>
> Its value should be an alist of elements (*group* . *method*), where *group* is a symbol specifying a group of characters, and *method* is a symbol specifying how to display them.
>
> *group* should be one of the following:
>
> `c0-control`
> > ASCII control characters U+0000 to U+001F, excluding the newline and tab characters (normally displayed as escape sequences like '`^A`'; see Section "How Text Is Displayed" in *The GNU Emacs Manual*).
>
> `c1-control`
> > Non-ASCII, non-printing characters U+0080 to U+009F (normally displayed as octal escape sequences like '`\230`').
>
> `format-control`
> > Characters of Unicode General Category [Cf], such as 'U+200E' (Left-to-Right Mark), but excluding characters that have graphic images, such as 'U+00AD' (Soft Hyphen).
>
> `no-font` Characters for there is no suitable font, or which cannot be encoded by the terminal's coding system.
>
> The *method* symbol should be one of `zero-width`, `thin-space`, `empty-box`, or `hex-code`. These have the same meanings as in `glyphless-char-display`, above.

37.23 Beeping

This section describes how to make Emacs ring the bell (or blink the screen) to attract the user's attention. Be conservative about how often you do this; frequent bells can become irritating. Also be careful not to use just beeping when signaling an error is more appropriate (see Section 10.6.3 [Errors], page 148).

`ding` &optional *do-not-terminate*   [Function]

> This function beeps, or flashes the screen (see `visible-bell` below). It also terminates any keyboard macro currently executing unless *do-not-terminate* is non-`nil`.

`beep` &optional *do-not-terminate*   [Function]

> This is a synonym for `ding`.

`visible-bell`   [User Option]

> This variable determines whether Emacs should flash the screen to represent a bell. Non-`nil` means yes, `nil` means no. This is effective on graphical displays, and on text terminals provided the terminal's Termcap entry defines the visible bell capability ('`vb`').

`ring-bell-function`   [User Option]
> If this is non-`nil`, it specifies how Emacs should ring the bell. Its value should
> be a function of no arguments. If this is non-`nil`, it takes precedence over the
> `visible-bell` variable.

37.24 Window Systems

Emacs works with several window systems, most notably the X Window System. Both
Emacs and X use the term "window", but use it differently. An Emacs frame is a single
window as far as X is concerned; the individual Emacs windows are not known to X at all.

`window-system`   [Variable]
> This terminal-local variable tells Lisp programs what window system Emacs is using
> for displaying the frame. The possible values are
>
> | | |
> |---|---|
> | `x` | Emacs is displaying the frame using X. |
> | `w32` | Emacs is displaying the frame using native MS-Windows GUI. |
> | `ns` | Emacs is displaying the frame using the Nextstep interface (used on GNUstep and macOS). |
> | `pc` | Emacs is displaying the frame using MS-DOS direct screen writes. |
> | `nil` | Emacs is displaying the frame on a character-based terminal. |

`initial-window-system`   [Variable]
> This variable holds the value of `window-system` used for the first frame created by
> Emacs during startup. (When Emacs is invoked with the `--daemon` option, it does not
> create any initial frames, so `initial-window-system` is `nil`, except on MS-Windows,
> where it is still `w32`. See Section "Initial Options" in *The GNU Emacs Manual*.)

`window-system` &optional *frame*   [Function]
> This function returns a symbol whose name tells what window system is used for
> displaying *frame* (which defaults to the currently selected frame). The list of possible
> symbols it returns is the same one documented for the variable `window-system` above.

Do *not* use `window-system` and `initial-window-system` as predicates or boolean flag
variables, if you want to write code that works differently on text terminals and graphic
displays. That is because `window-system` is not a good indicator of Emacs capabilities on
a given display type. Instead, use `display-graphic-p` or any of the other `display-*-p`
predicates described in Section 28.24 [Display Feature Testing], page 669.

37.25 Tooltips

Tooltips are special frames (see Chapter 28 [Frames], page 630) that are used to display
helpful hints (a.k.a. "tips") related to the current position of the mouse pointer. Emacs
uses tooltips to display help strings about active portions of text (see Section 31.19.4
[Special Properties], page 738) and about various UI elements, such as menu items
(see Section 21.17.1.2 [Extended Menu Items], page 417) and tool-bar buttons (see
Section 21.17.6 [Tool Bar], page 423).

`tooltip-mode`   [Function]
    Tooltip Mode is a minor mode that enables display of tooltips. Turning off this mode causes the tooltips be displayed in the echo area. On text-mode (a.k.a. "TTY") frames, tooltips are always displayed in the echo area.

When Emacs is built with GTK+ support, it by default displays tooltips using GTK+ functions, and the appearance of the tooltips is then controlled by GTK+ settings. GTK+ tooltips can be disabled by changing the value of the variable `x-gtk-use-system-tooltips` to `nil`. The rest of this subsection describes how to control non-GTK+ tooltips, which are presented by Emacs itself.

Since tooltips are special frames, they have their frame parameters (see Section 28.4 [Frame Parameters], page 642). Unlike other frames, the frame parameters for tooltips are stored in a special variable.

`tooltip-frame-parameters`   [Variable]
    This customizable option holds the frame parameters used for displaying tooltips. Any font and color parameters are ignored, and the corresponding attributes of the `tooltip` face are used instead. If `left` or `top` parameters are included, they are used as absolute frame-relative coordinates where the tooltip should be shown. (Mouse-relative position of the tooltip can be customized using the variables described in Section "Tooltips" in *The GNU Emacs Manual*.) Note that the `left` and `top` parameters, if present, override the values of mouse-relative offsets.

The `tooltip` face determines the appearance of text shown in tooltips. It should generally use a variable-pitch font of size that is preferably smaller than the default frame font.

`tooltip-functions`   [Variable]
    This abnormal hook is a list of functions to call when Emacs needs to display a tooltip. Each function is called with a single argument *event* which is a copy of the last mouse movement event. If a function on this list actually displays the tooltip, it should return non-`nil`, and then the rest of the functions will not be called. The default value of this variable is a single function `tooltip-help-tips`.

If you write your own function to be put on the `tooltip-functions` list, you may need to know the buffer of the mouse event that triggered the tooltip display. The following function provides that information.

`tooltip-event-buffer` *event*   [Function]
    This function returns the buffer over which *event* occurred. Call it with the argument of the function from `tooltip-functions` to obtain the buffer whose text triggered the tooltip. Note that the event might occur not over a buffer (e.g., over the tool bar), in which case this function will return `nil`.

Other aspects of tooltip display are controlled by several customizable settings; see Section "Tooltips" in *The GNU Emacs Manual*.

37.26 Bidirectional Display

Emacs can display text written in scripts, such as Arabic, Farsi, and Hebrew, whose natural ordering for horizontal text display runs from right to left. Furthermore, segments of Latin script and digits embedded in right-to-left text are displayed left-to-right, while segments of right-to-left script embedded in left-to-right text (e.g., Arabic or Hebrew text in comments or strings in a program source file) are appropriately displayed right-to-left. We call such mixtures of left-to-right and right-to-left text *bidirectional text*. This section describes the facilities and options for editing and displaying bidirectional text.

Text is stored in Emacs buffers and strings in *logical* (or *reading*) order, i.e., the order in which a human would read each character. In right-to-left and bidirectional text, the order in which characters are displayed on the screen (called *visual order*) is not the same as logical order; the characters' screen positions do not increase monotonically with string or buffer position. In performing this *bidirectional reordering*, Emacs follows the Unicode Bidirectional Algorithm (a.k.a. UBA), which is described in Annex #9 of the Unicode standard (`http://www.unicode.org/reports/tr9/`). Emacs provides a "Full Bidirectionality" class implementation of the UBA, consistent with the requirements of the Unicode Standard v8.0.

`bidi-display-reordering`   [Variable]

> If the value of this buffer-local variable is non-`nil` (the default), Emacs performs bidirectional reordering for display. The reordering affects buffer text, as well as display strings and overlay strings from text and overlay properties in the buffer (see Section 37.9.2 [Overlay Properties], page 907, and see Section 37.16 [Display Property], page 945). If the value is `nil`, Emacs does not perform bidirectional reordering in the buffer.

> The default value of `bidi-display-reordering` controls the reordering of strings which are not directly supplied by a buffer, including the text displayed in mode lines (see Section 22.4 [Mode Line Format], page 451) and header lines (see Section 22.4.7 [Header Lines], page 458).

Emacs never reorders the text of a unibyte buffer, even if `bidi-display-reordering` is non-`nil` in the buffer. This is because unibyte buffers contain raw bytes, not characters, and thus lack the directionality properties required for reordering. Therefore, to test whether text in a buffer will be reordered for display, it is not enough to test the value of `bidi-display-reordering` alone. The correct test is this:

```
(if (and enable-multibyte-characters
         bidi-display-reordering)
  ;; Buffer is being reordered for display
)
```

However, unibyte display and overlay strings *are* reordered if their parent buffer is reordered. This is because plain-ASCII strings are stored by Emacs as unibyte strings. If a unibyte display or overlay string includes non-ASCII characters, these characters are assumed to have left-to-right direction.

Text covered by `display` text properties, by overlays with `display` properties whose value is a string, and by any other properties that replace buffer text, is treated as a single unit when it is reordered for display. That is, the entire chunk of text covered by these properties is reordered together. Moreover, the bidirectional properties of the characters in such a chunk of text are ignored, and Emacs reorders them as if they were replaced with a single character U+FFFC, known as the *Object Replacement Character*. This means that placing a display property over a portion of text may change the way that the surrounding text is reordered for display. To prevent this unexpected effect, always place such properties on text whose directionality is identical with text that surrounds it.

Each paragraph of bidirectional text has a *base direction*, either right-to-left or left-to-right. Left-to-right paragraphs are displayed beginning at the left margin of the window, and are truncated or continued when the text reaches the right margin. Right-to-left paragraphs are displayed beginning at the right margin, and are continued or truncated at the left margin.

By default, Emacs determines the base direction of each paragraph by looking at the text at its beginning. The precise method of determining the base direction is specified by the UBA; in a nutshell, the first character in a paragraph that has an explicit directionality determines the base direction of the paragraph. However, sometimes a buffer may need to force a certain base direction for its paragraphs. For example, buffers containing program source code should force all paragraphs to be displayed left-to-right. You can use following variable to do this:

bidi-paragraph-direction   [Variable]
>   If the value of this buffer-local variable is the symbol **right-to-left** or **left-to-right**, all paragraphs in the buffer are assumed to have that specified direction. Any other value is equivalent to **nil** (the default), which means to determine the base direction of each paragraph from its contents.
>
>   Modes for program source code should set this to **left-to-right**. Prog mode does this by default, so modes derived from Prog mode do not need to set this explicitly (see Section 22.2.5 [Basic Major Modes], page 440).

current-bidi-paragraph-direction &optional *buffer*   [Function]
>   This function returns the paragraph direction at point in the named *buffer*. The returned value is a symbol, either **left-to-right** or **right-to-left**. If *buffer* is omitted or **nil**, it defaults to the current buffer. If the buffer-local value of the variable **bidi-paragraph-direction** is non-**nil**, the returned value will be identical to that value; otherwise, the returned value reflects the paragraph direction determined dynamically by Emacs. For buffers whose value of **bidi-display-reordering** is **nil** as well as unibyte buffers, this function always returns **left-to-right**.

Sometimes there's a need to move point in strict visual order, either to the left or to the right of its current screen position. Emacs provides a primitive to do that.

move-point-visually *direction*   [Function]
>   This function moves point of the currently selected window to the buffer position that appears immediately to the right or to the left of point on the screen. If *direction* is positive, point will move one screen position to the right, otherwise it will move one screen position to the left. Note that, depending on the surrounding bidirectional context, this could potentially move point many buffer positions away. If invoked at the end of a screen line, the function moves point to the rightmost or leftmost screen position of the next or previous screen line, as appropriate for the value of *direction*.

The function returns the new buffer position as its value.

Bidirectional reordering can have surprising and unpleasant effects when two strings with bidirectional content are juxtaposed in a buffer, or otherwise programmatically concatenated into a string of text. A typical problematic case is when a buffer consists of sequences of text fields separated by whitespace or punctuation characters, like Buffer Menu mode or Rmail Summary Mode. Because the punctuation characters used as separators have *weak directionality*, they take on the directionality of surrounding text. As result, a numeric field that follows a field with bidirectional content can be displayed *to the left* of the preceding field, messing up the expected layout. There are several ways to avoid this problem:

- Append the special character U+200E, LEFT-TO-RIGHT MARK, or LRM, to the end of each field that may have bidirectional content, or prepend it to the beginning of the following field. The function `bidi-string-mark-left-to-right`, described below, comes in handy for this purpose. (In a right-to-left paragraph, use U+200F, RIGHT-TO-LEFT MARK, or RLM, instead.) This is one of the solutions recommended by the UBA.

- Include the tab character in the field separator. The tab character plays the role of *segment separator* in bidirectional reordering, causing the text on either side to be reordered separately.

- Separate fields with a `display` property or overlay with a property value of the form `(space . PROPS)` (see Section 37.16.2 [Specified Space], page 946). Emacs treats this display specification as a *paragraph separator*, and reorders the text on either side separately.

`bidi-string-mark-left-to-right` *string*   [Function]
    This function returns its argument *string*, possibly modified, such that the result can be safely concatenated with another string, or juxtaposed with another string in a buffer, without disrupting the relative layout of this string and the next one on display. If the string returned by this function is displayed as part of a left-to-right paragraph, it will always appear on display to the left of the text that follows it. The function works by examining the characters of its argument, and if any of those characters could cause reordering on display, the function appends the LRM character to the string. The appended LRM character is made invisible by giving it an `invisible` text property of `t` (see Section 37.6 [Invisible Text], page 896).

The reordering algorithm uses the bidirectional properties of the characters stored as their `bidi-class` property (see Section 32.6 [Character Properties], page 766). Lisp programs can change these properties by calling the `put-char-code-property` function. However, doing this requires a thorough understanding of the UBA, and is therefore not recommended. Any changes to the bidirectional properties of a character have global effect: they affect all Emacs frames and windows.

Similarly, the `mirroring` property is used to display the appropriate mirrored character in the reordered text. Lisp programs can affect the mirrored display by changing this property. Again, any such changes affect all of Emacs display.

The bidirectional properties of characters can be overridden by inserting into the text special directional control characters, LEFT-TO-RIGHT OVERRIDE (LRO) and RIGHT-TO-LEFT OVERRIDE (RLO). Any characters between a RLO and the following newline or POP DIRECTIONAL FORMATTING (PDF) control character, whichever comes first, will be displayed as if they were strong right-to-left characters, i.e. they will be reversed on display. Similarly, any characters between LRO and PDF or newline will display as if they were strong left-to-right, and will *not* be reversed even if they are strong right-to-left characters.

These overrides are useful when you want to make some text unaffected by the reordering algorithm, and instead directly control the display order. But they can also be used for malicious purposes, known as *phishing*. Specifically, a URL on a Web page or a link in an email message can be manipulated to make its visual appearance unrecognizable, or similar to some popular benign location, while the real location, interpreted by a browser in the logical order, is very different.

Emacs provides a primitive that applications can use to detect instances of text whose bidirectional properties were overridden so as to make a left-to-right character display as if it were a right-to-left character, or vise versa.

`bidi-find-overridden-directionality` *from to* **&optional** *object*   [Function]
> This function looks at the text of the specified *object* between positions *from* (inclusive) and *to* (exclusive), and returns the first position where it finds a strong left-to-right character whose directional properties were forced to display the character as right-to-left, or for a strong right-to-left character that was forced to display as left-to-right. If it finds no such characters in the specified region of text, it returns `nil`.
>
> The optional argument *object* specifies which text to search, and defaults to the current buffer. If *object* is non-`nil`, it can be some other buffer, or it can be a string or a window. If it is a string, the function searches that string. If it is a window, the function searches the buffer displayed in that window. If a buffer whose text you want to examine is displayed in some window, we recommend to specify it by that window, rather than pass the buffer to the function. This is because telling the function about the window allows it to correctly account for window-specific overlays, which might change the result of the function if some text in the buffer is covered by overlays.

When text that includes mixed right-to-left and left-to-right characters and bidirectional controls is copied into a different location, it can change its visual appearance, and also can affect the visual appearance of the surrounding text at destination. This is because reordering of bidirectional text specified by the UBA has non-trivial context-dependent effects both on the copied text and on the text at copy destination that will surround it.

Sometimes, a Lisp program may need to preserve the exact visual appearance of the copied text at destination, and of the text that surrounds the copy. Lisp programs can use the following function to achieve that effect.

`buffer-substring-with-bidi-context` *start end* **&optional**   [Function]
> *no-properties*
> This function works similar to `buffer-substring` (see Section 31.2 [Buffer Contents], page 697), but it prepends and appends to the copied text bidi directional control characters necessary to preserve the visual appearance of the text when it is inserted at another place. Optional argument *no-properties*, if non-`nil`, means remove the text properties from the copy of the text.

38 Operating System Interface

This chapter is about starting and getting out of Emacs, access to values in the operating system environment, and terminal input, output.

See Section E.1 [Building Emacs], page 1067, for related information. See Chapter 37 [Display], page 886, for additional operating system status information pertaining to the terminal and the screen.

38.1 Starting Up Emacs

This section describes what Emacs does when it is started, and how you can customize these actions.

38.1.1 Summary: Sequence of Actions at Startup

When Emacs is started up, it performs the following operations (see `normal-top-level` in `startup.el`):

1. It adds subdirectories to `load-path`, by running the file named `subdirs.el` in each directory in the list. Normally, this file adds the directory's subdirectories to the list, and those are scanned in their turn. The files `subdirs.el` are normally generated automatically when Emacs is installed.

2. It loads any `leim-list.el` that it finds in the `load-path` directories. This file is intended for registering input methods. The search is only for any personal `leim-list.el` files that you may have created; it skips the directories containing the standard Emacs libraries (these should contain only a single `leim-list.el` file, which is compiled into the Emacs executable).

3. It sets the variable `before-init-time` to the value of `current-time` (see Section 38.5 [Time of Day], page 999). It also sets `after-init-time` to `nil`, which signals to Lisp programs that Emacs is being initialized.

4. It sets the language environment and the terminal coding system, if requested by environment variables such as `LANG`.

5. It does some basic parsing of the command-line arguments.

6. If not running in batch mode, it initializes the window system that the variable `initial-window-system` specifies (see Section 37.24 [Window Systems], page 979). The initialization function for each supported window system is specified by `window-system-initialization-alist`. If the value of `initial-window-system` is *windowsystem*, then the appropriate initialization function is defined in the file `term/`*windowsystem*`-win.el`. This file should have been compiled into the Emacs executable when it was built.

7. It runs the normal hook `before-init-hook`.

8. If appropriate, it creates a graphical frame. This is not done if the options '`--batch`' or '`--daemon`' were specified.

9. It initializes the initial frame's faces, and sets up the menu bar and tool bar if needed. If graphical frames are supported, it sets up the tool bar even if the current frame is not a graphical one, since a graphical frame may be created later on.

10. It use `custom-reevaluate-setting` to re-initialize the members of the list `custom-delayed-init-variables`. These are any pre-loaded user options whose default value depends on the run-time, rather than build-time, context. See Section E.1 [Building Emacs], page 1067.

11. It loads the library `site-start`, if it exists. This is not done if the options '-Q' or '--no-site-file' were specified.

12. It loads your init file (see Section 38.1.2 [Init File], page 988). This is not done if the options '-q', '-Q', or '--batch' were specified. If the '-u' option was specified, Emacs looks for the init file in that user's home directory instead.

13. It loads the library `default`, if it exists. This is not done if `inhibit-default-init` is non-nil, nor if the options '-q', '-Q', or '--batch' were specified.

14. It loads your abbrevs from the file specified by `abbrev-file-name`, if that file exists and can be read (see Section 35.3 [Abbrev Files], page 834). This is not done if the option '--batch' was specified.

15. It calls the function `package-initialize` to activate any optional Emacs Lisp package that has been installed. See Section 39.1 [Packaging Basics], page 1026. However, Emacs doesn't initialize packages when `package-enable-at-startup` is `nil` or when it's started with one of the options '-q', '-Q', or '--batch'. To initialize packages in the latter case, `package-initialize` should be called explicitly (e.g., via the '--funcall' option).

16. It sets the variable `after-init-time` to the value of `current-time`. This variable was set to `nil` earlier; setting it to the current time signals that the initialization phase is over, and, together with `before-init-time`, provides the measurement of how long it took.

17. It runs the normal hook `after-init-hook`.

18. If the buffer `*scratch*` exists and is still in Fundamental mode (as it should be by default), it sets its major mode according to `initial-major-mode`.

19. If started on a text terminal, it loads the terminal-specific Lisp library (see Section 38.1.3 [Terminal-Specific], page 989), and runs the hook `tty-setup-hook`. This is not done in --batch mode, nor if `term-file-prefix` is `nil`.

20. It displays the initial echo area message, unless you have suppressed that with `inhibit-startup-echo-area-message`.

21. It processes any command-line options that were not handled earlier.

22. It now exits if the option --batch was specified.

23. If the `*scratch*` buffer exists and is empty, it inserts (`substitute-command-keys initial-scratch-message`) into that buffer.

24. If `initial-buffer-choice` is a string, it visits the file (or directory) with that name. If it is a function, it calls the function with no arguments and selects the buffer that it returns. If one file is given as a command line argument, that file is visited and its buffer displayed alongside `initial-buffer-choice`. If more than one file is given, all of the files are visited and the `*Buffer List*` buffer is displayed alongside `initial-buffer-choice`.

25. It runs `emacs-startup-hook`.

26. It calls `frame-notice-user-settings`, which modifies the parameters of the selected frame according to whatever the init files specify.

27. It runs `window-setup-hook`. The only difference between this hook and `emacs-startup-hook` is that this one runs after the previously mentioned modifications to the frame parameters.

28. It displays the *startup screen*, which is a special buffer that contains information about copyleft and basic Emacs usage. This is not done if `inhibit-startup-screen` or `initial-buffer-choice` are non-`nil`, or if the '`--no-splash`' or '`-Q`' command-line options were specified.

29. If the option `--daemon` was specified, it calls `server-start`, and on Posix systems also detaches from the controlling terminal. See Section "Emacs Server" in *The GNU Emacs Manual*.

30. If started by the X session manager, it calls `emacs-session-restore` passing it as argument the ID of the previous session. See Section 38.18 [Session Management], page 1014.

The following options affect some aspects of the startup sequence.

`inhibit-startup-screen`   [User Option]

> This variable, if non-`nil`, inhibits the startup screen. In that case, Emacs typically displays the `*scratch*` buffer; but see `initial-buffer-choice`, below.
>
> Do not set this variable in the init file of a new user, or in a way that affects more than one user, as that would prevent new users from receiving information about copyleft and basic Emacs usage.
>
> `inhibit-startup-message` and `inhibit-splash-screen` are aliases for this variable.

`initial-buffer-choice`   [User Option]

> If non-`nil`, this variable is a string that specifies a file or directory for Emacs to display after starting up, instead of the startup screen. If its value is a function, Emacs calls that function which must return a buffer which is then displayed. If its value is `t`, Emacs displays the `*scratch*` buffer.

`inhibit-startup-echo-area-message`   [User Option]

> This variable controls the display of the startup echo area message. You can suppress the startup echo area message by adding text with this form to your init file:
>
> ```
> (setq inhibit-startup-echo-area-message
>       "your-login-name")
> ```
>
> Emacs explicitly checks for an expression as shown above in your init file; your login name must appear in the expression as a Lisp string constant. You can also use the Customize interface. Other methods of setting `inhibit-startup-echo-area-message` to the same value do not inhibit the startup message. This way, you can easily inhibit the message for yourself if you wish, but thoughtless copying of your init file will not inhibit the message for someone else.

`initial-scratch-message`   [User Option]

> This variable, if non-`nil`, should be a string, which is treated as documentation to be inserted into the `*scratch*` buffer when Emacs starts up. If it is `nil`, the `*scratch*` buffer is empty.

The following command-line options affect some aspects of the startup sequence. See Section "Initial Options" in *The GNU Emacs Manual*.

`--no-splash`
> Do not display a splash screen.

`--batch`   Run without an interactive terminal. See Section 38.17 [Batch Mode], page 1014.

`--daemon`   Do not initialize any display; just start a server in the background.

`--no-init-file`
`-q`   Do not load either the init file, or the `default` library.

`--no-site-file`
> Do not load the `site-start` library.

`--quick`
`-Q`   Equivalent to '`-q --no-site-file --no-splash`'.

38.1.2 The Init File

When you start Emacs, it normally attempts to load your *init file*. This is either a file named `.emacs` or `.emacs.el` in your home directory, or a file named `init.el` in a subdirectory named `.emacs.d` in your home directory.

The command-line switches '`-q`', '`-Q`', and '`-u`' control whether and where to find the init file; '`-q`' (and the stronger '`-Q`') says not to load an init file, while '`-u` *user*' says to load *user*'s init file instead of yours. See Section "Entering Emacs" in *The GNU Emacs Manual*. If neither option is specified, Emacs uses the `LOGNAME` environment variable, or the `USER` (most systems) or `USERNAME` (MS systems) variable, to find your home directory and thus your init file; this way, even if you have su'd, Emacs still loads your own init file. If those environment variables are absent, though, Emacs uses your user-id to find your home directory.

An Emacs installation may have a *default init file*, which is a Lisp library named `default.el`. Emacs finds this file through the standard search path for libraries (see Section 15.1 [How Programs Do Loading], page 244). The Emacs distribution does not come with this file; it is intended for local customizations. If the default init file exists, it is loaded whenever you start Emacs. But your own personal init file, if any, is loaded first; if it sets `inhibit-default-init` to a non-`nil` value, then Emacs does not subsequently load the `default.el` file. In batch mode, or if you specify '`-q`' (or '`-Q`'), Emacs loads neither your personal init file nor the default init file.

Another file for site-customization is `site-start.el`. Emacs loads this *before* the user's init file. You can inhibit the loading of this file with the option '`--no-site-file`'.

`site-run-file`   [User Option]
> This variable specifies the site-customization file to load before the user's init file. Its normal value is `"site-start"`. The only way you can change it with real effect is to do so before dumping Emacs.

See Section "Init File Examples" in *The GNU Emacs Manual*, for examples of how to make various commonly desired customizations in your `.emacs` file.

inhibit-default-init   [User Option]

> If this variable is non-**nil**, it prevents Emacs from loading the default initialization library file. The default value is **nil**.

before-init-hook   [Variable]

> This normal hook is run, once, just before loading all the init files (**site-start.el**, your init file, and **default.el**). (The only way to change it with real effect is before dumping Emacs.)

after-init-hook   [Variable]

> This normal hook is run, once, just after loading all the init files (**site-start.el**, your init file, and **default.el**), before loading the terminal-specific library (if started on a text terminal) and processing the command-line action arguments.

emacs-startup-hook   [Variable]

> This normal hook is run, once, just after handling the command line arguments. In batch mode, Emacs does not run this hook.

window-setup-hook   [Variable]

> This normal hook is very similar to **emacs-startup-hook**. The only difference is that it runs slightly later, after setting of the frame parameters. See Section 38.1.1 [Startup Summary], page 985.

user-init-file   [Variable]

> This variable holds the absolute file name of the user's init file. If the actual init file loaded is a compiled file, such as **.emacs.elc**, the value refers to the corresponding source file.

user-emacs-directory   [Variable]

> This variable holds the name of the **.emacs.d** directory. It is **~/.emacs.d** on all platforms but MS-DOS.

38.1.3 Terminal-Specific Initialization

Each terminal type can have its own Lisp library that Emacs loads when run on that type of terminal. The library's name is constructed by concatenating the value of the variable **term-file-prefix** and the terminal type (specified by the environment variable TERM). Normally, **term-file-prefix** has the value "**term/**"; changing this is not recommended. If there is an entry matching TERM in the **term-file-aliases** association list, Emacs uses the associated value in place of TERM. Emacs finds the file in the normal manner, by searching the **load-path** directories, and trying the '.**elc**' and '.**el**' suffixes.

The usual role of a terminal-specific library is to enable special keys to send sequences that Emacs can recognize. It may also need to set or add to **input-decode-map** if the Termcap or Terminfo entry does not specify all the terminal's function keys. See Section 38.13 [Terminal Input], page 1010.

When the name of the terminal type contains a hyphen or underscore, and no library is found whose name is identical to the terminal's name, Emacs strips from the terminal's name the last hyphen or underscore and everything that follows it, and tries again. This process is repeated until Emacs finds a matching library, or until there are no more hyphens or underscores in the name (i.e., there is no terminal-specific library). For example, if the terminal name is 'xterm-256color' and there is no term/xterm-256color.el library, Emacs tries to load term/xterm.el. If necessary, the terminal library can evaluate (getenv "TERM") to find the full name of the terminal type.

Your init file can prevent the loading of the terminal-specific library by setting the variable term-file-prefix to nil.

You can also arrange to override some of the actions of the terminal-specific library by using tty-setup-hook. This is a normal hook that Emacs runs after initializing a new text terminal. You could use this hook to define initializations for terminals that do not have their own libraries. See Section 22.1 [Hooks], page 429.

term-file-prefix   [User Option]
> If the value of this variable is non-nil, Emacs loads a terminal-specific initialization file as follows:
>
> ```
> (load (concat term-file-prefix (getenv "TERM")))
> ```
>
> You may set the term-file-prefix variable to nil in your init file if you do not wish to load the terminal-initialization file.
>
> On MS-DOS, Emacs sets the TERM environment variable to 'internal'.

term-file-aliases   [User Option]
> This variable is an an association list mapping terminal types to their aliases. For example, an element of the form ("vt102" . "vt100") means to treat a terminal of type 'vt102' like one of type 'vt100'.

tty-setup-hook   [Variable]
> This variable is a normal hook that Emacs runs after initializing a new text terminal. (This applies when Emacs starts up in non-windowed mode, and when making a tty emacsclient connection.) The hook runs after loading your init file (if applicable) and the terminal-specific Lisp file, so you can use it to adjust the definitions made by that file.
>
> For a related feature, see Section 38.1.2 [Init File], page 988.

38.1.4 Command-Line Arguments

You can use command-line arguments to request various actions when you start Emacs. Note that the recommended way of using Emacs is to start it just once, after logging in, and then do all editing in the same Emacs session (see Section "Entering Emacs" in *The GNU Emacs Manual*). For this reason, you might not use command-line arguments very often; nonetheless, they can be useful when invoking Emacs from session scripts or debugging Emacs. This section describes how Emacs processes command-line arguments.

command-line   [Function]
> This function parses the command line that Emacs was called with, processes it, and (amongst other things) loads the user's init file and displays the startup messages.

command-line-processed   [Variable]
> The value of this variable is t once the command line has been processed.

If you redump Emacs by calling `dump-emacs` (see Section E.1 [Building Emacs], page 1067), you may wish to set this variable to `nil` first in order to cause the new dumped Emacs to process its new command-line arguments.

`command-switch-alist`   [Variable]

This variable is an alist of user-defined command-line options and associated handler functions. By default it is empty, but you can add elements if you wish.

A *command-line option* is an argument on the command line, which has the form:

        `-option`

The elements of the `command-switch-alist` look like this:

    `(option . handler-function)`

The CAR, *option*, is a string, the name of a command-line option (not including the initial hyphen). The *handler-function* is called to handle *option*, and receives the option name as its sole argument.

In some cases, the option is followed in the command line by an argument. In these cases, the *handler-function* can find all the remaining command-line arguments in the variable `command-line-args-left` (see below). (The entire list of command-line arguments is in `command-line-args`.)

The command-line arguments are parsed by the `command-line-1` function in the `startup.el` file. See also Section "Command Line Arguments for Emacs Invocation" in *The GNU Emacs Manual*.

`command-line-args`   [Variable]

The value of this variable is the list of command-line arguments passed to Emacs.

`command-line-args-left`   [Variable]

The value of this variable is the list of command-line arguments that have not yet been processed.

`command-line-functions`   [Variable]

This variable's value is a list of functions for handling an unrecognized command-line argument. Each time the next argument to be processed has no special meaning, the functions in this list are called, in order of appearance, until one of them returns a non-`nil` value.

These functions are called with no arguments. They can access the command-line argument under consideration through the variable `argi`, which is bound temporarily at this point. The remaining arguments (not including the current one) are in the variable `command-line-args-left`.

When a function recognizes and processes the argument in `argi`, it should return a non-`nil` value to say it has dealt with that argument. If it has also dealt with some of the following arguments, it can indicate that by deleting them from `command-line-args-left`.

If all of these functions return `nil`, then the argument is treated as a file name to visit.

38.2 Getting Out of Emacs

There are two ways to get out of Emacs: you can kill the Emacs job, which exits permanently, or you can suspend it, which permits you to reenter the Emacs process later. (In a graphical environment, you can of course simply switch to another application without doing anything special to Emacs, then switch back to Emacs when you want.)

38.2.1 Killing Emacs

Killing Emacs means ending the execution of the Emacs process. If you started Emacs from a terminal, the parent process normally resumes control. The low-level primitive for killing Emacs is `kill-emacs`.

kill-emacs &optional *exit-data*   [Command]
>   This command calls the hook `kill-emacs-hook`, then exits the Emacs process and kills it.
>
>   If *exit-data* is an integer, that is used as the exit status of the Emacs process. (This is useful primarily in batch operation; see Section 38.17 [Batch Mode], page 1014.)
>
>   If *exit-data* is a string, its contents are stuffed into the terminal input buffer so that the shell (or whatever program next reads input) can read them.

The `kill-emacs` function is normally called via the higher-level command *C-x C-c* (`save-buffers-kill-terminal`). See Section "Exiting" in *The GNU Emacs Manual*. It is also called automatically if Emacs receives a `SIGTERM` or `SIGHUP` operating system signal (e.g., when the controlling terminal is disconnected), or if it receives a `SIGINT` signal while running in batch mode (see Section 38.17 [Batch Mode], page 1014).

kill-emacs-hook   [Variable]
>   This normal hook is run by `kill-emacs`, before it kills Emacs.
>
>   Because `kill-emacs` can be called in situations where user interaction is impossible (e.g., when the terminal is disconnected), functions on this hook should not attempt to interact with the user. If you want to interact with the user when Emacs is shutting down, use `kill-emacs-query-functions`, described below.

When Emacs is killed, all the information in the Emacs process, aside from files that have been saved, is lost. Because killing Emacs inadvertently can lose a lot of work, the `save-buffers-kill-terminal` command queries for confirmation if you have buffers that need saving or subprocesses that are running. It also runs the abnormal hook `kill-emacs-query-functions`:

kill-emacs-query-functions   [Variable]
>   When `save-buffers-kill-terminal` is killing Emacs, it calls the functions in this hook, after asking the standard questions and before calling `kill-emacs`. The functions are called in order of appearance, with no arguments. Each function can ask for additional confirmation from the user. If any of them returns `nil`, `save-buffers-kill-emacs` does not kill Emacs, and does not run the remaining functions in this hook. Calling `kill-emacs` directly does not run this hook.

38.2.2 Suspending Emacs

On text terminals, it is possible to *suspend Emacs*, which means stopping Emacs temporarily and returning control to its superior process, which is usually the shell. This allows you to resume editing later in the same Emacs process, with the same buffers, the same kill ring, the same undo history, and so on. To resume Emacs, use the appropriate command in the parent shell—most likely `fg`.

Suspending works only on a terminal device from which the Emacs session was started. We call that device the *controlling terminal* of the session. Suspending is not allowed if the controlling terminal is a graphical terminal. Suspending is usually not relevant in graphical environments, since you can simply switch to another application without doing anything special to Emacs.

Some operating systems (those without `SIGTSTP`, or MS-DOS) do not support suspension of jobs; on these systems, suspension actually creates a new shell temporarily as a subprocess of Emacs. Then you would exit the shell to return to Emacs.

suspend-emacs &optional *string* [Command]

    This function stops Emacs and returns control to the superior process. If and when the superior process resumes Emacs, `suspend-emacs` returns `nil` to its caller in Lisp.

    This function works only on the controlling terminal of the Emacs session; to relinquish control of other tty devices, use `suspend-tty` (see below). If the Emacs session uses more than one terminal, you must delete the frames on all the other terminals before suspending Emacs, or this function signals an error. See Section 28.2 [Multiple Terminals], page 631.

    If *string* is non-`nil`, its characters are sent to Emacs's superior shell, to be read as terminal input. The characters in *string* are not echoed by the superior shell; only the results appear.

    Before suspending, `suspend-emacs` runs the normal hook `suspend-hook`. After the user resumes Emacs, `suspend-emacs` runs the normal hook `suspend-resume-hook`. See Section 22.1 [Hooks], page 429.

    The next redisplay after resumption will redraw the entire screen, unless the variable `no-redraw-on-reenter` is non-`nil`. See Section 37.1 [Refresh Screen], page 886.

    Here is an example of how you could use these hooks:

```
(add-hook 'suspend-hook
          (lambda () (or (y-or-n-p "Really suspend? ")
                         (error "Suspend canceled"))))
(add-hook 'suspend-resume-hook (lambda () (message "Resumed!")
                                (sit-for 2)))
```

    Here is what you would see upon evaluating (`suspend-emacs "pwd"`):

```
---------- Buffer: Minibuffer ----------
Really suspend? y
---------- Buffer: Minibuffer ----------

---------- Parent Shell ----------
bash$ /home/username
bash$ fg

---------- Echo Area ----------
Resumed!
```

Note that 'pwd' is not echoed after Emacs is suspended. But it is read and executed by the shell.

suspend-hook   [Variable]
>   This variable is a normal hook that Emacs runs before suspending.

suspend-resume-hook   [Variable]
>   This variable is a normal hook that Emacs runs on resuming after a suspension.

suspend-tty &optional *tty*   [Function]
>   If *tty* specifies a terminal device used by Emacs, this function relinquishes the device
>   and restores it to its prior state. Frames that used the device continue to exist, but
>   are not updated and Emacs doesn't read input from them. *tty* can be a terminal
>   object, a frame (meaning the terminal for that frame), or nil (meaning the terminal
>   for the selected frame). See Section 28.2 [Multiple Terminals], page 631.
>
>   If *tty* is already suspended, this function does nothing.
>
>   This function runs the hook suspend-tty-functions, passing the terminal object as
>   an argument to each function.

resume-tty &optional *tty*   [Function]
>   This function resumes the previously suspended terminal device *tty*; where *tty* has
>   the same possible values as it does for suspend-tty.
>
>   This function reopens the terminal device, re-initializes it, and redraws it with that
>   terminal's selected frame. It then runs the hook resume-tty-functions, passing the
>   terminal object as an argument to each function.
>
>   If the same device is already used by another Emacs terminal, this function signals
>   an error. If *tty* is not suspended, this function does nothing.

controlling-tty-p &optional *tty*   [Function]
>   This function returns non-nil if *tty* is the controlling terminal of the Emacs session;
>   *tty* can be a terminal object, a frame (meaning the terminal for that frame), or nil
>   (meaning the terminal for the selected frame).

suspend-frame   [Command]
>   This command *suspends* a frame. For GUI frames, it calls iconify-frame (see
>   Section 28.11 [Visibility of Frames], page 658); for frames on text terminals, it calls
>   either suspend-emacs or suspend-tty, depending on whether the frame is displayed
>   on the controlling terminal device or not.

38.3 Operating System Environment

Emacs provides access to variables in the operating system environment through various functions. These variables include the name of the system, the user's UID, and so on.

system-configuration   [Variable]
>   This variable holds the standard GNU configuration name for the hardware/software
>   configuration of your system, as a string. For example, a typical value for a 64-bit
>   GNU/Linux system is '"x86_64-unknown-linux-gnu"'.

`system-type` [Variable]

The value of this variable is a symbol indicating the type of operating system Emacs is running on. The possible values are:

aix　　　　IBM's AIX.

berkeley-unix

Berkeley BSD and its variants.

cygwin　　Cygwin, a Posix layer on top of MS-Windows.

darwin　　Darwin (macOS).

gnu　　　　The GNU system (using the GNU kernel, which consists of the HURD and Mach).

gnu/linux

A GNU/Linux system—that is, a variant GNU system, using the Linux kernel. (These systems are the ones people often call "Linux", but actually Linux is just the kernel, not the whole system.)

gnu/kfreebsd

A GNU (glibc-based) system with a FreeBSD kernel.

hpux　　　Hewlett-Packard HPUX operating system.

irix　　　Silicon Graphics Irix system.

nacl　　　Google Native Client (NaCl) sandboxing system.

ms-dos　　Microsoft's DOS. Emacs compiled with DJGPP for MS-DOS binds `system-type` to `ms-dos` even when you run it on MS-Windows.

usg-unix-v

AT&T Unix System V.

windows-nt

Microsoft Windows NT, 9X and later. The value of `system-type` is always `windows-nt`, e.g., even on Windows 10.

We do not wish to add new symbols to make finer distinctions unless it is absolutely necessary! In fact, we hope to eliminate some of these alternatives in the future. If you need to make a finer distinction than `system-type` allows for, you can test `system-configuration`, e.g., against a regexp.

`system-name` [Function]

This function returns the name of the machine you are running on, as a string.

`mail-host-address` [User Option]

If this variable is non-`nil`, it is used instead of `system-name` for purposes of generating email addresses. For example, it is used when constructing the default value of `user-mail-address`. See Section 38.4 [User Identification], page 998. (Since this is done when Emacs starts up, the value actually used is the one saved when Emacs was dumped. See Section E.1 [Building Emacs], page 1067.)

getenv *var* **&optional** *frame*   [Command]

This function returns the value of the environment variable *var*, as a string. *var* should be a string. If *var* is undefined in the environment, **getenv** returns **nil**. It returns '""' if *var* is set but null. Within Emacs, a list of environment variables and their values is kept in the variable **process-environment**.

```
(getenv "USER")
     ⇒ "lewis"
```

The shell command **printenv** prints all or part of the environment:

```
bash$ printenv
PATH=/usr/local/bin:/usr/bin:/bin
USER=lewis
TERM=xterm
SHELL=/bin/bash
HOME=/home/lewis
...
```

setenv *variable* **&optional** *value substitute*   [Command]

This command sets the value of the environment variable named *variable* to *value*. *variable* should be a string. Internally, Emacs Lisp can handle any string. However, normally *variable* should be a valid shell identifier, that is, a sequence of letters, digits and underscores, starting with a letter or underscore. Otherwise, errors may occur if subprocesses of Emacs try to access the value of *variable*. If *value* is omitted or **nil** (or, interactively, with a prefix argument), **setenv** removes *variable* from the environment. Otherwise, *value* should be a string.

If the optional argument *substitute* is non-**nil**, Emacs calls the function **substitute-env-vars** to expand any environment variables in *value*.

setenv works by modifying **process-environment**; binding that variable with **let** is also reasonable practice.

setenv returns the new value of *variable*, or **nil** if it removed *variable* from the environment.

process-environment   [Variable]

This variable is a list of strings, each describing one environment variable. The functions **getenv** and **setenv** work by means of this variable.

```
process-environment
⇒ ("PATH=/usr/local/bin:/usr/bin:/bin"
   "USER=lewis"
   "TERM=xterm"
   "SHELL=/bin/bash"
   "HOME=/home/lewis"
   ...)
```

If **process-environment** contains multiple elements that specify the same environment variable, the first of these elements specifies the variable, and the others are ignored.

initial-environment   [Variable]

This variable holds the list of environment variables Emacs inherited from its parent process when Emacs started.

`path-separator`   [Variable]

    This variable holds a string that says which character separates directories in a search path (as found in an environment variable). Its value is `":"` for Unix and GNU systems, and `";"` for MS systems.

`parse-colon-path` *path*   [Function]

    This function takes a search path string such as the value of the `PATH` environment variable, and splits it at the separators, returning a list of directory names. `nil` in this list means the current directory. Although the function's name says "colon", it actually uses the value of `path-separator`.

> ```
> (parse-colon-path ":/foo:/bar")
>      ⇒ (nil "/foo/" "/bar/")
> ```

`invocation-name`   [Variable]

    This variable holds the program name under which Emacs was invoked. The value is a string, and does not include a directory name.

`invocation-directory`   [Variable]

    This variable holds the directory in which the Emacs executable was located when it was run, or `nil` if that directory cannot be determined.

`installation-directory`   [Variable]

    If non-`nil`, this is a directory within which to look for the `lib-src` and `etc` sub-directories. In an installed Emacs, it is normally `nil`. It is non-`nil` when Emacs can't find those directories in their standard installed locations, but can find them in a directory related somehow to the one containing the Emacs executable (i.e., `invocation-directory`).

`load-average` **&optional** *use-float*   [Function]

    This function returns the current 1-minute, 5-minute, and 15-minute system load averages, in a list. The load average indicates the number of processes trying to run on the system.

    By default, the values are integers that are 100 times the system load averages, but if *use-float* is non-`nil`, then they are returned as floating-point numbers without multiplying by 100.

    If it is impossible to obtain the load average, this function signals an error. On some platforms, access to load averages requires installing Emacs as setuid or setgid so that it can read kernel information, and that usually isn't advisable.

    If the 1-minute load average is available, but the 5- or 15-minute averages are not, this function returns a shortened list containing the available averages.

> ```
> (load-average)
>      ⇒ (169 48 36)
> (load-average t)
>      ⇒ (1.69 0.48 0.36)
> ```

The shell command `uptime` returns similar information.

`emacs-pid`   [Function]

    This function returns the process ID of the Emacs process, as an integer.

`tty-erase-char`   [Variable]

>   This variable holds the erase character that was selected in the system's terminal driver, before Emacs was started.

38.4 User Identification

`init-file-user`   [Variable]

>   This variable says which user's init files should be used by Emacs—or `nil` if none. `""` stands for the user who originally logged in. The value reflects command-line options such as '`-q`' or '`-u `*user*'.
>
>   Lisp packages that load files of customizations, or any other sort of user profile, should obey this variable in deciding where to find it. They should load the profile of the user name found in this variable. If `init-file-user` is `nil`, meaning that the '`-q`', '`-Q`', or '`-batch`' option was used, then Lisp packages should not load any customization files or user profile.

`user-mail-address`   [User Option]

>   This holds the nominal email address of the user who is using Emacs. Emacs normally sets this variable to a default value after reading your init files, but not if you have already set it. So you can set the variable to some other value in your init file if you do not want to use the default value.

`user-login-name &optional `*uid*   [Function]

>   This function returns the name under which the user is logged in. It uses the environment variables `LOGNAME` or `USER` if either is set. Otherwise, the value is based on the effective UID, not the real UID.
>
>   If you specify *uid* (a number), the result is the user name that corresponds to *uid*, or `nil` if there is no such user.

`user-real-login-name`   [Function]

>   This function returns the user name corresponding to Emacs's real UID. This ignores the effective UID, and the environment variables `LOGNAME` and `USER`.

`user-full-name &optional `*uid*   [Function]

>   This function returns the full name of the logged-in user—or the value of the environment variable `NAME`, if that is set.
>
>   If the Emacs process's user-id does not correspond to any known user (and provided `NAME` is not set), the result is `"unknown"`.
>
>   If *uid* is non-`nil`, then it should be a number (a user-id) or a string (a login name). Then `user-full-name` returns the full name corresponding to that user-id or login name. If you specify a user-id or login name that isn't defined, it returns `nil`.

The symbols `user-login-name`, `user-real-login-name` and `user-full-name` are variables as well as functions. The functions return the same values that the variables hold. These variables allow you to fake out Emacs by telling the functions what to return. The variables are also useful for constructing frame titles (see Section 28.6 [Frame Titles], page 654).

user-real-uid [Function]

This function returns the real UID of the user. The value may be floating point, in the (unlikely) event that the UID is too large to fit in a Lisp integer.

user-uid [Function]

This function returns the effective UID of the user. The value may be floating point.

group-gid [Function]

This function returns the effective GID of the Emacs process. The value may be floating point.

group-real-gid [Function]

This function returns the real GID of the Emacs process. The value may be floating point.

system-users [Function]

This function returns a list of strings, listing the user names on the system. If Emacs cannot retrieve this information, the return value is a list containing just the value of `user-real-login-name`.

system-groups [Function]

This function returns a list of strings, listing the names of user groups on the system. If Emacs cannot retrieve this information, the return value is `nil`.

38.5 Time of Day

This section explains how to determine the current time and time zone.

Most of these functions represent time as a list of four integers (*sec-high sec-low microsec picosec*). This represents the number of seconds from the *epoch* (January 1, 1970 at 00:00 UTC), using the formula: $high * 2^{16} + low + micro * 10^{-6} + pico * 10^{-12}$. The return value of `current-time` represents time using this form, as do the timestamps in the return values of other functions such as `file-attributes` (see [Definition of file-attributes], page 510). In some cases, functions may return two- or three-element lists, with omitted *microsec* and *picosec* components defaulting to zero.

Function arguments, e.g., the *time* argument to `current-time-string`, accept a more-general *time value* format, which can be a list of integers as above, or a single number for seconds since the epoch, or `nil` for the current time. You can convert a time value into a human-readable string using `current-time-string` and `format-time-string`, into a list of integers using `seconds-to-time`, and into other forms using `decode-time` and `float-time`. These functions are described in the following sections.

current-time-string &optional *time zone* [Function]

This function returns the current time and date as a human-readable string. The format does not vary for the initial part of the string, which contains the day of week, month, day of month, and time of day in that order: the number of characters used for these fields is always the same, so you can reliably use `substring` to extract them. You should count characters from the beginning of the string rather than from the end, as the year might not have exactly four digits, and additional information may some day be added at the end.

The argument *time*, if given, specifies a time to format, instead of the current time. The optional argument *zone* defaults to the current time zone rule. See Section 38.6 [Time Zone Rules], page 1000.

> (current-time-string)
> ⇒ "Wed Oct 14 22:21:05 1987"

current-time [Function]

This function returns the current time, represented as a list of four integers (*sec-high sec-low microsec picosec*). These integers have trailing zeros on systems that return time with lower resolutions. On all current machines *picosec* is a multiple of 1000, but this may change as higher-resolution clocks become available.

float-time &optional *time* [Function]

This function returns the current time as a floating-point number of seconds since the epoch. The optional argument *time*, if given, specifies a time to convert instead of the current time.

Warning: Since the result is floating point, it may not be exact. Do not use this function if precise time stamps are required.

`time-to-seconds` is an alias for this function.

seconds-to-time *time* [Function]

This function converts a time value to list-of-integer form. For example, if *time* is a number, (`time-to-seconds` (`seconds-to-time` *time*)) equals the number unless overflow or rounding errors occur.

38.6 Time Zone Rules

The default time zone is determined by the `TZ` environment variable. See Section 38.3 [System Environment], page 994. For example, you can tell Emacs to default to Universal Time with (`setenv "TZ" "UTC0"`). If `TZ` is not in the environment, Emacs uses system wall clock time, which is a platform-dependent default time zone.

The set of supported `TZ` strings is system-dependent. GNU and many other systems support the tzdata database, e.g., '`"America/New_York"`' specifies the time zone and daylight saving time history for locations near New York City. GNU and most other systems support POSIX-style `TZ` strings, e.g., '`"EST+5EDT,M4.1.0/2,M10.5.0/2"`' specifies the rules used in New York from 1987 through 2006. All systems support the string '`"UTC0"`' meaning Universal Time.

Functions that convert to and from local time accept an optional *time zone rule* argument, which specifies the conversion's time zone and daylight saving time history. If the time zone rule is omitted or `nil`, the conversion uses Emacs's default time zone. If it is `t`, the conversion uses Universal Time. If it is `wall`, the conversion uses the system wall clock time. If it is a string, the conversion uses the time zone rule equivalent to setting `TZ` to that string.

current-time-zone &optional *time zone* [Function]

This function returns a list describing the time zone that the user is in.

The value has the form (*offset abbr*). Here *offset* is an integer giving the number of seconds ahead of Universal Time (east of Greenwich). A negative value means west of Greenwich. The second element, *abbr*, is a string giving an abbreviation for the time zone, e.g., '"CST"' for China Standard Time or for U.S. Central Standard Time. Both elements can change when daylight saving time begins or ends; if the user has specified a time zone that does not use a seasonal time adjustment, then the value is constant through time.

If the operating system doesn't supply all the information necessary to compute the value, the unknown elements of the list are `nil`.

The argument *time*, if given, specifies a time value to analyze instead of the current time. The optional argument *zone* defaults to the current time zone rule.

38.7 Time Conversion

These functions convert time values (see Section 38.5 [Time of Day], page 999) into calendrical information and vice versa.

Many 32-bit operating systems are limited to system times containing 32 bits of information in their seconds component; these systems typically handle only the times from 1901-12-13 20:45:52 through 2038-01-19 03:14:07 Universal Time. However, 64-bit and some 32-bit operating systems have larger seconds components, and can represent times far in the past or future.

Time conversion functions always use the Gregorian calendar, even for dates before the Gregorian calendar was introduced. Year numbers count the number of years since the year 1 B.C., and do not skip zero as traditional Gregorian years do; for example, the year number -37 represents the Gregorian year 38 B.C.

decode-time &optional *time zone*   [Function]

> This function converts a time value into calendrical information. If you don't specify *time*, it decodes the current time, and similarly *zone* defaults to the current time zone rule. See Section 38.6 [Time Zone Rules], page 1000. The return value is a list of nine elements, as follows:
>
> > (*seconds minutes hour day month year dow dst utcoff*)
>
> Here is what the elements mean:

> | | |
> |---|---|
> | *seconds* | The number of seconds past the minute, as an integer between 0 and 59. On some operating systems, this is 60 for leap seconds. |
> | *minutes* | The number of minutes past the hour, as an integer between 0 and 59. |
> | *hour* | The hour of the day, as an integer between 0 and 23. |
> | *day* | The day of the month, as an integer between 1 and 31. |
> | *month* | The month of the year, as an integer between 1 and 12. |
> | *year* | The year, an integer typically greater than 1900. |
> | *dow* | The day of week, as an integer between 0 and 6, where 0 stands for Sunday. |
> | *dst* | `t` if daylight saving time is effect, otherwise `nil`. |
> | *utcoff* | An integer indicating the Universal Time offset in seconds, i.e., the number of seconds east of Greenwich. |

Common Lisp Note: Common Lisp has different meanings for *dow* and *utcoff*.

`encode-time` *seconds minutes hour day month year* **&optional** *zone*   [Function]

> This function is the inverse of `decode-time`. It converts seven items of calendrical data into a list-of-integer time value. For the meanings of the arguments, see the table above under `decode-time`.
>
> Year numbers less than 100 are not treated specially. If you want them to stand for years above 1900, or years above 2000, you must alter them yourself before you call `encode-time`.
>
> The optional argument *zone* defaults to the current time zone rule. See Section 38.6 [Time Zone Rules], page 1000. In addition to the usual time zone rule values, it can also be a list (as you would get from `current-time-zone`) or an integer (as from `decode-time`), applied without any further alteration for daylight saving time.
>
> If you pass more than seven arguments to `encode-time`, the first six are used as *seconds* through *year*, the last argument is used as *zone*, and the arguments in between are ignored. This feature makes it possible to use the elements of a list returned by `decode-time` as the arguments to `encode-time`, like this:
>
> > `(apply 'encode-time (decode-time ...))`
>
> You can perform simple date arithmetic by using out-of-range values for the *seconds*, *minutes*, *hour*, *day*, and *month* arguments; for example, day 0 means the day preceding the given month.
>
> The operating system puts limits on the range of possible time values; if you try to encode a time that is out of range, an error results. For instance, years before 1970 do not work on some systems; on others, years as early as 1901 do work.

38.8 Parsing and Formatting Times

These functions convert time values to text in a string, and vice versa. Time values are lists of two to four integers (see Section 38.5 [Time of Day], page 999).

`date-to-time` *string*   [Function]

> This function parses the time-string *string* and returns the corresponding time value.

`format-time-string` *format-string* **&optional** *time zone*   [Function]

> This function converts *time* (or the current time, if *time* is omitted or `nil`) to a string according to *format-string*. The conversion uses the time zone rule *zone*, which defaults to the current time zone rule. See Section 38.6 [Time Zone Rules], page 1000. The argument *format-string* may contain '%'-sequences which say to substitute parts of the time. Here is a table of what the '%'-sequences mean:
>
> | | |
> |---|---|
> | '%a' | This stands for the abbreviated name of the day of week. |
> | '%A' | This stands for the full name of the day of week. |
> | '%b' | This stands for the abbreviated name of the month. |
> | '%B' | This stands for the full name of the month. |
> | '%c' | This is a synonym for '%x %X'. |

'%C'   This has a locale-specific meaning. In the default locale (named C), it is equivalent to '%A, %B %e, %Y'.

'%d'   This stands for the day of month, zero-padded.

'%D'   This is a synonym for '%m/%d/%y'.

'%e'   This stands for the day of month, blank-padded.

'%F'   This stands for the ISO 8601 date format, i.e., '"%Y-%m-%d"'.

'%g'   This stands for the year corresponding to the ISO week within the century.

'%G'   This stands for the year corresponding to the ISO week.

'%h'   This is a synonym for '%b'.

'%H'   This stands for the hour (00–23).

'%I'   This stands for the hour (01–12).

'%j'   This stands for the day of the year (001–366).

'%k'   This stands for the hour (0–23), blank padded.

'%l'   This stands for the hour (1–12), blank padded.

'%m'   This stands for the month (01–12).

'%M'   This stands for the minute (00–59).

'%n'   This stands for a newline.

'%N'   This stands for the nanoseconds (000000000–999999999). To ask for fewer digits, use '%3N' for milliseconds, '%6N' for microseconds, etc. Any excess digits are discarded, without rounding.

'%p'   This stands for 'AM' or 'PM', as appropriate.

'%r'   This is a synonym for '%I:%M:%S %p'.

'%R'   This is a synonym for '%H:%M'.

'%S'   This stands for the seconds (00–59).

'%t'   This stands for a tab character.

'%T'   This is a synonym for '%H:%M:%S'.

'%u'   This stands for the numeric day of week (1–7). Monday is day 1.

'%U'   This stands for the week of the year (01–52), assuming that weeks start on Sunday.

'%V'   This stands for the week of the year according to ISO 8601.

'%w'   This stands for the numeric day of week (0–6). Sunday is day 0.

'%W'   This stands for the week of the year (01–52), assuming that weeks start on Monday.

'%x'   This has a locale-specific meaning. In the default locale (named 'C'), it is equivalent to '%D'.

'%X'   This has a locale-specific meaning. In the default locale (named 'C'), it
          is equivalent to '%T'.

'%y'   This stands for the year without century (00–99).

'%Y'   This stands for the year with century.

'%Z'   This stands for the time zone abbreviation (e.g., 'EST').

'%z'   This stands for the time zone numerical offset (e.g., '-0500').

You can also specify the field width and type of padding for any of these '%'-sequences.
This works as in **printf**: you write the field width as digits in the middle of a '%'-
sequences. If you start the field width with '0', it means to pad with zeros. If you
start the field width with '_', it means to pad with spaces.

For example, '%S' specifies the number of seconds since the minute; '%03S' means to
pad this with zeros to 3 positions, '%_3S' to pad with spaces to 3 positions. Plain
'%3S' pads with zeros, because that is how '%S' normally pads to two positions.

The characters 'E' and 'O' act as modifiers when used between '%' and one of the
letters in the table above. 'E' specifies using the current locale's alternative version of
the date and time. In a Japanese locale, for example, %Ex might yield a date format
based on the Japanese Emperors' reigns. 'E' is allowed in '%Ec', '%EC', '%Ex', '%EX',
'%Ey', and '%EY'.

'O' means to use the current locale's alternative representation of numbers, instead
of the ordinary decimal digits. This is allowed with most letters, all the ones that
output numbers.

This function uses the C library function **strftime** (see Section "Formatting Calendar
Time" in *The GNU C Library Reference Manual*) to do most of the work. In order
to communicate with that function, it first encodes its argument using the coding
system specified by **locale-coding-system** (see Section 32.12 [Locales], page 788);
after **strftime** returns the resulting string, **format-time-string** decodes the string
using that same coding system.

format-seconds *format-string seconds*   [Function]
     This function converts its argument *seconds* into a string of years, days, hours, etc.,
     according to *format-string*. The argument *format-string* may contain '%'-sequences
     which control the conversion. Here is a table of what the '%'-sequences mean:

'%y'
'%Y'   The integer number of 365-day years.

'%d'
'%D'   The integer number of days.

'%h'
'%H'   The integer number of hours.

'%m'
'%M'   The integer number of minutes.

'%s'
'%S'   The integer number of seconds.

'%z'   Non-printing control flag. When it is used, other specifiers must be given in the order of decreasing size, i.e., years before days, hours before minutes, etc. Nothing will be produced in the result string to the left of '%z' until the first non-zero conversion is encountered. For example, the default format used by `emacs-uptime` (see Section 38.9 [Processor Run Time], page 1005) `"%Y, %D, %H, %M, %z%S"` means that the number of seconds will always be produced, but years, days, hours, and minutes will only be shown if they are non-zero.

'%%'   Produces a literal '%'.

Upper-case format sequences produce the units in addition to the numbers, lower-case formats produce only the numbers.

You can also specify the field width by following the '%' with a number; shorter numbers will be padded with blanks. An optional period before the width requests zero-padding instead. For example, `"%.3Y"` might produce `"004 years"`.

Warning: This function works only with values of *seconds* that don't exceed `most-positive-fixnum` (see Section 3.1 [Integer Basics], page 34).

38.9 Processor Run time

Emacs provides several functions and primitives that return time, both elapsed and processor time, used by the Emacs process.

`emacs-uptime` **&optional** *format*   [Command]
       This function returns a string representing the Emacs *uptime*—the elapsed wall-clock time this instance of Emacs is running. The string is formatted by `format-seconds` according to the optional argument *format*. For the available format descriptors, see Section 38.8 [Time Parsing], page 1002. If *format* is `nil` or omitted, it defaults to `"%Y, %D, %H, %M, %z%S"`.

       When called interactively, it prints the uptime in the echo area.

`get-internal-run-time`   [Function]
       This function returns the processor run time used by Emacs as a list of four integers: (*sec-high sec-low microsec picosec*), using the same format as `current-time` (see Section 38.5 [Time of Day], page 999).

       Note that the time returned by this function excludes the time Emacs was not using the processor, and if the Emacs process has several threads, the returned value is the sum of the processor times used up by all Emacs threads.

       If the system doesn't provide a way to determine the processor run time, `get-internal-run-time` returns the same time as `current-time`.

`emacs-init-time`   [Command]
       This function returns the duration of the Emacs initialization (see Section 38.1.1 [Startup Summary], page 985) in seconds, as a string. When called interactively, it prints the duration in the echo area.

38.10 Time Calculations

These functions perform calendrical computations using time values (see Section 38.5 [Time of Day], page 999). A value of `nil` for any of their time-value arguments stands for the current system time, and a single integer number stands for the number of seconds since the epoch.

time-less-p *t1 t2*   [Function]
>   This returns `t` if time value *t1* is less than time value *t2*.

time-subtract *t1 t2*   [Function]
>   This returns the time difference *t1 − t2* between two time values, as a time value. If you need the difference in units of elapsed seconds, use `float-time` (see Section 38.5 [Time of Day], page 999) to convert the result into seconds.

time-add *t1 t2*   [Function]
>   This returns the sum of two time values, as a time value. One argument should represent a time difference rather than a point in time, either as a list or as a single number of elapsed seconds. Here is how to add a number of seconds to a time value:
>
>    ```
>    (time-add time seconds)
>    ```

time-to-days *time-value*   [Function]
>   This function returns the number of days between the beginning of year 1 and *time-value*.

time-to-day-in-year *time-value*   [Function]
>   This returns the day number within the year corresponding to *time-value*.

date-leap-year-p *year*   [Function]
>   This function returns `t` if *year* is a leap year.

38.11 Timers for Delayed Execution

You can set up a *timer* to call a function at a specified future time or after a certain length of idleness. A timer is a special object that stores the information about the next invocation times and the function to invoke.

timerp *object*   [Function]
>   This predicate function returns non-`nil` of `object` is a timer.

Emacs cannot run timers at any arbitrary point in a Lisp program; it can run them only when Emacs could accept output from a subprocess: namely, while waiting or inside certain primitive functions such as `sit-for` or `read-event` which *can* wait. Therefore, a timer's execution may be delayed if Emacs is busy. However, the time of execution is very precise if Emacs is idle.

Emacs binds `inhibit-quit` to `t` before calling the timer function, because quitting out of many timer functions can leave things in an inconsistent state. This is normally unproblematical because most timer functions don't do a lot of work. Indeed, for a timer to call a function that takes substantial time to run is likely to be annoying. If a timer function needs to allow quitting, it should use `with-local-quit` (see Section 20.11 [Quitting], page 382).

For example, if a timer function calls `accept-process-output` to receive output from an external process, that call should be wrapped inside `with-local-quit`, to ensure that *C-g* works if the external process hangs.

It is usually a bad idea for timer functions to alter buffer contents. When they do, they usually should call `undo-boundary` both before and after changing the buffer, to separate the timer's changes from user commands' changes and prevent a single undo entry from growing to be quite large.

Timer functions should also avoid calling functions that cause Emacs to wait, such as `sit-for` (see Section 20.10 [Waiting], page 382). This can lead to unpredictable effects, since other timers (or even the same timer) can run while waiting. If a timer function needs to perform an action after a certain time has elapsed, it can do this by scheduling a new timer.

If a timer function calls functions that can change the match data, it should save and restore the match data. See Section 33.6.4 [Saving Match Data], page 811.

`run-at-time` *time repeat function &rest args*   [Command]
> This sets up a timer that calls the function *function* with arguments *args* at time *time*. If *repeat* is a number (integer or floating point), the timer is scheduled to run again every *repeat* seconds after *time*. If *repeat* is `nil`, the timer runs only once.
>
> *time* may specify an absolute or a relative time.
>
> Absolute times may be specified using a string with a limited variety of formats, and are taken to be times *today*, even if already in the past. The recognized forms are '`xxxx`', '`x:xx`', or '`xx:xx`' (military time), and '`xxam`', '`xxAM`', '`xxpm`', '`xxPM`', '`xx:xxam`', '`xx:xxAM`', '`xx:xxpm`', or '`xx:xxPM`'. A period can be used instead of a colon to separate the hour and minute parts.
>
> To specify a relative time as a string, use numbers followed by units. For example:
>
> '`1 min`'   denotes 1 minute from now.
>
> '`1 min 5 sec`'
> > denotes 65 seconds from now.
>
> '`1 min 2 sec 3 hour 4 day 5 week 6 fortnight 7 month 8 year`'
> > denotes exactly 103 months, 123 days, and 10862 seconds from now.
>
> For relative time values, Emacs considers a month to be exactly thirty days, and a year to be exactly 365.25 days.
>
> Not all convenient formats are strings. If *time* is a number (integer or floating point), that specifies a relative time measured in seconds. The result of `encode-time` can also be used to specify an absolute value for *time*.
>
> In most cases, *repeat* has no effect on when *first* call takes place—*time* alone specifies that. There is one exception: if *time* is `t`, then the timer runs whenever the time is a multiple of *repeat* seconds after the epoch. This is useful for functions like `display-time`.
>
> The function `run-at-time` returns a timer value that identifies the particular scheduled future action. You can use this value to call `cancel-timer` (see below).

A repeating timer nominally ought to run every *repeat* seconds, but remember that any invocation of a timer can be late. Lateness of one repetition has no effect on the scheduled time of the next repetition. For instance, if Emacs is busy computing for long enough to cover three scheduled repetitions of the timer, and then starts to wait, it will immediately call the timer function three times in immediate succession (presuming no other timers trigger before or between them). If you want a timer to run again no less than *n* seconds after the last invocation, don't use the *repeat* argument. Instead, the timer function should explicitly reschedule the timer.

timer-max-repeats   [User Option]

> This variable's value specifies the maximum number of times to repeat calling a timer function in a row, when many previously scheduled calls were unavoidably delayed.

with-timeout (*seconds timeout-forms...*) *body...*   [Macro]

> Execute *body*, but give up after *seconds* seconds. If *body* finishes before the time is up, **with-timeout** returns the value of the last form in *body*. If, however, the execution of *body* is cut short by the timeout, then **with-timeout** executes all the *timeout-forms* and returns the value of the last of them.

> This macro works by setting a timer to run after *seconds* seconds. If *body* finishes before that time, it cancels the timer. If the timer actually runs, it terminates execution of *body*, then executes *timeout-forms*.

> Since timers can run within a Lisp program only when the program calls a primitive that can wait, **with-timeout** cannot stop executing *body* while it is in the midst of a computation—only when it calls one of those primitives. So use **with-timeout** only with a *body* that waits for input, not one that does a long computation.

The function **y-or-n-p-with-timeout** provides a simple way to use a timer to avoid waiting too long for an answer. See Section 19.7 [Yes-or-No Queries], page 337.

cancel-timer *timer*   [Function]

> This cancels the requested action for *timer*, which should be a timer—usually, one previously returned by **run-at-time** or **run-with-idle-timer**. This cancels the effect of that call to one of these functions; the arrival of the specified time will not cause anything special to happen.

38.12 Idle Timers

Here is how to set up a timer that runs when Emacs is idle for a certain length of time. Aside from how to set them up, idle timers work just like ordinary timers.

run-with-idle-timer *secs repeat function* **&rest** *args*   [Command]

> Set up a timer which runs the next time Emacs is idle for *secs* seconds. The value of *secs* may be a number or a value of the type returned by **current-idle-time**.

> If *repeat* is **nil**, the timer runs just once, the first time Emacs remains idle for a long enough time. More often *repeat* is non-**nil**, which means to run the timer *each time* Emacs remains idle for *secs* seconds.

> The function **run-with-idle-timer** returns a timer value which you can use in calling **cancel-timer** (see Section 38.11 [Timers], page 1006).

Emacs becomes *idle* when it starts waiting for user input, and it remains idle until the user provides some input. If a timer is set for five seconds of idleness, it runs approximately five seconds after Emacs first becomes idle. Even if *repeat* is non-`nil`, this timer will not run again as long as Emacs remains idle, because the duration of idleness will continue to increase and will not go down to five seconds again.

Emacs can do various things while idle: garbage collect, autosave or handle data from a subprocess. But these interludes during idleness do not interfere with idle timers, because they do not reset the clock of idleness to zero. An idle timer set for 600 seconds will run when ten minutes have elapsed since the last user command was finished, even if subprocess output has been accepted thousands of times within those ten minutes, and even if there have been garbage collections and autosaves.

When the user supplies input, Emacs becomes non-idle while executing the input. Then it becomes idle again, and all the idle timers that are set up to repeat will subsequently run another time, one by one.

Do not write an idle timer function containing a loop which does a certain amount of processing each time around, and exits when (`input-pending-p`) is non-`nil`. This approach seems very natural but has two problems:

- It blocks out all process output (since Emacs accepts process output only while waiting).
- It blocks out any idle timers that ought to run during that time.

Similarly, do not write an idle timer function that sets up another idle timer (including the same idle timer) with *secs* argument less than or equal to the current idleness time. Such a timer will run almost immediately, and continue running again and again, instead of waiting for the next time Emacs becomes idle. The correct approach is to reschedule with an appropriate increment of the current value of the idleness time, as described below.

`current-idle-time`   [Function]
> If Emacs is idle, this function returns the length of time Emacs has been idle, as a list of four integers: (*sec-high sec-low microsec picosec*), using the same format as `current-time` (see Section 38.5 [Time of Day], page 999).
>
> When Emacs is not idle, `current-idle-time` returns `nil`. This is a convenient way to test whether Emacs is idle.

The main use of `current-idle-time` is when an idle timer function wants to "take a break" for a while. It can set up another idle timer to call the same function again, after a few seconds more idleness. Here's an example:

```
(defvar my-resume-timer nil
  "Timer for `my-timer-function' to reschedule itself, or nil.")

(defun my-timer-function ()
  ;; If the user types a command while my-resume-timer
  ;; is active, the next time this function is called from
  ;; its main idle timer, deactivate my-resume-timer.
  (when my-resume-timer
    (cancel-timer my-resume-timer))
  ...do the work for a while...
```

```
(when taking-a-break
  (setq my-resume-timer
        (run-with-idle-timer
          ;; Compute an idle time break-length
          ;; more than the current value.
          (time-add (current-idle-time) break-length)
          nil
          'my-timer-function))))
```

38.13 Terminal Input

This section describes functions and variables for recording or manipulating terminal input.
See Chapter 37 [Display], page 886, for related functions.

38.13.1 Input Modes

set-input-mode *interrupt flow meta* **&optional** *quit-char*   [Function]
> This function sets the mode for reading keyboard input. If *interrupt* is non-`nil`, then
> Emacs uses input interrupts. If it is `nil`, then it uses CBREAK mode. The default
> setting is system-dependent. Some systems always use CBREAK mode regardless of
> what is specified.
>
> When Emacs communicates directly with X, it ignores this argument and uses inter-
> rupts if that is the way it knows how to communicate.
>
> If *flow* is non-`nil`, then Emacs uses XON/XOFF (*C-q*, *C-s*) flow control for output to
> the terminal. This has no effect except in CBREAK mode.
>
> The argument *meta* controls support for input character codes above 127. If *meta* is
> `t`, Emacs converts characters with the 8th bit set into Meta characters. If *meta* is
> `nil`, Emacs disregards the 8th bit; this is necessary when the terminal uses it as a
> parity bit. If *meta* is neither `t` nor `nil`, Emacs uses all 8 bits of input unchanged.
> This is good for terminals that use 8-bit character sets.
>
> If *quit-char* is non-`nil`, it specifies the character to use for quitting. Normally this
> character is *C-g*. See Section 20.11 [Quitting], page 382.

The `current-input-mode` function returns the input mode settings Emacs is currently
using.

current-input-mode   [Function]
> This function returns the current mode for reading keyboard input. It returns a list,
> corresponding to the arguments of `set-input-mode`, of the form (*interrupt flow
> meta quit*) in which:
>
> *interrupt*   is non-`nil` when Emacs is using interrupt-driven input. If `nil`, Emacs is
>   using CBREAK mode.
>
> *flow*   is non-`nil` if Emacs uses XON/XOFF (*C-q*, *C-s*) flow control for output to
>   the terminal. This value is meaningful only when *interrupt* is `nil`.
>
> *meta*   is `t` if Emacs treats the eighth bit of input characters as the meta bit;
>   `nil` means Emacs clears the eighth bit of every input character; any other
>   value means Emacs uses all eight bits as the basic character code.

quit   is the character Emacs currently uses for quitting, usually *C-g*.

38.13.2 Recording Input

`recent-keys`   [Function]
> This function returns a vector containing the last 300 input events from the keyboard
> or mouse. All input events are included, whether or not they were used as parts of
> key sequences. Thus, you always get the last 300 input events, not counting events
> generated by keyboard macros. (These are excluded because they are less interesting
> for debugging; it should be enough to see the events that invoked the macros.)
>
> A call to `clear-this-command-keys` (see Section 20.5 [Command Loop Info],
> page 355) causes this function to return an empty vector immediately afterward.

`open-dribble-file` *filename*   [Command]
> This function opens a *dribble file* named *filename*. When a dribble file is open, each
> input event from the keyboard or mouse (but not those from keyboard macros) is
> written in that file. A non-character event is expressed using its printed representation
> surrounded by '`<...>`'. Be aware that sensitive information (such as passwords) may
> end up recorded in the dribble file.
>
> You close the dribble file by calling this function with an argument of `nil`.

See also the `open-termscript` function (see Section 38.14 [Terminal Output], page 1011).

38.14 Terminal Output

The terminal output functions send output to a text terminal, or keep track of output sent
to the terminal. The variable `baud-rate` tells you what Emacs thinks is the output speed
of the terminal.

`baud-rate`   [User Option]
> This variable's value is the output speed of the terminal, as far as Emacs knows.
> Setting this variable does not change the speed of actual data transmission, but the
> value is used for calculations such as padding.
>
> It also affects decisions about whether to scroll part of the screen or repaint on text
> terminals. See Section 37.2 [Forcing Redisplay], page 886, for the corresponding
> functionality on graphical terminals.
>
> The value is measured in baud.

  If you are running across a network, and different parts of the network work at different
baud rates, the value returned by Emacs may be different from the value used by your local
terminal. Some network protocols communicate the local terminal speed to the remote
machine, so that Emacs and other programs can get the proper value, but others do not.
If Emacs has the wrong value, it makes decisions that are less than optimal. To fix the
problem, set `baud-rate`.

`send-string-to-terminal` *string* **&optional** *terminal*   [Function]
> This function sends *string* to *terminal* without alteration. Control characters in
> *string* have terminal-dependent effects. (If you need to display non-ASCII text on

the terminal, encode it using one of the functions described in Section 32.10.7 [Explicit Encoding], page 784.) This function operates only on text terminals. *terminal* may be a terminal object, a frame, or `nil` for the selected frame's terminal. In batch mode, *string* is sent to `stdout` when *terminal* is `nil`.

One use of this function is to define function keys on terminals that have downloadable function key definitions. For example, this is how (on certain terminals) to define function key 4 to move forward four characters (by transmitting the characters `C-u` `C-f` to the computer):

```
(send-string-to-terminal "\eF4\^U\^F")
     ⇒ nil
```

open-termscript *filename*   [Command]

> This function is used to open a *termscript file* that will record all the characters sent by Emacs to the terminal. It returns `nil`. Termscript files are useful for investigating problems where Emacs garbles the screen, problems that are due to incorrect Termcap entries or to undesirable settings of terminal options more often than to actual Emacs bugs. Once you are certain which characters were actually output, you can determine reliably whether they correspond to the Termcap specifications in use.

```
(open-termscript "../junk/termscript")
     ⇒ nil
```

> You close the termscript file by calling this function with an argument of `nil`.
>
> See also `open-dribble-file` in Section 38.13.2 [Recording Input], page 1011.

38.15 Sound Output

To play sound using Emacs, use the function `play-sound`. Only certain systems are supported; if you call `play-sound` on a system which cannot really do the job, it gives an error.

The sound must be stored as a file in RIFF-WAVE format ('`.wav`') or Sun Audio format ('`.au`').

play-sound *sound*   [Function]

> This function plays a specified sound. The argument, *sound*, has the form (`sound` *properties*...), where the *properties* consist of alternating keywords (particular symbols recognized specially) and values corresponding to them.
>
> Here is a table of the keywords that are currently meaningful in *sound*, and their meanings:
>
> `:file` *file*
>
>> This specifies the file containing the sound to play. If the file name is not absolute, it is expanded against the directory `data-directory`.
>
> `:data` *data*
>
>> This specifies the sound to play without need to refer to a file. The value, *data*, should be a string containing the same bytes as a sound file. We recommend using a unibyte string.

:volume *volume*

> This specifies how loud to play the sound. It should be a number in the range of 0 to 1. The default is to use whatever volume has been specified before.

:device *device*

> This specifies the system device on which to play the sound, as a string. The default device is system-dependent.

Before actually playing the sound, `play-sound` calls the functions in the list `play-sound-functions`. Each function is called with one argument, *sound*.

play-sound-file *file* &optional *volume device*   [Command]

> This function is an alternative interface to playing a sound *file* specifying an optional *volume* and *device*.

play-sound-functions   [Variable]

> A list of functions to be called before playing a sound. Each function is called with one argument, a property list that describes the sound.

38.16 Operating on X11 Keysyms

To define system-specific X11 keysyms, set the variable `system-key-alist`.

system-key-alist   [Variable]

> This variable's value should be an alist with one element for each system-specific keysym. Each element has the form (*code* . *symbol*), where *code* is the numeric keysym code (not including the vendor-specific bit, -2^{28}), and *symbol* is the name for the function key.
>
> For example (168 . mute-acute) defines a system-specific key (used by HP X servers) whose numeric code is -2^{28} + 168.
>
> It is not crucial to exclude from the alist the keysyms of other X servers; those do no harm, as long as they don't conflict with the ones used by the X server actually in use.
>
> The variable is always local to the current terminal, and cannot be buffer-local. See Section 28.2 [Multiple Terminals], page 631.

You can specify which keysyms Emacs should use for the Meta, Alt, Hyper, and Super modifiers by setting these variables:

x-alt-keysym   [Variable]
x-meta-keysym   [Variable]
x-hyper-keysym   [Variable]
x-super-keysym   [Variable]

> The name of the keysym that should stand for the Alt modifier (respectively, for Meta, Hyper, and Super). For example, here is how to swap the Meta and Alt modifiers within Emacs:
>
> ```
> (setq x-alt-keysym 'meta)
> (setq x-meta-keysym 'alt)
> ```

38.17 Batch Mode

The command-line option '-batch' causes Emacs to run noninteractively. In this mode, Emacs does not read commands from the terminal, it does not alter the terminal modes, and it does not expect to be outputting to an erasable screen. The idea is that you specify Lisp programs to run; when they are finished, Emacs should exit. The way to specify the programs to run is with '-l *file*', which loads the library named *file*, or '-f *function*', which calls *function* with no arguments, or '--eval *form*'.

Any Lisp program output that would normally go to the echo area, either using `message`, or using `prin1`, etc., with `t` as the stream, goes instead to Emacs's standard descriptors when in batch mode: `message` writes to the standard error descriptor, while `prin1` and other print functions write to the standard output. Similarly, input that would normally come from the minibuffer is read from the standard input descriptor. Thus, Emacs behaves much like a noninteractive application program. (The echo area output that Emacs itself normally generates, such as command echoing, is suppressed entirely.)

Non-ASCII text written to the standard output or error descriptors is by default encoded using `locale-coding-system` (see Section 32.12 [Locales], page 788) if it is non-`nil`; this can be overridden by binding `coding-system-for-write` to a coding system of you choice (see Section 32.10.7 [Explicit Encoding], page 784).

`noninteractive`   [Variable]
>   This variable is non-`nil` when Emacs is running in batch mode.

38.18 Session Management

Emacs supports the X Session Management Protocol, which is used to suspend and restart applications. In the X Window System, a program called the *session manager* is responsible for keeping track of the applications that are running. When the X server shuts down, the session manager asks applications to save their state, and delays the actual shutdown until they respond. An application can also cancel the shutdown.

When the session manager restarts a suspended session, it directs these applications to individually reload their saved state. It does this by specifying a special command-line argument that says what saved session to restore. For Emacs, this argument is '--smid *session*'.

`emacs-save-session-functions`   [Variable]
>   Emacs supports saving state via a hook called `emacs-save-session-functions`. Emacs runs this hook when the session manager tells it that the window system is shutting down. The functions are called with no arguments, and with the current buffer set to a temporary buffer. Each function can use `insert` to add Lisp code to this buffer. At the end, Emacs saves the buffer in a file, called the *session file*.
>
>   Subsequently, when the session manager restarts Emacs, it loads the session file automatically (see Chapter 15 [Loading], page 244). This is performed by a function named `emacs-session-restore`, which is called during startup. See Section 38.1.1 [Startup Summary], page 985.
>
>   If a function in `emacs-save-session-functions` returns non-`nil`, Emacs tells the session manager to cancel the shutdown.

Here is an example that just inserts some text into *scratch* when Emacs is restarted by the session manager.

```
(add-hook 'emacs-save-session-functions 'save-yourself-test)

(defun save-yourself-test ()
  (insert "(save-current-buffer
  (switch-to-buffer \"*scratch*\")
  (insert \"I am restored\"))")
  nil)
```

38.19 Desktop Notifications

Emacs is able to send *notifications* on systems that support the freedesktop.org Desktop Notifications Specification and on MS-Windows. In order to use this functionality on Posix hosts, Emacs must have been compiled with D-Bus support, and the **notifications** library must be loaded. See Section "D-Bus" in *D-Bus integration in Emacs*. The following function is supported when D-Bus support is available:

notifications-notify &rest *params*   [Function]
> This function sends a notification to the desktop via D-Bus, consisting of the parameters specified by the *params* arguments. These arguments should consist of alternating keyword and value pairs. The supported keywords and values are as follows:

> :bus *bus*   The D-Bus bus. This argument is needed only if a bus other than :session shall be used.

> :title *title*
> > The notification title.

> :body *text*
> > The notification body text. Depending on the implementation of the notification server, the text could contain HTML markups, like '"bold text"', hyperlinks, or images. Special HTML characters must be encoded, as '"Contact <postmaster@localhost>!"'.

> :app-name *name*
> > The name of the application sending the notification. The default is **notifications-application-name**.

> :replaces-id *id*
> > The notification *id* that this notification replaces. *id* must be the result of a previous **notifications-notify** call.

> :app-icon *icon-file*
> > The file name of the notification icon. If set to **nil**, no icon is displayed. The default is **notifications-application-icon**.

> :actions (*key title key title ...*)
> > A list of actions to be applied. *key* and *title* are both strings. The default action (usually invoked by clicking the notification) should have a key named '"default"'. The title can be anything, though implementations are free not to display it.

`:timeout` *timeout*

> The timeout time in milliseconds since the display of the notification at which the notification should automatically close. If −1, the notification's expiration time is dependent on the notification server's settings, and may vary for the type of notification. If 0, the notification never expires. Default value is −1.

`:urgency` *urgency*

> The urgency level. It can be **low**, **normal**, or **critical**.

`:action-items`

> When this keyword is given, the *title* string of the actions is interpreted as icon name.

`:category` *category*

> The type of notification this is, a string. See the Desktop Notifications Specification (`http://developer.gnome.org/notification-spec/#categories`) for a list of standard categories.

`:desktop-entry` *filename*

> This specifies the name of the desktop filename representing the calling program, like '`"emacs"`'.

`:image-data` (*width height rowstride has-alpha bits channels data*)

> This is a raw data image format that describes the width, height, rowstride, whether there is an alpha channel, bits per sample, channels and image data, respectively.

`:image-path` *path*

> This is represented either as a URI ('`file://`' is the only URI schema supported right now) or a name in a freedesktop.org-compliant icon theme from '`$XDG_DATA_DIRS/icons`'.

`:sound-file` *filename*

> The path to a sound file to play when the notification pops up.

`:sound-name` *name*

> A themable named sound from the freedesktop.org sound naming specification from '`$XDG_DATA_DIRS/sounds`', to play when the notification pops up. Similar to the icon name, only for sounds. An example would be '`"message-new-instant"`'.

`:suppress-sound`

> Causes the server to suppress playing any sounds, if it has that ability.

`:resident`

> When set the server will not automatically remove the notification when an action has been invoked. The notification will remain resident in the server until it is explicitly removed by the user or by the sender. This hint is likely only useful when the server has the `:persistence` capability.

`:transient`

> When set the server will treat the notification as transient and by-pass the server's persistence capability, if it should exist.

:x *position*
:y *position*

> Specifies the X, Y location on the screen that the notification should point to. Both arguments must be used together.

:on-action *function*

> Function to call when an action is invoked. The notification *id* and the *key* of the action are passed as arguments to the function.

:on-close *function*

> Function to call when the notification has been closed by timeout or by the user. The function receive the notification *id* and the closing *reason* as arguments:
>
> - expired if the notification has expired
> - dismissed if the notification was dismissed by the user
> - close-notification if the notification was closed by a call to notifications-close-notification
> - undefined if the notification server hasn't provided a reason

Which parameters are accepted by the notification server can be checked via notifications-get-capabilities.

This function returns a notification id, an integer, which can be used to manipulate the notification item with **notifications-close-notification** or the :replaces-id argument of another **notifications-notify** call. For example:

```
(defun my-on-action-function (id key)
  (message "Message %d, key \"%s\" pressed" id key))
    ⇒ my-on-action-function

(defun my-on-close-function (id reason)
  (message "Message %d, closed due to \"%s\"" id reason))
    ⇒ my-on-close-function

(notifications-notify
 :title "Title"
 :body "This is <b>important</b>."
 :actions '("Confirm" "I agree" "Refuse" "I disagree")
 :on-action 'my-on-action-function
 :on-close 'my-on-close-function)
    ⇒ 22


A message window opens on the desktop.  Press ``I agree''.
    ⇒ Message 22, key "Confirm" pressed
       Message 22, closed due to "dismissed"
```

notifications-close-notification *id* &**optional** *bus*   [Function]

> This function closes a notification with identifier *id*. *bus* can be a string denoting a D-Bus connection, the default is :session.

notifications-get-capabilities &optional *bus*   [Function]

Returns the capabilities of the notification server, a list of symbols. *bus* can be a string denoting a D-Bus connection, the default is `:session`. The following capabilities can be expected:

`:actions`   The server will provide the specified actions to the user.

`:body`   Supports body text.

`:body-hyperlinks`
              The server supports hyperlinks in the notifications.

`:body-images`
              The server supports images in the notifications.

`:body-markup`
              Supports markup in the body text.

`:icon-multi`
              The server will render an animation of all the frames in a given image array.

`:icon-static`
              Supports display of exactly 1 frame of any given image array. This value is mutually exclusive with `:icon-multi`.

`:persistence`
              The server supports persistence of notifications.

`:sound`   The server supports sounds on notifications.

Further vendor-specific caps start with `:x-vendor`, like `:x-gnome-foo-cap`.

notifications-get-server-information &optional *bus*   [Function]

Return information on the notification server, a list of strings. *bus* can be a string denoting a D-Bus connection, the default is `:session`. The returned list is (*name vendor version spec-version*).

name   The product name of the server.

vendor   The vendor name. For example, '`"KDE"`', '`"GNOME"`'.

version   The server's version number.

spec-version
              The specification version the server is compliant with.

If *spec_version* is `nil`, the server supports a specification prior to '`"1.0"`'.

When Emacs runs on MS-Windows as a GUI session, it supports a small subset of the D-Bus notifications functionality via a native primitive:

w32-notification-notify &rest *params*   [Function]

This function displays an MS-Windows tray notification as specified by *params*. MS-Windows tray notifications are displayed in a balloon from an icon in the notification area of the taskbar.

Value is the integer unique ID of the notification that can be used to remove the notification using `w32-notification-close`, described below. If the function fails, the return value is `nil`.

The arguments *params* are specified as keyword/value pairs. All the parameters are optional, but if no parameters are specified, the function will do nothing and return `nil`.

The following parameters are supported:

`:icon` *icon*

> Display *icon* in the system tray. If *icon* is a string, it should specify a file name from which to load the icon; the specified file should be a `.ico` Windows icon file. If *icon* is not a string, or if this parameter is not specified, the standard Emacs icon will be used.

`:tip` *tip*   Use *tip* as the tooltip for the notification. If *tip* is a string, this is the text of a tooltip that will be shown when the mouse pointer hovers over the tray icon added by the notification. If *tip* is not a string, or if this parameter is not specified, the default tooltip text is '`Emacs notification`'. The tooltip text can be up to 127 characters long (63 on Windows versions before W2K). Longer strings will be truncated.

`:level` *level*

> Notification severity level, one of `info`, `warning`, or `error`. If given, the value determines the icon displayed to the left of the notification title, but only if the `:title` parameter (see below) is also specified and is a string.

`:title` *title*

> The title of the notification. If *title* is a string, it is displayed in a larger font immediately above the body text. The title text can be up to 63 characters long; longer text will be truncated.

`:body` *body*

> The body of the notification. If *body* is a string, it specifies the text of the notification message. Use embedded newlines to control how the text is broken into lines. The body text can be up to 255 characters long, and will be truncated if it's longer. Unlike with D-Bus, the body text should be plain text, with no markup.

Note that versions of Windows before W2K support only `:icon` and `:tip`. The other parameters can be passed, but they will be ignored on those old systems.

There can be at most one active notification at any given time. An active notification must be removed by calling `w32-notification-close` before a new one can be shown.

To remove the notification and its icon from the taskbar, use the following function:

`w32-notification-close` *id*   [Function]

> This function removes the tray notification given by its unique *id*.

38.20 Notifications on File Changes

Several operating systems support watching of filesystems for changes of files. If configured properly, Emacs links a respective library like `inotify`, `kqueue`, `gfilenotify`, or `w32notify` statically. These libraries enable watching of filesystems on the local machine.

It is also possible to watch filesystems on remote machines, see Section "Remote Files" in *The GNU Emacs Manual* This does not depend on one of the libraries linked to Emacs.

Since all these libraries emit different events on notified file changes, there is the Emacs library `filenotify` which provides a unique interface.

file-notify-add-watch *file flags callback*   [Function]

Add a watch for filesystem events pertaining to *file*. This arranges for filesystem events pertaining to *file* to be reported to Emacs.

The returned value is a descriptor for the added watch. Its type depends on the underlying library, it cannot be assumed to be an integer as in the example below. It should be used for comparison by `equal` only.

If the *file* cannot be watched for some reason, this function signals a `file-notify-error` error.

Sometimes, mounted filesystems cannot be watched for file changes. This is not detected by this function, a non-`nil` return value does not guarantee that changes on *file* will be notified.

flags is a list of conditions to set what will be watched for. It can include the following symbols:

change   watch for file changes

attribute-change
                watch for file attribute changes, like permissions or modification time

If *file* is a directory, changes for all files in that directory will be notified. This does not work recursively.

When any event happens, Emacs will call the *callback* function passing it a single argument *event*, which is of the form

        (descriptor action file [file1])

descriptor is the same object as the one returned by this function. *action* is the description of the event. It could be any one of the following symbols:

created   *file* was created

deleted   *file* was deleted

changed   *file*'s contents has changed; with `w32notify` library, reports attribute changes as well

renamed   *file* has been renamed to *file1*

attribute-changed
                a *file* attribute was changed

stopped   watching *file* has been stopped

Note that the `w32notify` library does not report `attribute-changed` events. When some file's attribute, like permissions or modification time, has changed, this library reports a `changed` event. Likewise, the `kqueue` library does not report reliably file attribute changes when watching a directory.

The `stopped` event reports, that watching the file has been stopped. This could be because `file-notify-rm-watch` was called (see below), or because the file being watched was deleted, or due to another error reported from the underlying library.

file and *file1* are the name of the file(s) whose event is being reported. For example:

```
(require 'filenotify)
     ⇒ filenotify

(defun my-notify-callback (event)
  (message "Event %S" event))
     ⇒ my-notify-callback

(file-notify-add-watch
  "/tmp" '(change attribute-change) 'my-notify-callback)
     ⇒ 35025468

(write-region "foo" nil "/tmp/foo")
     ⇒ Event (35025468 created "/tmp/.#foo")
        Event (35025468 created "/tmp/foo")
        Event (35025468 changed "/tmp/foo")
        Event (35025468 deleted "/tmp/.#foo")

(write-region "bla" nil "/tmp/foo")
     ⇒ Event (35025468 created "/tmp/.#foo")
        Event (35025468 changed "/tmp/foo")
        Event (35025468 deleted "/tmp/.#foo")

(set-file-modes "/tmp/foo" (default-file-modes))
     ⇒ Event (35025468 attribute-changed "/tmp/foo")
```

Whether the action `renamed` is returned, depends on the used watch library. Otherwise, the actions `deleted` and `created` could be returned in a random order.

```
(rename-file "/tmp/foo" "/tmp/bla")
     ⇒ Event (35025468 renamed "/tmp/foo" "/tmp/bla")

(delete-file "/tmp/bla")
     ⇒ Event (35025468 deleted "/tmp/bla")
```

file-notify-rm-watch *descriptor*   [Function]
> Removes an existing file watch specified by its *descriptor*. *descriptor* should be an object returned by `file-notify-add-watch`.

file-notify-valid-p *descriptor*   [Function]
> Checks a watch specified by its *descriptor* for validity. *descriptor* should be an object returned by `file-notify-add-watch`.

A watch can become invalid if the file or directory it watches is deleted, or if the watcher thread exits abnormally for any other reason. Removing the watch by calling `file-notify-rm-watch` also makes it invalid.

```
(make-directory "/tmp/foo")
     ⇒ Event (35025468 created "/tmp/foo")

(setq desc
      (file-notify-add-watch
        "/tmp/foo" '(change) 'my-notify-callback))
     ⇒ 11359632

(file-notify-valid-p desc)
     ⇒ t

(write-region "bla" nil "/tmp/foo/bla")
     ⇒ Event (11359632 created "/tmp/foo/.#bla")
        Event (11359632 created "/tmp/foo/bla")
        Event (11359632 changed "/tmp/foo/bla")
        Event (11359632 deleted "/tmp/foo/.#bla")

;; Deleting a file in the directory doesn't invalidate the watch.
(delete-file "/tmp/foo/bla")
     ⇒ Event (11359632 deleted "/tmp/foo/bla")

(write-region "bla" nil "/tmp/foo/bla")
     ⇒ Event (11359632 created "/tmp/foo/.#bla")
        Event (11359632 created "/tmp/foo/bla")
        Event (11359632 changed "/tmp/foo/bla")
        Event (11359632 deleted "/tmp/foo/.#bla")

;; Deleting the directory invalidates the watch.
;; Events arrive for different watch descriptors.
(delete-directory "/tmp/foo" 'recursive)
     ⇒ Event (35025468 deleted "/tmp/foo")
        Event (11359632 deleted "/tmp/foo/bla")
        Event (11359632 deleted "/tmp/foo")
        Event (11359632 stopped "/tmp/foo")

(file-notify-valid-p desc)
     ⇒ nil
```

38.21 Dynamically Loaded Libraries

A *dynamically loaded library* is a library that is loaded on demand, when its facilities are first needed. Emacs supports such on-demand loading of support libraries for some of its features.

`dynamic-library-alist`   [Variable]

This is an alist of dynamic libraries and external library files implementing them.

Each element is a list of the form (*library files*...), where the `car` is a symbol representing a supported external library, and the rest are strings giving alternate filenames for that library.

Emacs tries to load the library from the files in the order they appear in the list; if none is found, the Emacs session won't have access to that library, and the features it provides will be unavailable.

Image support on some platforms uses this facility. Here's an example of setting this variable for supporting images on MS-Windows:

```
(setq dynamic-library-alist
      '((xpm "libxpm.dll" "xpm4.dll" "libXpm-nox4.dll")
        (png "libpng12d.dll" "libpng12.dll" "libpng.dll"
             "libpng13d.dll" "libpng13.dll")
        (jpeg "jpeg62.dll" "libjpeg.dll" "jpeg-62.dll"
              "jpeg.dll")
        (tiff "libtiff3.dll" "libtiff.dll")
        (gif "giflib4.dll" "libungif4.dll" "libungif.dll")
        (svg "librsvg-2-2.dll")
        (gdk-pixbuf "libgdk_pixbuf-2.0-0.dll")
        (glib "libglib-2.0-0.dll")
        (gobject "libgobject-2.0-0.dll")))
```

Note that image types `pbm` and `xbm` do not need entries in this variable because they do not depend on external libraries and are always available in Emacs.

Also note that this variable is not meant to be a generic facility for accessing external libraries; only those already known by Emacs can be loaded through it.

This variable is ignored if the given *library* is statically linked into Emacs.

38.22 Security Considerations

Like any application, Emacs can be run in a secure environment, where the operating system enforces rules about access and the like. With some care, Emacs-based applications can also be part of a security perimeter that checks such rules. Although the default settings for Emacs work well for a typical software development environment, they may require adjustment in environments containing untrusted users that may include attackers. Here is a compendium of security issues that may be helpful if you are developing such applications. It is by no means complete; it is intended to give you an idea of the security issues involved, rather than to be a security checklist.

File local variables

A file that Emacs visits can contain variable settings that affects the buffer visiting that file; See Section 11.11 [File Local Variables], page 177. Similarly, a directory can specify local variable values common to all files in that directory; See Section 11.12 [Directory Local Variables], page 180. Although Emacs takes some effort to protect against misuse of these variables, a security hole can be created merely by a package setting `safe-local-variable` too optimistically, a problem that is all too common. To disable this feature for both files and directories, set `enable-local-variables` to `nil`.

Access control

Although Emacs normally respects access permissions of the underlying operating system, in some cases it handles accesses specially. For example, file names can have handlers that treat the files specially, with their own access checking. See Section 24.11 [Magic File Names], page 529. Also, a buffer can be read-only even if the corresponding file is writeable, and vice versa, which can result in messages such as 'File `passwd` is `write-protected; try to save anyway?` (yes or no)'. See Section 26.7 [Read Only Buffers], page 558.

Authentication

Emacs has several functions that deal with passwords, e.g., `read-passwd`. See Section 19.9 [Reading a Password], page 340. Although these functions do not attempt to broadcast passwords to the world, their implementations are not proof against determined attackers with access to Emacs internals. For example, even if Elisp code uses `clear-string` to scrub a password from its memory after using it, remnants of the password may still reside in the garbage-collected free list. See Section 4.4 [Modifying Strings], page 53.

Code injection

Emacs can send commands to many other applications, and applications should take care that strings sent as operands of these commands are not misinterpreted as directives. For example, when using a shell command to rename a file *a* to *b*, do not simply use the string `mv a b`, because either file name might start with '`-`', or might contain shell metacharacters like '`;`'. Although functions like `shell-quote-argument` can help avoid this sort of problem, they are not panaceas; for example, on a POSIX platform `shell-quote-argument` quotes shell metacharacters but not leading '`-`'. See Section 36.2 [Shell Arguments], page 841. Typically it is safer to use `call-process` than a subshell. See Section 36.3 [Synchronous Processes], page 842. And it is safer yet to use builtin Emacs functions; for example, use `(rename-file "a" "b" t)` instead of invoking `mv`. See Section 24.7 [Changing Files], page 514.

Coding systems

Emacs attempts to infer the coding systems of the files and network connections it accesses. See Section 32.10 [Coding Systems], page 773. If Emacs infers incorrectly, or if the other parties to the network connection disagree with Emacs's inferences, the resulting system could be unreliable. Also, even when it infers correctly, Emacs often can use bytes that other programs cannot. For example, although to Emacs the null byte is just a character like any other, many other applications treat it as a string terminator and mishandle strings or files containing null bytes.

Environment and configuration variables

POSIX specifies several environment variables that can affect how Emacs behaves. Any environment variable whose name consists entirely of uppercase ASCII letters, digits, and the underscore may affect the internal behavior of Emacs. Emacs uses several such variables, e.g., `EMACSLOADPATH`. See

Section 15.3 [Library Search], page 247. On some platforms some environment variables (e.g., `PATH`, `POSIXLY_CORRECT`, `SHELL`, `TMPDIR`) need to have properly-configured values in order to get standard behavior for any utility Emacs might invoke. Even seemingly-benign variables like `TZ` may have security implications. See Section 38.3 [System Environment], page 994.

Emacs has customization and other variables with similar considerations. For example, if the variable `shell-file-name` specifies a shell with nonstandard behavior, an Emacs-based application may misbehave.

Installation

When Emacs is installed, if the installation directory hierarchy can be modified by untrusted users, the application cannot be trusted. This applies also to the directory hierarchies of the programs that Emacs uses, and of the files that Emacs reads and writes.

Network access

Emacs often accesses the network, and you may want to configure it to avoid network accesses that it would normally do. For example, unless you set `tramp-mode` to `nil`, file names using a certain syntax are interpreted as being network files, and are retrieved across the network. See *The Tramp Manual*.

Race conditions

Emacs applications have the same sort of race-condition issues that other applications do. For example, even when (`file-readable-p "foo.txt"`) returns `t`, it could be that `foo.txt` is unreadable because some other program changed the file's permissions between the call to `file-readable-p` and now. See Section 24.6.1 [Testing Accessibility], page 505.

Resource limits

When Emacs exhausts memory or other operating system resources, its behavior can be less reliable, in that computations that ordinarily run to completion may abort back to the top level. This may cause Emacs to neglect operations that it normally would have done.

39 Preparing Lisp code for distribution

Emacs provides a standard way to distribute Emacs Lisp code to users. A *package* is a collection of one or more files, formatted and bundled in such a way that users can easily download, install, uninstall, and upgrade it.

The following sections describe how to create a package, and how to put it in a *package archive* for others to download. See Section "Packages" in *The GNU Emacs Manual*, for a description of user-level features of the packaging system.

39.1 Packaging Basics

A package is either a *simple package* or a *multi-file package*. A simple package is stored in a package archive as a single Emacs Lisp file, while a multi-file package is stored as a tar file (containing multiple Lisp files, and possibly non-Lisp files such as a manual).

In ordinary usage, the difference between simple packages and multi-file packages is relatively unimportant; the Package Menu interface makes no distinction between them. However, the procedure for creating them differs, as explained in the following sections.

Each package (whether simple or multi-file) has certain *attributes*:

Name
: A short word (e.g., 'auctex'). This is usually also the symbol prefix used in the program (see Section D.1 [Coding Conventions], page 1053).

Version
: A version number, in a form that the function `version-to-list` understands (e.g., '11.86'). Each release of a package should be accompanied by an increase in the version number so that it will be recognized as an upgrade by users querying the package archive.

Brief description
: This is shown when the package is listed in the Package Menu. It should occupy a single line, ideally in 36 characters or less.

Long description
: This is shown in the buffer created by *C-h P* (`describe-package`), following the package's brief description and installation status. It normally spans multiple lines, and should fully describe the package's capabilities and how to begin using it once it is installed.

Dependencies
: A list of other packages (possibly including minimal acceptable version numbers) on which this package depends. The list may be empty, meaning this package has no dependencies. Otherwise, installing this package also automatically installs its dependencies, recursively; if any dependency cannot be found, the package cannot be installed.

Installing a package, either via the command `package-install-file`, or via the Package Menu, creates a subdirectory of `package-user-dir` named *name-version*, where *name* is the package's name and *version* its version (e.g., `~/.emacs.d/elpa/auctex-11.86/`). We call this the package's *content directory*. It is where Emacs puts the package's contents (the single Lisp file for a simple package, or the files extracted from a multi-file package).

Emacs then searches every Lisp file in the content directory for autoload magic comments (see Section 15.5 [Autoload], page 249). These autoload definitions are saved to a file named *name*-autoloads.el in the content directory. They are typically used to autoload the principal user commands defined in the package, but they can also perform other tasks, such as adding an element to auto-mode-alist (see Section 22.2.2 [Auto Major Mode], page 435). Note that a package typically does *not* autoload every function and variable defined within it—only the handful of commands typically called to begin using the package. Emacs then byte-compiles every Lisp file in the package.

After installation, the installed package is *loaded*: Emacs adds the package's content directory to load-path, and evaluates the autoload definitions in *name*-autoloads.el.

Whenever Emacs starts up, it automatically calls the function package-initialize to load installed packages. This is done after loading the init file and abbrev file (if any) and before running after-init-hook (see Section 38.1.1 [Startup Summary], page 985). Automatic package loading is disabled if the user option package-enable-at-startup is nil.

package-initialize &optional *no-activate*   [Command]
> This function initializes Emacs' internal record of which packages are installed, and loads them. The user option package-load-list specifies which packages to load; by default, all installed packages are loaded. If called during startup, this function also sets package-enable-at-startup to nil, to avoid accidentally loading the packages twice. See Section "Package Installation" in *The GNU Emacs Manual*.
>
> The optional argument *no-activate*, if non-nil, causes Emacs to update its record of installed packages without actually loading them; it is for internal use only.

39.2 Simple Packages

A simple package consists of a single Emacs Lisp source file. The file must conform to the Emacs Lisp library header conventions (see Section D.8 [Library Headers], page 1063). The package's attributes are taken from the various headers, as illustrated by the following example:

```
;;; superfrobnicator.el --- Frobnicate and bifurcate flanges

;; Copyright (C) 2011 Free Software Foundation, Inc.

;; Author: J. R. Hacker <jrh@example.com>
;; Version: 1.3
;; Package-Requires: ((flange "1.0"))
;; Keywords: multimedia, frobnicate
;; URL: http://example.com/jrhacker/superfrobnicate

...

;;; Commentary:

;; This package provides a minor mode to frobnicate and/or
;; bifurcate any flanges you desire.  To activate it, just type
```

```
          ...

          ;;;###autoload
          (define-minor-mode superfrobnicator-mode
          ...
```

The name of the package is the same as the base name of the file, as written on the first line. Here, it is 'superfrobnicator'.

The brief description is also taken from the first line. Here, it is 'Frobnicate and bifurcate flanges'.

The version number comes from the 'Package-Version' header, if it exists, or from the 'Version' header otherwise. One or the other *must* be present. Here, the version number is 1.3.

If the file has a ';;; Commentary:' section, this section is used as the long description. (When displaying the description, Emacs omits the ';;; Commentary:' line, as well as the leading comment characters in the commentary itself.)

If the file has a 'Package-Requires' header, that is used as the package dependencies. In the above example, the package depends on the 'flange' package, version 1.0 or higher. See Section D.8 [Library Headers], page 1063, for a description of the 'Package-Requires' header. If the header is omitted, the package has no dependencies.

The 'Keywords' and 'URL' headers are optional, but recommended. The command describe-package uses these to add links to its output. The 'Keywords' header should contain at least one standard keyword from the finder-known-keywords list.

The file ought to also contain one or more autoload magic comments, as explained in Section 39.1 [Packaging Basics], page 1026. In the above example, a magic comment autoloads superfrobnicator-mode.

See Section 39.4 [Package Archives], page 1029, for a explanation of how to add a single-file package to a package archive.

39.3 Multi-file Packages

A multi-file package is less convenient to create than a single-file package, but it offers more features: it can include multiple Emacs Lisp files, an Info manual, and other file types (such as images).

Prior to installation, a multi-file package is stored in a package archive as a tar file. The tar file must be named *name-version*.tar, where *name* is the package name and *version* is the version number. Its contents, once extracted, must all appear in a directory named *name-version*, the *content directory* (see Section 39.1 [Packaging Basics], page 1026). Files may also extract into subdirectories of the content directory.

One of the files in the content directory must be named *name*-pkg.el. It must contain a single Lisp form, consisting of a call to the function define-package, described below. This defines the package's attributes: version, brief description, and requirements.

For example, if we distribute version 1.3 of the superfrobnicator as a multi-file package, the tar file would be superfrobnicator-1.3.tar. Its contents would extract into the directory superfrobnicator-1.3, and one of these would be the file superfrobnicator-pkg.el.

define-package *name version* **&optional** *docstring requirements* [Function]

    This function defines a package. *name* is the package name, a string. *version* is the version, as a string of a form that can be understood by the function `version-to-list`. *docstring* is the brief description.

    requirements is a list of required packages and their versions. Each element in this list should have the form (`dep-name dep-version`), where *dep-name* is a symbol whose name is the dependency's package name, and *dep-version* is the dependency's version (a string).

If the content directory contains a file named `README`, this file is used as the long description.

If the content directory contains a file named `dir`, this is assumed to be an Info directory file made with `install-info`. See Section "Invoking install-info" in *Texinfo*. The relevant Info files should also be present in the content directory. In this case, Emacs will automatically add the content directory to `Info-directory-list` when the package is activated.

Do not include any `.elc` files in the package. Those are created when the package is installed. Note that there is no way to control the order in which files are byte-compiled.

Do not include any file named **name-autoloads.el**. This file is reserved for the package's autoload definitions (see Section 39.1 [Packaging Basics], page 1026). It is created automatically when the package is installed, by searching all the Lisp files in the package for autoload magic comments.

If the multi-file package contains auxiliary data files (such as images), the package's Lisp code can refer to these files via the variable `load-file-name` (see Chapter 15 [Loading], page 244). Here is an example:

```
(defconst superfrobnicator-base (file-name-directory load-file-name))

(defun superfrobnicator-fetch-image (file)
  (expand-file-name file superfrobnicator-base))
```

39.4 Creating and Maintaining Package Archives

Via the Package Menu, users may download packages from *package archives*. Such archives are specified by the variable `package-archives`, whose default value contains a single entry: the archive hosted by the GNU project at `http://elpa.gnu.org`. This section describes how to set up and maintain a package archive.

package-archives [User Option]

    The value of this variable is an alist of package archives recognized by the Emacs package manager.

    Each alist element corresponds to one archive, and should have the form (`id . location`), where *id* is the name of the archive (a string) and *location* is its *base location* (a string).

    If the base location starts with '`http:`', it is treated as a HTTP URL, and packages are downloaded from this archive via HTTP (as is the case for the default GNU archive).

    Otherwise, the base location should be a directory name. In this case, Emacs retrieves packages from this archive via ordinary file access. Such local archives are mainly useful for testing.

A package archive is simply a directory in which the package files, and associated files, are stored. If you want the archive to be reachable via HTTP, this directory must be accessible to a web server. How to accomplish this is beyond the scope of this manual.

A convenient way to set up and update a package archive is via the `package-x` library. This is included with Emacs, but not loaded by default; type *M-x load-library RET package-x RET* to load it, or add (`require 'package-x`) to your init file. See Section "Lisp Libraries" in *The GNU Emacs Manual*. Once loaded, you can make use of the following:

`package-archive-upload-base`   [User Option]

> The value of this variable is the base location of a package archive, as a directory name. The commands in the `package-x` library will use this base location.
>
> The directory name should be absolute. You may specify a remote name, such as `/ssh:foo@example.com:/var/www/packages/`, if the package archive is on a different machine. See Section "Remote Files" in *The GNU Emacs Manual*.

`package-upload-file` *filename*   [Command]

> This command prompts for *filename*, a file name, and uploads that file to `package-archive-upload-base`. The file must be either a simple package (a `.el` file) or a multi-file package (a `.tar` file); otherwise, an error is raised. The package attributes are automatically extracted, and the archive's contents list is updated with this information.
>
> If `package-archive-upload-base` does not specify a valid directory, the function prompts interactively for one. If the directory does not exist, it is created. The directory need not have any initial contents (i.e., you can use this command to populate an initially empty archive).

`package-upload-buffer`   [Command]

> This command is similar to `package-upload-file`, but instead of prompting for a package file, it uploads the contents of the current buffer. The current buffer must be visiting a simple package (a `.el` file) or a multi-file package (a `.tar` file); otherwise, an error is raised.

After you create an archive, remember that it is not accessible in the Package Menu interface unless it is in `package-archives`.

Maintaining a public package archive entails a degree of responsibility. When Emacs users install packages from your archive, those packages can cause Emacs to run arbitrary code with the permissions of the installing user. (This is true for Emacs code in general, not just for packages.) So you should ensure that your archive is well-maintained and keep the hosting system secure.

One way to increase the security of your packages is to *sign* them using a cryptographic key. If you have generated a private/public gpg key pair, you can use gpg to sign the package like this:

```
gpg -ba -o file.sig file
```

For a single-file package, *file* is the package Lisp file; for a multi-file package, it is the package tar file. You can also sign the archive's contents file in the same way. Make the `.sig` files available in the same location as the packages. You should also make your public key available for people to download; e.g., by uploading it to a key server such as `http://pgp.mit.edu/`. When people install packages from your archive, they can use your public key to verify the signatures.

A full explanation of these matters is outside the scope of this manual. For more information on cryptographic keys and signing, see Section "GnuPG" in *The GNU Privacy Guard Manual*. Emacs comes with an interface to GNU Privacy Guard, see Section "EasyPG" in *Emacs EasyPG Assistant Manual*.

Appendix A Emacs 24 Antinews

For those users who live backwards in time, here is information about downgrading to Emacs version 24.5. We hope you will enjoy the greater simplicity that results from the absence of many Emacs 25.2 features.

A.1 Old Lisp Features in Emacs 24

- The requirement that `setq` and `setf` must be called with an even number of arguments has been removed. You can now call them with an odd number of arguments, and Emacs will helpfully supply a `nil` for the missing one. Simplicity rules!

- *M-x shell* and *M-x compile* set the `EMACS` environment variable, as they should, to indicate that the subprocess is run by Emacs. This is so packages that took years to learn how to work around that setting could continue using their code to that effect.

- The `save-excursion` form saves and restores the mark, as expected. No more need for the new `save-mark-and-excursion`, which has been deleted.

- We have removed the `text-quoting-style` variable and the associated functionality that translates quote characters in messages displayed to the user and in help buffers. Emacs now shows exactly the same quote characters as you wrote in your code! Likewise, `substitute-command-keys` leaves the quote characters alone. As you move back in time, Unicode support becomes less and less important, so no need to display those fancy new quotes the Unicode Standard invented.

- Regular expressions have been simplified by removing support for Unicode character properties in regexp classes. As result, `[:alpha:]` and `[:alnum:]` will match any character with a word syntax, and `[:graph:]` and `[:print:]` will match any multibyte character, including surrogates and unassigned codepoints. Once again, this is in line with diminishing importance of Unicode as you move back in time.

- Evaluating '`(/ n)`' will now yield *n*. We have realized that interpreting that as in Common Lisp was a bad mistake that needed to be corrected.

- The `pcase` form was significantly simplified by removing the UPatterns `quote` and `app`. To further simplify this facility, we've removed `pcase-defmacro`, since we found no need for letting Lisp programs define new UPatterns.

- We've removed the text properties `cursor-intangible` and `cursor-sensor-functions`, replacing them by the much simpler `intangible`, `point-entered`, and `point-left` properties. The latter are implemented on a much lower level, and therefore are better integrated with user expectations. For similar reasons, `cursor-intangible-mode` and `cursor-sensor-mode` were removed; use the hook variable `inhibit-point-motion-hooks` which is no longer obsolete.

- Process creation and management functions were significantly improved and simplified by removing `make-process` and the `pipe` connection type. Redirecting `stderr` of a subprocess should be done with shell facilities, not by Emacs.

- We decided that shutting up informative messages is bad for user interaction, so we've removed the `inhibit-message` variable which could be used to that effect.

- Support for generators and for finalizers has been removed, as we found no real need for these facilities.

- Due to excessive complexity and the diminishing need for Unicode support, the functions `string-collate-lessp` and `string-collate-equalp` were removed. Their locale-independent counterparts `string-lessp` and `string-equal` are so much more simple and yield predictable results that we don't see any situation where the locale-dependent collation could be useful in Emacs. As result, the `ls-lisp.el` package sorts files in a locale-independent manner.

- In preparation for removal in some past version of Emacs of the bidirectional editing support, we started by deleting two functions `bidi-find-overridden-directionality` and `buffer-substring-with-bidi-context`.

- Time conversion functions, such as `current-time-string`, no longer accept an optional *zone* argument. If you need to change the current time zone (why?), do that explicitly with `set-time-zone-rule`.

- As part of the ongoing quest for simplicity, many other functions and variables have been eliminated.

Appendix B GNU Free Documentation License

Version 1.3, 3 November 2008

Copyright © 2000, 2001, 2002, 2007, 2008 Free Software Foundation, Inc.
`http://fsf.org/`

Everyone is permitted to copy and distribute verbatim copies
of this license document, but changing it is not allowed.

0. PREAMBLE

The purpose of this License is to make a manual, textbook, or other functional and
useful document *free* in the sense of freedom: to assure everyone the effective freedom
to copy and redistribute it, with or without modifying it, either commercially or non-
commercially. Secondarily, this License preserves for the author and publisher a way
to get credit for their work, while not being considered responsible for modifications
made by others.

This License is a kind of "copyleft", which means that derivative works of the document
must themselves be free in the same sense. It complements the GNU General Public
License, which is a copyleft license designed for free software.

We have designed this License in order to use it for manuals for free software, because
free software needs free documentation: a free program should come with manuals
providing the same freedoms that the software does. But this License is not limited to
software manuals; it can be used for any textual work, regardless of subject matter or
whether it is published as a printed book. We recommend this License principally for
works whose purpose is instruction or reference.

1. APPLICABILITY AND DEFINITIONS

This License applies to any manual or other work, in any medium, that contains a
notice placed by the copyright holder saying it can be distributed under the terms
of this License. Such a notice grants a world-wide, royalty-free license, unlimited in
duration, to use that work under the conditions stated herein. The "Document",
below, refers to any such manual or work. Any member of the public is a licensee, and
is addressed as "you". You accept the license if you copy, modify or distribute the work
in a way requiring permission under copyright law.

A "Modified Version" of the Document means any work containing the Document or
a portion of it, either copied verbatim, or with modifications and/or translated into
another language.

A "Secondary Section" is a named appendix or a front-matter section of the Document
that deals exclusively with the relationship of the publishers or authors of the Document
to the Document's overall subject (or to related matters) and contains nothing that
could fall directly within that overall subject. (Thus, if the Document is in part a
textbook of mathematics, a Secondary Section may not explain any mathematics.) The
relationship could be a matter of historical connection with the subject or with related
matters, or of legal, commercial, philosophical, ethical or political position regarding
them.

The "Invariant Sections" are certain Secondary Sections whose titles are designated, as
being those of Invariant Sections, in the notice that says that the Document is released

under this License. If a section does not fit the above definition of Secondary then it is not allowed to be designated as Invariant. The Document may contain zero Invariant Sections. If the Document does not identify any Invariant Sections then there are none.

The "Cover Texts" are certain short passages of text that are listed, as Front-Cover Texts or Back-Cover Texts, in the notice that says that the Document is released under this License. A Front-Cover Text may be at most 5 words, and a Back-Cover Text may be at most 25 words.

A "Transparent" copy of the Document means a machine-readable copy, represented in a format whose specification is available to the general public, that is suitable for revising the document straightforwardly with generic text editors or (for images composed of pixels) generic paint programs or (for drawings) some widely available drawing editor, and that is suitable for input to text formatters or for automatic translation to a variety of formats suitable for input to text formatters. A copy made in an otherwise Transparent file format whose markup, or absence of markup, has been arranged to thwart or discourage subsequent modification by readers is not Transparent. An image format is not Transparent if used for any substantial amount of text. A copy that is not "Transparent" is called "Opaque".

Examples of suitable formats for Transparent copies include plain ASCII without markup, Texinfo input format, LaTeX input format, SGML or XML using a publicly available DTD, and standard-conforming simple HTML, PostScript or PDF designed for human modification. Examples of transparent image formats include PNG, XCF and JPG. Opaque formats include proprietary formats that can be read and edited only by proprietary word processors, SGML or XML for which the DTD and/or processing tools are not generally available, and the machine-generated HTML, PostScript or PDF produced by some word processors for output purposes only.

The "Title Page" means, for a printed book, the title page itself, plus such following pages as are needed to hold, legibly, the material this License requires to appear in the title page. For works in formats which do not have any title page as such, "Title Page" means the text near the most prominent appearance of the work's title, preceding the beginning of the body of the text.

The "publisher" means any person or entity that distributes copies of the Document to the public.

A section "Entitled XYZ" means a named subunit of the Document whose title either is precisely XYZ or contains XYZ in parentheses following text that translates XYZ in another language. (Here XYZ stands for a specific section name mentioned below, such as "Acknowledgements", "Dedications", "Endorsements", or "History".) To "Preserve the Title" of such a section when you modify the Document means that it remains a section "Entitled XYZ" according to this definition.

The Document may include Warranty Disclaimers next to the notice which states that this License applies to the Document. These Warranty Disclaimers are considered to be included by reference in this License, but only as regards disclaiming warranties: any other implication that these Warranty Disclaimers may have is void and has no effect on the meaning of this License.

2. VERBATIM COPYING

You may copy and distribute the Document in any medium, either commercially or noncommercially, provided that this License, the copyright notices, and the license notice saying this License applies to the Document are reproduced in all copies, and that you add no other conditions whatsoever to those of this License. You may not use technical measures to obstruct or control the reading or further copying of the copies you make or distribute. However, you may accept compensation in exchange for copies. If you distribute a large enough number of copies you must also follow the conditions in section 3.

You may also lend copies, under the same conditions stated above, and you may publicly display copies.

3. COPYING IN QUANTITY

If you publish printed copies (or copies in media that commonly have printed covers) of the Document, numbering more than 100, and the Document's license notice requires Cover Texts, you must enclose the copies in covers that carry, clearly and legibly, all these Cover Texts: Front-Cover Texts on the front cover, and Back-Cover Texts on the back cover. Both covers must also clearly and legibly identify you as the publisher of these copies. The front cover must present the full title with all words of the title equally prominent and visible. You may add other material on the covers in addition. Copying with changes limited to the covers, as long as they preserve the title of the Document and satisfy these conditions, can be treated as verbatim copying in other respects.

If the required texts for either cover are too voluminous to fit legibly, you should put the first ones listed (as many as fit reasonably) on the actual cover, and continue the rest onto adjacent pages.

If you publish or distribute Opaque copies of the Document numbering more than 100, you must either include a machine-readable Transparent copy along with each Opaque copy, or state in or with each Opaque copy a computer-network location from which the general network-using public has access to download using public-standard network protocols a complete Transparent copy of the Document, free of added material. If you use the latter option, you must take reasonably prudent steps, when you begin distribution of Opaque copies in quantity, to ensure that this Transparent copy will remain thus accessible at the stated location until at least one year after the last time you distribute an Opaque copy (directly or through your agents or retailers) of that edition to the public.

It is requested, but not required, that you contact the authors of the Document well before redistributing any large number of copies, to give them a chance to provide you with an updated version of the Document.

4. MODIFICATIONS

You may copy and distribute a Modified Version of the Document under the conditions of sections 2 and 3 above, provided that you release the Modified Version under precisely this License, with the Modified Version filling the role of the Document, thus licensing distribution and modification of the Modified Version to whoever possesses a copy of it. In addition, you must do these things in the Modified Version:

A. Use in the Title Page (and on the covers, if any) a title distinct from that of the Document, and from those of previous versions (which should, if there were any, be listed in the History section of the Document). You may use the same title as a previous version if the original publisher of that version gives permission.

B. List on the Title Page, as authors, one or more persons or entities responsible for authorship of the modifications in the Modified Version, together with at least five of the principal authors of the Document (all of its principal authors, if it has fewer than five), unless they release you from this requirement.

C. State on the Title page the name of the publisher of the Modified Version, as the publisher.

D. Preserve all the copyright notices of the Document.

E. Add an appropriate copyright notice for your modifications adjacent to the other copyright notices.

F. Include, immediately after the copyright notices, a license notice giving the public permission to use the Modified Version under the terms of this License, in the form shown in the Addendum below.

G. Preserve in that license notice the full lists of Invariant Sections and required Cover Texts given in the Document's license notice.

H. Include an unaltered copy of this License.

I. Preserve the section Entitled "History", Preserve its Title, and add to it an item stating at least the title, year, new authors, and publisher of the Modified Version as given on the Title Page. If there is no section Entitled "History" in the Document, create one stating the title, year, authors, and publisher of the Document as given on its Title Page, then add an item describing the Modified Version as stated in the previous sentence.

J. Preserve the network location, if any, given in the Document for public access to a Transparent copy of the Document, and likewise the network locations given in the Document for previous versions it was based on. These may be placed in the "History" section. You may omit a network location for a work that was published at least four years before the Document itself, or if the original publisher of the version it refers to gives permission.

K. For any section Entitled "Acknowledgements" or "Dedications", Preserve the Title of the section, and preserve in the section all the substance and tone of each of the contributor acknowledgements and/or dedications given therein.

L. Preserve all the Invariant Sections of the Document, unaltered in their text and in their titles. Section numbers or the equivalent are not considered part of the section titles.

M. Delete any section Entitled "Endorsements". Such a section may not be included in the Modified Version.

N. Do not retitle any existing section to be Entitled "Endorsements" or to conflict in title with any Invariant Section.

O. Preserve any Warranty Disclaimers.

If the Modified Version includes new front-matter sections or appendices that qualify as Secondary Sections and contain no material copied from the Document, you may at your option designate some or all of these sections as invariant. To do this, add their titles to the list of Invariant Sections in the Modified Version's license notice. These titles must be distinct from any other section titles.

You may add a section Entitled "Endorsements", provided it contains nothing but endorsements of your Modified Version by various parties—for example, statements of peer review or that the text has been approved by an organization as the authoritative definition of a standard.

You may add a passage of up to five words as a Front-Cover Text, and a passage of up to 25 words as a Back-Cover Text, to the end of the list of Cover Texts in the Modified Version. Only one passage of Front-Cover Text and one of Back-Cover Text may be added by (or through arrangements made by) any one entity. If the Document already includes a cover text for the same cover, previously added by you or by arrangement made by the same entity you are acting on behalf of, you may not add another; but you may replace the old one, on explicit permission from the previous publisher that added the old one.

The author(s) and publisher(s) of the Document do not by this License give permission to use their names for publicity for or to assert or imply endorsement of any Modified Version.

5. COMBINING DOCUMENTS

You may combine the Document with other documents released under this License, under the terms defined in section 4 above for modified versions, provided that you include in the combination all of the Invariant Sections of all of the original documents, unmodified, and list them all as Invariant Sections of your combined work in its license notice, and that you preserve all their Warranty Disclaimers.

The combined work need only contain one copy of this License, and multiple identical Invariant Sections may be replaced with a single copy. If there are multiple Invariant Sections with the same name but different contents, make the title of each such section unique by adding at the end of it, in parentheses, the name of the original author or publisher of that section if known, or else a unique number. Make the same adjustment to the section titles in the list of Invariant Sections in the license notice of the combined work.

In the combination, you must combine any sections Entitled "History" in the various original documents, forming one section Entitled "History"; likewise combine any sections Entitled "Acknowledgements", and any sections Entitled "Dedications". You must delete all sections Entitled "Endorsements."

6. COLLECTIONS OF DOCUMENTS

You may make a collection consisting of the Document and other documents released under this License, and replace the individual copies of this License in the various documents with a single copy that is included in the collection, provided that you follow the rules of this License for verbatim copying of each of the documents in all other respects.

You may extract a single document from such a collection, and distribute it individually under this License, provided you insert a copy of this License into the extracted document, and follow this License in all other respects regarding verbatim copying of that document.

7. AGGREGATION WITH INDEPENDENT WORKS

A compilation of the Document or its derivatives with other separate and independent documents or works, in or on a volume of a storage or distribution medium, is called an "aggregate" if the copyright resulting from the compilation is not used to limit the legal rights of the compilation's users beyond what the individual works permit. When the Document is included in an aggregate, this License does not apply to the other works in the aggregate which are not themselves derivative works of the Document.

If the Cover Text requirement of section 3 is applicable to these copies of the Document, then if the Document is less than one half of the entire aggregate, the Document's Cover Texts may be placed on covers that bracket the Document within the aggregate, or the electronic equivalent of covers if the Document is in electronic form. Otherwise they must appear on printed covers that bracket the whole aggregate.

8. TRANSLATION

Translation is considered a kind of modification, so you may distribute translations of the Document under the terms of section 4. Replacing Invariant Sections with translations requires special permission from their copyright holders, but you may include translations of some or all Invariant Sections in addition to the original versions of these Invariant Sections. You may include a translation of this License, and all the license notices in the Document, and any Warranty Disclaimers, provided that you also include the original English version of this License and the original versions of those notices and disclaimers. In case of a disagreement between the translation and the original version of this License or a notice or disclaimer, the original version will prevail.

If a section in the Document is Entitled "Acknowledgements", "Dedications", or "History", the requirement (section 4) to Preserve its Title (section 1) will typically require changing the actual title.

9. TERMINATION

You may not copy, modify, sublicense, or distribute the Document except as expressly provided under this License. Any attempt otherwise to copy, modify, sublicense, or distribute it is void, and will automatically terminate your rights under this License.

However, if you cease all violation of this License, then your license from a particular copyright holder is reinstated (a) provisionally, unless and until the copyright holder explicitly and finally terminates your license, and (b) permanently, if the copyright holder fails to notify you of the violation by some reasonable means prior to 60 days after the cessation.

Moreover, your license from a particular copyright holder is reinstated permanently if the copyright holder notifies you of the violation by some reasonable means, this is the first time you have received notice of violation of this License (for any work) from that copyright holder, and you cure the violation prior to 30 days after your receipt of the notice.

Termination of your rights under this section does not terminate the licenses of parties who have received copies or rights from you under this License. If your rights have been terminated and not permanently reinstated, receipt of a copy of some or all of the same material does not give you any rights to use it.

10. FUTURE REVISIONS OF THIS LICENSE

The Free Software Foundation may publish new, revised versions of the GNU Free Documentation License from time to time. Such new versions will be similar in spirit to the present version, but may differ in detail to address new problems or concerns. See `http://www.gnu.org/copyleft/`.

Each version of the License is given a distinguishing version number. If the Document specifies that a particular numbered version of this License "or any later version" applies to it, you have the option of following the terms and conditions either of that specified version or of any later version that has been published (not as a draft) by the Free Software Foundation. If the Document does not specify a version number of this License, you may choose any version ever published (not as a draft) by the Free Software Foundation. If the Document specifies that a proxy can decide which future versions of this License can be used, that proxy's public statement of acceptance of a version permanently authorizes you to choose that version for the Document.

11. RELICENSING

"Massive Multiauthor Collaboration Site" (or "MMC Site") means any World Wide Web server that publishes copyrightable works and also provides prominent facilities for anybody to edit those works. A public wiki that anybody can edit is an example of such a server. A "Massive Multiauthor Collaboration" (or "MMC") contained in the site means any set of copyrightable works thus published on the MMC site.

"CC-BY-SA" means the Creative Commons Attribution-Share Alike 3.0 license published by Creative Commons Corporation, a not-for-profit corporation with a principal place of business in San Francisco, California, as well as future copyleft versions of that license published by that same organization.

"Incorporate" means to publish or republish a Document, in whole or in part, as part of another Document.

An MMC is "eligible for relicensing" if it is licensed under this License, and if all works that were first published under this License somewhere other than this MMC, and subsequently incorporated in whole or in part into the MMC, (1) had no cover texts or invariant sections, and (2) were thus incorporated prior to November 1, 2008.

The operator of an MMC Site may republish an MMC contained in the site under CC-BY-SA on the same site at any time before August 1, 2009, provided the MMC is eligible for relicensing.

ADDENDUM: How to use this License for your documents

To use this License in a document you have written, include a copy of the License in the document and put the following copyright and license notices just after the title page:

```
Copyright (C)  year  your name.
Permission is granted to copy, distribute and/or modify this document
under the terms of the GNU Free Documentation License, Version 1.3
or any later version published by the Free Software Foundation;
with no Invariant Sections, no Front-Cover Texts, and no Back-Cover
Texts.  A copy of the license is included in the section entitled ``GNU
Free Documentation License''.
```

If you have Invariant Sections, Front-Cover Texts and Back-Cover Texts, replace the "with...Texts." line with this:

```
with the Invariant Sections being list their titles, with
the Front-Cover Texts being list, and with the Back-Cover Texts
being list.
```

If you have Invariant Sections without Cover Texts, or some other combination of the three, merge those two alternatives to suit the situation.

If your document contains nontrivial examples of program code, we recommend releasing these examples in parallel under your choice of free software license, such as the GNU General Public License, to permit their use in free software.

Appendix C GNU General Public License

Version 3, 29 June 2007

Copyright © 2007 Free Software Foundation, Inc. http://fsf.org/

Everyone is permitted to copy and distribute verbatim copies of this
license document, but changing it is not allowed.

Preamble

The GNU General Public License is a free, copyleft license for software and other kinds of
works.

The licenses for most software and other practical works are designed to take away your
freedom to share and change the works. By contrast, the GNU General Public License is
intended to guarantee your freedom to share and change all versions of a program—to make
sure it remains free software for all its users. We, the Free Software Foundation, use the
GNU General Public License for most of our software; it applies also to any other work
released this way by its authors. You can apply it to your programs, too.

When we speak of free software, we are referring to freedom, not price. Our General
Public Licenses are designed to make sure that you have the freedom to distribute copies
of free software (and charge for them if you wish), that you receive source code or can get
it if you want it, that you can change the software or use pieces of it in new free programs,
and that you know you can do these things.

To protect your rights, we need to prevent others from denying you these rights or asking
you to surrender the rights. Therefore, you have certain responsibilities if you distribute
copies of the software, or if you modify it: responsibilities to respect the freedom of others.

For example, if you distribute copies of such a program, whether gratis or for a fee, you
must pass on to the recipients the same freedoms that you received. You must make sure
that they, too, receive or can get the source code. And you must show them these terms so
they know their rights.

Developers that use the GNU GPL protect your rights with two steps: (1) assert copyright on the software, and (2) offer you this License giving you legal permission to copy,
distribute and/or modify it.

For the developers' and authors' protection, the GPL clearly explains that there is no
warranty for this free software. For both users' and authors' sake, the GPL requires that
modified versions be marked as changed, so that their problems will not be attributed
erroneously to authors of previous versions.

Some devices are designed to deny users access to install or run modified versions of the
software inside them, although the manufacturer can do so. This is fundamentally incompatible with the aim of protecting users' freedom to change the software. The systematic
pattern of such abuse occurs in the area of products for individuals to use, which is precisely where it is most unacceptable. Therefore, we have designed this version of the GPL
to prohibit the practice for those products. If such problems arise substantially in other
domains, we stand ready to extend this provision to those domains in future versions of the
GPL, as needed to protect the freedom of users.

Finally, every program is threatened constantly by software patents. States should not allow patents to restrict development and use of software on general-purpose computers, but in those that do, we wish to avoid the special danger that patents applied to a free program could make it effectively proprietary. To prevent this, the GPL assures that patents cannot be used to render the program non-free.

The precise terms and conditions for copying, distribution and modification follow.

TERMS AND CONDITIONS

0. Definitions.

   "This License" refers to version 3 of the GNU General Public License.

   "Copyright" also means copyright-like laws that apply to other kinds of works, such as semiconductor masks.

   "The Program" refers to any copyrightable work licensed under this License. Each licensee is addressed as "you". "Licensees" and "recipients" may be individuals or organizations.

   To "modify" a work means to copy from or adapt all or part of the work in a fashion requiring copyright permission, other than the making of an exact copy. The resulting work is called a "modified version" of the earlier work or a work "based on" the earlier work.

   A "covered work" means either the unmodified Program or a work based on the Program.

   To "propagate" a work means to do anything with it that, without permission, would make you directly or secondarily liable for infringement under applicable copyright law, except executing it on a computer or modifying a private copy. Propagation includes copying, distribution (with or without modification), making available to the public, and in some countries other activities as well.

   To "convey" a work means any kind of propagation that enables other parties to make or receive copies. Mere interaction with a user through a computer network, with no transfer of a copy, is not conveying.

   An interactive user interface displays "Appropriate Legal Notices" to the extent that it includes a convenient and prominently visible feature that (1) displays an appropriate copyright notice, and (2) tells the user that there is no warranty for the work (except to the extent that warranties are provided), that licensees may convey the work under this License, and how to view a copy of this License. If the interface presents a list of user commands or options, such as a menu, a prominent item in the list meets this criterion.

1. Source Code.

   The "source code" for a work means the preferred form of the work for making modifications to it. "Object code" means any non-source form of a work.

   A "Standard Interface" means an interface that either is an official standard defined by a recognized standards body, or, in the case of interfaces specified for a particular programming language, one that is widely used among developers working in that language.

The "System Libraries" of an executable work include anything, other than the work as a whole, that (a) is included in the normal form of packaging a Major Component, but which is not part of that Major Component, and (b) serves only to enable use of the work with that Major Component, or to implement a Standard Interface for which an implementation is available to the public in source code form. A "Major Component", in this context, means a major essential component (kernel, window system, and so on) of the specific operating system (if any) on which the executable work runs, or a compiler used to produce the work, or an object code interpreter used to run it.

The "Corresponding Source" for a work in object code form means all the source code needed to generate, install, and (for an executable work) run the object code and to modify the work, including scripts to control those activities. However, it does not include the work's System Libraries, or general-purpose tools or generally available free programs which are used unmodified in performing those activities but which are not part of the work. For example, Corresponding Source includes interface definition files associated with source files for the work, and the source code for shared libraries and dynamically linked subprograms that the work is specifically designed to require, such as by intimate data communication or control flow between those subprograms and other parts of the work.

The Corresponding Source need not include anything that users can regenerate automatically from other parts of the Corresponding Source.

The Corresponding Source for a work in source code form is that same work.

2. Basic Permissions.

All rights granted under this License are granted for the term of copyright on the Program, and are irrevocable provided the stated conditions are met. This License explicitly affirms your unlimited permission to run the unmodified Program. The output from running a covered work is covered by this License only if the output, given its content, constitutes a covered work. This License acknowledges your rights of fair use or other equivalent, as provided by copyright law.

You may make, run and propagate covered works that you do not convey, without conditions so long as your license otherwise remains in force. You may convey covered works to others for the sole purpose of having them make modifications exclusively for you, or provide you with facilities for running those works, provided that you comply with the terms of this License in conveying all material for which you do not control copyright. Those thus making or running the covered works for you must do so exclusively on your behalf, under your direction and control, on terms that prohibit them from making any copies of your copyrighted material outside their relationship with you.

Conveying under any other circumstances is permitted solely under the conditions stated below. Sublicensing is not allowed; section 10 makes it unnecessary.

3. Protecting Users' Legal Rights From Anti-Circumvention Law.

No covered work shall be deemed part of an effective technological measure under any applicable law fulfilling obligations under article 11 of the WIPO copyright treaty adopted on 20 December 1996, or similar laws prohibiting or restricting circumvention of such measures.

When you convey a covered work, you waive any legal power to forbid circumvention of technological measures to the extent such circumvention is effected by exercising rights under this License with respect to the covered work, and you disclaim any intention to limit operation or modification of the work as a means of enforcing, against the work's users, your or third parties' legal rights to forbid circumvention of technological measures.

4. Conveying Verbatim Copies.

   You may convey verbatim copies of the Program's source code as you receive it, in any medium, provided that you conspicuously and appropriately publish on each copy an appropriate copyright notice; keep intact all notices stating that this License and any non-permissive terms added in accord with section 7 apply to the code; keep intact all notices of the absence of any warranty; and give all recipients a copy of this License along with the Program.

   You may charge any price or no price for each copy that you convey, and you may offer support or warranty protection for a fee.

5. Conveying Modified Source Versions.

   You may convey a work based on the Program, or the modifications to produce it from the Program, in the form of source code under the terms of section 4, provided that you also meet all of these conditions:

   a. The work must carry prominent notices stating that you modified it, and giving a relevant date.

   b. The work must carry prominent notices stating that it is released under this License and any conditions added under section 7. This requirement modifies the requirement in section 4 to "keep intact all notices".

   c. You must license the entire work, as a whole, under this License to anyone who comes into possession of a copy. This License will therefore apply, along with any applicable section 7 additional terms, to the whole of the work, and all its parts, regardless of how they are packaged. This License gives no permission to license the work in any other way, but it does not invalidate such permission if you have separately received it.

   d. If the work has interactive user interfaces, each must display Appropriate Legal Notices; however, if the Program has interactive interfaces that do not display Appropriate Legal Notices, your work need not make them do so.

   A compilation of a covered work with other separate and independent works, which are not by their nature extensions of the covered work, and which are not combined with it such as to form a larger program, in or on a volume of a storage or distribution medium, is called an "aggregate" if the compilation and its resulting copyright are not used to limit the access or legal rights of the compilation's users beyond what the individual works permit. Inclusion of a covered work in an aggregate does not cause this License to apply to the other parts of the aggregate.

6. Conveying Non-Source Forms.

   You may convey a covered work in object code form under the terms of sections 4 and 5, provided that you also convey the machine-readable Corresponding Source under the terms of this License, in one of these ways:

a. Convey the object code in, or embodied in, a physical product (including a physical distribution medium), accompanied by the Corresponding Source fixed on a durable physical medium customarily used for software interchange.

b. Convey the object code in, or embodied in, a physical product (including a physical distribution medium), accompanied by a written offer, valid for at least three years and valid for as long as you offer spare parts or customer support for that product model, to give anyone who possesses the object code either (1) a copy of the Corresponding Source for all the software in the product that is covered by this License, on a durable physical medium customarily used for software interchange, for a price no more than your reasonable cost of physically performing this conveying of source, or (2) access to copy the Corresponding Source from a network server at no charge.

c. Convey individual copies of the object code with a copy of the written offer to provide the Corresponding Source. This alternative is allowed only occasionally and noncommercially, and only if you received the object code with such an offer, in accord with subsection 6b.

d. Convey the object code by offering access from a designated place (gratis or for a charge), and offer equivalent access to the Corresponding Source in the same way through the same place at no further charge. You need not require recipients to copy the Corresponding Source along with the object code. If the place to copy the object code is a network server, the Corresponding Source may be on a different server (operated by you or a third party) that supports equivalent copying facilities, provided you maintain clear directions next to the object code saying where to find the Corresponding Source. Regardless of what server hosts the Corresponding Source, you remain obligated to ensure that it is available for as long as needed to satisfy these requirements.

e. Convey the object code using peer-to-peer transmission, provided you inform other peers where the object code and Corresponding Source of the work are being offered to the general public at no charge under subsection 6d.

A separable portion of the object code, whose source code is excluded from the Corresponding Source as a System Library, need not be included in conveying the object code work.

A "User Product" is either (1) a "consumer product", which means any tangible personal property which is normally used for personal, family, or household purposes, or (2) anything designed or sold for incorporation into a dwelling. In determining whether a product is a consumer product, doubtful cases shall be resolved in favor of coverage. For a particular product received by a particular user, "normally used" refers to a typical or common use of that class of product, regardless of the status of the particular user or of the way in which the particular user actually uses, or expects or is expected to use, the product. A product is a consumer product regardless of whether the product has substantial commercial, industrial or non-consumer uses, unless such uses represent the only significant mode of use of the product.

"Installation Information" for a User Product means any methods, procedures, authorization keys, or other information required to install and execute modified versions of a covered work in that User Product from a modified version of its Corresponding Source.

The information must suffice to ensure that the continued functioning of the modified object code is in no case prevented or interfered with solely because modification has been made.

If you convey an object code work under this section in, or with, or specifically for use in, a User Product, and the conveying occurs as part of a transaction in which the right of possession and use of the User Product is transferred to the recipient in perpetuity or for a fixed term (regardless of how the transaction is characterized), the Corresponding Source conveyed under this section must be accompanied by the Installation Information. But this requirement does not apply if neither you nor any third party retains the ability to install modified object code on the User Product (for example, the work has been installed in ROM).

The requirement to provide Installation Information does not include a requirement to continue to provide support service, warranty, or updates for a work that has been modified or installed by the recipient, or for the User Product in which it has been modified or installed. Access to a network may be denied when the modification itself materially and adversely affects the operation of the network or violates the rules and protocols for communication across the network.

Corresponding Source conveyed, and Installation Information provided, in accord with this section must be in a format that is publicly documented (and with an implementation available to the public in source code form), and must require no special password or key for unpacking, reading or copying.

7. Additional Terms.

"Additional permissions" are terms that supplement the terms of this License by making exceptions from one or more of its conditions. Additional permissions that are applicable to the entire Program shall be treated as though they were included in this License, to the extent that they are valid under applicable law. If additional permissions apply only to part of the Program, that part may be used separately under those permissions, but the entire Program remains governed by this License without regard to the additional permissions.

When you convey a copy of a covered work, you may at your option remove any additional permissions from that copy, or from any part of it. (Additional permissions may be written to require their own removal in certain cases when you modify the work.) You may place additional permissions on material, added by you to a covered work, for which you have or can give appropriate copyright permission.

Notwithstanding any other provision of this License, for material you add to a covered work, you may (if authorized by the copyright holders of that material) supplement the terms of this License with terms:

  a. Disclaiming warranty or limiting liability differently from the terms of sections 15 and 16 of this License; or

  b. Requiring preservation of specified reasonable legal notices or author attributions in that material or in the Appropriate Legal Notices displayed by works containing it; or

  c. Prohibiting misrepresentation of the origin of that material, or requiring that modified versions of such material be marked in reasonable ways as different from the original version; or

   d. Limiting the use for publicity purposes of names of licensors or authors of the material; or

   e. Declining to grant rights under trademark law for use of some trade names, trademarks, or service marks; or

   f. Requiring indemnification of licensors and authors of that material by anyone who conveys the material (or modified versions of it) with contractual assumptions of liability to the recipient, for any liability that these contractual assumptions directly impose on those licensors and authors.

All other non-permissive additional terms are considered "further restrictions" within the meaning of section 10. If the Program as you received it, or any part of it, contains a notice stating that it is governed by this License along with a term that is a further restriction, you may remove that term. If a license document contains a further restriction but permits relicensing or conveying under this License, you may add to a covered work material governed by the terms of that license document, provided that the further restriction does not survive such relicensing or conveying.

If you add terms to a covered work in accord with this section, you must place, in the relevant source files, a statement of the additional terms that apply to those files, or a notice indicating where to find the applicable terms.

Additional terms, permissive or non-permissive, may be stated in the form of a separately written license, or stated as exceptions; the above requirements apply either way.

8. Termination.

You may not propagate or modify a covered work except as expressly provided under this License. Any attempt otherwise to propagate or modify it is void, and will automatically terminate your rights under this License (including any patent licenses granted under the third paragraph of section 11).

However, if you cease all violation of this License, then your license from a particular copyright holder is reinstated (a) provisionally, unless and until the copyright holder explicitly and finally terminates your license, and (b) permanently, if the copyright holder fails to notify you of the violation by some reasonable means prior to 60 days after the cessation.

Moreover, your license from a particular copyright holder is reinstated permanently if the copyright holder notifies you of the violation by some reasonable means, this is the first time you have received notice of violation of this License (for any work) from that copyright holder, and you cure the violation prior to 30 days after your receipt of the notice.

Termination of your rights under this section does not terminate the licenses of parties who have received copies or rights from you under this License. If your rights have been terminated and not permanently reinstated, you do not qualify to receive new licenses for the same material under section 10.

9. Acceptance Not Required for Having Copies.

You are not required to accept this License in order to receive or run a copy of the Program. Ancillary propagation of a covered work occurring solely as a consequence of using peer-to-peer transmission to receive a copy likewise does not require acceptance.

However, nothing other than this License grants you permission to propagate or modify any covered work. These actions infringe copyright if you do not accept this License. Therefore, by modifying or propagating a covered work, you indicate your acceptance of this License to do so.

10. Automatic Licensing of Downstream Recipients.

Each time you convey a covered work, the recipient automatically receives a license from the original licensors, to run, modify and propagate that work, subject to this License. You are not responsible for enforcing compliance by third parties with this License.

An "entity transaction" is a transaction transferring control of an organization, or substantially all assets of one, or subdividing an organization, or merging organizations. If propagation of a covered work results from an entity transaction, each party to that transaction who receives a copy of the work also receives whatever licenses to the work the party's predecessor in interest had or could give under the previous paragraph, plus a right to possession of the Corresponding Source of the work from the predecessor in interest, if the predecessor has it or can get it with reasonable efforts.

You may not impose any further restrictions on the exercise of the rights granted or affirmed under this License. For example, you may not impose a license fee, royalty, or other charge for exercise of rights granted under this License, and you may not initiate litigation (including a cross-claim or counterclaim in a lawsuit) alleging that any patent claim is infringed by making, using, selling, offering for sale, or importing the Program or any portion of it.

11. Patents.

A "contributor" is a copyright holder who authorizes use under this License of the Program or a work on which the Program is based. The work thus licensed is called the contributor's "contributor version".

A contributor's "essential patent claims" are all patent claims owned or controlled by the contributor, whether already acquired or hereafter acquired, that would be infringed by some manner, permitted by this License, of making, using, or selling its contributor version, but do not include claims that would be infringed only as a consequence of further modification of the contributor version. For purposes of this definition, "control" includes the right to grant patent sublicenses in a manner consistent with the requirements of this License.

Each contributor grants you a non-exclusive, worldwide, royalty-free patent license under the contributor's essential patent claims, to make, use, sell, offer for sale, import and otherwise run, modify and propagate the contents of its contributor version.

In the following three paragraphs, a "patent license" is any express agreement or commitment, however denominated, not to enforce a patent (such as an express permission to practice a patent or covenant not to sue for patent infringement). To "grant" such a patent license to a party means to make such an agreement or commitment not to enforce a patent against the party.

If you convey a covered work, knowingly relying on a patent license, and the Corresponding Source of the work is not available for anyone to copy, free of charge and under the terms of this License, through a publicly available network server or other readily accessible means, then you must either (1) cause the Corresponding Source to be so available, or (2) arrange to deprive yourself of the benefit of the patent license for this particular work, or (3) arrange, in a manner consistent with the requirements of this License, to extend the patent license to downstream recipients. "Knowingly relying" means you have actual knowledge that, but for the patent license, your conveying the covered work in a country, or your recipient's use of the covered work in a country, would infringe one or more identifiable patents in that country that you have reason to believe are valid.

If, pursuant to or in connection with a single transaction or arrangement, you convey, or propagate by procuring conveyance of, a covered work, and grant a patent license to some of the parties receiving the covered work authorizing them to use, propagate, modify or convey a specific copy of the covered work, then the patent license you grant is automatically extended to all recipients of the covered work and works based on it.

A patent license is "discriminatory" if it does not include within the scope of its coverage, prohibits the exercise of, or is conditioned on the non-exercise of one or more of the rights that are specifically granted under this License. You may not convey a covered work if you are a party to an arrangement with a third party that is in the business of distributing software, under which you make payment to the third party based on the extent of your activity of conveying the work, and under which the third party grants, to any of the parties who would receive the covered work from you, a discriminatory patent license (a) in connection with copies of the covered work conveyed by you (or copies made from those copies), or (b) primarily for and in connection with specific products or compilations that contain the covered work, unless you entered into that arrangement, or that patent license was granted, prior to 28 March 2007.

Nothing in this License shall be construed as excluding or limiting any implied license or other defenses to infringement that may otherwise be available to you under applicable patent law.

12. No Surrender of Others' Freedom.

If conditions are imposed on you (whether by court order, agreement or otherwise) that contradict the conditions of this License, they do not excuse you from the conditions of this License. If you cannot convey a covered work so as to satisfy simultaneously your obligations under this License and any other pertinent obligations, then as a consequence you may not convey it at all. For example, if you agree to terms that obligate you to collect a royalty for further conveying from those to whom you convey the Program, the only way you could satisfy both those terms and this License would be to refrain entirely from conveying the Program.

13. Use with the GNU Affero General Public License.

Notwithstanding any other provision of this License, you have permission to link or combine any covered work with a work licensed under version 3 of the GNU Affero General Public License into a single combined work, and to convey the resulting work. The terms of this License will continue to apply to the part which is the covered work, but the special requirements of the GNU Affero General Public License, section 13, concerning interaction through a network will apply to the combination as such.

14. Revised Versions of this License.

The Free Software Foundation may publish revised and/or new versions of the GNU General Public License from time to time. Such new versions will be similar in spirit to the present version, but may differ in detail to address new problems or concerns.

Each version is given a distinguishing version number. If the Program specifies that a certain numbered version of the GNU General Public License "or any later version" applies to it, you have the option of following the terms and conditions either of that numbered version or of any later version published by the Free Software Foundation. If the Program does not specify a version number of the GNU General Public License, you may choose any version ever published by the Free Software Foundation.

If the Program specifies that a proxy can decide which future versions of the GNU General Public License can be used, that proxy's public statement of acceptance of a version permanently authorizes you to choose that version for the Program.

Later license versions may give you additional or different permissions. However, no additional obligations are imposed on any author or copyright holder as a result of your choosing to follow a later version.

15. Disclaimer of Warranty.

    THERE IS NO WARRANTY FOR THE PROGRAM, TO THE EXTENT PERMITTED BY APPLICABLE LAW. EXCEPT WHEN OTHERWISE STATED IN WRITING THE COPYRIGHT HOLDERS AND/OR OTHER PARTIES PROVIDE THE PROGRAM "AS IS" WITHOUT WARRANTY OF ANY KIND, EITHER EXPRESSED OR IMPLIED, INCLUDING, BUT NOT LIMITED TO, THE IMPLIED WARRANTIES OF MERCHANTABILITY AND FITNESS FOR A PARTICULAR PURPOSE. THE ENTIRE RISK AS TO THE QUALITY AND PERFORMANCE OF THE PROGRAM IS WITH YOU. SHOULD THE PROGRAM PROVE DEFECTIVE, YOU ASSUME THE COST OF ALL NECESSARY SERVICING, REPAIR OR CORRECTION.

16. Limitation of Liability.

    IN NO EVENT UNLESS REQUIRED BY APPLICABLE LAW OR AGREED TO IN WRITING WILL ANY COPYRIGHT HOLDER, OR ANY OTHER PARTY WHO MODIFIES AND/OR CONVEYS THE PROGRAM AS PERMITTED ABOVE, BE LIABLE TO YOU FOR DAMAGES, INCLUDING ANY GENERAL, SPECIAL, INCIDENTAL OR CONSEQUENTIAL DAMAGES ARISING OUT OF THE USE OR INABILITY TO USE THE PROGRAM (INCLUDING BUT NOT LIMITED TO LOSS OF DATA OR DATA BEING RENDERED INACCURATE OR LOSSES SUSTAINED BY YOU OR THIRD PARTIES OR A FAILURE OF THE PROGRAM TO OPERATE WITH ANY OTHER PROGRAMS), EVEN IF SUCH HOLDER OR OTHER PARTY HAS BEEN ADVISED OF THE POSSIBILITY OF SUCH DAMAGES.

17. Interpretation of Sections 15 and 16.

    If the disclaimer of warranty and limitation of liability provided above cannot be given local legal effect according to their terms, reviewing courts shall apply local law that most closely approximates an absolute waiver of all civil liability in connection with the Program, unless a warranty or assumption of liability accompanies a copy of the Program in return for a fee.

END OF TERMS AND CONDITIONS

How to Apply These Terms to Your New Programs

If you develop a new program, and you want it to be of the greatest possible use to the public, the best way to achieve this is to make it free software which everyone can redistribute and change under these terms.

To do so, attach the following notices to the program. It is safest to attach them to the start of each source file to most effectively state the exclusion of warranty; and each file should have at least the "copyright" line and a pointer to where the full notice is found.

```
one line to give the program's name and a brief idea of what it does.
Copyright (C) year name of author

This program is free software: you can redistribute it and/or modify
it under the terms of the GNU General Public License as published by
the Free Software Foundation, either version 3 of the License, or (at
your option) any later version.

This program is distributed in the hope that it will be useful, but
WITHOUT ANY WARRANTY; without even the implied warranty of
MERCHANTABILITY or FITNESS FOR A PARTICULAR PURPOSE.  See the GNU
General Public License for more details.

You should have received a copy of the GNU General Public License
along with this program.  If not, see http://www.gnu.org/licenses/.
```

Also add information on how to contact you by electronic and paper mail.

If the program does terminal interaction, make it output a short notice like this when it starts in an interactive mode:

```
program Copyright (C) year name of author
This program comes with ABSOLUTELY NO WARRANTY; for details type 'show w'.
This is free software, and you are welcome to redistribute it
under certain conditions; type 'show c' for details.
```

The hypothetical commands 'show w' and 'show c' should show the appropriate parts of the General Public License. Of course, your program's commands might be different; for a GUI interface, you would use an "about box".

You should also get your employer (if you work as a programmer) or school, if any, to sign a "copyright disclaimer" for the program, if necessary. For more information on this, and how to apply and follow the GNU GPL, see http://www.gnu.org/licenses/.

The GNU General Public License does not permit incorporating your program into proprietary programs. If your program is a subroutine library, you may consider it more useful to permit linking proprietary applications with the library. If this is what you want to do, use the GNU Lesser General Public License instead of this License. But first, please read http://www.gnu.org/philosophy/why-not-lgpl.html.

Appendix D Tips and Conventions

This chapter describes no additional features of Emacs Lisp. Instead it gives advice on making effective use of the features described in the previous chapters, and describes conventions Emacs Lisp programmers should follow.

You can automatically check some of the conventions described below by running the command *M-x checkdoc RET* when visiting a Lisp file. It cannot check all of the conventions, and not all the warnings it gives necessarily correspond to problems, but it is worth examining them all. Alternatively, use the command *M-x checkdoc-current-buffer RET* to check the conventions in the current buffer, or `checkdoc-file` when you want to check a file in batch mode, e.g., with a command run by *M-x compile RET*.

D.1 Emacs Lisp Coding Conventions

Here are conventions that you should follow when writing Emacs Lisp code intended for widespread use:

- Simply loading a package should not change Emacs's editing behavior. Include a command or commands to enable and disable the feature, or to invoke it.

  This convention is mandatory for any file that includes custom definitions. If fixing such a file to follow this convention requires an incompatible change, go ahead and make the incompatible change; don't postpone it.

- You should choose a short word to distinguish your program from other Lisp programs. The names of all global symbols in your program, that is the names of variables, constants, and functions, should begin with that chosen prefix. Separate the prefix from the rest of the name with a hyphen, '-'. This practice helps avoid name conflicts, since all global variables in Emacs Lisp share the same name space, and all functions share another name space[1]. Use two hyphens to separate prefix and name if the symbol is not meant to be used by other packages.

  Occasionally, for a command name intended for users to use, it is more convenient if some words come before the package's name prefix. And constructs that define functions, variables, etc., work better if they start with '`defun`' or '`defvar`', so put the name prefix later on in the name.

  This recommendation applies even to names for traditional Lisp primitives that are not primitives in Emacs Lisp—such as `copy-list`. Believe it or not, there is more than one plausible way to define `copy-list`. Play it safe; append your name prefix to produce a name like `foo-copy-list` or `mylib-copy-list` instead.

  If you write a function that you think ought to be added to Emacs under a certain name, such as `twiddle-files`, don't call it by that name in your program. Call it `mylib-twiddle-files` in your program, and send mail to '`bug-gnu-emacs@gnu.org`' suggesting we add it to Emacs. If and when we do, we can change the name easily enough.

  If one prefix is insufficient, your package can use two or three alternative common prefixes, so long as they make sense.

---

[1] The benefits of a Common Lisp-style package system are considered not to outweigh the costs.

- Put a call to **provide** at the end of each separate Lisp file. See Section 15.7 [Named Features], page 253.

- If a file requires certain other Lisp programs to be loaded beforehand, then the comments at the beginning of the file should say so. Also, use **require** to make sure they are loaded. See Section 15.7 [Named Features], page 253.

- If a file *foo* uses a macro defined in another file *bar*, but does not use any functions or variables defined in *bar*, then *foo* should contain the following expression:

    ```
    (eval-when-compile (require 'bar))
    ```

  This tells Emacs to load *bar* just before byte-compiling *foo*, so that the macro definition is available during compilation. Using **eval-when-compile** avoids loading *bar* when the compiled version of *foo* is *used*. It should be called before the first use of the macro in the file. See Section 13.3 [Compiling Macros], page 219.

- Avoid loading additional libraries at run time unless they are really needed. If your file simply cannot work without some other library, then just **require** that library at the top-level and be done with it. But if your file contains several independent features, and only one or two require the extra library, then consider putting **require** statements inside the relevant functions rather than at the top-level. Or use **autoload** statements to load the extra library when needed. This way people who don't use those aspects of your file do not need to load the extra library.

- If you need Common Lisp extensions, use the **cl-lib** library rather than the old **cl** library. The latter does not use a clean namespace (i.e., its definitions do not start with a 'cl-' prefix). If your package loads **cl** at run time, that could cause name clashes for users who don't use that package.

  There is no problem with using the **cl** package at *compile* time, with (**eval-when-compile (require 'cl)**). That's sufficient for using the macros in the **cl** package, because the compiler expands them before generating the byte-code. It is still better to use the more modern **cl-lib** in this case, though.

- When defining a major mode, please follow the major mode conventions. See Section 22.2.1 [Major Mode Conventions], page 432.

- When defining a minor mode, please follow the minor mode conventions. See Section 22.3.1 [Minor Mode Conventions], page 446.

- If the purpose of a function is to tell you whether a certain condition is true or false, give the function a name that ends in 'p' (which stands for "predicate"). If the name is one word, add just 'p'; if the name is multiple words, add '-p'. Examples are **framep** and **frame-live-p**.

- If the purpose of a variable is to store a single function, give it a name that ends in '-function'. If the purpose of a variable is to store a list of functions (i.e., the variable is a hook), please follow the naming conventions for hooks. See Section 22.1 [Hooks], page 429.

- If loading the file adds functions to hooks, define a function *feature*-unload-function, where *feature* is the name of the feature the package provides, and make it undo any such changes. Using **unload-feature** to unload the file will run this function. See Section 15.9 [Unloading], page 257.

- It is a bad idea to define aliases for the Emacs primitives. Normally you should use the standard names instead. The case where an alias may be useful is where it facilitates backwards compatibility or portability.

- If a package needs to define an alias or a new function for compatibility with some other version of Emacs, name it with the package prefix, not with the raw name with which it occurs in the other version. Here is an example from Gnus, which provides many examples of such compatibility issues.

```
(defalias 'gnus-point-at-bol
  (if (fboundp 'point-at-bol)
      'point-at-bol
    'line-beginning-position))
```

- Redefining or advising an Emacs primitive is a bad idea. It may do the right thing for a particular program, but there is no telling what other programs might break as a result.

- It is likewise a bad idea for one Lisp package to advise a function in another Lisp package (see Section 12.11 [Advising Functions], page 204).

- Avoid using `eval-after-load` and `with-eval-after-load` in libraries and packages (see Section 15.10 [Hooks for Loading], page 257). This feature is meant for personal customizations; using it in a Lisp program is unclean, because it modifies the behavior of another Lisp file in a way that's not visible in that file. This is an obstacle for debugging, much like advising a function in the other package.

- If a file does replace any of the standard functions or library programs of Emacs, prominent comments at the beginning of the file should say which functions are replaced, and how the behavior of the replacements differs from that of the originals.

- Constructs that define a function or variable should be macros, not functions, and their names should start with '`define-`'. The macro should receive the name to be defined as the first argument. That will help various tools find the definition automatically. Avoid constructing the names in the macro itself, since that would confuse these tools.

- In some other systems there is a convention of choosing variable names that begin and end with '`*`'. We don't use that convention in Emacs Lisp, so please don't use it in your programs. (Emacs uses such names only for special-purpose buffers.) People will find Emacs more coherent if all libraries use the same conventions.

- The default file coding system for Emacs Lisp source files is UTF-8 (see Section 32.1 [Text Representations], page 761). In the rare event that your program contains characters which are *not* in UTF-8, you should specify an appropriate coding system in the source file's '`-*-`' line or local variables list. See Section "Local Variables in Files" in *The GNU Emacs Manual*.

- Indent the file using the default indentation parameters.

- Don't make a habit of putting close-parentheses on lines by themselves; Lisp programmers find this disconcerting.

- Please put a copyright notice and copying permission notice on the file if you distribute copies. See Section D.8 [Library Headers], page 1063.

D.2 Key Binding Conventions

- Many special major modes, like Dired, Info, Compilation, and Occur, are designed to handle read-only text that contains *hyper-links*. Such a major mode should redefine `mouse-2` and RET to follow the links. It should also set up a `follow-link` condition, so that the link obeys `mouse-1-click-follows-link`. See Section 31.19.8 [Clickable Text], page 746. See Section 37.19 [Buttons], page 963, for an easy method of implementing such clickable links.

- Don't define `C-c letter` as a key in Lisp programs. Sequences consisting of `C-c` and a letter (either upper or lower case) are reserved for users; they are the **only** sequences reserved for users, so do not block them.

  Changing all the Emacs major modes to respect this convention was a lot of work; abandoning this convention would make that work go to waste, and inconvenience users. Please comply with it.

- Function keys `F5` through `F9` without modifier keys are also reserved for users to define.

- Sequences consisting of `C-c` followed by a control character or a digit are reserved for major modes.

- Sequences consisting of `C-c` followed by `{`, `}`, `<`, `>`, `:` or `;` are also reserved for major modes.

- Sequences consisting of `C-c` followed by any other ASCII punctuation or symbol character are allocated for minor modes. Using them in a major mode is not absolutely prohibited, but if you do that, the major mode binding may be shadowed from time to time by minor modes.

- Don't bind `C-h` following any prefix character (including `C-c`). If you don't bind `C-h`, it is automatically available as a help character for listing the subcommands of the prefix character.

- Don't bind a key sequence ending in ESC except following another ESC. (That is, it is OK to bind a sequence ending in *ESC ESC*.)

  The reason for this rule is that a non-prefix binding for ESC in any context prevents recognition of escape sequences as function keys in that context.

- Similarly, don't bind a key sequence ending in `C-g`, since that is commonly used to cancel a key sequence.

- Anything that acts like a temporary mode or state that the user can enter and leave should define *ESC ESC* or *ESC ESC ESC* as a way to escape.

  For a state that accepts ordinary Emacs commands, or more generally any kind of state in which ESC followed by a function key or arrow key is potentially meaningful, then you must not define *ESC ESC*, since that would preclude recognizing an escape sequence after ESC. In these states, you should define *ESC ESC ESC* as the way to escape. Otherwise, define *ESC ESC* instead.

D.3 Emacs Programming Tips

Following these conventions will make your program fit better into Emacs when it runs.

- Don't use `next-line` or `previous-line` in programs; nearly always, `forward-line` is more convenient as well as more predictable and robust. See Section 29.2.4 [Text Lines], page 676.

- Don't call functions that set the mark, unless setting the mark is one of the intended features of your program. The mark is a user-level feature, so it is incorrect to change the mark except to supply a value for the user's benefit. See Section 30.7 [The Mark], page 691.

  In particular, don't use any of these functions:

  - `beginning-of-buffer`, `end-of-buffer`
  - `replace-string`, `replace-regexp`
  - `insert-file`, `insert-buffer`

  If you just want to move point, or replace a certain string, or insert a file or buffer's contents, without any of the other features intended for interactive users, you can replace these functions with one or two lines of simple Lisp code.

- Use lists rather than vectors, except when there is a particular reason to use a vector. Lisp has more facilities for manipulating lists than for vectors, and working with lists is usually more convenient.

  Vectors are advantageous for tables that are substantial in size and are accessed in random order (not searched front to back), provided there is no need to insert or delete elements (only lists allow that).

- The recommended way to show a message in the echo area is with the **message** function, not **princ**. See Section 37.4 [The Echo Area], page 888.

- When you encounter an error condition, call the function **error** (or **signal**). The function **error** does not return. See Section 10.6.3.1 [Signaling Errors], page 148.

  Don't use **message**, **throw**, **sleep-for**, or **beep** to report errors.

- An error message should start with a capital letter but should not end with a period.

- A question asked in the minibuffer with **yes-or-no-p** or **y-or-n-p** should start with a capital letter and end with '? '.

- When you mention a default value in a minibuffer prompt, put it and the word 'default' inside parentheses. It should look like this:

  ```
  Enter the answer (default 42):
  ```

- In **interactive**, if you use a Lisp expression to produce a list of arguments, don't try to provide the correct default values for region or position arguments. Instead, provide **nil** for those arguments if they were not specified, and have the function body compute the default value when the argument is **nil**. For instance, write this:

  ```
  (defun foo (pos)
    (interactive
     (list (if specified specified-pos)))
    (unless pos (setq pos default-pos))
    ...)
  ```

  rather than this:

  ```
  (defun foo (pos)
    (interactive
     (list (if specified specified-pos
               default-pos)))
    ...)
  ```

This is so that repetition of the command will recompute these defaults based on the current circumstances.

You do not need to take such precautions when you use interactive specs 'd', 'm' and 'r', because they make special arrangements to recompute the argument values on repetition of the command.

- Many commands that take a long time to execute display a message that says something like 'Operating...' when they start, and change it to 'Operating...done' when they finish. Please keep the style of these messages uniform: *no* space around the ellipsis, and *no* period after 'done'. See Section 37.4.2 [Progress], page 890, for an easy way to generate such messages.

- Try to avoid using recursive edits. Instead, do what the Rmail *e* command does: use a new local keymap that contains a command defined to switch back to the old local keymap. Or simply switch to another buffer and let the user switch back at will. See Section 20.13 [Recursive Editing], page 386.

D.4 Tips for Making Compiled Code Fast

Here are ways of improving the execution speed of byte-compiled Lisp programs.

- Profile your program, to find out where the time is being spent. See Section 17.5 [Profiling], page 301.

- Use iteration rather than recursion whenever possible. Function calls are slow in Emacs Lisp even when a compiled function is calling another compiled function.

- Using the primitive list-searching functions `memq`, `member`, `assq`, or `assoc` is even faster than explicit iteration. It can be worth rearranging a data structure so that one of these primitive search functions can be used.

- Certain built-in functions are handled specially in byte-compiled code, avoiding the need for an ordinary function call. It is a good idea to use these functions rather than alternatives. To see whether a function is handled specially by the compiler, examine its `byte-compile` property. If the property is non-`nil`, then the function is handled specially.

  For example, the following input will show you that `aref` is compiled specially (see Section 6.3 [Array Functions], page 101):

```
    (get 'aref 'byte-compile)
         ⇒ byte-compile-two-args
```

  Note that in this case (and many others), you must first load the `bytecomp` library, which defines the `byte-compile` property.

- If calling a small function accounts for a substantial part of your program's running time, make the function inline. This eliminates the function call overhead. Since making a function inline reduces the flexibility of changing the program, don't do it unless it gives a noticeable speedup in something slow enough that users care about the speed. See Section 12.13 [Inline Functions], page 212.

D.5 Tips for Avoiding Compiler Warnings

- Try to avoid compiler warnings about undefined free variables, by adding dummy `defvar` definitions for these variables, like this:

```
(defvar foo)
```

Such a definition has no effect except to tell the compiler not to warn about uses of the variable `foo` in this file.

- Similarly, to avoid a compiler warning about an undefined function that you know *will* be defined, use a `declare-function` statement (see Section 12.15 [Declaring Functions], page 214).

- If you use many functions and variables from a certain file, you can add a `require` for that package to avoid compilation warnings for them. For instance,

```
(eval-when-compile
  (require 'foo))
```

- If you bind a variable in one function, and use it or set it in another function, the compiler warns about the latter function unless the variable has a definition. But adding a definition would be unclean if the variable has a short name, since Lisp packages should not define short variable names. The right thing to do is to rename this variable to start with the name prefix used for the other functions and variables in your package.

- The last resort for avoiding a warning, when you want to do something that is usually a mistake but you know is not a mistake in your usage, is to put it inside `with-no-warnings`. See Section 16.6 [Compiler Errors], page 265.

D.6 Tips for Documentation Strings

Here are some tips and conventions for the writing of documentation strings. You can check many of these conventions by running the command *M-x checkdoc-minor-mode*.

- Every command, function, or variable intended for users to know about should have a documentation string.

- An internal variable or subroutine of a Lisp program might as well have a documentation string. Documentation strings take up very little space in a running Emacs.

- Format the documentation string so that it fits in an Emacs window on an 80-column screen. It is a good idea for most lines to be no wider than 60 characters. The first line should not be wider than 67 characters or it will look bad in the output of `apropos`.

  You can fill the text if that looks good. Emacs Lisp mode fills documentation strings to the width specified by `emacs-lisp-docstring-fill-column`. However, you can sometimes make a documentation string much more readable by adjusting its line breaks with care. Use blank lines between sections if the documentation string is long.

- The first line of the documentation string should consist of one or two complete sentences that stand on their own as a summary. *M-x apropos* displays just the first line, and if that line's contents don't stand on their own, the result looks bad. In particular, start the first line with a capital letter and end it with a period.

  For a function, the first line should briefly answer the question, "What does this function do?" For a variable, the first line should briefly answer the question, "What does this value mean?"

  Don't limit the documentation string to one line; use as many lines as you need to explain the details of how to use the function or variable. Please use complete sentences for the rest of the text too.

- When the user tries to use a disabled command, Emacs displays just the first paragraph of its documentation string—everything through the first blank line. If you wish, you can choose which information to include before the first blank line so as to make this display useful.

- The first line should mention all the important arguments of the function, and should mention them in the order that they are written in a function call. If the function has many arguments, then it is not feasible to mention them all in the first line; in that case, the first line should mention the first few arguments, including the most important arguments.

- When a function's documentation string mentions the value of an argument of the function, use the argument name in capital letters as if it were a name for that value. Thus, the documentation string of the function `eval` refers to its first argument as 'FORM', because the actual argument name is `form`:

      Evaluate FORM and return its value.

  Also write metasyntactic variables in capital letters, such as when you show the decomposition of a list or vector into subunits, some of which may vary. 'KEY' and 'VALUE' in the following example illustrate this practice:

      The argument TABLE should be an alist whose elements
      have the form (KEY . VALUE). Here, KEY is ...

- Never change the case of a Lisp symbol when you mention it in a doc string. If the symbol's name is `foo`, write "foo", not "Foo" (which is a different symbol).

  This might appear to contradict the policy of writing function argument values, but there is no real contradiction; the argument *value* is not the same thing as the *symbol* that the function uses to hold the value.

  If this puts a lower-case letter at the beginning of a sentence and that annoys you, rewrite the sentence so that the symbol is not at the start of it.

- Do not start or end a documentation string with whitespace.

- **Do not** indent subsequent lines of a documentation string so that the text is lined up in the source code with the text of the first line. This looks nice in the source code, but looks bizarre when users view the documentation. Remember that the indentation before the starting double-quote is not part of the string!

- When a documentation string refers to a Lisp symbol, write it as it would be printed (which usually means in lower case), surrounding it with curved single quotes (' and '). There are two exceptions: write `t` and `nil` without surrounding punctuation. For example: 'CODE can be 'lambda', nil, or t'. See Section "Quotation Marks" in *The GNU Emacs Manual*, for how to enter curved single quotes.

  Documentation strings can also use an older single-quoting convention, which quotes symbols with grave accent ' and apostrophe ': 'like-this' rather than 'like-this'. This older convention was designed for now-obsolete displays in which grave accent and apostrophe were mirror images.

  Documentation using either convention is converted to the user's preferred format when it is copied into a help buffer. See Section 23.3 [Keys in Documentation], page 488.

  Help mode automatically creates a hyperlink when a documentation string uses a single-quoted symbol name, if the symbol has either a function or a variable definition. You do not need to do anything special to make use of this feature. However, when a symbol has both a function definition and a variable definition, and you want to refer to just one of them, you can specify which one by writing one of the words 'variable', 'option', 'function', or 'command', immediately before the symbol name. (Case makes no difference in recognizing these indicator words.) For example, if you write

> This function sets the variable `buffer-file-name'.

then the hyperlink will refer only to the variable documentation of `buffer-file-name`, and not to its function documentation.

If a symbol has a function definition and/or a variable definition, but those are irrelevant to the use of the symbol that you are documenting, you can write the words 'symbol' or 'program' before the symbol name to prevent making any hyperlink. For example,

> If the argument KIND-OF-RESULT is the symbol `list',
> this function returns a list of all the objects
> that satisfy the criterion.

does not make a hyperlink to the documentation, irrelevant here, of the function `list`.

Normally, no hyperlink is made for a variable without variable documentation. You can force a hyperlink for such variables by preceding them with one of the words 'variable' or 'option'.

Hyperlinks for faces are only made if the face name is preceded or followed by the word 'face'. In that case, only the face documentation will be shown, even if the symbol is also defined as a variable or as a function.

To make a hyperlink to Info documentation, write the single-quoted name of the Info node (or anchor), preceded by 'info node', 'Info node', 'info anchor' or 'Info anchor'. The Info file name defaults to 'emacs'. For example,

> See Info node `Font Lock' and Info node `(elisp)Font Lock Basics'.

Finally, to create a hyperlink to URLs, write the single-quoted URL, preceded by 'URL'. For example,

> The home page for the GNU project has more information (see URL
> `http://www.gnu.org/').

- Don't write key sequences directly in documentation strings. Instead, use the '\\[...]' construct to stand for them. For example, instead of writing 'C-f', write the construct '\\[forward-char]'. When Emacs displays the documentation string, it substitutes whatever key is currently bound to `forward-char`. (This is normally 'C-f', but it may be some other character if the user has moved key bindings.) See Section 23.3 [Keys in Documentation], page 488.

- In documentation strings for a major mode, you will want to refer to the key bindings of that mode's local map, rather than global ones. Therefore, use the construct '\\<...>' once in the documentation string to specify which key map to use. Do this before the first use of '\\[...]'. The text inside the '\\<...>' should be the name of the variable containing the local keymap for the major mode.

  It is not practical to use '\\[...]' very many times, because display of the documentation string will become slow. So use this to describe the most important commands in your major mode, and then use '\\{...}' to display the rest of the mode's keymap.

- For consistency, phrase the verb in the first sentence of a function's documentation string as an imperative—for instance, use "Return the cons of A and B." in preference to "Returns the cons of A and B." Usually it looks good to do likewise for the rest of the first paragraph. Subsequent paragraphs usually look better if each sentence is indicative and has a proper subject.

- The documentation string for a function that is a yes-or-no predicate should start with words such as "Return t if", to indicate explicitly what constitutes truth. The word "return" avoids starting the sentence with lower-case "t", which could be somewhat distracting.

- If a line in a documentation string begins with an open-parenthesis, write a backslash before the open-parenthesis, like this:

```
The argument FOO can be either a number
\(a buffer position) or a string (a file name).
```

This prevents the open-parenthesis from being treated as the start of a defun (see Section "Defuns" in *The GNU Emacs Manual*).

- Write documentation strings in the active voice, not the passive, and in the present tense, not the future. For instance, use "Return a list containing A and B." instead of "A list containing A and B will be returned."

- Avoid using the word "cause" (or its equivalents) unnecessarily. Instead of, "Cause Emacs to display text in boldface", write just "Display text in boldface".

- Avoid using "iff" (a mathematics term meaning "if and only if"), since many people are unfamiliar with it and mistake it for a typo. In most cases, the meaning is clear with just "if". Otherwise, try to find an alternate phrasing that conveys the meaning.

- When a command is meaningful only in a certain mode or situation, do mention that in the documentation string. For example, the documentation of `dired-find-file` is:

```
In Dired, visit the file or directory named on this line.
```

- When you define a variable that represents an option users might want to set, use `defcustom`. See Section 11.5 [Defining Variables], page 161.

- The documentation string for a variable that is a yes-or-no flag should start with words such as "Non-nil means", to make it clear that all non-`nil` values are equivalent and indicate explicitly what `nil` and non-`nil` mean.

D.7 Tips on Writing Comments

We recommend these conventions for comments:

`;` Comments that start with a single semicolon, `;`, should all be aligned to the same column on the right of the source code. Such comments usually explain how the code on that line does its job. For example:

```
(setq base-version-list                 ; There was a base
      (assoc (substring fn 0 start-vn)   ; version to which
             file-version-assoc-list))   ; this looks like
                                         ; a subversion.
```

`;;` Comments that start with two semicolons, `;;`, should be aligned to the same level of indentation as the code. Such comments usually describe the purpose of the following lines or the state of the program at that point. For example:

```
(prog1 (setq auto-fill-function
              ...
              ...
   ;; Update mode line.
   (force-mode-line-update)))
```

We also normally use two semicolons for comments outside functions.

```
;; This Lisp code is run in Emacs when it is to operate as
;; a server for other processes.
```

If a function has no documentation string, it should instead have a two-semicolon comment right before the function, explaining what the function does and how to call it properly. Explain precisely what each argument means and how the function interprets its possible values. It is much better to convert such comments to documentation strings, though.

';;;'   Comments that start with three semicolons, ';;;', should start at the left margin. We use them for comments which should be considered a heading by Outline minor mode. By default, comments starting with at least three semicolons (followed by a single space and a non-whitespace character) are considered headings, comments starting with two or fewer are not. Historically, triple-semicolon comments have also been used for commenting out lines within a function, but this use is discouraged.

When commenting out entire functions, use two semicolons.

';;;;'   Comments that start with four semicolons, ';;;;', should be aligned to the left margin and are used for headings of major sections of a program. For example:

```
;;;; The kill ring
```

Generally speaking, the M-; (comment-dwim) command automatically starts a comment of the appropriate type; or indents an existing comment to the right place, depending on the number of semicolons. See Section "Manipulating Comments" in *The GNU Emacs Manual*.

D.8 Conventional Headers for Emacs Libraries

Emacs has conventions for using special comments in Lisp libraries to divide them into sections and give information such as who wrote them. Using a standard format for these items makes it easier for tools (and people) to extract the relevant information. This section explains these conventions, starting with an example:

```
;;; foo.el --- Support for the Foo programming language

;; Copyright (C) 2010-2017 Your Name

;; Author: Your Name <yourname@example.com>
;; Maintainer: Someone Else <someone@example.com>
;; Created: 14 Jul 2010
;; Keywords: languages
;; Homepage: http://example.com/foo

;; This file is not part of GNU Emacs.

;; This file is free software...
...
;; along with this file.  If not, see <http://www.gnu.org/licenses/>.
```

The very first line should have this format:

```
;;; filename --- description
```

The description should be contained in one line. If the file needs a '-*-' specification, put it after *description*. If this would make the first line too long, use a Local Variables section at the end of the file.

The copyright notice usually lists your name (if you wrote the file). If you have an employer who claims copyright on your work, you might need to list them instead. Do not say that the copyright holder is the Free Software Foundation (or that the file is part of GNU Emacs) unless your file has been accepted into the Emacs distribution. For more information on the form of copyright and license notices, see the guide on the GNU website (`http://www.gnu.org/licenses/gpl-howto.html`).

After the copyright notice come several *header comment* lines, each beginning with ';; *header-name*:'. Here is a table of the conventional possibilities for *header-name*:

'`Author`' This line states the name and email address of at least the principal author of the library. If there are multiple authors, list them on continuation lines led by ;; and a tab or at least two spaces. We recommend including a contact email address, of the form '`<...>`'. For example:

```
;; Author: Your Name <yourname@example.com>
;;         Someone Else <someone@example.com>
;;         Another Person <another@example.com>
```

'`Maintainer`'
This header has the same format as the Author header. It lists the person(s) who currently maintain(s) the file (respond to bug reports, etc.).

If there is no maintainer line, the person(s) in the Author field is/are presumed to be the maintainers. Some files in Emacs use '`FSF`' for the maintainer. This means that the original author is no longer responsible for the file, and that it is maintained as part of Emacs.

'`Created`' This optional line gives the original creation date of the file, and is for historical interest only.

'`Version`' If you wish to record version numbers for the individual Lisp program, put them in this line. Lisp files distributed with Emacs generally do not have a '`Version`' header, since the version number of Emacs itself serves the same purpose. If you are distributing a collection of multiple files, we recommend not writing the version in every file, but only the main one.

'`Keywords`'
This line lists keywords for the **finder-by-keyword** help command. Please use that command to see a list of the meaningful keywords. The command *M-x checkdoc-package-keywords RET* will find and display any keywords that are not in **finder-known-keywords**. If you set the variable **checkdoc-package-keywords-flag** non-**nil**, checkdoc commands will include the keyword verification in its checks.

This field is how people will find your package when they're looking for things by topic. To separate the keywords, you can use spaces, commas, or both.

The name of this field is unfortunate, since people often assume it is the place to write arbitrary keywords that describe their package, rather than just the relevant Finder keywords.

'Homepage'

This line states the homepage of the library.

'Package-Version'

If 'Version' is not suitable for use by the package manager, then a package can define 'Package-Version'; it will be used instead. This is handy if 'Version' is an RCS id or something else that cannot be parsed by version-to-list. See Section 39.1 [Packaging Basics], page 1026.

'Package-Requires'

If this exists, it names packages on which the current package depends for proper operation. See Section 39.1 [Packaging Basics], page 1026. This is used by the package manager both at download time (to ensure that a complete set of packages is downloaded) and at activation time (to ensure that a package is only activated if all its dependencies have been).

Its format is a list of lists on a single line. The `car` of each sub-list is the name of a package, as a symbol. The `cadr` of each sub-list is the minimum acceptable version number, as a string that can be parse by version-to-list. An entry that lacks a version (i.e., an entry which is just a symbol, or a sub-list of one element) is equivalent to entry with version "0". For instance:

```
;; Package-Requires: ((gnus "1.0") (bubbles "2.7.2") cl-lib (seq))
```

The package code automatically defines a package named 'emacs' with the version number of the currently running Emacs. This can be used to require a minimal version of Emacs for a package.

Just about every Lisp library ought to have the 'Author' and 'Keywords' header comment lines. Use the others if they are appropriate. You can also put in header lines with other header names—they have no standard meanings, so they can't do any harm.

We use additional stylized comments to subdivide the contents of the library file. These should be separated from anything else by blank lines. Here is a table of them:

';;; Commentary:'

This begins introductory comments that explain how the library works. It should come right after the copying permissions, terminated by a 'Change Log', 'History' or 'Code' comment line. This text is used by the Finder package, so it should make sense in that context.

';;; Change Log:'

This begins an optional log of changes to the file over time. Don't put too much information in this section—it is better to keep the detailed logs in a version control system (as Emacs does) or in a separate ChangeLog file. 'History' is an alternative to 'Change Log'.

';;; Code:'

This begins the actual code of the program.

`';;; filename ends here'`

> This is the *footer line*; it appears at the very end of the file. Its purpose is to
> enable people to detect truncated versions of the file from the lack of a footer
> line.

Appendix E GNU Emacs Internals

This chapter describes how the runnable Emacs executable is dumped with the preloaded Lisp libraries in it, how storage is allocated, and some internal aspects of GNU Emacs that may be of interest to C programmers.

E.1 Building Emacs

This section explains the steps involved in building the Emacs executable. You don't have to know this material to build and install Emacs, since the makefiles do all these things automatically. This information is pertinent to Emacs developers.

Building Emacs requires GNU Make version 3.81 or later.

Compilation of the C source files in the `src` directory produces an executable file called `temacs`, also called a *bare impure Emacs*. It contains the Emacs Lisp interpreter and I/O routines, but not the editing commands.

The command `temacs -l loadup` would run `temacs` and direct it to load `loadup.el`. The `loadup` library loads additional Lisp libraries, which set up the normal Emacs editing environment. After this step, the Emacs executable is no longer *bare*.

Because it takes some time to load the standard Lisp files, the `temacs` executable usually isn't run directly by users. Instead, as one of the last steps of building Emacs, the command '`temacs -batch -l loadup dump`' is run. The special '`dump`' argument causes `temacs` to dump out an executable program, called `emacs`, which has all the standard Lisp files preloaded. (The '`-batch`' argument prevents `temacs` from trying to initialize any of its data on the terminal, so that the tables of terminal information are empty in the dumped Emacs.)

The dumped `emacs` executable (also called a *pure* Emacs) is the one which is installed. The variable `preloaded-file-list` stores a list of the Lisp files preloaded into the dumped Emacs. If you port Emacs to a new operating system, and are not able to implement dumping, then Emacs must load `loadup.el` each time it starts.

You can specify additional files to preload by writing a library named `site-load.el` that loads them. You may need to rebuild Emacs with an added definition

```
#define SITELOAD_PURESIZE_EXTRA n
```

to make *n* added bytes of pure space to hold the additional files; see `src/puresize.h`. (Try adding increments of 20000 until it is big enough.) However, the advantage of preloading additional files decreases as machines get faster. On modern machines, it is usually not advisable.

After `loadup.el` reads `site-load.el`, it finds the documentation strings for primitive and preloaded functions (and variables) in the file `etc/DOC` where they are stored, by calling `Snarf-documentation` (see [Accessing Documentation], page 488).

You can specify other Lisp expressions to execute just before dumping by putting them in a library named `site-init.el`. This file is executed after the documentation strings are found.

If you want to preload function or variable definitions, there are three ways you can do this and make their documentation strings accessible when you subsequently run Emacs:

- Arrange to scan these files when producing the `etc/DOC` file, and load them with `site-load.el`.

- Load the files with `site-init.el`, then copy the files into the installation directory for Lisp files when you install Emacs.

- Specify a `nil` value for `byte-compile-dynamic-docstrings` as a local variable in each of these files, and load them with either `site-load.el` or `site-init.el`. (This method has the drawback that the documentation strings take up space in Emacs all the time.)

It is not advisable to put anything in `site-load.el` or `site-init.el` that would alter any of the features that users expect in an ordinary unmodified Emacs. If you feel you must override normal features for your site, do it with `default.el`, so that users can override your changes if they wish. See Section 38.1.1 [Startup Summary], page 985. Note that if either `site-load.el` or `site-init.el` changes `load-path`, the changes will be lost after dumping. See Section 15.3 [Library Search], page 247. To make a permanent change to `load-path`, use the `--enable-locallisppath` option of `configure`.

In a package that can be preloaded, it is sometimes necessary (or useful) to delay certain evaluations until Emacs subsequently starts up. The vast majority of such cases relate to the values of customizable variables. For example, `tutorial-directory` is a variable defined in `startup.el`, which is preloaded. The default value is set based on `data-directory`. The variable needs to access the value of `data-directory` when Emacs starts, not when it is dumped, because the Emacs executable has probably been installed in a different location since it was dumped.

`custom-initialize-delay` *symbol value*   [Function]

> This function delays the initialization of *symbol* to the next Emacs start. You normally use this function by specifying it as the `:initialize` property of a customizable variable. (The argument *value* is unused, and is provided only for compatibility with the form Custom expects.)

In the unlikely event that you need a more general functionality than `custom-initialize-delay` provides, you can use `before-init-hook` (see Section 38.1.1 [Startup Summary], page 985).

`dump-emacs` *to-file from-file*   [Function]

> This function dumps the current state of Emacs into an executable file *to-file*. It takes symbols from *from-file* (this is normally the executable file `temacs`).
>
> If you want to use this function in an Emacs that was already dumped, you must run Emacs with '`-batch`'.

E.2 Pure Storage

Emacs Lisp uses two kinds of storage for user-created Lisp objects: *normal storage* and *pure storage*. Normal storage is where all the new data created during an Emacs session are kept (see Section E.3 [Garbage Collection], page 1069). Pure storage is used for certain data in the preloaded standard Lisp files—data that should never change during actual use of Emacs.

Pure storage is allocated only while `temacs` is loading the standard preloaded Lisp libraries. In the file `emacs`, it is marked as read-only (on operating systems that permit this), so that the memory space can be shared by all the Emacs jobs running on the machine at once. Pure storage is not expandable; a fixed amount is allocated when Emacs is compiled, and if that is not sufficient for the preloaded libraries, `temacs` allocates dynamic memory for the part that didn't fit. The resulting image will work, but garbage collection (see Section E.3 [Garbage Collection], page 1069) is disabled in this situation, causing a memory leak. Such an overflow normally won't happen unless you try to preload additional libraries or add features to the standard ones. Emacs will display a warning about the overflow when it starts. If this happens, you should increase the compilation parameter `SYSTEM_PURESIZE_EXTRA` in the file `src/puresize.h` and rebuild Emacs.

purecopy *object*   [Function]

> This function makes a copy in pure storage of *object*, and returns it. It copies a string by simply making a new string with the same characters, but without text properties, in pure storage. It recursively copies the contents of vectors and cons cells. It does not make copies of other objects such as symbols, but just returns them unchanged. It signals an error if asked to copy markers.

> This function is a no-op except while Emacs is being built and dumped; it is usually called only in preloaded Lisp files.

pure-bytes-used   [Variable]

> The value of this variable is the number of bytes of pure storage allocated so far. Typically, in a dumped Emacs, this number is very close to the total amount of pure storage available—if it were not, we would preallocate less.

purify-flag   [Variable]

> This variable determines whether **defun** should make a copy of the function definition in pure storage. If it is non-**nil**, then the function definition is copied into pure storage.

> This flag is **t** while loading all of the basic functions for building Emacs initially (allowing those functions to be shareable and non-collectible). Dumping Emacs as an executable always writes **nil** in this variable, regardless of the value it actually has before and after dumping.

> You should not change this flag in a running Emacs.

E.3 Garbage Collection

When a program creates a list or the user defines a new function (such as by loading a library), that data is placed in normal storage. If normal storage runs low, then Emacs asks the operating system to allocate more memory. Different types of Lisp objects, such as symbols, cons cells, small vectors, markers, etc., are segregated in distinct blocks in memory. (Large vectors, long strings, buffers and certain other editing types, which are fairly large, are allocated in individual blocks, one per object; small strings are packed into blocks of 8k bytes, and small vectors are packed into blocks of 4k bytes).

Beyond the basic vector, a lot of objects like window, buffer, and frame are managed as if they were vectors. The corresponding C data structures include the **struct vectorlike_header** field whose **size** member contains the subtype enumerated by **enum pvec_type** and an information about how many **Lisp_Object** fields this structure contains and what the size of the rest data is. This information is needed to calculate the memory footprint of an object, and used by the vector allocation code while iterating over the vector blocks.

It is quite common to use some storage for a while, then release it by (for example) killing a buffer or deleting the last pointer to an object. Emacs provides a *garbage collector* to reclaim this abandoned storage. The garbage collector operates by finding and marking all Lisp objects that are still accessible to Lisp programs. To begin with, it assumes all the symbols, their values and associated function definitions, and any data presently on the stack, are accessible. Any objects that can be reached indirectly through other accessible objects are also accessible.

When marking is finished, all objects still unmarked are garbage. No matter what the Lisp program or the user does, it is impossible to refer to them, since there is no longer a way to reach them. Their space might as well be reused, since no one will miss them. The second (sweep) phase of the garbage collector arranges to reuse them.

The sweep phase puts unused cons cells onto a *free list* for future allocation; likewise for symbols and markers. It compacts the accessible strings so they occupy fewer 8k blocks; then it frees the other 8k blocks. Unreachable vectors from vector blocks are coalesced to create largest possible free areas; if a free area spans a complete 4k block, that block is freed. Otherwise, the free area is recorded in a free list array, where each entry corresponds to a free list of areas of the same size. Large vectors, buffers, and other large objects are allocated and freed individually.

> **Common Lisp note:** Unlike other Lisps, GNU Emacs Lisp does not call the garbage collector when the free list is empty. Instead, it simply requests the operating system to allocate more storage, and processing continues until `gc-cons-threshold` bytes have been used.
>
> This means that you can make sure that the garbage collector will not run during a certain portion of a Lisp program by calling the garbage collector explicitly just before it (provided that portion of the program does not use so much space as to force a second garbage collection).

`garbage-collect`   [Command]

This command runs a garbage collection, and returns information on the amount of space in use. (Garbage collection can also occur spontaneously if you use more than `gc-cons-threshold` bytes of Lisp data since the previous garbage collection.)

`garbage-collect` returns a list with information on amount of space in use, where each entry has the form '(*name size used*)' or '(*name size used free*)'. In the entry, *name* is a symbol describing the kind of objects this entry represents, *size* is the number of bytes used by each one, *used* is the number of those objects that were found live in the heap, and optional *free* is the number of those objects that are not live but that Emacs keeps around for future allocations. So an overall result is:

```
((conses cons-size used-conses free-conses)
 (symbols symbol-size used-symbols free-symbols)
 (miscs misc-size used-miscs free-miscs)
 (strings string-size used-strings free-strings)
 (string-bytes byte-size used-bytes)
 (vectors vector-size used-vectors)
 (vector-slots slot-size used-slots free-slots)
```

```
(floats float-size used-floats free-floats)
(intervals interval-size used-intervals free-intervals)
(buffers buffer-size used-buffers)
(heap unit-size total-size free-size))
```

Here is an example:

```
(garbage-collect)
     ⇒ ((conses 16 49126 8058) (symbols 48 14607 0)
         (miscs 40 34 56) (strings 32 2942 2607)
         (string-bytes 1 78607) (vectors 16 7247)
         (vector-slots 8 341609 29474) (floats 8 71 102)
         (intervals 56 27 26) (buffers 944 8)
         (heap 1024 11715 2678))
```

Below is a table explaining each element. Note that last **heap** entry is optional and present only if an underlying **malloc** implementation provides **mallinfo** function.

cons-size   Internal size of a cons cell, i.e., **sizeof (struct Lisp_Cons)**.

used-conses
    The number of cons cells in use.

free-conses
    The number of cons cells for which space has been obtained from the operating system, but that are not currently being used.

symbol-size
    Internal size of a symbol, i.e., **sizeof (struct Lisp_Symbol)**.

used-symbols
    The number of symbols in use.

free-symbols
    The number of symbols for which space has been obtained from the operating system, but that are not currently being used.

misc-size   Internal size of a miscellaneous entity, i.e., **sizeof (union Lisp_Misc)**, which is a size of the largest type enumerated in **enum Lisp_Misc_Type**.

used-miscs
    The number of miscellaneous objects in use. These include markers and overlays, plus certain objects not visible to users.

free-miscs   The number of miscellaneous objects for which space has been obtained from the operating system, but that are not currently being used.

string-size   Internal size of a string header, i.e., **sizeof (struct Lisp_String)**.

used-strings
    The number of string headers in use.

free-strings
    The number of string headers for which space has been obtained from the operating system, but that are not currently being used.

byte-size   This is used for convenience and equals to **sizeof (char)**.

used-bytes   The total size of all string data in bytes.

vector-size   Internal size of a vector header, i.e., `sizeof (struct Lisp_Vector)`.

used-vectors
            The number of vector headers allocated from the vector blocks.

slot-size   Internal size of a vector slot, always equal to `sizeof (Lisp_Object)`.

used-slots   The number of slots in all used vectors.

free-slots   The number of free slots in all vector blocks.

float-size   Internal size of a float object, i.e., `sizeof (struct Lisp_Float)`. (Do
            not confuse it with the native platform `float` or `double`.)

used-floats
            The number of floats in use.

free-floats   The number of floats for which space has been obtained from the operat-
            ing system, but that are not currently being used.

interval-size
            Internal size of an interval object, i.e., `sizeof (struct interval)`.

used-intervals
            The number of intervals in use.

free-intervals
            The number of intervals for which space has been obtained from the
            operating system, but that are not currently being used.

buffer-size   Internal size of a buffer, i.e., `sizeof (struct buffer)`. (Do not confuse
            with the value returned by `buffer-size` function.)

used-buffers
            The number of buffer objects in use. This includes killed buffers invisible
            to users, i.e., all buffers in `all_buffers` list.

unit-size   The unit of heap space measurement, always equal to 1024 bytes.

total-size   Total heap size, in *unit-size* units.

free-size   Heap space which is not currently used, in *unit-size* units.

If there was overflow in pure space (see Section E.2 [Pure Storage], page 1068),
`garbage-collect` returns `nil`, because a real garbage collection cannot be done.

`garbage-collection-messages`   [User Option]
    If this variable is non-`nil`, Emacs displays a message at the beginning and end of
    garbage collection. The default value is `nil`.

`post-gc-hook`   [Variable]
    This is a normal hook that is run at the end of garbage collection. Garbage collection
    is inhibited while the hook functions run, so be careful writing them.

`gc-cons-threshold`   [User Option]
> The value of this variable is the number of bytes of storage that must be allocated for
> Lisp objects after one garbage collection in order to trigger another garbage collection.
> You can use the result returned by `garbage-collect` to get an information about
> size of the particular object type; space allocated to the contents of buffers does not
> count. Note that the subsequent garbage collection does not happen immediately
> when the threshold is exhausted, but only the next time the Lisp interpreter is called.
>
> The initial threshold value is `GC_DEFAULT_THRESHOLD`, defined in `alloc.c`. Since it's
> defined in `word_size` units, the value is 400,000 for the default 32-bit configuration
> and 800,000 for the 64-bit one. If you specify a larger value, garbage collection will
> happen less often. This reduces the amount of time spent garbage collecting, but
> increases total memory use. You may want to do this when running a program that
> creates lots of Lisp data.
>
> You can make collections more frequent by specifying a smaller value, down to 1/10th
> of `GC_DEFAULT_THRESHOLD`. A value less than this minimum will remain in effect only
> until the subsequent garbage collection, at which time `garbage-collect` will set the
> threshold back to the minimum.

`gc-cons-percentage`   [User Option]
> The value of this variable specifies the amount of consing before a garbage collection
> occurs, as a fraction of the current heap size. This criterion and `gc-cons-threshold`
> apply in parallel, and garbage collection occurs only when both criteria are satisfied.
>
> As the heap size increases, the time to perform a garbage collection increases. Thus,
> it can be desirable to do them less frequently in proportion.

The value returned by `garbage-collect` describes the amount of memory used by Lisp
data, broken down by data type. By contrast, the function `memory-limit` provides information on the total amount of memory Emacs is currently using.

`memory-limit`   [Function]
> This function returns the address of the last byte Emacs has allocated, divided by
> 1024. We divide the value by 1024 to make sure it fits in a Lisp integer.
>
> You can use this to get a general idea of how your actions affect the memory usage.

`memory-full`   [Variable]
> This variable is `t` if Emacs is nearly out of memory for Lisp objects, and `nil` otherwise.

`memory-use-counts`   [Function]
> This returns a list of numbers that count the number of objects created in this Emacs
> session. Each of these counters increments for a certain kind of object. See the
> documentation string for details.

`memory-info`   [Function]
> This functions returns an amount of total system memory and how much of it is free.
> On an unsupported system, the value may be `nil`.

`gcs-done`   [Variable]
> This variable contains the total number of garbage collections done so far in this
> Emacs session.

`gc-elapsed`   [Variable]
> This variable contains the total number of seconds of elapsed time during garbage collection so far in this Emacs session, as a floating-point number.

E.4 Stack-allocated Objects

The garbage collector described above is used to manage data visible from Lisp programs, as well as most of the data internally used by the Lisp interpreter. Sometimes it may be useful to allocate temporary internal objects using the C stack of the interpreter. This can help performance, as stack allocation is typically faster than using heap memory to allocate and the garbage collector to free. The downside is that using such objects after they are freed results in undefined behavior, so uses should be well thought out and carefully debugged by using the `GC_CHECK_MARKED_OBJECTS` feature (see `src/alloc.c`). In particular, stack-allocated objects should never be made visible to user Lisp code.

Currently, cons cells and strings can be allocated this way. This is implemented by C macros like `AUTO_CONS` and `AUTO_STRING` that define a named `Lisp_Object` with block lifetime. These objects are not freed by the garbage collector; instead, they have automatic storage duration, i.e., they are allocated like local variables and are automatically freed at the end of execution of the C block that defined the object.

For performance reasons, stack-allocated strings are limited to ASCII characters, and many of these strings are immutable, i.e., calling `ASET` on them produces undefined behavior.

E.5 Memory Usage

These functions and variables give information about the total amount of memory allocation that Emacs has done, broken down by data type. Note the difference between these and the values returned by `garbage-collect`; those count objects that currently exist, but these count the number or size of all allocations, including those for objects that have since been freed.

`cons-cells-consed`   [Variable]
> The total number of cons cells that have been allocated so far in this Emacs session.

`floats-consed`   [Variable]
> The total number of floats that have been allocated so far in this Emacs session.

`vector-cells-consed`   [Variable]
> The total number of vector cells that have been allocated so far in this Emacs session.

`symbols-consed`   [Variable]
> The total number of symbols that have been allocated so far in this Emacs session.

`string-chars-consed`   [Variable]
> The total number of string characters that have been allocated so far in this session.

`misc-objects-consed`   [Variable]
> The total number of miscellaneous objects that have been allocated so far in this session. These include markers and overlays, plus certain objects not visible to users.

intervals-consed [Variable]

    The total number of intervals that have been allocated so far in this Emacs session.

strings-consed [Variable]

    The total number of strings that have been allocated so far in this Emacs session.

E.6 C Dialect

The C part of Emacs is portable to C99 or later: C11-specific features such as '`<stdalign.h>`' and '`_Noreturn`' are not used without a check, typically at configuration time, and the Emacs build procedure provides a substitute implementation if necessary. Some C11 features, such as anonymous structures and unions, are too difficult to emulate, so they are avoided entirely.

At some point in the future the base C dialect will no doubt change to C11.

E.7 Writing Emacs Primitives

Lisp primitives are Lisp functions implemented in C. The details of interfacing the C function so that Lisp can call it are handled by a few C macros. The only way to really understand how to write new C code is to read the source, but we can explain some things here.

An example of a special form is the definition of `or`, from `eval.c`. (An ordinary function would have the same general appearance.)

```
DEFUN ("or", For, Sor, 0, UNEVALLED, 0,
  doc: /* Eval args until one of them yields non-nil, then return
that value.
The remaining args are not evalled at all.
If all args return nil, return nil.
usage: (or CONDITIONS...)  */)
  (Lisp_Object args)
{
  Lisp_Object val = Qnil;

  while (CONSP (args))
    {
      val = eval_sub (XCAR (args));
      if (!NILP (val))
        break;
      args = XCDR (args);
      QUIT;
    }

  return val;
}
```

Let's start with a precise explanation of the arguments to the `DEFUN` macro. Here is a template for them:

    DEFUN (*lname*, *fname*, *sname*, *min*, *max*, *interactive*, *doc*)

lname   This is the name of the Lisp symbol to define as the function name; in the example above, it is `or`.

fname   This is the C function name for this function. This is the name that is used in C code for calling the function. The name is, by convention, 'F' prepended to the Lisp name, with all dashes ('-') in the Lisp name changed to underscores. Thus, to call this function from C code, call `For`.

sname This is a C variable name to use for a structure that holds the data for the subr object that represents the function in Lisp. This structure conveys the Lisp symbol name to the initialization routine that will create the symbol and store the subr object as its definition. By convention, this name is always *fname* with 'F' replaced with 'S'.

min This is the minimum number of arguments that the function requires. The function `or` allows a minimum of zero arguments.

max This is the maximum number of arguments that the function accepts, if there is a fixed maximum. Alternatively, it can be `UNEVALLED`, indicating a special form that receives unevaluated arguments, or `MANY`, indicating an unlimited number of evaluated arguments (the equivalent of `&rest`). Both `UNEVALLED` and `MANY` are macros. If *max* is a number, it must be more than *min* but less than 8.

interactive

This is an interactive specification, a string such as might be used as the argument of `interactive` in a Lisp function. In the case of `or`, it is 0 (a null pointer), indicating that `or` cannot be called interactively. A value of `""` indicates a function that should receive no arguments when called interactively. If the value begins with a '"(', the string is evaluated as a Lisp form. For example:

```
DEFUN ("foo", Ffoo, Sfoo, 0, UNEVALLED,
       "(list (read-char-by-name \"Insert character: \")\
              (prefix-numeric-value current-prefix-arg)\
              t))",
       doc: /* ... /*)
```

doc This is the documentation string. It uses C comment syntax rather than C string syntax because comment syntax requires nothing special to include multiple lines. The 'doc:' identifies the comment that follows as the documentation string. The '/*' and '*/' delimiters that begin and end the comment are not part of the documentation string.

If the last line of the documentation string begins with the keyword 'usage:', the rest of the line is treated as the argument list for documentation purposes. This way, you can use different argument names in the documentation string from the ones used in the C code. 'usage:' is required if the function has an unlimited number of arguments.

All the usual rules for documentation strings in Lisp code (see Section D.6 [Documentation Tips], page 1059) apply to C code documentation strings too.

After the call to the `DEFUN` macro, you must write the argument list for the C function, including the types for the arguments. If the primitive accepts a fixed maximum number of Lisp arguments, there must be one C argument for each Lisp argument, and each argument must be of type `Lisp_Object`. (Various macros and functions for creating values of type `Lisp_Object` are declared in the file `lisp.h`.) If the primitive has no upper limit on the number of Lisp arguments, it must have exactly two C arguments: the first is the number of Lisp arguments, and the second is the address of a block containing their values. These have types `int` and `Lisp_Object *` respectively. Since `Lisp_Object` can hold any Lisp object of any data type, you can determine the actual data type only at run time; so if you want a primitive to accept only a certain type of argument, you must check the type explicitly using a suitable predicate (see Section 2.6 [Type Predicates], page 28).

Within the function `For` itself, the local variable `args` refers to objects controlled by Emacs's stack-marking garbage collector. Although the garbage collector does not reclaim objects reachable from C `Lisp_Object` stack variables, it may move non-object components of an object, such as string contents; so functions that access non-object components must take care to refetch their addresses after performing Lisp evaluation. Lisp evaluation can occur via calls to `eval_sub` or `Feval`, either directly or indirectly.

Note the call to the `QUIT` macro inside the loop: this macro checks whether the user pressed *C-g*, and if so, aborts the processing. You should do that in any loop that can potentially require a large number of iterations; in this case, the list of arguments could be very long. This increases Emacs responsiveness and improves user experience.

You must not use C initializers for static or global variables unless the variables are never written once Emacs is dumped. These variables with initializers are allocated in an area of memory that becomes read-only (on certain operating systems) as a result of dumping Emacs. See Section E.2 [Pure Storage], page 1068.

Defining the C function is not enough to make a Lisp primitive available; you must also create the Lisp symbol for the primitive and store a suitable subr object in its function cell. The code looks like this:

```
defsubr (&sname);
```

Here *sname* is the name you used as the third argument to `DEFUN`.

If you add a new primitive to a file that already has Lisp primitives defined in it, find the function (near the end of the file) named `syms_of_something`, and add the call to `defsubr` there. If the file doesn't have this function, or if you create a new file, add to it a `syms_of_filename` (e.g., `syms_of_myfile`). Then find the spot in `emacs.c` where all of these functions are called, and add a call to `syms_of_filename` there.

The function `syms_of_filename` is also the place to define any C variables that are to be visible as Lisp variables. `DEFVAR_LISP` makes a C variable of type `Lisp_Object` visible in Lisp. `DEFVAR_INT` makes a C variable of type `int` visible in Lisp with a value that is always an integer. `DEFVAR_BOOL` makes a C variable of type `int` visible in Lisp with a value that is either `t` or `nil`. Note that variables defined with `DEFVAR_BOOL` are automatically added to the list `byte-boolean-vars` used by the byte compiler.

If you want to make a Lisp variables that is defined in C behave like one declared with `defcustom`, add an appropriate entry to `cus-start.el`.

If you define a file-scope C variable of type `Lisp_Object`, you must protect it from garbage-collection by calling `staticpro` in `syms_of_filename`, like this:

```
staticpro (&variable);
```

Here is another example function, with more complicated arguments. This comes from the code in `window.c`, and it demonstrates the use of macros and functions to manipulate Lisp objects.

```
DEFUN ("coordinates-in-window-p", Fcoordinates_in_window_p,
  Scoordinates_in_window_p, 2, 2, 0,
  doc: /* Return non-nil if COORDINATES are in WINDOW.
  ...
```

```
    or `right-margin' is returned.  */)
    (register Lisp_Object coordinates, Lisp_Object window)
{
  struct window *w;
  struct frame *f;
  int x, y;
  Lisp_Object lx, ly;

  CHECK_LIVE_WINDOW (window);
  w = XWINDOW (window);
  f = XFRAME (w->frame);
  CHECK_CONS (coordinates);
  lx = Fcar (coordinates);
  ly = Fcdr (coordinates);
  CHECK_NUMBER_OR_FLOAT (lx);
  CHECK_NUMBER_OR_FLOAT (ly);
  x = FRAME_PIXEL_X_FROM_CANON_X (f, lx) + FRAME_INTERNAL_BORDER_WIDTH(f);
  y = FRAME_PIXEL_Y_FROM_CANON_Y (f, ly) + FRAME_INTERNAL_BORDER_WIDTH(f);

  switch (coordinates_in_window (w, x, y))
    {
    case ON_NOTHING:              /* NOT in window at all.  */
      return Qnil;

    ...

    case ON_MODE_LINE:            /* In mode line of window.  */
      return Qmode_line;

    ...

    case ON_SCROLL_BAR:           /* On scroll-bar of window.  */
      /* Historically we are supposed to return nil in this case.  */
      return Qnil;

    default:
      abort ();
    }
}
```

Note that C code cannot call functions by name unless they are defined in C. The way to call a function written in Lisp is to use `Ffuncall`, which embodies the Lisp function `funcall`. Since the Lisp function `funcall` accepts an unlimited number of arguments, in C it takes two: the number of Lisp-level arguments, and a one-dimensional array containing their values. The first Lisp-level argument is the Lisp function to call, and the rest are the arguments to pass to it.

The C functions `call0`, `call1`, `call2`, and so on, provide handy ways to call a Lisp function conveniently with a fixed number of arguments. They work by calling `Ffuncall`.

`eval.c` is a very good file to look through for examples; `lisp.h` contains the definitions for some important macros and functions.

If you define a function which is side-effect free, update the code in `byte-opt.el` that binds `side-effect-free-fns` and `side-effect-and-error-free-fns` so that the compiler optimizer knows about it.

E.8 Object Internals

Emacs Lisp provides a rich set of the data types. Some of them, like cons cells, integers and strings, are common to nearly all Lisp dialects. Some others, like markers and buffers, are quite special and needed to provide the basic support to write editor commands in Lisp. To implement such a variety of object types and provide an efficient way to pass objects between the subsystems of an interpreter, there is a set of C data structures and a special type to represent the pointers to all of them, which is known as *tagged pointer*.

In C, the tagged pointer is an object of type `Lisp_Object`. Any initialized variable of such a type always holds the value of one of the following basic data types: integer, symbol, string, cons cell, float, vectorlike or miscellaneous object. Each of these data types has the corresponding tag value. All tags are enumerated by **enum `Lisp_Type`** and placed into a 3-bit bitfield of the `Lisp_Object`. The rest of the bits is the value itself. Integers are immediate, i.e., directly represented by those *value bits*, and all other objects are represented by the C pointers to a corresponding object allocated from the heap. Width of the `Lisp_Object` is platform- and configuration-dependent: usually it's equal to the width of an underlying platform pointer (i.e., 32-bit on a 32-bit machine and 64-bit on a 64-bit one), but also there is a special configuration where `Lisp_Object` is 64-bit but all pointers are 32-bit. The latter trick was designed to overcome the limited range of values for Lisp integers on a 32-bit system by using 64-bit **long long** type for `Lisp_Object`.

The following C data structures are defined in `lisp.h` to represent the basic data types beyond integers:

struct `Lisp_Cons`
>   Cons cell, an object used to construct lists.

struct `Lisp_String`
>   String, the basic object to represent a sequence of characters.

struct `Lisp_Vector`
>   Array, a fixed-size set of Lisp objects which may be accessed by an index.

struct `Lisp_Symbol`
>   Symbol, the unique-named entity commonly used as an identifier.

struct `Lisp_Float`
>   Floating-point value.

union `Lisp_Misc`
>   Miscellaneous kinds of objects which don't fit into any of the above.

These types are the first-class citizens of an internal type system. Since the tag space is limited, all other types are the subtypes of either `Lisp_Vectorlike` or `Lisp_Misc`. Vector subtypes are enumerated by **enum pvec_type**, and nearly all complex objects like windows, buffers, frames, and processes fall into this category. The rest of special types, including markers and overlays, are enumerated by **enum `Lisp_Misc_Type`** and form the set of subtypes of `Lisp_Misc`.

Below there is a description of a few subtypes of `Lisp_Vectorlike`. Buffer object represents the text to display and edit. Window is the part of display structure which shows the buffer or used as a container to recursively place other windows on the same frame. (Do not confuse Emacs Lisp window object with the window as an entity managed by the user interface system like X; in Emacs terminology, the latter is called frame.) Finally, process object is used to manage the subprocesses.

E.8.1 Buffer Internals

Two structures (see `buffer.h`) are used to represent buffers in C. The `buffer_text` structure contains fields describing the text of a buffer; the `buffer` structure holds other fields. In the case of indirect buffers, two or more `buffer` structures reference the same `buffer_text` structure.

Here are some of the fields in `struct buffer_text`:

`beg`   The address of the buffer contents.

`gpt`
`gpt_byte`   The character and byte positions of the buffer gap. See Section 26.13 [Buffer Gap], page 566.

`z`
`z_byte`   The character and byte positions of the end of the buffer text.

`gap_size`   The size of buffer's gap. See Section 26.13 [Buffer Gap], page 566.

`modiff`
`save_modiff`
`chars_modiff`
`overlay_modiff`

> These fields count the number of buffer-modification events performed in this buffer. `modiff` is incremented after each buffer-modification event, and is never otherwise changed; `save_modiff` contains the value of `modiff` the last time the buffer was visited or saved; `chars_modiff` counts only modifications to the characters in the buffer, ignoring all other kinds of changes; and `overlay_modiff` counts only modifications to the overlays.

`beg_unchanged`
`end_unchanged`

> The number of characters at the start and end of the text that are known to be unchanged since the last complete redisplay.

`unchanged_modified`
`overlay_unchanged_modified`

> The values of `modiff` and `overlay_modiff`, respectively, after the last complete redisplay. If their current values match `modiff` or `overlay_modiff`, that means `beg_unchanged` and `end_unchanged` contain no useful information.

`markers`   The markers that refer to this buffer. This is actually a single marker, and successive elements in its marker `chain` are the other markers referring to this buffer text.

`intervals`

> The interval tree which records the text properties of this buffer.

Some of the fields of `struct buffer` are:

`header`   A header of type `struct vectorlike_header` is common to all vectorlike objects.

`own_text`   A `struct buffer_text` structure that ordinarily holds the buffer contents. In indirect buffers, this field is not used.

`text`   A pointer to the `buffer_text` structure for this buffer. In an ordinary buffer, this is the `own_text` field above. In an indirect buffer, this is the `own_text` field of the base buffer.

`next`   A pointer to the next buffer, in the chain of all buffers, including killed buffers. This chain is used only for allocation and garbage collection, in order to collect killed buffers properly.

`pt`
`pt_byte`   The character and byte positions of point in a buffer.

`begv`
`begv_byte`
              The character and byte positions of the beginning of the accessible range of text in the buffer.

`zv`
`zv_byte`   The character and byte positions of the end of the accessible range of text in the buffer.

`base_buffer`
              In an indirect buffer, this points to the base buffer. In an ordinary buffer, it is null.

`local_flags`
              This field contains flags indicating that certain variables are local in this buffer. Such variables are declared in the C code using `DEFVAR_PER_BUFFER`, and their buffer-local bindings are stored in fields in the buffer structure itself. (Some of these fields are described in this table.)

`modtime`   The modification time of the visited file. It is set when the file is written or read. Before writing the buffer into a file, this field is compared to the modification time of the file to see if the file has changed on disk. See Section 26.5 [Buffer Modification], page 556.

`auto_save_modified`
              The time when the buffer was last auto-saved.

`last_window_start`
              The `window-start` position in the buffer as of the last time the buffer was displayed in a window.

`clip_changed`
              This flag indicates that narrowing has changed in the buffer. See Section 29.4 [Narrowing], page 684.

`prevent_redisplay_optimizations_p`
              This flag indicates that redisplay optimizations should not be used to display this buffer.

`overlay_center`

> This field holds the current overlay center position. See Section 37.9.1 [Managing Overlays], page 904.

`overlays_before`
`overlays_after`

> These fields hold, respectively, a list of overlays that end at or before the current overlay center, and a list of overlays that end after the current overlay center. See Section 37.9.1 [Managing Overlays], page 904. `overlays_before` is sorted in order of decreasing end position, and `overlays_after` is sorted in order of increasing beginning position.

`name`   A Lisp string that names the buffer. It is guaranteed to be unique. See Section 26.3 [Buffer Names], page 553.

`save_length`

> The length of the file this buffer is visiting, when last read or saved. This and other fields concerned with saving are not kept in the `buffer_text` structure because indirect buffers are never saved.

`directory`

> The directory for expanding relative file names. This is the value of the buffer-local variable `default-directory` (see Section 24.8.4 [File Name Expansion], page 522).

`filename`   The name of the file visited in this buffer, or `nil`. This is the value of the buffer-local variable `buffer-file-name` (see Section 26.4 [Buffer File Name], page 554).

`undo_list`
`backed_up`
`auto_save_file_name`
`auto_save_file_format`
`read_only`
`file_format`
`file_truename`
`invisibility_spec`
`display_count`
`display_time`

> These fields store the values of Lisp variables that are automatically buffer-local (see Section 11.10 [Buffer-Local Variables], page 171), whose corresponding variable names have the additional prefix `buffer-` and have underscores replaced with dashes. For instance, `undo_list` stores the value of `buffer-undo-list`.

`mark`   The mark for the buffer. The mark is a marker, hence it is also included on the list `markers`. See Section 30.7 [The Mark], page 691.

`local_var_alist`

> The association list describing the buffer-local variable bindings of this buffer, not including the built-in buffer-local bindings that have special slots in the buffer object. (Those slots are omitted from this table.) See Section 11.10 [Buffer-Local Variables], page 171.

`major_mode`
> Symbol naming the major mode of this buffer, e.g., `lisp-mode`.

`mode_name`
> Pretty name of the major mode, e.g., `"Lisp"`.

`keymap`
`abbrev_table`
`syntax_table`
`category_table`
`display_table`
> These fields store the buffer's local keymap (see Chapter 21 [Keymaps], page 391), abbrev table (see Section 35.1 [Abbrev Tables], page 832), syntax table (see Chapter 34 [Syntax Tables], page 816), category table (see Section 34.8 [Categories], page 829), and display table (see Section 37.22.2 [Display Tables], page 974).

`downcase_table`
`upcase_table`
`case_canon_table`
> These fields store the conversion tables for converting text to lower case, upper case, and for canonicalizing text for case-fold search. See Section 4.9 [Case Tables], page 64.

`minor_modes`
> An alist of the minor modes of this buffer.

`pt_marker`
`begv_marker`
`zv_marker`
> These fields are only used in an indirect buffer, or in a buffer that is the base of an indirect buffer. Each holds a marker that records `pt`, `begv`, and `zv` respectively, for this buffer when the buffer is not current.

```
mode_line_format
header_line_format
case_fold_search
tab_width
fill_column
left_margin
auto_fill_function
truncate_lines
word_wrap
ctl_arrow
bidi_display_reordering
bidi_paragraph_direction
selective_display
selective_display_ellipses
overwrite_mode
abbrev_mode
mark_active
enable_multibyte_characters
buffer_file_coding_system
cache_long_line_scans
point_before_scroll
left_fringe_width
right_fringe_width
fringes_outside_margins
scroll_bar_width
indicate_empty_lines
indicate_buffer_boundaries
fringe_indicator_alist
fringe_cursor_alist
scroll_up_aggressively
scroll_down_aggressively
cursor_type
cursor_in_non_selected_windows
```
> These fields store the values of Lisp variables that are automatically buffer-local (see Section 11.10 [Buffer-Local Variables], page 171), whose corresponding variable names have underscores replaced with dashes. For instance, `mode_line_format` stores the value of `mode-line-format`.

`last_selected_window`
> This is the last window that was selected with this buffer in it, or `nil` if that window no longer displays this buffer.

E.8.2 Window Internals

The fields of a window (for a complete list, see the definition of `struct window` in `window.h`) include:

`frame`   The frame that this window is on.

`mini_p`   Non-`nil` if this window is a minibuffer window.

parent   Internally, Emacs arranges windows in a tree; each group of siblings has a parent window whose area includes all the siblings. This field points to a window's parent.

Parent windows do not display buffers, and play little role in display except to shape their child windows. Emacs Lisp programs usually have no access to the parent windows; they operate on the windows at the leaves of the tree, which actually display buffers.

hchild
vchild   These fields contain the window's leftmost child and its topmost child respectively. `hchild` is used if the window is subdivided horizontally by child windows, and `vchild` if it is subdivided vertically. In a live window, only one of `hchild`, `vchild`, and `buffer` (q.v.) is non-`nil`.

next
prev   The next sibling and previous sibling of this window. `next` is `nil` if the window is the right-most or bottom-most in its group; `prev` is `nil` if it is the left-most or top-most in its group.

left_col   The left-hand edge of the window, measured in columns, relative to the leftmost column in the frame (column 0).

top_line   The top edge of the window, measured in lines, relative to the topmost line in the frame (line 0).

total_cols
total_lines
      The width and height of the window, measured in columns and lines respectively. The width includes the scroll bar and fringes, and/or the separator line on the right of the window (if any).

buffer   The buffer that the window is displaying.

start   A marker pointing to the position in the buffer that is the first character displayed in the window.

pointm   This is the value of point in the current buffer when this window is selected; when it is not selected, it retains its previous value.

force_start
      If this flag is non-`nil`, it says that the window has been scrolled explicitly by the Lisp program. This affects what the next redisplay does if point is off the screen: instead of scrolling the window to show the text around point, it moves point to a location that is on the screen.

frozen_window_start_p
      This field is set temporarily to 1 to indicate to redisplay that `start` of this window should not be changed, even if point gets invisible.

start_at_line_beg
      Non-`nil` means current value of `start` was the beginning of a line when it was chosen.

`use_time`   This is the last time that the window was selected. The function `get-lru-window` uses this field.

`sequence_number`
A unique number assigned to this window when it was created.

`last_modified`
The `modiff` field of the window's buffer, as of the last time a redisplay completed in this window.

`last_overlay_modified`
The `overlay_modiff` field of the window's buffer, as of the last time a redisplay completed in this window.

`last_point`
The buffer's value of point, as of the last time a redisplay completed in this window.

`last_had_star`
A non-`nil` value means the window's buffer was modified when the window was last updated.

`vertical_scroll_bar`
This window's vertical scroll bar.

`left_margin_cols`
`right_margin_cols`
The widths of the left and right margins in this window. A value of `nil` means no margin.

`left_fringe_width`
`right_fringe_width`
The widths of the left and right fringes in this window. A value of `nil` or `t` means use the values of the frame.

`fringes_outside_margins`
A non-`nil` value means the fringes outside the display margins; othersize they are between the margin and the text.

`window_end_pos`
This is computed as `z` minus the buffer position of the last glyph in the current matrix of the window. The value is only valid if `window_end_valid` is not `nil`.

`window_end_bytepos`
The byte position corresponding to `window_end_pos`.

`window_end_vpos`
The window-relative vertical position of the line containing `window_end_pos`.

`window_end_valid`
This field is set to a non-`nil` value if `window_end_pos` is truly valid. This is `nil` if nontrivial redisplay is pre-empted, since in that case the display that `window_end_pos` was computed for did not get onto the screen.

`cursor`   A structure describing where the cursor is in this window.

`last_cursor`
> The value of **cursor** as of the last redisplay that finished.

`phys_cursor`
> A structure describing where the cursor of this window physically is.

`phys_cursor_type`
`phys_cursor_height`
`phys_cursor_width`
> The type, height, and width of the cursor that was last displayed on this window.

`phys_cursor_on_p`
> This field is non-zero if the cursor is physically on.

`cursor_off_p`
> Non-zero means the cursor in this window is logically off. This is used for blinking the cursor.

`last_cursor_off_p`
> This field contains the value of **cursor_off_p** as of the time of the last redisplay.

`must_be_updated_p`
> This is set to 1 during redisplay when this window must be updated.

`hscroll` This is the number of columns that the display in the window is scrolled horizontally to the left. Normally, this is 0.

`vscroll` Vertical scroll amount, in pixels. Normally, this is 0.

`dedicated`
> Non-**nil** if this window is dedicated to its buffer.

`display_table`
> The window's display table, or **nil** if none is specified for it.

`update_mode_line`
> Non-**nil** means this window's mode line needs to be updated.

`base_line_number`
> The line number of a certain position in the buffer, or **nil**. This is used for displaying the line number of point in the mode line.

`base_line_pos`
> The position in the buffer for which the line number is known, or **nil** meaning none is known. If it is a buffer, don't display the line number as long as the window shows that buffer.

`column_number_displayed`
> The column number currently displayed in this window's mode line, or **nil** if column numbers are not being displayed.

`current_matrix`
`desired_matrix`
> Glyph matrices describing the current and desired display of this window.

E.8.3 Process Internals

The fields of a process (for a complete list, see the definition of **struct Lisp_Process** in `process.h`) include:

name   A string, the name of the process.

command   A list containing the command arguments that were used to start this process. For a network or serial process, it is **nil** if the process is running or **t** if the process is stopped.

filter   A function used to accept output from the process.

sentinel A function called whenever the state of the process changes.

buffer   The associated buffer of the process.

pid   An integer, the operating system's process ID. Pseudo-processes such as network or serial connections use a value of 0.

childp   A flag, **t** if this is really a child process. For a network or serial connection, it is a plist based on the arguments to **make-network-process** or **make-serial-process**.

mark   A marker indicating the position of the end of the last output from this process inserted into the buffer. This is often but not always the end of the buffer.

kill_without_query
> If this is non-zero, killing Emacs while this process is still running does not ask for confirmation about killing the process.

raw_status
> The raw process status, as returned by the **wait** system call.

status   The process status, as **process-status** should return it.

tick
update_tick
> If these two fields are not equal, a change in the status of the process needs to be reported, either by running the sentinel or by inserting a message in the process buffer.

pty_flag   Non-**nil** if communication with the subprocess uses a pty; **nil** if it uses a pipe.

infd   The file descriptor for input from the process.

outfd   The file descriptor for output to the process.

tty_name The name of the terminal that the subprocess is using, or **nil** if it is using pipes.

decode_coding_system
> Coding-system for decoding the input from this process.

decoding_buf
> A working buffer for decoding.

decoding_carryover
> Size of carryover in decoding.

`encode_coding_system`
> Coding-system for encoding the output to this process.

`encoding_buf`
> A working buffer for encoding.

`inherit_coding_system_flag`
> Flag to set `coding-system` of the process buffer from the coding system used to decode process output.

`type` Symbol indicating the type of process: `real`, `network`, `serial`.

E.9 C Integer Types

Here are some guidelines for use of integer types in the Emacs C source code. These guidelines sometimes give competing advice; common sense is advised.

- Avoid arbitrary limits. For example, avoid `int len = strlen (s);` unless the length of `s` is required for other reasons to fit in `int` range.

- Do not assume that signed integer arithmetic wraps around on overflow. This is no longer true of Emacs porting targets: signed integer overflow has undefined behavior in practice, and can dump core or even cause earlier or later code to behave illogically. Unsigned overflow does wrap around reliably, modulo a power of two.

- Prefer signed types to unsigned, as code gets confusing when signed and unsigned types are combined. Many other guidelines assume that types are signed; in the rarer cases where unsigned types are needed, similar advice may apply to the unsigned counterparts (e.g., `size_t` instead of `ptrdiff_t`, or `uintptr_t` instead of `intptr_t`).

- Prefer `int` for Emacs character codes, in the range 0 .. 0x3FFFFF. More generally, prefer `int` for integers known to be in `int` range, e.g., screen column counts.

- Prefer `ptrdiff_t` for sizes, i.e., for integers bounded by the maximum size of any individual C object or by the maximum number of elements in any C array. This is part of Emacs's general preference for signed types. Using `ptrdiff_t` limits objects to `PTRDIFF_MAX` bytes, but larger objects would cause trouble anyway since they would break pointer subtraction, so this does not impose an arbitrary limit.

- Avoid `ssize_t` except when communicating to low-level APIs that have `ssize_t`-related limitations. Although it's equivalent to `ptrdiff_t` on typical platforms, `ssize_t` is occasionally narrower, so using it for size-related calculations could overflow. Also, `ptrdiff_t` is more ubiquitous and better-standardized, has standard `printf` formats, and is the basis for Emacs's internal size-overflow checking. When using `ssize_t`, please note that POSIX requires support only for values in the range −1 .. `SSIZE_MAX`.

- Prefer `intptr_t` for internal representations of pointers, or for integers bounded only by the number of objects that can exist at any given time or by the total number of bytes that can be allocated. Currently Emacs sometimes uses other types when `intptr_t` would be better; fixing this is lower priority, as the code works as-is on Emacs's current porting targets.

- Prefer the Emacs-defined type `EMACS_INT` for representing values converted to or from Emacs Lisp fixnums, as fixnum arithmetic is based on `EMACS_INT`.

- When representing a system value (such as a file size or a count of seconds since the Epoch), prefer the corresponding system type (e.g., `off_t`, `time_t`). Do not assume that a system type is signed, unless this assumption is known to be safe. For example, although `off_t` is always signed, `time_t` need not be.

- Prefer the Emacs-defined type `printmax_t` for representing values that might be any signed integer that can be printed, using a `printf`-family function.

- Prefer `intmax_t` for representing values that might be any signed integer value.

- Prefer `bool`, `false` and `true` for booleans. Using `bool` can make programs easier to read and a bit faster than using `int`. Although it is also OK to use `int`, `0` and `1`, this older style is gradually being phased out. When using `bool`, respect the limitations of the replacement implementation of `bool`, as documented in the source file `lib/stdbool.in.h`. In particular, boolean bitfields should be of type `bool_bf`, not `bool`, so that they work correctly even when compiling Objective C with standard GCC.

- In bitfields, prefer `unsigned int` or `signed int` to `int`, as `int` is less portable: it might be signed, and might not be. Single-bit bit fields should be `unsigned int` or `bool_bf` so that their values are 0 or 1.

Appendix F Standard Errors

Here is a list of the more important error symbols in standard Emacs, grouped by concept. The list includes each symbol's message and a cross reference to a description of how the error can occur.

Each error symbol has an set of parent error conditions that is a list of symbols. Normally this list includes the error symbol itself and the symbol `error`. Occasionally it includes additional symbols, which are intermediate classifications, narrower than `error` but broader than a single error symbol. For example, all the errors in accessing files have the condition `file-error`. If we do not say here that a certain error symbol has additional error conditions, that means it has none.

As a special exception, the error symbol `quit` does not have the condition `error`, because quitting is not considered an error.

Most of these error symbols are defined in C (mainly `data.c`), but some are defined in Lisp. For example, the file `userlock.el` defines the `file-locked` and `file-supersession` errors. Several of the specialized Lisp libraries distributed with Emacs define their own error symbols. We do not attempt to list of all those here.

See Section 10.6.3 [Errors], page 148, for an explanation of how errors are generated and handled.

error   The message is 'error'. See Section 10.6.3 [Errors], page 148.

quit   The message is 'Quit'. See Section 20.11 [Quitting], page 382.

args-out-of-range
           The message is 'Args out of range'. This happens when trying to access an element beyond the range of a sequence, buffer, or other container-like object. See Chapter 6 [Sequences Arrays Vectors], page 89, and See Chapter 31 [Text], page 696.

arith-error
           The message is 'Arithmetic error'. This occurs when trying to perform integer division by zero. See Section 3.5 [Numeric Conversions], page 39, and See Section 3.6 [Arithmetic Operations], page 40.

beginning-of-buffer
           The message is 'Beginning of buffer'. See Section 29.2.1 [Character Motion], page 674.

buffer-read-only
           The message is 'Buffer is read-only'. See Section 26.7 [Read Only Buffers], page 558.

circular-list
           The message is 'List contains a loop'. This happens when a circular structure is encountered. See Section 2.5 [Circular Objects], page 27.

cl-assertion-failed
           The message is 'Assertion failed'. This happens when the `cl-assert` macro fails a test. See Section "Assertions" in *Common Lisp Extensions*.

`coding-system-error`

> The message is 'Invalid coding system'. See Section 32.10.3 [Lisp and Coding Systems], page 776.

`cyclic-function-indirection`

> The message is 'Symbol's chain of function indirections contains a loop'. See Section 9.1.4 [Function Indirection], page 126.

`cyclic-variable-indirection`

> The message is 'Symbol's chain of variable indirections contains a loop'. See Section 11.13 [Variable Aliases], page 182.

`dbus-error`

> The message is 'D-Bus error'. This is only defined if Emacs was compiled with D-Bus support. See Section "Errors and Events" in *D-Bus integration in Emacs*.

`end-of-buffer`

> The message is 'End of buffer'. See Section 29.2.1 [Character Motion], page 674.

`end-of-file`

> The message is 'End of file during parsing'. Note that this is not a subcategory of **file-error**, because it pertains to the Lisp reader, not to file I/O. See Section 18.3 [Input Functions], page 304.

`file-already-exists`

> This is a subcategory of **file-error**. See Section 24.4 [Writing to Files], page 502.

`file-date-error`

> This is a subcategory of **file-error**. It occurs when **copy-file** tries and fails to set the last-modification time of the output file. See Section 24.7 [Changing Files], page 514.

`file-error`

> We do not list the error-strings of this error and its subcategories, because the error message is normally constructed from the data items alone when the error condition **file-error** is present. Thus, the error-strings are not very relevant. However, these error symbols do have **error-message** properties, and if no data is provided, the **error-message** property *is* used. See Chapter 24 [Files], page 495.

`compression-error`

> This is a subcategory of **file-error**, which results from problems handling a compressed file. See Section 15.1 [How Programs Do Loading], page 244.

`file-locked`

> This is a subcategory of **file-error**. See Section 24.5 [File Locks], page 504.

`file-supersession`

> This is a subcategory of **file-error**. See Section 26.6 [Modification Time], page 557.

`file-notify-error`
> This is a subcategory of `file-error`. It happens, when a file could not be watched for changes. See Section 38.20 [File Notifications], page 1020.

`ftp-error`
> This is a subcategory of `file-error`, which results from problems in accessing a remote file using ftp. See Section "Remote Files" in *The GNU Emacs Manual*.

`invalid-function`
> The message is 'Invalid function'. See Section 9.1.4 [Function Indirection], page 126.

`invalid-read-syntax`
> The message is 'Invalid read syntax'. See Section 2.1 [Printed Representation], page 8.

`invalid-regexp`
> The message is 'Invalid regexp'. See Section 33.3 [Regular Expressions], page 793.

`mark-inactive`
> The message is 'The mark is not active now'. See Section 30.7 [The Mark], page 691.

`no-catch` The message is 'No catch for tag'. See Section 10.6.1 [Catch and Throw], page 145.

`scan-error`
> The message is 'Scan error'. This happens when certain syntax-parsing functions find invalid syntax or mismatched parentheses. Conventionally raised with three argument: a human-readable error message, the start of the obstacle that cannot be moved over, and the end of the obstacle. See Section 29.2.6 [List Motion], page 681, and See Section 34.6 [Parsing Expressions], page 824.

`search-failed`
> The message is 'Search failed'. See Chapter 33 [Searching and Matching], page 790.

`setting-constant`
> The message is 'Attempt to set a constant symbol'. This happens when attempting to assign values to `nil`, `t`, and keyword symbols. See Section 11.2 [Constant Variables], page 157.

`text-read-only`
> The message is 'Text is read-only'. This is a subcategory of `buffer-read-only`. See Section 31.19.4 [Special Properties], page 738.

`undefined-color`
> The message is 'Undefined color'. See Section 28.21 [Color Names], page 666.

`user-error`
> The message is the empty string. See Section 10.6.3.1 [Signaling Errors], page 148.

`void-function`

> The message is 'Symbol's function definition is void'. See Section 12.9 [Function Cells], page 202.

`void-variable`

> The message is 'Symbol's value as variable is void'. See Section 11.7 [Accessing Variables], page 164.

`wrong-number-of-arguments`

> The message is 'Wrong number of arguments'. See Section 12.2.3 [Argument List], page 189.

`wrong-type-argument`

> The message is 'Wrong type argument'. See Section 2.6 [Type Predicates], page 28.

Appendix G Standard Keymaps

In this section we list some of the more general keymaps. Many of these exist when Emacs is first started, but some are loaded only when the respective feature is accessed.

There are many other, more specialized, maps than these; in particular those associated with major and minor modes. The minibuffer uses several keymaps (see Section 19.6.3 [Completion Commands], page 326). For more details on keymaps, see Chapter 21 [Keymaps], page 391.

2C-mode-map
> A sparse keymap for subcommands of the prefix *C-x 6*.
> See Section "Two-Column Editing" in *The GNU Emacs Manual*.

abbrev-map
> A sparse keymap for subcommands of the prefix *C-x a*.
> See Section "Defining Abbrevs" in *The GNU Emacs Manual*.

button-buffer-map
> A sparse keymap useful for buffers containing buffers.
> You may want to use this as a parent keymap. See Section 37.19 [Buttons], page 963.

button-map
> A sparse keymap used by buttons.

ctl-x-4-map
> A sparse keymap for subcommands of the prefix *C-x 4*.

ctl-x-5-map
> A sparse keymap for subcommands of the prefix *C-x 5*.

ctl-x-map
> A full keymap for *C-x* commands.

ctl-x-r-map
> A sparse keymap for subcommands of the prefix *C-x r*.
> See Section "Registers" in *The GNU Emacs Manual*.

esc-map   A full keymap for *ESC* (or *Meta*) commands.

facemenu-keymap
> A sparse keymap used for the *M-o* prefix key.

function-key-map
> The parent keymap of all local-function-key-map (q.v.) instances.

global-map
> The full keymap containing default global key bindings.
> Modes should not modify the Global map.

goto-map   A sparse keymap used for the *M-g* prefix key.

help-map   A sparse keymap for the keys following the help character *C-h*.
> See Section 23.5 [Help Functions], page 491.

`Helper-help-map`

   A full keymap used by the help utility package.

   It has the same keymap in its value cell and in its function cell.

`input-decode-map`

   The keymap for translating keypad and function keys.

   If there are none, then it contains an empty sparse keymap. See Section 21.14 [Translation Keymaps], page 410.

`key-translation-map`

   A keymap for translating keys. This one overrides ordinary key bindings, unlike `local-function-key-map`. See Section 21.14 [Translation Keymaps], page 410.

`kmacro-keymap`

   A sparse keymap for keys that follows the *C-x C-k* prefix search.

   See Section "Keyboard Macros" in *The GNU Emacs Manual*.

`local-function-key-map`

   The keymap for translating key sequences to preferred alternatives.

   If there are none, then it contains an empty sparse keymap. See Section 21.14 [Translation Keymaps], page 410.

`menu-bar-file-menu`
`menu-bar-edit-menu`
`menu-bar-options-menu`
`global-buffers-menu-map`
`menu-bar-tools-menu`
`menu-bar-help-menu`

   These keymaps display the main, top-level menus in the menu bar.

   Some of them contain sub-menus. For example, the Edit menu contains `menu-bar-search-menu`, etc. See Section 21.17.5 [Menu Bar], page 422.

`minibuffer-inactive-mode-map`

   A full keymap used in the minibuffer when it is not active.

   See Section "Editing in the Minibuffer" in *The GNU Emacs Manual*.

`mode-line-coding-system-map`
`mode-line-input-method-map`
`mode-line-column-line-number-mode-map`

   These keymaps control various areas of the mode line.

   See Section 22.4 [Mode Line Format], page 451.

`mode-specific-map`

   The keymap for characters following *C-c*. Note, this is in the global map. This map is not actually mode-specific: its name was chosen to be informative in *C-h b* (`display-bindings`), where it describes the main use of the *C-c* prefix key.

`mouse-appearance-menu-map`

   A sparse keymap used for the *S-mouse-1* key.

`mule-keymap`

   The global keymap used for the *C-x RET* prefix key.

`narrow-map`

> A sparse keymap for subcommands of the prefix *C-x n*.

`prog-mode-map`

> The keymap used by Prog mode.
> See Section 22.2.5 [Basic Major Modes], page 440.

`query-replace-map`
`multi-query-replace-map`

> A sparse keymap used for responses in **query-replace** and related commands;
> also for **y-or-n-p** and **map-y-or-n-p**. The functions that use this map do
> not support prefix keys; they look up one event at a time. **multi-query-
> replace-map** extends **query-replace-map** for multi-buffer replacements. See
> Section 33.7 [Search and Replace], page 812.

`search-map`

> A sparse keymap that provides global bindings for search-related commands.

`special-mode-map`

> The keymap used by Special mode.
> See Section 22.2.5 [Basic Major Modes], page 440.

`tool-bar-map`

> The keymap defining the contents of the tool bar.
> See Section 21.17.6 [Tool Bar], page 423.

`universal-argument-map`

> A sparse keymap used while processing *C-u*.
> See Section 20.12 [Prefix Command Arguments], page 384.

`vc-prefix-map`

> The global keymap used for the *C-x v* prefix key.

`x-alternatives-map`

> A sparse keymap used to map certain keys under graphical frames.
> The function **x-setup-function-keys** uses this.

Appendix H Standard Hooks

The following is a list of some hook variables that let you provide functions to be called from within Emacs on suitable occasions.

Most of these variables have names ending with '-hook'. They are *normal hooks*, run by means of **run-hooks**. The value of such a hook is a list of functions; the functions are called with no arguments and their values are completely ignored. The recommended way to put a new function on such a hook is to call **add-hook**. See Section 22.1 [Hooks], page 429, for more information about using hooks.

The variables whose names end in '-functions' are usually *abnormal hooks* (some old code may also use the deprecated '-hooks' suffix); their values are lists of functions, but these functions are called in a special way (they are passed arguments, or their return values are used). The variables whose names end in '-function' have single functions as their values.

This is not an exhaustive list, it only covers the more general hooks. For example, every major mode defines a hook named '*modename*-mode-hook'. The major mode command runs this normal hook with **run-mode-hooks** as the very last thing it does. See Section 22.2.6 [Mode Hooks], page 440. Most minor modes have mode hooks too.

A special feature allows you to specify expressions to evaluate if and when a file is loaded (see Section 15.10 [Hooks for Loading], page 257). That feature is not exactly a hook, but does a similar job.

```
activate-mark-hook
deactivate-mark-hook
```
> See Section 30.7 [The Mark], page 691.

```
after-change-functions
before-change-functions
first-change-hook
```
> See Section 31.28 [Change Hooks], page 759.

```
after-change-major-mode-hook
change-major-mode-after-body-hook
```
> See Section 22.2.6 [Mode Hooks], page 440.

```
after-init-hook
before-init-hook
emacs-startup-hook
window-setup-hook
```
> See Section 38.1.2 [Init File], page 988.

```
after-insert-file-functions
write-region-annotate-functions
write-region-post-annotation-function
```
> See Section 24.12 [Format Conversion], page 534.

```
after-make-frame-functions
before-make-frame-hook
```
> See Section 28.1 [Creating Frames], page 631.

```
after-save-hook
before-save-hook
write-contents-functions
write-file-functions
```
          See Section 24.2 [Saving Buffers], page 499.

```
after-setting-font-hook
```
          Hook run after a frame's font changes.

```
auto-save-hook
```
          See Section 25.2 [Auto-Saving], page 544.

```
before-hack-local-variables-hook
hack-local-variables-hook
```
          See Section 11.11 [File Local Variables], page 177.

```
buffer-access-fontify-functions
```
          See Section 31.19.7 [Lazy Properties], page 745.

```
buffer-list-update-hook
```
          Hook run when the buffer list changes (see Section 26.8 [Buffer List], page 560).

```
buffer-quit-function
```
          Function to call to quit the current buffer.

```
change-major-mode-hook
```
          See Section 11.10.2 [Creating Buffer-Local], page 172.

```
command-line-functions
```
          See Section 38.1.4 [Command-Line Arguments], page 990.

```
delayed-warnings-hook
```
          The command loop runs this soon after `post-command-hook` (q.v.).

```
focus-in-hook
focus-out-hook
```
          See Section 28.10 [Input Focus], page 656.

```
delete-frame-functions
```
          See Section 28.7 [Deleting Frames], page 655.

```
delete-terminal-functions
```
          See Section 28.2 [Multiple Terminals], page 631.

```
pop-up-frame-function
split-window-preferred-function
```
          See Section 27.15 [Choosing Window Options], page 603.

```
echo-area-clear-hook
```
          See Section 37.4.4 [Echo Area Customization], page 893.

```
find-file-hook
find-file-not-found-functions
```
          See Section 24.1.1 [Visiting Functions], page 495.

```
font-lock-extend-after-change-region-function
```
          See Section 22.6.9.2 [Region to Refontify], page 473.

`font-lock-extend-region-functions`
> See Section 22.6.9 [Multiline Font Lock], page 472.

`font-lock-fontify-buffer-function`
`font-lock-fontify-region-function`
`font-lock-mark-block-function`
`font-lock-unfontify-buffer-function`
`font-lock-unfontify-region-function`
> See Section 22.6.4 [Other Font Lock Variables], page 468.

`fontification-functions`
> See Section 37.12.7 [Automatic Face Assignment], page 926.

`frame-auto-hide-function`
> See Section 27.18 [Quitting Windows], page 607.

`kill-buffer-hook`
`kill-buffer-query-functions`
> See Section 26.10 [Killing Buffers], page 563.

`kill-emacs-hook`
`kill-emacs-query-functions`
> See Section 38.2.1 [Killing Emacs], page 992.

`menu-bar-update-hook`
> See Section 21.17.5 [Menu Bar], page 422.

`minibuffer-setup-hook`
`minibuffer-exit-hook`
> See Section 19.14 [Minibuffer Misc], page 343.

`mouse-leave-buffer-hook`
> Hook run when about to switch windows with a mouse command.

`mouse-position-function`
> See Section 28.15 [Mouse Position], page 661.

`prefix-command-echo-keystrokes-functions`
> An abnormal hook run by prefix commands (such as C-u) which should return a string describing the current prefix state. For example, C-u produces 'C-u-' and 'C-u 1 2 3-'. Each hook function is called with no arguments and should return a string describing the current prefix state, or nil if there's no prefix state. See Section 20.12 [Prefix Command Arguments], page 384.

`prefix-command-preserve-state-hook`
> Hook run when a prefix command needs to preserve the prefix by passing the current prefix command state to the next command. For example, C-u needs to pass the state to the next command when the user types C-u - or follows C-u with a digit.

`pre-redisplay-functions`
> Hook run in each window just before redisplaying it. See Section 37.2 [Forcing Redisplay], page 886.

```
post-command-hook
pre-command-hook
```
        See Section 20.1 [Command Overview], page 345.

```
post-gc-hook
```
        See Section E.3 [Garbage Collection], page 1069.

```
post-self-insert-hook
```
        See Section 22.3.2 [Keymaps and Minor Modes], page 448.

```
suspend-hook
suspend-resume-hook
suspend-tty-functions
resume-tty-functions
```
        See Section 38.2.2 [Suspending Emacs], page 993.

```
syntax-begin-function
syntax-propertize-extend-region-functions
syntax-propertize-function
font-lock-syntactic-face-function
```
        See Section 22.6.8 [Syntactic Font Lock], page 471. See Section 34.4 [Syntax Properties], page 823.

```
temp-buffer-setup-hook
temp-buffer-show-function
temp-buffer-show-hook
```
        See Section 37.8 [Temporary Displays], page 900.

```
tty-setup-hook
```
        See Section 38.1.3 [Terminal-Specific], page 989.

```
window-configuration-change-hook
window-scroll-functions
window-size-change-functions
```
        See Section 27.27 [Window Hooks], page 628.

```
window-text-change-functions
```
        Functions to call in redisplay when text in the window might change.

Index

B

C

F

M

O

P

S

X

Y

Z